WORLD ENCYCLOPEDIA OF POLITICAL SYSTEMS

Volume I
Afghanistan—Mozambique

WORLD ENCYCLOPEDIA OF POLITICAL SYSTEMS

Volume I
Afghanistan—Mozambique

Edited by
George E. Delury

Longman

World Encyclopedia of
Political Systems & Parties

by George E. Delury
© 1983 copyright by George W. Delury

Published exclusively in the United Kingdom, the Com-
monwealth (except Canada), Europe and Africa by
Longman Group Limited, Longman House, Burnt Mill,
Harlow, Essex, CM20 2 JE, UK.

ISBN 0-582-90254-1

First published in the United States by
Facts On File, Inc., New York

World encyclopedia of political systems.

1. Political science—Dictionaries
I. Delury, George E.
320' 03'21   JA61
ISBN 0-582-90254-1
         0-582-90258-4 (v. 1)
         0-582-90259-2 (v. 2)

TABLE OF CONTENTS

VOLUME II

Smaller Countries & Microstates

CONTRIBUTORS

Diego Abente is a doctoral candidate in Political Science at the University of New Mexico in Albuquerque. He received his M.A. from Ohio University in 1980 and is the author of "Uruguay and Paraguay" in *Introduction to Latin American Politics,* by Jan K. Black, ed. (Boulder, Colo.: Westview Press, 1983). PARAGUAY

Marvin Alisky is professor of Political Science at Arizona State University. He received his Ph.D. from the University of Texas and is the author of numerous books and articles on Latin American affairs, particularly Mexico. MEXICO.

Philip M. Allen is professor of Humanities at Johnson State College in Johnson, Vermont. He received his Ph.D. from Emory University. A specialist in Indian Ocean affairs, he is the author of several books on that subject and on Africa. COMOROS, MADAGASCAR, MALDIVES, MAURITIUS, REUNION, SEYCHELLES.

Rolando Alum, Jr., is professor at John Jay College of Criminal Justice in New York City and received his doctoral education in Social and Cultural Anthropology at the University of Pittsburgh. A specialist in Latin American political anthropology, he is also senior policy analyst at International Research Consultants, Inc. (IRCI). DOMINICAN REPUBLIC, EQUATORIAL GUINEA.

Helen E. Andrews is the Asia Coordinator of the Human Rights Internet in Washington, D.C. TAIWAN (REPUBLIC OF CHINA).

William G. Andrews is professor of Political Science at State University College in Brockport, N.Y. He received his Ph.D. in Comparative Government from Cornell University and has since specialized in Western European governments and the U.S. presidency. He has traveled widely throughout Europe and is the author of many books and articles on European government. FRANCE, UNITED KINGDOM.

Donald Barry is professor of Government at Lehigh University in Bethlehem, Pa. He received his Ph.D. from Syracuse University. He is co-author of *Contemporary Soviet Politics,* (Englewood Cliffs, N.J.: Prentice-Hall, 1982). SOVIET UNION.

Judy Barsalou is assistant program officer in the Developing Countries Programs of The Ford Foundation. A doctoral candidate at Columbia University, she specializes in Middle East comparative politics and has written articles on agriculture and land reform in that area. LEBANON, SYRIA.

Michael Bernhard is a Ph.D. candidate in Political Science at Columbia University. He received his M.A. in Russian and East European Studies from Yale University. POLAND.

Robert E. Biles is professor of Political Science at Sam Houston State University in Huntsville, Texas. He received his Ph.D. from The Johns Hopkins University School of Advanced International Studies. His research and publications have concentrated on the issue of political participation in Latin America. COLOMBIA.

Jan Knippers Black is professor of Public Administration and lecturer in Political Science at the University of New Mexico in Albuquerque. She received her Ph.D. in International Relations from American University in Washington, D.C. She is the author, co-author, or editor of more than twenty books on Latin American affairs and U.S. foreign policy. PORTUGAL, SPAIN.

John A. Booth is associate professor of Political Science (Latin America) at the University of Texas in San Antonio. He received his Ph.D. from the University of Texas at Austin. He is the co-editor of *Political Participation in Latin America,* 2 vols. (New York: Holmes and Meier, 1978, 1979) and author of *The End and the Beginning: The Nicaraguan Revolution* (Boulder, Colo.: Westview Press, 1982). NICARAGUA.

Marcia M. Burdette is assistant professor of Political Science and Economy at Fordham University in New York City. She received her Ph.D. from Columbia University, and has taught at the University of Zambia. She is the author of "Zambian Foreign Policy" in *The Political Economy of African Foreign Policies,* Tim Shaw, ed. (Farnborough, Hants, England: Gower Publishing, forthcoming). ZAMBIA.

Thomas M. Callaghy is professor of Political Science at Columbia University. He received his Ph.D. from the University of California and specializes in comparative and African politics. He has authored several articles and books on Zaire. ZAIRE.

Louis Cantori is associate professor and department chairman of Political Science at the University of Maryland, Baltimore County. He received his Ph.D. from the University of Chicago and has traveled throughout the Middle East and North Africa. He is co-editor of *Local Politics and Development in the Middle East* (Boulder, Colo.: Westview Press, 1982) and editor of *Comparative Political Systems* (London: Holbrook & Allyn-Bacon, 1974.). EGYPT.

Ronald H. Chilcote is professor of Political Science at the University of California, Riverside. He was the founder and since 1974 has been the editor of *Latin American Perspectives,* a quarterly. He is also the author of *Theories of Comparative Politics* (Boulder, Colo.: Westview Press, 1981) and of *The Brazilian Communist Party: Conflict and Integration, 1922-72* (Oxford: Oxford University Press, 1974). BRAZIL.

Jeanne Marie Col is associate professor in Public Administration with the Illinois Legislature Studies Center and Public Administration Program at Sangamon State University in Springfield, Illinois. She received her Ph.D. in Political Science from the University of South Carolina. A specialist in economic development administration in Africa, she is the author of *Uganda: A Profile of National Integration,* (Boulder, Colo.: Westview Press, 1982). UGANDA.

Richard Collings is chairman of the Department of Political Science at Southeast Missouri State University at Cape Girardeau. He received his Ph.D. from Tulane University and specializes in Uruguayan and Peruvian politics as well as Latin American international relations. URUGUAY.

Lucie Gallistel Colvin is associate professor in African American Studies at the University of Maryland, Baltimore County. She received her Ph.D. from Columbia University. A specialist in francophone African social and economic history, she is the author of the *Historical Dictionary of Senegal* (Metuchen, N.J.: Scarecrow Press, 1981) and of *The Uprooted of the Western Sahel: Migrants Quest for Cash in the Senegambia* (New York, Praeger, 1981). SENEGAL, SENEGAMBIA.

Jill Crystal is a doctoral candidate at Harvard University, where she also received her M.A. She has traveled throughout the Middle East and lived in Egypt and Saudi Arabia. KUWAIT.

Richard Dale is associate professor of Political Science at Southern Illinois University at Carbondale. He received his Ph.D. from Princeton University. His specialities are comparative, African, and civil-military politics and African international politics. He is the co-editor of *Southern Africa in Perspective: Essays in Regional Politics* (New York: The Free Press, 1972) and a member of the Council of the South African Institute of Race Relations. NAMIBIA.

Peter Dawson is lecturer in Political Science and Public Administration at the London School of Economics and Political Science. He received his M.A. from Cambridge University. A specialist in government and administration in Third World states, he has traveled widely in Southeast Asia, West Africa, and Latin America. MALAYSIA.

Juan Manuel del Aguila is assistant professor of Political Science at Emory University. He received his Ph.D. from the University of North Carolina and is the author of "Cuban Foreign Policy in the Caribbean and Central America," in *Latin American Foreign Policies,* E. Ferris and J. Lincoln, eds. (Boulder, Colo.: Westview Press, 1981). CUBA.

Mark W. DeLancey is associate professor of African Politics at the University of South Carolina. He received his Ph.D. from Indiana University and is a specialist in comparative and African politics. He has lived in west Africa for extended periods and has written extensively on Cameroon and Nigerian politics. CAMEROON.

George E. Delury is an editor and writer of reference materials in politics and economics. He received his doctoral education in Modern European History at Stanford University. He has been editor of *Deadline Data on World Affairs* (1969-72) and *The World Almanac* (1972-80). ALBANIA, BHUTAN, BRUNEI, CHANNEL ISLANDS, ISLE OF MAN, PAPUA NEW GUINEA.

David W. Dent is associate professor of Political Science at Towson State University in Baltimore. He received his Ph.D. from the University of Minnesota. A specialist in the comparative politics of Latin America, he is the co-editor of the *Handbook of Latin American Studies* (Austin: University of Texas, semi-annual). VENEZUELA.

Henry A. Dietz is associate professor of Government at the University of Texas in Austin. He received his Ph.D. from Stanford University. He was a Peace Corps volunteer in Peru from 1964 to 1966 and has since concentrated on Latin American comparative politics, with particular interest in civil-military relations and the voting behavior of the urban poor. He is the author of numerous books and articles on Peru and other Latin American topics. PERU.

Kanak Mani Dixit is a doctoral candidate in Political Science at Columbia University, where he also received his M.A. A graduate of New Delhi University in India, he taught Jurisprudence and International Law at Tribhuvan University in Katmandu, Nepal, for two years. NEPAL.

Timothy Dunmore is lecturer in Comparative Government at the University of Essex in Colchester, England, where he received his Ph.D. in Soviet Politics. He is a specialist in Soviet and African politics and is the author of *The Stalinist Command Economy* (London: Macmillan, 1981). ETHIOPIA, MALAWI, ZIMBABWE.

David B. Edwards is a journalist and a doctoral candidate in Anthropology at the University of Michigan. A specialist in refugee settlement and ethnicity, he has lived in Afghanistan for eighteen months and traveled extensively in the Middle East, North Africa, and South Asia. AFGHANISTAN.

Neil C.M. Elder is senior lecturer in Politics at the University of Hull, North Humberside, England. He received his education at Oxford University. A specialist in Swedish politics he is the

author of numerous books and articles on that topic, and co-author of *The Consensual Democracies? The Government and Politics of the Scandinavian States* (London: Oxford University Press, 1982). SWEDEN.

Nadine Epstein is a doctoral candidate at Columbia University, specializing in politics and development problems in the Third World, particularly east Africa. TANZANIA.

Martin Farrell is associate professor of Politics and Government and chairman of that department at Ripon College in Wisconsin. He received his Ph.D. in Political Science from the University of Chicago. A specialist in comparative politics and political philosophy, he has written several articles on Eurocommunism and on fascism in Finland. FINLAND.

Lois F. Fenichell is a writer and teacher specializing in policies toward indigenous peoples in the United States and elsewhere. She received her Ph.D. from Columbia University and is the author of numerous articles in ethnic history. NEW ZEALAND.

Elizabeth Ferris is assistant professor of Government at Lafayette College in Easton, Pa. She received her Ph.D. from the University of Florida and specializes in the foreign policies and governments of the Andean countries. She is the editor of several books and numerous articles on Latin America. BOLIVIA, CHILE.

Charles R. Foster is executive secretary of the Committee on Atlantic Studies in Washington, D.C. A specialist on microstates and ethnic minorities, he is the editor of *Nations Without States: Ethnic Minorities in Western Europe* (New York: Praeger, 1980). ANDORRA, FIJI, KIRIBATI, LIECHTENSTEIN, MALTA, MONACO, NAURU, SOLOMONS, TONGA, TUVALU, VANUATU, WESTERN SAMOA.

Norman Frankel is assistant professor and government documents librarian at Western Michigan University in Kalamazoo. He holds three M.A.'s (Political Science, Humanities, Library Science) from the State University of New York at Buffalo. He is a specialist in political science bibliography and in studies of terrorism, and was a guest lecturer at Queens University in Belfast in 1981. NORTHERN IRELAND.

Emil Freund is a doctoral candidate and research assistant at Columbia University's Institute on East Central Europe where he received his M.A. in Eastern European Politics. He is the author of "Nascent Dissent in Romania," in *Dissent in Eastern Europe,* Jane Curry, ed. (New York: Praeger, forthcoming). HUNGARY.

Albert L. Gastmann is professor of Political Science at Trinity College, Hartford, Conn. He received his Ph.D. at Columbia University in Political Science. A specialist in international law and Caribbean and comparative politics, he has authored several books and articles on Caribbean nations. SURINAME.

Valerie J. Griffith is a specialist in the art and culture of northwest Africa and has been a consultant to U.S. and African organizations in both cultural and political affairs. MALI, MAURITANIA.

Terrie R. Groth is a doctoral candidate in Political Science at the University of California, Riverside. He is an associate of *Latin American Perspectives,* a journal, and a recipient of a fellowship from the Organizations of American States. While writing the article, he was in Brazil doing research on the *abertura* to democracy. BRAZIL.

Olafur Th. Hardarson is lecturer in Political Science at the University of Iceland. He earned his M.Sc. in Political Sociology from the London School of Economics and Political Science. His areas of speciality are electoral behavior, party systems, and Icelandic politics. ICELAND.

Sally Healy is a doctoral candidate at the London School of Economics and Political Science, from which she received her M.Sc. in International Politics. Her speciality is the process of state formation in the Horn of Africa. DJIBOUTI, SOMALIA.

Shephen Heder is a doctoral candidate at Cornell University. An expert on Cambodian politics, he lived in Cambodia from 1973 to 1975, lived on the Cambodian border with Thailand during 1979-81, and visited the Cambodian capital in 1980 and 1981. KAMPUCHEA.

Joseph M. Hiatt earned his Ph.D. from the University of Pennsylvania in Social Anthropology, with particular emphasis on the Middle East. He spent two years in Jordan (1978-79) studying Bedouin social life and the trend toward sedentarization. JORDAN.

H. Monte Hill is assistant professor of Political Science at the University of North Carolina at Pembroke State University. He earned his Ph.D. from Northern Illinois University at DeKalb. He has written and lectured extensively on Philippine and other Southeast Asian subjects. LAOS, PHILIPPINES.

Tony Hodges is a freelance journalist on African affairs. He received his B.A. from Oxford and has studied at the London University School of Oriental and African Studies. A specialist in lusophone Africa and the Western Sahara, he has published several books on those and other subjects and written extensively for the *Economist* Intelligence Unit, *The Financial Times, The Observer, Le Monde Diplomatique,* and *Africa Report.* CAPE VERDE, GUINEA-BISSAU, MOROCCO, SÃO TOMÉ & PRINCÍPE, and WESTERN SAHARA (SAHARAN ARAB DEMOCRATIC REPUBLIC).

Paul V. Hyer is professor of History at Brigham Young University. He received his Ph.D. in Asian History and Social Institutions from the University of California at Berkeley. He has traveled, studied, and taught in Taiwan, China, Japan, and Mongolia and has written many books and articles on East Asian subjects. MONGOLIA.

Indira Jhappan has worked with several organizations which specialize in Caribbean affairs. She earned her M.A. in International Affairs from the School of Advanced International Studies of The Johns Hopkins University. BAHAMAS, BARBADOS, BELIZE, DOMINICA, GRENADA, JAMAICA, ST. LUCIA, ST. VINCENT, and TRINIDAD and TOBAGO.

M. Glen Johnson is professor of Political Science at Vassar College. He received his Ph.D. in Political Science from the University of North Carolina. He is the author (with Howard Bliss) of *Beyond the Water's Edge: America's Foreign Policies* (New York: Harper & Row, 1975) and has written several articles on Indian politics. He has traveled extensively throughout India and was Fulbright Visiting Professor at the University of Poona in 1978-79. INDIA.

Owen V. Johnson is assistant professor of Journalism at Indiana University. He received his Ph.D. in Eastern European History from the University of Michigan. A specialist in Eastern European media, he has published several articles on Czechoslovak education and the intelligentsia and has traveled widely in that country. CZECHOSLOVAKIA.

Isola O. Kokumo is visiting lecturer in African Studies at Rutgers University and a Ph.D. candidate in Political Science at Columbia University, where he also received his M.A. A resident of Lagos, Nigeria, he is the founder of the U.S. branch of the Unity Party of Nigeria. NIGERIA.

Michel S. Laguerre is assistant professor of Caribbean Anthropology at the University of California at Berkeley. He received his Ph.D. from the University of Illinois at Urbana in Social Anthropology. He is the author of several books and articles on the Caribbean and Haiti. HAITI.

Fred H. Lawson is assistant professor in the Department of Government at Smith College. He received his Ph.D. from the University of California at Los Angeles in International Relations. A specialist in Middle Eastern politics, he has traveled and studied in the region. BAHRAIN, QATAR, UNITED ARAB EMIRATES.

Keith Legg is professor of Political Science at the University of Florida. He received his Ph.D. from the University of California. He is the author of *Politics in Modern Greece* (Stanford University Press, 1969) and of *Patrons, Clients, and Politicians* (Institute of International Studies, University of California, Berkeley, 1975). GREECE.

René Lemarchand is professor of Political Science at the University of Florida at Gainesville. He received his Ph.D. from the University of California at Los Angeles. He has specialized in rural development issues, political violence, and political clientelism in Africa and is the author of numerous articles and books on those topics. CHAD.

R. William Liddle is professor of Political Science at Ohio State University. He received his Ph.D. from Yale University. He has traveled extensively in Indonesia and is the author of *Ethnicity, Party,* and *National Integration: An Indonesian Case Study* (Yale University Press, 1970), as well as several articles on Indonesia. INDONESIA.

Maleeha Lodhi is lecturer in Political Sociology at the London School of Economics and Political Science where she received her Ph.D. A specialist in South Asian politics, she is the author of several articles on India and Pakistan and of a forthcoming book on Pakistani politics during the Bhutto era. BANGLADESH.

Scott MacDonald is a doctoral candidate in Political Science at the University of Connecticut. He received his M.A. from the University of London's School of Oriental and African Studies. He is a specialist in the economic and political development of the Caribbean. ANTIGUA AND BARBUDA, SURINAME.

John T.S. Madeley is lecturer in Government at the London School of Economics and Political Science and a doctoral candidate at the University of Glasgow. A specialist in Scandinavian politics, he is the author of several articles in that field. NORWAY.

Paul J. Magnarella is professor of Anthropology at the University of Florida. He received his Ph.D. in Anthropology and Middle East Studies from Harvard University. A specialist in political anthropology and modernization in the Middle East, he is the author of *Tradition and Change in a Turkish Town* (Cambridge, Mass: Schenkman, 1974, 1982) and of *The Peasant Venture* (ibid., 1979). TURKEY.

Robert H. Manley is professor of Political Science at Seton Hall University in South Orange, N.J. He received his Ph.D. in Political Science from the State University of New York in Albany. A specialist in international public policy and international law as well as in Third World development, he is the author of *Guyana Emergent: The Post-Independence Struggle for Non-Dependent Development* (Boston: G.K. Hall, 1979, and Cambridge: Mass., Schenkman, 1982, rev. ed.) GUYANA.

Stephen C. Markovich is professor of Political Science at the University of North Dakota. He received his Ph.D. in Government from the University of Virginia. He specializes in comparative Communist systems and international relations and has written several articles on those topics. YUGOSLAVIA.

Steven Metz is instructor in Political Science at Towson State University in Baltimore, Md., and a doctoral candidate at The Johns Hopkins University. He is a specialist in the politics of west Africa and in U.S. policy in Africa. GABON, GAMBIA, GUINEA, IVORY COAST, SIERRA LEONE, TOGO.

Miltos C. Miltiadou is a doctoral candidate in International Relations at The Johns Hopkins University School of Advanced International Studies in Washington, D.C. His doctoral thesis is entitled *The International Dimensions of the Cyprus Conflict.* CYPRUS.

Waltraud Queiser Morales is assistant professor of Comparative and International Studies at the University of Central Florida in Orlando. She received her Ph.D. from the University of Denver Graduate School of International Studies. A specialist in Latin American, particularly Andean, politics, she is the author of several articles in that field. PANAMA.

David Morell has been research political scientist and lecturer in Politics at Princeton University where he also received his Ph.D. A specialist in the politics of Thailand and military rule, he is the author of numerous articles and books on those subjects, including *Political Conflict in Thailand* (Cambridge, Mass: Oelgeshlager, Gunn & Hain, 1982). THAILAND.

Anne Nelson reports on Caribbean and Central American affairs for *MacLean's* magazine and has published articles in the *Los Angeles Times, Newsday,* and *Nation.* Her work has also been broadcast by the Canadian Broadcasting Company and by National Public Radio. COSTA RICA, EL SALVADOR, GUATEMALA.

Thomas J. Nossiter is senior lecturer in Government at the London School of Economics and Political Science. He received his Ph.D. in Modern History from Oxford University. A specialist in South Asian and international affairs, he has traveled extensively throughout the area and written many books and articles in that field. SRI LANKA.

Thomas P. Ofcansky is wing historian of the 436th Military Airlift Wing and has been a lecturer in History at the University of West Virginia where he received his Ph.D. in African History. A specialist in east Africa environmental and medical issues, he is the author of several articles on those topics. BURUNDI, KENYA, RWANDA.

Cornelius O'Leary is professor of Political Science at The Queen's University in Belfast, Northern Ireland. He received his Ph.D. from Oxford University and has specialized in the electoral history of the United Kingdom and the Irish Republic. He is the author of *Irish Elections 1918-1977* (Dublin: Gill and Macmillan, 1979) and other books. IRELAND.

Thomas O'Toole is the program director of Studies in International Development at the University of Minnesota in Minneapolis. He received his Doctor of Arts degree in African History from Carnegie-Mellon University. He is a specialist in development issues in francophone Africa, has traveled widely in that area, and has written several books in the field. CENTRAL AFRICAN REPUBLIC.

Andrew Parkin is senior lecturer in Politics at Flinders University of South Australia. He received his Ph.D. in Government from Harvard University. His specialities are urban politics, public policy, and Australian politics, and he is the author or editor of several books on those subjects. AUSTRALIA.

Jack Parson is assistant professor of Political Science at The College of Charleston in South Carolina. He received his Ph.D. in Comparative Politics from the University of Sussex in England. A specialist in eastern and southern Africa, he has traveled and lived in the area and is the author of several articles and a book on southern African politics. BOTSWANA, LESOTHO, SWAZILAND.

William D. Pederson is assistant professor and Political Science coordinator at Louisiana State University in Shreveport. He received his Ph.D. in Political Science from the University of Oregon. He has specialized in presidential behavior and public justice systems in the Soviet Union and East Europe. Research for his article in this volume was done under a grant for the Summer Research Lab at the Russian and East European Center of the University of Illinois at Urbana. EAST GERMANY.

Daniel Pipes is a research associate in the Department of History at the University of Chicago. He received his Ph.D. in History from Harvard University. He has traveled widely in the Middle East, including Saudi Arabia, and is the author of *Islam and Modern Politics* (New York: Basic Books, 1983). SAUDI ARABIA.

D. Sterett Pope is a doctoral candidate in Political Science at Harvard University. He has traveled in North Africa and the Arabian Peninsula and lived in Tunisia and Egypt. OMAN, TUNISIA, YEMEN ARAB REPUBLIC, PEOPLES DEMOCRATIC REPUB-

LIC OF YEMEN.

Lawrence Potter is a doctoral candidate in Middle East History at Columbia University. He has traveled extensively in the Middle East and lived in Iran for several years. His doctoral dissertation deals with state/religion relationships in medieval Persia. IRAN.

Dennis Quinn is a doctoral candidate in Political Science at Columbia University. A specialist in the relations between government and heavy industry, his doctoral dissertation will study the role of the U.S. and Canadian governments in the support of a major automotive company. CANADA.

Michael Radu is a research associate at the Foreign Policy Research Institute in Philadelphia. He received his Ph.D. in International Relations from Columbia University and his M.A. from the Universtiy of Cluj in Romania. He is the editor of *Eastern Europe and the Third World* (New York: Praeger, 1981). ANGOLA, BENIN, CONGO, MOZAMBIQUE, ROMANIA.

Bernard Reich is professor of Political Science and International Relations at George Washington University. He received his Ph.D. in Foreign Affairs from the University of Virginia. A specialist in Middle East politics and foreign relations, he is the author or editor of many books and articles on those subjects, U.S. Middle East policy, and the Arab-Israeli conflict. ISRAEL.

Hewson A. Ryan is Edward R. Murrow Professor of Public Diplomacy and director of the Murrow Center at the Fletcher School of Law and Diplomacy at Tufts University. He received his Ph.D. from the University of Madrid. He spent twenty-six years in the U.S. Foreign Service and has been Ambassador to Honduras and deputy director of the U.S. Information Agency. HONDURAS.

Ronald Bruce St John is associated with the institute of International Studies at Bradley University in Peoria, Illinois. He received his Ph.D. in International Relations from the University of Denver. He traveled and worked in Libya for four years during the present regime and has written many articles on international affairs, including several on Libya. LIBYA.

David W. Schodt is professor of Economics at St. Olaf College in Northfield, Minn. He received his Ph.D. in Economics from the University of Wisconsin. A specialist in public finance and the political economy of development, he lived for several years in Ecuador and has lectured widely on Latin American topics. ECUADOR.

Charles F. Schuetz is assistant professor of Political Science at Carleton University in Ottawa, Canada, where he also received his Ph.D. His speciality is comparative federalism. SWITZERLAND.

Donald M. Seekins is associate research scientist in the Asia Division of the Foreign Area Studies Group at The American University. He received his Ph.D. in Political Science from the University of Chicago. A specialist in political philosophy and East Asian comparative politics, he is the author of portions of several of American University's country studies. BURMA, CHINA, HONG KONG, NORTH KOREA, SOUTH KOREA, SINGAPORE.

Reeva S. Simon received her Ph.D. in History (Middle East) from Columbia University. She is the author of *The Modern Middle East: A Guide to Research Tools in the Social Sciences* (Boulder, Colo.: Westview Press, 1978). IRAQ.

Hazel Sirett is assistant editor of the *Human Rights Internet Reporter* in Washington, D.C. and was an assistant in the Latin American Research Department of Amnesty International in London, where she specialized in Argentina, Mexico, and Brazil. ARGENTINA.

Martin Slater is lecturer in the Department of Government of the University of Essex in England. He received his Ph.D. in Political Science from the Massachusetts Institute of Technology. He is the author of several articles on West European comparative politics, integration, and migration. ITALY, SAN MARINO,

VATICAN CITY.

Joseph P. Smaldone is chief of the Arms Licensing Division in the Office of Munitions Control, U.S. State Department, and adjunct professor at the University of Maryland and Georgetown University. He received his Ph.D. in African Studies at Northwestern University and is the author of several books and numerous articles in that field. LIBERIA, SUDAN. (The views and conclusions contained in Dr. Smaldone's contributions are those of the author and do not necessarily represent those of the U.S. State Department or the U.S. government.)

Gordon Smith is a reader in Government at the London School of Economics and Political Science. He received his Ph.D. in German Politics from the University of London. A specialist in European party systems, he is the author of books on that subject and is co-editor of the quarterly journal *West European Politics.* BELGIUM, WEST GERMANY, LUXEMBOURG, NETHERLANDS.

Vladimir Socor received his Ph.D. in Eastern European Affairs from Columbia University and is the author of numerous articles on that topic and on Soviet foreign policy. He is presently with the Broadcast Analysis Division of Radio Free Europe in Munich, West Germany. BULGARIA.

David E. Spiro is a doctoral candidate in International Political Economy and Middle Eastern Politics at Princeton University. He has traveled widely in North and west Africa. ALGERIA.

Melanie Ann Sully is senior lecturer in History at North Staffordshire Polytechnic in Stafford, England. She received her Ph.D. from the University of Keele and is the author of several books and articles on Austrian politics, including *Political Parties and Elections in Austria* (London: Hurst, 1981). AUSTRIA.

Alastair H. Thomas is head of the Division of Political Science at Preston Polytechnic in England. A specialist in Scandinavian comparative politics, he is co-author of *The Consensual Democracies? The Government and Politics of the Scandinavian States* (London: Oxford University Press, 1982). DENMARK.

Dayna M. Tolley received her M.A. in Political Science and African Studies from the University of Indiana and was assistant project manager of Nigerian Projects of the State Legislative Leaders Foundation in Denver, Colo. She has traveled widely in west Africa. GHANA.

William S. Turley is associate professor of Political Science at Southern Illinois University in Carbondale. He received his Ph.D. from the University of Washington in Seattle. He is the editor of a book and author of several articles on his speciality, Vietnamese Communism. He taught at Saigon University in 1972-73. VIETNAM.

Richard Vengroff is director of the Center for Applied International Development Studies and professor of Political Science at Texas Technical University in Lubbock. He received his Ph.D. in Political Science from the Maxwell School of Syracuse University. A specialist in African politics and rural development, he has traveled widely in south and west Africa and written several books and many articles on those areas. NIGER, UPPER VOLTA.

Kal Wagenheim is a journalist and author who specializes in Puerto Rican topics. He is the author of *Puerto Rico: A Profile* and *The Puerto Ricans: a Documentary Profile* (both New York: Praeger, 1975 and 1973, respectively) as well as many newspaper and magazine articles on the subject. PUERTO RICO.

Martin E. Weinstein is associate professor of Political Science at the University of Illinois in Urbana. He received his Ph.D. in International Politics and Japanese Studies at Columbia University. He has lived six years in Japan and is the author of several books and numerous articles on Japanese foreign and defense policy and U.S.-Japanese relations. JAPAN.

Graham K. Wilson is lecturer in Government at the University of Essex in England. He received his Ph.D. in British and American Politics from Oxford University. He is the author of *Interest Groups in the United States* (London: Oxford University Press, 1981), *Unions in American National Politics* (New York: Macmillan, 1979), and other writings. He has twice been Visiting Associate Professor at the University of Wisconsin. UNITED STATES.

N. Brian Winchester is assistant director of African Studies at Indiana University where he received his Ph.D. in Political Science. He is the author of several articles on African political issues, particularly those of southern Africa. SOUTH AFRICA.

Lawrence Ziring is director of the Institute of Government and Politics and professor of Political Science at Western Michigan University in Kalamazoo. He received his Ph.D. from Columbia University. A specialist in South Asian and Middle Eastern foreign and comparative politics, he is the author of several books on these topics. PAKISTAN.

INTRODUCTION

The study of politics is a study of conflict. Whenever a few people gather to decide on common aims and means, some degree of conflict appears. Individual ambitions, more or less incompatible social and economic interests, and ideals that are often mutually exclusive compete for the resources of the group. When confined to a small institution—a church, a fraternal order, a business—the means by which such conflict can be pursued are limited and the potential gains and losses are relatively small. When the conduct of a sovereign state is at issue, however, the potential gains in wealth, prestige, and economic and physical power can be immense and the potential losses proportionately severe. Furthermore, the full resources of the state and society can be brought to bear on the conflict—money, people, institutions, and if necessary, weapons. National politics is a serious business, often deadly serious.

The business of politics is conducted within a system of interacting elements which include the state and its government with executive, legislative, and judicial functions and customary and/or written rules of procedure; a variety of social and economic interests which may or may not express themselves through political parties; and processes through which political parties or interests bring their influence to bear on the government. This encyclopedia describes these elements of the political systems of 169 sovereign nations and eight dependent territories in a relatively narrow cross-section of time, roughly the summer and fall of 1982.

The standard format of an article begins with an introductory section that provides a basic description of the institutions of government along with the historical background necessary to understand the present political arrangement in the country. This section looks first at the executive functions, the formal locus of policy- and decision-making power in the country. It then outlines the structure and powers of the legislature or any similar body that purports to represent at least some of the population, and that discusses, debates, and approves new laws. The judiciary is examined with particular concern for its independence from political pressures or control and its relative power vis-a-vis the other branches of government. Finally, this section briefly describes regional and local structures of government and tries to assess the degree of local autonomy and political-party activity.

The next section takes up the electoral system. It notes the extent of suffrage, registration and balloting procedures, whether voting is compulsory, and the level of voter turnout for elections. It describes how the country is geographically organized for elections and usually assesses the relative fairness and honesty of elections. Most importantly, this section describes the way in which election winners are determined in the state under consideration; this is important, for there are several systems, which differ markedly from one another. Proportional representation systems, which are used in many countries, require a special explanation.

The simple plurality system now used in most English-speaking countries met with serious objections on the European continent when the suffrage was expanded to include the vast mass of working people who tended to vote socialist. The traditional parties were faced with the possibility that socialist parties could consistently win large parliamentary majorities, even if they did not win a majority of the votes nationwide. It was also noted that a small party which represented an important but scattered minority in the country could be closed out of the legislative process altogether.

To overcome these objections, proportional representation (PR) systems were introduced, beginning with Denmark in 1855. After considerable debate over what constituted a fair system, Victor d'Hondt in 1878 devised a method that is still in common use, although with many variations. At its simplest, the d'Hondt method works as follows. Assume that three parties are competing for nine legislative seats in a multimember district. Voters, who in PR systems usually vote for party lists of candidates rather than for individuals, give Party A 10,000 votes; Party B, 7,000; and Party C, 3,000. The first seat goes to Party A, and its vote is divided by 2. Each time Party A wins another seat, its total vote is divided by the next highest number—2, 3, 4 and so on. In some countries the process ends there, but in others leftover votes (1,750

	Party A		Party B		Party C	
Seat 1	10,000	(50%)	7,000	(35%)	3,000	(15%)
Seat 2	÷ 2	5,000		7,000		3,000
Seat 3		5,000	÷ 2	3,500		3,000
Seat 4	÷ 3	3,333		3,500		3,000
Seat 5		3,333	÷ 3	2,333		3,000
Seat 6	÷ 4	2,500		2,333		3,000
Seat 7		2,500		2,333	÷ 2	1,500
Seat 8	÷ 5	2,000		2,333		1,500
Seat 9		2,000	÷ 4	1,750		1,500
	5 seats (55%)		3 seats (33%)		1 seat (12%)	

for party B for example) are pooled at the national level and additional seats are distributed by the same process.

The d'Hondt system tends to favor larger parties at the expense of small ones and can still elect a government that is not supported by a plurality of the voters. To overcome these problems, a variation called the Sainte-Laguë method (developed in 1910) was introduced. The essential difference between the systems is that the Sainte-Laguë method divides the party's total vote by 3, 5, 7 and so on. This makes it progressively harder for a large party to win each successive seat and reduces the advantages of electoral alliances, which in turn discourages the formation of very small parties. The three Scandanavian countries adopted the Sainte-Laguë method, with variations, in the early 1950s.

Another PR system, used in some English-speaking countries, is called the single transferable vote (STV). The STV method requires the setting of a quota—the number of votes needed to win a seat in a multimember district. Sometimes the simple formula—votes divided by number of seats—is used to determine the quota. Most STV systems, however, use "Droop's quota," devised in 1868, which employs the formula $(V \div [S + 1]) + 1$, where V is the total vote and S the number of seats to be distributed. If for example, the total vote was 10,000 in a race for four seats, a candidate would need 2,001 votes to win a seat. If a candidate gets 5,000 votes, the STV method distributes all the second-preference votes on those ballots to their respective recipients on the basis of the following formula: $(V - Q) \div V$, where V is the total vote for the winning candidate and Q is the quota. (In the example: $(5,000 - 2,001) \div 5,000 = 60$ percent.) If a candidate got 1,000 second-preference votes on the winning candidate's ballots, for example, 600 votes would be added to

his first-preference votes. The advantage of this system is that it allows the voters to vote for individuals and makes nearly every vote count. A variation on the STV system counts second-preference votes only if the voter's first preference fails to get enough votes to get elected.

Articles on countries with multiparty systems turn next to a general description of the system—when and how the parties originated, how they are supported or restricted by law, and their common elements of organization or lack of it. This section then briefly describes the general tone and methods of election campaigns in the country; it ends, where appropriate, with a look at the issue of voter loyalty to or independence of parties.

Each major party is then described in terms of its history, organization, policy, membership and electoral support, financing, leadership, and its prospects for remaining in government or gaining power. The major parties in some of the smaller countries are not treated in quite this detail, not only because of lack of space, but also because reliable information was simply not to be found. Even for major and thoroughly studied countries, there is often little or no information on either the sources of funds or the expenditures of political parties. Over most of the world, party financing, the life's blood of politics, is as much of a mystery to political scientists as the circulatory system was to the medical profession in the sixteenth century.

Reasonably reliable membership figures are also unavailable in many cases. Where such numbers are thought to indicate its basic strength, a party will often inflate them or keep them secret. In other countries, while some or all parties purport to have formal memberships, the rules of enrollment and dues-paying are laxly enforced and no accurate counts of members are made. In most one-party states, membership means little or nothing politically; it is simply a means of career advancement.

Following the description of the party in a one-party state, the next section of the article is found only where significant opposition is known to exist either in the country or in exile. Opposition here does not refer to scattered individuals or small groups of like-minded acquaintances—that phenomenon is better labelled dissent. Opposition, in this context, refers to more or less formally organized groups bent either on resisting the power of the one-party state and/or on radically altering the form of government or its leadership.

In many countries, major political roles are played by institutions or social groups that are not primarily political but which have considerable influence in the political system. Chief among these *other political forces* are the armed forces, which dominate the political process in many countries. Other such political forces are organized labor, religious institutions, ethnic groups, students, and occasionally foreign governments, international organizations, and even individuals. Each of these groups, where appropriate, is identified, and some indication of their role is provided.

Finally, each article briefly summarizes the nation's prospects for continuing or attaining political stability through the mid-1980s. These opinions must necessarily be speculative and can only extrapolate from known political facts. The sudden death of a commanding political figure, the rapid rise of a hitherto little-recognized political group (such as the Iranian clergy), and unforeseen catastrophe—economic, physical, military—can play no role in such predictions.

The length of the articles is determined more by the importance of the country than by the complexity of its political system. If the complex roles of all elements in a country's political system were clearly understood, two volumes of this size would scarcely suffice to deal with it fully.

Because of this complexity and our incomplete understanding, the classification of systems as authoritarian, democratic, multiparty, etc., while useful, must always be regarded critically. The reader is advised to study an article thoroughly before accepting a classification as anything other than a rough indicator of political appearances. A nation with parties and elections is not necessarily a democracy (e.g., Paraguay), nor is a country without those institutions necessarily a dictatorship (e.g., Somalia, Jordan).

Nevertheless, after examining these articles, I have concluded that there are four broad categories in which political systems might be placed more or less accurately. These categories refer not to the political systems themselves, but to the common attitudes and expectations—the political ethos—in which these systems function. The four categories can be called "no losers," "winner-take-all," "winner-took-all," and "single arbiter."

Perhaps a third of the world's countries have a "no losers" political ethos. Political conflict is channeled into more or less open and effective policy debates and relatively fair electoral processes. Every interested group can bring some degree of influence to bear on the government. Political actors find that it is in their own best interests to pursue moderate aims and to avoid any abuse of power that would seriously threaten the opposition. No single group seeks massive gains, and none faces massive losses. Generally, there is a widespread and deep respect for civil and human rights and for the rule of law. A key element in maintaining a "no losers" ethos is an economic prosperity—or its promise—sufficient to satisfy popular expectations, which can vary from pathetically low to unreasonably high.

The "winner-take-all" political ethos is more common than "no losers." It is found largely, but not exclusively, in countries numbered among the less economically developed. In this ethos, each contending political force more or less reasonably sees any loss of political or economic power as a threat to its continued existence. Conversely, any gain may be used to further limit or destroy the power of opposing forces. Such systems face the continuing possibility of severe civil strife between ethnic groups (Northern Ireland, South Africa, Nigeria), or classes (El Salvador, Iran), or ideologies (Poland, Chile), or between urban and rural interests (Philippines, Afghanistan). Usually, more than one of these divisive elements are factors in the conflict. Often such conflicts are made virtually unresolvable by religious or ideological dogmas that make the destruction of the opposition a virtuous act. A commonplace solution to the threat of civil strife is the imposition of some form of dictatorial rule by the military, a preeminent political leader, an elite, or even by an outside force. Many states that appear to have developed a "winner-took-all" ethos (some of the "Marxist" states in Africa, for example) are in reality relatively superficial impositions of military or elite power on a political ethos in which the contending forces would otherwise destroy the country.

About 10 percent of the world's nations seem to fit the "winner-took-all" category, in which there are no apparent bases for major civil conflict, because potential opposition has been destroyed in an earlier "winner-take-all" struggle. Stable, post-revolutionary regimes—the Soviet Union, Cuba, Vietnam—are clear examples.

Finally, the "single arbiter" ethos refers to those societies which accept the more or less benign rule of a traditional authority—a king or an emir—who is the final arbiter of any social conflict. The ruler usually seeks a balance between competing economic and social forces, few of which are threatened with political extinction. Some societies with apparently more "modern" regimes—Egypt, for example—might be seen as continuing the "single arbiter" ethos in a new guise.

When reading about the political system of any country, the reader should keep in mind that the political ethos in which the system functions may not be supportive of that system. Over much of the world, European government and party systems, both democratic and communistic, are often fragile and nearly irrelevant overlays on patterns of social power that are seldom clearly understood even by the participants. A professedly democratic system with regular and apparently open processes of political debate and resolution of conflict can be and often is an oligarchic system in which members of the elite only superficially represent the interests of the otherwise politically impotent groups. On the other hand, a system in which the "winner-took-all" can still retain or develop processes by which social interests effectively compete for influence (Hungary might be an example).

The contributors have demonstrated great commitment to the ideal of knowledge for its own sake. All showed a deep concern to make clear to the general reader the essential political elements operating in each country. Many submitted far more information and expended much greater time and energy on the project than the editor asked for. The editor thanks them heartily for their support, understanding, and patience.

Carol Simon, Muriel Bennet, Tina and A. La Russo, and the editorial staff of Facts on File, Inc., have also contributed to the success of this project. Most particularly, the encouragement and unrelenting demands of Ed Knappman have given this encyclopedia its extra measure of thoroughness.

George E. Delury
January 1983

DEMOCRATIC REPUBLIC OF AFGHANISTAN

(*Jamhuriat Democratek-E Afghanistan* [Dari]; *Afghanistan Democrateek Jamhuriat* [Pashto])

by David B. Edwards, M.A.

The System of Government

Afghanistan is a one-party communist state fighting a civil war against a dissident tribal population which refuses to recognize the government as legitimate. This situation has been a persistent one in Afghanistan. The tribes traditionally have been reluctant to relinquish their independence and accept the sovereignty of the government in Kabul. Regimes successful in exerting their authority, such as that of Amir Abdur Rahman in the late nineteenth century, maintained their position by manipulating tribal feuds and ethnic rivalries in order to divide their opposition. Governments which have been unsuccessful—notably the reform-minded administration of Amanullah Khan which ruled in the 1920s—failed because they attempted to exert too much control over the population.

Since the *coup d'état* of April 27, 1978, which placed the People's Democratic Party of Afghanistan (PDPA) in power, the authority of the state also has been eroded by factionalism within the party, unpopular reform programs, and defections in the military. Most importantly, the Afghan people have opposed the influence of the Soviet Union, which installed the current regime of Babrak Karmal on December 27, 1979, and which continues to oversee most activities of the government and armed forces.

The formal system of government in Afghanistan is outlined in "The Fundamental Principles of the Democratic Republic of Afghanistan," which is a provisional constitution promulgated on April 21, 1980. According to this document, final authority for establishing and executing state policy is invested in the Revolutionary Council and its executive committee, the Presidium. Both of these bodies are presided over by a president who serves for an indefinite term of office. Executive power is vested primarily in the Council of Ministers whose members are responsible to the Revolutionary Council. The third principal element in the Afghan political system is the Central Committee of the PDPA and its executive Politburo. Although its exact role is not spelled out in the constitution, the party has a major voice in establishing policy directives and in carrying out social and economic programs through its local party cadres. In addition, the PDPA directs the activities of the National Fatherland Front, which was founded in June 1981 to mobilize popular support for the government and its Soviet sponsors.

Executive

According to the constitution, the Revolutionary Council is "the highest organ of state power" until the election of a national assembly (*Loya Jirgah*). Since such an assembly has not been convened and elections are unlikely in the current circumstances, the Revolutionary Council remains the ultimate authority in the political system.

The Revolutionary Council meets in session every year in August and February; at all other times the business of the Council is conducted by the Presidium. The number of members of the Council and Presidium and their manner of selection are not fixed by the constitution; however, the first Revolutionary Council installed under Babrak Karmal had fifty-eight members, seven of whom also served on the Presidium. The membership of both bodies has fluctuated considerably since 1979. As of January 1982, the Presidium contained eleven members.

The Revolutionary Council and Presidium are presided over by the president, with one or more deputies and a secretary, all of whom are elected by the Council from among its members. As head of state, the president is also the commander of the armed forces and is charged with accepting the credentials of all foreign missions and with ratifying all laws and decrees approved by the Council and Presidium. President Karmal has followed the precedent set by past presidents—Hafizullah Amin and Nur Mohammad Taraki—of holding the principal party post of secretary general.

The general responsibilities of the Revolutionary Council include the ratification of legislation submitted by the Council of Ministers; the formation of governmental and judicial bodies; the approval of ministerial and judicial appointments; and the ratification or abrogation of all international agreements, treaties, and declarations of war. In addition, the Council determines the basic principles of government policy and approves all social and economic development programs. Between sessions of the Revolutionary Council, the Presidium assumes all of the aforementioned responsibilities while also fulfilling other administrative and ceremonial functions: setting dates for meetings of the Council; establishing jurisdictional boundaries within the system of provincial administration; granting decorations, titles, and military ranks; and announcing military emergencies and expeditions.

The Council of Ministers is "the supreme executive organ of state power" with the constitutional responsibility for implementing government policy. The Council is composed of a prime minister, two deputy prime ministers (each of whom has a ministerial portfolio), and the heads of the various government ministries, who are responsible for implementing the policy directives of the Revolutionary Council. As a body, the Council of Ministers is charged with establishing budgetary expenditures, submitting legislative proposals, and organizing the execution of development programs through the ministries under its control. Under the provisional constitution, the Council of Ministers is also responsible for han-

dling state security and for providing guidance in defense matters, although in both of these areas authority has been relinquished to the Soviet command, which dictates basic policy with respect to military and security matters.

Judiciary

The provisional constitution calls for the formation of an independent judiciary regulated by secular and religious (shari'ah) law and supervised by a supreme court which is authorized to "secure uniformity in the enforcement of law by the courts." Despite these assurances, however, the judicial system in Afghanistan remains a branch of the Revolutionary Council, which controls its activities and appoints its judges. The absence of an independent judiciary has been noted by organizations like Amnesty International which have protested the government's continuing practice of arbitrary arrest, imprisonment without trial, torture, and unlawful execution.

Regional & Local Government

Since 1964, Afghanistan has been divided into twenty-eight provinces (wilayat), each of which is subdivided into districts (woleswali) and subdistricts (alakadari). Governors are appointed for each province with subordinate administrators taking responsibility for the smaller jurisdictions. In addition, the provisional constitution authorizes the formation of provincial councils (jirgahs) to assist the government in implementing its programs and to handle local problems.

Although this system is apparently intact in most provinces of Afghanistan, the dissolution of a strong central power in Kabul has resulted in the assertion of regional autonomy, particularly in areas which are isolated from major roads and administrative centers. For example, Hazara tribesmen, who are part of an ethnic and religious minority group which has long been abused in Afghanistan, have taken advantage of the civil war to establish an independent government in the rugged mountains of central Hazarajat region.

In response to this situation, a new administrative system reportedly has been instituted by the government and its Soviet advisors. Under this system, the country has been divided into seven military zones, each of which is administered by a Soviet military officer and a political officer of the PDPA, who is responsible for working with local party committees to increase popular support for the government and implement reform programs.

People's Democratic Party of Afghanistan (PDPA; *Jamiyat-i Democratiqi-yi Khalq-i Afghanistan*)

History

The PDPA emerged in 1965 during a period of constitutional experimentation inaugurated by King Zaher Shah. Although the PDPA did not become a major political force at that time, the party did develop a degree of public visibility through the publication of its newspaper, *Khalq* (Masses), and established an organizational nucleus under the leadership of Nur Mohammad Taraki. In July 1967, however, the party was fractured by a dispute which was centered around the issue of how to develop a popular base of support. On the one side, Taraki and his Khalq faction advocated class struggle and rejected cooperation with other established political parties. On the other side, Babrak Karmal and the Parcham (Banner) faction favored a coalition approach which included working within the parliamentary framework.

The different strategies of the two factions were tested in 1973 when former prime minister Mohammad Daoud staged a successful *coup d'état* and overthrew the ineffectual constitutional monarchy. Believing Daoud's promises of socialist reform and an open political system, Parcham backed the new government and consequently was damaged when the regime turned increasingly repressive and autocratic. Khalq, however, stayed outside the governing coalition and pursued a program of covert organization which focused particularly on the military officer corps and civil service. As a result of this strategy, Khalq was able to mount a successful *coup d'état* in response to Daoud's imprisonment of leftist leaders in April 1979.

Once in power, the Khalq leadership under Taraki and his chief deputy, Hafizullah Amin, quickly turned against moderate elements in their ruling coalition, including Babrak Karmal and Abdul Qadir, one of the officers who had staged the coup. To overcome their lack of a popular base, Khalq instituted a series of sweeping reforms designed to fragment traditional social and economic structures and to mobilize the landless poor, which the Khalq perceived to be its natural constituency.

The reforms, which included measures to regulate marriage payments and impose coeducational classes, were resented as unwarranted intrusions on popular customs. Other symbolic acts such as changing the national flag to a solid red banner were perceived as anti-Islamic, despite the government's proclamations of religious belief. Within six months of their coming to power, the Khalq government faced widespread opposition, to which they responded with increasingly repressive security measures and vigorous enforcement of reform decrees.

By March 1979, opposition had spread to the military, and the Khalq leadership found itself faced with a choice between its hardline tactics and moderation. With the election of Amin to the post of prime minister in March 1979, and his subsequent assumption of the presidency of the Revolutionary Council in September (after a power dispute in which Taraki was killed), the government was clearly in the hands of the more militant members of the Khalq party. However, the collapse of the armed forces and Amin's inability to quiet the growing opposition left the government in a hopeless position, and the Soviet Union, which was already in control of the military counteroffensive against the rebels, moved in on December 27, 1979, to install Babrak Karmal as Amin's successor.

Organization

Since the change in power, the PDPA has adopted a coalition strategy. Whether by the design of Karmal or his Soviet sponsors, the party is now intended to serve as the vanguard of a revolutionary movement which draws its strength across the political spectrum. This approach can be seen both in the composition of the principal party organs, which include Parcham loyalists and former allies of Amin, and in the inclusion of nonparty members—including one former cabinet minister under Mohammad Daoud—in the Council of Ministers and other government bodies.

The main focus of the party's efforts to broaden its base of support is the National Fatherland Front, which was constituted in June 1981 "to propagate and explain on a broad scale the policy of the PDPA, the Revolutionary Council and the Government of the Democratic Republic of Afghanistan." In addition, the government has convened numerous tribal *jirgahs* and religious conferences to counter its antitribal and anti-Islamic image. The government also supports auxiliary party organizations such as the Democratic Organization of Afghan Women and the Democratic Organization of Afghan Youth.

At the same time, the government is attempting

to rally ethnic minority groups to its cause by publishing newspapers and broadcasting radio programs in the native languages of these groups. The effort to reach minority groups is one facet of a general campaign undertaken by the government to improve its dissemination of propaganda and fragment resistance efforts. This campaign is directed by the party through the Bakhtar news agency, which was elevated to the level of a government ministry in an apparent attempt to centralize and coordinate propaganda under the aegis of the PDPA. The principal vehicles for party and government propaganda include Radio Afghanistan and the government-controlled newspapers *Anis* (Pashto and Dari languages), *Hewad* (Pashto), *The Kabul New Times* (English), and *Haqiqat-e Enqelab-e Saur* (Dari).

Policy

The policy adopted by the Karmal regime has also been designed to encourage popular support. One aspect of this has been the public vilification of Hafizullah Amin by Karmal and other government officials. Political prisoners arrested by Amin have been released while many of the radical Khalq reforms have been either modified or eliminated. The land-reform program has been altered to allow greater private ownership, and certain individuals, such as religious and tribal leaders, have been permitted to keep their larger holdings. Refugees have also been encouraged to return with promises that their land will be turned over to them, and the much-despised flag introduced under Taraki has been redesigned to include the traditional red, black and green color scheme and prominent Islamic motifs.

With respect to foreign policy, the PDPA has proceeded in lockstep with its Soviet patrons. Like other client states, it has joined the non-aligned movement and has established trading relations with most of the Eastern European nations. Relations with Pakistan have been severely strained by the Pakistani government's support of the Afghan refugees (estimated at over two million in June 1981), and this situation is unlikely to change unless an agreement is reached to seal the border between the two countries. Afghanistan and Iran have also maintained some distance from each other, largely because of their mutual preoccupation with domestic matters.

Membership & Constituency

According to government sources, the Afghan people have been responsive to the conciliatory policies of the Karmal regime, and, at the seventh plenum of the PDPA, which was held in December 1981, it was announced that 10,000 new members had joined the party in the last ten months of 1981. It was further claimed that 75 percent of these new recruits are workers, artisans, and peasants living in provincial areas. Whatever validity these figures might have, the fact remains that the PDPA is building its numbers from a small nucleus of supporters that was severely fragmented by the purges of the Amin regime. Estimates of the size of this group are speculative at best, but it is generally assumed that party membership at the time of the Soviet invasion was under 10,000 and that many who have joined since then have done so for opportunistic reasons. The loyal core of Karmal's support is urban, middle class, educated, and, in many cases, associated with the university or one of the professions. Among the rural peasantry, which comprises the majority of the Afghan population, the party continues to have little support.

Financing

Although little is known about the specific mechanics of party financing, it can be assumed that the party—like the government as a whole—is being sustained by the Soviet Union. Because of the prolonged civil war, agricultural output has been greatly diminished, and the government has been forced to import wheat and other basic commodities from the Soviets. Traditional export items such as fruit, karakul wool, and the natural gas produced in the northern area of the country are sent to the Soviet Union in repayment for loans and credits and therefore do not earn any foreign revenues.

Leadership and Prospects

Babrak Karmal, president of the Revolutionary Council and secretary general of the PDPA, was born in Kabul Province in 1929. Karmal is the son of an army general who was a long-time supporter of the former royal family. Like other families of influence in Afghan government circles, Karmal's family spoke Dari Persian, and he was provided with an excellent education by Afghan standards. During the parliamentary period, Karmal was elected a deputy from Kabul in the *Wolesi Jirgah* (lower house), from which position he gained considerable notoriety as an articulate opponent of then prime minister, Mohammad Yousuf.

Other Parcham leaders also began their political activism during the chaotic period of the sixties. These include Dr. Anahita Ratebzad, who was also a parliamentary deputy from Kabul and, like Babrak, an early and vocal Marxist. One of the few women in politics in Afghanistan, Dr. Anahita has remained a close ally of Karmal's and currently serves on the Presidium and Politburo of the PDPA Central Committee. Other survivors from the original PDPA are Sultan Ali Keshtmand, the current prime minister; Nur Ahmad Nur, who serves as secretary of the PDPA Central Committee and is a member of the Presidium; and Dr. Saleh Mohammad Zeri, a Khalqi who has survived to become one of the secretaries of the PDPA Central Committee and chairman of the National Committee of the National Fatherland Front.

Despite the presence of Khalq members in important posts, the government and party continue to be divided by internal factionalism, and a stable coalition still has not been found. One principal source of resentment among Parcham members was the inclusion in Karmal's first government of Assadullah Sarwari, who was appointed deputy prime minister. Under Amin, Sarwari had been minister of the interior and head of the security force (AQSA), in which capacities he gained a reputation for brutal repression of political opponents, including members of the Parcham faction. Sarwari eventually was ousted from the government when he opposed Karmal's policy of reconciliation, but he remains in Kabul and must be considered a political force.

Other Khalq loyalists continue their opposition from within the government. It recently has been reported that Saleh Mohammad Zeri, Interior Minister Sayyid Mohammad Golabzoi, Communications Minister Mohammad Aslam Watanjar, and Transportation Minister Sherjan Mazduryar have been warned by the Soviet ambassador in Kabul to end their attacks on Karmal or face removal by the Soviets. At the same time, occasional reports suggest that other forces may be emerging to challenge Karmal's regime for Soviet support. These include a faction known as the Work (*Kar*) movement, which is reputedly headed by Dastigir Panjshiri, a long-time member of the PDPA and member of the PDPA Politburo.

Opposition

While a great deal of the opposition against the Afghan government is conducted on a local basis, a number of opposition parties have emerged in exile in Pakistan. Some of these groups have little backing within Afghanistan, although they may have influence in the numerous refugee camps

which have sprung up along the Afghan Pakistan border.

The two parties which are the oldest resistance organizations and probably also the most important are the *Hizb-e Islami* faction headed by Gulbuddin Hekmatyar and *Jamiat-e Islami*, which is run by Professor Burhanuddin Rabbani. Both of these men were associated with the fundamentalist *Ikhwan-e Musalamin* (Muslim Brotherhood) and fled Afghanistan after the suppression of the *Ikhwan* by President Daoud during the mid-seventies. Both groups appeal to a mixture of ethnic groups and social classes. Hekmatyar's group is reputed to be better armed and better organized. Its ideology is Islamic fundamentalism, and its centers of strength are in Wardak, Ghazni, Kabul, and Kunduz provinces. Rabbani's group is ideologically similar to *Hizb-e Islami*, but popular with non-Pushtun minority groups, especially Tajiks in northeastern Badakhshan Province and in the Panjsher Valley, where some of the fiercest resistance fighting has occurred.

Two less important fundamentalist groups are the *Hizb-e Islami* faction of Mohammad Yunus Khalis and *Harakat-e Enqelab-e Islami*, which is directed by Mohammad Nabi Mohammedi. Both Khalis and Mohammedi are in their sixties, long-time religious teachers, and less charismatic than Hekmatyar and Rabbani, who are also much younger men. The center of Khalis's support is in the eastern provinces, especially around Jalalabad, while Mohammedi's faction is particularly strong in the southwestern provinces of Farah and Nimroz.

Two other principal resistance organizations—*Jabha-ye Nejat-e Milli-ye Afghanistan* (Afghan National Liberation Front) and *Mahaz-e Milli-ye Islami-ye Afghanistan* (National Islamic Front of Afghanistan)—do not espouse a fundamentalist ideology, although both are led by men (Sibghatullah Mojaddedi and Sayyid Ahmad Gailani, respectively) whose authority derives in part from their association with well-known religious families. Both men are also shrewd politicians who, on the basis of their more moderate political stance, have gained financial backing from the West and from the Arabian oil states. Gailani's group is popular in Kandahar and with the powerful Mangal tribe of Paktia province, while Mojaddedi has support in the Kohistan and Kohedaman regions and in parts of Paktia.

Non-Islamic groups which deserve consideration are the *Afghan Mellat* party, which is popular among Afghan and Western Intellectuals because of its social democratic political orientation, and two leftist parties—*Settem-e*

Milli (Against National Oppression) and *Sazman-e Azadibakhsh-e Mardom-e Afghanistan* (Afghan People's Liberation Organization; SAMA) *Settem-e Milli*, which was founded by Taher Badakhshi, one of the original members of the Parcham party, is an extreme leftist party favoring rural mobilization along Maoist lines. This group is alleged to have been responsible for the abduction of U.S. Ambassador Adolph Dubbs, who was slain in a shootout between Afghan security forces and *Settem-e Milli* militants on February 14, 1979. The main center of support for this party is in the northeast among Tajiks and Uzbeks.

SAMA was founded by Majid Kalakani, a Tajik who is said to have been assassinated by the Soviets in June 1980. The organization is a successor to another Khalq splinter group, *Shu'la-ye Jawed* (Eternal Flame), which was especially strong among Afghan students and intellectuals in the 1960s.

National Prospects

Any realistic assessment of the Afghan situation must conclude that whatever changes occur in the Kabul regime will not affect the dominant position of the Soviet Union, which is committed to holding Afghanistan and has little reason to leave. Despite widespread opposition and some significant military successes by the Afghan resistance, the Soviet position has not been seriously challenged. At the same time, Soviet efforts to widen the popularity of the PDPA have been stymied by continued factionalism between Khalq and Parcham loyalists and by the necessity of bolstering the Afghan military through forced conscription of school-age boys. Such practices have crippled attempts to project a progressive image and have swelled the ranks of those who have chosen exile over cooperation with the regime.

The most significant loss for the PDPA has been the defection of educated families from Kabul and other cities. This has prevented effective administration, especially at the provincial level. In addition, the disaffection of the countryside has left the Karmal regime dependent upon the Soviets not only for economic credits but also for wheat and other basic staples.

Despite these problems, the situation for the resistance is probably even more tenuous, especially if one considers the continued presence of over two million refugees in Pakistan. This population cannot remain in its present dependent condition indefinitely, and it is fair to assume that the Pakistani authorities will eventually want a political compromise with the Kabul regime in order to dislodge the refugees from their country.

Because of the refugee situation and the general impoverishment of the Afghan provinces after three years of war, time is on the side of the Soviet Union. As long as their client regime in Kabul has sufficient manpower to bear the brunt of a low-level war of attrition, the Soviets will most likely hold to their current policy of passive control while awaiting further developments in neighboring countries. In this regard, it is worth remembering the words of Amir Abdur Rahman who effectively ruled Afghanistan in the late nineteenth century and who warned his successor of the dangers of involvement with the Russians to the north: "The Russian policy of aggression is slow and steady, but firm and unchangeable. If once they make up their minds to do a thing, there is no stopping them, and no changing their policy. . . . Their habit of forward movement resembles the habit of the elephant, who examines a spot thoroughly before he places his foot upon it, and when once he puts his weight there, there is no going back, and no taking another step in a hurry until he has put his full weight on the first foot, and has smashed everything that lies under it."

Further Reading

Dupree, Louis. *Afghanistan.* Princeton, N. J.: Princeton University Press, 1973.

———. "Afghanistan under the Khalq." *Problems of Communism, July-August, 1979.*

———. "Red Flag over the Hindu Kush." *American University's Fieldstaff Reports,* No. 44 (Asia), 1979.

Gregorian, Vartan. *The Emergence of Modern Afghanistan.* Stanford, Calif.: Stanford University Press, 1969.

Halliday, Fred. "War and Revolution in Afghanistan." *The New Left Review,* No. 119, January-February, 1980.

Middle East Research and Information Project. "Afghanistan." *MERIP Reports,* No. 89, July-August, 1980.

Newell, Richard S., and Newell, Nancy P. *The Struggle for Afghanistan.* Ithaca, N. Y.: Cornell University Press, 1981.

Poulos, John W. "Afghanistan." In *Constitutions of the World.* Albert P. Blaustein and Crisbert H. Flunz, ed., vol. I. Dobbs Ferry, N. Y.: Oceana Publications, July, 1980.

PEOPLE'S SOCIALIST REPUBLIC OF ALBANIA

(*Republika Popullore Socialiste e Shqipërisë*)

by George E. Delury

The System of Government

Albania, a nation of about 2.75 million people located on the Adriatic Sea between Yugoslavia and Greece, is a one-party communist state whose leaders lay claim to a special ideological purity which has isolated the nation from all other communist states. The smallest and poorest communist country in Europe, Albania relied on foreign support until 1977, but since then has pursued an independent course despite severe economic difficulties. The Party of Labor of Albania (PLA) dominates the country absolutely.

From 1941 to 1948, the Albanian communists relied heavily on the Yugoslav party for aid and organizational expertise. The threat of domination by the next-door neighbor and Tito's break with Stalin put Albania in the Soviet camp from 1948 to 1961, although relations with the USSR cooled after Nikita Khrushchev's de-Stalinization program began in 1955. With the Sino-Soviet split in 1961, Albania turned to even more distant China for aid and diplomatic support, a relationship that lasted until 1977 when the radical Maoist leadership was deposed in China. Even before 1977, Albania was noted for its hermitlike existence, closed to most foreign contacts and unusually secretive even for a communist state.

Executive

Executive powers are vested in the Council of Ministers (cabinet). Its chairman and head of government (premier) along with the cabinet are formally elected by the People's Assembly. Cabinet members are, in fact, chosen by the PLA and are usually PLA members. The head of state, a largely ceremonial position, is the chairman of the Presidium of the People's Assembly, a post held since 1953 by Haxhi Leshi, a member of the PLA Central Committee.

Legislature

The 250 members of the People's Assembly are elected every four years from single-member districts. Officially, the Assembly is the highest organ of state authority, but since it meets briefly only twice a year, its real function is to demonstrate unanimous approval for legislation prepared in the Council of Ministers under PLA direction. The fifteen-member Presidium, elected by the Assembly, exercises all the Assembly's powers when it is not in session.

Judiciary

Supreme Court judges are elected to four-year terms by the People's Assembly. They and the judges in local people's courts are responsible for imposing the law as interpreted by the party. Albania is unusual in that its Ministry of Justice has been combined with the Interior Ministry, thus placing the courts and police under a single administration.

Regional & Local Government

Albania is divided into twenty-six districts. Districts and localities are administered by executive committees chosen by people's councils which are "popularly" elected every three years. Council and executive committee members are selected by the PLA; many are party members. The executive committees are responsible to the next-highest government organ, and their work is supervised by the local or district party secretariats.

The Electoral System

Suffrage is universal for Albanian citizens age eighteen and over. The Democratic Front, a mass organization under PLA control, selects one candidate from each district for election to the People's Assembly. According to official Albanian figures, out of 1,627,960 voters only one voted against the party slate in 1982, and there were only eight invalid ballots.

Party of Labor of Albania (PLA)
(*Partia e Punës se Shqipërisë*)

History

Between the two world wars, Albania went through several types of government, both monarchial and republican, and even spent some ten years (1914–25) without effective national government. Before World War II, fragmented groups of students, intellectuals, and a few workers engaged in haphazard socialist opposition against the prevailing regimes. The occupation of the country by Italy in 1939 and by Germany in 1943, gave radical groups the opportunity to mobilize patriotic elements into a National Front dominated by the Party of Labor of Albania (PLA), which was founded November 8, 1941, with Yugoslav communist help. A new Albanian government under PLA first secretary Enver Hoxha was recognized by the major powers in November 1945. Controlled elections a month later resulted in a PLA-dominated assembly.

Party history after 1945 in part reflected Albania's foreign policy. A ruthless purge followed the shift to the Soviet camp in 1948, and milder purges accompanied the moves into and out of the relationship with China. Other party shakeups occurred periodically, indicating some factionalism within the party, but the very top rung of leadership remained remarkably stable until the death of Premier Mehmet Shehu in December 1981, after twenty-seven years in that office.

Shehu's death occurred six weeks after the Eighth Party Congress in November 1981. The Albanian government announced that Shehu, who had been in poor health, had shot himself. Official notice of his death was minimal, and he was buried without honors. The Yugoslav press reported rumors of heated arguments between Shehu and Hoxha that culminated in an exchange of gunfire. Hoxha was not seen in public for nearly a month after Shehu's death, and there were some indications that his unquestioned preeminence in the party might have been under attack. Hoxha later asserted that Shehu had been an agent of Yugoslavia. Speculation about these "events" suggests deep fissures in PLA unity.

Organization

The PLA is a tightly knit, highly disciplined, and hierarchically structured body ruled by the party elite. According to the party statutes, the party congress is theoretically the highest party organ. It meets every five years to decide on policies and elect the leadership. In practice, it serves as a sounding board for the leaders, whose policies and candidates it approves unanimously. The congress elects the Central Committee whose function is to guide the party in periods between congresses. The Central Committee was last chosen at the 1981 congress.

The Politburo, elected by the Central Committee, is the ultimate seat of power. It is generally composed of twelve full and five candidate members. (The latter group can participate in debates but cannot vote.) The basic decisions governing the party and state are made in the Politburo. Another important party organ is the Secretariat which is in charge of party administration and supervises all operations of the state. First Secretary Enver Hoxha and several other secretaries, most of them Politburo members, run the Secretariat.

City and district committees constitute the intermediate level of party structure. They supervise party activities and state bodies in their areas. Town and village committees carry out the wishes of the party at the local level. Rank-and-file members belong to basic party organizations which exist in every factory, farm, and office.

Policy

Despite tactical changes in the party line, the leadership has consistently followed a basic policy; modernization with an emphasis on steady economic growth based on nationalized heavy industries and forced collectivization within a planned economy. Consumer goods production is neglected. Real and imagined opponents of the regime are persecuted; the old fuedal social order has been smashed, and tribal and religious loyalties (Albania was once predominantly Muslim) replaced by loyalty to the party and state.

Hoxha declared, at the 1981 party congress, that Albania was prepared to improve its relationship with the United States and the Soviet Union, but added that the latter must cease its "war-mongering" before Albania would seek a rapprochement. The party tries to cultivate the good will of

Marxist splinter groups around the world. The 1981 congress was attended by twenty-three foreign delegations, nearly all of them representing minor communist factions and only one, the Vietnamese, representing a ruling party.

Membership & Constituency

The party has grown steadily since 1945. At the 1981 congress, Hoxha announced that total party membership including candidate members, had reached 122,600, about 4.5 percent of the total population and an increase of some 20,000 since 1976. The membership was reported to be 38 percent workers, 32.6 percent white-collar employees, and 29.4 percent farmers. Thirty percent were women. Party and state bureaucrats, military officers, and intelligentsia are, for the most part, included in the figure for white-collar employees and are clearly overrepresented in the party.

Financing

The party is financed by membership dues based on a percentage of income, sales of party publications, and probably subsidies from the state.

Leadership

Enver Hoxha (born 1908) has been first secretary of the party since its founding. He has been in power longer than any other governing communist leader. Educated in France and once a teacher, Hoxha is reputed to be tough and intelligent.

Until his death, Shehu was the second most powerful man in Albania. At the time of his death, a close relative, Fecor Shehu, was interior minister and his brother-in-law, Kadri Hasbiu, was defense minister. In the new cabinet created January 14, 1982, Fecor Shehu lost his post, but Hasbiu retained his.

The new premier, Adil Carcani (born 1920) had been first deputy chairman of the Council of Ministers since 1974. He had not previously been mentioned as a member of the first rank of leaders and may represent a temporary compromise among competing factions.

Other important veteran Politburo members are Hysni Kapo (born 1915), who specializes in party organization; Ramiz Alia (born 1925), an expert in ideological and cultural affairs; and Hasbiu (born 1920). One of these men is likely to be Hoxha's successor.

National Prospects

Albania's political and economic isolation is in the long run untenable, and the country may be preparing to emerge from its shell, if only slightly. Its lack of a powerful distant ally increases the leadership's concern over potential Yugoslav influence and has led it to make some vague public statements indicating an interest in better relations with Turkey and Western Europe. It is also possible that Albania will try to establish a relationship with the Soviet bloc that would fall short of membership in COMECON and the Warsaw Pact. While the country can probably continue to manage for a while without outside help, it cannot do much to improve its economic base without some foreign aid.

Hoxha, though reportedly healthy, is in his midseventies and cannot be expected to remain in power too much longer. The ensuing struggle for supremacy could create even more serious problems for the nation. It is highly unlikely, however, that the PLA will be replaced as the sole political force in the country.

Further Reading

Griffith, William E. *Albania and the Sino-Soviet Rift.* Cambridge, Mass.: MIT Press, 1963.

Logorechi, Anton, *The Albanians: Europe's Forgotten Survivors.* Boulder, Colo.: Westview Press, 1978.

Marmullaku, Ramadan. *Albania and the Albanians.* Hamden, Conn.: Archon Books, 1975.

Pano, Nicholas C. *The People's Republic of Albania.* Baltimore: Johns Hopkins University Press, 1968.

Prifti, Peter R. *Socialist Albania Since 1944.* Cambridge, Mass.: MIT Press, 1978.

Skendi, Stavro, ed. *Albania.* New York: Praeger, 1958.

DEMOCRATIC AND POPULAR REPUBLIC OF ALGERIA

(*Al-Jumhuriya al-Jaza'iriya al-Dimugratiya al-Sha'biya*)

by David E. Spiro, M.A.

The System of Government

Algeria, a nation of nearly twenty million people, has been an independent republic with a strongly centralized government since July 5, 1962, following a particularly violent and protracted war of independence with France. In 1965, after a bloodless *coup d'état* by Colonel Houari Boumedienne, Algeria's fledgling constitution was suspended and its democratic National Assembly dissolved. A new national charter was approved by 91 percent of the nation's resident voters in 1976. It affirmed "Islamic Socialism" to be the guiding principle of the state and paved the way for a referendum to promulgate a new constitution.

Somewhat later the same year, the new constitution was approved by 99.2 percent of the electorate (93 percent of registered voters). The constitution provides for a single-party socialist state with Islam as the state religion and Arabic as the official language. Political ideology is the province of the National Liberation Front (*Front de Libération Nationale;* FLN), which the constitution calls "a vanguard force, guiding and organizing the people for the building of socialism." The constitution also established the National Popular Assembly, to be selected every five years; an executive branch led by a president, who serves an unlimited number of five-year terms; and a judiciary, which is partly responsible to the executive.

Actually, the 1976 constitution simply legitimized the military government that had been ruling Algeria by decree since the 1965 coup. Under the constitution, Boumedienne became secretary general of the FLN and the head of a powerful executive branch that dominates the National Assembly.

Political institutions in Algeria are a facade with little importance; they do not reflect the authority patterns of Algerian society. The party system and government bureaucracy are simply European screens, behind which the new political elites govern with the traditional Islamic methods of consultation (*shura*) at various levels of the stratified society. The new elites have diverged from traditional Algerian political practice only by instituting a system of state capitalism which involves the governing authorities in the day-to-day lives of the peasantry.

Executive

Every five years, a candidate nominated by the FLN congress is to run unopposed in an election for the presidency. The candidate must be at least forty years of age, Algerian by birth, and Muslim. The president is the head of state, head of the armed forces, and minister of defense. He appoints the Council of Ministers (over which he presides), the prime minister, and one or more vice presidents. After Boumedienne's death in 1978, the president of the National Assembly, Rabah Bitat, assumed the presidency, as provided for in the constitution. Legally, Bitat was not allowed to run for the presidency and had to organize elections within forty-five days. The election was won (unopposed) by Colonel Chadli Benjedid, who is currently the head of state.

Because the president of the country is also the chairman of the FLN, he has immense power. The head of state may dissolve the National Assembly and call early elections or extend the mandate of the Assembly and delay elections. He may legislate by decree when the Assembly is not in session, although all such legislation must be submitted to the Assembly during its next session. Legislation may be initiated by the president, as well as by the Assembly. Extensive emergency powers allow the president to rule by decree, should he deem it necessary after conferring with party officials. During a state of emergency, siege, or war, the constitution is suspended.

Legislature

Although it serves as Algeria's main legislative body, the National Popular Assembly (*al-Majlis al-Sha'bi al-Jaza'iri*) is extremely limited in power. Its 261 members are elected every five years by universal, direct, secret suffrage, from a list of candidates nominated by the party. On February 25, 1977, voters chose from among 783 candidates (three for each seat) who had been selected by the FLN—the first time a national legislature had been elected since 1964.

The Assembly ordinarily meets for no more than six months a year, in two three-month sessions. Between its sessions, the Assembly is legally suspended, enabling the president to rule by decree. Though the Assembly may afterwards choose to disagree with (and thus nullify) any decrees made by the president between sessions, a flagrant contradiction of the president's policy objectives can lead to a dissolution of the Assembly and early elections. In its short life as an institution, the present National Assembly has not been dissolved by presidential order.

After it is elected, responsibility for validating the elections remains with the National Assembly itself. It is also the responsibility of the Assembly to judge retroactively the eligibility of its deputies for election, as well as to decide whether to revoke the mandate of those deputies who have "committed treason against the confidence of the people, or committed an act that disgraces them in their function." The Assembly elects a president of the legislature to a five-year term and four vice presidents each year, and convenes eight permanent commissions that deal with the affairs of state (except for national defense). Thus, the Assembly would appear to be a strong, autonomous body; in fact it has no jurisdiction over affairs that are defined by the head of state to be within the realm of national security, and it may be disbanded at any time.

Judiciary

All of the 132 courts in Algeria are answerable to the Supreme Court, which is under the Ministry of Justice. A High Court is presided over by the president of the republic, and his minister of justice is the vice president of the Court. Judges are instructed by the constitution to defend the socialist revolution.

Under the Supreme Court are *wilaya* (district) courts and over 100 courts of first instance. All judges, as well as justices of the peace, are appointed by the Ministry of Justice. Three special courts have been set up by the Ministry of Justice to hear cases on economic crimes against the state. Defendants in those courts have no right of appeal. The Court of State Security tries cases that involve state security.

Regional & Local Government

Algeria is divided into thirty-one administrative districts (*wilayat*), which are further divided into subdistricts (*da'irat*) and 676 communes. Elective assemblies in the *wilayat* and communes have gained importance since the 1960s, but their ability to affect government policy is still relatively miniscule. Communal popular assemblies (with ten to eighty members) and *wilayat* assemblies (around thirty members each) are elected directly by universal suffrage from lists of candidates made up by the FLN. These assemblies are under the direct supervision of the minister of the interior (in late 1982, Boualem Benhamuda), who is responsible for appointing local administrators and a *wali* (governor) for each administrative district.

The Electoral System

In preparation for the 1977 Assembly elections, candidate selection was initiated by a commission established in each *waliya*. By presidential directive, the commission consisted of the national commissioner of the party, the *wali* (governor), the sectoral army chief, the president of the *waliya* popular assembly, and general secretaries of local mass organizations. Each commission was presided over by an appointee of the central echelon of the party. Nominations for candidates to the National Assembly were considered by this *waliya* commission, which then passed them down to a group at the *da'ira* level. That group consisted of an assembly of *kasmat* councils (commune-level councils of the FLN), leaders of mass organizations at the *da'ira* level, and the chief of the *da'ira*. Supervised by a member from the *waliya* commission, the *da'ira* group, voting by secret ballot, pared down the group of candidates, which could not exceed four times the number of seats available to the specific *da'ira*. (Each *da'ira* of less than 80,000 inhabitants is entitled to one seat, those with 100,000 get two seats, those with 120,000 three seats, etc.) The list approved by the *da'ira* was then sent back to the *waliya* commission, which judged the merit of each candidate. The final list of candidates was approved by a national commission appointed by the central echelon of the party.

All Algerians eighteen years of age and over are eligible to vote. Turnout in 1977 was 78.5 percent.

National Liberation Front (*Front de Libération Nationale; FLN*)

History

Ahmed Messali Hadj headed a succession of radical Muslim organizations in Algeria between 1926 and 1963, all of which called for the violent expulsion of France from Algeria. However, the Messalist organizations, first the *Etoile Nord-Africain*—which successively became the *Parti du Peuple Algerien*, the *Amis du Manifeste et de la Liberte* (which Messali formed with Ferhat Abbas), and finally the *Mouvement pour le Triomphe des Libértes Démocratiques*—tended to emphasize the religious and traditionalist elements in Algerian political culture; during the post-World War II period, a younger group moved toward a socialist viewpoint.

In 1954, a breakaway group of Messalists formed the FLN and assumed responsibility for the political direction of the revolution, which was carried out by the *Armée de Libération Nationale* (ALN), the FLN's military branch. Within a few years after the opening of the liberation struggle, competing organizations were either coopted by the FLN or ceased to be significant actors. In 1958, FLN leaders formed a provisional government—the *Gouvernement Provisoire de la République Algérienne* (GPRA). Ferhat Abbas, a French-educated moderate, was appointed the first premier of the GPRA, which based its government-in-exile in Tunis.

Under pressure from the United Nations General Assembly and the North Atlantic Treaty Organization, French president de Gaulle accepted the principle of national self-determination for Algeria in September 1959. In March 1962, the French and the FLN finally agreed to an immediate cease-fire, and France recognized the FLN as the sole legal representative of the Algerian people.

Ben Youssef Ben Khedda, a pharmacist and former secretary general of the *Mouvement pour le Triomphe des Libértes Démocratiques* (MTLD), had become president of the GPRA in 1960. He and his "centralist" cabinet moved the provisional government to Algiers. However, they faced the opposition of several more radical FLN leaders who had just been freed from French prisons. Two such leaders, Ahmed Ben Bella and Colonel Houari Boumedienne, set up a *Bureau Politique* in Tlemcen to compete with the GPRA. When independence formally came to Algeria in July 1962, Ben Khedda and the *wilaya* leaders who supported him controlled Algiers, while Ben Bella and his ALN backers held much of the rest of the country. The ALN forces loyal to Ben Bella advanced on Algiers in September. Civil war was averted when it became obvious that the tide of events had moved against Ben Khedda and the centralists. He and his followers were purged from a single list of candidates to the new Constituent Assembly, as were members of the Communist Party, Messalists, and left-wing socialists who followed Muhammad Boudiaf.

A new constitution, shaped by Ben Bella, declared the FLN to be the single party of the new state. It was approved in September 1963 by a National Assembly that was itself largely appointed by Ben Bella. On June 19, 1965, Boumedienne overthrew the Ben Bella government in a military coup. The FLN continued to be the only legal party in Algeria, but its role in government was markedly diminished. Algeria was still a one-party state, but the party was essentially a tool of the government rather than its guiding force.

Boumedienne's creation to replace the National Assembly, the Council of the Revolution (*Conseil de la Révolution*), was controlled by his military colleagues, but it also contained a disorganized opposition of former guerrillas and leftists within the FLN. In 1967, Boumedienne escaped harm in a poorly executed coup attempt led by army chief of staff Colonel Taher Zbiri, which was presumably instigated by party leftists. If the FLN had previously been in decline, this marked its almost total eclipse. Boumedienne used the attempt as an excuse to consolidate the power of his military-backed government, and from that time on the FLN represented government policy rather than the converse.

Organization

Though it has been dominated by the executive and military throughout Algeria's independent history, the FLN did play a significant role in effecting a smooth transition of power following Boumedienne's death in 1978. Party organization, therefore, is particularly significant to Algerian politics in the event of a president's death or loss of power. At present, the principal party organs are the Secretariat, the Central Committee, and the Political Bureau. At the local level, the party structure is divided into federations for each *waliya, da'irat,* and commune.

Shortly after the death of Boumedienne, the FLN held its first congress in over fifteen years, revamping the party structure. The congress elected the Central Committee of 160 members, which in turn elected Colonel Chadli Benjedid secretary general. Benjedid nominated a Political Bureau of seventeen members, who were then confirmed by the Central Committee. Since, by law, the secretary general is also head of state, the party congress effectively named Benjedid president of Algeria.

At a special FLN congress in June 1980, Benjedid was given a mandate of "full power" to make major changes in the structure of the party's upper echelon. He reduced the membership of the Political Bureau from seventeen to seven, reduced the frequency of its meetings from weekly to monthly, and transferred much of its power to the office of the president. Benjedid also nominated a new national commission to be responsible for formulating lists of candidates for election to the National Assembly.

While mass organizations of labor, students, women, peasants, and veterans exist in Algeria and have a marginal role in politics, all are formally part of the FLN. Though these organizations may serve to increase popular participation in FLN policymaking, it is more accurate to view these groups as means by which the FLN reduces social conflict and divides Algerian society into corporate bodies.

The principal mass organizations include the General Union of Algerian Workers (*Union Générale des Travailleurs Algériens;* UGTA), the General Union of Algerian Muslim Students (*Union Genérále des Etudiants Musulmans Algériens;* UGEMA), the National Union of Algerian Women (*Union Nationale des Femmes Algériennes;* UNFA), the National Union of Algerian Peasants (*Union Nationale des Paysans Algériens;* UNPA), and the National Organization of Veterans (*Organisation Nationale des Mujahidin;* ONM). Except for the UGTA, which was taken over by the party in 1963, all of the organizations were formed by the FLN and remain subservient to it.

Policy

Officially, FLN policy is state policy. In fact, however, the FLN is highly factionalized and the policy statements of the Central Committee and Political Bureau usually reflect only the views of the state leadership. Since its founding, the ideology of the FLN has been Islamic socialism. Under Boumedienne especially, this translated into state capitalism, with most Algerian industries owned and managed by the appropriate ministries. Nationalization of industry reached its peak under Boumedienne and has been deemphasized somewhat under Benjedid. The FLN congress in 1979 criticized previous economic policy for creating trade deficits, shortages, and a corrupt bureaucracy.

Though the party has always been strongly nationalist, attempts to Arabize the country have become more prominent since 1979. Education in state-run schools is now in Arabic, which has prompted student unrest. The students feel that they are at a disadvantage because public affairs at high levels are largely conducted in French. Berbers, who make up one-sixth of the population (and have a language of their own), have also expressed displeasure with Arabization and rioted over the issue in May 1980. Benjedid, while condemning Berber protests as a threat to national unity instigated by foreign influence, made concessions by instituting Berber-language radio programs and university chairs.

In matters of foreign policy, the FLN is decidedly radical. It is a strong proponent of Third World nonalignment and has taken a vociferous role in that movement. The FLN also calls for a massive redistribution of wealth in the world economic order and advocates higher prices for the exhaustible resources that are produced in many developing countries. As a party that evolved during a war against colonialism, the FLN supports organizations that it recognizes as "national liberation movements." It is a strong supporter of the Palestinian Liberation Organization and nationalist groups in southern Africa. Algeria has served as a supplier and refuge for the Polisario (*Frente Popular para la Liberaçion de Saquia el Hamra y Rio de Oro*), which is currently at war with Morocco over independence for the Western Sahara. Moroccan troops have reported engagements with the Algerian army throughout the conflict, but the Algerian government has denied direct involvement.

Membership & Constituency

Initially, full party membership was restricted to those over the age of eighteen who had fought in the war for independence, adhered to the socialist ideology of the party, worked actively to spread party programs, paid regular dues, and were considered to be of good moral character.

Such members were called "militants." They were admitted into cells by vote at the commune level, and once accepted they were able to participate in all party functions. "Adherents" were associate members of the party not subject to any entrance requirements. They were formed into their own cells under the tutelage of militants and could not vote or serve on party committees. Although specific requirements for membership have changed since the early 1960s (e.g., having to be a veteran of the war), the general procedure for initiating new recruits has not.

In 1963 the FLN faced the choice of remaining an elite vanguard force or becoming a mass organization. It was Ben Bella who wanted the former, while the party's secretary general, Mohamed Khider, supported the latter. Because Khider left for Switzerland with large amounts of party funds, and Ben Bella was brought down by a coup not long after, the issue was never really resolved. It would seem that official party ideology calls for it to be an elitist vanguard force, but it has not restricted its membership and has at times actively encouraged mass participation. In 1973 Boumedienne warned publicly that "every person who believes in the revolution and its objectives must be a member of the party from this day. Otherwise, quite frankly, he will not be given a place at any level of political leadership." However, top-level industrial managers and administrators have not been required to belong to the party.

Financing

So far as is known, the FLN is financed entirely by the state.

Leadership

With each change in regime, the type of leaders who fill elite positions within the FLN has changed. During the Ben Bella government, intellectuals and revolutionaries comprised the core of the FLN elite. Boumedienne's tenure saw many positions filled by members of the military.

Benjedid was selected as secretary general of the FLN in what most observers saw as a political compromise between a pragmatic faction of the party, which wished to liberalize Algeria's politics and economy, and a radical leftist faction, which supported a continuation of state capitalism and advocated party-dominated politics. Although those factions are still represented in the Central Committee and Political Bureau, Benjedid has ousted most of the leftists from ministerial positions.

The members of the FLN Political Bureau in late 1982 are listed below.

Colonel Chadli Benjedid (born 1925 in Bouteldja) has been secretary general since 1979. He was formerly commander of the Oran military region.

Rabah Bitat (born 1925 in Ain Kerma) is the only one of the nine "historic leaders" of the Algerian revolution who is still in power. He is president of the National Popular Assembly.

Colonel Abdellah Belouchet (born 1924 near Sedrata) joined Boumedienne's Council of the Revolution in 1978 after a career in the military.

Muhammad Salah Yahioui, leader of the radical faction in the FLN, has held ministerial portfolios and was on the Council of the Revolution.

Abdelaziz Bouteflika (born 1937 in Morocco) is the leader of FLN moderates. Formerly foreign minister, he is now a minister without portfolio.

Boualem Benhamouda (born 1929 in Constantine) is minister of the interior and has held other portfolios.

Muhammad Said Mazouzi was formerly minister of work and social affairs.

Other Political Forces

Military

Although the army plays a major role in Algerian politics and many top-level leaders have military backgrounds, increasing internal stability has obviated the need for the army to keep the Algerian regime in power. In 1978, during an orderly transfer of power after the death of Boumedienne, the lack of military-political strife was credited to the professionalism of the Algerian officer corps.

In the 1960s, army factions centered around former guerrillas and professional officers (many of whom were trained in France before the war). After the coup attempt in 1967, the guerrillas were purged, and the army was unified. Early political factions were sometimes known by geographic names (e.g., Ben Bella and Boumedienne were called the Tlemcen Group in 1963, and Boumedienne's supporters were called the Oujda Group in 1967). Partly because the regional groups from the revolution are now retired and partly because such names were misnomers to begin with, the army is not divided by regional loyalties. Differences of political opinion in the army are not serious, posing no threat to elite politics.

According to the Algerian government, "in 1978 the typical Algerian career soldier was the son of a peasant or an urban laborer. He had the reputation of being tough, hardy, and amenable to discipline." Reliable sources of information, other than informal impressions, that document the composition and morale of the Algerian military are not available.

National Prospects

It is difficult to tell what Algeria resembles more: a single-party state or a military regime that makes use of the party for legitimacy. Because the FLN has freely nominated candidates for national leadership, and that leadership was confirmed in popular elections, Algeria is technically a one-party state. However, most of those leaders came to power by virtue of a military *coup d'état,* and the FLN is under the firm control of the executive branch.

The FLN will continue to enjoy a monopoly status as Algeria's only political party for the foreseeable future, no matter what its functional role in government really is. Despite occasional signs of popular unrest, no political opposition has formed.

Liberalization measures (such as the freeing of Ben Bella in 1980 after fifteen years of confinement) may point to a resurgence in the importance of the FLN. On the other hand, those measures may simply indicate the regime's feeling of security in its strong control of the party.

Further Reading
Nelson, Harold D., et al. *Algeria: A Country Study.* 3rd ed. Washington, D.C.: U.S. Government Printing Office, for Foreign Area Studies, American University, 1979.
Leca, J., and Vatin, J. C. "Algérie: le système politique." In *Développements Politiques au Maghreb: Aménagements Institutionnels et Processus Électoraux.* J. Leca, ed. Paris: Éditions du Centre National de la Recherche Scientifique, 1979.
———. *L'Algérie Politique: Institutions et Régime.* Paris: Presses de la Fondation Nationale des Sciences Politiques, 1975.
Ottoway, David and Marina. *Algeria: The Politics of a Socialist Revolution.* Berkeley and Los Angeles: University of California Press, 1970.
Quandt, William B. *Revolution and Political Leadership: Algeria, 1954–68.* Cambridge, Mass.: MIT Press, 1969.

PEOPLE'S REPUBLIC OF ANGOLA
(*Republic Popular de Angola*)
by Michael Radu, Ph.D.

The System of Government

Angola, a nation of over seven million people, achieved its independence from Portugal on November 11, 1975, after fourteen years of guerrilla warfare by nationalist groups. Until November 1980 the country was ruled by a nonelected Revolutionary Council, an organ under the direct control of the sole legal party, the *Movimento Popular de Libertação de Angola* (MPLA). Following elections to a Popular Assembly in 1980, the government of Angola became a full-fledged one-party communist state organized on democratic centralist principles.

Potential sources of antiregime activity have either been taken over or sharply restricted by the government, except in areas in the south and east, where anticommunist guerrilla forces continue to wage sporadic conflict with the MPLA government. The media is government owned and censorship is omnipresent. Churches, while still legal, are not permitted to engage in any but purely religious activities; their organizations for youth and women have been banned and they are not permitted to own or operate schools. The bureaucracy, though small and relatively powerless, is regarded with suspicion by the party and the population because it is mostly Portuguese educated. An abortive coup in May 1977 was based, in part, on opposition to this *mestiço* element.

After 1976, the state took control of all Angolan- and Portuguese-owned enterprises—large, medium, and small—in most cases without compensation. The state also took a majority share in the large oil and mineral companies operating in Angola. Peasants were forced into a growing number of collective farms, and they along with the urban population can be sent far from their homes at any time to harvest crops at government-imposed wages.

The army has a very strong influence over the political life of the country through its strong representation in the MPLA leadership and its control over the administration of the provinces.

A peculiar and important part of the political situation in Angola is the large number of foreigners who are, in fact, the main source of strength of the regime. At least 20,000 Cuban and several thousand East German, Soviet, and other East European troops are in Angola; as well as a similar number of civilian advisors, technicians, doctors, teachers, and other professionals. They operate in all ministries, train and control both the army and the security apparatus, have a major role in economic planning, and help in party organization. Much, if not most, of the daily operations of the government are carried out by these foreign cadres.

Executive

The government consists of a president, twenty-two ministers, and seventeen provincial commissioners. The office of prime minister was abolished in 1978 to allow the president to exercise direct control over the activity of the government. The president is head of state and government and is also the president of the MPLA. The power and influence of the ministers depends on their position in the party, rather than on the importance of their government office. Thus, the foreign affairs, planning, and security ministers are less influential than the defense, interior, and provincial coordination ministers, because the last three are also members of the party's supreme executive body, the Politburo.

Legislature

Between August and November 1980, the first national elections ever held in Angola selected a Popular Assembly. The Assembly's 206 members were elected indirectly by provincial assemblies previously elected—also indirectly—by electoral colleges meeting at workplaces and in neighborhoods. Only the party had the right to propose candidates, and all candidates were party militants. The Popular Assembly's only prerogative is to approve laws proposed by the government.

Judiciary

The old Portuguese legal system was dismantled by 1976 and replaced with a "socialist" legal structure. The court system includes local, provincial, and central courts, with the first two including a combination of elected judges and appointed ones. The Supreme Court is formed of judges appointed by the president, who can also dismiss them. A Supreme Revolutionary Tribunal, with exclusive jurisdiction over crimes against state security also exists; it usually summarily tries antigovernment guerrillas, generally imposing the death penalty.

The trial of the authors of the May 1977 attempted coup, if there were a trial, was held *in camera*, and the sentences never made known; such instances may still occur.

Regional & Local Government

Since the government does not effectively control extensive areas in the south and southeast of the country, and its hold over the central regions, outside the cities, is precarious, local and provincial administration is limited to the northern areas. The country is divided into ten provinces, each led by a governor appointed by the president and enjoying extensive civilian and military prerogatives over the region. Neighborhood committees exist in the capital of Luanda, and are used as vigilante groups and a source of informers. Other institutions, such as the trade union, are established only in isolated cities. An attempt at decentralization was halted after the 1977 attempted coup.

Popular Movement for the Liberation of Angola—Labor Party (*Movimento popular de libertação de Angola—Partido de Trabalho;* MPLA-PT)

History

The MPLA was founded in 1956 as a "liberation movement" with the primary goal of obtaining independence from Portugal. The founders were a group of Portuguese-speaking, mixed-blood intellectuals, the most prominent of which were Agostinho Neto, Viriato da Cruz, Mario de Andrede, and Lucio Lara. In November 1975, when Portugal turned the country over to the MPLA and two Western-oriented liberation groups, the MPLA, which was in control of Luanda, the capital, proclaimed the People's Republic and, by February 1976, had taken full control of most of the northern and western areas of the country.

At its First Ordinary Congress, December 4–11, 1977, the party proclaimed itself a "vanguard party" and formally adopted Marxism-Leninism as its ideology. As a liberation movement, it had claimed to represent all anti-Portuguese sections of the population, but after 1977 it referred to itself as the sole representative of the working class. In keeping with its new character and structure, the party added the phrase Partido de Trabalho (Labor Party) to its name in 1977.

Organization

The supreme ruling body of the party is, in theory, the congress, which must ordinarily convene at least once every ten years. Extraordinary congresses may be convened by the party's Central Committee. The congress elects the Central Committee, which in turn elects the Secretariat. The Politburo is selected from among the members of the Secretariat. Between congresses the party is supposedly led by the Central Committee, but that body is only convened by the Politburo, on average, once a year for a few days.

Real power within the party is in the hands of the ten-member Politburo and the Secretariat. The Secretariat has nine departments, each of them supervising a number of ministries or social organizations. Some of the Secretariat and Politburo members are also members of the government. All Politburo members are or were at some time military leaders or have had military training. Over one-third of the Central Committee members are also military. Membership in the Central Committee, and thus in the Politburo and Secretariat, is restricted to those party members who joined before independence.

Because ultimate political power in Angola lies with the ten-member Politburo, all essential policy disputes are resolved within that body. Whenever those disputes involve critical issues, the losing side is expelled. (Such purges occurred in 1976 and 1978, when those favoring extreme radical social and economic reorganization were expelled, and in 1980; the issue and consequences of the latest purge are not clear.) The power of the president, then, depends on his ability to control a majority in the Politburo.

Through its total control of the government, the MPLA-PT is also in control of the entire political, social, and cultural life of the society. In practice, this control is exercised through a number of mass organizations which reach the large majority of the population in the areas under MPLA-PT domination. The single trade union, the National Union of Angolan Workers (*União Nacional de Trabalhadores de Angola*; UNTA) is under the leadership of a Politburo member. Theoretically, only UNTA can approve a strike, but since the government is virtually the sole employer, strikes are automatically considered antigovernment actions and harshly suppressed. The sole youth organization, *Juventude de MPLA* (JMPLA), is under direct control of the Secretariat, of which its leader is a member, and of the minister of education and culture, who is a Politburo member. The Organization of Angolan Women (*Organização de Mulheres de Angola*; OMA), is similarly controlled; it was restructured in 1977 according to the ideas of and under the supervision of Lucio Lara, the second-ranking Politburo member.

Policy

Immediately after the end of the civil war in the spring of 1976, the MPLA engaged in a campaign of thorough nationalization of private property, largely belonging to the over 300,000 Portuguese. The nationalization was most often tantamount to confiscation, the only major exceptions being the large multinational corporations, which were allowed to continue their operations, particularly in the oil industry, and were paid for the majority share taken over by the government. The policy toward the foreign oil companies was one of the reasons for Agostinho Neto's dismissal in 1978 of powerful Vice-President Carlos Rocha "Dilolwa" and of Prime Minister Lopo do Nascimento, both of whom were opposed to the multinationals' presence. Ever since independence the GNP has declined steadily, and the oil industry remains the only major source of revenues for an economy which, until 1974, was one of the most balanced in Africa.

Although Angola claims to be a nonaligned country and is a member of the Nonaligned Movement, the party's foreign policy is completely aligned to that of the Soviet Union. Angola has vocally supported the Vietnamese occupation of Kampuchea (Cambodia), the Soviet invasion of Afghanistan, and the imposition of marital law in Poland; and has signed treaties of friendship and cooperation with the USSR, Cuba, the German Democratic Republic (East Germany), Romania, Bulgaria, and North Korea. The presence of over 30,000 military and civilian personnel from the Soviet bloc on its territory seems to ensure that Angola's international alignment will not change in the foreseeable future.

Membership and Constituency

After the Third Extraordinary Congress, December 4–11, 1980, the party claimed a membership of 30,000 full and candidate members. Workers and soldiers are encouraged to join the party. Because of the small number of wage earners and college graduates in the country, the social basis of the MPLA-PT is extremely narrow. The membership is largely of peasant origin, though most members now live in the cities. The leadership is strictly of urban origin, foreign-trained, and in most cases of military background. The only ethnic group which actively supports the MPLA-PT in significant proportions is the Mbundu of the Luanda area and the northeastern provinces. The Mbundu, however, are only about 30 percent of the total population, the third-largest ethnic group in the country. Many Mbundu, however, as well as the poorest strata of the Luanda population, were alienated from the party after their most popular leader, Nito Alves, was arrested and disappeared after his failed coup in May 1977.

Financing

All MPLA-PT members pay dues according to their income, but party finances are not covered by the dues, and the origins of the additional funds are unclear. Moreover, since all the party members also occupy top government or military positions, party and state expenditures are difficult to separate.

Leadership

The president of Angola and of the MPLA-PT is José Eduardo dos Santos. Born in 1942, the son of a stonemason, dos Santos was educated as a geological engineer in Yugoslavia and received training as a radar operator in the Soviet Union. He joined the MPLA in 1961, and after independence became a member of the government as foreign minister, as second deputy prime minister until 1978, and as planning minister until 1979. He was elected president by the Central Committee on September 21, 1979, succeeding Agostinho Neto, who had died of natural causes a few days before. His wife is Russian.

Lucio Rodrigo Leite Barreto de Lara is the second-ranking Politburo member and the party's ideologue. Born in Luanada, April 9, 1929, son of a wealthy mestiço plantation owner, Lara studied in Angola and Portugal. He led the movement during Neto's imprisonment. Closely linked to the Portuguese Communist Party since his youth, Lara spent most of the 1960s in the USSR. Lara was one of the most powerful leaders of Neto's MPLA faction, and the most powerful representative of the Leninist tendency. Between 1978 and 1979, during Neto's illness, he often made the major decisions.

Opposition

Because there is no institutional opportunity for any political opposition in Angola, and because of the historical cleavages in the Angolan society—between ethnic groups as well as between races—the political life of the country is dominated by the permanent use of violence by both the government and its opponents. There are three major types of opposition to the present MPLA-PT leadership.

The first, which may be defined as internal and ideological, comes from within the party itself, and expresses the dissatisfaction of the black members with the mixed racial background of most of the postindependence leaders, all of whom were also Portuguese educated. This antipathy to the Portuguese element played a role in Nito Alves's attempted coup in 1977, when some army units were joined by segments of the capital's poor and youths. The attempt was crushed by Cuban troops and the security police, but a number of its supporters remain active. Ideologically, this opposition group was far to the left of the present leadership. The shock of the coup attempt led the party leadership to try to attract more blacks and to purge, in time, many of the nonblacks from the leadership.

The second source of opposition is the secessionist movement in the oil-rich province of Cabinda. Although the secessionist organization—the Front for the Liberation of the Enclave of Cabinda (FLEC)—is militarily very weak and politically divided, it enjoys large popular support within the province. Almost half the population of the province has chosen to live in exile rather than accept MPLA-PT's rule. Gulf Oil, the Cabinda concessioniare, supports the government.

The third and by far the strongest and most dangerous source of opposition to the government comes from the two other liberation movements which fought the Portuguese and were defeated by MPLA's Cuban allies in the civil war which followed the proclamation of independence. Both movements—the Front for the National Liberation of Angola (FNLA) and the National Union for the Total Independence of Angola (UNITA)—receive support from South Africa. The FNLA, sporadically active in the northern provinces, enjoys significant support from the Bakongo, the second-largest ethnic group in Angola.

By far the most formidable opponent of the government, UNITA enjoys very strong support among the Ovimbundu ethnic group of the central and most populous provinces, as well as among the smaller groups in the southeast and south. Its political aim is the creation of the government of popular unity (to include also the FNLA and the MPLA-PT), the expulsion of all foreign troops from the country, and a foreign policy of nonalignment. UNITA is structured along the usual lines of a guerrilla movement.

As a political party, it has a political bureau, selected from among the members of the Party's Central Committee, themselves elected by popular assemblies, which in turn are elected by local assemblies. As in the case of MPLA-PT, the elections are indirect, and it is doubtful that, amidst a civil war, they could take place on any regular basis. UNITA also claims to have women's, youth, and labor organizations under its control, but these claims are impossible to verify.

UNITA's Twelfth Annual Conference took place in 1979 in the south of Angola. It decided to create a revolutionary council of twenty-five members as the movement's executive organ. The Revolutionary Council is an adjustment to the situation of civil war and includes several military leaders as well as Central Committee members. UNITA's armed forces are estimated at between 8,000 and 12,000 men.

The president of UNITA is Jonas Malhiero Savimbi. Born in 1934, the son of a railroad-station master, Savimbi is from a prominent Ovimbundu family. After studying medicine in Portugal, he obtained a degree in political science at the University of Lausanne, Switzerland. In 1961, he joined the FNLA and later became the foreign minister of the government in-exile established by that movement. He broke with the FNLA and in 1966 founded UNITA, whose president and most charismatic leader he has remained ever since.

Miguel Nazu Puna (born 1939), a Cabindan from one of the aristocratic families of the province, is the second-ranking leader of the movement. He is the chief administrator and handles the delicate problem of relations with South Africa. The UNITA military commander, Sam Chivale (born 1944), and UNITA's foreign representative, Jorge Sangumba (born 1942), are from minor ethnic groups.

National Prospects

The prospects of Angola are at this time very difficult to assess because of the decisive role played by factors outside the control of either the government or the people of the country. If it is true that without the Cuban, Soviet, and East German troops the MPLA-PT could not remain in power, it is equally true that without South African support UNITA would be militarily defeated. Neither side seems interested in compromise. The result is not only economic collapse but also a steady sharpening of social and ethnic tensions.

Further Reading

Brown, Kevin. "Angolan Socialism." In *Socialism in Sub-Saharan Africa*, Carl G. Rosberg and Thomas M. Callaghy, eds. Berkeley: Institute of International Studies, University of California, 1979.

Gabriel, Claude. *Angola: Le tournant Africain?* Paris: Éditions La Brèche, 1978.

Marcum, John A. *The Angolan Revolution, Volume II; Exile Politics and Guerrilla Warfare (1962–1976)*. Cambridge, Mass.: M.I.T. Press, 1978.

Ottaway, David and Marina. *Afrocommunism*. New York: Africana Publishing House, 1981.

Young, Crawford. *Ideology and Development in Africa*. New Haven and London: Yale University Press, 1982.

REPUBLIC OF ARGENTINA
(*República de Argentina*)
by Hazel Sirett

The System of Government

Traditionally, Argentina, a nation of twenty-eight million people, is a federal republic with a representative form of government, with power divided between the national government, twenty-two provinces, and one national territory. The Argentine military seized power in a bloodless coup on March 24, 1976, and disposed of all democratic institutions.

The Military Government

When the military seized power on March 24, 1976, deposing the government of María Estela Martínez de Perón, Argentina's democratic system was still in effect, the legislative and executive branches of government were fully operative, and political parties were permitted to organize and to publish their opinions. Upon taking power, the military regime assumed extraordinary powers in violation of the 1853 constitution, and substantially altered the political and judicial organization of the Argentine state.

The armed forces offered two principal justifications for their takeover: to save Argentina from "subversion and corruption" and to restore stability to a chaotic economy, with the ultimate aim of restoring democracy. International observers feel that they have failed on both counts. The regime has succeeded in eliminating armed opposition, but only at enormous social and human cost. The failure of the military's economic program has been drastic; by mid-1982 Argentina was in even worse financial straits than prior to the 1976 coup.

The military regime's basic guiding philosophy and objectives for the organization and operation of state authorities were stated in their Act for the National Reorganization Process (*El Acta Para el Proceso de Reorganización Nacional*), issued on the day of the coup. Pursuant to this act, they established a three-man military junta composed of the commanders-in-chief of the army, navy, and air force to assume the "political power of the Republic." The act declared the terms of office of the president, vice president, governors, and vice governors to be null and void. It dissolved Congress, the provincial legislatures, the House of Representatives of the city of Buenos Aires, and the municipal councils. It removed and replaced all members of the Supreme Court with military officials and dismissed the attorney general and members of the higher provincial courts. Military officials took over most key ministerial posts and, with three men from each branch of the armed forces, filled all nine positions on the newly established Legislative Advisory Committee (*Comisión de Asesoramiento Legislativo*), empowered to intervene in the drafting and approval of laws.

Finally, the military installed army commander-in-chief General Jorge Rafael Videla as president, the tenth Argentine president in this century to assume power as the result of a military coup. On March 29, 1981, five days after the fifth anniversary of the 1976 coup, Videla was replaced by General Roberto Eduardo Viola, who had held key positions in the army since 1976. On November 20, 1981, President Viola stepped down from office "temporarily" due to alleged heart problems; on December 22, General Leopoldo Fortunato Galtieri succeeded Viola as president.

Like his immediate predecessor, Galtieri was considered a "hardliner," and even less likely than Viola to encourage civilian political expression. Galtieri retained his post as commander-in-chief of the army, thereby giving his presidency greater weight. Upon assuming the presidency, however, Galtieri made some vague attempts to dispel his hardline reputation. He appointed a number of civilians to provincial governorships, and discussed the possible introduction of some form of democracy in the not-too-distant future. However, Argentina's military defeat by Great Britain in the Malvinas (Falklands) episode resulted in Galtieri's dismissal in mid-June 1982 and in the installation on July 1, 1982, of General Reynaldo Bignone as president, the fourth since the military coup.

The president may be removed by the military

junta whenever it is considered desirable for reasons of state. In addition to his functions as head of the executive, the military president now exercises the duties constitutionally reserved for Congress, including the power to appoint Supreme Court justices, the attorney general, and judges of the provincial Superior Courts.

The Statute for the National Reorganization Process (*El Estatuto para el Proceso de Reorganización Nacional*), adopted on March 26, 1976, reiterated what had been established by the Act for the National Reorganization Process.

Although the fundamental text of the 1853 constitution is still in effect, the military regime has amended it by a series of decrees with the force of law and subordinated it to their Statute for the National Reorganization Process. With respect to those provisions not amended by the military, the constitution is invoked and applied, providing it is not contrary to the basic objectives declared by the armed forces when they took power.

The military junta has maintained the state of siege introduced by decree on November 6, 1974, by the government of María Estela Martínez de Perón, even though there is no real justification for its continued existence. The state of siege has enabled them to suspend many of the civil liberties guaranteed by the constitution. On April 13, 1981, the conservative Argentine Federation of Bar Associations (*Federación de Colegios de Abogados;* FACA) called for the lifting of the state of siege. More recently, in June 1982, some 400 individuals, including Nobel laureate Adolfo Pérez Esquivel, filed a lawsuit in Buenos Aires demanding a judicial termination to the state of siege. This lawsuit has so far gone unanswered.

In their quest for social order and the eradication of subversion, the junta enacted an arsenal of antisubversive legislation after the coup, much of which is in direct violation of specific articles of the 1853 constitution. The junta decreed the dissolution of Marxist political parties and related organizations, closed their establishments, blocked their bank accounts, and incorporated their assets into the state treasury. They suspended the activities of all political parties, labor unions, business associations, and professional organizations; and compelled all such groups to withdraw all identifying symbols from their offices and meeting places. Labor unions lost the right to strike. The junta also placed constraints on academic freedom and brought the educational system under direct state control. Forty-nine political and community groups declared illegal in 1976 are still under an absolute ban on any activity of any sort.

The junta introduced the death penalty for political misdemeanors, in direct violation of the constitution, and reduced the age of criminal responsibility to sixteen years. On the day of the coup, strict press censorship was introduced by Communiqué 19: Crime of the Press (*Delito de Prensa*) which prescribes severe prison terms for anybody reporting on the activities of "illicit organizations notoriously dedicated to subversive activities" or divulging information "with the purpose of disrupting, prejudicing or lessening the prestige of the Armed Forces." A little less than a month later, such crimes were broadened to include reporting on "the appearance of bodies and the deaths of subversive elements and/or members of the armed or security forces. . . . This includes kidnappings and disappearance."

The exercise of freedom of opinion, expression, and information has been limited by the enactment of emergency laws, and labor rights have been severely affected by decrees prejudicial to trade-union activity and by military interference. Organizations within Argentina working for the protection and promotion of human rights have encountered serious obstacles, including arrests, imprisonment, and raids on their offices.

Councils of War (*Consejos de Guerra*) were established to try cases involving subversion or violent activity. These trials are conducted without civilian lawyers and generally take place *in camera.*

Both domestic and international human rights organizations consider that the military government of Argentina has perpetrated numerous serious violations of fundamental human rights since the 1976 takeover. In particular, such organizations cite the right to life (it is estimated that since the coup some 10,000 to 15,000 people have "disappeared" after their detention by the Argentine security forces); the right to personal freedom; the right to personal security (torture has been commonplace); and the right to a fair trial and due process. However, such abuses have declined since 1979.

The following paragraphs describe the Argentine political system before the military takeover. Argentina's constitution—the oldest in Latin America and closely modeled after that of the United States—was adopted in Santa Fé on May 1, 1853, by the General Constituent Congress of the Argentine Confederation. It provides for a system based on the principle of separation of powers: legislative, executive, and judicial. The constitution may only be amended by a convention summoned for that purpose by a two-thirds vote of members of Congress. Amending conventions met in 1880, 1890, 1898, 1949, 1957, and 1972.

Executive

Under the constitution, the executive branch of government consists of the president, the vice president, and a cabinet. Executive power is vested in the "President of the Argentine Nation," who is directly elected for a maximum term of four years and may not be immediately reelected. He must have been born in Argentina or be the child of native-born Argentines. Both the president and the vice president must profess the Roman Catholic faith and be at least thirty years old. The vice president is elected at the same time as the president and may succeed him "in case of his illness, absence from the capital, death, resignation, or removal from office." If the vice president is also incapacitated, the line of succession is the president pro tempore of the Chamber of Senators, the president of the Chamber of Deputies, and the president of the Supreme Court. If the presidency is filled by anyone other than the vice president, the constitution requires that a new election be called within thirty days.

Because the authors of the 1853 constitution wanted to create a strong presidency in line with the Spanish tradition of the *caudillo* (political strongman), the constitution endows the Argentine president with extensive powers, including the general administration of the country, execution of its laws, broad powers of appointment, the conduct of foreign affairs, and the power to approve or veto all legislative acts of Congress. The president's broad legislative powers enable him, in the majority of cases, to take the initiative in introducing legislation to Congress. He nominates the bishops of the Roman Catholic Church from a list of three names submitted by the Senate and, with the exception of judges and members of the diplomatic corps who must be confirmed by the Senate, is the sole judge of the qualifications of his appointees.

Of great importance is the president's power to declare a state of siege "in times of internal upheaval," thereby effectively suspending most of the civil liberties guaranteed under the constitution. He can only do so when Congress is in recess and within certain constitutional limitations. Congress also has the power to declare a state of siege in one or several areas of the nation in case of internal disturbance, and it may suspend a state of siege declared by the executive during a congressional recess.

The constitution provides that the president is also commander-in-chief of the armed forces. However, this has not always been the case: for example, when Argentina was under military rule from 1966 to 1973, the president and the commander-in-chief of the armed forces were not always the same person. Although the president may not formally declare war, he is able to use his military and diplomatic powers in such a way that Congress is virtually forced to go along.

Legislature

The legislature is responsible for drafting and enacting laws. As provided for by the constitution, the legislature consists of a Congress (*Congreso Nacional*), composed of two chambers: the Chamber of Deputies (*Cámara de Diputados*) and the Senate (*Senado*). The Chamber is composed of 243 representatives directly elected by the citizens of the provinces and of the capital, one for every 85,000 inhabitants. The Senate is composed of three senators from each province and the capital—a total of sixty-nine. Before 1973, senators from the Federal District were elected by an electoral college chosen for that purpose, but in 1973 this was abolished and they are now elected by direct vote.

Senators must be at least thirty years old, have been Argentine citizens for six years, and must either be natives of the province from which elected or have resided there during the two preceding years. They serve for nine years and one-third are elected every three years. The vice president presides over the Senate and votes only in case of a tie. Deputies must be twenty-five years old, have been an Argentine citizen for at least four years, and must have resided for at least two years in the province in which they seek election.

Under the constitution, both houses meet from September 30 to May 1 of each year. The president may call special sessions which deal solely with matters specified in the call. Each house makes its own rules, and parliamentary immunity is granted for opinions and speeches. Bills may be introduced in either house, then sent to appropriate standing committees for consideration and amendment, and returned to the house floor for debate and a final vote. A bill must be approved by both houses to become law. A presidential veto can be overridden by a two-thirds majority vote in both houses.

A member of Congress enjoys a number of privileges—including immunity from arrest, which can only be removed by a two-thirds vote of the member's house.

The Chamber of Deputies, with the Senate sitting in judgment, has the exclusive right to impeach the president, vice president, ministers, and members of the Supreme Court.

Judiciary

The Argentine judiciary functions as a separate and independent branch of government. Judicial power is exercised by the Supreme Court and a series of lower courts established by Congress. The national territory is divided into several judicial districts—each of which is assigned one federal judge. Each province has its own judicial system, including courts of first instance and appellate courts. The five judges of the Supreme Court and those of the lower federal courts are appointed for life by the president, with the Senate's consent. Traditionally, these positions have been political appointments with low pay.

The Supreme Court selects its chief justice from among its own members for a three-year term. Although the Supreme Court in the past has declared legislation or acts of the executive to be unconstitutional, the practice of judicial review is not carried out as extensively as in the United States. In general, the requirement that all judicial actions be presented in writing makes the process somewhat lengthy. Most cases are read rather than heard by a judge. The jury system, although mentioned in the constitution, is rarely used except in a few provinces, including Buenos Aires and Cordoba. In no case may the president exercise judicial functions, assume jurisdiction over pending cases, or reopen those decided.

Regional & Local Government

The 1853 constitution divides power between the national government, the twenty-two provinces, and one national territory (Tierra del Fuego, Antarctica, and the South Atlantic Islands), stipulating that the provinces "retain all power not delegated by the national constitution to the federal government." (Argentina also lays claim to the *Islas Malvinas* [Falkland Islands], a group of desolate islands some 300 miles off the Patagonian coast which have been occupied by Great Britain since 1833. On April 2, 1982, Argentine military forces occupied the islands and, after a brief war, were forced to surrender to British forces on June 14, 1982.)

Each province has its own constitution which is similar in nature, although more detailed, to the federal constitution and usually includes a bill of rights and amendments. Such amendments are made in the same manner as those to the federal constitution in the national government. The provinces elect their own legislatures and governors, who are "regents of the federal government for the exercise of the constitution and law of the nation."

The chief provincial executive is the governor. In all provinces, the governor's term is four years, and he may not be immediately reelected. In the majority of provinces, the governor is elected by direct suffrage; a few provinces retain electoral colleges.

Like the president, a governor enjoys extensive powers of appointment and removal. He is able to call special legislative sessions, to introduce and veto bills, and to issue executive decrees. He is responsible for the preparation and execution of the provincial budget, and, as the direct agent of the national government, is charged with the enforcement in his province of all national laws. The governor is also commander-in-chief of the local militia.

Structurally, provincial legislatures vary. Only those provinces with a population with a population of more than half a million have bicameral legislatures, with the result that almost two-thirds of the provincial legislatures are unicameral. Members usually serve for four years in the lower house and six years in the upper, if there is one. Most legislative sessions last four to five months and focus on such topics as taxation, approval of the provincial budget, and the promotion of education and health-related activities.

In the majority of provinces, the governor appoints city mayors; however, the president, with the approval of the Senate, appoints the mayor of Buenos Aires. Each mayor heads an elected council. In some small towns, the governor appoints an assisting commission of three to five persons.

Argentina has had a long history of federal intervention in provincial affairs. The federal government is constitutionally empowered to intervene in order "to guarantee the republican form of government, repel foreign invasion and, at the request of the constituted authorities, to support or reestablish those authorities, should they have been deposed by sedition or invasion by another province"—a power subject to frequent abuse. The president or Congress may remove all government officials in a province and replace them with federal appointees or "intervenors," responsible only to the president and Congress. From 1966 to March 1973, the provinces were directly controlled by such intervenors, who exercised both executive and legislative power in the name of the president. They were removed from power in October 1973. However, federal control was re-imposed after the 1976 military coup.

The Electoral System

Until passage of the Saenz Pena Law in 1912, the Argentine electorate was firmly controlled by the political hegemony of the ruling oligarchy located in Buenos Aires. This law (named after a president elected in 1910) provided for universal and compulsory male suffrage, a secret ballot, and permanent registration. Minority representation in the Chamber of Deputies was ensured by a rule that one-third of a province's representatives must come from the province's second-strongest party. In 1972, the same rule was applied to the Senate. The Argentine Congress approved a law granting women the vote on September 9, 1947, and they were able to vote for the first time in the elections of 1951.

International observers mark the passage of the Saenz Pena law as "the point from which the conditions necessary for the operation of a representative democracy" began in Argentina. Ballot rigging declined substantially and voter participation increased dramatically from about 190,000 in 1910 to 640,000 in 1912 and to 1.46 million in 1928. Argentina's first bona fide elections were held in 1916. In 1963, the Saenz Pena law was replaced by a combination of earlier electoral practices, decrees of several governments since 1955, and a system of proportional representation, the last requiring a party to gain a minimum of 3 percent of the vote in order to obtain a seat.

Voting always takes place on a Sunday and is compulsory for all Argentina citizens between the ages of eighteen and seventy. Failure to vote may be punished with a small fine or brief imprisonment, but the rule is only occasionally enforced. Of those eligible to vote, 85 to 90 percent have done so at most elections. Recognized political parties have poll watchers at the polling places, where detailed regulations safeguard the secrecy of the ballot. Each precinct processes a maximum of 250 voters, except those located in cities with more than 30,000 inhabitants, where 300 is the maximum number.

The Electoral Department of the Interior Ministry appoints a federal judge, known as an "electoral judge," and an electoral board to administer elections. The electoral judge is responsible for the registration list and oversees the eligibility and actions of political parties. The electoral board names polling place officials and adjudicates any irregularities that arise regarding voting.

The Party System

Origins of the Parties

The origins of the modern party system can be traced back to 1891 and the founding of the first radical party in opposition to the conservative oligarchs who had ruled Argentina until then. For the next fifty years, Argentine politics was largely a struggle between Radicals and Conservatives who, respectively, can be characterized very roughly as representing new Argentine business vs. old agricultural and business interests with strong European ties. The system changed radically in the mid-1940s with the appearance of the Peronist movement and the emerging clash between the old elites, largely represented by the Radicals, and the electoral power of labor. Marxist socialism, moderate or revolutionary, while not unrepresented in Argentina, has played very little role in its politics.

The Parties in Law

Parties were suspended and party activity was banned when the military took over in 1976. In December 1979, President Videla announced that political parties would soon be allowed to function again, although those professing totalitarian ideologies (i.e., communists) would remain banned. At the same time the junta issued a document outlining steps for the introduction of the parties into the military's National Reorganization Process.

While still legally banned, party activity resumed openly in 1981 and began to reach prejunta proportions in the wake of the Malvinas (Falklands) debacle. The legal ban was lifted soon after the end of hostilities. At the same time, a proposed new law for parties was circulated for discussion. The law would require parties to register their memberships with the central government. A party of 35,000 members organized in at least five districts would be recognized as a national party. The law would require that party leaders be elected by direct vote of the whole membership every four years.

Party Organization

Argentine parties are marked by factionalism and personalism and are usually dependent on a strong leader for cohesion and effectiveness. In the absence of such a leader, local and personal political organizations are often stronger than the national body, reflecting the strength of independent individuals with local, regional, or institutional power bases. The Radicals have generally permitted a loose relationship between the local organization and the center, but the Peronists usually have tried to impose strict centralized control. Even when Perón was alive, however, but out of power, he was often forced to negotiate with independent local Peronist leaders. By and large, the major political groups do not have coherent or distinctive policies, and divisions between the parties and between intraparty factions are based as much or more on personalities as on ideology. Both major movements, Peronist and Radical, contain groups and individuals whose political ideologies differ sharply.

This incoherence, combined with the fact that the parties have been openly active for only three of the last sixteen years, has made their detailed and comprehensive study virtually impossible, resulting in information that is often vague, contradictory, and incomplete. Because of this paucity of trustworthy information and the parties' general incoherence, the two major political tendencies, Peronist and Radical, will be discussed below as general movements, rather than as sets of distinct parties.

The Peronist Movement

History

The Argentine political process was transformed radically by the election of Colonel Juan Domingo Perón to the presidency in 1946. Until his overthrow and eventual exile in 1955, Perón succeeded in mobilizing the overwhelming support of the large and previously uncommitted labor sector of the Argentine electorate. His ideas and supporters, who split into various factions, remain the dominant ideological force in Argentine politics.

After participating in a military coup in 1943, Perón appointed himself minister of labor and social planning at a time when Argentina was undergoing a profound economic and social transformation. The Second World War had forced the country toward self-sufficiency, accelerating the rate of industrial development. Since 1930, a growing exodus from rural to urban areas, particularly to Buenos Aires, greatly enlarged the working class, which began to demand greater opportunities and social reforms. The traditional parties failed to recognize the full extent of these claims, and were unable to obtain sufficient support from the urban and rural proletariat to win the elections of 1946.

Prior to the elections, Perón won considerable support from the working class by using his ministerial post to reform the labor movement and to enact a series of social measures, including paid vacations, protection against arbitrary dismissal, and a pension system. He also won increased salaries for labor, helped in labor's organizational efforts, and appointed labor leaders to government office. Paradoxically, Perón also managed to gain the backing of the emerging industrial elite, who saw in Perón a strong leader who advocated an authoritarian, nationalistic government which would work toward economic independence and the development of a strong industrial sector.

During the Perón presidency, labor gained more than it had in half a century of association with the Radical and Socialist parties. Labor's real income increased from 30 percent to 53 percent of the gross national product. The ranks of the labor movement swelled to three million, with the majority affiliated with the General Confederation of Labor (*Confederación General de Trabajo;* CGT) where Perón's influence was strongest. Although Perón sought active support from the country's economic elite, by offering them benefits in exchange, his real power base rested with the working class, which was the principal beneficiary of his policies.

After the overthrow of Perón by the military in 1955, the Peronist Party was dissolved by decree. Weakened by the loss of their leader, the Peronist movement became fractionalized by personal rivalries, tactical disputes, and factional differences. Perón further complicated attempts to reorganize the party by discrediting from his place of exile anyone who aspired to the leadership of the party. Furthermore, the army threatened the overthrow of any government which permitted the Peronist Party to reconstitute itself freely or participate in local and national elections. In 1962, President Frondizi was deposed by the army because Peronists polled one-third of the popular vote in that year's elections, winning forty-seven national deputies and ten provincial governorships. The government set up by the army annulled the election and dissolved Congress.

When new elections were held in July 1963, the Radical candidate, Arturo Illia, was elected with only one-fourth of the popular vote. Eighteen percent of the ballots cast were blank, an expression of Peronist strength. The remaining votes were divided among six other major parties.

In 1966, Illia was ousted by the military, which remained in power until March 1973, when new balloting, the first in ten years, elected Hector Cámpora president. Cámpora was the candidate of a new party created by the Peronists and a Radical faction under the leadership of former president Frondizi. The party was set up solely to support the candidacy of Cámpora.

Cámpora resigned in July 1973 with the statement that "my election was for no other reason than to restore to General Perón the mandate that was taken from him unjustly." Perón, who had been allowed to return to Argentina in November 1972, was elected president in September 1973. His second wife, María Estela (Isabel) Martínez de Perón, became vice president.

Peron died July 1, 1974, and his widow succeeded him. In the following two years, the Peronists split into warring factions which covered the political spectrum from radical and populist left-wing urban guerrillas to radical and paternalistic right-wing groups. Amid a climate of rising violence, Isabel Perón continued to attempt to carry out her husband's policies until the 1976 military coup.

Organization

Better described as a movement than a structured party, Peronism suffered from a dispersal of votes after Perón's exile and the dissolution of the party in 1955. However, the majority of Peronist supporters were not absorbed into other parties, and they remained the most important political force in the country.

While other parties were divided on their policies toward the Peronists, the Peronists were divided on how to treat the rest of the political system. The movement split into two groups: The largest group, known as the Orthodox Peronists, remained loyal to Perón and the original party platform, forming the Popular Union (*Unión Popular*). A smaller group, known as the Neo-Peronists, were more willing to collaborate with other parties and opposed direct action against the government. The latter group represented the right wing of the movement and lacked strong ties with the CGT. Under the slogan "Peronism Without Perón," the Neo-Peronists formed the Popular Provincial Parties (*Partidos Populares Provinciales*).

The ability of the Peronist movement to survive in spite of its factionalism has been attributed to the "vertical form of organization and the extremely rigid structure" within the various Peronist parties. These structures enabled Perón to exercise leadership from abroad through personal representatives within the top leadership of most of the parties. Where Perón was unable to maintain control, particularly among the Neo-Peronists and the Peronist unions (who during the late 1960s sought autonomy from the party leaders, and increasingly, from Perón himself), his representatives were instructed to try negotiating with the dissidents.

Peronism often benefited indirectly from government policies. The banning of all political parties during the three military presidencies from 1966 to early 1973 put all parties on an equal footing; the Peronists took advantage of the situation by appealing for support from the working classes, who were also suffering from restrictions on trade-union activities. Furthermore, the military regimes gradually alienated most major sectors of Argentine society, resulting in widespread opposition to military rule. Because of its size and organizational foundation in the union movement, Peronism was able to achieve greater visibility than other groups and was seen by many as the only viable alternative to military rule. These factors played a key role in the return of Juan Perón as president in October 1973.

Policy

Since the organization of the movement in 1947, the various Peronist parties and groups have followed Juan Perón's domestic policies: the formation and support of unions, social legislation, and the participation of workers in the economy and government. Following the dissolution of the Peronist Party in 1955 and until Perón's return to power in 1973, the Peronist leadership, especially within the CGT, increasingly neglected purely social demands to embark on a political offensive opposing the various military regimes.

During his second presidency, Perón buttressed the national aspirations of his supporters by adopting a foreign policy favoring economic independence and excluding alliances with the United States and the Soviet Union. While assuming a neutralist position (*tercera posición*) toward world powers, Perón worked vigorously to promote Argentine leadership in Latin America and to gain prestige for his country among its closest neighbors and trading partners.

Since the 1976 military takeover and the severe curtailment of all political activity, it is unclear whether the policies of the Peronist movement have undergone any radical change in face of the present economic crisis, which has severely affected the working class. However, given the persistence of Peronist policies in the past, it seems probable that the movement's supporters still pursue the original goals.

Membership & Constituency

The mainstay of Peronist support comes from the urban and rural working class and the lower middle classes with a relatively low level of education. Although the Peronist electorate is distributed fairly evenly over all the provinces, the bulk of its membership is found in urban and industrial areas such as Córdoba and Buenos Aires. There is also considerable Peronist support in rural areas—particularly in the provinces of Salta, Santiago del Estero, and Tucumán—where there is a high proportion of agricultural laborers and seasonal workers.

The Popular Union of the 1960s retained the electoral support of the industrial areas and the more densely populated provinces (the federal capital, Córdoba, Santa Fé), while the Peronists in the agricultural provinces (Mendoza, Salta, Jujuy, Tucumán, Chaco, Neuquen and Río Negro) favored the Popular Provincial Parties.

Financing

No reliable information is available on the sources of Peronist funds.

Leadership

The movement has been unable to fill the vacuum left by the death of Perón, whose personal dynamism maintained the loyalty and cohesion of the movement's key leaders. The central Peronist organization, now called the *Justicialistas*, is led by Deolindo Bittel. A left-wing leader, Juan Manuel Abal Medina, now in exile after spending six years (1976–82) in asylum in the Mexican Embassy in Buenos Aires, is sometimes mentioned as a potential force in the movement. Other leading figures are Mario Cámpora, nephew of the former president, and Jorge Vásquez, who was in jail from 1976 to 1981.

Prospects

It is believed that the Peronists still command the highest percentage of electoral support and are most likely to replace the military government in free elections.

The Radical Parties

History

The formation of the Radical Civic Union (*Unión Cívica Radical;* UCR) in 1891 was the result of strong opposition to the ruling oligarchy who controlled the principal commercial and landowning interests in the country. Hipólito Irigoyen dominated the Radicals, and it was due largely to his powerful personality that he was elected to the presidency in 1916 with 45.9 percent of the vote. The Radicals remained in power until 1930, when conservatives regained control following a military coup which deposed Irigoyen. During the next two decades, the Radicals split into factions as a result of differences over issues and power struggles among party leaders.

The Radical Congress of 1956 nominated Arturo Frondizi as its presidential candidate. A faction led by Ricardo Balbín broke with the party in opposition to Frondizi's desire to gain the support of Peronists and other groups. Balbín founded the People's Radical Civic Union (*Unión Cívica Radical del Pueblo;* UCRP). Frondizi's faction then adopted the name of Intransigent Radical Civic Union (*Unión Cívica Radical Intransigente;* UCRI) and went on to win the elections of 1958, with the support of the Peronists, Communists, and splinter parties. Frondizi campaigned on a platform calling for nationalism, agrarian reform, and an independent economic and foreign policy.

In 1962, the armed forces—alarmed at the rise in Peronist power in the Chamber of Deputies and provincial governments, as well as the worsening economic situation—deposed and arrested President Frondizi. Arturo Umberto Illia, leader of the UCRP, was elected president the following year. Illia's government was unable to solve the country's economic problems or control the military who forced Illia out of office in 1966.

Organization

Traditionally, the Radicals have maintained local committees in the provinces in an attempt to assure geographical balance. However, the large measure of autonomy exercised by the local committees has often limited central control of the membership by national party leaders. Although party leaders are democratically elected, upward mobility within the party hierarchy is based on a candidate's proven commitment to maintaining a party career. The Radicals, like the Peronists, are divided into several more or less distinct factions which are often bitterly at odds.

Policy

The Radicals' ideological position has been defined by their standing as an opposition group for much of their existence. At the turn of the century, the Radicals campaigned against the close European ties of Argentina's ruling oligarchy and European control of the country's commerce. The Radicals have consistently opposed military rule, and on some occasions have compromised on issues with the Peronists in order to force the military to set a timetable for elections. The Radicals still adhere to most of the party programs adopted by its leadership in the first half of this century: economic nationalism, including tariff protection and state intervention in oil and mining interests, as well as an independent foreign policy.

Membership & Constituency

Since its foundation, the Radicals have sought to present a program which would involve all sectors of the population in the exercise of political power. However, according to an electoral survey in 1962 in the federal capital, where the Radicals enjoy their strongest support, 78 percent of the party's supporters came from the middle class, both upper and lower.

Women also ranked high among the Radical electorate. Despite restrictions on their activities by the various military governments, the Radicals have maintained support in the provinces of Buenos Aires, Córdoba, Entre Ríos, Santa Fé, and Santiago del Estero.

Financing

No reliable information is available on Radical finances, but it can probably be safely assumed that their income is largely derived from contributions by wealthy individuals and corporations.

Leadership

Internal power struggles among party leaders have often split the movement into factions. For the past two decades national leadership of the Radicals was in the hands of Ricardo Balbín. In September 1981, Balbín died at the age of seventy-seven, and was replaced by Antonio Troccoli.

The preeminent Radical leader (UCRP) from 1961 to 1981 was Ricardo Balbin. Upon his death in 1981, Antonio Troccoli briefly took over the party until mid-1982, when a party meeting marked by scuffles elected Carlos Contín (born 1916) party leader. His primary opponent was Raúl Alfonsín (born 1927).

Prospects

While the Radicals do not apparently have the same degree of popular support as the Peronists, they are slightly more cohesive and could mount a more coordinated election campaign. At the same time, elements of the Radicals favor an alliance with the Peronists to present a presidential candidate who could win a clear popular majority and so inhibit further military intervention.

Minor Parties

In addition to the Peronists and the Radicals, Argentina's political landscape has supported several minor parties, whose relatively small numbers, especially among the conservatives, have come from one specific sector of the population and have generally tended toward single-issue politics in their own interest.

An exception is the Movement for Integration and Development (*Movimiento de Integración y Desarrollo;* MID), a small but significant splinter group from the Radicals led by former president Frondizi. Organized in 1963, it achieved its major success when it joined with Peronists and several minor parties to support Cámpora's candidacy in 1973. The MID wants to incorporate Peronism fully into the nation's political life and put an end to its position as an often banned and potentially revolutionary force. The MID also calls for greater industrialization, particularly in heavy industry, stimulation of domestic saving, encouragement of foreign investment, and a foreign policy that would open new markets. The party's position as a cohesive swing group with a respected national leader gives it a more important role than its numbers and popular support would suggest.

The conservative parties have represented the large landowners as well as those among the urban upper middle class who favor free trade and economic liberalism. In the first half of this century, the conservatives strove to retain close ties with Europe. Conservatives governed the country from 1874 until 1916 and again from 1930 to 1943. The party now operates under the name National

Democratic Party (*Partido Demócrata Nacional;* PDN). Although in recent years electoral support for the conservatives has been weak, many party leaders have been appointed to government posts under the various military governments.

In August 1980, a coalition of eight minor political organizations, representing the center to moderate left, founded the Center Democratic Federation (*Federación Centro Democrática;* FCD) to challenge the "domestic monopoly of the populist movements." The major groups in the coalition were the Christian Democratic Union (*Unión Cristiano Democrática;* UCD), the Progressive Democratic Party (*Partido Demócrata Progresivo;* PDP), and the Socialist Democratic Party (*Partido Social Democrática;* PSD). In July 1981, many of these groups joined with the Radicals and Peronists to demand a return to democratic rule.

Other Political Forces

Military

The roots of the power of the Argentine armed forces date back to the early nineteenth century, when elite figures from Buenos Aires and other provinces established private armies to protect their property and power. By the end of the century, a professional army had evolved. Today, the Argentine armed forces, with some 140,000 troops, are the second largest and among the most sophisticated in Latin America.

The armed forces were loyal to the various conservative presidents who ruled between 1862 and 1916, but major conflicts between the government and the armed forces began when the Radicals assumed power in 1916. The "military party" which exists today, and which provides political leadership and strength for the interests of Argentina's traditional oligarchy, has been a force in Argentine politics since 1930, the date of the first successful military intervention. Since that time, well over half of all Argentine presidents have been generals, and every chief executive in the three decades prior to the 1973 elections either assumed or lost power through force of arms. Indeed, over the years, the active support of the military has been essential to the existence of any civilian government in Argentina.

As pretexts for their takeovers, the armed forces usually cite civilian government corruption, immorality, and inability to maintain law and order and control subversion and "the spread of communism." Additionally, although not stated by the military, it appears that some of the overthrown administrations attempted to assert some control over military affairs. The 1976 intervention may be considered distinct from prior takeovers in that the military intended to maintain control of government for the duration and did not contemplate an early return to civilian rule.

Widespread anti-Peronism among the armed forces has been a contributing factor in the last four takeovers. The reasons for this opposition are complex. The vastly increased power of the labor unions under Perón concerned the military, who felt threatened by a popular power base outside their control. The military was also violently opposed to a series of measures carried out by Perón in 1954 and 1955 including the legalization of divorce and prostitution and abrogation of religious instruction in schools. Perón's anticlerical campaign probably went a long way to costing him his position in 1955. The military also took a personal dislike to Perón's first wife, Evita, and her openly antimilitary stance. After Perón's death, the military's continued opposition to Peronism was, in large part, due to its alleged connections with the Montoneros, an urban guerrilla group which was creating domestic havoc at the time of the 1976 takeover.

The ideology of the armed forces in Argentina, as in much of Latin America, has undergone substantial changes in the past two decades. It is no coincidence that these changes have occurred at the same time as an expansion of U.S. training programs and military aid to a number of Latin American military regimes. Such training programs have been marked by anticommunist and anti-Castro indoctrination and by stress on the military's role as guardian of internal security and economic stability. As a consequence, the military now considers itself responsible for the definition and delegation of political authority.

The officer corps has reportedly been strongly influenced by the teachings of Jordán Bruno Genta, a long-time educator in the military's officers schools and author of *Guerra Contrarevolucionaria* (*Counterrevolutionary War*), published in 1962. In this book, Genta argued that the ills of the modern world can be traced to the French Revolution (1789), which paved the way for liberal democracy. Liberal democracy, according to Genta, is a front for the Masonic orders and is supported by a cabal of international financiers, mostly Jews. Genta argued that, outside the Church, the military was the last repository of spiritual values and should transform itself into a "mystical body" in order to carry out its mission. Genta denied that the military should be subordinate to a liberal democratic constitution and its corrupt laws and declared that the military's higher responsibility to God and the motherland required direct intervention in politics. Genta was assassinated in 1974.

Surveys carried out in Argentina in the 1960s revealed that some 70 percent of Argentina generals come from the upper middle class (with the largest proportion coming from families with business and military backgrounds) and with almost half born in the Greater Buenos Aires area. Many generals have been second-generation Argentines of Italian or Spanish descent. (This is true of all four of Argentina's presidents since the 1976 coup: Videla, Viola, Galtieri, and Bignone.)

Argentine troops are essentially conscripts, that is, citizen soldiers serving for one to two years. Military service is compulsory; all males must register for service upon attaining their eighteenth birthday. Some 80,000 young men are inducted annually. There is also a large number of noncommissioned officers, who are volunteers and of proven capability. Noncommissioned officers come from all regions of the country and varied social backgrounds. Thus, the ranks of the Argentine armed forces are very much a "melting pot."

The armed forces are as ridden with factionalism as the civilian political parties. In spite of the officers' general antipathy to Peronism, there are elements in the military with Peronist inclinations. According to some reports, this is particularly true among armored units and junior officers. Interservice rivalries are also common. Both the navy and air force disagreed with the choice of president after the Malvinas (Falklands) defeat and withdrew from the junta for several weeks. Air force general Basilio Lami Dozo and many other leading air force officers resigned in the wake of the war, in which the air force performed creditably in comparison with the army and navy. Lami Dozo reportedly wanted the military to set up a political party to carry forward its National Reorganization Process when the military stepped down. Additional divisions apparently stem from inter- and intraservice disputes over the apportionment of blame for the defeat.

Armed Movements (Guerrillas)

During the 1970s, two organized urban guerrilla movements increased their activities in Argentina: the Montonero Peronist Movement (*Movimiento Peronista Montonero;* MPM), commonly known as the "Montoneros"; and the People's Revolutionary Army (*Ejército Revolucionario del Pueblo;*

ERP), a Marxist-Leninist organization. These two groups were crushed by assassination, "disappearance," imprisonment, and exile; they have not presented a threat to national security or the social order since 1977.

Organized Labor

The Argentine constitution recognizes the right to work, the rights of association and collective bargaining, and the right to strike. Argentina's labor movement is the oldest and most experienced in Latin America: the Buenos Aires printers' union, constituted as a mutual society in 1857, was the first real trade union on the continent.

Prior to the 1976 military takeover, Argentina's most powerful labor union was the General Confederation of Labor (*Confederación General del Trabajo;* CGT). A forty-eight-hour general strike called by the CGT in July 1975 paralyzed the country and forced the government to dismiss Social Welfare Minister José López Rega, the man behind the formation and functioning of the notorious AAA (Argentine Anti-Communist Alliance [*Alianza Argentina Anti-Comunista*] or "Triple A" death squad, allegedly responsible for the assassination of large numbers of trade unionists and political militants.

The military government in 1976 suspended by decree all trade-union activity, including the right to strike, and appointed military officers to take charge of the CGT and all important unions. (Currently, some fifty national union syndicates are controlled by appointed military officers.) In addition, several labor unions were dissolved and declared illegal; their bank accounts were closed, and their stocks and assets were incorporated into the state treasury. Furthermore, the military government's long-awaited labor code, published in November 1979, abolished national labor confederations, including the CGT, banned all political activity by labor groups, outlawed the closed shop, and took over all labor-union social welfare activities.

Despite physical intimidation—trade unionists figure heavily in the lists of those who have "disappeared" since the military takeover—and restrictive measures imposed on all labor activity, it appears that the Argentine labor movement still retains its traditional strength and can mobilize its members when necessary. Strikes have taken place in several sectors since 1976. In April 1979, government repression and soaring inflation provoked a general strike involving 30 percent of all workers in Argentina. A recent CGT demonstration was held on March 30, 1982, shortly before the Argentine invasion of the Malvinas (Falkland) Islands. The police arrested some 2,700 demonstrators in Buenos Aires; in Mendoza, the police fired into crowds of demonstrators, killing one person and injuring several others.

Physical repression, accompanied by an economic policy which has slashed the real wages of the working class, continue to provoke scattered strikes.

Press

Despite strict censorship laws imposed by the military since the 1976 coup, the press has increasingly spoken out against the government's policies, reported instances of disappearance, etc. As a result, journalists have been one of the groups singled out for repression and intimidation and large numbers have disappeared. Even the conservative daily *La Prensa* has been attacked for its strong criticism of the military government: in June 1981 the government removed all official advertising from its pages, branding its onslaughts as "harmful" and "malicious."

Human Rights Groups

Human rights groups in Argentina—of which eight are significant—are becoming increasingly bold and vocal, demanding that the military regime account for the whereabouts of an estimated 10,000 to 15,000 people who have disappeared since the coup, especially in the years 1976 to 1979. When Adolfo Pérez Esquivel—head of the Buenos Aires-based Service for Justice and Peace in Latin America (*Servicio Paz y Justicia en América Latina*)—received the 1980 Nobel Peace Prize, the widespread international support and visibility increased the credibility and strength of the Argentine human rights movement.

Roman Catholic Church

Until recently, Argentina's traditionally conservative Roman Catholic Church hierarchy had not openly opposed the military government. In July 1981, however, the church hierarchy issued a seventy-four-page document calling for greater respect for human rights and expressing concern for the "anguished situation of the relatives of disappeared people." The Church has also criticized declining living standards brought about by the military's conservative economic policies.

Moreover, Church criticism has been accompanied by a number of well-publicized activities, including participation in meetings with political parties.

In August 1982, the Argentine Roman Catholic Church called on the military to address the plight of the disappeared and asked that the state of siege be lifted.

National Prospects

The prospects for a return to civilian rule in Argentina were probably better in late 1982 than at any other time since the 1976 coup. Not only has the military regime failed to meet many of its economic and social objectives and engaged in acts of brutality unprecedented in Argentine history, it has lost a war which it initiated. As a result, the regime has become increasingly isolated. After years of relative silence, the press, political parties, labor, human rights groups, and even the Church are demanding a return to civilian government.

On July 1, 1982, President Bignone announced that the ban on political activity had been lifted; an act that was only a recognition of reality. The parties had already begun to act together a year earlier, when Peronists, Radicals, the Christian Democrats, MID, and smaller groups joined in multiparty talks to push for a timetable for elections.

Despite these developments and the military's previously declared intent "to ensure the later restoration of a republican, representative, and federal democracy," there are no indications that the country will be allowed to return to democratic rule in the immediate future. The end of Bignone's term in 1984 is most often mentioned as a likely date for a transfer of power. Furthermore, many Argentine politicians believe that even if the military does turn over the government to civilians, it will expect to continue to play a special role and will resist any attempt to establish civilian control over the armed forces.

Given the disarray and intense factionalism of Argentine politics, it is likely that only the appearance of an individual or political party with strong support among both the general public and the armed forces will make possible a peaceful and stable transfer of power. A far more probable prognosis would be that the instability that has dominated Argentine political life for half a century will continue.

Further Reading

Ciria, Alberto. *Parties and Power in Modern Argentina (1930–1946)*. Albany, N. Y.: State University of New York Press, 1974.

Fernandez, Julio A. *The Political Elite in Argentina*. New York: New York University Press, 1970.

Goldwert, Marvin. *Democracy, Militarism, and Nationalism in Argentina, 1930–1966: An Interpretation*. Austin: University of Texas Press, 1972.

Graillot, Helene. "Argentina." In *Guide to the Political Parties of South America*. Middlesex, England: Penguin Latin American Library, 1973.

Kirkpatrick, Jeane. *Leader and Vanguard in Mass Society: A Study of Peronist Argentina*. Cambridge, Mass.: MIT Press, 1971.

Lewis, Paul H. *The Governments of Argentina, Brazil, and Mexico*. New York: Crowell, 1974.

Organization of American States. *Report on the Situation of Human Rights in Argentina*. Washington, D.C.: Organization of American States, 1980.

Potash, Robert A. *The Army and Politics in Argentina, 1945–62*. Stanford, Calif.: Stanford University Press, 1980.

———. *The Impact of Professionalism on the Twentieth-Century Argentine Military*. Amherst, Mass.: University of Massachusetts, Program in Latin American Studies, 1977.

Snow, Peter G. *Political Forces in Argentina*. New York: Praeger, 1979.

Stover, Eric. *Scientists and Human Rights in Argentina Since 1976*. Washington, D.C.: American Association for the Advancement of Science, 1981.

COMMONWEALTH OF AUSTRALIA

by Andrew Parkin, Ph.D.

The System of Government

Australia, a nation of 14.7 million people, is both a federal and a parliamentary democracy. Federalism reflects the circumstances of Australia's colonial origins. On January 1, 1901, six self-governing British colonies—New South Wales, Victoria, Queensland, South Australia, Western Australia and Tasmania—federated to form the Commonwealth of Australia. The six colonies remained as component states of the federal system. There are also now two territories—the Northern Territory and the Australian Capital Territory—directly administered for most of their history by the Commonwealth (national) government.

The Act of the British Parliament which authorized federation also provided Australia with a written constitution. The constitution specifies the allocation of powers between the Commonwealth and the states. The Commonwealth powers are mainly the obvious "national" ones—currency, defense, foreign affairs, immigration, international trade, postal service, and so on. Few of these powers are exclusive, most being "concurrent" with continuing state powers—though Commonwealth law prevails in any case of inconsistent concurrent legislation. The states retain all powers not exclusively transferred to the Commonwealth, leaving them with immediate authority over most personal and property matters.

Over the years, there has been a gradual expansion of the significance of the Commonwealth government, partly achieved by constitutional amendment. Amendments are difficult to approve, requiring the passage of a referendum by a majority of voters nationwide *and* a majority of voters in at least four of the six states. Only eight out of thirty-six proposed amendments submitted to referendum have passed into law. Some of these, however, have increased Commonwealth power, such as a 1946 expansion of its authority to provide welfare benefits and a 1967 amendment providing powers to assist Aborigines.

The High Court, which exercises judicial review over constitutional matters, also has assisted the increasing prominence of the Commonwealth government. The Commonwealth has been permitted to use the primacy of its concurrent legislation to monopolize the collection of income taxes and, in turn, make the states dependent on the "reimbursement" of these funds through a revenue-sharing arrangement. In addition, the constitution enables the Commonwealth to "grant financial assistance to any state on such terms and conditions as the Parliament thinks fit." This has been interpreted by the High Court to allow "terms and conditions" which control powers otherwise "reserved" to the states. As the chief justice of the High Court noted in 1942, a situation in which "all state powers would be controlled by the Commonwealth . . . cannot be prevented by any legal decision." The federal "balance" is thus largely (though not entirely) a political rather than a strictly constitutional matter. The question of the appropriate balance has been one of the political controversies of recent decades.

This federal system coexists with parliamentary institutions originally developed under the British unitary system. The British Westminster model was followed in the nineteenth-century colonies (and thus persists in all states). Its melding with federalism required use of North American as well as British precedents. The national legislature (Parliament) consists of two chambers: a House of Representatives in which the majority party (following Westminster conventions) forms the government, and a Senate in which there is an equal allocation of seats to each state.

Sixty percent of Australians live in five great metropolitan areas with sprawling suburbs, and the population is overwhelmingly English-speaking. A massive influx of European immigrants in the 1950–1975 period (about 35 percent of Australians are first- or second-generation immigrants, about half of these from a Continental European source) has been absorbed into the older British and Irish stock without much social dislocation.

In fact, ethnic groups have had a surprisingly muted impact, though recently there have been appeals to the ethnic vote through such avenues as the promotion of multicultural media networks and bilingual education programs. There are embryonic signs of ethnic-based interest groups.

Executive

The Australian head of state is technically the British monarch. Except when this monarch is actually visiting Australia, however, the role is carried out by the governor-general (appointed by the monarch on the advice of the Australian government). It is the firm convention of the parliamentary system that this head of state acts only on the advice of his ministers and, in particular, of the prime minister.

The prime minister is, also by convention, the leader of the majority party or coalition in the House of Representatives. Other ministers are drawn from either house of Parliament, mostly from the House of Representatives. The parties vary in how they choose ministers: in the Australian Labor Party (ALP), it is by ballot of all parliamentary caucus members; in the Liberal Party (LP), the leader is elected by caucus, but then is empowered to appoint his ministerial colleagues. In most governments, the cabinet is composed of the prime minister plus a small number of senior ministers.

As of 1982, for example, the governing coalition of the Liberal Party and the National Country Party (NCP) had the LP leader, Malcolm Fraser, as prime minister, and the NCP leader, Doug Anthony, as deputy prime minister. There were twenty-four other ministers, nineteen LP and five NCP. Only twelve ministers joined the prime minister and his deputy in the cabinet, though other ministers attended cabinet meetings on matters relating to their portfolios. In the ALP government of 1972 to 1975, all twenty-seven ministers were included in a rather unwieldy cabinet.

The cabinet, chaired by the prime minister, is the central organ of government. All major decisions about policy and legislation are dealt with at this level. Because the government, by definition, controls the House of Representatives (and usually the Senate as well), the cabinet is able to operate as the effective locus of decision making within the constraints of broad party expectations. Technically, under the constitution, executive power is wielded by the Executive Council, consisting of the governor-general and his ministers. In practice, the Executive Council meets only to satisfy this technical requirement, providing a forum in which the governor-general follows ministerial advice in assenting to legislation, making proclamations and appointments, and so on.

Ministers are nearly always given particular responsibility for a department or departments within the Commonwealth bureaucracy. While ministers appoint a small number of personal advisers, these departments are staffed by a permanent civil service.

The Commonwealth bureaucracy has expanded considerably in the past decades. Some departments, because of their key coordinating role or traditional prestige, are regarded as the more significant. The Department of Prime Minister and Cabinet, for example, is becoming increasingly important as a source of policy advice to the prime minister on cabinet submissions from other departments. The Treasury has long been a powerful institution, being responsible not only for the formulation of economic policy but also, with the Department of Finance, exercising oversight of the expenditure of all other departments and drawing up the annual budget. There are also a large number of statutory authorities which operate outside the civil-service structure with varying degrees of financial and policy independence. Among the more significant authorities are Australia Post, Telecom (the public telecommunications monopoly), Trans Australia Airlines (competing with privately owned Ansett Airlines as the only Australian national airlines), and the Australian Broadcasting Commission (national TV and radio network). As in other Western countries, there has been concern expressed about the degree of accountability of the vast bureaucracy to the government.

Legislature

The House of Representatives is the forum from which the government emerges. Under the constitution, it must be "as nearly as praticable" double the size of the Senate, and each of the six states must have at least five members. Apart from the latter provision, which gives Tasmania an overrepresentation, and a more recent provision of two members for the Australian Capital Territory and one for the Northern Territory, electoral districts are allocated between states in proportion to population. Each of the 125 members of the House of Representatives presently represents a district averaging about 120,000 people. The House is elected for a maximum term of three years. An earlier election may be held if the government loses its parliamentary majority and no alternative party or coalition can build a majority, or, more commonly, if the government perceives some electoral advantage in going to the polls early.

Each state has ten senators, elected at-large for six-year terms, half of them retiring every three years. Senate elections are customarily arranged to coincide with House of Representatives elections, but this is not always possible when the House is dissolved early. There were attempts to resolve this in both 1974 and 1977 through a constitutional amendment fixing the senatorial term to two House terms, but the necessary referendum was defeated on both occasions. Since 1975, the two territories have each had two senators who, unlike their colleagues, must all seek reelection at the same time as every House of Representatives election.

Although the Senate acts generally as a "house of review" on legislation originating in the House of Representatives, the constitution states that the two Houses "shall have equal power" except in a few specific instances; the Senate, for example, cannot originate money bills. For a bill to become law, it must be passed in identical language by both houses. There are cumbersome mechanisms provided in the case of a very prolonged disagreement. Within certain time constraints, if the Senate twice fails to pass a bill, there can be a so-called double dissolution (if the government is prepared to fight an election on the issue). This means that the *entire* membership of *both* houses must face simultaneous reelection. If there is still a deadlock after the elections, there can be a *joint* sitting of both houses (in which senators are outnumbered two to one) to consider the disputed bill(s). Double dissolutions occurred most recently in 1974 and 1975 when an ALP government faced a hostile Opposition-controlled Senate. The only joint sitting took place after the 1974 double dissolution returned both the ALP government and the Opposition-controlled Senate.

In discussing Parliament, it is necessary to separate its key constitutional position from the rather subsidiary role which it now performs. Constitutionally, Parliament is the linchpin of the democratic system, a great debating forum in which legislation is discussed and amended, in which policies are debated and criticized, and in which the actions of the government are overseen.

In practice, however, the locus of power is with the executive. There are several reasons for this development. Probably the most important has been the retrenchment in Parliament of disciplined political parties, making for no clear separation between the executive and its origins in the legislature. Backbench members of the majority party identify closely with the government. They realize that they were elected because of their party label and that their chances of reelection depend largely on the performance of the government. If they were to oppose their own party's government in Parliament, the result might be the defeat of the government, its enforced resignation, and an early election. Without reendorsement by the same party, the backbenchers would have little hope of success. It is much safer for criticisms and misgivings to be expressed within the secrecy of the party caucus. In the ALP, in fact, members of parliament are pledged always to vote in accordance with the majority decision of the caucus. Party discipline is almost as rigid in the Senate as in the House of Representatives, even though the fate of the government is not at stake and despite the original intention that the Senate represent the interests of the states.

A further cause of the decline of Parliament has been the enormous growth of governmental activity, necessarily supervised through the executive. The scale and complexity of the bureaucracy and the expanding range of government programs mean that it is not possible to scrutinize more than a fraction of this empire. Ministers themselves take "responsibility" for their departments only in the broadest sense, this in turn weakens the accountability of ministers to Parliament. The common practice of delegated legislation, where general authorization is given to a minister or some public authority to make regulations, is both a recognition and an exacerbation of the problem.

A third cause of Parliament's weakness is sometimes held to be the internal procedures of the Parliament itself. Parliamentary debates involve many anachronistic rituals irrelevant to the substantive questions under consideration. The government, through its majority, can restrict debating time and force the rapid passage of legislation. Members of Parliament have few staff or research facilities. The "committee" stage of legislative procedure, in which a bill can be examined clause by clause, has proved ineffective as a means of scrutinizing the huge volume of legislation. The few committees, such as the Public Accounts Committee, depend on information supplied by the executive.

It would be dangerous, however, to dismiss Parliament as insignificant. Parliament remains the formal and symbolic focus for the democratic system and remains in the public spotlight. It is the arena from which national leaders are drawn. It provides regular publicity for the Opposition, whose leader is provided salary and privileges equivalent to those of a minister, and whose so-called shadow cabinet mirrors the portfolio responsibilities of the cabinet. The initial period of each day of a sitting Parliament is devoted to "questions without notice" during which any minister can be questioned about his portfolio. While ministers often evade probing questions from the Opposition and indulge themselves in self-congratulation invited by friendly queries from their own backbenchers, this question period does provide a well-publicized arena for the "cut-and-thrust" of political debate.

There have been recent attempts to upgrade the oversight and investigatory capacities of Parliament, particularly in the Senate. In the early 1970s, the Senate established a number of permanent and ad hoc committees, along the lines of those in the United States Congress. However, party loyalty remains the primary motivating force in the legislature, even in the Senate.

When the governing party or coalition does not have a Senate majority—and, given the different electoral bases of the two houses, this has not been uncommon—then the significance of the Senate increases markedly. While the defeat of ordinary legislation in the Senate does not compel the government to resign, obviously its functioning is impaired if such defeats become regular. In this case, some accommodation needs to be sought with the Opposition majority or perhaps with a minor party holding the "balance of power" between the major-party blocs. The actions of all parties depend partly on the perceived political advantages of compliance or confrontation. A government confident of its electoral support may threaten the Senate with a double dissolution; the Opposition in the Senate may recognize a governmental "mandate" to implement election promises; or some compromise may be reached in which Opposition amendments are accepted by the government.

The most controversial aspect of this problem concerns the Senate's power with respect to the government's budget. Under the constitution, the Senate is prohibited from "amending" bills dealing with taxation or financial appropriations (though it is assumed that it can *defeat* them, and thereby effectively force the House of Representatives to make amendments). Until 1975, the Senate had never voted to defeat the government's budgetary legislation (known as supply), without which a government cannot operate. In 1975, however, the Opposition, which controlled the Senate, decided to force what it perceived as an unpopular government to resign and contest a new election. It refused to pass the budget in the Senate.

The government, however, refused to resign, consistent with the Westminster convention that a government which retains the confidence of the House of Representatives stays in office. A stalemate—a "constitutional crisis," as it was called—developed.

The most appropriate solution would seem to have been a political one, with the stalemate persisting until public funds started to run out and the pressure of the crisis, or public opinion, or perceived political advantage produced a compromise on one or both sides. Instead, the situation was "resolved," dramatically and controversially, by the unprecedented intervention of the head of state. The governor-general, contrary to the tradition that he act only on the advice of his ministers, but consonant with a literal reading of the constitution, dismissed the prime minister and his government. He installed the leader of the Opposition as prime minister of a caretaker government, even though the leader of the Opposition had only minority support in the House of Representatives. After a double dissolution, an election a month later returned the caretaker government with an overwhelming majority in both houses. Debate still continues, however, over the propriety of various events in the constitutional crisis and particularly over the action of the governor-general.

Since the 1975 election, two additional elections have again returned the same governing coalition of the Liberal Party and the National Country Party, keeping the ALP in opposition. The most recent (1980) election results for the House of Representatives are produced in Table 1, which

Table 1
THE 1980 HOUSE OF REPRESENTATIVES ELECTION

		Distribution of Seats by Party		
Number of Parliamentary Seats by State or Territory		Liberal Party	National Country Party	Australian Labor Party
New South Wales	43	16	9	18
Victoria	33	13	3	17
Queensland	19	7	7	5
South Australia	11	5	—	6
Western Australia	11	8	—	3
Tasmania	5	5	—	—
Australian Capital Territory	2	—	—	2
Northern Territory	1	—	1	—
TOTAL	125	54	20	51

Table 2
THE 1980 SENATE ELECTION

Number of Senate Vacancies per State or Territory		Distribution of Senators by Party				
		Liberal Party	National Country Party	Australian Labor Party	Australian Democrats	Independent
New South Wales	5	1	1	3	—	—
Victoria	5	2	—	2	1	—
Queensland	5	1	1	2	1	—
South Australia	5	2	—	2	1	—
Western Australia	5	3	—	2	—	—
Tasmania	5	2	—	2	—	1
Australian Capital Territory	2	1	—	1	—	—
Northern Territory	2	1	—	1	—	—
TOTAL	34	13	2	15	3	1

also shows the distribution of parliamentary seats between the states. With seventy-four seats to the ALP's fifty-one, the LP and NCP coalition enjoys a comfortable twenty-three–seat majority.

Five senators from each state and both the senators from each territory were also up for election in 1980. Table 2 shows the results of that election. The senators elected in 1980 joined the thirty senators who were still serving a six-year term beginning in 1977 (the composition of the full Senate is portrayed in Table 3).

In the Senate, the coalition government presently commands only thirty-one of the sixty-four seats. Because a Liberal senator has been elected president of the Senate, officiating (like his counterpart, the speaker of the House of Representatives) over the business of the chamber and casting a vote only in the event of a tie, the gov-

ernment's position is effectively thirty senators out of sixty-three. The five senators from the Australian Democrats, a relatively minor party, and one independent senator hold the balance of power between the government and the twenty-seven ALP senators. Another constitutional crisis is possible, though politically very unlikely.

Judiciary

The High Court exercises judicial review over matters relating to the constitution as well as being a final court of appeal from other jurisdictions. In many respects, the High Court was directly modeled on the United States Supreme Court and exercises a similar capacity to invalidate legislation which the court has deemed unconstitutional. The Australian constitution, however, has no "bill

Table 3
CURRENT SITUATION IN THE SENATE AS A RESULT OF THE 1980 ELECTION

Number of Senate Seats by State or Territory		Distribution of Senators by Party				
		Liberal Party	National Country Party	Australian Labor Party	Australian Democrats	Independent
New South Wales	10	3	1	5	1	—
Victoria	10	4	—	4	2	—
Queensland	10	3	2	4	1	—
South Australia	10	5	—	4	1	—
Western Australia	10	6	—	4	—	—
Tasmania	10	5	—	4	—	1
Australian Capital Territory	2	1	—	1	—	—
Northern Territory	2	1	—	1	—	—
TOTAL	64	28	3	27	5	1

of rights" component. Apart from the Federal Court of Australia (responsible for a range of matters such as bankruptcy and trade practices) and the family court (divorce settlements, etc.), no further system of federal courts has been established. The court systems of the states are vested with jurisdiction over federal law, though final appeals are made to the High Court rather than to state supreme courts in matters of federal law.

As noted earlier, High Court interpretations have been a factor in the increasing prominence of the Commonwealth government. It is common to demarcate four phases in the history of the court, two of them (1900–20, 1942–71) being periods in which a court majority exercised restraints on Commonwealth powers and the other two (1920–42, 1971 to the present) revealing a court majority more inclined to loosen those restraints.

That High Court decisions have a political impact was perhaps most apparent during the 1942 to 1949 term in office of an ALP government which sought to establish a national health scheme and to nationalize the airlines and the banks. Through an adroit interpretation of the constitution which says, ambiguously, that "trade, commerce and intercourse among the States . . . shall be absolutely free," the High Court declared all such actions invalid on the grounds of abrogating the "freedom" of interstate trade. The government, despite being popularly elected with a majority in both houses, was simply not empowered to implement such policies. Through such judicial review, exercised in many other less dramatic cases, the High Court is a significant, though often inconspicuous, political actor.

The justices of the High Court—the chief justice and six associate justices—are appointed by the cabinet. No parliamentary ratification is required. All justices appointed have had legal experience. Under a new constitutional amendment of 1977, newly appointed justices must retire at the age of seventy. Otherwise, they can be removed only by a resolution of both houses of Parliament on the grounds of "proved misbehavior or incapacity"; this has never happened. However, when a seat on the High Court does open, the government will appoint a justice whose views are expected to be compatible with its own. Conservative governments (who have, in fact, appointed the vast majority of justices) have had a somewhat easier task in this, since leading members of the legal profession commonly share a conservative political disposition. Appointed justices occasionally have had party or parliamentary associations. Both conservative and ALP governments

have appointed former attorney-generals to the High Court.

Regional & Local Government

In terms of providing essential services and of maintaining direct contacts with citizens, the states are the most visible level of government in Australia. The present state governments are the historical successors to the colonial governments whose federation created the nation. The states thus have historical roots and traditions which predate nationhood. State identification remains fairly strong among Australians. This identification is assisted, in part, by a peculiar social geography which sees 60 percent of Australians residing in the five metropolitan areas which also happen to be the seats of state governments. The parochial focus of the state-based mass media also contributes to citizen identification with the state.

Services which in many Western countries would be provided by national or local authorities are in Australia firmly entrenched at the state level. State governments provide the public school systems, with state education departments responsible for most aspects of teacher allocation, school location, finance, curriculum at the primary and secondary levels. Education is the biggest single state function, but the states also tend to provide the major public hospitals, personal welfare services, general law and order, public housing, regulation of industry and labor, highways, ports, various agricultural services, subsidies to industrial development, electricity and gas networks, and other property services. States differ a little in the style, standard, and range of public services, though standards are remarkably uniform by comparison with other federations. Political behavior varies more, with different states commonly controlled by different political parties, with the variation partly explained by moderate social and demographic differences and by the greater influence of charismatic politicians in these smaller polities.

State governments operate under their own constitutions, most of which date from the 1850s and which must now adapt to the existence of the Australian constitution. Each state operates, like the Commonwealth, under a parliamentary system. In five of the states, the parliament is bicameral, with the composition of the government being determined in the lower house. The sixth state, Queensland, abolished its Upper House in 1922. For most of its history, the upper house has generally not been democratically elected, being appointed in New South Wales and elected on a property-based franchise in most other states.

Much of what has been observed above, at the Commonwealth level, about the supremacy of the executive, the importance of the bureaucracy, and the decline of Parliament applies also to the states. The premier (the state equivalent of the prime minister) and his cabinet are the visible focus of government, though again a governor sits as the formal representative of the monarch.

Table 4 shows the current parliamentary situation in the lower houses in each of the six states. The party or coalition with the majority of seats forms the government, and parliaments normally have a maximum three-year term in office.

The two territories have been administered directly by the Commonwealth. The Northern Territory, however, recently has won a large degree of self-government, though there are no immediate plans to confer statehood. The Northern Territory legislature is presently controlled by the Country Liberal Party (a nomenclature unique to the territory) with eleven seats, versus seven for the Australian Labor Party and one independent member. Various tentative proposals for self-government in the Australian Capital Territory have been largely ineffectual.

Except for some sparsely populated areas which remain unincorporated, Australia is divided into a patchwork of local government jurisdictions. These local governments possess many of the superficial characteristics of "political sys-

tems," with an elected legislature (the Council) generally based on American rather than Westminster procedures (with, for example, a fixed term of office and a separately elected mayor as chief executive). Local government as a whole, however, only accounts for about 7 percent of total public-sector activity and it is of far lesser significance than in most other Western countries. Local councils principally are involved with mundane property services—garbage, parking, street lighting, sanitation, minor roads, and so on— though in some states there is also some involvement in water, sewage, electricity, and gas services. Some municipalities have a minor, though perhaps growing, role in such welfare areas as kindergartens, child-care centers, aged-person homes, recreational facilities, and so on.

There is a long history of property restrictions on the local voting franchise, though some states have introduced full adult franchise in recent years. There is also a long history of nonpartisanship in local elections, though there are no legal prohibitions on party involvement. Party involvement at the local level has been virtually nonexistent in South Australia, Western Australia, and Tasmania, and is not a common feature in the other states. The Australian Labor Party is involved in some inner-city and industrial municipalities in Sydney and Melbourne, and also controls the City of Brisbane which is Australia's only consolidated metropolitan local authority. Conservative councillors sometimes form partylike coalitions in opposition to the Australian Labor Party.

Table 4
STATE PARLIAMENTS, LOWER HOUSE

State	Most Recent Election	Parliamentary Seats by Party						Governing Party or Coalition
		Liberal Party	National Country Party	National Party*	Australian Labor Party	Australian Democrats	Inde-pendent	
New South Wales	1981	14	14	—	69	—	2	Australian Labor
Victoria	1982	24	8	—	49	—	—	Australian Labor
Queensland	1980	22	—	35	25	—	—	National/ Liberal
South Australia	1979	25	1	—	19	1	—	Liberal
Western Australia	1980	27	3	3	22	—	—	Liberal/ National Country
Tasmania	1982	19	—	—	14	1	1	Liberal

* In Queensland, the National Party is the local branch of the National Country Party; in Western Australia, it is a breakaway group from the official National Country Party.

The Electoral System

Australians directly elect representatives to a number of legislative bodies—two houses at the Commonwealth level, two (except in Queensland) at the state level, and the local council. Different electoral systems may be in operation for each ballot. There are, however, a number of common features.

First, except in most (though not all) local government elections, registration and voting are *compulsory.* Noncompliance without sufficient reason (such as illness) attracts a nominal fine. Turnouts of around 98 percent of eligible voters at Commonwealth and state elections are not uncommon. Second, except for some state upper houses and some local-government systems, there has been a long history of universal adult suffrage, which Australia pioneered. The eligibility age for voting is now eighteen years. Third, the Australian colonies also were pioneers in the use of secret ballots displaying the names of all candidates (still sometimes termed "the Australian ballot" in the United States). Fourth, electoral boundaries generally are drawn up by independent commissioners, so that blatant gerrymandering is virtually unknown.

Malapportionment, however, has been quite common, with the commissioners instructed to ensure a disproportionate representation of rural voters. In several instances, state governments have held office for lengthy periods because of malapportionment, even though a majority of voters supported the Opposition. There have been recent reforms in South Australia and New South Wales, which now join Tasmania in providing "one vote, one value," but electoral bias remains significant in Queensland, Western Australia, and, to a lesser extent, Victoria. For the Commonwealth House of Representatives, the commissioners can take into account geographical size in determining electoral boundaries, but they must keep the variation in the number of voters per district to within 10 percent of the average.

The most common electoral system—used for elections for the House of Representatives and for all state lower houses except Tasmania—is based on *preferential* voting in *single-member* districts. Under preferential voting, voters must rank all candidates on the ballot in numerical order. If no candidate wins an absolute majority of first-preference votes, then the lowest-scoring candidate is eliminated and his votes redistributed according to the second preference of his supporters. This process of elimination and redistribution continues until one candidate wins by acquiring an absolute majority of votes. The necessity for all ballots to show a rank preference for all candidates in order to be valid means that all parties issue "how to vote" instruction cards with a recommended order of preference.

Although only major parties can hope to win a seat, the single-member preferential system allows some role for minor parties. Minor parties may influence the outcome through the distribution of their preference votes. In exchange for recommending a particular ranking of their candidates, minor parties sometimes hope to win policy concessions from the government or potential government.

The preferential system also allows two allied parties to endorse separate candidates for the same district without harming the alliance. For example, the Liberal Party (LP) and National Country Party (NCP) sometimes field separate candidates for the same district. These candidates "exchange preferences," i.e., each places the other in the second position on his how-to-vote recommendation card. This ensures that the higher vote-winner of the two will effectively benefit from their combined vote when and if the preferences are distributed during the counting of votes. It means that the electoral prospects of the LP–NCP coalition as a whole are not harmed by rivalry between the parties in the electoral districts themselves.

The election system for the Australian Senate is a little more complicated since five members (ten in a double dissolution) are elected at-large from each state. Candidates are elected if they receive a quota of votes calculated as one-sixth (one-eleventh in a double dissolution) plus one of the total votes. A preferential system is again used: candidates with more than a quota have their "surplus" votes distributed according to the indicated preferences. In this way, and with the elimination of the lowest-scoring candidates if necessary, the requisite number of winning candidates is determined. Because candidates are grouped on the ballot paper in (unlabelled) party columns and because most voters follow the party how-to-vote instructions in numbering preferences, the effect is somewhat similar to proportional representation. The system, however, is best described as multimember preferential.

Casual vacancies, caused by the death or resignation of an elected member during a term, are handled differently for each house. In the House of Representatives, a by-election is conducted in the local district. In the Senate, a replacement senator is chosen at a joint sitting of the particular *state* houses of parliament. By convention, irrespective of the partisan composition of the state parliament, the Senate vacancy has usually been filled by a nominee of the same political party as the departing occupant, thus preventing an arbitrary alteration to the party balance in the Senate. This convention was broken twice in 1975, however, when two state parliaments controlled by the Liberal and National Country parties refused to replace vacancies with the ALP nominees. This action was taken with the express intention of curtailing the national ALP government, and without it the constitutional crisis of the same year could not have developed. In 1977, with the ironic support of all major parties, a constitutional amendment was passed which explicitly required the filling of Senate vacancies with a candidate from the same political party.

The Party System

Origins of the Parties

Australia waited some forty years after the expansion of the franchise in the 1850s for its first modern parties. In the colonial parliaments of the later nineteenth century, cadrelike groupings did appear, often around a leading personality, but these were loose and unstable alliances.

The emergence and almost immediate success of the Australian Labor Party in the 1890s also served to solidify conservative interests. By the time of federation in 1901, the ALP was opposed by two relatively coherent groups, the Free Traders and the Protectionists, which fused in 1910 to form the Liberal Party. Thereafter, the major party on the right underwent several changes in structure and name, absorbing various breakaways from the ALP, until in 1945 the modern Liberal Party (LP) was established. The ALP and the LP remain the two most important parties today. The LP, however, operates in coalition with the National Country Party (NCP), which remains a significant force. No other parties have won seats in the House of Representatives since the Second World War. In the Senate, multimember elections enable some minor-party representation.

The Parties in Law

Until 1977, the Australian constitution was silent on the subject of political parties. In that year, an amendment specified that casual Senate vacancies should be filled by a member of the same political party. Nowhere, however, is a party defined or made subject to any constitutional provisions. Neither are the Australian parties subject to any particular legal forms or requirements. In law, they are simply voluntary associations with the same legal status and obligations as any other voluntary association. Thus their internal rules and procedures are largely matters for self-control. Any candidate paying a nominal fee, which is refundable if he wins a specified proportion of the vote, is placed on the ballot. Party affiliation is not listed, but most candidates publicize themselves through a party label. Only major party candidates have any real prospects of success. Recently, public financing of party election expenses has been debated, but only the state of New South Wales actually has instituted such a system for its state elections.

Party Organization

The major parties share some structural similarities and could be loosely described, in the organizational sense, as mass parties. Most importantly, they are primarily federal in nature. Most organizational activity takes place within the states, and national umbrella bodies typically are surprisingly weak.

Within the states, the basic unit is the local branch to which dues-paying members belong. Local-branch members tend to be inactive most of the time, except during elections when they assist with publicity, distribute how-to-vote cards at polling booths, and so on. Delegates from local branches meet, typically annually, in state conferences, at which platforms for the state parties are debated. Delegates from the states then attend periodic national conferences which are responsible for national party platforms, with states usually being equally represented despite their varying populations. This federal basis has important ramifications for national politics, for it means that national politicians have their prime organizational bases at the state level.

The parties differ in the procedures used to select candidates for election to Parliament. Some variation exists among the parties in the relative formal status of the parliamentary caucus vis-à-vis the party organization.

Campaigning

Compulsory voting means that election campaigns in Australia differ slightly from those in other Western democracies. Parties are not forced to "get out the vote"—what matters is influencing the actual vote itself.

Today's election campaigns indicate a significant drift away from the mass-party model of mobilization. Increasingly, campaigns are centered on the media image of the parties and particularly of the party leaders. The major parties direct a large proportion of their funds into media advertising, especially television. Laws which place limits on campaign spending by individual candidates are so full of loopholes (such as not regulating expenditure *on behalf* of a candidate) that they are effectively ignored. It is estimated that the ALP and LP/NCP coalition each spend in the region of $A 4 million (about $US 3.7 million) on a national election campaign. Besides emphasizing the image of their leaders, the parties pitch their campaign at what they perceive to be the typical undecided voter—from lower-white-collar or upper-blue-collar, suburban, home-buying households.

Local campaigning by candidates in their districts is of far less significance than the national campaign. It may be possible for politicians to attract a personal following worth a few percentage points (possibly crucial in a close election), and occasionally local issues assume some significance, but generally variations in electoral support can be explained by national or state factors rather than local ones. Most House of Representatives seats are quite safe for one or another of the major parties; only about 30 percent of seats could conceivably change hands in any one election. Intensive campaigning by the parties, involving visits by national leaders and targeted advertising in the local media, is largely restricted to these marginal seats, but it is unlikely that such campaigns have a dramatic effect on the outcome.

Most of the mass-media outlets can be relied upon to support the Liberal Party during elections, though the effect of this is difficult to determine. The Australian mass media are characterized by ownership oligopolies. Three companies own all sixteen metropolitan daily newspapers and, with a fourth, most television stations, most weekly magazines, and many radio stations. With few exceptions, the media are state-based and fairly parochial.

Independent Voters

Surveys suggest that about 85 percent of adult Australians identify with a political party, and this identification is a reasonably accurate, though certainly not perfect, predictor of voting support. The best predictor of party identification is occupational class—about 60 percent of adults with a blue-collar background support the ALP, and about 70 percent with a white-collar background support the LP—but these figures are somewhat volatile. The overall relationship seems to be weakening in what is, for most people, a mobile, suburban, and affluent society.

A majority of voters consistently vote for the same party, at least in the short term, but there are still many crossovers between elections even though the *net* swing from party to party is rarely more than about 5 percent. Because most voters rely on how-to-vote instruction cards, ticket splitting is probably less common. An indication, however, of both the relative complexity of the ballot and of the indifference of some citizens compelled to vote is that 2 or 3 percent of voters simply number their ballot paper from top to bottom. This so-called donkey vote means that there is a 2 or 3 percent advantage in being the top candidate on the ballot paper. Since candidates are listed alphabetically for the House of Representatives, candidates with names starting early in the alphabet are overrepresented, particularly among minor parties.

Table 5 provides an indication of change in party support since the Second World War in national House of Representatives elections.

Table 5 PARTY VOTING FOR THE HOUSE OF REPRESENTATIVES: 1946–1980			
	Australian Labor Party	Liberal Party	National Country Party	Others
1946	50%	33%	11%	6%
1949	46	39	11	4
1951	48	41	10	2
1954	50	39	9	3
1955	45	40	8	8
1958	43	37	9	11
1961	48	34	9	10
1963	46	37	9	9
1966	40	40	10	10
1969	47	35	9	10
1972	50	32	9	9
1974	49	35	11	5
1975	43	42	11	4
1977	40	38	10	12
1980	45	37	9	9

Note: All elections except 1946, 1972, and 1974 won by LP/NCP coalition.

Australian Labor Party (ALP)

History

The Australian Labor Party emerged in the 1890–91 period when the failure of maritime and shearers' strikes during this recessionary period persuaded trade unions to seek parliamentary representation. By 1899, a minority Labor government—the first in the world—held office in the Queensland colony, albeit for only five days before being defeated in Parliament. The ALP held the balance of power in the first Commonwealth Parliament, formed a minority national government for four months in 1904, and then won clear control of both houses in 1910. Since those early decades, the ALP's history has been varied and volatile. At the national level, it has enjoyed only a few short periods in office, primarily because of three devastating splits in the party.

The first split came in 1916 over opposition within the party to conscription (particularly among Irish Catholic elements opposed to helping the English war effort), which caused the ALP prime minister to leave the party with many of his ministerial and parliamentary colleagues. They joined the Opposition in a new National Party which kept the ALP out of office until 1929. The Labor government which acceded in that year ruptured over the appropriate policy response to the Depression, losing office in 1932. Again, some ALP parliamentarians formed a new anti-Labor grouping (the United Australia Party) in combination with the conservatives. After another decade in the wilderness, the ALP in the 1941–49 period enjoyed its longest period of national government under prime ministers Curtin and Chifley, producing innovative policies in social welfare, national development, economic management, public enterprise, and immigration. The third major fissure took place in 1955 to 1957 when a strongly anti-communist and predominantly Catholic group broke away to form the Democratic Labor Party, which again helped to keep the ALP in opposition for many years. Only in the 1972–75 period did Labor again assume national office, under Prime Minister Whitlam, for another brief period of government terminating with the constitutional crisis.

This national history is interwoven with varied experiences in the states, although generally the ALP has enjoyed greater success at that level. It has governed for long periods in New South Wales (forty-two years this century), Queensland (thirty-nine years), Western Australia (thirty-five years), Tasmania (fifty-two years) and, to a lesser extent mainly due to malapportionment, South Australia (twenty-two years). Victoria (eight years) is the conspicuous exception.

Organization

The ALP is a federal party with its historical origins in the trade unions. Both aspects are essential for understanding its organization.

The key components of the ALP organization are its relatively autonomous state branches. The national components are largely umbrella bodies made up of delegates from the states, and the real life of the party remains at the state level. The trade-union connection manifests itself in the formal affiliation of unions to the party in the states. Thus there is a basic dualism in party membership: dues-paying voluntary members of local branches and members of trade unions affiliated to the party. State conferences, usually annual, are the supreme policymaking bodies in each state. Some variation in how voting power is arranged exists at these conferences, but generally delegates from affiliated unions easily can outvote delegates from local branches. State conferences debate and amend the party platform, elect the smaller state executives which meet more frequently, and elect a full-time secretary and other staff. State branches differ in their procedures for selecting parliamentary candidates: in some states such selection is conducted at state conferences, while in others there are selection panels consisting of conference delegates and local members, or, in New South Wales only, a plebiscite of all members.

Until 1981, the annual National Conference and more regular National Executive meetings of the ALP were composed of equal representations from each of the states plus smaller delegations from ALP branches in the two territories. (The effect of a 1981 decision to accord representation in proportion to population cannot yet be assessed.) In theory, the national bodies are the supreme organs of the party, able to impose their will on state branches. In recent years, the state branches in Victoria and Queensland, regarded as electoral liabilities, have been forcibly reconstructed. Mostly, however, state interests have been paramount for delegates to these national bodies. There is a small national secretariat and the position of federal ALP president has been prominent recently, but the party's most visible *national* presence is its representation in the national Parliament.

In the ethos and formal rules of the ALP, parliamentarians are subordinate to the organization, and all party candidates are pledged to uphold the party platform. In practice, however, the parliamentary caucus enjoys a greater degree of autonomy, especially in matters of political strategy and priority, than this formal pledge might suggest. Potential conflict between politician and organization is also somewhat attenuated by the influence of some members of Parliament in the party organization and, conversely, by the granting of endorsement for parliamentary seats to influential figures in the organization. Some awkward conflicts have occurred in the past, but in an endeavor to minimize such conflict, parliamentary leaders are now ex officio members of bodies like the National Conference and National Executive. Certainly the parliamentary leaders are the most visible symbols of the party.

The ALP cannot be understood only in terms of its formal organization. In all states, a relatively small group of influential people, sometimes described pejoratively as "the machine," can be identified as exerting disproportionate influence. Certain union leaders, for example, are able to command large blocs of votes at party conferences. Others have personal followings among unions or local branches or represent a particular ideological grouping. In most states, a number of factions represent loose alliances based on ideological affinity, power groupings, personality, pragmatism, and, occasionally, patronage. Some factions have their own caucuses, publications, and internal voting tickets. It is common to describe the factions on a left–right spectrum though this may exaggerate their ideological coherence. Broadly speaking, there is a socialist left faction (strongest in Victoria and drawing heavily on middle-class activists), a traditional left (based in some of the unions), a center group (with disproportionate influence in the parliamentary caucuses), and a right faction (often Irish Catholic, strongest in New South Wales).

The ALP national headquarters are located at John Curtin House, 22 Brisbane Avenue, Barton, ACT.

Policy

The ALP always has purported to be a reformist party. Like all such parties, however, its ideological and policy positions are complex, contentious, and sometimes volatile. As a complex coalition of ideologues, pragmatists, factions, and personalities which needs to seek electoral majorities, the ALP is best described as a social democratic party. Its platform states that it seeks the "democratic socialization of industry, distribution, production and exchange," though this is immediately qualified by the rider "to the extent necessary to eliminate exploitation and other anti-social features in these fields."

The essential elements guiding ALP policy can be briefly, though simplistically, summarized. The ALP maintains a critical view of capitalism as generating maldistribution and injustice, though this critique probably owes more to Christian and humanist sources than to Marxism. The party does accept private enterprise within a mixed economy. The party generally supports redistribution to promote equalization. Today, this is more likely to be expressed in terms of equality of opportunity and nondiscrimination in education, ethnic, and urban policy, as well as in industrial and welfare policy. In industrial matters, the ALP lends general support to the trade unions. It promotes a rationalistic and benevolent view of government as an instrument for reform. The party is committed to parliamentary democracy, distinguishing itself from the extreme left at this point. It promotes a form of Australian nationalism which is skeptical of traditional international alliances—such as with the United States—and of foreign investment. Particularly within the federal parliamentary caucus, federalism is viewed distastefully in so far as it weakens the power of the national government, a position shared by few state ALP politicians. In foreign policy, the ALP sympathizes with other reformist movements (such as anticolonialism) and is disinclined to take a militantly anticommunist position.

In practice, these party principles are reflected in some of the policies of the 1972 to 1975 national ALP government under Prime Minister Whitlam. The government instituted a national health scheme, greatly increased federal spending on welfare and education (even where this trespassed on traditional state responsibilities), instituted new urban policies, imposed stricter controls on foreign investment, instituted some constraints on prices, and in foreign policy formally recognized the People's Republic of China, East Germany, North Korea, and North Vietnam.

Membership & Constituency

The total number of local branch members is estimated at around 50,000, or roughly one member for every sixty-five supporting voters. Another 1.3 million unionists are affiliated through their unions, this figure representing slightly less than half of all union members. Both membership figures have been reasonably steady in recent years, though there appeared to be an upsurge in local branch membership following the constitutional crisis of late 1975. Branch members are typically from a more middle-class background than are the unionists passively affiliated through their union. Only a minority (20 to 35 percent) of branch members are women, though this proportion is increasing. Paradoxically, some of the most active local branches are located in middle-class areas which safely return Liberal Party candidates to Parliament.

The party's voting support is strongest in urban, industrial, working-class districts. About 60 percent of blue-collar Australians vote ALP (though this proportion is decreasing) compared with 40 percent of lower-white-collar and 25 percent (increasing) of middle-class professionals. Rural support for ALP is low, even in the towns; its support among women has been lower than among men of similar social background; and there is a tendency for its support to be lower in older age cohorts. Among ethnic groups, the ALP receives good support from Southern European groups but performs poorly among Eastern Europeans.

Union strength within the party organization means that there is still a substantial number of ALP legislators from a union background. Increasingly, however, the ALP parliamentary caucus is dominated by lawyers, teachers, and other professionals.

The ALP is still closely identified in its public image with the trade unions, which cover 57 percent of the work force. Seventy percent of all unionists also are represented through the Australian Council of Trade Unions, an umbrella organization which is a highly visible political factor and which participates in centralized national wage determinations.

Financing

All political parties maintain tight secrecy about their financial affairs. The main sources of finance for the ALP are membership dues, periodic fundraising events organized by branches, affiliation fees paid by unions, and donations, usually by unions, though support from some business sources has not been unknown. Financial resources never seem sufficient to cover costs, and the ALP is consistently in the position of trying to pay off the debt from previous election campaigns.

Leadership

Many of the prominent ALP leaders in the past have been powerful figures in the state branch organizations. Increasingly, however, the parlia-

mentary leaders—some of them also holding key organizational positions—monopolize public attention. In the past twenty years, parliamentary leadership in the ALP has gradually shifted from more traditional men, often with a Catholic and trade union background, to professionals. This was typified by the accession to national parliamentary leadership of Gough Whitlam, a lawyer, in 1967. Whitlam has retired, but present notable figures include:

Bill Hayden (born 1933), leader of the Opposition, Commonwealth Parliament, since 1978. From Queensland, Hayden is regarded as a pragmatist from the center-left.

Bob Hawke (born 1928), formerly both president of the ALP and president of the Australian Council of Trade Unions. Now shadow minister for industrial affairs, Hawke is a nationally known figure and regarded as a potential leader. Identified with the center-right, Hawke is from Victoria.

Neville Wran (born 1927), electorally successful premier of New South Wales and national president of the ALP. His possible move to national politics remains a topic of repeated speculation. He is pragmatic and right of center.

Paul Keating (born 1944) is federal shadow minister for minerals and energy, but also a power in the New South Wales party machine. He is right of center.

Prospects

The ALP has enjoyed only brief periods in national office, followed by years in opposition. The party has remained unified since it lost office in 1975, however, and has a reasonable chance of returning to office at the next federal election given the continuing economic recession. At the state level, the party seems entrenched in New South Wales. It won office in Victoria in 1982 after a long period in opposition and has a good chance of taking over South Australia. It suffered a rare defeat in Tasmania in 1982 and seems to have little hope in Western Australia and Queensland.

Liberal Party (LP)

History

The Liberal Party was founded in 1945, but it is the fourth in a continuous succession of anti-Labor parties. Its creation was largely the achievement of its first leader, Robert Menzies, who brought together the non-Labor members of Parliament during a time of solid ALP government and fashioned a mass organization to sustain them. His success is reflected in the unbroken twenty-three years in office which the LP enjoyed in coalition with the (National) Country Party from 1949 until 1972, the first seventeen years under Menzies's prime ministership. Some instability developed after Menzies's retirement, and the coalition lost office in 1972. It was returned under Prime Minister Malcolm Fraser in 1975 after the constitutional crisis, and two elections since have confirmed the comfortable electoral victory won in that year. The party has been less dramatically successful at the state level, but it has long dominated the state of Victoria without any coalition assistance from the NCP.

Organization

The Liberal Party has managed to graft a cadre-like parliamentary party onto a mass-party base. This has allowed the relatively autonomous parliamentary party to respond pragmatically to the electorate, within a broadly conservative ethos, while giving it the organizational support necessary for electoral success. Far more than the ALP, the members of Parliament are the essence of the LP. The party organization is strongly federalist, with each state Liberal Party enjoying a large measure of autonomy. Some variation exists in organizational structure, but generally local branches within the states, combined where necessary to cover each parliamentary electorate, have a primary role in selecting candidates and running their campaigns. At the state level, state councils representing local branches, members of Parliament, LP women's organizations (a feature of the party), and Young Liberal associations consider matters of general state party business and policy, though their decisions usually do not bind the members of Parliament.

State executives administer such business on a more continuous basis. National business and policy are considered by the LP Federal Council, which has equal representation from each state (including delegates from the women's and Young Liberal organizations), and by the Federal Executive. Rarely, such extraparliamentary bodies attempt to influence the members of Parliament, but generally the parliamentary party sustains its autonomy.

Within the parliamentary caucus, the elected leader assumes great significance. He chooses his own cabinet or shadow cabinet, in contrast to the ALP where those positions are elective. In theory,

LP members are free to vote as they choose in Parliament—and there have been a few cases of nonconformity, especially in the Senate—but the party line usually is as firm as in the ALP.

The LP structure does not appear to promote factionalism. Some divisions occur within the parliamentary caucus—based on personalities, on the mentor–protege relationships built by contending leaders, on disagreements about the degree to which the LP should appease its NCP coalition partner, and on policy differences. Generally, the LP has been able to accommodate a range of views from right to center.

National headquarters are located at Blackwell and Macquarie Streets, Barton, ACT.

Policy

The Liberal Party features a mixture of classic liberalism, conservatism, and pragmatism. The range of opinions within its parliamentary caucus varies from ultraorthodox free-market advocates to those more tolerant of the welfare state, from social libertarians to the advocates of strict censorship, from protectionists to free-traders.

A brief listing of the important elements of LP policy would begin with individualism, a belief in the sanctity and rights of the individual. The individual is believed to respond to incentives, such as profits, which stimulate greater effort and productivity. The party has a benevolent view of private enterprise, though in practice it supports a significant degree of public intervention and regulation. It accepts moderate inequality as inevitable and perhaps socially necessary. Stability and order are recurring themes. Its foreign policy includes a strong anticommunism and a belief in the appropriateness and efficacy of traditional alliances, such as with the United States.

Some guide to policy can be seen in the actions of the Fraser government. Many ALP initiatives have been reversed. Public support for education and urban programs were cut, the national health scheme significantly revised to revert to private insurance, and responsibility handed back to the states in many policy areas. In foreign policy, American positions on Afghanistan, Poland, and elsewhere have been supported publicly, though Fraser has surprised many observers by his strong support for black-majority rule in Zimbabwe and for continuation of the north-south dialogue.

Membership & Constituency

The LP has the largest local-branch membership of any party, estimated at a fairly stable figure of 100,000 (or one for every thirty supporting voters). Members are disproportionately middle class and Protestant, often with a private-school background. A large proportion are women. The main function of the membership is to provide financial and election assistance.

Electoral support for the Liberals is socially more widespread than for the ALP, though it is strongest among those with a professional or managerial background (about 70 percent) or lower white collar (60 percent) than among blue collar (40 percent). The safest Liberal seats are in affluent residential suburbs, though the party's electoral success can be gauged by its general ability to win in lower-middle-class suburbs as well. Women, members of Eastern European ethnic groups, and older age cohorts support the LP in disproportionate numbers. Liberal members of Parliament are overwhelmingly from professional, managerial, and business backgrounds.

The LP also is identified through an affinity of interests, social contacts, and overlapping membership—with the main business organizations. The principal national umbrella organizations are the Confederation of Australian Industry and the Australian Chambers of Commerce.

Financing

Membership dues range up to about $10 per annum and local branches also engage in various fundraising social activities. It is certain that the party benefits from substantial business donations, but, as with other parties, secrecy is maintained about such matters.

Leadership

The parliamentary leader holds the preeminent party position, and unsuccessful LP leaders are quickly replaced. Current prominent figures are:

Malcolm Fraser (born 1930), prime minister since 1975 and winner of three comfortable election victories. Fraser is from a rural Victorian background and is thought to be close to his Country Party coalition partners.

John Howard (born 1929), deputy parliamentary leader, is from New South Wales. Identified with the party's free-market advocates, he is considered a possible leadership successor.

Andrew Peacock (born 1939), from Victoria, is leader of an embryonic progressive/pragmatic faction in Parliament. He was a flamboyant minister of foreign affairs before resigning from a domestic cabinet portfolio after a disagreement with Fraser. He is known to have leadership ambitions.

Prospects

Despite the continuing recession, the LP remains the dominant governing party. It seems to have monopolized a mantle of legitimacy as Australia's "natural" government and benefits from its sound administrative and businesslike image. While the ALP could win the next election, the LP should remain a powerful force. It is less solid at the state level, and lost control of its Victorian bastion in 1982 while winning the less significant Tasmanian state elections.

National Country Party (NCP)

History

The NCP can be understood largely as the political representative of Australia's rural sector. It originated in farmer and grazier organizations in the period 1914 to 1922. Because its voting strength is concentrated geographically in rural areas, it has maintained a continual parliamentary presence since 1919, despite consistently winning only about 10 percent of the national vote. In 1922, it agreed to form a coalition with the larger anti-Labor party; this arrangement has continued ever since, except in Victoria. In Queensland, the NCP (under the local name of National Party) is the majority party in the coalition state government. It also is quite strong in New South Wales and Western Australia, but very weak in South Australia and Tasmania.

Organization

Considerable autonomy, even over candidate endorsement, is delegated to local branches. Within the states, the hierarchy is fairly simple. Local branches send delegates to electoral councils, while chairmen of electoral councils form most of the state executive. As in the LP, NCP members of Parliament enjoy a large degree of freedom in pursuing policies and electoral strategies.

The NCP national headquarters are located at McEwen House, National Crescent, Barton, ACT.

Policy

As a representative of rural interests, the NCP supports public intervention to provide services to rural areas, to coordinate the marketing of agricultural products, and to guarantee incomes in the rural sector. On other matters, however, it tends to be conservative. Because it is crucial to the survival of the coalition, the NCP is able to secure substantial policy concessions from the Liberal Party.

Partly in an endeavor to broaden electoral support (for which purpose the prefix National was added to its name in 1975), NCP leaders also have taken a strong interest in cabinet portfolios dealing with mining and manufacturing, the latter being an urban activity. Some policy tensions are thereby created, such as the manufacturers' interest in tariff protection clashing with the free-trade interests of agricultural- and mining-product exporters.

In foreign policy, the NCP supports the LP's strong pro-Western line, though it is no coincidence that proposed trade boycotts of the Soviet Union and Iran, both prime markets for Australian agriculture, did not materialize.

Membership & Constituency

The NCP is estimated to have about 80,000 members, producing a high ratio of one member to every nine supporting voters. The majority of them are primary producers, and all the party's parliamentary seats are outside the metropolitan areas. The NCP remains closely associated with the national farmer and grazier organizations.

Financing

Membership dues vary between states, reaching a high of $20 in New South Wales. The NCP has developed the extensive use of a bank-order scheme whereby members authorize direct payments from bank accounts, guaranteeing a fairly steady source of party income. The NCP also has an arrangement with an insurance company which pays a commission to the party for group insurance sold to party members. While the NCP may be less dependent on outside funding than other parties, it almost certainly receives considerable unpublicized donations.

Leadership

Doug Anthony (born 1929), deputy prime minister, parliamentary leader of the NCP, and minister for trade and resources, is from New South Wales.

Johannes Bjelke-Petersen (born 1911) is National Party premier of Queensland and a controversial figure who might be described as a populist conservative. He is militantly anticentralist.

Prospects

Commentators have been predicting the demise of the NCP for years in the face of steady urbanization. However, the party has maintained its share of the vote and its ability to be indispensible to the Liberals. It is unlikely to weaken significantly in the near future.

Minor Parties

Geographical concentration translates the NCP's 10 percent share of the vote into a solid parliamentary presence. Other minor parties have achieved a similar level of national support but have found it much more difficult to win seats. Such parties can, however, wield some influence through the direction of preferences in House of Representatives elections and have a better chance of winning seats in the multimember Senate elections.

Australian Democrats (AD)

A party which seeks to exploit the middle ground between the major party groupings, it is led by Don Chipp (born 1925), a former LP minister who left the party in 1977 after a public disagreement with the Fraser government. Chipp was elected to the Senate in 1977 as a Victorian representative. After the 1980 elections, the AD party has five senators and holds the balance of power. Its voting support is found mainly in middle-class areas. Apart from a general advocacy of consensus and moderation, AD policies are not very specific. The party can be seen as supporting individualism within the context of a welfare state. Its particular interests in such policy areas as education, the environment, industrial democracy, foreign aid, and opposition to the export of uranium identifies the party as the moderate parliamentary expression of ideas which have also produced some activism among environmentalist and student groups in the past fifteen years.

The AD national headquarters are located at 18 Pavonia Street, Rivett, ACT.

Communist Parties

Communism has had some industrial significance in Australia, but it has never been an electoral force, though Communist candidates periodically stand for election. The Australian Communist Party was founded in 1922 and has followed a generally pro-Moscow line. The party was strongest in the 1930–50 period, at one point claiming 20,000 members and controlling a number of trade unions. It also had an indirect influence on the ALP, both as a rival for support within the unions and as a tarbrush with which opponents could blacken the ALP by association. Splits since the 1950s, precipitated by such matters as de-Stalinization, the Sino–Soviet conflict, the New Left, and Euro–Communism, have weakened the movement and produced a number of competing sects: the Communist Party of Australia (following a Euro-Communist model), the CPA (Marxist-Leninist, a Maoist offshoot), the Socialist Party of Australia (generally pro-Moscow), and various Trotskyite factions. None has any electoral importance.

National Prospects

Whichever party controls the Australian government in the foreseeable future, it will be concerned primarily with managing the national economy. While Australia's mineral and energy resources should make its long-term prospects fairly secure, it faces increasing pressure from international competition and the vagaries of world markets. In the short-term, there are no easy solutions to problems of unemployment and inflation which, though less serious than in most other developed countries and partly caused by international factors, are (by Australia's historical standards) at worrying levels.

Although the major party blocs—the LP/NCP coalition and the ALP—will differ somewhat in policies about public job creation, control of foreign investment, welfare relief and so on, there is little prospect of radically different economic policies arising from any change in government. Even the ALP seems resigned to a period of relative austerity. Australia is likely to remain a politically stable and still relatively affluent European outpost.

Further Reading

Aitkin, Don and Jinks, Brian. *Australian Political Institutions.* Melbourne: Pitman, 1980.

Emy, Hugh V. *The Politics of Australian Democracy.* 2d ed. Melbourne: Macmillan, 1978.

Jupp, James. *Party Politics Australia 1966–81.* Sydney: George Allen & Unwin, 1982.

Mayer, Henry and Nelson, Helen, eds. *Australian Politics: A Fifth Reader.* Melbourne: Longman Cheshire, 1980.

Parkin, Andrew. *Governing the Cities: The Australian Experience in Perspective.* Melbourne: Macmillan, 1982.

_____; Summer, John; and Woodward, Dennis, eds. *Government, Politics and Power in Australia.* 2d ed. Melbourne: Longman Cheshire, 1980.

_____ and Warhurst, John, eds. *Machine Politics in the Australian Labor Party.* Sydney: George Allen & Unwin, 1982.

Penniman, Harold A., ed. *The Australian National Elections of 1977.* Washington, D.C.: American Enterprise Institute, 1979.

Starr, Graeme; Richmond, Keith; and Maddox, Graham. *Political Parties in Australia.* Melbourne: Heinemann, 1978.

REPUBLIC OF AUSTRIA
(Republik Österreich)
by Melanie A. Sully, Ph.D.

The System of Government

The Austrian republic is a democratic federal state consisting of nine provinces (*Bundesländer*). According to the 1981 census, it has a population of more than seven and one-half million, one fifth of which lives in Vienna, the capital and center of most political activity.

The present political system rose from the ruins of the Austro-Hungarian Empire, which collapsed in 1918. The weak First Republic foundered in a new environment, surrounded by hostile successor states (Hungary, Yugoslavia, parts of Poland, for example), and beset by economic disintegration and political polarization between the Social Democratic—Marxist camp and the right-wing clerical-conservatives and semifascists. A civil war in 1934 resulted in a heavy defeat for the Social Democrats. From 1934 to 1938 a corporate state ruled Austria under an authoritarian system which stressed loyalty to the nation and Christian morals. The Nazis, Communists, and Social Democrats were outlawed. In 1938, the country was annexed by Nazi Germany.

Austria was liberated by the Allies in 1945 and was divided into four zones of Allied occupation. A provisional government was set up under Karl Renner, a Social Democratic leader who had also been premier of the first provisional government after the collapse of the Empire. The first national elections of the Second Republic (based on the 1920 and 1929 constitution of the First Republic, which is still in force) were held in November 1945. Renner became president, and a coalition government, called the Great Coalition, was set up under a People's Party premier with extensive participation by the Social Democrats.

The Great Coalition lasted until 1966. In the meantime, Austria had regained its full sovereignty and independence (1955), in exchange for a policy of permanent neutrality between East and West. After 1966, the People's Party (ÖVP) governed alone until 1970; the Social Democrats (SPÖ) have governed alone since then.

Executive

The federal president is the official head of state, but his duties are mainly ceremonial. He appoints the federal chancellor, normally the leader of the strongest party in the legislature, and on the chancellor's recommendation, appoints the other members of the federal government. The president's official acts require the countersignature of the chancellor and/or the appropriate federal minister. Technically, the president is commander-in-chief of the army, although the constitution also says that the "supreme command of the federal army is exercised by the competent federal minister." If the president is incapacitated, his powers pass to the chancellor until he recovers or new elections can be arranged.

The president is popularly elected by direct vote every six years. The winner is the candidate who gains more than half of all the valid votes cast. If a candidate does not receive the required majority, a runoff election is held between the two most successful vote-getters. The president can only serve a maximum of two terms. All of Austria's presidents since 1945 have been Socialist Party of Austria (SPÖ) candidates. The current president, Rudolph Kirchschläger, was reelected in May 1980 with almost 80 percent of the vote.

The chancellor is the head of government. Acting through the president, he has the power to appoint and dismiss individual members of his government. The Austrian constitution does not accurately describe the power of the chancellor; since 1945, the chancellor's role has become increasingly powerful and independent.

Legislature

Primary legislative power is vested in the *Nationalrat* (National Assembly), which consists of

NATIONALRAT (1966–1979) ELECTION RESULTS

	SPÖ		ÖVP		FPÖ	
	% Votes	Seats	% Votes	Seats	% Votes	Seats
1966	42.56	74	48.35	85	5.35	6
1970	48.42	81	44.69	78	5.52	6
1971*	50.04	93	43.11	80	5.54	10
1975	50.42	93	42.95	80	5.41	10
1979	51.03	95	41.90	77	6.06	11

* An electoral reform in 1970 increased the number of seats from 165 to 183.

183 deputies who are elected directly on the basis of proportional representation every four years. The *Nationalrat* holds two sessions each year, one in the spring and the other in the fall; combined, the two sessions must last at least six months. These sessions are open to the public and receive some television coverage. The *Nationalrat* is chaired by three presidents, who reflect the strength of the parties in the chamber and take turns chairing the debates. In 1982, the first and third presidents were members of the SPÖ and the second a member of the Austrian People's Party (ÖVP). The president of the *Nationalrat* is empowered to nominate the employees of the Chancellory and has extensive powers on other personnel matters. In consultation with the leaders of the official parliamentary blocs or *Klubs* (these must have at least five members), the three presidents draw up the agenda and arrange the business of the chamber.

Special "constitutional laws" require a two-thirds majority to pass and at least half of the members must be present. An absolute majority with one-third of the members present is sufficient to pass most legislation. Legislation is usually initiated by the government, but individual members also have this right. Much of the work in the *Nationalrat* is carried out by committees. For each area of legislation, a main committee (elected by the *Nationalrat*) and a standing subcommittee (elected by the main committee) reflect the strength of the parties. If the chamber is dissolved, power devolves upon the standing subcommittee until the *Nationalrat* can meet again.

Since 1955 there have only been three parties in the *Nationalrat*—the SPÖ, the ÖVP, and the small, right-wing Freedom Party (FPÖ). In 1979 the two main parties together accounted for 94 percent of the seats. Over 80 percent of legislation is adopted unanimously; this basic consensus has not altered significantly since the SPÖ gained an absolute majority in 1971.

Theoretically, the *Bundesrat* (Federal Assembly) represents the interests of the nine federal provinces; in practice, the *Bundesrat* represents the interests of the parties rather than the separate provinces. The number of deputies from a province depends on its populations. The constitution stipulates that the province with the largest number of citizens is entitled to twelve members and that every province must have at least three members. The fifty-eight members of the *Bundesrat* are elected indirectly by the provincial legislatures (*Landtage*) in accordance with the principle of proportional representation. The chairmanship of the *Bundesrat* rotates among the federal provinces every six months in alphabetical order. This can be important when the number of deputies from each party is the same, since the chairman has no voting rights.

The *Bundesrat* has little power. The constitution states that every enactment of the *Nationalrat* shall without delay be conveyed by the president to the chancellor, who is to inform the *Bundesrat*. The latter can object to the legislation and must communicate this in writing to the *Nationalrat* via the chancellor. If the *Nationalrat* with at least half of its members present carries its original resolution, the bill becomes federal law. The *Bundesrat* cannot object to laws pertaining to appropriations within federal budget estimates, the sanction of the final federal budget accounts, the raising or conversion of federal loans, or the disposal of federal property. Legislative motions emanating from the *Bundesrat* for discussion in the *Nationalrat* have to be submitted in the first instance to the federal government. When the Great Coalition was in operation, the *Bundesrat* played a very modest role, objecting to only sixteen resolutions of the *Nationalrat* in just over twenty years. With the single-party ÖVP government (1966–70), greater opportunity existed for dissent, but there was a reluctance to embark on a policy of confrontation. Successes in provincial elections in 1968 gave the SPÖ, for the first time, a majority in the *Bundesrat*, which thus faced a conservative majorty in the *Nationalrat*. This resulted in an increase in objections from the *Bundesrat*; but because of limitations on its power, no major conflicts ensued and controversial legislation was merely delayed. Since 1973 the SPÖ has had the same number of seats in the *Bundesrat* as the ÖVP. When the Socialist-led provinces of Burgenland, Carinthia, and Vienna chair the proceedings, the ÖVP has an advantage. The SPÖ has a lead of one when members from the six ÖVP-governed provinces are in the chair. Both chambers meet together as a federal assembly for the affirmation of the federal president and to adopt a resolution on the declaration of war.

The interests of business, labor, and agriculture are organized and represented more formally in the governing process than is usual in European democracies. The Chambers of Commerce, Labor, and Agriculture are public corporations organized at each administrative level throughout the nation. Membership is compulsory and automatic for every employer, employee, and farmer, so that with the exception of civil servants (including teachers) nearly every adult working Austrian is a voting member of a chamber. (In addition to these three primary chambers there are smaller chambers for professions and special categories, such as agricultural laborers.) Elections to the chambers' councils take place every five years after hard-fought partisan campaigns.

The chambers maintain research facilities, review draft legislation, and assist in implementation. They serve their members by providing legal advice and other information.

Representatives of the chambers, the Trade Union Federation (*Österreicher Gewerkschaftsbund;* ÖGB), and the government meet about once a month in the Parity Commission under the chairmanship of the chancellor. This body has no statutory authority, but it reviews proposed economic legislation, approves or denies requests for wage and price increases, and is instrumental in shaping Austria's economic policy.

This system of interest-group cooperation and participation in government is called the "social partnership." It developed after World War II as a way to avoid the violent internecine conflict which had marked pre-war Austrian politics. The system has effectively incorporated labor into the policymaking process and has contributed greatly to Austria's social peace and economic health.

Judiciary

Austria possesses an administrative court and a constitutional court. The administrative court ensures the legality of all acts of public administration. The constitutional court can pronounce judgment in disputes between or among the provinces, or between a province and the federal government, and between the courts and the administrative authorities. Any citizen who feels that his rights have been violated by an administrative act or that his basic rights as guaranteed by the constitution have been encroached on may appeal to the administrative and constitutional courts. An example of this was when Otto Hapsburg, the eldest son of the banished imperial family, put his case to return to Austria before both the constitutional and administrative courts in the early 1960s. The ruling, although favorable for Otto, was blocked because of hostility from SPÖ and FPÖ members in the *Nationalrat*.

The constitutional court consists of a president,

DISTRIBUTION OF SEATS IN THE BUNDESRAT (1981)

	ÖVP	SPÖ	Total
Burgenland	1	2	3
Carinthia	1	3	4
Lower Austria	6	5	11
Upper Austria	5	4	9
Salzburg	2	1	3
Styria	5	4	9
Tyrol	3	1	4
Vorarlberg	2	1	3
Vienna	4	8	12
	29	29	58

PERCENTAGE OF PARTY REPRESENTATION IN THE ECONOMIC CHAMBERS (1981)

	ÖVP	SPÖ	FPÖ	KPÖ	Independent
Chamber of Commerce	86	13	—	—	—
Chamber of Agriculture	84	9	2	—	5
Chamber of Labor	31	64	3	1	—

vice-president, twelve other members, and six substitutes. The president and vice-president, six members and three substitutes are appointed by the federal president on the recommendation of the government. The remaining members are appointed by the president on the basis of recommendations from the two chambers.

In 1977 a law was passed establishing an ombudsman; when no other means of appeal is available, a citizen who feels that he has been a victim of maladministration may file a complaint with the ombudsman. There are three ombudsmen elected by the *Nationalrat* for six years. If they consider a case justified they can recommend that appropriate action be taken by the relevant authority. Such action must be carried out within eight weeks or written justification given for ignoring the ombudsman's advice. Extensions of this time limit can be obtained in cases of serious difficulty. On average, 25 percent of cases investigated can expect a positive result. In 1981, 5,055 cases were examined by the ombudsmen; most complaints were registered in Vienna and Salzburg.

Regional & Local Goverment

Each of the nine provinces has its own parliament (*Landtag*), which closely resembles in organization that of the federal parliament. Burgenland has had a socialist provincial governor (*Landeshauptmann*) since 1964. Apart from this province, and Vienna and Carinthia, the rest have ÖVP governors. Elections take place in the provinces on the basis of proportional representation.

Although technically a federal state, Austria exhibits a high degree of centralization. The federal provinces do have a say on regional planning, hospitals, electricity, and agriculture, but education, the police, administration of the postal service, the railways, and fiscal and social policies are within the competence of the federal government. Some small changes in 1974 granted the provinces executive powers over inland shipping and the river police, but the central government continues to be of prime importance given the chronic financial weakness of the provinces, which have few revenue-raising powers. Local loyalty is strongest in the western provinces, particularly in Vorarlberg where "control" from Vienna is most resented.

It is on the local level that the domination of the established parties is most threatened. Citizens' initiatives have been successful against highway-building plans in the Styrian capital of Graz, and organized citizen groups are actively fighting to preserve the scenic beauty of the Alpine countryside, particularly from the noise and exhaust of European juggernaut trucks. A citizens' initiative in Innsbruck has so far been unsuccessful in campaigning for a reduction in noise levels from the local airport.

The Electoral System

The distribution of *Nationalrat* seats is based on the number of citizens, including children, not simply on the number of voters. This procedure has tended to favor the rural, Catholic areas with larger families who are more likely to be ÖVP supporters.

An electoral law passed by the SPÖ in 1970 increased the number of deputies from 165 to 183 and reduced the number of electoral districts from twenty-five to nine. The reform did not alter the bias towards areas with large families, but did make the number of votes needed to win a seat more equal and potentially helped small parties. After 1970, each federal province became a separate electoral district or *Wahlkreis*. Combinations

RECENT ELECTIONS TO THE LANDTAGE

Province	Year	ÖVP %	ÖVP Seats	SPÖ %	SPÖ Seats	FPÖ %	FPÖ Seats	KPÖ %	KPÖ Seats
Burgenland	1977	45.1	16	51.9	20	2.2	—	0.3	—
Carinthia	1979	31.8	12	54.0	20	11.7	4	1.0	—
Lower Austria	1979	49.6	29	45.4	27	3.2	—	0.8	—
Upper Austria	1979	51.6	29	41.4	23	6.4	4	0.6	—
Salzburg	1979	45.4	17	39.1	14	13.3	5	0.4	—
Styria	1981	50.9	30	42.7	24	5.1	2	1.3	—
Tyrol	1979	63.1	25	29.3	10	6.6	1	0.4	—
Vorarlberg	1979	57.4	22	29.1	10	12.5	4	1.0	—
Vienna	1978	33.8	35	57.2	62	6.3	3	1.8	—

of these form two larger units known as *Wahlkreisverbände*. Burgenland, Vienna, and Lower Austria, the three eastern provinces, form *Wahlkreisverband I*, and the rest of the country constitutes the second. The steady shift in population away from the east means that districts like Vienna will in future be entitled to fewer parliamentary deputies. These seats will be allocated to provinces with expanding populations such as Vorarlberg and Tyrol, both ÖVP strongholds in the past.

Election to the *Nationalrat* is determined by proportional representation. The allocation of seats takes place in two stages. In the first, the total vote in a *Wahlkreis* is divided by the total number of seats alloted to that district. The result is the electoral quota, the number of votes required to win a seat in that district. A party must win at least one seat (*Grundmandat*) at this level somewhere in the nation in order to be eligible to receive additional seats at the second stage. (This quota has not been met by the Communist Party since 1956.) Seats and votes not allocated in the first stage are carried over to the second, which is based on the larger *Wahlkreisverbände*. Here, again, the seats are distributed proportionately. The second stage benefits the smaller parties, because it brings together votes that were scattered across the districts. In 1979, the FPÖ gained four of its eleven seats in the second stage, the SPÖ picked up six of its ninety-five, and the ÖVP gained two of its seventy-seven.

The system is not precisely proportional. Over the last three elections, the parties have received about 25,000 votes per seat won. Usually, the FPÖ has slightly more votes per seat won than the average, while the SPÖ has slightly less. In 1979, for example, FPÖ votes per seat won were 26,068 compared to the SPÖ's 25,402. That 666-vote disparity was over twice the size of the disparities in 1971 and 1975.

All Austrian citizens over the age of nineteen are entitled to vote. An official ballot paper lists the names of the parties in their order of strength in the last election. The voter puts a cross against the preferred party list. Voting in *Nationalrat* elections is compulsory only in Styria, Tyrol, and Vorarlberg, but turnout is very high throughout the country and has not fallen below 92 percent since the war. Voting in presidential elections is compulsory for all and failure to vote can result in a fine of 3,000 schillings (about $175). The 1980 turnout was 91.6 percent.

Proposals for further reform of the electoral system are under discussion. Beside the bias toward areas with large families and the disparity of votes per seat, there have been complaints that the strict party-list system is too remote from the voters and too controlled by the party machines. Reformers have suggested adoption of the West German system in which a voter casts one ballot for a specific candidate and another for a party list. It is felt that this might improve the voter's sense of immediate participation and influence.

The Party System

Origins of the Parties

Traditionally the Austrian party system has been dominated by three *Lager* or encampments: the Social Democratic-Marxist; the Catholic-conservative; and the weakest of the three, the pan-German nationalist. These *Lager* originated in the nineteenth century and have been powerful forces in shaping political structures. After both world wars, the parties stepped into the political vacuum to revive political life. In the Second Republic, the *Lager* have managed to coexist in contrast to their battles of the interwar period; the coalition between the ÖVP and the SPÖ reflected this new mood. Some observers believe that personal links established between early ÖVP and SPÖ leaders in Nazi concentration camps contributed to the new spirit of cooperation and compromise which now characterizes contemporary Austrian politics. Since the war, the two main parties have increased their share of the vote, and together in 1979 gained 93 percent of the vote compared with 83 percent thirty years earlier.

This close cooperation between the parties has been the dominant theme in postwar Austrian politics and extends to all areas of government. During the Great Coalition, the two governing parties established a system of distributing appointive offices on the basis of electoral strength. This *Proporz* (proportion) system continues to determine who will gain leading administrative posts in many Austrian institutions, including the nationalized banks and industries. The system gives the two dominant parties not only a secure influence in all administrative bodies, but also a dependent clientele of significant social and political personalities and an important means to repay party loyalty.

The Parties in Law

In July 1975, a Party Law was passed which granted federal financial support to parties, especially for publicity and campaigning. The law stated that "the existence and diversity of political parties is an essential component of the democratic order of the Republic of Austria." Each recognized party—those with at least five deputies in the *Nationalrat*—receives a lump sum; additional money is distributed annually, depending on the number of votes acquired in the previous election. Political parties which have contested but not won seats in the *Nationalrat* and have received one percent of the valid votes also are entitled to financial support in proportion to their votes. All parties must be officially registered with the Ministry of the Interior and demonstrate that they have comprehensive statutes defining the rights and duties of their members. The Party Law has been important in granting funds to smaller parties like the FPÖ, which is less able to rely on contributions from industry or members than the SPÖ and the ÖVP. In 1980 the three parties in Parliament each received a lump sum of 5 million schillings (about $300,000). In addition, the SPÖ received 23.6 million schillings, the ÖVP 19.3 million, and the FPÖ 2.8 million. Supervision of expenditures is carried out by a department of the Ministry of the Interior. In spite of the fact that the Party Law has brought relatively more financial benefits to the FPÖ, the domination by the SPÖ and the ÖVP shows little signs of radical change.

It is difficult for a new party to get on the ballot; three parliamentary deputies must support a party's application. If this support is not forthcoming, a new party must get between two hundred and five hundred voters' signatures in each of the various provinces within thirty days before the election. While this would appear to be a small task, most voters are reluctant to associate their names (and addresses) with a nonestablished party. Whether a petition signer's future would be affected adversely is very uncertain, but many Austrians are not prepared to test the issue.

Party Organization

Two kinds of party organization prevail in Austria. The FPÖ and SPÖ have the usual direct membership organized by locality and province. The ÖVP, however, has an indirect membership system in which adherents, with few exceptions, are first of all members of six functional or age-group organizations for farmers, workers, businessmen, women, youth, and retirees. It is these six organizations which are the real constituents of the ÖVP.

While the national conference of elected delegates is technically the ultimate authority in each party, in practice, the conferences rarely alter policy decisions by the leadership and tend to serve as instruments of support for the party leaders. Nevertheless, local and provincial party organizations are jealous of their prerogatives, maintain some control over candidate selection and ranking, and do influence the party leadership and policymaking.

Years of party work and seniority are the bases for the selection of party leaders at all levels. Incumbents in party office and in the *Nationalrat* tend not to be challenged from within the party, while the stability of party identification among voters assures most elective office holders of consistent reelection. The parties do give extra consideration and respect to experts and technocrats, and on occasion the swift rise of such people through party ranks has caused resentment among members of the parties' parliamentary groups.

All three parties maintain political academies which organize seminars, lectures, and other educational activities for their members and supporters. Much of this activity is aimed at youth and is designed to acquaint them with the history and philosophy of the party. Research centers associated with the academies examine both government and party activity and publish pamphlets for the general public and for members to discuss at local party meetings. At a higher level, the research staffs, classes, and publications inform party functionaries of contemporary government and party issues and help them to convey this information to the rank and file.

Campaigning

Election interest first makes its appearance about a year before the event, although it is usually very mild in the early stages. If an election is scheduled for late autumn, most political activity is suspended during the summer. Normally, organizing and campaigning get underway a few months before election day. In general, Austrian election campaigns are quiet and ethical.

Issues play a minor role, especially since Kreisky has been such a dominant figure; the SPÖ's slogan in 1974 was "Kreisky—who else?" The ÖVP also attempts to project the image of its leader, and the FPÖ tries to appear as a respectable potential partner for any coalition that may develop. In recent years, the main issue has been whether the SPÖ will retain its absolute majority and, if not, whether it will go into coalition with the FPÖ or the ÖVP.

The style of campaigning has become more "Americanized" in recent years. Media shows and popular entertainment are the norm now for mass meetings. Items of all sorts are given away—pens, candles, books, carnations, flags, badges, etc. The leaders of the parties meet on television in a series of discussions before election day, with the press rating their performances the next day. The influence of the news media on election results is problematic. In 1979, both the press and television commentators were skeptical of SPÖ's chances to retain its absolute majority; this obviously had little impact on the voters.

Independent Voters

Party identification is traditionally strong in Austria. Independent or "floating" voters constitute only an estimated 5 or 6 percent of the electorate. Membership in parties is high; a quarter of the population belongs to a political party. This attachment is often believed to be a result of the pervasive influence of the parties on hiring and advancement in the bureaucracy at all levels and in major nationalized industries. Though there are signs that party identification may be weakening, polls show that most voters—80 percent of the supporters of the SPÖ, the ÖVP, and the Communists and 60 percent of FPÖ supporters—have made firm decisions about their vote well before an election. With the exceptions of the 1966 and 1970 elections, voting behavior has been consistently predictable and stable.

Freedom Party of Austria (*Freiheitliche Partei Österreichs; FPÖ*)

History

The FPÖ was founded in 1955 by a former Nazi, Anton Reinthaller, as the heir of the national-liberal tradition in Austrian political history. Frequent factional disputes flare up between right-wing nationalists and moderate liberals. It has not participated in government in the Second Republic. The FPÖ contested the presidential election for the first time in 1980 and won 17 percent of the vote. The party had put up a joint candidate with the ÖVP in 1957, but that effort failed.

Organization

Provincial congresses elect delegates to the national conference, which in turn elects the leader and his chief deputies. The leader is responsible for all party activities and appoints most of the senior party office holders. However, the party is not as highly centralized as the leader's formal authority would suggest. Factional and regional interests play a part behind the scenes in the selection of the leader, and once elected he must continue to play factions off against each other. The FPÖ consciously tries to avoid excessive centralization and tolerates a high degree of independent activity in its local organizations.

The FPÖ has a youth organization, the Ring of Free Youth, for those under thirty years of age; its membership is thought to be about 5,000. The youth group is overtly pan-German and rejects the idea of an "Austrian" nation. The FPÖ student organization, which takes a similar line, won 7 percent of the vote in university student-body elections in 1979.

The party has a weekly newspaper, *Neue Freie Zeitung* (New Free News), and a quarterly theoretical journal, *Freie Argumente* (Free Debate).

Party headquarters are at Kärntnerstrasse 15, A-1010 Vienna.

Policy

The FPÖ presents itself as an advocate of law and order and a defender of "German" interests, a conveniently vague concept that appeals to German (as opposed to Austrian) national sentiment and rejects the continuation of non-German, mostly Slavic, cultural traditions in Austria. (These traditions are particularly strong among the small group of Slovenes in Carintha on Austria's border with Yugoslavia.) Foreign workers, largely Slavic, also are seen as a threat to "German Austria."

The party is strongly in favor of individual achievement within a free-enterprise system. It objects to excessive government regulation and especially to the proportional system by which the two major parties monopolize most significant management positions. The FPÖ not only opposes "red" socialism, but also "black" Catholic clericalism, which it sees as a constraint on individual liberty. Only 30 percent of the party's parliamentary group describe themselves as Catholics.

The party is riven by disputes between the older, right-wing nationalists and a younger wing of free-enterprise liberals. The party leader, Norbert Steger, is identified with the latter group, but he has not been able to establish his authority over all branches of the party.

Membership & Constituency

Membership is estimated to be around 35,000. Compared to the other parties, the FPÖ has a low ratio of voters to members, about eight to one. Most support for the FPÖ comes from small towns, and the bulk of its voters are self-employed or white-collar workers and civil servants. The province of Salzburg consistently has been the stronghold of the party and gave the FPÖ 11.4 percent of the province's vote in 1979. The western Alpine provinces of *Wahlkreisverband II* also give the FPÖ its firm support.

Financing

The FPÖ has weak links with the major economic interest groups and depends more than the ÖVP and the SPÖ on financial aid from the state to run its programs and campaigns.

Leadership

Anton Reinthaller, the FPÖ founder, died in 1958 and was succeeded by Friedrich Peter, a former Waffen SS officer. Peter attempted to give the party a more liberal image and fostered relations with the SPÖ. In 1978, Peter was replaced by a right-wing candidate, Dr. Alexander Goetz, who adopted a more aggressive campaign style, without result. The liberal wing forced a new leader on the party in 1980—Dr. Norbert Steger. Steger (born 1944) is from Vienna and his power base within the party is fragile. Although not a serious contender to regain party leadership, Goetz remains a major political force in Styria; and Peter, who remains leader of the FPÖ parliamentary *Klub*, could make a comeback, particularly if a coalition with the SPÖ became possible. Dr. Joerg Haider (born 1950) is seen as a rising party star. A deputy from Carinthia, he is in charge of FPÖ social-policy formulations.

Prospects

Right-wing groups in Austria, including the FPÖ, are especially prone to internal strife, personal rivalries, and schisms, so there is always some danger of FPÖ disintegration. The party hopes eventually to hold the balance of power between the two main parties, but this assumes that the SPÖ will both lose its absolute majority *and* reject another coalition with the ÖVP.

Austrian People's Party
(*Österreichische Volkspartei;* ÖVP)

History

The ÖVP was founded in April 1945 as a revival of the Catholic conservative *Lager*. The movement originated in the late nineteenth century as an antiliberal and antisocialist force outside the political mainstream. In the 1920s, however, the ÖVP's immediate predecessor, the Christian Social Party, was the core of a series of antisocialist blocs which formed governments under the guidance of Ignaz Seipel, a Catholic priest. The brief civil war of 1934 found the Christian Socials allied with the fascist paramilitary *Heimwehr* and other groups of a Christian, fascist, or authoritarian stamp against the Socialists, who were soundly defeated. These groups were seldom united on any other question; economic policy, church policy, and policy toward Mussolini's Italy and Hitler's Germany were all major points of contention.

The ÖVP's first leaders and members had taken part in these pre-annexation struggles. Leopold Figl, one of the founders, had been director of the prewar peasant's league and a local leader of a paramilitary organization. Julius Raab, the party's leader from 1952 to 1960, led the *Heimwehr* in Lower Austria. Alfons Gorbach, who succeeded Raab, had been a leader of the Fatherland Front in Styria. Figl, Gorbach, and many others were imprisoned in Dachau and other concentration camps after the Nazi annexation.

The new ÖVP was an immediate success and led the Austrian government from 1945 to 1966. Since then, however, it has steadily lost ground to the SPÖ.

Organization

The party consists of six separate organizations, each of which is organized in the nine provinces, making a total of fifty-four units that require coordination. Each province also has an organization of the ÖVP itself, as do local districts. The six components of ÖVP include three powerful economic leagues—farmers, business, and workers—and three weaker groups based on status—women, youth, and retirees.

The ÖVP puts a high priority on intraparty democracy, a priority enforced by the independent strength of the suborganizations. These units are entitled to send twenty-five delegates each to the national party conference, where they are joined by at least ten delegates from each ÖVP provincial organization, the party's *Nationalrat* members, and ÖVP members of the provincial governments.

Tensions between the parliamentary *Klub* and local organizations (especially those of Styria and Tyrol), between the *Klub* and the leagues, and among the leagues themselves are common and public. For example, the Business League and the employees' group have been at odds over the suggestion by the latter that a shortened workweek and longer vacations might help alleviate the unemployment problem.

Candidate selection and ranking on the party list is a complex process in the ÖVP. Candidates are first proposed at the district level and discussed with the provincial party leaders, who in turn carry their proposals to the national directorate. The national leaders can veto candidate proposals, but at least 5 percent of all nominations remain the sole prerogative of the provincial organizations. Ranking of candidates is also primarily a provincial prerogative, but the relative strength of the provincial suborganizations plays a major role in determining the ranking of their representative's names on the ballot. The national leadership can reject provincial rankings, but such disputes are rare and usually resolved by negotiation.

In 1975, the ÖVP experimented with primaries as a basis for candidate selection and ranking. The party's return to the usual methods in 1979 suggests that the primaries only exacerbated one of problems of the ÖVP, i.e., making room for the ambitions and opinions of its disparate groups, while at the same time trying to achieve the unity necessary for electoral success.

The ÖVP has numerous auxilliary organizations such as the League of Academics with 8,900 members and a Tenants' League, which represents the interests of both tenants and landlords and numbered some 60,000 in its membership in 1980. The ÖVP does not have direct contact with Catholic organizations, because the Church, since the disasters of the prewar period, has tried to remain at a distance from party politics.

Party headquarters are at Kärntnerstrasse 51, A-1010 Vienna.

Policy

The postwar ÖVP stressed its commitment to democracy and its distance from the authoritarian corporate state with which the old Catholic *Lager* had been associated. The early postwar programs put great emphasis on the peasantry as the moral backbone of society. The general welfare of the nation was thought to be linked inextricably with the fate of the rural community; this was too narrow a focus for the business interests in the party, who supported the idea of a "social market economy" with minimal state organization of economic affairs. The social-market-economy policy was adopted in the Salzburg Program of 1972.

The farming community wants to preserve the family unit, which it feels is threatened by increasing modernization and industrialization. To that end it is keen to gain state subsidies to alleviate difficult conditions on the land and stop the drift of labor, especially young people, to the towns. The farmers also have strong regional loyalties which they place above the federal party. Conservative and staunchly Catholic, the farmers are inclined to resist changes in the structure and ideology of the ÖVP, believing that change will only lead to a dilution of the party's commitment to Christian teachings. The business and commercial interests in the party are more interested in attacking the Socialist government for its wasteful welfare and educational programs.

In recent years, the Workers' and Employees' League has come more to the forefront of the ÖVP, sometimes supporting the farmers, sometimes the Business League. The issues of unemployment and working conditions are critical for the workers' wing of the party. The same problems affect the farming community.

In spite of the ÖVP's attempts to develop a coherent and distinctive ideology, a survey in 1975 revealed that 42 percent of the electorate found it difficult to detect any major differences between the ÖVP and the SPÖ. Of the 56 percent that did see a clear distinction (2 percent did not respond), most saw the ÖVP's attachment to the Catholic Church and its opposition to abortion as the party's distinguishing characteristics. The party has been working on a revision of its policy and program statements (as well as its structure) in an attempt to present a united and forward-looking image to the voters in 1983.

Membership & Constituency

Members are recruited to the party indirectly through the appropriate suborganizations. Direct membership is possible but not significant. According to the ÖVP's own report for 1980, membership totaled 1,167,888. Although these figures are in dispute, in part because some people belong to more than one suborganization, it is clear

ÖVP SUBORGANIZATIONS AND MEMBERSHIP (1981)	
Farmers' League (*Bauernbund*)	388,800
Business League (*Wirtschaftsbund*)	152,900
Workers' and Employees' League (*Arbeiter und Angestellterbund*)	272,000
Women's Movement (*Frauenbewegung*)	76,500
Young People's Party (*Junge Volkspartei*)	104,500
Senior Citizens' League (*Seniorenbund*)	172,800
Individual members	300

that the party has a substantial membership. Most members are practicing Catholics, and 80 percent of the party's deputies in the *Nationalrat* describe themselves as Catholic.

Staunch Catholics and wealthy farmers are the most faithful members of the ÖVP: in 1979, the party won 55 percent of the vote in both Vorarlberg and Tyrol. Elsewhere the party is on the defensive, suffering from a decline in the peasant-farmer population and losing in agricultural areas where SPÖ policies of full employment have had an impact on farmers who must supplement their farm income with other jobs.

Financing

Dues paid to the party's suborganizations amounted to about 131 million shillings (nearly $8 million) in the late 1970s, but only a small portion of this was passed on to the federal party. These funds represented about 30 percent of the party's income. Another 9 percent, about 42.5 million shillings, came from functionaries who owe their positions to the party and pay a party tax for the privilege. Additional funds came from donations, mostly from industry, and from the government. Total annual expenses run in the neighborhood of 400 million shillings (about $25 million).

Leadership

The ÖVP has difficulty maintaining continuity at the top: since 1960, the party has had six leaders. Before 1960, the party leader was Julius Raab. When his health failed, Alfons Gorbach took over, but he could not manage the competing interests in the party as well as Raab had. Gorbach was ousted by younger men eager for reform in the party, who put Josef Klaus in the office. Klaus met with the similar difficulties, and was replaced by Karl Schleinzer, who was killed in a car accident in 1975, shortly after the general election. The party settled on a young leader, Josef Taus, but when the ÖVP lost the 1979 election, it replaced Taus with Alois Mock.

Mock was born in Lower Austria in 1934 and is a member of the Workers' and Employees' League. As the organizer of the party's business in the *Nationalrat*, he has shown skill as a parliamentarian, but he is not a dynamic figure. His appeal to voters lies in his image as a sincere, hardworking, and modest politician.

If the ÖVP should lose the 1983 elections, there are several figures who might be called upon to replace Mock. Among them are Herbert

Kohlmaier, born in Vienna in 1934, currently deputy leader of the party and a member of the Workers' League, and Dr. Michael Graff, the new general secretary of the party. Graff is a technocrat and administrator as well as a politician. He is a member of both the Business and Workers' leagues.

Prospects

The ÖVP has a chance to break SPÖ's absolute majority in the spring 1983 elections, particularly if Kreisky's health continues to deteriorate and the SPÖ is unable to weather a recent series of internal disputes and scandals. The SPÖ may also manage to keep its position if the economy and unemployment remain major issues. In any case, even with a victory, the ÖVP would probably have to have a coalition partner to be able to govern.

Socialist Party of Austria (*Sozialistische Partei Österreichs; SPÖ*)

History

The SPÖ was founded in April 1945, but is the successor of the former Social Democratic Party which was established in Lower Austria in 1888. This party became identified in the First Republic with "Austro-Marxism" which emphasized unity in the labor movement. In spite of ideological radicalism, the party's actions were pragmatic and reformist. In 1934 an illegal group of Revolutionary Socialists was formed after the party's defeat in the civil war. The SPÖ of the Second Republic was less concerned with ideology, and its responsible partnership with the ÖVP in the 1945–66 government gained it increasing popularity.

Organization

The SPÖ is much more centrally organized and managed than either the FPÖ or the ÖVP. The party congress, which must meet every two years, almost always endorses the decisions of the leadership. While this is equally true of the other parties, the SPÖ leadership has much less need to compromise with the kind of ideological, regional, and special-interest divisions which beset the other parties.

Delegates to the party conference are elected by local party organizations on the basis of their membership strength. Provincial party organizations send at least two delegates each with additional delegates allotted according to party strength in the province. The provincial delegates are selected by the provincial executive. The Austrian Trade Union (*Österreichischer Gewerkschaftsbund;* ÖGB) sends fifty delegates, the youth organization sends six, and additional delegates from a variety of auxiliary organizations also attend. *Nationalrat* members and editors of the party's press organs are also delegates.

Candidate selection and ranking is done by a special party council convened by the party leader. Consultations with provincial and district organizations are common, but the council makes the final decision. One-fifth of the places on the ballot are allocated without regard to place of residence and are given to people, mostly experts, who can contribute to the party's work in Parliament.

The SPÖ has a wealth of auxiliary organizations, including a Sports Association with over 800,000 members, a parents' association of 30,000, and a group for children, the Red Falcons. Other party-associated groups include special-interest clubs for stamp collectors, amateur musicians, gardeners, etc., and an Abstinence Society.

The Austrian Socialist Youth (*Sozialistischer Jugend Österreichs;* SJÖ) is the most significant of these auxiliaries, because it stands well to the left of the parent body. In foreign policy it advocates closer Austrian association with the Third World, and it is sharply critical of the "social partnership" system which, it argues, essentially denies the class struggle and assumes that workers and employers have common interests. An associated group, the Students' Association, was suspended by the party leadership in the late 1970s on suspicion of having Trotskyite leanings. Suspension means that the party no longer provides financial support to the group and does not permit it to send delegates to the national conference. The SPÖ hopes that a new generation of students will enable the party to resume full relations.

The party publishes a daily newspaper, *Die AZ,* once called the *Arbeiterzeitung* (Worker News), but changed when the SPÖ wanted to broaden its image. The newspaper is in financial difficulties. The SPÖ also has a monthly theoretical journal, *Die Zukunft* (The Future).

Party headquarters are at Lowelstrasse 18, A-1010 Vienna.

Policy

In government, the SPÖ has tried to implement its manifesto pledge to create a modern and hu-mane Austria. The most recent program was adopted in 1978. The SPÖ has maintained a full-employment policy and has managed to keep inflation under control. Unemployment was kept to an average of below 2 percent in the 1970s, although current projections indicate that it will increase. The working week has been reduced to forty hours and all workers are now entitled to a minimum of four weeks annual holiday. Modernization of the communications network, hospitals, and schools have provided better services. The chancellor has won contracts abroad for Austrian firms and has fostered good relations with the Arab world and Eastern Europe. These advances have created a feeling that the "Kreisky era" has brought stability and prosperity.

Membership & Constituency

The SPÖ is a mass-membership party. Membership is direct and individual and in 1980 was 719,881, over 9 percent of the total population. The party has a high ratio of members to voters; in 1979, 29.68 percent of Socialist voters were also party members. Women comprise just over a third of the total membership.

The party is popular with women, who make up over 54 percent of the electorate, and the "floating voter." In the 1979 elections, the SPÖ won forty-five out of the eighty-one seats in the three eastern provinces of *Wahlkreisverband I.* The SPÖ has been increasingly successful in rural communities and Catholic areas, while maintaining its strength in traditional working-class areas. In spite of the party's Marxist tradition, 47 percent of the party's deputies in the *Nationalrat* describe themselves as Catholics.

The SPÖ relies heavily on young voters and, at the same time, finds them least amenable to direction by the party's leadership. Young people were instrumental in securing a negative vote in a national referendum on nuclear power in 1978. Against the advice of the SPÖ government, organized labor, and industry, the vote indefinitely delayed the commissioning of Austria's sole nuclear reactor, already built near Vienna.

Young voters have put the SPÖ under greatest pressure in Vienna, where the party took 61 percent of the *Nationalrat* vote in 1979. The ÖVP hopes to mobilize the youth by pointing out the inadequacies in the city and criticizes the SPÖ government of Vienna for mismanaging public funds. The SPÖ at the national level recognizes the importance of Vienna in its overall fortunes, but is reluctant to become entangled in the mistakes and tribulations of the party in the municipality. The party hopes that local problems will remain isolated and not damage the party's impressive performance in national elections.

The antinuclear and ecological concerns shown by the urban electorate, especially the youth, have caused some prominent SPÖ members to shift their support to this "green" movement. This is a new development in Austrian politics and its impact on the 1983 elections and the SPÖ is unpredictable.

Financing

At the end of the 1970s, around 135 million schillings were received every year by the party from membership dues. A further 42.5 million schillings came from the party tax on functionaries, and 170 million shillings were provided by public funding.

Leadership

The personality of the leader, Bruno Kreisky, has been an important factor in the party's success. Kreisky (born 1911) has led the party since 1967, and in a 1979 poll was preferred by 57 percent of voters compared with only 23 percent who favored the ÖVP leader. Kreisky has become a kind of father-figure for many Austrians at a time of international insecurity. His outlook is undogmatic, and he values democracy and the freedom of the individual. Among potential successors is the current vice chancellor, Fred Sinowatz (born 1929), from Burgenland. As minister of education since 1971, he is highly regarded as the author of important reforms in educational policy. It is felt that he could best hold the party together in the difficult post-Kreisky period. Other leading party figures are Erwin Lanc (born 1930), minister of the interior since 1977 with a power base in Vienna's SPÖ organization; Heinz Fischer (born 1938), *Klub* leader since 1975; and Karl Blecha (born 1933), central secretary of the party since 1976 and a member of the *Nationalrat* since 1970.

Prospects

The SPÖ continues to do well in local and provincial elections and is confident of the future. Kreisky's health and a recent breath of scandal in the party may cause some decrease of support in the 1983 elections, but continued perception of the SPÖ as competent to handle the country's economic difficulties should continue. If the SPÖ were to lose its absolute majority in the *Nationalrat*, the event could mark a turning point in Austrian political history.

Minor Parties

Christian Social Working Group (*Christlich-Soziale-Arbeitsgemeinschaft*)

Based in Tyrol, this party won only 0.66 percent of the votes cast in that province in the 1979 elections. It is antipornography and committed to Catholic moral and family values.

Communist Party of Austria (*Kommunistische Partei Österreichs; KPÖ*)

The KPÖ was founded in Vienna on November 3, 1918, in the turmoil which accompanied the collapse of the Hapsburg Empire. It was a weak political force before World War II and has steadily declined in influence in the Second Republic. Under the Occupation, the KPÖ became identified as the unpopular "party of the Russians," and the SPÖ retained the loyalty of the working class.

The KPÖ had one seat in the *Bundesrat* from 1949 to 1954. In elections to the *Landtage*, the KPÖ lost its last seats in Vienna in 1969 and in Carinthia and Styria in 1970. The KPÖ lost its three remaining seats in the *Nationalrat* in 1959.

The organization of the KPÖ is based on the Marxist-Leninist principle of democratic centralism. The party conference meets once every three years and elects the Central Committee which in turn elects the Politburo, the party chairman, and the central secretaries. The Politburo makes decisions between meetings of the Central Committee.

The KPÖ aims to establish a new socialist order. Its loyalty to the Soviet Union has been put under some strain since the invasion of Czechoslovakia in 1968, but dissidents have either resigned or have been expelled. The KPÖ is generally uncritical of the USSR and rejects "Eurocommunism."

Most support for the party in 1979 was in Vienna (1.5 percent), which provides the KPÖ with over a third of its total votes. Official figures for membership are not available, but it is believed to be under 20,000. The KPÖ has a high ratio of members to voters; in 1979, 44 percent of Communist voters were also party members. In 1974, 49 percent of the membership was over sixty, 20 percent were aged between fifty and sixty, and only 6.6 percent were under thirty.

The party attracts only a small portion (1.2 percent) of the vote in elections for the central council of the Chamber of Labor and only a little more in the ÖGB leadership. Its strength was undercut in the Chamber by the appearance of a rival list of candidates put up by members who were alienated from the party in the wake of the Soviet invasion of Czechoslovakia. At present the party has four members in the Chamber, two from Vienna and one each from Lower Austria and Styria. In the labor-union central committee, the KPÖ holds 7 percent of the seats, and on the executive board, elected by the committee, they hold only two seats compared to the Socialists' thirty-nine and the ÖVP's thirteen.

Membership dues could not finance the numerous activities of the party; it relies on the "goodwill" of the Soviet Union. It once qualified for state support, but rejected "bourgeois" capital.

Franz Muhri (born 1924) has led the party since 1965. His power base is in Vienna.

The KPÖ's chances of making a major impact on political life in Austria seem very remote.

Group of Revolutionary Marxists (Gruppe Revolutionäre Marxisten)

Founded in 1972, the Group has a membership of about 100, produces a monthly paper *Die Rotfront* (The Red Front) and describes itself as the Austrian section of the Trotskyite Fourth International. It contested the general election of 1975 with a list in Vienna, gaining 1,024 votes. In 1979 it was unable to obtain the signatures necessary to put up a list of candidates. This was due, in part, to poor organization.

Marxists-Leninists of Austria (Marxisten-Leninisten Österreichs)

Founded in 1965, this Maoist group split from the KPÖ. The leader is Franz Strobl, who started the party's newspaper *Rote Fahne* (Red Flag). In 1966 the party contested one constituency in Vienna and won 486 votes. The radical left parties are permanently engaged in polemical and personal feuds. Their influence is negligible.

National Democratic Party (Nationaldemokratische Partei; NDP)

Founded in 1966, this radical right-wing party stands for the reintroduction of the death penalty, the abolition of abortion, and the withdrawal of civil rights from conscientious objectors. It is violently anticommunist and anti-Slav, and opposes the presence of foreign workers in Austria. In 1970, it gained only 0.07 percent of the vote in the *Nationalrat* election; and in 1978, in Vienna's local elections, only 133 people voted for its candidates. In 1980, however, its leader, former FPÖ

member Dr. Norbert Burger, won 3.2 percent of the vote in the presidential elections with the slogan "Austria must stay German." Commentators have assumed that these were protest votes in areas of high unemployement. The party also did well in areas where Austria borders communist nations.

Other Political Forces

Organized Labor

The Austrian Trade Union Federation (*Österreicher Gerwerkschaftsbund*; ÖGB) is a strong, centralized body with the primary responsibility of bargaining for workers' demands. In spite of voluntary membership, it has enrolled nearly two-thirds of Austria's work force. The central Federation leadership is elected indirectly by workers' councils which are chosen by the employees of individual firms. In the last elections, the socialists won 75 percent of the vote and the ÖVP, which has a small union affiliate associated with the ÖGB, won 17 percent. The communists won only 7 percent. Though dominated by the SPÖ, with which most of the unions have historic ties, the ÖGB has no formal links with the party. The party leadership takes the federation into consideration when nominating candidates for public office and there is a large membership overlap between the SPÖ and ÖGB.

National Prospects

There are two primary unknowns in assessing Austria's fortunes in the next few years—the outcome of the 1983 elections and, assuming the SPÖ wins, how long thereafter Kreisky can continue to serve as the chancellor. Whatever the answers to these questions, Austria will have to cope with zero economic growth, greater inflation, and an increase in unemployment, especially in the construction trades. The country will not be able to avoid the budget cutbacks that have been forced on other industrialized nations, even though Kreisky does not want to reduce government expenditures on education and welfare schemes. Austria has been active and successful in securing business relations with Saudi Arabia and East Europe and hopes to ride out the economic recession by further development of this trade.

While Austria in the pre-World War II period displayed extreme political instability in face of economic crisis, the Austrians of today are proud of their economic achievements and will not want to risk those advances by making radical changes in either economic or political arrangements.

Further Reading

Barker, Elisabeth. *Austria 1918–1972*. London: Macmillan, 1972.

Fischer, Heinz, ed. *Das politische System Österreichs*. Vienna: Europa Verlag, 1977.

Kadan, Albert, and Pelinka, Anton, eds. *Die Grundsatzprogramme der österreichischen Parteien*. St. Poelten: Niederösterreichisches Pressehaus, 1979.

Stadler, fKarl R. *Austria*. London: Ernest Benn, 1971.

Steiner, Kurt. *Politics in Austria*. Boston: Little Brown & Co., 1972.

_____ ed. *Modern Austria*. Palo Alto, Calif.: Society for the Promotion of Science and Scholarship, 1981.

Sully, Melanie A. *Political Parties and Elections in Austria*. London: Hurst, 1981.

COMMONWEALTH OF THE BAHAMAS

by Indira Jhappan

The System of Government

The Commonwealth of the Bahamas, a nation of 260,000 people, consists of over 700 islands and many more cays extending over 600 miles (from about fifty miles off the coast of Florida southeast nearly to Haiti). It is a parliamentary democracy in the British style, having gained its independence from Great Britain in 1973. Although the Bahamas have recently developed as a thriving offshore financial center, the economy remains heavily dependent on tourism. The population is predominantly of black and mixed descent, but there is a large white presence in the form of tourists and immigrant retired people.

Executive

The head of state is the British monarch who is represented in the commonwealth by a governor-general. Real executive power is exercised by the prime minister and his cabinet. The prime minister, ceremonially appointed by the governor-general, is the leader of the majority party in the House of Assembly. The cabinet oversees all the affairs of state and originates nearly all legislation. The prime minister may advise the governor-general to dissolve the Parliament at any time.

Legislature

Parliament is divided into two houses: the Senate and the House of Assembly. Of the Senate's sixteen members, nine are appointed by the governor-general on the advice of the prime minister, four on the advice of the leader of the opposition, and three on the advice of the prime minister after consultation with the leader of the opposition. Appointments are for five years and may be renewed. The Senate's political power is limited; it serves primarily as a consultative body with some power to delay the passage of legislation.

The House of Assembly consists of forty-three members (thirty-eight before 1982) elected to five-year terms. Bills can be introduced in either the House or Senate, but money bills can only be in-troduced in the House. If a bill is rejected twice by the Senate after it has been passed twice by the House, it can nevertheless be sent to the governor-general for formal approval. To change the constitution, each chamber must pass the amendment by a three-fourths majority, and the amendment must then be submitted to a national referendum.

In the 1982 elections, the ruling Progressive Labour Party (PLP) won thirty-two House seats and the opposition Free National Movement (FNM) won eleven.

Judiciary

The system of justice is based on English common law and is administered by the Supreme Court and the Court of Appeal. The Supreme Court consists of a chief justice, appointed by the governor-general on the advice of the prime minister in consultation with the leader of the opposition, and two additional judges. Decisions of the Supreme Court can be appealed to the Court of Appeal, consisting of a president and two judges, also appointed by the governor-general on the advice of the prime minister. The ultimate court of appeal is the Judicial Committee of the Privy Council in London.

Regional & Local Government

Local divisions are based on eighteen natural island groupings and are, with two exceptions, administered by centrally appointed district commissioners. The islands of New Providence, site of the capital of Nassau, and Grand Bahama have elected local governing bodies.

The Electoral System

Elections in the Bahamas are held at least every five years and within ninety days after the dissolution of Parliament. Bahamians eighteen years of age and over are eligible to vote. Each of forty-three constituencies returns one representative elected by a simple plurality. Turnout commonly exceeds 90 percent. Elections have generally been fair, but after the 1982 elections, the opposition charged fraud and challenged the election results in eight constituencies where PLP candidates won by very narrow margins. In a countermove, the PLP challenged the results in five constituencies won by the opposition FNM.

The Party System

Political competition in the Bahamas began in the early 1950s, when a movement to organize the black working class developed its own political party, the PLP, to compete against the predominantly white and light-colored elite group representing the business interests in the United Bahamian Party (UBP), which dominated the government until 1967. The PLP came to power in that year and has remained the dominant party since then.

The formation of political parties is easy, and a variety of opposition parties have competed against the PLP from time to time. They have not mounted effective challenges because of their inability to organize a united front.

The major parties have been well organized with local organizations in every constituency and frequent national conventions. Campaigning is lively and serious and concentrates on personalities, since the ideological differences between the parties are minor.

Free National Movement (FNM)

The FNM was formed in late 1971 as a merger between the old UBP and dissidents from the PLP who called themselves the Free PLP. In the 1972 elections, the FNM won nine seats to the PLP's twenty-nine. In December 1976, the party suffered a split with most of the old UBP members forming a new party, the Bahamian Democratic Party (BDP). In the 1977 elections, the FNM won only two seats, while the BDP won five. In 1979, four BDP members of Parliament left to form the Social Democratic Party (SDP), which briefly became the official opposition. The remaining BDP member of Parliament and, later, one of the SDP men rejoined the FNM. Going into the 1982 elections, the FNM had four seats in the House and the SPD three. The SPD disbanded before the elections, from which the FNM emerged with eleven seats and 44 percent of the vote.

A major factor in the reunification of the opposition forces in 1981 was the return to politics of Kendal Isaacs (born 1925), who had retired for reasons of health in the early 1970s. He resolved the leadership disputes between the former Free PLP and UBP leaders and, as a former attorney general and senator, brought the party renewed respect.

The FNM's campaign issues in 1982 were the need for a change, charges of corruption against the PLP, and the need to move the country's economy forward by making foreign investment more welcome.

In the 1982 elections the FNM lost three seats by less than twenty-five votes each and five other seats by less than 150 votes each. Thus a shift of less than 900 votes among the total of 76,098 would have given the FNM nineteen seats to the PLP's twenty-four. If the economy remains sluggish and the tourist business does not improve by the time of the next election, the FNM stands a fair chance of putting the PLP in opposition.

Progressive Labour Party (PLP)

The Progressive Labour Party was formed in 1953 by Lynden O. Pindling (born 1930), a black attorney who is still the party's leader. Outside of a leadership dispute in 1967 between Pindling and Cecil Whitfield, who then formed the Free PLP, the party has shown excellent unity and organization. With the exception of a brief period in the mid-1970s, it has always had the firm support of the Trade Union Congress (TUC), the labor organization out of which the PLP originally sprang.

The party is slightly to the left of center in the Bahamian political spectrum, but is basically a moderate, pro-American party with a free-enterprise point of view. Pindling maintains that in times of economic difficulties, the Bahamas must try to become more self-reliant and less dependent on foreign investment.

Vanguard Party

The Vanguard, an avowedly socialist party, first competed in the 1977 elections when it ran four candidates who won fifty-five votes among them. In 1982, it ran fifteen candidates and won 173 votes. While Bahamian voters obviously have little interest in socialism, the Vanguard's apparent growth over those five years suggests that the party may have the necessary organizational ability to take advantage of a severe economic downturn and extensive unemployment if they should occur.

Other Political Forces

Organized Labor

The Trade Union Congress (TUC) was firmly associated with the PLP until 1975, when it moved toward the FNM. After that party split in December 1976, the TUC negotiated an agreement with the PLP under which the party promised to give TUC views greater weight in forming party policy. These rapid changes in direction occurred before the 1977 elections and thus failed to weigh the TUC's power in the electoral scale. However, the brief experiment did demonstrate the TUC's potential independence from the PLP. Given the increased threat of the FNM in the 1982 elections, the PLP is likely to make greater efforts to ensure the loyalty of organized labor, which it has always depended on for its electoral majorities.

National Prospects

With the unemployment rate hovering at 20 percent and the tourist industry depressed by the economic recession, the PLP faces severe problems. If it does not find adequate solutions and the economy does not improve, its majority position could be in jeopardy.

Further Reading
Hughes, Colin A. *Race and Politics in the Bahamas.* New York: St. Martin's Press, 1981.

STATE OF BAHRAIN
(*Dawlat al-Bahrain*)
by Fred H. Lawson, Ph.D.

The System of Government

Bahrain, an island in the Persian Gulf, is a non-party autocracy whose ruler governs the country's 380,000 people in consultation with a small group of advisers that includes members of the royal family and professional administrators associated with them. This elite is descended from a branch of the Bani 'Utub tribal confederacy that arrived in the islands around 1780 and set up a commercial, estate-holding aristocracy over the local inhabitants. These class distinctions were reinforced by religious ones, as the new rulers were Sunni Muslims, and the indigenous farmers, pearl-divers and fisherpeople were Shi'a Muslims.

Serious outbreaks of political violence have occurred repeatedly in the country from at least 1911 to the present. These protests can be grouped into three distinct waves on the basis of the political forces which have been most actively involved in them. During the 1910s and 1920s, local merchants and tradespeople joined together in opposition to economic regulations proposed by British colonial officials. From the 1930s to the 1950s, a similarly broad coalition of social forces demonstrated against continued British domination, against the presence of large numbers of foreign workers in the country, and in favor of allowing local labor to unionize. After the 1950s, riots and strikes pitting Bahrain's working class against its government have continued to occur quite frequently. Some violence has taken on sectarian overtones, appearing as conflicts between Sunni and Shi'a; however, these incidents have for the most part been characterized as well by consistent demands for changes in the country's economy to benefit poorer workers. Partly as a result of a major general strike by construction, shipyard and aluminum-plant workers in March 1972 that threatened the rulers' industrialization programs, Bahrain's emir (ruler) authorized the establishment of the country's first, but very short-lived, electoral system, in which he assumed the role of a constitutional monarch and his council of advisers operated as an appointed cabinet.

Executive

Shaikh 'Isa bin Salman Al Khalifa (born July 3, 1933) became ruler of Bahrain in 1961 upon the death of his father. According to the constitution adopted in 1973, the office of emir passes from father to eldest son unless the ruler chooses someone else to succeed him. This section of Bahrain's constitution is not subject to amendment. Other parts of this document authorize the emir to act as head of state, to serve as commander-in-chief of the country's armed forces, and to "conclude treaties by decree." These legal prerogatives are buttressed by tribal authority within the Al Khalifa clan.

Close relatives of the emir fill the most important posts in the country's cabinet. The family ties among cabinet ministers are illustrated in Figure 1.

Ministers who are not members of the royal family are drawn largely from among those sons of the country's established rich merchant community who have received specialized training in Western universities. Mahmud Ahmad al-Alawi, the minister of finance and national economy, and Yusif Ahmad Shirawi, the minister of development and industry, are the most notable. Bahrain's largest industrial concerns are managed by this group of royal family members and influential civil servants.

Legislature

Bahrain's first national elections were held in December 1972. Twenty-two representatives to a constitutional assembly were chosen by the country's native-born male citizens twenty years of age and older, grouped into nineteen electoral districts centered on the cities and towns. Several candidates ran for office within each district, with

Figure 1

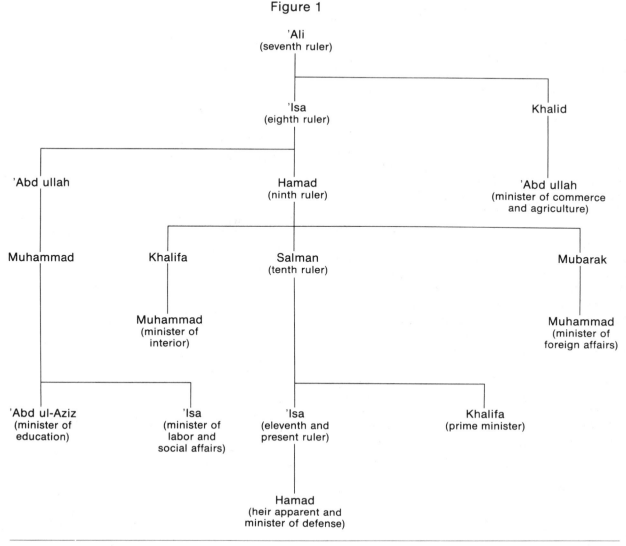

Source: Fuad I. Khuri, *Tribe and State in Bahrain* (Chicago: University of Chicago Press, 1980), p. 127, Fig. 4.

the winner in single-member districts being the one who received a plurality of the votes cast. In each of the three two-member districts in Manama and Muharraq, the two candidates getting the most votes were the winners. Candidates ran as individuals or as part of informal, personalist slates of candidates headed by such prominent local businessmen as 'Abd al-Aziz Shamlan and Hisham ash-Shahabi. These procedures also were followed in December 1973, when Bahrain's first National Assembly was elected.

College-educated professionals, shopkeepers, middle-income merchants, and the owners of the country's newspapers were the strongest supporters of the new electoral system. The merchant elite remained noncommital on the issue of a popularly elected parliament and did not participate in the elections either as candidates or as voters. Employees of the state bureaucracy also avoided becoming involved with the assemblies, as they would have had to resign their government posts in order to run for seats.

Radical groups, such as the local branch of the Popular Front for the Liberation of Oman and the Arab Gulf (PFLOAG), actively tried to convince potential voters not to go to the polls on the grounds that the new assemblies represented only a façade for the continuation of autocratic rule. These groups—whose members were largely workers and students, both indigenous and expatriate—demanded more comprehensive freedoms of press and assembly, the release of those they claimed were political prisoners of the regime and laws permitting trade unionization as first steps toward the establishment of a democratic regime in the country.

Purely by chance, these radical proposals coincided with the last-minute withdrawal of the ash-Shahabi slate from the constitutional assembly elections of 1972. This led the cabinet to suspect some sort of collusion between these two forces and created a measure of opposition within the ruling class to the election process in general. As a result, when a group of younger radical representatives led by Dr. 'Adb al-Hadi Khalaf of the banned National Liberation Front–Bahrain and Yusif Hasan al-Ajaji emerged as winners in the elections of 1973, the government prevented many of them from taking their seats in the Assembly on the basis of technicalities in the election law.

Despite the fact that the National Assembly was authorized only to give advice and consent to laws initiated in the cabinet, and was thus not a true legislature, its members began seriously to debate two volatile issues during 1974. One issue was the formulation of a general labor law that would have allowed trade union organization and restricted the importation of foreign workers. The other major issue was the continuation of a strict Public Security Law that had been used to suppress the PFLOAG, Ba'thists, and local communists. It became clear by mid-1975, however, that the two largest informal blocs of delegates within the Assembly, the People's and the Religious blocs, acting together could not force the government to cancel the Public Security Law. At the same time, the cabinet and the Religious Bloc could not find any grounds for cooperation. Consequently, the National Assembly became virtually deadlocked. In August of 1975, the prime minister submitted the cabinet's resignation to the emir, who dissolved the Assembly but reinstated the government, giving the cabinet "full legislative powers."

Presently, no popularly elected governmental body exists in Bahrain. Each Friday, the emir holds an open public meeting (*majlis*) at which he hears requests from individuals. These requests are referred directly to agencies of the state bureaucracy for appropriate action.

Judiciary

Bahrain's system of autonomous religious courts has gradually been incorporated into a more centralized judiciary closely linked to the government bureaucracy. Sunni courts have a history of subservience to tribal custom and thus to the interests of the rulers. Shi'a courts have resisted integration into a central structure, but

have been forced to accept a secondary role by their need for state subsidies to fund religious schools and other institutions.

The Party System

Political parties, like trade unions, are prohibited by law. What little party system there is in Bahrain only began to emerge during the brief life of the National Assembly.

Three informal blocs appeared in the Assembly in the early part of 1974. The first of these, the People's Bloc, advocated traditional labor demands for unionization, worker participation in economic policy making, and higher wages. Its members came from poorer families of Manama and Muharraq (Bahrain's largest urban centers) and included Ba'th, communist, and PFLOAG sympathizers. The Religious Bloc also supported a wide range of labor reforms but tied these to demands for puritanical restrictions on the licensing of youth clubs, the sale of alcoholic beverages, and various aspects of relations between men and women in public places. Its members came from rural and suburban districts in which the Shi'a community was predominant and they were supported—directly and indirectly—by Bahrain's Shi'a religious authorities. Finally, the Independents advocated a great number of diverse proposals and programs that were largely in line with the maintenance of an unregulated market economy on the islands and the advocates' individual vested interests. These representatives were almost all middle-income merchants, contractors, and employers who had the support of their business associates, families, and social clubs.

Other Political Forces

Radical Organizations

Since mid-1974, when the local section of the Popular Front for the Liberation of Oman and the Arab Gulf (PFLOAG) split with the more active parts of the movement based in Dhofar in southern Oman, there has been little overt political activity by the new Popular Front in Bahrain (PFB). Regionally oriented movements, such as the PFLOAG and the Palestine Liberation Organization, are tolerated by the regime; predominantly local organizations are increasingly harassed and suppressed. When 'Abd ullah Madani, the owner-editor of Manama's conservative *al-Mawaqif,* was found murdered in November 1976, the government accused those responsible of being PFB members. This connection was never proved. It appears that both the PFB and the more radical National Liberation Front–Bahrain have gone completely underground in the wake of the dissolution of the National Assembly and in the face of efforts by governments in the southern Gulf to expand their armed forces and cooperate on matters of internal security.

Student & Youth Groups

Youth and athletic-social clubs continue to provide forums for political discussion and agitation. In March 1977, Bahrain's interior minister announced the closing of two youth clubs he claimed had been "infiltrated" by "some destructive elements." Members of two student organizations, the National Bahraini Club and the Bahraini Students' Union, clashed at Kuwait University in January 1978, apparently as a result of political disagreements. This precipitated a number of arrests of students and other young people within Bahrain the following month.

Religious Groups

Antigovernment agitation by Shi'a mullahs (religious leaders) sympathetic to the regime of the Ayatollah Khomeini in Iran finds fertile ground among the poorer workers. Attempts to arrest or deport these preachers resulted in widespread demonstrations in the fall of 1979. At least one Shi'a secret society, as-Sanduq al-Husaini, was raided and a number of its members were arrested by the police during the summer of 1980. But political demonstrations again broke out in Jidd Hafs—a working-class, Shi'a suburb of Manama—in early December of that same year. Quick action by state security forces appears to have been necessary to prevent the rioting from spreading to Zararia, a poor district of Manama populated by unskilled foreign laborers.

Bahrain's rulers have tried to undercut the social and economic appeal of radical political organizations and the Shi'a mullahs by authorizing the establishment of joint worker-management councils in the country's larger industries. Councils of this sort already existed at Bahrain Petroleum Company, Bahrain Shipways, and Aluminum Bahrain; in mid-1980 they were extended to plants operated by Gulf Air, the Arab Shipbuilding and Refitting Yards, and other larger firms. Whether or not these councils will succeed in reconciling workers to the existing regime and defusing radical political activity within the country remains to be seen.

National Prospects

Inflation continues to increase the cost of living on the islands, and the influx of foreign workers shows no sign of abating. Traditional occupations such as farming, fishing, and shrimping are suffering both from the environmental damage that accompanies heavy industrial projects and from competition from foreign goods.

Tensions created by these economic problems, as well as those arising from class and religious divisions, provide a number of issues around which organized political parties and trade unions with fairly well-defined programs for social change could emerge. But the government's ban on political and labor organizations has throttled peaceful political competition in the country. The ruling elite's refusal to submit its authority to the uncertainties of public debate and compromise no doubt increases the likelihood that political unrest will become more widespread and violent.

Further Reading
Fischer, Michael M. J. "Competing Ideologies and Social Structure in the Persian Gulf." *The Persian Gulf States: A General Survey,* Alvin J. Cottrell, ed. Baltimore: Johns Hopkins University Press, 1980.
Halliday, Fred. *Arabia Without Sultans.* Harmondsworth, England: Penguin, 1974.
Khuri, Fuad I. *Tribe and State in Bahrain.* Chicago: University of Chicago Press, 1980.
Nakhleh, Emile A. *Bahrain.* Lexington, Mass.: D. C. Heath, 1976.

PEOPLE'S REPUBLIC OF BANGLADESH

(*Ganarojatantri Bangladesh*)

by Maleeha Lodhi, Ph.D.

The System of Government

Bangladesh is a unitary state comprised of the former Eastern Province of Pakistan. With a population of nearly ninety million people, it is one of the most densely populated countries in the world. Since independence in 1971, Bangladesh has been subjected to persistent, often violent, political strife which has not enabled governmental selection and policymaking processes or the norms of office to become well established.

Executive

The military's seizure of power on March 24, 1982, led to the suspension of the constitution and the dissolution of Parliament. The new military junta named a civilian, A. M. Choudhury, a retired Supreme Court chief justice, as the country's new president. Real power, however, resides with the army chief of staff, General Hossain Mohammed Ershad, as chief martial-law administrator and the two deputy martial-law administrators appointed by him, who are the chiefs of staff of the navy and air force. A council of advisors functions as a cabinet, comprised predominantly of both retired and serving senior military officers and a few civilian figures.

Until the military takeover, the system of government that had functioned for the longest period was a presidential one. This was established by General Ziaur* Rahman who assumed power in November 1975 after the third of three bloody military coups that began with the killing of Sheikh Mujibur Rahman, the country's founder, in August 1975. Zia* was assassinated in May 1981 in an abortive coup, but the mode of governance devised by him survived until 1982. This was essentially a partnership between the military and the civilian bureaucracy marked by the progressive induction of political personalities agreeable to the regime. Zia gradually moved towards civilian democracy, choosing a strong presidential system as the vehicle for his own transition to civilian political leadership. The rudiments of such a system already existed in actions undertaken by Mujib in 1975. Prior to this the country had functioned under a parliamentary system in accordance with the constitution promulgated on November 4, 1972. In 1975, however, Mujib proclaimed a state of emergency, replaced the parliamentary system with a presidential one, and became president. Parliament (in which his Awami League party held a majority) was dissolved and a one-party state established.

Zia retained the presidential system announced by Mujib, assuming the presidency in April 1977. He then strengthened the presidential office through a series of decrees and amendments to the 1972 constitution—adaptations which created a system often likened to the French presidential system. The fifth constitutional amendment of 1978 provided for an omnipotent president, in whom was vested all executive authority and who was also the constitutional head of state, directly elected for a five-year term by all citizens over the age of eighteen.

Two presidential elections were held under Zia's system. In the first in June 1978, Zia defeated the joint opposition candidate, retired general M. A. G. Osmany, with 76.63 percent of the votes to Osmany's 21.70 percent in a poll with a 53.5 percent turnout. The second election was held in November 1981. Thirty-one candidates competed but the real contest pitted the acting president, Abdus Sattar (former chief justice of the Supreme Court who had been Zia's vice-president since 1977), leader of Zia's Bangladesh Nationalist Party

---

* Bengali usage dictates that certain given names end in "ur" when used with the surname, but not when used alone.

(BNP) and the military's nominee, against Dr. Kamal Hussain, the Awami League candidate. Sattar won with 65.8 percent of the votes against Hussain's 26.35 percent.

Legislature

The fifth amendment also provided for a unicameral legislature (*Jatiya Sangsad*), also elected directly, with normal legislative powers but subservient to the president. Unlike Mujib's intended one-party system, however, this amendment provided for a multiparty polity.

Elections to the 300 seats in Parliament were held in February 1979. Zia's BNP secured more than two-thirds of the seats. The results of the election were as follows:

BANGLADESH PARLIAMENTARY ELECTIONS (1979)		
	Seats	% Votes
Bangladesh Nationalist Party (BNP)	210	41.16
Awami League (Ukil)	39	24.55
Muslim League-Islamic Democratic League Alliance	18	10.08
Jatiya Samajtantrik Dal (JSD)	8	4.84
Awami League (Mizan)	2	2.78
Other parties	7	6.23
Independents	16	10.36
TOTAL	300	100.00

An additional thirty seats reserved for women were filled by a special election by elected members of Parliament. The BNP won all thirty seats.

Judiciary

The Supreme Court headed by the chief justice is the highest judicial body in the country and is comprised of high court and appellate divisions. In addition there are subordinate courts at district, subdivisional, and other levels. The president appoints the chief justice and all other judges, including those in the appellate courts, high courts, and special administrative and military tribunals. Under Zia's system, the subservience of the judiciary to the president was assured by the president's powers to appoint or remove any judge, and his immunity from court proceedings. There is also a clause in the fifth constitutional amendment providing that any advice tendered by the president to his Council of Advisors is beyond the jurisdiction of any court. Following the military takeover of March 1982, several military courts were established, headed by senior army officers. Martial-law regulations have given these courts far-reaching judicial powers, including the imposition of the death penalty for officials found guilty of corruption. Some 300 people, including several former BNP ministers, senior civil servants, industrialists, and politicians were arrested in April 1982 on charges of corruption, misuse of power, or "antistate" activities. They will be tried in the special military courts. A former BNP deputy prime minister, Jamaluddin Ahmed, has already been convicted of corruption by one such court, which sentenced him to pay a heavy fine in default of which he would undergo a year's rigorous imprisonment.

Regional & Local Government

A major innovation in local government was introduced by President Zia in 1980 with the announcement of a *Gram Sarkar* (village government) scheme. This system was grafted on the existing local-government system of directly elected local councils in the rural areas (the Union *Parishads*, totaling 4,353 and each covering a population of approximately 20,000 and thus several villages) and municipal councils in the urban areas (some 108). During 1980 and 1981, *Gram Sarkars* were organized in the country's estimated 68,385 villages. Each *Gram Sarkar* covered a maximum of 5,000 people. In theory each village was to have its own *Sarkar*, but in practice several small villages were sometimes combined to form one *Sarkar*, while bigger villages were divided. These *Gram Sarkars* were selected by a "consensus" evolved at village meetings, with the nature of that consensus being determined by *thana*-level officials representing the central government. (A *thana* is an administrative unit roughly equivalent to a county.) *Gram Sarkars* are distinguished by their unique membership, since two of their twelve members must be from the landless classes, two from among women, two from the landed peasantry, two from shopkeepers, and two from among fishermen or artisans. The eleventh and twelfth members are the chairman (*prodhan*) and secretary, chosen by the other ten members. The *Gram Sarkars* are charged with a number of specific functions—taking care of local problems, controlling population growth, increasing food production and maintaining law and order (by functioning as local courts and by controlling the Village Defense Force, a rural quasivoluntary police force set up by Zia). Many of these functions overlap with those performed by the Union *Parishads*. While there has not yet been a clear delineation of powers between the two institutions, the authority of the *Gram Sarkars* is expected to be greater than the Union *Parishads* in the future. Although opposition parties, notably the Awami League and the JSD, have participated in the *Gram Sarkar* "elections" (and control a number of these village bodies), they have argued that the *Gram Sarkar* scheme is intended not to increase the degree of local self-government, but to provide new centers of influence and patronage for the government much like the Union Councils functioned in Ayub Khan's Basic Democracy scheme in the 1960s (see PAKISTAN, Regional & Local Government). While it is not yet clear whether this will eventually occur, recent developments suggest that the *Gram Sarkars* have not merely become a pliable arm of the government, but have emerged as significant sources of local opinion and pressure.

The Electoral System

The parliamentary elections of 1979 were based on a universal adult (age eighteen) franchise and saw a 51 percent turnout. Legislators were elected in single-member constituencies by simple pluralities. The 1981 presidential elections had a turnout of 55.5 percent of 39 million eligible voters.

Opposition parties repeatedly have questioned the fairness of elections, and charges of ballot rigging have accompanied every election. While independent observers reported several instances of vote fraud in the 1978, 1979, and 1981 elections, it was generally agreed that such electoral irregularities were not so widespread as to have materially affected the result.

The Party System

Origins of the Parties

Political parties in Bangladesh originated during the struggle against British colonial rule which culminated in independence and the establishment of Pakistan in 1947. In the early years following independence, disagreements between the East and West Pakistani sections of the various national parties (notably the independence party,

the Muslim League), particularly over the issue of political autonomy for East Bengal eventually led to the rise of exclusively East Pakistani political organizations, either as breakaway factional groupings or new parties. The east-west breach was accentuated when five Bengali parties that had combined to form the United Front in 1953 defeated the ruling West Pakistani–dominated Muslim League in the 1954 provincial elections in East Pakistan. Thereafter, efforts to organize national parties were largely unsuccessful.

The Parties in Law

Political party activity was banned following the November 1975 coup. In July 1976 the Political Parties Regulation Order was promulgated, requiring political parties desirous of participating in politics to submit their constitutions and programs to the government for its approval. Of over fifty parties which sought permission to operate, twenty-two were officially recognized. This regulation was repealed in November 1978, and the ban imposed in 1977 on three parties (the National Socialist Party, the pro-Moscow Bangladesh Communist Party, and the Democratic League) was lifted. Government approval was no longer required to organize political parties. However, under a decree issued in December 1978, a ban was imposed on all parties organized with foreign financial assistance, affiliated to any foreign organization, propagating views detrimental to the sovereignty and security of the country, or maintaining an underground armed organization. All parties were required to keep their accounts in recognized banks in Bangladesh. After the coup of March 1982, a ban was imposed on political activity, which means that at present political parties cannot undertake any political action.

Party Organization

In general Bangladeshi parties are "hybrid" types combining mass- and cadre-party characteristics. In large part, party adherence reflects traditional patron-client relationships, particularly in the rural countryside (where the majority of the population lives). Kinship groups such as *gushti* ("patrilineage") and *poribar* ("family of procreation"), and their residential distribution in the *bari* (cluster of households with a common courtyard), play a central role in local political alignments. Typically, political parties mobilize support from dominant lineages and much of local political activity centers on recruiting locally powerful men who head economically (ownership of land being an important indicator of this) or demographically dominant lineages that can activate a host of kin-group ties in their political activities. The various Marxist and left-wing parties also use kinship ties to mobilize support, often by capitalizing on tensions between rich and poor *baris* and on intralineage disputes which typically reflect conflicts over land ownership.

Campaigning

Policy or ideological issues play little part in party campaigning except in the urban areas. Of greater importance is the role played by personalities and their manipulation of traditional patron-client structures. Violence has been a common feature in campaigning.

Bangladesh has over fifty parties of varying size and strength, many of which are little more than projections of personalities. The following are the most important.

Awami League (AL)

History

Founded in 1949 by Abdul Hamid Bhashani (who subsequently broke away to form another party) as the Awami Muslim League, the AL headed coalition governments in East Pakistan from 1956 to 1958 and was represented in the central government in 1956 and 1957 and 1958. In elections held in 1970, it won 151 of the 153 East Pakistan seats in the Pakistan National Assembly and 268 of the 278 seats in the East Pakistan Assembly. Subsequently, under Sheikh Mujibur Rahman's leadership, it led the movement for independence and was the ruling party in Bangladesh from 1971 to 1975. After Mujib's overthrow the party was temporarily banned and its leader, Abdul Malek Ukil, was jailed until 1977. In the 1978 presidential election the AL was the leading element in the five-party alliance which unsuccessfully campaigned for Osmany's election. In August 1978 the party split when a small group led by Mizanur Rahman formed its own AL. In February 1981, Mujib's daughter, Hasina Wajed, assumed the party's leadership.

Organization

Because of the personalized nature of the party and from the severity of factional conflict, the organizational structure of the party is weak. Factionalism was to some extent inherent in the "umbrella" nature of the AL: as the party of independence, it was composed of divergent interests. Factionalism can also be attributed to what is often characterized as the Bengali propensity for political schism, illustrated in the popular saying, "Where you have two Bengalis, you have four political parties." During its years in power Mujib was able to keep the warring factions together by judicious balancing and using patronage to cement the party. But with Mujib's demise and the party's loss of power, factional conflict erupted and led to the 1978 split. Currently the party is divided into two major factions led by Abdur Razzak and Tofael Ahmed, reflecting a mixture of policy and personal differences.

Factionalism has also been rampant in the various fronts organized by the party among students (Bangladesh Students League), labor (Jatio Sramik League), peasants (Jatio Krishak League) and youth (Awami Jubo League).

National headquarters are at 660/B, Road No. 32, Dhanmandi R/A, Dacca.

Policy

An advocate of moderate socialism, AL in practice has been highly pragmatic. The party's major campaign issue in both the 1979 and 1981 elections was a demand for the restoration of parliamentary democracy. Its foreign policy is staunchly pro-India and pro-Moscow.

Membership & Constituency

Initially emerging as a middle-class body representing urban professionals (lawyers, businessmen, teachers, doctors) and students, its support base expanded during the independence movement to incorporate a wide variety of interests. Popular support for the party (strongest in 1971) diminished rapidly in the face of its poor record in office and the growth of corruption in its ranks. While the elections of 1979 and 1981 demonstrated the reemergence of considerable support for the AL, its defeat indicated that the vast majority of people still recall its record in office uneasily. As a party advocating secularism, it appeals strongly to the Hindu minority (approximately 10 percent of the population).

No membership figures are available.

Financing

No information is available on party financing.

Leadership

Party leadership is dominated by persons in their late thirties or early forties. Present leaders are:

Hasina Wajed (born 1947), president; no specific power base.

Abdur Razzak (Naokhali, birthdate not available), secretary general; power base in Faridpur.

Tofael Ahmed (born 1947), organizing secretary; power base in Barisal.

Kamal Hossain (born 1937), presidential candidate in 1981; no specific power base.

Prospects

The party has failed to establish an issue to capture the imagination of the masses, particularly in the countryside (where 89 percent of the population lives). This failure, coupled with renewed factionalism and the political inexperience of its current leader, indicates that the party's potential for growth is limited.

Bangladesh Nationalist Party (BNP; *Bangladesh Jatiyabadi Dal*)

History

The BNP was formed in September 1978 by Zia from sections of the six parties that had supported his candidacy in the 1978 presidential elections: the National Democratic Party (launched in February 1978 under Sattar's leadership with Zia's blessing), the pro-Peking National Awami Party (NAP), the United People's Party, the Muslim League, and an organization representing Hindu scheduled castes ("untouchables"). After Zia's death, power struggles in the BNP, particularly over the selection of its presidential candidate in 1981, seriously threatened its unity. A split was averted by the timely intervention of the army chief, General Ershad, who persuaded Acting President Sattar to stand for election as a compromise candidate. Despite his election victory, Sattar was unable to control intraparty factionalism, thus provoking the military to depose him.

Organization

The BNP is a hastily assembled, loosely structured party comprising three distinct strands: (1) Zia's own factional followers who formerly belonged to the military and bureaucracy; (2) the bulk of the leadership and party cadres of the Muslim League and Islamic fundamentalist parties, which had previously been banned by Mujib for alleged collaboration with Pakistan; and (3) Bhashani's faction of NAP. Bhashani had advocated an eclectic melding of Marxism and Islam; after his death in 1975, his successor, Mashiur Rahman, brought the bulk of Bhashani's followers into the BNP. Fissures in the BNP were thus inherent in its heterogeneous composition and focused on divisions such as retired military/civilian bureaucrats versus politicians; socialists versus nonsocialists; Islamists versus secularists freedom fighters (*Mukti Bahini*) versus "collaborators." It was Zia's personality and official patronage that held this uneasy coalition together.

The party has a student wing (*Jatiyotabadi Chhatra Dal*) which attracted several dissidents from the AL student front. However, this body, too, has been subject to intense factionalism.

BNP's national headquarters are at 19-A, Road No. 16, Dhanmandi, Dacca.

Policy

Vague exhortations to nationalist commitment have constituted the party's principal platform. While Zia attempted a delicate policy balancing act in response to the dual elements of Bangladeshi nationalist identity—Islam and Bengali ethnicity—he increasingly stressed the former, rejecting secularism. The BNP's foreign policy generally has been less favorable to Delhi and Moscow with a pro-Peking and pro-Islamic slant.

Membership & Constituency

The BNP draws support from a broad cross section of society, but its primary constituencies are Muslim conservative elements and the military and bureaucratic factions loyal to Zia. Although the party won a two-thirds majority in Parliament in the 1979 elections, it did so with only 41.16 percent of the votes. In the 1981 presidential poll the BNP (with a 67 percent vote) was unable to retain the strong popular support accorded to Zia (76 percent) in 1978. This can partly be attributed to the growth of corruption in the BNP ranks which had begun to tarnish its reputation even under Zia.

Financing

No information is available on party financing.

Leadership

With the exception of Sattar, BNP leaders are in their late forties or early fifties. Current leaders are:

Abdur Sattar (born Calcutta, 1906). Leader, no specific power base.

Shah Azizur Rahman (born Kushtia, 1925), former prime minister; power base in Kushtia.

Badrudoza Choudhury (born Dacca, 1932), secretary general; no specific power base.

Moudud Ahmed (born Noakhali, 1940), former deputy prime minister; power base in Dacca.

Prospects

Given Sattar's failing health and with no leader of Zia's stature to hold the party together, the BNP is liable to disintegrate. Its loss of power is likely to hasten this process.

National Socialist Party
(*Jatiya Samajtantrik Dal;* JSD)

History

Soon after independence, leading dissidents from the AL student and labor branches (including Abdur Rab and Serajul Alam) established an underground party, the Bangladesh Communist League (BCL) under Seraj's leadership. When the BCL established its own parallel organizations, splits developed in the AL's student, labor, and peasant branches, and its affiliated Association of Freedom Fighters. The JSD was formed in October 1972 as a mass political front of these organizations; it was led by a former army major, M. A. Jalil, a guerrilla leader in the liberation struggle. In 1974 the JSD recruited Colonel Abu Taher, another former guerrilla commander, under whose leadership it organized a secret armed wing, the Revolutionary People's Army (*Biblopi Gono Bahini*) in the army. Taher was the principal figure behind the November 7, 1975, "Sepoy mutiny" which brought Zia to power. Zia, however, turned on his leftist benefactors, jailing Taher and other JSD leaders and subsequently executing Taher. In October 1971 the JSD's armed wing reportedly was disbanded. In October 1977 the JSD was banned, but in November 1978 this ban was lifted and several JSD members were released from prison. In November 1980, the party split with a smaller group, the Bangladesh Samajtantrik Dal (BSD), which claimed that the JSD leadership had pursued an opportunistic line to secure their release from prison.

Organization

Although the JSD does not have a nationally comprehensive structure, it is the best organized of all leftist parties in terms of the breadth of its national coverage and the degree of real organizational structure. Information about the affiliated BCL is sparse, but it reportedly has a tightly controlled organization with party cells in the various districts of its operation. It publishes a Bengali daily, *Gonokantha* (Voice of the People) which periodically has been banned. The JSD is governed by a Central Committee and has student, labor, peasant, and freedom-fighter associations affiliated to it.

JSD headquarters are at 23 D.I.T. Road, Malibagh, Dacca.

Policy

The JSD is a Marxist party which aims at establishing socialism. While it has engaged in armed struggle in the past, it seeks to work within existing institutions. In light of changing circumstances, however, this position is likely to be modified, as it was in 1975 with the Taher coup. While anti-Indian, anti-Soviet, and pro-Peking, it has resisted following any international communist line.

Membership & Constituency

The major constituency of JSD is youth, particularly students; it also enjoys the support of sections of urban labor, peasants, and radicalized *Mukti Bahini* (former freedom fighters) elements in the military. No membership figures are available.

In the 1979 elections, its electoral strength, while not substantial, was sufficient to make it the second-largest opposition party in Parliament. In 1981, its presidential candidate, M. A. Jalil, polled only 1.14 percent of the vote.

Financing

No information is available on the party's sources of income.

Leadership

Leadership is predominantly in the late thirties; Jalil is regarded as the oldest of the JSD leaders. Current leaders are:

M. A. Jalil (born 1936), president since the party's inception, appeals strongly to former freedom fighters.

A. S. M. Abdur Rab, general secretary since the party's inception, power base in Dacca.

Shahjahan Sirah (born 1943), member of parliament, power base in Tangail.

Prospects

The JSD is widely regarded as the party of the future. Some view it as a potential Bangladesh counterpart of the Khalq or Parcham factions of the Afghani Communist Party, a view difficult to substantiate given the lack of information on the party's proselytizing campaign in the army in the post-Taher period. However, JSD's continued appeal to radical sections of the army indicates its potential if electoral politics remain suspended.

Minor Parties

The Muslim League

The Muslim League was constituted out of the various factions of the Pakistan Muslim League, which was the ruling party in East Pakistan in 1947 to 1954. It was banned under Mujib's regime for its alleged support of Pakistan during the Bangladeshi war of independence, but it returned to legality in 1977. It was formally a part of the coalition that supported Zia in the 1978 elections, but the party itself was divided over the issue of supporting Zia and factionalized soon after. One section led by Shah Azizur Rahman (who subsequently became Zia's prime minister) went into the BNP. The other and probably larger faction led by Khan Abdus Sobur (until his death in early 1982) retained its identity. The Muslim League is a right-wing party favoring Islamization of the country.

The Islamic Democratic League

The Islamic Democratic League (IDL) is comprised of members of Islamic fundamentalist organizations, notably the *Nizam-e-Islam* and the *Jamaat-e-Islami*, which were also banned by Mujib for alleged collaboration with Pakistan, but were allowed to operate again in 1977. The organizational backbone of the IDL is the *Jamaat-e-Islami*, a well-knit, tightly organized party with highly disciplined cadres, modeled on the lines of the Muslim Brotherhood (prominent in many Arab countries, particularly Egypt, where it was founded). The IDL is vehemently opposed to westernization and secularization, and advocates the establishment of an Islamic state. (For further details on *Jamaat-e-Islami*, see PAKISTAN, The Islamic Assembly.)

Other Political Forces

Military

Having acquired its sovereign status through a civil war, Bangladesh began its independent existence with a highly politicized military. The army was comprised of Pakistani military personnel who had defected to the freedom movement in 1971 and of selected recruits from irregular volunteer troops, which together formed the *Mukti Bahini* or freedom fighters, as well as approxmiately 28,000 soldiers (including 1,100 officers) who were stranded in West Pakistan in 1971 and repatriated in 1973.

Immediately after independence the military was subordinated to civilian authority as Mujib stood forth as undisputed leader of the new nation. However, the military became increasingly restive as it witnessed the country's rapid slide into economic and political disorder. It was particularly resentful of Mujib's creation of a well-equipped paramilitary force (the *Rakhi Bahini*) personally loyal to him. Adding to the military's displeasure was what they saw as Mujib's efforts to turn Bangladesh into a satellite of India. Grievances in the military were accentuated when the repatriated personnel returned to find that important posts have been given to junior colleagues or irregulars claiming special favor as freedom fighters or through close relationship to the ruling party. Despite mounting tension between him and the military in 1974, Mujib employed the army and navy to fight smuggling and corruption. However, the army was abruptly ordered back into the barracks when its investigations threatened to implicate Mujib's close political associates.

Against this background, the coup of August 1975 came as little surprise. There then followed the coup–countercoup sequence of November 1975 in which the regime established in August was overturned by Brigadier Khalid Musharaf, reportedly loyal to Mujib. The widespread feeling that Musharaf's coup was Indian-inspired provoked the uprising of junior officers and sepoys in which Musharaf and his associates were killed and which eventually brought General Zia to power. That the prime mover of the third coup was Colonel Taher acting on behalf of the Marxist JSD indicated the emergence of a powerful radical force within the army. Viewing this unprecedented development as a dangerous portent for the future, Zia jailed Taher and JSD leaders and subsequently purged the army of their supporters. He later ordered Taher's execution.

Zia undertook a major reorganization of the military to restore discipline and consolidate his power. Although a *Mukti Bahini* officer himself, Zia brought repatriated officers into important positions to balance the more politicized liberation elements. Nevertheless, serious divisions persisted in the military and exploded repeatedly in several coup attempts and lesser mutinies. In May 1981 Zia was killed in a mutiny which was eventually crushed (and the coup leader killed) by army chief of staff, General Ershad, who took over the government himself in March 1982.

Although there are no significant ethnic, religious, or regional differences in the military, the estimated 63,000-man force is not a homogeneous entity. Divisions in the military are based on a number of cleavages. Although currently almost the entire senior hierarchy is composed of officers who did not participate in the liberation struggle, the schism between freedom fighters and non-freedom fighters remains significant. The rivalry between these groups was a major factor in Zia's assassination. Another source of cleavage is that between pro-Islamic soldiers and those who advocate secularism. Then there are ideological polarizations along left-right lines and pro-Indian and anti-Indian divisions. Added to these are divisions reflecting personal rivalries. Finally, the tumultuous events of 1975 and the subsequent rounds of trials and executions superimposed additional divisions on the multitude of existing ones. Thus factionalism in the military has been endemic, seriously affecting its professionalism, morale, and discipline.

Bureaucracy

The Bangladesh civil service was organized from Bengali personnel belonging to the former East Pakistan provincial administration and from those in the central administration (the "elite" cadre known as the Civil Service of Pakistan or CSP) who were repatriated from Pakistan in 1973. During Mujib's rule, the professional bureaucracy lost many of its former privileges. It no longer played the dominant role in public policy-making that it had done under British colonial and

Pakistani rule. Senior bureaucrats who returned to Bangladesh in 1973 were not given important administrative posts; many were removed or downgraded for alleged collaboration with Pakistan. Mujib abolished the CSP and selected, largely on a political basis, more than 500 top administrators with little or no experience. They were part of a special "freedom fighters" pool, a concession that made it possible for them to enter the bureaucracy without training and with only perfunctory examinations. These policies bred resentment among career bureaucrats; few of them lamented Mujib's fall.

Zia initially relied heavily on members of the old CSP and other bureaucrats shunted aside by Mujib, and on professionals and technocrats whom Mujib had similarly alienated. Initially, Zia was popular with senior bureaucrats as he purged the administration of many Mujib appointees; reimposed rigorous examinations and training requirements; and by rationalizing promotion and retirement policies, restored some semblance of order in the ranks. Above all he restored the senior bureaucracy's policymaking role, albeit in subordination to the military. In 1979 Zia pushed through a major reform, creating a fourteen-cadre administrative arrangement, a Bangladesh Civil Service, and a Senior Policy Pool, comprising 625 top administrative posts. A special feature of this system was that it allowed civil servants from all cadres to reach, through talent and efficiency, positions in the Senior Service Pool. Former officers of the CSP and the Provincial Service were unhappy with these changes as they threatened their recently restored privileged position. Bureaucrats also were resentful of the growing introduction of army personnel into the administration. Moreover, as Zia moved increasingly towards involving politicians in the governmental process, bureaucrats feared that their policymaking role would again be diminished. The return of Bangladesh to direct military rule in 1982 portends a revival of that partnership between the civil and military bureaucracy that marked the first half of Zia's rule.

Factionalism in the bureaucracy has been pervasive, seriously undermining its coherence and efficiency. Tension and rivalry between officials who had defected to the liberation movement ("patriots") and those who had stayed in their posts ("collaborators") or were repatriated from Pakistan remains a continuing source of disunity. The former division of the administration into federal and provincial services provides another source of cleavage. Since the civil service has long functioned as a political group it also mirrors many of the political cleavages in the country.

National Prospects

The present military regime reportedly favors
institutionalizing the military's role in government
by amending the constitution (suspended at
present) or devising a new one. Whatever system
is eventually adopted and whether or not politicians and political parties are allowed a role in it,
the military is likely to exercise effective power in
Bangladesh for some time to come. However, reconciling the divided military is going to be a formidable task; if this proves as elusive as it has in the
past, there is a high probability of violent upheavals to come. Given the conservative cast of the
present ruling junta, the reemergence of a radical
force in the army cannot be ruled out.

Further Reading

Franda, Marcus. "Bangladesh Nationalism and
Ziaur Rahman's Presidency." *American Uni-
versity Field Staff Reports*, South Asia Series,
No. 7, 1981.
Jahan, Rounaq. *Bangladesh Politics: Problems
and Issues*. Dacca: University Press Ltd., 1980.
Lifschultz, Lawrence. *Bangladesh: The Unfin-
ished Revolution*. London: Zed Press, 1979.
Talukder, Maniruzzaman. *Radical Politics and the
Emergence of Bangladesh*. Dacca: Bangladesh
Books, 1975.

BARBADOS

by Indira Jhappan

The System of Government

Barbados, east of the Windward Islands at the outer edge of the Caribbean Sea, is a parliamentary democracy which gained its independence from Great Britain in 1966. The population of Barbados, which now stands at about 250,000, is predominantly of mixed origin and, in comparison with the rest of the Caribbean, has a high percentage of whites. The island's elite group is composed mainly of professionals, businessmen, and technocrats, and there is a significant middle class. The island is heavily dependent on tourism as an earner of foreign exchange and generator of employment.

Executive

The formal head of state is the British monarch represented by a governor-general. The latter appoints as prime minister the leader of the party with the most seats in the National Assembly. In practice, the prime minister exercises the executive power in the system.

Legislature

The bicameral legislature consists of the Senate and the House of Assembly. The Senate has twenty-one members appointed by the governor-general—twelve on the advice of the prime minister; two on the advice of the leader of the opposition; and seven on the advice of religious, economic, cultural and community organizations.

The House of Assembly consists of twenty-four members elected to five-year terms in direct elections. Parliament has the power to make and to change laws and can alter the constitution with a two-thirds majority. Bills can be introduced in both houses, with the exception of money bills, which can only be introduced in the House and only with the approval of the cabinet. Bills can be sent to the governor-general for his assent without passing the Senate if they pass the House in two consecutive sessions and are rejected twice by the Senate. The exception to this rule are money bills, which can be sent for approval at the discretion of the House. Votes of no confidence result in the dissolution of Parliament and new elections.

Judiciary

The Barbadian judicial system is based on English common law. The law is administered by a system of courts of summary jurisdiction and the Supreme Court of the Judicature. The latter consists of the High Court and the Court of Appeal. The chief justice is appointed by the prime minister in consultation with the leader of the opposition and is chairman of the Judicial and Legal Service Commission, which makes appointments in the system. The Court of Appeal is the highest court in the land; further appeals may be sent to the Privy Council of the British monarch.

Regional & Local Government

Barbados is divided into eleven parishes and one municipality, Bridgetown, the capital; all local-government units are under the control of the central government. This system replaced the pre-1966 system of elected local governments.

The Electoral System

Barbadians eighteen years of age and over are eligible to vote. Parliamentary candidates are elected by simple plurality in single-member districts. In elections held between 1951 and 1976, electoral turnout averaged about 70 percent.

The Party System

Although the party system began with several parties and still permits easy entry for new parties, the trend since 1951 has been towards consolidation in a two-party system. Between 1951 and 1966, votes and Assembly seats were divided among the Barbados Labour Party (BLP), the Democratic Labour Party (DLP), and a variety of conservatives. The share of votes won by the BLP and the DLP began to increase after 1956 in proportion to a decline in the number of independent candidates. In 1956, there were eleven independents; after 1966 there were none. Although there have been party shifts among the politicians, the general trend is towards stable affiliations; it was common in the past for candidates to change party allegiance often.

The Barbadian electorate is highly literate and politically conscious and campaigns are hard fought by well-organized constituency groups. Although democratic organization is strong within the parties, charismatic leadership continues to play a major role in setting party policy.

Barbados Labour Party (BLP)

The BLP traces its origins to the Barbados Progressive League which was formed in 1938. The League founded the Barbados Workers' Union in 1941 and the BLP in 1946. Sir Grantley Adams, founder of the League and head of the Union, became the leader of the new party. The BLP first entered the government in 1951 and remained there until 1961, when it lost to the DLP. In 1954, when Adams assumed the leadership of the fledgling new government, he was the first prime minister in the British West Indies. From 1958 to 1962, he also served as prime minister of the short-lived West Indies Federation.

The party returned to power in 1976 with seventeen of the House of Assembly seats and retained the same number of seats in the 1981 elections. Under the leadership of Grantley Adams's son, John Michael Geoffrey "Tom" Adams (born 1931), since 1971, the party has pursued a conservative domestic and foreign policy, supporting free enterprise and encouraging foreign investment. Although moderately socialist, it has generally opposed leftist activities in the region and has been sharply critical of the leftist government in Grenada.

The BLP has a strong organizational base in party branches in each of the constituencies. The party is managed by a national executive committee of about thirty-six members elected at an annual conference of delegates. Membership in 1982 was estimated at about 10,000. Prospects are excellent that the party will complete its five-year term which expires in 1986. Whether it will then be reelected will depend largely on whether the island continues to prosper.

Democratic Labour Party (DLP)

The DLP was founded in 1955 under the chairmanship of F. G. Smith and consisted primarily of dissidents from the BLP. The party, which was closely allied with the island's major trade union, came to power in 1961 under the leadership of Errol Barrow. It remained in power until 1976, when it was defeated by the BLP and became the opposition party with seven seats in the House. In that year also, Barrow resigned as leader of the party, then returned briefly only to leave again. The party is currently led by Branford Mayhew Taitt. The party has a strong organizational base in a network of party branches in the constituencies. Administrative functions are performed by an executive council elected at annual conventions. Party membership is estimated at about 9,000. Once to the right of the BLP, the DLP adopted a more progressive stance in the 1970s. The DLP will remain a strong opposition force with some chance of returning to government in 1986.

People's Political Alliance (PPA)

The new, moderately leftist PPA ran eight candidates in the 1981 elections. Its failure to elect any probably means that it will not reappear in 1986.

National Prospects

Traditionally an island of stability in the Caribbean, there is every sign that Barbados will continue to remain so. The country is dependent on tourism and, with the world recession, this dependence could prove to be a problem. However, the government's encouragement of foreign investment should ameliorate many of the economic problems which afflict the rest of the Caribbean.

Further Reading
Barriteau, Eudine. "The 1981 General Elections in Barbados—Some Comments." *Bulletin of Eastern Caribbean Affairs*, Vol. 7, No. 2, May–June, 1981.
Gooding, Earl. *The West Indies at the Crossroads: The Search for a Viable Future.* Cambridge, Mass.: Schenkman, 1981.
Will, W. Marvin. "Mass Political Party Institutionalization in Barbados." *Journal of Commonwealth and Comparative Politics*, Vol. 19, No. 2, July 1981.

KINGDOM OF BELGIUM
(*Koninkrijk België; Royaume de Belgique*)
by Gordon Smith, Ph.D.

The System of Government

Belgium is a constitutional monarchy with a parliamentary system of government. Originally a part of the Netherlands, the southern provinces of the state seceded, after a revolution in 1830, and formed the state of Belgium, which also incorporated a part of Luxembourg. The constitution of Belgium, adopted in 1831, was characterized by its liberal and relatively democratic system of government in reaction to the strong executive authority that had been a feature of the Netherlands monarchy.

The constitution prescribed a unitary state, and a degree of national unity was found in the dominant Roman Catholic Church. However, there was a sharp linguistic cleavage in the new state between the French-speaking population of Wallonia and the Flemish, Dutch speakers, in Flanders in the north. The "language frontier" (at present, 55 percent Flemish and most of the remainder French-speaking in a population of almost ten million) was masked by the predominance of French-speaking elites in all walks of life—industry, culture, and government—and was buttressed by the fact that Wallonia was the center of industry. The supremacy of French also applied to the capital, Brussels, which although within Flanders became a predominantly French-speaking enclave. It was not until the 1960s that the linguistic issue became the all-important question for the political system and threatened to fragment the political and constitutional structure. As a consequence, the Belgium constitution has recently undergone large-scale revision to grant greater economic and cultural powers to the linguistic communities.

Executive

The 1831 constitution established a limited constitutional monarchy, so that from the outset the king could only govern through his prime minister and cabinet ministers who were recruited from and responsible to Parliament. The principle was also instituted that the government should have the support of both houses of the bicameral legislature.

Governments have a maximum life of four years, corresponding to the four-year term of the lower house, the Chamber of Representatives. Between the two world wars and until the 1960s, a stable three-party system (Social Christians, Liberals, and Socialists) produced an equally stable pattern of government. But with the fragmentation of the party system in the 1960s, short-lived governments have now become the rule, with governments collapsing through the break up of coalitions, not because of adverse votes in Parliament. In this situation, the King of Belgium is a unifying symbol, but his active political function is limited to encouraging the formation of broad coalitions.

Legislature

The lower house, the Chamber of Representatives, consists of 212 members elected by proportional representation. The upper house, the Senate, is made up of 181 members (106 directly elected, fifty elected by provincial councils, and a further twenty-five coopted members). Most legislation is government-sponsored, submitted first to the Council of State (an administrative body) for scrutiny and then introduced into Parliament. Amendments to bills are made in committee, and the final form must be agreed by both houses. The procedure for constitutional change requires that once an affirmative vote has been taken an automatic dissolution of the Chamber of Representatives follows, and the newly elected Parliament must pass the amendment by a two-thirds majority in both houses.

Elections to the Chamber of Representatives					
	1974 %	1977 %	1978 %	1981 %	Seats
Christian Peoples	23.3	26.2	26.1	19.3	43
Christian Social	9.1	9.8	10.1	7.1	18
Socialist (French)	14.2	13.4	13.0	12.7	35
Socialist (Flemish)	12.6	13.0	12.4	12.4	26
Freedom and Progress	10.0	8.5	10.4	12.9	28
PRL Liberal Reform	5.1	7.0	6.0	8.6	24
Volksunie	10.1	10.0	7.0	9.8	20
RW* FDF*	11.0	7.2	7.1	4.2	8
Others**	4.7	4.9	7.9	13.0	10

* The chief Francophone party in Wallonia is the *Rassemblement Walton* (RW). In Brussels, its equivalent is the *Front Démocratique des Francophones* (FDF). They are not in a competitive position, so their percentage vote is aggregated.
** This category includes a variety of parties, only one of which is primarily a community party: the extreme *Vlaamsche Blok,* which is more radical than the Flemish *Volksunie.* It won 1.1 percent in 1981. The other parties are the Communist Party (2.3 percent in 1981); the Ecologists (4.8 percent in 1981) and the economically conservative "protest" party, outbidding the Liberals, *Union Démocratique pour le Respect du Travail/Respekt voor Arbeid en Demokratie* (2.7 percent in 1981).

Judiciary

The highest ordinary court in Belgium is the Court of Cassation. Judges are appointed for life by the cabinet from nominations submitted by the Senate and by the Court itself. The Court has no power of judicial review with respect to legislation. It can examine administrative decrees to see that they are in conformity with the law, but this function is largely exercised by the Council of State (established in 1946) which has general oversight of all administrative bodies. In the Belgian tradition, the absence of judicial review regarding parliamentary legislation is not regarded as a deficiency, because all important legislation requires considerable interparty agreement in the legislature and cabinet, and all proposed legislation is subject to an extensive process of consultation with affected interests.

Regional & Local Government

Until the 1970s, the Belgian constitution had been remarkably free from basic amendment, and the unitary state form had not been seriously under attack, despite the coexistence of two main linguistic communities in clearly defined geo-graphical areas. However, the Flemish had been discontented with French-speaking dominance for a long time. As Flanders made rapid economic progress after 1945, the demand for parity and autonomy became more insistent, and the ethnic conflict began to determine the political agenda. The 1960s saw the rise of the specifically linguistic parties and linguistic dissension within the traditional parties. It appeared that only a fundamental restructuring of the Belgian state could satisfy the various claims.

The amendments to the constitution, which gave a large measure of decentralization but did not create a federal state, were originally passed in the 1967–71 period, but these changes only specified general principles; their detailed application required legislation, itself also subject to the two-thirds majority stipulation. That legislation, a complex package, was largely completed in 1980 when definitive regionalization laws were approved; certain issues—especially those relating to the position of Brussels—were unresolved.

The constitutional revision divided Belgium into four linguistic regions: the French, Dutch, bilingual Brussels, and the small German-speaking area. Further, three cultural communities were recognized: Francophone, Flemish, and German. As far as the linguistic regions were concerned, provisions were made to set up elected regional councils for Wallonia, Flanders, and Brussels. These councils are to have primarily economic responsibility for their respective regions. The regional councils for Wallonia and Flanders have now been established, but Brussels remains a stumbling block, with Francophones holding out for full regional status while the Flemish parties are unwilling to see this happen.

In addition to the regional councils, each of the three cultural communities is respresented by a cultural council with responsibility for education, cultural affairs, and social-welfare provisions. Each of the two major language communities also includes the community's members in the Brussels area. Some simplification has been achieved in the case of Flanders, where the regional council has effectively been merged with the Flemish cultural council. Finally, with regard to national legislation, there is now a special procedure in Parliament whereby laws dealing with community matters require the positive support of a majority of representatives from both major language communities, and either one can apply a suspensory veto to delay consideration if community interests are felt to be threatened.

Local government proper—that is, excluding the new bodies set up as a result of the constitutional changes—consists of two tiers, both established by the terms of the 1831 constitution. The upper tier consists of nine provinces, each with a provincial assembly from which an executive council is elected to work alongside a governor appointed by the central government. The powers of the provinces are limited, and the recent creation of regional and cultural bodies may well make them redundant in the long term.

More important are the communes which rest on very old traditions and serve as a source of recruitment for national politics as well as expressing local interests. Before a reorganization of local government in 1971, there were over 2,500 communes, but since then there has been some rationalization, in particular by the creation of intercommunal "urban areas" and "federations." Each commune has an elected council from which a board of aldermen is chosen, headed by a burgomaster who, though centrally appointed and paid, is in practice a nominee of the commune. The communes have extensive powers, but their activities are subject to a veto imposed by the provincial governor, with the Council of State having the final say. At a local level, one or other of the national parties will usually be dominant, but the communal councils are elected by proportional representation so that one-party government does not result.

The Electoral System

Elections to the Chamber of Representatives take place at least every four years. The number of members and their distribution among the provinces is adjusted periodically according to the results of a decennial census. The voting age was lowered from twenty-one to eighteen in 1981. Universal male suffrage was introduced after World War I, with women obtaining the vote only in 1949. Voting is compulsory, which brings a high turnout of some 95 percent, but there is also a high proportion of spoiled ballots, often amounting to over 5 percent of total votes cast.

The Chamber of Representatives has been elected by proportional representation since 1900. Voters may vote either for the whole party list or select a preferred candidate from the list, but it is not possible to split votes between parties. Party lists are presented at the district (*arrondissement*) level. Provinces have from two to five *arrondissements*. Seats are first distributed according to the size of the party votes within the *arrondissement*, and any remainders are carried over for a further distribution within the province.

Proportionality is thus secured on a provincial basis, but not necessarily for the country as a whole. The effect of the electoral system is a slight bias in favor of the larger parties, but smaller ones are not unduly penalized. The small linguistic parties, which tend to have regional concentrations of support, have not had their growth impeded by the system.

The Party System

Origins of the Parties

In the early period there were no well-defined parties, but rather loose associations of Liberals and Catholics who formed informal coalitions, so-called "union" cabinets which met the king's desire for political unity. With the dispute over the papal ban on Freemasonry in 1846, the Liberals became an anticlerical party, and majoritarian government became the rule. The establishment of the Socialists in 1885 as a second secular party and the extension of the franchise in 1894 sharply cut the proportion of support the Liberals had enjoyed. Unwilling to be left alone with the Socialists, the dominant Social Christians introduced proportional representation in 1900, and this led to a stable three-party system. After women gained the vote in 1949, the Social Christians gained a decisive edge on the Socialists.

The shape of the party system changed radically in the 1960s with the emergence of the language issue. "Community" parties, based on the demands of the French- and Flemish-speaking activist groups, were successful in winning up to 20 percent of the vote by 1971, consolidating their position subsequently at a lower level (14 percent in 1981). The impact of the conflict was just as profound in its effect on the traditional parties: with the exception of the small Communist Party, they were all soon forced to split into separate linguistic parties. Thus the Social Christians, Socialists, and Liberals each now constitute two distinct parties. As a result, Belgian politics is characterised by an advanced multipartism; no fewer than thirteen parties had seats in the Chamber of Representatives following the 1981 election.

The Parties in Law

Apart from the operation of the electoral laws, the Belgian parties are relatively free from legal regulation, with no restrictions on the nature of parties that can compete. In the 1977 election, for example, one small independent party presented its list under the title "Snow White and the Seven Dwarfs." The freedom of party activity tends to be limited by the language issue, since it is important that a party not appear to discriminate against any linguistic demands. The amended constitution also effectively gives linguistic parties an entrenched status.

Parties actually represented in either house benefit from an annual, direct state subsidy at the rate of 280,000 Belgian francs ($7,775) per deputy and 480,000 francs ($13,330) for every senator. Perhaps more important is the fact that the state provides a large number of jobs which the parties can distribute to their loyal adherents. All the linguistic councils at the various levels, the regular civil service, and other institutions such as the state schools are part of this patronage system. Moreover, since the bulk of social security schemes are administered by party-affiliated organizations, the parties have a highly privileged position at both local and national levels.

Party Organization

The structure of Belgian parties has been largely determined by the strong "associational" features of the society. Party membership is important and there is a fairly high ratio of members to voters, with an average member/voter ratio for the traditional parties of around twelve per 100. At the same time, the links the parties maintain with organized interest groups are of considerable importance. Of particular interest in this respect is organized labor, which has three unions—Christian, socialist, and liberal—each linked to the respective party. The Social Christians benefit most from "association" since there are numerous ties with Catholic organizations; the Flemish *Boerenbond* (Farmers' League) is a particularly important source of Social Christian support. The organizational strength of the parties also depends on their linguistic homogeneity, although this development came at the cost of the break up of the traditional parties.

The larger parties have similar national structures: a supreme congress of delegates from the districts which meets yearly and a small executive national committee or bureau which manages party affairs. Between the congress and the national committee is a general council, consisting of members of both bodies, which has a general watchdog function. There is a marked "separation of powers" between the national party organization and the parliamentary bloc, with the result that both have a degree of independence. The party's president will not be a government office-holder (elected or appointed), but nevertheless ranks in status somewhat above a cabinet minister. The party leader's status is based largely on his role as chief negotiator in intraparty disputes over linguistic issues. Once such a dispute is resolved, the party's ministers in government have little or no freedom of action. Failure to resolve such disputes has regularly caused the collapse of governing coalitions. The linguistic splits in the older parties mean that the two parts (Flemish and Wallonian) retain only tenuous links with one another and cooperate only on policy questions not related to the linguistic issue. Selection of candidates is made locally, with the central organization having veto power. Something like party primaries has been used for candidate selection, but that practice has declined in recent years.

The smaller community parties do not have the powerful organizational base of the larger ones. largely because all the major organized economic and cultural interests are preempted by the major parties. The smaller parties do benefit from strong local concentrations of support.

Campaigning

Elections to the Chamber of Representatives take place every four years, at least. In fact, they have become much more frequent in the recent past: the 1981 election was the third in a period of five years, and it was the sixth in succession that had been called before time. The Belgian electorate is "election weary," despite the apparent intensity and intractability of the linguistic issue. Indications from survey data suggest that most Belgians place its resolution lower down on the list of priorities than, say, the economic situation of the country. Nonetheless, it is very difficult for the average voter to ignore the linguistic appeal, and the ramifications spill over to the economic sector because of the varying economic fortunes of the two major regions.

Much of the campaign momentum is preserved by party activists and elites rather than the mass of the electorate. Voters are well aware that a forthcoming election will not have a decisive outcome, and campaigning centers on mobilizing existing support to increase a party's representation and thus to enhance its bargaining power. It is not particularly difficult for a party to enter government if it so wishes, because gaining broad interparty support with an "excess majority" is a feature of coalitions.

Campaigns are media-dominated, each region in its own language. The powerful press in the regions is largely formally independent of the parties, but committed to definite political directions. The role of personalities is important, because of the "personalized" vote. Although voting is compulsory, interest is high and voters are made to feel they should not "let down" their particular language community.

Independent Voters

Traditionally, party identification has been strong in Belgium and cuts across the linguistic boundaries. Thus the Social Christians could rely on the Catholic vote throughout the nation, particularly in rural Flanders. The stability of party identification was weakened in the 1960s: thus while the three major parties took 95 percent of the vote between them in 1958, this fell to about 75 percent in 1971, and still further in 1981.

To some extent the initial growth of support for the new community parties was in the nature of a protest vote which was weakened as the major parties themselves divided into their linguistic wings. It is difficult to say how far the new parties have been able to build up a stable identification with parts of the electorate. Their radicalism is an antidote to the immobilism of the political system, on economic as well as linguistic matters. But a resolution of some of the outstanding problems could still lead to a partial return to former voting loyalties.

Belgian Socialist Party (Francophone: *Parti Socialiste Belge;* PSB) (Flemish: *Belgische Socialistische Partij;* BSP)

History

These two parties, the PSB and the BSP, had a common origin and history until the linguistic division of the Socialist Party was made formal in October 1978. The party was founded in 1885 as the Belgian Workers' Party, and it soon became a political force by winning manhood suffrage through the pressure of a general strike. During the interwar years the party participated in government both with the Catholic party and in "tripartite" governments which included the Liberals. The party sought a wider appeal, changing its name to Socialist in 1944, but always found it difficult to compete successfully with the Social Christians, since the latter could rely on the wide connections of the Catholic Church. Nonetheless, the two parties showed a high compatibility and regularly joined in coalition governments after 1945.

Organization

Even before the final break in 1978, the two wings of the party had developed separately. From 1971 two party presidents were elected, one Francophone and the other Flemish, and the two sections of the party contested elections in Brussels on competing lists. The structure of the two parties is similar: both have an annual congress, an executive, and a general council which (composed of delegates, parliamentary deputies, and members of the executive bureau) has a coordinating function. A feature of party organization is the relative independence of the regional federations of the parties, and this applies particularly to the selection of parliamentary candidates, in which the institution of primaries is still of importance.

PSB headquarters are at Boulevard de L'Empereur 13, 1000 Brussels; BSP headquarters are at Keizerslaan 13, 1000 Brussels.

Policy

The party in Wallonia was more traditionally socialist, while in Flanders it tended to be moderate and reformist. These contrasts were later joined by the constitutional disputes relating to the linguistic problem, especially concerning the position of Brussels. The PSB argues that Brussels should be an entirely distinct region, whereas the BSP is unable to accept full regional status for it. Both parties support European Community membership and NATO, although they are inclined to oppose an increase of nuclear arms in western Europe.

Membership & Constituency

The Socialists in Wallonia were more strongly organized around the centers of coal mining and the steel industry and consistently recorded a much higher share of the regional vote than the party did in Flanders. The composition of support was biased much more to the manual occupations, and the party was more uniformly anticlerical or secular. In Flanders, the Socialists lacked a solid base of industrial support and had to compete with the Social Christians, who had a strong organization. A further difference was that total membership of the two parties is about 260,000, in roughly equal proportions, which represents a ratio of membership to voting support of some 17 percent.

Financing

Both parties rely heavily on high membership dues and trade-union sources. Mutual-aid societies associated with the parties also contribute to its support.

Leadership

The parliamentary leader of the PSB is Guy Spitaels (born 1931), while the BSP is led by Karel van Miert (born 1942).

Prospects

While there is no likelihood of the two parties merging again, they do cooperate in questions of national policy and in discussions on coalition participation; a formal coordinating committee with representatives from both parties exists for this purpose.

Christian Social Party
(*Parti Social Chrétien;* PSC)
Christian People's Party
(*Christelijke Volkspartij;* CVP)

History

Catholic political organizations developed between 1846 and 1884, coalescing in that year to form the Catholic Party, which then became the dominant force in Belgium for the next thirty years and the leading one until the present. When the party was reconstituted in 1945, changing its title to the Christian Social Party, an attempt was made to move away from a strict confessional appeal. Since then the Christian Socialists have participated in almost all coalition governments, with either or both of the Liberals and Socialists. Even though the party was made up of the two distinctive linguistic elements, it maintained a unitary structure. This remained substantially true until 1968 when the two "wings" held separate party congresses; the common presidency fell into disuse from 1972 onwards.

Organization

The formal structure of the PSC and CVP is similar, with annual national congresses functioning as the supreme policymaking organs, a party president, and an executive bureau. Both also have a national council, consisting of members elected from the congress and selected members, which oversees party policy between congresses. Although the PSC and CVP are now separate parties, there is fairly close liaison between them, and they still share the same party headquarters in Brussels. They coordinate their activities through an unofficial presidium which consists of the leading officials of the parties from Parliament and the national party organizations. However, the decisions of the presidium have to be ratified by the bureaus of the two parties. Local organizations exist from the *arrondissement* downwards. They are active and enjoy a degree of autonomy, especially in candidate selection for which local primaries are held, although central approval is required for the candidate lists.

The parties share headquarters at Rue des Deux Eglises 41, B-1040 Brussels.

Policy

Both parties believe in "an economy in the service of man" and favor policies of social responsibility and justice, a high level of employment tempered by a need to secure price stability, and an avoidance of waste. The PSC tends to be more conservative than its Flemish counterpart, for the latter is strongly influenced by its trade-union connections. Both parties fully support Belgium's membership in the European Community and NATO.

Membership & Constituency

Neither the PSC or the CVP is particularly strong as a membership party: the CVP has just over 100,000 and the PSC some 45,000. But the question of membership cannot be considered in isolation from the contribution made by organized interests at a local level, particularly in Flanders, where three groupings stand out: the trade-union Christian Workers' Movement, the Farmers' League (*Boerenbond*), and the so-called National Association of the Christian Middle Classes. In both Flanders and Wallonia the support of these and similar groups is vital for party success: for mobilizing Catholic voters and as a source of money.

There are significant disparities between the Flanders CVP and the Wallonian PSC, not least in the degree of support they can muster. Thus, in the 1981 election the CVP took 19.3 percent of the national vote and forty-three seats (competing in Flanders and Brussels), while the PSC recorded only 7.1 percent and eighteen seats (competing in Wallonia and Brussels). The great difference in strength, which is not a new occurrence, can be ascribed to the greater interclass unity of the

Catholic community in rural Flanders; in Wallonia the PSC has a less-structured base and also has to compete with a strong Socialist party for the working-class vote.

Financing

The two parties receive substantial support from various social and economic organizations. This support supplements their income from membership dues.

Leadership

The CVP has a strong national leadership with considerable governing experience, and the party usually holds the prime ministership in governing coalitions. Thus even though the CVP and PSC both lost about a quarter of their seats at the 1981 election, the new prime minister (and former party leader) Wilfried Martens (born 1936) came from the CVP. Martens had previously held the same office from 1978 to 1981, and Leo Tindemanns (born 1922), who was CVP prime minister from 1974 to 1978, is now foreign minister. The present party leader of the CVP is Mark Eyskens (born 1934). In contrast, the PSC has to be content with a junior position, and the resignation of the party's former leader, Paul Vanden Boeynants (born 1919), in 1981 has set the PSC somewhat in disarray. The PSC parliamentary leader is Gerard Deprez; his CVP counterpart is Frank Swaelen.

Prospects

The difference in size of the two parties means that, with full autonomy, there is little likelihood that either would wish to give up its independence. Nevertheless, the CVP/PSC in combination represents the pivot of all likely coalition formations, and for this reason the two parties cooperate closely in government.

Liberal Reform Party
(*Parti Réformateur Libéral;* PRL)
Freedom and Progress Party
(*Partij voor Vrijheid en Vooruitgang;* PVV)

History

The PVV and PRL are the two successor parties to the old Liberal Party, and they are therefore part of the "traditional" party system. The Liberal Party was the first to be established, in 1846. It was bourgeois in nature and strongly anticlerical. The Liberals were adversely affected by the widening of the franchise and only rescued by the adoption of proportional representation in 1900; during the interwar years it was the smallest party in the three-party system. In 1961, the party underwent a rejuvenation, dropping its old title to become the Party of Liberty and Progress; its progressive nature was shown chiefly in the party's renunciation of anticlericalism. Otherwise it retained its attachment to economic liberalism and orthodox financial management. At the same time, party organization was strengthened with greater authority given to the party's president, a considerable change for the party of individualists. The reforms increased the party's electoral attraction, increasing its representation from twenty to forty-eight seats in the 1965 election, although even before the reforms the Liberals had regularly served in government prior to 1961. In fact, the changes made the party more conservative and meant that it was less inclined to serve with the Socialists in government. The Liberals at first managed to avoid a split over the linguistic problem and stood for the preservation of a unitary state, but in 1970 the Flemish PVV effectively became a separate party. In Wallonia a new party was formed in 1976, combining with the French-speaking Brussels Liberals in 1979 to form the PRL.

Organization

The parties have a similar structure, with an annual delegate congress, a chairman for the PVV and a president for the PRL, executive bureaus, and administrative councils. Despite their separation, the two parties cooperate with regard to coalition policies and in research.

Liberal policy was one of economic *laissez-faire* until the 1961 party renewal when it became more progressive. However, in recent years, the Liberals have returned somewhat to market orthodoxy in economic policy, especially as opposed to the Socialists. There are important differences in emphasis between the PRL and the PVV: the PRL represents declining heavy industry in Wallonia and is more inclined to favor government subsidies and rescue operations, unlike the PVV in more prosperous Flanders. In foreign policy, both parties are highly supportive of NATO and the European Common Market.

PVV headquarters are at Regentlaan 47-8, 1000 Brussels; and PRL headquarters are at Centre International Rogier, Place Rogier, 1000 Brussels.

Membership & Constituency

Of the two present-day parties, the PVV is the stronger, although neither has been able to match the previously united party's performance in the respective regions. The PVV has a membership of 50,000 against 40,000 for the PRL. Support for the party comes primarily from urban upper and middle classes and from old-line anticlericals who also oppose the Socialists.

Financing

The parties have traditionally relied on contributions from commercial and industrial interests. While direct membership support is increasing, it still provides a relatively small portion of the parties' annual budgets.

Leadership

The PVV's parliamentary leader is Guy Verhofstadt; the PRL's is Louis Michel.

Prospects

With the worsening economic situation in Belgium, especially since the late 1970s, the Liberal economic philosophy shows a renewed appeal. The two Liberal parties won a place in government with the Social Christians (to the exclusion of the Socialists) subsequent to the 1981 election. They may well retain their government role as long as the electorate does not move to the left in face of greater economic distress.

Minor Parties

Communist Party of Belgium (*Kommunistische Partij van België/Parti Communiste de Belgique;* KPB/PCB)

The Belgian Communist Party was formed in 1921 as a breakaway from the Workers' Party. It has never succeeded in becoming a mass party. For a brief period after 1945, after playing a part in the wartime resistance movement, the Communists verged on becoming a popular force and served in government from 1946 until 1947. Thereafter its electoral fortunes declined. The party dropped its early hard-line communist strategy in 1954, but it now obtains only a handful of seats (in 1981 2 seats and 2.3 percent). In Flanders, the Communists have only a minute following, but in Wallonia there are local bastions of support. Total membership is 15,000, and the party's daily newspaper has a similar circulation. Unlike the other older parties, the Communist Party has preserved its unified structure—a central committee with a political bureau—but it also has regional councils together with twenty-three federations. The party supports a Belgium of three regions, and it is fully supportive of the parliamentary road to socialism and cooperation with other democratic parties. Party headquarters are at Avenue de Stalingrad 18/20, 1000 Brussels.

Democratic Union for the Respect of Labor (*Union Démocratique pour le Respect du Travail/Respect voor Arbeid en Democratie;* UDRT/RAD)

The UDRT/RAD, formed in 1978, is a typical "anti-tax" protest party with middle-class support. It advocates a return to sound monetary policy, and demonstrates the fact that sections of the electorate see the economy as a more important issue than the linguistic one. Its radical stance represents a potential threat to the more orthodox liberals. With a membership of 4,000 throughout the country, the UDRT/RAD won a single seat in 1978 and three in 1981 with 2.7 percent of the vote. Party headquarters are at Chaussée de Boondael 548, 1050 Brussels.

Flemish Bloc (*Vlaamsche Blok;* VLBL)

The *Vlaamsche Blok* is one of the more extreme linguistic parties. It was established in 1978 as an alliance of two earlier offshoots from the more moderate *Volksunie* (see below). The VLBL is against the compromises involved in the constitutional reforms, especially relating to Brussels; it also represents separatist inclinations. However, the *Vlaamsche Blok* has had limited success, winning only one seat in both the 1978 and 1981 elections.

Francophone Democratic Front (*Front Démocratique des Francophones;* FDF)

The FDF, founded in 1964, is the party of French speakers in the Brussels area, strongly supporting the claims of Brussels as a third region on par with the other two. It also argues that Brussels's city limits should be extended to take account of the overspill of French-speakers into surrounding Flemish districts, a demand which is especially related to the problem of providing a French-speaking education in Flemish areas. The FDF is closely allied to the *Rassemblement Wallon,* and like the *Rassemblement,* appeals to voters who might otherwise vote for one of the traditional parties. The FDF wins about a third of the Brussels vote and now has built up a consistent following; however, it experienced a reverse in the 1981 election, winning only five seats compared with eleven in 1978. A significant feature of the FDF is its willingness to undertake government responsibility: it entered the 1977 coalition which produced a constitutional agreement, and again after the 1978 election, the FDF joined the government only to withdraw subsequently when the party's demands for full regional status for Brussels were not met. Its headquarters are at 42 rue P.E. Janson, B-1050 Brussels.

People's Union (*Volksunie*)

Flemish nationalism began primarily as a cultural movement in the nineteenth century, but during World War II—under the German occupation of Flanders and encouraged by the Germans—it became an active political force and led to a separatist movement. In the interwar years there were several specifically Flemish parties; they were little more than pressure groups, but strong enough to cause considerable political dissension. *Volksunie* emerged in 1954 as a result of a fusion of a number of smaller parties, but the party did not make an electoral breakthrough until 1965 when it won twelve seats, reaching a high point in 1974 with twenty-two seats. It declined somewhat after 1974, taking about 15 percent of the vote in Flanders. *Volksunie* is a "people's" party in the sense that it draws support from all social classes. Its general political orientation is moderate. Its success was the primary catalyst in bringing about the total restructuring of the Belgian party system. *Volksunie's* demands for constitutional changes to secure a measure of Flemish autonomy have been largely met; the party was a member of a coalition government in 1977–78 which reached a constitutional agreement. However, *Volksunie* strongly resists the creation of a Brussels region, since that would effectively ensure Francophone predominance in two of three regions. Moreover, it sees no reason why Flanders should be asked to subsidize the ailing Wallonian economy. *Volksunie* has a relatively high membership of 60,000, with 400 local branches, a national council of 100, and a national executive committee of fifteen members. Its headquarters are at Barrikadenplein 12, 1000 Brussels.

Walloon Rally (*Rassemblement Wallon;* RW)

The Walloon Rally, formed in 1968 from the merger of a number of smaller Francophone groupings, was a direct reaction to the success of the Flemish *Volksunie.* The RW is much more a regional party than a linguistic one; a fact demonstrated by its primary concern with Wallonian economic problems. The party is more left leaning than the other community parties, drawing some of its support from previous adherents to the Socialist Party, but differing from the Socialists in its greater appeal to practicing Wallonian Catholics. The party served in government from 1974 to 1977, but is more at home taking an opposition stance. The party is linked with the Brussels FDF, but follows an independent course, for instance, in its attitude to government participation. Its main unifying platform is that Brussels and Wallonia should enjoy a "special relationship," a demand which is naturally anathema to the Flemish. Despite RW's identification with Wallonian economic interests and that region's economic problems, the party has steadily declined since the early 1970s. It has a strong organizational structure and a membership of 9,500. It appears that the RW is unable to offer sufficient credibility in comparison with the traditional parties, especially the Socialist Party. Its headquarters are at 42 rue Rogier, 5000 Namur.

Minor parties which have not played a significant role in Belgian politics include:

Ecological Party (*Ecolo-Agalev*)

The ecology movement in Belgium first contested a national election in 1978 in Wallonia but was unsuccessful, winning only 0.8 percent of the vote. In 1981, however, it joined forces with the Flemish equivalent, *Anders Gaan Leven* (Live Differently), and won four seats with 4.8 percent of the national vote (289,000). This achievement indicates that a significant section of the electorate is turning away from an exclusive preoccupation with the linguistic issue.

Party of German-Speaking Belgians (*Partei der deutschsprachigen Belgier;* PDB)

There is a very small German-speaking minority of about 60,000 people in Belgium, concentrated in the border area in the eastern region. Although the PDB has never won representation nationally, it has seven of the twenty-one seats on the German Cultural Council.

Party of Labor (*Partij van de Arbeid;* PdvA)

The PdvA is a Marxist-Leninist party which

stands in opposition to the orthodox Communist Party. Previously, the PdvA called itself "All power to the Workers;" it became the PvdA in 1979. It contested the 1981 election and had the support of 0.8 percent of voters.

National Prospects

The high instability of Belgian coalition governments and the fragmentation of the party system have become endemic features of the system, even though substantial progress has been made in meeting linguistic demands and in securing a substantial decentralization of legislative and executive authority. Two underlying problems remain unresolved. One concerns the position of Brussels which is subject to the incompatible claims of the linguistic protagonists. The other relates to the increasing economic imbalance between Wallonia and Flanders, with the relative prosperity of Flanders and the structural problems of Wallonian industry readily translatable into the rivalry of the two linguistic areas. However, the economic difficulties also constitute a national problem: Belgium has the highest rate of unemployment in Western Europe (about 13 percent) together with a high rate of inflation and a weak currency. The practice of wage indexing has also made it difficult to secure economic stabilization. The outcome of the 1981 election was a center-right coalition of Social Christians and Liberals committed to a program of financial austerity. Yet the new government was based on a coalition that held only forty-two of the ninety-one French-speaking seats, in other words, government measures which would inevitably adversely affect Wallonia did not enjoy a popular mandate from that region. There are indications that these problems are causing greater political polarizaion as the Socialist parties object vehemently to the economic retrenchment advocated by the Liberals.

Further Reading

Covell, M. "Ethnic Conflict and Elite Bargaining: The Case of Belgium." *Western European Politics*, Vol. 4, No. 3, October 1981.

Day, A. J., and Degenhardt, H. W. *Political Parties of the World.* Harlow, Essex, England: Longman, 1980.

Hill, K. "Belgium." In *European Political Parties*, S. Henig and J. Pinder, eds. London: George Allen & Unwin, 1969.

———. "Belgium: Political Change in a Segmented Society." In *Electoral Behavior: A Comparative Handbook*, R. Rose, ed. New York: Collier, 1974.

Irving, R. *The Christian Democratic Parties of Western Europe.* London: George Allen & Unwin, 1979.

Lorwin, V. "Belgium: Religion, Class and Language in National Politics." In *Political Oppositions in Western Democracies*, R. A. Dahl, ed. New Haven, Conn.: Yale University Press, 1966.

Mabille, X., and Lorwin, V. "The Belgian Socialist Party." In *Social Democratic Parties in Western Europe*, W. Paterson and A. Thomas, eds. London: Croom Helm, 1977.

———. "Belgium." In *Political Parties in the European Community*, S. Henig, ed. London: George Allen & Unwin, 1979.

MacMullen, A. L. "The Belgian Election of November 1981." *Parliamentary Affairs*, Vol. 35, No. 2, Spring 1982.

———. "Belgium." In *Government and Administration.* F. F. Ridley, ed. Oxford: Martin Robertson, 1979.

BELIZE

by Indira Jhappan

The System of Government

Belize (until 1973, British Honduras) is a parliamentary democracy which gained its independence from Great Britain on September 21, 1981. The population of Belize, about 145,000, is characterized by unusual racial diversity, a fact in which the Belizeans take some pride. For the sake of simplicity, the society can be divided into three major groups: the Creoles, of African and English descent; the *mestizos*, of Spanish-Indian (largely Mayan) descent; and the Caribs, the native Indians. There are also several smaller groups: Chinese, East Indians, and Lebanese and Syrians. Color and social class are interrelated, with lighter color associated with higher social class. Nevertheless, there have been no serious racial or other social disorders.

Executive

The head of state is still the British monarch represented by a governor general whose powers are largely ceremonial. The governor general appoints as prime minister the leader of the party with a parliamentary majority. It is the prime minister who, as head of government, wields real executive power. The prime minister may call early elections before the five-year term of the legislature has expired.

Legislature

The House of Assembly consists of an appointed Senate and an elected House of Representatives. The latter body is composed of eighteen members elected by universal suffrage from single-member districts by simple pluralities. Eight of the representatives are elected from the Belize City area. The Senate has eight members, five appointed by the prime minister, two by the leader of the opposition, and one by the governor in consultation with social organizations and individuals of his choice. Senators are drawn from the party organizations, the business and professional communities, and from other social leaders.

Bills may be introduced in either house, with the exception of money bills, which may not be introduced in the Senate. Normally, bills passed by both houses become law, but if the Senate fails to consider a money bill within thirty days of its passage by the lower house, the bill may be sent directly to the governor general for his formal assent. Bills receive two readings and votes in the House of Assembly. Since the introduction of universal suffrage in 1954, Prime Minister George Price and his People's United Party (PUP) has been in firm control of both houses.

Judiciary

The judicial system is based on English common law, which means that the courts cannot overturn an act of Parliament, but otherwise exercise considerable independence from political influence. The chief justice of the Supreme Court is appointed by the governor general on the advice of both the prime minister and the leader of the opposition. The final Court of Appeal is the judicial committee of the British Privy Council.

Regional & Local Government

Local government elections are contested as fiercely as national elections. Although it is generally true that PUP has dominated municipal councils, opposition parties have sometimes made inroads. This was particularly true in 1979, when thirty-nine of fifty-eight council seats and six of eight cities and towns went to the United Democratic Party (UDP).

The Electoral System

House of Representative members are elected by simple majority vote in eighteen single-member districts. Elections are held every five years and citizens eighteen years of age and older are eligible to vote. Voter participation since 1954 has shown considerable fluctuations. In 1954, 70 percent of the eligible voters turned out. In 1957, this figure fell to 53 percent. By 1974, it had climbed back to 68 percent, and in 1979 reached a peak of 90 percent. Turnout in urban areas tends to be greater than in rural areas. Independent candidates have usually failed to gain election.

The Party System

The party system in Belize is well developed. In theory it is a multiparty system which new groupings can enter without restriction, but in practice it has been dominated by the PUP. The PUP's success can be traced to superior organization through its connections with organized labor and the Roman Catholic Church, as well as to excellent leadership with solid political expertise. Another factor which inadvertently helped the PUP gain dominance was the eagerness of the British to grant self-government to Belize. This desire coincided with the rise of the PUP and the demands of its leaders for greater autonomy and constitutional concessions. The PUP's apparent ability to win British approval increased its popularity.

People's United Party

The PUP was founded in 1950 by members of an informal political group called the People's Committee. The founders—Philip Goldson, George Price, John Smith, and Leigh Richardson—soon split up: Smith resigned in 1954, and Richardson and Goldson left in 1956 to form the Honduran Independence Party, which merged with the National Independence Party in 1958. These departures shook the party, but also left George Price in firm control. Price's quiet statecraft and charisma brought the party through this period with no damage to its preeminent position.

The PUP's share of the national vote has never fallen below 51 percent. In 1954, it won 70 percent of the vote. In 1969, it won seventeen of the eighteen seats in the lower house and lost only one seat in 1974. In the 1979 elections it won only 51.8 percent of the vote, the poorest showing since it was founded, but still won thirteen of the seats.

The PUP has been known for its nationalist policies. It has always fought for Belizean independence. It favors improving the country's ties with the rest of Central America and with the rest of the English-speaking Caribbean. More recently, the party has cautiously advanced economic and social policies that are slightly to the left of center.

The links between the ruling elite of the party and the mass of dues-paying members are weak. Annual party conventions which elect party leaders are, in fact, small gatherings of local political notables. Nevertheless, the party draws its support from all groups in the society, especially from the *mestizos*, and from both rural and urban areas.

In the early stages of its development, the PUP drew its leadership from the middle and upper classes, primarily Creole groups. This component in the leadership group increased as the British attitude towards the party became increasingly conciliatory and more members of the professional classes and wealthy businessmen began to join. George Price is Creole and a devout Catholic. He is in his early sixties.

The PUP faces an uncertain future. Election returns since 1954 show a slowly rising strength among the opposition parties, which have recently begun to pay increased attention to improved organization. Analysis of voting patterns suggest that Creole groups may be shifting their allegiance to the opposition. Now that independence has been gained, the common cause that held rich and poor, Creole and *mestizo* together in the PUP is no longer a unifying issue.

United Democratic Party (UDP)

Founded in 1973, the UDP is an alliance of a number of opposition parties: the Liberal Party, the People's Development Movement, the National Independence Party, and the United Black Association for Development. Unable to challenge PUP's supremacy separately, these parties finally pooled their efforts with relative success. In 1974, the party won six seats. In 1979, it won only five seats but nearly half the total vote. It also won a majority of municipal council seats, including the majority in Belize City, the capital and largest urban area. Led by Theodore Aranda, the UDP has the support of wealthy, conservative businessmen and those who dislike either Price's policies or his long dominance of the political scene. Beyond the opposition to Price, there is little ideological coherence in the UDP. Nevertheless, if the party maintains its unity, it appears ready to offer the PUP stiff competition in coming years.

National Prospects

Because it is a new state, it is difficult to predict the prospects for stability in Belize. In the short run, Price's PUP can thrive on its pro-independence record, but if popular expectations of independence fail to materialize, the reaction may give the UDP greater strength or lead to more militant opposition. The possibility of racial conflict cannot be ruled out, but it does appear unlikely. An unknown factor in Belize's future is the Guatemalan government. Guatemala claims Belize as its territory and a strong government in Guatemala, whether of the right or the left, might press that claim in the future.

Further Readings

Blaustein A., and Flanz, Gisbert H., eds. *Constitutions of the World.* Dobbs Ferry, N. Y.: Oceana Publications, 1971.

Dobson, Narda. *A History of Belize.* London: Longman Caribbean Ltd., 1973.

Grant, C. H. *The Making of Modern Belize. Politics, Society and British Colonialism in Central America.* London: Cambridge University Press, 1976.

PEOPLE'S REPUBLIC OF BENIN
(*République Populaire du Bénin*)
by Michael Radu, Ph.D.

The System of Government

Benin, a West African country of over three million people, has a presidential, one-party, Marxist–Leninist political system, in which the military plays a very strong role.

The country was proclaimed independent from France on August 1, 1960, as the Republic of Dahomey, with a multiparty, presidential government structure. The three major political figures—Justin Ahomadegbe, Sourou-Migan Apithy, and Hubert Maga—all of whom had served as president by 1972, were supported by the three most important ethnic groups in the country, the Fon, Yoruba, and Bariba, respectively. From October 28, 1963, when the first military coup occurred, until 1972, the country was known as the most unstable and coup-prone in Africa. Since October 26, 1972—when a group of military officers led by Major Mathieu Kerekou staged a coup—Kerekou has been president.

On November 30, 1974, the military regime proclaimed its allegiance to Marxism-Leninism. Exactly one year later it proclaimed the People's Republic of Benin and founded the Popular Revolution Party of Benin (*Parti de la Révolution Populaire du Bénin;* PRPB). According to the August 26, 1977, constitution, all social activities of Benin are to be organized under the centralized leadership of the PRPB, defined as "the vanguard detachment" and "leading nucleus" of the people and revolution of Benin.

Executive

The president of the republic is elected by the National Revolutionary Assembly, but is nominated by the PRPB Central Committee. He is, at the same time, president of the party, and chief of the National Executive Council, i.e., chief of government. In addition to his offices as chief of state, party, and government, Mathieu Kerekou is also commander-in-chief of the armed forces and defense minister. The presidential term is three years and renewable.

The National Executive Council (*Conseil Exécutif National*) is composed of the president, ministers, and the leaders of the six provinces. Both the ministers and the provincial administrators are appointed and removed from office by the president. On the other hand, since the holders of the key ministerial offices—interior, finance, foreign affairs, planning, ideological orientation, and justice—are all members of the PRPB Politburo as well, it is Kerekou's control over the party itself which enables him to remove from office influential ministers with high party offices. His ability to do so was demonstrated after the November 1979 PRPB Congress, when he downgraded the government positions of the second- and third-ranking Politburo members (Foreign Minister Michel Alladaye and Propaganda Minister Martin Dohou Azonhiho) and again in March 1982, when he replaced Politburo member and foreign minister Simon Iffèdé Ogouma.

Legislature

The 336 members of the National Revolutionary Assembly (*Assemblée Nationale Révolutionaire*) are elected every three years. They elect the Permanent Committee which has complete control over the National Executive Council, i.e., the cabinet. All candidates for the Assembly are nominated by the PRPB Central Committee.

Judiciary

The judicial system and law is based roughly on that of France. Judges have no real independence from the dictates of the regime.

Regional & Local Government

Local revolutionary councils are elected by the populace every three years at the provincial, district, and village or municipal level. They are under the direct control of the Permanent Committee of the National Assembly.

The Electoral System

Suffrage extends to all citizens eighteen years of age or over. The elections are organized and supervised by the Permanent Committee.

Popular Revolutionary Party of Benin
(*Parti de la Révolution Populaire du Bénin;* PRPB)

History

The PRPB is a Marxist–Leninist party, founded November 30, 1975. Its first (extraordinary) congress was held May 15–17, 1976, and the second (first ordinary) November 13–15, 1979.

The PRPB was established to legitimize what was, at the time, a military junta with little popular support; and to attract the support of radicalized students, unionists, and intellectuals. On the other hand, the most radical of the initial junta members, such as Michel Aikpe and Nestor Beheton, were eliminated early. Only after the 1979 congress did the party succeed in attracting significant civilian support.

Organization

Although the party congress is formally the supreme body, it is the Central Committee which actually controls the party; the Committee's decisions are simply approved by the seldom-convened congress. The congress elects the Central Committee, which in turn elects its own president. Party organization is extremely weak outside of the three major cities of Cotonou, Porto Novo, and Abomey.

Policy

Despite its Marxist–Leninist rhetoric, the PRPB has moved cautiously in domestic affairs. Nationalization of foreign companies was limited and generally followed by compensation. The minis-cule industrial sector is under state control, but agriculture remains largely private.

Benin's external policies, while strongly anti-Western in rhetoric, are a mixture of support for Third World radical causes, friendship with Libya and the Soviet bloc, as well as with China, and economic dependence on France and general Western aid.

Membership & Constituency

The PRPB, while claiming to represent the entire people, is actually a very small group dominated by intellectuals and military figures. It is essentially an instrument of Mathieu Kerekou's personal rule. Although no reliable figures for membership exist, it is likely that the party amounts to only a few thousand people.

Financing

No information is available on the party's finances. Extensive state support is probable.

Leadership

Mathieu Kerekou was born September 2, 1933, in northwestern Benin, a member of the minor Somba tribe. He received his military training at Kati, Mali, and at Saint Louis, Senegal, before undergoing training in France, at Fréjus and the École Militaire de Saint-Raphael. In 1960, he served in the French army. He was Hubert Maga's aide de camp in 1961 and 1962, and was one of the main leaders of the 1967 military coup. In 1968 and 1969, he had further training as a staff officer in France. Appointed major and commander of the elite commando units at Ouidah in 1969, he became chief of staff in 1970. After his coup, he promoted himself to colonel.

Opposition

Small and fragmented opposition groups in exile, mostly in France, pose no threat to the regime.

National Prospects

The considerable stability achieved by the Kerekou regime is due largely to the application of Leninist techniques of power consolidation, and for this very reason the official rhetoric and institutional structure of Benin can be expected to last for years to come. The pragmatic domestic and, in economic terms at least, foreign policies of Kerekou probably will remain stable as well, given Benin's economic dependence on the West and close security ties with the Soviet bloc and a number of Third World radical regimes.

Further Reading

Decalo, Samuel. *Coups and Army Rule in Africa*, New Haven and London: Yale University Press, 1976.

————. "Ideological Rhetoric and Scientific Socialism in Benin and Congo/Brazzaville." In *Socialism in Sub-Saharan Africa*, Carl G. Rosberg and Thomas M. Callaghy, eds. Berkeley: Institute of International Studies, University of California, 1979.

Young, Crawford. *Ideology and Development in Africa*, New Haven and London: Yale University Press, 1982.

REPUBLIC OF BOLIVIA
(*Republica de Bolivia*)
by Elizabeth G. Ferris, Ph.D.

The System of Government

Bolivia, a nation of nearly six million people with a history of political instability, authoritarian rule, frequent military governments, and few legitimate institutions, has been ruled almost continuously by military juntas from 1964 to late 1982, when the last legitimately elected president, Hernán Siles Zuazo, was permitted to take control of the government in face of the failure of the military to govern effectively.

Since achieving independence in 1825, Bolivia has had sixteen constitutions and more than 190 extraconstitutional changes in government. While most of these changes in government were little more than rotations of like-minded strongmen, Bolivia is one of the few Latin American nations to have experienced a true national revolution. Its revolution of 1952 fundamentally altered the Bolivian power structure, creating new political actors who challenged the economic and political dominance of the few elite families which had governed Bolivia since independence. The failure of the revolutionary party and government to implement its policies led to a military takeover in 1964.

Bolivia's weakness relative to surrounding nations has led to conflicts in which Bolivia has lost territory to all of its neighbors. Economic dependence on exports of a few primary products, particularly tin and other minerals, has made Bolivia vulnerable to fluctuations in prices and to shifts in the international financial system.

The Bolivian Revolution had its origin in the Chaco War (1932–35), when Bolivia was soundly defeated by Paraguayan forces. The defeat led to intense self-examination by the leadership groups, while urban and rural laborers began to question the competence of that leadership. In the decade which followed, the growth of labor unions and new political parties, most notably the National Revolutionary Movement (*Movimiento Nacional Revolucionario*; MNR), challenged the fundamental assumptions of Bolivian government. From 1932 to 1952, there were numerous revolts culminating in short-lived military regimes.

In April 1952, the MNR overthrew the government. The MNR governments, under Victor Paz Estenssoro and Hernán Siles Zuazo, carried out redistributive measures: giving land to the peasants, nationalizing the mines, expanding educational opportunities, providing universal adult suffrage, limiting foreign investment, and stripping the military of its power. Urban and rural unions acquired their own weapons and developed their own militias. As economic conditions worsened, the revolutionary government was forced by the requirements of international financial institutions to take unpopular austerity measures. These measures hurt the labor and peasant sectors—which were precisely the groups most supportive of the revolution. As the MNR governments became less popular and as economic conditions deteriorated, MNR leaders slowed down their reforms and built up the military once again. In 1964, after elections marked by widespread fraud, Victor Paz Estenssoro was overthrown in a military coup by General René Barrientos. Barrientos oversaw the formation of a new constitution and abortive "elections," but military coups continued to be the only real means for transferring power in the country.

Following two short-lived military governments (General Ovando Candía, 1969–70; General Juan José Torres, 1970–71), General Hugo Banzer Suárez took power in August 1972 and ruled with the support of the MNR. In 1973, the coalition was dissolved and Banzer ruled without the MNR, using both repression and astute manipulation of various civilian groups to maintain power. Under pressure from the United States, Banzer agreed to hold elections in 1978. The results of the elections were annulled by the military and followed by a military coup led by General Juan Pereda Asbun. Pereda was in turn overthrown by General David Padilla Arancibio, who presided over new presidential elections in July 1979. No clear victor emerged, and Congress selected a compromise interim president. Three months later, the civilian president was overthrown by General Natusch Busch whose rule was so violent and inept that civilians were able to oust him in only two weeks.

The next interim president, Lidia Gueiler, presided over new elections in 1980. Every major civilian institution—unions, peasant organizations, universities, and the Roman Catholic Church—publicly committed itself to democracy and formed the Committee for the Defense of Democracy (*Comité Nacional para la Defensa de la Democracia*; CONADE) in alliance with several political groups. This time the electoral system did produce a clear victor—Hernán Siles Zuazo, the candidate of a center-left coalition. As soon as the result became clear, however, the military under General Luís García Meza seized power. Given the earlier commitment to democracy and the military's ineptness and corruption (it has been closely linked with an extensive traffic in cocaine), civilian society has been thoroughly alienated. Subsequent coups have not made any real difference in the quality of government or the degree of corruption. At the same time, the military now has added reasons to hang on to power—it fears major criminal charges against many military leaders if civilians ever gain control of the machinery of state.

The constitution of 1967 is still the official charter of the nation, and although it has been suspended since 1969, the military regime has stated its intention of restoring it.

Executive

The constitutional executive is a president, elected for a four-year term by direct suffrage and a simple majority. If no candidate obtains a majority, Congress chooses between the two top candidates. A president may not succeed himself. The formal powers of the president are extensive, but patronage is the most widely used source of political control. The president appoints a Council of Ministers which serves as his cabinet. In the June 1980 elections there were thirteen candidates for president. Those receiving the most votes were Hernán Siles Zuazo (MNRI), 500,000; Victor Paz Estenssoro (MNR), 260,000; Hugo Banzer Suárez (ADN), 218,000, and Marcelo Quiroga Santa Cruz (PS-1), 112,000.

Legislature

The legislature consists of a Senate (twenty-seven members) and a Chamber of Deputies (130 members). The electoral rules provide that each department will be represented by three senators, two from the leading party in the province and one from the second party.

Judiciary

The Supreme Court consists of ten justices, elected by the Chamber of Deputies from nominees submitted by the Senate. The Supreme Court either nominates or directly appoints the judges of the district and local courts. It has no independent power presently, since judges can be appointed and dismissed at will.

Regional & Local Government

Bolivia is a unitary system with nine departments, divided into ninety-six provinces and 940 *cantones*. The president appoints department prefects who in turn appoint officials on the local level. The separatist tendencies in the department of Santa Cruz, in the eastern part of the country, have contributed to Bolivia's political instability. Santa Cruz, agriculturally rich and politically conservative, has long felt that the central government in La Paz is unresponsive to its development needs. Military leaders seeking to overthrow the government in La Paz have frequently started their rebellions in Santa Cruz.

The Electoral System

Since the 1952 election, there has been universal adult suffrage for all citizens over the age of twenty-one (eighteen if married). There is no literacy requirement. Voting is compulsory; in the 1980 elections, nonvoters faced loss of legal privileges (including use of banks, schools, etc.) for up to three months.

Elections for president, vice-president, and the legislature are direct, unless no presidential candidate wins an absolute majority, in which case Congress determines the outcome. In 1979, Congress was unable to decide between the two leading candidates and selected a compromise candidate, Walter Guevara Arce.

Although balloting is secret, each party's ballot has a distinctive color and symbol. The administration of the electoral system is overseen by a theoretically impartial electoral court including representatives of the legislature, the Supreme Court, the executive, and the principal political parties. In practice, however, there has been widespread fraud and considerable violence associated with elections. Election results take weeks or months to be announced, the results are usually close, and it is traditional for the losing candidate to accuse the winner of fraud.

The Party System

Origins of the Parties

During the 1880s, the Conservative and Liberal movements struggled for control of the national government. The Conservatives—representing the southern silver-mining institutions, the traditional landed elite, and the Sucre region—were eventually defeated by the Liberals in a civil war. The Liberals represented the tin interests, the emerging urban middle class, and La Paz. These Liberal elites dominated the country until the 1930s, although they alternated rule with the Republican Party (which came to represent Conservative interests). The Liberal program for the nation—liberal democracy, rapid economic development, and peace—was shattered by the Chaco War.

Since 1952, party formation has been predominantly of two kinds—splits off the MNR to the right and left and the development of personalist parties to serve as the electoral machinery of former coup leaders attempting to retain power and legitimize their rule.

The Parties in Law

There are few restrictions on the freedom to form political parties in normal times, and despite the prevalence of fraud and manipulation in the elections, dozens of parties usually form up in anticipation of elections. As many as sixty parties appeared before the 1980 elections. Their existence is highly ephemeral as they merge and splinter, change their names and points of view, join tenuous coalitions, and withdraw. In an effort to reduce the number of parties on the ballot, the electoral court imposes fines and possible jail sentences on leaders of parties which fail to get 50,000 votes. To avoid this fate, several parties withdrew their candidates in the weeks preceding the 1980 election.

All parties were dissolved after the 1980 military coup and the leaders of most of the leftist parties were either killed in the coup, imprisoned, or exiled.

Party Organization

Bolivian political parties are small, personalistic, loosely structured associations. Due to frequent periods of repression, most parties have little permanent organization. The parties have relatively few dues-paying members, but they can count on larger numbers of supporters during elections. The dominant characteristic of most current party leaders in Bolivia is that they all stem from the revolutionary period and from the original revolutionary party, the MNR. The splits and factions which have developed since the revolution stem largely from personal disputes among the leaders rather than from ideological differences.

Campaigning

In the 1980 elections, campaigning lasted only one month. All of the presidential candidates, except former president Hugo Banzer Suárez, suffered from a severe shortage of funds. In the period preceding the election, the military announced that an "extremist" government would not be acceptable and speculation on the possibility and timing of a coup was intense.

Authentic Revolutionary Party (*Partido Revolucionario Auténtico*; PRA)

One of the first revolutionary leaders to split with the MNR and the leadership of Victor Paz Estenssoro was Walter Guevara Arce (born 1912), who in 1960 formed the groups which became the PRA. Guevara felt that the MNR was becoming too socialist and feared the growing power of the unions. The PRA draws its strength from small businessmen and the middle class. In 1978, Guevara rejoined Paz Estenssoro as vice-presidential candidate of the MNR-H (Histórico) coalition and in 1979 participated in another MNR coalition. In 1979 when Congress was unable to choose between Paz Estenssoro and Siles Zuazo, Guevara Arce was selected as a compromise president. He ruled from August 6, 1979, until November 1, when he was overthrown in a military coup.

Bolivian Socialist Falange
(*Falange Socialista Boliviana*; FSB)

The Bolivian Socialist Falange was founded in 1937 in Chile by a group of Bolivian students seeking to emulate the fascist Spanish Falange. With the defeat of the Axis powers in 1945, the FSB dropped many of its overtly fascist trappings. The FSB has played an important role in Bolivian politics by serving as a rallying point for conservative interests. Drawing its strength primarily from the upper and middle classes, the FSB does not have a well-developed ideological base. During the years of MNR dominance, the FSB served as the only organized opposition group. The party suffered sporadic reprisals at the hands of the MNR and usually found an ally in the military. However, when Hugo Banzer Suárez took power in 1971, the FSB found itself in the short-lived government coalition which included the MNR. In 1978, the FSB split over whether or not to support the military's candidate for president since the government refused to allow the FSB to run its own candidate. The FSB is led by Dr. Mario Gutiérrez of Santa Cruz (born 1917) and has worked with the other small right-wing parties in the past. Members of the FSB served in the military government of General García Meza.

Leftist Nationalist Revolutionary Movement
(*Movimiento Nacionalista Revolucionario Izquierdo*; MNRI)

The most important split in the revolutionary party was between the two former presidents, Paz Estenssoro and Siles Zuazo (born 1914), who founded the MNRI in 1971. Siles opposed Paz's support of the Banzer government. In the elections of 1978, Paz and Siles were pitted against each other. In the 1979 and 1980 elections, the MNRI was the principal organization in the Democratic and Popular Unity coalition (*Unidad Democrática y Popular*; UDP). The UDP was more openly antimilitary than the MNR coalition and advocated more nationalistic policies and greater redistribution of wealth.

In 1978, Paz's forces apparently won a majority in the legislature, while Siles obtained the most votes for president. In the 1980 election, Siles Zuazo was the clear winner, receiving 34 percent of the vote to Paz's 18 percent. Siles Zuazo and his vice-presidential candidate, Jaime Paz Zamora of the Leftist Revolutionary Movement, currently are leading the oppositon from exile. They have formed a Government of National Unity as an opposition force to the current military government.

Nationalist Democratic Action
(*Acción Democrática Nacionalista*; ADN)

The ADN was formed in 1979 by former president Banzer who sought to continue his hold on government through his chosen ADN candidate, General Juan Perada Asbun. The ADN's inability to secure more support than either the UDP or the MNR coalition signaled the end of the brief military-peasant alliance which Banzer had tried to create during his regime.

National Revolutionary Movement
(*Movimiento Nacional Revolucionario*; MNR)

The MNR was founded in 1941 by Victor Paz Estenssoro (born 1907) and continues to be an important force in Bolivian politics. During the 1940s, the MNR developed a reformist ideology which incorporated socialist, indigenous, and nationalist philosophies. The MNR drew its leadership almost exclusively from the educated middle class, but sought to unite peasants and workers in a multiclass party.

When it came to power in 1952, the MNR moved to integrate the Indians (the majority of the population) into full citizenship, reform the agricultural system, nationalize the mines, develop the region of Santa Cruz, and implement other reforms. The MNR's policy toward the Indian population created a reservoir of loyalty among the peasants which continues to this day. The MNR sought to establish a revolutionary party in which key functional groups—labor, peasants, small business, etc.—would be integrated into corporatist party structures. These groups, however, were more effective in presenting their demands to government than in mobilizing support for the MNR regime. A declining economic situation, electoral fraud, the reluctance of Paz Estenssoro to leave office, and growing popular opposition to the party led the military to intervene in 1964. The party returned to government briefly from 1971 to 1973 when it supported Hugo Banzer Suárez. The consequent split between Paz and Siles has condemned the MNR to second-class status since then, and it continues to be regarded with deep suspicion by those who firmly oppose military intervention in politics.

Revolutionary Party of the Nationalist Left (*Partido Revolucionario de la Izquierda Nacionalista*; PRIN)

In late 1963, in a dispute over who would be the MNR's presidential candidate, Juan Lechín (born 1915), leader of the powerful mineworkers' union, withdrew from the MNR and formed the PRIN. This party has consistently advocated more leftist measures than either of the two center-left coalitions. The party draws its support from the trade unions and is very powerful in the mining regions.

Socialist Party-One (*Partido Socialista-Uno*; PS-1)

The Socialist Party was organized in 1971 as a small personalist party associated with former military president Ovando Candía. Under the leadership of Marcelo Quiroga Santa Cruz, it developed increasing strength in the elections of 1978, 1979, and 1980, receiving 15 percent of the vote in the 1980 election. The military opposed the PS-1, fearing its Marxist orientations, and the party's leadership, including Quiroga Santa Cruz, was killed in the 1980 military takeover. The PS-1 still exists underground, but nothing is know of its size or leadership.

Minor Parties

Christian Democratic Party (*Partido Demócrata Cristiano*; PDC)

A center-left Catholic party, factions of which supported the Banzer regime, the PDC supported the MNRH parties in the 1979 elections.

Committee of National Unity (*Comité de Unidad Nacional;* CUN)

An organization of moderate conservative business and technocrat groups formed in 1978.

Communist Party (*Partido Comunista Boliviano*; PCB)

A Moscow-line party established in 1952, the PCB has little appeal to the radical left because of its refusal to support popular revolutionary forces. It supported the UDP and Siles Zuazo in recent elections.

Leftist Revolutionary Movement (*Movimiento Izquierda Revolucionario*; MIR)

A Marxist party which split from the PDC, MIR supported the UDP in the last elections. One of its leaders, Jaime Paz Zamora, was Siles Zuazo's running mate in the 1980 elections.

Popular Christian Movement (*Movimiento Popular Cristiano*; MPC)

The MPC is a right-wing party originally created, in 1964, to support the presidential aspirations of René Barrientos.

National Barrientista Movement (*Movimiento Nacional Barrientista*; MNB)

The MNB is another right-wing party associated with the ideas of René Barrientos.

Social Democratic Party (*Partido Social Demócrata*; PSD)

A small party of middle-class intellectuals organized in 1945, the PSD supported the UDP until it was expelled in 1979 for failure to back the coalition fully.

Other Political Forces

Military

In 1952, following the revolution, the MNR forced the retirement of approximately 80 percent of the military's officers, and the armed forces as an institution was so weakened that it could no longer wielded significant political power. Military expenditures dropped from 23 percent of the budget in 1952 to 6.7 percent in 1957. In 1953, President Paz began a project to restore the military and give it a new image by encouraging its participation in civil-improvement activities such as public works projects. Members of the lower classes were also drawn into the military hierarchy at that time. By the late 1950s, however, the MNR was forced to restore the military to its former strength to defend the government against new worker and peasant militias. There are currently 22,500 men in the armed forces: 17,000 in the army, 4,000 in the air force, and 1,500 in the navy.

For the most part, military intervention in politics has followed rather predictable patterns. Conspiracies within the military to overthrow the government are commonplace and lead to direct intervention when economic and social order breaks down, when political leaders lack clear popular support, or when left-wing leaders *do* have clear popular support. Military leaders have generally sought to limit political activity by outlawing or suppressing political organizations, but brutal institutionalized repression so far has not been the norm.

The armed forces have been riddled with personalistic cliques, interservice rivalries, and ideological factions. The lack of institutional solidarity makes it difficult for any particular military leader to stay in power very long. In the 1980 overthrow of Lidia Gueiler, fighting broke out between army and navy units, reflecting their leaders' inability to agree on the nature and timing of the coup. Throughout 1981, the leadership of General García Meza was repeatedly challenged by military officers organizing forces to overthrow his government. García Meza responded by relieving some generals of their commands and by stationing others in isolated areas. Finally, in August 1981, the forces opposing García Meza were able to coalesce enough to force him to step down from the presidency. But he, like other former military leaders, undoubtedly will continue to influence current policies and seek to regain power in the future.

The fact that military leaders seek political power to further their own personal ambitions as well as to restore national order makes continuity in policies difficult. Leaders are unwilling to take unpopular economic measures which may provide an opportunity for rival military leaders to unite and form a new government. In other Latin American countries, permanent ministerial personnel and technical experts provide a degree of continuity in spite of changes in leadership, but in Bolivia, these functionaries usually are replaced following a coup. During difficult negotiations with the International Monetary Fund in 1981, for example, the Bolivian government finally announced that there simply was no representative available to represent the Bolivian position in the negotiations.

Corruption in the armed forces weakens the institution's credibility and morale. Fear of civilian investigations into alleged corruption in the Banzer regime was a key factor in the military's decision not to allow a return to civilian rule. Charges of drug trafficking have plagued the military regimes since then.

Morale is reportedly low among enlisted personnel. The troops usually are drawn from the lower classes and experience personal conflict when used to put down popular uprisings. In August 1980, eighty members of one army regiment reportedly were shot for refusing to fire on striking mineworkers in Corocoro. About the same time, three truckloads of troops deserted their posts near La Paz after reportedly killing their officers.

Organized Labor

Urban labor unions began among Bolivia's mineworkers in the 1920s and were an important part of the revolutionary movement which brought the MNR to power in 1952. The strongest single union was the mineworkers' (*Federación Sindical de Trabajadores Mineros Bolivianos*; FSTMB) under the leadership of Juan Lechín. Labor unions and, to a lesser extent, rural peasant unions were organized into the Confederation of Bolivian Workers (*Confederación de Obreros Bolivianos*; COB), the single most important component of the revolutionary government. During the early years of that government, the COB obtained a system of cogovernment which gave the unions veto power over important decisions and power to directly name the ministers of mines, labor, public works, and peasant affairs.

Much of the labor sector split with MNR in the early 1960s as the result of arguments over whether Lechín or Paz should be the party's nominee in 1963. Paz ended up with the nomination, Lechín left the party, and the military soon stepped in. Under the Barrientos regime, the military invaded the mines, destroyed the unions and worker militias, and supplanted the COB with a more acquiescent group of labor leaders. The military regimes since that time have sought both to repress the labor movement and to incorporate it into government-controlled groups. The 1980 coup was opposed violently and vigorously by labor, which staged strikes and seized highways. The military put down this dissent with an unusual degree of repression; labor unions have either been outlawed or suppressed since then. Juan Lechín was imprisoned and then sent into exile.

Although peasants were virtually excluded from political participation before the 1952 revolution, they have exercised, albeit intermittently, some power since then. The rural peasant unions were extremely important in the period following the revolution and served as a vital link between national political leaders and isolated rural areas. By the early 1960s, the National Confederation of Rural Workers of Bolivia (*Confederación Sindical Unica de Trabajadores Campesinos de Bolivia*; CSUTCB) claimed two million members. Under military government, peasant unity and power declined, although military leaders sought peasant support. General Banzer, in particular, was very astute in organizing peasant unions which were responsive to his personal leadership and supportive of MNR, but the peasants had minimal impact on the government. The peasant unions supported a return to democratic rule and bitterly opposed the military coups of 1979 and 1980. Following the 1980 coup, the leader of the CSUTCB, Genaro Flores, was the highest-ranking labor leader at large in the country until his capture by the government in June of 1981.

Roman Catholic Church

Traditionally the Roman Catholic Church has played only a minor role in Bolivian politics. However, since the 1980 military coup, it has become more involved. Archbishop Jorge Manrique of La Paz set up an office to help political prisoners and their families, and church leaders have attempted to mediate conflicts among military leaders. In 1980 and 1981, the government on several occasions closed down the offices of a Catholic newspaper in La Paz, *Presencia*. Although its power is limited, particularly in comparison with the Church in other Latin American nations, the Bolivian Church remains the principal opposition force to the military.

National Prospects

The principal political issue in Bolivia is the question of rescheduling the nation's massive foreign debt. Approximately 60 percent of the nation's export earnings is needed to service the debt. Agreement with the International Monetary Fund, a prerequisite to renegotiating the debt with private bankers, requires the imposition of austerity measures which are extremely unpopular with the peasants and workers. A government already unsure of its political support is reluctant to impose such measures. The larger questions of development—such as agricultural reform, international investment, and industrial development—are overshadowed by the country's precarious financial position and by the recurrent political instability. The recurring separatist movement in Santa Cruz, efforts to obtain a corridor to the Pacific Ocean through negotiations with Chile and Peru, and corruption in government are other principal difficulties faced by the nation. The United States broke off relations with Bolivia following the 1980 coup, and did not restore them until the fall of 1981 due to Bolivia's inability (or unwillingness) to reduce cocaine production and to prosecute drug dealers.

Continued political instability and authoritarian rule seem to be Bolivia's certain prospects in the coming years. The nation is in such economic difficulties that there seems to be little possibility that Bolivia can meet its obligations to the international financial system and also meet the demands of the underprivileged. Both the aspirations and the political muscle of groups previously excluded from political participation have increased since 1952, but after seventeen years of military rule, the forces favoring democracy are fragmented and isolated. The lack of a unified military and the difficulty in putting together a military government that has the support of most factions in the armed forces make it unlikely that even military regimes will be long lasting.

Further Reading

Malloy, James. *Bolivia: The Uncompleted Revolution*. Pittsburgh, Pa.: University of Pittsburgh Press, 1970.

——— and Thorn, Richard, eds. *Beyond the Revolution: Bolivia Since 1952*. Pittsburgh, Pa.: University of Pittsburgh Press, 1971.

Mitchell, Christopher. *The Legacy of Populism in Bolivia: From the MNR to Military Rule*. New York: Praeger Special Studies, 1977.

———."The New Authoritarianism in Bolivia." *Current History*, February 1981.

REPUBLIC OF BOTSWANA

by Jack Parson, Ph.D.

The System of Government

Botswana, a country of 820,000 people just north of South Africa, is a parliamentary republic and unitary state. Formerly the British protectorate of Bechuanaland, the country became fully independent on September 30, 1966. The first president, from independence until his death in 1980, was Sir Seretse Khama. He was succeeded by Quett Masire, formerly vice president.

Leading external entities which must be taken into account in Botswana's political system are mining companies and South Africa. Botswana imports most of its goods from or through its powerful neighbor to the south and some 45,000 Botswana nationals work in South Africa on short-term contracts. The Anglo-American Corporation of South Africa, together with the American Metal Climax Corporation (AMAX), operate a copper-nickel mine; and the DeBeers Diamond Mining Company, a subsidiary of Anglo-American, operates three diamond mines in Botswana. These mines provide the base for Botswana's development expenditure. The government has a significant shareholding in the mines and must take their operations into account when formulating policy.

Executive

Executive power is vested in the president. At the time of their nomination, National Assembly candidates declare their support for a presidential nominee. Whichever presidential candidate has majority support in the Assembly after the election becomes president. Presidential nominees have been leaders of their respective parties, but this is not required by law.

The president is assisted by a cabinet drawn largely, but not exclusively, from the Assembly. Members of the cabinet are individually responsible to the president and National Assembly. The president has significant authority, including the power to dissolve the Assembly. All bills dealing with raising revenue must have his assent to be introduced.

Legislature

Legislative power is vested in a Parliament composed of the president and National Assembly. The Assembly is made up of thirty-two directly elected members, the attorney general, a speaker, and four specially elected members. The special members are nominated by the president and chosen by the elected members of the Assembly, who may also nominate candidates for the special seats.

Judiciary

The judicial system is composed of customary and statutory courts. Customary courts are presided over by chiefs and exercise minor powers, most significantly in cases of cattle theft. Common law courts include magistrates courts, circuit courts of appeal, and the High Court, located in Lobatse.

Regional & Local Government

Local government consists of nine district and four town councils, created by Parliament, each with an elected governing body. The councils have the basic responsibility for providing primary education, licensing, and collecting local-government taxes. They also play a role in development planning and expenditure. National supervision of local government is organized and coordinated by the Ministry of Local Government and Lands through its officers, particularly the district commissioners, and through district development committees and land boards.

Each of the eight principal tribes are headed by a chief and each has a statutory body of headmen. These parallel the local and national governments. However, the chiefs and headmen are now under the jurisdiction of national government and have no independent power. Chiefs play a significant role on district councils and land boards, as well as through the holding of public meetings (*kgotla*) and the exercise of minor judicial functions.

RESULTS OF 1979 ELECTIONS

Party	Number of Seats Won	% of Votes	Number of Votes Cast
Botswana Democratic Party (BDP)	29	75.2	101,098
Botswana National Front (BNF)	2	13.0	17,480
Botswana Peoples' Party (BPP)	1	7.4	9,983
Botswana Independent Party (BIP)	0	4.2	5,657

The Electoral System

Elections for local councils and the Assembly, in single-member districts with plurality winners, must be held at least once every five years. These elections are competitive and conducted in an open way, free from all but insignificant forms of manipulation and corruption. The ballot is secret. Suffrage is extended to all citizens twenty-one years of age and older. Voter turnout in 1979 was 58.4 percent of those registered. General elections were held in 1969, 1974, and 1979.

The Party System

Botswana has a multiparty system dominated by one party, the Botswana Democratic Party. Four political parties are registered and carry on political activities. Of the four only the Botswana Democratic Party is well organized nationally. The other three are mainly regional parties, although the Botswana National Front does hold regular meetings outside its regional base, mainly in urban areas.

Botswana Democratic Party (BDP)

History & Organization

Founded in 1962, the BDP has held the vast majority of seats in the Assembly and overall in the councils, although it has not always had an elected majority in every council. It has a nominal grass-roots organization, but it functions as an entity mainly during election campaigns. The party's members in Parliament have significant power in their districts and hold primary responsibility for district party organization. The day-to-day work of the party is conducted by the party's parliamentary caucus and at an annual general meeting. National headquarters are at Tsholetsa House, Gaborone.

Policy

The policies of the BDP are moderate. It advocates a mixed economy, the role of government being that of stimulating private enterprise. Its goals include maximizing mining revenues to reinvest in agricultural and industrial growth.

Membership & Constituency

The party's primary supporters are the community of private businesspeople, mainly foreign, organized in the Botswana Employers Federation; a small trade-union movement; and large-scale cattle owners. Many of the last group are members of district councils and the National Assembly and exercise considerable power through their ability to mobilize the populations of rurual areas.

Financing

The BDP is financed through dues, contributions, and rent from offices in its headquarters building. Its resources are limited and reach significant levels only during election campaigns.

Leadership

The party leader is president Quett Masire (born 1926) whose personal power derives from his long association with the first president, Seretse Khama, and his tenure as vice president and minister of finance and development planning. Other prominent leaders include Daniel Kwelagobe, M. Nwako, and L. Seretse.

Minor Parties

Botswana Independence Party (BIP)

The creation of M. Mpho, the BIP is most active in the northwest among the Bayei. Its appeal has been based on the historial subordination of the Bayei to the BaTawana.

Botswana National Front (BNF)

Nominally socialist, the BNF was founded by Kenneth Koma in 1965. Its supporters are primarily the urban working class. It also has a regional base in the BaNgwaketse area around the personality of ex-chief Bathoen Gaseitsiwe.

Botswana Peoples' Party (BPP)

The BPP has its primary strength among minorities in northeast Botswana. Associated with the personality of P. G. Matante until his death in 1981, the party is now nominally led by K. M. Nkhwa.

Other Political Forces

Civil Service

Some 2,000 civil servants, among them a significant number of foreigners (English and American), play a role in policy making, particularly in the "senior" ministries: the Office of the President, incorporating the Directorate of Personnel; and the Ministry of Finance and Development Planning.

National Prospects

Despite signs of tension over land and cattle, Botswana's nearly unique stability, resting on the connection made between an educated and economic elite in the BDP and the mass of the population, will probably be maintained. The electoral strength of the BDP shows no sign of being seriously challenged. However, Botswana's future is closely tied to the changing situation of southern Africa and particularly to the fate of South Africa.

Further Reading
Carter, Gwendolen and Morgan, E. Phillip, eds. *From the Frontline: The Speeches of Sir Seretse Khama.* London: Rex Collings, 1980.
Colclough, Christopher and McCarthy, Stephen. *The Political Economy of Botswana: A Study of Growth and Distribution.* London: Oxford University Press, 1980.
Morgan, E. Phillip. "Botswana: Democratic Politics and Development." In *Sourthern Africa in Crisis.* Gwendolen Carter and Patrick O'Meara, eds. Bloomington, Ind.: Indiana University Press, 1977.
Parson, Jack. *Botswana: An Introduction.* Boulder, Colo.: Westview Press, 1983.

FEDERATIVE REPUBLIC OF BRAZIL
(*República Federativa do Brasil*)
by Ronald H. Chilcote, Ph.D., and Terrie R. Groth

The System of Government

A federal system of twenty-three states, three territories, and a federal district, Brazil, a nation of over 123 million people, has alternated between authoritarian military rule and parliamentary democracy. Since 1964, the military has dominated the office of the president. The military has nominated the sole candidate for president, who was then approved by an electoral college. These military presidents were Humberto Castello Branco (1964), Artur da Costa e Silva (1967), Emílio Garrastazú Médici (1969), Ernesto Geisel (1974), and João Baptista Figueiredo (1979).

Since 1979, initiatives in the direction of an *abertura* or democratic "opening" provided for elections to Congress, state governors, and to municipal offices in 1982 and for president in 1985.

Executive

Under the constitution, the power granted to the president allows his dominance over the legislative and judicial branches of government. He is the supreme commander of the armed forces, issues decrees and regulations implementing existing legislation, may declare a state of emergency, prepares and executes a national budget, proposes legislation to Congress, and appoints and removes cabinet ministers as well as the governors of the Federal District and Federal Territories. The president also usually wields influence over a major party.

In addition the military government imposed several institutional acts which expanded the president's powers. The first act (April 9, 1964) permitted the president to cancel the mandates of elected members of Congress, state assemblies, and municipal councils. Another act (October 27, 1965) allowed the president to suspend Congress, dismiss elected officials, and deprive a citizen of political rights for up to ten years. A new constitution, promulgated January 24, 1967, expanded press censorship and permitted federal interven-

tion in state government. The powers of the presidency continued to be expanded until 1974, when popular pressures induced the Geisel administration to adopt a strategy of *distensão* (liberalization) and *descompressão* (easing).

Presidents since 1965 have been indirectly elected (currently to six-year terms) and were not immediately eligible for reelection. In the 1982 elections, the government party won enough Electoral College seats to ensure its control of the presidential election in 1985.

Legislature

The National Congress consists of a Chamber of Deputies and a Senate. As of early 1982, the Chamber had 420 members (increasing to 479 in the 1982 elections) elected for a term of four years and representing each of the states and territories in proportion to population. There were sixty-seven members of the Senate (increasing to sixty-nine with the admission of Rondônia as a state), three from each state and one holdover from the fusion of two states in 1975. Senators are elected for a term of eight years, with elections every four years, alternately for one-third and two-thirds of the members.

The powers of Congress include participation in the Electoral College for selection of the president and vice president and approval of legislation, budgets, taxes, treaties, etc. The memberships of the Chamber and the Senate each elect a president, two vice presidents, and four secretaries. Each house has twelve permanent committees with membership ranging from five to thirty-seven in the Chamber and three to fifteen in the Senate. Under military rule, both houses have been controlled by the official National Renovating Alliance (*Aliança Renovadora Nacional;* ARENA) with the Brazilian Democratic Movement (*Movimento Democrático Brasileiro;* MDB) in opposition.

Unofficial returns from the November 15, 1982, elections gave the four new opposition parties 245

LEGISLATIVE ELECTION RESULTS (1966–1978)

Years	Federal Senate				Chamber of Deputies				State Assemblies			
	% of Votes				% of Votes				% of Votes			
	ARENA	MDB	Blank & Null Votes	Total	ARENA	MDB	Blank & Null Votes	Total	ARENA	MDB	Blank & Null Votes	Total
1966	44.7	34.2	21.2	17,259,598	50.5	28.4	21.0	17,285,556	52.2	29.2	18.6	17,260,382
1970	43.7	28.6	27.7	46,986,492	48.4	21.3	30.3	22,435,521	51.0	22.0	26.8	22,435,521
1974	34.7	50.0	15.1	28,981,110	40.9	37.8	21.3	28,981,015	42.1	38.8	18.9	28,922,618
1978	35.0	46.4	18.6	37,775,212	40.0	39.3	20.7	37,629,180	41.1	39.6	19.3	37,449,488

LEGISLATIVE ELECTION RESULTS (1966–1978) BY REGION

Regions	Years	% of Votes			Total
		ARENA	MDB	Blank & Null Votes	
North	1966	60.0	18.8	21.2	431,682
	1970	45.4	21.9	32.7	551,525
	1974	45.3	30.7	24.0	826,632
	1978	44.1	30.4	25.5	1,272,326
Northeast	1966	67.8	20.3	11.9	3,819,040
	1970	55.4	16.5	28.1	5,037,464
	1974	59.2	20.4	20.3	6,370,642
	1978	57.8	22.1	20.1	8,677,800
Central-West	1966	54.0	27.6	18.4	675,094
	1970	49.9	22.4	27.7	913,941
	1974	50.3	27.9	21.8	1,284,454
	1978	46.2	34.2	19.6	1,819,817
Southeast	1966	40.8	31.7	27.5	8,977,985
	1970	44.4	21.4	34.2	11,389,252
	1974	32.8	44.4	22.8	14,638,221
	1978	29.7	47.9	22.4	18,662,465
South	1966	55.0	30.2	14.8	3,381,755
	1970	51.0	26.0	23.0	4,543,489
	1974	38.7	43.4	17.9	5,861,066
	1978	43.0	40.8	16.2	7,196,772

Sources: Tribunal Superior Eleitoral, and Maria D'Alva Gil Kinzo, "Novos Partidos: O Início do Debate," in Bolivar Lamounier, (org.), Voto de Desconfiança: Eleições e Mudança Política no Brasil: 1970–1979. São Paulo, 1980, pp. 223 (top) and 225 (bottom).

of the Chamber's 479 seats and twenty-three Senate seats.

Judiciary

Judicial power is exercised through the federal Supreme Court, federal appeals courts, military courts, electoral courts, and labor courts. The Supreme Court, located in Brasilia, is composed of sixteen judges appointed by the president and approved by the Senate.

Prior to 1937, a dual system of federal and state courts prevailed, but today the court system is integrated with the Supreme Court as the highest court. It has jurisdiction over common crimes committed by the president, attorney general, and its own members; over conflicts between a state government and the federal government or between state governments; over litigation between the government and a foreign nation; and over some other matters.

In certain instances, for example the pretext of national security after the 1964 coup, the jurisdiction of the military courts has been extended to civilians.

Regional & Local Government

Each of the twenty-three states has a constitution, generally modeled after the federal constitution. Under the military regime, each state's governor was nominated by the president and elected to a four-year term by an electoral college, consisting of members of the state legislature and representatives of municipal councils. Governors were directly elected in late 1982. Each state has a unicameral legislature whose membership varies (from a low of fifteen in Acre to a high of 115 in São Paulo).

In the 1982 elections, the opposition parties won the governorships of eleven states, putting 60 percent of Brazilian territory and 58 percent of the population under opposition governments. The government party won in Pernambuco and Rio Grande do Sul, states once considered firmly in the opposition camp, but it lost in Acre, Pará, and Mato Grosso do Sul, where government victories had been expected. The opposition parties also won in the large industrial states of Minas Gerais, Rio de Janeiro, and São Paulo.

The territorial governments of Amapá, Roraima, and Fernando de Noronha are administered by governors appointed by the president. Fernando de Noronha, an archipelago off the northeast coast, is a military dependency and has no representative in the Chamber of Deputies.

The Federal District, consisting of 2,400 square miles in eastern Goiás, has a limited form of self-government with a governor appointed by and directly responsible to the president.

There are more than 3,000 municipalities, the unit of local government. Elections for city councils are based on proportional representation. A party wins seats in proportion to the size of its vote, and individual candidates are seated on the basis of the number of votes they won for their party.

The 1946 constitution provided for decentralization of administrative procedures and allowed for some flexibility and autonomy in organization according to local needs. Theoretically, the range of functions at the local level was similar to that at the state level, yet state and federal governments were reluctant to provide municipalities with sufficient resources.

The 1967 constitution reduced the autonomy of municipalities. They were permitted to elect their mayors and councilmen, to collect some taxes, and to organize local affairs according to needs, but these activities were usually subject to close scrutiny by military officers residing in the local area as well as by government officials in the state and federal capitals. The municipalities were subject to intervention where financial obligations were not met. There were regulations concerning the scheduling of elections and controls on municipal budgets.

The Electoral System

Members of legislative bodies are elected directly by a simple proportional representation system: the percentage of seats won is in direct ratio to the percentage of the vote a party receives. For elections to Congress and state legislatures, each state is one multimember electoral district in which candidates compete at large. Municipalities also constitute single districts for municipal council elections. All candidates must appear on official party lists; no independent lists are permitted.

In 1982, elections for mayors, governors, and all legislative bodies took place at the same time, but because mayoral and municipal council terms have been lengthened to six years, local elections will not coincide with the state and federal elections in 1986. Another change planned for 1986 is the election of half the Chamber of Deputies in single-member districts.

Representation in proportion to population has worked to the disadvantage of some of the more populous states. Each state is entitled to one federal deputy for every 300,000 persons up to twenty-five deputies and to one additional seat for every one million inhabitants thereafter. Consequently, the states of São Paulo, Mina Gerais, Rio de Janeiro, Paraná, and Rio Grande do Sul, which together contain 60 percent of the country's population, have considerably less than 60 percent of the Chamber's seats.

In 1985, the presidential Electoral College will consist of the entire Congress and six representatives from each state legislature chosen by the majority party in each legislature.

All Brazilians between the ages of eighteen and sixty-five are required to vote, but there is little enforcement of the compulsory rule. In the 1982 elections, voters were required to write in the names or numbers of one party's candidates. In the past, voters had been able to vote either for a straight party list or for individual candidates and could vote for different parties for local, state, and federal offices.

The Party System

Origins of the Parties

Historically, and to some extent today, the Brazilian political system was built on the power of the local landowner or political boss. Known as *coronelismo*, this patron-client system thrived in rural areas where the electorate tended to be illiterate, impoverished, and dispersed. During the empire (1822–89), elections were controlled by local political chiefs; cooperative arrangements between them and the central government in Rio de Janeiro were necessary to assure support for the government, fair distribution of government resources and patronage, and the avoidance of violence. During this period, the electorate constituted less than 1 percent of the population and was determined by the ruling rural families. The political class of each region thus controlled the electoral system. Eventually, the ruling class organized its national political interests around two parties located in Rio de Janeiro—the Liberal and Conservative parties.

Under the Old Republic (1889–1930), some accommodation between local power and federal authority was established despite efforts to grant greater autonomy to the states. The political problem remained of resolving the remaining discrepancies in power between the weak national administration in Rio de Janeiro and the stronger political forces in the states, especially São Paulo,

Minas Gerais, Rio Grande do Sul, and powerful forces in the interior. Well into the twentieth century, the dominant clans controlled the electoral system and bartered their blocks of votes to state and national leaders.

With the political system in the hands of a few men centered in São Paulo and the south, opposition to this oligarchy developed in the states of the northeast and especially in Rio Grande do Sul in the south. Disaffected younger army officers, known as *tenetes* or lieutenants, led an abortive revolt at the Copacabana fort in Rio de Janeiro in July 1922, later joining with the opposition in occupying the city of São Paulo from July 9 to 27, 1924. Forced to retreat, the rebels formed the Prestes Column, led by Luís Carlos Prestes, and began a two-year march of 14,000 miles through the interior. The revolts and the march symbolized the opposition to the ruling oligarchy and a desire for a more democratic order. Further, the *tenentes* were able to usher Getúlio Vargas into power after declaring the 1930 elections fraudulent.

Under Vargas during the early thirties, there were two major attempts to organize politics on a national level. The first of these political movements was known as Brazilian Integralist Action (*Acão Integralista Brasileira;* AIB), formed in 1932 under Plínio Salgado and modeled after European fascism. The *Integralistas* stressed organic unity and nationalism, discipline and order, and eventually influenced Vargas to consolidate his regime under the New State (*Estado Novo*) and a corporatist constitution which denied the possibility of representative and popularly elected government. The second of the movements was known as the National Liberation Alliance (*Aliança Nacional Libertadora;* ANL), established in 1935 under Prestes as a popular-front organization along lines advocated by the Communist International. The ANL aimed to fight fascism and mobilize liberal and progressive elements along with the growing labor movement. After abortive revolts during November 23 to November 27 in Rio de Janeiro, Recife, and Natal—planned principally by communist leaders—Vargas repressed the ANL and arrested thousands of ANL and communist leaders; Prestes was imprisoned until 1945. In 1937, Vargas dismantled the AIB and all other parties.

In 1945 Vargas left office under pressure from the army. Immediately, an array of superficially organized political parties appeared, and Brazil entered an era of representative or bourgeois democracy. Six presidents came to power through popular elections: General Eurico Dutra (1946–

50); Getúlio Vargas (1951 until his suicide in 1954); João Café Filho (1954–55); Juscelino Kubitschek (1956–61); Jânio Quadros (1961 until his resignation in August); João Goulart (1961 as succeeding vice president under new rules that shifted power to a prime minister). Goulart regained full presidential power after a 1963 plebiscite, but was ousted by the military in April 1964.

Thirteen parties were represented in the system from 1945 to 1964. Three of them—a labor party, a social-democratic party, and a center-conservative party—came close to being truly national parties although each was constituted by a loose coalition of regional interests. The only party organized around a clear set of ideas and structures at a national level appeared to be the communist party, which operated clandestinely except for a brief period of legality from 1945 to 1947. Even the spirit of nationalism and sentiment against outside capitalist influence and imperialism was not accompanied by the emergence of any significant legal popular party of national scope. Brazilian parties in large measure were formed in the tradition of regional entities, organized around personalist leadership with links to local *coronelismo* and the patriarchical families of the interior.

In order to understand the evolution of political parties after 1964, it is essential to identify the parties during the previous periods of bourgeois democracy from 1945 to 1964. The influence of these parties was to continue through the period of military rule and even into the period of reformulation of party structure that began in the late seventies and carried into the early eighties.

The Brazilian Labor Party (*Partido Trabalhista Brasileiro;* PTB) was originally formed in 1945 in support of Vargas as a rival of the PCB in labor circles; the party included urban labor as well as some wealthy individuals. Its center of support was in Rio Grande do Sul, but it was also influential in Rio de Janeiro, Bahia, and Paraná states. The party had conservative, moderate, and radical elements and was beset by ideological and personal factionalism. Nationalism was the main cohesive element in the party. Its leadership included João Goulart, Leonel Brizola, Almino Afonso, Miguel Arraes. After 1964 it supported the MDB opposition until 1979 when it reemerged under Ivette Vargas.

The Social Democratic Party (*Partido Social Democrático;* PSD) was established in 1945 in support of Getúlio Vargas, the PSD combined moderate and conservative elements. It was primarily a coalition of state machines with ties to major politicians and rural landowners in some local areas. The PSD held substantial representation in Congress and with Dutra and Kubitschek gained the presidency. It tended toward pragmatic compromise in its relations with the government and other major parties. Its leadership also included Amaral Peixoto, Ranieri Mazzilli, and Auro Moura Andrade. Its strength was in Minas Gerais.

The National Democratic Union (*União Democrática Nacional;* UDN) was formed in 1945 as an anti-Vargas coalition of politicians, military, and professional men, the UDN successfully backed Quadros for the presidency in 1960, and was the second leading party until 1964. Its strength was in Minas Gerais, Bahia, Santa Catarina, and the northeast. It was backed by center-conservative and commercial and industrial interests. It was supportive of the military regime. Among its leaders were Carlos Lacerda, Magalhães Pinto, and Juracy Magalhães. Most members of the UND joined the ARENA after 1964 and the PDS after 1979.

The Social Progressive Party (*Partido Social Progressista;* PSP) was an amalgamation of three splinter parties under Governor Adhemar de Barros of São Paulo, known for his personalism and corruption. Considered a conservative and populist party, its main strength was in São Paulo, although in 1962 it elected twenty-three deputies in eight states.

The Christian Democratic Party (*Partido Democrata Cristão;* PDC) was founded in 1948 as a reformist party with connections to the international Christian Democratic movement. The PDC's ideological platform included the thrust of the *Mater et Magistra* papal encyclical. It supported Jânio Quadros in 1960. In 1962, the PDC elected nineteen federal deputies and with 5.7 percent of the vote became the fourth-ranked party. Its leadership included Paulo de Tarso, leader of the leftist faction, Juárez Tavora, Ney Braga, and Franco Montoro. Generally, it supported the military regime after 1964.

The National Labor Party (*Partido Trabalhista Nacional;* PTN) elected six deputies in São Paulo and a total of eleven throughout Brazil in 1963. It supported Quadros in 1954 and 1960. Its leadership included Emilio Carlos.

The Social Labor Party (*Partido Social Trabalhista;* PST) was a small party of uncertain ideology. Its members tended to side with ARENA in the post-1964 period.

The Republican Party (*Partido Republicano;* PR), with roots going back to the 1870s and the Old Republic, was conservative and nationalist in outlook after 1945. It received between 4 and 6 percent of the vote in elections from 1954 to 1962

PARTY AFFILIATIONS OF FEDERAL DEPUTIES (1963–1982)

Parties pre-1966	1963–65	1966–67			1967–71			1971–75			1975–79			1979–82		
		ARENA	MDB	Total	ARENA	MDB	Total	ARENA	MDB	Total	ARENA	MDB	Total	ARENA	MDB	Total
1 PTB	119	34	75	109	34	50	84	17	32	49	13	42	55	16	36	52
2 PSD	118	80	44	124	83	39	122	52	22	74	64	28	92	60	37	97
3 UDN	91	84	10	94	105	14	119	79	8	87	69	14	83	70	13	83
4 PSP	21	20	4	24	13	8	21	12	4	16	8	6	14	9	7	16
5 PDC	20	15	5	20	18	5	23	16	3	19	13	5	18	14	8	22
6 PTN	11	8	5	13	6	7	13	3	5	8	—	5	5	1	3	4
7 PST	7	3	1	4	1	2	3	2	—	2	—	3	3	2	—	2
8 PR	4	4	—	4	4	—	6	8	2	10	10	3	13	10	3	13
9 PL	5	3	—	3	4	2	6	3	—	3	3	—	3	—	—	—
10 PRP	5	6	—	6	4	—	4	3	—	3	3	—	3	4	—	4
11 PSB	5	1	2	3	2	1	3	2	2	4	1	2	3	1	4	5
12 PRT	3	2	2	4	1	—	1	2	—	2	2	2	4	2	2	4
Total	409	260	148	408	275	128	403	199	78	277	186	110	296	189	113	302
Other	—	—	—	1	1	5	6	25	8	33	18	50	68	42	76	118
Total	409	260	148	409	276	133	409	224	86	310	204	160	364	231	189	420

Source: David V. Fleischer, "Evolucão do bipartidarismo brasileiro 1966–1979," Revista Brasileira de Estudos Politicos, No. 51, July 1980, p. 160. A forthcoming book by Fleischer and Robert Wesson, to be published by Praeger, will contain an important analysis presently available only in Brazilian journals. That analysis has been invaluable in preparing this article.

with particular strength in Bahia and Minas Gerais. In 1962 it elected ten deputies.

The Liberation Party (*Partido Libertador;* PL) was a pre-Vargas party founded to advocate secret ballots and parliamentary government. With less than 2 percent of the vote, it elected five seats in the Chamber of Deputies in 1962. Its strength was in Rio Grande do Sul under Raúl Pilla, an intellectual of that state.

The Popular Representation Party (*Partido de Representação Popular;* PRP) was an extreme rightist party that evolved from the Integralist movement of the 1930s. The PRP was led by the former Integralist leader, Plínio Salgado, who organized the PRP in 1945. It advocated a corporative state and claimed to be anticommunist and antiliberal. Its strength was in São Paulo and Rio Grande do Sul.

The Brazilian Socialist Party (*Partido Socialista Brasileiro;* PSB), formed in 1946 out of the left wing of the UDN, comprised disparate elements. It never won more than 3 percent of the vote between 1954 and 1962. Its leadership included Francisco Julião, deputy from Pernambuco and leader of the Peasant Leagues during the early 1960s.

The Republican Labor Party (*Partido Republicano Trabalhista;* PRT) gained a small congressional representation in 1962 through electoral alliances and pulled 1.8 percent of the vote for federal deputies, especially in São Paulo and Rio de Janeiro states.

The Brazilian Communist Party (*Partido Comunista Brasileiro;* PCB), founded in 1922, led an abortive uprising in November 1935 and was repressed until 1945 when it became legal. It participated in the December 1945 elections, winning fifteen seats in the Chamber and one in the Senate. Although outlawed in May 1947, the party remained openly active until 1964 when it went underground. Its leadership included Luís Carlos Prestes.

On April 9, 1964, thirty-nine deputies and one senator were deprived of their political rights, and a few days later several hundred more politicians were purged from the system. Changes were made in the electoral code to ensure that candidates acceptable to the military would be elected. Constraints were placed on party activity and the number of eligible parties was reduced. The institutional act of October 27, 1965, dissolved the political parties; ended direct elections for the presidency; and established a new, two-party system. The official government party, ARENA, absorbed most of the UDN and the PSD and some smaller parties, while the opposition group, the MDB, was

made up of the PTB and remnants of other parties. The military government continued to exercise its power to oust elected members of Congress under the institutional act of December 13, 1968; many MDB deputies were removed in late 1968 and 1969.

The two-party system established by the government was new to Brazil, except in the state of Rio Grande do Sul where a tradition of two rival parties had prevailed since the Old Republic and the ARENA and MDB could be founded on past legacies. At the national level, the system permitted only minor opposition skirmishes with the military government.

The moderate success of the MDB in the elections of 1974, especially in the south and southeast, required a shift in the government control of the political system. Once ARENA lost total control in the Congress, President Geisel was compelled (in April 1977) to change the constitution to permit amendments by simple majority rather than a two-thirds vote. The international petroleum crisis of 1973 had brought an end to rapid economic growth, resulting in further controls on the economy and pressures on the business community. In May 1978, the first labor strikes in nearly a decade were initiated in São Paulo, the major industrial area. In March 1979, President Figueiredo took office with a promise to restore democracy. In August an amnesty bill became law, and in November the two-party system was abandoned. In March 1980, the government promised direct elections for state governors in 1982 and repealed the 1968 institutional act.

The Brazilian Democratic Movement (*Movimento Democrático Brasileiro;* MDB), created largely from members of the original PTB and dissident remnants of other parties, was to play the role of a "responsible opposition." As increasingly vocal critics of the military regimes during the 1960s, MDB members suffered *cassações* (suspension or cancellation of political rights) under Castello Branco and Costa e Silva; some 20 percent of the MDB congressional representatives were purged prior to the November 1966 elections. Its leaders included Freitas Nobre, Marcos Freire, Jarbas Vasconcellos, Ulysses Guimarães, and Franco Montoro. Congressional representatives tended to divide into a right wing of *adhesionistas* (collaborators with the government), a group of moderates, and a radical wing of *autênticos* (authentic opposition).

By 1969, the party leadership had been seriously weakened by government purges. In the 1970 elections, electoral manipulation brought the MDB to its lowest point. Four years later, with sentiment favoring the MDB, direct elections for state governors were cancelled. However, in the Congressional elections of November 1974, the MDB won sixteen of twenty-two available Senate seats and increased its number of deputies from eighty-six to 160. The party successfully channeled the opposition vote and campaigned against null voting. In the state legislative elections, it received 50 percent of the vote and won majorities in six states, including São Paulo, Rio Grande do Sul, and Rio de Janeiro. As the *distensão* of Geisel slowed, further *cassações* and government pronouncements cooled MDB political activity in 1976. Further manipulations of the system guaranteed the government a majority party in the November 1978 elections. While the MDB outpolled the ARENA in votes for senators, it won only eight seats in contrast to sixteen for ARENA, further, since a third of the Senate seats were chosen by special electoral colleges in each state, ARENA won twenty-one of those twenty-two seats. In the Chamber, ARENA won 231 seats compared to 189 seats for the MDB, even though its margin of votes was less than 2 percent.

The primary political program of the MDB was to end rule by the military and return to a pluralist democratic electoral system and a state of law. The party favored repeal of all repressive legislation, general amnesty for political exiles, control of national resources and multinational corporations, and other economic measures that would lessen foreign dependency. Among fundamental principles advocated by the party were defense of human rights; right to participation; involvement in base communities; establishment of a democratic state; and economic development that would concentrate on meeting social needs, not on growth for growth's sake.

The National Renovating Alliance (*Aliança Renovadora Nacional;* ARENA), formed by nearly all former UDN and most former PSD members, was conceived as parliamentary support for the military regime. However, it was not always a mere front organization. Castello Branco had to replace some recalcitrant ARENA state governors, and some ARENA members of Congress tried to dissociate themselves from the image or performance of the regime as early as the first postcoup elections in 1966. About ninety also voted against the *cassação* of MDB Deputy Márcio Moreira Alves in December 1968, and some ARENA members lost their political rights in 1969. Under Médici, ARENA party conventions ratified presidential choices for state governors.

While ARENA political platforms contained many of the same objectives and similar language

as those of the MDB, the role of the party was clearly to approve legislation submitted by the Brazilian executive. The party program called for the implementation of representative democracy; economic development in the direction of increased production, and growth as well as changes in social sectors such as health, education, work, housing, and welfare. Emphasis was placed on national sovereignty and national integration. Although the ARENA dominated Congress after the purging of many opposition representatives, and it easily won the 1970 elections, it was able to keep its majority in 1974 and 1978 elections only after electoral engineering by the government. Among prominent ARENA leaders were Jarbas Passarinho, José Sarney, Nilo Coelho, Luís Viana Filho, and Petrônio Portela.

During the second half of the 1978 legislative session, the ARENA majority voted to end some of the objectionable aspects of presidential exceptional powers and provide for another period of party reform after the November 1978 elections. Under President Figueiredo's Minister of Justice, Petrônio Portela, the government adopted a series of measures providing for a general amnesty, the extinction of the enforced two-party system, and direct elections for state governors. The Portela strategy envisioned a "divide to conquer" reorganization of the party structure.

From 1980 into the first half of 1981, there was considerable political maneuvering as new parties formed and congressmen shifted their allegiances, realigning along preexisting ideological divisions and/or on the basis of personal rivalries at the state level. In late 1981 and in 1982, the government issued new laws altering the electoral system and the rules of party organization and eligibility. As a result, each party's constitution and electoral behavior were conditioned in most instances more by expedient adaptation to shifts in the regime's political strategy than by the parties' own initiatives and plans. Ultimately, five parties emerged to contest the November 1982 elections, four of them opposition parties.

The Parties in Law

New parties can be formed in the same "top-down" method as in the period before 1979, but the number of deputies and senators required to join as signators of a new party was reduced to forty-two and seven, respectively.

In 1981 and 1982, two important electoral "packages" emerged that conditioned party organization and electoral activity. The "November package" of 1981 prohibited electoral coalitions, mandated that the voter must select candidates for all offices from within one party only, and obliged the parties to present complete slates. The key aspect of this package for the government party was the tying of the individual vote (*voto vinculado*) to one party. Since the electoral strength of the new government party remained predominantly rural, it was hoped that local voting for mayor would "pull" the vote across the ticket for the party's state and federal candidates.

The "June package" of 1982 aimed at consolidating the government position after the 1982 elections. After some confusion as to its specific features and the attachment of the riders necessary to secure some opposition support, the package allowed minor parties to participate until the 1986 elections, when their survival would depend on their polling the minimum number of votes in 1982 (5 percent of the total votes cast for the Chamber, with a minimum of 3 percent of the votes cast in each of nine states).

Party Organization

In general, Brazilian parties are weakly organized and tend to manifest themselves nationally, regionally, and locally only at election times. In 1982, some appear to be coalitions of interests (PMDB) while others seem more mass-based and clearly ideological (PT). All have elements of personalism in their composition and conduct. Party leaders are usually members of Congress.

In spite of weak organization and personalist leadership, party structures are usually well-defined by individual party statutes and charters. All parties attempt to coordinate activities nationally and extend their organization to the state and local levels.

In all cases, parties must tailor their strategies to the relative electoral strengths and leadership disputes of a given state. Formally, candidates are chosen in accord with procedures set down in party rules, which usually require conventions at each government level for the selection of candidates at that level.

Party activities are typically restricted to those associated with campaigning. Local committees work to recruit and motivate neighborhood campaign workers. Party adherents are often neighborhood association activists, church-group members, or union militants; overlap in membership appears to be great among these groups. Regionally and nationally, most parties restrict their activities to the coordination of partisan information campaigns.

All the parties maintain their national headquarters in Brasilia, and some have significant branch offices in Rio de Janeiro and São Paulo.

Campaigning

Contemporary campaigning is remarkably similar to that found in Western democracies in spite of careful government control of electoral contests. While other nations may not employ samba bands in their retinue of campaign gimmicks, Brazil is quickly adopting other familiar methods, for example, the use of electronic media; celebrity endorsements; campaign planning and coordination by public relations firms; and the customary arsenal of billboards, posters, graffiti, and handbills. Expenditures on individual campaigns have increased commensurately.

In the sixty days prior to elections, candidates may not appear on radio and television; before that period, the media must reserve two hours of free time each day for candidates. With the large number of candidates in the 1982 election it was not possible to provide all with access to the media, thereby limiting opposition propaganda. Paid advertising and partisan appeals were not permitted.

The national hierarchy of each party usually attempts some general control of the various races through the implementation of a campaign timetable, general platform themes, and common literature for distribution. Locally, candidates are usually left to develop their own style and campaign on the issues most persuasive to their constituency.

Independent Voters

In nearly all elections there are blank or null votes. Generally, the degree of null voting (e.g., defacing the ballot, voting for a noncandidate, or writing in obscene words) has been considered a barometer of protest. Elections held between 1945 and 1962 resulted in a percentage of blank and null votes that ranged from 2.3 to 17.8 percent (the latter figure for the 1962 election for federal deputies). In the 1966 elections, null votes comprised 7 percent and blank votes were 14 percent of the total. In the 1970 elections, opposition groups campaigned in favor of null-and-blank balloting; and the total of absentee, blank, and null votes ranged from 25 to 30 percent. In 1974 and 1978 blank and null votes totalled 15 to 20 percent of the total vote. In the 1982 elections, given the confusion over the appearance of the ballot and lack of time for voter education, the null vote might achieve the highest total, by default. Under current provisions, if null voting exceeds 50 percent, elections would be invalidated and must be restaged within twenty to forty days. In addition, the requirement that the elector vote for a single party precluded the possibility of ticket splitting, a practice common to Brazilians in past elections.

Brazilian Labor Party
(*Partido Trabalhista Brasileiro; PTB*)

History

The original PTB was formed in 1945 and eventually was subsumed into the MDB. Reformulation of the new PTB began with promulgation of a party statute and program on March 26, 1979. The process was marked by a schism between Leonel Brizola (ex-governor of Rio Grande do Sul and a participant in the Goulart government, who had returned from fifteen years in exile) and Ivette Vargas, the niece of Getúlio and a former MDB deputy. The original bloc consisted of twenty-three deputies and one senator, most of whom were from the states of Rio Grande do Sul, Bahia, and Rio de Janeiro. Brizola and Vargas left the resolution of their differences to the Supreme Electoral Court, which awarded the PTB acronym to the Vargas faction in May 1980. Five Brizola deputies defected to the newly sanctioned PTB, as Brizola formed the PDT; other Brizola supporters defected to the PMDB. By January 1982, the PTB had benefited from a split in the PDS in Pará and gained the support and followers of Governor Alacid Nunes. Also joining the PTB was ex-president Jânio Quadros, who was the party's 1982 candidate for governor of São Paulo. Other important adherents included the Rio de Janeiro gubernatorial candidate, Sandra Cavalcanti, and the ex-deputy from Pará, Américo Silva.

The PTB did not fare well in the 1982 elections. Early returns showed that it retained four Chamber seats from Rio de Janeiro and won eight from São Paulo, but lost one of its nine seats in the Rio de Janeiro state legislature and won only two municipalities.

Organization

The party is organized around its congressional membership and through a loose network of state and municipal offices. The national convention and executive committee are the highest party or-gans. The PTB sponsors the Getúlio Vargas Institute of Political Studies and maintains student and worker affiliates, although its influence in these sectors is minimal.

Policy

Party objectives include the struggle for a new constitution; national unity; a democratic, multiparty system; and political representation and rights for workers and students.

Membership & Constituency

Very little information on membership is available, but the party draws its constituency primarily from former supporters of Getúlio Vargas.

Financing

No information is available.

Leadership

Party officers are: Ivette Vargas, president; Ario Theodoro, first vice president; Fernando Alberto da Costa Leandro, second vice president; and Roberto Marcos Frati, secretary general.

Prospects

Just prior to the November 1982 election the PTB was represented by twelve federal deputies from Rio de Janeiro and two from Paraná. Given its electoral showing, its future possibilities are dim.

Democratic Labor Party
(*Partido Democrático Trabalhista; PDT*)

History

The party was formed on June 26, 1980, by the Brizola faction in the Brizola-Vargas dispute over leadership of the new PTB. It was comprised initially of about ten deputies. Later it attracted other known progressive politicians and intellectuals such as sociologists Theotônio dos Santos and Vania Bambirra, ex-Deputy Armindo Marcílio Doutel de Andrade, and ex-ministers Darcy Ribeiro and Neiva Moreira.

Brizola handily won the Rio de Janeiro gubernatorial election in 1982 along with his running mate, Darcy Ribeiro, and Roberto Saturnino Braga won a Senate seat from Rio. The party also ran strongly in the Rio state legislature and in the city of Rio de Janeiro.

Organization

In addition to its national, regional, and municipal conventions and committees, the PDT organized an Institute of Political, Economic, and Social Studies; a Women's Department; and workers' and students' movements.

Policy

The party manifesto calls for defense of democracy, nationalism, and socialism and departs from the *trabalhismo* (laborism) inspired by João Goulart in the early sixties. Nevertheless, the party assumes a social-democratic stance and considers itself a democratic workers' party. The party calls on Brazilians to struggle against privileged national and foreign groups and to oppose imperialism and exploitation. The PDT advocates a program of full employment and redistribution of income to eliminate inequality, struggle against internal colonialism, land reform to benefit the masses, and industrial and agricultural production in accordance with popular needs.

Membership & Constituency

The PDT's primary strength is in Rio Grande do Sul and Rio de Janeiro, although it has fielded candidates for elections in other states.

Financing

No information is available.

Leadership

In addition to Brizola, Ribeiro, Dos Santos, and other intellectuals as well as popular politicians such as Alceu Collares, the party executive included Deputy João Satte, and Deputy Carlos Augusto de Souza, secretary-general and president.

Prospects

By running popular and highly visible candidates for the governorship and federal deputy seats in Rio de Janeiro and Rio Grande do Sul, the PDT obtained significant victories in those states. While some military figures openly expressed anxiety over Brizola and his promised reforms, it is unlikely that he could bring about substantial change in face of the military government's control of the political system.

Party of the Brazilian Democratic Movement
(*Partido do Movimento Democrático Brasileiro;* PMDB)

History

Formed between December 1979 and March 1980, the PMDB was a direct descendent of the old MDB. It was a victim of the multiparty strategy of the regime, losing seventy of its original federal deputies and five of its senators to other newly formed opposition parties (PP, PTB, and PT). Additionally, twenty-four deputies and one senator went over to the government party, PDS. The PMDB gained only a handful of legislators in return. Eventually its strength stabilized at ninety-four deputies and seven senators. As the largest opposition party in the Congress and in most states, it regained some adherents in 1981 (rising to 113 in the Chamber and twenty in the Senate).

In the November 1982 elections, the PMDB won the governorships of Amazonas, Acre, Espírito Santo, Goiás, Mato Grosso do Sul, Minas Gerais, Pará, Paraná, and São Paulo. It improved its position as the largest opposition party in both the Chamber and Senate. Its defeat of the PDS in São Paulo was devastating: the PMDB emerged with forty-two of eighty-four seats in the state legislature, thirty of the sixty federal deputies, two of the three senators, and 308 of the 565 mayors in municipalities.

Organization

Facing the 1982 elections, PMDB displayed great heterogeneity as it was supported in some states by traditional political machines and in others by radical reform groups. Intraparty disagreements usually centered around personal rivalries for state governor or federal senator candidacies. Prestigious members included: Miguel Arraes, ex-governor and recently elected federal deputy from Pernambuco; Mário Covas, president of the party in São Paulo, who was purged as a federal deputy in 1969 and reelected in 1982; Marcos Freire, former senator and recently defeated candidate for governor in Pernambuco; Fernando

Henrique Cardoso, noted political sociologist and senator from São Paulo; Franco Montoro, a former senator recently elected governor of São Paulo; and Almino Afonso, former labor minister. In addition to its national convention and national, regional, district, and municipal committees, the PMDB maintains the Pedroso Horta Institute of Political Studies. Beyond these formal structures, the party in practice was an amalgamation of diverse groups, including liberal ARENA elements that had formed the PP, moderates of the old PSD, and leftists in the MDB, as well as representatives of such illegal leftist groupings as the PCB, PC do B, and MR-8 whose ability to organize and mobilize intellectuals and workers is substantial.

Policy

The PMDB position is moderate and reformist, with primary demands to end the military dictatorship, convoke a national constituent assembly to write a new constitution, and return to a state of law. Economically, the party favors nationalist controls on resources and foreign capital, creation of a larger domestic market, and more equitable distribution of national income to the middle class and workers. It calls for a foreign policy of independence and self-determination, less emphasis on a military definition of national security, and more attention to internal socioeconomic strength and reduction of foreign structural dependency. Its program specifically refers to the concerns of workers, women, blacks, youth, and illiterates (the last about 30 percent of the population).

Membership & Constituency

The general base of support for the PMDB is in the expanded middle stratum produced by the "economic miracle" of 1967 to 1973. The party is also supported by some moderate factions of the military, intellectuals, workers, and students. It can be characterized as a broad-based center-left party.

Financing

Elected members of the party must contribute 3 percent of income received as officials. Members are expected to donate money to the party, with members on executive committees and district and municipal committees owing an annual contribution determined by their respective entities. Financial contributions are also made by op-position business leaders, especially those formerly connected to the PP.

Leadership

Party officials are Deputy Ulysses Guimarães, president; recently elected governor of Minas Gerais, Tancredo Neves, first vice president; Miguel Arraes, second vice president; Senator Pedro Simon, third vice president; Deputy Francisco Pinto, secretary-general; Humberto Lucena, leader in the Senate; and Odacir Klein, leader in the Chamber of Deputies.

Prospects

In spite of manipulation of the electoral system by the government, the PMDB made strong electoral gains in urban and rural Brazil in 1982. The fact that the party is a coalition of diverse elements, however, left open the possibility that some on the left wing of the party might join a new socialist party, while some on the right might join a center party representing business and the middle class.

Party of the Workers
(*Partido dos Trabalhadores;* PT)

History

The PT is the only avowedly class-based socialist party. Its origins and initial leadership come from the new labor movement of the late 1970s that attempted to end the co-optation of labor by the traditional parties and the state. While seeking to organize committees in fifteen states in order to achieve government recognition, the PT was able to form a presence in Congress with five ex-MDB deputies and one senator. Early 1982 election returns gave the party eight representatives in Congress.

Organization

Unique in the party system, the PT was committed to mass participation and to organizing local committees from the "bottom up." While not involved in all electoral contests in all states in 1982, the national organization of the party made great strides after 1979. The base of party strength remains in the independent labor movement of the industrial belt of the state of São Paulo and in leftist movements of students and intellectuals. The formal organs of the party include the national convention and national committee and executive committees. In practice, the party is organized around a number of less formal groupings on the left, including such illegal parties as MEP, *Frente Operária, Convergência Socialista*, PCBR, PC do B dissidents, and APML do B.

Policy

In spite of early worker suspicion of explicitly socialist politics, the current platform of the PT clearly argues for direct worker participation in and control of the state. Domestically, the PT favors a complete end of the military regime, an end to fixed salaries, establishment of a free trade-union movement independent of state control, and democracy within the parties. The platform argues for an independent, anti-imperialist foreign policy.

Membership & Constituency

The constituency of the party includes the marginal urban and rural poor, which the PT has been actively organizing. Militants and voters tend also to be involved in progressive neighborhood, church, and labor groups at the local level.

Financing

Party financing is based on donations by party committees at all levels for distribution to electoral campaigns and party publications.

Leadership

Party officials are Luís Inácio da Silva (Lula), president, who won only about 10 percent of the 1982 vote for the governorship of São Paulo; Olívio Dutra, vice president and defeated candidate for governor of Rio Grande do Sul; peasant leader Manoel da Conceição, vice president: Apolônio de Carvalho, vice president; and Jacó Bittar, secretary-general and defeated candidate for the Senate from São Paulo. Key party figures also include social scientists José Álvaro Moisés and Francisco Weffort, while Deputy Airton Soares is party leader in the Chamber.

Prospects

The party will continue to play only a minor role in national politics.

Democratic Social Party (*Partido Democrático Social;* PDS)

History

The PDS is the direct descendant of the old ARENA, having lost much less in the period of party reorganization than the old MDB. While about two dozen deputies initially were lost in the formation of the PP, about the same number defected from PMDB and joined the PDS. The PDS was very much the largest party in both houses of Congress before and after the 1982 elections.

Organization

In practice, the PDS is more hierarchical than other parties and has the strongest national coverage. While continuing as the majority party in government, it suffers from the same regional internal divisions as its predecessor, the ARENA, and before that, the UDN. Disagreements are usually resolved by the party leadership and in critical cases by personal intervention of the president of the republic. Military and bureaucratic figures continue to command the party.

Policy

On paper, the party's policy appears remarkably similar to the PMDB (as that of ARENA did to MDB). In practice, domestic policy rests on the maintenance of the military regime while relaxing overt political controls; economic development through salary control and attraction of foreign capital; and continued tacit support of U.S. objectives in the region, even though the party's formal foreign policy position supports nonalignment.

Membership & Constituency

PDS membership and support come primarily from urban business and upper- and middle-class leaders and the traditional rural strongholds where *coronelismo* continues to command allegiance and votes.

Financing

Party money comes from the upper bourgeois and propertied classes of Brazilian industry and agriculture that support the military regime.

Leadership

Party officials and major leaders are Senator José Sarney, president; Deputy Prisco Vianna, secretary-general; Minister of Justice Ibrahim Abi-Ackel; Minister of Planning Antônio Delfim Netto; Senator Luís Viana Filho; Senator Jarbas Passarinho; and Deputy Nelson Marchezan. Other key political figures include: Paulo Maluf, ex-governor of São Paulo and candidate for deputy; Reynaldo de Barros, ex-mayor of São Paulo and defeated candidate for governor; Antônio Carlos Magalhães, governor of Bahia; Deputy Thales Ramalho, a crossover from the PP; Ney Braga, governor of Paraná; Marco Maciel, former governor and recently elected senator from Pernambuco; and Senator Nilo Coelho, leader in the Senate. In the 1982 election-year climate, Brazilian President João Figueiredo assumed a more public role as symbolic head of the PDS.

Prospects

In spite of gains by the opposition PMDB in 1982, the real exercise of state power lies outside the competition of the party system, i.e., the regime's ability to change the political "rules of the game" all but guarantees that the government party will continue to command the primary role in government.

Popular Party
(*Partido Popular;* PP)

History

The PP had a temporary role among Brazilian parties, beginning about mid-1979 and ending in early 1982. Its origins laid in an attempt by Deputy Magalhães Pinto to organize a centrist party of dissident ex-ARENA members and ex-MDB moderates. The PP was officially born in January 1980 with support of Senator Tancredo Neves and Deputy Thales Ramalho. Its initial membership was perhaps as high as ninety deputies. The party was intended to be a centrist group which would support conservative military government at the state level and align with the government party on national questions in the Congress.

Subsequent machinations by General Golbery do Couto e Silva after Petrônio Portela's death limited ARENA defections in Minas Gerais, the prime source of PP strength, and slowed the growth of PP in other states. Eventually, party strength stabilized at sixty-six deputies and ten senators by 1981. Regionally concentrated in Minas Gerais and Rio de Janeiro, party influentials included Rio Governor Chagas Freitas; Miro Teixeira, PP general-secretary and later Rio PMDB candidate for governor; Olavo Setúbal, ex-ARENA and ex-mayor of São Paulo; and key ex-governors such as Sinval Guazelli (Rio Grande do Sul) and Roberto Santos (Bahia).

Ten PP adherents joined the PMDB in February–March 1982; a few returned to the ranks of the PDS after feeling their personal ambitions were thwarted in states where the PMDB was most powerful. While formally inactive after its incorporation in the PMDB, the PP might seek a new coalition in the future. With its liberal bourgeois orientation such a reorganization is a clear possibility.

Minor Illegal Parties

During the late 1960s, a number of revolutionary parties and movements carried on radical political agitation, largely in the form of urban guerrilla warfare. By the early 1970s, the government had succeeded in curtailing these activities, imprisoning or killing most of the radical leadership. Nevertheless, some of these groups and individual members survived and were still active in 1982. Many of them joined or worked with the official parties, especially the PMBD and the PT.

Action for National Liberation
(*Ação Libertadora Nacional;* ALN)

The ALN was founded in late 1967 by Carlos Marighella, who broke with the PCB over its policy of peaceful coexistence. Marighella was killed in September 1969 and his successor, Câmara Ferreira, suffered the same fate in October 1970. The party continued underground for some time, but was inactive in 1982.

Armed Revolutionary Vanguard-Palmares
(*Vanguarda Armada Revolucionária-Palmares;* VAR Palmares)

See **Students** below.

Brazilian Communist Party
(*Partido Comunista Brasileiro;* PCB)

The Communist Party, now the oldest politically active party in Brazil, is still illegal, but as part of the PMDB ran several candidates in the 1982 elections. It suffered numerous schisms in the late 1960s and early 1970s, when radical activist groups disagreed with its less revolutionary course. The party leaders now lean toward a Eurocommunist position and several old guard Moscow "hardliners," including Luís Carlos Prestes, have been dropped from the leadership.

Brazilian Revolutionary Communist Party (*Partido Comunista Brasileiro Revolucionário;* PCBR)

Under the leadership of Jacob Gorender and Mário Alves, the PCBR broke from the PC do B in the 1960s. It was involved in armed struggle in 1969 when its militants in Rio aligned with the *Movimento Revolucionário-26.* In 1982, the party was sympathetic to the PT; the PCBR's leader, Apolônio de Carvalho, served as a member of the PT executive committee. It publishes *Voz da Unidade* (Voice of Unity) in São Paulo.

Communist Party of Brazil (*Partido Comunista do Brasil;* PC do B)

This dissident pro-Chinese and later pro-Albanian faction of the PCBR broke away in 1962. One faction split off in 1966 to form the PCR, and another faction called the ALA (Red Wing or ALA Vermelha) broke off in the same year. After 1979, the PC do B, and especially its youth, tended to support the PMDB, while PC do B dissidents joined the PT. The PC do B publishes *Tribuna Operária;* the dissidents publish *Teoria e Política.*

Communist Workers Party (*Partido Operário Comunista;* POC)

Formed in 1967 by POLOP militants in Rio Grande do Sul and PCB dissidents, the POC was inactive in 1982.

Marxist Leninist Popular Action of Brazil (*Ação Popular Marxista-Leninista do Brasil;* APML do B)

Originally a leftist Catholic movement active during the early 1960s, this group became part of the urban armed struggle in late 1960s. By 1980, it was involved in the PT and the minority left of the student union, UNE.

Movement of Emancipation of the Proletarist (*Movimento de Emancipação do Proletariado;* MEP)

This organization was active in the UNE and PT in 1982.

Revolutionary Communist Party (*Partido Comunista Revolucionário;* PCR)

A dissident splinter of the PC do B, the PCR joined MR-8 and supported the PMDB in the early 1980s; it holds some strength in the UNE.

Revolutionary Movement of the Eighth of October (*Movimento Revolucionário de Oito de Outubro;* MR-8)

A dissident group of the PCB that took up armed struggle in October 1968 under Carlos Lamarca, MR-8 survived despite police repression. It was aligned with the ALN for a time, and later emerged openly under the democratic *abertura.* During the early 1980s, the MR-8 assimilated the PCR, the *Organização Comunista do Sol,* the *Fração Operaria Comunista,* and the *Grupo Companheiro.* In 1982, it tended to support the opposition PMDB.

Revolutionary Peoples Vanguard (*Vanguarda Popular Revolucionária;* VPR)

See **Students** below.

Socialist Convergence (*Convergência Socialista*)

A Trotskyite group active in the São Paulo strikes of the late 1970s, this organization worked within the PT in 1982.

Workers Front (*Frente Operária*)

A Trotskyite current inspired by the late J. Posadas, the group publishes a newspaper of the same name.

Workers Politics (*Política Operária;* POLOP)

POLOP was formed in 1961, and broke up over the question of armed struggle at its congress in São Paulo in 1967. Many of its members were involved in the urban armed struggle, while others were imprisoned or lived in exile. It was inactive in 1982.

Other Political Forces

Military

The empire of Dom Pedro II was ended by a military coup in 1889, and the military has played an influential or decisive role in the political crises of 1930, 1945, 1954, 1955, and 1961. The military remains the central political institution in Brazilian society, having directly commanded the state apparatus since 1964. As in most other Latin American nations, the army has been the leading political branch of the armed forces. It is broadly divided into four command regions: the First Army in Rio de Janeiro, the Second in São Paulo, the Third in Pôrto Alegre, and the Fourth in Recife. The First Army has been most significant in that it dominates the political center of the nation, the state of Rio de Janeiro.

Officers are mainly recruited from sons of officers and from geographic areas in which they later command, thus maintaining continuity in the rural *coronelismo* system. Mainly lower middle class in social origins, officers are selected and promoted through a rigid system of competitive examinations and review in tune with an emphasis on professionalization which began in 1966. Of particular importance in this system is the Higher War School (*Escola Superior da Guerra;* ESG), an advanced training program for senior colonels and junior generals.

The factionalism within the military has tended to center around adherents to and dissenters from the ideological training of the ESG. The pro-ESG current of the military, the so-called Sorbonnists, argue that planning and technocratic efficiency are necessary for national development and national security. Politics, in their view, should be guided by a developmental ideology in tune with transnational capital, technology, and foreign aid. Politically moderate, this wing of the military emphasizes technical competence as the basis of legitimate rule. Their objective in politics is to at least maintain democratic forms and institutions and to reserve the option of eventually returning to civilian rule. The hardliners within the military favor repression of democratic processes and share the ESG values of security and nationalism while disputing the high degree of foreign political and economic dependence necessary for their attainment. Such officers are not generally anxious to return to civilian rule in any form.

These ideological differences generally become noticeable to the Brazilian public when certain issues (presidential succession, economic stabilization and foreign balance-of-payments problems, and the role of the state in the economy, etc.) become hotly contested within the relative secrecy of the military institution.

The military apparatus functions as a vast information and control system with roots invading all key aspects of federal, state, and local bureaucratic operations. Of particular importance is the National Information Service (*Serviço Nacional da Informação;* SNI) which, in addition to its activity as an intelligence network, usually provides army candidates for the presidency, generals Médici and Figueiredo being recent examples of this practice.

Organized Labor

In Brazil, a distinction must be made between organized labor as a political group and the political activities of the working class. As part of the legacy of corporatism under Vargas, the Brazilian state controls the political life of the official labor unions by sanctioning their existence, intervening in leadership selection, controlling union budgets and expenditures, and prohibiting union organization across professional categories. Thus official labor representation in politics has been characterized by paternalism, manipulation, and repression.

In the post–1964 period, wage demands were perceived as exorbitant and union activities in general as subversive. An official policy of wage control (*arrocho salarial*) replaced collective bargaining in 1965 with a sophisticated formula which automatically adjusted occupational wages on an annual (and later, semiannual) basis. Replacement of union leaders and other forms of official tampering in labor politics existed with direct military repression of strikes.

In spite of this history of official co-optation and repression, wage laborers as a whole have been a growing force in Brazilian society, with a long history of political action culminating in a new challenge to the official labor-union system in 1977. In mid-1977, the government revealed that it had lied regarding official data used for calculating the wage increases for industrial workers in 1973 and 1974. This disclosure touched off a labor campaign, largely spearheaded by the Metalworkers Union of São Bernardo do Campo under the leadership of Luís Inácio da Silva (Lula), to regain the lost wages and agitate for changes in labor-union structure. During 1978 and 1979 over 130 strikes occurred, involving nearly four million workers in fifteen states. Significantly, the demands of this period were not restricted to wages alone, but involved desires for direct collective bargaining at the factory level, job security, rank-and-file union democracy, and an end to state control of union spending (a mandatory payroll tax is used for health and education programs rather than for direct political and economic action). In spite of repression, the new labor movement remains a potent force in contemporary Brazilian politics.

Religious Groups

Closely related to the reemergency of working-class political activism is the progressive action of the Brazilian Catholic Church and its "political arm," the National Conference of Brazilian Bishops (*Conferência Nacional dos Bispos Brasileiros;* CNBB).

Deeply influenced by the positions of Pope John XXIII (1958–63); the social-justice orientation of the Second Vatican Council (1962–65); and the Latin American Bishops' Conferences in Medellín, Colombia (1968), and Puebla, Mexico (1979), the Brazilian Church has demonstrated a preference for political activism. In the 1950s and 1960s, the Church was heavily involved in organizing peasants in the northeast and later provided opposition to the Castello Branco regime. Church groups involved in social and political action in 1960s and 1970s were distrusted by the military regimes, reflected by official opposition to human rights groups and the Movement for Basic Education (MEB), a grass-roots literacy campaign in the northeast that used the revolutionary pedagogical methods of Paulo Freire. In the same period, Archbishop Dom Helder Câmara became and remains a progressive Catholic leader. Official harassment led to clashes between Church groups and the military in the late 1960s, as well as to the torture and deportation of foreign priests active in the Brazilian ministry.

The contemporary political significance of the Brazilian Church is found in its continuing grass-roots activity on a number of social issues. In May 1967, the CNBB supported land redistribution and other reforms which it viewed to be necessary to stave off widespread social violence. In July 1968, Dom Helder formed the Action: Peace and Justice Movement, a human rights group with broad clerical and lay support. Today, the CNBB, at the diocesan and archdiocesan levels, organizes and promotes the work of *pastorais* (ministry groups) involved in aiding the poor; improving work, housing, and health conditions; helping abandoned children; and struggling with a range of socioeconomic questions plaguing the countryside. Regime responses to such activism have varied. During the Médici government, the state counterattacked with a public relations campaign downplaying Church criticism of the social effects of the "economic miracle," the period of rapid economic growth which was markedly slowed in 1973. Geisel attempted a reconciliation with Church officials. CNBB headquarters (as well as those of other opposition groups) were bombed by right-wing groups during the elections of 1976.

The lay community of the Church has also been active since the 1960s through the Ecclesiastical Base Communities (*Comunidades Eclesiais de Base;* CEBs). Arising originally as a response to the lack of trained clergy in rural and some urban areas, the CEBs were small groups of citizens organized by priests or bishops to perform ceremonies associated with the Catholic faith and to act in projects to alleviate social problems. Groups may number from a dozen or two to 100 or more persons in a neighborhood afflicted by poverty or other problems. Approximately 80,000 CEBs currently exist throughout the nation. In the late 1970s, the CEBs provided a base for political consciousness raising, for the practice of neighborhood democracy, and for the organization of concrete programs for community action. Their memberships probably closely overlap those of hundreds of neighborhood associations and *favela* (slum) associations and societies and involve millions of lower- and middle-class citizens.

Students

As a reflection of middle- and upper-middle-class discontent, students as a political group have played the role of dissenters in authoritarian Brazil. The major organization for the expression of student interest has been the National Union of Students (*União Nacional de Estudantes;* UNE).

Generally, manifestations of student political opinion have been nationalist and leftist. The UNE supported President Goulart until a coup ended his term. At the time, the UNE also opposed the political and economic role of the United States in Brazil.

Students were vocal opponents of the military regimes that followed. They especially agitated against Castello Branco during the last sixteen months of his term. Immediately after the coup, many student leaders were arrested, and the regime attempted to bring student organizations under state control and outlawed the UNE.

Widespread demonstrations, interventions, some deaths, and thousands of arrests characterized the period of August 1967 to September 1968. During this period, some students were involved in *Política Operária* (POLOP) which divided to become the *Vanguarda Popular Revolucionária* (VPR) and the *Vanguarda Armada Revolucionaria* (VAR-Palmares), two resistance movements involved in the armed urban struggle of the period.

Contemporaneous with the militancy of the labor movement and other popular groups in the 1970s, students renewed their protests to military rule after mid-1977. While the UNE officially continues to be illegal, it has been allowed to organize at state and campus levels. At the UNE Congress of October 1980, two coalitions were evident. A majority coalition included delegates of the PC do B, MR-8, and the PCR, while a minority coalition comprised the dissidents of the PC do B, MEP, and the APLM do B. The former coalition was aligned with the PMDB, the latter with the PT. Student activism continues to be a target of regime counterpressure, e.g., the Ministry of Justice successfully campaigned to deport the former UNE president Francisco Javier Alfaya, a Spanish-born, twenty-five-year-old architecture student from Bahia, resident in Brazil since age six.

National Prospects

The prospects of the Brazilian political system depend in part upon the economy. The government has launched a series of projects, including nuclear power plants; construction of large dams for hydroelectric energy; agricultural irrigation projects; and the controversial Carajás Project, designed to tap large reserves of iron ore, manganese, gold, and other minerals. The state participation in these sectors has not been without repercussions, however. The main problems have been an annual inflation rate of more than 100 percent, recession and high unemployment due to monetary constraints, and a foreign debt that reached more than $80 billion in 1982. The government strategy was to arrange long-term credit and loans to finance the development of natural and agricultural resources, increase industrial capacity, and augment exportable products. The so-called economic miracle that once brought an annual growth rate of more than 10 percent was undermined by the petroleum crisis of 1973, so that in 1982 oil imports cost some $11 billion. These problems—and the large foreign debt in particular—became major issues for the political opposition and its nationalistic appeals to reduce Brazilian dependence on the outside world.

Further Reading

Alves, Márcio Moreira. "New Political Parties." *Latin American Perspectives*, Vol. 6, No. 2 (Fall 1979).

Bruneau, Thomas C. *The Political Transformation of the Brazilian Catholic Church.* London: Cambridge University Press, 1974.

Chilcote, Ronald H. *The Brazilian Communist Party: Conflict and Integration, 1922–1972.* New York: Oxford University Press, 1974.

Erickson, Kenneth Paul. *The Brazilian Corporate State and Working-Class Politics.* Berkeley: University of California Press, 1977.

Fiechter, Georges André. *Brazil since 1964—Modernization under a Military Regime.* London: Macmillan, 1975.

Flynn, Peter. *Brazil: A Political Analysis.* Boulder, Colo.: Westview Press, 1979.

McDonough, Peter. *Power and Ideology in Brazil.* Princeton, N. J.: Princeton University Press, 1981.

Schmitter, Philippe C. *Interest Conflict and Political Change in Brazil.* Stanford, Calif.: Stanford University Press, 1971.

Schneider, Ronald M. *The Political System of Brazil: Emergence of a "Modernizing" Authoritarian Regime, 1964–1970.* New York: Columbia University Press, 1971.

Skidmore, Thomas. *Politics in Brazil, 1930–1964: An Experiment in Democracy.* New York: Oxford University Press, 1967.

Stepan, Alfred, ed. *Authoritarian Brazil: Origins, Policies, and Future.* New Haven, Conn.: Yale University Press, 1973.

PEOPLE'S REPUBLIC OF BULGARIA
(Narodna Republika Bulgaria)
by Vladimir Socor, Ph.D.

The System of Government

Bulgaria, a nation of nearly nine million people, is a one-party communist state in which the leadership of the Bulgarian Communist Party (BCP) holds the monopoly of political power. Because the BCP is the real decision-making center, the formal constitutional setup is essentially irrelevant to the real policymaking process. The current Bulgarian constitution, promulgated at the tenth party congress in 1971, proclaims the BCP "the leading force in society and the state." The constitution also enshrines the country's ties to the Soviet Union.

Executive

Executive power is formally vested in the Council of Ministers headed by the prime minister. The Council, with thirty-two members in late 1982, functions primarily as an implementing body to carry out the policy decisions of the BCP leadership. The prime minister in late 1982 was Grisha Filipov (born 1919).

Legislature

The "highest organ of state power" is officially the National Assembly (*Narodno Subranie*). The Assembly consists of 400 members who meet a few times each year for a few days at a time to unanimously approve the decisions of the party leadership and confirm its choices for the Council of Ministers and the State Council. When the Assembly is not in session, its standing presidium, the State Council, performs the formal legislative function. The head of the State Council is Bulgaria's head of state; since 1971 this office has been held by the general secretary of the BCP, Todor Zhivkov.

Judiciary

The Supreme Court has fifty members appointed by the National Assembly. The judiciary has no independent authority, because justice is considered an instrument of party policy in the service of socialist development.

Regional & Local Government

Local administrative power is formally vested in the village, town, city, and district people's councils which are formally elective bodies. In practice, local power is exercised primarily by the local and regional committees of the BCP under their secretaries. The committees, in turn, are controlled by the party central apparatus. However, there is a tradition of regionalism in Bulgarian politics which gives the district party committees greater influence than is the case in most other communist states.

The Electoral System

The National Assembly is elected every four years in a ceremonial presided over by the Fatherland Front, the BCP's national mass organization. Nominally all candidates are chosen by the Front; in fact, they are selected and approved by the BCP. The candidates run unopposed on a single slate and are routinely attributed 99 percent of the vote or more.

Bulgarian Communist Party (BCP; *Bulgarska Komunisticheska Partiya*)

History

The BCP was founded in 1919, and for the ensuing quarter century existed largely underground or in exile in the Soviet Union. Due to the caliber of its leaders (the most prominent of whom, Georgi Dimitrov, was secretary general of the

Communist International and later the first communist ruler of Bulgaria), the party played an important role in international communist affairs, far out of proportion to its or Bulgaria's size. At home, however, the party consistently failed to win sizable political support, and its repeated resort to armed struggle failed to achieve any political gains. When Bulgaria was occupied by the Soviet army in 1944, the BCP captured political power and by the late 1940s had established a totalitarian polity, using mass-scale violence in the process. Following the liquidation of all organized opposition, including independent-minded groups within the BCP itself, the use of terror abated. By the late 1950s, the current system of repressive controls combined with political mobilization was firmly in place.

Organization

The BCP, whose latest party statute was issued in 1962, is hierarchically structured on the basis of "democratic centralism." At the bottom of the pyramid, the basic party unit, called the primary organization, exists in every place of work (including factories, farms, schools, offices, and military and police units) where there are at least three party members. It is directly subordinate to the local party committee. There is a party organization for every administrative unit—village, town, city, district—each one run by a bureau whose members are full-time party functionaries. Ostensibly elected, bureau members, in fact, are appointed by the party organization immediately above.

The highest nominal authority in the party is the national congress, which is summoned every five years, the delegates having been selected at each level by the next higher level. In theory the congress elects members of the Central Committee; in practice it merely confirms those members preselected by the party's leadership. The congress also ratifies the party's basic policies as presented to it by the leadership. While playing an entirely passive role, it is the congress which, through ratification, confers legitimacy on the party leadership and its basic policy line.

The Central Committee confirms the party's top leadership: the Politburo and the Secretariat. The Central Committee is, theoretically, the party's policymaking body. In fact, it meets only about four times a year for one or two days at a time to endorse decisions made by the Politburo. During the intervals between congresses, the Central Committee constitutes the source of legitimacy for Politburo decisions and also for important personnel changes. The Central Committee's size has steadily grown with every party congress and in recent years has exceeded 300 people, including both full and candidate members.

The Secretariat normally consists of eight to ten secretaries, some managing party affairs and others duplicating or streamlining the functions of government ministries or agencies over which they have supervisory control. The Secretariat's work includes both party and government (including industry) personnel policy; the appointment of officials at all levels is a prerogative of the party (the *nomenklatura* system).

At the pinnacle of the party is the Politburo. Its size varies, but it usually consists of about twelve members. The most important members of the Secretariat, the prime minister, and key members of the Council of Ministers are ex officio members of the Politburo. The Politburo is a standing body and the seat of party and state policymaking authority.

The BCP maintains several mass organizations including the Bulgarian Communist Youth Union (Komsomol), trade unions, and professional and cultural organizations. These groups are component organizations of the Fatherland Front, whose membership of over four million embraces most of the country's employed adult population. The Front presides over national and local elections, mobilizes the population behind BCP policies, and promotes communist ideological values in the society.

Among the Front's constituent organizations, one possesses all the trappings of an independent political party, the Bulgarian Agrarian Union (BAU). Once Bulgaria's largest political movement, the BAU was destroyed by the Communist Party in the early postwar years; a rump of it has been formally maintained under party control. It functions as a mass organization in the countryside. Its membership is permanently set at 120,000, and it is allocated a fixed quota of 100 seats in the National Assembly, five seats on the Council of Ministers, and one deputy chairmanship on the State Council. The Union's by-laws commit it to full support of BCP policy and programs, and its leadership is selected by the Communist Party.

Policy

The basic policies of the BCP are characterized by adherence to the Soviet model of political organization and socioeconomic development, alignment on ideological positions with the Soviet party, and active support for Soviet foreign policy in the Balkans and beyond. Bulgarian political, economic, and international policies are influenced by and responsive to Soviet policy guidance. The Soviet Union has consistently praised the BCP for its adaptation of the Soviet development model, and has repeatedly described Bulgarian-Soviet relations as exemplary of correct relations between communist states.

In its domestic policies the BCP is among the least innovative and most doctrinaire of East Europe's ruling communist parties. Measures introduced since the late 1970s for a limited decentralization of economic management have not affected the system of command economy, although investment policy is less weighted toward heavy industry as against consumer goods and agriculture than is the case in other communist states. Economic performance in recent years and for the seven-year plan which ended in 1981 has fallen short of plan figures in most categories; the new plan announced in 1981 showed a substantial scaling down of economic-growth targets. The BCP continues to wage an intensive but thus far sterile campaign to infuse Bulgarian society with communist ideological values and to bring about the emergence of the communist "new man."

Bulgaria's foreign policy is based on the country's membership in the Warsaw Pact, the Soviet-led alliance system in eastern Europe. Bulgarian diplomacy is an active promoter of the Soviet project for turning the Balkans and adjacent areas into a nuclear-free zone and detaching Greece and Turkey from NATO. In recent years, Bulgaria has been increasingly involved in supportive or proxy roles in a variety of operations in the Third World alongside the Soviet Union. Close links exist between the Bulgarian and Soviet military and security establishments. Bulgaria's long-standing dispute with Yugoslavia over Slavic Macedonia is not a factor in official Bulgarian foreign policy, although it does receive an indirect airing in cultural propaganda.

The official celebrations in 1981 of the 1300th anniversary of Bulgarian statehood provided the framework for a vigorous reassertion of Bulgarian national consciousness and patriotism. Events organized by the regime showed an effort to relate the communist government to national values and advance its claim to legitimacy by projecting itself as the heir to the nation's historic heritage.

Membership & Constituency

As of its twelfth congress in April 1981, the BCP had 826,000 members, amounting to about 13 percent of the adult population. Admission no longer presupposes a personal, internalized commitment by the individual rank-and-file member to the party's policies and ideology. Indeed, admission has been facilitated by a dilution of the political and

ideological requirements for membership. Since the post-Stalin period, the party has adopted a recruitment policy designed to offer a stake in the political order to growing sections of society, particularly the bureaucratic, managerial, and professional groups. As a result the ranks of the party have grown faster than the country's adult population.

According to official figures of 1976, government, economic, administrative, cultural, and military personnel make up 35.6 percent of the membership, far in excess of their proportion in society. "Workers," probably defined so as to inflate their numbers, are said to form 41.3 percent of the party's ranks; their share has been growing more slowly than that of the other groups. Peasants, with 23.1 percent in 1979, were greatly underrepresented. Revised figures in 1981, put the figure at 42.7 percent, but failed to specify the shares of other parties. The party leadership has shown itself to be keenly aware of the imbalances in the party's class composition. Repeated programs for bringing more industrial workers into the party have consistently fallen short of their goals.

The relative preponderance of bureaucratic-managerial groups, along with the erosion of ideological commitment, has been responsible for a marked decline in the share of youth in the party; only 15 percent of party members are under thirty. Women, who form a slight majority of the nation's population, supply only 27.5 percent of party members. The Turkish minority is severely underrepresented, apparently as a matter of policy since no special effort has been made to increase the percentage of Turks.

The leadership has tried to solve the problem of inadequate communist consciousness in the party's ranks by adopting a more discriminating admissions policy and by a closer monitoring of the performance and conduct of members. As a result, between 1976 and 1981, the party's membership expansion rate was only about one-third that of the preceding five-year period—down from 13 to 4.6 percent. While the party has continued to show a net growth, over 38,000 or 3.7 percent of its members were weeded out as ideologically or otherwise unfit in the course of an exchange of party cards conducted in 1978 to 1980.

Financing

The BCP finances its operations primarily by drawing on the resources of the national economy which the party itself administers. Membership dues are a lesser source of the party's income. No figures are available on party finances; they are kept secret and are never a subject of public discussion.

Leadership

In 1982, the Central Committee counted 197 full members and 139 candidate members. The average age was 58.5 years in 1982. At least one-third of the members, most of them part of the older generation of revolutionaries, lack formal education beyond the secondary level. Nevertheless, the Central Committee is now numerically dominated by the generations who have received a formal higher education under the communist system. The occupational breakdown of the Central Committee shows an overwhelming predominance of party and government officials, including a large representation of military and police officials. The category of economic managers remains only marginally represented, as do women and the virtually unrepresented Turkish minority.

The Politburo consisted of eleven full members and three candidate members in 1982. Among the full members, at least five have Soviet ties through previous residence there and through education or marriage. The Politburo is about evenly divided between the older generation or revolutionaries and system-builders and the younger generation of party *apparatchiki*. The average age in 1982 was slightly over sixty years.

Todor Zhivkov, an uneducated man, has headed the party (first secretary 1954–81; general secretary 1981–) since 1954, which makes him the senior Communist Party leader in the Warsaw Pact. Born in 1911, he is still fully active and in robust health.

While official BCP doctrine and Zhivkov himself routinely pay homage to the idea of collegial leadership and repudiate the cult of personality, Zhivkov's leadership style features elements of personal rule. He is the object of adulatory treatment by the party and the state, and arrogates to himself alone the prerogative of addressing the nation directly. His speeches are prolix and didactic, and are regarded as a source of guidance and inspiration. In what appeared to be a relapse into dynasticism (discernible also in such communist states as neighboring Romania and North Korea), Zhivkov's daughter, chairwoman of the State Committee on Culture, was made a member of the Politburo, despite her youth (born 1942) and lack of proper credentials (her education was English and humanistic, not Russian and technical). She appeared to play an influential role with her father and was the object of a strong propaganda

buildup, possibly with an eye to the succession, until her unexpected death in 1981.

Like other communist parties, the BCP has no established procedure to provide for succession at the pinnacle of power. At present there is no visible front-runner for Zhivkov's place. Zhivkov has a consistent record of purging or easing out those who have emerged as the second most powerful figure in the party. Boris Velchev in 1977 was the latest casualty.

Those who by virtue of institutional power base, personal background, and age are at present in a strong position to succeed Zhivkov, include Central Committee secretaries Ognyan Doynov, Alexander Lilov, and Prime Minister Grisha Filipov. More distant possibilities are First Deputy Prime Minister Todor Bozhinov and Foreign Minister Petur Mladenov, who are also Politburo members. Filipov, who was born in the Soviet Union of Bulgarian communists, is the oldest of these; the rest are all members of the younger Politburo generation, approaching fifty years of age. Only Doynov holds a post that is generally considered a direct stepping stone to leadership of the party. Soviet endorsement will be the indispensable prerequisite to the emergence of any new BCP leader.

Other Political Forces

While there is no sign at all of opposition to the government, either in the society at large or within the party, the party has a tradition of factionalism, compounded by military involvement in politics. This tradition has not been noticeable, however, since the early 1970s and appears to have been overcome as the old revolutionary leaders left the scene.

One potential source for the emergence of a pressure group within the system may be the sizeable contingent of party and government officials of Macedonian origin. These men have been numerous and prominent in the BCP, have a group identity, and have been systematically promoted to positions of influence in recent years. The potential of this group may turn on the historic dispute between Yugoslavia and Bulgaria over Slavic Macedonia, most of which is in Yugoslavia. Yugoslavia and, more especially, Soviet foreign policy will determine whether the Macedonians exert a direct influence, as a group, on national policy.

A more material and recurring concern, in line with the tradition of patron-client relationships and regionalism in Bulgarian political culture, is the possible emergence within the party apparatus of influential individual leaders who command a personal following. This potential source of system disruption has so far been successfully managed by the top leadership's ultimate control of access to rewards and prerogatives.

National Prospects

Outside of the official political process, no social forces or political groups are discernible that might in the near future demand to be included in the formulation of national policy. Although Bulgaria experienced a few stirrings of intellectual dissent and social unrest in 1978, these were successfully isolated and contained by the authorities. Prospects for the emergence of religious or ethnically based opposition movements are practically nil. The Bulgarian Orthodox Church has a tradition of close identification with the state and lacks the political, organizational, and intellectual potential for emerging as a competing ideological power center. The Turkish minority is isolated and inward-looking and completely inert politically.

The destruction of civil society and elimination of political opponents (both democratic and intraparty) by the BCP in its early years continues to pay political dividends. Effective wielding of the instruments of political, social, and economic control by the party has firmly consolidated its posi-

tion. The prognosis for the near future is for stability and continuity of the system in its present form.

Further Reading

Brown, James F. *Bulgaria under Communist Rule.* New York: Praeger, 1970.

Chary, Frederick B. "Bulgaria: The Solace of History." *Current History*, Vol. 80, No. 465, April 1981.

Dellin, L. A. D. "The Communist Party of Bulgaria." In *The Communist Parties of Eastern Europe*, Stephen Fischer-Galati, ed. New York: Columbia University Press, 1979.

King, Robert R. "Bulgaria." In *Communism in Eastern Europe*, Teresa Rakowska-Harmstone and Andrew Gyorgi, eds. Bloomington, Ind.: Indiana University Press, 1979.

Oren, Nissan. *Revolution Administered: Agrarianism and Communism in Bulgaria.* Baltimore: Johns Hopkins University Press, 1973.

U.S. Congress, House of Representatives Committee on Foreign Affairs and Senate Committee on Foreign Relations. "Bulgaria." In *Country Reports on Human Rights Practices Submitted by the Department of State.* Washington, D.C.: U.S. Government Printing Office, 1981 and 1982.

Yearbook on International Communist Affairs. 1976–82. Stanford, Calif.: Hoover Institution Press, annual.

SOCIALIST REPUBLIC OF THE UNION OF BURMA

(*Pyidaungsu Socialist Thammada Myanma Naingngandaw*)

by Donald M. Seekins, Ph.D.

The System of Government

Burma has been a one-party socialist republic under military rule since the coup d'état of March 2, 1962, led by General Ne Win, toppled the civilian government of Prime Minister U Nu.

The population, estimated at 33,310,000 in 1980, is ethnically diverse. The largest group, about 70 percent of the total, are the Burmans, who predominate in the agriculturally rich central river valley and southern coastal and delta regions. They have largely supplanted another ethnic group, the Mons or Talaings, in the delta regions. Other ethnic minorities are found in the mountainous border areas: the Karens and the Kayahs in the southeast, the Shans in the east, the Kachins in the north, and the Chins and Arakanese in the west. Other indigenous groups include the Nagas, the Wa, the Palaung, and the Lolo. There are also overseas Chinese and Indian communities who came into the country largely during the period of British colonial rule. The Burmans are dominant culturally and politically, although all Burmese governments since independence have espoused principles of minority rights (the term "Burmese" is used to refer to any citizens of Burma, including non-Burmans). Suspicion and hostility between Burmans and minorities, however, have persisted, hindering the development of genuine national unity.

Buddhism of the southern or Theravada School—of Sri Lanka, Thailand, Laos, and Cambodia—is the dominant religion, and has inspired Burmese cultural life for over a millenium. Many of the minority peoples are Christian or animist,

and there are Muslims in the western part of the country, bordering Bangladesh.

Burma has a political tradition going back to the unification of the country under the Burman Pagan dynasty (1044–1287). During the nineteenth century, the British made Burma a colony, completing their takeover in 1885, when the northern remainder of the country, Upper Burma, was annexed and the last king of the Konbaung dynasty, Thibaw, was deposed and exiled. Burma became a province of British India. Because Burma had a long history as an independent nation, outside rule was deeply resented, especially by the Burmans. The British granted limited self-government in the 1930s, but the nationalist *Dobama Asiayone* (We Burmans Association) pressed for complete independence. The association's leaders included Aung San (assassinated in 1947 and now venerated as a national hero), U Nu, and Ne Win. Burma was occupied by the Japanese from 1942 to 1945, and a nominally independent Burmese state was set up at that time under Japanese auspices. The British returned in 1945, and full independence was acheived January 4, 1948.

Between 1948 and 1958, Burma had a parliamentary government, mostly under the prime ministership of U Nu. Several political parties existed of which the most important was U Nu's Anti-Fascist People's Freedom League (AFPFL). Growing unrest, particularly in the minority regions, led U Nu to ask General Ne Win, commander of the armed forces, to form a "caretaker government" in 1958. This lasted until 1960, when U Nu was returned to power in an election. Continued instability, however, led the military under Ne Win to seize power on March 2, 1962. A Revolutionary Council of military officers, claiming that parliamentary government was unworkable in Burma, suspended the 1948 constitution. In July 1962, they established the Burma Socialist Program Party (BSPP; *Lanzin* in Burmese), and in March 1964, the Law to Protect National Solidarity made all other political parties illegal. Opponents of the military, especially university students and Buddhist monks, were suppressed.

A new constitution, which was to mark the transition from military to "civilian" rule, was drawn up by the BSPP and approved by the people in a referendum in December 1973. It went into effect in January 1974 and provided for a new government structure to replace the Revolutionary Council. The name of the country was changed from the Union of Burma to the Socialist Republic of the Union of Burma. Top leaders shed their military titles and uniforms, but the military continued to keep a tight grip on the reins of power.

Executive

Under the 1974 constitution, executive power is vested in two councils: the Council of State and the Council of Ministers, both of which are selected by the national legislature, the People's Assembly. The Council of State has twenty-nine members, consisting of one legislator from each of the country's fourteen states or divisions; fourteen others selected from the People's Assembly at large; and the prime minister, elected by the Council of Ministers. The chairman of the Council of State, elected by its members, becomes the president of the republic who is recognized as head of state. In 1982, the president was San Yu, and the prime minister Maung Maung Kha. The Council of State has broad powers: the ratification of treaties, military command during national emergencies (including the proclamation of martial law), the convening of special sessions of the People's Assembly, and the assumption of powers of government when the Assembly cannot be called together. When the legislature is not in session, the Council of State can issue ordinances that have the force of law. The council also nominates members of the Council of People's Inspectorates, which has broad and undefined powers and serves as a monitoring agency for all government bodies. The terms of the president and the Council of State are four years, coinciding with that of the People's Assembly.

The civil service and ministries are the responsibility of the Council of Ministers. In 1982, there were eighteen ministers, including the prime minister. They are elected by the People's Assembly from a list submitted by the Council of State.

Legislature

Under the 1974 constitution, the People's Assembly (*Pyithu Hluttaw*), a unicameral legislature, "exercises sovereign power on behalf of the people." It is responsible for the national budget, can declare war or peace, selects and delegates power to the executive and judicial bodies, and has the power to dissolve local-level people's councils. It has a term of four years, although a vote by at least three-quarters of the legislators may dissolve it earlier and set new elections. Two regular sessions of the Assembly are held annually. Fourteen presiding officers are drawn from each of the fourteen states or divisions, and the chairmanship of the Assembly is rotated among them. It had 473 members in 1982, elected from constituencies based on the township unit of local government. Each township has at least one representative, plus additional ones in proportion to the population. The first election for the People's Assembly was held in January and February 1974; the second between January 1 and 15, 1978; and the third between October 4 and 19, 1981. The Burma Socialist Program Party chooses candidates for the Assembly, and no one can run without its approval.

Judiciary

The Council of State nominates members of the Council of People's Justices, which is the highest judicial organ, and the Council of People's Attorneys, who are then approved by the Assembly. These judicial bodies have four-year terms and are accountable to the Council of State; thus, the principle of judicial autonomy is not recognized.

Regional & Local Government

The 1974 constitution provides for a four-tiered government structure. The top tier is the national government, and below that are seven state and seven division governments (the term "state" is used for minority areas and "division" for Burma proper.) These are subdivided into townships, which are further subdivided into village tracts or urban wards. Each of the units of the three levels of regional and local government elects a people's council which, like the People's Assembly, has a four-year term. The executive committees of the people's councils are responsible for administration on the local level and the formation of judges' committees, which are the subnational judicial bodies. The autonomy of regional and local units is limited by the priniciple of democratic centralism which assures that they will not deviate from policy lines laid down by the central government.

The new constitution changed the nature of regional government concerning the status of ethnic minorities. The 1948 constitution established a limited federal system in which states belonging to and created especially for the Shan, Karen, Kachin, Chin, and Kayah peoples had autonomous governments, with their own heads of state and legislatures: the heads of state were chosen by the national prime minister (with the exception of the Chin State) and state legislators were simultaneously members of the national legislature. The minority states had their own budgets. The Burman areas were governed directly by the national government. The new system abolished the federal status and special privileges of the minority states. Many observers interpreted this change in terms of the military's desire to "Burmanize" the minorities, undercutting the regional independence of non-Burman groups.

The Electoral System

Elections for the People's Assembly and the people's councils are held every four years simultaneously. All Burmese citizens over eighteen can vote, with the exception of members of religious orders, such as Buddhist monks, and certain other groups defined by law. Voting is by secret ballot. Voters are given a token to deposit in a box which represents the candidate the voter wants to win. If only one candidate is running, which apparently is the usual case, an extra box allows the voter to indicate a negative vote.

Candidates on all levels are chosen by the BSPP in conjunction with the workers' and peasants' mass organizations (People's Peasants Council and Workers Council). Persons both of whose parents are citizens can run for election to village tract, ward, and township people's councils at age twenty, to state or division people's councils at age twenty-four, and to the People's Assembly at age twenty-eight.

Burma Socialist Program Party (BSPP)

History

The military established the Burma Socialist Program Party in 1962 as their political arm, to bridge the gap between themselves and the people. According to the 1974 constitution, which the BSPP drafted, the party is the only legal one. It perceives itself as a revolutionary vanguard, embodying the will of the working people. The ideology of the BSPP, as found in documents such as *The Burmese Way to Socialism* (1962) and *The System of Correlation of Man and His Environment* (1963), emphasizes two goals: national unity and the construction of a socialist society. Like Marxist theories, it espouses collective ideas and the need to struggle against the exploitation of man by man; unlike Marxism, however, it does not acknowledge economic or materialist theories of historical development or progress. If anything, its metaphysical base is more closely allied to the Buddhist doctrines of the impermanence and changeability of all things. The party has asserted its differences with Marxism and its willingness to learn from non-Marxist sources. In the words of a 1964 official statement, "What is good and useful for the human society in the Union of Burma will be extracted in its essence, adapted and applied."

Organization

In its structure, however, the BSPP resembles the Leninist model of party organization. The Central Committee, consisting in 1982 of 260 members, is elected by the party congresses, there having been four of these since the first was held in 1971, the latest in August 1981. The Central Committee is controlled by the Central Executive Committee of fifteen men. The Central Committee includes a secretariat responsible for the day-to-day business of the party center and committees dealing with inspection, discipline, and policy formation. Party branches or units exist at each level of state and division, township and village tract government.

The BSPP maintains a number of training institutes for party cadres, including the Central Institute of Political Science at Chawdwigon, and the Academy for the Development of National Groups at Ywathitgyi, for the training of minority cadres. The Party Education Committee of the armed forces gives political training courses to military personnel.

Mass organizations established by the party to mobilize the general population include the People's Peasant Councils and the People's Worker Councils. Three youth organizations contain members from five to twenty-five years old: the Lanzin youth, Shesaung youth, and Teza youth.

Policy

In the area of policy, the BSPP-military leadership has established a centrally controlled, socialist economic system in which even the smallest shops are state-run enterprises. Although agriculture is not collectivized, farmers are required to sell their crops—principally rice—to the state at a fixed price. These rigid policies have led to decreased production, shortages of consumer goods, and a thriving black market. In recent years, however, economic controls have been loosened with some positive results.

In foreign policy, the military has continued the strict neutralist stance initiated by U Nu after independence. Burma has steered clear of involvement with the superpowers where possible, even at the price of economic isolation. Most recently, Burma renewed its commitment to neutrality by resigning from the Non-Aligned Movement, which U Nu had helped to establish, because of what was perceived as its excessive "tilt" toward the Soviet Union at its conference in Havana in 1979. Relations with the People's Republic of China are perhaps the most important and sensitive for Burma. They generally have been good in recent years, though strained over the Chinese Communist Party's support for the insurgent Burma Communist Party.

In line with its redefinition of state and division governments, the regime has attempted to draw minorities into the political system and convince them to think of themselves as citizens of a single country. Minorities are encouraged to join the BSPP, and several members of the Central Committee are from minority groups. A proposed two-tier citizenship policy, under consideration in mid-1982, however, would give full citizenship to Burmans and indigenous minorities, but only restricted citizenship rights to Chinese and Indian minorities, thus preventing them from having any political influence.

Membership & Constituency

Membership in principle is open to all citizens over eighteen who have committed themselves to the BSPP ideology, although candidate members must pass a two-year probationary period before becoming full members. In 1978, there were 281,617 full members, less than one percent of the total population despite party efforts to transform itself from a cadre-style to a mass party. By January 1981, however, it had increased to 1,500,912, according to the BSPP's own statistics, consisting of 1,275,498 men and 225,414 women. This figure, however, probably includes candidate as well as full members. Statistics in 1972 showed that at that time almost sixty percent of the full members and a quarter of the candidate members were military personnel. In 1981, however, they comprised only 9 percent of membership. They remain prominent in the upper ranks of the party. Thus, sixty of the 260 Central Committee members are officers (forty of these having been elected at the 1981 Fourth Party Congress), as are four of the fifteen members of the Central Executive Committee.

Financing

The sources of party revenues are not clear; direct state support is probably a sizeable portion of party income.

Leadership

The head of the Central Executive Committee and Chairman of the BSPP is Ne Win. Born on May 24, 1911, and educated at Rangoon University, he was a member of the *Dobama Asiayone* and gained military experience during the 1942–45 Japanese period and the postwar years. He held a number of high military posts before becoming prime minister and defense minister in 1958–60, chairman of the Revolutionary Council from 1962 to 1974, and president of Burma from 1974 until 1981.

Observers see Brigadier General San Yu as Ne Win's most probable successor. Born in 1919 and educated at Rangoon University, he entered military life in 1942 and served under Ne Win. After the 1962 coup, he was a member of the Revolutionary Council and served as secretary general of the BSPP from 1973 and secretary of the State Council from 1974. San Yu was so popular among party members that at the 1977 Party Congress, he received more votes for Central Committee membership than Ne Win himself; this led to the purging of some San Yu supporters, and at the 1981 Party Congress, San Yu himself was obliged to step down as BSPP secretary general and member of the Central Executive Committee. Nevertheless, after the October 1981 People's Assembly elections, he was named chairman of the State Council and president of Burma.

Other Political Forces

Military

During the colonial period, the army was organized along ethnic lines, with strong minority representation (as in the British Indian army). After independence, its units were desegregated and Burman elements became more predominant. Observers see it as "Burmanized," with the minority groups playing a subordinate role.

The military have perceived themselves as the guardians of the nation's welfare since preindependence times. Their roots go back to the prewar period when thirty members of the *Dobama Asiayone*, including Ne Win, were trained by the Japanese, whom they accompanied in the Japanese invasion of Burma in 1942 but revolted against in March 1945. These "thirty comrades" formed the postindependence armed forces. The fact that the leadership shares a common history of participation in the independence struggle invests the military with a strong sense of unity, although cracks in this unity were perceived when a plot to assassinate Ne Win and other top leaders was uncovered in 1976. The plot, by younger army officers, ostensibly arose from dissatisfaction with Burma's stagnant economy and its supposed cause, one-party socialist rule. Yet in the words of two observers, F. N. Trager and W. L. Scully, "The army is the strongest institution—in fact the *only* institution in the society that has any kind of cohesiveness. No civilian has risen to eminence since the coup of 1962."

Minority Opposition

Insurgent movements in the minority border areas do not pose a direct threat to the government, which is firmly entrenched in the Burman heartland, but the movements are costly in terms of lives and resources and reveal the fragility of the "Burmese nation." The largest in the early 1980s were the guerrilla forces of the Burma Communist Party, operating in the Shan State and numbering from 14,000 to 20,000. In recent years, government armed forces have engaged the communists in pitched battles, but have yet to break the back of the Chinese-supported movement. Campaigns also have been launched against the Karen National Liberation Army on the Thai border. Other insurgent groups include the Kachin Independence Army and the Shan State Army, which have allied at times with the communists.

Other Opposition

Within Burma proper, no civilian group has emerged to challenge military rule in any effective way. University students and Buddhist monks, however, have had a history of opposition to the government. In December 1974, for instance, they protested with such vehemence against the government's refusal to give appropriate honors to United Nations Secretary General U Thant, a popular figure who had died the month before, that the military declared martial law. In May 1980, in an attempt to co-opt, or at least to neutralize the Buddhist church, the government sponsored a convention, attended by over 1,200 representatives of the clergy, at which a constitution was drafted recognizing nine major sects. An authoritative body was established to discipline the country's many, often unruly, monks. Monks were required to carry identity cards issued by the Ministry of Home and Religious Affairs.

National Prospects

Although Ne Win's retirement from the presidency in late 1981 probably does not signal any basic change in the nature of military rule, especially as he intends to stay on as BSPP party chairman, an orderly succession would strengthen the political system and the regime's credibility. In the near future, the most pressing problems will be familiar ones: those of drawing the minorities into a single "Burmese" political system, of neutralizing insurgents, and lifting the economy out of its stagnation. Getting the 1974 constitutional system to stand on its own without the support of the military will be a most important task, one that will require the more active participation of civilians in the political process.

Further Reading
Asia 1981 Yearbook. Hong Kong: Far Eastern Economic Review, Ltd., 1980.
Cady, John F. *The United States and Burma.* Cambridge, Mass.: Harvard University Press, 1976.
Henderson, John W., et al. *Area Handbook for Burma.* Washington, D.C.: U.S. Government Printing Office, 1971.

McBeth, John. "Ne Win's Time of Change." *Far Eastern Economic Review*, September 25, 1981.

Scully, William L., and Trager, Frank N. "The Third Congress of the Burma Socialist Program Party: 'The Need to Create Continuity and Dynamics of Leadership.' " *Asian Survey*, Vol. 17, No. 9, Sept. 1977.

Silverstein, Josef. *Burma: Military Rule and the Politics of Stagnation.* Ithaca, N. Y.: Cornell University Press, 1977.

————. "Burma in 1980: An Uncertain Balance Sheet." *Asian Survey*, Vol. 21, No. 2, February 1981.

————. "Burma in 1981: The Changing of the Guardians Begins." *Asian Survey*, Vol. 22, No. 2, February 1982.

————. *Burmese Politics: The Dilemma of National Unity.* New Brunswick, N. J.: Rutgers University Press, 1980.

Steinberg, David I. *Burma's Road Toward Development: Growth and Ideology under Military Rule.* Boulder, Colo.: Westview Press, 1981.

UNITED REPUBLIC OF CAMEROON
(République Unie du Cameroun)
by Mark W. DeLancey, Ph.D.

The System of Government

The United Republic of Cameroon, a country of 8.5 million people in west central Africa, is a highly centralized, one-party state. The major institutions of government are the president and the party—the Cameroon National Union (CNU)—the bureaucracy, and the legislature. Cameroon was a German colony from 1884 to 1914 and then was a mandate/trust territory under France and Great Britain. The French section gained independence on January 1, 1960, and was joined on October 1, 1961, by the British section, becoming the bilingual Federal Republic. The present status as the United Republic began on June 2, 1972, after an intensive government drive for unity.

Executive

The president of the republic serves as head of state and government. He is directly elected to a five-year term by a majority of the votes cast and is reelectable without limit. President Ahmadou Ahidjo, Cameroon's first president, had been in office since independence. In the last election (May 1980), Ahidjo, the only candidate, received 99.99 percent of the vote. On November 6, 1982, he stepped down, reportedly for health reasons and was replaced by Paul Biya, who had been prime minister.

The constitution grants great power to the president, and Ahidjo assumed even greater power through his personality, his immense political skills, and the unfolding of events. The president is responsible for the conduct of the affairs of the republic and for ensuring national unity. He may initiate legislation and require a second reading of legislation he opposes. In fact, all significant legislation originates in the presidency. He is the head of the armed forces, is responsible for negotiating and ratifying treaties, appoints all major civil and military posts, and directs the administration. He appoints the prime minister (who replaces the president in case of death or disablement) and all ministers and vice ministers, and presides over the Council of Ministers. He can also proclaim a state of emergency or siege, both of which grant extraordinary powers to the president.

President Ahidjo ruled the country in a rather stern fashion. His presidential powers, his position as president of the party, and his political skills enabled him to build a system in which all power and authority emanate from the president; the presidency is essentially the government. He used a variety of techniques to divide and rule, such as constantly shifting ministers so that no one could build a machine to compete with him. Cabinet reshuffles, for example, took place in June 1978, November 1979, August 1980, and February 1982. Potential leaders were bought off with high posts or reduced to inactivity through various pressures. It is expected that the style of government will not change appreciably under Biya, and that Ahidjo will continue to play an important role in day-to-day policy making and the selection of government and party leaders.

Unconfirmed and strongly denied reports from Amnesty International suggest that there are political prisoners in Cameroon. An extensive net of patron-client relationships spreads from the president to the ministers (plus a few others) and downward into the villages. The complex multinational population of the country finds representation in the capital of Yaoundé through a system of ethnic balancing at the ministerial and vice-ministerial level.

Legislature

The National Assembly has 120 members and is elected for a five-year term, which may be shortened or lengthened in agreement with a request from the president. As with presidential elections, voters are encouraged to turn out. In the last election (May 1978), 98.7 percent of registered voters voted and 99.8 percent of them voted for party candidates; the Assembly consists entirely of CNU members. The Assembly meets in two sessions per year, each limited to a maximum of thirty days; the president may call special sessions.

Bills may be introduced by the president or by members of the Assembly and require a simple majority vote of members present to become law. The president may require a second reading, and then a majority of all members must vote in favor of passage. Constitutional amendment is the prerogative of the Assembly, requiring a simple majority in favor or a two-thirds majority in case of a second reading. The president may request a national referendum on an amendment, and he may call on the Supreme Court to judge the constitutionality of any law.

The Economic and Social Council, consisting of sixty-five members appointed by the president, and a small bureaucracy play an important role in the writing of legislation and in examining (and amending) legislation in respect to its impact on social and economic development.

Certain areas of legislation are reserved to the Assembly, but these may be turned over to the president at his request, unless the Assembly specifically rejects that request. These areas are citizen rights and obligations, labor law, general matters of defense, property law, civil and commercial law, nationality, local government, some aspects of criminal law, taxation, education, economic and social planning, and currency. The Assembly must also approve the budget. All other matters are reserved to the president who issues statutes in those areas.

The constitution clearly gives the president a powerful influence over legislative matters, and through his control of the party, he is in a position to completely dominate the Assembly.

Judiciary

The Supreme Court is appointed by the president. The Court's role is limited, but the constitution does give it certain responsibilities of possible significance. The Court may determine that the president is "permanently prevented from attending to his duties." Also, at the request of the president, the Court can determine the constitutionality of any law. The Court can also decide any disputes on the admissibility of a bill or amendment before the National Assembly. However, in any of the above instances, the size of the Court is to be doubled by the addition of persons designated by the president. There is also a court of impeachment (*la Haute Cour de Justice*) to try cases against the president, prime minister, and ministers for high treason. Its organization and

membership are set by law, not by constitution and are thus amenable to control by the president.

Regional & Local Government

Cameroon is divided into seven administrative units or provinces and these are subdivided into *départments* (divisions). A hierarchy of administrators appointed by and reporting to the president governs each of these units. Each ministry has representatives at each of these levels, who report to the presidential representative of the same level as well as upward to their ministry.

Local governments consisting of locally elected personnel play a very limited role. The CNU is responsible for nominating these persons and in some areas the CNU local organs play an active part as a sounding board for citizen demands and complaints and as a means of citizen control. In rural areas, traditional authorities (derived to some extent from precolonial political systems) are active, although they are largely dependent upon government and CNU support and appointment for their existence. Local rule is very weak in this highly centralized system. In essence, decisions and control emanate from Yaoundé, the capital; local government merely implements Yaoundé's decisions and instructions.

The Electoral System

The president is directly elected by the nation as a whole, as is the National Assembly. Although the constitution makes provision for the existence of multiple parties, the electoral system (as well as the weight of the government) reinforces a single-party system. Nominees are from single-member districts based on population, but the party with the most votes nationally takes all of the seats. The ballot is secret and suffrage is universal for all persons twenty-one years or older.

Cameroon National Union (CNU; *L'Union Nationale Camerounaise*)

History

At independence there were numerous political parties of various types in anglophone and francophone Cameroon, including one major organization, the francophone Union of Cameroon Populations (*l'Union des Populations du Cameroun;*

UPC), that had been driven underground and into rebellion by the colonial administration. By 1962, the parties in East Cameroon, the Francophone state, had coalesced voluntarily and under government pressure into the ruling party, *l'Union Camerounaise* (UC) under President Ahidjo. In West Cameroon, a similar process of amalgamation was occurring, with the Kamerun National Democratic Party (KNDP) emerging as the major party. On September 1st, 1966, the UC and the parties of the West joined to become the Cameroon National Union, the single party of the country. Ahmadou Ahidjo and John Foncha, head of the KNDP, were major figures in this merger. This party was more like an elite party than a mass party; it was a union of notables, each of whom brought his followers into the new party, rather than an organization consisting of members who had joined of their own accord.

Today, there is only the CNU, which is registered with the Ministry of Territorial Administration, as required by law. The ties between the CNU and the government are numerous and in many respects the party and the government are synonomous. "The Government of the United Republic of Cameroon is nothing but an offspring of the Party," according to a recent Party publication.

Over time, the coalition nature of the early party has altered in the direction of a mass party, though powerful individuals still bring their followers to the party.

Organization

The cell is the basic structure. Cells are grouped into branches, into subsections, and then into sections. Party sections coincide with the *département*. In 1979, there were forty-two sections (including those in France and Great Britain), 226 subsections, 7,474 branches, and 32,619 cells. Each unit has officers elected by its members.

The ruling bodies of the CNU are the congress, the National Council, the Central Committee, and the National Political Bureau. The congress meets every fifth year, most recently in 1980. The reports of these congresses are important documents, for they describe the general policy outlines of party and government. The National Council meets every two years (if called by the president) to supervise the implementation of the decisions of the congress. The Central Committee of no more than sixty members is responsible for directing the affairs of the party and for the nomination of all candidates for election. It, too, meets at the request of the president.

The National Political Bureau consists of twelve members, nominated by the president from the Central Committee and elected by the Committee. It is the true ruling body of the party and meets at the request of the president.

There are two significant affiliates of the CNU: the Women's Organization of the Cameroon National Union (WCNU) and the Youth Organization of the Cameroon National Union (YCNU). The national trade-union organization, the National Union of Cameroonian Workers (NUWC), although not an affiliate of the party, is closely aligned and coordinated with the CNU.

In addition to the reports of the party congresses, the CNU publishes collections of Ahidjo's speeches; party manuals; and a bilingual monthly magazine, *L'Unite*.

Policy

The policies of the party are those of the government: national unity, social and economic improvement through "planned liberalism" and "self-reliant development," cultural development, and bilingualism in the domestic sphere; nonalignment, respect for the sovereignty of all nations, African unity, and the liberation of Namibia and South Africa in the international sphere.

National unity is the prime goal in this country where differences in religion (Muslim, Christian and animist), geographic and cultural affinity (north and south and a welter of ethnic groups), and the French and English languages and other colonial heritages, provide plenty of reason for separatist movements and fears of domination by one category or another. In a country with an annual GDP per capita of $747, development is also a prime focus of the government. Planned liberalism—"private initiative within the framework of the conditions of the national development plan"—and self-reliant development—"the determination of the Cameroonian people to depend first and foremost on their endeavors"—are the means to that end.

Membership & Constituency

At present there are about three million members of the CNU, YCNU, and WCNU, an increase of 50 percent since 1975. Incomplete statistics indicate that actual paid membership of the WCNU is larger than that of either the CNU or YCNU, with about 45 percent of the total party membership in the women's wing alone. Some 23 percent is in the YCNU and 22 percent in the main party body. As females are also members of the CNU and YCNU as well as the WCNU, it appears that they play a predominant role in party membership. Of the 600,000 CNU members, 332,000 are defined as "militants," the really active members as opposed to those who merely pay dues. Membership is widespread throughout the country, although some sections fall far below the average in proportion of their population in the party.

Financing

Revenues are derived from membership fees, annual subscriptions, special contributions from members (especially militants), and proceeds from the sale of publications and other items. Membership fees are 200 francs (60 cents); CNU and WCNU subscriptions are 150 francs (43 cents); and YCNU subscriptions are 100 francs (29 cents). Large but unknown amounts of support are provided by government and business by allowing vehicles and other property, as well as personnel, to be used for party activities without charge. No overall financial figures are available.

Leadership

The prime figure in the party is still Ahidjo, a member of the Fulani group that dominates much of the Northern Province. Born in 1924, he has been in power since 1958, and appears willing to remain in power for years to come. Other significant figures in the CNU include Sadou Daoudu, another northerner and somewhat older than Ahidjo. He holds a cabinet-level position and was minister of armed forces for eighteen years. Moussa Yaya Sardifaka, another Fulani northerner and like Ahidjo and Daoudu, a Muslim, is about Ahidjo's age. He is a deputy and vice president of the National Assembly and is secretary for labor, social, and women's affairs in the CNU. A younger man, Thomas Ebongalame, represents southern and Anglophone interests. He is a deputy in the National Assembly and administrative secretary of the CNU. The new president, Paul Biya, was an *ex officio* member of the party's Central Committee, but not a prominent leader.

Opposition

There are no competitors to the CNU or to Ahidjo, though two political groups, the Cameroon Action Movement (CAM) and the remnants of the old UPC, would like to claim such a position. CAM represents the discontent of the Anglophone population. Both groups exist only in exile and consist of small, but difficult to number, memberships. They wish to return to the federal system or possibly to form a separate Anglophone state linked only loosely in a confederal relationship with the Francophone state. The discovery and development of petroleum largely in the Anglophone areas has encouraged their discontent.

The UPC originated in 1948 in coastal areas of Francophone Cameroon. Its radical nationalism has since that time been a rallying point for left-wing, socialist, and anti-French youths, but its activities are limited. Its ideas may appeal to a larger group in and out of Cameroon, but the leadership under Woungly Massaga has been unable to put this appeal to serious effect.

National Prospects

The CNU and its present leadership will remain in control of the country for years to come. No clear long-term successor to Ahidjo is apparent, but Biya would appear to have a slight advantage over other contenders.

Further Reading
Azarya, Victor. *Aristocrats Facing Change: The Fulbe in Guinea, Nigeria and Cameroon.* Chicago and London: University of Chicago, 1978.
Bayart, Jean-François. *L'Etat au Cameroun.* Paris: Foundation Nationale des Sciences Politiques, 1979.
Beti, Mongo. *Main Basse sur le Cameroun.* Paris: François Maspero, 1972.
Cameroon National Union. *CNU in the Nation.* Douala: Cameroon Public-Expansion, 1980.
_____. *L'Unite: Actes du Troisieme Congres.* Yaoundé: CNU, 1981.
Joseph, Richard A., ed. *Gaullist Africa: Cameroon under Ahmadu Ahidjo.* Enugu, Nigeria: Fourth Dimension, 1978.
_____. *Radical Nationalism in Cameroun: Social Origins of the U.P.C. Rebellion.* Oxford: Clarendon, 1977.
Kofele-Kale, Ndiva, ed. *An African Experiment in Nation-building: The Bilingual Cameroon Republic Since Reunification.* Boulder, Colo.: Westview Press, 1980.

Le Vine, Victor. *The Cameroon Federal Republic.* Ithaca and London: Cornell University Press, 1971.

Nelson, Harold D., et al. *Area Handbook for the United Republic of Cameroon.* Washington, D.C.: U.S. Government Printing Office, for Foreign Area Studies, American University, 1974.

Nkwi, Paul N. *Traditional Government and Social Change: A Study of the Political Institutions among the Kom of the Cameroon Grassfields.* Fribourg, Switz.: University Press, 1976.

DOMINION OF CANADA

by Dennis Quinn, M.A.

The System of Government

The Dominion of Canada, a nation of over twenty-four million people, is a multiparty parliamentary democracy. It is comprised of ten provinces and two territories; each province has its own parliament and premier. The provinces retain an unusual degree of autonomy and self-direction in political matters. Whether Canada is or ought to be a relatively loose confederation of provinces or a unified nation is the central issue in Canadian politics.

Colonial Canada developed as a union of French Canada, which came under British suzerainity in 1763, and the English-speaking colonies, which remained loyal to Britain during the American War of Independence (1775–83). Many thousands of American colonists (known as United Empire Loyalists) who had supported the Crown during the war fled to Canada during and after the war. The traditions of these settlers, in conjunction with nineteenth-century United States' threats to Canadian territory and Canadian independence, help to define the political culture of contemporary Canada.

The basic forms of Canadian government (an elected lower house, an appointed upper house, cabinet responsibility, etc.) are derived directly from Canada's historical status as a colony of Great Britain. Political self-government began with the grant of an assembly to the colony of Nova Scotia in 1758. By 1791, all the Canadian colonies had been granted assemblies. They had relatively little authority, however; decision making rested with the governor of the individual colony, who was always appointed from London.

Canada's government is based on the British North America Act of 1867 which confederated the colonies of Nova Scotia, New Brunswick, Ontario (Upper Canada), and Quebec. Manitoba joined in 1870, British Columbia in 1871, Prince Edward Island in 1873, and Alberta and Saskatchewan in 1905. Newfoundland was governed directly from Great Britain until 1949. The central government of the confederation was charged with primary responsibility in the areas of foreign affairs, defense, commerce, finance, and criminal justice. All other areas, including education, social services, and civil justice, were reserved to the provincial governments.

The expansion of Canada changed the nature of Canadian political problems. Prior to the admission of the prairie provinces (Alberta, Manitoba, Saskatchewan) and British Columbia, the primary political division had been over the cultural and religious differences between English and Protestant Ontario and French and Catholic Quebec. These two old provinces had agreed, however, on the use of high tariff walls to encourage the development of industry. The economies of the new western provinces were based on the sale of primary goods like wheat, mining products, and timber (now, oil and gas, as well) and the import of cheap manufactured goods. Thus a second political division, between east and west, between a manufacturing-based economy and a primary-goods economy developed in Canada. One manifestation of this split has been the rise of third parties (Progressive, Social Credit, the Cooperative Commonwealth Federation, and the Western Canada Concept Party) in opposition to the Liberal and Conservative parties which shared control of the eastern provinces and the federal government.

These geographic divisions are reinforced by Canada's electoral system, which puts considerable political power in the hands of local and regional electorates. As a result, the province has been the primary agency of resistance by both the French and the West to Ontario's dominance of Canada. Both federal and provincial governments have developed programs in education, health, and other areas. And not only do the two levels of government and their programs compete for public revenues, they also frequently evolve spending plans with diametrically opposed aims. For example, both the federal government and Ontario made public funds available to Chrysler Corporation in 1980. The funds from Ontario were aimed at persuading Chrysler to maintain its production and employment levels in Ontario, while one of the federal government's aims was that Chrysler move some of its production into other provinces.

One of the most serious federal-provincial disputes concerned Alberta and was waged over the price of gas and petroleum and the division of oil and gas tax revenues between the provincial and federal governments. The federal government claimed authority to set the price of domestic crude and did so at well under half the prevailing world price. Alberta, where most of Canada's oil and gas is located, is heavily dependent for its revenues on the price of oil and the subsequent higher tax revenues. Alberta demanded an increase in the oil price to near the world level. To force the federal government to go along with this, Alberta delayed approval of new oil projects and imposed production cuts on gas output. The bargaining between the two layers of government, which resulted in a compromise, resembled negotiations between two sovereign nations.

The Canadian east-west confrontation, the continuing English-French confrontation over the possible separation of Quebec from the rest of Canada, and the problem of competition over public funds and policy led Liberal Prime Minister Pierre Trudeau to propose constitutional reforms that would increase the power of the central government. Parliament passed the Trudeau reforms despite the opposition of nearly every provincial and municipal government. Of the major provincial governments, only the Ontario government (ironically, Conservative) supported Trudeau. An unlikely coalition of provincial premiers, including the Quebec separatist party leader, the Conservative leader of Alberta, and the New Democratic (socialist) leader of Saskatchewan, challenged the proposals at every turn.

Trudeau and nine of the provincial premiers (Levesque of Quebec being the exception) came to a compromise formula in November of 1981. Trudeau's proposal for a Canadian Bill of Rights was accepted with some modifications concerning the rights of "native Canadians," i.e., Indians. The original proposal for amending the constitution was changed to require the favorable votes of the federal Parliament and of seven of the ten provincial legislatures. The seven approving provinces must also contain more than 50 percent of the population of the nation. Any province not accepting an amendment may opt out for renewable five-year periods.

The reforms were then submitted to debate in the British House of Commons, which had the right of final approval of any change in the Canadian constitution. The constitutional reform was approved by the British Parliament and received final royal assent on March 29, 1982. Among the reforms was a provision to enable Canada to amend its constitution without British approval in future.

Executive

The head of state is the monarch of the United Kingdom, represented in Canada by a governor general and in each of the provinces by a lieutenant governor. As in Great Britain, the role of the monarch is formal, involving no real political power; the primary functions of the monarch's representatives are ceremonial in nature. The appointment of the governor general and lieutenant governors is technically made from London; but, in practice, the appointments are made in close consultation with the political leaders of Canada, particularly the prime minister. The current governor general, Edward Schreyer, has served since 1976.

Executive power in Canada rests with the prime minister and his cabinet who are members of Parliament. In effect, the executive branch in Canada, as in most parliamentary systems, is part of the legislature and is directly and collectively responsible to Parliament. This political arrangement is legitimized by tradition, not by law; the British North America Act makes no mention of either a prime minister or a cabinet.

The prime minister is the leader of either the largest party in Parliament, or of the senior party in a coalition of parties that control the majority of votes and has the "confidence of Parliament." Trudeau is prime minister by virtue of his leadership of the Liberal Party, which currently holds 146 of the 282 seats in the House of Commons. The prime minister makes all appointments to the cabinet, controls its agenda, and is ultimately responsible for the decisions of the government. The prime minister is a more powerful and politically important figure both for the nation and for his party than is the president of the United States in the American political system.

Technically, the prime minister is chosen by the governor general. In practice, the prime minister is usually, but not always, the elected leader of his party's parliamentary bloc. The party choice is strongly influenced by the preferences of the party elite, particularly by the retiring leader. The leader who emerges need not be a current member of Parliament. The Progressive Conservatives have occasionally chosen a provincial premier to lead the party. Nevertheless, if the chosen leader is to become prime minister, he must be elected to

Parliament from a specific electoral district (riding). When necessary, this election can be managed through a by-election in a safe district within a matter of weeks.

The cabinet is usually chosen from the members of the House of Commons. Each minister has a defined area of responsibility within the cabinet, as well as responsibilities for the collective decisions of the cabinet.

Much of the actual decision making occurs in meetings of the eleven cabinet committees, such as the committee on priorities and planning, chaired by the prime minister. These committee meetings include ministers, parliamentary secretaries (MPs who serve as chief aides to the minister), and senior civil servants. Any minister, even one who is not a member of the committee in question, may object to a decision, which elevates the issue to the level of cabinet discussion. This gives each minister the opportunity to structure government decisions so as to avoid politically insensitive directives.

To some extent, ministers are chosen to represent various regions and groups. Every government attempts to have each province represented in the cabinet. Given the regional divisions of Canada, this is not always an easy task. The Conservative Party, through its sometime French affiliate, Union Nationale, was able to win only two of the seventy-five possible seats from Quebec in 1979, despite winning a plurality of Commons seats. The Conservative government of Joe Clark was obliged to appoint a defeated candidate from Quebec to the Senate in order to make him a minister. The Liberal Party has for years reached into the Senate for cabinet members from the Canadian west.

Two agencies, the Prime Minister's Office and the Privy Council Office, have become important for the operation of the cabinet during the Trudeau years. The Privy Council Office is an ostensibly nonpartisan agency manned by civil servants whose primary function is the coordination of cabinet activities and cabinet committee meetings. The Prime Minister's Office is comprised of politically appointed staff whose primary loyalty is to the prime minister. This office is an agency of political control, following through on decisions as they move from cabinet policy to implementation. Like the cabinet, these agencies have no constitutionally defined role and vary in purpose with the desires of the prime minister.

The civil service staffs the departments of the Canadian government, usually up to the level of deputy minister. In theory, only the minister and the parliamentary secretary are politically ap-

pointed. The civil service is intended to be politically neutral, providing expert advice and carrying out political commands. While the vast majority of civil servants are unaffected by a change in government, a handful who have been closely associated with the previous government are often asked to resign or are reassigned. The extent to which the bureaucracy as a whole is politically neutral is a subject of some debate. Joe Clark claimed that the civil service as an institution was politically too powerful and called for a redress in power towards Parliament.

Legislature

The legislature of Canada is divided into two branches, an elected lower house, the Commons, and an appointed upper house, the Senate. As in Great Britain, the Commons produces the prime minister, most of the cabinet, and most of the politically important legislation. The Senate, though constitutionally a nearly co-equal branch of government, in practice defers to the Commons on most matters, reserving for itself the roles of reconciling legal inconsistencies in Commons legislation and holding hearings on major social and political issues.

The House of Commons has 282 members, each representing a single district. The seats are allotted to the provinces in proportion to population, though smaller provinces like Prince Edward Island and Newfoundland receive more than their due.

Parliamentary sessions are variable in length, depending on the amount of legislation that the government is prepared to introduce. Sessions are usually held twice a year, commencing in October and January. The end of sessions is not fixed; the opposition can extend the length of a session by refusing to support adjournment. The opposition leader, Joe Clark, did exactly that in the summer of 1981, refusing to permit Parliament to adjourn until a strike by workers of the Canadian Post had been settled.

The formal powers of the House of Commons are substantial. Yet, political power in Canada rests not with Parliament itself, but with the prime minister, the cabinet, and the majority-party caucus. Individual MPs can introduce private member's bills, but none pass without government support. Parliamentary committees exist and members of all parties have places on these committees, but legislation is generally prepared within a government ministry and presented to the parliamentary committees as more or less a *fait accompli*. Members of the governing party without government responsibility (backbenchers) could theoretically oppose the party leadership, but strict party discipline is maintained by patronage, the threat of dissolution (calling an early election), and possible rejection of the renegade as a candidate of the party.

The opposition has several devices at its disposal. The government is obliged periodically to endure a question period in Commons in which members of the opposition raise questions about government actions; the government must respond. The opposition also participates in parliamentary debates and in committee meetings. Opposition parties also maintain "shadow cabinets" in which leading MPs develop and present opposition-party policy in the various areas for which real cabinet ministers are responsible. The opposition can defeat the governing party on a major vote in Parliament, as it did in 1979. Such a defeat need not be followed by new elections but invariably is.

Parliamentary elections must be held at least every five years. In practice, the governing party usually calls for an election after three and a half to four years, at a moment the prime minister believes to be most favorable to his party. The power to set the date of an election is one of the prime minister's most potent tools. The two most recent elections were held within the space of a year, in February 1980 and May 1979. The results were as follows:

PARLIAMENTARY SEAT DISTRIBUTION AFTER 1980 ELECTIONS						
Province	Seats	Liberal	Conservative	New Democrat	Social Credit	Vacant
Ontario	95	52 (32)*	37 (57)	5 (6)	0 (0)	1 (0)
Quebec	75	73 (67)	1 (2)	0 (0)	0 (6)	1 (0)
Nova Scotia	11	5 (2)	6 (8)	0 (1)	0 (0)	0 (0)
New Brunswick	10	7 (6)	3 (4)	0 (0)	0 (0)	0 (0)
Manitoba	14	2 (2)	5 (7)	7 (5)	0 (0)	0 (0)
Saskatchewan	14	0 (0)	7 (10)	7 (4)	0 (0)	0 (0)
Alberta	21	0 (0)	21 (21)	0 (0)	0 (0)	0 (0)
British Columbia	28	0 (1)	16 (19)	12 (8)	0 (0)	0 (0)
Prince Edward I.	4	1 (0)	2 (4)	0 (0)	0 (0)	1 (0)
Newfoundland	7	5 (4)	2 (2)	0 (1)	0 (0)	0 (0)
Northwest Territory	2	0	1 (1)	1 (1)	0 (0)	0 (0)
Yukon Territory	1	0	1 (1)	0 (0)	0 (0)	0 (0)
Total**	282	145 (114)	102 (136)	32 (26)	0 (6)	3 (0)

*The results of the 1979 election are enclosed in parentheses.
**As of August 1982, the Liberals had 146 seats, the Conservatives 100, and the New Democrats 32. There was one independent member and three vacant seats.

The Senate has 104 seats. All senators are appointed by the prime minister. Except for those from Quebec, senators are appointed from their provinces at large; Quebec senators are appointed from specific districts. Provincial representation is sharply disproportional: Newfoundland and British Columbia, for example, have equal representation even though B.C. has nearly five times the population. Ontario and Quebec have twenty-four seats each; Nova Scotia and New Brunswick, ten each; Prince Edward Island has four; and Manitoba, Saskatchewan, Alberta, British Columbia, and Newfoundland each have six. The two territories, the Northwest Territories and Yukon Territory, have one each.

The disparities in party representation are even more striking. In 1981 the Liberal Party had sixty-seven of the seats; the New Democratic Party, which receives between 13 and 18 percent of the popular vote and has governed several provinces, had none. Twenty-six seats were held by the Progressive Conservatives, two by independents, one by an independent Liberal, one by a member of the Social Credit Party. Several seats may be vacant at any given time.

Many commentators have noted that, in recent

years, the Senate has become little more than a combination of a retirement ground for older politicians, a reward for diligent party work, and a haven for cabinet ministers who have been unsuccessful candidates for a Commons seat. Because senators are selected by the prime minister for the duration of their careers (new appointees must now retire at 75) and are unremovable, appointment is more a matter of social prestige and a lobbying opportunity than a way of advancing one's political career. The Senate does have the authority to block Commons legislation or amend it, but the overrepresentation of Liberals and the absence of partisan politics means that, in practice, Trudeau's government has had little political difficulty with the upper house.

Judiciary

Canada's federal political system is mirrored by a federal judicial system. Provincial courts are responsible for civil-law matters and such areas as civil and linguistic rights. The federal courts are assigned jurisdiction over criminal and interprovincial matters. The highest court is the Supreme Court, the final court of appeal for both provincial and federal matters and the ultimate arbiter of federal versus provincial government disputes. The Supreme Court is also an advisory body. The government can and does ask the Supreme Court to rule on the constitutionality of a wide range of issues without the necessity of having a specific case at law before the bench.

The Supreme Court is comprised of eight judges and the chief justice. Traditionally, judges are selected both for their legal ability and for their ethnic and regional backgrounds. In recent years, appointments to both the Supreme Court and the federal courts have been screened by the Canadian Bar Association before submission of the appointments to Parliament for approval. Legal scholars believe that the consequence has been a more qualified and less politicized judiciary.

Regional & Local Government

Provincial elections are important events in Canada, since the provincial governments control such central elements of everyday life as education, civil rights, and civil law. For instance, laws made by the provincial governments of Quebec and Ontario concerning language rights in the schools have been among the most controversial in the nation. Often, a province is more effective

in its opposition to the national governing party than the opposition party in Parliament.

Newfoundland

The Province of Newfoundland and Labrador is the most culturally and socially isolated province in Canada. Newfoundland was the last of the provinces to break ties with Great Britain and join Canada. Prior to its entrance into the Dominion in March 1949, the people of Newfoundland had been governed directly from Great Britain following the suspension of the Newfoundland legislature in 1933 (due to a series of financial and political scandals). The province's 600,000 people are overwhelmingly located on the island; Labrador is sparsely peopled by Inuits (Eskimos), Indians, and transient miners and loggers.

Newfoundland politics is dominated by the Progressive Conservatives and the Liberals. Brian Peckford, leader of the province's Conservatives, is premier. The Conservatives have won the past two elections; in 1979 they captured thirty-four and in 1982 won forty-four of the fifty-two seats. The Liberal Party held the remainder.

The province is split on religious lines. Those of Irish and Catholic descent tend to vote Liberal; those of English or Scottish and Protestant descent tend to vote Conservative. Not surprisingly, the major opposition to Canadian union came from the anglophile Conservative Party.

The Maritimes

New Brunswick, Nova Scotia, and Prince Edward Island—Canada's three Atlantic provinces—are commonly known as the Maritimes. Their common political and economic history has, in the past, generated discussion of a provincial union. The Maritimes have produced a surprisingly large number of federal political leaders.

The three provinces are politically dominated by the Liberal and Conservative parties. Neither New Brunswick nor Prince Edward Island has elected provincial representatives from a third party since 1920. Nova Scotia has a significant New Democratic Party which gathers between 10 and 15 percent of the popular vote, but political power still rests with the two dominant parties. The three provinces share a common occupational structure. Manufacturing (excepting the Sydney region of Cape Breton, Nova Scotia) is rare; catering to tourists, fishing, and farming are the most common activities.

New Brunswick is unique among Canadian provinces in that the population of 700,000 is nearly evenly divided between French and English speakers; both languages are used in government and business. As in Canada as a whole, most of the support for the Liberal Party comes from those who are Catholic and/or French; the English and/or Protestants support the Conservatives. Though the Conservatives have governed since 1970, elections in New Brunswick are closely contested; the opposition Liberals are more than a paper force, with twenty-eight of the fifty-eight provincial assembly seats.

Prince Edward Island has an unusual electoral system; the thirty-two members of the Assembly are divided between assemblymen and councillors. The sixteen electoral districts select one of each in separate ballots. The Conservative Party controls twenty-one of the seats. The eleven Liberals elected are not representative of the real strength of the party; the Liberals usually win about 45 percent of the popular vote and actually won the elections of 1970 and 1974. Party switching is rare among PEI's 110,000 citizens.

Nova Scotia and Cape Breton Island also have a competitive, two-party-dominant electoral system. The province's fifty-two seats are divided among the Conservatives (thirty-three seats, 46 percent of the 1978 vote), the Liberals (fifteen seats, 39 percent of the vote), and the New Democratic Party (four seats, 15 percent of the vote). The 1978 vote reversed that of 1974, when the Liberals won thirty-one of the then forty-six seats. As in the other Maritime provinces, party loyalty is strong. Varying voter turnout and a small floating group of voters account for changing electoral outcomes.

Quebec

The Province of Quebec contains nearly one quarter of the population of Canada. Quebec's 6.25 million people are split between the French-speaking majority (80 percent) and the English-speaking population (nearly 29 percent).

The political scene in Quebec has changed dramatically during the past twenty years. Quebec has changed from a rural, conservative province dominated by the Roman Catholic Church and by Maurice Duplessis's Union Nationale Party to a more urban, modern, and liberal province where a neosocialist party committed to Quebec's independence, the *Parti Quebecois*, has won the past two elections. The changes in Quebec affect not just Quebec, but are a burning issue throughout Canada.

Under both the Liberal Party and the now-governing *Parti Quebecois* (PQ), Quebec has exercised a degree of autonomy that has seldom been challenged by the federal government. For example, Quebec legislation (Bill 101) which mandates that new settlers in Quebec send their children to French-speaking schools, went unchallenged by the federal government under Trudeau even though this francophile policy runs counter to the Liberal government's policy of bilingualism.

Despite the PQ defeat in a referendum on renegotiating Quebec's position in the Dominion, and even though early opinion polls showed the provincial Liberal Party leading the PQ by a wide margin, in April 1981 the PQ actually increased its percentage of the popular vote over the previous election. Of Quebec's 122 seats, the PQ took eighty with only 49 percent of the popular vote. The Liberals with 46 percent of the vote won only 40 seats, and the once-powerful Union Nationale won none. This result confirmed the polarization of Quebec politics between the independence-seeking PQ and the federally oriented Liberals. In the 1976 vote, the Union Generale had won eleven seats with 18 percent of the vote, and another small party had taken one seat with 5 percent of the vote.

Ontario

Ontario is the most populous (8,543,000 in 1980), wealthiest, and politically most important of Canada's provinces. Ontario can be seen as a microcosm of Canadian society. Given the regional split in Canadian politics, the party that carries Ontario in the federal elections has the best chance of dominating the government.

Ontario's party system is the only true three-party system in Canada. Although the Progressive Conservative Party has governed by itself or in coalition since 1943, the electorate is split between the Conservatives, Liberals, and New Democrats at roughly 40, 35, and 25 percent, respectively. The provincial premier, William Davis, has governed since 1971. Davis was forced into a coalition government following the 1977 election when the Conservatives captured fifty-eight of the 125 seats (39.7 percent of the vote). The Liberals and the NDP each took 33 seats, though the Liberals' vote count was higher (31.5 percent to 28). The 1981 elections restored Davis to a majority position with seventy seats (44.5 percent of the vote). The NDP suffered a major drop in the vote (21 percent) and seats (twenty-one). The vote of the Liberals increased slightly to 33.6 percent (thirty-four seats). Davis (along with Nova Scotia's John Buchanan) supported Trudeau's recentralization measures. Because Ontario is a major financial beneficiary of the Dominion, such a stand is politically popular in Ontario. Davis's stand puts him at odds with the national Progressive Conservative policy, but he is firmly supported within the provincial party.

Manitoba

Manitoba has an economy split between manufacturing (around Winnipeg) and prairie farming. It is an ethnically diverse province with long-settled French and Ukranian populations.

In recent years, the province has been politically dominated by the Conservatives and the New Democrats. In November 1981, Premier Howard Pawley led the NDP to victory, winning thirty-four seats to the Conservatives' twenty-three. Previously, the Conservatives had ended eight years of NDP rule with their 1977 election victory. The Liberal Party won only one seat in 1977 and none in 1981.

Manitoba has had a long tradition of socialist and communist party activity. The city of Winnipeg, which contains half of Manitoba's population, has been the scene of much working-class political organization, and the New Democrats have always been well organized there. A member of the Winnipeg city council is the only elected official in Canada who is a Communist Party member.

Saskatchewan

Although some oil and gas have recently been found in the province, Saskatchewan as a whole is heavily dependent on agricultural products, especially wheat, for its prosperity. Recent years have seen a stagnant population, a collapse of the Liberal Party, a period of political domination by the New Democratic Party, and an unexpected resurgence of the Progressive Conservative Party.

Until April of 1982, the New Democratic Party had governed Saskatchewan for all but seven years since 1944 (the Liberals were in power between 1964 and 1971). Provincial NDP leader Allan Blakeney had been premier since 1971. The 1978 election had given Blakeney forty-four seats (48 percent of the vote), the Conservatives fifteen seats (38 percent of the vote) and the Liberals two seats (14 percent of the vote). In a major upset in April 1982, the PC, led by Grant Devine, won fifty-seven of the provincial assembly's sixty-four seats; the NDP won the other seven. The separatist Western Canada Concept Party fielded forty candidates, none of whom came close to winning.

Alberta

Alberta is the fastest-growing province in Canada. Major deposits of oil, natural gas, and tar sand have changed Alberta from a predominantly agricultural province to one in which energy matters are the primary political issues. Alberta, along with Quebec, has taken the lead among the provinces in challenging Ottawa's decisions.

Although Alberta's occupational structure has changed, important aspects of the political culture remain. Alberta is a one-party-dominant electoral system. Every election since 1921 has produced an overwhelming assembly majority for one of the major parties, always a party (excepting Clark's seven-month reign) which has not been in power in Ottawa at the same time. Alberta seems to be in perpetual opposition to central Canada. In the 1979 elections, the Conservatives won 57 percent of the vote, compared to Social Credit's 20 percent, and the Liberal's 6 percent. The current premier, Peter Lougheed, commands a Conservative majority of seventy-four seats, Social Credit has three, and the NDP and Western Canada Concept Party one each.

A provincial by-election in February 1982 dramatized the hostility felt by some Albertans towards the Ottawa government. Gordon Kessler, the leader of the separatist Western Canada Concept Party, won a close election to replace a Social Credit candidate, thus becoming the party's first elected official. Alberta hostility has surfaced before. In 1977, several Calgary businessmen set up a foundation, West-Fed, which agitated for Albertan independence. Despite these signs of anger, few Albertans actually support separatism.

British Columbia

Canada's westernmost province is heavily dependent on resource-extraction industries like mining and lumbering. The population is heavily concentrated in Vancouver, Victoria, and other industrial towns. Vast sections of British Columbia remain unpopulated despite the province's 2.6 million people, the third-largest provincial population in Canada.

British Columbia has an elaborate electoral system whereby fifty constituencies elect fifty-seven representatives with some of the larger districts electing several legislators.

Neither of Canada's two dominant parties are important in British Columbia. The Social Credit Party of William Bennett governs with thirty-one out of fifty-seven seats. The remainder fall to the NDP. The Social Credit Party has been the majority in British Columbia since 1953, excepting the 1972–75 period when the NDP governed.

The Electoral System

Elections to the House of Commons and provincial legislatures are direct. Canadians eighteen years of age or older are eligible to vote by secret ballot in the parliamentary district in which they reside. Voter turnout for provincial and federal elections ranges from 60 to 85 percent of registered voters.

Canadian electoral rules specify single-member districts. The effect of this is twofold: minority political parties or positions which are regionally based will be overrepresented, and parties and issues which are both minority-based *and* diffused throughout the country will be underrepresented. For example, the New Democratic Party, with substantial support everywhere except Quebec, generally receives 15 to 18 percent of the vote, but only 8 to 12 percent of the seats in Parliament. The electoral system also dramatically overstates trends in the electorate. In the 1981 Quebec election for example, the *Parti Quebecois* won 64 percent of the provincial seats with only 49 percent of the vote. The Liberal Party's 46 percent of the vote entitled them to only 36 percent of the seats. The Progressive Conservative's dominance over Alberta (92 percent of the provincial seats) obscures the fact that 40 percent of Albertans vote for parties other than the Conservatives. Many commentators have called for proportional representation as a way out of Canada's continuing regional crises.

The Party System

Origins of the Parties

The first Canadian political parties emerged directly out of Canada's experience as a British colony. The Conservative Party of John Macdonald consciously used the ideology and symbols of the British Conservative Party. The Canadian variant—strongly Protestant, pro-British and anti-American—evolved its own policies based on Canada's unique conditions. The main features of the Canadian Conservative Party, an emphasis on social order and close ties to Britain, dominated the party until 1960.

The Liberal Party also consciously imitated its English forebear. The reform tradition applied to Canada meant a commitment to anticlericalism, free trade, and profarmer policies. The Liberal Party has placed less emphasis on Canada's British heritage. Liberal prime minister Lester Pearson, for example, was a particular devotee of "Canadianization" and was responsible for the introduction of a distinctive Canadian flag.

The more recent New Democratic Party (formerly the Cooperative Commonwealth Federation) was influenced by the rise of the British Labour Party. Though the NDP contains a large agrarian element not found in the Labour Party, both parties share a commitment to democratic socialism, government control of the economy, and redistribution of national income.

Not all Canadian parties have roots in British political culture: Social Credit, the *Parti Quebecois*, and the Union Nationale grew out of the problems faced by subcultures of the Canadian population. These parties, creations of the mid-twentieth century, are part of a well-established tradition in Canada of the rapid rise (and often rapid fall) of third and fourth political parties.

The Parties in Law

Political parties are among the important institutions in Canadian politics which have no constitutional standing. The Canadian state does register political parties and provides them with financial support if they meet the basic requirements. However, individual candidates who wish to stand for Parliament need only make an election deposit of $200, which is forfeited if a candidate fails to receive 15 percent of the vote. Independent candidacies are very common, but seldom successful.

The Election Expenses Act of 1974 altered the basic financing of election campaigns. The Act enables the state to subsidize campaigns indirectly by allowing individuals tax credits for gifts up to $500. The Act requires that a party have either one representative in Parliament or field candidates in at least fifty electoral districts to be eligible for the indirect subsidies. These requirements are met by the Liberal Party, the Conservative Party, the New Democratic Party, the Social Credit Party, the Communist Party, and the Marxist-Leninist Party. The Act also limits campaign expenditures: parties may spend no more than 80 cents per voter in a district and candidates are subject to a sliding scale based on the number of votes received. (Some provinces have also placed limits on the size of individual campaign donations.) Candidates may be directly reimbursed by the state for a percentage of electoral costs if they receive at least 15 percent of the votes cast and meet all other requirements, including publication of the names of donors of over $100. The three larger parties have benefited most by this arrangement.

Party Organization

Canadian political parties share a number of common organizational features. Each of the parties is dominated by a handful of politicians who have relatively high visibility for voters. The domination by notables extends even to so-called mass-based parties like the *Parti Quebecois*, whose leader, René Levesque, is widely credited with PQ's success.

Parties in Canada are essentially associations which band together for elections. No Canadian party shows evidence of emerging into a "way of life" in the fashion of the French Communist Party with its social and cultural organizations and activities. Neither the Liberal Party nor the Conservative Party are tightly bound to voluntary associations in the community, though both have close ties to the business community and depend on the middle class for support. The New Democratic Party does have links with the Canadian Labour Congress (CLC) and various farmer groups, but neither has a decisive voice in NDP politics.

Each of the major national parties maintains separate provincial and federal party systems; even the local-level constituency associations are separate. The main reason for this, of course, is that each province has its own legislature with its own powers and issues. Neither the timing of the provincial elections nor the electoral districts (excepting Ontario's) coincide with those of the federal system. The provincial premier is a powerful figure in his own right and is usually unresponsive to federal party pressures. His base of support is restricted to the province, and his main concern is the electoral success of the provincial party. That success may well require advocating policies in conflict with those of the federal party. For example, in 1980, the issue of constitutional reform saw each of the three major federal parties at odds with some of their provincial counterparts. At the national level the Progressive Conservative Party opposed Trudeau's original proposals, but the PC premier of Ontario backed those proposals, which were popular in Ontario. New Democratic premier Blakeney of Saskatchewan opposed the pro-

posals, despite the federal party's support of them. In Quebec, the provincial Liberal Party, after much debate, came out against fellow Liberal and Quebecker Trudeau. Nine Liberal members of the provincial assembly, mostly from English-speaking districts, did back Trudeau, however, fearing the wrath of their constituents more than that of the provincial party leader. In each case, provincial- and/or local-constituency considerations were the decisive factor in placing the provincial party at odds with the national one.

The organizational strength of the political parties rests on the local, or constituent, level. The constituency associations of the major parties are club-based electoral associations of volunteers who are particularly active in times of elections. The NDP does have a dues-paying membership, but their constituency associations also are most active during elections.

Generally speaking, constituency parties are largely responsible for nominating electoral candidates (usually through a local convention or committee meeting), raising funds for candidates and for the party, and canvassing the electorate. Where the constituency party is weak (the Conservatives in parts of Quebec, for instance) the national and provincial party cannot compensate, and electoral success is highly unlikely.

Candidates need not be residents of the districts in which they run, but most are. Candidates who are important to the national party, but who have been defeated in recent elections, are often placed in "safe" constituencies. When Prime Minister Mackenzie King failed to win election in his own district, another member of Parliament resigned, and King ran and won a by-election in the former MP's district. In 1981, a political ally of Trudeau, Jim Coutts, was placed in a "safe" district in Toronto, and lost.

The various branches of each party meet in a national party convention (each of the three major parties requires such a convention "at least" every two years), and each has a national council or executive where provincial and national party people try to coordinate policy and, more effectively, plan national election campaigns. Each party has a president, not the party leader, who is in charge of general administration of day-to-day party affairs.

The constituency organizations are not accorded the power that their electoral influence might warrant. Canadian parties are dominated at the national level by the parliamentary party leader and at the provincial level by the provincial assembly party leader. The power accorded to party leaders arises from the nature of parliamentary government and gives them wide discretion regarding the rank-and-file member of Parliament and local leaders.

The party leader's power evolves significantly from his critical importance to the electoral success of the party. Trudeau's resignation as Liberal Party leader following the party's defeat in 1979 was quickly followed by party demands for his return. No other figure in the Liberal Party had Trudeau's stature with the electorate. One of the consequences of the importance of the party leader is that one is rarely displaced; Canadian party leaders show a longevity rare in Western democracies. John Macdonald led the Conservative Party for twenty-four years; Wilfred Laurier led the Liberals for thirty years; and William Mackenzie King was the Liberal leader for twenty-nine years. Pierre Trudeau has governed both the Liberals and Canada since 1968, with an interlude of only seven months as leader of the opposition.

Campaigning

Electoral campaigns in Canada are increasingly staged through the media, with particular attention focused on the competing party leaders. Now that parts of House of Commons sessions are televised, voters have a much stronger sense of who the major leaders are. The media play a decisive role in communicating new faces and policies since election campaigns are comparatively short (usually two to three months). However, the media is unlikely to replace the constituency association as the most important element in a campaign because of the ceiling on campaign expenditures imposed by the 1974 Election Expenses Act.

Independent Voters

Campaigns in Canada tend to be aimed at the relatively small number of undecided (or "swing") votes located in "swing" provinces: This is the result of two factors. First, to a high degree voters identify with the parties and not with the candidates themselves (leadership excepted). For instance, Jack Horner, a Progressive Conservative MP from Alberta was defeated in the 1980 general election (23,491 to 4,761) after he switched parties and became a Liberal cabinet minister. Horner had had a 14,571-vote margin of victory in 1974 as a Conservative. Second, election is based on a "winner take all" system which causes parties to ignore constituencies where the electorate has shown consistent preference for one party. The dividing lines of culture (French and Catholic [Liberal] versus English and Protestant [Conser-vative]) and region mean that party efforts are often concentrated heavily in Ontario, where no one culture or party is dominant.

Liberal Party of Canada

History

The Liberal Party emerged as the colonial counterpart of the British Liberal Party after Canada gained Dominion status in 1867. The party was based on anticlericism in Quebec; on anticonservative, free-trade Ontario English (Grits); and on anglophone farmers. It was characterized by a strong free-trade and anticolonial policy. The Liberal Party under Laurier and King openly welcomed American capital for industrial development.

The Liberal Party had had only seven leaders since 1867, six of whom were prime ministers. Among the prominent Liberal leaders have been Sir Wilfred Laurier, the first French Canadian prime minister (1896–1911) and head of the party for thirty years; William Lyons MacKenzie King; Louis St. Laurent, leader and prime minister from 1948 to 1957; Lester Pearson; and Pierre Trudeau. Liberal Party prime ministers have led the government for well over half of Canada's history since 1867. Since the days of Laurier, Liberal Party tradition requires that the leadership of the party alternate between French and English Canadians.

Organization

The Liberal Party is the only one of the three major parties which attempts to unite the national party constituency associations with the provincial party organizations. Although they are separate organizations, the constituency associations of the national party belong to the provincial-level member organizations. The youth and women's commissions are branches of the provincial party organizations, not the national.

A national convention meets every two years to set policy and elect national officers. It is broadly representative of party adherents with delegates from Parliament, the provincial organizations, the provincial legislatures, the constituency associations, and the youth and women's commissions. The delegates to the convention serve as a consultative council between conventions. Party by-laws stipulate that they must be consulted by the National Executive twice a year; this is usually done by mail.

The thirty-four-person National Executive consists of national party officers and the administrative leaders of the provincial party organizations and the youth and women's commissions. The selection of national officers is heavily influenced by the presidents of the provincial member organizations and the two affiliated commissions.

National party headquarters are at 102 Bank Street, Ottawa, Ontario.

Policy

Trudeau has reversed some traditional Liberal policies. With Walter Gordon at the finance ministry, the Liberals in the 1970s began to oppose the further "Americanization" of Canada. The Foreign Investments Review Act and 1981 legislation concerning energy companies are aimed at developing an autonomous Canadian economy in certain sectors. The basic tenor of Canadian foreign policy—close relations with the United States and the NATO alliance—remains unchanged.

Membership & Constituency

The national party is comprised primarily of the Quebec, Ontario, and Maritime parliamentary delegations. West of Ontario, only two Commons seats are held by Liberals. This structure is partly the result of the political strengths and weaknesses of Pierre Trudeau. His popularity in Quebec is matched by his lack of appeal in the west; the next liberal leader, most probably an English speaker, may change this trend. The primary social bases of support for the Liberals lie within Quebec (especially among the French), among English-speaking central Canadians who have benefited from long years of Liberal rule, among city inhabitants, and among the well-educated and the middle- and upper-middle classes.

Financing

Liberal Party expenditures in the 1979 fiscal period, according to reports made by the party to the government, amounted to C$2,770,623 (about US$2.33 million), while income was C$6,302,033 (about US$5.3 million). Nearly 83 percent of income came from contributions, and almost 75 percent of that amount was donated by corporations. Individual contributions to the Liberals came from far fewer people and amounted to far less than similar contributions to the other two major parties (C$1,184,755 from 13,025 contributors).

Leadership

The leadership of the Liberal Party is drawn overwhelmingly from the Quebec, Ontario, and Maritime professional classes. Very rarely is anyone from a nonprofessional background a candidate for party positions. Among the significant members of the Liberal Party are Pierre Trudeau (born 1919 in Quebec), prime minister; John Turner (born 1929 in the United Kingdom), candidate for leader and based in Ontario; Allan MacEachon (born 1921 in Nova Scotia), external affairs minister; Jean Chretien (born 1934 in Quebec), energy minister; Mark MacGuigin (born 1931 in PEI), justice minister; and Marc Lalounde (born 1929 in Quebec), finance minister.

Prospects

The Liberal Party has dominated Canadian politics since the turn of the century, in large part, because no party has successfully challenged the national party's position in Quebec. Liberal dominance in Quebec has compensated for the sharp decline in support that the party has experienced in the western provinces. Whatever negative implications this fact has for Canada as a whole, it means that the Liberals need only carry Ontario as well as Quebec to govern. The development of a Quebec separatist movement threatens the base of the Liberal Party. The *Parti Quebecois* has suggested that it will challenge the Liberals in Quebec in the next general election. Should the PQ deny the Liberals a significant number of Quebec's seats, the chances of the Liberals governing alone would depend upon a nearly complete Liberal sweep in Ontario, an unlikely prospect in Ontario's three-party system. However, even a weakened Liberal Party would be the most likely coalition partner for either the NDP or the Conservatives since the Liberals are Canada's center party.

New Democratic Party (NDP)

History

The New Democratic Party (known prior to 1961 as the Cooperative Commonwealth Federation) developed in 1933 out of the United Farmers Party, the Socialist Party of Canada, and a number of small political groups whose members were European immigrants. The party committed itself to socialism and the end of capitalism. The party had then, as now, two sources of political strength: farmers in Manitoba and Saskatchewan and members of the working class in Ontario and British Columbia. Political power has often been achieved in the prairies (1971–82 in Saskatchewan) and from 1972 to 1975 in B.C. The NDP has participated in a national coalition from 1972 to 1975 and in several coalitions in Ontario.

Organization

The NDP federal and provincial constituency associations are strictly separate units, the provincial associations relating to the national party only indirectly through the provincial party organizations. The party's biannual federal convention includes delegates from the provincial organizations, the federal constituency associations, the Young New Democrats, and some trade unions and farmers' groups.

Between conventions, the Council is the chief governing authority. Its membership of over 100 includes twenty elected by the convention, twenty elected by provincial party conventions, and provincial party officers. The associated trade unions and farm groups also elect members to the Council. The Council, in turn, elects from among its members the Executive of twenty-eight members. The Executive is the center of power in the party and meets frequently.

The NDP is a member of the Socialist International.

National headquarters are at 301 Metcalfe Street, Ottawa, Ontario.

Policy

In the course of governing, the NDP has lost some of its rhetorical commitment to tenets of socialism (the party now supports state "control," not necessarily ownership, of industry) and has suffered some ideological splits. (The Waffle, or New Left faction, was expelled from the party in the late 1970s.) In its domestic policy, the NDP is the most nationalistic of the three main parties and has called for a gradual ouster of foreign (i.e., American) capital. NDP foreign policy is similar to the independent stands taken by the French Socialist Party. The NDP, for example, has been highly critical of the U.S. role in El Salvador.

Membership & Constituency

The NDP is organizationally strong in Manitoba, Saskatchewan, British Columbia, and Ontario. The party has some support in Alberta and Nova Scotia (rarely more than 10 percent of the electorate), but very little at all in Quebec or in the rest of the Atlantic Provinces. Because the party is so closely tied to agrarian and British Labour Party socialism, in areas where groups of prairie farmers and English-speaking industrial workers do not exist, neither does the NDP.

Financing

Expenditures by the New Democratic Party in the 1979 fiscal period, according to party reports to the government, amounted to C $4,677,836 (nearly US $4 million), while income was C $4,741,281. Nearly 97 percent of income came from contributions, and 37 percent of that amount came from labor unions. Nearly 60 percent of contributed monies came from 63,655 individual donations.

Leadership

The major figures in the NDP are Ed Broadbent (born 1936 in Ontario), the party leader, and Allan Blakeney (born 1925), the premier of Saskatchewan from 1971 to 1982.

Prospects

In the long term, while the NDP will continue to be important provincially, the electoral system will guarantee their underrepresentation on the national level. Unless the party can find new issues which will gain it strength in Quebec against the Liberals and in Ontario against the Conservatives, the party is unlikely to ever govern alone.

Progressive Conservative Party of Canada (PC)

History

The Conservative Party governed Canada for most of the first thirty years of Dominion status (1867–97). The early Conservative Party appealed to a staunch pro–British Empire, anti-American, English Canadian constituency and to religious and highly conservative Quebec. The Conservatives were associated with policies meant to develop an autonomous Canadian manufacturing base, e.g., the "National Policy" of tariffs and trade restrictions. The Conservative Party suffered a major loss of electoral support in Quebec (nearly 60 percent of its votes) following the 1917 conscription crisis when Canadians were drafted to fight in the First World War. French Canadians opposed the war, blaming the Conservative government for Canada's involvement. The Conservatives also had the misfortune to be governing Canada as the Great Depression began.

For many voters, Conservatives' actions during these two periods is cause enough to vote for another party. The Conservative Party became the Progressive Conservative Party in 1942 when John Bracken, premier of Manitoba and head of the Progressive Party, joined the Conservative Party as its leader. The party, once considered antifarmer, has built a strong following in the prairie provinces ever since.

Organization

The PC provincial and national constituency associations, like those of the NDP, are quite separate, the local provincial bodies relating to the national party only indirectly through the provincial party organization. The party's semiannual general meeting includes delegates from the federal constituency associations, their youth and women's auxilliaries, and the provincial organizations. The general meeting elects the major party officers.

The National Executive of some 125 people, nearly all appointed by the party leadership, meets at least once a year. The center of power in the party is the Steering Committee of about twelve members. It includes the top party officers and meets frequently.

National headquarters are at 178 Queen Street, Ottawa, Ontario.

Policy

The Progressive Conservative Party differs only in degree from the Liberal Party, especially in foreign affairs, where both are pro-NATO and seek good relations with the United States. The major issues of substance between them were over Trudeau's constitutional proposals (the Conservatives were opposed) and over energy policy, where the PC supported Alberta in its dispute over pricing.

Membership & Constituency

The contemporary PC is structured around English-speaking Canada. The party, in each of the regions where it has support, depends on rural voters (especially farmers), Protestants, and part of the working and lower middle classes. The prai-

ries and the Atlantic provinces are especially important Conservative strongholds.

Financing

Conservative Party expenditures in the 1979 fiscal period, according to reports to the government from the party, amounted to C$5,083,350 (about US$4.27 million), while income was C$8,375,716 (just over US$7 million). The party reported that its entire income came from contributions, of which 60 percent of the total amount was donated by corporations. Nearly all the rest, C$3,182,897, came from 35,952 individual donations.

Leadership

The Conservative Party leadership is drawn from a wider social base than that of the Liberal Party; many more provinces and many more occupations are represented. Following the Conservatives' defeat in the 1980 election (they lost thirty-four seats), challenges to Joe Clark's leadership emerged. Though Clark (born 1919 in Alberta) survived the March 1981 Conservative convention as a party leader, nearly one-third of the convention sought to have him removed, usually citing his "colorlessness" and his lack of popular appeal. Clark's reputed "colorlessness" is in sharp contrast to Pierre Trudeau's "charisma."

Other major party figures are Brian Mulrooney (born 1939), Quebec challenger for party leadership; William Davis (born 1929), premier of Ontario since 1971; John Crosbie (born 1931), former Newfoundland finance minister; Peter Lougheed (born 1928), premier of Alberta since 1971.

Prospects

As long as the Conservatives have no representation in Quebec, they must depend on English Canada, especially Ontario, if they are again to regain power.

Regional or Minor Parties

Parti Quebecois (PQ)

The *Parti Quebecois* achieved power in Quebec in 1976, eight years after its founding. Most of the credit for its meteoric rise belongs to its leader René Levesque (born 1921), a journalist who broke with the Liberal Party in order to work for

Quebec independence. The PQ was created from three organizations, *Mouvement Souveraineté* (Levesque and other breakaway Liberals), the *Ralliement National,* and the *Rassemblement pour l'Indépendance Nationale.* These three organizations were divided on every issue except their commitment to Quebec independence.

The PQ has won the past two Quebec provincial elections; they have not competed on the national level, but they will run candidates from Quebec in the next general election. The party has not fought elections on a platform of independence for Quebec, but has pushed instead its claim of better management of the provincial government. In practice, this means that the PQ conforms to the laws and traditions of the Canadian confederation (the PQ ministers even take the oath of loyalty to the Queen of Canada), while agitating among the Quebec population for *"souverainité";* for an independent Quebec linked to the rest of Canada through economic agreements. In a referendum in May 1980, Levesque sought permission from the electorate to begin negotiations with the federal government over the issue of sovereignty. The electorate turned him down, 59 percent to 41 percent. The anglophone population, about 20 percent of the total, voted overwhelmingly against the proposal, while the francophone community also voted no by a very slight margin.

The paradox of electoral success without the achievement of the goal of independence has created much tension within the party. Levesque, as leader of the moderate wing of the party, suffered a political defeat in December 1981 when the majority of delegates to the party convention voted to fight the next provincial elections on the issue of sovereignty and to interpret a victory as a mandate to separate the province from Canada. Levesque appealed to the rank-and-file members of the party (estimated at 290,000) to write to party headquarters expressing their views on the issue and later announced that 95 percent of those who responded supported his position. A follow-up convention in February 1982 effectively realigned the party's position with that of Levesque. The squabble, combined with Levesque's inability to block Trudeau's constitutional proposals, has meant increasing isolation for the party both in Canada and within the province. Levesque, however, remains personally popular with Quebec voters.

Other important figures in the PQ include Jacques-Yvan Morin (born 1931), minister for intergovernmental affairs; Marc-André Bedard (born 1935), minister of justice; and Jacques Parizeau, minister of finance.

Party headquarters are at 8790 Avenue du Parc, Montreal, Quebec, H2N 1Y7.

It does not appear likely that the PQ will realize its goal of independence for Quebec. A large majority of the provincial electorate is opposed to the idea and its rejection even by francophones would seem to rule it out for the time being. The party, however, will continue to have a major role in defending provincial rights and French culture against encroachments by the federal government and the Canadian anglophone majority. Heavy-handed or careless federal policies toward Quebec could give new life to the "free Quebec" movement.

Western Canada Concept Party (WCCP)

Founded in Alberta in 1981, this party aims at the withdrawal of Manitoba, Saskatchewan, Alberta, and British Columbia from the Dominion of Canada, and the creation of a new state from these provinces. To date, the party has had limited electoral success despite much attention from the domestic and international press. In the party's only major electoral test, the party won no seats in the 1982 Saskatchewan provincial elections. The chairman of the party, Gordon Kessler, a member of the Albertan provincial assembly, is the party's only officeholder. Another prominent party figure, Brian Westwood, is the former provincial leader of the PC in British Columbia.

Social Credit Party—*Ralliement des Créditistes*

Social Credit emerged in Alberta in 1935 as a direct response to the distress among farmers during the Depression. The party won fifty-six seats in the Alberta legislature that year and dominated politics in the province until the 1960s. The party also developed strength in British Columbia (where it currently governs) and in Quebec. The party in recent years has been reduced to its British Columbia rump, lead by William Bennett (born 1932, premier since 1975), the son of an earlier B.C. premier. The Quebec wing of the Social Credit party left the national party to form the *Ralliement des Créditistes* in the early 1960s, and the Alberta wing has been buried by the Conservatives. The party won no seats in the 1980 federal elections, and the Quebec party won no seats in the provincial elections.

Union Nationale (UN)

This once-powerful party failed to win any seats in the 1981 Quebec provincial elections, having fallen victim to the leftward shift in Quebec politics. The party emerged in 1936 when dissident Liberals joined Duplessis's Conservative Party. The social forces upon which UN rested, the Catholic Church and rural Quebec, no longer dominate Quebec politics, and the party is unlikely to survive the next decade.

Communist Party of Canada

The CP in Canada has only 2,000 members, overwhelmingly concentrated in Winnipeg and Toronto. The party elects no one to Parliament and receives only about 1.7 percent of the votes for its efforts. The party has a pro-Moscow orientation.

Marxist-Leninist Party of Canada

This party is a splinter group from the Communist Party and is Maoist in orientation. The party receives slightly less than 1 percent of the electoral vote. It has never won a seat in Parliament.

Other Political Forces

Canadian Corporate Elite

The wealth and political influence of the families that dominate the Canadian economy are hard to measure. What is clear is that the Bronfman, Desmarais, Thompson, Black, Weston and other prominent families and individuals wield great influence in the Canadian political system through a system of campaign contributions, personal ties, and interlocking directorates that include many prominent former Canadian politicians. While there is no conclusive evidence to substantiate the left's claim that Canada is run by 1,000 people, the Canadian economy is characterized by a degree of private centralization rare in Western democracies.

Organized Labor

The Canadian labor movement has been beset by troubles in recent years. High unemployment, splits in the labor movement between Quebec and the rest of Canada, and a breakaway movement led by the construction unions have plagued the major labor federation, the Canadian Labor Congress (CLC). Perhaps more distressing has been the inability of the CLC to deliver the votes of its members to the party with which it is allied, the New Democrats. The CLC provides money, volunteer workers, and organizing skills to the NDP, but it does not dominate the party like the British Trade Union Congress dominates the Labour Party, in part because of the legal limits on contributions to the party. Like its American counterpart, the AFL-CIO, the CLC is uncertain about its future political course.

National Prospects

Canada's stability as a nation is strongly affected by economic factors partially beyond its control. Canada's economy, though one of the largest in the world, is dwarfed by the American economy, with which Canada does nearly 70 percent of its trade. Of particular difficulty for Canada are the facts that Canada's interest rate follows the American rate; that Americans own or control approximately half of Canada's major industrial firms; and that Canada has run, on average, a $4 billion current-account deficit since 1977. The ability of the Canadian state to influence its own future is constrained by these economic ties.

Ironically, Canada's "weakness" with regard to the American economy may provide some national "glue" by giving all Canadians a greater sense of nation and national purpose. The next few years will show whether or not Canada's new federal constitution can provide a flexible enough framework to dampen tensions between English and French, east and west.

Further Reading

Bellamy, David J., et al. *The Provincial Political System.* Toronto: Methuin Press, 1976.

Cambell, Colin, and Szablowski, George. *The Superbureaucrats; Structure and Behavior in Cultural Agencies.* Toronto: Macmillan, 1979.

Clement, Wallace. The *Canadian Corporate Elite.* Toronto: McClelland and Stuart, 1975.

Doern, G. Bruce, and Wilson, V. Seymour, eds. *Issues in Canadian Public Policy.* Toronto: Macmillan, 1974.

Engelman, F. C., and Schwartz, M. A. *Canadian Political Parties*. Scarborough, Canada: Prentice-Hall, 1975.

Fox, Paul, ed. *Politics: Canada*. 4th ed. Toronto: McGraw-Hill Ryerson, 1977.

French, Richard. *How Ottawa Decides*. Ottawa: Canadian Institute for Economic Policy, 1980.

Hockin, T. A. *Government in Canada*. Toronto: McGraw-Hill Ryerson, 1976.

Neilson, W. A. W., and MacPherson, James, eds. *The Legislative Process in Canada*. Montreal: Institute for Research on Public Policy, 1978.

Winn, C., and McMenemy, J. *Political Parties in Canada*. Toronto: McGraw-Hill Ryerson, 1976.

REPUBLIC OF CAPE VERDE
(*República de Cabo Verde*)
by Tony Hodges

The System of Government

With a population of 320,000 (and as many emigrants living abroad), this former Portuguese colony (1587-1974) of ten islands and several islets of the Cape Verde archipelago, some 385 miles west of Senegal, is now ruled, under a one-party system of government, by the *Partido Africano da Independência de Cabo Verde* (PAICV).

Executive

The president of Cape Verde is head of state and commander-in-chief of the People's Revolutionary Armed Forces (*Forças Armadas Revolucionárias do Povo*; FARP). A prime minister heads the Council of Ministers. Both the president and the prime minister are elected by the National Popular Assembly for a five-year term of office. Under the 1980 constitution, the government is subordinate to the ruling party, and this is reflected in the overlapping of state and party posts. The president is secretary general of the PAICV, and the prime minister is the party's deputy secretary general.

Legislature

The National Popular Assembly (*Assembleia Nacional Popular*) has sixty-three members, elected for five-year terms. It normally meets only twice a year for sessions lasting only a few days. All deputies are members of the ruling party, and the Assembly is apparently a rubber-stamp body for legislation drafted by the Council of Ministers under the party's guidance.

Judiciary

The highest court is the National Court of Justice (*Conselho Nacional da Justiça*). At the local level there is a network of people's tribunals.

Regional & Local Government

The country is divided into fourteen municipalities, each of which is supervised by an appointee of the Ministry of the Interior. He is assisted by a deliberative council.

The Electoral System

The PAICV is the only party allowed to contest elections. At the first postindependence elections, held in December 1980, the party, which was then known as the PAIGC (see below) presented a single slate of candidates for the sixty-three seats in the Assembly. A quarter of the electorate did not bother to vote.

African Party for the Independence of Cape Verde
(*Partido Africano da Independencia de Cabo Verde*; PAICV)

History

Founded in January 1981, the PAICV is the successor to the Cape Verdian wing of the African Party for the Independence of Guinea and Cape Verde (*Partido Africano da Independência de Guiné e Cabo Verde*; PAIGC). The PAIGC was founded in 1956 to lead the struggle for independence in both the Cape Verde Islands and mainland Guinea-Bissau; but while it conducted an effective guerrilla war against Portugal in Guinea-Bissau, it was unable to establish a presence in the remote Cape Verdes until after the downfall of the Caetano dictatorship in Portugal in April 1974. Portugal set up a transitional government, including PAIGC ministers, in December

1974. Cape Verde became independent under a PAIGC government on July 5, 1975. The PAIGC became the country's sole legal party and was given supremacy over government structures. This was confirmed by the constitution adopted in July 1980. Since its founding, the PAIGC had been a binational party and had the unification of Guinea-Bissau and Cape Verde into a single state as one of its principal policy objectives. However, the party's unity was shattered by a coup d'état in Guinea-Bissau in November 1980 which had marked anti–Cape Verdian overtones. The Cape Verdian wing of the party then held an extraordinary congress in January 1981, changed its name to the PAICV, and formally abandoned the goal of unification with Guinea-Bissau.

Organization

The party is headed by a nine-member Supreme Council, including the president, the prime minister, the president of the National Popular Assembly, and six other senior party officials.

The party is divided into five regions (the islands of Santo Antão, São Vicente, São Nicolau, Santiago, and Fogo) and five autonomous sectors (the islands of Sal, Boavista, Maio and Brava, and the capital, Praia, on the island of Santiago). The regions are divided into sectors, the sectors into sections, and sections into local party groups (numbering 449 in 1976), in a pyramidal structure. The party is flanked by three mass organizations—for youth, workers, and women—which are intended to mobilize broad support for government policies.

Policy

The PAICV is committed to what it calls "national revolutionary democracy," which it claims differs from both Western liberal democracy and Marxist socialism, and is supposedly based on an alliance of all social classes, united to promote economic development. In practice, the ruling party has been very careful to avoid alienating powerful privileged social groups, such as rural landowners. Reform of the islands' archaic and stratified landholding system has been slow and modest in scope. In foreign policy, the party is committed to a highly pragmatic brand of nonalignment in order to attract as much aid as possible for its development program and to relieve the effects of the terrible drought which has ravaged the islands almost without interruption since 1968.

Membership & Constituency

The party is numerically small. Membership criteria are fairly stringent, and in 1977 there were only 1,130 members. In 1976, 40 percent were salaried workers, 40 percent public employees, 10 percent farmers, and 4 percent students. Only 12 percent were women. About 60 percent were under thirty years old, and 35 percent were between the ages of thirty and fifty.

Financing

No information is available on party financing, but government funding is assumed to be substantial.

Leadership

Aristides Pereira (born 1924 on the island of Boavista) was head of the telecommunications service in Guinea-Bissau when, in 1956, he helped found the PAIGC. In 1964, he was elected deputy secretary general of the PAIGC and, in 1973, became secretary general following the death of Amilcar Cabral. He was elected president of Cape Verde at independence, and elected secretary general of the PAICV at its founding congress in January 1981.

Pedro Pires is deputy secretary general of the PAICV and prime minister.

Other Political Forces

Landed interests were prominent in an anti-PAIGC movement, the Democratic Union of Cape Verde (*União Democrático de Cabo Verde*; UDCV) in 1974–75. The UDCV became illegal in 1975 and some of its leaders were deported shortly before independence. However, about forty rightists, some with former UDCV connections, were jailed in 1977 after the discovery of an alleged coup. They were released in 1979. A Maoist group, the Union of the People of the Cape Verde Islands (*União dos Povos das Ilhas de Cabo Verde*; UPICV), was also active in 1974–75, and a Trotskyite faction, which included two government ministers, was expelled from the PAIGC in 1979. The Cape Verde League of Human Rights was founded in Portugal in 1982 and accuses the government of suppressing opposition.

National Prospects

The governing party, which appears to have a genuinely collective leadership, does not face significant opposition and continues to enjoy the prestige of having led the country's struggle for independence. However, economic conditions in this drought-scarred country will inevitably be very difficult for many years.

Further Reading

"Cape Verde Islands, The End of a Dream for Drought-Stricken Islanders." In *Africa Contemporary Record.* Colin Legum, ed. Vol. 13, 1980-81. New York: Holmes and Meier, 1981.

"Cape Verde, The Sahel in the Sea." *The Courier*, No. 65, January-February 1981.

Hodges, Tony. "Cape Verde under the PAIGC." *Africa Report*, May-June 1977.

CENTRAL AFRICAN REPUBLIC
(*République Centraficaine*)
by Thomas O'Toole, D.A.

The System of Government

The Central African Republic, a country of nearly three million people, is a unitary state under military rule. The current government dates from September 1, 1981, when army units took over the capital, Bangui, in a bloodless coup which probably was prearranged with the French government and the ousted president, David Dacko, who was allowed to retire to his farm on the pretense of poor health.

By a referendum on February 1, 1981, the Central African Republic had accepted a new constitution which provided for a democratic multiparty state governed by the Council of Ministers headed by a prime minister appointed by an elected president. The National Assembly was to have been elected democratically every five years. Dacko was elected president on March 15, 1981, with only 1,712 votes more than necessary to avoid a runoff election out of a total vote of 757,430 (77 percent of registered voters).

Complaints of election rigging and riots in Bangui and elsewhere were followed by Dacko's declaration of a state of siege. The political situation had changed little since September 22, 1979, when Dacko, who had presided over the country in an increasingly authoritarian manner from 1960 to 1966, was returned to power in a French-backed coup against the disastrous regime of Emperor Jean-Bedel Bokassa.

RESULTS OF THE 1981 ELECTION		
Candidate	Votes	Percent
David Dacko (UDC)	374,027	50.23
Ange Patasse (MLPC)	283,739	38.11
Francois Pehoua (GIRA)	39,661	5.33
Henri Maidou (PRP)	24,007	3.23
Abel Goumba (FPO-PT)	10,512	1.42
Blank, null	12,742	1.68

The September 1981 coup was probably a step toward a more open regime. Dacko's crony-packed party, the Central African Democratic Union (*Union Démocratique Centrafricaine;* UDC), had created a private militia which was armed by the state but restricted to members of Dacko's ethnic group, the M'Baka. In April 1981, Dacko forbade the use of the state-controlled radio and television systems by the opposition parties on the grounds that they were appealing to tribalism. In May, he announced that parliamentary elections would not take place as scheduled because of an alleged need to reorganize procedures and check voter lists. In the wake of a May 15 strike, Dacko dissolved the main trade union, the General Union of Central African Workers (*Union Générale des Travailleurs Centrafricaine;* UGTC), and replaced it with a new official body, the National Confederation of Central African Workers (*Confédération Nationale des Traivailleurs Centraficaine;* CNTC). In July, he briefly suspended the activities of several of the opposition parties. The military government halted these attempts to turn Central Africa into a one-party state.

Executive

In August 1982, the president was Army Chief of Staff André Kolingba, who presided over the Military Commmittee of National Recovery (*Comité Militaire de Redressement National;* CMRN), a body of about thirty members which exercised full executive and legislative powers. The new constitution and political parties were suspended. The military government has made no move to schedule new elections or to turn government back to civilian control.

Legislature

The National Assembly was to have been elected in the spring or summer of 1981. Because such matters have been largely irrelevent in Central African affairs, constitutional details regarding the size and powers of the Assembly, the method of the proposed elections, and other constitutional details are not available.

Judiciary

The new constitution provided for an independent judiciary. In the past, while the Supreme Court and lesser courts were theoretically free of political influence, they seldom showed any independence. The courts are not necessarily obedient to the government, however, and may be responsive to the political interests of major opposition groups or to public opinion. A lower court sentenced six Bokassa functionaries to death in early 1980. The Supreme Court, perhaps under pressure from the Dacko government, set aside the sentences and ordered retrials. In spite of the fact that some of the defendants were related to Dacko, a lower court again found the men guilty and sentenced them to death. The sentences were only carried out, however, after a sharp change in the political climate put Dacko on the defensive.

Regional & Local Government

The republic is divided into fourteen prefectures administered by appointees from the capital. Traditional ethnic forms of local government predominate over most of the country.

The Electoral System

Outside the referendum of the constitution and the presidential election in early 1981, no elections have been held in Central Africa since the mid-1960s. Regulations governing the referendum and presidential election are not available.

The Party System

Parties are very loosely organized groups centering around personalistic leaders. None have strong nationwide appeal, but base their strength on ethnic groups and regions or on the disaffected urban lower classes. Most political party activity is limited to Bangui and vicinity.

Central African Democratic Union (*Union Démocratique Centrafricaine;* UDC)

This party, created with David Dacko's blessing in an attempt to legitimize his regime in the spring of 1980, represents little more than an extension of the same ruling M'Baka clique which has dominated this country since independence. Yet rural election returns of March 15 did show that the anti-French nationalism exhibited by anti-Dacko students and urban populations is far less important in the countryside. Dacko's election was probably a legitimate choice of the unsophisticated majority.

Central African People's Liberation Movement (*Mouvement de Libération du Peuple Centrafricaine;* MLPC)

Founded in opposition to Bokassa by a former prime minister under Bokassa, Ange Patasse, in the spring of 1979, this party showed considerable strength in Bangui among the urban poor and students, as well as in Patasse's Sara home area in the northwestern part of the country near the Chad and Cameroon borders. No accurate information on actual members or financing of this party is available, but since he is in exile in Togo after an abortive coup attempt in March 1982, Patasse is no longer a political force. His popularity was largely the result of his being made into a martyr by Dacko's use of French military force against him in the fall of 1979. Bombing his house and imprisoning him made this left populist—who held numerous interests in wood, cotton, and coffee—the darling of the street crowd in Bangui. Patasse was long on violent rhetoric, but very short on political organization and theory.

Minor Parties
Movement for Democracy and Independence (*Mouvement pour la*

This group, formed by former minister of justice François Gueret, in 1981, represented little more than a personal vehicle. Given an almost total lack of support for its virulent anti-Soviet stance, it did not run a candidate in the 1981 elections and, for all practical purposes, has ceased to exist.

Independent Grouping for Reflection and Action
(*Groupement Indépendant du Réflexion et d'Action;* GIRA)

François Pehoua ran unsuccessfully as the candidate of this group in the 1981 election. Founded by him in 1981, the group represents moderate bureaucrats who will continue to play a role in Central African politics because they are necessary components of any future government.

Progressive Republican Party
(*Parti Républicain du Progrès;* PRP)

The PRP was formed in 1981 and represents little more than the personal ambitions of Henri Maidou, its presidential candidate in 1981. As prime minister under Bokassa and a close ally of conservative French factions, Maidou has little influence in the present politics of CAR.

Ubangian Patriotic Front Worker's Party
(*Front Patriotique Oubanguien-Parti du Travail;* FPO-PT)

Founded by Dr. Abel Goumba, now rector of the University of Bangui and once the original president of the French colonial Ubangui-Shari government council and a close collaborator with Barthelemy Boganda, founder of the Central African Republic, this party was created in exile to oppose Bokassa. It has only limited support within the country. Its militant nationalistic and leftist stance has gained it a small dedicated following among students, teachers, urban workers, the unemployed, and some civil servants. The FPO-PT also has considerable support from French socialists. Goumba's outspoken faith in the ability of the Central African people to develop a grass-roots democracy under a more open regime is predicted on a program that, in relation to other Central African political groups, is the most clearly articulated. Yet even in this case, though the party cuts across ethnic lines more than any other, most of its support derives from Goumba's personal prestige as an honest and dedicated leader rather than real organizational linkages.

Provisional Political Committee
(*Comité Politique Provisoire*)

Prior to the military takeover, the four losing candidates in the 1981 elections and Gueret's MDI formed this committee to fight the legislative elections. United in opposition to Dacko's ambitions, it is uncertain if these politicians and their followers will again work together and whether they will be called on by the ruling military committee to help return the country to civilian rule.

Central African Movement for National Liberation
(*Mouvement Centrafricain de Libération National;* MCLN)

A clandestine, radical left group of unknown size, the MCLN was led by Iddi Lala. Its activities included terrorist actions such as the bombing of the popular Cinema Le Club in central Bangui, which killed three persons and wounded over thirty in July 1981. This event gave Dacko a pretext for a severe, if brief, crackdown on legitimate political activity.

Other Political Forces

Military

The army of Central Africa is a key political actor in the nation. Shortly before the coup against Dacko, the president attempted to buy the military commanders' allegiance by promoting Kolingba to a full general and four colonels to the rank of brigadier general. The army, however, is an independent force with its own contacts with the French government. French advisors and training personnel and French supplies have raised the standards of the army slightly since 1979, but it remains a small (2,000 regulars; 1,000 paramilitary) and relatively ineffective military force. The new leadership is basically Yakoma as opposed to the previous M'Baka predominance.

France

France has some 1,100 troops stationed in the CAR, most of them in the northwest of the country, but with a small contingent in Bangui, the French government can play the role of ultimate arbiter; for example, French assistance enabled Dacko to oust Bokassa, and French refusal to act against Kolingba's coup sealed Dacko's fate. It is thought that the new socialist government of François Mitterand in France will be less interventionist than its predecessors, while perhaps increasing the economic aid on which this desperately poor country depends.

National Prospects

The stability of any government in Central Africa is very uncertain. The economy is in shambles, and even if the dreams of a generation of Central African leaders were to come true and uranium, oil, and other minerals were to become important exports within the next few years, severe problems would remain. Corruption, mismanagement, poor health, insufficient food supplies, transportation problems, and a general malaise are so pervasive that this poor landlocked country seems incapable of generating self-sustained development for many years.

Massive unemployment, a declining rural economy, and years of instability have created conditions in Bangui which work against political stability. Whether the nation is governed by the army, a civilian dictatorship, or a popularly elected government, the urban underclass represents a potential threat to any government in power; there is little likelihood that there will be sufficient employment and upward mobility to satisfy its growing demands. Contemplation of the political future of the Central African Republic provides little ground for optimism.

Further Reading

Ballard, J. A. "Politics and Government in Former French West and Equatorial Africa: A Critical Bibliography." *Journal of Modern African Studies*, Vol. 3, No. 4 (1965).

Kalck, Pierre. *Central African Republic.* London: Pall Mall, 1971.

———. *Historical Dictionary of the Central African Republic.* Metuchen, N. J.: Scarecrow Press, 1980.

REPUBLIC OF CHAD
(*République du Tchad*)
by René Lemarchand, Ph.D.

The System of Government

Only by diplomatic courtesy can violence-torn Chad be called a state. Twenty-two years after its independence from France, this country of 4.5 million people remains a perfect example of a crippled polity, too weak to respond creatively to the challenge of nation-building, yet strong enough to keep trying. The off-and-on civil war that has been going on since 1968 has resulted in a situation of ethnic and regional fragmentation virtually unparalleled elsewhere in Africa. Tens of thousands have perished in the course of seemingly endless factional strife, and to the human costs of civil violence must be added widespread economic dislocation and a catastrophic decline in agricultural output. As the country entered a new phase in its turbulent political history in June 1982, the task of national reconstruction appears quite beyond the capacity of its new leadership.

Anarchy is a pervasive feature of the Chadian political system, yet even anarchy has a certain logic of its own and reflects the very nature of factionalism as a political phenomenon. Factions are notoriously fluid and unstable; today's friend may be tomorrow's enemy and vice versa. Ideology, ethnic ties, even family ties have relatively little to do with factional alliances. Much depends on the pragmatic choices made by faction leaders in their attempt to consolidate their power base and weaken that of their opponents. In this highly fluid environment, personalities are all-important, and so are the personal resources of faction leaders—their access to cash, cattle, and guns—along with their personal connections, ethnoregional affiliations, and strategic skills. Short-term calculations inevitably take precedence over long-run policies. Structural innovations, long-term planning, or economic reform are hardly likely to emerge from factional fighting. Opportunism, bribery, revenge, and assassination, on the other hand, figure prominently in the arsenal of factions. And because factional systems tend to discourage the rise of strong leaders, political fragmentation is likely to persist.

Twice the size of Texas and stretching almost a thousand miles from the Libyan desert in the north to the tropical grasslands of the Logone valley in the south, Chad forms a huge rectangle of arid and semi-arid lands inhabited by a variety of populations whose lifestyles, social organizations, and political cultures reflect a similarly wide range of variations between north and south. At least four major population groups must be noted. The Toubou, or Teda, located in the extreme north in and around the Tibesti massif, number anywhere from 15,000 to 30,000. Individualistic and contentious, they are a nomadic people, organized in a variety of clans, all supposedly owing nominal allegiance to a paramount chief, the *Derdei*. The Arabs, estimated at about half a million, are subdivided into several small nomadic and sedentary communities dispersed throughout the country, but primarily concentrated in the Sahelian belt. The so-called "Sahelian" populations, an extremely loose and arbitrary grouping, include a number of groups spread across the Sahel from east to west. The most important, historically, are the sultanates of Baguirmi, Kanem, and Waddai. The Sara people, heavily concentrated in the extreme south, number approximately a million and a half. Originally a set of discrete but linguistically related subgroups (Madjingaye, Mbaye, Ngama, Kaba, etc.), their sense of "Saraness" is a relatively recent phenomenon.

Creating a sense of national loyalty out of this complex cultural mosaic is made more arduous still by the uneven spread of Islam and the heavy concentration of modern Western influences in the south. Historically, the principal carrier of Islam has been the Senusiyya brotherhood, whose influence in Chad became dominant in the late nineteenth century; yet it remained essentially a northern phenomenon. The old sultanates of Baguirmi, Kanem, and Waddai were and still are widely Islamicized; indeed much of the animus felt by the Sara towards Islam must be attributed to the periodic slave-raiding activities conducted by these precolonial states among the populations of the south. In the minds of most Sara, Islam is largely synonymous with slave raiding. The important fact, at any rate, is that the Christian-Muslim cleavage in contemporary Chad tends to coincide with the Sara–non-Sara division, thus greatly accentuating the potential for conflict between north and south.

An additional source of tension stems from the effective monopoly of most of the country's economic and social resources, including cotton, by the Sara. Although Chad as a whole remained one of the most neglected of France's former colonies, nowhere was this neglect more apparent than in the north. What little effort was made to promote primary and secondary education occured primarily in the south, and then largely through missionary activity. Thus while the north remained almost totally insulated from the forces of social change released by the colonial state, the south underwent a substantial transformation of its traditional social structures. To this day, the Sara have the largest percentage of Western-educated and urbanized people, the highest concentration of cash crops and processing industries, and the most extensive transportation network. Political mobilization in the south occurred earlier and on a much wider scale than in the north; for this reason, southerners came to dominate the administrative and political institutions of Chad for several years after independence, thereby creating the conditions that led to the civil war. The systematic exclusion of northern elements from effective political participation made their recourse to violence almost inevitable.

Executive

Since the reentry of Hissène Habré into the capital city, Njamena (formerly Fort Lamy), by force of arms in June 1982, the country has been nominally governed by the State Council consisting of eighteen commissioners and twelve vice commissioners in charge of running the ministries. Pending general elections and the establishment of "definitive institutions," the State Council is expected to act as the provisional executive of the Republic of Chad, and Habré as its president. Habré's State Council also has full legislative and judicial powers in the areas where Habré's troops hold sway.

Although the previous "transitional executive," the so-called Transitional Government of National Unity (GUNT), has been formally dissolved, the vice president of the GUNT, Abdelkader Kamougue, remains the recognized leader of the Sara-dominated south. The five southern prefectures of Moyen-Chari, Logone Occidental, Logone Oriental, Tanjile, and Mayo Kebbi, are in a state of de facto secession, and are administered by the all-Sara "Permanent Committee" headed by Kamougue. Although the north-south division seems to have once again reemerged as the central element in Chadian politics, the evidence points to a somewhat more complex situation. Just as factional splits continue to pit northerner against northerner, similar divisions threaten the cohesiveness of the southern region.

Legislature

The National Assembly has not met since 1971. The last Assembly had 105 deputies elected to five-year terms from single-member districts. Fifty-four deputies were from the north, while fifty-one represented the six Sara prefectures in the south, which constituted one-fifth of the country's territory and about a third of its population.

Judiciary

Justice, generally of a summary nature, depends on which factional army controls a particular area. The national judiciary has functioned only sporadically since 1975 and has never been free of political manipulation.

Regional & Local Government

Chad is supposedly divided into fourteen prefectures administered by governors appointed by the president. In fact, traditional forms of clan and tribal government continue in most regions, subject to intermittent interference from the factional armies.

The Electoral System

There have been no elections in Chad since 1969. Even those were dominated by a single legal party and were not competitive. According to the constitution, suffrage extends to all citizens eighteen years of age and over. The National Assembly was directly elected, while the president was elected to a seven-year term by an electoral college consisting of the Assembly, heads of communities, and tribal leaders.

The Factional System

Origins of the Factions

The forces in conflict in Chad are not political parties but loosely organized private armies loyal to individual leaders. Roughly speaking, the armies represent ethnic groups and/or regions, sometimes in alliance. The leaders have few policies, if any, beyond domination of the state if possible, and personal, ethnic, and regional defense if not.

At the time of independence in 1960, the Sara-dominated Chadian Progressive Party (*Parti Progressiste Tchadien;* PPT) controlled fifty-seven of the eighty-five seats in the National Assembly, and the majority of ministerial posts. With the rapid Africanization of the civil service, Sara hegemony quickly expanded into the bureaucratic sectors; furthermore, the massive recruitment of Sara elements into the army and the gendarmerie also insured the loyalty of the security forces. Under the leadership of the late president Tombalbaye, the PPT eventually emerged as the dominant force in Chadian politics.

In 1966, opposition to the Sara-dominated Tombalbaye regime was channelled into the National Liberation Front (*Front de Liberation National;* Frolinat) initially led by Ibrahim Abatcha. Structurally, the Frolinat was the product of a fusion of several minor opposition parties (the *Union Nationale Tchadienne,* the *Union Generale des Fils du Tchad,* and the *Mouvement National de Liberation du Tchad*) and directed its appeal to a large number of ethnic constituencies. Their common resentment of Sara rule failed to produce anything like a lasting sense of solidarity among their presumptive spokesmen. Thus, the death of Abatcha in 1968 triggered a bitter struggle for leadership among his lieutenants, only temporarily resolved by the appointment of Dr. Abba Siddick as secretary general of the Frolinat in 1969.

By then, however, the insurgency had reached alarming proportions. Following riots by Moubi tribesmen in Mangalme in October 1965, violence quickly spread to the central and northern prefectures, and in 1968 Tombalbaye called upon the French to restore "peace and order." French intervention took the form of a large-scale civilian-military counterinsurgency effort, which lasted until 1979. Through the combined efforts of the *Mission de Réforme Administrative* (MRA), consisting of approximately thirty civilian and military "technical assistants," and a military task force involving at its peak some 3,000 men, mostly drawn from the Foreign Legion, the French gave a

new lease on life to their client state. The political costs, however, were hardly worth the gamble. The French intervention gave substance to Frolinat accusations that Tombalbaye was a "stooge of French imperialists." The pacification of rebel strongholds was accompanied by considerable brutality and unnecessary bloodshed, thus casting further discredit on a regime whose legitimacy had already been seriously eroded by its own incompetence, corruption, and systematic discrimination against non-Sara.

Meanwhile, the sheer ineptitude of Tombalbaye's "Chadization" policies (including the requirement that all civil servants undergo the traditional Sara initiation ceremony, the so-called *yondo*) paved the way for the rise of an intra-Sara opposition to the regime. With the arrest, at Tombalbaye's request, of the army chief of staff, General Félix Malloum, in June 1973, discontent spread to the armed forces. On April 13, 1975, units of the gendarmerie and the army moved against the presidential residence and overthrew the regime. For the next three years, government responsibilities were entrusted to a civilian-military junta headed by Malloum.

Precisely at this juncture cracks began to appear in the facade of the Frolinat. By 1975 at least three rebel armies claimed the mantle of revolutionary legitimacy: Hissène Habré's "second army" (in contrast to Frolinat's first army), later renamed Northern Armed Forces (*Forces Armées du Nord;* FAN), in the Borkou-Ennedi-Tibesti area; Abba Siddick's Popular Liberation Forces (*Forces Populaires de Liberation;* FPL) in the extreme northeast along the Sudan border; and Mahamat Baghlani's "eastern army" in the Waddai region in the east. A year later, Habré's army suffered a major split when his immediate rival and Toubou kinsman, Goukouni Weddei, backed by Libya, asserted himself as leader of the Popular Armed Forces (*Forces Armées Populaires;* FAP).

Despite fragmentation, the rebel forces were able to score decisive victories against the Njamena regime. The crunch came in early 1978 with the capture of Fada and Faya-Largeau by Habré. The first of many abortive attempts at national reconciliation occurred in August 1978 in the form of a compromise worked out in Khartoum between Malloum and Habré; Habré became prime minister. The arrangement led to a total deadlock, ultimately resolved by a major trial of strength in Njamena in February 1979. Overwhelmed by Habré's FAN and with the French adopting a posture of neutrality, Malloum's armed forces, under the command of Kamougue, withdrew from the capital to the south. By then, Kamougue had effectively displaced Malloum as the leading Sara personality in the south, and with the appointment of a de facto Sara-dominated government in Moundou, in May 1979, the so-called Permanent Committee, the southern prefectures joined to form a separate political entity.

It was in this climate of utter anarchy that the first Kano conference was held (March 10–16, 1979) in an effort to arrive at a compromise among the contestants. The resulting accord called for a cease-fire, demilitarization of the capital within a sixty-mile radius, and the creation of a national transitional union government.

Another Kano conference followed (April 3–11, 1979) to discuss the means of implementing the agreement; both proved totally ineffective in containing civil violence. The next step towards reconciliation took place in Lagos from August 12 to August 18, in what turned out to be a replay of Kano I. Ironically, though intended to offer a basis for reunification, the Lagos accord injected yet another source of discord among the signatories, each blaming the other for his lack of cooperation. The rebellion had spawned a veritable alphabet soup of factions and "tendances": no less than eleven such factions took part in the Lagos Accord of August 1979 that led to the Transitional Government of National Unity (GUNT) nominally headed by President Goukouni Weddei.

Mutual suspicion eventually reached such a level of paranoia between the GUNT president, Goukouni Weddei, and his minister of state in charge of national defense, Habré, that on March 22 a full-scale battle erupted in Njamena between FAP and FAN. By May 1980, the death toll had reached 2,000, with at least 5,000 wounded.

The "war of position" dragged on through most of 1980, and with the French by now out of the game, Goukouni Weddei turned to Libya. On December 14, 1980, Libyan tanks backed by units of Muammar Qaddafi's Islamic Legion took Njamena by storm, and what was left of the battle-scarred capital was soon delivered into the hands of Goukouni's FAP. As the guns fell silent, the GUNT inherited a devastated capital, a state ripped apart by factional strife, and a crippled economy. It also inherited a Libyan presence of some 12,000 troops.

It seems clear, in retrospect, that until their sudden and unexpected withdrawal from Chad in November 1981, the Libyan forces played a decisive stabilizing role in the fluctuating power equations among the several Chadian warlords. Not the least of the ironies attached to the Libyan pullout—for which much of the credit must go to Goukouni Weddei—is that it created in its wake a

political vacuum that was immediately filled by Habré's forces. Habré, not Goukouni, gained the largest strategic dividends from the Libyan withdrawal.

Despite the serious setback inflicted to Habré's FAN by the combined Libyan-FAP attack on Njamena, the Toubou leader managed to recoup his losses after seeking refuge in the Sudan. As Quaddafi's bitterest opponent, he had little trouble persuading Egypt and the Sudan to provide him with military and political assistance. It can be reasonably assumed that Habré also received considerable covert assistance from the United States, if for no other reason that he is perceived in Washington as the "safest bet" against Qaddafi's expansion into Sub-Saharan Africa. This, however, in no way detracts from his superb skills as a warlord-politician. To have taken on as many challengers as he had and, despite some calamitous setbacks, still be able to operate a spectacular strategic retreat across 600 miles of parched savannah into the Sudan, and months later reemerge triumphant in the capital city is little short of astonishing.

The Factions in 1982

Among the many armed fctions, four groups stand out.

Northern Armed Forces (Forces Armées du Nord; *FAN*)

Under Habré's command, the FAN developed out of Frolinat's "second army" and was initially recruited almost exclusively among Toubou elements. It is now the largest and ethnically most diversified of all existing armies, numbering anywhere from 6,000 to 8,000 men. It is in control of much of the northern and eastern regions and the capital city, and will presumably form the nucleus of the future Chadian army.

Popular Armed Forces (Forces Armées Populaires; *FAP*)

Headed by Goukouni Weddei until June 1982, the FAP now consists of a handful of dipersed Toubou warriors trying to hold their ground in a few isolated enclaves in the extreme north, principally in the Tibesti. Its significance appears marginal.

Democratic Council of the Revolution (Conseil Democratique de la Revolution; *CDF*)

Led by Ahmat Acyl until his death in July 1982, the CDR developed out of Frolinat's "first army," founded by Ibrahim Abatcha in 1966. Its bases of support are essentially among the Arabs of the Lake Chad region. It is the only faction which remains openly pro-Libyan. Decimated after its engagements with the FAT in late 1981 and early 1982, the CDR, now led by Acheick ibn Oumar, has probably the smallest following claimed by any faction leader.

Chadian Armed Forces (Forces Armées Tchadiennes; FAT)

Formally under the command of Abdelkader Kamougue, the FAT is the remaining "hard core" of the national Chadian armed forces, once numbering some 12,000 men. Today they number approximately 3,000 and are concentrated in the south. Within the FAT, however, two splinter groups have emerged, one headed by Colonel Rodai, a Sara Nar from Moissala, and the other by Kamougue, a Mbai also from Moissala. Shortly before the capture of Njamena by Habré, on June 7, violent clashes were reported between Kamougue's gendarmerie (a rural constabulary force which also doubles as a praetorian guard) and Colonel Rodai's supporters. Although Kamougue's faction emerged triumphant, the incident suggests that the bonding glue of ethnicity that once held the FAT together has now dissolved into intra-Sara squabbles centering on personalities.

National Prospects

The real test of Habré's leadership is yet to come. His most urgent task to to piece together a reasonably dependable security force out of the many private armies. None of the existing private armies appear ready to give up their political and operational autonomy, although some, at this point, have little to surrender.

The next most challenging order of business is to bring the southern prefectures effectively back into the fold of the central government. As the situation in the south continues to deteriorate, new opportunities may arise for working out a *modus vivendi* with Saraland. Aware that power may soon slip from his hands, Kamougue may

well settle for a compromise solution that would enable him to hold a portfolio in the central government in exchange for a promise of "loyalty" to the Habré government on the part of his faction.

With their bases of support deeply eroded, Habré's rivals will have to face the option of either staying out of the game, with the risk of political and military annihilation, or joining the winner on his own terms. The chjoice of alternatives depends in part on the play of external forces. Another Libyan intervention, though unlikely, could drastically alter the existing balance of forces. A more desirable and plausible alternative, however, would be for France and the United States to offer the Habré regime not just the benefit of the doubt, but the economic and financial support which it desperately needs to set about the task of national reconstruction.

Against the continuing threats posed by Libya to his political survival, Habré can rely on the diplomatic support of the Sudan, Egypt, the United States, and, most probably, France. In fact, no other Chadian government has ever enjoyed such widespread external sympathy. In an environment where success is its own vindication, these assets are clearly convertible into domestic support. Whether Habré will seize upon this opportunity and display the same astuteness and determination in the arena of domestic politics as he once did on the battlefield remains an open question.

Further Reading

Bouquet, Christian. *Tchad: Genèse d'un conflit.* Paris: Editions L'Harmattan, 1982.

Buijtenhuis, Robert. *Le Frolinat et les révoltes populaires du Tchad, 1965–1976.* Paris: Mouton, 1978.

Chapelle, Jean. *Le peuple tchadien.* Paris: Editions L'Harmattan, 1980.

Decalo, Samuel. *Historical Dictionary of Chad.* Methuchen, N. J.: The Scarecrow Press, 1977.

Lemarchand, René. "The Politics of Sara Ethnicity: A Note on the Origins of the Civil War in Chad." *Cahiers d'Etudes Africaines*, Vol. 20, No. 4 (1980).

Thompson, Virginia, and Adloff, Richard. *Conflict in Chad.* Institute of International Studies. Berkeley: University of California Press, 1981.

REPUBLIC OF CHILE
(*República de Chile*)
by Elizabeth G. Ferris, Ph.D.

The System of Government

Since 1973, Chile has been governed by a four-man military junta, under the leadership of General Augusto Pinochet.

The junta consists of the leaders of the four branches of the armed forces. In mid-1982, besides Army General Augusto Pinochet Ugarte, it was comprised of Air Force General Fernando Malthei Aubel, Admiral José Torribio Merino, and Carabinero Director-General César Mendoza. The dominance of the army within the armed forces is reflected in Pinochet's position of leadership. General Pinochet's original title was president of the *Junta del Gobierno*, but in June 1974, it was officially changed to president of the republic.

The 1973 coup which overthrew President Salvador Allende also destroyed the Chilean democratic political system. Unlike most Latin American nations, Chile had a long tradition of stable democratic government. Its political institutions were based on law and largely untarnished by political corruption. The presidency, the Congress, the judicial system, and the bureaucracy were legitimate and authoritative and the people accepted their right to govern. By the middle of the twentieth century, Chile stood apart from virtually all Latin American nations in terms of both its stable democratic system and its high standard of living. Chile's ten million people were among the most educated and most aware citizens in the Third World. Although economic disparities existed, and indeed were very visible due to the openness of the system, they did not seem to pose the kinds of challenges usually associated with such inequalities. Labor unions were powerful actors on the political scene, and the government had substantial power as the major source of capital investment and the major employer.

Reflecting the power of the state and the political awareness of the population, numerous interest-group organizations worked to influence governmental policies. These organizations were pervasive; they represented not only the demands of labor, but also of numerous middle-class and professional groups. Chilean politics was a process of compromise and coalition building among a variety of these groups. The stability of Chilean democracy depended on the willingness of various powerful interests and parties to compromise and to work toward consensus. By 1970, this willingness to compromise had broken down. Bitterness between groups grew more virulent and political institutions became politicized for narrow partisan advantage.

During the 1960s, groups which had been largely excluded from the political system were mobilized into political activity on a very large scale. Party competition and unionization of rural workers were the main causes of such mobilization. By 1970, this competition had become so intense that Chile had become a polarized society. Changes in party alignments (rather than a growth in power on the left) led to the 1970 victory of Salvador Allende, the candidate of a leftist coalition, Popular Unity. Allende's campaign promised a transition to socialism while preserving Chilean democracy. Allende's term was marked by further polarization, by unprecedented economic woes, and by Allende's inability to keep his promise of maintaining democracy while creating a socialist state. The causes of his failures are many: the unwillingness to compromise by both left and center parties, both government and private intervention from the United States, and the difficulties involved in efficiently implementing policies in a context in which even technical details were seen as politically significant. For the junta which took power on September 11, 1973, the message was clear: the chaos of the Allende years was the product not of one man's or one party's policies, but of a failure of the system as a whole. The Chilean political process which had functioned smoothly for decades was to be dismantled. The chaos of the Allende years, according to the military, must never be repeated.

While many had expected a military coup—and indeed many Chilean moderates had openly advocated military intervention—few expected the military government to be so brutal. Allende was killed during the coup, and in the first few years of the Pinochet regime, thousands of Chileans were killed, torture was commonplace, and civil liberties virtually ceased to exist. Political parties were outlawed, labor unions restricted, censorship imposed, and the fundamental rights of the person repeatedly violated. From the military's perspective, these measures were necessary to prevent the resurgence of leftist activity. Since leftists made up over one-third of the population, sweeping measures of repression were seen as essential.

Executive

Until the 1973 military coup, Chile was governed under the constitution of 1925, which established a unitary representative democracy. The Chilean executive was elected for a six-year term by direct vote and prohibited from reelection. If no candidate received a majority of the votes, Congress was to choose between the top two contenders. In practice, Congress always selected the candidate receiving the most votes. There was no vice president.

The president traditionally was given extensive power, and yet his power was much more limited than the power of executives in other Latin American nations. The main limit was the existence of powerful competing political institutions and interest groups. Congress, for example, could impeach the president's cabinet ministers. In times when Congress was controlled by opposition forces, this power to impeach cabinet ministers proved to be a serious limit to presidential power. Several of President Allende's cabinet ministers resigned when congressional impeachment was threatened.

The president had extensive powers of appointment and thus had some ability to control the bureaucracy, but the proliferation of government agencies and departments—many of which were independent of direct executive control and financing—served as an additional restraint on presidential power. During the previous half century, informal rules were developed which provided for a sharing of political patronage within the bureaucracy regardless of the party in power.

One institution which was not susceptible to political control was the *contraloría general* (comptroller general), an independent auditing agency which reviewed all government actions under the direction of a comptroller appointed for life by the president with the Senate's approval.

Other government agencies, political parties, and private-interest groups could request the comptroller to investigate any aspect of government and give an informal opinion of its efficiency and rectitude. The agency was scrupulously above politics and enjoyed a reputation for independent judgment. However, in the postcoup environment, these institutions which previously had not been susceptible to executive control—including the comptroller general—are subservient to the military government's power.

Today, the principal political issues in Chile are the nature of economic development programs, particularly the control of inflation, and the restructuring of the economy along capitalist lines. The military government not only destroyed any vestige of the previous political system, but also undid the pattern of state involvement in the economy—a pattern which had evolved over a fifty-year period and had been greatly accelerated under Allende. The economic policies of the Pinochet regime have been based on the monetarist, free-market ideas of Milton Friedman; technical experts—the so-called Chicago Boys—acquired increased political importance. The success of these hard-line policies has been mixed. The imposition of free-trade policies coupled with drastic reductions in public spending have led to a notable decline in the inflation rate, increases in GNP, and rapid growth in foreign investment. But these policies have also been accompanied by increasing unemployment and a steady worsening of the position of the lower classes due to the curtailment or eradication of major social programs. The government's commitment to reducing and eliminating tariffs on manufactured goods has also hurt small businessmen and increased the number of bankruptcies.

With overall leadership supplied by the junta, military government is now pervasive throughout Chile. Military officers have replaced their civilian predecessors at all levels of government. With the single exception of economic planning, in which civilian technicians play a major policy role, all government institutions, including the foreign service, the educational establishment, and local governments, are now headed and controlled by military personnel.

In the mid-1970s, the international outcry over Chile's human-rights violations was at its height. Foreign governments (particularly the United States and in Europe), international organizations, and private organizations all condemned the Chilean military. The Chilean government reacted to these pressures by alleging the existence of an international conspiracy designed to weaken the government's will to continue the battle against communism. The Chilean government also denounced efforts to influence its policies as hypocritical (given the existence of far worse situations in other parts of the world) and as interventionist. Chile significantly reduced its involvement in international relations, sharply curtailing its bilateral relations and withdrawing from the Andean Common Market in 1976. Conflicts with Argentina over the Beagle Channel and continuing difficulties with Bolivia and Peru over Bolivian access to the ocean have increased Chile's diplomatic isolation.

In an effort to gain some legitimacy for the junta's goals, General Pinochet called a plebiscite in 1978 to demonstrate popular support for the military government and to consolidate his personal position of power. Voting in the plebiscite was mandatory and the election was called at such short notice that there was little opportunity to develop opposition. When the comptroller general denounced the plebiscite as without legal basis, he was replaced the next day by a new comptroller who, not surprisingly, declared the plebiscite legal. Pinochet reported that 75 percent of the Chilean people had voted in support of his government. This plebiscite met with widespread skepticism, both at home and abroad.

On September 11, 1980, another plebiscite was held to ratify the long-awaited constitution drawn up by the miltary with the advice of the Council of State. The constitution was approved by a vote of 4,203,615 (which included one million abstentions counted as yes) to 1,891,332, although there has been considerable criticism of the plebiscite and of the constitution itself.

The new constitution establishes a timetable for the restoration of democratic rule in Chile. General Pinochet will remain as president until 1989. Political parties will not be permitted to resume their political activities until that time. In 1989, the junta will designate a president to hold power until 1997. The new constitution may be changed by General Pinochet with the approval of the junta. (Pinochet has said that he will not be a candidate in 1989.)

Legislature

In December 1975, the government announced the formation of a Council of State to be composed of all former Chilean presidents and sixteen other prominent individuals. These individuals included representatives of different groups, such as labor, universities, and women. The Council first met in July 1976 and was composed primarily of retired government functionaries. Former president Eduardo Frei, leader of the Christian Demo-

PRESIDENTIAL ELECTIONS (1952–1970)	
	%
1952	
Carlos Ibáñez (Independent)	46.8
Arturo Matte (Right: Conservative, Liberal)	27.8
Pedro E. Alfonso (Center: Radical)	19.9
Salvador Allende (Left: Socialist)	5.5
1958	
Jorge Alessandri (Right: Conservative, Liberal)	31.6
Salvador Allende (Left: Socialist, Communist)	28.9
Eduardo Frei (Center: Christian Democrat)	20.7
Luis Bossay (Center: Radical)	15.6
Antonio Zamorano (Independent Left)	3.3
1964	
Eduardo Frei (Center-Right: Christian Democrat, Conservative, Liberal)	56.09
Salvador Allende (Left: Socialist, Communist)	38.93
Julio Durán (Center-Right: Radical)	4.99
1970	
Salvador Allende (Left: Socialist, Communist)	36.6
Jorge Alessandri (Right: Independent, National)	35.2
Radomiro Tomic (Center: Christian Democrat)	28.1

crats, refused to participate. The Council meets from time to time in an advisory capacity. It is usually perceived as a facade for authoritarian rule with little independent power.

Prior to the coup, Chile had a bicameral legislature with an upper house, the Senate, consisting of forty-five members (five from each of the nine districts) who were elected, in staggered elections, for eight-year terms. The Chamber of Deputies consisted of 147 deputies elected every four years. The Chilean Congress was one of the most professional legislative bodies in Latin America, but its power was primarily the power to block legislation. While Congress could initiate legislation, its ability to amend legislation proposed by the executive was limited. In cases in which the president declared a proposal to be urgent, the Congress had to act on the matter within thirty days.

Judiciary

While the executive and the legislative bodies traditionally jockeyed for power with one another, both branches displayed considerable respect for the judiciary. The courts had a long tradition of independence and integrity, and the

CONGRESSIONAL ELECTIONS, 1969 AND 1973

Party	1969 Number of Votes	%	1973 Number of Votes	%
Popular Unity				
Socialists	294,448	12.2	678,674	18.4
Communists	383,049	15.9	595,829	16.2
IC			41,432	1.1
API			29,977	0.8
MAPU			90,620	2.5
Radical	313,559	13.0	133,751	3.6
UP List			46,100	1.3
Others	65,378	2.8		
Total	1,056,434	43.9	1,616,383	43.9
Opposition				
Christian Democrats	716,547	29.8	1,049,676	28.5
National	480,523	20.0	777,084	21.1
PIR			65,120	1.8
DR			70,582	1.9
CODE ticket			33,918	0.9
Total	1,197,070	49.8	1,996,380	54.2
Other				
USOPO	51,904	2.2	10,371	0.3
Blank and Void	98,617	4.0	57,770	1.6
Registered	3,244,892		4,510,060	
Voting	2,406,129		3,680,307	
Abstaining	838,763	16.5	829,753	18.4

IC   = Christian Left (*Izquierda Cristiana*)
API   = Popular Independent Action (*Acción Popular Independiente*)
MAPU = United Popular Action Movement (*Movimiento de Acción Popular Unitario*)
PIR   = Left Radical Party (*Partido Izquierda Radical*)
DR   = Radical Democracy (*Democracia Radical*)
CODE = Democratic Confederation (*Confederación Democrática*)
USOPO = Popular Socialist Union (*Unión Socialista Popular*)

junta exercised considerable caution in dealing with it. From the outset the military promised to respect the rights of the court and, on September 12, 1973, the Supreme Court issued a statement giving its approval to the new government. In 1976, however, the new chief justice, José María Eyzaguirre, adopted a much more critical attitude toward the junta, and the independence of the courts was subsequently limited.

The Supreme Court is made up of thirteen justices who are appointed for life by the president from lists submitted by the Supreme Court. Appointments at all levels of the judicial hierarchy are determined primarily by the judiciary itself as judicial appointments are made from lists submitted by the courts. The Supreme Court can declare the enforcement of a given law unconstitutional, but not the law itself.

Regional & Local Government

Chilean politics are dominated by national concerns and by Santiago, the capital city. Chile is divided into twenty-five provinces which are further divided into departments, subdelegations, and districts. Municipal councils are generally composed of five council members (or *regidores*), but the councils are larger in larger cities. The councils have little power. The mayors and governors are generally appointed by the Ministry of Interior in Santiago. While municipal elections are important in assessing national political attitudes, they are of much less significance in local self-government.

The Electoral System

Before 1973, the Chilean electoral system was respected throughout Latin America for its integrity. Regular elections were held for president, national legislators, and municipal councils, the last two groups being elected through a system of proportional representation. Citizens eighteen years of age and over were required to register and vote, and proof of registration was required for many governmental and financial transactions. Literacy requirements were dropped in 1970.

The Party System

Origins of the Parties

Political parties began in Chile as elite organizations during the mid-nineteenth century. The Conservative Party protested the expanding state sector, the anticlerical actions of the government, and challenges to the power of the major rural landowners. The Liberal and Radical parties, representing urban professional classes, were committed to a stronger government. By the turn of the century, political parties were changing their fundamental nature by turning to the masses for popular support and party networks penetrated all social levels. The Communist and Socialist parties were formed in the 1920s. A new growth of centrist political parties—the Christian Democrats and the Radical parties—was accompanied by the slower growth of the conservative parties.

The Parties in Law

Political parties no longer legally exist in Chile. They were outlawed by the military regime in stages: first, on September 11, 1973, all Marxist parties were outlawed, and all other parties were recessed (and thus could not hold public meetings or meetings of leaders or maintain headquarters). In 1977 the remaining parties—the Christian Democrats, National Party, and two small radical splinter groups—were dissolved.

Under the precoup constitution, any party could list its candidates on the ballot once it had filed certain information with the electoral authorities. The main requirement for participating in elections was that a party be endorsed on a petition by 10,000 registered voters. These provisions made it relatively easy for parties to organize.

Party Organization

Prior to the 1973 coup, Chilean political parties provided an important link between local communities and national political structures. Party organization generally provided for varying degrees of input from local levels. The Christian Democrats and the Radicals, particularly, stressed local involvement more than parties on either the right or the left. All parties, however, centered

their national organizations in Santiago and concentrated their organizational efforts in the major cities. Although varying significantly by time and party, party membership generally required formalized adherence to party principles and/or a probation period before full membership was conferred. Recruitment of party candidates tended to be dominated by local party leaders while regional and national assemblies met periodically to consider questions of policy and organization. Party funding came from a variety of sources, including membership dues, voluntary contributions, legislators' assessed contributions and special election-year fundraising efforts. Most local-party organizations raised their own income, though the national party provided some campaign support during election years.

Several characteristics of the party system contributed to the suspension of democratic institutions in Chile. The parties were extremely important in the power structure of the country. They dominated the legislature and the links between local and national levels of government, but they were also fragmented, highly competitive, and by the mid-1960s sharply polarized. Coalitions were essential if leaders were to be elected and the nation governed. Support for the left (Socialists and Communists) averaged only 21.5 percent from 1925 to 1973, while votes for the right averaged only 30.1 percent. This meant that the cooperation of the center parties was essential to any government.

Cooperation, however, required compromise and three factors made compromise difficult. Party cohesion depended in part on securing government jobs and other benefits for party members. Interparty compromises over these "spoils" led to intraparty feuds which reduced support for party leaders and contributed to the creation of many small splinter parties, which in turn made coalition politics that much more difficult. Finally, ideology—both as genuine moral commitment and as smoke screen for personal ambition—tended to make compromise morally suspect and politically unprofitable.

Campaigning

Although campaigning was offically limited to the six months prior to a presidential election and to two months before a congressional election, in practice campaigning began much earlier. Since elections for municipal council members, for Congress, and for president were held on different dates, there were many opportunities to assess popular opinion and electoral trends. Elections were hotly contested and served an important mobilization function. Chileans discussed politics with an intensity unique on the continent, rallies and demonstrations for all parties were commonplace, and election results were anxiously anticipated. One of the first acts of the Pinochet regime was to order the destruction of the basis of the system—the records of the Electoral Registry.

Christian Democrat Party (*Partido Demócrata Christiano;* PDC)

History

The Christian Democratic Party began as an offshoot of the Conservative Party in the 1930s, but remained a tiny organization until it merged with another small center party in 1957. After that the PDC enjoyed a meteoric rise to power when in 1964, the party's candidate, Eduardo Frei Montalva, was elected president with the largest majority (56 percent) in recent Chilean history. In fact he was the only president to be elected with a majority since 1950. The PDC together with the National Party and other small opposition parties held a majority in Congress during the Allende administration. Several factions split with the party during that period over the question of how much support to give Allende. The PDC's persistent opposition to Allende was an important factor in the military's decision to take power.

Organization

The PDC organization was well developed with local, provincial, and national deliberative bodies and an effective interchange of opinion between leaders and the rank and file.

Policy

The PDC general policy was social reform along democratic Christian humanist lines. They advocated a mixed economy with an important role for government, nationalistic policies in opposition to the United States, agrarian reform, and a more open democracy.

Since the 1973 coup, the Christian Democrats have been the most active party in domestic politics. Initially, the PDC accepted the coup as a *fait accompli*; indeed, many party leaders welcomed the coup. However, the party was soon disillusioned; by 1975 even the conservative wing of the party under Eduardo Frei was in opposition to the government. Frei refused to serve in the Council of State, charging that it lacked meaningful political power. As the only opposition group of any significance allowed to function, if only semi-legally, PDC leaders were in an awkward position. Dissident groups within the party, notably one led by Renan Fuentealba, wanted more militant opposition to the regime. The majority of the party's leadership argued that confrontation with the military would only destroy the party without achieving real political concessions. With the dissolution of all remaining parties in 1977, former PDC members grew more openly critical. Debate continues within the party over whether or not the PDC should work with the parties of the old Popular Unity alliance in opposition to the junta.

Membership & Constituency

The membership of the Christian Democrats came from the Catholic middle class, including professionals and intellectuals. Although not as strong as the left with urban and rural labor, the PDC attracted considerable support from some unions and from the poorest agricultural workers. The PDC had support in all regions of the country.

Financing

The PDC was generously supported by contributions from wealthy individuals and businesses, as well as by membership dues.

Leadership

The current head of the PDC is Gabriel Valdez (born 1919), whose election as party president in April 1982 indicated a shift to the left. The previous leader, Andrés Zaldivar, was expelled from the party in disputes over the extent to which the party should cooperate with the junta.

Prospects

The death of Eduardo Frei in January 1982 left the party without a preeminent leader, but the PDC will undoubtedly continue as a major factor in Chilean politics even under the junta. While the military remains in power, the party will probably experience some splintering and disorganization, but if the military steps down, the Christian Democrats will emerge as the most likely alternative national leadership.

Communist Party
(*Partido Comunista de Chile*)

History

Since its creation in 1921, the Chilean Communist Party has undergone several periods of governmental repression and almost constant conflicts with other leftist parties. Disputes between the Communists and Socialists, encompassing both ideological and personal issues, have been particularly acrimonious. However, the Communist Party has worked with other leftist parties in forming electoral coalitions. In 1970, the Communist Party joined with other leftist political parties to support the candidacy of Salvador Allende through the Popular Unity coalition.

Like the other leftist political parties, the Communist Party was harshly repressed by the military. Its leaders were either killed, imprisoned, or sent into exile. The Communists' previous experience as an underground political party gave it an advantage over other leftist parties.

Organization

The party was tightly organized in spite of factional disputes, and the central leadership dominated decision making. Although information on current leftist activity in Chile is sketchy, there are reports that some party organization still exists.

Policy

The Communist Party platform stressed the need for nationalist revolutionary measures to counter perceived U.S. imperialism and the entrenched power of the Chilean oligarchy. Specifically, the Communists advocated the nationalization of industries, the transfer of land to peasant cooperatives, and worker control of industries. The Chilean Communist Party had close relations with European Communist parties and with the Soviet Union. The party's leader, Luis Corvalan, broke with other leftist leaders over the issue of transferability of the Cuban revolution to other Latin American nations. While other leftist groups saw the Cuban example as the desired model for revolutionary change, the Communist Party continued to stress the possibility of peaceful transition to socialism. The Communists in exile have been more receptive than the Socialists or the other leftist parties to overtures from the PDC to forge a united front against the military regime.

Membership & Constituency

The party had approximately 30,000 members before the 1973 coup; current membership is unknown. The party drew steady support from the north and far south of Chile, from the industrial city of Concepción, and from the capital of Santiago.

Financing

Membership dues were probably the primary source of the party's income. Sale of publications, union support, and contributions from highly placed professionals and intellectuals provided additional funds. Support from the Soviet bloc, while rumored, was never acknowledged or proven.

Leadership

Luis Corvalán, party secretary general, is now in exile.

Prospects

The Communist Party is likely to reappear as a major political force, legal or illegal, as soon as the junta steps down. It is not inconceivable, in fact, that the longer the junta stays in power, the more influential the Communist Party and other leftist parties will become as a counterweight. If the military's economic policies are seen as failures, the party's position will be even more enhanced.

National Party
(*Partido Nacional*)

History

The National Party was formed in 1965 when the Liberal and Conservative parties merged. Although the two parties had historic differences (particularly on the role of the Church and on the need for industrialization), they supported the same candidates and felt similarly threatened by the growing leftist political parties. The National Party came to be the major organized political party on the right, drawing its strength from the upper and middle classes. Party leadership was drawn from powerful confederations of industrial interests.

Organization

Traditionally less highly organized than parties to its left, the National Party relied on local political leaders and their clients to advance the party's interests. The importance of local leadership meant that the party faced many factional disputes over personalities and economic policies.

Policy

The party was opposed to extensive state involvement in the economy, although its rural, landowning wing favored subsidies for agriculture. Presently, party leaders are cooperating with the regime.

Membership & Constituency

Support for the National Party was concentrated in the old elite and the upper classes, but middle-class entrepreneurs and some small farmers also gave their votes to the party. The party's stronghold was the agricultural areas of the center-south.

Financing

The party was well financed by wealthy landowners and industrialists.

Leadership

Sergio Unoçre Jarpa, president, and Mario Anello, secretary general, were the principal party leaders throughout the 1970s.

Prospects

The future of the right wing in Chile depends largely on the success of the junta's policies. If in the long run their economic policies work without extensive social dislocation and political repression, the right will prosper. If the junta's policies fail, however, or the military becomes involved in corruption scandals, the right wing will have to pay the price of collaborating with the regime.

Socialist Party
(Partido Socialista)

History

The Socialist Party was founded in 1934 and quickly developed a sizable following among the working class and intelligentsia. It did not begin to have a real impact on Chilean politics until the 1950s, when the leadership of Salvador Allende brought the various factions of the party into working unity and provided a rallying point for wider popular appeal. With the overthrow and death of Allende, the party organization shattered and factionalism asserted its dominant role in party life.

Organization

The party was well organized at all levels of society, but was not cohesive. At local and regional levels, factions fought for control of the organization and found unity only in Allende's electoral prospects, whose leadership was partly based on his ability to moderate the intraparty disputes.

Policy

The Socialists were generally agreed that the use of the democratic political process to gain power was fraught with danger, but they preferred that process to violence or civil war. They had supported the Cuban revolution and were not, in theory, opposed to following that example to achieve a socialist state, but they were prepared to try their luck at the polls first. Unlike the Communists, they were not committed to a theory which held that a genuine Marxist victory could only come after a failure of liberal reforms had paved the way. In short, in the Chilean context, the Socialists appeared more radical than the Communists.

The Socialists called for rapid transfer of agricultural land and factories from the owners to the workers, the nationalization of major industries, a greatly reduced role for foreign capital, and the development of a new, socialist culture. When rural laborers and urban workers moved quickly to put the first of these policies into practice, the Allende government accepted their takeovers.

In opposition to U.S. investment in Chilean businesses and influence in Chilean politics, the Allende regime's aim was to exclude the United States from both as much as possible, and to align itself with the left wing of the nonaligned movement.

The party is now sharply divided over questions of responsibility for the failure of the Allende regime and the coup, as well as over the best tactics to adopt for the future.

Membership & Constituency

The party's primary support came from urban and rural labor and from ideologically committed professionals and intellectuals. Support was found in every region. In 1972, the party membership was estimated at some 100,000.

Financing

Membership dues and small contributions were the party's primary sources of revenue. Additional support came from left-wing labor unions. How much foreign support the party received, whether from West Europe or the Soviet bloc, is unknown.

Leadership

The party's leadership is now in exile. Its two principal spokesmen, Carlos Altamirano and Clodomire Almeyda (born 1923), are in Europe and Venezuela, respectively. Altamirano represents a more radical view, advocating more active and violent opposition to the junta and a rejection of Allende's gradualist approach to seizing power.

Prospects

Because of its association with the failures of the Allende government and the political disaster which followed, the prospects of the Socialist Party, as such, are weak. Unless a new leader emerges who can pull the factions together and provide a convincing rationale for the 1973 debacle, the Socialists are unlikely to emerge again as a coherent force in the near future.

Minor Parties

Among the many minor parties which appeared and disappeared, two in particular stand out—the leftist MIR and the centrist Radicals.

Movement of the Revolutionary Left (*Movimiento de la Izquierda Revolucionaria*; MIR)

The MIR was founded in 1966 when a small group of dissatisfied Socialists broke away from the party in opposition to Allende's gradualism. The pro-Castro MIR advocated rapid revolutionary change through direct confrontation and armed struggle. It gained considerable support among urban and rural laborers. The MIR refused to support Allende's Popular Unity coalition, preferring instead to exert pressure on the Allende government from an independent position. The MIR consistently pushed the Allende regime to adopt more revolutionary measures and was a major element in the peasant and worker takeover of land and factories. Many of the government's programs were thus upstaged by MIR activities. The MIR also advocated arming the workers. After the 1973 coup, the MIR leadership was decimated and very little was heard of the party for several years. In 1980 and 1981, however, the MIR claimed responsibility for various violent acts against the military government. Andrés Pascal Allende, nephew of the slain president, is secretary general of the MIR.

Radical Party (*Partido Radical*)

The Radical Party, together with the Christian Democrats, was one of the major political parties in the center of the Chilean political spectrum. Founded in the 1860s as an offshoot of the Liberal Party, the Radicals initially represented the frustrations of provincial elites over continued domination by the capital, Santiago. However, the Radical Party grew to encompass the expanding middle class and to advocate secular reforms. The party supported government employment programs, and government employees were a major source of Radical Party support. Public education and moderate working-class programs also figured in party policy. The radical coalition of rural elites and urban workers, together with the more dominant professional middle classes, proved an unworkable combination. The Radical Party, by the late 1950s, lost many of its more progressive elements to the more liberal Christian Democrats and to leftist political parties. The Radicals, however, were pragmatic, perhaps even opportunistic. They supported the Allende candidacy in the 1970 elections and were rewarded with several cabinet positions. The decision to support the Allende candidacy cost the party considerable support as many more conservative members left the party.

Other Political Forces

Military

Before 1973, the Chilean military's involvement in governing the nation had been limited. The last *coup d'état* had taken place in 1932, when the military briefly intervened to restore political and social order. After serving in government for a short time, the military devoted its energies to upgrading itself as an institution.

Although both top leadership and the vast majority of military officers were committed to civilian rule throughout the 1932–73 period, military conspiracies did surface from time to time, but for lack of support, rarely amounted to more than brief flare-ups. The military was, however, concerned with politics and, like its counterparts throughout the world, lobbied hard for increases in military spending. The military was concerned with the fact that between 1948 and 1968 the military share of the budget dropped from 18 percent to 9 percent. The drop was particularly acute in the case of the army which, although the largest branch of the armed forces, saw the navy and air force increase their share of appropriations much more rapidly.

The Chilean armed forces (including the police) today number approximately 109,000 personnel in four branches: the army, navy, air force, and carabineros (national police). The navy was clearly the most elitist of the branches and, together with the air force, enjoyed the highest prestige. These two branches, because of their traditions and emphasis on sophisticated technologies, were the most politically conservative branches, opposing radicalism of both left and right. They drew their officers from the upper classes. By 1950, the carabineros were increasingly being drawn from the lower middle classes as were many in the army; both forces were considered more liberal than the navy and air force, although their officers—of upper-middle-class backgrounds—were opposed to the "excessive" freedoms usually associated with moderen liberalism.

The armed forces' leadership did not seriously consider a military takeover when Salvador Allende was elected president. Although they feared the effects of Allende's election on law and order in the nation and were strongly anti-Marxist in principle, adherence to constitutional norms prevailed in spite of right-wing pressures to intervene. Allende's Popular Unity government was keenly aware of these pressures and was generous in dealing with the armed forces: salaries were increased, government officials were careful to praise the military in public, and, indeed, military officials were even brought into the government to win support for its programs. However, many military officers opposed this political role and felt that it weakened the power and the prestige of the armed forces. A further consequence of the incorporation of military men into the government was increased military awareness of the in-

efficiency of civilian leaders and a growing awareness that military leaders could do as well if not better.

On June 29, 1973, an attempted military coup failed for lack of broad-based support. The Allende government responded with greater efforts to increase military participation in the government. As the leftist political parties called for arming the workers and as political violence from both the left and right reached an all-time high, the military leaders became more alarmed at the disintegration of the Chilean social fabric. By August 1973, a coup seemed inevitable with not only the right but also some of the center calling for military intervention. After the September 11 takeover, the officer corps itself was purged, as some 2,000 officers were forced out of positions of power.

The ruling military forces have little in the way of a coherent ideology and important factions have developed within the military. One faction, the duros or hard-liners, see protracted military rule as essential. The duros are nationalistic and reject measures which are perceived to give foreign companies or other international interests too large a share in the Chilean economy. While they support the free-market ideas of the economic technocrats and favor returning nationalized industries to the private sector, they are suspicious of both foreign investors and of Chilean elite groups. The duros feel that the military is the only group whose loyalty to the nation is unquestioned. The other faction, the blandos or soft-liners, favor a quicker transition to civilian rule and rapid increases in foreign investment, and are much more sympathetic to the needs of Chilean industrialists than the duros. Most of the blandos have come from the air force and, to a lesser extent, the navy. Many military officers saw the 1978 plebiscite as a rather crass effort by Pinochet to increase his personal power. Air Force general Gustavo Leigh, while a member of the junta, was most vocal in his opposition. He called the voting "the biggest mockery in Chilean history" and resigned from the junta. Leigh has continued his verbal attacks on the junta and is popularly known as the "dissident general."

The policies pursued by the military government have been a curious amalgam of blando and duro views. The duros, led by Pinochet, have been fairly successful in minimizing popular political participation and in institutionalizing military rule. However, the economic politicies pursued by the government seem to reflect the blando belief in the need for foreign capital and for strong domestic industrialists.

Economic Elites

Wealthy industrialists are becoming an increasingly powerful force in Chilean politics. Government policies reducing tariffs on imported manufactured goods and the process of returning formerly state-owned industries to the private sector has had the effect of concentrating wealth in the hands of large corporations. A recent study published in Chile showed that in 1978 six economic "clans" controlled two-thirds of the assets of the nation's top 250 corporations. The clans are interrelated and have considerable influence in the rural sectors as well. Given Chile's economic development model, the power of the industrialists seems likely to increase, although the current economic problems of the regime are causing severe financial difficulties for some of the clans.

Organized Labor

Unions were firmly established in Chile by the 1920s. Competition between leftist parties, particularly the Socialists and the Communists, to gain control over the unions was intense. In 1952, the two parties agreed to set aside their differences and established the United Central of Chilean Workers (*Central Unica de Trabajadores de Chile*, CUT). The CUT increased labor's power by incorporating white-collar workers, but it was constantly challenged by the Christian Democratic Party which supported other unions. The CUT was also highly politicized, and alienated some workers with its leftist political positions.

By 1970 there were approximately 500,000 union members, representing approximately 30 percent of the Chilean work force. However, 70 percent of the workers in industries having more than twenty-five employees were unionized. Approximately 65 percent of Chilean unions were affiliated with the CUT. Under Allende, the labor unions became even more powerful and more politicized. The CUT became the main organizational base of the government and attained a major voice in labor policy and in the public sector of the economy. Workers were given large wage increases, but local union leaders demanded still higher ones. Local unions began taking over their factories without prior government approval. By 1973, these *cordones* or worker-controlled factories exercised considerable power within the labor movement.

When the military took over, the CUT was dissolved and union activity greatly restricted. Union elections could not be called, collective bargaining was suspended, many labor leaders were either killed or disappeared, and the right to assemble and to strike were for all practical purposes withdrawn. Protests from international labor organizations were of no avail. Rigid wage controls, inflation, repression, high unemployment, and a drastic reduction in social benefits made labor one of the biggest losers under military rule. In 1979 some labor reforms were announced, culminating in August 1979 with a new labor code. The new code guaranteed the right of all workers to organize, but placed severe limitations on the ability of unions to negotiate collectively. For example, all strikers are considered to have resigned after sixty days and new workers can be hired.

Roman Catholic Church

Traditionally, the Roman Catholic Church in Chile has been a moderate-conservative force in society. The Church hierarchy opposed the Allende government on the grounds that it was Marxist, contributed to social decay, and challenged the Church's authority, particularly with its emphasis on public education. However, there were Christian groups, most notably Christians for Socialism, which supported Allende. Following the coup, the Church leadership initially took a noncommittal policy, but increasing conflicts over human rights brought it into open opposition to the government. In 1975, government pressures led to the dissolution of the *Comité de Cooperación para la Paz* (Committee of Cooperation for Peace), the principal ecumenical group working in human rights. This was replaced in 1976 with the Vicarate of Solidarity which performed similar functions including legal aid, help in finding jobs, and more traditional social services. The archbishop of Santiago, Cardinal Raul Silva Henriquez, has displayed a willingness to use the resources of the Church to counter the military's power. The Church opposed the plebiscites called by the government to legitimate its rule, and has supported various protest groups. The government has attacked the Church, albeit in a veiled fashion, for supporting what it terms "Marxist acts" and "demonstrated superficial judgments." The Church offers one of the few sources of opposition to the government.

Students

Throughout the 1960s, and during the Allende regime, university students played an important role in Chilean politics. University students were active in the political parties and elections in universities reflected—or presaged—political coalitions in national politics. After the 1973 coup, student organizations were disbanded and students active in leftist political parties were imprisoned or exiled. The military subsequently permitted the formation of "acceptable" student organizations. However, in the University of Chile elections in 1980, only 32 percent of the students voted for the official candidates. Beginning in 1980, the government began a process of reform which increased government control of the university decisions. This has triggered discussion and protests by both faculty and students.

Opposition

In comparison with the years before the military coup, current political activity in Chile seems minimal. But opposition to the government is expressed through musical performances (particularly in traditional Chilean *penas*, or folklore clubs), theater, and increasingly through political institutes and foundations. The largest of these groups is known as the Group of Constitutionalist Studies (or the Group of 24) and consists of opposition leaders from across a broad political spectrum under the leadership of Manuel Sanhueva, former head of the law faculty. The *Instituto Chileno de Estudios Humanísticos* consists primarily of former Christian Democrats while the *Centro de Estudios Social–Democráticos* attracts Social Democrats. The socialist-oriented press of *Talleres Socialistas* has published several books. The *Corporación de Estudios Nacionales*, led by Lucía Pinochet (daughter of the president), is a powerful institute which reflects conservative interests, while the *Academia de Humanismo Cristiano* was created by Archbishop Silva Henriquez.

National Prospects

Military rule in Chile seems likely to continue for at least the next decade. The military's control of political institutions is secure and popular political participation has been effectively limited. Certainly power will not be transferred to civilian leaders until the military is convinced that leftist political forces will not play a role. The military will also be reluctant to turn power over to civilian leaders without some assurance that the civilians will not seek retribution from the military for acts committed during the early years of military rule.

While Chile's military rulers will undoubtedly continue in power, they will probably move toward some relaxation of restrictions on political activity. Given the economic and political impact of their policies, they will be unlikely to tolerate much mobilization of the working classes—either in urban unions or in rural areas. However, limited participation of these sectors—under government control—will probably be permitted. Increased participation of middle-class sectors, particularly those supporting centrist political parties in the past, will be more likely. By permitting limited participation, the military rulers can increase their legitimacy, overcome some of the hostile international criticism which has plagued the regime, and control the "transition to democracy." However, that democracy, when and if it emerges, will be far different than the Chilean democracy destroyed in 1973.

Further Reading

Alexander, Robert J. *The Tragedy of Chile*. Westport, Conn.: Greenwood Press, 1978.

Caviedes, César. *The Politics of Chile: A Sociogeographical Assessment*. Boulder, Colo.: Westview Press, 1979.

Loveman, Brian. *Chile: The Legacy of Hispanic Capitalism*. New York: Oxford University Press, 1979.

Marcella, Gabriel. "The Chilean Military Government and the Prospects for Transition to Democracy." *Inter-American Economic Affairs*, Vol. 33, No. 2, Autumn 1979.

North, Liisa. "The Military in Civilian Politics." *Studies in Comparative International Development*, Vol. II, No. 2, Summer 1976.

Remmer, Karen. "Pinochet's Chile." *Worldview*, October 1979.

———. "Political Demobilization in Chile, 1973–1978." *Comparative Politics*, Vol. 12, No. 3, April 1980.

Sigmund, Paul E. *The Overthrow of Allende and the Politics of Chile, 1964–1976*. Pittsburgh: University of Pittsburgh Press, 1979.

Valenzuela, Arturo. *The Breakdown of Democratic Regimes: Chile*. Baltimore: Johns Hopkins University Press, 1978.

——— and Valenzuela, J. Samuel, eds. *Chile: Politics and Society*. New Brunswick, N. J.: Transaction Books, 1976.

PEOPLE'S REPUBLIC OF CHINA
(*Zhonghua Renmin Gongheguo*)
by Donald M. Seekins, Ph.D.

The System of Government

The People's Republic of China is, according to its 1978 state constitution, "a socialist state of the dictatorship of the proletariat led by the working class and based on the alliance of workers and peasants." It was established formally on October 1, 1949, after communist armed forces successfully defeated those of the Nationalists or Guomindang (Kuomintang) under Jiang Jyeshi (Chiang Kai-shek) after four years of civil war.

China's territory can be divided into two geographic and historic regions: the provinces of China proper, located south of the Great Wall, which were unified under the Qin (Ch'in) and Han (Han) Dynasties (221 to 207 B.C. and 206 B.C. to 220 A.D., respectively) and which have been under Chinese rule ever since; and a much larger region consisting of the three provinces of the northeast, Julin, Liaoning, and Heilongjiang (Kirin, Liaoning, and Heilungkiang, commonly known as Manchuria), Nei Monggol (Inner Mongolia), Xinjiang (Sinkaing), Qinghai (Ch'inghai), and Xizang (Tibet) added to the Chinese empire during the Manchu Qing (Ch'ing) Dynasty (1644–1911). China has over 20,000 kilometers (12,400 miles) of land frontier, 6,452 kilometers (4,000 miles) of which form the border with the Soviet Union. Border disputes, particularly with the Soviet Union and India, have been prominent in China's relations with its neighbors, as it strives to regain territory lost during the nineteenth century period of "unequal treaties" with Russia and the Western powers.

In 1982, the population was approximately one billion, up from an estimated 583 million in 1953, the largest in the world. It is concentrated in the eastern part of the country, particularly in the coastal provinces south of the Great Wall, while vast mountainous and desert areas of Xinjiang, Xizang, Qinghai, and Nei Monggol are virtually uninhabited. Of the total population, 94 percent is ethnically Chinese (officially designated the Han nationality). In the remaining 6 percent, there are fifty-five officially recognized minority nationalities, of which the largest include the Zhuang (Chuang), Hui, Uygur (Uighur), Tibetans, Manchus, Mongols, and Koreans. Most of the minority groups are concentrated in the border regions.

The structure and process of government which evolved during the more than twenty-two centuries between the beginning of the Han Dynasty (206 B.C.) and the end of the Qing Dynasty (1911) combined, in a unique fashion, the rational and the despotic. At the apex of the system was the emperor (*huangdi; huang-ti*), who combined in himself the roles of ceremonial head of state with almost divine charismatic powers, chief executive, and supreme legislator. During the Qing Dynasty, he made the final decision on all policy matters of importance, enacted laws, and supervised the government bureaucracy on all levels. He was served by a sophisticated and functionally specific hierarchy of civil servants. The historian Albert Feuerwerker estimates that during the eighteenth century, the high point of Qing power and prestige, a cadre of 20,000 civil servants governed a population of 300,000,000. For most common people, the government was a distant (though often threatening) entity. Lower-level officials had to rely on the cooperation of local "gen-

Note: Chinese names and terms are given in the official *pinyin* transliteration: the Wade-Giles or commonly used transliteration follows in parentheses for items of the pre-1949 period, for example, Qing (Chi'ng) Dynasty, Beijing (Peking).

try" and larger numbers of usually rapacious functionaries (not themselves professional civil servants) in order to maintain public order, raise tax revenues, and complete public projects like canals and irrigation works. The constructive influence of even the most enlightened officials on the villages and hamlets of China was thus much diluted by local interests.

An element of central importance in the continuity of the imperial system was Confucianism which from the Han Dynasty on served as the moral basis of the state and defined the culture and way of life of the ruling classes. As formulated by Kongfuzi (K'ung Fu-tzu or Confucius, 541–479 B.C.) and Mengzi (Meng-tzu or Mencius, 372–289 B.C.) in the late Zhou and elaborated by Han Dynasty scholars, this body of thought was at once a philosophy of human nature, a system of ethics, and a political ideology. For Confucianists, society was not an aggregate of self-interested, private individuals, but a highly interdependent system consisting of a complex and tightly drawn network of reciprocal (though not equal) social bonds regulated by the principles of *ren* (*jen;* humanity, or benevolence) and *li* (rites, or ceremony).

On the political level, the Confucian ruler, assisted by able and loyal officials, was responsible for preserving and promoting this social network, both by providing for the people's basic material welfare and by furthering "moral education" through the power of good example and the sponsoring of educational and cultural institutions. Moral (or ideological) mobilization was especially stressed. Virtuous rulers and conscientious officials could, according to Confucian doctrine, inspire the people to live up to the ideals embodied in *ren* and *li*, and the empire as a whole would prosper and be happy. Superior and inferior were defined sharply, but the right of the former to rule was conditioned by the principle that they possessed superior merit and had an attitude of benevolent paternalism toward the latter. This was an ideal, however, and the growth of the emperor's absolute power in the Ming (1368–1644) and Qing dynasties led to terrible abuses of power. For the common people, the repressive aspects of government—harsh laws and punishments, heavy taxes and *corvees*, as well as corruption—were often more apparent than Confucian benevolence.

The inability of the Manchu Dynasty to maintain internal peace and China's humiliation at the hands of the Western powers, Russia, and Japan in the nineteenth and early twentieth centuries led to the dynasty's overthrow and the dissolution of the imperial system itself in 1911. The period between 1912, when the first Republic of China was formally established, and 1949 was largely one of disunity and civil war, exacerbated by the Japanese invasion of China in the 1930s. In 1949, the Chinese communists were finally able to fill the political vacuum that had been left by the fall of the Qing thirty-eight years before.

The structure of political institutions in the People's Republic of China, as defined in the 1977 constitution of the Chinese Communist Party (CCP) and the 1978 state constitution, with subsequent revisions, is based upon the Soviet model of a hierarchy of dual and parallel party and state organs extending from the center to the local level. In such an arrangement, the party, in conformity with the principle found in the 1978 constitution that "the working class exercises leadership over the state through its vanguard, the Communist Party of China," is the formulator of policy, while the state administration is charged with its implementation. The principle of "dual rule," adopted at the Eighth Party Congress in 1956, defines the CCP's dominant role by stipulating that state organs are not only responsible to the state organs above them, but are also responsible to the party organ on their own level. For example, the provincial state administration is subordinate both to the central state administration and the provincial party committee.

The history of the Chinese revolution, however, has left its mark on political institutions and accounts for some divergence from the Soviet model. During the periods of resistance to the Guomindang and the Japanese, the party and its armed force, the People's Liberation Army, were virtually identical. An emphasis was placed on mobility, flexibility, and the need to maintain broad popular support in the face of much more powerful adversaries. Fixed and functionally defined hierarchies of state and party organizations were seen as much less effective under these conditions than "guerrilla administrations" which combined state, party, and military functions in relatively simple organizations. The result was in 1949 a movement in which party, state, and army were blended both in terms of personnel and functions. Drawing a parallel with Cuba, Franz Schurmann, in *Ideology and Organization in Communist China*, states that "organizationally speaking, it was the revolution which created the party, and not the party that created the revolution." Even after the founding of the People's Republic, when party and state bureaucracies were set up on a permanent basis, the interchangeability of party and state personnel continued. Leaders belonged, and still belong, to the top levels of both party and state hierarchies. During the Cultural Revolution (1966–69), party and state organizations, after coming under attacks from groups of Red Guards, were dissolved on the subnational level and replaced by revolutionary committees, coalitions of the People's Liberation Army, "revolutionary mass organizations," and "revolutionary state and party cadres" designed to unite party and state functions. Separate party organizations on the provincial, county, and local levels were reestablished in 1971, but the revolutionary committees continued to be responsible for state administration until 1979, when they were replaced by people's governments. Recent years have seen a new emphasis on defining and separating party and state personnel and functions.

In early 1982, a special Committee for the Revision of the Constitution of the Standing Committee of the Fifth National People's Congress approved a draft revision of the 1978 constitution which would alter the state structure in significant ways. Its final approval by the Congress seems assured.

Executive

Although the constitution does not state it precisely, the chairman of the Standing Committee of the National People's Congress acts as the head of state, receiving foreign ambassadors, promulgating laws and decrees, and ratifying treaties with foreign countries. In 1982, the chairman was Ye Jianying. The chairman is assisted by a secretary general and a number of vice chairmen (twenty in 1981).

China's central executive body is the State Council, whose members are selected by the Standing Committee or by the National People's Congress, if it is in session. It is headed by a premier (technically the head of government) selected by the National People's Congress in consultation with the Central Committee of the Communist Party. In 1982, the premier was Zhao Ziyang, who was assisted by a secretary general and two vice premiers, reduced from thirteen in April 1982. The number of State Council ministries, commissions, and agencies was also reduced from ninety-three to forty-one, in a move to streamline state administration and retire senior bureaucrats. A new body, the Standing Committee of the State Council, consisting of the premier, vice premiers, ministers, and heads of agencies, was established.

The responsibilities of the State Council include the submission of proposals for laws to the National People's Congress or its Standing Committee, supervision of the work of the different organizations under its jurisdiction, and the drafting of economic plans and the national budget.

A major change which appears in the 1982 constitutional revision is the creation of the office of the chairman of the People's Republic of China. Elected for a five-year term by the National People's Congress, he will serve as head of state for a maximum of two terms. The office is equivalent to that of the president, which fell vacant with the purge of Liu Shaoqi in 1967 and was abolished during the Cultural Revolution period.

Legislature

The National People's Congress (NPC) is defined as the "highest organ of state power," in both the 1978 Constitution and the 1982 draft revision. Its members are elected by province-level people's congresses and units of the People's Liberation Army for a term of five years, although this term may be shortened or extended if necessary. Five national people's congresses have been elected: in 1954, 1959, 1965, 1975, and 1978. It is supposed to meet once a year, although it held no meetings in the ten years between January 1965 and January 1975, a period which included the Cultural Revolution. Because it is a large body (the 1978 NPC had 3,459 deputies) and meets for only a few days, its role is largely symbolic, although the 1978 constitution and the draft revision give it broad powers including legislation, the amendment of the consitution, approval of economic plans and the national budget, and deciding "on matters of war and peace." It is also responsible for choosing the premier, cabinet ministers, and the highest judicial officials.

When the Congress is not in session, its duties are carried out by the Standing Committee of the National People's Congress, elected by the Congress (176 members in 1978). The Standing Committee has the power to conduct elections for the National People's Congress and convene its sessions, to "interpret the constitution and laws and to enact decrees," to nullify "inappropriate" decisions made by lower-level government organs, to appoint and remove government officials, including cabinet ministers, and in general to oversee the operation of the executive and judicial apparatus.

Judiciary

The 1978 consitution provides for people's courts on the levels of provincial, county, and local government, and a Supreme People's Court at the center, whose judges are chosen by the National People's Congress or its Standing Committee. Parallel with the court system is the Supreme People's Procuratorate and its corresponding lower-level branches. It is responsible for seeing that the courts operate in conformity with lawful procedure, and represents the state in criminal trials, similar to a district attorney's office. The procuratorates were abolished during the Cultural Revolution, and their restoration is a sign of the recent great concern with reestablishing "socialist legality." China's first criminal code and law of criminal procedure were approved in 1980. Following years of neglect, law courses are being established in China's universities, and a new generation of legal specialists is being trained.

The 1978 constitution devotes sixteen articles to "the Fundamental Rights and Duties of Citizens," and many observers interpreted this as a sign that the leadership had a new commitment to the protection of individual rights. Perhaps the most significant was Article Forty-five, which enumerated the "four big rights": the right to "speak out freely, to air views fully, hold great debates, and write big-character posters." When the constitution was promulgated, there was an effervescence of discussion and free expression, of which the most prominent sign was the "Democracy Wall" in Beijing (Peking), where people hung "big-character posters" criticizing government officials and policies. Deng Xiaoping, then vice premier of the State Council and vice chairman of the CCP, at first encouraged the democratic movement, apparently to enlist popular support in his struggle against his radical foes, but a clampdown began in 1979 and 1980. "Democracy Wall" was closed in late 1979, and two leading dissidents, Wei Jingsheng and Fu Yuehua, were convicted of "anti-state activities." Deng announced in 1980 that the democracy movement had gone too far and that the constitution would be amended to abolish the "four bigs." Ironically, billboards carrying advertisements for consumer goods were put up, covering "Democracy Wall," a sign of the government's intention to shelve political in favor of economic development.

Although the 1982 draft revision lists twenty-two articles under the "Fundamental Rights and Duties of Citizens," the "four bigs" are not included. Article forty-eight states that when "exercising their freedom and rights, citizens . . . must not infringe upon the interests of the state, of society and of the collective, or upon the lawful freedoms and rights of other citizens."

Regional & Local Government

The constitution defines three levels of government below the national level. First, the country is divided into twenty-one provinces (the eighteen provinces of China Proper and the three northeast provinces of "Manchuria"), five autonomous regions (Xinjiang Uygur, Ningxia Hui, Nei Monggol, Xizang and Guangxi-Zhuang), and three large municipalities (Beijing, Tianjin [Tientsin], and Shanghai). These are subdivided into some 2,138 counties, 190 cities, a number of autonomous counties and prefectures, and the districts of the three municipalities. On the lowest level of government, there are towns, districts within cities, and some 54,000 people's communes in the rural areas. The term "autonomous" is applied to those administrative districts in which there is a large proportion of minority peoples. They have special privileges in regard to the preservation of their national cultures and ways of life, but are in no sense really self-governing.

Government on the three subnational levels is organizationally the same as that at the center. People's congresses of the provinces, autonomous regions, and municipalities are elected for five-year terms, while county-level and commune-level people's congresses are elected for three and two years, respectively. Each congress appoints a standing committee which in turn appoints a people's government responsible for regional or local administration.

A major change found in the 1982 constitutional revision is the reestablishment of the township (xiang) level of government, to replace the commune as a unit of local administration in rural areas. Each xiang will have its own people's congress, standing committee, and people's government.

In the cities and municipalities there is a network of neighborhood committees, containing from 2,000 to 10,000 families, subdivided into residents' committees containing 100 to 600 families, further subdivided into residents' small groups of fifteen to forty families. These units work closely with police and perform a social-control function. Work units such as factories, offices, and schools are also centers for control and surveillance. City life is thus tightly regulated, in part a reflection of the traditional role of the Chinese city as a center of control and administration. Close surveillance of the urban population also facilitates the government's policy of preventing unwanted immigration from the countryside, a potentially serious problem since standards of living in cities are much higher than those of rural villages.

In the countryside, by contrast, the production-brigade and production-team units below the people's commune level are primarily economic units, although the brigade is delegated certain responsibilities related to health and education.

OUTLINE OF GOVERNMENT STRUCTURE (as defined in the 1982 draft constitutional revision)

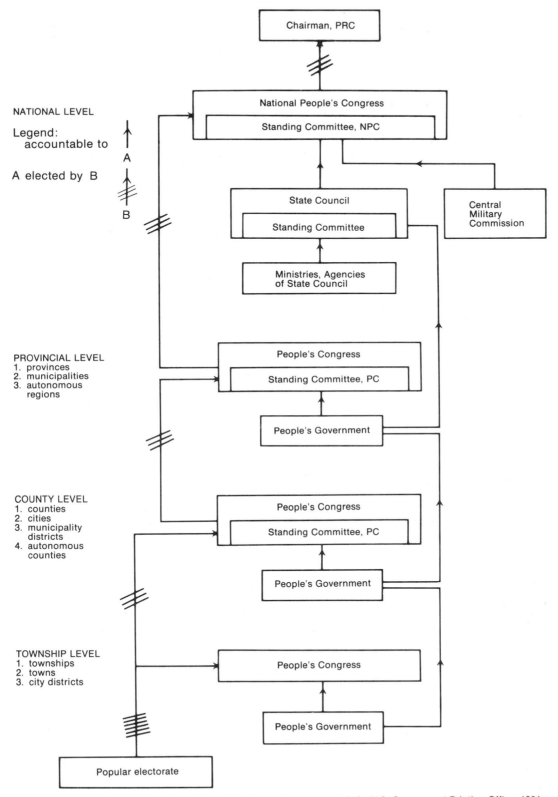

Sources: Frederica M. Bunge and Rinn-sup, Shinn *China: A Country Study.* Washington, D.C.: U.S. Government Printing Office, 1981, p. 337.
"Draft of the Revised Constitution of the People's Republic of China—Committee for the Revision of the Constitution of the PRC," *Beijing Review,* Vol. 25, No. 19, 10 May 1982, pp. 27–47.

Overall, control in rural areas is less pervasive, and the state must work through local leaders and groups to insure cooperation on the grass-roots level. In the past, during periods when class struggle was stressed, the state has enlisted the support of poor peasants against more conservative middle-class and upper-middle-class peasants in orde: to exert its influence in the villages.

Article 113 of the 1982 draft revision labels urban "neighborhood committees" as "mass organizations of self-government at the primary level." "Villagers' committees" (in the rural areas) are also mentioned. They are probably expected to take over some of the grass-roots-level responsibilities formerly delegated to the brigade unit of the People's Commune.

The Electoral System

Until recently, direct popular elections were held only at the basic level, for town, city district, or commune people's congresses. Elections for county-level and provincial-level people's congresses and the National People's Congress were indirect: deputies at each level elected deputies to the one directly above it. In July 1979, the National People's Congress passed the "Electoral Law of the People's Republic of China for the NPC and Local People's Congresses At All Levels," which went into effect on January 1, 1980. It embodied significant reforms, with the object of promoting "socialist democracy." One of these was direct popular election of county-level people's congresses, which was being carried out throughout the country by late 1980. Another reform was the encouragement of electoral competition. Previously, voters had to "rubber-stamp" candidates preselected by the party. New rules stipulated that for direct elections the number of candidates had to be 50 to 100 percent more than the number of offices to be filled, and for indirect elections, 20 to 50 percent more. Ordinary citizens, not necessarily members of the Communist Party, could nominate candidates and the secret ballot was instituted. According to one observer, 370,000 voters in Tongxiang County in Zhejiang Province elected 494 representatives to the people's congress from between 750 to 1,000 candidates. It also was reported that the weighting of electoral districts was strongly in favor of city voters, with only 400 needed to elect a deputy, compared to 1,600 rural voters to elect one. National minorities have also been favored. Large factories, mines, and other production units formed electoral constituencies, as did residential areas. Suffrage is universal and the minimum age for voting and running for office is set at eighteen years.

The experimentation with direct county-level elections seems to mark a departure from the "dual role" principle, at least insofar as non-CCP candidates have a chance of being nominated and elected to office. It was reported in 1980 that independent and even openly non-Marxist candidates defeated party-backed opponents in some contests. In Hunan Province, 4,000 students and young people demonstrated after the authorities barred a non-Marxist student from running in an election; eighty-seven of his fellow students held a hunger strike until the central government agreed to hear their grievances. China has no genuine parliamentary tradition, however, and the future of open elections is highly uncertain.

Chinese Communist Party (CCP; *Zhongguo Gongchandang*)

History

The party was established in Shanghai in 1921 by a small group of young Chinese intellectuals inspired by the example of the Bolshevik revolution in Russia. During its early years, it sought the support of workers in China's urban centers. Under orders from the Communist International (Comintern) in Moscow, the CCP formed a united front with the Guomindang led by Sun Zhongshan (Sun Yat-sen), a much larger and more powerful organization. In 1927, Jiang Jyeshi (Chiang Kai-shek), Guomindang's leader after Sun's death, ordered a bloody purge of Communists that virtually destroyed the CCP's urban base. It was at this time that certain elements of the party, notably Mao Zedong (then thirty-four years old), began transforming the movement from an urban-based workers' party into a rural peasants' army similar in many ways to the peasant rebel armies of the imperial period. At the heart of the movement was the People's Liberation Army which, based in "liberated areas" in remote parts of the country, was able to resist Japanese and Guomindang foes and finally go on the offensive. The most important base was at Yan'an (Yenan) in southern Shaanxi (Shensi) Province, established after the epic 10,000 kilometer Long March in 1934 and 1935. Although the Communists and the Guomindang established a fragile united front to resist the Japanese during World War II, the end of the war saw a renewal of civil war and the Guomindang's defeat.

Like other successful revolutionary movements, the Chinese Communist Party had to face the problem of converting itself from an insurrectionist army into a national government. The difficulties attending this conversion were an important factor in the establishment and the reform of political institutions. The period from 1949 to 1954, known as the period of the Common Program, saw China governed by a "united front" of Communists and non-Communist "progressive" elements represented on the highest level by the Chinese People's Political Consultative Conference. This united front was replaced by the Soviet-style party-state apparatus when the first state constitution was ratified in 1954. A five-year plan, emphasizing heavy industry in the Soviet manner, was implemented between 1953 and 1957. The party moved to eliminate the conservative "gentry" and rich peasant class in the countryside, executing many of them, distributing their land to poorer peasants, and organizing agricultural producers' cooperatives. Gradually, the party secured control over all sections of the population. Thus urban intellectuals, after being allowed a great measure of freedom during the 1956 "let a hundred flowers bloom" period, were harshly disciplined during the Anti-Rightist Campaign held the following year. Dominance was asserted over all of mainland China, including border regions, such as Xizang (Tibet), which had slipped out of Chinese control in the early twentieth century.

The years between 1949 and 1981 have witnessed power struggles between top leaders and periods of great instability. China analysts trace a continuing conflict between "radicals" or "leftists" and "pragmatists" or "rightists" during this period.

The Great Leap Forward of 1958 to 1960 marked an abrupt transformation from a pragmatic to a radical policy line. Mao was impatient with the slow pace of socialist construction in the countryside and pressed for a program of radical collectivization and grass-roots mobilization. Large-scale collectively owned economic enterprises, known as people's communes, were set up in all parts of China. Each contained an average of 5,000 households and over 20,000 individuals. The unpopularity and economic failure of Great Leap crash programs led to a reversal in the collectivization process, and the communes were reduced to administrative units. Between 1960 and 1965, the CCP pursued moderate and cautious policies of "readjustment and recovery," emphasizing economic rather than ideological incentives for increased production.

The second radical attempt to implant the principle of "continuous revolution" was the Great Proletarian Cultural Revolution, which began in 1966 and ended in 1969, although the ten years from 1966 to 1976 are often referred to as the "Cultural Revolution decade" in Chinese publications. The now-notorious "Gang of Four"—Jiang Qing, Mao's wife, and her associates, Wang Hongwen, Yao Wenyuan, and Zhang Chunqiao— as well as Lin Biao were extremely influential during this period. The purpose of the Cultural Revolution was the complete transformation of the consciousness of the people. This could be accomplished, it was argued, only through an almost complete overthrow of the status quo. Mao encouraged millions of young Red Guards— students and other young people—in the colorful language of the times, to "bombard the headquarters" of state and party authorities in Beijing and the provinces. Pragmatist leaders such as Liu Shaoqi, labelled "China's Khrushchev" and "the number-one capitalist roader," were purged and publicly humiliated. Many state and party organizations on all levels were abolished. Though radical, the Cultural Revolution was also in a sense conservative: the radicals wished to restore the revolutionary way of life of the Yen'an and civil-war period. At the height of the Cultural Revolution, many parts of China were plunged into anarchy and the army was called in to restore order. Institutions were slowly rebuilt after 1969, although the legacy of the Cultural Revolution would not be renounced until the rise to power of Deng Xiaoping and his pragmatist followers after 1977.

Organization

The structure of the party is hierarchical. It operates on the Leninist principle of "democratic centralism": lower levels are subordinate to higher levels, and, within party units, the minority submits to the decision of the majority in all issues and observes party discipline.

Party levels of organization, being parallel with those of the state administration, are four in number. At the highest level is the National Party Congress, convened once every five years, although, like the National People's Congress, it can be convened earlier or later if necessary. There have been eleven national party congresses since the first one was held in 1921, the latest being in August 1977. The party congress is a large body—the eleventh had 1,510 delegates—and it meets for only a week. By secret ballot, it elects the central committee, which in 1977 had 213 full and 131 alternate members. The Central Committee meets in plenary session about once a year, but is too large to be effective in decision making. The Committee elects a Political Bureau (Politburo) which had twenty-four full and two alternate members in 1977. The politically most powerful group at the party center, a small, collegial group of top leaders, is the Politburo's Standing Committee, with seven members, including the chairman of the Central Committee of the Communist Party (Hu Yaobang), in 1982. All of these groups, as well as the Central Committee's chairman and vice chairman, are chosen by the Central Committee in its plenary session.

Other important party organizations at the center include the Secretariat, abolished during the Cultural Revolution but reestablished in 1980, which is responsible for day-to-day administration of the party's business. It is headed by a secretary general who is assisted by eleven secretaries. The Central Commission for Inspecting Discipline, founded in 1978, is responsible, as its name implies, for curbing abuses by party members such as were claimed to have been excessive during the Cultural Revolution.

Below the center, each subnational unit has its own party congress, party committee, standing committee and secretariat, structurally analogous to those at the center. There are also subnational unit branches of the commission for inspecting discipline. Basic-level party organizations—known as party branches, general party branches, and primary party committees—are set up in villages, schools, workplaces, and neighborhoods, and play an important role in maintaining, in the words of the 1977 party constitution, "close ties with the masses," educating them in ideology, and mobilizing them for political campaigns.

The most important party publications are *Honggi* (Red Flag), a theoretical journal, and *Renmin Ribao* (The People's Daily), the official party newspaper.

Policy

The CCP is defined in the 1978 state constitution as "the core of the leadership of the whole Chinese people." The 1982 consitutional revision does not contain this phrase, although in the Preamble, it states that "led by the Communist Party of China . . . the Chinese people will continue to uphold the people's democratic dictatorship and the socialist road. . . ." Ideology, described as "Marxism-Leninism-Mao Zedong Thought," is central to the party's identity. Marxism-Leninism provides what could be called the theoretical basis for the party's existence, a set of universal principles of historical development and revolutionary change supposed to be operative in any human society; "Mao Zedong Thought" is seen as an application of these universal principles to the specific historical context of China.

Official interpretations of CCP history published in 1981 continue to affirm the relevance and validity of Mao Zedong's ideas, even while criticizing Mao himself for certain excesses, particularly during the Great Leap Forward and Cultural Revolution. Mao is seen as a leader capable of grasping concrete reality and evolving practical principles of revolutionary strategy that remain true to basic Marxist-Leninist orthodoxy. The strategies of the "peasant line" and the "new democratic revolution"—a united front of peasants, workers, and patriotic bourgeoisie against the reactionary classes—and the building of the People's Liberation Army are seen as three of his greatest achievements, although Mao is never taken to be the equal of Marx or Lenin.

Although the written works of Marx, Lenin, and Mao are available to party members and the general public, the gap between ideology and actual policy is a wide one, and the question of interpreting even the practical applications of Mao Zedong Thought over the years has been fraught with controversy. Overall, ideology serves not only to legitimize party rule, but also as a medium through which points of view are expressed. It becomes what Franz Schurmann calls a "system of communication" through which the initiated are informed about current issues and decisions made at the top.

Political communication within the party and the country as a whole is maintained through a sophisticated and extensive system of newspapers and other mass media which conveys information from the top to the grass roots in the form of ideological language. Thus a newspaper reader following the philosophical discussion on "two combine into one" versus "one divides into two," if he knew the ideological language, would understand that the issue at stake was the appropriateness of class struggle at that particular historical stage, a classic bone of contention between pragmatists and radicals. Deng Xiaoping's stated principle of "practice is the only criterion for judging truth" in 1980, a reflection of Mao Zedong's own theories on the value of practice, was interpreted as an argument for more flexible policies of economic development and an attack on "whateverism," the alleged belief held by his leftist opponents that whatever Mao Zedong said or did was right.

As noted above the party's policy has a history of division between "radicals" and "pragmatists." At the risk of great oversimplification, it can be said that the radicals have advocated mass mobilization, radical collectivization, social experimentation, and class struggle. The pragmatists advocate the construction and preservation of stable institutional frameworks and "rational" methods of planning and administration. At the heart of the conflict are two differing interpretations of the process and stages of revolution. For pragmatists, the states of mass mobilization and class struggle have essentially been completed. Socialist construction requires the building of modern political, economic, and social systems based on the socialist mode of production (state planning and state or collective ownership of the means of production). For radicals, class struggle has to continue, and established state and party organizations can themselves become instruments of exploitation if not purified through the process of "continuous revolution."

The year 1976 was traumatic for the Chinese. Three of her most important leaders—Mao Zedong, Zhou Enlai, and Zhu De—died. A devastating earthquake in July, centered at Tangshan near Beijing, killed almost a quarter of a million people. For some, it had an ominous significance beyond the tragedy of so many casualties: natural catastrophes traditionally were believed to mark the end of dynasties. The arrest of the "Gang of Four," including Mao's wife, Jiang Qing, in October marked the decisive round in the struggle between pragmatists and radicals and the beginning of the end of radical power. The party *apparat* had at first been cautious about criticizing Mao and the "new things" of the Cultural Revolution. But under the influence of Deng Xiaoping and his followers, who gradually gained strength at the expense of Mao's designated successor, Hua Guofeng, the party by 1981 had completed a reconstruction of its image and a reorientation of its policy lines.

The break with the past was marked on the personnel level with the reinstatement of party and state officials on all levels who had been purged during the Cultural Revolution, including Deng himself. Numerous pre-Cultural Revolution organizations were revived. A new interpretation of party history was published by the sixth plenum of the eleventh Central Committee in July 1981. The history claimed that the Cultural Revolution "was responsible for the most severe setback and the heaviest losses suffered by the party,

the state, and the people since the founding of the People's Republic." Mao's old opponents, Liu Shaoqi and General Peng Dehuai, purged in 1959 for criticizing certain excesses of the Great Leap Forward, were rehabilitated.

At their trial, held from November 1980 to January 1981, the "Gang of Four" were charged with crimes ranging from plots to assassinate top leaders to causing the deaths of over 30,000 people. Jiang Qing and Zhang Chunqiao were given the death sentence, suspended, and their companions and six other defendants received long prison sentences. The removal of Mao's portrait from public places marked a watershed in party history comparable to Khrushchev's denunciation of Stalin in the late 1950s.

New experiments in election procedures and the restoration of "socialist legality" have already been discussed. Overall, foreign observers noted a freer, more relaxed atmosphere in China, despite Deng's crackdown on dissidents and the "four big freedoms." Artists, writers, and musicians, freed from the stranglehold of Jiang Qing's "revolutionary" cultural policies, had greater opportunities for free expression, and cultural contacts with foreign countries increased. There was a reevaluation of China's traditional cultural heritage, revealed in the decision to hold an academic conference on Confucian philosophy in 1981. Scientists were encouraged to pursue original research, and a campaign to encourage appreciation of their work was promoted nationwide.

Changes in the economic system were especially significant, even if their real impact will not be known for some time. Deng committed the party to the program of the "four modernizations" (agriculture, industry, science and technology, and defense) and to the improvement of the people's living standards. This involved opening the country to foreign investment (negating the radical emphasis on self-reliance), promoting efficiency and technological innovation in factories and on farms, and tolerating, within limits, free enterprise and entrepreneurial autonomy. Private markets sprang up in all parts of China, particularly in the cities, and peasants were encouraged to engage in private sideline production. A mild form of consumerism was prevalent in the cities, as people queued to buy watches, bicycles, and televisions. One foreign observer in Beijing was amused to discover a long line of people waiting to be photographed standing next to a small automobile, obviously the ultimate in status symbols.

What appears to be a very significant reform is the *baochan* (fixed amount of production) system, approved by the fifth plenum of the eleventh Central Committee in February 1980. Under the *bao-chan* system, production teams contract out land, equipment, and seed stock to small agricultural groups, families, and even individuals. In return, the production teams get a fixed amount of the harvest (not a percentage), and the workers keep the surplus to sell on the free market if they wish. The old "work-point" system which made farmers wage earners or "rural proletarians" who received their income from the collective was abolished in those areas where the *baochan* system was fully implemented. This system of "sharecropping" transformed the countryside in 1980 and 1981. According to the China analyst Jürgen Domes, "the level of collectivization . . . is now everywhere lower than at the time of the advanced agricultural 'producers' cooperatives' in 1956–57." In mid-1982, the dismantling of the communes was being carried out on an experimental basis in three counties in Sichuan Province and one in Anhui Province. Not only have *xiang* or townships been established to replace communes as political units, but the responsibilities of production brigades have been returned to rural villages. Analysts believe that the complete abolition of China's communes may occur in the near future.

Among the most significant Cultural Revolution changes were those in the area of education. Schools were politicized: ideological rather than academic or scientific subjects were stressed, and people's management of schools, decentralization, and a high degree of egalitarianism were promoted. These policies have been completely reversed, with stress now being placed on scientific and technical courses, academic performance, the "tracking" of bright and average students into different educational paths, and the support of elite "key schools" on all levels. "Moral education" courses emphasizing "socialist decorum" have been established. The reestablishment of the entrance-examination system for secondary schools and universities has brought to China the ultra-competitive rigors of "examination hell," similar to that endured by students in Japan, South Korea, and Taiwan. The highly unpopular *xiafang* system, through which some seventeen million urban youth were resettled in the countryside or in border regions between 1968 and 1978, has been curtailed and may be abolished.

A perpetual issue for the party has been the quality and commitment of cadres, administrators, and managers in party and state organs who numbered some eighteen million in 1980. The present leadership is committed to "breaking the iron ricebowl" (that is, tenure in employment) and firing corrupt or incompetent officials. Evaluation of cadres will be on the basis of technical and administrative competence rather than the old stress on "revolutionary consciousness."

The Chinese political system is riddled from top to bottom with personalistic networks (*guanxi* or relationships) through which favors and support are exchanged. The present government is committed to uprooting these. Thus, the *Far Eastern Economic Review* reports that senior state officials who have been obliged to retire in the 1982 streamlining of the State Council will keep their old salaries and privileges; they will not, however, be allowed to have telephones, which would enable them to keep old *guanxi* alive.

China's foreign policy is based on its self-perceived role as a developing nation of the Third World rather than a member of the "socialist camp"—which, China believes, no longer exists. Since the early 1970s, the Chinese perception has been that it must oppose the "hegemonism" of both major powers, the United States and the Soviet Union, on all fronts, but that with the supposed decline of U.S. military power, it is the Soviet Union which poses the greatest threat. The Chinese see themselves as encircled by Soviet power, particularly since that country has gained influence with the Socialist Republic of Vietnam. Although Sino-Soviet borders generally have been quiet since the armed clashes of the late 1960s, fighting broke out between China and Vietnam in February 1979. Tension between the two Asian nations continues.

The Soviet Union has been seeking to reduce tensions with China, however, and observers believe that in the near future the two countries may restore some of the technological and economic links which were severed in 1960. A move to make China more equidistant from the Soviet Union and the United States, rather than an ally of the latter, would be consistent with its basic policy line of not favoring either of the superpowers. A restoration of close Sino-Soviet collaboration, as existed during the 1950s, however, is highly unlikely.

China and the United States exchanged ambassadors on January 1, 1979, seven years after President Nixon's trip to Beijing and the issuing of the Shanghai Communique, which laid the groundwork for normalization of relations. Relations between the two countries have been generally friendly, although soured by Reagan Administration plans to sell jet-fighter parts to Taiwan. China has also been developing closer diplomatic, trade, and cultural relations with Japan and the countries of Western Europe. Overall, foreign policy, marked by stridency and militance in the late 1960s, when China's closest overseas friend was the hermit socialist state of Albania, has evolved along distinctly moderate and pragmatic lines.

Membership & Constituency

The CCP's thirty-eight million members in 1980 make it the world's largest Communist Party, but it is actually a very small elite composing only 3 percent of the country's population. The 1977 party constitution states that any working person above the age of eighteen who does not have a history of counterrevolutionary activity may apply to join. Candidates are examined and screened carefully and must serve a one-year probationary period. Breaches of discipline, i.e., behavior contrary to the principle of democratic centralism, may be punished with expulsion. Members are required to pay party dues. Overall, they are not only expected to work efficiently at their tasks, but to serve as good examples for the whole population.

The role of the party in society reveals a striking continuity between traditional and contemporary China. Both Confucian and Communist elites are defined in terms of a socially oriented ideology in which collective duties are stressed over individual freedoms. Just as the ideal Confucian ruler had the mission of transforming society according to the principles of *ren* and *li*, so the good Communist works to raise the consciousness and enthusiasm of the masses, to a great extent through the power of personal example. Liu Shaoqi's 1939 lectures on "How To Be a Good Communist," recently republished, emphasize "self-cultivation" and "self-perfection" in ways that consciously reflect Confucian precedents.

The youth arm of the CCP is the Communist Youth League, which in 1979 had fifty million members between the ages of fifteen and twenty-five. Its purpose is to educate and train future party members. It was inactive during the Cultural Revolution decade, being revived in 1978. Children under fifteen years of age belong to the Young Pioneers of China.

Financing

The sources of party financing are unclear, although at least some of it must be from membership dues, as the 1977 party constitution states that individuals who fail to pay their dues are considered to have terminated their membership.

Leadership

Mao Zedong, chairman of the Communist Party from 1936 until his death in September 1976, used his tremendous charisma and prestige to impose his will on the party and state in a manner reminiscent of the most vigorous emperors. Mao is generally regarded as the guiding light of the radicals, deeply suspicious of institutions and concerned about the rise of a "new class" like the party and technocratic elite of the Soviet Union. Liu Shaoqi, president of the People's Republic of China until he was purged in 1967 (the office itself being abolished), and Deng Xiaoping, in 1981 vice chairman of the Communist Party and considered the most powerful man in China today, were the principal leaders of the pragmatist faction. Zhou Enlai, premier from 1954 until his death in 1976, was a durable and much-respected mediator between radicals and pragmatists. The radical-pragmatist polarization within the leadership was exacerbated and complicated by personal rivalries and animosities comparable to those of the old imperial palace. It ranged over the broadest possible scope of issues, from abstract philosophical controversies pursued with amazing vehemence by top party intellectuals to concrete policy problems such as agricultural collectivization, the structure of the education system, wages and incentives for workers and peasants, the treatment of cadres (party and state management personnel), and the role and mission of the People's Liberation Army.

The leadership of the Communist Party has been drawn, with few exceptions, from the revolutionary generation which shared the common experience of the struggle to seize power. Many received their baptism of fire in the Long March of 1934 to 1935. Regionally, the central and western provinces of Hunan and Sichuan have been strongly represented, with Mao, Zhou, and Liu Shaoqi coming from the former and Deng Xiaoping from the latter. The regional bias of the party prompted Mao once to remark humorously that the cooking of these two provinces, which uses lots of hot peppers, was conducive to making good revolutionaries. There has been no institution of retirement in the PRC (in the traditional system, Confucian scholar-officials retired to the countryside, often as a form of protest), and party and state leaders have tended to serve until death. Thus, the leadership is primarily one of old men, such as Deng, born in 1904, and Ye Jianying, born in 1899. With the move toward establishing a younger leadership, however, the practice of retiring older leaders has been initiated. Top leaders, members of the Standing Committee of the Politburo, in 1982 included Hu Yaobang, CCP chairman; Deng Xiaoping; Zhao Ziyang (who was also premier); Li Xiannian; Ye Jianying; and Chen Yun.

Mass Organizations & "Democratic Parties"

Although the Chinese People's Political Consultative Conference no longer has a governing role, as it did up to 1954, it still exists as an advisory body on matters concerning mass organizations and "united front work." It held its fifth national congress in 1978. Mass organizations exist to educate and mobilize the nonparty "progressive" elements in the population. The most important of these include the All-China Federation of Trade Unions, the All-China Women's Federation, the All-China Federation of Literary and Art Circles, and the All-China Federation of Youth. There are a number of small "democratic parties" which are allowed to exist, including the Revolutionary Committee of the Guomindang; the anti-Jiang Jyeshi "left" Guomindang; the China Democratic League; and the Taiwan Democratic Self-Government League, committed to the "liberation" of Taiwan. In recognition of the constitutional principle of freedom of religion (which also gives the right "not to believe in religion and to propagate atheism"), there are token Buddhist, Taoist, Christian, and Islamic associations.

Other Political Forces

Military

The People's Liberation Army (PLA) in 1980 had some 3.6 million members, divided among the ground forces, which had the great majority, and the armor, artillery, air, engineer, navy, and telecommunications service arms. Since the establishment of the People's Republic of China, it has been not simply a military force organized for national defense, but an important political actor, a reflection of the pre-1949 "army-party" tradition. The close ties between the PLA and the CCP are expressed in the principle, enunciated in the 1978 state constitution, that the chairman of the CCP is the commander of the armed forces. The 1982 draft revision, however, establishes a Central Military Commission whose chairman will be respon-

sible to the National People's Congress. Party leadership is exercised through the Military Affairs Commission of the Central Committee and political departments in each of the PLA's units. Under Lin Biao, the PLA's commander until his death in September 1971, its ideological and revolutionary roles were stressed. Model soldiers such as Lei Feng were held up as paragons of Communist virtue, and the people were exhorted to "learn from the PLA." The abolition of ranks within the PLA is a further expression of its role as a revolutionary model espousing egalitarianism. During the Cultural Revolution, the armed forces assumed an administrative role in many parts of China after the collapse of party and state organization. With the exposure of Lin's plot to assassinate Mao and other top leaders, however, more moderate military leaders gained influence and the PLA's political role was apparently circumscribed. What it will be in the 1980s remains a question mark. The present leadership would like to see it give up its political role and assume a more "professional" stance concomitant with the modernization of its weaponry, part of the "four modernizations" program, but the reentry of the PLA onto the political stage is by no means precluded.

National Prospects

The rapid reversal of Cultural Revolution policies between 1978 and 1981, the new stress on institutional stabilization, the rule of law and economic development, the reinterpretation of party history, and the diminution of Mao's role as a leader, if not as a thinker, in his later years, apparently has gained widespread and genuine support for the new leadership, especially among those who stand to gain from a liberalization of policies. Yet certain groups, particularly elements in the People's Liberation Army and the large number of cadres who feel threatened by Deng Xiaoping's determination to "break the iron ricebowl" (especially those who supported or gained office through the Cultural Revolution), may become more active in the protection of their interests and resist further pragmatist policies. The announcement in February 1982 that Deng had retired to "the second line of leadership" has aroused much speculation among analysts, some of whom suggested that this was the result of a "bloodless coup" carried out by elements in the army and bureaucracy who had lost much, and had more to lose, with the implementation of Deng's policies.

Yet it became clear by mid-1982 that Deng's step-down was only the result of his desire to make way for younger leaders, principally Zhao Ziyang and Hu Yaobang. The publication of the draft revision of the constitution shows that the program of reforms he initiated continues. China's prospects for the future, however, remain highly uncertain.

Further Reading

Beaufort, Simon de. *Yellow Earth, Green Jade: Constants in Chinese Political Mores.* Center for International Affairs. Cambridge, Mass.: Harvard University Press, 1978.

Bunge, Frederica M. and Shinn, Rinn-sup, eds. *China: A Country Study.* Washington, D.C.: U.S. Government Printing Office, 1981.

Chan, Wing-tsit. *A Sourcebook in Chinese Philosophy.* Princeton, N. J.: Princeton University Press, 1963.

Domes, Jürgen. *China after the Cultural Revolution: Politics Between Two Congresses.* Berkeley: University of California Press, 1977.

————. "New Policies in the Communes: Notes on Rural Societal Structures in China, 1976–1981." *Journal of Asian Studies*, Vol. 41, No. 2, February 1982.

Eckstein, Alexander. *China's Economic Revolution.* Cambridge, England: Cambridge University Press, 1977.

Goodman, David S.G. "The Provincial Revolutionary Committee in the People's Republic of China, 1967-1979: An Obituary," *China Quarterly,* No. 85, March 1981.

————. "The Sixth Plenum of the 11th Central Committee of the CCP: Look Back in Anger?" *China Quarterly,* No. 87, September 1981.

Perolle, Pierre M., ed. *Fundamentals of the Chinese Communist Party.* White Plains, N. Y.: International Arts and Sciences Press, 1977.

Qi Xin (Chi Hsin), et al. *China's New Democracy.* Hong Kong: Cosmos Books, 1979.

Saich, Tony. *China: Politics and Government.* New York: St. Martin's Press, 1981.

Scalapino, Robert A., ed. *Elites in the People's Republic of China.* Seattle: University of Washington Press, 1972.

Schram, Stuart. *Mao Tse-tung.* New York: Simon and Schuster, 1966.

————, ed. *Authority, Participation and Cultural Change in China.* Cambridge, England: Cambridge University Press, 1973.

Schurmann, Franz. *Ideology and Organization in Communist China.* 2nd ed. Berkeley: University of California Press, 1970.

Townsend, James R. *Political Participation in Communist China.* Berkeley: University of California Press, 1968.

————. *Politics in China.* 2nd ed. Boston: Little, Brown, and Company, 1980.

Wilson, Dick, ed. *Mao Tse-tung in the Scales of History.* Cambridge, England: Cambridge University Press, 1977.

REPUBLIC OF COLOMBIA
(*Republica de Colombia*)
by Robert E. Biles, Ph.D.

The System of Government

Colombia is a unitary republic with a strong president and a long liberal-democratic history centered on competition between two traditional political parties. Although some governments, such as that of Laureano Gómez (1950–53), have been authoritarian, Colombia has experienced intransigent dictatorship only five times in its history: 1830–31, 1854, 1884 to 1894, 1904 to 1909, and 1953 to 1957. Since 1960, surveys of U.S. specialists in Latin America have ranked Colombia from the third to the fifth most democratic nation in Latin America.

Colombia's recent political history has been marked by three key elements: the dominance of the two parties, political violence, and the National Front coalition. The major cleavage in the nation—more powerful than those of class and ethnicity—is identification with the Liberal Party or Conservative Party. Not only have the two parties won an average of over 95 percent of the vote for the Chamber of Representatives in the period from 1945 to 1982, but feuds between families and struggles for the patronage of the two parties have engendered bloody violence. The greatest bloodshed came in the War of a Thousand Days (1899–1902) and *La Violencia* (very roughly, 1948–58) in which 100,000 and 100,000 to 200,000, respectively, died. Presently, Colombia is plagued by violence from several leftist guerrilla groups and by high levels of criminal violence involving both street criminals and the drug mafias. In response to the period of *La Violencia* and the 1953–57 Rojas dictatorship, the two parties formed the National Front coalition in which the Liberals and Conservatives alternated the presidency and split evenly the congressional seats and the bureaucracy for sixteen years from 1958 to 1974. This coalition succeeded in reducing the level of partisan violence and over the long run reduced the role of the political parties.

On July 20, 1810, the citizens of Bogotá created the first representative council to defy Spanish authority. The Vice-Royalty of New Granada gained its independence from Spain in 1819. The Republic of Greater Colombia split into Venezuela, Ecuador, and New Granada in 1830. *Nueva Granada* became the *Confederación Granadina* in 1858, the *Estados Unidos de Colombia* in 1863, and the *República de Colombia* on August 5, 1886, with the centralization of governmental power in Bogotá. Although it has been so substantially amended as to bear little resemblance to the original, the 1886 constitution is still in effect. Under it, power is distributed among the executive, a bicameral legislature, and the judiciary.

Colombia has an estimated population of over twenty-seven million, of which 64 percent are urban and 65 to 80 percent literate. The capital, Bogotá, has a population of 4.3 million. Medellín, Cali, and Barranquilla also have over one million inhabitants.

Executive

The president is both chief of state and head of government. The formal and informal powers of the presidency make the president the center of the political system with far more power than the Congress or the judiciary, a typical Latin American pattern. The president has extensive appointive and removal powers not requiring congressional approval; frequent congressional authorization to issue decree-laws; the power (used by every government since World War II) to invoke a state of siege under which decrees may be issued and exising laws suspended; a tradition of implementing broadly phrased legislation (much in the U.S. mode); strong budgetary powers such as the item veto; and the tools to gain congressional action through the power to declare a matter urgent, ministerial participation in congressional debate, and introduction of legislation by cabinet ministers. The president has extensive powers to make foreign and economic policy. Presidential leadership is enhanced by the culture's emphasis on personalism, by the role of the government in providing employment and status, and by the role of the president as commander-in-chief of the military (which serves primarily an internal security function). On the other hand, the president's power is limited by democratic traditions; the power of the legislative and judicial branches to block or impede presidential initiatives; the strength of the Church, the military, and elite interest groups; public opinion as expressed in election results; and, most importantly, the weakness of the state in this less developed nation. As a consequence, presidential power has been more limited in Colombia than in almost any other Latin American nation.

The president is chosen in a direct popular election for a four-year term. He cannot serve consecutive terms but may seek reelection later, a feat several ex-presidents have unsuccessfully attempted since Lleras Camargo's reelection in 1958. In the 1982 elections, Belisario Betancur Cuartas, the Conservative Party candidate, was elected president with 47 percent of the vote over expresident Alfonso López Michelsen (40 percent) and Senator Luis Carlos Galán Sarmiento (11.5 percent), both of the Liberal Party, and Gerardo Molina (1 percent), backed by a coalition of communists and socialists.

The vice presidency as such does not exist. Every two years Congress elects a "designate" from the president's party to become acting president in the event of the president's ill health, death, or resignation. If the president's inability to serve is permanent, the designate must call new elections within three months. The designate has no duties or salary and may fill other public or private positions. After the president, the most powerful members of the government are the cabinet ministers, the most important of which generally are the ministers of government (national police and departmental affairs), defense (in recent decades, a general), and finance (economic affairs and planning).

Legislature

Colombia's legislature is one of the strongest in Latin America, exceeded in power only by those of Venezuela and Costa Rica. And much more so than in the United States, Colombia's legislature is a reflection of the political parties. Congress has the power of initiation, amendment, interpretation, and repeal of legislation; taxation and reve-

---

PRESIDENTS SINCE 1945

1945–46—Alberto Lleras Camargo (Liberal)

1946–50—Mariano Ospina Pérez (Conservative)

1950–53—Laureano Gómez (Conservative)

1953–57—Gen. Gustavo Rojas Pinilla (military dictator)

1957–58—Military Junta (Maj. Gen Gabriel París and four others)

1958–62—Alberto Lleras Camargo (National Front/ Liberal)

1962–66—Guillermo León Valencia (National Front/ Conservative)

1966–70—Carlos Lleras Restrepo (National Front/ Liberal)

1970–74—Misael Pastrana Borrero (National Front/ Conservative)

1974–78—Alfonso López Michelsen (Liberal)

1978–82—Julio César Turbay Ayala (Liberal)

1982–86—Belisaro Betancur Cuartas (Conservative)

---

nue; budget; legislative oversight through interpellation (questioning) of cabinet ministers and other public officials; selection of a small range of officials and approval of appointment of high-ranking military officers; impeachment; and authorization of declarations of war and entry of foreign troops. In practice, however, these powers are relatively weak. In the area of legislation, for example, most authorities see Congress primarily as legitimizing or blocking initiatives taken by the executive.

The Colombian Congress is composed of two houses, the Senate (Senado) and the Chamber (Cámara) of Representatives. The Congress meets annually from July 20 to December 16, and the president of the republic may call special sessions at other times. The presidents of both houses are elected for sixty-day terms.

Congress has played a key role in the integration of new groups into the political system and serves as the major forum for regional and party conflicts. Ambitious local politicians gain national exposure for themselves and their interests in Congress. The orientation of Colombian legislators toward their regions as opposed to the nation is probably stronger than in most legislatures. Congressmen battle particularly over regional politics and their electoral fiefdoms. The particular role of the parties in Congress can be seen in the variability of party discipline. Party unity is required on issues seen to be of "stragegic" importance for the party (e.g., patronage and electoral advantage), but not on "program" issues such as fiscal or social policy. Similarly, effective opposition to the president's program has tended to come not from struggles for power between the executive and legislative branches as such, but from conflicts between the president and the political parties or factions over "strategic" issues. The relationship between Congress and the parties is symbolized by the fact that the parties sometimes hold their conventions in the Congress building.

The level of professionalism and institutionalization is low. Turnover, for example, is quite high, especially in the Chamber of Representatives (60 to 80 percent from term to term since the 1920s). Congress has been criticized for high absenteeism (over 25 percent even on close, important issues), a weak committee system, and lack of expertise. Generally, congressmen are viewed more as effective brokers with the executive than as legislative agents. Colombian congressmen come from elite backgrounds. One study found that 35 percent were from the upper class, 53 percent from the upper middle class, and none from the lower classes.

Members of both houses are elected from the twenty-three departments on the basis of population. The size of the legislature is a function of the population and varies from election to election. In 1982, the Senate had 113 members and the Chamber of Representatives 199. Members are elected for four-year terms in the same year but at a different time than the president. They may be reelected indefinitely.

In the 1982 elections, the Liberals maintained their majorities in both houses, with the López faction winning 47.4 percent of the Senate and 47.7 percent of the Chamber seats and the Galán faction winning 7 percent of the Senate and 9.1 percent of the Chamber seats. The Conservatives won 44.7 percent of the Senate and 42.2 percent of the Chamber seats. A leftist coalition headed by

Consuelo de Mantejo won about 3 percent of the vote and one seat in each house.

Judiciary

The Colombian court system is headed by the Supreme Court of Justice. However, there is also an important system of administrative courts headed by the Council of State. The method of selection of Supreme Court justices has alternated in recent decades between appointment by Congress from lists presented by the president and selection by the high court itself. Terms have also varied between five years (with unlimited reelection) and service to retirement age. The Supreme Court may rule on the constitutionality of legislation challenged by the president or any citizen, try high government officials, deal with legal questions concerning foreign governments, and deal with other cases assigned by law. In 1981, the Supreme Court struck down a major series of constitutional changes, including the method of appointment of judges and provisions underpinning key parts of the Turbay government's economic program. In spite of strong executive pressures, the decision stood. Colombian lower courts tend to be overburdened and slow. Following the Roman Law tradition, juries are employed infrequently.

Regional & Local Government

Colombia is currently divided into twenty-three departments, the special district of Bogotá, and eight territories (intendencias and comisarias). Within each department and territory, the lowest level of government is the municipality (Municipio), roughly equivalent to the U.S. county. The president appoints the mayor of Bogotá and the governors of the departments, who in turn appoint the mayors of the municipalities. Departments also have popularly elected unicameral assemblies, and councils are elected within the municipalities. In the 1982 elections, the Liberals maintained control of a majority of the assemblies and councils.

While most authorities feel that nationalism is weak and regionalism is strong in Columbia, government is highly centralized in Bogotá. In administering the departments, the governors are constitutionally and politically agents of the national government. Moreover, most bureaucrats are national employees reporting back to Bogotá. The departmental assemblies are relatively weak, but do have some administrative and financial powers. The mayors may come from entirely different areas than those they serve and are fre-

COMPOSITION OF CONGRESS, 1978 AND 1982				
	Chamber		Senate	
	1978	1982	1978	1982
Liberals	111	114	62	62
Conservatives	83	84	49	51
Leftists				
UNO-ANAPO	4	—	1	—
FUP	1	—	—	—
Coalition		1		1

Source: Colombian Registraduría del Estado Civil; preliminary data.

quently rotated. Quite often, the municipal councils exist in name only and do not meet. Almost all major municipal decisions must be made at the departmental level or at least have the governor's approval.

The Electoral System

Colombians choose their president, legislature, departmental assemblies, and municipal councils in direct popular elections. The president is chosen by plurality, while the legislative bodies are chosen by a list system of proportional representation. Contests for Congress and departmental assemblies are at large within the department; those for councillor at large within the municipality.

Prior to each election, party directorates at the appropriate level, departmental or municipal, prepare lists of candidates which are sent to the national directorate for approval. However, the faction-ridden departmental directorates often cannot agree and so send several lists to Bogotá. The national directorate, sensitive to local power groupings, usually accepts the departmental recommendations, seeks compromises, or accepts several competing lists. Even without the national directorate's blessing, dissident factions may print their own ballots and campaign successfully. As a result, there tend to be several lists within each major party. The power of party leaders is enhanced by their roles in creating the lists but reduced by the ease of forming competing lists. Candidates need not reside in the districts from which they run, and it is common practice for key leaders to be placed in safe departments. Lists include principals and alternates.

If a list does not receive the electoral quotient (which is equal to the total number of department or district votes divided by the total number of congressional or assembly seats to be filled), then the votes of that list go to the list with the same party label with the most votes. This encourages multiple lists, since no votes in legislative races are "lost" to other parties. In the Chamber elections for 1968, there was an average of 9.7 lists per department. In the March 1982 elections, there were 100,000 candidates for 9,000 congressional and departmental assembly seats. The candidates themselves win election according to their order on the list. Alternates also replace the principals according to their order on the list. About 20 percent of the principals give up their seats to alter-

nates, although technically they may reclaim the seats if they wish. With the system of alternates, there is no need for by-elections. It is not unusual for a prominent individual to run for several offices in various departments at the same time in order to attract votes to the lists. This system is generally thought to reduce responsiveness to constituents.

All citizens eighteen years of age and over are eligible to vote except members of the armed forces on active duty, the national police, and individuals deprived of their political rights. Women voted for the first time in 1957. There have been no literacy or property requirements for voting since 1936. Prior registration is not required for voting. Simply by showing their *cédula* (identification card) on election day, voters can cast their ballots in electoral posts located in the center of each municipality. In larger urban areas, they may preregister and vote in a polling place in their neighborhood. For those who have moved, the preregistration process is complicated, and going to the town center and finding the polling station that corresponds to their *cédula* is bothersome for many, thus contributing to abstention.

The parties print their own ballots according to legal requirements. These may be clipped from a newspaper or obtained from a party worker in the neighborhood or at the polls. The voter may not indicate a preference for individual candidates, but must choose an entire list. However, the voter may choose different lists within or across party lines for different offices. To preserve secrecy, the ballot is placed in an envelope before being dropped into the official urn. Men and women vote separately.

Elections are held on Sunday, with polls opening at 8:00 A.M. for eight hours. Local elections are held every two years. There are frequent charges of fraud by both parties, and by U. S. standards there is considerable violence associated with the elections.

Voting is not compulsory in Colombia, and nonvoting is a major concern. In the period 1945 to 1982, turnout for elections to the Chamber have varied from 34 percent in 1978 to 69 percent in 1958. Average turnout from 1935 to 1949 was 48 percent, during the National Front period 51 percent, and 44 percent in the post-National Front period. Turnout is higher in national elections; in rural areas and small cities; and among the middle aged and older, middle and upper classes, and men. Survey date indicates abstention is related more to the interest generated by an election than to political discontent (as is often argued).

The Party System

Origins of the Parties

The Conservative and Liberal parties have their origins in the conflicts between the followers of, respectively, Simon Bolívar and Francisco Paula de Santander, the first president and vice president. The term Liberal was used at least from the 1830s, but it did not clearly distinguish the contending groups until the 1848 election when the incumbents adopted the Conservative label. The organizational base of the parties can be traced to the formation in 1838 of two competing electoral societies: the *Sociedad Católica (Sociedad Popular)* and the *Sociedad Democrática de Artesanos*. The year 1848 is widely accepted as the point at which these societies became, respectively, the Conservative and Liberal organizations. The Liberals dominated national politics from 1861 to 1886, while the Conservatives were dominant from 1886 to 1930. Although the Liberals have been the majority party since 1930, splits in the Liberal leadership allowed Conservative presidents to win in 1946 and 1982, and Liberal abstention in the face of authoritarian measures gave Conservatives the victory in 1949.

The intense partisan competition has often degenerated into violence. In order to decrease the violence and to rule effectively, the leaders of the parties often form coalitions. From 1854 to 1956, there were twelve such coalitions covering thirty-two years. In 1957, to quell the bloodshed of *La Violencia* and to return to civilian rule after the Rojas military dictatorship, the last Liberal and Conservative presidents, Alberto Lleras Camargo and Laureano Gómez, negotiated the Sitges Agreement, creating the National Front. Approved by a plebiscite later in the year, the agreement provided for alternation of the presidency between the two major parties for sixteen years; parity within legislative bodies and the bureaucracy at all levels; and to force cooperation, a requirement of a two-thirds majority in legislative bodies. The requirements were phased out between 1968 and 1978. Since then, however, the nongovernment party must receive "adequate and equitable representation" in the cabinet and bureaucracy. (President Turbay responded to this requirement in 1978 by appointing a cabinet of seven Liberals, five Conservatives, and one military general officer.)

The National Front is generally viewed as successful. The military returned to less overt involvement in politics; partisan violence was substantially eliminated; elections became competitive again; and the economy improved. The National Front has also had a major continuing impact on party politics. Prior to the *Frente*, there was intense party competition, strong party government often involving persecution of the opposition, and a fairly high degree of integration of the political and governmental areas. Since the Front, observers note a decline in party influence and activism; weakened, more intermittent party organization; and less difference between the parties' policies.

The Parties in Law

With some historical exceptions, there have been few legal restrictions on Colombian parties. Lists are easily formed either within existing parties or for new parties. During the National Front, when public offices were constitutionally divided between the two major parties, third parties simply presented themselves as lists within the major parties. (The ANAPO candidate for president, for example, almost defeated the National Front candidate in 1970, with both running as Conservatives.) While government does not officially subsidize the parties, the patronage system has traditionally given advantage to the party in office, and obstacles are often placed in the way of third parties. The government, for example, for some time descreetly impeded the importation of newsprint for the creation of an ANAPO newspaper.

Party Organization

The two major parties are frequently described as clientele-based, multiclass parties with weak organizations held together by long-standing patterns of party identification, personal relationships, and the quest for government power as a means to patronage. They are seen as falling somewhere between cadre and mass parties. Both resemble the mass model in that they have long been successful in mobilizing the population for political activity and violence. In most other respects, however, they more closely resemble cadre parties, dominated by relatively independent individual activists. Traditional party structures are poorly differentiated. Organizational activity is centered particularly in Congress, resting upon regionally based *politicos* tied to a national faction or leader. Decision-making tends to be concentrated in the hands of a closed circle of professional politicians. The major limitation on the leadership is the relative ease in forming dissident factions, even though most such factions are short lived.

According to their rules, each party has biennial national conventions attended by its government and party officials and delegates from the departments. The national conventions select the national party directorates and nominate their party's candidate for president. There are also departmental conventions. These and related provisions give the parties a decentralized appearance.

The Liberal Party, in theory, adds a substantial measure of popular participation. In reality, however, these formal provisions are meaningless: party elections and conventions frequently are not held; party leaders sometimes nullify results they do not like. Real control of both parties rests with the party directorates. One author describes the process as the "wheel of fortune": departmental party directorates designate municipal directorates; members of municipal directorates serve as delegates, or name them, to departmental conventions; the conventions select the candidates; the candidates are named to departmental directorates. The upshot is that the departmental directorates, often faction-ridden, select the candidates and control the local party mechanisms. National party directorates are generally unable or unwilling to intervene in candidate selection.

While there is considerable turnover in many other positions, there is substantial stability in both departmental and top national party leadership, the so-called natural bosses (*jefes naturales*). There is a strong relationship between social class and party position, with the top national leadership being composed particularly of former presidents, relatives of former national leaders, and other elites. Exceptions are President Betancur, whose father was an illiterate peasant, and President Turbay, who came from the middle class.

Organizational coverage for both parties is national but incomplete within any given department, because many communities are overwhelmingly Liberal or Conservative and lack organized opposition. Since the onset of the National Front period, party organizations have become more intermittent, coming to life during elections and declining sharply in activity at other times. During periods of inactivity, the regional and national leadership keep the party alive. There is also a division of labor, with the *barrio* (neighborhood) leaders handling the routine and mechanical matters, while the top leadership makes most of the decisions. *Barrio* leaders may go door to door to urge support. In a survey of Bogotá after the 1978 presidential election, 38 percent of those polled in the general public said they had been contacted by someone to interest them in the campaign. Local and regional leaders also play a brokerage role, trading votes for government assistance.

The two parties traditionally have been the basis of Colombia's two major subcultures. Some self-segregation exists in small communities—where people show a tendency to divide along party lines into clubs, unions, and newspaper readership—but there is more contact with supporters of other parties than there is in Switzerland or Belgium. Elites are much less isolated by party.

Over the years, both parties have sought to increase their influence through affiliated organizations of women, youths, students, lawyers, and intellectuals. They have formed *barrio*-improvement associations and have close relations with the two major labor confederations. The Liberals have gone further in this area, but most of the organizations have been short lived or sporadic, showing greatest life during campaigns. In this sense, the Colombian parties have not been parties of integration, have not given members a voice in party decisions. Women, for example, participate in party affairs, but they tend to be found in those sections aimed specifically at women and to be involved more in campaign execution than strategy, with the notable exceptions of Conservative Bertha Hernández de Ospina and 1974 ANAPO presidential candidate María Eugenia Rojas.

Campaigning

Much of the potential vote for a party is determined by party identification. However, there is such great variability in turnout that winners may be determined by whose supporters go to the polls. Traditionally, heavy reliance is placed upon local and regional leaders (called *caciques* or *gamonales*) to deliver the vote. However, long, intense campaigns are also waged to stir interest and to win the "floating" vote (the independent). Recent presidential campaigns have lasted up to a year. Betancur, for example, launched his campaign in June 1981 for the May 1982 presidential election. His campaign was aided by the decision of his chief rival for the Conservative nomination,

Alvaro Gómez Hurtado, to withdraw after the first round of voting at the party convention. In 1978, the Liberals used the February congressional elections as a primary, with Lleras Restrepo withdrawing when Turbay's list outpolled his own. No such agreement was reached for 1982. López Michelsen's tactics in winning the Liberal nomination and his long rivalry with Liberal expresident Lleras Restrepo, created the alternate Liberal candidacy of Luis Carlos Galán, who drew enough Liberal votes to throw the victory to the Conservative Betancur.

Throughout the campaign, much more emphasis is generally placed on the presidential candidates than the congressional and local candidates. Direction of the campaigns tends to be in the hands of the candidates and national leadership. The presidential candidates normally travel throughout the country to give speeches and appear at rallies, dinners, and benefits. In recent elections, the electronic media have become increasingly important. In 1978, 81 percent of Bogatá respondents said they had followed the campaign in the media: 32 percent on radio, 31 percent on television, and 18 percent in newspapers. In 1982, all three major candidates made a populist appeal, presenting similar programs to increase social welfare measures. All expressed concerns about inflation, government corruption, crime, and guerrilla violence. In both 1978 and 1982, the official Liberal candidate was identified with the incumbent government. In 1978, Turbay, as the candidate of the majority party, made a highly partisan appeal, while Betancur made a more national appeal. Betanur presented himself in both elections as unpretentious, while Turbay was often seen as turgid, and López as highly confident or arrogant.

The long campaigns are known to be expensive, but the amounts and sources of party funds—as well as the relationship between contributions and favors rendered—are far from clear. Finance is of primary concern during campaigns. Party headquarters, even at the national level, are not elaborate, and expenditures appear low. Funds are raised through contributions by affluent party supporters at the request of the party treasurer and the candidates. Some official funds undoubtedly are used; government employees are commonly involved in spite of legal provisions to the contrary. Nevertheless, it appears that the bulk of funds comes from the candidates themselves and their friends and relatives. Funds for congressional campaigns are raised primarily within the respective departments.

Independent Voters

Traditionally, it was believed that most Colombians identified with one of the two major parties and that the identification was very strong. However, a survey of five regions of Colombia in 1977 indicated that 36 percent of the respondents did not identify with a political party, a proportion similar to that of the United States at that time. Moreover, the proportion of party identifiers may be in decline. In Bogotá, surveys showed 86 percent identifying with a party in 1970, 79 percent in 1972, 81 percent in 1974, and 74 percent in 1978. The young are particularly likely to be independents. In 1978, 64 percent of Bogotanos identified with the two major parties, 10 percent with the minor parties. Among party identifiers, there is a strong tendency to vote for one's own party; 94 percent did so in 1974, 81 percent in 1978. The traditional bases of party identification in Colombia have been family tradition, patronage, and reactions to partisan violence.

The lack of an independent center group between the parties has made a peaceful transition of power from one party to another difficult. The minority party could win peacefully only if the majority party was split, as in 1946 and 1982. (If the dominant Liberals are able to run a single candidate, as in 1974 and 1978, they win). With strong party identification, presidential succession has frequently been challenged by violence. If, as seems the case, the process of urbanization and industrialization is breaking down party identification, transitions of power may become less traumatic.

Ticket splitting is not possible within lists, but different parties' lists may be chosen for different offices; however, this is not common. In 1974 in Bogotá, for example, 83 percent reported voting for the same party for president and local council. The fact that congressional and presidential elections are held at different times permits differing turnouts and choices. In 1978 in Bogotá, the Liberals improved their congressional majority in February, but lost to the Conservative presidential candidate in June.

Conservative Party
(*Partido Conservador*)

History

The Conservative Party's current factions had their beginnings in the broadening of the base of party support in the 1930s. They were intensified by the violence and military intervention of the 1940s and 1950s. By the beginning of the National Front in 1957, two major factions had emerged based on the personal rivalry between former presidents Mariano Ospina and Laureano Gómez. Gómez had been a dominant figure in the Conservative Party since the 1930s. Following his death in 1965, leadership of the faction passed to his son Alvaro Gómez Hurtado, who still leads it. The *Alvaristas* were called at different times *Laureanistas*, *Doctrinarios*, *Lauro-Alvaristas*, and *Independientes*. They were in opposition to the National Front and other Conservatives from 1960 to 1974, when Gómez Hurtado received the Conservative Party nomination.

Ospina's faction gained control of the party and provided the National Front candidate in 1962 and 1970. With Ospina's death in 1976, leadership passed to expresident Pastrana. The *Ospino-Pastranistas* (also known as *Unionistas*) joined with the *Alvaristas* in support of the presidential candidacies of Gómez Hurtado in 1974 and of Betancur in 1978 and 1982. Betancur had headed his own small faction in the early 1970s. The factions competed against each other in the 1978 congressional elections, but not in 1982.

Although the *Alvaristas* are slightly more conservative, the differences in ideology and class composition are not substantial. They are more clearly personalist factions with differences in rural-urban and regional support.

Organization

Of the two major parties, the Conservative Party probably has a more effective organizational structure at the regional and municipal levels. At each level, the party directorates tend to be responsive to the national directorate. In Congress and the executive branch, the two major factions exercise considerable control over members, and most of the power rests in the hands of the factional leaders. While the words used by leaders of the two factions in the heat of campaigns are often sharp, identification with the overall party remains strong and reconciliation does take place. In the last two presidential contests, factional conflict has been much less acrimonious than that within the Liberal Party. Differences tend to be resolved when it suits the personal and electoral interests of the top leadership.

Colombia's press traditionally has been affiliated with the parties and factions, often serving as the official voice of the leaders. *El Siglo* of Bogotá

has been directed by Laureano and Alvaro Gómez, while *El Colombiano* of Medellín and *La República* of Bogotá have been *Ospino-Pastranista*. Several other smaller dailies, such as *El País* and *Occidente* of Cali are also Conservative, as are a number of radio stations and programs. The party has no international affiliation, although it has some affinity to Christian democracy, particularly among elements of the *Ospino-Pastranistas*.

National headquarters are at Calle 36, No. 16-56, Bogotá.

Policy

In the nineteenth and early twentieth century, the Conservative Party advocated order, close alliance between government and the Roman Catholic Church, a strong executive, highly centralized government, limited suffrage, and the maintenance of class privilege; issues which are no longer paramount. Among Conservatives today there is somewhat less welfare-state orientation, more support of the institutional Church, and more orientation to private property in comparison with Liberals. A survey of congressmen found that Conservatives were significantly to the right of their Liberal colleagues in economic and political ideology and religiosity.

However, since the National Front, the differences in the actual policies pursued by the parties have been less significant and related more to the particular candidate. The presidential candidates of both parties took similar campaign positions in 1978 and 1982. In 1982, Betancur promised increased low-cost housing, eased credit, tax incentives for new business, and special tax and credit arrangements for foreign investment in Colombia. Betancur's rhetoric was far more populist than his basic, business-oriented policies. He differed with his Liberal opponents in opposing proposals to legalize divorce. The debates in Colombian politics—at both the elite and popular level—have consistently focused on domestic as opposed to international issues. There has been considerable continuity in foreign policy from one government to another, regardless of party, as Colombia has sought a more active international role in the post-War II period.

Membership & Constituency

The Conservative Party is clearly established as Colombia's second party, with an average of 41.5 percent of the vote for the Chamber in the 1945–82 period. Conservative support has varied, but has not increased or declined markedly, ranging from 30.8 percent in 1972 to 48.5 percent in 1964 and 1970. Conservative candidates receive some support from all segments of the population. The more traditional Conservative candidates Pastrana (1970) and Gómez Hurtado (1974) drew their strongest support from the middle and upper classes and from the older age groups. However, in 1978 the more populist Betancur drew significant support at all economic and age levels. Gender made little difference in party preference. And while the Conservative vote has historically come from rural and more traditional areas, Betancur won a plurality in Bogotá in 1978 and carried the major provincial cities in 1982.

Support varies considerably by department. The Conservative presidential candidate won Caldas, Nariño, and North Santander in both 1974 and 1978; in the latter year, five other departments were won including Cundinamarca and Antioquia. The party has traditionally drawn support from large landowners, the church hierarchy, the military, and the Union of Colombian Workers (UTC) labor federation. No reliable membership figures are available.

Financing

With the exception of election periods, party financial needs are low. Special fund-raising events, including fiestas, dinners, and lotteries cover regular expenses. Contributions from affluent supporters and from office holders are a major source of income. A congressional candidate may turn back to the party as much as half the expected income from the office. See also, **Campaigning,** above.

Leadership

Leadership has tended to be drawn from the elites, especially from the major political families. Top leadership at both the national and regional levels is relatively stable, but new entrants appear regularly. Lines of succession are not yet clear.

Present leaders are:

Belisario Betancur Cuartas (born 1923 in Antioquia), president of the republic since 1982, draws his support from *Ospino-Pastranista* faction.

Alvaro Gómez Hurtado (born 1919 in Bogotá), has led the *Alvarista* faction since 1965.

Misael Pastrana Borrero (born 1923 in Huila), is a former president and has led the *Ospino-Pastranista* faction since 1976.

Prospects

The increasing number of independents (primarily, it appears, at the expense of the Liberals) and the broader appeal of Betancur to the working class and urban dwellers may make the Conservatives more competitive over time. However, there is no clear trend. If the new government is effective in the management of the economy, it will give a considerable boost to the Conservative cause. Betancur will probably continue to broaden the Conservative appeal through populist-oriented strategies, but as a longtime professional politician, he is not expected to attempt major changes in the political system.

Liberal Party
(*Partido Liberal*)

History

The Liberal Party became the majority party with the broadening of the electorate in the 1930s. Particularly important in this process were the reforms carried out by Liberal President López Pumarejo (1934–38, 1942–45). As with the Conservatives, factionalism has a major role in the Liberal Party. Contemporary factionalism can be traced to the 1930s, when moderates broke with what they considered to be the more radical reformist policies of López Pumarejo. This moderate-reformist split sharpened with the rise of the populist reformer Jorge Gaitán in the 1940s. During the National Front, the factions became more personalist, although ideology continued to play some role. Until 1967, there were two major factions: the *Oficialista*, led by cousins Lleras Camargo and Lleras Restrepo, and the Liberal Revolutionary Movement (MRL), led by López Michelsen, the son of López Pumarejo. In 1967 López Michelsen and much of the MRL were reunited with the *Oficialistas*. By the 1970s, however, three essentially personalistic factions were again competing. The strongest was centered on Turbay Ayala and the second on Lleras Restrepo. In the 1973 party convention, the smallest faction—associated with López Michelsen—switched from the Lleras to the Turbay faction in order to further López's presidential ambitions. The *Turbayistas* then secured the presidential nomination of López in 1974 and Turbay in 1978, both against Lleras Restrepo. With the aid of the *Turbayistas,* López Michelsen was again the official nominee in 1982. He was opposed by Luis

Carlos Galán of the *Nuevo Liberalismo* faction supported by Lleras Restrepo.

Turbay's faction has been the best organized and most responsive to leadership decisions. The opposition factions have been less cohesive. In the last two elections, the faction associated with Lleras Restrepo has drawn the support of the party's left wing and has scored its major successes in Bogotá. Actual policy differences between the major factions are less clear.

Organization

The Liberal Party tends to be less well organized and to exercise less effective party discipline than does the Conservative Party, although during the Turbay government, his faction improved its capacity to deal with regional bosses. The party has been formally led by both individuals and directorates. Sitting Liberal presidents are considered party heads. However, much of the power of the formal leadership is dependent upon the cooperation of the factions. Power is thus dispersed among the president, the formal party leadership, and ex- and would-be presidents who head the factions, and regional leaders. The sharpness of internal conflict in recent years is reflected in the refusal of Lleras Restrepo to endorse López Michelsen in the 1978 presidential election, and the decision of Galán to remain in the 1982 race. When factional leaders reach personal agreement, one faction either returns to the larger group or disintegrates.

The Liberal Party has no international affiliation, although during the 1982 campaign, López Michelsen said he would take the party into the Socialist International, a surprising suggestion to many. Elements of the party have had an affinity to Venezuela's *Acción Democrática* and Peru's *Aprista* party.

Colombia's two largest circulation dailies are both Liberal in orientation. *El Tiempo* has a long history as the leading Liberal outlet. Its current competitor, *El Espectador*, is considered an independent Liberal newspaper (supporting Galán in 1982, for example). Both newspapers publish in Bogotá, as does *El Bogotano*, another Liberal-leaning newspaper. A number of smaller newspapers in other cities are also Liberal, as are various radio stations and programs. Television news is financed by the great financial groups in the country. As a consequence, there is considerable selective reporting. In 1982, the Grancolombiano group was supportive of López Michelsen, a cousin of its head.

National headquarters are at Avenida Jiménez 8-56, Bogotá.

Policy

Historically, the Liberals supported a decentralized government, state rather than Church control of education, and broadened suffrage. The Conservatives achieved a highly centralized government, but the Liberals eventually won universal adult suffrage and significant separation of Church and state. Today, the party tends to stress secular positions, such as legalized divorce, and to emphasize economic development and industialization. Since 1934, Liberal platforms have included calls for special incentives and protection for developing industries, social welfare measures, prolabor legislation, tax reform, agrarian reform, and public ownership of national resources. In 1982, López Michelsen supported Keynesian economic policies, increased social welfare measures, reincorporation of the guerrillas into normal political life, and reequipment of the armed forces. Some observers have noted a tendency of the party to have two faces: one leftist and popular when in opposition and one more centrist and elitist when in power.

Membership & Constituency

In spite of their 1982 presidential defeat, the Liberals are Colombia's majority party with a mean 54.6 percent of the vote for the Chamber in the 1945–82 period. These figures seem to be stable, with no apparent trend toward increase or decline. The party has had a majority or plurality in all of the Chamber elections since 1945.

Liberal candidates tend to draw support from a spectrum of the population. In 1974, López Michelsen ran strongly across all age groups and drew substantial support from all class levels, although he was strongest among lower-middle and middle-class voters. Turbay's support, however, was located particularly in the working and lower middle classes. Historically, the Liberal vote has come from the more urban, commercialized, industrialized, and less traditional areas. However, since early in the National Front, the Liberal percentage of the urban vote has decreased steadily; the two major parties' urban votes were quite close by 1978. Traditional bases of support are in Bogotá, the northern coastal departments, Chocó, Tolima, Cundinamarca, and to a lesser degree, Valle and Cauca. In most of these, however, victory is not assured. Although there is considerable overlap in leadership between the party and interest groups such as the Confederation of Colombian Workers (CTC) labor federation, most important groups are not formally associated with either party.

Financing

Party financing for the Liberals is much the same as for Conservatives, except that Liberals have at times collected membership dues. See also, **Campaigning,** above.

Leadership

In Colombia's political parties, the key figures are the so-called *jefes naturales*, the prominent figures who lead because of their status and connections. They may or may not hold formal positions. The top leadership is composed particularly of expresidents and presidential candidates. Common formal positions held are cabinet minister, ambassador to a major nation, and, in particular, congressman. If a major figure accepts formal party leadership, the position is often used to strengthen his faction and increase the likelihood of a presidential nomination, as was demonstrated by Turbay in 1978 and López Michelsen in 1981. The current top Liberal leaders—especially in terms of Colombian politics whose leaders tend to enter and leave politics at a younger age than in the United States—are relatively old. Barring unforeseen circumstances, the top leaders will retain great power. Potential presidential candidates, for the moment, are impossible to predict.

Present leaders are:

Julio César Turbay Ayala (born 1916 in Bogotá), was president from 1978 to 1982; he leads the Turbayista faction.

Alfonso López Michelsen (born 1913 in Bogotá), is an expresident with a long history as a party and factional leader.

Carlos Lleras Restrepo (born 1908 in Bogotá), is also an expresident and longtime factional leader. His position is weakened by his long-standing conflict with Turbay and López.

Prospects

A major party realignment which would cost the Liberals majority status does not appear likely. With control of Congress and a majority of departmental and local assemblies, the party has a forum for its role of loyal opposition. However, Congress cannot compete with the presidency as a focal point of public attention. Moreover, the decline in party identification appears to be at the Liberals' expense in particular, and the Conservatives are increasingly able to challenge the Liberals in urban areas. Liberal prospects depend upon the success or failure of the Conservative government and the ability of the Liberals to unify behind a single presidential candidate in 1986.

Minor Parties

Except for ANAPO, minor parties have had little success in contemporary Colombia. Combined, they never gained as much as 6 percent of the vote for Congress in the period from 1945 to 1982. Most of the minor parties are part of the highly fractured left. Never strong, the left declined in 1982 because of the stigma of subversion associated with the leftist guerrilla movements. The major area of voting strength for the left is in urban areas, particularly Bogotá. All parties listed below are headquartered in Bogotá. The percentages given are for the 1978 national presidential vote.

Colombian Communist Party (*Partido Comunista Colombiano;* PCC)

Pro-Soviet, dominated UNO, supported Gerardo Molina in 1982.

Front for the Unity of the People (*Frente por la Unidad del Pueblo;* FUP)

Vote: 0.5 percent. Marxist, anti-Soviet, Maoist, comprised of elements of the Independent Revolutionary Labor Movement and the National Popular Alliance.

Independent Revolutionary Labor Movement (*Movimiento Obrero Independiente y Revolucionario;* MOIR)

Marxist, anti-Soviet, part of FUP in 1978, once a part of UNO.

National Opposition Union (*Unión Nacional de Oposición;* UNO) Vote: 1.9 percent

Left-wing coalition dominated by the Communist Party and including remnants of ANAPO and MOIR.

National Popular Alliance (*Alianza Nacional Popular,* ANAPO)

Begun in 1961 in opposition to the National Front and as a personal instrument of former dictator Rojas Pinilla, ANAPO ran candidates under both Conservative and Liberal labels. It drew support from the urban lower class and traditionally Conservative rural areas. In rhetoric it was populist, but its ideology was never clearly developed. ANAPO peaked in 1970 when Rojas almost defeated the National Front candidate Pastrana, 39.1

percent to 40.7 percent. It began to decline after declaring itself a distinct party in 1971, winning only 19 percent of the vote in 1972 and 9.5 percent in 1974. It did not run as a separate party in 1978 and lost all its congressional seats. Its leaders and supporters moved to other parties. The death of the party is generally viewed as a consequence of the strength of identification with the major parties (ANAPO prospered only under the traditional parties' labels) and its personalist nature (Rojas was ailing by 1972, and his daughter, the 1974 candidate, lacked her father's appeal).

National Renovation Movement (*Movimiento de Renovación Nacional*)

Vote: 1.3 percent. Formed to support the candidacy of former General Alvaro Valencia Tovar in 1978. Positions similar to those of major parties, with emphasis on morality. Half of its vote came from Bogotá.

Socialist Workers Party (*Partido Socialista de los Trabajadores;* PS)

Vote: 0.1 percent. Leftist.

Other Political Forces

There is debate among experts as to the exact nature of group influence in Colombian politics. Historically, the Catholic Church and the military have played important roles. Associational interest groups, such as those of industrialists and coffee growers, appear to have influence in proportion to the wealth and status of their members. However, the degree of influence on and independence from government is unclear. Many organizations are closely connected to government through official appointments to their boards, group representation on government boards, and government subsidies to the group. Colombian political parties do little to arrange for compromise and consensus on the demands of interest groups. More so than in the United States, interest-group access to government is through the executive branch, however, recent evidence suggests that such access has become more difficult in the last decade because of the increasing prominence of technocrats. Currently, a large number of interest groups are in existence, most representing upper- and middle-class interests.

The vast majority of the working class and peasantry do not belong to organizations, and those groups representing them have tended to be relatively ineffectual, weakly organized and often co-opted. For example, the organizations of *campesinos* created in the 1960s to provide a popular rural base for government programs became radicalized and lost access to the presidency. Peasants have never had a significant say in the agrarian-reform programs.

Interest-group behavior tends to be reactive and defensive, often coming after government proposals or enactments; they commonly seek exceptions or redress, rather than bargain over policies before they are formulated. When petitions are denied, major economic interests as well as students and labor often take direct action in the form of strikes and boycotts.

A survey at the beginning of the 1970s found that congressmen ranked the most influential groups, in descending order, as follows: ANDI (industrialist), FEDECAFE (coffee growers), the clergy, the UTC and CTC labor federations, and the military.

Economic Groups

The National Association of Industrialists (*Asociación Nacional de Industrialistas;* ANDI) is comprised of more than 500 of the country's largest enterprises. Its power comes from the wealth of its members, their high status, overlap with agrarian interests, the national priority on industrialization, and official representation on a half-dozen government boards. ANDI advocates free enterprise, is a leader on questions of taxation, and advises the government on business and industry. Similar to ANDI in power and policy orientation is the National Federation of Merchants (*Federación Nacional de Comerciantes;* FENALCO). Comparable to the National Chamber of Commerce in the United States, it is well organized and has substantial resources. The National Federation of Coffee Growers (*Federación Nacional de Cafeteros;* FEDECAFE) tends to be dominated by the larger producers and exporters. Because of the role of coffee exports as the principal source of foreign exchange, the association and its members have great influence, particularly over policies affecting coffee. It has close government ties, including government ministers serving ex officio on its national board. ANDI, FENALCO, and FEDECAFE have broad influence on economic matters through close ties to both parties, substantial access to the presidency, and generally close association with finance and development ministers. Less homogeneous and less influential is the Colombian Association of Small

Industrialists (*Asociación Colombiana Popular de Industrialistas*; ACOPI). Large landowners have traditionally been quite influential and are represented in federations of producers of sugarcane, cotton, cattle, and rice.

Roman Catholic Church

The Roman Catholic Church is probably stronger politically in Colombia than in any other Latin American nation. It has a favored position in the constitution, significant influence within the Conservative Party, close relations with the UTC labor federation, a major role in public and private education, an impact on most charitable activities and social legislation, and a substantial political role in rural areas. The Church's power comes in part from the large proportion of Catholics (95 percent of the population is at least nominally Catholic), the upper-middle to upper-class status of most of the Church hierarchy, its strong organization and discipline, and the strength of tradition. The Colombian Church has historically been quite conservative and orthodox. Today, it still has some of the most conservative clergy in Latin America, but it also has a minority of activist, reform-oriented priests. The contemporary Church seeks to maintain its institutional prerogatives and continues its traditional opposition to such things as divorce, but it is moving toward more support for social change. The hierarchy has not had to deal with a significant lay social Christian party; rather, it has long been closely associated with the Conservative Party. Until quite recently, some bishops have threatened to excommunicate Liberals. However, the National Front coalition freed the Church from narrow partisanship and even enabled it to embrace Liberal presidents, who in turn treated the Church well.

Organized Labor

Labor began to emerge as a significant factor in politics as a consequence of the Liberal labor legislation passed in the 1930s and 1940s. The first major labor federation was the Confederation of Colombia Workers (*Confederación de Trabajadores Colombianos*; CTC), founded in 1935 by the Liberal party. It is now the second-largest labor federation. Largest is the Union of Colombian Workers (*Unión de Trabajadores Colombianos*; UTC), founded in 1946 through efforts of the Jesuits. Although neither federation belongs formally to the parties, the CTC is closely aligned with the Liberals and UTC with the Conservatives and the Church. However, during the 1970s, labor militancy increased and along with it dissatisfaction with the parties and the growth of new, independent unions. Many believe that labor is less powerful than congressmen perceived in the survey cited above. Government exercises significant control over the unions, and there is selective law enforcement against communist-led unions. Moreover, neither major federation has achieved the institutionalized position of labor in Venezuela or Mexico, and neither has an effective access to the presidency. The third major union is the militant Trade Union Confederation of Workers of Colombia (*Confederación Sindical de Trabajadores de Colombia*; CSTC), founded in 1966 by several communist-controlled unions expelled from the CTC.

Military

Both historically and currently, the Colombian military has been less involved in politics than is the case in most of Latin America. It is constrained by strong traditions of being apolitical and subordinate to civilians, by antimilitarism among both elites and masses, and by legal and constitutional prohibitions. On only three occasions has the military seized power: 1830, 1854, and 1953. Only in the last case did military rule last more than a year, and that was ended by the military in response to civilian demands. The military has been active in the twentieth century, but more as a tool of government leadership than as an independent actor, in the suppression of Liberals during the Ospina and Gómez governments, the ending of the *Violencia*, and in counterguerrilla warfare since the 1960s. Presidents have on several occasions dismissed top military leaders for political involvement (e.g., in 1965, 1969, and 1975).

In spite of these limitations, the military does play a major political role—a role which increased significantly during the Turbay government—and the use made of the military has increased its political involvement. For example, it has become common practice to name military men as governors in areas of substantial violence. And, there have been sufficient rumors of coups in recent years to cause the civilian leadership to pay close attention to military feelings.

The military has developed an effective veto power in matters of internal security and an important voice in the military budget, in policy in the frontier areas and territories, and in some areas of foreign policy. For example, it forced a break in relations with Cuba in 1981 over Cuban aid to the M-19 guerrillas.

Unlike the political, economic, and Church leadership, the generals do not have elite backgrounds. Rather, they tend to come from the middle class and, in this highly status-conscious society, are looked down upon by the elites. Since the 1960s, the military has sought to increase its prestige by increasing its professionlism and competence. It has been more successful in the last intentions than the first.

Bureaucracy

In Colombia, as in much of Latin America, it is struggle within government bureaucracy that determines the course of policy and the areas and levels of appropriations. Beginning in the 1920s and accelerating during the National Front period, Colombia has come to rely heavily on autonomous decentralized agencies to make policy decisions and to expend the majority of government funds. In 1976, the autonomous agencies spent 60 percent of the national budget. They have had 36 percent of government employees compared to only 8 percent directly under the cabinet ministers. This has produced a sharp increase in the importance of the *técnicos*, the experts within the bureaucracy. The *técnicos*' role is reinforced by the focus of interest groups on the bureaucracy and the importance of the international financial agencies, which have espoused a depoliticized development model that enhances the scope and resources of the bureaucracy. Lacking group cohesion and organization, the bureaucracy serves a variety of interests: its own, elite, and to a lesser degree popular. The orientation of the *técnicos* toward development and policy implementation contrasts sharply with the orientation of the *políticos* toward partisan and factional advantage.

Guerrillas

Colombia has experienced leftist guerilla activity since the 1960s. A serious challenge in the mid-1960s was repressed, but there has been a resurgence in recent years. The guerrillas are fragmented by personal rivalries and ideology, and it appears that no group currently has the popular support or military capability to mount a serious threat. However, they do have the ability to effect spectacular actions such as the 1980 takeover of the Dominican embassy and to carry on guerrilla action in such sparsely populated areas as the southeastern jungles. How to deal with the guerrillas is the subject of a major political debate and the central concern of the military. Amnesty International and many Colombians have been quite critical of human rights violations by the army during the counterguerrilla campaign.

The major guerrilla organizations include:

The Army of National Liberation (*Ejército de Liberación Nacional*; ELN), founded 1964 by Fabio Vásquez, was the most successful guerrilla group in the 1960s, but is less active today. It is Castroite in ideology. The most active group in the early 1980s was M-19, which operated on both urban and rural fronts. It originated in 1974 in the radical wing of ANAPO over the "stolen" election of April 19, 1970. Led by Jaime Bateman, it is Marxist and receives Cuban aid. It has cooperated in military actions with FARC, but maintains its own staff and areas of operation. There are internal divisions in M-19, particularly between hard and soft lines.

The Popular Liberation Army (*Ejército Popular de Liberación*; EPL), founded in 1967, is Maoist.

The Revolutionary Armed Forces of Colombia (*Fuerzas Armadas Revolucionarias de Colombia*; FARC), emerged in 1966. It was the second most successful group in the 1960s and was quite active in the early 1980s. Seen by many as the military wing of the Communist Party, it nevertheless includes non-Communists.

The Workers Self-defense Movement (*Movimiento de Autodefensa Obrera;* MAO or ADO) is small and leftist.

Students

Colombian students have been far more willing than their North American counterparts to demonstrate and to challenge openly a wide range of government policies. In Colombia, while students have had their greatest impact as articulators of popular discontent, their specific policy successes have been few. Political activism is strongest among university students, particularly in the public universities, but also occurs among secondary students. Students have joined with other groups, such as labor, but have had difficulty in coordinating their own efforts, and working in tandem with other groups.

Drug Traffic

The illegal drug traffic is second only to coffee as a foreign-exchange earner. Using both physical threats and their financial resources, the drug "mafias" have a significant if unclear impact on Colombian politics. Charges of drug connections have touched judges, governors, and even President Turbay. Medellín gangs are alleged to have financed a right-wing death squad (MAS) used against guerrillas and labor leaders.

National Prospects

A number of major changes are possible in Colombia, but not probable. A military coup could take place if the ranking officers perceive that the civilian government is too soft or ineffective in dealing with the guerrillas. However, the likelihood is that the military will not intervene. In fact, the military may play less of a role under Betancur than under Turbay. Hopes were raised during and after the 1982 elections that Betancur might reach a truce with the major guerrilla groups, but an escalation of guerrilla activity is also possible, although not to the point of threatening a revolutionary takeover.

Colombia's economy has suffered the malaise affecting other Latin American nations in the early 1980s, but by the middle of the decade, a number of primary exporting projects in such fields as coal, nickel, and oil should come into production and relieve some of the major economic problems now facing the nation. Economic improvement, however, will do little to reduce the substantial inequality in the distribution of income which has long plagued the nation.

Politically, no major changes appear likely; much the same cast of leaders will continue to dominate through much the same mechanisms. Periodically, analysts predict the demise of Colombia's traditional parties, yet they continue to survive. Over the next few years, the Conservative party may become more competitive; and, with a Conservative president the Liberal Party may move somewhat to the left, particularly in its rhetoric. In short, Colombia's strong traditions, elite, and institutions will probably—but not certainly—maintain substantial continuity.

Further Reading

Berry, Albert; Hellman, Ronald G.; and Solaún, Mauricio. eds. *Politics of Compromise: Coalition Government in Colombia.* New Brunswick, N. J.: Transaction Books, 1980.

Blustein, Howard, et al. *Area Handbook for Colombia.* 3rd ed. Washington, D.C.: U.S. Government Printing Office, for Foreign Area Studies, American University, 1977.

Dix, Robert H. *Colombia: The Political Dimensions of Change.* New Haven and London: Yale University Press, 1967.

Hoskin, Gary; Leal, Francisco; and Kline, Harvey. *Legislative Behavior in Colombia.* 2 vols. Buffalo, N. Y.: International Studies Series, 1976.

PEOPLE'S REPUBLIC OF CONGO
(*République Populaire du Congo*)
by Michael Radu, Ph.D.

The System of Government

Congo, a central West African country of over 1.5 million people, has a one-party, presidential, Marxist–Leninist political system, with the military playing an essential political role.

Between August 15, 1960, when it obtained independence from France, and August 15, 1963, when a popular uprising overthrew President Fulbert Youlou, Congo had a presidential system of uncertain ideology and a primary political base in the Lari, a southern ethnic group. Following the 1963 revolution, a radical regime led by Alphonse Massémba-Debat was installed, one-party rule was imposed, and a new Marxist party, the National Revolutionary Movement, was created. Under the combined pressure of radical youth and discontented army officers, the Massémba-Debat regime was overthrown on August 29, 1968, in a military coup led by Captain Marien Ngouabi, a member of the northern Kouilou ethnic group. Since 1968 the northerners, although a minority, have retained their control over the government, the army, and the ruling party. On December 30, 1969, Congo was proclaimed a people's republic, and on December 29 to 31 of the same year, the new ruling party, the Congolese Labor Party (*Parti Congolais du Travail*; PCT) was founded. Ngouabi remained national president, party president, and commander-in-chief until his assassination on March 18, 1977. He was succeeded in all these functions by Joachim Yhomby-Opango, who was deposed on February 5, 1979, and succeeded by President Denis Sassou-Ngouesso.

Since the creation of the PCT, Congo's political system has been dominated by conflict between the military and the radical civilians, as well as by attempts to defuse the ethnic tensions between the northerners and the two major southern Bakongo groups, the Lari and the Vili. These tensions were reflected in the adoption of no less than three successive constitutions—in 1969, 1973, and 1979—by repeated purges of the party, and countless failed coups.

Executive

Denis Sassou-Ngouesso is president of the state, president of the Council of Ministers, and president of the ruling party. The government itself is under the direct control of the Politburo, because Sassou-Ngouesso and Sylvain-Goma, the prime minister, are Politburo members. Moreover, most sensitive government positions also are filled by Politburo members: defense, interior, finance, foreign affairs, propaganda, and information. The members of the government are appointed and removed by the PCT Central Committee.

Legislature

The official supreme legislative body is the People's National Assembly, elected by universal vote from the list of candidates presented by the PCT. Elections, however, only took place twice in the last decade, in 1974 and 1979. The Assembly was summarily suspended in April 1977. Its role is basically that of approving laws proposed by the government.

Judiciary

All the Supreme Court judges, as well as those of the Revolutionary Court of Justice, which rules on cases involving the state security, are appointed by the PCT Central Committee.

Regional & Local Government

Congo is divided into nine regions and the capital district, all under the direct control of the central government. Traditional authorities still play minor leadership roles among some of the ethnic groups.

Congolese Labor Party
(Parti Congolais du Travail; PCT)

History

After the party's founding at the end of 1969, both Ngouabi and Opango, wary of the potential threat to themselves of an ideological institution controlled by ideologues and civilians, treated the PCT as secondary to their interests, which were better promoted by the military. Thus, following a failed coup led by leftist officer Ange Diawara in February 1972, Ngouabi purged the PCT to such an extent that he practically dismantled it. At Ngouabi's death, the Central Committee and the Politburo virtually were forced to hand power to an eleven-man Military Committee, and until February 1979 the PCT remained a minor force. Opango's disregard for the party, however, may have cost him his office, since it was the Central Committee which, in February 1979, was used by his rivals to put him in the minority and to implement what amounted to a palace coup. The March 1979 Congress, the third after those of 1969 and December 1974, reinvigorated the PCT. The PCT's revival was only possible because the military radicals and their civilian counterparts had by then succeeded in eliminating all alternatives, including the institutional military influence.

Organization

The 1979 Congress shaped the PCT into an orthodox Leninist party. Power formally rests in the Congress, which is required to meet every five years. A thirty-member Central Committee is the supreme body between congresses, and a ten-member Politburo is in actual control of both the PCT and, both directly and indirectly, the government as well.

The mass organizations the PCT was supposed to control and use for the implementation of its policies and for popular mobilization suffered from the same irrelevance as the party itself. When, in March 1976, the unions organized a general strike, it was suppressed by the army and the leaders arrested. Three relatively important mass organizations are the Congolese Trade Union Confederation (Confédération Syndicale Congo-

laise), the Revolutionary Union of Congolese Women (Union Révolutionnaire des Femmes Congolaises), and the Union of Congolese Socialist Youth (Union de la Jeunesse Socialiste Congolaise). The second was never important, while the first and third were at various times used as power bases by ambitious radical politicians. Since 1979, all three appear to be under firm PCT control.

Policy

The domestic policies of the Congolese regime are characterized by a permanent attempt to placate the large urban population, the PCT's popular base, at the expense of the peasantry. Most of the economy is under state control, although the regime, despite its radical rhetoric, welcomes foreign, mostly French, investments. In its foreign policy, while claiming to be nonaligned, Congo supports most Soviet-bloc policies; in May 1980 it signed a treaty of friendship and cooperation with the Soviet Union.

Membership & Constituency

By the end of 1972, following Ngouabi's purges, the party had a total of about 160 to 230 members; the Central Committee had only five members left, and the Politburo only three. By 1974, membership had grown to 1,427, according to official data, and it reached about 3,000 by 1981.

Financing

Nothing is known of party financing. Because of the interlocking of party and state functions and personnel, state funds probably are used extensively in party work.

Leadership

The ten Politburo members represent a better than usual balance between northerners and southerners and between civilians and military, although the northern military retain their majority. Denis Sassou-Ngouesso, the first-ranking Politburo member, shares a significant part of his powers with the rest of the Politburo in general, and with two of its members in particular. These are the PCT ideologue and second-ranking member, Jean-Pierre Thystère-Tchicaya, and Prime Minister Louis Sylvain-Goma. Thystère-Tchicaya is a civilian, as is Pierre Nze, the foreign minister. Sylvain-Goma, Nze, and Thystère-Tchicaya are all southerners.

Denis Sassou-Ngouesso was born in 1942 in northern Congo and received training as a paratrooper officer in France, Cuba, and the USSR. He became involved in politics in 1968 and was a member of the first PCT Politburo. In 1971, suspected of involvement in student disturbances, he was dismissed from the Politburo, but after being promoted to major, was appointed defense minister in 1973. After Ngouabi's death, he became leader of the Military Committee and was generally expected to succeed Ngouabi. Under Opango, he was the second-ranking party member and was promoted to colonel.

Jean-Pierre Thystère Tchicaya was born in 1936 to a wealthy family of Pointe Noire. He received his higher education in France. Until 1971, when he was appointed minister of higher education, he was director and professor at a Brazzaville high school. He had close relations with the radical intellectuals in Brazzaville and with the Soviet Union. By the end of Ngouabi's rule, he was generally considered the most influential ideologue of the PCT.

Opposition

Small and fragmented opposition groups in exile, mostly in France, pose no threat to the regime.

National Prospects

Given the accession to power of Sassou-Ngouesso and the subsequent strengthening of the PCT position, and considering the young age of the Congolese leadership, one may expect the present ruling group to remain in power for an extended period. In addition, and regardless of the person of the president, present balances between southerners and northerners, civilians and military, close economic ties with the West and diplomatic and military alignment with the Soviet bloc are very likely to continue since such balances have become a structural characteristic of the Congolese system.

Further Reading
Decalo, Samuel. *Coups and Army Rule in Africa.* New Haven and London: Yale University Press, 1976.
_____. "Ideological Rhetoric and Scientific Socialism in Benin and Congo/Brazzaville." In *Socialism in Sub-Saharan Africa,* Carl G. Rosberg and Thomas M. Callaghy, eds. Berkeley: Institute of International Studies, University of California, 1979.
Young, Crawford. *Ideology and Development in Africa.* New Haven and London: Yale University Press, 1982.

REPUBLIC OF COSTA RICA
(*Republica de Costa Rica*)
by Anne Nelson

The System of Government

Costa Rica, a nation of 2.25 million people, is one of the most stable democracies in Latin America, with a strong parliamentary and presidential system. Costa Rica's present political system dates from the bloody revolution of 1948, in which the ruling military dictatorship was defeated by a wide range of opposition. Constitutional government was restored under the military leadership of José "Don Pepe" Figueres, who then dissolved the country's army and surrendered power to civilian authorities. He quickly regained control of the government, however, as leader of the National Liberation Party (known as *Liberación*), which he helped to found in 1949. Figueres was the party's victorious presidential candidate in 1953 and again in 1970. He remains the "grand old man" of Costa Rican politics, just as *Liberación* has been the dominant organization in Costa Rican political life. The February 1982 election of *Liberación* candidate Luis Alberto Monge, another cofounder of 1949, restored the party's rule with a full congressional majority after a four-year hiatus.

Executive

The president is elected every four years by a national secret ballot. He has broad powers to instigate economic programs and appoint government officials, but most of his decisions are subject to approval by the Legislative Assembly. The president, in turn, has both modifying and unconditional veto powers over Assembly votes. When the president and the majority of the Assembly are from the same party, as they have been through most of Costa Rica's recent past, conflicts are naturally reduced.

Legislature

The Legislative Assembly is a unicameral body of fifty-seven members directly elected to four-year terms. In 1982 the National Liberation Party won thirty-three of the seats; the Unity party (*Unidad*) eighteen; the leftist coalition, People United (*Pueblo Unido*), four; and the National Movement (*Movimiento Nacional*) won one seat. A new party based in Alajuela won an Assembly seat for the first time after campaigning only in that province. Members of the Assembly cannot be dismissed by the president and enjoy legal immunity against house searches and confiscation. The legislative body requires a two-thirds majority to amend the constitution. Taxation, budgetary concerns, and a wide range of other powers are exercised through an absolute majority vote.

Judiciary

A Supreme Court of seventeen judges is appointed by the president subject to approval by the Legislative Assembly. Its members, who serve six-year terms and are almost always reappointed, form the final court of appeal. The court operates under a code law system and does not have the right of constitutional review.

Regional & Local Government

Costa Rica is divided into seven provinces which are further divided into a total of eighty cantons, which are in turn divided into districts. Each province has a governor and an executive (*ejecutivo*). Provincial governors are appointed by the president, while the executive, who is responsible for local programs, is named by and answerable to the municipal councils (*muni-*

cipes). The members of the *municipes* are elected by direct and secret ballot and have the power to impose local taxes.

The Electoral System

Elections take place every four years on the first Sunday in February. A paper ballot bears the names of the presidential and vice presidential candidates, party names and party colors, and a photograph of the presidential candidate. A separate ballot contains ranked lists of names, by party, of candidates for the Assembly, who are elected from the province at large by a proportional representation system. Additional ballots are used for provincial and local offices. There is universal suffrage in Costa Rica, and at the age of eighteen a citizen is automatically registered and given a voter's *cédula*, or identity card.

Votes are cast by placing a thumbprint beneath the candidate's name in the vertical strip on the ballot representing his party. After dropping the ballot in a box the voter has his right index finger stained with indelible ink to prevent his voting twice.

Although Costa Ricans call their elections a *fiesta cívica*, fewer and fewer voters are coming to the gala. In 1979 there was an abstention rate of 19 percent, which rose to 25 percent in 1982. Local observers blamed the low 1982 turnout on lackluster campaigns, the similar platforms of the two leading parties, and widespread confusion and anxiety over the country's economic crisis. It should be noted, however, that even with the rise in abstentions, Costa Rica's is by far the highest turnout in Central America.

The Party System

Origins of the Parties

The modern Costa Rican political system began with the revolution of 1948, though the characterizations of the different participants tends to be a subjective matter among Costa Ricans. The groups allied around Rafael Angel Calderón and those following José Figueres all claimed to be reformist and progressive. Calderón had won the presidency in 1940 as candidate for the now-defunct National Republican Party (PRN), but his social reforms and his alliance with the communist Popular Vanguard led to the formation of two opposition parties, one led by Figueres and one led by conservative Otilio Ulate Blanco. Calderón's party had won a narrow victory in 1944, but in 1948 his victory was challenged by charges of electoral fraud. After Figueres overthrew Calderón, he turned the government over to Ulate, the actual victor.

Since 1948, electoral politics have been contested by Figueres, Calderón, and Ulate and their political heirs. Figueres's party has been the only one of the three, however, to achieve a lasting party structure and is the only party to continue under the same name. Calderón's PRN has undergone many different formations and alliances, most recently taking shape as the Unity party. Unity won the 1978 elections with presidential candidate Rodrigo Carazo Odio, but suffered defeat under Calderón's namesake son (popularly known as "Junior.") Ulate's conservative National Union Party (*Partido Unión Nacional*; PUN) was the antecedent of the National Movement. Although the National Movement's founder, Mario Echandi, won the presidency as a PUN candidate in 1958, he appears to be losing his appeal and made a dismal showing in 1982.

The Parties in Law

To form a party for local elections in Costa Rica one need only collect twenty-five signatures and decide upon a name and a flag. To offer a candidate for national office a party must present three thousand signatures. (In 1982, for example, there were six parties on the presidential ballot, while the municipality of San José had a total of ten parties fielding candidates on a local level.) Costa Rica's campaign finance law states that if a party gets at least 5 percent of the vote, the government will help to subsidize its campaign expenses in the following election on a per vote basis. If the party then loses votes, it must reimburse the government for the difference.

Party Organization

To a great extent the National Liberation Party is the only cohesive party structure in Costa Rica today, its opposition consisting of hastily assembled coalitions or parties formed as the personal political vehicles of individual candidates. The parties that have rallied around the Calderón family have been united only in their opposition to *Liberación* and its leading personalities. *Liberación*'s nomination process begins with the selection of representatives who form a cantonal assembly in each of the eighty cantons. Each cantonal assembly names ten party representatives to the provincial assembly, where delegates from the seven provinces nominate candidates for the presidential offices and deputies. The other parties and coalitions do not have comparable grass-roots organizations. In 1982 Unity held a convention to approve rather than decide on the nomination of Calderón; Mario Echandi formed the National Movement directly for the purposes of advancing his own candidacy. Rodrigo Gutiérrez was the compromise candidate of the leaderships of the three parties making up the leftist coalition, People United.

Campaigning

Campaigning in Costa Rica depends on mass rallies, extensive newspaper coverage, and dense media advertisements. Party T-shirts, banners, and paper visors proliferate in the capital and to a lesser extent in the countryside.

As the election date nears, groups of teenagers in party regalia collect on the street to exchange good-natured insults with their opponents and form horn-honking caravans of cars. The candidates keep their campaign rhetoric on a fairly high level, concentrating on mismanagement and political blunders committed by their opponents rather than on broad personal slurs, although slurs freely circulate as gossip.

Independent Voters

Although it is simple to form an independent or provincial party in Costa Rica, such parties do not play a major role in the country's political life. It is possible to vote for different parties in national, provincial, and local elections. Although no detailed studies have been made, it appears that such ticket splitting is very rare.

National Liberation Party
(*Partido Liberación Nacional;* PLN)

The National Liberation Party (PLN) was legally founded October 12, 1951, although it began to form at the end of the 1948 revolution, and was the first party to install an elected constitutional government in the aftermath of the conflict. *Liberación* administrations have been characterized by extensive public spending and fierce anticommunism. Its most notable gains have been in the

fields of health care and education, contributing greatly to the country's political stability.

The two terms of office of José "Don Pepe" Figueres (1953–1958, 1970–74) saw the country move into the vanguard of social democracy in the Caribbean Basin, impelled by Figueres's close working relationship with Luís Muñoz Marín of Puerto Rico, Rómulo Betancourt of Venezuela, and Juan Bosch of the Dominican Republic. Figueres, like the others in this movement, derived much of his social vision from Roosevelt's New Deal in the United States, infused with an unbridled enthusiasm for the United States that also helped to attract U. S. aid and investment capital. *Liberación* is a long-standing member of the Socialist International, tending towards the right wing of that organization; the party has begun to deemphasize the affiliation in recent years.

The party entered the 1980s with a gradual transfer of power from the old guard, embodied by Figueres (born 1906), to a slightly younger group. Figueres's political heir, Luis Alberto Monge, was born in 1925 in Palmares to a peasant family and has a background in national and regional labor-union activity (this in contradistinction to Figueres's aristocratic Spanish origins and his lifestyle as a gentleman farmer). Monge made an unsuccessful bid for the presidency on the *Liberación* ticket in 1978. Monge's combined rural, university, and labor experience made him popular with the party regulars, who find their strongest support in the Worker's Confederation, the educators' association (ANDE), and the public employees' union (ANEP).

Unity
(*Unidad*)

The Unity Party, the incumbent in the 1982 elections, was formed in 1978 by Rodrigo Carazo. It is self-described as "a coalition of the Democratic Renovation party (*Renovación Demo-crática*), the Calderonist Republican Party (*Partido Republicano Calderónista*), the Popular Union party (*Unión Popular*), and the Christian Democratic Party (*Partido Demócrata Cristiano*)." Its origins lie with the National Republican Party founded by Rafael Angel Calderón Guardia, which peaked in the 1940s. Following his defeat in the revolution of 1948, Calderón went into exile. The party—and Calderón—made a gradual political comeback over the next two decades, but did not win the presidency until 1978, as part of Christian Democrat Rodrigo Carazo's coalition. The Unity party won 50 percent of the vote in 1978, but Carazo's administration was bedeviled by a grave economic crisis and widespread charges of mismanagement and corruption in his government. Carazo's record was the greatest obstacle to Unity's 1982 presidential candidate, Rafael Calderón Fournier (born 1950, son of the late president).

National Movement
(*Movimiento Nacional*)

The National Movement was formed in May 1981 as a personal vehicle for former president Mario Echandi (born 1915, served 1958–62), who had previously run on the since-dissolved National Democratic Union ticket. Echandi, a major proponent of the private sector, has been the conservative archrival of Figueres for decades, but drew only 10 percent of the vote in 1982. It is uncertain whether the National Movement will survive to compete in the 1986 elections or whether it will dissolve and/or reappear under another name.

People United
(*Pueblo Unido*)

The Costa Rican left was represented in the 1982 elections by the People United (*Pueblo Unido*), a coalition of the Popular Vanguard (*Vanguardia Popular*), the traditional Moscow-line Communist Party; the Socialist party (*Partido Socialiste Costarricense*), and some smaller leftist groups. The Popular Vanguard grew out of the Communist Party, organized in 1929 and officially founded two years later. Declared illegal in 1948, a constitutional reform permitted it to participate in the 1974 elections, when it won two assembly seats. The People United coalition, formed in 1978, fielded its first presidential candidate in 1982 with Rodrigo Gutiérrez, a socialist defector from *Liberación*. Although Gutiérrez ran an active campaign, the party failed to win 10 percent of the vote. Most of its support was drawn from the capital and the banana workers of the Atlantic coast.

National Prospects

Although the Costa Ricans like to consider their nation an island of peace and prosperity in the Central American maelstrom, both their peace and prosperity are increasingly dependent on regional factors beyond their control. The Central American economy is a shambles brought about by low commodity prices, high oil prices, worldwide recession, as well as by destruction from civil wars and capital flight. The loss of regional markets has halted Costa Rican economic growth, and the stringent measures imposed by the International Monetary Fund in response to the country's insupportable deficits and public debt will have a profound impact. The spending cuts will undermine the very social programs that most Costa Ricans credit with heading off social unrest. All the same, Costa Rica's democratic system has the advantage of virtually no organized revolutionary or military opposition. The dissolution of the country's military in 1948 leaves only a constabulary force to oversee public order. Nearly all of the armed guerilla activity in Costa Rica to date has been the work of fugitive Salvadorans and Guatemalans.

Much of Costa Rica's continued tranquility will depend on the degree to which it can maintain neutrality amid the rising tensions of the region. The most immediate concern has been Nicaragua. Figueres was an early mentor of the Sandinistas and members of the Carazo administration made considerable profits in selling them arms. But Nicaragua's leftward drift has disconcerted many of the Sandinista's old supporters, and Costa Rica's traditional anticommunism has revived in face of the revolutionary movements of El Salvador and Guatemala. Costa Rica's economic crisis has made it more susceptible to political pressure from the United States; it broke diplomatic relations with Cuba in 1981. Costa Rica's relatively unpopulated northern reaches have been used as a refuge by Nicaraguan counterrevolutionaries (as they were by the Sandinistas when they were fighting Somoza's forces), and relations with Nicaragua have been further strained by accusations of Nicaraguan incursions into the area.

Costa Rica's economic future depends on the success of austerity measures and the turn of the world economy. The country's democratic system, however, remains the best insurance against the spirals of repression and revolution tormenting its neighbors to the north.

Further Reading
Alexander, Robert J. "The *Partido Liberación Nacional* of Costa Rica." In *Latin American Political Parties*, New York: Praeger, 1973.

Ameringer, Charles. *Don Pepe*. Albuquerque: University of New Mexico Press, 1978.

Blutstein, Howard I., ed. *Area Handbook for Costa Rica*. Washington, D.C.: U.S. Government Printing Office, for Foreign Area Studies, American University, 1970.

Busey, James L. "Notes on Costa Rican Democracy." University of Colorado Series in Political Science, No. 2. Boulder: University of Colorado Press, 1967.

Guess, George. "Narrowing the Base of Costa Rican Democracy." *Development and Change*. Vol. 9, No. 4, October 1978.

Mijeski, Kenneth J. "Costa Rica: The Shrinking of the Presidency," In *Presidential Power in Latin American Politics*, Thomas V. DiBacco, ed. New York: Praeger, 1977.

Tomasek, Robert D. "Costa Rica." In *Political Forces in Latin America*. Ben G. Burnett and Kenneth F. Johnson, eds. 2nd ed. Belmont, Calif.: Wadsworth Publishing Co., 1970.

REPUBLIC OF CUBA
(*República de Cuba*)
by Juan Manuel del Aguila, Ph.D

The System of Government

Cuba, a nation of ten million people, is a one-party socialist republic and the only Latin American country subscribing to Marxism-Leninism as its official ideology. Since 1976, Cuba has been governed under a socialist constitution, which declares in its preamble that Cuba's citizens have "started the construction of socialism and under the direction of the Communist Party continues said construction with the objective of building a communist society." It is a well-integrated polity, where no organized political opposition is tolerated and where the basic means of production, except small plots of private land, are owned and administered by the state.

The triumph of Fidel Castro's revolutionary movement in January 1959 ushered in basic transformations in Cuba's political, economic, social, and cultural systems. Cuba's foreign economic, trade, and defense policies were shifted away from the United States and Latin America and integrated into the socialist bloc. Cuba is a full member of COMECOM (the Soviet bloc economic community) and has not had normal diplomatic relations with the United States since January 1961.

During the first years of the Cuban revolution, important measures such as agrarian reform, urban reform, national education campaigns, and extensive nationalization of U.S. properties were undertaken. Confiscation of Cuban-owned properties also took place, along with the collectivization of agriculture and the creation of state farms. Dozens of state agencies were created in order to administer state enterprises. By the mid-1960s, the basic transition to socialism had been accomplished.

During the late 1960s, remnants of capitalism in the commercial and retail sector were abolished; the country was fully mobilized and partially militarized as Castro committed his own and the revolution's prestige to harvesting ten million tons of sugar in 1970. Castro himself admitted failure when the harvest reached only eight and one-half million tons. Economically and psychologically, it was a debacle and led to a reassessment of Cuba's domestic economic policies as well as its political institutions. In the mid-1970s, a process of "institutionalization" was launched, leading to the establishment of a new set of economic, political, and administrative institutions modeled on similar structures in the Soviet Union and other East European countries. Most importantly, the Cuban Communist Party (PCC) assumed its "vanguard" role, acquiring direct though not absolute control over the new political, administrative, and juridical structures.

Despite Castro's declaration in April 1961 that Cuba's would be a "socialist revolution" and his subsequent public conversion to Marxism-Leninism in December 1961, his character, temperament, and charisma have shaped the revolution more than any ideological or organizational factor. His ability to survive internal economic setbacks, political challenges, external aggression, and diplomatic isolation underscores his shrewdness and political astuteness. Furthermore, the process of institutionalization has not curbed Castro's personal power, it has simply formalized and structured it. The Maximum Leader—a man of action and a pragmatist rather than a Marxist ideologue—continues to personify the revolution, and his word is final on critical domestic and foreign-policy matters.

Executive

Cuba's highest executive and administrative organ is the Council of Ministers (CM), composed of the head of state and government, several vice-presidents, the president of the Central Planning Board, ministers, and "others that the law determines." Fidel Castro is president of the council as well as the formal head of state and government, thus holding Cuba's top executive and administrative positions. His brother Raúl is the Council's first vice-president.

According to the constitution, the Council is accountable to the National Assembly and has powers to "organize and conduct the political, economic, cultural, scientific, social, and defense activities outlined by the Assembly." The Council is empowered to conduct foreign relations and trade, maintain internal security, and draw up bills for submission to the National Assembly. Vice-presidents and members of the CM are appointed or removed by the Assembly at Castro's initiative. The Council has an executive committee whose members control and coordinate the work of ministries and other central organizations; for example, the Central Planning Agency (JUCEPLAN), formal ministries (education, defense, domestic trade), as well as institutes such as ICAP (Cuban Institute of Friendship with Peoples) fall under its jurisdiction. In practice, the CM is subordinate to the Assembly's Council of State, but it does centralize top bureaucratic authority in a cabinetlike structure.

Legislature

Elected for a period of five years (1976–81; 1981–86), the National Assembly of People's Power is the only national body invested with constituent and legislative authority. During the 1976–81 period, the Assembly had 481 deputies, of whom 55.5 percent were elected from Cuba's 169 municipal assemblies. The rest of the deputies were government and party officials nominated by the party for appointment to the Assembly by the municipal assemblies. For the 1981–86 *quinquento* (five-year term), the Assembly has 499 deputies elected and appointed in roughly similar proportions. The current Assembly first met in December 1981. Fidel Castro, who was elected a deputy from Oriente province, was duly elected president once again.

The fact that the deputies are not elected directly by the people and meet only for two brief sessions a year limits their autonomy and freedom of action. In addition, the composition of the Assembly remains elitist, with peasants, workers, and women underrepresented. The current Assembly includes 386 men and 113 women; the average age of members is forty-four. According to the Cuban government, 38 percent are workers, technicians, clerks, professors, and teachers; 32 percent are administrators; 20 percent are political and mass-organization leaders; 7 percent are members of the armed forces or police; and 2 percent are peasants. Some 58 percent have com-

pleted a secondary education, and another 35 percent have attended university. All but a handful are party members.

Among its powers, the Assembly can decide on constitutional reforms, discuss and approve the national budget as well as plans for economic and social development, declare war, approve the general outlines of foreign and domestic policy, and elect judges of Cuba's Supreme Court and the attorney general. In practice, legislative initiative is not exercised, votes are unanimous or nearly so, partisanship is nonexistent, debate is unpolemical, and the Assembly is subordinated to the will of higher state and party organs. The National Assembly is neither a policymaking institution nor an equal branch of government; it is inconceivable that it would defy or overrule policies initiated and desired by the political leadership. It listens and ratifies, offering a sense of individual participation to its members and a largely symbolic sense of representation to the masses. Notions such as "representing district interests" or even the representation of functional groups, such as the peasantry, are absent.

The Assembly does serve as a forum for citizens' grievances against the bureaucracy, and deputies may on occasion propose slight modifications to bills which will later become laws; deputies may also render constituent services. Deputies can and have made inquiries of ministers and may call for explanations or information about economic or nonsensitive matters; they are also constitutionally bound to "explain state policies to the electors" and "periodically render accounts to them of the result of their activities."

The Council of State (CS) functions as the executive committee of the National Assembly between its sessions. Its president is the head of state and government. The CS can decree laws on its own, exercise legislative initiative, decree general mobilization, replace ministers, and issue general instructions to the courts. Its president, Fidel Castro, can assume direct control of and supervise ministries and other agencies, as well as assume command of the Revolutionary Armed Forces (FAR), making Castro in effect commander-in-chief. Reacting to major problems in sectors of the Cuban economy, transportation, and internal security, Castro assumed direct control of the interior and defense ministries in late 1979. Broader personnel changes at the top of the economic administrative/executive hierarchy took place in early 1980 with the ousting of several ministers in an apparent attempt to overcome deficiencies and make the bureaucracy more responsive to political leadership.

Judiciary

The People's Supreme Court is the foremost judicial unit; its decisions are final. Supreme Court justices are elected by the National Assembly, as are its president and vice-president, but the latter two have to be nominated by the Cuban president. According to the constitution, the Court's objectives are to maintain and strengthen socialist legality; and to safeguard the legitimate interests of state agencies, other institutions, and the masses.

Cuba has 169 municipal courts and fourteen provincial courts exercising jurisdiction on criminal and civil matters, with the latter acting as appellate courts. Military courts also exist, as well as labor councils with some quasijudicial functions. Professional and lay judges for the municipal and provincial courts are elected by the respective assemblies following nominations from the Ministry of Justice.

Through the 1960s and early 1970s, popular courts operated outside the formal court structure. They acquired broad but ill-defined jurisdiction over civil, political, and criminal matters, but their proceedings often degenerated into personal and political vendettas in the highly charged atmosphere of the period. These tribunals imposed sentences ranging from public admonishments to incarceration, and in many of their cases the distinction—if any—between delinquency and political crimes was unclear. These courts were abolished following reorganization of the court system in 1973 and 1977.

Cuban courts do not constitute an independent branch of government which could presumably check abuses of executive, legislative, or Communist Party authority. They are not charged with protecting individual rights and freedoms. Article 61 of the Cuban constitution states that "none of the freedoms which are recognized for citizens can be exercised contrary to the existence and objectives of the socialist state, or contrary to the decision of the Cuban people to build socialism and communism." The courts are in fact subordinate to the National Assembly and the Council of State. Least of all are they immune from interference from the Communist Party or the political leadership.

Regional & Local Government

Since 1976, Cuba has been divided into fourteen provinces. The city of Havana is a separate province. Each province and municipality is governed by an Assembly of Delegates of People's Power; these are the local organs of state power. Delegates serve for two and one-half years.

Provincial and municipal assemblies act in close coordination with social and mass organizations and are charged with management of local services, as well as recreational, cultural, and educational activities. The assemblies are led by executive committees elected from the membership. An interesting feature is the provision that the president of each municipal executive committee (169 individuals) is by right a delegate to the provincial assembly.

According to Cuba's National Electoral Commission, 843 or 8 percent of the 10,735 elected municipal delegates in 1982 were women and 2,429 or 23 percent were workers, both groups registering minor gains in comparison to 1979 results.

The Electoral System

In October 1981, according to figures released by the Cuban government, 6,097,639 citizens elected 10,735 delegates out of 22,726 candidates to the Municipal Assemblies of People's Power. The turnout represented 97 percent of all those registered to vote. All Cubans sixteen years of age and older can vote through secret ballot to elect these delegates; that is the extent of their direct participation.

Candidates are nominated in public assemblies. Nonparty candidates can be nominated, but the electoral process is stacked against them. Party monitoring and ultimate approval of nominees inhibits competition and reduces the number of nonparty contestants presented to the electorate. A nominee's political behavior, his standing in the community, his commitment to the revolution, and his moral attributes are important factors determining party approval of his candidacy. No campaigning or discussion of the issues is allowed.

Municipal delegates in turn elect provincial-assembly delegates and a significant proportion of deputies to the National Assembly. One does not have to be elected to a municipal assembly to be eligible to run for a National Assembly seat. Nominees for the higher assemblies are determined entirely by party commissions. Regulations covering nomination and the two-tiered system of selecting national officials ensures that party members will be elected in large numbers at all levels. For example, 92 percent of the deputies elected to the National Assembly for the 1976–81 period were either PCC members or candidate members; 71 percent of those elected to the Havana provincial assembly in 1976 were party members.

Elections in Cuba are not meant for citizens to

choose among competing candidates or policy alternatives; instead, they serve to legitimize established institutions, offering citizens the opportunity to ratify the leadership's choice of both candidates and policies. They are also meant for external consumption. Neither can one take seriously claims by the Cuban leadership that since 97 percent of those eligible to vote did so, Cuba's system is one of the most democratic in the world. Sociocultural pressures to vote combine with subtle forms of coercion to make nonvoting suspect behavior. A revolutionary, highly mobilized society frowns on apathy and political indifference, and voting is one more test of one's political commitment. This is not to suggest that large numbers of Cubans turn out to vote against their will, but the costs of noninvolvement are substantial.

Cuban Communist Party (*Partido Communista Cubano*; PCC)

Castro came to power in Cuba as the charismatic leader of a political movement with substantial popular and middle-class support; for all practical purposes, his guerrilla forces in combination with an urban underground overthrew the preceding regime without assistance from the Communist Party. In fact, the party subordinated itself to Castro's leadership and subsequently supported his policies and governing style.

The PCC today is a Castroite party which occupies the central role in Cuba's government and institutions. Its position is recognized in the constitution, which describes it as "the organized Marxist-Leninist vanguard of the working class" and "the highest leading force of the society and the state."

History

Founded in 1925 by Julio A. Mella, Carlos Baliño, and others, some of its members participated in radical and nationalistic struggles in the 1920s and 1930s. Its activities were often outlawed by governments in the 1930s. During the 1940s, the PSP (*Partido Socialista Popular*), as it became known in 1943, collaborated with Batista's constitutional government (1940–44), gradually gaining some support from the working class during that decade. The PSP suffered setbacks at the hands of the governments between 1944 and 1952, and its leaders never reached positions of influence after 1944.

Castro's first blow against the Batista dictatorial regime, the attack on the Moncada barracks in July 1953, was denounced by the PSP as "putschist." The party viewed the subsequent July 26 Movement as bourgeois, and did not actively participate in the anti-Batista campaign. In 1958, when it appeared that the revolution might very well succeed, PSP leaders made contact with Castro in the mountains. However, the number of actual communists among Castro's guerrillas remained quite small and a united front against Batista was never formally established. When the Castro's guerrillas entered Havana on January 1, 1959, the PSP still had no clear policy regarding the movement or its leader.

Tactical imperatives rather than ideological commitment or revolutionary comradeship led Castro to the communists in the 1960–62 period, as liberal, democratic, and pro-American elements within the revolutionary movement were purged, exiled, incarcerated, or killed. The communists accepted Castro's leadership, capitalizing on the political opportunities he offered, and providing Castro with a sound organizational network which he used to consolidate his power. The communists also provided solid contacts with the Soviet Union (the party had always been orthodox and pro-Moscow), a well-elaborated antiimperialist ideology, dedicated militants, and access to international propaganda resources. In other words, Castro's marriage to the communists during the first years was one of strict convenience for both.

Nevertheless, the old guard of the PSP found Castro's methods and ideological training offensive and anarchistic. Unsuccessful challenges to Castro's authority were mounted in 1962, 1964, and 1968. In each case, many communists were purged, and the party lost much of its influence. Economic failure and Soviet pressure led to the PCC's revitalization in the early 1970s. In brief, the party accepted periodic humiliation in exchange for participation and political legitimacy.

In 1961, the old PSP was merged into the broad Integrated Revolutionary Organization (ORI), replaced in turn in 1963 by the United Party of the Socialist Revolution (PURS), and finally by the Cuban Communist Party (PCC) in 1965. In 1965 the party had neither statutes nor a written program, and Castroites from the guerrilla period controlled its top organs.

The PCC's first congress was announced for 1967 but never took place; it was rescheduled and cancelled again in 1969. It finally was held in December 1975. A second congress took place at the stipulated five-year interval in December 1980.

Organization

As is the case with other Communist parties and in keeping with the Leninist method, the principle of democratic centralism governs intraparty affairs. Top organs and leaders decide crucial policy matters, make critical appointments, assess trends in foreign and domestic politics, and then obtain ratification and approval for their decisions from lower party organs. Structurally, the PCC's top organs are the Political Bureau, the Secretariat, and the Central Committee.

In addition to being top party men, several members of the Political Bureau also occupy high positions either in the state bureaucracy, the party Secretariat, or the armed forces, illustrating the interlocking nature of party and state characteristic of communist regimes. In sum, in terms of power and influence, the Political Bureau is "the elite of the elite," with its members assuming major roles due to their party positions, their integrity and ability, and their personal loyalty to Fidel Castro.

The Central Committee of the PCC has assumed new importance and has begun to meet regularly. Besides "electing" the top party leadership and on occasion serving as a deliberative body, its primary function is to serve as a channel through which party policy is announced and disseminated to provincial and local party organs. Its work involves party affairs, national economic matters, budgets, and the review of foreign-policy issues. It is organized in departments, e.g., America Department, Department of Revolutionary Orientation, Department of Economy, through which the party monitors government activities and offers guidance in specific areas. Following the second party congress total membership expanded from 112 to 148 individuals, with members coming from the party organization, the government, the military and police, and the mass organizations.

The third top party organ is the Secretariat. Its membership fluctuates between six and eleven members, and the Castro brothers are its first and second national secretaries. Although information on the Secretariat's activities is extremely difficult to find and is seldom disclosed by the regime, it is reasonable to assume—based on what other communist parties' secretariats do—that it is responsible for party organization at all levels and that it may well have enforcement capabilities, both in terms of disciplining members and guiding policy. Unlike the Political Bureau, the Secretariat is not a policymaking body. It clearly serves as a mechanism through which compliance with party decisions is monitored at all administrative and functional levels. The Secretariat has provincial and municipal branches which supervise the party cells in work centers, factories, state farms, government offices, and military units.

Policy

A direct result of institutionalization has been an increase in influence of the PCC in all areas of life and society, which in turn has brought ideological orthodoxy, dogmatism, and bureaucratization. Revolutionary change has meant politicization of secular areas, including arts, culture, literature, cinema, and other forms of expression. Castro's line still holds in these matters: "within the Revolution, everything; against the Revolution, nothing." Artists' and intellectuals' organizations, such as the state-sponsored National Union of Writers and Artists of Cuba, further ensure party control over cultural and intellectual affairs. As is the case in other Marxist societies, religious beliefs and practices are openly discouraged and religious education is proscribed. Relatively few priests remain in the island, the Catholic Church is weak, and atheism is the official doctrine.

All available evidence suggests that major foreign- and domestic-policy decisions are reached in the Politburo. Its proceedings are highly secret, and one can only speculate about the real nature of the decision-making process; there is no doubt whatsoever that once decisions are made, they are fully supported and there is no available evidence of intense factionalism on these matters within the ruling elite. It is likely that some Politburo members (e.g., Carlos Rodriguez) favor moderately pragmatic policies in some cases, whereas Castro himself is inclined to promote vigorous internationalism.

Although central planning dominates the Cuban economy, recent changes point away from economic centralization and towards greater reliance on market mechanisms for production, distribution, and planning purposes. For example, since the late 1970s the new System of Economic Management and Planning has taken into account supply-and-demand factors as well as market mechanisms such as credit, interest, prices, and taxes to regulate and evaluate economic activities. Improvements also are expected in terms of state enterprises' performance, with profits, quality of output, managerial capabilities, and labor productivity used as indicators of efficiency. These changes are designed to increase the relative autonomy of economic units, providing greater flexibility for planners and local managers.

Finally, in February 1982, legislation was passed designed to attract new foreign investment in Cuba. Companies from any country are welcome to form joint ventures, acquiring up to 49 percent equity with no limits on profit repatriation and gaining substantial tax breaks from the state. This measure reflects Cuba's acute capital shortage and may bring in needed resources in exchange for access to the local market, a reliable labor pool, and new opportunities for expansion and profits.

Cuba's military intervention in Angola and Ethiopia are seen by Castro as assertions of Cuba's own interests, though Soviet strategic interests may have influenced the decision to intervene in Ethiopia. Raúl Castro works closely with the Soviet Union on military affairs. The top ranks of the military seem committed to the existing system and to Cuba's role abroad. Party cells in the military ensure the leadership's political control.

Membership & Constituency

Party membership has risen dramatically since the 1960s. In 1965, membership was 70,000, but by 1969 it had declined to 55,000; it rose to 170,000 in 1973 and 202,807 in 1975. Nevertheless, membership in the PCC has been highly restricted. Belonging to the Communist Youth Union increases one's probability of someday becoming a party member. Candidates from the Youth Union can become party members provided they are at least twenty-four years old and have belonged to the Union for three years; for others, there is a mandatory one-year probationary period. In recent years, efforts have been made to broaden the PCC's social base by lifting some restrictions regarding nomination of candidates by party cells.

As of 1979, 44.6 percent of all party members were workers in material production and services; 26.2 percent were administrative leaders; 13.5 percent were small farmers; 9.6 percent were administrative, professional, and technical workers. The rest were political leaders and others. According to figures disclosed by Castro in 1981, current membership stands at about 400,000, or 4.1 percent of Cuba's total population. In addition, the proportion of workers (47 percent) and women (17.5 percent) in the party has risen, though not dramatically.

Financing

Little is known about party finances. Membership dues paid by party members are not made public. There is no evidence that the party lacks resources to carry out its programs.

Leadership

The party is ruled by Fidel Castro Ruz (born August 13, 1926 or 1927—the year is in dispute), who was trained as a lawyer at the University of Havana in the late 1940s. Second in command and heir apparent is Raúl Castro Ruz, who is four years younger than his brother.

Continuity at the top characterizes the party's ruling elite. Following the 1975 party congress, thirteen individuals made up the Political Bureau, with the Castro brothers as first and second secretaries. After the 1980 congress, Political Bureau membership rose to fifteen, but control was retained by a small clique of Castroite loyalists, most of whom were duly "reelected."

The Cuban leadership is made up of Castroite loyalists (civilian and military) and old-line Communists, with the former a solid majority in the Political Bureau. Rodriguez and Milian are former PSP members; Dorticos was nominally affiliated with the party in the 1950s and was president of Cuba from 1959 to 1976. Garcia, Almeida, Cienfuegos, del Valle, Valdes, and Machado are military men. Hart and Risquet are former civilian members of the 26th of July Movement; Miret is an old Castro loyalist who has alternated between civilian and military roles. Some of these men have government responsibilities: Hart is cur-

MEMBERSHIP IN PCC POLITICAL BUREAU (1976 and 1981)		
Name	1976	1981
Fidel Castro	1st Secretary	1st Secretary
Raúl Castro	2nd Secretary	2nd Secretary
Juan Almeida	Member	Member
Osvaldo Dorticós	Member	Member
Guillermo García	Member	Member
Armando Hart	Member	Member
Ramiro Valdés	Member	Member
Sergio del Valle	Member	Member
Blas Roca	Member	(died)
José R. Machado	Member	Member
Carlos R. Rodríguez	Member	Member
Pedro Miret	Member	Member
Arnaldo Milián	Member	Member
Jorge Risquet	—	Member
Julio Camacho	—	Member
Osmany Cienfuegos	—	Member

rently minister of culture; Almeida, Rodriguez, and Valdez are vice presidents of the Council of State; Valdes is also minister of the interior, and Milian is minister of agriculture. Cienfuegos is a member of the Council of State and vice president of the Council of Ministers.

TOTAL CDR MEMBERSHIP	
Year	Total Membership
1961	798,000
1966	2,237,652
1971	3,500,125
1976	4,800,000
1981	5,500,000

Mass Organizations

Cuba is a highly mobilized and partially controlled society where citizen participation is encouraged. Participation through membership in the Committees for Defense of the Revolution (CDR), the Federation of Cuban Women (FMC), labor unions, or the Communist Youth Union (UJC) means discussing local affairs, doing volunteer work, receiving "guidance" from party officials, marching in the streets against fellow citizens who choose to emigrate, attending mass rallies, and engaging in other revolutionary duties. Individual participation signals the depth of one's commitment to the new order: social apathy and political indifference are scorned by the revolutionary ethos, which demands "full integration" and punishes political bystanders.

The limits of political participation are explicit; antisocialist or dissident conduct is proscribed, and it is the regime which defines acceptable and intolerable behavior. Mass participation is neither an influence nor a restraint on the behavior of the political elite.

The Committees for the Defense of the Revolution (*Comités para la Defensa de la Revolución;* CDR) constitute the revolutionary organization *par excellence*, serving a variety of purposes and generating popular mobilization when the occasion requires it. Founded in 1960 as neighborhood committees designed to protect the revolution from its internal enemies and emphasizing vigilance against or outright persecution of suspected counterrevolutionaries, the CDR gradually assumed other functions without ever giving up their original mission. The CDR have organized neighborhood work campaigns, political discussion circles, and educational and cultural activities. Leaders of CDR also have encouraged voluntarism, helped in public-health campaigns, and called for unremitting revolutionary consciousness. Militants have hounded "nonintegrated" individuals, denouncing and condemning all forms of "parasitic" and antisocial behavior, as well as collaborating with local authorities in policing neighborhoods. In 1980, according to eyewitness accounts from recent refugees, the CDR sponsored "repudiation meetings" designed to chastise, browbeat, and humiliate citizens who wanted to leave Cuba. Often, these meetings turned vituperative and sometimes even led to violent mob action.

Membership in the CDR has risen dramatically since 1960; roughly 56 percent of Cuba's total population of 9.7 million are members. The CDR draw their members from both sexes, all ages, and every social group, but their hardcore followers disproportionately come from the popular sectors. It would be misleading to conclude that every CDR member is a dedicated militant; many belong to the organization for practical rather than political or ideological reasons. Local CDR leaders are normally politically correct individuals with solid revolutionary credentials; they are firmly controlled by the party. National CDR coordinator is Armando Acosta, an old PSP member and, from 1965 to 1975, a member of the party's Central Committee. Not an important figure, he is presently an alternate member of the Politburo.

The Federation of Cuban Women (*Federación de Mujeres Cubanas;* FMC) was founded in 1960 to mobilize the skills and energy of women in the service of the revolution. Membership has grown to include some two million women, or over 80 percent of the adult female population. Vilma Espín, Raúl Castro's wife, is FMC president and a member of the party Central Committee. While the role of women in Cuban society has changed since the revolution, particularly for younger members of the first revolutionary generation— economic, political, and social equality was written into the 1976 constitution—Cuba continues to be a society dominated by deeply held values and beliefs asserting the superiority of the male.

The Confederation of Cuban Workers (*Confederación de Trabajadores Cubanos*—CTC) was founded in 1939, and currently is led by Roberto Veiga, who is also a new member of the Council of

State and an alternate member of the Political Bureau.

The objectives of CTC are in line with the official view that workers should promote society's collective interests rather than pursue selfish, gain-oriented aims. Statutes unveiled at labor congresses and subsequently endorsed by the leadership in the early 1970s defined union objectives as support of the government, participation in vigilance and defense activities, cooperation to improve managerial efficiency, maintenance of labor discipline, and raising workers' political consciousness.

Undoubtedly, the CTC is a captive organization; nevertheless, workers are often consulted about proposed laws, regulations, production goals, and administrative matters affecting labor. At other times, they are asked to ratify government measures. Cuban labor has gained benefits in terms of health care, vacations, pension coverage, and other rewards. Wage differentials have been introduced, and workers are constantly urged by officials to increase their productivity, make greater sacrifices, and improve workmanship and efficiency.

Opposition

There is no substantial or organized opposition to the Castro regime in Cuba. The government and party have been efficient and effective in isolating and crushing any concerted opposition. What remains are various forms of discontent which lack focus and coherence and cannot be equated with opposition.

Opposition to the regime in the Cuban community in exile is highly fragmented. Disputes over strategy, tactics, and ideology, personality clashes, and age-group differences make it difficult if not impossible for exile opposition groups to develop a program that could command the support of the exile community as a whole. In addition, the younger generation of that community is less committed to the idea of returning to Cuba. Periodically, attempts are made to develop a common program for liberating the island. The latest of these, the *Junta Patriotica Cubana*, was formed in 1980. While it is still trying to achieve some cooperation among the exile groups, there is little sign of progress.

The most active exile group, Alpha '66, is a very militant organization which promotes direct military attacks against the Castro regime. It does not emphasize any ideology, merely stating that its objective is "to establish a free, independent and democratic Cuba." Its secretary for a number of years has been Andrés Nazario Sargén. It is based in Miami.

National Prospects

Cuba's socialist system confronts several problems as the 1980s unfold; none of these problems, however, threatens to undermine either the fundamental political stability of the regime or its survival. Cuba's economy did not perform up to expectations in the 1976–80 period and the 4 percent growth rate fell well short of planned objectives. Castro's report to the second party congress did not envision dramatic improvements in growth rates for the next five-year period. In addition, rationing is still in effect, the housing shortage is critical, labor productivity is low, the economy is still dependent on sugar, and the country's economic dependence on the USSR cannot be effectively reduced without a major restructuring of Cuba's productive capabilities as well as its policies regarding foreign trade and external credit and finance. As of 1980, Cuba owed $8 billion to the USSR, the highest per-capita debt ratio of any country in Latin America; in that year, 57 percent of Cuba's exports went to the USSR and 62 percent of its imports came from there as well.

Recent experiments designed to increase the supply of goods available, especially food, may alleviate some shortages, but are not likely to satisfy pent-up demand. The introduction of the Economic Management System in all 441 state enterprises, emphasizing profits, material incentives, decentralization, and quasimarket mechanisms, may increase domestic output in some sectors and improve labor productivity, but it will not solve the island's basic problems. Since 1959, one million Cubans have left the country and the desire to leave is still quite strong even among the popular sectors, as the 1980 exodus demonstrated.

Finally, the charisma, shrewdness, ruthlessness, and sheer tenacity of Fidel Castro baffles adversary governments, holds the system in place, and seduces naive visitors. To underestimate his political skills would be a grave mistake.

Further Reading
Bonachea, Ramón L. and San Martín, Marta. *The Cuban Insurrection, 1952–1959.* New Brunswick, N. J.: Transaction Books, 1974.

Domínguez, Jorge I. *Cuba: Order and Revolution.* Cambridge, Mass.: Belknap Press of Harvard University Press, 1978.

Fagen, Richard. *The Transformation of Political Culture in Cuba.* Stanford, Calif.: Stanford University Press, 1969.

Franqui, Carlos. *Diary of the Cuban Revolution.* New York: Viking Press, 1980.

Gonzales, Edward. *Cuba under Castro: The Limits of Charisma.* Boston: Houghton Mifflin Co., 1974.

Halperin, Maurice. *The Taming of Fidel Castro.* Berkeley: University of California Press, 1981.

Mesa-Lago, Carmelo. *Cuba in the 1970s.* Albuquerque: University of New Mexico Press, 1978.

————. The Economy of Socialist Cuba: A Two-Decade Appraisal. Albuquerque: University of New Mexico Press, 1981.

Montaner, Carlos Alberto. *Secret Report on the Cuban Revolution.* Translated by E. Zayas-Bazan. New Brunswick, N. J.: Transaction Books, 1981.

Salas, Luis. *Social Control and Deviance in Cuba.* New York: Praeger Publishers, 1979.

Suárez, Andrés. *Cuba: Castroism and Communism, 1959–1966.* Cambridge, Mass.: M.I.T. Press, 1967.

Thomas, Hugh. *Cuba: The Pursuit of Freedom.* New York: Harper & Row, 1971.

REPUBLIC OF CYPRUS

(*Dimokratia Kyprou* [Greek]; *Kibris Cumhuriyeti* [Turkish])

by Miltos C. Miltiadou, M.A.

The System of Government

The Republic of Cyprus, an island country of nearly 700,000 people in the eastern Mediterranean, has been an independent, sovereign state, with a democratic presidential government, since 1960. Both the constitution and the international status of Cyprus derived from a series of accords known as the Zurich-London agreements reached by Britain, Greece, and Turkey in 1959. They were designed as a compromise solution to conflicting aspirations between the Greek (80 percent of the population) and Turkish (18 percent) communities.

The bicommunal 1960 constitution devised by the Zurich-London agreements was never submitted to a referendum by the Cypriots or to ratification by an elected Cypriot legislature. Its complexity and rigidity inevitably led to an impasse in the implementation process. According to the 1960 constitution Cyprus should have a Greek president and a Turkish vice president elected by their respective communities. Both were granted the power of final veto over any decision of the Council of Ministers or the House of Representatives in matters concerning foreign affairs, defense, and security. Since the president appointed 70 percent of the ministers, who served at his pleasure, he faced no problems with the Council of Ministers. The veto, therefore, became in essence a vice presidential prerogative. The president recommended in his constitutional proposals of 1963 that the veto power be abolished. He also recommended that the vice president should assume the duties of the president in case of the latter's temporary incapacity or absence. The 1960 constitution provides that it is the president of the House of Representatives (a Greek) who should assume the president's duties. All the constitutional proposals were turned down by the Turkish community. The vice president's post has been vacant since 1964 when the Turks withdrew from the government.

The Greeks of Cyprus once sought to unite the island with Greece. When the British rejected this demand, they fought a guerrilla war in the mid-fifties in order to unite with Greece. The Turkish Cypriots opposed unification with Greece. They preferred either the status quo or partition of the island between the two communities. The 1959–60 London-Zurich agreements expressly prohibit both *enosis* (union) with Greece and *taksim* (partition).

Since independence the Greek Cypriots (a small right-wing faction excepted) seem to have turned away from the idea of *enosis*, for several reasons. First, they thought it was not feasible even if it was desirable. Second, as Cyprus began to modernize and prosper as an independent state they realized the advantages of independence; i.e., given the small size of Cyprus, the central government was more immediately and directly involved with problems that would have to wait if Cyprus was part of Greece and only one of many districts of another country. People began to realize that it was not absolutely essential for them to be part of the state of Greece in order for them to be Greeks. Thus, a more sophisticated definition of Greekness began to emerge that distinguished between cultural and political identities. Finally, the military junta that ruled Greece from 1967 to 1974 was not attractive to the democratic Cypriots.

The Turkish Cypriots never believed that the Greeks had given up the idea of *enosis*, and their suspicion played a major role in shaping their policies. The Turkish Cypriots interpreted the constitution as guaranteeing them the status of an equal partner in the government. They regard themselves as one of two communities in the island with equal claim to political power. The constitution was indeed bicommunal and gave the Turks disproportionate power relative to their numbers.

The Greeks felt they were discriminated against. After the constitutional crisis and the intercommunal violence of the sixties both sides recognized the need for revising the 1960 constitution. That was the purpose of the 1968–74 intercommunal talks. Although no concrete, final agreements were reached, substantial progress was made on various important issues. Everything was changed with the events of 1974 when Turkey invaded Cyprus.

Unlike the Greek Cypriots, who were independent of Greece in their policymaking, the Turkish community depended heavily on Ankara for political direction and economic aid, illustrated by the history of the intercommunal talks of 1967 to 1974. In January 1974, the Turkish prime minister in Ankara announced that the new structure in Cyprus should be along federal lines. This was a major reason for the disruption of the talks. Furthermore, Turkey's postinvasion policies in Cyprus point to the conclusion that Turkey always wanted to physically control at least a part of Cyprus so that it could play a major role in determining the direction of the country through the Turkish community.

In mid-1974, the military junta which ruled Greece instigated a coup against the Cypriot government of Archbishop Makarios. The Turkish government responded to the apparent move toward *enosis* by invading the island and occupying the northern third of it. It then instituted a massive population transfer in which all Greeks in the Turkish occupied area were forced to move south, while Turks in the south fled north to escape the possibility of a Greek backlash. The island has remained rigidly partitioned since then.

Turkey declared a Turkish Cypriot Federated State (TCFS) in the occupied area and does not recognize the government of the republic. The 1960 constitution, as amended, is still the legitimate legal structure of the state even though Turkey's occupation of northern Cyprus prevents its operation there. Therefore, the TCFS is an extraconstitutional entity that lacks legal foundation as far as the government of Cyprus is concerned. The TCFS has never been granted international recognition, and internationally, Cyprus is represented by the Greek-controlled government.

Executive

The president of the republic is the head of state and government. He is elected by universal suffrage for a five-year term, with no limit on the number of terms he may serve. Executive powers are exercised by the president through a Council of Ministers appointed by him and serving at his pleasure. There is no prime minister. The Council has executive power on all matters except those expressly reserved for the president, i.e., appointment of ministers, the attorney general, and other high officials and the granting of pardons and clemency. The president may convene meetings of the Council, set the agenda, and preside over them. He does not have the right to vote in such meetings.

The Council's powers include the general direction and control of the government; direction of general policy; defense and security; foreign affairs; the coordination and supervision of all public services; consideration of bills to be introduced in the legislature; consideration of the budget, etc. The decisions of the Council are taken by absolute majority. They are binding on the president, but in practice, since the Council serves at the president's pleasure, it also serves as his instrument.

Archbishop Makarios was president from 1960 until his death in 1977. He dominated the political life of the country and commanded widespread support. Makarios was succeeded by Spyros Kyprianou, leader of the Democratic Party (DIKO). He faces his first election in February 1983. He lacks a strong, personal political base, but will have the support of the Communist Party (AKEL); his major opponent will be the leader of the Democratic Rally (DISI). The election is regarded as very important for the future of the country with the problem of intercommunal negotiations being the dominant issue.

Legislature

The legislative body of the republic is a unicameral House of Representatives, elected for a term of five years. Of the nominal fifty members of the House, thirty-five are elected by the Greeks and fifteeen by the Turks. The latter have boycotted the House since 1964. According to the constitution, the president (speaker) of the House is elected by the Greek legislators.

A simple majority vote of those members present and voting is required for all laws and decisions to pass. The power to veto or return for consideration of any law or decision is vested in the president with regard to foreign affairs, security, and defense. Although this limits the power of the House, the independence of the legislature is expressly recognized and protected by the constitution. For example, the president of the republic does not have the power to dissolve the legislature.

The last legislative elections took place in May

HOUSE OF REPRESENTATIVES ELECTIONS (1981)

Party	% of Total Vote	Seats	% of Constituency Vote					
			Nicosia	Larnaca	Kyrenia	Paphos	Limassol	Famagusta
AKEL	32.769	12	29.40	36.28	34.34	20.81	35.71	39.11
DIKO	19.500	8	19.12	15.01	26.76	27.41	21.51	14.84
DISI	31.918	12	32.78	33.83	24.38	20.04	30.13	38.35
EDEK	8.169	3	10.62	8.33	9.44	11.30	6.33	3.68
EK	2.738	—	4.23	4.10	1.61	0.96	1.73	1.37
NEDIPA	1.919	—	2.22	0.70	1.26	5.66	1.21	1.26
PAME	2.787	—	1.49	1.75	1.44	13.81	2.87	1.38
Independents	0.29	—						

DISTRIBUTION OF SEATS (1981)*

	Nicosia	Larnaca	Kyrenia	Paphos	Limassol	Famagusta	Total
AKEL	4	1	1	1	2	3	12
DIKO	3	—	1	1	2	1	8
DISI	4	2	—	1	2	3	12
EDEK	1	—	—	1	1	—	3
TOTAL	12	3	2	4	7	7	35

* In early 1982, a DISI member died. The DIKO won that seat in a by-election.

1981 under a new, rather complex proportional representation system. No single party emerged as a dominant force. The electorate manifested a tendency towards the ideological poles. The right-wing Democratic Rally (DISI) and the communist AKEL gained twelve seats (out of thirty-five) with the latter polling not quite 1 percent more votes. AKEL and the Democratic Party (DIKO) formed a legislative alliance and elected the latter's candidate as president of the House.

Judiciary

The ten-member Supreme Court is the highest appellate court for all criminal and civil matters. It also adjudicates exclusively and finally on all matters of constitutionality. The judges are appointed by the president and may be impeached by the House. The assize courts have unlimited criminal jurisdiction. The district courts exercise original civil and criminal jurisdiction. The Supreme Council of Judicature (the attorney general, the judges of the Supreme Court, and a member of the Cypriot Bar), is entrusted with appointment, promotion, transfers, termination, and disciplinary control over all judicial officers, other than the judges of the Supreme Court.

There are also Greek ecclesiastical and Turkish family courts.

Regional & Local Government

Administratively, Cyprus is divided into six districts: Nicosia, Paphos, Larnaca, Limassol, Famagusta and Kyrenia. The last two have been under military occupation by Turkey since 1974. The administrative center for each district is the principal city of the district and has the same name. Most of the departments of the central government have offices in these cities. Each district is administered by a district officer appointed by the Ministry of Interior. He is the coordinator of all government activities in his district, including the supervision of all elections. His general duties include advice and guidance to local authorities, i.e., municipal corporations, village improvement boards, and village commissions.

The mayors and councils for the municipalities are appointed by the central government. The political parties, especially AKEL, would like to have them elected.

Village affairs are administered by five-member commissions appointed by the Ministry of Interior. Recent legislation provides for the election of these authorities in future.

Government in the Turkish Zone

All of Kyrenia, most of Famagusta, and parts of Nicosia comprise the Turkish Federated State of Cyprus (TFCS), which is not formally defined as an independent entity and has never sought or been granted any international recognition. It has a constitution providing for a president, a prime minister with a cabinet, a legislative assembly, and a separate judiciary. The Turkish government has stated that the TFCS will remain in place until it is superseded by a new federal constitution for the whole of Cyprus. Rauf Denktash was elected president of the TFCS in 1976.

In spite of the constitutional structures of the TFCS, it is under the control of Turkish military forces and major policy decisions for the area are made in Turkey. The economy of the rich agricultural area of the north has stagnated, while the southern part of the island continues to experience solid economic growth.

Since 1974, Turkey has tried to change the population ratio in Cyprus by importing settlers from Turkey. Turkish press reports estimated the number of these colonists at 50,000 to 60,000 by the spring of 1979. There have also been reports of serious discontent with the "colonists" on the part of the Cypriot Turkish community. Apparently, large numbers of the settlers come from eastern Turkey and are far less sophisticated and law abiding than the Turkish Cypriots.

The major political parties of the Turkish community are:

National Unity Party (Ulusal Birlik Partisi; UBP)

Established in 1975 by the Turkish-Cypriot leader Rauf Denktash and headed by Mustafa Cagatay, UBP advocates a bicommunal federal state in Cyprus. It won eighteen seats in the legislative assembly in the 1981 elections.

Communal Liberation Party (Toplumcu Kurtulus Partisi; TKP)

Recently renamed the Socialist Salvation Party, this party advocates policies similar to the UPB's. It won thirteen seats in the 1981 legislative elections. Its leader is Alpay Durduran.

Republican Turkish Party (Cumhuriyetci Turk Partisi; CTP)

A leftist party headed by Ozker Ozgur, the CTP has six seats in the legislative assembly.

Democratic People's Party (Demokratik Halk Partisi; DHP)

Founded by Nejat Konuk and Osman Orek in 1979 following their split from the UBP, the DHP platform calls for an independent, nonaligned, biregional state in Cyprus.

The Turkish Unity Party

Formed in 1978 by Ismail Tezer, a retired Turkish Air Force colonel, it holds one seat in the legislative assembly. The party derives its support primarily from the "colonists" and advocates partition of Cyprus and the creation of an independent Cyprus Turkish republic closely allied with Turkey. All founding members of the party were settlers from Turkey.

The Electoral System

Voter registration and voting are compulsory for all citizens twenty-one years of age and older. Voter turnout is usually high. In the 1981 legislative elections, 93 percent of the eligible Greek voters went to the polls. Heavy participation is also expected in next year's presidential election. Voting is by secret ballot.

The president is elected through universal suffrage by an absolute majority. If no candidate receives more than 50 percent of the vote, a second round of elections takes place between the top contestants.

So far four candidates have officially declared for next year's presidential election. It will be the first time in the history of the republic that several candidates, representing organized political parties, will be competing. Until his death, Makarios was guaranteed victory and faced only nominal opposition.

For legislative elections Cyprus is divided into six electoral districts: Nicosia, Famagusta, Limassol, Paphos, Larnaca and Kyrenia. Each is allocated a number of seats based on population. Greeks who formerly lived in Famagusta and Kyrenia vote for the representatives from those districts.

A new and complex proportional representation system was used for the first time in the 1981 elections for the House. In the first round of counting, seats are distributed within each district to parties which gather more votes than the district's electoral quotient (the total votes divided by the seats available). Parties with less than 10 percent of the total vote (8 percent if one of their candidates gets elected) are eliminated. In a second round of counting, surplus votes are added together and the remaining seats are distributed on the basis of a new quotient (the total number of surplus votes divided by the number of seats remaining). The leftover votes from the second distribution are used to allocate the remaining seats. Seats are then allocated to parties for the districts in which they polled best, ensuring that all elected legislators represent the districts in which they run as candidates. Through the elimination of the smaller parties from the second distribution, the larger parties enlarge their representation.

The Party System

Until recently, political life was divided along communal lines: The Turks were represented by the Turkish Cypriot Labor Federation; on the Greek side, the Patriotic Front and its splinter factions along with AKEL supported the Makarios regime until the mid-seventies. Multiparty activity expanded following the abortive coup against Makarios and Turkey's invasion of Cyprus in 1974. In the Turkish community, the National Unity Party of the Turkish Cypriot leader Rauf Denktash became the largest party. In the Greek community, opposition to Makarios and his successor centered around the right-wing Democratic Rally.

All parties except AKEL are essentially the creatures of their founders and reflect the personality and orientation of their leaders. They are supported by membership dues and donations. Although regional and local branches exist, they are centrally controlled. Reliable data on party membership and finances is scarce.

Party rallies in the squares of the big cities and extensive speechmaking by the party leader and candidates are the major modes of political campaigning. While there is no political advertising on television or the radio, party leaders are invited to debate their views through these media. Most newspapers are party instruments and promote their party's candidates.

Democratic Party (*Demokratico Komma*; DIKO)

The DIKO was founded by President Kyprianou in 1976 and follows the policies of Makarios. Internal disputes caused the defection of prominent members prior to last year's elections. It is allied with AKEL in the legislature and in next year's presidential elections; however, this alliance has been widely criticized. DIKO supports a non-

aligned foreign policy and resolution of the intercommunal problem through the United Nations. Spyros Kyprianou (born 1932) has served as foreign minister and president of the House, and is now president of the republic. He is a moderate-centrist, a nonideologue, and not favored by the West. Party headquarters are at 13 Diagoras Street, Nicosia, Cyprus.

Democratic Rally (*Dimokratikos Synagermos*; DISI)

DISI was organized by Glafkos Clerides (born 1919) in 1976 after a disagreement with Makarios. It is a right-wing party with some extremist members in its ranks. It favors a pro-Western policy contending that only the United States and the European community can pressure Turkey to make concessions on Cyprus. It supports a free-enterprise system and is favored by the business community. DISI has been critical of the handling of the intercommunal talks by the government, accusing it of missing opportunities to come to an agreement. It is the second-largest party and appears to be gaining strength. The party is affiliated with the European Christian Democratic Union. Clerides served as president of the House, with one brief interruption, from 1960 to 1976, and has been the Greek representative in the intercommunal talks. For many years he was considered as the heir apparent to Makarios. He is conservative but not extremist and is highly respected in the West. Party headquarters are at 4 C. Palama Str., Nicosia, Cyprus.

Progressive Party of the Working People (*Anorthotikon Komma Ergazomenou Laou*; AKEL)

The oldest and most effectively organized party, AKEL, succeeded the Communist Party of Cyprus in 1941. Internationally a pro-Moscow party, it follows a pragmatic domestic program. It has traditionally supported nonalignment and prefers welfare reformism within the free-enterprise system rather than revolutionary transformation of society. It claims the support of more than half of organized labor, and its following is fairly evenly distributed geographically. While it espouses a more flexible approach to the intercommunal talks than the socialists or, until recently, DIKO, opponents charge that this policy reflects Moscow's wish to have good relations with Turkey. Although AKEL's position has been bolstered by what are perceived as negative Western policies toward the Greek community, Moscow's flirtations with Turkey embarrass AKEL. Ezekias Papaioannou (born 1908) has been regularly elected general secretary of the party since 1949. AKEL's leadership is the oldest of all parties and, like the party itself, represents an element of continuity and stability in the country's political history. AKEL participates in international communist conferences and promotes cultural exchanges between Eastern-bloc countries and Cyprus. It publishes the daily *Haravgi* (*Dawn*) and the weekly *Demokratia* (*Democracy*). Party headquarters are at 10 Akamantos Street, Nicosia, Cyprus.

Unified Democratic Union of the Center (*Eniea Demokratiki Enosis Kyprou*; EDEK)

This socialist party was founded in 1969. It is anti-NATO, favors nonalignment, and strongly opposed the interference of the Greek junta (1967–74) in Cyprus. It advocates a long struggle to liberate Cyprus from foreign influence. It has called for the nationalization of foreign-owned mines and banks and favors socialized medicine. It attracts noncommunist leftist youth and intellectuals. EDEK is active internationally, especially in Third World forums. It is a consultative member of the Socialist International and a member of the Afro-Asian People's Solidarity Organization. Vassos Lyssarides, born 1920, EDEK's founder and leader, is the finest political orator in Cyprus. He has strong affiliations in the Arab countries and is anti-Moscow. A daily paper, *Ta Nea* (*The News*), and a weekly paper, *Anexartitos* (*Independent*) are the party instruments. Party headquarters are at Constantinou Paleologou 23, Nicosia, Cyprus.

Minor Parties

None of the smaller parties are represented in the legislature. They are centrist in orientation and do not seem to have a bright future although their leaders may emerge in important government positions.

The Center Union (*Enosis Kentrou*; EK) was founded in 1976 by T. Papadopoulos, who has served as labor minister, Greek representative in the intercommunal talks, and legislator.

The New Democratic Camp (*Nea Dimokratiki Parataxis*; NEDIPA) was formed in 1980 by A. Michaelides, former president of the House while in the DIKO party. NEDIPA is very similar to DIKO.

The Pancyprian Renewal Front (*Pankyprion Ananeotikon Metopon*; PAME) was organized in 1979 by former education minister, Ch. Sofianos after he broke from DIKO. He is left of center and extremely critical of DISI.

Other Political Forces

Ethnic Groups

Turks and Greeks lived in partially intermingled communities for years under the British with little ethnic tension, but without ever developing a distinct Cypriot identity. Each group retained a primary identification to its homeland and culture.

The Greek community may be roughly characterized as urban and cosmopolitan with extensive business dealings throughout the Mediterranean. Greek Cypriots have generally been more prosperous, better educated, and more inclined to expend the energy and take the risks required by entrepreneurship. Nearly all the Greeks have an Orthodox Christian background.

The Turkish community, once associated with the Turkish rulers of the island until it was ceded to Britain in 1878, have traditionally been more rural, less prosperous, and less educated than the Greeks. Conservative in lifestyle, they have not been as self-assertive as the Greeks. The Turks are generally Sunni Moslem.

Approximately 2 percent of the population is made up of three other ethnoreligious groups— Armenians, Maronites, and Latins, all Christians. Most Maronites are of Lebanese Arab descent, while the Latins are largely of Italian origin. All three groups have harmonious relations with the Greek community.

United Nations

Following Turkey's invasion in 1974, the Cyprus government worked through the United Nations to restore the unity of the country and free the northern third from Turkish control. General Assembly Resolution 3212, the basic document, was adopted unanimously (including Turkey) on November 5, 1974. It calls for the withdrawal of all foreign troops and the safe return of all refugees to their homes. Neither this nor any other U.N. resolution on Cyprus has been implemented. A U.N. peacekeeping force controls a buffer zone of about 3 percent of the island between the two communities.

National Prospects

After several rounds of intercommunal negotiations under United Nations auspices, no agreement has been reached. A bizonal, bicommunal, federal state appears to be a likely basis of agreement. There is, however, strong disagreement as to the particular provisions of such a framework.

The major issue in the Cyprus situation is whether outside powers wish to see Cypriots resolve their differences in an independent state run by Cypriots for Cypriots. Greece generally has supported such a conclusion. Turkey apparently wants substantial influence in at least a portion of the island. The North Atlantic Treaty Organization is not comfortable with the idea of an independent Cyprus which might well be nonaligned. United States military planners are particularly concerned about this possibility as Cyprus would be a key strategic area in any general conflict in the Middle East. In short, outside forces and contending interests complicate Cypriot internal problems and present the country with the possibility of an imposed settlement that will satisfy neither community.

Further Reading

Adams, T. W. "The First Republic of Cyprus: A Review of an Unworkable Constitution." *Western Political Quarterly*, Vol. 19, No. 3 (Sept. 1966).

Day, A. J., and Degenhardt, H. W., eds. *Political Parties of the World*. Detroit: Gale Research Company, 1980.

Kyriakides, S. *Cyprus: Constitutionalism and Crisis Government*. Philadelphia: University of Pennsylvania Press, 1968.

Markides, K. C. *The Rise and Fall of the Cyprus Republic*. New Haven and London: Yale University Press, 1977.

Polyviou, P. G. *Cyprus: Conflict and Negotiation 1960–1980*. London: Gerald Duckworth, and New York: Holmes and Meier, 1980.

———. *Cyprus—In Search of a Constitution: Constitutional Negotiations and Proposals, 1960–1975*. Nicosia, Cyprus: Chr. Nicolaou and Sons, 1976.

Public Information Office. *Parliamentary Elections, May 24, 1981: The New Electoral System*. Nicosia, Cyprus: P.I.O., 1981.

Stephens, R. *Cyprus—A Place of Arms: Power Politics and Ethnic Conflict in the Eastern Mediterranean*. London: Pall Mall, 1966.

Tornaritis, C. G. *Cyprus and Its Constitutional and Other Legal Problems*. 2nd ed. Nicosia, Cyprus: n.p. 1980.

CZECHOSLOVAK SOCIALIST REPUBLIC
(*Československá Socialistická Republika*)
by Owen V. Johnson, Ph.D.

The System of Government

The Czechoslovak Socialist Republic (CSSR), a nation of 15.4 million people, is a socialist state which since 1948 has been under the control of the Communist Party of Czechoslovakia (KSC). Under the Constitution of 1960, as amended in 1968 and 1970, it is a federated republic of two equal states—the Czech Socialist Republic (CSR) and the Slovak Socialist Republic (SSR)—each with its own prime minister, cabinet, and legislature. The governmental structure, partially influenced by the pre-Communist Czechoslovak system, has a bicameral Federal Assembly, elected every five years, which formally elects the president. He in turn appoints the members of the government, including the prime minister, but they are responsible only to the Federal Assembly. Ultimate political control is located in the Presidium of the Communist Party, which has been led since April 1969 by Gustáv (née Augustin) Husák, who since 1975 has been concurrently the president of Czechoslovakia.

Executive

The executive includes the president, the premier, deputy premiers, and the federal cabinet.

In the constitution, the prime minister and the cabinet are preeminent. In reality, the president has far more authority and prestige. This situation reflects the tremendous prestige of Thomas G. Masaryk, the country's founder and first president (1918–35). The president, who resides in the Prague Castle, is formally elected by the Federal Assembly to a five-year term as head of state and may be reelected. He represents the country in affairs of state, receives and appoints ambassadors, calls the Federal Assembly into session, and signs laws. He is commander-in-chief of the armed forces and appoints the premier and his cabinet as well as other officials, including generals and university professors. He may attend and preside over Federal Assembly meetings, but he has neither vote nor veto. In addition, he may exercise powers not specifically delineated in the constitution if the Federal Assembly approves.

In the event of the president's death, the prime minister becomes acting president until the Federal Assembly chooses a new president; there is no vice-president. The present occupant of the office is Gustáv Husák (born 1913), who was first elected in 1975, and reelected in 1980, both times unanimously. He is the seventh president since Czechoslovakia was formed in 1918, but the first Slovak to hold that position. Husák succeeded General Ludvík Svoboda, who had been chosen president during the Prague Spring (1968), but resigned in 1975 for reasons of health.

In the constitution, the premier and cabinet are collectively referred to as "the government" (*vláda*), the "highest executive organ of the state," responsible to the Federal Assembly. The government is composed of the premier (*předseda vlády*), eight deputy premiers, fourteen ministers, and three representatives of national commissions. Lubomír Štrougal, a Czech, has been prime minister since 1969. He is considered a moderate within the leadership.

The number of ministries and the division of responsibilities among them has varied. In 1982, there were fourteen federal ministries. In addition, the government includes the vice-chairman of the State Planning Commission (the chairman is a deputy premier), and the chairmen of the People's Control Board (which monitors the execution of policy) and the Federal Price Office. The State Planning Commission is of particular importance. It is responsible for drawing up and implementing the state economic plan.

The federal government is responsible for defense, national security, foreign policy, economic development, the implementation of measures passed by the Federal Assembly, and the control of the federal ministries and offices. Key decision-making power is vested in the presidium, a kind of inner cabinet, composed of the prime minister and the eight deputy premiers. The constituent

Czech and Slovak republics are responsible for education, culture, justice, health, trade, construction, and forest and water resources. In certain areas—including industry, agriculture, and food—the federal government and the two national governments share responsibilities. In reality, the government is only an executive: policymaking is a function of the Communist Party.

Although theoretically separate, the government and the Communist Party are tied closely together. Most, if not all, members of the cabinet are party members and several are members of the ruling presidium of the party. In addition, the party has supervisory organs which parallel those of the government.

Legislature

According to the constitution, the Federal Assembly is the highest organ of power in the state. It consists of two houses with equal powers: the House of the People with 200 deputies chosen by direct election from the country as a whole; and the House of Nations, made up of 150 directly elected deputies, 75 each from the Czech and Slovak republics. Deputies, who must be twenty-one years old, are elected to five-year terms, with all terms beginning and ending at the same time. Elections are usually held several months after the quinquennial Communist Party Congress. The Assembly holds two annual sessions, one in the fall and one in the spring, each usually lasting only a few days. However, if at least a third of the deputies independently request an Assembly session, it must be convened within thirty days.

Legislation must be approved by both houses, a process often speeded up by the holding of joint sessions. On certain matters, legislation passed by the House of Nations requires a majority vote of representatives from each of the two republics. Specific matters of special importance—election of the president, constitutional amendments, and a declaration of war—require a 60 percent majority in each half of the House of Nations as well as a 60 percent vote in the House of the People.

A forty-member presidium, twenty from each house, is empowered to act on the Assembly's behalf when the Assembly is not in session. The twenty representatives from the House of Nations must be equally divided between representatives from the Czech and Slovak republics. The entire Assembly elects the chairman and deputy chairman of the presidium who must not be from the same republic. Each house also elects its own presidium of three to six members. The presidium may not elect a president, amend the constitution, or dissolve the government, and, except under ex-traordinary circumstances, may not declare war. The next regular session of the Federal Assembly must approve the presidium's actions or they become inoperative. Since 1970 this has been a formality. The presidium normally schedules the semiannual sessions of the Assembly.

The constitution gives the Federal Assembly exclusive jurisdiction in foreign and domestic policy, economic planning and control of the executive. If either house of the Assembly should withhold its approval of a government program, theoretically the president would be directed to recall the government. In reality, the Assembly only approves measures placed before it. Such influence as its individual members might have is wielded behind the scenes.

The most recent elections to the Assembly were held June 5–6, 1981. Nearly one-third (109) of its members were elected for the first time, sixty-eight in the House of the People (34 percent) and forty-one in the House of Nations (27 percent); there were ninety-nine women in the two houses (28 percent).

The Communist Party held more than two-thirds of the seats (237) in the Assembly elected in 1976. However, there were also seventeen deputies from the Czechoslovak Socialist Party (CSS), eighteen from the Czechoslovak People's Party (CSL), four from the (Slovak) Party of Freedom (SSI), four from the Party of Slovak Renewal (SSO), and seventy deputies without party affiliation.

Judiciary

The judiciary includes the Supreme Court and republic, regional, district, local, and military courts.

The Supreme Court's primary function is to adjudicate conflicts between citizens. It also supervises the activities of lower courts, including the supreme courts of the Czech and Slovak Republics. Although military courts have special regulations, the Supreme Court is also the highest military court. Members of the Court, who must all be legally trained, are elected to ten-year terms by the Federal Assembly. The chief justice and his deputy may not be from the same republic.

Republic and regional judges are elected by the corresponding legislative body, while lower courts are elected directly by the public. In all but the federal Supreme Court, both legal professionals and lay people serve as judges, to suggest popular participation in the judicial process. Lay members are elected to four-year terms, legally trained persons to ten-year terms. Elections are held at different times than legislative elections.

PROFILE OF CZECHOSLOVAKIA'S FEDERAL ASSEMBLY

Occupation	Total	Percent	Percentage Change from Previous Assembly
Workers	92	26.3	−9.8
Agriculturists (i.e., farming sector)	51	14.6	+8.5
Technical and economic employees	63	18.0	+21.2
Party & other political functionaries	113	32.3	+2.7
Intellectuals, armed forces, & others	31	8.9	−20.5
Nationality			
Czech	202	57.7	+1.5
Slovak	122	34.9	−0.8
Hungarian	18	5.1	−5.3
Ukrainian	4	1.1	0.0
Polish	2	0.6	−33.3
German	2	0.6	0.0
Age			
Under 35	60	17.1	−3.2
36–50	127	36.3	−19.1
51–60	133	38.0	+16.7
Over 60	30	8.6	+76.5

There is no federal minister of justice since that function is the responsibility of the two republic governments. Federal legal responsibility is vested in the Office of the Procurator, whose head is the procurator general. He is appointed by the president and responsible to the Federal Assembly. He supervises the prosecution of dissidents; there are also procurators at the republic, regional, and district level, and in the military.

In addition to adjudication, courts and legal offices in Czechoslovakia are assigned functions of education and criticism.

Regional & Local Government

One of the keys to understanding postinvasion Czechoslovakia is the federal structure of the state adopted in October 1968 and instituted in January 1969. It is one of the few reforms of the Prague Spring that remains in effect. It marked the culmination of half a century of Slovak efforts to achieve equality with the Czechs.

Each of the newly formed constituent republics created unicameral legislative and executive bodies. Each republic has a cabinet (government) consisting of a premier (Josef Korčak in the Czech Republic; Peter Colotka in Slovakia), three deputy premiers (one of which in each case is the chairman of the republic planning commission), the chairman of the republic people's control board, and thirteen department heads (agriculture and nutrition, building, construction and technology, culture, education, finance, forestry and water conservation, health, industry, interior, justice, labor and social welfare, and trade).

The legislative body, known as the National Council, is the highest organ of state power in each republic. The Czech National Council has 200 members and the Slovak National Council has 150 members. Deputies are elected to five-year terms. Each council holds two annual sessions and elects a presidium. Relations between the councils and the republic governments parallel those between the federal government and the Federal Assembly. The republic government, however, is appointed by the National Council presidium. The government's program must then be approved by the entire council. All matters not reserved to the federal government or to joint federal–republic jurisdiction are handled by the republics.

While it is true that the failure to federalize the Communist Party structure has removed most of the independent power of the republic governments, it is also true that for Slovaks the possession of a national government has been a source of enormous pride. This explains in large part the lack of Slovak opposition to the present regime.

Below the republics, Czechoslovakia is divided into 12 regions (kraje), two of which are the cities of Prague and Bratislava; 112 districts (*okresy*); and about 10,000 local units. These are all governed by "national committees" which vary in size from 15 to 150 members, depending on the population and the level of government. Each committee elects a council to coordinate its work. As the constitution assigns to national committees responsibility for organizing and directing economic, cultural, health and social services, it is with the local national committee that the average citizen of Czechoslovakia has the greatest contact.

The Electoral System

Representative bodies at all levels are elected from single-member districts every five years in a two-day election extending over twenty-four hours. The constitution says little about the election process. The elections are supervised by the National Front, an umbrellalike organization coordinating political and social groups. Candidates for all offices must be twenty-one years of age or older. Not all candidates are Communists, but all must be approved by the National Front, which is subordinate to the Communist Party. In some cases at the lowest levels, voters may be presented with a choice of candidates; otherwise there is a single candidate. Voting is legally secret. Voters may abstain by crossing names off the ballot, but this takes an extra step at the voting station, which by its visibility could jeopardize the livelihood of the voter and/or his family. Each voter casts six ballots, a different color for each level of representation.

All citizens aged eighteen and over are eligible to vote. Voter turnout regularly exceeds 99 percent of eligible voters, and the candidates usually receive at least 99 percent of the vote. On several occasions, it appears that voting results were determined before the votes were counted. In the 1981 elections, 99.51% of eligible voters cast ballots. The slates for both the House of the People and the House of Nations received 99.96% of the votes cast. Only one of the 197,169 candidates at the six levels was not elected.

When vacancies occur in the Federal Assembly, the Assembly presidium schedules by-elections. This procedure is not mandatory, however, if the vacancy occurs in the last year of the term.

While the elections may seem perfunctory, they do test the Communist Party's organizational and supervisory capabilities with the public at large. There is an exchange of ideas, too, especially at the local level, a process which has a modest impact on policymaking.

The Party System

Politics in Czechoslovakia are directed by the National Front, an umbrella organization founded in 1945. Brought under Communist control in 1948, the National Front coordinates both political activities and the election process. The constitution refers to the Front as the "political expression of the ties of workers of the city and the countryside." Represented in it are five political parties and numerous mass organizations which theoretically can influence government policy in its discussions. Since 1968, it has been organized along federal lines under the chairmanship of Gustáv Husák, who holds the office by virtue of the fact that he is the leader of the Communist Party. In addition to the Communist Party, seventeen other organizations, such as the Czechoslovak Union of Women, the Czechoslovak Red Cross, the Czechoslovak Union of Journalists, the Union of Czechoslovak Stamp Collectors, and the Socialist Union of Youth, are members. There are thirty members in the National Front of the Czech Republic, chaired by Josef Kempný, and twenty-seven members in the Slovak National Front, led by Josef Lenárt. The four non-Communist Czech and Slovak political parties are represented in the respective national committees.

In 1968, there was some effort made to overcome the monolithic nature of policy by revitalizing the Front. It could potentially play that role again in the future.

The National Front screens all candidates for elections to legislative bodies at every level and offers its approval to a slate. It also provides a platform for the slate to run on.

National Front headquarters are at Škretova 6, 120 59, Prague 2.

Communist Party of Czechoslovakia (*Komunistická strana Československa;* KSC)

The Communist Party of Czechoslovakia has ruled the fortunes of Czechoslovakia for more than half of that country's existence, although the Soviet Union and its East European allies have occasionally influenced its activities.

History

The roots of the KSC lie in the Czechoslovak Social Democratic Party, founded in 1897. The left wing of the Social Democrats, led by Bohumír

Šmeral, broke away from the party in 1920, and founded the KSC in May 1921. Operating legally, it was one of six major parties in the interwar Czechoslovak Republic, drawing as much as 13 percent of the vote. It was the largest party not to join any of the interwar cabinets. Its success waxed and waned in the interwar period, but its long-term strength was aided by the fact that it was one of the few parties in Czechoslovakia at that time that was multiethnic, a policy dictated largely by the Communist International.

The party's social-democratic antecedents persisted in party policy until the triumph of the "Boys from Karlin" under Klement Gottwald at the 1929 party congress resulted in the Bolshevization of the party and committed it to overthrowing the capitalist system. Membership in the first eight years after 1929 declined from 350,000 to 25,000. The Depression helped the party recover its image as did the party turnabout in 1936 when it urged cooperation with bourgeois parties in Popular Front activities to defend the republic. Membership rose to 90,000 by 1938. The Nazi–Soviet pact and the breakup of Czechoslovakia in 1939 forced another reversal of policy, one which supported the country's dismemberment. When Hitler attacked the Soviet Union, the KSC went underground and resumed its support for a renewed Czechoslovak state. A separate Communist Party of Slovakia (KSS), operating illegally in the semi-independent Slovak State, occasionally pursued different goals.

The KSC was reconstituted in 1945 with a massive influx of members. After receiving 38 percent of the national vote in free elections in 1946, it apparently began to lose influence. After a dress-rehearsal semicoup in Slovakia in late 1947, the party seized power in February 1948 when the non-Communist members of the government resigned, and the party, with a massive show of force in the streets, persuaded President Edvard Beneš to accept the resignations and call on the Communists under Gottwald to organize a new government. Party membership soared to nearly 2.5 million members.

As did most East European Communist parties, the KSC underwent a purge in Stalin's last years (1950–52). More than a half million members were dropped from the party rolls, hundreds were imprisoned, and some, including former party leader Rudolf Slánský, were even executed on false charges. The party's present leader, Húsák, was imprisoned for ten years as a "Slovak nationalist." During this period, Antonín Novotný took over the leadership of the party, and remained in control until 1968.

In the mid-'60s, Czechoslovakia became the first East European country to face a postwar economic crisis. A reform group within the party pressed for economic decentralization and the implementation of a more rational and efficient system of management. The party leadership, however, resisted these reform efforts because of justified fears of a loss of political power. Other reform forces *within* the party—including dissatisfied writers and intellectuals, students, and Slovaks who sought equality with the Czechs—helped precipitate the removal of Novotný from the leadership and his replacement by Alexander Dubček, which unleashed the Prague Spring of 1968. A plan of action adopted in April 1968 had the KSC abandoning the monopoly of power, but maintaining its leading role while cooperating with a wide range of groups in society. These plans were never carried out: no new parties were chartered, no new election law passed. Ironically, the Communist Party might have won a fair and free election in 1968.

The Soviet invasion eventually brought about the elimination of most of the reforms and shattered the public's faith in the party. The party has not succeeded in winning back the enthusiastic support of the populace.

Organization

The KSC, which operates under a system of democratic centralism, is organized in 45,564 cells across the country. These basic party units are organized in places of work and residence where there are at least five party members. They are joined together under larger factory, village, or city committees. The local units are involved in directing economic enterprises; training members and keeping them informed of party policy; participating in local social, economic, and cultural activities; and propagandizing nonmembers. The membership in each local organization meets monthly. With prior approval from higher authorities, it selects its own officers, including a chairman and secretaries, and names delegates to conferences at higher organizational levels.

The next higher unit, the district organization, guides local offices in their work, and a regional organization guides the district offices. The district and regional party officials handle affairs related to economic development, ideological work, personnel selection, and the implementation of party policy. In the spirit of democratic centralism, these groups also on occasion make proposals to higher bodies.

District conferences attended by representatives of local-party organizations generally are held twice every five years. Between conferences, a district committee led by a presidium and a secretariat handle district affairs. District committee members must have been party members for at least four years, and the district secretary at least eight years.

The district conferences, in turn, elect delegates (who must have been party members at least five years) to regional conferences. Again, a regional presidium, which meets at least every two months, and a secretary handle affairs between conference sessions. The leading secretary must have been a member of the party for at least ten years.

At the pinnacle of the party is the party congress, which now meets in a week-long session once every five years. The most recent congress, the sixteenth, met in April 1981 and was attended by 1,421 delegates. (Three other unnumbered congresses have also been held.) The congress only ratifies decisions of the party Presidium and its Central Committee. The congress formally elects the latter two bodies, although in fact the Presidium and the Secretariat choose the Central Committee membership. The Presidium and members of the Secretariat are self-appointed.

The party and the country basically are run by the twenty-two people who make up these two groups. They make the important policy decisions and outline legislation. They have direct institutionalized influence on the holders of about 80,000 positions, and a strong influence on another 600,000 posts. The general secretary is the party's chief executive. Husák has held that post since April 1969. The Central Committee is charged with party activities and policy implementation between congresses, and meets at least three times a year to conduct its work.

The party's main organs are the Czech daily newspaper *Rudé právo;* the economic weekly *Hospodářské noviny;* the ideological and political weekly *Tribuna;* the political, scientific, and cultural weekly *Tvorba;* the ideological and organizational weekly *Život strany;* the theoretical and political monthly *Nová mysl;* the theoretical and informational weekly *Otázky míru a socializmu;* and the pictorial weekly *Kvety.*

Policy

Party policy has been fairly constant for the last decade: "an ever fuller application of the interests of the working class" and "a strengthening of the socialist system and of the power of the working class, and the deepening of the leading role of the Communist Party and of its link with the people." As these general statements suggest, the party concentrates on propaganda activities in the do-

mestic sphere. Internationally, the party stands solidly behind the USSR in support of proletarian internationalism, Leninist principles, and the Brezhnev doctrine. This last doctrine specifies that no decision regarding a country's development by its ruling Communist Party can be allowed to damage Communist hegemony in that country or any other Communist-ruled country.

While some observers perceive a pragmatic technocratic faction led by Lubomír Štrougal and an ideological faction led by Vasil Bilàk engaged in mortal battle in the party Presidium, in fact the groupings at the top seem to be fluid.

Membership & Constituency

Today's party membership approximates that of the mid-1960s. While in 1966, there were 1,698,002 members and candidate members (about 12.7 percent of the population), that figure had dropped to 1.1 million by 1975 (about 7.4 percent of the population). Since then nearly a half million members have been added.

COMMUNIST PARTY MEMBERSHIP		
Year	Members	% of Population
1976	1,382,660	9.3
1978	1,473,112	9.9
1981	1,538,179	10.3

Every sixth adult is a party member. A party official has estimated that fully committed members number about 300,000 or 3 percent of the adult population.

Of the 321,000 members admitted in the last five years, 61 percent were workers, 22.1 percent intelligentsia, and 7.8 percent farmers. The new members have reduced the average age of members from 46 to 44 years as more than 90 percent of the new members were under age 35; overall, 20 percent of the membership is under age 35. Over 40 percent of the membership joined the party after the Soviet invasion. Women make up 27.5 percent of the current membership and workers 45 percent.

At the last party congress in 1981, 35.8 percent of the delegates were active members, and 67.3 percent workers by origin. Ethnic representation was 71.2 percent Czech, 25 percent Slovak, 2.4 percent Hungarian, 1.1 percent Ukrainian, and 0.3 percent Polish, German, and Serb.

The Central Committee now numbers 123 full members and 55 candidate members, or one member or candidate for every 8,641 party members.

Thirty-four Central Committee members are women, forty are party officials, twenty are members of government and Parliament, eight are military, three are from the trade union, and eleven are from other mass organizations. Sixteen are workers, eight farmers, eight managers, and sixteen are from the fields of education and culture; the occupations of forty-eight were undetermined.

Sixty different people have been members of the KSC Presidium in the 1946–82 period. Of these, forty-one were Czech, fifteen Slovak, one German, one Ruthenian (the present chief ideologist Vasil Bilàk), one Gypsy (Emil Rigo), and one unknown.

Financing

How the party is financed is not clear. One source indicates a modest dues of three crowns a month (against an average monthly salary now approaching 3,000 crowns, about $300) which would generate 4.5 million crowns a month (about $450,000 at a fair exchange rate). A report of the 1981 KSS Congress noted that the Slovak branch of the party had covered all of its expenses from its own revenue since 1977. One estimate puts the number of full-time party employees in the country at 10,000. If even a conservative 2,000 were estimated to be in Slovakia, the stated dues would hardly be enough to pay labor costs, let alone capital and overhead.

Leadership

Membership in the party Presidium has been remarkably stable over the last decade. Since 1971, there have been only two changes, one of them representing only an addition, and the other the departure of the late president of the republic, Ludvík Svoboda. As a group, they are still comparatively young, most being in their fifties and early sixties. Husák, who turns seventy in 1983, is the senior in age by four years. His tenure owes much to his being a centrist among the leadership. His removal would leave a vacuum and create potential for turmoil. His health has suffered from the ten years he spent in prison. He had an eye operation several years ago and now wears thick lenses.

Present leaders are:

Gustáv Husák, born Dúbravka, Slovakia, January 10, 1913—general secretary of KSC and president of CSSR as well as chairman of the National Front; a moderate.

Lubomír Štrougal, born in Czech Lands, 1924, member of KSC Presidium and prime minister; a moderate.

Vasil Bilàk, born Krajná Bystrá, August 11, 1917,

member of KSC Presidium, secretary for international politics and agitprop. A hardliner, whose Ruthenian nationality makes him an unlikely holder of the top spot.

Jozef Lenárt, born Liptovská Porubka, April 3, 1923, general secretary of the Communist Party of Slovakia, member of KSC Presidium, and chairman of Slovak National Front; a former prime minister and a moderate.

Václav Hulá, born 1925 in Czech Lands, member of Presidium, and until 1981, chairman of State Planning Commission. He may be on the way down, perhaps for reasons of health; a hardliner.

Miloš Jakeš, born 1923 in Czech Lands, member of KSC Presidium and Secretariat; a hardliner.

Josef Kempný, born 1920 in Czech Lands, member of KSC Presidium and secretary for economic affairs.

The party's headquarters are located at Nábr. Ludvíka Svobody 12, 125 11 Prague 1.

Communist Party of Slovakia (*Komunistická Strana Slovenská;* KSS)

While the government of Czechoslovakia has been converted to a federal structure, the party remains asymmetrical because Leninist doctrine dictates there can only be one Communist Party in a country. The separate Communist Party of Slovakia (KSS) operates as "the territorial organization of the KSC in Slovakia." Led since 1969 by First Secretary Jozef Lenárt, the KSS implements KSC policy in Slovakia and coordinates the regional Slovak party organizations. The KSS meets in congress every five years several weeks prior to the KSC congress. It approves the Central Committee report, elects a new Central Committee report, elects a new Central Committee and other Republic-level officials, and listens to speeches. The Central Committee in turn elects a Presidium and a Secretariat. The KSS publishes the daily newspaper *Pravda* and the lively political and cultural weekly *Nové slovo*. Headquarters are located at Hlboká 2, 883 83 Bratislava.

During World War II there was an independent KSS operating underground in the semiindependent Slovak State. After the war, a separate KSS was maintained because it gave the Communists an additional vote within the National Front, but this fiction was ended after the Communists seized power in February 1948.

The KSS played an important role in the liberalization of the 1960s. Alexander Dubček led the Slovak party for five years prior to taking over the helm in Prague, a path his successor Gustav Husák later followed. The always reliable Lenárt may well have remained as the head of the Slovak party for so long because Husák knows Lenárt is not likely to challenge him at the federal level.

For much of its existence, the KSS included a wide variety of views about the proper role of the party and of the relationship of Czechs and Slovaks in the party and in the state. There were right-wingers and left-wingers, doubting intellectuals, Czechoslovak centralists, Slovak nationalists, and those who thought Slovakia should become a republic of the Soviet Union. In 1968 the Slovak Communists were split between those who thought democratization should be the first priority and those who thought federalization was most important. While such broad divisions are not visible among the Slovak party leadership today, it would not be surprising to find them under the surface.

It should be noted that the KSS avoided much of the post–1968 purging. While 500,000 members were dropped in Czechoslovakia as a whole, only 50,000 were removed in Slovakia. And while a fifth of the Czechs lost their political and civil rights and were subjected to employment discrimination, that rarely happened in Slovakia. As of January 1, 1981, the KSS had 388,543 members and candidate members, 70,477 of which had joined the party in the previous five years. Of the new members, 64 percent were workers and 31 percent were women. The Central Committee has ninety-one full and thirty candidate members.

Several weeks before the Soviet invasion of Czechoslovakia in 1968, proposals were set forth creating an equal Communist Party of the Czech Lands. Some experts believe that particular proposal actually triggered the invasion. In fact, a "Bureau for the Conduct of Party Work in the Czech Lands" did operate for a while after the invasion and then quietly went out of business. (Note that there is no separate Communist Party of Russia in the Soviet Union, although republic communist parties operate in all other Soviet Republics.)

Minor Parties & Organizations

Czechoslovak People's Party
(*Československá strana lidová*)

Founded in 1918, this party is based in the Czech Republic. It supports the building of socialism and recognizes the leading role of the KSC. It is a voluntary select organization of "Christian-thinking citizens." Its organ is the daily *Lidová*

demokracie. Its chairman is Zbyněk Zalman. Address: nám. Republiky 7, 111 49 Prague 1.

Czechoslovak Socialist Party
(*Československá strana socialisticka*)

Founded in February 1948 from a rebirth of the Czechoslovak National Socialist Party, it was originally founded in 1897. This party has no relationship to the interwar German party of the same name; rather, it was basically a socialist party with a greater emphasis on nationalism. Its membership seems to include mostly Czech white-collar workers and the urban middle class, reflecting the membership of the prewar party. The party's leader is Bohuslav Kučera; its organ is the daily *Svobodné slovo*. Address: Revoluční 5, 110 15 Prague 1.

The membership of both of the above parties is limited by statute. They are thought to have about 10,000 members each.

Slovak Freedom Party
(*Strana slobody*)

Founded in 1946, it is led by Michal Žakovic and publishes the weekly *Sloboda*. Address: Štefániková 6C, 892 18 Bratislava.

Party of Slovak Rebirth
(*Strana slovenskej obrody*)

Founded in 1948 from the remnants of the postwar Slovak Democratic Party, its chairman is Jozef Mjartan and it publishes the daily *L'ud*. Address: Sedliárska 7, 801 00 Bratislava.

Both the Slovak parties are rather insignificant with only a few hundred active members each. They have seven members in the Slovak National Council of 150 members.

Satellite Organizations

There are a number of mass organizations in Czechoslovakia. Their membership expanded dramatically during the 1970s to the point where being a member of such an organization does not imply any compromise with the system. Not to be a member is a needless challenge to the system. The most important mass organizations include the following:

The Revolutionary Trade Unions (*Revoluční odborové hnutí*), founded in 1945, enrolls nearly all workers in Czechoslovakia as members. Headquartered in Prague (nám. A. Zápotockého 2, 113

59 Prague 3), it has 7,300,000 members. It has the dual duty of supporting state and member interests. In response to the possible influence of the Polish Solidarity movement, it became a little more active in 1981. It holds a congress every five years which elects a Central Council of Unions. The head of the organization is Karel Hoffmann. It publishes the daily newspaper *Práce* in Prague and *Práca* in Bratislava, as well as the weekly *Svět Práce* and the biweekly *Odborář*.

The Socialist Youth Union (*Socialistický svaz mládeže;* SSM) was founded in 1970 to replace the discredited Czechoslovak Youth Union. It includes as members persons aged fourteen to thirty. The leaders are frequently in their forties. The SSM now claims 1.5 million members. The head of the organization is Miloslav Dočkal, and the organization's central headquarters are at nám. M. Gorkého 24, 116 47 Prague 1. It publishes the daily newspapers *Mladá fronta* and *Smena* and the weekly *Mladý svět*, among other publications. The Young Pioneers, which enrolls nearly all children ages six to fifteen, is run by the Youth Union. It claims 1.3 million members.

The Union for Cooperation with the Army (*Svazarm*) claims 900,000 members. It is a voluntary civil and military defense, technical, and sports organization. One of its most important functions in Czechoslovakia is conducting driver's training classes. The chairman is Václav Horaček. It publishes a weekly *Svět motorú*.

The Czechoslovak Union of Women (*Československý svaz žen;* CSZ) was founded in 1974 to assert and protect the interests of working women. Its chairman is Marie Kabrhelová, who sits on the KSC Secretariat. The Czech section of CSZ publishes the weekly *Vlasta*, and the Slovak section the weekly *Slovenka*.

The Union of Czechoslovak–Soviet Friendship (*Svaz Československo–Sovětského Přátelství*), founded in 1948, is devoted to increasing knowledge of and affection for the Soviet Union. Chaired by Václav David, it prints the weekly *Svět socialismu* in both Czech and Slovak editions.

German nationals are represented by the Cultural Union of Citizens of Czechoslovakia of German Nationality (*Kulturní sdružení občanu CSSR německé národnosti*) which publishes the weekly *Prager Volkszeitung.* Hungarian nationals are represented in Csemadok. A Union of the Gypsy population begun in 1968 was closed down five years later. For Polish citizens, there is the Polish Cultural and Adult Education Union *Polský kulturno-osvétovy svaz,* (PZKO) and for Ukrainians, the Cultural Union of Ukranian Workers (*Kultúrny zväz ukrajinských pracújucich*).

Religion

The constitution of Czechoslovakia guarantees religious freedom and the right to exercise religion insofar as it does not involve illegal practices. Religious belief or conviction, for example, may not be used to justify the refusal to perform legal obligations. Eighteen religious groups are recognized, the most important of which are Roman Catholic, Greek Catholic (Uniate), the Czechoslovak Hussite Church, Russian Orthodox, Czech Brethren, Lutheran, and Jewish. Clergy who actively support the party and government are organized in *Pacem in terris* (Catholic) and Christian Unity (Protestant). There are frequent reports of an underground Catholic Church, especially in Slovakia, which opposes the regime. Clergy for the eighteen legal groups are trained at six small theological seminaries.

National Prospects

The policy followed by KSC leaders since the ending of the 1968–69 reform movement will be tested in the 1980s. The party seeks popular participation in the system. Mass organizations now enroll practically all eligible people, and it is implicitly understood by the populace that to oppose the party can be personally costly. In return, the party offers a secure life: guaranteed employment and an improving standard of living. In particular, the party has taken aim at the consumers in the age eighteen-to-fifty population. Cars, housing, color televisions, and country cottages are obtainable. In the decades after Husak came to power, there were no critical shortages of important items. The number of privately owned cars doubled (and tripled in Slovakia). The dissident movement centered in Chapter 77 seems to have little popular support.

The increase in world energy prices has jeopardized this tradeoff. Aging industrial machinery, low labor productivity, energy shortages, and reduced East-West trade caused by the martial-law crackdown in Poland point to serious economic problems and a probable increase in dissatisfaction. The country's leaders in early 1982 raised prices on food by as much as 50 percent, and other prices have also gone up. Any decline in the standard of living could threaten the unspoken agreement with the populace.

There is little potential for change in the Communist Party leadership. In time, the 40 percent of the party that is new will hanker for greater influence, but the men who came to power with Husák, who are still mostly in their fifties, are unlikely to welcome competitors for power. Even very limited reform proposals are drowned in a sea of criticism because of fears a new Prague Spring might result. Economic change and modernization cannot be delayed much longer, however. In the interim, inertia holds the system together.

Further Reading

Korbel, Josef. *Twentieth Century Czechoslovakia: The Meaning of Her History.* New York: Columbia University Press, 1977.

Kusin, Vladimir. *From Dubček to Chapter 77: A Study of "Normalization" in Czechoslovakia 1968–1978.* New York: St. Martin's Press, 1978.

Mamatey, Victor S. and Luža, Radomír, eds. *A History of the Czechoslovak Republic, 1918–1948.* Princeton: Princeton University Press, 1973.

Paul, David W. *The Cultural Limits of Revolutionary Politics: Change and Continuity in Socialist Czechoslovakia.* New York: Columbia University Press, 1979.

Skilling, H. Gordon. *Czechoslovakia's Interrupted Revolution.* Princeton: Princeton University Press, 1976.

Suda, Zdenek. *Zealots and Rebels: A History of the Ruling Communist Party of Czechoslovakia.* Stanford, California: Hoover Institute Press, Stanford University, 1980.

Taborsky, Edward A. *Communism in Czechoslovakia 1948–1960.* Princeton: Princeton University Press, 1961.

Ulč, Otto. *Politics in Czechoslovakia.* San Francisco: W. H. Freeman & Co., 1974.

DENMARK
(*Kongeriget Danmark*)
by Alastair H. Thomas, Ph.D.

The System of Government

Denmark is a constitutional monarchy. The current constitution, which dates from 1953, consolidated broadly agreed changes of detail made in the country's political institutions as part of a process of peaceful development, the main lines of which can be traced back to the adoption of the 1665 June Constitution. The monarchical dynasty goes back even further and is the oldest in Europe; the national flag *Dannebrog*, a white cross on a red ground, traditionally dates from 1219.

The unitary constitution applies to Denmark proper and to the Faroe Islands and Greenland, with a total population of 5.1 million (1981). The Faroe Islands, north of Britain, have been a "self-governing community within the kingdom of Denmark" since 1948. Greenland, "an equal part of the kingdom of Denmark" since 1953, has had home rule since 1979. The sparse populations of both territories are heavily dependent on fishing, and number some 50,000 (mostly Eskimos) in Greenland and 42,000 in the Faroes.

Executive

Denmark has a parliamentary system of cabinet government. The parliamentary principle has operated since 1901, and the constitution requires that "No Minister shall continue in office after the Parliament [*Folketinget*] has expressed no confidence in him." The cabinet of about twenty members is headed by the prime minister (*Statsminister*), and is officially appointed by the monarch after consultation with the leaders of all the political parties represented in Parliament. In practice, the parliamentary party groups make a recommendation based upon their assessment of the political situation (usually following a parliamentary election) and of the prospects of forming a government which will incorporate their own views and those of their close allies. The parties usually indicate one of the two or three party leaders capable of forming such a government. Based on her assessment of this advice, the monarch then appoints one such leader to form a government. Initially, a condition of the appointment is that the government should have a parliamentary majority. If this proves impossible in the complex multiparty relationships which prevail, an alternative party leader may be appointed, or the condition may be reduced to "a broadly based government." A single-party minority government may be accepted finally as the only real possibility.

Politically, the main limitation on the powers of the government is imposed by the multiparty system and the fact that no party in this century has obtained a parliamentary majority. Therefore, governments must seek the support of at least one and probably several other parties for their policies. This support may take the form of a majority coalition (1957–64, 1968–71), a minority coalition (1950–53, 1978–79, 1982–) or a minority government with the parliamentary support of several parties for an agreed set of policies for an agreed period. For example, the Jorgensen Social Democratic (SD) government of 1975 to 1978 relied on the parties of the center-right—Radical Liberals (RV), Christian People's Party (KF), Center Democrats (CD), and Liberals (V)—for its financial policies, but exchanged the support of the Radical Liberals for that of the Conservative People's Party (KF) on military expenditure.

Additional limitations on executive power are imposed by constitutional referendum provisions, introduced in 1953 when the upper house was abolished. These come into effect if sovereignty is ceded, even in part, to an international authority (as in 1972 when Denmark joined the European Communities), or if a change in voting age is proposed. Constitutional amendment also requires that a proposal must be passed by two successive parliaments, with an intervening election. The amendment must then be put to a referendum in

DANISH GOVERNMENTS (1968 TO PRESENT)		
Years	Parties	Prime Minister
1968–71	Conservative, Liberal, Radical majority	Hilmar Baunsgaard (RV)
1971–72	Social Democrat minority	Jens Otto Krag (SD)
1972–73	Social Democrat minority	Anker Jorgensen (SD)
1973–75	Liberal minority	Poul Hartling (V)
1975–78	Social Democrat minority	Anker Jorgensen (SD)
1978–79	Social Democrat, Liberal minority	Anker Jorgensen (SD)
1979–82	Social Democrat minority	Anker Jorgensen (SD)
1982–	Conservative, Liberal, Center Democrat, Christian People's minority	Poul Schlüter (KF)

which a majority of those voting *and* at least 40 percent of those entitled to vote must approve the amendment if it is to take effect. The constitution has not been amended since 1953.

The hereditary monarch, Queen Margrethe II, succeeded her father in 1972. She appoints the cabinet, within the limits of the parliamentary circumstances, and presides over the Council of State which gives formal assent to legislation. Otherwise her functions are ceremonial and representational. Ministers have sole responsibility for government decisions, but bills and government orders acquire legal validity when signed by the monarch with the countersignature of one or more ministers. Constitutionally, legislative power is vested jointly in the monarch and the *Folketing*, executive power in the monarch, and judicial powers in the courts. In political reality, these powers are only exercised through a cabinet responsible to a popularly elected Parliament or through a judiciary independent of legislature and executive.

Legislature

The unicameral *Folketing* has a maximum term of four years, but elections have been held every second year since 1971. Of the 179 members, two each are elected from the Faroes and Greenland and the remaining 175 by a closely proportional electoral system. The newly elected Parliament convenes autonomously after an election, determines the validity of its members' election, and chooses its own presiding officer (*formand*) and his deputies—in practice by election on the nomination of the parties. Parliamentary sessions begin on the first Tuesday in October and average 300 plenary sitting hours per year (1963–74), spread over about 117 days through to May. Parliament recesses at Christmas, Easter, and for sessions of the transnational Nordic Council in Feb-

ruary and March. Much of the work is done in the twenty-three standing committees which have areas of competence broadly complementary to those of the main ministries; there are also committees on standing orders, proof of elections, scientific research, energy policy, and Common Market policy. One-third of the members of Parliament may force a referendum on legislation within three days of its final parliamentary reading. The referendum must then be held within eighteen days, and the bill is rejected only if the majority against it comprises at least 30 percent of those entitled to vote. Financial and nationality legislation is excluded from this referendum procedure. This opposition device was used once, in 1963, to reject a group of four bills seeking to change certain aspects of land law.

Within Parliament, party groups play an essential role, although they are not mentioned in law or standing orders. They choose members of committees, party floor leaders, and spokesmen; they meet each day of a parliamentary session to determine the party's view on forthcoming business; and they maintain the high levels of party cohesion and discipline which are characteristic of Danish parliamentary behavior.

The Social Democrats have predominated in cabinet office since 1929, but have had to seek support from nonsocialist parties. Until 1973, this support came from the Radical Liberals. Only two periods, 1966 to 1968 and 1971 to 1973, saw an aggregate socialist majority in the *Folketing*, but in neither case were the SD and the Socialist People's Party (SF) able to agree on EEC and NATO policy. The SD was forced to seek parliamentary support from other parties on an issue-to-issue basis.

Jens Otto Krag, SD prime minister, successfully negotiated Danish EEC membership. While doing so he was secured in office by the Liberals and some Radical Liberals, the agrarian supporters of

DENMARK *FOLKETING* ELECTIONS (1971–1981)

	1971 Votes %	1971 Seats Won	1973 Votes %	1973 Seats Won	1975 Votes %	1975 Seats Won	1977 Votes %	1977 Seats Won	1979 Votes %	1979 Seats Won	1981 Votes %	1981 Seats Won
Center Democrats (SD)		—	7.8	14	2.2	4	6.4	11	3.2	6	8.3	15
Christian People's Party (KrF)		—	4.0	7	5.3	9	3.4	6	2.6	5	2.3	4
Communists (DKP)		—	3.6	6	4.2	7	3.7	7		—		—
Conservative People's Party (KF)	16.7	31	9.2	16	5.5	10	8.5	15	12.5	22	14.4	25
Justice Party (DRF)		—	2.9	5		—	3.3	6	2.6	5	1.4	0
Left Socialists (VS)		—		—	2.1	4	2.7	5	3.6	6	2.6	5
Liberals (Venstre; V)	15.6	30	12.3	22	23.3	42	12.0	21	12.5	22	11.3	21
Progress Party (FP)		—	15.9	28	13.6	24	14.6	26	11.0	20	8.9	16
Radical Liberals (RV)	14.4	27	11.2	20	7.1	13	3.6	6	5.4	10	5.1	9
Social Democrats (SD)	37.3	70	25.7	46	29.9	53	37.1	65	38.2	68	32.9	59
Socialist People's Party (SF)	9.1	17	6.0	11	5.0	9	3.9	7	6.0	11	11.3	21
Faroese representatives		2		2		2		2		2		2
Greenland representatives		2		2		2		2		2		2
Total seats		179		179		179		179		179		179
Turnout, percent	87.2		88.7		88.2		88.7		85.6		82.7	

both parties being keen to benefit from the agriculture policy of the European Economic Community (EEC); and also by the Conservative, whose industrialist supporters also foresaw substantial benefits from membership. Entry into the EEC was opposed by some Radical Liberals, by some trade unionists within the Social Democrats, and by the Socialist People's Party.

The Social Democrats were continuously in power from 1975 to 1982—in coalition with the Liberals in 1978–79—but otherwise with the parliamentary acquiescence of shifting majorities from the small parties of the center-left: Center Democrats, Christian People's Party, Radical Liberals, and, on various issues, Liberals or Conservatives.

The period since 1973 has seen a highly fragmented Parliament with about ten parties represented, as opposed to the four or five of earlier times. Electoral opinion has been volatile, continuity of parliamentary membership low, and the problem of government formation difficult and sometimes protracted. In 1975 thirty-five days elapsed between the election date and the formation of the government; a period of one to two weeks is more common.

Judiciary

As a logical consequence of the codified constitution, there is a right of judicial review of legislation alleged to be unconstitutional. The courts do not refuse such cases, but in each of the instances (about ten so far this century) the Supreme Court has always found the law to be constitutional. Executive orders which do not conform to the enabling legislation have been struck down, but the courts cannot override the discretionary decisions of the executive unless the influence of extraneous considerations can be shown. The judiciary assert their independence of the other branches of government by maintaining an apolitical stance. The most effective remedy available to citizens in dispute with the administration is through the *Ombudsmand* of the *Folketing*, whose opinions are usually accepted by the authorities.

Regional & Local Government

The country is divided into 277 districts (*kommuner*), each having a council elected every four years and headed by a mayor (*borgmester*) who acts as chairman and heads the local administration of schools, social welfare, homes for the aged, child care, and visiting nurses. Mayoral authority is shared with committees appointed by the council, usually proportionally representative of the party composition of the council. Fourteen county districts (*amtskommuner*) have broader responsibilities for hospitals, highways, and aspects of social welfare and education. Fourteen counties (*amter*), each headed by an *amtmand*, are mainly concerned with administering family law and deciding appeals on social-welfare cases. The capital, Copenhagen, has a fifty-five–member council (*borgerrepraesentation*) elected for four years and an eleven-member executive (*magistrat*). The latter is elected by the council for an eight-year term and is comprised of a mayor, five *borgmestre* and five aldermen. Party lists for council elections are usually created by the national parties, but they sometimes reflect a bipartisan alliance or special consideration of a specific local issue. Turnout is generally lower (60 percent for county elections, 49 percent in Copenhagen in 1974) than in parliamentary elections (89 percent three months earlier).

The Faroe Islands have had home rule since 1948, with an elected *Løgtingid* or assembly of thirty-two members to which a four-member *Landsstyrid* (cabinet) headed by a *Lagmand* (prime minister) is responsible for the devolved administration of local affairs. Foreign affairs, civil and criminal law, social welfare, church affairs, and education are regulated by the central Danish government; the islands elect two representatives to the *Folketing*. Similar arrangements for Greenland came into effect in 1979.

The Electoral System

The *Folketing* is elected directly by secret ballot within a party-list system of proportional representation in multimember constituencies. The number of members per constituency varies from two in Bornholm to fifteen for the capital. The Danish electoral system is one of the most complex in the world and cannot be fully explained here. It allows parties to use three different types of party lists, plus combinations of those three, and to use different types in different constituencies. It also permits the voter to choose one of three different ways of registering a preference. Finally, a two-tier allocation procedure first distributes 135 seats in the seventeen constituencies by a complex formula (modified St. Laguë). Forty supplementary seats are distributed on the basis of the total national vote received by each party, taking into account the allocation of the 135 constituency mandates. Two percent is the effective threshold for the representation of small parties, but otherwise very closely proportional results are achieved through the allocation of the supplementary mandates. Revision of constituency boundaries, most recently in 1970, helps to ensure equivalence of number of votes per seat, as does the supplementary seat system.

The ballot itself shows a list of candidates grouped under party names, and the parties are also lettered (A for the Social Democrats through Z for the Progress Party) to facilitate identification. Candidates are nominated from and associated with one of the 103 nomination districts within the seventeen constituencies. Normally parties nominate a candidate in each district, but smaller parties may have fewer candidates. Nonparty candidates can also stand.

Names on each list may be arranged in one of three different ways. The usual form, by its arrangement of names, permits the voter to cast his vote in one of three different ways: for the party, for the candidate nominated in the voter's own district, or for one of the candidates from another district within the constituency. Both party votes and personal votes are attributed to the party's candidates and the candidate(s) of the party with the largest number of votes is/are elected. The party-list form, where a party ranks candidates according to its own priorities, is also used. A simultaneous-list arrangement of names permits all of a party's candidates to be nominated simultaneously in all the nomination districts of the constituency. Thus, within a closely proportional overall result, candidates may still retain a clear identification with a nomination district (averaging 35,000 voters in size), and a voter may exercise both an effective personal vote for candidates and a party preference.

There are no by-elections, as vacancies are filled by the candidate of the same party having the next-largest number of votes, so that the party balance of the Parliament remains fixed from one election to the next, unless *Folketing* members break away from their party.

All Danish citizens of eighteen or over have the vote provided they have not formally been declared incapable of managing their own affairs and if they are permanently resident in the kingdom. This has been extended to include the diplomatic service abroad and people working for the state in such international organizations as the European Communities. The voting age was reduced from twenty-five to twenty-three in 1953, to twenty-one in 1961, to twenty in 1971, and to eighteen in 1978.

Voting normally is conducted at polling stations, but voters in prison, hospital, aboard ship, on remote islands, abroad, or housebound may vote by post. The voter marks a cross on the ballot paper against the preferred party or candidate. Blank or invalid votes are not more than about 0.6 percent of the poll. Voter turnout ranges between 80 and 90 percent. A turnout of 82.7 percent in

1981 was the lowest since 1953 and is attributed partly to heavy snow on polling day and partly to increased apathy among voters. The electoral register is kept by each municipal authority. It is renewed every January and interim changes are also noted, so there is little reason for omissions.

The Party System

Origins of the Parties

The Danish party system began to emerge in the last thirty years of the nineteenth century. The Liberal Party originated in opposition to the conservatism of large landowners and a professional class who dominated the upper house (*Landstinget*) of Parliament. Despite growing opposition to their policies in the lower house (*Folketinget*), the king continued to choose his ministers from this conservative group, which organized in 1876 as the United Right (*Højre*). The Liberal aim of constitutional and democratic government, based on the principle that a government should at least not face majority opposition in the lower house, was conceded in 1901.

In 1905 the Radical Liberals broke away from the Liberals primarily over the taxation of smallholders, although it also differed from the parent party in other respects. The Social Democrats, Radicals, Liberals, and Conservatives are known as "the four old parties." Ranging ideologically from left to right, respectively, they have dominated the process of government formation during the twentieth century. In the 1946–81 period, Social Democrats have been represented in government 75 percent of the time, Radicals and Liberals 31 percent, and Conservatives 19 percent. The only other party to share in cabinet formation during this period was the Justice Party (DRF), which was represented in the 1957–60 majority coalition with the Social Democrats and Radicals, when its main function was to give the coalition its minimal majority.

The 1973 election marked an end to the system of four or five parties. The Communist Party (DKP), the Left Socialists (VS), and the Justice Party (unrepresented since 1960) were returned to Parliament. In addition three new parties gained representation for the first time: the Center Democrats, which had just broken away from the Social Democrats; the Christian People's Party, which sought to make a moral stand against "permissiveness"; and the Progress Party (FP), a populist movement against taxation and "paper-shuffling bureaucracy." A consequence of this fragmentation has been that Denmark has not had a majority government since 1971; legislation is enacted by the government party with parliamentary support partly based on specific policy agreements and partly ad hoc.

The Parties in Law

Parties are not mentioned in the constitution and receive very little mention elsewhere in the law. Individual candidates require the signatures of only twenty-five local voters for nomination. To take part in elections, a party must meet one of two conditions. If it was represented in Parliament after the previous election and remains so when an election is called, the Interior Ministry is formally notified of this fact by Parliament's presiding officer; no other formality is required. Other parties, including those formed in Parliament by a party split, must apply to the Interior Ministry for recognition, accompanied by the signatures of a number of voters corresponding to 1/175 of the total valid votes cast at the previous election—about 18,000 after the 1979 election.

State support for political parties is in the form of an annual grant to the parliamentary group calculated as a basic amount plus a sum related to the size of the group, in total about 8 million kroner ($1 million). This grant finances the work of the group and is spent on office equipment and supplies, to appoint experts, or commission research, etc. It is generally not used to support party organizations outside Parliament.

Party Organization

Since the establishment in the 1920s of mass-party organizations based on individual membership, especially by the Social Democratics, this pattern has been followed by the other parties. During the 1920s and 1930s related youth organizations were also established and, at least for the larger parties, are still important for recruiting members and giving them early experience of political participation and responsibility. With the exception of the Progress Party, whose populist origins and iconoclastic attitude to established practices have been its distinguishing features and which has therefore attracted individuals who have not previously been involved in party politics, most leading politicians hold a party position early in their careers. A successful politician's career also frequently shows close involvement in local politics and/or related professional or interest organizations. Danish party leaders' authority rests on election to office, usually by their parliamentary colleagues with subsequent confirmation from the party's national conference.

Party activity has shifted somewhat from the local to the national level. The Social Democrats and the Liberals, with distinctive social bases among, respectively, blue-collar workers and farmers, have remained the best organized at the local level, where they have retained a strong membership base and a network of branches. In the 1950s, all the party organizations together enrolled about one-third of the voters as members. Since then, party membership has declined markedly, although less for Liberals and Social Democrats. Local party branches are nevertheless important for raising funds and nominating candidates for election, and they jealously protect their rights from the national party.

The national party seeks to involve the local branches in forming party programs, which in Denmark take the form of a set of broad principles intended to stand for a decade rather than a detailed manifesto prepared for each election. The Social Democrats have permitted party branches to reconsider their choice of candidate before each election. The result has been to increase the turnover of local party representatives and the number of personal votes received by their candidates. The need for local party organizations was reduced, in part, by television campaigning, introduced in 1954. The large gains by the Radical Liberals in 1968 were attributed to the success of their leader, Hilmar Baunsgaard, on television. The personalities of their leaders were notable factors in the success of the Center Democrats and the Progress Party during the 1970s. Indeed, the newer parties have not built up the mass structures of their older counterparts. They have relied instead on locally organized and financed campaigns and have then had to accommodate the national aspirations of local activists, sometimes giving rise to party factionalism and swings in the parties' electoral fortunes. In structure, these newer parties are closer to cadre parties than to mass parties.

Party discipline within Parliament is maintained mainly by a strongly held norm of party solidarity which requires dissident views to be made known, and justified, to the parliamentary group meeting held before each day's parliamentary session. In the 1970s, 87 percent of bills were passed without any break in the unity of any of the parties. The socialist parties were least likely to be internally divided, but even the Radical Liberals, with the highest level of internal divisions of any of the parties, were united in 94 percent of the final votes on all bills during the decade.

Campaigning

While campaign posters are much in evidence and there is some newspaper advertising, a modern electoral campaign relies heavily on media coverage in the neewspapers and, especially, on television. An equal-time rule ensures that each party obtains equal television coverage: this tends to favor the smaller parties and the parties with leaders who perform well on television.

The "four old parties" each used to publish their own daily newspaper in most of the larger towns. In 1945 there were 130 such newspapers, but by 1979 there were only forty-nine, ten of them published in Copenhagen. The Liberal Party's newspapers have best resisted decline, and twenty-three are still published. Seven papers originally affiliated to the Conservatives remain, as do four linked to the Radical Liberals, and two to the Social Democrats. The process of concentration has been especially marked in the Social Democrats' case. Newspapers' political ties are also much less pronounced than earlier, and more than half are now wholly or largely independent of political parties, although still appealing to opinions held by specific sections of the population.

Campaign funds are raised largely from membership dues, which generally are collected by local branches and a proportion transferred to the national party. The basic dues may be supplemented by donations, but these do not attract tax concessions and therefore are generally not large. Special-interest organizations are an important source of finance—trade unions for the Social Democrats, industry and the employers for the Conservatives and the Liberals. The trade-union donations are usually for a specific purpose such as an election campaign or to support an affiliated newspaper. The possibility that such trade-union donations might go to one of the parties to the left of the Social Democrats has been raised intermittently during the 1970s. Clearly dependence on organizational sources of finance may at times be

ESTIMATED TOTAL PARTY EXPENDITURE ON THE 1979 ELECTION

	Danish kroner	U.S. $ (approx.)
Conservatives	1,500,000	188,000
Liberals	2,000,000	250,000
Social Democrats	4,500,000	563,000
Other parties (in total)	3,000,000	375,000
TOTAL	11,000,000	1,375,000

a significant sanction in the hands of the organizations.

Independent Voters

Greater use of television has increased the tendency for voters to be influenced by issues rather than social allegiances. Opinion has become more volatile than in the 1950s and a much higher proportion of voters change their voting intention during the election campaign than in the past.

Independent candidates are insignificant in a system which sets such low barriers to party formation. In 1977, nine of the 1,129 candidates were independent of a party, and they obtained 317 votes altogether, about 0.01 percent of the poll.

Center Democrats
(*Centrum-Demokraterne;* CD)

History

The CD broke away from the Social Democrats—and thus precipitated the 1973 election—in opposition to the SD's move to the left and, in particular, to protest the way that taxation bore more heavily on a person who owned rather than rented his house. Support comes from a younger and more middle-class sector than those who vote for SD and has fluctuated from election to election.

Organization

The basic units of organization are local clubs and discussion groups, each of which can send one delegate for each fifteen members to the party's national assembly. The national assembly is the highest authority in organizational matters and the body which elects the thirty-one–member National Council and the nine-member National Executive. The parliamentary group is independent of these bodies but is represented on the National Council and nominates the party chairman for election by the assembly. Choices of parliamentary candidates are made within a year after each parliamentary election in a way which makes it easy to include new nominees. The structure thus encourages participation by members in the choice of leaders and the discussion of issues, but imposes few policy constraints on elected representatives.

The party headquarters are at Laksegade 12, 1063 Copenhagen K.

Policy

While drawing on "bourgeois" occupational groups for support, the CD opposes the formation of bourgeois and socialist party blocs. In this it justifies its centrist name, supporting the SD minority governments which prevailed during the 1970s as long as they recognized the center-right predominance of opinion in the *Folketing*. The difficulty for the leadership is to hold together the leftward tendency implied by this support for SD and the more rightward inclinations of the party's electorate. The latter has led the party to join the Conservative group in the European Parliament.

In domestic policy, the CD opposes the corporatism of trade-union influence on political parties and wishes to maintain a balance between public and private sectors of the economy. The party has extensive policies on education and culture and advocates standards of minimum competence in both intellectual and practical subjects. The CD wishes to ensure that state grants to cultural activities are made independently of their political content and that time on the state radio is allocated with fair and comprehensive regard to the political and other viewpoints of society, and with a right of reply guaranteed.

In foreign policy the party supports membership in both NATO and the EEC, higher defense spending, and closer European cooperation in economic and especially political matters.

Membership & Constituency

The CD claimed 2,100 members for the period 1981–82, a ratio to its voters of 1 to 100, the lowest such ratio of any party. The party is also the most heavily dependent on nonmanual employees and those in the 40–61 age range for support. It gains slightly more of its votes from the provincial towns than any of the other parties and appeals less to rural voters. The party has attracted the more middle-class, white-collar, better-educated, and middle-aged groups who might otherwise have supported the Social Democrats.

Financing

Annual membership dues for the period 1981–82 were 90 kroner (about $11), or 120 kroner for a married couple, 30 for junior members, and 15 for pensioners. Additional funds came from state support for the parliamentary party group.

Leadership

The party's founder and chairman is Erhard Jakobsen (born 1917), a well-known radio and tele-

DEMOGRAPHIC BASIS OF PARTY SUPPORT

Party	Minor Socialist Parties: SF, VS, DKP %	SD %	FP %	V %	KF %	CD %	Socialist Parties: RV, KrFP, DRF %	Whole Sample %
Occupation								
Manual workers	38	56	35	16	4	19	22	37
Nonmanual employees	45	36	30	26	46	58	47	39
Urban employers	3	5	20	7	30	17	12	10
Farmers	1	1	13	50	8	3	17	11
Students, etc.	13	2	2	1	2	3	2	3
Education								
Primary only	44	78	74	74	47	48	61	68
More than primary	56	22	26	26	53	52	39	32
Age								
20–29	49	15	21	14	7	14	19	19
30–39	23	21	25	19	16	24	19	21
40–61	20	35	43	39	39	45	36	36
Over 61	8	29	11	28	39	17	26	24
Sex								
Male	47	45	56	51	43	50	43	47
Female	53	55	44	49	57	50	57	53
Residence								
Rural	17	27	27	71	25	22	39	35
Provincial towns	31	43	43	23	41	46	35	37
Copenhagen area	52	30	30	6	38	32	26	28
N =	(171)	(697)	(185)	(208)	(122)	(107)	(168)	(1,164)

vision personality who has been active in politics for many years. He was mayor of Gladsakse (a suburb of Copenhagen) from 1958 to 1974, chairman of the European Movement in Denmark from 1964 to 1973, and one of the founders of a media pressure group (Active Listeners and Viewers) in 1976. The Center Democrats' fluctuating electoral fortunes have discouraged the emergence of an obvious successor, but Arne Melchoir (born 1924) has held important offices in the party and the *Folketing* over the past five years. In the Conservative-led coalition in 1982, Melchior was minister of public works.

Prospects

The Party's prospects are dependent on the ability to counter pressures from left and right, to retain voter support for its issue-orientation to politics, and to move away from undue reliance on the leadership of its founder.

The Conservative People's Party (*Det konservative folkeparti;* KF)

History

The origins of the party can be traced to the United Right (*Højre*), a grouping formed in 1876 from the landowners and their upper-class supporters in the *Landsting* (upper house), together with the more numerous National Liberals, intellectuals and academics who became increasingly conservative as the farmers in the Liberal Party became increasingly influential. The United Right lost its dominance in 1901 and its residues joined with a group called Free Conservatives to form the KF in December 1915, a party which explicitly accepted the constitutional and tax reforms of its opponents.

Apart from the united front wartime coalitions of 1940 to 1943 and 1945, the KF had to wait until 1950 to enter government. Its minority coalition with the Liberals (*Venstre*) successfully carried through a major reform of the constitution, which also had the support of the Radicals and the Social Democrats. Thereafter, the SD reasserted its dominance and the KF was out of office again until 1968. In that year, the KF joined with *Venstre* again, and the two parties were able to persuade the Radicals to make up a Radical-led majority coalition. Participation in this government associated the KF with pay-as-you-earn taxation, introduced by a Conservative finance minister, and with the abolition of censorship of obscene publications, carried through by Knud Thestrup as minister of justice and Conservative Party leader. Elements of the party were alienated by both these measures, and their votes were lost to the Progress Party and the Christian People's Party, respectively, in 1973.

In 1982 Poul Schlüter became the first Conservative prime minister since 1901, at the head of a government comprising eight Conservatives, eight Liberals, four Center Democrats, and one member of the Christian People's Party. With the backing of sixty-six of the 179 members of Parliament this government will have to attract support from the Progress Party and the Radicals, or the Social Democrats, in order to survive.

Organization

The party is branch based, but direction of its affairs is centralized. The parliamentary group proposes directions for party policy for debate by the national council, a relatively large body which is the party's highest authority in political matters and which elects its own director and the chairman of the party. The directorate (*repraesentska-bet*) is the highest organizational authority, linked through county committees to local branches. The branch is expected to report at least annually to the head office. Its purpose is defined as being a meeting place for conservative electors and a base for spreading conservative policy. It nominates parliamentary and local council candidates, but must first allow the county committee an opportunity to discuss its choice.

The party headquarters are at Vesterbrogade 40, 1620 Copenhagen V.

Policy

As in Norway and Sweden, the Danish Conservative Party has had to compete for existence with a substantial Liberal party and with parties of the center. At the same time, it has sought to avoid the reactionary label which conservatism has implied elsewhere in Europe. Its only prospect of power was in cooperation with Liberals, but it also wished to remain distinct from them.

The party wishes to reduce the role of the state, to reduce and simplify taxation and legislation, to reward individual initiative, and to encourage trade in free and equal competition. It is KF policy that all should be able to save money and to own property; to encourage this, an anti-inflation policy should be pursued. Tax law should help to extend share ownership to employees of large companies, who should also have a say in decisions affecting their workplace and community.

Conservatives have always advocated substantial defense expenditure within NATO, with increases to cover continuous modernization and to meet a perceived increase in the threat to NATO countries. The party, supported by employers and industrialists, is a keen supporter of EEC membership as another way of ensuring external security and the expansion of trade. It also wishes to see a common energy policy developed by the EEC and in the Organization for Economic Cooperation and Development, with less reliance on oil, more nuclear power, and greater energy conservation.

Membership & Constituency

Membership in 1982 was reported at 50,000, a figure which was on the increase after a decline during the 1970s. The KF thus has just less than half as many members as *Venstre* and numerically is the third-largest party. The ratio of members to voters is 11 percent, a relatively low figure which reflects KF's steady and rapid electoral growth since the heavy losses of the 1975 election. The party is strongly supported by urban employers and also attracts a disproportionately large share of nonmanual employees, including upper-level white-collar workers. Supporters tend to be well educated, over forty, and residents of Copenhagen or provincial towns rather than rural areas. The party organizational structure includes an educational association, the Conservative Women's Organization, and the Young Conservatives. Despite the efforts of the Young Conservatives, the party's appeal to younger voters is very low in comparison to the other main parties.

Financing

The party is financed by subscriptions and donations from members. Typically these are at the rate of 100 kroner ($12) annually, but vary among party branches. Branches contribute 18 kroner per member to the national party. The other significant source of income is the state grant to all parliamentary party groups.

Leadership

Leadership disputes in the late 1960s and early 1970s left the party weak, so weak that Erik Ninn-Hansen, then a leading member of the party and now the senior member of the *Folketing*, proposed an amalgamation of nonsocialist parties in 1975. Poul Schlüter (born 1929) was elected chairman of the parliamentary group in 1974 and has consolidated his position as party leader and chief spokesman, taking the office of prime minister in 1982. He also held office as national chairman from 1974 to 1977. He was succeeded as national chairman by Ib Stetter (born 1917), who has also been vice chairman of the parliamentary group since 1971.

Prospects

Patient tactics of giving conditional support for some of the policies of the minority SD government—while at the same time offering the electorate a center-right alternative in cooperation with Liberals, CD, and Krf—have brought electoral rewards. The right-wing Progress Party has declined, and in 1981 the KF regained their 1971 position as the second largest party in the *Folketing* and as the leading nonsocialist party. But the nonsocialists remain fragmented and even the KF and *Venstre* together are far smaller than the SD. In the Danish pattern of flexible interparty cooperation, the 1982 Conservative-led coalition government could choose to rely on the Progress Party and the Radicals, or on the SD, for support.

Liberal Party
(*Venstre, Danmarks liberale parti;* V)

History

The Liberals were founded in 1870, the first organized modern political party in Denmark, and led the struggle against the monarchy to secure recognition of the principle of parliamentary majoritarian government. This they achieved in 1901 after increasingly bitter struggles with the Conservatives. Since 1945, the Liberals have participated in five governments: alone in minority governments twice (1945–47; 1973–75); with the

Conservatives in minority coalition (1950–53); in majority coalition with the Conservatives and the Radical Liberals (1968–71); and in minority coalitions under Social Democratic leadership (1978–79), and under the Conservatives in 1982. In the 1982 government, they held the key ministries of finance and foreign affairs, as well as those of economy, energy, and education.

Organization

With its large and flourishing membership, the party is organized at four levels: local associations in *kommunes* (the smallest units of local government); constituency organizations formed of the local associations within the constituency; county organizations, with the task of extending local activities and putting on political meetings and courses; and at the national level, the Executive Committee and an annual national meeting. The national meeting decides the party program and the activities of affiliated organizations. It comprises constituency representatives, the National Executive, the parliamentary group, ministers, and parliamentary candidates, European Parliament members and candidates, members of the youth organization, and Liberal newspaper editors. The Executive Committee is chaired by the national chairman and is a large body, including the chairmen and vice chairmen of county, parliamentary, editorial, youth, and other organizational structures within the party. Although subsidiary only to the national meeting, the Executive Committee has authority to discuss policy and to negotiate with the parliamentary group on policy matters.

The party's headquarters are at Søllerødvej 30, 2840 Holte.

Policy

The party's guiding principles include freedom, exercised responsibly, to think, believe, and speak, expressed as the wish to be able to test one's opinions in free debate. Individual freedom is limited only by the rights of others to freedom and the vital interests of the community, the task of which is to care for the weak, establish a common framework for society, and ensure that it is respected and maintained.

The detailed application of these principles has been worked out at great length, as befits a party which has been in government three times during the 1970s. In particular, men and women are accorded equal rights; cooperative housing is encouraged; a high priority is given to education, culture, and the church, with support for the established church and freedom for minority beliefs.

In economic policy, the party stands for full employment and economic growth, with a reduction of public-sector consumption; greater equality of distribution of capital; and better opportunities for individual employees to become co-owners and coresponsible for their work. Although illiberal, an incomes policy may be necessary to ensure competitiveness and a balance between consumption and investment. (The 1978–79 government broke up over the Liberals' advocacy of a freeze on wages and prices, which the SD opposed.) Monetary policy should attempt to expand production and improve foreign-exchange earnings, so as to reduce interest rates and improve the supply of capital. Energy policy should encourage conservation and the development of wind and sun power to supplement greater use of coal and natural gas. Nuclear power should only be developed when its safety is guaranteed for the population.

In foreign policy, the Liberals have always been strongly internationalist. The Nordic Council should be expanded. The EEC should be open to all democratic European countries, with policies carried out in ways which do not make its institutions an end in themselves and with stronger links to the wider world. Development aid should benefit the poorest countries and should be coupled with an open trade policy, and Denmark should seek greater involvement in the U.N. Security policy rests on membership in NATO, the EEC, and the U.N. A real chance of relaxing tensions between East and West is seen to lie in a balance of military forces.

Membership & Constituency

The Liberals are second only to the SD in membership. Both parties have built their strength on the clearly defined social sectors whose interests they represent, farmers in the case of *Venstre* and workers in the case of SD. However, both parties have seen these sectors decline in homogeneity and numbers, especially during the 1970s. This decline is reflected in *Venstre's* membership which fell from 129,000 in 1971 to 95,000 in 1981. Yet, the ratio of members to voters is 27 percent—only the Communist Party, which claims 29 percent, is better organized in this respect.

The strength which the members-to-voters ratio suggests has helped the Liberals to hold a leading position among the nonsocialist parties during the 1970s (they were surpassed electorally by the Conservatives in 1981). Liberal support is drawn heavily from the farming and rural community. The party is often referred to as the Agrarian Liberals, the Danish counterpart of the center parties in Finland, Norway, and Sweden. In 1970, it added to its name to emphasize its liberalism, but has had only limited success in attracting urban voters. The party and its parliamentary group maintain close links with the large interest organizations, especially in the agricultural sector, in part formally and in part through membership of working groups established by the party.

Financing

Membership dues are set by each branch and range from 50 to 125 kroner annually (about $6 to $15); of this, 38 kroner ($5) goes to the national party. The party also receives donations from individuals and organizations, and benefits from its still large network of provincial newspapers.

Leadership

Venstre was led by Poul Hartling from 1965 until his appointment as U.N. High Commissioner for Refugees in 1977. He was succeeded as national party chairman by Henning Christophersen (born 1939), who had been party spokesman (floor leader) since 1973. Hartling's relationship with Anker Jørgensen, the SD leader, had been antagonistic. Christophersen was much more prepared to be cooperative and took his party into coalition with the SD, an arrangement which lasted only fourteen months. It was entered into in the hope of longer-term agreement on economic policy and ended when this proved elusive and when *Venstre* found itself less influential over government policy than it had hoped. In the 1982 Conservative-led coalition, Christopherson became deputy prime minister and finance minister.

Prospects

Liberal prospects depend on its ability to retain the support of farmers, high-school teachers, and the cooperative movement while broadening its urban base and attracting issue-oriented voters. The 1981 election was fought on a joint economic plan developed with the KF, and the two parties are in cooperative competition for leadership of the nonsocialist bloc. The Liberals will continue to be better placed than their conservative rivals either to put together an alternative to the SD or to cooperate with them.

Progress Party
(*Fremskridtspartiet;* FP)

History

The Progress Party was started in 1972 on a platform of demands for an end to taxation and "paper-shuffling bureaucracy," even to the extent of a defense policy comprised of a phone-answering machine with the message "We surrender" in Russian. The founder of this overtly populist movement was a tax lawyer, Mogens Glistrup, whose claim was that he and many of his clients paid no income tax at all. In the 1973 election the party gained 16 percent of the vote to become the second-largest party in the *Folketing*, but support has declined sharply since then. Largely ostracized by the other parties, the FP has never participated in government, but its presence has constrained the other parties to take some account of its policy demands.

Organization

Its populism initially led FP to operate without a formal national structure or membership, and meetings of the parliamentary party group are still open to the public. But local organizations were soon necessary to raise money and campaign support. The party is largely held together by Glistrup.

The party's headquarters are at Prinsesse Mariesallé 1, 1980 Copenhagen V.

Policy

The Progress Party claims to offer a real alternative to 1770s liberalism and 1870s socialism, seeing the most urgent tasks as its campaigns against income taxes, overadministration, and confusion in the laws. Income taxes would be replaced by taxes on consumption, and the tax-free income level would be raised in progressive stages over seven years to achieve this. The income tax is opposed because of the large bureaucracies required to collect it and because of the temptation it offers politicians to increase taxation. They also are said to be a cause of the social problems of those who lack the gift of economic management. Public expenditure should be regulated strictly according to income, with a checking account in the National Bank for each expenditure heading.

The country's economic problems would be solved by moving labor from administrative to productive jobs, and there should be freedom of action for trade unions in pursuit of this aim. Workers should be free to invest savings where they please, and the compulsory contributions to a trade-union-controlled fund (advocated by the SD) are opposed.

Further reductions of administration would be achieved by adopting a unitary administrative structure and abolishing the county level of government. The party has iconoclastic ideas about representative government: Parliament would be reduced from 179 to forty members, one retiring each month, with elections in a single national constituency, at which voting would be for individuals, not parties. *Folketing* members would have a bloc vote equal to the number of votes by which they were elected, and the referendum would be used for any law which did not receive a 60 percent majority.

The 1979 program does not mention foreign policy. The party has advocated entirely replacing the country's diplomatic service by electronic or personal communication, except for a single delegation to secure the country's interests within the European Community.

Membership & Constituency

The party does not have members as such. In 1974 there were about 25,000 readers of the party's journal, a figure estimated to have fallen to 15,000 by 1977, equivalent to about 3 percent of the party's vote. Support comes mainly from self-employed businessmen in urban industry—middle aged, middle income, not many educated beyond the legal minimum, and living in small towns rather than in the capital. It has few supporters of pensionable age, and its appeal is much stronger to men than to women. Its opposition to income tax and bureaucracy gave it a clear image which drew initial support almost equally from that of the four old parties.

Financing

There are no data on party finance, but income is thought to come mainly from small individual donations.

Leadership

The founder of the party, Mogens Glistrup (born 1926), was prosecuted for tax fraud soon after forming the party. After an eight-year court case, he was sentenced to four years imprisonment and a fine of four million kroner (over $500,000). If the Supreme Court confirms the conviction, he will most likely be declared unworthy to continue as a member of the *Folketing*. He has been give the title of "campaign leader and extraordinary honorary life member of the executive committee," a practice unknown to the other Danish parties. The party has claimed that his prosecution was politically motivated, and sees him as a martyr to his cause. Neither the party's national chairman, Alvar Roland Petersen, nor the chairman of the parliamentary party, Ove Jensen (born 1933), are likely to fill the role in Glistrup's absence.

Prospects

The Progress Party has seen some reduction in the burden of taxation as a result of the prominence it has given this issue, while at the same time its radical populism has been tempered during its ten-year existence. These two factors, combined with the possible imprisonment of its leader, must reduce the party's prospects. Nevertheless, it may continue to attract some support from the disaffected lower middle class and to have a role as a conservative critic of Danish "politics as usual." Paradoxically, its presence in the *Folketing* may also block the formation of a united opposition to the Social Democrats.

Social Democrats
(*Socialdemokratiet;* SD)

History

The party was founded in 1871 on Marxist principles, although there was little initial contact with other such parties. In its early years, it concentrated on trade-union organization, achieving its first parliamentary representation in 1884. Participation in the government during 1916 to 1920 and the predominance of the parliamentary over the labor wing in 1920 has attracted voters and members from outside the labor movement made it the largest party in the *Folketing* ever since 1924, although it has never attained a majority. The Social Democrats have dominated the process of cabinet formation since forming their first cabinet in 1924 to 1926 and laying the foundations of the welfare state while in office with the Radical Liberals during 1929 to 1943. Since 1945, SD

has given Denmark five of its nine prime ministers and has led twelve of the sixteen governments.

Organization

The highly developed organization of the Social Democrats builds on some 700 local branches which are represented in the 103 constituency organizations, fifteen county organizations, and in the party congress which is held at least every four years. A meeting of representatives from counties and constituencies, the youth organization, the executive of the cooperative association, the business committee of the national trade-union organization, and the party's Executive Committee is held annually. The party is also represented on trade-union, cooperative, youth, arts, leisure, press, and workers' educational wings of the labor movement. The congress approves the party's program of principles after debate in the branches and elects the party chairman, political and organizational vice-chairmen, and the party secretary. The party is managed by a business committee, responsible to the Executive Committee, which meets about twice per month. Party members may not hold seats in both *Folketing* and the European Parliament and county or local councils.

The party's headquarters are at Nyropsgade 26, 1602 Copenhagen V.

Policy

The party's most recent program of principles was adopted in 1977 after extensive debate with voters and within the party.

The party is democratic in its advocacy of freedom of expression, association, assembly, the right to strike and to demonstrate, public access to the administrative process, and direct elections and cabinet responsibility. It is socialist in advocating democratic control of economic decisions and, ultimately, communal ownership of all means of production. The party aims at a society based on equality and solidarity, with an equal right for all to do their share in production and to achieve a materially secure life.

In employment the individual should be able to take part in decisions about his job. Arrangements for economic democracy should include a joint fund, with wage earners as part owners, which would collect investment capital (perhaps from pension-fund contributions) and support democratic control of investment policy. Implementation of this originally Swedish idea, while supported by SF and most unions, has been opposed by the nonsocialist parties. Other aims include the gradual takeover by society of land for housing; state employment of all welfare and health workers, including doctors and dentists; state control of pharmacies and pharmaceutical production; a general and uniform pension scheme; communal ownership of national energy sources; and taxation and subsidized recycling of scarce resources. Most taxes should be raised through excise duties and a proportional income tax paid by employers. Greater equality of distribution should be achieved by taxes on property, land, capital gains, and inheritance.

In foreign policy, SD supports a strengthened United Nations, Scandinavian cooperation, and active efforts for realistic solutions to common problems within the EEC. Membership of NATO is supported as long as NATO aims at ensuring a balanced basis for détente and cooperation between East and West. The party also expresses support for popular movements fighting against economic and political oppression, and would like to see more assistance for developing countries.

Membership & Constituency

The Social Democrats claimed 125,000 members in 1980 and has long been the largest party in Denmark. Membership has been declining since the peak in 1948, when it represented 38 percent of SD voters, but has recovered slightly since 1974; the ratio is now 10 percent. Support is concentrated heavily among manual workers and employees, both blue and white collar. Supporters are more likely than in any other party to have only a minimal education. The socialist parties farther to the left have been far more successful in attracting the age group under thirty, the better educated, and inhabitants of the capital. Social Democrats are more likely to live in provincial towns.

Financing

The annual subscription is about 150 kroner (about $19) per member, but pensioners pay less than half that and both figures are indexed to inflation. This rate is under half that of the Communist Party, but higher than other Danish parties. Thus, given the size of its membership, the SD is the best-financed party in the country. Contributions also are received from trade unions, although there is increasing competition for these funds from other socialist parties.

Leadership

The leader of the SD since 1972, for most of that time as prime minister, has been Anker Jørgensen (born 1922). Before that he had been leader of the largest trade union in the country and had no previous cabinet experience. In 1973, the CD split from the right of SD, and SD had the lowest proportion of the vote since 1906. Jørgensen's leadership has seen a steady rebuilding of the party's support until a further, much smaller, setback in 1981. As prime minister of successive minority governments, he has also shown skill in building parliamentary support for his policies, mainly from the smaller parties of the center and right. After the 1981 election, support came from the Socialist People's Party and the Radical Liberals, but he has never relied on the Left Socialists or the Communist Party on the left or on the Progress Party on the right. There is no lack of potential successors, should Jørgensen retire.

Prospects

The SD's support has been aging during the past decade, and the party has found it difficult to recruit the growing proportion of young, well-educated voters of the professional and public-service sector. Unless it is able to improve its share of the vote, SD risks losing its dominant position in the Danish party system.

Socialist People's Party
(*Socialistisk folkeparti;* SF)

History

The SF was founded in 1959 by Aksel Larsen, who had been the leader of the Danish Communist Party (DKP) for twenty-six years before being expelled for advocating socialism on Danish lines rather than on lines laid down by Moscow. The new party won eleven *Folketing* seats the following year and eclipsed DKP. It has never sat in the cabinet, primarily because of its opposition to NATO and the EEC, but it has joined in supporting arrangements for SD governments in 1966 to 1968, 1971 to 1973, and 1981 and 1982.

Organization

Unlike the Communist Party, SF aims to be "a real mass party . . . and not a steel-hard militant sect." One consequence has been far greater electoral success. Another has been recurrent faction-alism: the Left Socialists broke away in 1967; in 1974 and 1976, there were serious disagreements between the parliamentary group and the rest of the party, leading to leadership changes; and there have also been disagreements about the relative emphasis to be given to parliamentary or trade-union activities.

The party's small size makes for a less elabo-rate formal structure than the larger parties have, but the normal democratic procedures are fol-lowed: the party congress of delegates from local branches must approve the party program, usually after lively debate, and elect all party leaders. In spite of factional disagreements within the party, its parliamentary bloc is highly disciplined.

The party's headquarters are at Christiansborg, 1218 Copenhagen K.

Policy

The SF began by advocating clearly socialist solutions to Danish problems, but, unlike the Communist Party, not dictated by a leadership trained in and controlled from Moscow. From the outset, SF gained substantial popular support for its anticapitalist position and its emphasis on common ownership of the means of production under self-administration. The party recognizes the dangers of state socialism, arguing that expan-sion of the state in the 1960s and early 1970s merely postponed the crisis of capitalism. The SF therefore gives equal weight with its parliamen-tary activities to its work in trade unions, coopera-tive housing, environmental groups, and other popular movements.

The socialist society advocated by the SF will be one of equality between the sexes, each person being his or her own master so far as possible, with people and not the party as the end. Just as capitalists have no right to power, socialism can-not be reconciled with a system which gives power to civil servants, politicians, or an all-pow-erful state. Workers should run their own affairs within a common, compulsory plan for produc-tion and expansion worked out by popular coun-cils within the firm or locality or among inhabit-ants and consumers. A clearly decentralized society is envisaged.

Internationally, SF seeks freedom from great power and capitalist interference, and therefore would take the country out of the EEC, preferring instead to work for solidarity with the labor move-ments of other countries. On similar grounds, the party opposes NATO.

Membership & Constituency

With only about 5,000 members in 1977, the SF is one of the smaller parties, but this membership represents only about 4 percent of its electoral strength. The party appeals more successfully to white-collar and service workers than the SD, and has been more successful also in attracting young and well-educated voters. The bulk of its strength is concentrated in the Copenhagen area.

Financing

Few data are available, but the party has at-tracted some trade-union donations in addition to membership dues and state support for the parlia-mentary group.

Leadership

After the death in 1971 of the party's founder, Aksel Larsen, the SF had a period of difficulty in establishing a stable leadership. Gert Petersen (born 1927) had helped to form the party. In 1972 he became party spokesman (floor leader) and has been national chairman since 1974. The par-liamentary group has been chaired since 1977 by Ms. Ebba Strange (born 1929).

Prospects

The party has had to compete with the VS and the DKP for the limited space to the left of the SD, offering a style of leadership and participation be-tween the near anarchy of the VS and the tight discipline of the DKP. The party has been most successful when offering constructive criticism rather than outright opposition to the SD. But even if the SD and the SF were to gain a joint majority, which would be the SF's most plausible route to power, the record of past relationships between the two parties does not indicate a likeli-hood of smooth cooperation between them.

Minor Parties

Parties designated here as "minor" are those which polled 5 percent or less in the 1981 parlia-mentary election. This classification should not mislead: in the multiparty system in which no party has a majority, these parties are able to in-fluence legislation by giving or withholding sup-port. At times they have also been significant in government formation: the Radical Liberals were customarily partners of the Social Democrats from 1929 to 1964 and were again relied on in

1981–82 period; and the Justice Party joined the RV and the SD in the 1957–60 cabinet.

Christian People's Party (*Kristeligt Folkeparti;* KrF)

Founded in 1970 and first represented in the *Folketing* in 1973, this party is one of religious and moral protest and of cultural defense—comparable to its sister parties in Norway, Finland, and Sweden—rather than with the catchall Christian Democratic parties which form a moderate right in Germany and elsewhere. Initial support came from the low-church Inner Mission, but the party has built up support from other wings of the state church as well as from Catholics and the free churches.

The policies of the KrF emphasize respect for life, peace, and property in a just society which recognizes the importance of the family. Its origins were in opposition to the "moral permissiveness" of legislation, especially on pornography and abortion, passed by the 1968–71 nonsocialist government and supported by other parties. On economic issues the party stands in the progressive center with the CD and the RV, giving conditional parliamentary support to SD minority governments.

In foreign policy, the KrF emphasizes aid to developing countries, extending this priority to cover trade and cooperative production, even at the cost of reorganizing Danish trading patterns. The party argues that the policy should be pursued within the EEC and that Denmark should act as a bridge between the EEC and the Nordic countries. NATO membership should be continued until a better alternative can be found.

In 1981, KrF had 11,500 members, approximately 16 percent of its total electoral support. Membership dues are 90 kroner (about $11) annually.

After solving conflicts between an initially co-opted leadership and the attitudes of party members to the other parties (which were not necessarily seen as un-Christian), KrF was led by Jens Møller until 1978, and since then by Flemming Kofoed-Svendsen as national chairman and by Christian Christensen (born 1925) as chairman of the parliamentary group since 1973. Party headquarters are at Skindergade 24, 1159 Copenhagen K.

Danish Communist Party (*Danmarks kommunistike parti;* DKP)

This small, Moscow-oriented party was founded in 1919 and first gained parliamentary representation in 1932, but has generally been overshadowed by the SD. It experienced a brief period of growth after World War II but declined again after 1947, when the role of the U.S.S.R. in Eastern Europe became clear. The party's determination to maintain its ties with Moscow and the consequent breakaway of SF in 1959 isolated DKP on the far left. It regained parliamentary representation from 1973 to 1979, due to the prevailing mood of political mistrust of the established parties and the effective television performance of its party chairman and leading spokesman, Knud Jespersen (born 1926). The SD has been able to ignore DKP's efforts to have policies implemented by the left rather than the center-right. Those efforts have been further frustrated by the existence of at least three parties to the left of the SD, all in dogmatic disagreement. The DKP's opposition to both NATO and the EEC has brought it some votes from beyond the ranks of its members, but most Danes prefer Danish solutions to their problems. The party claimed about 10,000 members in 1981, about 29 percent of its electoral support. Party dues are 360 kroner annually (about $45), the highest in Denmark.

Justice Party (*Danmarks retsforbund;* DRF)

Founded in 1919 but not represented in Parliament until 1926, the party is based on the economic and political ideas of the American, Henry George, whose *Progress and Poverty* (1879) provoked extensive discussion in Denmark and inspired Social Credit parties in Canada and New Zealand. The party has three main aims: a single tax on increases in land values to ensure that those values are treated as common property for the benefit of all (hence the party's alternative name of Single-Tax Party); the security of individual rights against the state—the only task of the just state is to ensure personal freedom within limits which secure the freedom of others; complete freedom of trade. The first of these aims amounts to a radical economic innovation which attracts the support of the lowest income and occupational groups and the opposition of property owners. The other two aims place the party with extreme *laissez-faire* liberals, an uneasy combination of attitudes which makes it impossible to place the party on a conventional left-right spectrum.

The party's inclusion in the 1957–60 RV-SD government was a temporary measure to exclude Liberals and Conservatives from office. Its failure to achieve distinctive policy objectives led to electoral oblivion until 1973, when it gained from its opposition, on free trade grounds, to EEC membership. Support for the 1973–75 Liberal government's economic policies again lost it support, and it now rejects bloc politics and seeks a broadly based government. In 1981 the party had some 3,000 members and about 45,000 voters. As a long-standing and distinctive feature of the Danish party system, it is likely neither to disappear nor to play a crucial role in government formation.

Left Socialists (*Venstresocialisterne;* VS)

This party originated in 1967 as a splinter group from the left wing of SF and opposed the then SD minority government's anti-inflationary policies to limit cost-of-living increases in wages. It is libertarian-socialist in outlook. It criticizes SF's ability to attract professionals and student voters, which it stigmatizes as a tendency toward *embourgeoisement*. Skeptical of the parliamentary and state institutions which it sees as the consequences of class conflict, the VS has tended to pursue its revolutionary socialist aims in workplaces, convinced that the institutions of capitalism and the state will melt away as a result of their own internal contradictions. The party does not cooperate much with others in Parliament, but uses its time allocation to propagate its ideas, occasionally proposing imaginative policies, for example, on energy conservation.

Radical Liberals (*Det radikale venstre;* RV)

One of the "four old parties," RV split from the Liberals in 1905 and soon held cabinet office, first in the 1909–10 government and then in 1913 to 1920. The party has occupied a pivotal position between socialist and nonsocialist blocs. In intermittent alliance with the SD from the 1920s until 1964, it exerted a liberalizing influence on its socialism. In 1968 to 1971, the Radical, Hilmar Baunsgaard, led a majority coalition government of Radicals, Liberals, and Conservatives. Since 1973 this pivotal function was also performed by the CD, the KrF, and other parties of the center-right, while the RV has declined correspondingly in importance. Party membership has also declined, from 25,000 in 1974 to 13,400 in 1980, a ratio of 8 percent of its voters. Dues income averaged 27 kroner per member ($3.50) and was substantially exceeded by donations, none of which came from business organizations.

RV is social-liberal in outlook, equidistant from state socialism and unrestrained liberalism. It stands for intellectual, personal, and political freedom and against misuse of organized or monopoly power. It supports economic freedom within limits set by the state to ensure the general good.

In foreign policy, much emphasis is given to Danish membership in the United Nations and the EEC and on working with the other Nordic countries in pursuit of cooperation, internationally controlled disarmament, and aid to the least-developed countries. The Radicals have always opposed excessive military spending; favor neutralism; and wish to see NATO, the Warsaw Pact, and other such alliances dissolved.

The RV's domestic policies are formulated very generally. It wants to increase equality and reduce restrictive practices at workplaces, to encourage participation in local affairs, to reduce differences between theoretical and practical aspects of education, to search for ways to remove the causes of crime, and to increase the powers of popularly elected bodies over the forces which influence decision making—technological development, special-interest organizations, experts and administrators, and concentrations of economic power.

The Radicals' parliamentary leader is Niels Helveg Petersen (born 1939), a member of a well-known Radical family. Party headquarters are at Christianborg, 1218 Copenhagen K.

National Prospects

The Danish economy has suffered severely from the slackening of world economic activity and from both main rounds of oil price rises, in 1973 and 1979. The main objectives of economic policy have been to eliminate the balance-of-payments deficit (running at an estimated $550 million in 1981 and at six times that level in 1979) and to reduce inflation (11.7 percent in 1981). Especially since 1979, governments have pursued restrictive economic policies, including high interest rates, devaluation of the *krone* (twice in 1979 and again in 1982), incomes policies to limit wage increases, and several rises in direct and indirect taxation. As a result, the gross national product (GNP) declined slightly in 1980 (with private consumption down a record 4.1 percent) and is estimated to have remained unchanged in 1981. Although one of the wealthiest countries in the EEC in terms of GNP per capita, the tax burden is also one of the heaviest and tax increases produce diminishing returns.

Some relief from oil-import costs (amounting to about 15 percent of consumption) will be obtained from North Sea oil production in 1982, and gas from the same source will come on stream in late 1984. Total output should satisfy one-third of energy requirements by the late 1980s and half in the 1990s. More immediately the economy should benefit from construction of a major natural gas pipeline network.

Politically the task of governments will be to hold a balance between economic targets and domestic political pressures, and especially to avoid undue reliance on North Sea oil and gas as a panacea for economic difficulties. The 1981 election results gave no clear pointers to government formation and increased the level of party system fractionalization. On these results, no two-party majority coalition was possible and any three-party coalition would have to include the SD. The SD continued in office, relying on parliamentary support from the SF and the RV, although neither of these parties would negotiate directly with the other. This arrangement broke down in mid-1982. The minority coalition which took over in September 1982 aimed to help industry and increase export competitiveness by cutting public expenditure and limiting bureaucracy. It will have to obtain broader parliamentary support if it is to succeed in these aims.

Further Reading

Cerny, Karl H., ed. *Scandinavia at the Polls: Recent Political Trends in Denmark, Norway and Sweden.* Washington, D.C.: American Enterprise Institute, 1977.

Denmark: An Official Handbook. Copenhagen: Royal Danish Ministry of Foreign Affairs, 1974.

Elder, Neil; Thomas, Alastair H.; and Arter, David. *The Consensual Democracies? The Government and Politics of Scandinavian States.* Oxford: Martin Robertson and Co., Ltd., 1982.

Fitzmaurice, John. *Politics in Denmark.* London: C. Hurst and Co., 1981.

Johansen, Lars Nørby. "Denmark." In *European Electoral Systems Handbook*, Geoffrey Hand et al, eds. London: Butterworths, 1979.

Pedersen, Mogens N. *Denmark: The Breakdown of a "Working Multiparty System?"* Odense University, Institute of Social Science, Working Paper No. 11. Odense, Denmark, 1981.

Thomas, Alastair H. "Denmark: Coalitions and Minority Governments." In *Government Coalitions in Western Democracies*, Eric C. Browne and John Dreijmanis, eds. New York and London: Longman, 1982.

———. "Social Democracy in Denmark." In *Social Democratic Parties in Western Europe*, William E. Paterson and Alastair H. Thomas, eds. London: Croom Helm, 1977.

COMMONWEALTH OF DOMINICA

by Indira Jhappan

The System of Government

Dominica is a parliamentary republic which became independent of Great Britain on November 3, 1979, after over a decade of self-rule as a member of the West Indies Associated States. The Caribbean island's 80,000 people, nearly all African or mixed race, are mostly poor; the unemployment rate is consistently around 30 percent. The country's economy is heavily influenced by a few wealthy landowning families. Bananas account for 80 percent of the value of exports.

Executive

The head of state is a president elected to a five-year term by the House of Assembly after he is jointly nominated by the leaders of the majority and the opposition. His powers are largely formal. Real executive power belongs to the head of government, the prime minister, who is the leader of the House majority.

Legislature

The House of Assembly in 1982 consisted of twenty-one members elected to five-year terms and nine appointees. Of the latter, five are appointed by the prime minister and four by the leader of the opposition. The number of elected members can be changed by an independent Constituency Boundaries Committee. Party discipline in the House is unusually strict and government bills are seldom voted down.

Until June 1979, the House had been dominated by the Dominican Labour Party (DLP), a democratic socialist party led by Patrick John. For years, the DLP tried to push through major land-reform legislation, but was consistently thwarted by the conservative Freedom Party. In mid-1979, a series of scandals over graft brought down the Labour government, and the House chose Oliver Seraphin, a John associate, to lead a caretaker government and prepare for new elections. Elections were not held until July 1980, by which time the Seraphin government had also been tainted by scandal. The elections resulted in an overwhelming victory for the Freedom Party.

1980 ELECTION RESULTS

	Seats	Votes	%
Democratic Freedom Party (DFP)	17	16,083	52.34
Dominican Democratic Labour Party (DDLP)	2	5,944	19.34
Dominican Labour Party (DLP)	0	5,195	16.91
Democratic Liberation Movement Alliance (DLMA)	0	2,464	8.02
Independents	2	1,043	3.39

Judiciary

The judicial system is based on English common law and is part of the Eastern Caribbean Supreme Court, one of whose judges sits in Dominica.

Regional & Local Government

The only subnational governments are partially elected town and village councils which manage local affairs.

The Electoral System

Suffrage extends to all citizens age eighteen and older. Voting is by secret ballot in single-member districts. House seats are won by a simple plurality. The Electoral Commission oversees voter registration and the elections. Voter turnout has never fallen below 71 percent since the first election in 1951. In 1980, the turnout was 79.9 percent of eligible voters. Independent candidates have been very successful, in part because personality and charisma play a major role in determining the outcome of elections.

The Party System

The first election in Dominica to be contested by organized parties was in 1961. The oldest party in the system, the DLP, built its success on the organized-labor movement. The Freedom Party developed largely in reaction to the policies of the DLP, particularly DLP's advocacy of land reform and independence from Great Britain.

Party organization has been relatively loose and is built largely around the constituency organizations of candidates for the House. The parties do not have formal memberships. The Freedom Party shows signs of developing more formal party structures.

Dominican campaigns are characterized by simple rhetoric at rallies; the distribution of items, such at T-shirts, which display the party's name and symbol; and assorted publicity stunts. The 1980 elections were marked by charges from the Alliance Party that the U.S. Central Intelligence Agency had interfered in an attempt to split the labor vote and to tag the Alliance Party as "communist."

Democratic Freedom Party (DFP)

The DFP draws its leadership from the middle classes and represents the landed elite and other upper-class groups. In the 1980 election, however, it successfully appealed to the rural poor in spite of its conservative ideology. Founded in 1970, it has consistently supported pro-West, anticommunist policies. The party ran only nineteen candidates in the 1980 elections. The two elected independents in 1980 are said by at least one observer to be DFP supporters who dropped their affiliation for tactical reasons. The present leader, Eugenia Charles, was born in 1919. The party's financial strength and the control of the press by its supporters gives it considerable leverage in the political process.

Dominican Democratic Labour Party (DDLP)

The DDLP was founded by Oliver Seraphin in 1979 as a breakaway group from the Labour Party. Its sole aim was to dissociate its candidates from the scandals which had surrounded the John government. Although it won two House seats in 1980, its leader failed to get reelected.

Dominican Labour Party (DLP)

Founded in 1961 by Phyllis Shand Allfrey, a Fabian socialist, the DLP drew its leadership from the labor movement. Its decade long electoral success was based on promises of land reform and better working conditions on the banana plantations and docks. The charismatic leadership of Edward O. LeBlanc (1970–75) and Patrick John (1975–80) also gained the party considerable support. In 1981, John was arrested on charges of conspiring to overthrow the government in a coup which was to be carried out by hired American soldiers of fortune. The present party leader is Michael Douglas, the son of a wealthy landowner. With the party tainted by scandal and in possession of only two House seats, its prospects look bleak, barring blatant mismanagement by the Freedom Party government.

Dominica Liberation Movement Alliance (DLMA or Alliance)

The Alliance, a coalition of leftist groups, was founded in 1980 and led by Atherton (Athie) Martin. It ran sixteen candidates in the elections. Since Martin has moved to the United States, the future of the party is cloudy.

Other Political Forces

Organized Labor

The labor movement is well organized and has some role in influencing economic policy. However, in face of high unemployment, it cannot be militant.

Rastafarians

Since 1974, public order has been periodically disrupted by groups of Rastafarians, a West Indian religious-political sect. Operating out of the rugged central highlands of the island, these groups have engaged in terrorist activities with increasingly political overtones. Firebombings and attacks on homes and cars culminated in 1981 with the kidnapping of a wealthy landowner, the father of a member of the government. He was held hostage in exchange for the freedom of two Rastas in prison for murder and was later killed. While the Rastafarians probably do not constitute a serious threat to the government, emergency measures have been instituted to deal with them.

National Prospects

Although the present regime has faced serious challenges to its power from groups in the society which have threatened the stability of the government, there are signs that these trends are changing. The current regime is attempting to improve the economic situation, especially by encouraging foreign investment and strengthening its ties with the United States. The government is also committed to the development of the infrastructure, such as roads, and to the development of social and health services.

Further Reading
Emmanuel, Patrick. "Elections and Parties in the Eastern Caribbean: A Historical Survey." *Caribbean Review*, Vol. 10, No. 3, Summer 1981.
_____. *General Elections in the Eastern Caribbean: A Handbook.* Cave Hill, Barbados: Institute of Social and Economic Research, 1979.
Michaels, Robert A. "Changing the Guard in Dominica." *Caribbean Review*, Vol. 10, No. 3, Summer 1981.

DOMINICAN REPUBLIC
(*República Dominicana*)
by Rolando A. Alum, Jr.

The System of Government

The Dominican Republic is a unitary, multi-party, democratic state with a strong president. Although remarkable stability and social and economic development have been achieved since the mid-1960s, this Caribbean nation of 5.5 million people has had a history of political instability, undergoing foreign domination and invasions, native dictatorships, civil wars, and revolutions. The country occupies the eastern two-thirds of the island Columbus named Hispaniola, which is shared with the Republic of Haiti.

The United States occupied the Dominican Republic from 1916 to 1924. There followed six years of relatively democratic experimentation, until a mulatto army officer of humble origins, Rafael Trujillo, took power in 1930 with the support of the army and a coalition of political forces. Trujillo, while preserving a facade of constitutional legitimacy, ruled with an iron fist for thirty-one years, until May 1961, when he was assassinated by underground opposition forces. Apologists for Trujillo point to such alleged contributions as political stability, the instillment of a sense of nationhood based largely on fear of Haitian aggression and immigration, and the establishment of a semi-welfare state in the paternalistic style.

Trujillo's dictatorship was followed by a succession of temporary governments. The first free elections since the 1920s were held in 1962, and Juan Bosch, a gifted writer and leader of the Dominican Revolutionary Party (PRD), was elected president. Despite his initial widespread popularity, Bosch's administration was besieged by opposition from the extreme right and left, labor and peasant unrest, religious zealotry, and international intrigues. Witnesses claim that his own inflexibility and dogmatism invited the military coup that sent him into exile in September 1963.

Various provisional civilian-military juntas followed until April 1965, when a new coup triggered a civil war that was largely limited to the capital city of Santo Domingo on the southern coast. The coup-makers, known as Constitutionalists, included some military officers with varied motives who agreed on the return of Bosch to power. Most of the organized parties of the left and center sided with the Constitutionalists and distributed arms to a large number of young civilians. The anticoup forces, known as Loyalists, counted on the support of the overwhelming majority of the armed forces and the more conservative elements of the population. The fratricidal conflict ended when joint military forces of the Organization of American States (OAS) and the United States intervened.

In new elections held in 1966 under close international supervision, Joaquín Balaguer, head of the Reformist Party (PRef), an intellectual, and Trujillo protegé, defeated Bosch by a two-to-one margin, thus inaugurating the twelve-year "pax Balagueriana." Balaguer was reelected in 1970 and 1974, but lost in 1978 to a renewed PRD (which also won the 1982 elections).

The constitution of 1966, now in force, is the twenty-fifth in Dominican history. It was promulgated by a constitutional convention called by Balaguer. Drawing heavily from the Bosch-sponsored constitution of 1963, which had its sources in previous Dominican constitutions and in the Cuban constitution of 1940, it is considered one of the most progressive in the Americas. The 1966 constitution established a classic system of checks and balances among the branches of the government.

Executive

Executive power is exercised by the president with the assistance of a vice president and some fifteen appointed secretaries of state who form the cabinet. The president is head of state and government and his powers are extensive, in part because of the size of the enterprises which the state inherited from Trujillo's personal business empire. About half of all jobs in the country are ultimately controlled by the executive.

In 1978, Silvestre Antonio Guzmán of the PRD, a wealthy rancher, defeated Balaguer by a vote of 856,084 to 698,273. In contrast to Balaguer, who had the constitution amended to allow him to succeed himself, Guzmán lived up to his pledge not to seek reelection. Had he completed his term, he would have been the first elected president not to seek reelection and to hand over his office to an elected successor. In July 1982, two months after his successor, Salvador Jorge Blanco, became president-elect after a hard-fought campaign against Balaguer and several other candidates, Guzmán committed suicide. The term was completed by the vice president, Jacobo Majluta. Jorge assumed office in August, promising not to seek reelection.

Legislature

Legislative power is exercised by a bicameral congress consisting of the Senate and the Chamber of Deputies. Legislators may not hold any other public office. The Senate has twenty-seven members, one for each province and the National District, Santo Domingo. The 120 deputies are elected from multimember districts based on province boundaries.

The powers of Congress are similar to those given the United States Congress. Legislation may be introduced by legislators in either house or by the president. Money bills must be introduced by the president and cannot be altered except by a two-thirds majority in both houses. Passage of other legislation requires a majority vote in both houses and approval by the president. A presidential veto can be overridden with a two-thirds majority vote in both houses.

In his years in office, Balaguer was always able to count on full control of Congress, particularly since the opposition boycotted the 1970 and 1974 elections. During that period, some opposition independents were elected to Congress. Under Guzmán, the PRD had forty-eight seats in the lower house compared to forty-three for Balaguer's PRef; in the Senate, the PRef had a majority of sixteen to PRD's eleven. Under Jorge, the PRD was credited with sixty-two seats, the PRef with forty-seven, Bosch's Liberation Party (PLD) with nine, and two independents with the remainder. In the Senate, the PRD won seventeen seats and the PRef won the rest. Actual party allegiance remains unclear because deputies switch sides often.

Judiciary

The Supreme Court of nine justices, one of whom serves as chairman, is the highest court. There are seven courts of appeal, twenty-seven courts of first instance, and numerous lesser courts. There are also several special courts such as the land, labor, and electoral tribunals. All members of the judiciary are elected by the Senate to renewable four-year terms.

Regional & Local Government

The twenty-six provinces are each headed by a governor appointed by the president. Balaguer initiated a tradition of appointing women to all gubernatorial posts. There are no provincial legislatures, and the provinces have little financial independence. The provinces are subdivided into municipalities, each headed by a *síndico* (mayor) and a municipal council, both elected every four years.

The National District, which has about 20 percent of the national population, is a separate entity, also headed by an elected *síndico*. In 1982, the secretary general of the PRD, José Francisco Peña Gómez, was elected *síndico* of the District. The District also elects one senator, who is usually highly influential in Congress. President Jorge Blanco had been the District's senator and president of the Senate (1978–82); former vice president Majluta was elected District senator in the 1982 elections.

The Electoral System

Elections for national and local offices are held concurrently every four years. All citizens eighteen years of age and over (or those married if younger) are eligible to vote. It is estimated that at least 90 percent of eligible voters are registered, a high proportion by Latin American standards. According to the constitution, voting is compulsory, but this provision apparently is not enforced. Turnout commonly runs above 73 percent of registered voters.

Election days are national holidays, and the people treat the event as a festive occasion. Selected police and military personnel are assigned to safeguard the polling places and the ballots; all other military personnel are confined to barracks. Active members of the armed forces and police may not vote.

Voters are presented with two ballots for each party—one for local offices, the Chamber of Deputies, and the Senate, and one for the presidency. The ballots are color coded to indicate the party since over 40 percent of adult Dominicans are illiterate. In the local and Chamber of Deputies elections, voters choose a ranked party slate rather than an individual candidate. In the voting booth, voters insert the ballots of their choice in an envelope which goes into the ballot box. Voters' hands are then stamped with indelible ink to prevent their voting again.

One Senator is elected from each province and the National District by simple plurality. Deputies are elected by a proportional representation system in each province, which is treated as a multi-member electoral district.

The Party System

Origins of the Parties

Political parties began to develop in the late nineteenth and early twentieth centuries, but foreign intervention and Trujillo's one-party system prevented the full development of other political parties. Although some of the contemporary parties claim to have roots in pre-Trujillo times, and some were founded during the Trujillo period, none became effectively functioning entities until after the Trujillo dictatorship. Furthermore, most have gone through sweeping changes in leadership and cadre, so that, with the partial exception of the PRD, the present parties cannot be clearly associated with those existing before 1961. By 1982, there were several parties, but the system appeared to be moving toward a two-party arrangement.

The Parties in Law

The constitution declares that the organization of political parties shall not be restricted. A party may register with the government and appear on the ballot by the relatively simple process of filing a petition with a minimal number of signatures of qualified voters. A party must win at least 10 percent of the popular vote or repeat the petitioning process.

Party Organization

The major parties are effectively organized, with dues-paying members in localities nationwide, and run candidates in local elections. Most parties also have a formal structure with democratic procedures for the naming of delegates to the national conventions and for choosing candidates for office. In practice, however, only the PRD measures up to a democratic standard. The

PRef has been totally dominated by Balaguer; the PLD, by Bosch. All parties have been rocked by internal dissension that has sometimes resulted in public scandals and/or the creation of new parties.

Another feature of the Dominican system is the appearance in election years of alliance parties and of parties established as the independent personal vehicles of politicians usually associated with one of the major parties. Thus, in the 1982 election season, six leftist parties established the United Left (*Izquierda Unida*) with Rafael Tavares as their presidential candidate. José Rafael Abinader, normally associated with the PRD, utilized the Social Democratic Alliance (*Allianza Social Democrática*) to support his presidential candidacy; after the election he was appointed finance minister in the new PRD government. The Christian Popular Party (*Partido Popular Cristiana*) was established to support the candidacy of Rogelio Delgado Boegart when the main Christian party, the Christian Social Revolutionary Party, chose to support Balaguer. These tiny parties, together with the Communist Party and the personal party of General Wessin, shared less than 8 percent of the vote among them.

With the exception of the PRD and some communist groups, ideology remains vague, although nearly all parties espouse some degree of socialism. It is the personal views of the leader, rather than the formal party program, that determine the parties' position along the left-right spectrum. Members of the national elite may be found in the top leadership of all the parties, no matter how radical. This oligarchy is beginning to share those positions, albeit reluctantly, with members of the growing educated and well-to-do middle class. All social classes are represented in all the parties.

Campaigning

Campaigning has become strident, expensive, and professionalized. Vast amounts are spent on marketing strategies based on polling. Radio and rallies constitute the primary means for reaching voters. Caravans and posters and party decorations make campaigning quite colorful.

A new campaign element was added in 1978 and 1982, when the parties brought in sympathetic political figures from abroad to support their campaign. The PRD especially used this ploy to lend prestige to its candidates. Most campaigns and elections have been marked by violence and judicial and electoral irregularities (although these have declined in recent years). In 1978, there were some deaths and injuries reported as campaign related, and some activists were jailed. The 1982 campaign and elections, however, were conducted in a more peaceful and orderly manner.

Independent Voters

The ballot form encourages voting for one party only for all offices. Ticket splitting is practiced only in the larger urban areas, Santo Domingo and Santiago, where literacy and political sophistication are high.

Reformist Party
(*Partido Reformista;* PRef)

History

Balaguer founded the PRef while in exile in New York in 1964. The party grew rapidly, won the 1966 elections, and increasingly consolidated its power during the twelve years of Balaguer's rule. Nevertheless, rampant corruption and ostentation; neglect of the needs of the countryside; police and military heavy-handedness; and Balaguer's dominating style, age, and ill health caused party support to decline before 1978 and to diminish still further in 1982.

Organization

Although the party has maintained a representative democratic structure rising from local party organizations to the national conference, until recently it was effectively dominated by Balaguer, whose personality and political astuteness held the party factions together. Balaguer's dominant position was clearly illustrated in 1978, when Fernando Álvarez Boegart was nominated as the party's vice presidential candidate by democratic processes, but was later replaced at Balaguer's order. In 1982, Álvarez again won the party's nomination, but Balaguer was not able to unseat him a second time.

Policy

The PRef's ideology remains vaguely centrist and democratic. Factions within the party run all the way from former Trujillo supporters to democratic socialists, although moderates are the strongest force. The Balaguer administrations emphasized rapid economic development, which was largely based on foreign aid and investment. The program benefitted urban areas but neglected crucial rural interests.

Membership & Constituency

No reliable figures are available, but the party claims over 700,000 members. While the members and electoral support come from all social classes and areas, the urban middle class probably leans slightly more toward the PRef than toward the other parties. Most of the military favored the PRef until at least 1978.

Financing

No details on the sources of party funds are available. Membership dues are based on a sliding scale according to income, but they are not consistently collected nor is the scale enforced. Government resources were used extensively for the party's benefit during the Balaguer administrations.

Leadership

The party's greatest liability is the inability of its founder to permit the development of a capable leadership to succeed him. Joaquín Balaguer (born 1908) is partially blind, unwell, and apparently unable to lead the party to victory again. If the party remains unified once Balaguer leaves the scene, Fernando Álvarez Boegart (born 1934) seems a likely replacement.

Prospects

Balaguer has sought a merger with the Christian Democrats and is trying to transform the party into a Christian-democratic one before his departure. Whether he succeeds or not, there is little to prevent serious splits in the party once its founder and *raison d'être* is gone.

Dominican Revolutionary Party
(*Partido Revolucionario*
Dominicano; PRD)

History

The PRD was founded in Havana in 1939 by a group of anti-Trujillo exiles, among whom was Juan Bosch. It was in more than one way a copy of the populist Cuban Revolutionary Party (PRC), better known as the *Auténticos,* which reached power in 1944. The PRD became the PRC's protegé until Batista's coup in 1952. When Rómulo

Betancourt won the presidency of Venezuela in 1959, most of the PRD leadership went there.

The PRD did not become active on Dominican soil until after Trujillo's demise. In the first free elections (1962), Bosch, became the winning presidential candidate against the National Civic Union (*Unión Cívica Nacional;* UCN). His administration received the enthusiastic support of U.S. President John F. Kennedy. Bosch imported foreign talent from among his Latin American friends, including Cubans exiled by Fidel Castro. After the military coup that deposed him in 1963, Bosch went to Puerto Rico as a guest of Governor Munóz. He returned after the civil war of 1965, in which the PRD was an active participant, and ran unsuccessfully against Balaguer in 1966.

In 1970, the PRD abstained from the elections, claiming lack of civil liberties. By then Bosch had repudiated the traditional idea of representative democracy and proposed a "dictatorship with popular support." This policy alienated many PRD members, especially the founders. In 1973, Bosch finally walked out of the PRD, founding the PLD. The PRD leadership fell to Secretary General José Francisco Peña Gómez.

For the 1974 elections, the PRD organized an opposition coalition called the *Acuerdo* [Accord] *de Santiago,* embracing seven parties. Guzmán was the candidate for the presidency and General Elías Wessin for the vice presidency. Wessin had been the leader of the anti-Bosch coup in 1963 and of the anti-Constitutionalist and anti-Bosch forces in the 1965 civil war. At the last minute, the coalition, with the exception of one group, withdrew from the elections, charging Balaguer with "colossal fraud." In 1978, the party finally defeated Balaguer by itself with a wide margin that elected Guzmán president and Majluta vice president.

The PRD that came to power was very different from the earlier party. The well-dressed *Perredeistas* (PRDers) who paraded or drove expensive cars along Santo Domingo's ocean drive, waving the PRD's symbolic white flag in celebration, little resembled the *campesinos* that followed Bosch in 1962 or the ragged students that revolted in 1965. Important sectors of the middle and upper classes worked for the victory of the PRD, which still enjoyed the support of workers and peasants.

Organization

The PRD has come to be one of the most thoroughly modern political parties in Latin America. It is well organized and financed, sensitive to contemporary issues, committed to governing, and relatively pragmatic. Moreover, it has found a means of uniting the diverse elements, particularly in its leadership elite that comprise its organization, and it has provided for the institutionalization of competing national political interests within the party.

Policy

The PRD is ostensibly guided by center-liberal social-democratic values and is a member of the Socialist International. Guzmán's administration concentrated on the economy, international affairs and the military, and on strengthening democracy. In the economic sphere, Guzmán was less successful. The administration faced many inherited problems which could not be solved easily, and many people were disappointed. Hurricanes in 1979, increases in energy costs, declines in sugar prices, decreased international aid, and the worldwide economic crisis added to Guzmán's difficulties. In foreign affairs, Guzmán followed a course similar to Balaguer's, despite conflicting points of view within the party. Relations with Castro's Cuba were shunned; the republic normally voted with the United States in the United Nations; and relations with social-democratic governments were strengthened. Guzmán's greatest accomplishment was his depoliticizing of the military sector. His administration, however, was plagued by unexpected corruption and nepotism. Jorge's administration, while pursuing an economic policy of austerity, has made serious attempts to overcome the domestic policy deficiencies of his predecessor and to consolidate Guzmán's policies elsewhere.

Membership & Constituency

Like the other parties, the PRD draws its membership and support from all levels of the society. Reliable figures are not available, but the party claims to have over 700,000 members. Primary sources of the party's support are the urban working and professional classes and the peasantry. Sectors of the traditional oligarchy, the intelligentsia, and the expanding middle class also support the PRD.

Financing

The PRD is well financed, but no information as to its sources of funds is available. The party probably makes a greater effort to collect membership dues than do the other parties and European social democratic parties are said to have provided substantial assistance, especially in the 1978 campaign.

Leadership

Salvador Jorge Blanco (born 1926), as president of the republic, is the acknowledged leader of the party. He has been associated with the left wing of the party. Jacobo Majluta (born 1932) is of Christian Arab descent and has strong support in the Syrio-Lebanese business and professional community. He is seen as a moderate centrist. Hatuey DeCamps (born 1944) is a charismatic leader who was Chamber speaker in Guzmán's time and is secretary of the presidency under Jorge. Hugo Tolentino Dip (born 1930), a well-to-do historian and former chancellor of Santo Domingo University, succeeded DeCamps as Chamber speaker. An avowed neo-Marxist, he is resented by some PRD members as a latecoming opportunist because he did not join the party until after Guzmán's victory in 1978. PRD secretary general and Santo Domingo mayor, José Francisco Peña Gómez is a controversial figure who is thought by some to favor establishing the PRD as a permanent government party along the lines of the Institutional Revolutionary Party of Mexico. Majluta, DeCamps, and Peña are assumed to have presidential ambitions. Peña's aspirations may be limited, however. He is black and supposedly of Haitian descent. While the majority of the population is mulatto, negritude is considered undesirable in the popular mind. Furthermore, Peña has neither personal wealth nor a network of well-connected kinsmen, both of which are often decisive factors in Dominican politics.

Prospects

With a leadership that many foreign experts characterize as one of the most promising in Latin America and with a proven record at the polls, the prospects of the PRD for remaining in power are very bright. Only a severe economic crisis is likely to dislodge it.

Minor Parties

Dominican Liberation Party (*Partido de la Liberación Dominicana;* PLD)

Bosch founded the PLD after abandoning the PRD in 1973. The party received only 18,000 votes in the 1978 election and had to go through the registration process again to reestablish its legal status. In the 1982 elections, however, the PLD won nearly 10 percent of the vote and emerged as a definite third force, albeit a relatively weak one and probably ephemeral.

While the PLD is organized across the country, it is still dominated by Bosch, whose leadership style has led to party schisms. In 1978, Bosch's handpicked secretary general left the PLD to found his own party, the Democratic Union. Despite the fact that Bosch (born 1909) was a protegé of pre-Castro bourgeois governments and maintained close relations with Cuban liberal intelligentsia in exile (including relatives of his wife), Bosch has now become an apologist for the Castro government of Cuba and calls himself a Marxist-Leninist. He has never recovered the momentum he enjoyed in the early 1960s, and it is doubtful that the party will survive once he leaves the political scene.

Christian Social Revolutionary Party (*Partido Revolucionario Social Cristiano;* PRSC)

After Trujillo's assassination in 1961, several political groups emerged with a Christian, social, and democratic orientation. The PRSC soon became the major representative of this trend, gaining the recognition of the international Christian Democratic organizations of Europe and Latin America. In the 1960s, it looked as if the PRSC was going to become a significant force in Dominican politics. However, from a solid third place in the 1962 elections, it slipped to a poor fourth in 1978, as the electorate polarized behind the PRD and PRef. During Balaguer's last term, some PRSC leaders accepted government positions, especially in the diplomatic corps, and Balaguer proposed a merger of the PRef and PRSC. Although the party supported Balaguer in the 1982 elections, the merger has not yet occurred. If it does, it is expected that the PRSC will provide the ideology and international connections, while PRef will provide the voters.

Heavily influenced by the most progressive elements of Catholicism, the party's ideology is a complex center-left doctrine that rejects the excesses of both capitalism and Marxism-Leninism. The party has close ties to the Autonomous Confederation of Christian Syndicates (CASC), which controls the all-important unions of sugar workers. This tie probably makes the PRSC the most influential party in the still meagerly organized labor movement.

A multiclass party, the PRSC also has great appeal to intellectuals and students, and it is noted for the efforts it makes to impart its ideology to youth. In spite of its strong Catholic background, many of the PRSC leaders are Protestants. If a PRef-PRSC merger does take place, the new bloc would pose a formidable challenge to the PRD.

National Civic Union (Unión Cívica Nacional; UCN)

Middle-class professionals and businessmen clandestinely founded the UCN during the latter part of the Trujillo dictatorship. The party was a major force in the short-lived governments that followed the dictator's assassination. The UCN gained the reputation of being vindictively opposed to those who had collaborated with Trujillo; Bosch's PRD maintained a more conciliatory line and won the 1962 elections. The UCN promoted Bosch's overthrow later that year, but the party never regained its earlier momentum. Although the UCN opposed Balaguer for many years, its vestige supported him in 1978 and 1982.

Quisqueyan Democratic Party (Partido Quisqueyano Democrático; PQD)

General Elías Wessin y Wessin, leader of the anti-Bosch forces in 1963 and 1965, founded the PQD in 1968. (Quisqueya is the indegenous name of the island.) Implicated in a plot to overthrow Balaguer in 1973, Wessin was exiled for five years. In 1974, from exile, he ran as the vice presidential candidate of the Santiago Accord alliance. In 1978, Wessin joined forces with two minor parties. In 1982, running alone, Wessin received less than two percent of the vote. He continues to wield some influence in the officer corps.

Dominican Communist Party (Partido Comunista Dominicano; PCD)

Formerly the Dominican Popular Socialist Party, this Moscow-oriented group was founded by exiled Spanish Republicans in 1942. Although it suffered persecution under Trujillo, he used the PCD in the 1940s to create labor unrest in the U.S.-owned sugar enterprises, most of which he eventually succeeded in buying out. After periods under ban in the 1960s and 1970s, the PCD was legalized by Balaguer. The party draws its strength from among a few talented and well-educated young intellectuals and members of the urban upper-middle class. It appears to be an elitist, dogmatic Marxist-Leninist party playing the electoral game in a developing country. It is vociferously anti–United States and pro-Castro. It received very few votes in 1978 or 1982.

Communist Party of the Dominican Republic (Partido Comunista de la República Dominicana; PACOREDO)

PACOREDO is one splinter of the larger Dominican Popular Movement (Movimento Popular Dominicano; MPD), which was founded in Havana in 1956 by exiled Dominicans who had been expelled from the PCD. The MPD broke into three harshly contending factions, all claiming Maoist orientations in opposition to the original pro-Castro MPD. Of these three groups, PACOREDO is the only one that remains visible. PACOREDO became loudly critical of Castro, Moscow, and Balaguer. Comprised largely of young activists, the party has been considered subversive, but in the early 1980s seemed to have become more moderate.

Other Leftist Groups

There are several other minor political groups professing variants of communism, including Trotskyites and one group that takes its lead from North Korea. While all these groups, including the communists, loudly claim to represent the working class, none seems to have had any impact on the labor movement or the peasantry.

Other Political Forces

Military

From the founding of the Republic in 1844 until the arrival of the U.S. Marines in 1916, the republic was almost always under the control of the military. When the Marines left, the elected governments which followed tried to professionalize the armed forces and bring the independent-minded generals under a single command. Trujillo was given that command and a short time later used it to take control of the government and bring the military back to power. By the time Trujillo was assassinated, the military had become factionalized; several officers participated in the conspiracy that killed Trujillo. The civil war of 1965 saw officers fighting on both sides. Balaguer's regime was based in part on military support, with Balaguer successfully playing the military factions off against each other. The last coup attempt came in May 1978. When it became clear that the PRD was winning the elections, the officer corps attempted to stop the counting and prevent Guzman's victory. Under pressure from Balaguer, from international quarters, and from popular forces, the military backed down. Under Guzmán, many officers were transferred, retired, or assigned to adminstrative or diplomatic posts, and the power of the military was neutralized.

While the officers see themselves as the defenders of the nation against Cuban-supported domestic conspiracies and possible Haitian aggression, their individual behavior is largely self-serving, as they compete for power, privilege, and sinecures. A career in the military offers a poor Dominican a rather fast means to acquire status and wealth; almost all military personnel come from humble origins.

Organized Labor

The labor movement has not as yet played a significant role in Dominican politics, but the increasing membership and effectiveness of two union confederations may change that in years to come. The Autonomous Confederation of Classist Syndicates (*Confederación Autónoma de Sindicatos Clasistas;* CASC) claims a membership of some 70,000 and is particularly strong among workers in the sugar industry. It is ideologically, but not institutionally, aligned with the PRSC. One of its most prominent leaders is Henry Molina, a young activist who has served as Jorge's aide for labor affairs.

The General Union of Dominican Workers (*Unión General de Trabajadores Dominicanos;* UGTD) was founded with the sponsorship of the PRD after that party won the 1978 elections. The union claims about 35,000 members and will probably continue to grow.

The General Confederation of Work (*Confederación General de Trabajo*, CGT) is avowedly pro-communist. Although it claims a membership of some 40,000, it controls very few unions, and the majority of workers are not even aware of its existence. There are also a number of independent unions, some of which are organizations of small businessmen such as taxi drivers.

Unemployment of 15 percent and underemployment as high or higher make labor organization and activism unusually difficult; the movement has a long way to go to achieve any real power.

Students

Students were an important element on the side of the Constitutionalists in the 1965 civil war. Under Balaguer, student rallies, demonstrations, and violence often spilled into the streets from the campus of the public Santo Domingo Autonomous University. The university at times was sealed off and classes suspended. With the coming of the PRD to power, conflict between students and the government decreased substantially. PRD presidents, for example, have been able to visit the campus safely, whereas Balaguer could not.

Both the PRD and the PRSC have developed student affiliates with moderate and effective leadership, but the most active student groups are those of the radical left which are potentially violent.

Roman Catholic Church

Most leading Dominicans are nominal Catholics, including most PRD leaders, but the Church is not a major political actor in the republic. Lack of funds and personnel, particularly Dominican clergy, and increasing growth of Protestantism, have sharply weakened the Church's influence. The clearest signs of that weakness are the republic's liberal divorce law and the state-supported family-planning program, both initiated by Balaguer.

United States

The United States has played an important role in the politics of the Dominican Republic since the mid-nineteenth century. Besides direct intervention in 1904, 1916–24, and 1965, recent indirect interventions have included U.S. cooperation with the Organization of American States to isolate the Trujillo regime in 1961 and the strong stance taken against an attempted coup in 1978. All Dominican parties deplore such intervention, even when it supports stability and democracy, and parties routinely charge each other with collaborating with the American government, often exaggerating the degree of U.S. involvement in Dominican politics.

Private U.S. corporations have made extensive capital investments in the republic, especially since 1961. Whether these corporations have any significant influence on Dominican policy is doubtful. The Dominican government continues to court foreign investment and offers economic incentives to such investors.

National Prospects

Since 1966, the Dominican people have shown themselves capable of using their democratic freedom effectively to regularly elect governments by popular vote according to their own perceptions of their best interests. The principal parties seem to be committed to democratic procedures, civil rights, and peaceable alternation in power. While military figures and radical leftist groups stand ready to take advantage of any serious crisis, the stability of the present system appears to be secure for the next few years.

Much of the country's future depends on the economy. The republic is self-sufficient in basic needs and potentially rich, but it suffers seriously when the prices of its export products decline. The worldwide recession of the early 1980s has slowed the country's ability to deal with its social problems—illiteracy, poor public health facilities, substandard housing and housing shortages, unemployment, etc. Nevertheless, these problems and the recession probably will not constitute a threat to the present democratic system unless the recession gets much worse or persists for several more years.

Further Reading

Alum, Rolando. "Dominican Republic." In *Current History Encyclopedia of Developing Nations.* New York: McGraw-Hill, 1982.

Atkins, G. Pope. *Arms and Politics in the Dominican Republic.* Boulder, Colo.: Westview Press, 1981.

Bell, Ian. *The Dominican Republic.* Boulder, Colo.: Westview Press, 1981.

Moreno, José. *Barrios in Arms: Revolution in Santo Domingo.* Pittsburgh: University of Pittsburgh Press, 1970.

Moya-Pons, Frank. *Manual de Historia Dominicana.* Santiago, Dominican Republic: Catholic University, 1977.

Sharpe, Kenneth. *Peasant Politics: Struggle in a Dominican Village.* Baltimore: Johns Hopkins University Press, 1977.

Wiarda, Howard, and Michael Kryzanek. *The Dominican Republic: A Caribbean Crucible.* Boulder, Colo.: Westview Press, 1982.

REPUBLIC OF ECUADOR
(*República del Ecuador*)
by David William Schodt, Ph.D.

The System of Government

Ecuador, a nation of 8.5 million people, is a presidential democracy and a unitary state divided administratively into provinces, cantons, and parishes. There are separate executive, legislative, and judicial branches. Politics has been characterized traditionally by chronic instability and strong regional antagonisms. Ecuador has had seventeen constitutions since independence in 1830; the most recent was adopted in 1978. Prior to the 1978 constitution, a president was elected to a four-year term. However, because of military coups and political factionalism, the average president served for less than three years. In 1972, Ecuador became a petroleum-exporting country. Per capita incomes rose dramatically along with popular expectations. In 1979, a democratically elected government was installed after nine years of nonconstitutional rule. This government came into office promising to direct petroleum revenues toward much-needed social and economic reforms.

Executive

The president of Ecuador is chosen by majority vote in direct popular elections for a five-year term and cannot be reelected to a second term. The 1978 constitution grants considerable authority to the executive, reversing a historical trend which weakened the executive relative to the legislature and the bureaucracy. The most recently elected president was Jaime Roldós Aguilera who took office in 1979. He was killed in an airplane crash in March of 1981 and was replaced by his vice president, Osvaldo Hurtado Larrea. By a one-vote margin, Congress chose the late president's brother, León Roldós Aguilera, leader of the faction of the Concentration of Popular Forces (CFP) opposing Hurtado, to become the new vice president. Roldós won over Rodolfo Baquerizo,

the choice of the CFP faction led by Assad Bucaram.

Legislature

The National Chamber of Representatives (*Camàra Nacional de Representantes*) is unicameral (it was bicameral until the constitution of 1978). It consists of sixty-nine members selected in direct popular elections. Twelve are elected nationally, the remainder from the provinces. Representatives are selected from lists of candidates presented by legally recognized parties in proportion to the number of votes earned. They serve terms of five years and may be reelected only after an absence of one term. Provincial representatives must be natives of the province or have resided in the province for the preceding three years. The legislature elects its own president, who is currently Raúl Baca Carbó of the Democratic Left (ID) party.

The legislature meets each year on the tenth of August for a sixty-day session. Elected from the legislature are four legislative commissions made up of five members each. These commissions function when the legislature is not in session. Either the president of the republic or the president of the National Chamber has the power to call the legislature into extraordinary session to deal with particular issues not resolved during the regular session.

Judiciary

The highest court is the Supreme Court of Justice. Its members are selected by the legislature, hold office for six years, and may be reelected. Historically, the judiciary has remained remarkably aloof from the constant political quarrels which have characterized the legislative and administrative branches.

1978 PRESIDENTIAL ELECTION RESULTS (FIRST ROUND)

Candidate	Party	Percent of Vote
Jaime Roldós Aguilera	Concentration of Popular Forces (CFP)	31
Sixto Durán Ballén	National Constitutional Front (FNC)	22
Raúl Clemente Huerta	Radical Liberal Party (PLR)	21
Rodrigo Borja Cevallos	Democratic Left (ID)	11
Abdón Calderón Muñoz	Radical Alfarista Front (FRA)	9
René Maugé Mosquera	Left Broad Front (FADI)	5

Regional & Local Government

There are three subnational levels of government: nineteen provinces and the Galapagos Islands, 103 cantons or municipalities, and 846 parishes. Government is a curious mixture of

CHAMBER ELECTION RESULTS (1979) AND SEAT DISTRIBUTION (1981)

Party	Seats	Percentage of Total Vote
Concentration of Popular Forces (CFP)		26.84
Bucaram	12	
Roldós/PCD	12	
Democratic Left (ID)	12	14.23
Conservatives (PC)	6	7.15
Liberals (PLR)	4	7.56
Social Christians (PSC)	2	6.41
National Revolutionary (PNR)	2	5.18
Democratic Popular (MPD)	1	4.17
Democratic Union (UDP)	1	3.26
Velasquistas (PNV)*		2.40
Democratic Coalition (CID)*		5.25
Democratic Party (PD)**	1	
Independents**	9	
Popular Democrats (DP)***	7	

Note: Percentages do not total 100 because of blank and invalid votes.
*Parties not represented in 1981.
**New parties which did not compete in 1979 elections.
***The DP candidates ran on the CFP and ID lists.

appointed and elected officials. Officially, the president appoints provincial governors, canton political chiefs (*jefes politicos*), and parish political lieutenants (*tenientes politicos*). In practice, provincial governors normally make appointments to the last two offices.

In rural areas, the appointed officials, especially the *tenientes politicos*, are important sources of authority. In urban areas, elected officials play a more important role. All provincial capitals have an elected mayor who presides over an elected council (*consejo*) whose members are called *consejales*. The mayors of Quito and Guayaquil exercise considerable national as well as local power. Each province also has an elected council made up of provincial councilors (*consejeros*), presided over by the provincial governor.

The most recent provincial and municipal elections, which took place in 1980, were notable in that the leading party, the Radical Alfarista Front (FRA), had not previously demonstrated much electoral appeal. These elections were also significant because, for the first time in Ecuador's history, illiterates were allowed to vote.

The Electoral System

The president and vice president are directly elected in popular elections. A candidate must secure an absolute majority of the vote to win. If no candidate is able to win an absolute majority, runoff elections between the top two candidates are required. In the 1978 presidential elections, no candidate won an absolute majority: Jaime Roldós won 32 percent of the vote, followed by Sixto Durán with 22 percent. In the runoff election in April 1979, Roldós won with 62 percent of the vote. Representatives to the National Chamber are chosen in the following way: twelve are elected at large in a national vote and at least two are elected from each province, with the exception of those provinces containing less than 100,000 inhabitants which elect only one. An additional representative is elected for each 300,000 provincial residents or fraction greater than 100,000 residents (e.g., a province of 550,000 people would have four representatives). Voters choose among ranked lists of candidates presented by legally recognized parties. Where more than two seats are to be filled, they are allocated by a simple proportional system.

In an important change from previous systems of representation, the new system eliminates functional representatives. Since the constitution of 1929, functional representation had given dis-

PERCENTAGE OF TOTAL VOTE BY PARTY (1978–80)

Party	1978 (Provincial, Municipal)	1979 (Chamber)	1980 (Provincial, Municipal)
Conservative	10.34%	7.15%	4.59%
Liberal	15.77	7.56	6.42
CFP	18.13	26.84	6.50
Social Christians	3.20	6.41	1.98
CID	2.97	5.25	0.60
UDP	4.65	3.26	3.42
Velasquista	5.19	2.40	2.47
PNR	2.65	5.18	2.72
ID	2.65	14.23	14.10
FRA	2.23	—	18.85
MPD	—	4.17	4.23

Note: Percentages do not total 100 because of null and invalid ballots. Since eligible Ecuadoreans are legally required to vote, the percentage of null and invalid ballots has always been fairly high. The 1980 figure is particularly high since that is the first year illiterates voted. Elections for local office also produce a higher percentage of null votes.

proportionate representation to special interest groups such as agriculture, commerce, industry, labor, and the military. Under the 1967 constitution, fifteen of the fifty-four senators in the upper house were selected by a form of electoral college to represent different special interests.

All Ecuadorians eighteen years of age and over have the right to vote; literates under age sixty-five are required to vote. Illiterates were given the vote for the first time in the constitution of 1978 and exercised that right for the first time in the municipal and provincial elections in 1980. Qualified voters must register to vote and can vote only in the parish in which they register. A change in

RATES OF POLITICAL PARTICIPATION PRESIDENTIAL ELECTIONS

Year	Participation Rate (percent of population)	Year	Participation Rate (percent of population)
1888	3.0	1956	15.8
1924	11.0	1960	17.8
1931	3.1	1966	11.0
1932	4.2	1968	14.7
1933	3.1	1979	21.0
1948	9.1		

residence must be communicated to the Electoral Tribunal 135 days prior to an election in which the individual wishes to vote.

A significant feature of Ecuadorian politics has been extremely low levels of political participation. The literacy requirement in a country where, as recently as 1974, national rates of illiteracy were in excess of 25 percent, along with various other restrictions, have effectively disenfranchised large sectors of the population. Ecuadorian politics are best characterized as elite politics.

The Party System

Origins of the Parties

Ecuador's traditional parties emerged in the latter half of the nineteenth century. Their ideological orientations reflected the theocratic debates of the period and the regional conflicts which have continued to characterize Ecuadorian politics. The Conservative Party represented the interests of the Sierran landowning aristocracy, supporting close relationships between the Catholic Church and the state, centralized government, and state regulation of economic activity. The Liberal Party drew its primary support from Coastal (Costa) commercial and financial interests, particularly those of Guayaquil. It was anticlerical and advocated decentralized government along with *laissez-faire* economic policies. By the end of World War II, anticlericism had ceased to be an important issue. Differences between the two parties were drawn largely along regional lines. Neither party has won the presidency since the 1956 victory of Conservative candidate Camilo Ponce Enriquez.

Politics in the twentieth century saw an increasing fragmentation of parties, with the emergence of numerous splinter parties on both the left and the right. Highly personalistic politics, always a feature of Ecuadorian political competition, became even more prominent. No one better exemplified this characteristic than José María Velasco Ibarra (1893–1979), who held the presidency five times between 1933 and 1972. Velasco was a spellbinding orator with a charismatic appeal for the masses, but with little ability to govern once elected, as evidenced by his successful completion of only one of his five terms in office. Although supported by the Conservative Party during his early career, he resisted formal party affiliation until he formed the *Federación Na-*

cional Velasquista, a party which served only as a vehicle for its leader's personality.

The Parties in Law

The 1978 constitution took steps to restrict the growth of splinter parties and to increase their accountability in an effort to reduce the role of individual personalities, such as Velasco Ibarra. In mid-1982, there were thirteen legal parties.

The Law of Parties establishes the conditions under which a party will be recognized. A party wishing to compete in elections must submit information to the Supreme Electoral Tribunal, the most important of which includes the following: a declaration of ideological principles; a detailed government plan indicating the policies the party would undertake if successful in the presidential elections; certification of membership equal to at least 1.5 percent of the registered voters in the last elections; and evidence of national support demonstrating the existence of the party in at least ten provinces, including two of the three most populous provinces, which are dominated by the cities of Guayaquil, Quito, and Portoviejo. A party must submit this information and be qualified six months prior to an election it wishes to contest. This requirement does not apply to coalitions formed within six months of an election. Any party failing to obtain 5 percent of the vote in two successive elections loses its official recognition. Two parties have lost recognition since the passage of the Law of Elections in 1978.

According to the Law of Elections, parties are to be financed from obligatory membership contributions, donations, and state assistance. Traditionally, parties have depended heavily on private contributions from wealthy individuals and from organizations such as the Chambers of Commerce, Agriculture, and Industry, giving these groups disproportionate political leverage. Provision for state assistance is designed to counterbalance this influence. Two state funds have been established; each receives 0.05 percent of total government expenditures. The first fund provides yearly assistance to parties which received at least 10 percent of the vote in the most recent, national legislature elections. Sixty percent of this election fund is distributed in equal shares among the qualifying parties; 40 percent is distributed in proportion to the number of votes obtained in the most recent national elections. In election years, the second fund provides additional resources for election expenditures and is distributed in proportion to the number of votes obtained in the most recent national elections. According to the vote obtained in the 1979 congressional elections, only two parties, the CFP and the ID, qualified for state assistance.

Party Organization

Party organization in Ecuador has traditionally been very weak, reflecting the elite nature of politics. The very small size of the electorate has meant that parties have little need to be accountable. Personalistic domination of many parties has hindered the development of programmatic policies, and parties are not characterized by consistent ideological positions. Parties tend to appear before elections, campaign furiously, and disappear until the next round of elections. Party membership is very limited; there has been virtually no effort to create mass-based organizations. As a result, although party activity is intense, it takes place among small groups of elites and tends to involve Byzantine political maneuvering for short-term advantage. This tendency, when combined with the large number of parties, sets the stage for constantly shifting coalitions and alliances.

The 1978 constitution and the revised Law of Parties represented a serious effort to change the traditional conduct of politics. If enforced, these revisions should reduce the number of competing parties and force those remaining to adopt more programmatic policies. In addition, the enfranchisement of illiterates may increase the accountability of parties, particularly those that campaign on promises of social reform.

Campaigning

Campaigns are characterized by intense periods of political activity and traditionally have relied heavily on the oratorical skills of the candidates. Velasco Ibarra, an unparalleled performer in this arena, is said to have boasted, "give me a balcony and the people are mine." Given the elite character of parties, campaign donations have assumed great importance since dues have been an insignificant source of funds and state assistance was not legislated until 1978. As a result, the parties which the economic elites choose to support have a clear advantage.

Extremely weak party organizations and the extreme geographic isolation of many parts of the country discourages national party control of local campaigning. The traditional feudal structure, particularly in the Sierra, lends itself to the creation of political fiefdoms.

Independent Voters

Party identification in Ecuador is very weak. The majority of voters have learned that whichever party holds office, it has little concrete impact on their lives. Most of these voters tend to vote for personality rather than party. For the small group of elites who stand to gain or lose from the policies of different parties, there is somewhat greater party identification, but even this identification is largely opportunistic.

Concentration of Popular Forces (*Concentración de Fuerzas Populares;* CFP)

History

The large influx of rural migrants into Guayaquil, beginning in the 1920s, provided the base for the CFP, which was established in that city under Carlos Guevara Moreno in 1949. It represents the closest example of a populist movement to be found in Ecuadorian politics. The CFP under Guevara Moreno firmly controlled Guayaquil politics, but it was never able to compete successfully in national elections. Guevara Moreno ran for the presidency in 1953, but was defeated by the rightist candidate, Camilo Ponce. With this defeat, Guevara Moreno gradually withdrew from active political life.

Assad Bucaram assumed control of the CFP in 1960 and was elected mayor of Guayaquil in 1962. Under Bucaram, the CFP began to emerge as a significant national political force. One indication of the CFP's growing national strength was its capture of five of the sixteen provincial seats in the national congress in 1968. Bucaram was widely regarded as a certain victor in the presidential elections of 1978, but he was disqualified by the military on the grounds that neither of his parents was born in Ecuador. The CFP selected Jaime Roldós, the ultimate victor, as its candidate, and Bucaram was elected president of the new Chamber of Representatives.

Organization

The CFP is primarily a Coastal party which became a serious national force only with the election of Jaime Roldós to the presidency. From the beginning of the new administration, however, conflict between Roldós and Bucaram paralyzed the government and threatened to split the party. Roldós maneuvered to remove Bucaram from the Chamber presidency and to create his own political party, People, Change and Democracy (PCD). By 1981, the party had split into two factions. Bucaram's death in the same year further weakened the party and threatened to splinter it as potential successors competed for its leadership.

Policy

The CFP has traditionally been a personalistic, not an ideological, movement which has represented itself as strongly opposed to the privileges of the oligarchy. A statement of CFP philosophy emphasizes "its essence, which is profoundly democratic, progressive, antifeudal, contrary to the *caciquismo* of cliques and influential bigwigs, republican, law-abiding, and supportive of large-scale social and economic transformation."

In practice, the CFP is a moderate left-wing reformist party officially committed to ending the privileges of the oligarchy and to implementing programs in aid of the poor. Land reform is viewed as central to restructuring the agricultural sector. It supports expanded political participation of all groups in Ecuadorian society.

Membership & Constituency

The stronghold of CFP support has traditionally been the Guayaquil lower middle classes. In the most recent presidential elections, the party made a concerted effort to appeal to middle-class professionals, a group created by the petroleum boom of the 1970s.

Financing

The CFP was one of two parties to be awarded state assistance in 1980, receiving 8,464,120 sucres (about $338,500). No other details on party finances are available.

Leadership

With the deaths of Roldós and Bucaram, the party was left without a strong leader. Temporary leadership, pending a national party convention, was assumed by Rafael de la Cadena.

Prospects

The party's strength has diminished because of the conflict between Roldós and Bucaram and the latter's death. The new vice president, León Roldós, assumed leadership of the fledging PCD, withdrawing this group from the government coalition in 1982. In the same year, the opposing Bucaram faction of the CFP agreed to join the government. The CFP fell to third place in the 1980 provincial and municipal elections, losing heavily to the FRA in its traditional stronghold, Guayas province (Guayaquil). The CFP will have difficulty sustaining the strength it has demonstrated in the last three years and may soon cease to be an important national political force.

Conservative Party
(*Partido Conservador Ecuatoriano;* PC)

History

The Conservative Party, Ecuador's oldest political party, was founded in 1855 by Gabriel Garcia Moreno, an autocratic leader who dominated Ecuadorian politics until his assasination in 1875. The party has traditionally represented the landed elite of the Sierra. Although still influential, the party has not succeeded in winning the presidency since 1956. To broaden its base of support, the Conservative Party sought to modernize its platform in 1966 with a declaration of principles which softened its position on the unity of church and state and called for basic social reforms. With these changes some of its more traditional supporters defected to other parties on the political right.

Organization

The party has suffered from considerable factionalism in recent years. In 1976, the party split into left and right wings, with the former organizing as the Progressive Conservative Party, which later joined with another party to form Popular Democracy (DP).

Policy

The party is generally rightist, although loss of support and internal conflict have modified its traditional orientation somewhat. Ironically, it was the first party to introduce a bill into the legislature calling for land reform while at the same time

expressing its belief in an innate right to private property.

Membership & Constituency

The Conservative Party is a national party with its base in the Sierra. Its presidential candidates in 1956 and 1960 polled barely 9 percent of the Coastal vote. The Sierra vote was sufficient, however, to gain the victory of the Conservative candidate in 1956, when only a plurality of votes was needed to win. Support for the Conservative Party has declined in recent years.

Financing

No details of party financing are available. The party did not qualify for state subsidies after the 1979 elections.

Leadership

The leader of the party is Rafael Armijos Valdivieso. Born in 1918, he followed a military career, reaching the rank of colonel, before retiring. He was elected as a national representative to congress in 1979 and was chosen vice president of congress. He lost that position in 1981. Armijos represents the most traditional sectors in society.

Prospects

The party's prospects for active electoral participation are poor. It has lost both moderate and very conservative support to other parties.

Democratic Left
(*Izquierda Democratica;* ID)

History

The ID was formed in 1970 as the result of a Liberal Party split. Dissatisfaction with the Liberals' support of Velasco in 1969 and dissension within the party over candidates for mayor and municipal council of Quito in 1970 precipitated the division. The ID fielded its own candidates in the 1970 election and won a sound victory. In the first round of the presidential elections in 1978, the ID candidate won 11 percent of the vote; in the second round, it supported the victorious CFP candidate Jaime Roldós. In the congressional elections of 1979, the ID won twelve seats.

Organization

The ID has emerged as an important national force in spite of intraparty disagreement between a moderate group advocating reform and a more extreme group committed to radical structural solutions. The ID is affiliated with the Socialist International.

Policy

The ID is a moderate left-wing party which advocates democratic socialism and defines itself as "democratic-revolutionary." It supports land reform and proposes a nationally elected fourth branch of government, a review council, whose function would be to monitor the activities of the legislative and administrative branches. It would have authority to dismiss ministers and to impose sanctions on the president and legislators. The party also supports the creation of a new international economic order. Its government plan is the most detailed of all the parties, drawing on extensive statistics of social and economic conditions in Ecuador.

Membership & Constituency

The ID's main base of support is the province of Pinchincha (Quito), but its influence is growing as witnessed by its showing in the 1980 provincial elections where it took second place with 14 percent of the vote.

Financing

One of the two parties to be awarded state aid, the ID received 4,485,880 sucres (about $179,435) in 1980. No other information about its finances is available.

Leadership

The leader of the ID is Rodrigo Borja Cevallos (born 1936), a lawyer and former university teacher who led the 1970 split from the Liberal Party. He is currently a national representative in the legislature.

Prospects

Prospects for the ID appear to be excellent. The party has strong representation in the Chamber of Representatives and has demonstrated widespread support in the provincial elections. Con-flict within the party may cause some problems, but the ID has demonstrated remarkable party discipline compared to the other major parties.

Popular Democracy—Christian Democratic Union (*Democracia Popular—Union Demócrata Cristiana;* DP)

History

The DP was formed from an alliance of the Christian Democratic Party and the Progressive Conservative Party in early 1978. The former was originally formed in 1964 by university students, faculty, and young professionals. At the time of the alliance, it was led by Osvaldo Hurtado, who was elected vice president in 1979 and became president on Roldós's death in 1981. The Progressive Conservative Party was a progressive faction of the Conservative Party. In the presidential elections in 1978 and 1979, the DP was restricted in its participation by the military government and chose to support the CFP. In the 1979 National Chamber elections, the DP won five seats (three on the CFP list and two on the ID list); it currently holds seven seats.

Organization

With the succession of its leader to the presidency, the party has become a national force, in spite of its weak, urban-centered organization. It is affiliated with the Christian Democratic Organization of America and with the Christian Democratic World Union.

Policy

The DP is a center-left party which claims as its fundamental objective that of serving as a means of political expression for rural and urban popular organizations. It advocates "popular democracy" as opposed to "formal democracy": in the latter the people choose from an agenda presented to them by the dominant groups in society, while in the former, the agenda supposedly rises from the grass roots. In keeping with this view, the Roldós-Hurtado administration has sought to greatly increase political participation. The DP also advocates the establishment of *empresas comunitarias* or worker-controlled organizations.

Membership & Constituency

Support for the DP has grown in recent years as the party has emerged as a significant national electoral force. In the 1980 elections, it took a strong second place in Guayas province, which comprises one-quarter of the electorate. It draws its traditional support from urban intellectuals and professionals, but has clearly broadened its base in recent years.

Financing

No financial details are available. The party was not eligible for state subsidies after the 1979 elections.

Leadership

The party president is Dr. Julio César Trujillo (born 1931), a labor lawyer who led a split from the Conservative Party in 1976 and founded Popular Democracy in 1977. In 1979, he was elected to the National Chamber from Pinchincha province. Osvaldo Hurtado Larrea (born 1930) is leader of the Christian Democrats, which he founded in 1964. Hurtado was a professor of political sociology at the Catholic University in Quito, from which he graduated with a law degree in 1966.

Prospects

The DP's prospects for the future are synonomous with those of President Osvaldo Hurtado. The party has shown solid electoral strength in recent elections, but is experiencing heavy criticism from both the left and the right in the National Chamber and must struggle to maintain a governing coalition. In a country where personality plays an important role in politics, Hurtado's reserved, intellectual style may prove a serious drawback. The economy may also play an important role in the future of the DP. As the party in power, it must deliver on its reformist promises or face the threat of a loss of popular support. The recent decline in export earnings raises serious questions about the DP's ability to do this.

Radical Liberal Party
(*Partido Liberal Radical Ecuatoriano;* PLR)

History

The Liberal Party was founded in 1890 under the leadership of Pedro Carbo. In 1895, the Liberal Revolution ended the first period of Conservative rule and brought the Liberal Party to power under Eloy Alfaro. Liberals dominated Ecuadorian politics until the ouster of Carlos Arroyo del Río in 1944. The two constitutions introduced during the 1895–1944 period contained sweeping reforms such as the establishment of equality under law, a guarantee of free public education, separation of church and state, and provisions that commanded the state to assume responsibility for the protection of the indigenous Indians. There remained a considerable gap between this legislation and its effective implementation.

Since 1944, the Liberal Party has been plagued by disunity. It successfully backed Galo Plaza for president in 1948, but has not held the presidency since that time. In 1970, internal conflict caused liberal and socialist elements in the party to leave to form the Democratic Left Party; in 1972 Abdón Calderón left to form the Radical Alfarista Front (FRA).

Organization

The Liberal Party is a national party with its power base on the Coast. Intraparty disagreements have been serious and have seriously diminished the party's electoral effectiveness.

Policy

Historically the party has advocated separation of church and state, secular education, and a federal structure of government. The party has had difficulty developing a position with contemporary electoral appeal. It claims to have a leftist orientation but, in reality, is more accurately identified as centrist. Its most recent platform pledges the party to "authentic democracy," reaffirms its support for secular education, advocates private enterprise as long as this does not become exploitative, and supports land reform. Its government plan is detailed and makes considerable effort to analyze Ecuador's problems according to dependency theory, which emphasizes a developing country's relationship to the international economy.

Membership & Constituency

The Liberal Party has its strongest base of support on the Coast; support from the Sierra was eroded with the formation of the Democratic Left Party. The party has traditionally been supported by the financial and commercial elites of Guayaquil. Electoral support for the Liberal Party has been diminishing in recent years.

Financing

No information is available on party finances.

Leadership

Party leaders include Pedro José Areta and Francisco Hidalgo Villavicencio.

Prospects

The prospects for the Liberal Party are not promising. Continued intraparty conflict and the growth of the Democratic Left suggest that the party will not play a major role in future elections.

Minor Parties

Democratic Institutionalist Coalition (*Coalición Institutionalista Democrática,* CID)

A right-wing traditional political party which serves largely as a vehicle for the aspirations of former president Otto Arosemena Gómez (born 1922), the CID has little electoral support.

Democratic Party (*Partido Demócrata;* PD)

The leader of the PD is Francisco Huerta Montalvo, formerly of the Liberal Party, who was elected mayor of Guayaquil in 1970. The party is social democratic in orientation. Demonstrating increasing strength in the National Chamber, it claimed four representatives as of May 1982.

Left Broad Front (*Frente Amplio de Izquierda;* FADI)

A brief alliance of six left-wing parties, including the Ecuadorian Communist Party (PCE), formed to contest the presidential elections of 1978, the FADI's candidate and leader was René Maugé Mosquera.

Nationalist Revolutionary Party (*Partido Nacionalista Revolucionario;* PNR)

A personalistic party which has served as a political vehicle for former president Carlos Julio Arosemena Monroy (born 1919), the PNR is in danger of losing its official recognition as a legitimate party.

National Constitutional Front (*Frente Nacional Constitucionalista;* FNC)

The FNC was an alliance of eleven right-wing and center-right parties formed solely for the purpose of supporting a candidate, Durán Sixto Ballén, former mayor of Quito, in the 1978 presidential elections.

Nationalist Velasquista Party (*Partido Nacionalista Velasquista;* PNV)

The PNV is a personalistic, populist party which has served as a vehicle for the political ambitions of Velasco Ibarra. With Ibarra's death in 1979, the party's long-term survival is problematic.

People, Change and Democracy (*Pueblo, Cambio y Democracia;* PCD)

Formed by Jaime Roldós in 1980 with anti-Bucaram members of the CFP, the PCD withdrew from government coalition in 1981. The leaders include Aquiles Rigail and the former president's brother León Roldós Aguilera.

Democratic Popular Movement (*Movimiento Popular Democrático;* MPD)

A far-left party which is the legal vehicle for the radical Marxist-Leninist Communist Party, the MPD is led by Jaime Hurtado Gonzalez (born 1937), a national representative to congress. Based on its performance in the last two elections in which it failed to gain 5 percent of the vote, the MPD should lose its official recognition.

Popular Democratic Union (*Union Democrático Popular;* UDP)

The legal representative of the Ecuadorian Communist Party, the UDP is currently recognized by the Supreme Electoral Tribunal, but as it has failed to gain 5 percent of the vote in the last two elections, the UDP is likely to lose its recognition. Its leader is Pedro Saad Niyaim.

Radical Alfarista Front (*Frente Radical Alfarista;* FRA)

The FRA is a populist party formed when a group under the leadership of Abdón Calderón Muñoz split from the Liberal Party in 1968. Calderón was assassinated by the military junta in

November 1978. In January 1979, the FRA lost its official recognition. Under the leadership of Calderón's daughter, Cecilia Calderón (born 1950), the FRA regained recognition in 1980 and took first place in the provincial elections of that year with 19 percent of the vote. This success has been generally interpreted as a protest vote over the slow pace of reforms under the Roldós-Hurtado government and not as an indication of lasting political support for the FRA.

Social Christian Party (*Partido Social Cristiano;* PSC)

The PSC is a right-wing, personalistic party formed originally to serve the interests of former Conservative president Camilo Ponce Enriquez. In the 1978 presidential elections, the PSC's candidate was Guayas Chamber of Industry president León Febres Cordero (born 1931), a vehement opponent of the new constitution and the increased opportunities for democratic participation it promised. Febres Cordero is currently a national representative in congress.

Other Political Forces

Military

The military has played an active role in Ecuadorian politics; over 30 percent of Ecuador's presidents have been army officers. About six times as many military officers are from the Sierra as from the Coast and tend to come from middle-class families. Typically, the military has remained in power only briefly, viewing its role as caretaker and defender of the constitutional order. Even without direct involvement, the military plays a significant role since the threat of military intervention does much to shape the course of politics. Recently the military has taken power for longer periods of time.

Since 1960, military juntas have ruled Ecuador on two separate occasions. The first military junta took power in 1963, using the threat of Cuban communist intervention to justify its action. Its proposed policies were reformist. Its most notable achievement was the establishment of Ecuador's first land-reform legislation, but very little reform was actually realized. The military withdrew from power in 1966, under heavy criticism from nearly all sectors of society. In 1972, the military again entered politics, this time in response to its perception of threats of destabilization created by Ecuador's new petroleum wealth and from the almost certain victor in the presidential elections to be held that year, Assad Bucaram. The second junta proclaimed itself reformist and nationalist in the style of the Peruvian military at that time. Severe internal disagreements over the proper political model for the military and strong opposition from civilian elites prevented the realization of any significant reforms. Again under heavy criticism, the military withdrew from power in 1979. The military remains an important political force which can be expected to intervene if it perceives a need to safeguard constitutional order. It represents an important political constraint on what is possible for any party in office.

Students

Students in Ecuador, while not well organized, have often mounted major demonstrations which have served as the catalysts in every nonconstitutional change of government but one since 1944. Both secondary and university students are highly political and generally leftist in their political orientation. The two major student organizations are the Federation of University Students of Ecuador (*Federación de Estudiantes Universitarios del Ecuador;* FEUE) and the Federation of Secondary Students of Ecuador (*Federación de Estudiantes Secundarios del Ecuador;* FESE). Students at the Central University (several public campuses) tend to be the most radical and active.

Organized Labor

Labor unions in Ecuador have traditionally been weak, owing in large part to the low level of economic development. Union membership represents less than 10 percent of all workers. Certain unions, such as the professional drivers' association (*Federación del Choferes Profesionales del Ecuador*), hold considerable veto power over government policy through the effectiveness of their strikes. However, organized labor has not been particularly important either in deciding the agenda of politics or through disciplined support of parties.

Interest-Group Organizations

The economic elites in Ecuador play a very important political role. Indeed, until very recently politics was a game played almost exclusively by these classes. Although the land-owning Sierra aristocracy still wields considerable influence, the most important group today is undoubtedly the commercial, financial, and banking elite of the Coast. Both these groups exercise political influence through the Chambers of Commerce, Industry, and Agriculture.

National Prospects

The stability of any government in Ecuador is always uncertain. Opportunistic shifts of allegiance by elite groups and the constant threat of military intervention make for a highly unpredictable political environment. The present government of Osvaldo Hurtado has performed remarkably well given the numerous problems it has faced during its first three years in office. There are, however, some potentially serious problems ahead. Hurtado's party has become increasingly isolated in the Chamber of Representatives and faces difficulty assembling a governing coalition, particularly as other parties begin to position themselves for the 1984 presidential elections. Expectations have been raised by the petroleum boom, but declining export revenues make their realization difficult. The present government has followed a policy of greatly expanding the electorate and has committed itself to a program of social reforms. If the government finds itself unable to deliver on its promises of social reform, it is likely to find its position very unstable.

Further Reading
Blanksten, George I. *Ecuador: Constitutions and Caudillos.* Berkeley: University of California Press, 1951.
Cueva, Agustin. *The Process of Political Domination in Ecuador.* New Brunswick, N. J.: Transaction Books, 1982.
Fitch, John Samuel. *The Military Coup D'Etat as a Political Process: Ecuador 1948–1966.* Baltimore: Johns Hopkins University Press, 1977.
Hurtado, Osvaldo. *Political Power in Ecuador.* Alburquerque: University of Mexico Press, 1980.
Martz, John D. *Ecuador: Conflicting Political Culture and the Quest for Progress.* New York: Allyn and Bacon, 1972.
Tribunal Supremo Electoral. *Principios Ideologicos y Planes de Gobierno de los Partidos Politicos de la Republica del Ecuador.* Quito, Ecuador, August 1981.

ARAB REPUBLIC OF EGYPT
(*Gumhuriyya Misr al-Arabiyya*)
by Louis J. Cantori, Ph.D.

The System of Government

The Arab Republic of Egypt is a presidential authoritarian state with the largest population (forty-four million) and the largest army (350,000) of any Arab state. It is also the Middle Eastern state with the longest history of modernization (with the advent of Muhammad Ali who ruled Egypt from 1805 to 1848). From Pharonic times until the present, the irrigation system of agriculture in the country seems to have fostered authoritarian rule. The modernization process has perhaps even refined this basic authoritarianism, but it has also introduced democratic tendencies. The "modern" autocracy of Muhammad Ali and the creation of representative or councilior bodies from 1866 on joined to produce the pendulum swings between democracy and authoritarianism of contemporary political Egypt. A further heritage of modernization has been an intense and deeply internalized nationalism. This nationalism has seized upon Pharonic and Islamic roots to produce a durable (but occasionally violated) nonsectarian unity of Christian Coptic population (7 percent) and a Sunni Muslim population (93 percent).

From 1805 to 1882, when British forces occupied the country, the Muhammad Ali dynasty was Egypt's sole modernizing force. The unilateral granting of independence by the British in 1922 after the bloody revolution of 1919 was only nominal. A growing pattern of social injustice due to corruption and inequality of landholding became subordinated to a preoccupation with continued British meddling. The revolution of July 1952 by Gamal Abd al-Nasser and his Free Officers finally evicted the British by the end of the 1956 Suez War and made significant strides in correcting social and economic injustices.

Under both Anwar Sadat and Hosni Mubarak, the Egyptian ruling elite can be characterized today as technobureaucratic in character. It is a component of a middle class whose large size and dominant political role in fact defines Egypt as a "middle class" state. Under Nasser, the military, itself from the middle class, dominated the politics of Egypt. Under Sadat, a new civilian segment of the middle class has replaced the previous military one at the center of the political stage. Whether military or civilian, however, the middle class, with its privileges and its concept of what is good for the Egyptian masses, rules. Other segments of the middle class consist of the professionals (doctors, lawyers, etc.) as well as new entrepreneurial capitalists and students.

Egypt has had a geopolitically determined hegemonial role to play in the Middle East region from the time the Nile Valley inhabitants achieved a level of agriculture able to support a large population and create sufficient wealth to support a developed civilization.

Population, wealth, and sophistication remain relevant elements in Egypt's position today, but added to them is a regional sense of Arabness and the role of Islam. Nasser, in the anti-imperialism of his national and international policy from 1952 to 1958, asserted Egyptian leadership over the region. The creation of the United Arab Republic (1958–61), consisting of Egypt and Syria, also asserted Egyptian leadership, now in the name of Arab socialism. The June 1967 defeat and the loss of Sinai and the Suez Canal had the effect of reorienting Egyptian foreign policy from a preoccupation with inter-Arab rivalries to a primacy of concern with Israel. The defeat, however, had the effect of diminishing the stature of Egyptian leadership. The 1969–70 war of attrition across the Suez Canal helped restore it somewhat, but the Camp David accords and subsequent Israel-Egypt peace treaty isolated Egypt diplomatically in the Arab world. Virtually all of the Arab states broke relations with Egypt, and the Arab League headquarters, which had been in Cairo since 1945, moved to Tunis. Egypt's "natural" leadership role in the Arab state system, however, has led to expected efforts by Sadat's successor, Mubarak, to reverse this state of affairs.

Executive

The president of the republic epitomizes the authoritarianism of Egyptian political culture. The constitution of 1971 merely codifies the fact that a single person has wielded supreme authority in Egypt since the July 1952 revolution (Gamal Abd al-Nasser, 1952–70; Anwar al-Sadat, 1970–81; and Hosni Mubarak, 1981 to date). Moreover, the constitution, while delineating the considerable power of the office of president, has hardly ever served to exercise restraint upon the president himself. Instead, such restraint has tended to come from reactions of an often violent nature from the population, e.g., the February 1968 protests against the light sentences of generals held responsible for the disaster of the June 1967 war with Israel or the January 1977 "food riots" in protest against a decision to abolish food subsidies. The general pattern, however, has been one of acquiescence in even extreme abuses of executive authority.

The political position of Mubarak was strengthened by the anticipated regaining of Sinai from the Israelis on April 25, 1982. This date acted as a domestic constraint by putting a premium upon national unity and assisted Mubarak in the major task of consolidating his authority after Sadat's assassination on October 6, 1981. Mubarak has proceeded with a mixed policy of repression of the most extreme of the religious right wing and conciliation of the less extreme (e.g., release of the Muslim Brethren arrested earlier by Sadat). Mubarak has emerged as a synthesizer of Nasser and Sadat policies. Thus a renewed emphasis is to be put upon the public sector (Nasser), but foreign private investment is still encouraged (Sadat). In foreign policy, Egypt is to be positively neutral and nonaligned (Nasser), but Sadat's firm commitment to the Americans remains. The death of Sadat has had the effect of removing from the scene a focus of Arab anger over the peace treaty. Thus, for example, the meeting of Arab League heads of state in Rabat, Morocco, in November 1981, was notable for its lack of vituperation directed at Egypt. Subsequently, a meeting in Kuwait of the Non-Aligned Conference Executive Committee in April 1982 was attended by Egypt. The Iranian-Iraqi war has found the Egyptians providing the Iraqis with $800 million worth of Soviet equipment. Upon the death of King Khalid of Saudi Arabia, Mubarak payed a visit of condolence to the new king, Fahd. In fact, a pattern has emerged of Egyptian-Saudi Arabian consultation and communication.

The June 1982 Israeli invasion of Lebanon provided Egypt with a further opportunity to reestablish its Arab identification. From the beginning, Egypt was harsh in its criticism of Israel. Egypt retained diplomatic relations, but it put the normalization of economic, tourist, and cultural relations in a deep freeze. In the negotiations over the PLO evacuation from Beirut, Egypt wanted to relate the outcome of the Lebanese crisis to the West Bank issue. It said it would not accept any PLO members unless Israel agreed to withdraw from Lebanon as a whole. Furthermore, Egypt said it would not take part in the previously stalled Camp David autonomy talks until Israel had withdrawn from Lebanon and had agreed to the objective of autonomy for the people of the West Bank by 1985. In taking this position, Mubarak was placing some distance between himself and a United States policy viewed widely in the Arab world as either having colluded with Israel in the invasion or at least as having condoned it.

Legislature

Egypt has had a history of consultative or elected legislatures since 1866. As presently constituted, the People's Assembly (*Majlis al-Sha'ab*) consists of 392 members. Of these, 382 are elected and ten appointed. Sadat named Christian Copts to the appointive seats in order to alleviate religious tensions. In addition, in the thirty constituencies (mostly urban) which elect three members each to the legislature, one of those members must be a woman. The other constituencies elect two representatives each. In the 1979 elections, the government's National Democratic Party won 330 seats; the Socialist Labor Party, twenty-nine; the Socialist Liberal Party, three; and independents, ten.

Although the *Majlis* is constitutionally and practically subordinated to the personality and office of president, it would be wrong to dismiss its political importance. As an elected body, it symbolically represents the democratic strain within Egypt. As such, it can be seen as legitimizing any ruler in power. Furthermore, especially since the 1976 advent of political parties, it has acted in some degree as a safety valve for points of view at variance with those of the government. Members also serve the important functions of interceding for their constituents with the national bureaucracy and of presenting specific community needs to the government.

Judiciary

The Egyptian judicial system is based on the French system introduced into the country in 1854. It is extraordinary in that it has been able to preserve a relative degree of independence from political interference. This was especially true under Gamal Abd al-Nasser, but also under Anwar al-Sadat. As late in his rule as 1969, Nasser felt the need to attempt to purge the judiciary. The judiciary and the Egyptian Bar Association both opposed Sadat's effort to impose a three-person tribunal system called the Law of Shame (*ganun al-'aib*), which he intended to use against political opponents. Sadat forced the law through the Parliament in April 1980, but due to the strong opposition of the bar association, it was never really implemented. "Shame" referred to the shame of the family, and violations of the law were defined as acts of shame against the Egyptian "family," i.e., the nation. On the one hand, it was a law reflecting Egyptian authoritarianism, and yet on the other hand, it was constrained by Egyptian "democratic" pluralism.

Regional & Local Government

Local government in Egypt until 1975 had been heavily dominated by the national government. In that year, Law 52, calling for administrative decentralization as part of President Sadat's program of political liberalization, was promulgated. Other laws since have had the stated purpose of increasing the administrative independence of Egypt's twenty-six provincial governors. In addition, elected local popular councils increasingly are supposed to take policy initiatives. The outcome thus far appears to be mixed. It does appear that the authority of the governors has been increased, but there is a question of whether this has been accomplished at the expense of local village and urban elected councils.

The Electoral System

All Egyptians age eighteen and over are eligible to vote; voting is compulsory for men. Candidates for the legislature are put forth by the parties and the voter casts his or her vote for the party list, not for the individual candidate. If no party receives a majority in the constituency, a run-off election between the two leading parties takes place, usually a week later. Candidates are required to live in the districts they hope to represent.

The fact that the electoral law calls for the political parties to offer candidates is somewhat undercut by the requirement that candidates be approved by a three-person committee consisting of a member of the judiciary, a representative of the government, and a member of the security forces.

The Party System

Origins of the Parties

Egypt had a parliamentary multiparty system before the 1952 revolution, which was followed by a succession of single-party structures. The first of these, the Liberation Rally (1952–58), was ostensibly set up as a mass-mobilizational party, but in reality it was perhaps intended more to fill the gap left by the banned Wafd Party which had dominated Egyptian politics from 1918 until 1952. The Liberation Rally lasted until the advent of political union with Syria in 1958. It was replaced by the National Union Movement which became the official party of the Egyptian and Syrian regions of the United Arab Republic. Egypt's Arab Socialist ideological phase, which began in July 1961, was accompanied by the creation of a new organization, the Arab Socialist Union (ASU). Even more than its predecessors, this party was intended to be a disciplined, ideological, mass-mobilization party. In fact, however, with the possible exception of the so called "Vanguard" period (1965–68), the ASU, like its predecessors, was less an instrument of mobilization and more one of political control. This does not mean that the Egypt of Nasser was not progressive or did not meet the needs of the masses. It did so, but it carried out measures of land reform, nationalization, etc., in a paternalistic, authoritarian fashion. Sadat kept the ASU in existence until 1978, but in reality his commitment to economic and political liberalization was such that the party's position rapidly deteriorated. It was legally abolished by the *Majlis* in April 1980. In March 1976, Sadat began a new experiment with a multiparty system. In that year, he encouraged the formation of "forums" or "pulpits" (*al-manabir*) of left, right, and center opinions within the *Majlis*. By late 1976, these were permitted to take the identity of political parties and compete in that year's parliamentary elections.

Sadat was sincere in wanting to break out of the mold of Egypt's experience with a single-party structure. A reading of his autobiography, *In Search of Identity*, provides a clue to what his conception of such a party system was to be. One of the historical figures who inspired him was Kemal Attaturk, the great modernizer of Turkey. Like Attaturk, Sadat wanted to introduce democracy and yet retain control of the political process. Thus, it is not surprising that in late 1975, when the "forums" were under discussion, Egypt's parliamentary leaders invited two Turkish political scientists to Egypt in order to get information about Turkey's experience with political parties.

The first blush of party democracy was diminished, however, by events which appear to have shaken Sadat's democratic resolve. The first of these was the limited outburst of protest against price increases in January 1975, during which trains and buses were damaged or destroyed but no lives were lost. The second and more serious event was the January 1977 demonstrations against a threatened end to food subsidies. Like the 1975 disturbance, the 1977 disturbance appears to have been a spontaneous movement largely free of organization. Nonetheless, violence against government offices and police stations took place in all major cities and towns from the north to the south of Egypt. Over seventy persons were killed and the regime was shaken. The threatened cuts were rescinded, and the food subsidies of more than three billion dollars annually continued. Other events of a politically threatening kind followed, chiefly, acts of political violence by a right-wing religious group in June and July 1977.

In November 1977 President Sadat made his dramatic visit to Israel, setting in motion a peace process which was to result in the Camp David accords of 1978 with Israel and the peace treaty of March 1979. These foreign-policy ventures had the support of overwhelming numbers of Egyptians. Nonetheless, they gave his critics from the left and the right additional ammunition. These events and, especially, the necessity of asserting his control domestically as he attempted to meet the obligations of the peace treaty with Israel, led Sadat to tighten his political control. In early spring 1978—true to both authoritarian form and to the constitution—Sadat resorted to a plebiscite. Among questions asked of a devout Muslim/Christian population was whether they thought atheists should participate in politics. They also were asked if they thought that individuals associated with the pre-1952 corrupt political parties should be permitted to participate in politics. A nearly 100 percent "no" vote led to the "voluntary" withdrawal from the 1979 parliamentary elections of the National Union Progressivists

(the presumed Marxist leftists who "naturally" are atheists) and the New Wafd Party (the presumed "corrupt" individuals from pre-1952). The results of the election thus confirmed a political shift to the center and right. The seal upon the reassertion of executive authority came in a plebiscite in the following spring when the constitution was amended to allow the president (Sadat) to have more than two terms. Sadat then used his authority under the constitution to become both president and prime minister.

The attitude of the regime towards the new multiparty system has differed under Sadat's successor, Mubarak. Faced perhaps with the necessity to extend his appeal upon succeeding Sadat, Mubarak has adopted a distinctly less repressive attitude toward the political parties and, in fact, seems to have fallen into a pattern of consultation with them on policy matters.

The Parties in Law

Having launched the political-party experiment in November 1976, Sadat then began to act to restrict parties in the aftermath of the January 1977 food riots. In February 1977 a law was passed stating that there could be no more than three parties. In June 1977 an additional law stated that a party, in order to maintain existence, had to have at least twenty members in the *Majlis*. This would have eliminated all parties except the centrist Arab Socialist Party (after June 1978, the National Democratic Party) if the law had been implemented. A year later, after the plebiscite, atheistic (National Unionist Progressivist Party), pre-1952 parties (New Wafd Party), and all religious parties were excluded from legal electoral status. Finally, in April 1980, these restrictions were made part of the constitution, the Arab Socialist Union was abolished, and the Socialist Labor Party was designated the official opposition party.

Party Organization

With the partial exception of the leftist National Union Progressivist Party and the official National Democratic Party, Egyptian political parties have formal structures only on paper, if that. They are essentially congeries of upper- and middle-class urban elites and have little or no connection to the mass of the population beyond either ideological appeals or patron-client relationships, which most members of these elites maintain through their positions as bureaucrats, businessmen, or landowners.

The parties are not aimed at gaining control of the government, but at presenting to the government issues and alternatives that it may have overlooked. If not in clear opposition, party leaders also hope to aquire whatever favors or privileges may come their way if the government should adopt one or more of the policies they advocate. Even the leaders of the opposition parties are not without hope that a sudden change in state leadership or international conditions could catapult them into a position of major influence within the government.

In the absence of formal structures, the parties are dominated by family, peer group, and "old boy" ties. These ties provide the cohesiveness and dynamism of the parties and the society as a whole.

The extended family, including grandparents and aunts and uncles, is the most important of these ties. The authority of the father is absolute, an important clue to the persistence of Egypt's authoritarian culture. President Sadat made a practice of referring to the Egyptian nation as the Egyptian family. The Law of Shame, for example, was defined in terms of violations of the precepts of the Egyptian family. The family also represents an important network of influence, i.e., personal loyalty to the family and its collateral relationships precedes any other. Thus, the solidarity of the political elite surrounding Sadat was enhanced by patterns of intermarriage.

The peer group (*shilla*) is a second important informal grouping. Egyptian men, both young and old, belong to such groups. The *shilla*'s more egalitarian character perhaps offsets the authoritarianism of the family. The peer groups are bound by loyalty and constitute an additional influence network. In fact, in Egypt under Sadat, his elite associates were frequently referred to as his *shilla*, and as is the case throughout Egypt, marital bonds between *shilla* members tended to reenforce the solidarity of Sadat's *shilla*.

The old-boy network is related to the educational system. High school, college, and military graduating classes are referred to as the *dufa'a* of the graduating year. Thus in the July 1952 Revolution, Nasser, Sadat, and fifteen to twenty of the other Free Officers leading the revolution were members of the *dufa'a* of 1938 from the military academy. Likewise, at least three or four of the conspirators in the failed May 1971 coup attempt were members of the academy's 1947 graduating class. A *dufa'a* and peer group provide positions of influence in many different sectors of society and broad networks of contacts and patronage.

Campaigning

The campaign for the June 1979 elections was undertaken with some vigor by the political parties. All except the National Democratic Party, however, were handicapped by their lack of access to government-controlled television and radio. In addition, newsprint for the publication of newspapers and campaign materials was only sporadically available for the nongovernmental Socialist Labor and Socialist Liberal Parties. Political violence also attended the campaign; one person was killed and scores wounded.

National Democratic Party (NDP; *Hizb al-Dimuqratti al-Wattaniyya*)

The NDP is the official government party. When the "forums" were established in 1976, the regime did not seem intent upon establishing its own political party. The centrist party was the Egyptian Arab Socialist Party, and its leader was Abu Wafia. Wafia, although related by marriage to Sadat, was not an important personality in the regime itself. By 1978, the regime decided to identify itself more directly in the party system and changed the party's name to the National Democratic Party with then vice president Hosni Mubarak as its secretary general, a post he retained on suceeding Sadat as president of Egypt. From 1978 onwards, it appears that Sadat himself began to pay close attention to the party, demonstrated by his practice of speaking before regional meetings of the party and the use of the party newspaper *Mayu* (May, after the May 1971 corrective revolution) for statements of official policy.

The NDP, in contrast to the other parties, seems to have been able to erect an organizational structure from the top of the society to the local level. It has been assisted in this by two factors. First, it appears that administrative officials tend to identify with the party and, in fact, are beginning to operate a kind of patronage system at the local level in which economic assistance and government services become identified with the party. Second, and not surprisingly, the party seems to be utilizing former Arab Socialist Union officials to staff its organization. The adherence of government officials obviously reenforces the perception of the party as being official in nature and thus strengthens executive authority. The utilization of former ASU officials would appear to have the danger of reintroducing into the NDP the weaknesses of the former ASU: i.e., an overly bureaucratic mentality with its implications of "top down" authority and consequent stifling of political spontaneity and local initiative.

National Union Progressivist Party (NUPP; *Hizb al-Tajamaa al-Watani al-Taqaddam al-Wahdawi*)

The party of the left, the Progressivists stand for a social democratic and Marxist intellectual ideology. Under the leadership of Khalid Muhiyidin, one of the few Free Officers from July 1952 still prominent in politics, the party has supported a greater role for the public sector and a more neutral foreign policy. It has been critical of the 1978 Camp David accords and the March 1979 peace treaty with Israel. The party's appeal is primarily to the intellectual elite. In addition, however, it lays particular stress on its claim on being Nasserist and thus attempts to break out of its elitist confines. When not being harassed by the government, it has made some attempts at grassroots organization.

New Delegation Party (*Hizb al-Wafd al-Jadid*)

The Wafd was originally organized as a delegation to the Versailles peace conference of 1919 where it attempted to gain Egypt's independence from British control. It dominated Egyptian politics from then until 1952 when it was dissolved by the revolutionary regime. The New Wafd Party gains some strength from its association with the pre-1952 party, which enjoyed great popularity for its strenuous resistance to British interference in Egyptian government. On the other hand, the party has also been harmed by the fact that its leader, Fuad Seraq al-Din, was associated with the party's prior history of corruption. The New Wafd has placed itself just left of center. It has advocated a more balanced approach to the relationship of public and private sectors and has been critical of the government's encouragement of foreign investment.

Socialist Labor Party (*Hizb al-Amal al-Ishtiraki*)

The Socialist Labor Party is just right of center. Like the New Wafd, this party has pre-1952 origins, being related to a protofascist party, the Green Shirts (*Misr al-Fatat;* Egyptian Youth). Under the leadership of Ibrahim Shukri, it has generally subscribed to the liberalization policies of Sadat, while being especially critical of the peace treaty with Israel. It has been designated the official opposition party by the regime. Its labor connection appears to be an association with the higher echelon of organized labor, while the support of labor rank and file has been elusive. Thus, it is less a party of the socialist left than one with a commitment to the management of labor by the state and elite along corporatist of fascist lines.

Socialist Liberal Party (*Hizb al-Ahrar al-Ishtiraki*)

Farther to the right of the Socialist Labor Party, the Socialist Liberal Party is lead by Hilmi Murad. This party represents the point of view of liberal capitalism and as such subscribes to the Sadat-Mubarak liberalization policies while being mildly critical of peace with Israel. It differs from the other political parties in that it has no direct historical antecedents. It is very much an organizational expression of the nascent capitalism introduced by Sadat from 1974 onwards.

Other Political Forces

Military

The Egyptian army had carried out the Revolution of 1952 in a reasonably disciplined fashion. Thereafter, however, it fell into factionalism and corruption. It survived the Suez War of 1956 primarily because the combined forces of the Israelis, British, and French were seen as too overwhelming to judge its performance as a fighting force. The June 1967 War, however, revealed it to be incapable of fulfilling its military mission. The disastrous nature of that defeat led to its reconstitution as a disciplined force. Its later very satisfactory performance in the October 1973 War redeemed its reputation and set it in its present mold of professionalism, discipline, unity, and freedom from everyday political involvement. The *dufa'a* phenomenon, that is, Egypt's version of the old-boy network, is still present: President Mubarak and Defense Minister Abu Ghazaleh are members of the class of 1949. It is likely that the *dufa'a* as a political phenomenon will continue. Although not involved in daily politics, the army remains the ultimate factor in Egyptian politics, Mubarak was commander of the air force, General Kamal Hassan Ali is foreign minister, and General Abu Ghazallah is defense minister.

Interest Groups

Egypt, unlike other more typical Third World countries, possesses a substantial number of interest groups such as an active bar association, medical association, labor unions, etc. Not only is their number impressive, but they are neither superficial nor politically irrelevant as is often the case in underdeveloped countries. The effective political roots of such groups are anchored securely in class, (e.g., the bar association and the professional middle class or labor unions and the urban proletariat) and reinforced by family and other informal groupings. The vitality of such groupings can be seen in the case of the bar association's (founded prior to World War I) opposition to the Law of Shame as depriving Egyptians of the right of constitutional safeguards and due process. In addition, its opposition to the peace treaty resulted in Sadat's resorting to an internal coup of its executive committee in order to tame it. Likewise, the trade unions (there was a confederation of Egyptian trade unions by 1920) have proven to be militant—they took to the streets in February 1968 and there was some evidence of union activity in the January 1977 food riots. The result has been that government policy pays close heed to organized labor. In addition, there are an estimated 9,000 private voluntary organizations, e.g., daycare centers, orphanages, and Muslim charitable organizations.

Religious Right

A major contributing factor to an atmosphere of political instability developed when Sadat appealed to the religious right in order to legitimize and stabilize his government upon his accession to power. Additionally, the failed Nasserite coup of May 1971 made Sadat fearful of a threat from the left, which he attempted to counteract by the appeal to the religious right. The October War of 1973, for example, was termed Operation Badr (after the battle at the time of the Prophet Mu-

hammad against his Meccan opponents), and Egypt's domestic propaganda was full of religious appeals and symbols.

Sadat's autobiography revealed that he had always felt some sympathy for the Muslim Brotherhood (*Ikhwan al-Muslimin*), and from 1970 on he occasionally expressed that sympathy. The Brotherhood had been founded in Egypt in 1928 and became a formidable political factor before the 1952 revolution. Although it has long since been declared illegal, it is allowed to publish its newspaper, *al-Dawa* (The Call), from time to time. By 1975 Sadat had released hundreds of Brotherhood members who had been imprisoned after the assassination attempt on Nasser in 1954 and a coup attempt in 1965. The organization appears to have undergone an aging of its leadership, while at the same time being coopted by Sadat's sympathy (continued by Mubarak). The organization did not seem to be a factor in the religious turmoil of the 1970s and early 1980s.

Sadat's appeal to the religious right was occurring, however, in the context of an Islamic revival in the Middle East as a whole and in Egypt in particular. A number of factors have been adduced as to the reasons for this revival, but in Egypt one can speculate that it was a reaction to Nasserite socialism. The disastrous defeat of June 1967 signaled a failure of Nasser's socialism and at the same time sparked a turning inward in the effort to identify the causes of the defeat. Thus Sadat's encouragement of the religious right had the effect of generally inflaming religious sentiment.

There had already been scattered incidents of a religious nature, but in April 1974 the Islamic Liberation Organization launched an armed attack upon the Cairo Military Engineering College. The intention was to seize the college and then move on to kill President Sadat who was making a speech in the area. The attack was put down and the leaders eventually were executed. One of the individuals seized and then released in the ensuing crackdown was Shukri Mustafa, previously a member of the Muslim Brotherhood. He subsequently went on to form a militant group called *al-Takfir wa al-Higra* (Repentance and Migration) and was sought by the police. In July 1977, the group kidnapped and killed a former minister. By August, Mustafa and his group had been seized, brought to trial, and executed. However, the climate of religious political contentiousness continued.

By September 1981, harassed by a large number of such incidents, Sadat struck at all his opponents and put 1,500 under arrest. These included about 500 secular personalities, principally professors and journalists. The remaining 1,000 consisted of religionists, Muslim and Christian. While the Coptic Christian Pope Shenouda III was not arrested, Sadat exiled him to the countryside, and the Coptic Church was then headed by a committee of bishops. In cracking down on Muslims *and* Christians, Sadat was attempting to show his evenhandedness according to his principle "That there was to be no politics in religion and no religion in politics."

Sadat had thought that the July 1977 and the September 1981 crackdowns had dealt *al-Takfir* in particular and the Muslim fringe groups in general a death blow. But on October 6, 1981, *al-Takfir* struck back, assassinating Sadat and others on a reviewing stand during celebrations of the anniversary of the 1973 war. The assassins were brought to trial before a military court, convicted, and executed.

In the days following the assassination, another fringe organization, *al-Jihad* (Religious Struggle), led an insurrection in the southern city of Asyut; over seventy soldiers, police, and officers were killed. Once the uprising was put down, the new government under Mubarak began a process of reconciliation with the more secular political opposition, while continuing a crackdown upon the religious right, especially *al-Jihad*. The basis of the reconciliation with the secular groups was a tacit agreement that until the Israelis returned Sinai to the Egyptians on April 25, 1982, under the provisions of the peace treaty, there would be a show of national unity in order to deny the Israelis a pretext for not following through in their commitments.

The rightist religious groups represent and symbolize popular religious sentiment. And yet they appear to be recruited from educational groups (engineering, medicine, and religion) which consist of largely upwardly mobile individuals. What appears to have eluded them is widespread organizational capacity and, more importantly, mass popular support. Unless overall political circumstances change, it is unlikely that they will play more than an occasional episodic violent role.

Students

Among the elements of the dominant middle class are university students. Largely concentrated on two campuses in Cairo and a third in Alexandria, they are also increasingly important in provincial areas as well. Always a factor in Egyptian politics, especially during the Nasser pe-

riod, in Sadat's early years they became fragmented and politically diverse as political liberalization proceeded. From the beginning, however, Sadat began to appeal to the right-wing religious groups on the campuses in order to play them off against a perceived left-wing threat (i.e., the May 1971 coup attempt). These organizations, *jamiyyat al-Islam*, (religious organizations) have been a vocal, if perhaps a numerical, minority on the campuses.

Other Elites

Besides the dominant middle class, a powerful land-owning class and a religious elite are important elements in the Egyptian political process. About 1 percent of the landowning class possessed 20 percent of the land until the Nasser period, when much of its land was confiscated and redistributed to peasants. The maximum land holding was limited to fifty acres by 1969. Nevertheless, the landowning elite remained intact and in control of vast tracts and continues to play a significant role in the economy and the government.

The religious elite functions as a legitimizer of the government while acting as a bridge to the masses as a whole. This elite has not been particularly active in the recent rise of religious sentiment and radicalism.

Urban & Rural Masses

The urban masses, consisting of the unskilled and semiskilled urban population, are a complex phenomenon. They comprise both longtime urban dwellers and more recently arrived peasants. The common political denominator of both segments, however, is traditionalism and relative political quietism.

Peasants comprise 65 percent of the population. They have been politically passive, with the notable exception of occasional local rebellions against abusive landowners. Nonetheless, the imperatives of social justice in the 1952 Revolution, the peasants' importance to agricultural production, and the potential of political unrest have brought significant political attention to the peasantry. While their economic situation improved dramatically under Nasser, it was under Sadat that the chronic unemployment and underemployment of the countryside was most sharply relieved. For a time in the mid-1970s, it looked as if they were suffering an economic decline relative to the landowning class, who were receiving perhaps as much as two billion dollars in foreign economic assistance. More recently, however, the drain of 350,000 Egyptians to the Libyan and Persian Gulf labor markets has created further openings for Egyptian farmers in Jordanian agriculture and in the construction industry in Egypt. This shift has created a near labor shortage in the countryside and a consequent increase in wage levels.

National Prospects

Mubarak's tough line with Israel on the Camp David peace process and the Lebanese invasion has helped Egypt move closer to the moderate Arab states and perhaps has partially defused a domestic political opposition united in its criticism of United States policy and calling for the withdrawal of the Egyptian ambassador to Israel. Mubarak has also shifted focus to domestic policy to such a degree that even foreign policy can be said to be pursued with a close eye to domestic considerations.

Egypt under Mubarak is experiencing a low-keyed leadership style that projects energy and efficiency. Ultimately beholden to the military, Mubarak has also found it relatively easy to consult and communicate with the secular opposition. His foreign and domestic policies can be seen as being especially sensitive to that opposition. The religious extremists, however, have been met with unremitting repression. With the heightened religious consciousness of contemporary Egypt, Mubarak faces the problem of acquiring some degree of religious legitimacy while effectively stopping the most extreme expression of religious sentiment. Nevertheless, Mubarak has solid support in comparison to the fragmented religious opposition. There is no widespread general dissatisfaction with the government or Mubarak personally.

Further Reading

Akhavi, Shahrough. "Egypt: Diffused Elite in a Bureaucratic Society." In *Political Elites in Arab North Africa*, I. W. Zartman, ed. London: Longman, 1982.

Baer, Gabriel. *Studies in the Social History of Modern Egypt.* Chicago: University of Chicago Press, 1969.

Baker, Raymond W. *Egypt's Uncertain Revolution under Nasser and Sadat.* Cambridge: Harvard University Press, 1978.

Cantori, Louis. "Religion and Politics in Egypt." In *Religion and Politics in the Middle East*, Michael Curtis, ed. Boulder, Colo.: Westview Press, 1981.

Cooper, Mark. "The Demilitarization of the Egyptian Cabinet." *International Journal of Middle East Studies*, Vol. 14, No. 2., 1982.

Ibrahim, Saad Eddin. "Anatomy of Egypt's Militant Islamic Groups." *International Journal of Middle East Studies*, Vol. 12, No. 4, 1980.

Merriam, John. "Egypt after Sadat." *Current History*, Vol. 81, No. 471, 1982.

al-Sadat, Anwar. *In Search of Identity: An Autobiography.* New York: Harper & Row, 1978.

Springborg, Robert. "Patterns of Association in the Egyptian Political Elite." In *Political Elites in the Middle East*, G. Lenczowski, ed. Washington, D.C.: American Enterprise Institute, 1975.

Vatikiotis, P. J. *The History of Egypt from Muhammad Ali to Sadat.* 2nd ed. Baltimore: Johns Hopkins University Press, 1980.

Waterbury, John. *Egypt: Burdens of the Past/Options for the Future.* Bloomington: Indiana University Press, 1978.

REPUBLIC OF EL SALVADOR
(*República de El Salvador*)
by Anne Nelson

The System of Government

El Salvador, a Central American nation of nearly five million people, has been ruled by military dictatorships under the direction of a small but powerful oligarchy for much of its history. On October 15, 1979, a coup by a group of younger army officers overthrew the regime of General Carlos Romero and installed a military-civilian junta. Rather than establishing a stable new government, the coup was merely symptomatic of the general collapse of the traditional power structure in El Salvador and the beginning of a new level of U.S. involvement. Following the 1979 coup the Salvadoran government became highly volatile. The junta changed leadership on a revolving-door basis and many of the left, center-left, and Christian Democratic participants in the administration's first few months later went into exile.

The fraudulent outcomes of the 1972 and 1977 elections coincided with a growing guerrilla movement. By the late 1970s each of the five guerrilla organizations was also affiliated with its own mass organization, which worked to unite peasant groups, trade unions, and student movements in its revolutionary enterprise. In the first few months after the 1979 coup, the mass organizations were permitted to function openly, hold public demonstrations, and publish their positions. This period came to a close by the spring of 1980, when troops fired on demonstrations and Archbishop Oscar Arnulfo Romero (who had identified himself with the mass organizations) was assassinated. In this period, the guerrilla groups, the mass organizations, and other affiliates began to form centralized, unified structures of opposition, which eventually evolved into a political umbrella organization.

The guerrilla war escalated in January 1981, and in the ensuing months the United States rapidly stepped up its military aid to the regime, now headed by Christian Democrat José Napoleón Duarte. For the rest of 1981 the guerrillas, accused of receiving assistance from Cuba and Nicaragua, regrouped in their strongholds of the underdeveloped northern and northeastern provinces, locking the country in a military stalemate. The Salvadoran regime met increasing criticism for human rights violations on the part of the Salvadoran military.

Elections for a constituent assembly were announced for March 1982 amid international calls (primarily from Socialist International affiliates) for a negotiated settlement between government and guerrilla forces. An unexpectedly large turnout at the polls dampened international support for the guerrilla movement. But in the months following the elections it became apparent that little else had changed. The Constituent Assembly named as its president retired Major Roberto D'Aubuisson, who had been widely discredited under previous governments for his connections with right-wing "death squads." Alvaro Magaña, named as provisional president, had relatively little previous public experience and was known primarily for his role as the army's banking and financial advisor.

Executive

Alvaro Magaña, the acting president of El Salvador, was chosen by the Constituent Assembly following the March 1982 elections. He was regarded as a compromise candidate, with no history of active participation in any of the traditional parties. He will continue to hold office until the national elections slated for 1983. Magaña works closely with the military and the Constituent Assembly, serving as the regime's primary civilian spokesman. While the formal powers of the presidency are extensive, the political fragmentation of the country forces the president to play a mediating role among the military and the civilian political factions.

Legislature

El Salvador's sixty-member constituent assembly was elected March 28, 1982, and is charged with rewriting the country's constitution and laying the groundwork for national elections in 1983. The Assembly was elected on a national basis by party (individual candidates were not named on the ballot). In those elections, the Christian Democrats won 35.5 percent of the vote and twenty-four seats, the National Republican Alliance (ARENA) won 25 percent and nineteen seats, and the Popular Orientation Party (POP), Democratic Action, and the Salvadoran Popular Party (*Partido Popular Salvadoreño;* PPS) together won 27 percent of the vote and a total of seventeen seats between them. A postelection alliance between the parties of the right (PPS, POP, and ARENA) and Democratic Action, apparently planned in advance, left the Christian Democrats in a minority position.

Judiciary

Justice is administered by the Supreme Court which, in the past, has been appointed by the legislature for renewable three-year terms. The judiciary is subject to heavy political influence.

Regional & Local Government

The country is divided into fourteen departments administered by appointees of the central government. Major municipalities have elected mayors, but their functions are primarily administrative, not policy making.

The Electoral System

El Salvador traditionally has held direct national elections every five years. Election fraud in the recent past, however, contributed to the country's destabilization. The elections of March 1982 were undoubtedly the most honest in Salvadoran history on a technical basis, but the fact that there was no participation on the part of the left and center-left, both significant factors in Salvadoran political life, weakened their meaning.

The secret ballot contained the symbols and names of six political parties. Suffrage was universal for persons eighteen and over, but there was no special registration drive, and registration has been criticized as erratic in the past. While the count of the voter turnout in March 1982 approached 1.5 million, El Salvador's Catholic University charged that this figure was inflated. About 12 percent of the ballots cast were null or invalid. Members of the Salvadoran armed forces, numbering over 20,000, were not permitted to vote.

The Party System

While El Salvador was not without political parties prior to 1944, the modern party process has developed in response to the many coups since that year. Most parties since 1944 have been personal vehicles of military figures or leftist groups in opposition. Few of these gained any significant support, and the leftist groups were invariably banned and their leaders exiled, tortured, and killed. As a result, the quasi-official parties of the government in power dominated the scene—the Revolutionary Party of Democratic Unification (*Partido Revolucionario de Unificación Democrática;* PRUD) from 1950 to 1960, followed by the still-existent Party of National Reconcilition (PCN). Opposition parties began to gain ground in the 1960s; the first opposition member of the Legislative Assembly since 1931 was elected in 1964, and three years later the Christian Democratic Party (PDC) won fifteen seats with 22 percent of the vote. During the same period, opposition parties were gaining representation in municipal elections. Electoral fraud and repression in the 1970s held back further opposition party organization until the 1979 coup. Formal party organization remains rudimentary, heavily dependent on leading personalities, and primarily urban in membership and elitist in leadership.

National Republican Alliance (*Alianza Republicana Nacionalista;* ARENA)

The youngest and most controversial of the parties that participated in the 1982 elections, ARENA was founded in 1981 by Major Roberto D'Aubuisson (born 1944), former chief of intelligence for the National Guard and a popular figure of the extreme right. Former U.S. Ambassador to El Salvador Robert White had linked D'Aubuisson to the death squad that killed Archbishop Romero in 1980. The party launched the most aggressive campaign of the election and was the only party to hold large open rallies in the countryside under wartime conditions. Although ARENA won only 25 percent of the vote, D'Aubuisson emerged as the single most influential *caudillo* of the right and was elected president of the Constituent Assembly. ARENA promised aggressive prosecution of the war against the guerrillas and found most of its financing and support among landowners and businessmen fearful of losing their property in the course of the civil war.

Christian Democratic Party
(*Partido Democrata Cristiano;* PDC)

The PDC was founded in 1960 and gained strength through the 1960s, thanks in part to the efforts of the popular mayor of San Salvador, engineer José Napoleón Duarte. In 1972, the Christian Democrats joined with the legal arm of the illegal Communist Party, the National Democratic Union (*Unión Democrática Nacional;* UDN) and the socialist National Revolutionary Movement (*Movimiento Nacional Revolucionario;* MNR) to form the National Opposition Union (*Unión Nacional Opositora;* UNO). The UNO coalition won the 1972 elections with Duarte as its presidential candidate and MNR leader Guillermo Ungo as his running mate. They were defrauded of their victory by the military, however, and went into exile. The UNO attempted the same project with different candidates in 1977 with similar results. From the mid-1970s on, there was growing disenchantment with the electoral process, leading up to the 1979 coup. After the dissolution of several military-civilian juntas, Duarte was called from exile to serve as president by appointment in December 1980.

The 1982 elections were regarded as a defeat for his government, although the Christian Democrats won more than 35 percent of the vote, more than any other party. A controversial land-reform program had cost the Christian Democrats what little support they had among the upper classes, and the continuation of political violence created disillusionment among labor and peasant classes, traditionally their bedrock of support. More than forty Christian Democratic mayors were killed between 1980 and 1982, many of them presumed victims of right-wing death squads. The party's most promising survivor in government was Foreign Minister Fidel Chávez Mena, one of the few high-ranking members of the Duarte administration to retain his office in the new government.

Democratic Action
(*Acción Democrática;* AD)

The AD was organized specifically to participate in the March 1982 election. Its founder, Dr. René Fortín Magaña, was a prominent lawyer in San Salvador who briefly served as a member of a three-man "90-day" junta in 1960. He hoped to appeal to the country's center-right business sector, but failed to win 10 percent of the vote.

Renovating Action Party
(*Partido de Acción Renovadora;* PAR)

The PAR, founded in 1944, was billed as the only leftist party to participate in the March 1982 elections. It withdrew shortly before the election citing death threats received by its candidates. It has little support or presence in the country.

Party of National Reconciliation
(*Partido de Conciliación Nacional;* PCN)

The PCN was the official government party from 1969 to 1979. As such, it was able to use government mechanisms to promote its candidates, Generals Molina (1972) and Romero (1977), and is generally considered to have installed them in office through electoral fraud. The PCN was the third runner-up in the 1982 elections, campaigning under leadership largely carried over from the Romero administration. Prominent among these figures are Roberto Escobar García, Romero's labor minister, and Julia Castilla, who served as deputy minister of health. It played an unexpectedly strong role in the new Constituent Assembly as power broker between ARENA and the Christian Democrats. Its chief appeal is among the military, traditionalists, and parts of the business sector.

Salvadoran Popular Party
(*Partido Popular Salvadoreño;* PPS)

The PPS was founded in 1965 and has traditionally been supported by wealthy individuals and large corporations. Rightist and nationalist, it fielded José Antonio Rodríguez Porth as a presidential candidate in 1972. It has shown only the most insignificant electoral strength. The party's present leader is Francisco Quinoñez.

Popular Orientation Party (*Partido de Orientación Popular;* POP)

The POP is headed by General José Alberto "Chele" Medrano, also the founder of the National Democratic Organization (*Organización Democrática Nacional;* ORDEN), a right-wing vigilante group that collaborates with security forces. The POP was organized in 1981 specifically to take part in the 1982 elections as Medrano's personal political vehicle. It won a negligible number of votes and threw its support behind the coalition of the right against the Christian Democrats in the Constituent Assembly.

Other Political Forces

Military

The Salvadoran military has long been regarded as the true seat of political power, along with the handful of wealthy families referred to as the oligarchy. From the late 1970s on, the power of military cliques grew, due in part to an abdication on the part of the oligarchy as their families and their capital fled the country. Heavy infusions of military aid also increased the military's economic might. Minister of Defense General Guillermo Garcia and General Jaime Abdul Gutiérrez are the only prominent figures of government to have retained their positions since the 1979 coup; the head of the National Guard, Eugenio Vides Casanova, represents the third political force within the military. With the flight of President General Carlos Romero in the October 1979 coup, the military was "decapitated," with all of the generals temporarily forced into exile.

A new generation of colonels rose through the command structure accordingly. As the counterinsurgency war continues, however, it is apparent that little else in the military has changed. The military includes the army, estimated at at least 20,000 men, and the security forces made up of the National Guard, the Hacienda (or Treasury) Police, the National Police, and the Customs Police, totalling at least another 15,000. The officer corps has largely middle-class origins and receives its training at the national military academy. Enlisted men are usually forcibly conscripted from rural areas. Many are under the officially required age of eighteen, and there is a high percentage of illiteracy among them. Since 1981, counterinsurgency instruction from U.S. military advisory teams has become a major element in the training of both officers and enlisted men.

Organized Labor

The Salvadoran labor movement went through a period of rapid growth during the economic boom of the 1950s and 1960s. By the 1970s, it was clearly divided between those peasant and labor organizations that operated under government sanction and those affiliated with the left. By the end of the 1970s most of the independent labor organizations had close ties to two of the left's "popular organizations," the Popular Revolutionary Block (*Bloque Popular Revolucionario;* BPR) and the United People's Action Front (*Frente de Acción del Pueblo Unido;* FAPU.) In August 1980, a work stoppage carried out by electrical workers, one of the most militant leftist unions, was broken by widespread arrests. The left's labor organizations have since been further weakened by frequent assassinations and "disappearances" of members carried out by the security forces and the death squads. The government-approved unions, such as the Salvadoran Peasant Union (*Union Campesina Salvadoreña;* UCS), have also suffered political repression, though to a far lesser degree.

Religious Groups

The Catholic Church has played an enormous role in the recent political development of the country. The theology of liberation and the religious "base community" movements of the 1960s were forerunners of the popular organizations that developed during the next decade. Figures such as Jesuit Rutilio Grande and Archbishop Oscar Romero, both assassinated by the right for their identification with the popular movements, have been converted into revered symbols of the popular Church. Since Romero's death in March, 1980, however, a schism within the Church and among the bishops has become pronounced. Romero's temporary replacement, Bishop Arturo Rivera y Damas, has attempted to straddle the distance between the Church's traditional conservative wing and Romero's followers, with limited success. The situation has been complicated by the rapid expansion of evangelical Protestant movements in the country. These sects have benefited from the shortage of clergymen in the Catholic Church, as well as the fear and uncertainty in some rural communities over the trends of the Catholic liberationist movement.

The Left

The Salvadoran guerrilla movement had its origins in the Salvadoran Communist Party and the 1932 peasant uprising led by Farabundo Martí. The uprising failed, and in the aftermath more than 20,000 indigenous peoples and peasants were killed in the western provinces by the army. This was effectively the end of an identifiable indigenous culture in El Salvador. The Communist Party went underground, resurfacing in the 1950s in its legal form, the National Democratic Union (UDN), participating in elections with a standard pro-Moscow, reformist line. In the early 1970s, there was a major split in the party, and a group known as the Popular Liberation Front (*Frente Popular de la Liberación;* FPL) came into being under the leadership of Cayetano Carpio. Carpio, whose *nomme de guerre* is "Marcial," is considered the grand old man of the Salvadoran guerrilla movement. Within the next few years, two competing guerrilla organizations formed. These groups spent their first years evolving revolutionary strategies and conducting kidnapping-and-ransom operations to build their warchests. The FPL embarked on a program of mass recruitment early on in its history, through close ties with the Popular Revolutionary Block, an umbrella organization of religious, peasant, labor, and student groups. Its aim was to pursue a "prolonged popular war," known as the GPP strategy. An independent guerrilla movement, the Revolutionary Army of the People (*Ejercito Revolucionario del Pueblo;* ERP), representing the other radical option, pressed instead for a quick and decisive popular insurrection, stressing military preparedness as opposed to mass organization. Another independent group, the National Resistance (*Resistencia Nacional;* RN) broke off from the ERP after the killing in 1975 of revolutionary poet Roque Dalton in a policy dispute. The RN added the strategy of cultivating sectors of intellectuals and the military, while its mass organization, FAPU, concentrated much of its efforts among labor. By the late 1970s, another group, the Central American Revolutionary Workers Party (*Partido Revolucionario de los Trabajadores Centroamericanos;* PRTC) formed, along with its corresponding popular or-

ganization, the Popular Liberation Movement (*Movimiento Liberación Popular;* MLP). In 1980, the Communist Party, which had worked closely with the other groups in the late 1970s, formed its own armed branch, the Armed Forces for Liberation (*Fuerzas Armades de la Liberación;* FAL). Collaboration among the groups had always been problematical; it was not until 1980 that they formed a unified military command, the Farabundo Martí National Liberation Front (*Frente Farabundo Marti para la Liberación Nacional;* FMLN), and a unified structure for their noncombatant supporters, the Revolutionary Democratic Front (*Frente Revolucionario Democratico;* FDR). Estimates of guerrilla strength run from 5,000 to 10,000 active and armed troops with several thousand more ready to take up arms if weapons become available.

National Prospects

As 1982 drew to a close the guerrillas mounted another offensive. The power structures involved in El Salvador's conflict were obviously more divided according to social sector than to specific political parties. Besides the Constituent Assembly and the political parties represented within it, the army and the security forces, the guerrillas, and the left and center-left organizations and parties currently underground or in exile will all play a major part in the resolution of the civil war. Until most of these sectors are either vanquished or included in a compromise, no regime can expect to achieve a stable governmental structure.

Further Reading
Americas Watch Committee and the American Civil Liberties Union. *Report on Human Rights in El Salvador.* New York: Vintage Books, 1982.
Anderson, Thomas. *Matanza: El Salvador's Communist Revolt of 1932.* Lincoln, Neb.: University of Nebraska Press, 1971.
———. *The War of the Dispossessed.* Lincoln and London: University of Nebraska Press, 1981.
Armstrong, Robert, and Shenk, Janet. *El Salvador: The Face of Revolution.* Boston: South End Press, 1982.
Arnson, Cynthia. *El Salvador: A Revolution Confronts the United States.* Washington, D.C., and Amsterdam: Institute for Policy Studies, 1982.

Browning, David. *El Salvador, Landscape and Society.* Oxford, England: Clarendon Press, 1971.

Gettleman, Marvin, et al., eds. *El Salvador: Central America in the New Cold War.* New York: Grove Press, 1981.

Lernoux, Penny. *Cry of the People.* Garden City, N. Y.: Doubleday, 1980.

Webre, Stephen. *José Napoleon Duarte and the Christian Democratic Party in Salvadoran Politics: 1960–1974.* Baton Rouge: Louisiana State University Press, 1979.

White, Alistair. *El Salvador.* New York: Praeger, 1973.

ETHIOPIA
(*Etiyopiya*)
by Timothy Dunmore, Ph.D.

The System of Government

Ethiopia, a nation of over 33 million is a military dictatorship. Its history over the last twenty years, especially since the military came to power in 1974, has been one of armed struggle against the attempted secession of the province of Eritrea and against the incursions of Somalia in the west. In both of these struggles, the Ethiopian military council has recently had extensive assistance from Cuban troops and Russian advisors.

Ethiopia is the oldest independent state in Africa; save only for an Italian occupation from 1936 to 1941, it was never a colony. It was an autocratic monarchy under Haile Selassie until he was overthrown by the military in September 1974. Although much respected as an elder statesman by other African leaders, Haile Selassie lost much of his support because of his failure to deal with the Eritrean and Somali secessionist movements and to grapple with the country's chronic economic underdevelopment. The 1931 constitution was abolished by military decree in 1974.

The present military regime has its origins in the 1974 coup, although several changes of leading personnel since then can be regarded as countercoups. The last major change occurred in February 1977 when Lt. Colonel Mengistu Haile Mariam overthrew and executed Brig. General Teferi Benti. Mengistu has taken his country deeper into alliance with the Soviet Union than his predecessors. He also claims that his regime is more socialist, but his opponents regard it as simply more authoritarian than its predecessors. Various political organizations established since 1974 bear some similarity to the Soviet model. As in most Soviet-bloc countries, government and party leadership are so intertwined as to make it difficult to distinguish between them. This is particularly true of Ethiopa where the party organization is being built from the top down by the government.

Executive

The head of state, Colonel Mengistu, is chairman of the Provisional Military Administrative Council (PMAC) commonly known as the Dergue (*dergue* is the Amharic word for "committee"). Mengistu is also head of government by virtue of his position as chairman of the Council of Ministers. His dominance of Ethiopian politics is also based on his assumption of the post of commander-in-chief of the armed forces. In theory he is chosen by the Dergue; in practice Mengistu has based his power more on the elimination of his opponents.

He cannot rule, however, without the consent of the Dergue as a whole, an arrangement modelled along the lines of party structures in East Europe. The basic policymaking unit is meant to be the General Congress of the PMAC, consisting of about eighty members, mostly from the military. In practice, however, most day-to-day policymaking is done by the thirty-two-man Central Committee of the Dergue and especially by its eight-man Standing Committee. The Central Committee is chosen from the members of the General Congress and the Standing Committee from the members of the Central Committee.

While the Dergue is the main policymaking body, the civilian administration of the country is the responsibility of a twenty-seven-man Council of Ministers, only six of whom are officers of the armed forces.

In addition, there was created in 1977 the National Revolutionary Operations Command chaired by Colonel Mengistu. Its main responsibility seems to be to combat the organizations and movements that are seeking the overthrow of the military government. This command has its own committees at all regional levels.

Legislature

The Parliament was suspended by military decree in 1974.

Judiciary

The Supreme Court has appellate jurisdiction only. It consists of a president and two other judges and generally works within a European legal tradition. The High Court is the highest court in Ethiopia with original jurisdiction. Ethiopia also utilizes military tribunals; there is no appeal against the decisions of the Supreme Military Tribunal. In addition, the military regime has given itself the power to detain opponents for up to six months without trial. Especially since 1977, with the government beleaguered on all sides, there have been numerous arrests and executions of political opponents.

Regional & Local Government

Ethiopia is formally divided into fourteen provinces. However, where the government is in control of an area, government power is concentrated at the local level. In urban areas this means the *kebelles*, or urban dwellers' associations, of which there are now more than 1,000. The mass of Ethiopians (about 90 percent) live in the countryside, many of whom are now ruled by peasants' associations with wide-ranging administrative and judicial authority. The peasants' association have a national organization, the All-Ethiopia Peasants' Association. These local government units are very much the creation of the military leadership and remain subservient to it.

In several regions of Ethiopia—notably in the provinces of Eritrea, Tigre, Shoa, and Bale, and in the Ogaden—the government's authority is under strong challenge from ethnic minorities often backed by foreign powers, especially Somalia.

From 1952 to 1962 Ethiopia was a federation, with Eritrea having federal status within the union. Since 1962 it has been a unitary state.

Commission for Organizing the Party of The Working People of Ethiopia (COPWE)

History

For the first two years after the overthrow of the monarchy, all political parties were banned. In 1976, the Dergue established *Abyot Seded* (Revolutionary Flame) to undermine two other revolutionary parties, the Ethiopian People's Revolutionary Party, and the All-Ethiopian Socialist Movement. Two other small parties, the Marxist-Leninist Organization (*Malerid*) and the Labor League (*Woz Ader*), were made subservient to the *Seded*.

In 1979, the COPWE was formed as a cadre-preparatory organization which will form the core of a mass party. While many of the top leaders and workers of *Seded* were made part of the new organization, *Seded* itself remained unrelated to COPWE and the new party it began to form.

Organization

COPWE already has the regional infrastructure common to East European communist parties, but the full organization of the party has been delayed by the secessionist and economic problems that have dogged the regime. It is led by a seven-man committee, all of whom are Dergue members and five of whom are members of the Council of Ministers. A Central Committee of ninety-three members was chosen by the party's first congress in June 1980. Seventy-nine members of the Central Committee are military men or police.

Policy

COPWE is an avowedly Marxist-Leninist organization. The Dergue has carried this view of class conflict into reality by embarking (in 1979) on a campaign to collectivize agriculture and by establishing a Supreme Council to control the process of industrial development. Most sections of trade and industry have been nationalized. However, in spite of the propaganda devoted to them, neither of these schemes has yet succeeded.

On the ethnic and religious front, the Dergue seeks the forced reintegration of the country and leans heavily towards the Christian church and the Amharic peoples. Orthodox Christianity is officially recognized by the state, but the nation's constitution also guarantees religious freedom for Moslems and other religious groups. Nevertheless, there have been reports of severe persecution of the country's Jewish community, the Falashas.

Colonel Mengistu has been one of the Soviet Union's staunchest allies since he came to power. Since in November 1978, when he signed a treaty of friendship and cooperation with the USSR, Russian arms and economic aid have been poured into Ethiopia. In addition, upwards of ten thousand Cuban troops have been sent to help the Ethiopians defend the Ogaden against Somali forces. Cuban troops have apparently not been used against the other liberation movements, but their deployment in the west has allowed the Dergue to employ its own forces more effectively against the Eritreans, especially in a successful offensive begun in December 1980.

Membership & Constituency

COPWE has already begun to select "good communists" for the mass membership of the party. Only individuals are permitted to join; no organization, not even *Seded*, is allowed to affiliate. At a February 1981 meeting of the Central Committee, it was reported that the party had 1,500 members, of whom two-thirds were soldiers.

Financing

COPWE is financed by the government.

Leadership

Mengistu is the chairman of the party's executive committee and of the Central Committee. He was born in 1937.

Opposition

Opposition parties are of two types: those seeking to replace the existing military regime and those seeking to liberate their region or ethnic group from Ethiopian control. In both cases, the only means either has of achieving its objectives in the circumstances is by fighting a guerrilla war against the government.

The only avowedly antisocialist movement among the first group is the Ethiopian Democratic Union (EDU) which opposes the Dergue's social reforms. It is strongest in the west of the country. It was established in 1975 and unites many of the supporters of the old monarchy.

The All-Ethiopian Socialist Movement (AESM or *Me'ei Sone*) fell out with the regime in August 1977. Both it and its breakaway wing, the *Eech-At* (Revolutionary Movement for the Oppressed), were banned in 1978 by the Mengistu regime.

The most effective national opposition has come from the Ethiopian People's Revolutionary Party (EPRP) which was founded in 1972 to oppose the monarchy. It is equally adamant in its opposition to military rule, although, in theory, it shares the same Marxist philosophy with the Dergue and broadly supported it for its first two years. Several EPRP leaders were captured and shot in 1979, but the movement continues to work in urban areas.

The best known of the separatist groups are those fighting for the independence of Eritrea.

The original Eritrean Liberation Front (ELF) was founded in 1958; supported primarily by Muslims, it has Marxist sympathies. In 1970, the Eritrean People's Liberation Front (EPLF) split off from the parent organization and is less exclusively Muslim than the ELF. It is now much the most important of the Eritrean Liberation movements and is carrying out its own socialist program in the areas under its control. Also, the more conservative Eritrean Liberation Front–Popular Liberation Forces maintains an army which is less than one-fifth of the size of the EPLF's guerrilla forces.

The other major opponents of the Dergue are the two movements based on Somali minorities in Ethiopia. The Somali Abo Liberation Front (SALF) is active in Bale province. Much the larger organization, with several thousand men under arms, is the Western Somali Liberation Front (WSLF). The WSLF is politically and military backed by the Somali government. Its aim is to incorporate the Ogaden region with its Somali population into Somali.

Other liberation fronts have been organized in Afar, Oromo, and Tigre provinces. The main support for the regime comes from the urban areas and the southern peasants.

Other Political Forces

Organized Labor

The most important trade-union organization is probably the All-Ethiopian Peasants Association, set up in 1978 by the military government. Its aims are both political and economic. It seeks to promote literacy and to advance agricultural techniques as well as to make itself the umbrella organization for the 30,000 or so peasants' associations and their seven million members.

The All-Ethiopian Trade Union (AETU) unites about 350,000 (in 1978) industrial workers. It was set up to replace the old trade-union organization, the Confederation of Ethiopian Labor Unions (CELU). The CELU was held responsible for a general strike in 1975 and a further wave of industrial trouble in 1976. The AETU, like many of the official organizations in modern Ethiopia, was set up by the regime in a bid to engender support for itself.

Religious Groups

Religion is a major factor in Ethiopian politics. The country is nearly equally divided between Orthodox Coptic Christians and Sunni Muslims, with small groups of other religions and sects, and some traditional animists in the far south. Amharic-speaking Christians have dominated the Ethiopian government for many years, and although the military regime and many of the opposition movements profess Marxist beliefs, the Christian community continues to play a role in both the Dergue and its revolutionary opposition.

National Prospects

Ethiopia and its military regime have come very close to complete disintegration. However, there were signs in 1981 that they were at last winning the wars in the Ogaden and Eritrea, thanks mainly to Cuban and Russian help. The Dergue has also managed to ease its diplomatic isolation. It has support from Libya and Syria, two of the USSR's allies, and has found common ground with Kenya in the south which has also suffered from Somali claims on its territory.

The major problems facing the regime are economic. Civil war and several droughts have brought famine to many areas of Ethiopia. The Dergue seeks to combat food shortages by a program of land reform and by encouraging the adoption of modern agricultural techniques.

On several occasions, Colonel Mengistu has made mention of the possibility of a return to civilian rule in Ethiopia. The establishment of COPWE seems a concrete step towards this aim. However, the military battle for control has yet to be won in many regions. Only when the various opposition forces have been defeated can the military afford to relinquish power. The most likely means of introducing civilian rule in the near future would be the replacement of the Dergue by the leading organs of COPWE, while retaining the same people in senior positions. Such a move would bring Ethiopia's political structure very much into line with that of its East European allies.

Further Reading

Davidson, Basil; Cliffe, Lionel; and Selassie, Bereket, eds. *Behind the War in Eritrea.* Nottingham, England: Spokesman Books, 1980.

Goricke, Fred V. *Social and Political Factors Influencing the Application of Land Reform Measures in Ethiopia.* Saarbrucken, West Germany: Verlag Breitenbach, 1979.

Harsch, Ernst. *The Ethiopian Revolution.* New York: Pathfinder Press, 1978.

Legum, Colin, and Lee, Bill. *The Horn of Africa in Continuing Crisis.* New York: African Publishing Co., 1979.

Markakis, John, and Ayele, Nega. *Class and Revolution in Ethiopia.* Nottingham, England: Spokesman Books, 1978.

Selassie, Bereket H. *Conflict and Intervention in the Horn of Africa.* New York: Monthly Review Press, 1980.

Sherman, Richard. *Eritrea: The Unfinished Revolution.* New York: Praeger, 1980.

Spencer, John H. *Ethiopia, the Horn of Africa and United States Policy.* Cambridge, Mass.: Institute for Foreign Policy Analysis, 1977.

REPUBLIC OF FINLAND
(*Suomen Tasavalta*)
by Martin F. Farrell, Ph.D.

The System of Government

The Republic of Finland, a nation of nearly five million people, is a presidential-parliamentary republic and a unitary state, with limited local self-government and one autonomous province, the Aaland Islands. The present system is based upon the Form of Government Act of 1919 and several subsequent Fundamental Laws which together comprise the Finnish constitution.

Executive

Primary executive authority is vested in the president of the republic, who also serves as head of state. The president's relatively broad powers include the appointment and dismissal of the State Council (cabinet), including the prime minister, as well as other important executive, judicial, and even clerical officers; the dissolution of Parliament; the presentation of most bills for parliamentary consideration; the ratification or veto of all legislation; significant decree powers; supreme command of the armed forces; and leadership of the nation's foreign policy.

In most of these areas, the Finnish system attempts to place some checks on presidential power. All his decisions are supposed to be made in State Council meetings, emerging as Council decisions, and linked to parliamentary approval by the requirement that the cabinet retain parliamentary confidence. Presidential decisions made in the face of cabinet opposition have been quite rare. Also, his decree powers are limited largely to administrative matters and cannot involve a change in law, except in emergency conditions, when Parliament may vastly expand these powers. Even then, however, Parliament retains the authority to overturn such decrees, and it has granted such powers only for limited periods, generally one year. Similarly, Parliament can override a presidential veto by a simple majority vote, but only after an intervening general election. Such overrides have occurred only five times since 1919.

Despite these checks, the president retains far more authority than any other head of state in a parliamentary system. Of crucial importance is his power to form and dismiss governments. These governments need not receive a parliamentary vote of confidence at their inception, and they may be dismissed by the president even if they enjoy the support of a parliamentary majority. The president is not bound by election results. During the 1970s President Urho Kekkonen continued to appoint center-left coalition governments, even though those parties steadily lost ground to the conservative parties in the parliamentary elections.

The strength of the individuals who have held the office have also contributed to the development of its authority. Through the 1960s and 1970s, Kekkonen's leadership of domestic policy, especially in overseeing rapid industrial growth, so enhanced his prestige that by 1978 all six of Finland's largest parties endorsed his reelection for a fifth term.

The president is elected to a six-year term by a 300-member electoral college, itself selected by popular vote based upon proportional representation. The electors are not legally bound to support any particular candidate, and while no formal discussion is allowed, tough and extended negotiations between ballots have sometimes occurred.

The 1978 presidential election was the first held in Finland since 1968. In January 1973, the Parliament voted 170 to 28 (just over the five-sixths majority needed) to postpone the 1974 presidential contest, giving Kekkonen a four-year extension in office to allow him to conduct lengthy economic negotiations with the European Community. This was not the first time that regular constitutional procedures for presidential election had been bypassed; in 1919, 1944, and 1946 the president was selected by the Parliament, and in 1940 and 1943 the president was chosen by the same electoral college which had convened in 1937.

In January 1982, after Kekkonen retired for health reasons, eight candidates ran for the presidency. As expected, the easy winner was Social Democratic Party candidate Mauno Koivisto, who gained almost 44 percent of the popular vote and entered the electoral college voting with 145 of the 301 members. To these were added the votes of twenty-one Finnish People's Democratic League electors and one from the Rural Party, for a total of 167, as against fifty-eight for Harri Holkeri of the *Kokoomus* and fifty-three for Johannes Virolainen of Kekkonen's Center Party.

The State Council (*Valtioneuvosto*) or cabinet consists of a prime minister, deputy prime minister, and no more than fifteen other ministers. Its primary functions are to prepare legislation for submission to the Parliament and to supervise the implementation and administration of policies by the civil service. Over 90 percent of Finland's enacted bills originate with the State Council, whose legislative program is worked out in cooperation with the president.

The State Council occupies a precarious position: it is appointed and dismissed by the president, but also needs the confidence of the fractious, multiparty Parliament. Ministers are held legally, as well as politically, responsible for all their actions. As a result, Finland averaged almost exactly one government per year over the first sixty-two years of the republic. Nearly all of these have been coalitions of three or more parties. Since 1966 the governments have been almost exclusively center-left in composition (the "Red-Green Alliance"). However, given conservative gains in the 1975 and 1979 parliamentary elections and the absence of Kekkonen after 1981, there is some chance of returning to the pre-1966 pattern of center-right coalitions in the near future, despite Soviet opposition to such a move.

Due to the strength of the presidency and the principle of collegiality (equality of all ministers), the Finnish prime ministry is weaker than that of most parliamentary systems. The prime minister leads the day-to-day work of the State Council and serves as the government's spokesman in parliamentary debates and interpellations, but does not have the authority to command his ministers, that power being reserved to the president.

Legislature

Legislative power is vested in a 200-member unicameral Parliament known as the *Eduskunta*. Since 1955, its maximum term has been set at four years, one year more than previously. In recent years, it has met virtually throughout the year. Members are chosen by direct, secret election based on proportional representation. The body selects its own speaker, who is then expected to drop his partisan role and cannot vote.

Exceptions to a Fundamental Law can be enacted, as in the 1973 extension of President Kekkonen's term in office. However, the procedure required is the same as for enacting a Fundamental Law: namely, a two-thirds majority after a five-sixths declaration of an "urgent question," or two successive two-thirds majority votes with an intervening general election. Such exceptions have been much more common than formal amendment of a Fundamental Law.

Other than the limits of Fundamental Laws, there are in principle no restrictions on the powers of the *Eduskunta*, but in practice, its powers are exercised primarily at the behest of the president and State Council. Individual members may introduce legislation, but in recent years only 7 percent of members' bills have been approved, compared with 80 percent of those submitted by the government. The opposition of one-third of the body can force the deferral of an ordinary bill until general elections have been held.

Current representation in the *Eduskunta* is based on the 1979 elections, presented in the accompanying table, with changes from the 1975 election in parentheses; e.g., (−2) means the party lost two seats in the 1979 election; (n/c) indicates no change.

EDUSKUNTA REPRESENTATION AFTER 1979 ELECTIONS		
	Seats (200)	Popular Vote (%)
Social Democratic Party	52 (−2)	23.9 (−1.0)
National Coalition Party	47 (+12)	21.7 (+3.3)
People's Democratic League	35 (−5)	17.9 (−1.0)
Center Party	36 (−3)	17.3 (−0.3)
Christian Union	9 (n/c)	4.8 (+1.5)
Finnish Rural Party	7 (+5)	4.6 (+1.0)
Swedish People's Party	10 (n/c)	4.5 (−0.5)
Liberal People's Party	4 (−5)	3.7 (−0.6)
Constitutional Party	0 (−1)	1.2 (−0.4)
People's Unity Party	0 (−1)	0.3 (−1.4)
Others	0 (n/c)	0.1 (−0.6)

Judiciary

Judicial authority is exercised through a system of general courts, special courts, and administrative courts. The Supreme Court consists of a president and twenty-three permanent justices. As vacancies arise, they are filled by the president from among legally trained and experienced candidates. The Supreme Court fulfills its ordinary duties in sections. Only matters considered to be of highest principle or the trial of a sitting president for treason are heard in plenary session. Most notable of the rights and duties *not* granted to the Supreme Court is the judicial review of the constitutionality of legislation, which is left to the *Eduskunta*'s constitutional committee to decide.

Regional & Local Government

Although Finland is essentially a unitary state, its constitution recognizes a certain measure of local self-government, in accordance with practices extending back many centuries. Today, there are three such basic units, collectively known as communes: forty-nine cities (*kaupungit*), twenty-nine towns (*kaupplat*), and 443 rural communes (*maalaiskunnat*). Communal authority is vested primarily in a communal council, consisting of between thirteen and seventy-seven members, depending on the commune's population, directly elected by proportional representation every fourth year. This council selects an executive body, the communal board.

The commune's authority is exercised in matters delegated to it by the *Eduskunta* or not specifically assigned to other bodies: maintenance of order, local highways and transportation, primary and special schools, public health, social welfare, public-works employment, and land settlement. Communes are permitted to levy local taxes, primarily income taxes, to finance their activities. In recent years, total communal revenues have equalled about one-half of state revenues.

Party identification has been less clear-cut in communal elections than in national elections, but is becoming increasingly apparent. In recent years about one-third of the communes have been led by socialists, with two-thirds ruled by nonsocialists.

Finland's thirteen provinces also have their own provincial governments, each headed by a governor. These, however, function essentially as administrative units operating under the direction of the State Council. Since 1951 the Aaland Islands have constituted an autonomous province, which, while still subject to overall state control, enjoys broader self-governing authority than any other area in Finland.

The Electoral System

All three types of elections (presidential, parliamentary, and communal) are conducted in much the same way. All begin as direct, secret ballots based on proportional representation. For the two national elections, Finland is divided into fifteen electoral districts. These districts vary considerably in population, so that before each election the State Council apportions the number of seats in each, according to census figures (rather than size of the electorate). For the 200-member *Eduskunta*, the number of seats per district ranges from nine to twenty-one, except for the Aaland Islands, a separate district electing just one representative. Division of the 300-member electoral college is made in the same manner.

Two or more parties may join together to form an election bloc, but they still present separate lists. The voter casts his ballot for an individual candidate, but it is also tallied for the party list on which it appears. The number of votes for each list and/or bloc is recorded. Each candidate of a unified voting group (list or bloc) is then assigned a "comparison number" based on the following formula: the leading individual vote getter in each bloc is assigned the total vote of that bloc, the second-leading individual is assigned one-half the total vote of that bloc, the third receives one-third, and so on. Once these computations are made for each bloc, all candidates are ranked according to these figures, and the available seats are assigned on the basis of this ranking. In effect, then, the vote for the individual candidate helps determine his ranking within the bloc, while the simultaneous vote for the party list helps determine the party's proportion of the available seats. This system does discriminate somewhat against the very small parties, but it has not prevented ten or more parties from being represented in the *Eduskunta* in recent years.

All citizens who have reached age eighteen before the election year may vote. Registration is conducted by local election boards on the basis of the previous year's census. Voter turnout as a proportion of those eligible is relatively high. However, turnout for presidential voting lags about ten points below that for the *Eduskunta*. For example, parliamentary turnout since 1962 has ranged between 85.1 percent (1962) and 79.7 percent (1975), with the most recent election (1979) producing a turnout of 82 percent. Presidential turnout, on the other hand, was 70.2 percent in 1968 and 70 percent in 1978.

The Party System

Origins of the Parties

Modern party organizations date from the mid-nineteenth century. The original impetus was provided by ethnolinguistic divisions between Finnish- and Swedish-speaking Finns. Later, class and urban-rural cleavages also emerged, so that with Finland's first modern elections in 1906, a distinct multiparty system was evident. This pattern has persisted until today, with many Finns believing that this multiplicity of parties is preferable to what they would consider an "unhealthy" polarization of politics.

The Parties in Law

Political parties are not mentioned in any of the Fundamental Laws, and thus are generally considered civil organizations with the same legal status as other associations. There are no special state restrictions, except when extreme parties have been banned, as with the Communist Party in 1928 and the profascist People's Patriotic League (IKL) in 1944. Since 1970, nomination of candidates for the *Eduskunta* has been a legally recognized function of registered political parties. Legally defined seating in the Parliament is also by party grouping. Overall, there is a minimum of legal apparatus surrounding party formation or activity.

Party Organization

Today, all the major parties in Finland are considered mass parties, with large dues-paying memberships. However, they have not evolved into catchall parties on the American, British, or West German models. Rather, they remain rather narrowly based.

With the exception of the Finnish People's Democratic League, the political parties share the same basic pyramidal structure, with a large number of local base units, district (provincial) units, and the national party congress, executive organs, and central bureaus. The local units, usually defined residentially rather than functionally, have as their main tasks the recruitment of new members; the organization of meetings, study clubs and courses, and entertainment events; and the distribution of party literature. Local activities peak at the time of communal or national elections.

The district or provincial organization serves to coordinate and support the work of the base units and to link the base units with the party's central leadership. Authority is vested in district meetings, to which each base unit sends one representative. This meeting elects a district executive committee of ten to twenty members to direct the day-to-day work of the district organization.

The national party congress is the primary source of the party's program, rules, and finances. The delegates are chosen at the local and district levels either at meetings or by membership vote, the latter being more characteristic of the socialist parties. The congress also elects the executive council or board which exercises authority between congresses and which, in turn, chooses an even smaller committee to handle day-to-day affairs. The left parties tend toward a more centralized administration coupled with emphasis on democratic participation by the rank and file. The nonsocialist parties lean more toward territorial decentralization, but with greater passivity of members and reliance on party officials at various levels. Each party also sponsors parallel women's, youth, and auxiliary organizations.

The relationship between a party's members and its parliamentary bloc also tends to vary along the ideological spectrum, with the independence of the member of Parliament (MP) being greatest in the rightist parties and least on the left. Overall, it is still safe to say that the MPs represent their party organizations more than their electoral constituencies. Candidate lists are drawn up by the district party organizations, with the left parties seeking more and the center and right parties less rank-and-file participation.

Party leadership dominated by outstanding individuals is relatively rare in Finland. It is unusual for anyone to become the undisputed leader of a Finnish party. Thus, in the case of a cabinet crisis, a given party may well have several candidates for near equal stature for prime minister.

Campaigning

Campaign activity is centered on the permanent party organization, supplemented by special election committees and support organizations. Propaganda for candidates is conducted at all levels, but with a recent tendency toward centralized, uniform party propaganda. The shift to single-name candidate lists in 1965, however, has led to a significant growth in separate electioneering by individual candidates and voters' associations.

Campaign activities include speeches, rallies, newspaper and journal articles, mass mailings, door-to-door canvassing, posters, print media advertising, and broadcast debates.

Independent Voters

The number of independent voters, those not identifying with one particular party, is estimated at about 15 percent of the electorate. Even in the least-partisan elections, those for the communal councils, the party affiliation of most candidates can be discerned and voted upon. Given conditions of partisan stability and multipartism, elections are now often effectively won or lost with these floating independents, found disproportionately within the urban upper middle class.

Party Financing

As largely unregulated civil associations, Finnish parties are not required to divulge their sources of funds, so that detailed information is not readily available. Generally it can be said that the leftist parties rely more heavily on membership dues than do the others, but even here dues comprise less than 10 percent of revenues. Private contributions, raffles, entertainment, business activities, and income from publications and auxiliary organizations supplement state financing, which since 1967 has been set at 10 million marks (about $2.38 million) annually. This sum is distributed to parties on the basis of 50,000 marks (about $12,000) per MP.

Center Party
(Keskustapouloe)

History

The party was founded as the Agrarian Union in 1906 and adopted its present name in 1965. It has almost always been the leading nonsocialist party, with Eduskunta representation ranging from sixty seats in 1929 to thirty-five in 1972. It has also served as the nearly indispensable pivot in coalition formation, having served in over 90 percent of the noncaretaker governments. Similarly, it has supplied more presidents and prime ministers than any other party. However, with the sharp demographic decline of the farming population following World War II, the party's change of name in 1965 signalled its awareness of the need to broaden its appeal.

Organization

Center Party structure follows the general pattern for nonsocialist parties described above. In recent years, a distinct minority faction, known as the "Black Dozen" has emerged. A rightist group, the "Dozen" objects to Center Party participation in center-left coalition governments. Its members now include about one-fourth of the party's thirty-six representatives in the Eduskunta; however, party control rests securely in the hands of those favoring cooperation with the left and a moderate social-agrarian orientation. The party sponsors no fewer than eighteen official publications, led by Etela-Saimaa, Ilkka, and Iisalmen Sanomat.

Headquarters are at Pursimiehenkatu 15, 00150 Helsinki 15.

Policy

The policy of the Center Party was for decades that of a clear-cut interest party with a distinctly Arcadian flavor. More recently it has attempted to broaden its appeal as a moderate party of the democratic center. Favoring small-scale private enterprise, it objects both to socialism and to the concentration of economic power in a few private hands. State regulation, ownership, and planning are justified on pragmatic grounds as essential to balanced development, in which rural areas should share equally with urban.

In foreign policy, the party has supported and been identified with the "Kekkonen line," a posture of "active neutrality" in which Finland seeks to pursue its own interests in ways not considered unacceptable by the Soviet Union. On this issue, the Center Party has been less supportive of cultivating close relations with the Soviets than the Finnish People's Democratic League, but more supportive than the Social Democrats or the conservative parties.

Membership & Constituency

Party membership was reported at over 300,000 in 1979, by far the largest in the country. Every second voter for the party is thus a member. Socioeconomic characteristics of Center Party members are not specifically known, but is thought to approximate that of its voters: 60 percent independent farmers, 20 percent managerial upper white collar, 15 to 20 percent lower-white-collar and blue-collar workers. It does better with female voters than do the socialist parties, but not as well as the more conservative parties. Its electorate is definitely aging more rapidly than that of any other party, except the Swedish People's

Party. Geographically, the Center's support is spread fairly evenly, except in the southern, more urbanized districts of Häme, Uusimaa, and especially Helsinki, where it receives less than 5 percent of the vote. Its best showings are recorded in the northern provinces of Oulu and Lapland and in the southeast.

Interest groups closely associated with the Center Party include the Confederation of Agricultural Producers (MTK), the Confederation of Small Farmers (PVK), and the Central Association of Finnish Cooperatives (SOK).

Financing

See **Party Financing** above.

Leadership

The two leading contenders for de facto party leadership are Ahti Karjalainen (born 1923) and Johannes Virolainen (born 1914). Both have served as prime minister. Virolainen was the party's nominee in the 1982 presidential elections.

Prospects

The efforts of the party to broaden its appeal in the face of the continuing atrophy of the farming sector have not been successful to date. In 1979 it lost the only *Eduskunta* seat it held from Helsinki. Merger with the Liberal People's Party and/or the Swedish People's Party has long been in the air. In 1979 the Center and Liberal parties did not compete against each other in several districts and called on their supporters to vote for the other party's candidate. They even agreed on a ten-point Common Program. Alternatively, or in conjunction with a merger, the party may underscore its commitment to the ecology movement in a search for younger, urban support. With the resignation of Kekkonen in 1981 and the rise of the National Coalition Party, the Center Party's role in government formation looked less secure than ever before.

Finnish Christian Union
(*Suomen Kristillinen Liitto*)

History

The party was founded in 1958 in an attempt to give partisan expression to the Lutheran pietist tradition. It gained its first *Eduskunta* representa-

tive in 1966, expanding to four seats in 1972 and nine in 1976. In the 1979 election, the party increased its popular vote, but still won just nine seats.

Organization

A homogeneous party that draws support exclusively from devout Lutherans, there are no apparent major factions within the party. Pietist clergy are probably the most influential party group. Its major publication is the weekly *Kristityu Vastuu*.

Headquarters are at Toolonkatu 50 D, 00250 Helsinki 25.

Policy

The Christian Union slogan for the 1979 election was "to restore respect for basic values." The party emphasizes strengthening the values of the traditional family and its restoration as a God-fearing institution. The party has taken a more stridently rightist stance in recent years, prompting the leader of the National Coalition Party to suggest that the Christian Union MPs should be seated to the far right of the *Eduskunta* chamber, rather than just to the right of center. In the 1978 presidential election, it was the largest party to oppose the reelection of Kekkonen, indicating its nonacceptance of the Kekkonen line in foreign affairs. Its candidate, Raino Westerholm, received a creditable 8.8 percent of the vote.

Membership & Constituency

Party membership is listed at 20,000, or about one member for every seven votes in 1979. Although support seems fairly evenly spread in the country, its strongest representation is in the Pietist strongholds of Vaasa and Mikkeli.

Financing

See **Party Financing** above.

Leadership

Raino Westerholm (born 1919) is both the political leader and administrative head of the party.

Prospects

The party has never aspired to be a permanent fixture on the political scene, stating that a more overt Christian orientation in the Center or National Coalition parties would render its existence superfluous. These parties have remained hostile, however. The Union's prospects for entering a government are very slim, even in a nonsocialist-majority coalition.

Finnish People's Democratic League
(*Suomen Kansan Demokraattinen Liito;* SKDL)

History

Formed in 1944 by dissident Social Democrats, independent socialists, and Communists, the SKDL serves as an umbrella electoral vehicle for these groups. The Finnish Communist Party (*Suomen Kommunistinen Puolu;* SKP) is the leading group within the league, but a significant role is given to non-Communists and to the League's other two constituent organizations, the Democratic League of Finnish Women and the Socialist League of Students. Of its thirty-five seats in the 1979 *Eduskunta*, six belong to non-Communists, and their role is more important than this fraction would indicate.

A revolutionary group in exile formed the Finnish Communist Party in 1918 with Lenin's aid. Its adherents returned to Finland with the general amnesty of 1922. By 1929, its militancy had helped arouse the fascist Lapua Movement which, through legal pressure and illegal terror, crushed the Communist Party and eliminated it as an institutional force until 1944.

Working within the SKDL, the SKP has enjoyed considerable success, receiving an average over 20 percent of the vote. Since 1966, however, SKDL popularity has declined, and its *Eduskunta* representation has steadily fallen, from a peak of fifty in 1958 to thirty-five, lowest in its postwar history, in 1979. Since 1966, the SKDL has been included in all but two noncaretaker governments, and presently holds two cabinet portfolios (labor; transport and communication), with a third (the second minister of education) held by a non-Communist member.

Organization

The SKDL and SKP maintain separate organization networks and membership lists. They are different sorts of organizations, as well. The SKDL is a broadly based, open organization striving to fos-

ter cooperative mass action by people of differing viewpoints. The SKP remains a much smaller, more restrictive and exclusive group still organized somewhat along Leninist lines. In 1957, about 30 percent of the executive board members of SKDL associations were SKP members, a figure which the SKP leadership considered too high and has subsequently reduced. SKDL basic organizations are formed mainly on a territorial-residential pattern, while the SKP emphasizes workplace sections. Both organizations maintain nationwide coverage and organization. Supreme authority in the SKDL is vested in the sixty-member League Council and in the SKP in the Central Committee of thirty-five full members.

Since 1969, the SKP has been clearly divided into two factions, with the division by now virtually institutionalized. The minority "Stalinist" group, which includes eleven of the League's MPs, favors the retention of the party's commitment to ultimate revolution and opposes its participation in government or in any union of the left. The majority Eurocommunist faction currently includes eighteen of the League's MPs, who cooperate with the six non-Communist SKDL MPs.

The SKDL maintains seven major publications, including the daily *Satakunnan Työ* and the weekly *Folktidningen Ny Tid*. The SKP publishes the daily *Kansan Uutiset* and the monthly *Kommunisti*.

SKDL headquarters are at Simonkatu 8B, 00100 Helsinki 10. The SKP headquarters address is Sturenkatu 4A, 00510 Helsinki 51.

Policy

The major focus of the SKP program is on long-range goals, while the SKDL directs itself toward more immediate and tangible policy objectives. The SKP stresses the abolition of bourgeois domination of the state and society and its replacement, by degrees, with a socialist system. Since the mid-1960s the SKP has also stressed the importance of rights and freedom and the party's desire to achieve its revolution through peaceful means. The minority "oppositionist" group rejects these Eurocommunist tendencies.

The SKDL program stresses expanded state enterprises and planning, participation by workers in public and private enterprise management, enlargement of rural landholdings, keeping land out of the hands of speculators, and meeting the late 1970s economic slump by increasing unemployment benefits, instituting a thirty-five-hour work week with four rather than three work shifts per day, lowering the retirement age, and payment of a housewife's wage. These measures would be financed by increasing taxes on corporations, large landowners, and wealthy individuals.

In foreign policy, the SKDL has been a strong supporter of the Kekkonen line in all its ramifications. The minority "oppositionist" SKP faction differs from the rest of the SKDL in refusing to criticize virtually any action of the Soviet Union, even the invasion of Afghanistan.

Membership & Constituency

The SKDL is second only to the Center Party in membership, with 176,000 official members in 1980, or about one member for every third SKDL voter. The SKP is a much more restrictive organization with about 60,000 members. Around 10 to 15 percent of the SKDL members in basic units also belong to the SKP. In voting, the SKDL tends to split the industrial working class of the urban areas with the Social Democratic Party. A second pillar of SKDL support is found among the landless laborers and small holders of the north and east. This "backwoods radicalism" has mainly emerged since 1945 and in recent years has been a more encouraging base than the industrial workers, who are fading as a political force as Finland becomes more postindustrial in character. Some northern areas have become virtually two-party regions, with the SKDL and Center party taking 80 percent of the vote.

Financing

See **Party Financing** above.

Leadership

The SKDL leadership tends to be less dynamic and less well known than that of the SKP. Its chairman, Kalevi Kivistö (born 1941), currently serves as first minister of education. The SKP leaders are the chairman, Aarne Saarinen (born 1913), and secretary, Arvo Aalto (born 1932), who also serves as minister of labor.

Prospects

Despite its record as perhaps the most successful radical left party of Western Europe, the SKDL must take some immediate steps to reverse its recent slide. Four of the five seats lost by the League in 1979 were in the southern districts, where the League must improve its appeal to younger, better-educated salaried employees. The existence of the hardline faction within the SKP

also hurts the League. However, the hardline faction leader, Taisto Sinisalo, lost his parliamentary seat to a non-Communist People's Democrat in 1979. Party leaders hope for a continuation of this trend.

Finnish Rural Party
(*Suomen Maaseudun Puolue*)

History

The Finnish Rural Party was founded in 1956 by a group of dissident Agrarian (Center) Party members led by the colorful and outspoken Veikko Vennamo, who charged that the Agrarians were selling out the interest of the small farmers, laborers, and small businessmen, especially in the remote areas. The Rural Party achieved a stunning breakthrough in the *Eduskunta* elections of 1970, winning 10.5 percent of the vote and eighteen seats. It held this total in the 1972 poll. In 1975, however, it fell dramatically to 3.6 percent and two seats. The 1979 elections represented something of a comeback for the party, but it remains far short of its peak strength. As a protest party, it has not been asked to participate in any governments.

Organization

The Rural Party ranks fourth in Finland in the number of organizational units, with an impressive total of over 1,500 basic units, including 150 communal and fourteen district organizations. These units tend to function as a transmission belt, however, since party policy is decided by the central leadership, essentially Veikko Vennamo. The extensive organizational network of the party is an important reason for its success, however. The party's chief press organ is the *Suomen Uutiset*.

Party headquarters are at Pohjois-Rautatienkatu 15B, 00100 Helsinki 10.

Policy

The Rural Party program contends that the nation's largest population group has been unnecessarily divided by the ideology and propaganda of the old parties. In particular, it criticizes the Center Party for sacrificing "backwoods" interests to those of the more prosperous farmers of the south and west and urban dwellers. Its very effective

1970 platform was directed towards "promoting backwoods Finland."

Its means for achieving this goal include an unusual mixture of socialist and nonsocialist policies along with constant reference to the need to root out the misuse, abuse, and corruption of public power by the older parties. It calls for state action to abolish unemployment and to solve the housing shortage, but demands an end to state subventions for political parties. State power should be used more efficiently to compensate those who have suffered losses in face of industrialization.

Membership & Constituency

With membership listed at over 35,000 in 1980, the Rural Party maintained a ratio of approximately four voters per member. Voters are generally small businessmen and impoverished smallholders. Geographically, the party's chief stronghold has been in the eastern provinces, especially Kuopio and Pohjois-Karjala.

Financing

See **Party Financing** above.

Leadership

The fortunes of the Rural Party have turned to a large extent on the credibility and effectiveness of its founder and rather autocratic leader, Veikko Vennamo (born 1913). Following the party's successes of 1970 and 1972, it was riven by dissension over Vennamo's proclaimed willingness to join in a coalition with the SKDL and the Social Democratic Party. This announcement caused the departure of a significant portion of the party, including twelve of its eighteen MPs, which subsequently formed the People's Unity Party. Vennamo has continued his strong leadership, with his son, Pekka (born 1944) assuming the party chairmanship.

Prospects

The party's modest comeback of 1979 can probably be attributed to the economic slump of the preceding two years and the failure of the rival People's Unity Party to strike a responsive chord in the countryside. The continued foundering of the Center Party also aids the Rural Party. Prospects are not promising, however, due to widespread disillusionment with Vennamo and to the party's shrinking demographic base.

Finnish Social Democratic Party (SDP; *Suomen Socialidemokraattinen Puolue*)

History

The party was founded in 1899 as a direct outgrowth of the nascent labor movement. It rejected a reformist approach in favor of an uncompromising commitment to class struggle, as reflected in the radical Forssa Program of 1903. When the Tsar allowed elections to the 200-member Finnish Diet to be conducted by universal adult suffrage in 1907, the Social Democrats astonished nearly everyone by winning eighty seats, twenty-one more than any other party. In 1916, it won 103 seats, an absolute majority not nearly matched by any party since. (The Tsar refused to convene that Diet following this election.) With the collapse of the Russian Empire in 1917, the highly polarized Finnish political system erupted in civil war, with the Social Democrats leading the nearly victorious Red forces. With their defeat, the most radical Social Democrats were forced into exile, where they formed the Finnish Communist Party. When the Allied Powers vetoed the Finnish conservatives' plan to set up a monarchy, the remnants of the Social Democratic Party reconstituted themselves under the control of the reformist wing, led by Vaino Tanner. In the first postindependence elections, the party again won eighty seats, almost twice as many as any other party.

Since World War II, the SDP has had to face renewed competition on its left from the SKDL and SKP. Thus, its largest number of seats in this period has been fifty-five (1966, 1972). A period of intraparty tension culminated in 1958 when a group of more radical dissidents was expelled from the party. They formed the Social Democratic League of Workers and Small Farmers (TPSL), which was able to win seven *Eduskunta* seats in 1966, before fading away in the early 1970s. From its all-time low of thirty-eight seats in 1962, the SDP quickly rebounded, and has headed six governments since 1966. In 1979, its parliamentary leader, Mauno Koivisto, was named prime minister. When Koivisto became president in 1982, Kalevi Sorsa became prime minister.

Organization

As Finland's first truly mass party, the SDP seeks to recruit members on a broad basis. Its organization, covering all parts of the country, includes 1,350 basic units, 176 communal organizations, and sixteen district organizations. Three district organizations may request a partywide referendum on any question, although the results are no longer binding on the Executive Committee. Representatives to the triennial party congress are selected by a mail vote of the entire membership. Between congresses, party affairs are run by the fifty-member Party Council, meeting several times each year, and the fifteen-member Executive Committee, which handles day-to-day business. Despite its history of factionalism, the SDP today seems relatively united behind the Koivisto leadership.

Chief press organs include the *Turun Päivälehti* (daily) and the *Sosialistinen Aikakauslehti*.

SDP headquarters are at Saariniemenkatu 6, 00530 Helsinki 53.

Policy

The main tendency within the party since the 1920s has been in the mainstream of moderate, reformist social democracy. Although it has stressed anticommunism and opposes any "union of the left," the SDP's position on the pivotal issues of the 1979 campaign, unemployment and taxation, did not differ much from that of the SKDL. In agriculture, the SDP has condemned the postwar land-settlement policy for creating units too small to be economically viable. Hence, it favors expansion of small holdings and the creation of rural industry to sustain marginal workers. The party has also favored the democratization of production by giving workers a decisive voice in production decisions.

In foreign policy, the SDP remained openly hostile to the Soviet Union well into the 1960s. Only with the stepping down of Vaino Tanner did the party make itself more amenable to the Kekkonen line. This move was also required in order to make the party an acceptable part of a governing coalition.

Membership & Constituency

With about 100,000 members, unchanged since the mid-1960s, the SDP ranks third among the leading four parties, giving it a comparatively high seven voters per member. Party support is weakest in the northern provinces of Lapland, Oulu, and Kuopio, and in Vaasa province to the west. Support comes from older skilled and semiskilled workers, especially in the more prosperous and secure industries. The SDP also appeals to educated youth. Recent studies indicate that young white-collar workers are more likely to vote SDP than are their blue-collar cohort, who are more likely to vote for a nonsocialist party. The party has also recently attempted to appeal to one of its traditional enemies, small business.

A major source of strength is the party's close tie with the Confederation of Finnish Trade Unions (SAK). Although the SAK is formally independent of all parties, some 63 percent of its members identify with the SDP. In the 1979 campaign, each SAK activist was asked to recruit at least five previously passive voters for the SDP. This strong organizational link is a key factor in the consistent levels of support the party has achieved.

Financing

See **Party Financing** above.

Leadership

The undisputed leader of the SDP today is Mauno Koivisto (born 1923), a former dock worker who went on to earn his doctorate in economics. Following several years in politics, he became governor of the Bank of Finland. He returned to politics in 1979 and commanded widespread support, even among conservative voters.

Kalevi Sorsa (born 1930), prime minister from 1977 to 1979 and again in 1982, draws his greatest support from leftists and trade unionists. He was favored over Koivisto by SKDL for prime minister after the 1979 elections.

Prospects

The party has been losing ground of late. Many consider its program unambitious and uninteresting. The strong organizational support of the SAK has helped it maintain its leading position, but the decline of organized labor will necessitate a shift in emphasis. Capture of the presidency may help, but since the office is by tradition nonpartisan, there are limits to what Koivisto can do.

Liberal People's Party (*Liberaalinen Kansanpoulue*)

History

The party was formed in 1965 as a coalition of the Finnish People's Party and the small Liberal Union (also known as the League of Independents). Since its founding, the party has declined in popularity. It lost five *Eduskunta* seats in 1979, bringing its total to four, the lowest ever. Since 1970 it has usually joined in the center-left coalition governments. However, it decided to join the opposition to the 1979 Koivisto cabinet because it considered Koivisto's taxation policy too radical.

Organization

The party remains relatively homogeneous, made up of the urban and professional middle class. Like its predecessors, however, it suffers from organizational weakness. It maintains around 300 basic organizations, no communal organizations, and fourteen district organizations. Policy is set by the biennial party congress. The Party Board handles decision making between congresses. Its major publication is the weekly *Uusi Poettopiste.*

Party headquarters are at Fredrikinkatu 58A 6, 00100 Helsinki 10.

Policy

The party has recently shifted its appeal somewhat, from a rather disembodied attempt to formulate social-welfare policy on behalf of society as a whole to the representation of the interests of the urban middle classes. Part of this new strategy was the formulation of a ten-point Common Program and several electoral alliances with the Center Party. The party continues its progressive emphasis on state regulation and planning of a privately owned, but decentralized economy. The party sees itself as profoundly anticonservative, whether manifested in rightism, agrarianism, or even ossified socialism.

Membership & Constituency

Party membership was listed at 18,000 in 1980, giving it about six voters per member. Membership has grown 55 percent since 1965, while votes received declined by almost 50,000 in the same period. The urban middle-class voters sought by the Liberals and the Center Party have instead opted overwhelmingly for the conservative position of the National Coalition Party. Still, over two-thirds of the party's voters and supporters come from urban areas, especially Helsinki. It also gains above-average support in Lapland, Kymi, Uusimaa, southern Tarku and southern Häme provinces.

Financing

See **Party Financing** above.

Leadership

Current party leadership includes the chairman, M. A. J. Itälä (born 1933), and the leader of the parliamentary group, Aneli Kivitie (born 1934).

Prospects

Current prospects for the party are not bright. Historically, the party gained its influence more from providing key ministers than from organizational or voter support, but its small size now makes it less significant as a coalition partner. The possibility of merger with the Center Party may be the best remaining hope for the progressive-liberal tendency in Finnish politics.

National Coalition Party (*Kansallinen Kokoomus*)

History

The *Kokoomus* was founded in 1918 as a continuation of the pre-independence "Old Finns," a Finnish-language group less hostile to Russification than the "Young Finns." For decades, its electoral support was limited to less than 20 percent by its image as a rather extreme right-wing party. This image was reinforced by its support for the Lapua Movement, stopping just short of endorsing the attempted Lapuan *coup d'état* of 1932. However, other sources of strength gave it power far beyond that indicated by the election results. With its leader, P. E. Svinhufoud, serving as president from 1931 to 1937, the *Kokoomus* was largely able to implement its probusiness program for meeting the Great Depression. It participated in most governments between 1924 and 1946, supplying ten prime ministers. Since then, it has participated in only three governments (1958–59, 1962–63, and 1964–66). Once the dominance of the Kekkonen line was established, the *Kokoomus* was no longer considered an acceptable coalition partner.

Since its last participation in government, however, it has made by far the largest electoral gains of any party, increasing its popular vote from 326,928 (13.8 percent) in 1966 to 626,108 (21.7 percent) in 1979. Its *Eduskunta* representation increased from twenty-six to forty-seven in the same period. It has been by far the most success-ful party of the past decade, but this success has not won it a role in government.

Organization

For many years, the *Kokoomus* remained clos-est of all Finnish parties to the cadre type, with little emphasis on enrolling and mobilizing a mass membership. Even today it lists only 80,000 mem-bers, down from 83,000 in 1965. It thus ranks a rather poor fourth in total membership, with al-most eight voters per member. It maintains only 716 basic units, no communal organs, and sixteen district organizations. National policy is set by the biennial party assembly, the sixty-member Party Council, and the Executive Board. The party's par-liamentary group is undoubtedly the leading force in forging national party policy. However, local and district organs are free to act quite indepen-dently of the central leadership. Its chief press organs include *Aamulehti*, *Lansi-Suomi*, and *Nykpaiva* (a membership weekly).

Kokoomus headquarters are at Kansakoulukuja 3, 00100 Helsinki 10.

Policy

Coincident with the party's recent electoral success has been a shift in image from that of a rather extreme rightist party to that of a more moderate conservative group. A key move in this evolution occurred in 1968 when it joined the six-party front backing Kekkonen's reelection. Today, the party champions "people's capitalism," with as many citizens as possible becoming owners by dint of their own achievement. To aid in this pro-cess, the government's economic role should be trimmed to the barest minimum possible. Its pol-icy proposals to meet the late-1970s slump were to cut business taxes and social security and un-employment benefits. It also favors a shift from income taxes to taxes on consumption, in order to encourage saving. The *Kokoomus's* continued anti-communism and pro-Western orientation have rendered it unacceptable as a coalition part-ner of the left and center parties.

Membership & Constituency

Historically, membership and voting support came from big business, large landowners, and portions of the upper middle class (e.g., top bu-reaucrats). More recently, it has broadened its ap-peal to people of all kinds weary of fifteen years of uninterrupted center-left rule. Also, it has made gains in the new middle class of the larger south-ern cities and towns, displacing the SDP as the leading party in several such districts. Many first-time voters and disgruntled supporters of the smaller nonsocialist parties have also rallied to the *Kokoomus*.

Traditionally, interest-group support was a more significant contributor to *Kokoomus* power than membership or voters. As the party becomes more mass-based and catchall in nature, this bal-ance will shift. Still, the Federation of Finnish In-dustries, the Confederation of Finnish Employers, the Central Chamber of Commerce, the Confeder-ation of Agricultural Producers, and various alumni and veterans organizations maintain close, if informal, financial and political ties to the *Ko-koomus*.

Financing

See **Party Financing** above.

Leadership

Kokoomus leadership in recent years has been much less dominating than it was in the 1930s and 1940s. It has returned to the more typical Finnish pattern of fairly anonymous party leadership. Polls taken before the 1979 election indicated that a majority of *Kokoomus* voters favored the Social Democrat Koivisto as prime minister over their own leader Harri Holkeri (born 1937).

Prospects

The *Kokoomus* has many reasons to be optimis-tic. Above all, it has been the only party to make significant inroads into the burgeoning service-sector urban middle class. It now stands as the largest conservative party in Finnish history and as the leading party in the nonsocialist *Eduskunta* majority. However, hostility toward the *Ko-koomus* by the Center Party and the Soviet Union means that it will have to continue in opposition indefinitely. Party leaders also must wonder if they are approaching some "natural limits" of electoral strength in highly politicized Finland. Hence, its prospects for gaining a ruling position will remain dim unless President Koivisto takes a radically different tack in government formation from that of his predecessor.

Swedish People's Party (*Svenska Folkparteit*)

History

During the period of Swedish rule of Finland (1323–1809) thousands of Swedes became residents in the country and established themselves as an elite. By the mid-nineteenth century, the language and culture of this group had become dominant at the top of Finland's upper class. The party was founded in 1906 as the institutional continuation of the Swedish interest group (*Svecomen*) in the Diet and was aimed explicitly at promoting the interests of the Swedish-speaking minority. Even by the time of its founding, however, the language issue had been largely settled. Nevertheless, the party was able consistently to obtain between 10 and 14 percent of the vote through the 1930s. Since the war, its popularity has declined steadily, reaching the lowest total in its history in 1979. This decline reflects both a decrease in the proportion of Swedes in the population and the pull of other, more ideological, parties. Swedes now constitute only 6.2 percent of the population. Swedish-speaking Finns, if still somewhat privileged, are no longer considered a threat by the Finnish majority. The party has joined all of the center-left governments since 1968 and in 1982 held two cabinet positions, minister of justice and second minister of education. It has never contributed a prime minister or president, however.

Organization

Virtually all party members and supporters come from the Swedish-speaking minority, but with respect to other criteria, the party is heterogeneous and loosely organized. Factions within the party represent a broad range of opinions on concrete policy matters. The party maintains only ninety-seven basic units and only four district organizations limited to those areas with concentrated Swedish population. Ultimate authority is vested in the party assembly, the only major party congress in Finland to meet annually.

Chief press organs include the *Medborgarbladet, Hufvudstadsbladet,* and *Jakobstads Tidning.*

Headquarters are at Bulevarden 7A, P.B. 146, 00121 Helsinki 12.

Policy

Originally dominated by large landowners, the party has always tended toward a conservative stance. Today, it retains its firm attachment to private property, tempered, however, by the influence of social-liberalism. Because the party has difficulty taking firm stands on issues unrelated to the special position of the Swedish-speaking population, it is in a position to promote conciliation and unity in the multiparty system. The system has responded by making it common practice to include one or two Swedish-speaking ministers in most cabinets. In foreign policy, the party has been an eager supporter of the Kekkonen line.

Membership & Constituency

Party membership has held at the 50,000-member level over the past twenty years, ranking fifth among Finnish parties. This gives it a rather low ratio of 2.5 voters per member (1979). Geographically, members and supporters are concentrated overwhelmingly in Helsinki, in Uusimaa and Vasa provinces, and the Aaland Islands. In 1979, 85 percent of the party's vote came from these areas. In recent decades, there has been evidence of a drift of Swedish-speaking workers to the left parties and of youth to the left or to the *Kokoomus*. Major interest-group support comes from the 25,000-member Central Association of Swedish Agricultural Producers and the Swedish Cooperative Association.

Financing

See **Party Financing** above.

Leadership

Current leadership includes Foreign Minister and party chairman Par Stenbäck (born 1941) and Minister of Justice Christoffer Taxell (born 1948).

Prospects

Overall, the Swedish group would seem to be a somewhat privileged, rather than oppressed, minority. That lack of oppression and the passage of time have eroded its base of support. Merger with another center party, or with the *Kokoomus*, has been seriously entertained.

Minor Parties

Constitutional Party of the Right (*Perustuslaillinen Oikeistopuolue/Swedish Konstitutionella hogerpartiet*)

Founded in 1973 to oppose the exceptional legislative reelection of President Kekkonen in 1975, it won 1.6 percent of the vote and one *Eduskunta* seat. Membership numbers are not known. The backbone of the party is thought to be older, urban, anti-Soviets who dissented from the *Kokoomus* and the Swedish People's Party's support of Kekkonen. Its vote fell to 1.2 percent (34,707 votes) in 1979 and it lost its only seat.

People's Unity Party
(*Suomen Kansan Yhtenaisyyden Puolue*)

Founded in 1972 by former members of the Rural Party dissatisfied with Vennamo's autocratic leadership and his decision to cooperate with the left parties, the party's main backing was from small proprietors deeply hostile to socialism. Originally strong, with 15,000 members and twelve of the eighteen Rural Party MPs rallying to its banner, it won only 1.7 percent of the vote in 1975, good for just one *Eduskunta* seat. In 1979 it lost even that seat, falling to 0.3 percent (8,677 votes).

National Prospects

Despite suffering the economic problems of all the industrialized Western countries and charges that Finland's independence has been fatally compromised by its relations with the Soviet Union, the overall prospects for the country must be considered quite bright. Politically, the Finnish system has proved since World War II that stable and effective representative government can be achieved in a nation of many deep partisan cleavages. The replacement of the quasimonarchial Kekkonen with the more republican Koivisto attests to the further democratization and popularization of the system. With uniquely strong trade ties to both East and West, it seems well situated to make a relatively rapid economic recovery, some signs of which were already evident in mid-1982. Finland's position in foreign affairs is stable and comfortable, as indicated by overwhelming public support for the Kekkonen line. The sometimes hysterical charges from other countries that this policy amounts to a form of national serfdom is completely rejected by the Finns themselves, who know that it has accompanied the longest period of peace, democracy, and profound economic and social development their nation has ever seen. In this context, the Finnish people and their leaders have every reason to face the future with confidence and a realistic optimism.

Further Reading

Arter, David. "All Party Government for Finland?" *Parliamentary Affairs*, Vol. 31, No. 1, January 1980.

———. "The Finnish Center Party: Profile of a 'Hinge Group.'" *West European Politics*, Vol. 2, No. 4, January 1979.

———. "The Finnish Election of 1979: The Empty-Handed 'Winner'?" *Parliamentary Affairs*, Vol. 32, No. 1, Autumn, 1979.

Borre, Ole. "Electoral Instability in Four Nordic Countries, 1950–1977." *Comparative Political Studies*, Vol. 13, No. 2, July 1980.

Haranne, Markku. "Dialectics Between Occupational and Party Structures: Finland Since World War II." *Acta Sociologica*, Vol. 23, Nos. 2 and 3, 1980.

Kirby, D. G. *Finland in the Twentieth Century.* Minneapolis: University of Minnesota Press, 1980.

Nousiainen, Jaakko. *The Finnish Political System.* Translated by John Hodgson. Cambridge, Mass.: Harvard University Press, 1971.

Upton, A. F. *Communism in Scandinavia in Finland: Politics of Opportunity.* New York: Anchor Books, 1973.

Warwick, Paul. "The Durability of Coalition Governments in Parliamentary Democracies." *Comparative Political Studies*, Vol. 12, No. 2, January 1979.

REPUBLIC OF FRANCE
(*Republique Française*)
by William G. Andrews, Ph.D.

The System of Government

France, a nation of nearly fifty-four million people, is a unitary state ruled by a democratic republic that combines features of presidential and parliamentary government. The present regime is the Fifth Republic, based on a constitution drafted under the leadership of Premier Charles de Gaulle and ratified by popular referendum on September 28, 1958. The only major amendment to that constitution introduced direct popular election of the president in 1962.

The Fifth Republic is the most durable French regime since the fall of the absolute monarchy in 1789, excepting only the Third Republic (1875–1940). The Third and Fourth (1946–58) republics were parliamentary systems plagued by weak, unstable coalition governments and divided, indecisive assemblies. The inability of the latter regime to suppress an Algerian nationalist insurrection (1954) caused its collapse and the return to office of de Gaulle, who had been the leader of the French military and diplomatic resistance during World War II and who organized and led the provisional government of 1944 to 1946.

Executive

The Fifth Republic has a dual executive. The president of the republic is the chief of state, elected by popular vote for seven-year renewable terms. The prime minister, appointed for an indefinite term by the president, is head of the government; he must have the confidence of a majority in the National Assembly. Most formal business of the executive is transacted in a Council of Ministers, composed of the prime minister and other senior members of the government chaired by the president. The president gives the executive branch its general policy orientation and controls the composition of the government. The constitu-

tion gives the president special powers in foreign affairs and defense, but the president's position enables him to take a leading role in any area of government, depending on his interests and the circumstances. For instance, President Georges Pompidou (1969–74) was more involved in economic affairs than de Gaulle (1959–69).

The president has ample powers to carry out his duties. He can dissolve the National Assembly at any time and call new elections, although he may not do so a second time within a year. The president can call popular referenda, in certain circumstances, on laws or constitutional amendments and can invoke broad emergency powers in crisis situations. The constraints on these emergency powers include the right of the Assembly to meet without threat of dissolution; this proved to be so embarrassing the only time an emergency was invoked (1961) that the experiment has not been repeated.

Theoretically, the president can withhold his signature from decrees developed in the Council of Ministers. However, presidents have controlled the actions of the Council so thoroughly, that none has withheld his signature or, so far as is known publicly, threatened to do so.

In addition, the president has all the usual powers of a chief of state. He commands the armed forces, sends and receives diplomatic envoys, makes high-level civil and military appointments, promulgates laws, negotiates and ratifies treaties, and exercises the pardoning power. However, all those powers require the countersignature of the prime minister and, in most cases, the minister responsible for implementing the decision.

The original 1958 constitution provided that the president be elected for a seven-year term by an electoral college dominated by local elective officials, using a majority electoral system with runoff balloting, if necessary. The electoral college

PRESIDENTIAL ELECTIONS UNDER THE FIFTH REPUBLIC

	1st round	2nd round
1965		
de Gaulle (G.)	10,828,523 (44.6)	13,085,407 (55.2)
Mitterrand (S.)	7,694,003 (31.7)	10,623,247 (44.8)
Lecanuet (Cen.)	3,777,119 (15.6)	
Others	1,954,909 (8.1)	
1969		
Pompidou (G.)	9,763,428 (44.0)	10,686,498 (57.6)
Poher (Cons.)	5,202,271 (23.4)	7,870,601 (42.4)
Duclos (Comm.)	4,781,838 (21.5)	
Defferre (S.)	1,128,049 (5.1)	
Others	1,335,136 (6.0)	
1974		
Giscard d'Estaing (Cons.)	8,326,774 (32.6)	13,396,203 (50.8)
Mitterrand (S.)	11,044,373 (43.2)	12,971,604 (49.2)
Chaban-Delmas (G.)	3,857,728 (15.1)	
Others	2,309,761 (9.0)	
1981		
Mitterrand (S.)	7,505,960 (25.8)	15,714,598 (51.8)
Giscard d'Estaing (Cons.)	8,222,432 (28.3)	14,647,787 (48.2)
Chirac (G.)	5,225,846 (18.0)	
Marchais (Comm.)	4,456,922 (15.3)	
Others	3,626,876 (12.5)	

G. = Gaullist, S. = Socialist, Cons. = Conservative, Cen. = Centrist, Comm. = Communist

macy through popular election, (2) his consequent control over the prime minister and government, and (3) the constitutional powers they have.

The prime minister is responsible for leading and supervising the government on a day-to-day basis and for managing the parliamentary majority. Much of the work of the government in defining and implementing policy is performed within the framework of legislation through executive decrees and similar texts and oral decisions. The constitution has delineated a "domain of law" that covers the most important policy areas for which parliamentary statutes are required. All other areas, mainly the specification of detail and implementation measures, are reserved for governmental action. The procedures and practices for producing such action have become quite regularized and systematic.

In addition to routine exercise of normal regulatory powers by issuing executive decrees, the government may ask Parliament to delegate special legislative authority to it in a specified area of policy for an explicitly limited period of time subject to subsequent veto by Parliament. During the first twenty years of the Fifth Republic, thirteen such requests were made, granted, and used. Only four had substantial importance: in 1959 against alcoholism and other "social scourges"; in 1960 against an abortive insurrection in Algeria; in 1964, 1966, and 1969 to adapt the French economy to European Community decisions; and in 1967 to reform economic policies and the social security system. A fourteenth such request was made and granted in December 1981 in order to speed measures against unemployment.

Beyond its policymaking powers within the executive branch, the government has substantial authority to lead Parliament in the legislative process. The government's general policy declaration gives Parliament its overall orientation. It has the right to introduce legislation; in the first twenty-two years of the Fifth Republic nearly 31 percent of all bills considered by Parliament came from the government. In the same period, 87.3 percent of government bills became law compared to only 7.4 percent of private member's bills. As a result, 85.6 percent of all laws originated with the government.

The government can prevent MPs from introducing certain kinds of bills, namely those that would increase expenditures, reduce revenues, or trespass in the domain reserved for government regulations. About 8.7 percent of proposed MPs' bills have been excluded on those grounds. When the government dislikes an MP's bill that it cannot

was replaced by direct popular vote as a result of a 1962 referendum.

A majority of the votes cast is required for election on the first ballot. If no candidate receives a majority, a second round of balloting is held two weeks later. Only the two top first-round candidates who choose to remain in the running are eligible for the second balloting.

In practice, the president's power derives mainly from (1) his claim to democratic legiti-

exclude, it can kill it by keeping it off the agenda, a constitutional power that governments have wielded ruthlessly.

Ministers have full access to the parliamentary committee and floor deliberations, including the right to speak, but not to vote. Ministers make formal statements to the assemblies on behalf of the government and they lead and manage most parliamentary debates. Ministers take part in 100 to 150 National Assembly debates a year, often several times in a deliberation. Their remarks consume about eighty to ninety hours of Assembly time per year, one-fifth of the total. Ministers also appear before committees to explain the government's position, respond to questions and criticism, and work out disagreements. On a few occasions, the government has made a "declaration of general policy" as the basis for a vote of confidence by the Assembly, which the governments have always won.

The government's legislative leadership includes the amending process. It may propose amendments, require "blocked votes," and exclude certain types of amendments proposed by MPs. The "blocked vote" provision of the constitution authorizes the government to require that the Assembly or Senate "take a single vote on all or part of the bill under discussion, retaining only the amendments proposed or accepted by the government." This device has been used in the Assembly fairly often, 158 times through 1980. The government has been defeated on such votes only eight times. About three-fifths of the blocked votes concerned budgetary matters.

In exceptional circumstances, the government may declare bills urgent and require accelerated consideration. This happens in the Assembly eight to ten times a year on the average. If the Assembly and Senate disagree on the provisions of a bill, the government may require that it be referred to a special committee for reconciliation and can force adoption of the version it prefers if the Assembly agrees, despite the opposition of the Senate. Through 1980, fifty-six laws had been enacted through this procedure.

The government's most powerful and controversial special weapon is passive enactment. It can "engage its responsibility" on a bill. If no motion of censure is submitted within twenty-four hours and passed by an absolute majority of the Assembly, the bill has been adopted passively. Only four bills have been passed in that manner, all of them after motions of censure had been defeated. The government has never been defeated on such a vote. Finally, the government

may enact the annual budget by decree if Parliament fails to act on it in the allotted time. This has never happened because Parliament has always met its deadline.

The success of these devices has rested on the relationship of confidence between the Parliament and the government. The French system assumes that the government and a parliamentary majority share a common political and partisan interest. Though individual deputies may disagree with the government on particulars, the majority expects to benefit in the next elections from the overall success of the government's efforts. The parliamentary weapons are the government's means to ensure that the MPs act consistently in their own long-term general interest.

The National Assembly of the Fifth Republic has never expressed a lack of confidence in a newly appointed government or prime minister. Only once, has it changed its mind. In October 1962, the Assembly passed a motion of censure initiated by the opposition against the government of Georges Pompidou because of its intention to carry out de Gaulle's plan to revise the constitution by popular referendum. That experiment in overthrowing a government had a decidedly chilling effect on the overthrowers. President de Gaulle dissolved the rebellious Assembly and his supporters won a larger majority in the new Assembly than had ever before been elected in republican France. Since then, majorities have held firm. There have been grumbles, groans, and occasional splits, but the MPs have not endangered the government or themselves. Through the 1978–81 legislature, twenty-two motions of censure had been submitted in the National Assembly. Except for the 1962 motion, none was adopted and only four—in 1967–68—came close. The constitution states that only votes favorable to a censure motion are counted, thus avoiding a distinction between negative votes and abstentions. The highest of the 1967–68 censure votes was 237, seven short of the required majority.

Governments have been less successful in retaining the confidence of the president. Through 1981, eight men had served as prime minister. Seven of them had resigned because they lacked the confidence of either the president who had appointed them or the succeeding president. Also, prime ministers had submitted the resignations of their governments nine times and been reappointed immediately, usually with major reshuffling. Premiers have averaged 38.6 months in office, governments 16.9 months.

Under the constitution, individual ministers are

appointed by the president upon nomination of the prime minister. In practice, the composition of the governments has been the product of negotiations and deliberations between the president and prospective prime minister and between the prime minister and the leaders of the parties in the majority. All the governments have been coalitions, although the orthodox Gaullists (1968–73) and the Socialists (elected 1981) had single-party majorities. During the first legislature (1958–62), the coalition included all major parties except the Socialist and Communists; from 1962 to 1981 the Gaullists, Giscardians, and a fraction of the Centrists; and since 1981 the Socialists, Communists, and Left Radicals.

Legislature

The governments lead a Parliament that consists of two chambers: the National Assembly and the Senate. However, they give most of their attention to the Assembly and are responsible to it, not to the Senate. Although the executive is the more influential branch of government in the Fifth Republic, Parliament remains important.

The National Assembly has 491 seats, each deputy representing a single-member election district. Each of the ninety-six departments (large counties) is guaranteed at least two seats. Also, seventeen deputies represent French overseas possessions. Otherwise, the seats are allocated proportionate to population. The official leadership organ of the chamber is the steering committee (*bureau*). It administers the business, facilities, and resources of the Assembly but does not make major policy or political decisions. It consists of the president of the National Assembly, six vice presidents, three *questeurs* (financial officers), and twelve secretaries, all of whom are deputies elected to their Assembly offices by its membership. The constitution requires that the Assembly president be "elected for the duration of the legislature." That officer is chosen from the chamber's political majority and ensures the orderly conduct of its business, as well as performing other important functions. The vice presidents represent the major parties in the governance of the Assembly. The Assembly's agenda is prepared by the Conference of Presidents, which includes the president of the Assembly, its vice presidents, the chairs of the standing committees, the chairs of the party caucuses, the member of the Finance Committee responsible for reporting bills, and the chairs of special investigative committees. A representative of the government may attend its meetings. In fact, under the constitution, the government controls the agenda by requiring priority consideration of its bills.

Most of the legislative work of the Assembly is prepared by six standing committees, a number specified by the constitution. Their subjects are culture, family, and social affairs; production and exchange; constitutional law, legislation, and general administration; foreign affairs; finance, the economy, and planning; national defense and the armed forces. They range in size from sixty to 120 members and, invariably, are chaired by the government's supporters. Most bills are referred to those committees.

Partisan affairs in the Assembly are managed by caucuses, called parliamentary groups. Under Assembly rules, caucuses require at least thirty members. Recent Parliaments have had five caucuses: the Communists, the Socialists and Radicals, the Gaullists, followers of Giscard d'Estaing, and the Centrists. Some independent deputies have affiliated with those caucuses. The caucuses are represented proportionately on the committees and other Assembly organs and in the distribution of debating time.

By occupational background, French MPs are rather different from American congressmen. The largest single category in the 1981 Assembly (metropolitan France only) was secondary-school teacher, represented by 108 deputies, with college professors accounting for another 31 and elementary-school teachers 22. High civil servants were second with 107, while lawyers ranked fifth with 25, just behind physicians (27). Those standings vary somewhat by legislature, but teaching and the civil service rank at the top consistently.

Parliament attempts to control the government by threat of censure and by investigative committees. In addition, Parliament formally may question the government. As many as 20,000 written questions have been put to the government in one year and about 90 percent are answered, also in writing. Oral questions can be raised on the floor during special weekly sessions set aside for that purpose and the ministers to whom the questions are directed must respond immediately.

More important than censure, investigative committees, or questions in controlling the government on a day-to-day basis are informal means. The parliamentary majority and the government communicate constantly outside formal channels to ensure that their closely similar interests are well served. Such communications work more effectively than their public counterparts to main-

NATIONAL ASSEMBLY ELECTION RESULTS (1958–1981)
FIRST-ROUND VOTES, PERCENTAGES, AND TOTAL NUMBER OF SEATS WON

	1958*			1962*			1967*			1968*			1973			1978			1981		
	Votes	%	Seats	Votes	%	Seats	Votes	%	Seats	Votes	%	Seats	Votes	%	Seats	Votes	%	Seats	Votes	%	Seats
Communist	3,882	18.0	10	3,992	21.8	41	5,030	22.5	72	4,435	20.0	33	5,149	21.4	73	5,870	20.6	86	4,066	16.1	44
Socialist	3,167	14.8	40	2,320	12.6	65⎫	4,207	18.8	117	3,660	16.5	57	4,579	19.0	89	6,451	22.6	103⎫	9,433	37.4	269⎫
Radical	2,348	11.5	35	680	3.7	40⎭	—	—	—	—	—	—	—	—	—	604	2.1	10⎭	—	—	14
Other Left	347	1.4	2	705	3.8	4	507	2.3	4	1.037	4.7	2	1,457	6.0	20	1,879	6.6	1	800	3.2	6
MRP/Center	2,379	11.6	57	1,635	8.9	36	2,864	12.8	27	2,290	10.3	28	3,896	16.1	50	—	—	—	—	—	—
Moderates	4,250	19.9	132	1,661	9.1	28	—	—	—	—	—	—	—	—	—	—	—	—	—	—	—
Giscardians	—	—	—	798	4.4	20⎫	—	—	—	—	—	—	1,674	6.9	54	6,814	23.9	141	4,839	19.2	61
Gaullists	3,604	17.6	188	5,847	31.9	229⎭	8,454	37.8	233	10,585	47.8	350	5,760	24.9	185	6,462	22.6	148	5,250	20.8	85
Other Right	670	3.3	1	82	0.5	2	1,331	6.0	17	140	0.6	—	1,528	6.3	19	543	1.9	2	804	3.2	11
			465			465			470			470			490			491			490
Registered Voters	27,245,202			27,539,698			28,291,838			28,177,914			29,865,345			35,204,152			36,342,827		

* Metropolitan France only; popular votes in thousands.

tain the relationship of confidence between the two institutions that is the essential element of the parliamentarian aspect of the Fifth Republic.

Bicameralism is a long, deeply entrenched tradition in French government. Historically, the upper house has been principally a "chamber of reflection" and a means of ensuring representation of the *départements* (provinces) as governmental entities. Generally, it had somewhat less legislative authority than the lower house and no direct power to vote down governments. In 1958, de Gaulle and Michel Debré (a senator in the Fourth Republic) conceived of the Senate as one means to curb the power of the National Assembly and, therefore, sought to give it a more important role than it had had in the Fourth Republic. In fact, both before the 1981 Socialist victory and since, the Senate has tended to be less favorable to the governments than has been the Assembly, and, thus, has not served its intended purpose.

Originally, the Fifth Republic Senate had 283 seats. That number has been increased gradually since 1977 and will reach 316 in 1983, 296 from France and the rest from its overseas possessions or French citizens living abroad. The internal structure of the Senate is similar to that of the Assembly. The subject areas of the standing committees are delineated slightly differently and neither special committees nor investigative committees have been used as much. In recent years, seven party caucuses have been formed: Communist, Socialist, Radical, Centrist, Conservative, Gaullist, and Peasant. Sometimes, the Conservatives (Independents) and Peasants have formed a common caucus.

Because of its higher age requirement (thirty-five), its less political character, and the longer terms of its members, the Senate tends to attract local personages of the distinguished-elder-states-man type, rather than more active, ambitious politicians. Also, the partisan lineup in the Senate has been quite different from the Assembly. Neither the Gaullists nor the Socialists have ever held as many as one-quarter of the Senate seats, despite their clear majorities in the Assembly. Rather, the Senate's composition has remained remarkably similar to that of its Fourth Republic predecessor.

Judiciary

The 1958 constitution created, for the first time in France, a quasijudicial institution—the Constitutional Council—that can invalidate legislative and executive acts on grounds of unconstitutionality. Its authority is much more closely proscribed than that of the U.S. Supreme Court, but the Council has become somewhat more important than expected as a result of some of its decisions and a constitutional revision.

The Council is composed of nine appointed members. The president of the republic, the president of the Senate, and the president of the National Assembly each make three appointments. Members serve nine-year nonrenewable terms. In addition, former presidents of the republic are ex officio members. This last category has had little importance. The president of the Council is appointed by the president of the republic from among its members.

Besides ensuring the integrity of elections and referenda, the Council's most important function is that of determining the constitutionality of decrees and proposed legislation. It may make such determinations only on appeal by the president of the republic or by the president or sixty members of either chamber. By mid-1979, it had handed down 108 decisions on decrees and 115 on legislation and parliamentary rules. A number of these

APPROXIMATE NUMBER OF SENATORS, BY PARTY, AFTER EACH ELECTION (1958–80)									
	1958	1959	1962	1965	1968	1971	1974	1977	1980
Communists	16	14	14	14	18	18	20	23	23
Socialists	56	48	55	53	50	49	52	62	69
Radicals	65	51	50	48	43	38	35	40	42
MRP/Center	26	29	36	40	47	46	54	61	58
Independents	90	85	63	61	53	59	57	52	64
Gaullists	39	27	29	29	35	38	30	33	39
Peasants	—	—	20	18	19	16	15	15	—
Other	24	33	6	11	18	19	20	9	9
TOTAL	311	287	273	274	283	283	283	295	304

were important interpretations, especially those that have prevented the government from encroaching on the rights of other institutions and individuals. Nevertheless, the Council remains a relatively limited and weak institution.

The French judicial system itself rests on a codified system of law. It differs from Britain and the United States in organizing trials on an inquisitorial, rather than adversarial, basis. It lacks the power to review legislative and executive action for constitutionality.

The French have three main court systems— civil, criminal, and administrative. The civil-court structure has 475 *tribunaux d'instance* at the lowest level, and 172 *tribunaux de grande instance* at the departmental level. The criminal-court structure has police courts at the bottom, correctional courts at the next level, and an assize court for each department. Appeals from both civil and criminal courts go to the twenty-seven courts of appeal and, then, to the Court of Cassation. The administrative-court system adjudicates complaints against the state administration (though not the police). Thirty-one regional courts of general jurisdiction and several specialized administrative tribunals hear the cases initially. The Council of State receives them on appeal. A High Court of Justice may be constituted by Parliament to try a president for treason or members of the government for crimes or misdemeanors.

Regional & Local Government

The structure of French government below the national level has three main tiers. At the base are some 36,000 municipalities, called *communes*. They are grouped into ninety-six *départements* and twenty-two *régions*. The system of communes and departments dates to the French Revolution, but the regions have developed gradually as important governmental units only during the past twenty years.

Traditionally, the territorial units were less governmental than administrative, as their discretionary powers and budgetary authority were limited narrowly. The governmental powers of the communes and departments have long been vested in popularly elected councils headed by mayors (communes) or presidents (departments) chosen by the councilors from among themselves. The regional councils were composed of the deputies and senators representing the departments of each region in Parliament and of delegates from the cities and departmental councils of the region. The chief administrative officials have been regional and departmental prefects, with subprefects being responsible for major subdivisions of the departments, called *arrondissements*. Appointed from Paris, these officials had considerable power, including the authority to override decisions of the councils.

A sweeping reform of regional and local government was begun in 1981 and has shifted authority decisively in favor of regional and local bodies. In March 1983, regional councils will be directly elected. Primary executive powers have been transferred from the prefects, now called commissioners, to the presiding officers of the councils at each level. The discretionary powers and budgetary authority of the councils were increased substantially. Nevertheless, the state remains much more highly centralized in France than in the United States. Thus, about 99 percent of all governmental revenues in France are collected by the national government, compared to about two-thirds in the United States.

The Electoral System

Members of the National Assembly are chosen by direct, popular vote for five-year terms, all seats being filled at the same election. Single-member districts and a majority electoral system are used. If no candidate wins a majority of the votes in the first round of balloting in a district, a second is held a week later for which only a simple plurality is required to win. Candidates receiving fewer than 12.5 percent of the first-round vote may not compete in the second round. Usually, other candidates with no prospect of success withdraw.

In each election in a few districts, all but one of the eligible candidates withdrew from the second round. The remaining candidate's name then appears alone on the second-round ballot. Most of the second-round contests are duels between two rivals, usually one from the left and one from the center-right. In 1981, only one of the 310 second-round battles in metropolitan France involved more than two candidates. However, that was true in sixty-four of the 424 runoffs in 1978.

In general, perhaps one-fourth of the seats are "safe," in that one candidate is virtually assured of easy election on the first round. In most of the rest, the first ballot amounts to a primary election. When the parties of the left are allied (1973, 1981), they normally agree to support those of their candidates whose first-round performances are most promising of second-round success. The center-right allies are more selective in holding such "primaries." For instance, in 1981, they had that type of agreement in eighty-eight districts, but gave joint support to single candidates on the first round in 358 others.

An unusual feature of the French parliamentary electoral system is the constitutional requirement that each candidate designate a running mate (*suppléant*) who will represent the district if the candidate is elected and later resigns to accept governmental office, is elected to the Senate or appointed to the Constitutional Council, or dies. This provision was designed mainly to prevent MPs from also holding ministerial office and to avoid a rash of by-elections after the formation of a government.

In practice, a minister who was elected to Parliament before his appointment to the government uses his *suppléant*, the new deputy, as a parliamentary assistant, while the minister continues to function like a deputy in all but name. In spite of the *suppléant* system, by-elections are sometimes necessary, averaging over three a year.

The French ballot is a slip of white paper. One candidate's name, party affiliation, and public offices held are printed on one side. Ballots for all candidates are mailed by the government to registered voters in a given district (for the entire country in presidential elections) along with the candidates' campaign statements. On polling day (always Sunday), the voters take ballots for the candidates of their choice to the polling station. (Ballots are also available at the voting booth.) Election officials verify the registration of each voter, who then enters a voting booth, places one ballot in an official envelope, leaves the booth, has the envelope stamped by an official, and deposits it in the ballot box. Because of the nature of the electoral system, ticket splitting is not possible, although voters can and do vote for one party in local elections and another in national elections.

All French citizens at least eighteen years old are eligible to vote. The government registers all voters by mail. Registration lists are available for public perusal, verification, and correction well in advance of each election campaign.

Generally, voting turnout has been high. All but three of the seventeen national consultations have drawn between 75 and 85 percent of the registered voters. One exception (68.7 percent) was the 1968 Assembly elections that were held immediately after the May/June disorders and during the summer vacation. Another (61.4 percent) was the "unnecessary" 1972 referendum. The third was the 1981 parliamentary election, whose outcome was so clearly preordained by Mitterrand's presidential victory. French turnout figures are somewhat inflated, as about 6.5 percent of the voting-age population is not registered.

Senators are elected by thirds every three years for nine-year terms by electoral colleges in each department and overseas possession. Each college is composed of the mayors, municipal and departmental councilors, and deputies of that department. In addition, the councils of all municipalities with more than 30,000 inhabitants choose additional delegates roughly proportionate to their additional population. Under the 1975 census, the colleges contained a total of 119,000 municipal councilors and delegates, 3,529 departmental councilors, and 474 deputies. That allocation of electoral votes tends to favor the smaller, rural municipalities. Under that census, municipalities under 3,500 inhabitants have half the votes but only 35 percent of the population. The more rural departments tend to vote less for Communists, Centrists, and Gaullists, and more for Conservative Moderates and Radicals. Senate seats are allocated among the departments and possessions on the basis of one for the first 150,000 population or fraction thereof and one additional seat for each additional 250,000 or fraction thereof.

Four different electoral systems are used for senatorial elections. The fifteen departments and territories with one seat each choose their senators by the majority system with single-member districts and a runoff ballot the same day if no candidate wins a majority on the first round. The fifteen most populous departments with at least five seats each (a total of ninety-seven seats) use a proportional representation system. The remaining departments with from two to four seats each (198 seats), use the majority system with multi-member districts and a runoff ballot. Finally, the six senators who represent French citizens living abroad are nominated by an official governmental advisory council composed of representatives of their local associations. Its choices are ratified routinely by the Senate.

Senatorial candidates have *suppléants* analogous to those of the deputies. *Suppléants* for the candidates in the departments using the majority electoral systems are nominated as their running mates. In the departments that use proportional representation, the highest-ranking unsuccessful candidate on the senator's party list is the replacement.

In addition to presidential and parliamentary elections, popular consultations at the national level in France include referenda. This institution was introduced into modern France by de Gaulle in the aftermath of World War II, but was not

RESULTS OF REFERENDA (1958–1972)					
	9/28/1958	%	1/8/1961	%	4/8/1962	%
Registered voters	26,603,464		27,184,408		26,991,743	
Votes cast	22,596,850	84.9	20,791,246	76.5	20,401,906	75.6
Valid ballots	21,989,752		19,601,848		19,303,668	
Yes	17,668,790	79.2	15,200,073	75.2	17,508,607	90.7
No	4,624,511	20.8	4,996,474	24.8	1,795,061	9.3
	10/28/1962	%	4/27/1969	%	4/23/1972	%
Registered voters	27,582,113		28,655,692		29,312,637	
Votes cast	21,301,816	77.2	23,092,296	80.6	17,693,567	61.4
Valid ballots	20,742,058		22,457,618		15,628,328	
Yes	12,809,363	61.8	10,512,469	46.8	10,601,645	67.8
No	7,932,695	38.2	11,945,149	53.2	5,026,683	32.2

incorporated in the Fourth Republic system. De Gaulle insisted on including it in the 1958 constitution.

Referenda played an important role in the early years of the Fifth Republic. De Gaulle gave those early referenda a plebiscitary character by threatening to resign if his proposals were defeated. Since then, the referendum has faded badly. De Gaulle let it lapse for nearly six years. Then during the 1968 disorders, he attempted to revive its use—unsuccessfully. When he persisted in that ill-conceived effort in 1969, he was defeated and resigned. Pompidou called only one referendum, in 1972, to approve British admission to the European Community. He refrained from making it a plebiscite and the campaign and voting were so desultory and equivocal that the institution was badly discredited.

The Party System

Origins of the Parties

Organized political parties first appeared in France in the wake of the 1789 revolution. However, none of the present-day parties antedates 1901, and today's party system evolved from the one that emerged then. The Third Republic had a multiparty system with no party ever winning as many as one-quarter of the votes cast. On the left, the Socialists and, later, the Communists had well-organized parties with sizable memberships; the parties of the center and right were little more than loose alliances among personal orgnizations of leading politicians. The most important party during that period was the centrist Radical-Socialist. Hardly a government could be formed without support from a substantial part of that faction-ridden and undisciplined, but strategically placed, party. The parties of the center and right became somewhat better structured during the Fourth Republic, and the multipartism was less extreme. However, the general configuration of the system survived and the Radicals remained pivotal.

The ideological character of the party system underwent substantial change from the Third to the Fourth Republic. The Marxist Socialists and Communists were the only Third Republic parties to profess anything approaching common systems of doctrine. The Radical-Socialists rarely united on anything except resistance to the Church and the state, and the rest of the political landscape was occupied by pragmatic, personalist cliques. The ideological Marxist parties were joined in the Fourth Republic by the Christian democratic Popular Republican Movement (Mouvement Républican Populaire; MRP) and the nationalist Gaullists. Those four parties held 65 to 75 percent of the Assembly seats in the first three postwar Parliaments (1945–56), but their strength and ideological commitment waned toward the end of the Fourth Republic.

The Parties in Law

Both constitution and statute nominally regulate political parties in France; however, neither type of law has much impact on them. For all practical purposes, parties are virtually extralegal institutions. The 1958 constitution departed from French tradition by dealing explicitly with parties, but the clause has been a virtual dead letter.

Article 4 reads: "Parties and groups take part in the exercise of the suffrage. They may form and engage in their activities freely. They must respect the principles of national sovereignty and democracy."

The last sentence was directed at the Communist Party because of its close ties to the Soviet Union and its authoritarian internal structure. However, it has not been used to require the Communists or any other party to abide by its terms. In fact, the only application of Article 4 yet made was a Constitutional Council ruling that struck down parliamentary rules of order that restricted the freedom of MPs to form party caucuses. No laws or decrees rest on the authority of Article 4 nor has the Constitutional Council applied that provision to parties outside Parliament.

No laws deal expressly with parties as organizations. Thus, they are covered by a 1901 statute that governs all associations in France, however, the legislation regulating campaigns and elections refers to parties. For instance, certain types of parties are recognized as organizations eligible to receive governmental support in campaigns such as controlled access to radio and television and free mailings of candidates' flyers. Neither the associations laws nor the campaign laws restrict the behavior of parties significantly. The former is very permissive and the latter is easily and frequently evaded.

Similarly, the state provides no aid to political parties as such. Parties have some tax advantages as nonprofit associations, their candidates get electoral campaign subsidies, and their newspapers benefit from press subventions. In none of those cases do parties have special status. Nonparty associations, candidates, and newspapers receive the same assistance. Furthermore, the amount of this aid to the parties is quite modest.

To become a candidate for the National Assembly, an eligible person files a simple declaration at the prefecture of the appropriate *département* and pays a deposit of 1,000 frs. ($200), which is refunded to all candidates receiving at least 5 percent of the vote. A presidential nomination requires the signatures of 500 elected office holders from at least thirty different *départements*.

Party Organization

Historically, French political parties followed two basic patterns of organization: the center and right formed "cadre" parties; the left had mass-membership parties.

That dichotomous structural pattern was broken in the early Fourth Republic by the Christian democratic MRP and the Gaullist Rally of the French People (RPF). Both were center or right parties that built mass-membership organizations somewhat similar to those of the left. As the MRP waned late in the Fourth Republic and when the RPF dissolved into the Social Republicans after 1953, both movements adopted cadre structures. Nevertheless, when Gaullism rebounded in the Fifth Republic, it resumed its mass-membership orientation. Also, that model was followed, though less vigorously and enthusiastically, by Giscard d'Estaing's Republican Party after 1977. Thus, all four major parties in France today are, more or less successfully, mass-membership organizations, though the minor parties tend to remain in the cadre mold.

The activities of all French political parties center on elections. They spend most of their organizational time and effort working in local, parliamentary, and presidential campaigns: preparing for them or raising money to pay for them. Other activities, such as regular business meetings and conventions and discussion sessions, have the primary purpose of keeping the organization in shape for the next election. The Communist Party is somewhat exceptional in this regard. It engages in a much broader range of activities than the other parties.

The parties vary considerably, also, in the type of relationship between the membership organizations and the parliamentary caucuses. The Communists see their MPs as infiltrators into enemy territory and treat them like potential defectors. Communist MPs are held strictly accountable to the membership organization. Party policies and strategies are decided by the Central Committee and Policy Bureau and the MPs are expected to put them into effect loyally.

The Socialists subscribe to the same principle of authority, but Socialist MPs control the leading organs of the membership party. Thus, membership-party decisions differ little from those that the parliamentary caucus would make on its own. On the few occasions of conflict between the two branches of the party, the caucus has prevailed. That relationship is complicated by the faction-ridden character of the party. The resultant struggle for party unity leads to compromises that modify parliamentary dominance.

The highly authoritarian structure of the Gaullist Rally for the French Republic (RPR) determines the relationship between its membership and parliamentary wing. Party leader Jacques Chirac dominates both the membership organization and the parliamentary caucus. A similar situation existed in the Republican Party while Giscard d'Estaing was president of the republic. The Centrist and Radical membership parties have little say in the behavior of their caucuses.

Most parliamentary candidates are put forward by political parties. In all parties, the decisions on parliamentary candidates are made through consultations within the local party, among local and national party leaders, and by negotiations among the parties. The amount of influence of the local party in the nominating process is roughly proportionate to its strength. In a party's weakest districts, its main task is finding suitable candidates willing to run and the national party often takes the initiative. At the other extreme, a strong local party with a well-entrenched incumbent deputy who wants reelection is virtually immune to national party intervention. Also, the parties vary greatly in the degree of centralization of the nomination process. The national headquarters of the Communist Party maintains an iron grip on all nominations, though it usually ratifies the recommendations of the departmental federations. The national office of the Socialist Party decides in negotiation with the Left Radicals which seats to contest, but defers to the local federations on the choice of candidates. The center-right parties engage in a delicate process of analysis and bargaining to agree on where they will hold first-round "primaries," where they will back a single candidate, and who to nominate. The status and preferences of the local parties are considered, of course, but the decisions are made nationally. However, in every election, some local leaders defy national headquarters and run as mavericks; a few of them win. Most nominations, however, are uncontested, especially those sought by incumbent deputies.

In the early Fifth Republic, major presidential candidacies were launched independently of parties, though they were endorsed and supported by parties later. Indeed, de Gaulle had intended that presidential aspirants would be required to renounce party affiliation. However, that intention did not survive the drafting process for the constitution. As the republic has evolved, parties have played a more prominent role in presidential nominations, though their endorsements have remained largely pro forma. In each case, the top leader of a party has had its nomination for the asking. Nominations have been made with in-

creasing uniformity by special delegate conventions at the national level.

Campaigning

Election campaigns in France are regulated by the designation of permissible activities and the prohibition of all others. Among those permitted are posters that may be mounted only on official billboards, circulars that conform to government rules and are sent to all voters in official mailings, radio and television broadcasts on the state network, and meetings with voters in schools and town halls. Most candidates evade the prohibitions through a variety of subterfuges. For instance, they print and distribute posters that advertise their parties and themselves, but make no direct reference to the election. Also, they publish brochures in the form of ephemeral "newspapers" and mail printed "letters" appealing for votes under cover of constitutional guarantees of a free press and mail communications.

Until 1965, campaigning was almost exclusively local. Since the first direct, popular presidential election, however, national party leaders have campaigned across the country, in both presidential and parliamentary elections. Rallies drawing 100,000 people or more in large population centers are notable among the changes in recent elections. On the other hand, very little campaigning is conducted at the local level for presidential elections.

A substantial portion of campaign costs are covered by the government. Broadcasting is free but tightly controlled. All candidates winning at least 5 percent of the votes cast are reimbursed for the printing costs of their official posters and circulars. Postage for those circulars and meeting space in public buildings are provided without charge.

Nevertheless, substantial expenses remain. The RPR spent an estimated $14 million ($30,000 per candidate) for the 1978 parliamentary elections. None of the other parties spent as much. Reliable statistics are not available, although the total amounts for each party probably range between half and three-fourths of the Gaullists' spending.

Presidential elections cost even more. The 1981 vote cost the state about $54 million. In addition, the two finalists spent perhaps $15 million to $20 million each and the other two major candidates about $10 million each. Minor candidates added at least $6 million more to the total of over $50 million.

The Gaullist and Communist national parties

control local campaigning quite closely through direct instructions and subsidies. In the other parties, supervision is looser and less direct and results mainly from the campaign materials provided by the national organizations.

Independent Voters

Generally speaking, voter loyalty to parties is strong and there is a high level of consistency of partisanship between local and national elections. A prominent local personality, however, can overcome this pattern in local elections.

French Communist Party
(Parti communiste francais; PCF)

History

The PCP was founded as a result of a split in 1920 in the socialist party (*Section francaise de l'internationale ouvrière;* SFIO). A three-to-one majority at the SFIO's Tours Congress voted to accept Lenin's "twenty-one conditions" and join the Third Communist International. The conditions included adoption of the name "Communist," an intransigent revolutionary stance, an internal organization based on Lenin's principles of "democratic centralism," a pledge of unquestioning obedience to Moscow, and support of the "socialist motherland" of Soviet Russia above all considerations of French patriotism.

Maurice Thorez became general secretary in 1930 and ruled the party with an iron hand until his death in 1964. He was succeeded by Waldeck Rochet and, in 1972, Georges Marchais. From its beginning, the PCF has been among those Communist parties most loyal to Moscow, and its history has been determined by the foreign-policy positions of the Soviet Union.

During the Popular Front period, 1934 to 1939, it supported Leon Blum's governments, but did not join them. After World War II, its members served in de Gaulle's government and the "tripartite" ministries of the early Fourth Republic. The *détente* period produced an agreement with the Socialists and Left Radicals on a "Common Program" in 1972 and, eventually, membership in the Mauroy governments of 1981. Otherwise, the party has been in the opposition, although it supported some policies of some governments, e.g., de Gaulle's NATO withdrawal and Mendès-France's refusal to endorse the European Defense Community.

Organization

The PCF has the most elaborate structure among French political parties. Its base units are 23,000 to 25,000 cells at workplaces, in neighborhoods, or in rural villages. They are grouped in 2,500 "sections." All the sections in a *département* form a federation. Each unit in that structure has an executive committee (*bureau*) that includes a secretary and a treasurer. The sovereign organ is the national congress, which meets at approximately three-year intervals and is composed of delegates from the federations, roughly in proportion to their size. The congress elects the Central Committee of some 120 members, including twenty-four candidate-members. The Central Committee also elects the seven-member Secretariat and the 21-member Policy Office (*bureau politique*). The Secretariat is the cadre of professional managers who run the party on a day-to-day basis under the supervision of the Policy Office, a kind of board of directors. They are accountable periodically to the Central Committee, to which the authority of the congress is delegated between its meetings. In practice, the general secretary has been virtually unassailable, at least since Thorez consolidated his power in the early 1930s.

For decades, the party maintained the appearance of a monolith. Occasional dissidents were cast out individually without producing factions or affecting the party's unity. However, in recent years, muffled though open dissent has been expressed at party congresses and elsewhere within the party, and minority factions have appeared on both flanks, some peeling off and others forming loyal oppositions within the party.

L'Humanité, the party's flagship daily in Paris, with a distribution of 150,000 daily and 360,000 on Sunday, is the largest remaining political newspaper in France. However, most observers believe that the newspaper's survival has required constant infusion of party funds for at least twenty years. A few small provincial dailies maintain similarly tenuous existences, as do a score of local weeklies. The principal doctrinal journal of the party is *Cahiers du communisme,* a monthly, and *France-Nouvelle,* a weekly magazine. Specialized periodicals concern agriculture, philosophy, teaching, and economics.

Communist auxiliaries include large and vigorous youth, student, and women's associations. Also, the party is noted for its elaborate program to train and indoctrinate its prospective leaders. For instance, in one recent three-year period, its federation and central schools gave courses to over 6,000 members, and at a typical congress two-thirds to three-fourths of the delegates are their graduates.

Communist militants control or influence significantly a wide range of leftist organizations. The largest and most important is the General Confederation of Labor (*Confédération générale de travail;* CGT) with 2.5 million members. Also, it controls MODEF, the second-largest agricultural association, a war veterans' organization (ARAC), and the Movement of Peace (*Mouvement de Paix*). Its control of "fronts" is somewhat illusory. For instance, the power of the CGT depends on its ability to attract the votes of non-Communists in representational elections. Therefore, if it serves the PCF contrary to the interests of the workers as perceived by those non-Communists, it may lose their support.

National headquarters are at 2 place du Colonel Fabien, Paris 75019.

Policy

The party's policies are rooted in Marxist-Leninist ideology. In recent decades, that commitment had been obscured somewhat by the party's urgent desire to emerge from the political wilderness through an alliance with the Socialists. Thus, it expunged advocacy of a "dictatorship of the proletariat" from the party statutes in 1976 while denying any diminution of its revolutionary militancy. Also, it has renounced such concepts as democratic centralism and a one-party state without changing anything of substance in its operations. It continues to preach the overthrow of capitalism, though expressing new doubts that violence will be needed. It wants sweeping nationalization of productive property well beyond the compromise it accepted in the Common Program with the Socialists. Its views on foreign policy are Soviet diplomatic dispatches adapted to a French public. In other areas, it has argued consistently for the redistribution of wealth through confiscatory taxation and generous social-welfare programs, although it exempts peasant-owned farm land from its definition of capital.

Membership & Constituency

The PCF membership has fluctuated greatly over the decades. Despite its overwhelming majority at Tours in 1920, its membership lead was quickly overtaken by the Socialists and it remained much smaller than the SFIO until World War II. Capitalizing on its wartime resistance performance and the prestige of the USSR, it launched a spectacular recovery after the 1944 Liberation. By 1947, it was the largest party in France, claiming over 900,000 members, three times its prewar peak. That figure fell steadily through the Cold War period until it hit 250,000 in 1956. Since then, it has recovered; membership is now over 700,000. However, all those figures are official party statistics that are known to be grossly inflated. Probably, the actual 1982 number is no more than 500,000. In any case, the PCF and the RPR compete closely for the title of largest French party.

Because Communist voting strength has declined proportionately to its membership rise, the gap between them has narrowed substantially since 1956. In that year, it had twenty-two voters for every member claimed. By 1981, it had only about five and a half. Industrial workers account for about half of the party's members, clerical occupations provide another one-fifth, and "intellectuals" and farmers/farm workers one-tenth each. About 30 percent are women and a similar number are Catholics of occasional observance. The median age of party members is probably in the early 40s.

Geographically, the party has been strongest in the most heavily industrialized regions, especially Paris and its working-class suburbs. Other strongholds have included the industrial north and some of the poorer rural areas in the south.

Financing

The PCF is the wealthiest French party. Its official budget runs about $25 million in a nonelection year. About 40 percent comes from membership dues levied at the rate of about one percent of the member's annual income. An equal amount comes from special fund drives and donations and the remainder from the party's MPs and other elected officials, who contribute the difference between their salaries and the average annual wages of a skilled worker. In addition, the party earns profits on some of its publishing, commercial, and financial enterprises. It spends about half its income on propaganda and one-fourth each on administrative expenses and salaries and benefits for its 600 regular staff members.

Leadership

The PCF's penchant for secrecy and its refusal to admit the existence of factions within the party complicate the task of identifying its actual, rather than simply formal, leaders. In 1982, the most prominent leaders are:

Georges Marchais, general secretary since 1972, born in La Hoguette, 1920. He did not join the party until 1947, but rose rapidly as the protegé of Jeanette Thorez-Vermeesch, Thorez's common-law wife. He became a Central Committee member in 1956 and secretary for party organization in 1961. He is regarded generally as an opportunist Stalinist who has suppressed his Marxist-Leninist inclinations to lead the party into the union of the left.

Roland Leroy, editor of *L'Humanité* since 1974, born in Saint-Aubinles-Elbeuf, 1926. A member of the Policy Office (Politburo) since 1964, he is a leader of the diehard Stalinists in the party.

Paul Laurent, secretary for party organization since 1973, born in Génélard, 1925. A member of the Central Committee since 1956 and of the Policy Office since 1961; general secretary of Communist Youth (*Jeunesse Communiste*), 1954–62, he is leader of the party "liberals" and is responsible for party organization and relations with other parties.

Georges Séguy, CGT general secretary since 1967, born in Toulouse, 1927. A member of the PCF Central Committee since 1954 and of the Policy Office from 1956 to 1982, he leads the trade union wing of the party.

Charles Fiterman, secretary for economic affairs since 1976, born in Saint-Étienne, 1933. A member of the Policy Office since 1972, he was a leading negotiator for the Common Program and became minister of state and minister for transportation in the second Mauroy government, the top post held by a Communist.

Prospects

The 1981 elections placed the PCF in a paradoxical situation. On the one hand, its goal of the preceding quarter-century had been achieved. It held ministerial portfolios for the first time since 1947 in the most leftist government in the history of France. On the other, its share of the vote was the lowest since 1936 and it had lost ground to the Socialists in three consecutive parliamentary elections. The Socialists had surpassed the PCF for the second time in a row and held the first single-party parliamentary majority in the history of the French left. They could govern comfortably without the Communists, holding them virtually at their mercy. The Communist quandary was exacerbated by the likelihood that the government's success would redound to the benefit of the Socialists, but its failures might be blamed on the PCF if it showed a flicker of dissent or independence. This position was sorely uncomfortable for

a party that had an almost unrelieved history of intransigent opposition to every government.

French Socialist Party
(*Parti socialiste français;* PSF)

History

Modern French socialism dates to 1905, when most of the rival organizations in the movement united as the *Section française de l'internationale ouvrière* (SFIO). Although the party was reformist in practice, its initial policy program declared it to be a "class party whose goal is to transform capitalist society into a collectivist or communist society." That split between action and rhetoric marked the SFIO for the next forty-nine years.

From 1920 until 1969, the SFIO was dominated by Leon Blum (1920–46) and by Guy Mollet (1946–69). By the end of that half-century the party had withered in membership, voting strength, and doctrinal integrity, in spite of brief periods of government leadership (1936–38; 1946). By the time Mollet served as premier for sixteen months in 1956–57, the SFIO had become so "bourgeois" that the government's policies were virtually indistinguishable from those of its predecessors.

The transformation of the SFIO began in 1969 when Alain Savary succeeded Mollet as general secretary and its name was changed to PSF. Most party leaders at all levels were replaced over the next two years. In 1971, François Mitterrand brought his confederation of political clubs into the PSF and became its first secretary. In 1974, the PSF was enlarged further by about 4,000 militants from the left-wing Unified Socialist Party (*Parti socialiste unifié*; PSU) and the Democratic French Confederation of Labor (*Confédération française démocratique du travail*; CFDT).

One effect of those changes was the reorientation of French socialism. It moved decisively leftward from the opportunistic moderation of Molletism. Mitterrand at the head of the PSF pursued the same "Union of the Left" strategy he had followed consistently since 1958 in trying to mold the traditional parties of the left (Socialist, Radical, Communist) into a united opposition to Gaullism.

The fruits of that strategy ripened rapidly. A Common Program was negotiated with the PCF and the Left Radicals by 1972. That served as the basis for the alliance of those parties in the 1973 parliamentary elections when they gained 5.7 percentage points and seventy-eight seats over 1968. Those parties allied again for the 1974 presidential election, but not for the 1978 parliamentary elections.

The success of PSF's strategy was triumphantly evident in 1981. Mitterrand won the presidency with the essential help of Communist votes, and the PCF was outvoted by the PSF more than two-to-one in the parliamentary elections. The Socialists received a larger share of the poll than any left party in French history. The PSF, with the PCF securely and submissively in harness, had driven the Gaullist/Giscardian right from all the bastions of power in the French republic.

Organization

The French socialist movement has been characterized by rife factionalism throughout its history. Whether deep in the political swamp (before World War I or in the 1960s) or at the pinnacle of power (during Popular Front and "Union of the Left" governments), the party leadership has been subjected to continuous assault from both flanks of its own organization. After Mitterrand captured the party, Mollet's supporters, moderates, formed an organized faction, complete with officers and publications, now called *Bataille socialiste* and headed by Claude Fuzier. Those who consider Mitterrand too conservative constitute the CERES (*Centre d'études de recherchés et d'éducation socialistes;* Center of Socialist Studies, Research, and Education), led by Jean-Pierre Chevènement. Other major factions are grouped around Mauroy's federation in the north, Gaston Defferre's in Marseilles, and the former PSU groups associated with Jean Poperen and Michel Rocard. Party statutes ensure such factions proportionate representation in its leadership organs.

The basic structural unit of the PSF is the "section." It requires at least five members and may be formed by residence, workplace, or university. Sections send delegates to their departmental federations in proportion to the size of their membership. Federation representation in the regional coordinating committees, national congresses, and national conventions has similar bases. Traditionally, the four largest federations (Nord, Bouches-du-Rhone, Pas-de-Calais, and Paris) have dominated the national party. A national congress meets biennially as the sovereign decision-making body of the party. Conventions meet at least twice a year to supervise the leadership on behalf of the rank-and-file members. The congress elects the 131-member Steering Committee (*Comité directeur*) that runs the party between congresses. The Committee, in turn, elects and delegates day-to-day management to a first secretary and a twenty-seven-member Executive Office (*Bureau exécutif*). The first secretary appoints the members of the national Secretariat, which in 1982 numbered fifteen secretaries and twelve deputy secretaries. Most of them are designated as the party's official spokesmen in various policy areas. The PSF is a member of the Socialist International.

The most important, though unofficial, PSF publication is *Le Matin de Paris*, a daily newspaper founded in 1977 with the main purpose of promoting the party's candidate in the 1981 presidential elections. By 1981, its circulation had reached a respectable 121,000 copies. Defferre's *Le Provençal* (circ. 345,000) in Marseilles and the *Nord-Matin* (120,000) in Lille are the leading Socialist dailies in the provinces. *L'Unité* is the official party weekly paper. In addition, the party publishes several internal and specialized periodicals.

The largest organization associated with the PSF is the 750,000-member CFDT, the second-biggest French trade-union federation. Although its ties are looser than those of the CGT to the PCF, Socialists dominate its leadership, and form the largest bloc of members; the two organizations are reciprocally influential. Similar affinities bind the PSF to other trade unions, especially the largest teachers' organizations and the third major general-labor confederation (*FO, Force ouvrière;* Workers' Force). Also, the party sponsors youth, women's, and farm associations.

National Headquarters are at 10, rue de Solférino, Paris 75333.

Policy

The official statements of the PSF commit it to a radical reformist program. The most articulate intellectual current is Marxist, but the party's by-laws oblige it to encourage diversity of opinion in its ranks. State ownership of the principal financial and industrial enterprises is a key component of its domestic program. So are generous social-welfare programs, reduction of unemployment (even at the cost of greater inflation), and abolition of private, mostly Church-sponsored, schools. Despite some reduction in emphasis, it favors continuance of the French commitment to nuclear power and weapons. Another policy that has won increased support in the party in recent years is *autogestion*, worker management of industry. Perhaps because of its traditional distinction as the strongest party at the local-government level, it has pursued policies of reducing the power of the national government over the regional, departmental, and municipal administrations. It advocates greater protection for civil liberties and minority rights. Internationally, the party maintains a firm commitment to the Western alliance and the European Community, despite a loud neutralist minority. Also, it has come out strongly in favor of increased aid from the industrial countries to Third World nations.

Membership & Constituency

The party has about 250,000 members. This is a sixteenfold increase over the low point it hit in the late 1960s, when the number of actual members reportedly fell to 15,000 (although it claimed 75,000). However, it remains well below its peak of 355,000 in 1945. The party's resurgence is due to the vigorous leadership and clear leftist orientation provided by Mitterrand since 1971 and to the continuing embarrassment of the PCF. Still, Socialist parliamentary candidates in 1981 won about 50 times as many votes and Mitterand about 87 times as many as the party has members.

Support for PSF remains most solid among certain categories of state employees (teachers, postal employees, railroad workers), industrial workers in some regions (the north and Provence) and sectors (light and medium manufacturing), and farmers in the center and south. However, the party has become remarkably successful in recent years in broadening its appeal to most categories of the French, including practicing Catholics.

Geographically, the party is strongest in the north, parts of the east, and Provence. It does better south of the Loire River than north of it. It draws less than its share of women and more than its share of the young.

Financing

Revenues come mainly from three sources. The largest item is membership dues, which produce about $8 million annually for the national party. A second substantial amount comes from a levy it imposes on its MPs. Finally, the party collects considerable sums in special fund drives and individual contributions.

Leadership

The PSF leadership has undergone sweeping renewal since 1971. One result has been a lowering of the average age of its higher echelons. An even more striking characteristic is the predominance of teachers: 48.7 percent of its 1981 National Assembly delegation claimed that profession, as did eighteen of its thirty-five ministers.

Present leaders include:

François Mitterrand, former first secretary of the PSF and president of the French Republic, born in Jarnac, 1916. His original power base was in the confederation of left-wing political clubs he had organized and among Socialists who favored party reform and an alliance with the PCF.

Gaston Defferre, mayor of Marseilles, national secretary and member of the Executive Office, born in Marsillarques, 1910, minister of state in the government. His power base is in the Bouches-du-Rhone federation, largest in the party, and in the moderate wing of the party.

Pierre Mauroy, prime minister, national secretary and member of the PSF Executive Office, born in Cartignies, 1928. Former mayor of Lille, his power base is the two neighboring PSF federations in northern France, Nord and Pas-de-Calais.

Michel Rocard, minister of state, national secretary and member of the PSF Executive Office, born in Courbevoie, 1930. His power base is the former membership of the PSU and the advocates of *autogestion*.

Jean-Pierre Chevènement, national secretary and member of the PSF Executive Office, born in Belfort, 1939. His power base is the more radical CERES.

Lionel Jospin, first secretary since 1981, formerly secretary for the Third World, born in Meudon, 1937.

Pierre Joxe, president of the PS group in the National Assembly, is one of the party's "young Turks." He was born in Paris in 1934.

Jean Poperen is national secretary for coalition coordination and for elections.

Prospects

Presumably, the party's ability to remain in power will depend on its success at dealing with France's problems, but it has, at least, established the Union of the Left as a viable alternative to the center-right coalitions that had dominated French government previously.

Rally for the French Republic (*Rassemblement pour la République;* RPR)

History

The RPR, the "orthodox" Gaullist party originated in the program of democratic nationalism and strong central leadership of General Charles de Gaulle, leader of the Free French in World War II. The movement's first party, the Gaullist Union (founded 1946), was soon absorbed by de Gaulle's own Rally of the French People (RPF), which quickly became the largest party in France with some one million members. Nevertheless, the party was unable to carry out its program of constitutional reform and began to decline precipitously in the early 1950s. When de Gaulle retired from politics in 1955, only eighty deputies remained faithful to him.

With de Gaulle's return to power in 1958, the party was revived as the Union of the New Republic and won 188 seats in the 1958 Assembly elections. It retained the leadership of the Assembly for the next twenty years.

In 1974, after the party's candidate lost the presidential election, Prime Minister Jacques Chirac took over the party, now called the Union of Democrats for the Republic, with the express intent of making it more aggressive. After Chirac resigned as premier in 1976, he assumed the party's presidency, changed its name to the RPR, centralized its structure, and launched a massive membership drive. In spite of these efforts, the party lost its leadership of the Assembly in 1978 and was reduced to an opposition role in 1981.

Organization

The RPR is a mass organization with centralized leadership. In spite of an elaborate system of local, district, and *département* organizations, the secretaries of the department federations are appointed by the general secretary of the national party who is, in turn, appointed by the party president. National conferences (*assises nationales*), with voting delegates elected from the *département* federations, meet regularly every two years to rubber stamp the national leadership's policies.

Between conferences, party affairs are supervised by the Central Committee of about 250 members, composed of 100 national delegates and seventy regional delegates elected at conferences as well as the party's MPs and the members of the Policy Council (*Conseil politique*). The Policy Council, which makes day-to-day policy decisions, is composed of the party president and general secretary, some fifteen representatives of the Central Committee, former prime ministers, the presidents of the parliamentary caucuses, and at least fifteen others appointed by the president. The Executive Committee (*Commission éxécutive*), which is responsible for "assisting the president and general secretary" in the day-to-day management of the party, has about eight members, all nominated by the general secretary and appointed by the president, who, in turn, is elected or confirmed in office by the National Conference. This arrangement indicates the extent of Chirac's domination of the party. He was elected initially by 11,500 to zero, with 400 abstentions and spoiled ballots, and has not been challenged since, being reelected with 97 percent of the vote in 1979 and 99.1 percent in 1982.

The party distributes a daily newsletter, *La Lettre de la Nation*, and publishes a monthly, *Démocrates*, and a fortnightly *Les Cahiers*, magazine and a monthly internal newsletter, *La Lettre des Compagnons*.

The RPR has not done much toward forming auxiliary organizations. This may be partly because the youth affiliate of the Union of Democrats seceded from the party in October 1975 and attacked its parent organization for its continued support of Giscard d'Estaing. On the other hand, the RPR has made a considerable effort to build up party schools for its activists and candidates. Also, it has been associated closely with the autonomous Civic Action Service (*Service d'Action Civique;* SAC). This semiclandestine, paramilitary organization of some 5,000 members has aided the RPR by ensuring order at its meetings, disrupting its opponents' activities, and similar questionable work.

National headquarters are at 33, Ave. de Maine, Tour Maine-Montparnasse, Paris 75755.

Policy

The RPR professes to advocate policies in line with those pursued by de Gaulle. They include foreign policies intended to promote national independence and "grandeur." That means a defense policy based on the so-called independent nuclear striking force, aversion to entanglement in NATO's military system or any international organization not controlled by France, and cultivation of special ties with former French colonies and other French-speaking areas. It means a commitment to a strong state, especially through adherence to the constitutional principles of the original Fifth Republic and the traditional centralization of government. Finally, it includes domestic policies designed to cement French unity and strength. Among them are "participation" of workers in management, economic modernization, and hostility to ethnic particularism.

Membership & Constituency

In recent years, the RPR has claimed a membership of over 700,000, reaching 760,347 at the end of 1978. If its figures are about as inflated as those of the other parties, the RPR is the largest in France. That size has resulted from Chirac's recruitment drive. Using the 1978 figures, the ratio of members to voters in the 1981 elections was 1:6.9.

The RPR membership is predominantly masculine (58.6 percent), middle-aged (63 percent over forty), middle class, northern, and Catholic. The largest occupational category is "businessmen, tradesmen, and members of the fee-earning professions," 25.1 percent, compared to 19.9 percent for white-collar workers, 14.5 percent for middle management, 11.3 percent for workers, 11.1 percent farmers, and 4.5 percent for upper management. The party is strongest north of the Loire Valley, especially in Paris and its middle-class suburbs. Other areas of strength are such traditional Catholic regions as Alsace, Lorraine, and Brittany. Throughout France, practicing Catholics support Gaullism disproportionately.

The RPR voters fall into much the same pattern as its members. A 1977 survey showed that they split fifty-fifty between men and women and that 69 percent were over thirty-four. The largest occupational category was "inactive" (retired, housewives, and those with independent means) with 29 percent. Others were workers 20 percent; middle management and white-collar workers 19; upper management, fee-earning professions, industrialists, and big businessmen 13; farmers and farm workers 12; and small businessmen and tradesmen 7.

Financing

Detailed financial data are not available on the RPR. Given the size and relative affluence of its membership, it must receive a substantial income in members' dues and contributions. In addition, it can call on many prosperous French who choose not to join the party. Finally, its supporters tend to be more able than most to donate time, effort, and physical resources. In any case, the movement has never appeared to suffer from lack of funds. Its reports show an annual budget of over 20 million francs ($4 million) for operating expenses, over and above election-year costs. Especially while it held national office, its regular income was supplemented through the diversion of state resources such as staff time.

Leadership

As late as 1976, most top-rank party leaders had come out of "historic Gaullism," World War II, and the RPF. They included Jacques Chaban-Delmas,

Michel Debré, and Georges Pompidou. With the Chirac coup that changed. Most of today's leaders are too young to have figured importantly in the earlier movement. Although many of the earlier group remain active and even prominent members, they have been pushed out of the positions of power by the Chirac bulldozer. Current leading figures in the party, by prominence, power, or both are:

Jacques Chirac, former premier, founder and national president; born in Paris, 1932; 1981 presidential candidate.

Claude Labbé, official political advisor to Chirac, president of the RPR Assembly group, born in Argenteuil, 1920.

Bernard Pons, general secretary, born in Beziers, 1926.

Jean Méo, assistant general secretary, born in Vosne-Romanée, 1927.

Jacques Chaban-Delmas, former premier, former president of the National Assembly, born in Paris, 1915; 1974 presidential candidate.

Prospects

The Gaullist movement has always been a party of national office and power or seemed likely to be so very soon. When its leaders have held public office, the party has flourished at all levels. Out of office, it has suffered disastrously from defections, schisms, and internecine wrangling. Its return to the wilderness in 1981 is a severe test. Though Chirac is ambitious and driving, with a touch of charisma, he is no de Gaulle. Even de Gaulle failed to keep the RPF alive when his prospects of returning to office disappeared. Gaullism without office is even bleaker than Gaullism without de Gaulle.

Republican Party
(*Parti républicain;* PR)

History

The Republican Party has a dual character. In one respect, it belongs in the tradition of Orleanist conservatism, the moderate, reasonable, adaptable branch of the French right. In another, its existence, growth, and success derive solely from the ambition of one man, former president Valéry Giscard d'Estaing. The conservative movement's leading lights in the Third and Fourth republics were such men as Adolphe Thiers, Raymond Poincaré, Gaston Doumerque, Pierre-Etienne Flandin,

Paul Reynaud, and Antoine Pinay, who usually called themselves "moderates."

The Republican Party was founded as the Independent Republicans (*Republicains indépendents*; RI) during the great political battles of 1962. The leadership and overwhelming majority of the moderate deputies turned against de Gaulle and opposed his referendum proposal for direct election of the president. Most who did were defeated in the parliamentary elections that followed. Giscard remained loyal to de Gaulle and survived. He organized thirty-one fellow survivors into a parliamentary group that was separate from the orthodox Gaullist group, but closely allied to it.

At the time, Giscard was a young, highly ambitious junior minister. He had entered Parliament in 1956 at age thirty-five, winning the seat from which his grandfather had retired after an eleven-year tenure. He had joined the government in 1959.

Except during the 1968–73 Assembly, Giscard's followers were an essential but distinct part of all the non-Socialist governmental coalitions of the Fifth Republic. Under presidents de Gaulle and Pompidou, they sometimes voted differently from the orthodox Gaullists, but never so as to endanger the government. Giscard once characterized their attitude as "yes, but"—support with reservations.

The movement passed a major turning point when Giscard was dismissed from the government in January 1966. Six months earlier, he had organized a network of "political clubs," called Perspectives and Reality (*Perspectives et Realités*). He expanded it to fourteen clubs with 700 members in 1967, fifty-five clubs with 5,000 members in 1970, and 300 with 45,000 members in 1978. Also, in June 1966, he founded a political party called the National Federation of Independent Republicans (*Fédération nationale des républicains indépendents*; FNRI). In 1977, it became the Republican Party. Meanwhile, Giscard's fidelity to de Gaulle softened steadily until his defection provided the decisive votes in the 1969 referendum that forced the Old Hero's retirement.

Despite Giscard's somewhat hesitant support for Pompidou in the ensuing elections and his direction of the Ministry of Finance in the Chaban-Delmas and Mesmer governments, Giscard continued to prepare his own presidential campaign, which succeeded in 1974 after Pompidou's death.

The personalist character of the PR deserves emphasis. Indeed, even the RPR in its most Gaullist stage was less the creature of its leader. However, by the time of Giscard's fall, the PR had a structure and, to a lesser extent, a set of policies of its own.

Organization

The PR structure reflects its personalist origins and parliamentary basis. The general secretary has wide powers of appointment and is controlled closely by Giscard, although formally he is elected by a triennial delegate congress. The general secretary appoints the Political Office (*bureau politique*) and the National Secretariat (*sécretariat national*). The former has twenty-four members and defines the general lines of policy. The latter has twenty-one members, each the spokesman for a policy area. Below the national level, the structure consists of departmental federations, each with a secretary appointed by the national office, and weak constituency associations. At all levels, the real levers of power are held by two groups: Giscard's proteges and the party's MPs. The PR has no regular national newspaper or periodical, but gets along with internal newsletters and campaign literature.

In contrast, the PR is more than adequately endowed with auxiliary organizations. The most important remain the Perspectives and Realities clubs. Also, the PR has an active youth auxiliary, called Social and Liberal Generation (*Génération Sociale et Libérale*; GSL), but its efforts to organize a viable women's affiliate have never succeeded, despite its large female vote. From December 1976 to May 1981, a separate but allied organization, the National Commission of Support for the President of the Republic (*Comité nationale de Soutien pour le Président de la République*) worked to sustain the coalition that had supported Giscard in the 1974 elections. Finally, the Act for the Future club (*Agir pour l'Avenir*) ran a training program for the party's candidates for municipal and parliamentary office before being integrated into the central structure.

National headquarters are at 41, rue de la Bienfaisance, 75008 Paris.

Policy

The policies of so personal a party must be discussed with caution; they are subject to change at the leader's whim. This is especially true of a party undergoing the painful transition from power to opposition.

In any case, during its years in office, the policy characterization preferred most by the PR was "liberal." It stressed a commitment to promote the development of the individual and to pursue a generally centrist course. However, it repeatedly compromised its liberal professions in the face of the hard realities that its members and voters were solidly conservative and that it could do nothing without the Gaullists.

In practice, the party's policies were defined mainly in the ways they were distinguished from those of the Gaullists. They were more committed to European integration and NATO, less willing to push industrial modernization, less committed emotionally to such Gaullist gimmicks as the nuclear striking force, "participation," and the referendum. They would have preferred to denationalize some enterprises and to decentralize the state had the Gaullists been willing. The pragmatism of their liberalism is especially evident in their approach to civil liberties. After pushing freedom of information legislation, a more autonomous status for the state broadcasting network, curbs on wiretapping, and abortion reform, they forced through a "Security and Liberty" law that was widely regarded as a serious threat to procedural protections in criminal law.

Membership & Constituency

The PR claimed 160,000 to172,000 members at its height. That figure was probably inflated then and has surely declined since Giscard's defeat. The GSL had some 15,000 members, the Perspectives and Realities clubs about 30,000, and the National Committee of Support 47,000. Of course, those numbers include a lot of overlap. Probably, the Giscardian structure rested on no more than 150,000 to 160,000 individuals at the peak and has fallen well below that total since May 1981. Using the figure of 150,000, the ratio of members to voters was 1:46 in the 1978 and 1:32 in the 1981 parliamentary elections.

According to a 1977 poll, the largest occupational category of PR voters is "inactive" (35 percent); white-collar workers are next (17 percent), just ahead of workers (16 percent). Other groups are high-level administrators, fee-earning professionals, industrialists, and big businessmen (14 percent); farmers and farm workers (10 percent); and small shopkeepers and tradesmen (8 percent). This pattern parallels closely that of the RPR, the main differences being that the Republicans draw fewer workers and more "inactives."

The PR is the most elderly and feminine of the four major parties. Forty-eight percent of its electorate is fifty or older and only 26 percent are under twenty-five. Women constitute 54 percent of its supporters.

Financing

The PR relies heavily on contributions to cover a typical annual official budget of 8 million francs. As each member pays only 10 francs dues to the national organization (and 40 francs to the departmental federation), this produced only about 1,600,000 francs, even at the peak. The other 80 percent must come mainly in the form of donations from wealthy sympathizers and corporations. Also, some income may have come from some questionable financial manipulations, and while the party was in power, personnel was loaned to the party from government ministries.

Leadership

The leadership of the Giscardians underwent a very perceptible evolution during their years in power. Initially, the Independent Republicans (RI) were little more than a group of conservative MPs, all with local power bases and united by little more than a wish to support de Gaulle without joining his party. Giscard brought them together and was the most prominent of them, but was little more than the first among equals. As the movement became more structured and bureaucratized and as Giscard's career soared, he acquired greater authority over the party and its leadership changed. It came to be dominated by young, ambitious technocrats whose political careers depended on Giscard's personal patronage. The current leaders are:

Valéry Giscard d'Estaing, born in Koblenz, Germany, 1926; founder and probably still the dominant figure in the party, despite having resigned from it when he became a presidential candidate in 1974. He retreated further behind the scenes after his 1981 defeat.

Michel Poniatowski, born in Paris, 1922; Giscard's oldest and closest political associate and righthand man in party affairs. Founding general secretary of the RI, he succeeded Giscard as party president in 1974, but resigned in 1977.

Jean-Pierre Fourcade, born in Marmande, 1929; member of Giscard's ministerial staff, 1959–66, and of his government, 1974–77; president, Perspectives and Realities Clubs, 1975 to date.

Jacques Blanc, born in Rodez, 1939; general secretary, PR 1978; member Political Office of RI then of PR.

Jean-Pierre Soisson, born in Auxerre, 1934; vice president, RI and PR; general secretary, PR, 1977–78.

Prospects

The PR and the Union for French Democracy (see below) harnessed traditional French conservatism to the political career of one man. In the months following his defeat in the 1981 presidential elections, Giscard showed every sign of abandoning his ambitions, despite his relative youth. If that retirement continues and no leader of comparable stature emerges, the whole structure seems likely to collapse. In that case, traditional French conservatism would be likely to go mainly in two directions. One part would merge with the neo-Gaullism of Chirac. The other would become a loose collection of the personal followings of locally prominent conservatives, much as the French right had been before 1962. Even if Giscard resumes his career, the events of 1981 make it unlikely that he can restore the PR to anything close to the position it held during the previous eighteen years.

Minor Parties

Left Radical Movement (*Mouvement des Radicaux de Gauche;* MRG)

This minor party is the junior partner in the Union of the Left. It began in 1972 as a band of Radical-Socialist members disgruntled by the decision of their party to form an alliance with centrists. As the movement of the Radical-Socialist left, it signed the Common Program with the Communists and Socialists in July 1972. It fought the 1973 parliamentary elections allied with them and the 1978 elections in concert with the Socialists. Its first president was Robert Fabre, who defected after the 1978 defeat. Michel Crépeau succeeded him until he, in turn, resigned to accept ministerial portfolios in the Mauroy governments of 1981. Roger-Gérard Schwartzenburg replaced Crépeau as president. Another MRG member, François Abadie, became a junior minister at the same time. The MRG delegation to the National Assembly increased from ten in 1978 to fourteen in 1981. It claims about 20,000 members. Its national headquarters are at 11, rue de Grenelle, Paris 75007.

Union for French Democracy (*Union pour la democratie française;* UDF)

For the 1978 and 1981 parliamentary elections, the PR formed electoral alliances with several centrist parties under the label Union for French Democracy. The deputies elected under that banner joined a parliamentary group of the same name. Although Giscard and his PR dominated this coalition (Jacques Blanc was vice president), the president of the UDF in 1981 was Jean Lecanuet, also president of one of the smaller member parties, the Center of Social Democrats. At the time of the 1981 elections, the UDF claimed 300,000 members. About 60,000 were enrolled directly, the others belonging indirectly through the member parties. Besides the PR and Giscard's Perspectives and Realities clubs, those parties were:

Center of Social Democrats (*Centre des democrates sociaux;* CDS)

The current heir to the Christian democratic tradition in French politics, the CDS was formed in 1976 by a merger of two centrist parties: the Democratic Center and the Center for Democracy and Progress. It had thirty-six deputies before the 1981 elections and nineteen afterward. At the time of the election, it had 30,000 to 60,000 members. Its headquarters are at 207, blvd. Saint-Germain, Paris 75007.

Radical and Radical-Socialist Party (*Parti radical et Radical-specialist*)

This group is the right wing of the Radical-Socialist Party that was the leading political organization of the Third and Fourth Republics. Its most prominent leader in recent years has been former magazine publisher Jean-Jacques Servan-Schreiber, but the current president is Didier Bariani. The 1981 elections cost the Radicals six of their eight Assembly seats. It has 15,000 to 20,000 members. Party headquarters are at 1, place de Valois, Paris 75001.

Movement of French Social Democrats (*Mouvement des democrates sociaux français*)

This small party, founded in 1972, is mainly the personal following of former deputy Max Lejeune, and consists mostly of former Socialists disaffected by the leftward turn their party had taken. In 1981, it lost both of its Assembly seats. As the smallest of these parties, probably it has fewer than 10,000 members. Headquarters are at 110, rue de Sèvres, Paris 75015.

National Center of Independents and Peasants (*Centre national des Indépendants et Paysan;* CNIP)

This group comprises the surviving traditional conservatives who did not follow Giscard into the Gaullist camp in 1962. The party had one of the largest parliamentary groups in the late Fourth and early Fifth Republic, but has shrunk to almost nothing, with six seats in the 1981 Assembly: president, Philippe Malaud; general secretary, Maurice Ligot. Its national headquarters are at 106, rue de l'Université, Paris 75007.

National Prospects

The next four or five years in France will be a period of assessment and consolidation of the drastic changes effected by the Socialist government in 1981–82. A continuation of its heavy emphasis on reducing unemployment, even at the expense of increased inflation, will maintain great pressure on the franc internationally and on the economy in general. The expectation of the government that it can use the newly nationalized banks and industries to stimulate that economy and relieve that pressure will be tested thoroughly. Regional and local governments will be challenged to make effective use of the powers newly devolved upon them. The effects of the government's plan to abolish private education will become evident, including the possible renewal of the long and bitter quarrel over the church-state issue. On the other hand, the still-older constitutional issue of the form of the republican regime seems finally to have been settled and the present government seems unlikely to revive it.

The opposition will be deeply preoccupied with the task of becoming as highly unified as possible in preparation for the parliamentary elections that must be held by mid-1986. In part, this will turn on the rival ambitions of neo-Gaullist Jacques Chirac, former president Valéry Giscard d'Estaing, and former premier Raymond Barre. Similarly, the Socialists and Communists will confront difficult questions of coalition strategy as those elections approach. The Communists, especially, must decide how much principle they will sacrifice to remain in the government and whether their recent loss of voting strength can be better stemmed in office or out.

The surprising success of President Mitterrand and his government at sustaining a high level of popularity during the first year in office and the willingness to adopt some measures of economic austerity suggest that Mitterrand may be able to achieve most of his major objectives over the long run without excessive economic, social, or political disruption. In that case, the Communists are likely to continue to submit without reaping significant electoral rewards. The opposition could then face a loss in the next round of parliamentary elections. However, the government has embarked on a high-risk undertaking and a serious misstep could change the situation dramatically overnight.

Further Reading

Andrews, William G. *Presidential Government in Gaullist France.* Albany, New York: SUNY Press, 1982.

———, and Hoffmann, Stanley, eds. *The Fifth Republic at Twenty.* Albany, New York: SUNY Press, 1981.

Cerny, Philip G., and Schain, Martin A., eds. *French Politics and Public Policy.* New York: St. Martin's Press, 1980.

Frears, J. R. *France in the Giscard Presidency.* London: Allen and Unwin, 1981.

———. *Political Parties and Elections in the French Fifth Republic.* London: C. Hurst & Co., Ltd., 1977.

Hayward, Jack. *The One and Indivisible French Republic.* New York: Norton, 1973.

Penniman, Howard R., ed. *The French National Assembly Elections of 1978.* Washington, D.C.: American Enterprise Institute, 1980.

Safran, William. *The French Polity.* New York and London: Longmans, 1977.

Wright, Vincent. *The Government and Politics of France.* London: Hutchinson, 1978.

OVERSEAS DEPARTMENT OF REUNION
(*Département Outre-Mer de la Réunion*)
by Philip M. Allen, Ph.D.

Reunion lies in a strategic position in the Indian Ocean about 569 miles east of Madagascar. Reunion has been an integral component of the political and economic system of France since 1946.

The island's 510,000 people enjoy a relatively high standard of living, thanks to French markets and services, French and European Economic Community price supports, and large transfers of French public funds. The 968-square-mile (2,500-sq.-km.) island is surrounded by independent, economically beleaguered neighbors—Madagascar, Mauritius, and Seychelles—which are governed by nonaligned socialist regimes suspicious of the international strategic and economic systems in which Reunion participates through France. On the other hand, their neighbors' economic and political problems emphasize for Reunion's loyalist majority the advantages of continuing and secure dependence on France.

Reunion is represented in the French Parliament by three deputies and two senators. In 1982, the island was administered by a prefect appointed by and responsible to Paris. The thirty-six-member General Council on Reunion, elected by direct popular suffrage, had little power in the past, but will gain distinct executive powers in 1983 when the French government's decentralization program takes effect in the overseas departments. The Council will assume responsibilities for determining and executing priorities in spending, not only from locally collected taxes but also from the budgets of the technical ministries and the special funds provided by Paris. The thirty-six seats of the new General Council will be filled by a proportional-representation scheme which is expected to benefit the Socialists and Communists. Minor political parties, never of great importance under the old single-member district system, may also gain representation, thus fragmenting the political system still further and aggravating the problems of reaching consensus.

Reunion's political parties, to a large extent, are reflections of those in France. The right is dominated by the Gaullist Rally (RPR), in mildly competitive coalition with the Giscardist Union for French Democracy (UDF) and several moderate and conservative nonparty personalities. These groups held twenty-six of the General Council's seats in 1982. They also controlled twenty of the twenty-four municipal governments. The RPR mayor of St. Denis, the capital, was the president of the General Council; the island's two senators were RPR members; and of the three deputies, one was a nonparty conservative while another was a major Gaullist leader, former French premier Michel Debré, who has represented the island since adopting it as his electoral base in 1963.

These conservative "Réunion Française" forces appeal to a constituency of planters and merchants, urban professionals (many of them transplanted from France), and others anxious to keep Reunion's bonds with France as tight as possible. They tend to regard elections as referenda on the island's status within the Republic and to protest any French government measure which implies a difference in treatment for Overseas France. Those bonds are reinforced by the island's strategic position as headquarters of France's Southern Indian Ocean Command. Important units of the French navy, air force, and Foreign Legion operate out of Reunion and its tiny administrative dependencies, by and large avoiding anything more than symbolic involvement in local politics.

On the left, the Socialists and Communists (*Partie Socialiste Reunion* [PSR] and *Partie Communiste Reunion* [PCR], respectively) pursue an uneasy, one-sided coalition. In 1981, Socialist, Wilfred Bertele, the first leftist ever to be elected deputy from Reunion, won in large part because of Communist support, but the leading Communist candidate lost by a mere 500 votes in another district because the Socialists withheld their support in spite of a directive from the French Socialist Party to back the Communist candidate.

The PSR and PCR concentrate on eliminating class privilege in the island's white-dominated society (the majority of the work force and peasantry, to which the two parties appeal, is a "creole" mixture of African and Asian origins) and at correcting disparities between French and overseas living standards. The decentralization program of the French Socialist government is seen by the two parties as a precondition for restoring agricultural productivity, increasing industrial investment and employment, and creating relative self-sufficiency and diversification. The island's prosperity, impressive in most Third World contexts, is regarded by the left as artificial and socially debilitating, reducing Reunion to a "consumer colony" without productive vitality.

Cane sugar dominates an economy geared to specialized export production for the French market, but agriculture now represents only 12 percent of GDP, with three-fourths of the economy concentrated in trade and services, including the official bureaucracy needed to administer vast welfare and public services. Exports (83 percent of them raw sugar) cover only 20 to 25 percent of import costs, requiring massive subsidies from Paris to balance the island's accounts. Cane planters (many of them smallholders) and the larger estates which also mill the cane have benefited from French investment in improved facilities and technology, as well as from price supports, but the economy remains plagued by inefficiencies; remoteness from its trading part-

ner; migration of skilled labor to France and of rural labor to the towns; and the tendency of private capital to avoid productive investment in favor of real estate, trade, and other speculation. Unemployment has reached 30 percent, and equally serious underemployment plagues urban and rural areas alike.

Few Reunionnais politicians dare advocate substantive change in the islands departmental status. Even the CPR's call for "decolonization" entails only a measure of "autonomy" within the French Republic. A PSR-PCR governing coalition in the new General Council would aim at improving economic conditions and some income redistribution and provide support for the island's Creole culture, without jeopardizing Reunion's access to French consumer goods and economic and military protection.

GABONESE REPUBLIC
(République Gabonaise)
by Steven Metz, M.A.

The System of Government

Gabon, a nation of nearly 600,000 people, is a one-party republic with a presidential form of government. The current political system, created by the constitution of 1975, is one of the most democratic one-party governments in Africa. Although the constitution has been revised frequently since Gabon's independence in 1960, there have been few instances of the military intervention or political violence typical of other African states. This is largely due to the absence in Gabon of the two major problems faced by most African governments: overpopulation and poverty.

Executive

The president of Gabon is head of state, head of government, and head of the military. The presidency is by far the most powerful political office in the Gabonese political system. According to the constitution, the primary powers of the president are the determination of national policy and the exercise of exclusive executive power. Essentially, the president helps both to initiate laws and to enforce laws which are passed by the legislature.

The president appoints the prime minister, the cabinet, some members of the National Assembly, the Supreme Court, and many local officials. The president may also dissolve the National Assembly and call new elections. The power of the president, however, is strictly limited by the constitution, which remains the final authority.

The president is chosen by direct popular election for a seven-year term of office. The candidate for presidency is chosen by the only party allowed by law. The current president is El Hadj Omar Bongo, who assumed the presidency in 1967 upon the death of the president who had led Gabon to independence—Leon M'Ba. Bongo was reelected in 1973 and 1979.

The prime minister, the second most powerful executive officer, oversees the operations of the state bureaucracy. The prime minister is not the automatic successor to the president. If the president dies while in office, a college—composed of the prime minister, the president of the National Assembly, and a member of the Political Bureau of the national party—governs until new elections can be held.

Legislature

Legislative power in Gabon is vested in the unicameral National Assembly. Since 1979 the National Assembly has been composed of ninety-three members, of which eighty-four are elected and nine appointed. The appointed members are chosen by the president in consultation with the Political Bureau of the national party and are usually closely aligned with the president.

The elected members of the National Assembly are chosen from single-member districts by direct vote. Candidates are selected at the local level through a primary held by the national party, but they must be approved by the higher officials of the party.

The members of the National Assembly are elected at the same time as the president. Like the president, each member serves a seven-year term. The National Assembly can be dissolved by the president, in which case new elections must be held within twenty to forty days.

The National Assembly approves bills initiated by individual members or by the president by a simple majority. It also authorizes taxes and oversees a spectrum of government functions dealing with issues ranging from citizenship to economic planning.

Judiciary

The judiciary ranges from a series of local courts ruling on issues of tribal law to the Supreme Court created by the constitution. While the Supreme Court was granted wide powers by the constitution, including the right of judicial review, its members are appointed by the president, and thus seldom deviate from government policy.

Regional & Local Government

Gabon is divided into nine provinces, which are further divided into thirty-six prefectures and eight subprefectures. All governors, prefects, and subprefects are appointed by the president.

The Electoral System

Suffrage in Gabon is universal. All Gabonese nationals twenty-one years of age or older are eligible electors. Election is by secret ballot. Foreign nationals living in Gabon may also vote. Because of the vote of foreign nationals and because registration is not a prerequisite for voting, the votes actually cast in a national election often exceed the number of registered voters.

Although elections for National Assembly seats often are hotly contested, on national issues there is little factionalism along regional or economic lines or between the Gabonese nationals and the resident aliens.

Gabonese Democratic Party (*Partie Démocratique Gabonais;* PDG)

History

The PDG, the only party allowed by law, was formed in March 1968 when President Bongo dissolved the former ruling party—the *Bloc Démocratique Gabonais* (BDG)—and officially ended all party competition. Because of the limited number of Gabonese trained and experienced in political matters, party competition never had been an important element of national politics. The party competition that did exist entered a period of steep decline in 1963 when the ruling BDG forced members of the rival *Union Démocratique et Social Gabonais* (UDSG) to join the BDG or resign all political offices.

Bongo's purpose in creating a one-party state was to submerge regional and tribal rivalries. Many members of smaller tribes were afraid that the majority tribe, the Fang, would gain control of the government and utilize it to the Fang's benefit.

Bongo's control of the party and government eased these fears since he is from one of the smaller tribes.

Organization

The main organs of the PDG are the Central Committee, which rules on matters of party organization, including the selection of candidates for office, and the Political Bureau, which controls the policy decisions of the PDG.

In addition to his role as president, Omar Bongo is chairman of both the Central Committee and the Political Bureau of the PDG. Bongo recently has increased his control of the party by replacing many older party officials with younger members who are, for the time being, more loyal to him personally.

Policy

The major programs of the PDG focus on economic issues. The most important of these is the continuation of Gabon's economic growth and development, which has been spurred by the country's vast natural resources, including oil and uranium. While retaining close political and economic ties with Gabon's former colonial ruler, France, Bongo has sought to avoid any conflict with neighboring African states. This relative harmony is essential since guest workers from these states comprise a large proportion of Gabon's work force.

Membership & Constituency

Since the PDG is the only party and voter turnout is nearly 100 percent, the party claims that membership is universal. No statistics are available on the number of party activists.

Financing

Although no data is available on party finances, it can be assumed that direct government support is substantial.

Leadership

Omar Bongo (born 1933) is secretary general of the PDG. He is a member of the Bateke tribe, which is very small. He was educated at Brazzaville Technical College, and has spent his entire career as a civil servant.

Leon Mebiame (born 1934) holds the second

highest government position, that of prime minister, and is deputy secretary general of the party.

Other Political Forces

The large number of foreign workers in Gabon, including both French administrators and guest workers from neighboring African states, means that this group does affect government policy. Foreigners are allowed to vote in Gabonese elections, and thus tend to pose no real challenge to Bongo's rule.

The largest tribal group, the Fang, have held an inordinately large number of government positions, but since the elite of other tribal groups also have been given government positions, political rivalries have not splintered along tribal lines.

National Prospects

Through efforts to increase participation in the PDG at the local level, especially among the young, Bongo appears to have a firm grip on both the party and government. As long as the rapid economic development of Gabon continues, Bongo will probably face few serious challenges from rival leaders.

Further Reading
Hughes, Anthony J. "Interview with Omar Bongo, President of the Republic of Gabon." *Africa Report*, May–June 1977.
Weinstein, Brian. *Gabon: Nation Building on the Ogooue.* Cambridge, Mass.: MIT Press, 1966.
U.S. Dept. of State. *Gabon.* Background Notes Series, no. 7968.

REPUBLIC OF THE GAMBIA
by Steven Metz, M.A.

The System of Government

Gambia is a West African republic of over 600,000 people with a political system based on a separation of powers among executive, legislative, and judicial branches of the government. From 1965, when the nation became independent, until 1970, Gambia was a constitutional monarchy under the British sovereign. The republic was declared and the present constitution promulgated in 1970.

Following an attempted overthrow of the government by Marxist rebels in 1981, a loose confederation was formed with Senegal, which dwarfs Gambia in size and surrounds it geographically. While both nations are to remain sovereign under this plan, there is to be an integration of security functions, communications, and of the monetary and economic systems.

Executive

The primary executive officer in Gambia is the president, who is head of government, head of state, and commander-in-chief of the security forces. In addition to the usual executive functions dealing with the application of law, the president also has the power to dissolve the legislature and call new elections.

Candidates for the presidency must be at least thirty years old and must be registered voters. The president is chosen by a direct election with universal suffrage. A vice-president is chosen at the same time as the president. The term of office is five years.

The current president is Alhaji Sir Dawda Kairaba Jawara. He has served as leader of Gambia since 1962, and easily won reelection in the most recent national election, which was held in 1977. The current vice-president is Assan Musa Camara.

Legislature

The unicameral legislature of Gambia is composed of the House of Representatives, with forty-three members. Of these, thirty-five are selected by direct election from single-member districts; four are appointed by the president; four are selected by a council of tribal chiefs; and a speaker of the House is appointed by the president. The appointed members are nonvoting.

The legislative sessions are set by the president, but according to the constitution they may be no more than twelve months apart. The president may also call extraordinary sessions of the legislature.

All laws must be passed by a majority vote in the House of Representatives. A bill which receives majority support is then sent to the president for his signature. If the president chooses not to sign a bill, it can be resubmitted to him within six months if approved by a two-thirds vote of the House. If a bill receives the necessary support and is resubmitted, the president must either sign the bill or dissolve the legislature.

The normal term for the House of Representatives is five years. The most recent national elections were held in 1977, when the Progressive People's Party, which has dominated Gambian politics since the early 1960s, received its usual substantial majority.

Judiciary

The highest courts in Gambia are the Supreme Court and the Court of Appeals. Although the judges are appointed by the president, the constitution gives the courts an independent role in Gambia. Besides lower courts operating under Anglo-Saxon legal rules, native courts have both civil and criminal jurisdiction among the tribes.

Regional & Local Government

The form of local government in Gambia varies. Banjul, the capital and largest city, has an elected council, and many of the rural areas have ruling councils which are partially elected and partially appointed. Tribal chiefs have retained some authority, especially on matters dealing with customary law and tradition.

The Electoral System

Elections in Gambia are direct; suffrage is universal for citizens at least twenty-one years old; and secret ballots are used. While voter turnout in local elections is often under 50 percent of those registered, turnout for national elections is high, with 82 percent of those eligible voting in the 1977 elections. The Gambian electoral system is widely recognized as one of the most open and honest in Africa, with results seldom contested or questioned.

The Party System

Gambia is a rarity in Africa—a working multi-party system. While one party, the Progressive People's Party (PPP), has controlled the government since independence, active and vigorous opposition parties hold seats in the House of Representatives. The respective strength of the PPP, however, has increased during the last decade. Political parties in Gambia originally polarized around rural-urban splits, which also had tribal overtones. But during the 1970s, tribal and regional differences declined in importance, as political parties, especially the PPP, became national and multiethnic in nature.

Progressive People's Party (PPP)

The PPP, which was formed in 1959, was originally conceived as a rural-based competitor for the more urban-oriented United Party. But when the PPP merged with the urban-based Gambia Democratic-Congress Alliance (DCA) in the early 1960s, the party began to gain support from both the countryside and the cities. After the PPP won control of the government in the 1962 election, it became the only truly national party.

The PPP has been led since the early 1960s by Dawda Jawara (born 1924), a former veterinarian educated in Britain. Despite an unexpected loss in a 1976 by-election, the PPP appears solidly in control of the government and enjoys a wide base of support. Jawara was reappointed secretary general of the PPP in a 1979 party congress, and remains personally popular despite open criticism of the PPP leadership.

United Party (UP)

The UP is an urban-based party formed in the mid-1950s, most of whose support comes from Banjul. The UP is led by Pierre Sarr N'Jie (born 1909). Prior to the 1977 national elections, the UP was the primary opposition party in Gambia. Little effort was made to muster support for UP candidates in that election, however, which led to a great decline in support. The future status of the UP is unclear.

National Convention Party (NCP)

The NCP, led by former vice-president Sherif Dibba (born 1937), was formed by Dibba in the mid-1970s and emerged from the 1977 elections as the major opponent of the PPP. During that election, the NCP was accused of tribalism, since the vast majority of its support came from the rural Mandinka tribe. But since President Jawara is himself Mandinka, most of the NCP's support appears to have been instigated more by dissatisfaction with the condition of the Gambian economy than by tribal antagonism.

National Prospects

Gambia's political system—based on compromise, bargaining, and open elections—appears to be one of the more successful governments in Africa. The stability of the political system is fragile, however, for two reasons. First, high unemployment and inflation have slowed economic growth considerably; the government is often blamed for the stagnant state of the economy and becomes the focus of discontent. Second, Gambia is a tiny country with no military force. This means that armed dissident groups, even if small and lacking support, can challenge the government. The continuation of Gambian democracy therefore depends on two things: a rejuvenation of the economy and the continuation of military support from Senegal.

Further Reading
Daun, Holger. *Change, Conflict Potential and Politics: Two Gambian Case Studies.* Lund, Sweden: Stasvetenskapliga Institutionen, Lunds Universitet, 1974.
Nyang, Sulayman S. "Recent Trends in Gambian Politics." *L'Afrique et L'Asie,* Vol. 109, 1976.
———. "Ten Years of Gambia's Independence: A Political Analysis." *Présence Africaine,* Vol. 104, 1977.

SENEGAMBIA CONFEDERATION
(*Confederation de la Sénégambie*)
by Lucie Gallistel Colvin, Ph.D.

The Senegalese army moved into the Gambia on the night of July 29, 1981, at the request of Gambian president Sir Dawda Jawara, to put down a bloody coup attempt. During that tense moment, and perhaps as a condition to Senegalese assistance, the Gambian president agreed to a confederation with his country's geographically and demographically encompassing neighbor. It was the fruition of an idea with a long history, mooted when Britain and France conquered the neighboring river basins, and proposed again strongly at the time of Gambian independence. Commercial and ethnic ties have long united the two, in both complementarity and competition.

The confederation, officially in existence as of January 1982, is superimposed on but does not impair the sovereignty of the two nations. On these grounds, both presidents submitted it to the two parliaments for approval, rather than to referenda, effectively squelching opposition. The Senegalese president is ex officio president of the confederation and the Gambian president ex officio vice president. One key element of the proposal is the integration of the armed forces. Gambia's military consisted only of the 300-man Field Forces, most of whom were implicated in the coup, so the practical effect has been to leave Senegalese troops visibly occupying the Gambia. Other elements, all proceeding slowly towards implementation in the indefinite future, include a supranational Parliament and customs union, and harmonization of foreign policies, civil services, and currencies.

Further Reading

Colvin, Lucie Gallistel, et al. *The Uprooted of the Western Sahel: Migrants' Quest for Cash in the Senegambia*. New York: Praeger, 1981.

Jalloh, Abdul A. *Political Integration in French-Speaking Africa*. Berkeley: University of California, Institute of International Studies, 1973.

Robson, Peter. "Problems of Integration between Senegal and Gambia." In *African Integration and Disintegration*, Arthur Hazelwood, ed. London and New York: Oxford University Press, 1967.

GERMAN DEMOCRATIC REPUBLIC

(Deutsche Demokratische Republik)

by William D. Pederson, Ph.D.

The System of Government

The German Democratic Republic (GDR) is a communist state of about seventeen million people located in an area one-fourth the size of pre–World War II Germany, which makes it one of the most densely populated countries in Europe. Although it has a nominally parliamentary political system with five political parties, in reality East German political life is dominated by the Socialist Unity Party (*Sozialistische Einheitspartei Deutschlands;* SED). The pre–World War II repression of the German communists and the post–World War II presence of Soviet troops helps to explain why East German leaders identify strongly with the Soviet Union.

The German Democratic Republic was established on October 11, 1949. Its governmental structure is based on the constitution of April 6, 1968, which was amended in October 1974. The amended constitution is the work of Erich Honecker, the current leader of the GDR, who in 1971 replaced Walter Ulbricht, the "founding father" responsible for the 1949 and 1968 constitutions.

Executive

Two large political bodies, both with smaller auxilliary units, make up the most important institutions in the executive branch: the Council of Ministers with its Presidium and the State Council with its National Defense Council. In reality, these institutions operate as executive organs of the SED, which has majority membership on each of them.

As is true of most East German political institutions, the Council of Ministers is based on the Soviet model. In essence, it is an economic board of some forty members that roughly corresponds to a cabinet. The Council issues ordinances to the government apparatus that administers the national economy. Although the legislature formally elects the members of the Council for five-year terms, in reality the SED Central Committee selects them with the legislature merely formalizing the selection. According to the constitution, the chairman of the Council of Ministers (that is, the premier) is the formal head of government. Willi Stoph is the long-time chairman of the Council and the Presidium of the Council, which consists of sixteen council ministers who oversee the larger body.

The State Council (*Staatsrat*) replaced the office of the presidency in 1960. Walter Ulbricht created the new institution to serve as his chief executive agency, but after his death it lost much of its authority in the 1974 revisions to the constitution. It has twenty-four members, elected by the legislature; three-fifths (i.e., fifteen) are required to belong to the SED. Erich Honecker, as chairman of the State Council, is chief of state; he is also head of the Communist Party, once again following Soviet practice. He is also chairman of the twelve-member National Defense Council, an auxiliary organ of the State Council, set up in 1960 to monitor the defense and security needs of the GDR.

Legislature

Legislative power in the German Democratic Republic is vested in the People's Chamber (*Volkskammer*), a unicameral Parliament which meets at least twice yearly. It grew slightly in importance after the formal abolition of the upper legislative chamber, the States Chamber (*Länderkammer*), in 1958, and particularly after the 1974 constitutional revisions that strengthened it at the expense of the State Council. On the other hand, its constitutional description as the "supreme state authority" is misleading given the power of the SED.

The Chamber is elected every five years in elections based on a universal, direct, and secret vote. Quotas of assigned seats in the 500-member body reflect the SED's concern with East German public opinion: the Socialist Unity Party is assigned 127 seats; fifty-two are designated for each of the four minor political parties; and the remainder are allotted to the "mass organizations" (the Free German Trade Union Federation, sixty-eight seats; the Free German Youth, forty seats; the Democratic Women's League, thirty-five seats; and the Cultural League, twenty-two seats). These quotas have not changed since 1963.

On the whole, the People's Chamber tends to have only a formal ratification role to play in the policymaking process, although some debate occurs during the early stages of the legislation. The limited importance of the East German legislature is indicated by three facts: its sessions average four to eighteen days per year; it passes an average of only about twelve laws per year; and its votes are nearly always unanimous.

Judiciary

As in the cases of the executive and legislative branches of government, the East German judiciary is modeled increasingly along Soviet lines. The purpose of the law in such judicial systems is to achieve party goals and to maintain internal order rather than to limit state power. Although the GDR Supreme Court (Oberstes Gericht) is constitutionally responsible only to the People's Chamber, in reality, it follows the guidance of the SED.

The Supreme Court is elected by the People's Chamber. It is the highest organ of the administration of Justice in East Germany and mostly functions as a court of appeals. The decisions of the court are based on guidelines set by the party Presidium to ensure the uniform application of the law by the courts. Under the Supreme Court, there are fifteen district courts (Bezirksgerichte) and 249 county courts (Kreisgerichte). The judiciary employs some 1,200 professional judges with legal degrees and 50,000 lay judges. The SED recruits the latter to run for office, with the result that the entire judicial system is influenced by the party.

In addition to these courts, thousands of "social courts" of dispute commissions and arbitration committees (Konflikt Kommissionen and Schiedskommissionen) have been set up since 1968 and function outside the formal judiciary. These courts are located in residential areas and in production cooperatives to aid in the reduction of the case load in the state courts. More than one-third of all criminal cases are handled in the social court system.

Regional & Local Government

In 1952, the five traditional provinces (Länder) and their legislative bodies were abolished and replaced by fifteen administrative units (Bezirken), each consisting of fifteen or more counties. The purpose of this reorganization was to increase the power of the central government and to contribute to furthering a communist identity.

Each Bezirk is administered by an assembly (Bezirkstag), which is divided into standing committees on economic, cultural, and security matters. The assembly elects a council (Rat) that serves as the executive. The national People's Chamber has the power to override the decisions of the councils.

The Electoral System

All citizens age eighteen and over have the right to vote in direct elections of legislators to the People's Chamber. The five political parties and four "mass organizations" are required to align under the National Front, which is an outgrowth of the immediate post-war Antifascist Democratic Bloc. Although each of the bodies in the National Front participates in the electoral process, it is completely dominated by the Socialist Unity Party. For example, to conduct elections the Front forms constituency commissions which have the right to screen nominations by the political parties and mass organizations. The Front has a further right to veto any later efforts to change these approved nominations. During elections, the voters are presented with a so-called unity list, which since 1965 provides for the elimination of candidates only when more than one is listed for a given office. Otherwise, the list must be accepted or rejected as a whole. The electoral process is not designed to provide political choices, but to mobilize the masses and ratify the decisions of the Socialist Unity Party.

Theoretically, every voter has the right to vote in a private polling booth, but the usual practice is for work brigades and housing communities to vote in public as a group; this discourages both the use of the private voting booth and abstention. Consequently, voter turnout is nearly 100 percent, and the results nearly unanimous. The vote in favor of candidates to the People's Chamber in 1981 was 99 percent, the same as in 1976. Only 16,645 voted against the candidates in the last election. In any case, the composition of the People's

Chamber is unaffected since the quota of seats assigned to the parties and organizations remain the same. The 1981 elections saw the first direct elections of East Berlin delegates to the People's Chamber.

Socialist Unity Party (*Sozialistische Einheitspartei Deutschlands;* SED)

The Socialist Unity Party is not only the predominant political institution in the DDR but it is also the most monolithic party in Eastern Europe. As the westernmost outpost of the European communist states, the party has developed the most orthodox pro-Soviet ideology. Its traditional insecurities are also reflected in the complex and overlapping controls the party maintains on East German institutions and its citizenry.

History

The Socialist Unity Party was created in April 1946 out of the forced merger of the Socialist Party (*Sozialistische Partei Deutschlands;* SPD) with the Communist Party (*Kommunistische Partei Deutschlands;* KPD). Under Hitler, members of the Communist Party were either murdered, imprisoned, or forced into exile. Many members who had fled to the Soviet Union during this period returned after World War II to reestablish the KPD under the direction of the Soviet military administration in East Germany. The wartime experience of many East German leaders contributes to their extreme loyalty to the USSR.

During the period from 1956 to 1961, the SED went through a final phase of resolving internal disputes within the party and consolidating its control in East Germany. The repression needed to accomplish the latter led to a sharp increase of refugees fleeing to West Germany. After the Berlin Wall was built in August 1961, the repression abated and a limited de-Stalinization program followed. As a result, productivity increased and the East Germans soon achieved the highest standard of living in the socialist world.

Organization

The SED organization is based on the Soviet party model. The smallest units in the party are the 79,668 primary organizations, formerly known as cells, located in enterprises and residential areas. Although some of these may number hundreds of members, the average has twenty-six members and three candidates. Above the primary organization are the town, county, and district organizations. The 218 county and fifteen district organizations operate parallel to the administrative units of the government.

The SED Central Committee is elected by the party congress every five years and acts as the highest authority between congresses. Currently, the Central Committee has 156 members and fifty-seven candidates. It usually meets four times yearly and conducts its work through a variety of commissions. Neither the party congress, nor the Central Committee is a normal legislative body, since both serve mainly to ratify the decisions of the Politburo.

The Politburo is the most powerful body in the party hierarchy and the real decision-making center in the GDR. It is the only SED organ where issues are made on the basis of majority vote rather than with unanimous formal approval. Meeting weekly as a rule, it consists of seventeen members and eight candidates who are elected by the Central Committee from its own membership.

The Secretariat is also elected by the Central Committee to serve as the continuing administrative unit of the party. It is presently comprised of forty-one operational departments with a central administrative staff of over 1,000 persons located in East Berlin. The Secretariat is not an independent source of power, but merely serves to carry out the decisions of the Politburo. The general secretary chairs both the Secretariat and the Politburo. As the head of the party, the general secretary is the most powerful person in the GDR.

Four important mass organizations are state-sponsored interest groups which are, nevertheless, closely linked both in structure and staffing with the Socialist Unity Party. Lenin's description of these types of organizations as "transmission belts" suggests their function as "schools of socialism" and adjuncts of the party.

The Free German Trade Union Federation (*Freier Deutscher Gewerkschaftsbund;* FDGB), with more than nine million members, is the largest of the four mass organizations. Nearly all workers belong to one of its 250,848 trade-union groups. Although the FDGB has no real bargaining power for the improvement of wages and working conditions, recent efforts have been made to engage workers in discussion to gain their cooperation. The FDGB is represented in local assemblies and has representatives in the state economic planning and supervisory organs.

The unions attempt to increase production, organize industrial safety, and control professional qualifications. They also provide welfare services. The Federation is responsible for the administration of social security.

The Free German Youth (*Freie Deutsche Jugend;* FDJ) is the second-largest mass organization with over two million members ranging in age from fourteen to twenty-five. Many members also belong to the SED. The FDJ is represented on almost all state and political bodies. The purpose of the organization is to integrate East German youth into a socialistic state by providing them with a multitude of opportunities in sports, education, and other areas at home and abroad. It is based on earlier German models and the Soviet Komsomol with which it has affiliations. Party control over the FDJ has increased in recent years. With church-related youth associations banned, it appears to be an effective means of political socialization, especially since it is the only youth organization permitted. Children between the ages of five and fourteen belong to the Ernst Thälmann Pioneers, an organization named after the communist leader in the Weimar Republic. It has a membership of nearly two million members. About two-thirds of all children and youth belong to one of the two organizations.

Membership in both the FDJ and the Pioneers is promoted through the monopoly of opportunities in sports and education. Nonmembership or even poor performance in the Pioneers or the FDJ may limit opportunity for advancement in education and employment. On the other hand, because East Germany has one of the highest growth rates of higher education in the world, a growing problem facing the educational system is overeducation and underemployment. The number of graduates in the work force has doubled every decade in the GDR, so that about one in every five members of the work force is a university graduate.

The Democratic Women's League of Germany (*Demokratischer Frauenbund Deutschlands;* DFD) has a membership of approximately 1.3 million. It derives importance from the major role that women play in the GDR economy, which suffers from a chronic labor shortage. Almost 50 percent of the labor force is female, and more than 80 percent of all women between the ages of eighteen and sixty hold jobs.

The purpose of the organization is to work for the equal rights of women guaranteed by the constitution. Although there is nearly total integration of women in the labor force, only about 13 percent of the SED's Central Committee are women and less than one-third of the trade-union federation's presidium is female. On the other hand, the People's Chamber has four times more women in it than the West German Parliament does.

The smallest of the mass organizations is the Cultural League (*Kulturbund;* KB) which has 208,000 members and is used to promote official cultural policy.

Policy

Often to the dismay of its East European allies, the SED follows an orthodox Soviet approach on foreign and domestic issues; in fact, it sometimes advocates old Soviet positions when Moscow is adopting a new line. The starkest examples of this occurred during the early years of the Ulbricht era when de-Stalinization was resisted, and then during Ulbricht's final years when détente was resisted. The older generation of East German communists seems to have a need to overconform to the Soviets in order to prove their loyalty.

In domestic policy, the SED advocates the prosecution of the class struggle and the elimination of the remnants of capitalism. Economic planning, as well as defense and security planning, are closely coordinated with the Soviets. Generally, the GDR has followed the Soviet model of highly centralized planning. In recent years, however, there are some signs of a slow-moving trend toward slightly less centralization. The GDR is a member of the Council for Mutual Economic Assistance (COMECON) and the Warsaw Pact. Seventy percent of East Germany's trade remains with communist states, and the Soviet Union is its principal trading partner. It has a growing trade deficit with the Soviets and an estimated $12 billion debt with the West.

By the early 1970s, the GDR had achieved, at least on paper, its long search for international legitimacy through membership to the United Nations in 1973 and recognition by the United States in 1974. It no longer advocates reunification with West Germany, but focuses now on combating imperialism by providing economic and military aid to the Third World, especially to those countries in which Soviet aid might prove an embarrassment. While the GDR once strongly advocated a reunification of Germany, party policy has accepted the East-West division since 1975 and signing of the Helsinki agreement recognizing Europe's postwar borders.

Membership & Constituency

The Socialist Unity Party is not only the largest party in the GDR but also in Eastern Europe. Although it emphasized massive recruitment from 1946 to 1948, it purged many members in the years following and now pursues a limited membership policy. Even so, the party presently enrolls about 11 percent of East Germany's population. In April 1981, there were 2,172,110 members and candidates.

Membership requirements involve a candidacy and probationary period. A candidate must be recommended by party members or by the local youth organization's functionary if the candidate already belongs to the Free German Youth. In either case, a candidate must be no more than forty years old and must remain a candidate member for one year.

The social composition of the SED suggests a large white-collar and intelligentsia component, although efforts have been made to increase the membership of production workers. In 1981, the membership consisted of approximately 58 percent industrial workers, 22 percent officials and intelligentsia, and 5 percent farm workers. Membership demographics also reveal that approximately 31 percent of the party consists of women. The factor of an aging membership has been slowed in recent years, so that presently 20 percent of the members are under thirty and 43 percent are under forty years old. Some 27 percent of party members have had post–high school education.

Financing

No accurate information is available on party financing.

Leadership

For more than twenty-five years the dominant figure in East Germany was Walter Ulbricht. His tenure as the head of the party ended in May 1971 with a smooth transition to Erich Honecker, who for years had served as Ulbricht's loyal deputy. Honecker was born in 1912 in the Saar region. His father was a coal miner and a communist. Honecker joined the communist children's organization at the age of eight. After studying at the Lenin Academy in Moscow a decade later, he became the secretary of the youth movement for the Saar. In 1935, he was imprisoned by the Nazis and was not released until the Soviet armed forces arrived in 1945. He reached the power center in the SED as the leader of the Free German Youth, which he helped to establish and headed from 1946 to 1955. After spending about a year in the Soviet Union for political training, he was advanced to the position of Central Committee Secretary for Security, Military, Organizational, and Cadre Affairs. He became head of state in 1976. In

1982, he was awarded the title of "Hero of the Soviet Union," the highest Soviet state honor.

Willi Stoph (born 1914) has been chairman of the Council of Ministers (premier) since 1976. Although some observers view him as Honecker's major rival, there has been no open factional strife in the party.

Minor Parties

Christian Democratic Union (*Christlich-Demokratische Union Deutschlands;* CDU)

East Germany is the only predominantly Protestant communist state in the East European bloc. The existence of the Christian Democratic Union as one of the four minor political parties is recognition of the traditional role of religion in German life. The party was founded in 1945, but lost independent leadership within three years. Traditionally, the CDU has been the most important of the minor parties, and it has slightly increased in size recently, so that presently it has 150,000 members. An indicator of its strength is suggested in its vote against the government's abortion legislation in 1972 and in the election of a CDU member as the president of the People's Chamber in 1975.

Nevertheless, the role of communist socialization in the GDR has contributed to an overall decline in the importance of the CDU and religion. Only 20 percent of East Germans are practicing Christians. The Evangelical Lutheran Church, which claims the allegiance of eight million members, has recently tried to use the peace movement to make itself more attractive to youth. In fact, the GDR is the only East European state to recognize religiously motivated conscientious objectors, who have the option to serve in construction brigades rather than in the combat arms of the military. Although the Protestant churches are the only institutions allowed to remain outside the control of the state and the SED, recent occasions of church-connected dissent probably stem more from the Polish example and embarrassment over the churches' subservient past than from any real alternative vision for the future.

Democratic Farmers' Party of Germany (*Demokratische Bauernpartei Deutschlands;* DBD)

The importance of the DBD has grown in relation to the other minor parties due to the emphasis put on agriculture in East Germany. The party was founded in 1948 by the SED in order to gain the support of farmers for the agricultural policies of the government, such as collectivization. Although the party was originally meant to be only a temporary expedient, it has evolved into a regular feature of the system and has 92,000 members.

Liberal Democratic Party of Germany (*Liberal-Demokratische Partei Deutschlands;* LDPD)

The LDPD, like the Christian Democratic Union, was established in 1945; both parties drew support from the middle class in the Soviet Occupation Zone. The LDPD originally advocated constitutional government and private ownership, but the leadership of the party soon became dependent on the Communists. With a present membership of only 75,000, it is the smallest party in East Germany. Although the LDPD retains the quota of 52 seats reserved for each of the minor parties, it has decreased in importance with the decline of the private sector in East Germany.

National-Democratic Party of Germany (*National-Demokratische Partei Deutschlands;* NDPD)

The NDPD, like the Democratic Farmers' Party of Germany, was established in 1948 by the communists to gain the support of former Nazis and military officers and thereby weaken support of genuine noncommunist parties. Although it was designed to be only a temporary expedient, the NDPD has evolved into an integral feature of the party system and now has 85,000 members. The party favors a pro-Soviet policy and strong armed forces, for which it has furnished many officers.

Other Political Forces

Military

As in other East German institutions, the boundaries between the Socialist Unity Party and the military are blurred. The SED relies heavily on the military as another facet of political socialization. It attempts to obtain the broadest strata of citizens to identify with the state's defense. The extent and intensity of citizen participation in military activity is greater in the GDR than elsewhere in Eastern Europe. The number of paramilitary forces in East Germany reflects this: there are 46,000 border guards; 24,000 security troops; 400,000 members of the Fighting Units of the Working Class, the workers' militia; and 450,000 participants in the Society for Sports and Technology, a youth organization with paramilitary aspects. In fact, the GDR has the highest ratio of soldiers or armed militiamen per square kilometer in the world.

The regular National People's Army (*Nationale Volksarmee;* NVA) numbers some 143,000 troops, including 87,000 conscripts. It is composed of 98,000 in the army, 28,000 in the air force, and 17,000 in the navy. Although the NVA is small, it is superbly equipped. The status and pay of East German military officers is high, and they obtain advantageous postmilitary positions with the state. This reward system operates from youth to retirement and is effective in gaining strong support for the state.

The Soviet Army is recognized as the "basic model" for the NVA which is subordinated to the USSR to a greater extent than any other Warsaw Pact member's military. Moreover, it is the only East European military subordinated to the Warsaw Pact Command (i.e., Soviet command) even in time of peace. The presence of Soviet officers in GDR military bodies is also more pervasive than elsewhere in Eastern Europe; and more NVA officers seem to receive training in the USSR than those from other East European states. USSR influence on the GDR and the NVA is represented in the more than twenty Soviet divisions stationed on East German territory—by far the largest number the USSR maintains in any foreign state.

National Prospects

The only serious challenge to the SED occurred in 1953 when there was a widespread spontaneous revolt among leaderless workers. After several years of economic improvement and the death of Stalin in 1953, workers' expectations had been suddenly reversed when the gains they had made were threatened with the imposition of impossible production quotas.

The leadership of the SED is astute at dividing and neutralizing potential political opposition. In 1953, workers revolted alone, while the privileged intelligentsia and the middle class remained aloof. In 1982, the workers, now enjoying greater material gains, are aloof from the protests of intellectuals and the children of the middle class. Since the construction of the Berlin Wall, the SED has opened a small safety valve through an unofficial policy of exchanging its political prisoners for West German currency.

Since most East Germans now receive Western television programs in their homes, West Germany has become the largest indirect source of opposition in the GDR. As the westernmost outpost in the Eastern European bloc, the GDR has the best-informed citizenry in the communist world.

Possible reflections of a frustrated East German public include rises in alcoholism, divorce, and teenage criminality. College graduates face increasing underemployment. Applications for emigration continue along with escapes to West Germany. The GDR has the highest suicide rate in the world and the highest military-desertion rate, although the latter has declined over the last fifteen years. On the other hand, East German athletes seldom defect.

Most indicators suggest that, at least in terms of short-term prospects, the state is stable. It has achieved international legitimacy; the political socialization process appears to produce a supportive citizenry; and the first and only occasion of succession was smoothly handled. Although the economy faces uncertainties, the GDR still has the highest standard of living in Eastern Europe. The large presence of Soviet troops also tends to reinforce the authority of the party.

A key to the GDR's long-term prospects may lie in the inevitable replacement of an older generation of political leaders, who tend to be inflexible, with a newer generation which has less sense of historic insecurity. A future leadership might feel secure enough to permit some loosening of political constraints and greater traffic and cooperation with West Germany. If such a period of relaxation were then followed by new restrictions, the 1953 revolt could be repeated on the political plane.

Further Reading

Grote, Manfred. "The Socialist Unity Party." In *The Communist Parties of Eastern Europe*, Stephen Fischer-Galati, ed. New York: Columbia University Press, 1979.

Hanhardt, Arthur M., Jr. *The German Democratic Republic*. Baltimore: Johns Hopkins Press, 1968.

Johnson, A. Ross; Dean, Robert W.; and Alexiev, Alexander. *The East European Military Establishment*. New York: Crane, Russak, 1982.

Kohn, Walter S. *Governments of the German-Speaking Countries*. Chicago: Nelson-Hall, 1980.

Lippman, Heinz. *Honecker and the New Politics of Europe*. New York: Macmillan, 1973.

Merritt, Anna J., and Merritt, Richard L., eds. *Politics, Economics, and Society in the Two Germanies, 1945–1975: A Bibliography of English-Language Works*. Urbana: University of Illinois Press, 1978.

Schneider, Eberhard. *The G.D.R.: The History, Politics, Economy and Society of East Germany*. New York: St. Martin's Press, 1978.

Sontheimer, Kurt, and Bleck, Wilhelm. *The Government and Politics of East Germany*. New York: St. Martin's Press, 1976.

Staar, Richard F. *Communist Regimes of Eastern Europe*. 4th ed. Stanford, Calif.: Hoover Institution Press, 1982.

Starrels, John. "Political Development in the German Democratic Republic." *Government and Opposition*, Vol. 16, No. 2, Spring 1981.

FEDERAL REPUBLIC OF GERMANY
(*Bundesrepublik Deutschland*)
by Gordon Smith, Ph.D.

The System of Government

The Federal Republic of Germany came into existence in 1949 as a consequence of the division of Germany in 1945. The three western zones (American, British, and French) of the occupying powers made up the new state, with the later addition of the Saarland in 1957. The Basic Law (constitution) of 1949 established a federal system of ten states (*Länder*) with a parliamentary system of government.

The West German political system has shown great stability in the post-war period, but it began to undergo considerable change in late 1982. The coalition between the Social Democrats (SPD) and the Free Democrats (FDP), which had governed the country since 1969, collapsed when Free Democrat leaders shifted their support to the Christian Democrats (CDU) and helped oust the SPD prime minister and install a CDU-FDP government on October 1. In December, the new government parties deliberately arranged to lose a vote of confidence so as to provide a pretext for new national elections, which are scheduled for March 6, 1983.

At the same time, the FDP has seen a sharp fall-off in its support. It recently failed to win any seats in state elections in Hamburg and Hesse where its pivotal role between the two major parties has been taken over by a new ecological party, the Greens. The Greens, however, are reluctant to compromise their principles in order to form stable coalitions with the SPD. Since the SPD and CDU often do not win absolute majorities in either state or federal elections and have, in the past, depended on the FDP to provide a working majority, the decline of the latter party and the wariness of the Greens may mean that minority governments at the state and even federal level will have to be considered.

Executive

Executive authority rests with the federal chancellor who heads the federal government. He is elected by the members of the Bundestag, usually at the commencement of a new legislative term, and his dismissal can only be effected by the process of electing a successor. The head of state, the federal president, is elected for a five-year term by a Federal Assembly, consisting of the Bundestag and an equal number of representatives from the states. No president may serve more than two consecutive terms of office. The president's powers are very limited and his function is largely ceremonial.

Legislature

Legislative authority is shared between the directly elected Bundestag and a second body, the Bundesrat, which represents the interests of the state governments. All constitutional changes have to be approved by a two-thirds majority in both houses, and the Bundesrat has a power of veto over legislation which affects the powers of the states.

The Bundestag is elected for a maximum life of four years, and because it is difficult to call new elections, the Bundestag had only once been dissolved early before 1983. The Bundestag normally consists of 496 representatives, but because of the operation of the electoral system its size occasionally may be increased. In addition, there are twenty-two representatives from West Berlin, but since West Berlin is not an integral part of the Federal Republic, they do not have full voting rights.

The Bundestag at its first meeting of the legislative term elects a chancellor by secret ballot on the proposal of the president, although the latter has to nominate the person who is likely to secure an absolute majority in the Bundestag, that is, the "chancellor candidate" of the party able to secure a majority by itself or in coalition with another party.

Party discipline in the Bundestag is strong, each party being organized as a party group or *Fraktion*. The president and four vice-presidents

VOTE IN FEDERAL ELECTIONS BY PARTY,[1] 1949–1980

	CDU/CSU	SPD	FDP	Others
1949	31.0	29.2	11.9	27.9
1953	45.2	28.8	9.5	17.5
1957	50.2	31.8	7.7	10.3
1961	45.3	36.2	12.8	5.7
1965	47.6	39.3	9.5	3.6
1969	46.1	42.7	5.8	5.4
1972	44.9	45.8	8.4	0.9
1976	48.6	42.6	7.9	0.9
1980	44.5	42.9	10.6	2.0[2]

[1]Party names are abbreviated as follows: Christian Democratic Union/Christian Social Union—CDU/CSU; Social Democratic Party of Germany—SPD; Free Democratic Party—FDP; German Communist Party—DKP.
[2]"Others" in 1980 included: The Greens (1.5%); extreme right (0.2%); extreme left, principally the DKP (0.2%).

of the Bundestag are usually members of the majority coalition. This presidium, together with a further twenty-three members of the Bundestag selected according to the size of the party groups, make up the Council of Elders (*Ältestenrat*). The Council determines the business agenda of the house and appoints the chairmen of some twenty specialist committees. The great bulk of legislation is initiated by the federal government, and since the government has a disciplined party majority its bills invariably pass the Bundestag, although frequently in amended form.

The Bundesrat has a unique composition in that it is not elected directly but consists of government delegations from the individual *Länder* which act on instructions from those governments. *Land* representation varies roughly according to the size of the population. Thus Baden-Württemburg, Bavaria, Lower Saxony, and North Rhine-Westphalia each have five seats; Hesse, the Rhineland Palatinate, and Schleswig-Holstein each have four; and the smallest *Länder*—Bremen, Hamburg and the Saarland—have three each. In addition, West Berlin has four seats, but with voting rights only in committee. The size of the Bundesrat is thus forty-one seats, plus the four from West Berlin.

Votes of the delegations must be cast *en bloc*. The individual delegation—led by the *Land* head of government, the minister-president—is composed of *Land* members of government, although in practice, and especially in committees, they may be replaced by senior civil servants. Unlike the Bundestag, the Bundesrat cannot be dissolved, and its composition changes only with changes of government within the *Länder*.

In the early years of the republic, *Land* governments were controlled by a variety of parties so that clear party blocs did not exist in the Bundesrat. Gradually, with the disappearance of the multiparty system, the party composition of the Bundesrat has become of leading significance. This is particularly true of the period after 1969, during which the Christian Democrats had a majority in the Bundesrat while the Socialist-led coa-

BUNDESTAG ELECTIONS, 1980

Land	CDU Direct	CDU List	SPD Direct	SPD List	FDP List	Total
Baden-Wurttemburg	31	5	6	21	9	72
Bavaria (CSU)	40	12	5	25	7	89
Bremen	—	1	3	—	—	4
Hamburg	—	4	7	—	2	13
Hesse	3	16	19	3	5	46
Lower Saxony	8	18	23	7	7	63
North Rhine-Westphalia	27	33	44	26	17	147
Rhineland-Palatinate	10	5	6	8	3	32
Saarland	2	2	3	1	—	8
Schleswig-Holstein	—	9	10	1[1]	3	23
Federal Republic	121	105	127	91	53	497
West Berlin[2]	10		11		1	22

[1]An excess seat awarded in Schleswig-Holstein (see Electoral System).
[2]West Berlin delegates are elected by the West Berlin assembly.

lition controlled the Bundestag. In some cases the Bundesrat has been used to block government legislation or to secure important amendments. However, some 90 percent of all federal legislation is uncontested by the Bundesrat. Compromises on legislative variations between the two houses are made in a conciliation committee which consists of equal numbers of members from the Bundestag and Bundesrat, twenty-two in all.

Judiciary

In addition to the system of federal and *Länder* courts, and standing apart from the structure of the ordinary courts, West Germany has a Federal Constitutional Court. The Bundesrat and the Bundestag each appoint half its sixteen judges on the nomination of the parties. To be elected a judge requires a two-thirds vote in the Bundestag or in the appropriate Bundesrat committee. A number of appointments are reserved for serving members of the highest federal courts, but otherwise it is only necessary that candidates should have the standard legal qualification. Once appointed for the twelve-year term, none of the judges may be removed, except on the motion of the Court itself.

The Federal Constitutional Court, established by the 1949 Basic Law, has unlimited powers of constitutional interpretation. Its ruling on the constitutionality of federal legislation is final. Cases may be referred directly to the Court by the *Land* governments, one-third of the Bundestag deputies, the federal president, or by the federal government itself if it is in dispute with a *Land* government. If federal legislation is thought to be in conflict with the constitution, the Court may rule on the issue even before the legislation goes into effect, although it often hears cases from the federal courts where a constitutional issue is claimed to be integral to the issue. The Constitutional Court also rules on constitutional complaints brought to it by individual citizens who hold that their basic rights have been infringed.

The powers of the Constitutional Court are such that it is bound to become involved in contentious issues, but it has avoided becoming the subject of political controversy. Nor has the mode of appointment of the judges led to an overt political bias in its rulings. The Court's high standing is due, in large part, to the general respect which legal norms enjoy in Germany, a respect which extends to the Basic Law and to the Constitutional Court.

Regional & Local Government

Each *Land* has its own constitution, establishing parliamentary systems very similar to that of the federal government. A *Land* government is headed by a minister-president who is elected by and responsible to the *Land* assembly (*Landtag*). With the exception of Bavaria, the *Landtage* are all unicameral. *Landtag* elections take place at four-year intervals, except for the Saarland's five-year terms. These elections do not coincide with the federal elections, but are scattered throughout the federal legislative period. As a result, the elec-

LAND GOVERNMENTS AND THE PARTY VOTE

	Election Year	Party Vote (%)				Government
		CDU	SPD	FDP	Greens[1]	
Baden-Wurttemberg	1980	53.4	32.5	8.3	5.3	CDU
Bavaria	1978	59.1 (CSU)	31.4	6.2	—	CSU
Bremen	1979	31.9	49.4	10.8	6.5	SPD/FDP
Hamburg	June 1982	43.2	42.8	4.8[2]	7.7	SPD
	Dec. 1982	38.6	51.3	2.6[2]	6.8	SPD
Hesse	1982	45.6	42.8	3.1[2]	8.0	SPD
Lower Saxony	1982	50.7	36.5	5.9	6.5	CDU
North Rhine-Westphalia	1980	43.2	48.4	4.9[2]	—	SPD
Rhineland-Palatinate	1979	50.1	42.3	6.4	—	CDU
Saarland	1980	44.0	45.4	6.9	—	CDU/FDP
West Berlin	1981	47.9	38.4	5.6	7.2	CDU

[1] Vote given only where the Greens are represented in *Land* assembly; in West Berlin, "Alternative List" stood.
[2] FDP not represented.

tions in the *Länder* are taken to be important tests of the federal government's standing with the electorate. They are also significant in possibly altering the party balance in the Bundesrat.

Below the level of the *Länder*, counties, districts, and towns each elect their councils. The local party organizations are very active in these elections. The councils elect the chairmen or mayors, which means that the parties put forward and promote their best candidates for the job in very much the same manner as the national parties put forward a chancellor candidate. Towns and counties are entitled to set and collect property taxes and also receive a proportion of national and *Land* taxes. Generally, however, these revenues are insufficient to cover the costs of local responsibilities. The localities are thus forced to rely on *Land* revenues with the consequent *Land* control of key elements in local planning and development.

The Electoral System

The electoral system used in the Federal Republic is best described as a form of "personalized" proportional representation (d'Hondt). Half of the 496 members of the Bundestag are elected as individuals in local districts by plurality vote and the other half from lists presented by the parties in each *Land*. Each voter has two votes, one to choose the constituency representative and the other, the second vote or *Zweitstimme*, for the party list.

The second vote is decisive for determining a party's total number of seats in the Bundestag, while the first vote partly influences which members of the party will have seats. The distribution of seats is made on a *Land* basis, and there is no provision for securing overall national proportionality. For example, the Christian Democratic Union (CDU) in Hesse at the 1981 federal election recorded 39.8 percent of the total vote in that *Land* which (after the elimination of the vote for smaller parties who failed to clear the 5 percent electoral threshold) entitled the CDU to nineteen of the forty-six seats for Hesse. Since the CDU had won three district seats on the first vote, it received a further sixteen seats via its party list. A small party, such as the Free Democrats (FDP), may not win any district election outright, in which case all its members elected will be drawn from the party list. If, as occasionally happens, a party wins more district seats than it is entitled to on a proportional basis, it keeps the additional

seats and the size of the Bundestag is increased accordingly. In that case, of course, none of the party's elected members in that *Land* come from the party list.

Although the electoral system is proportional, a fairly high electoral threshold operates: a party which fails to win 5 percent of the federal vote (or three district seats) does not share in the proportional distribution at *Land* level (although if it won one or two district seats it would keep them). The 5-percent barrier operates strongly against small parties; since 1961 only three parties have been represented in the Bundestag. Those which do surpass the barrier benefit from the exclusion of those that do not, so that there is some distortion of the proportionality principle.

All German citizens eighteen years of age and over are eligible to vote and registration is virtually automatic. Voting is not compulsory, but there are very high levels of participation, usually approaching 90 percent. However, there is some ignorance as to how the electoral system works: polls show that up to a fifth of all voters are not aware that it is the "second vote" which is decisive in determining party strength in the Bundestag.

The Party System

Origins of the Parties

Following the defeat of Germany in May 1945, the occupying forces at first banned all political activity, but from August 1945 those parties judged to be "democratic" (i.e., anti-Nazi) were allowed to operate at a local level. Each party had to be licensed individually, giving rise to the description "democracy under license." Initially, only four party groupings were allowed: the Christian Democrats, Social Democrats, Liberals, and Communists. These parties dominated the first series of *Land* elections within each of the western zones of occupation in 1946 and 1947. As a result, these parties were also the ones to devise the constitutions of the *Länder* and later to be responsible for drawing up the Basic Law, since the Parliamentary Council responsible for that task was composed of representatives from the *Länder* parties. The Christian Democrats—with its Bavarian affiliate, the Christian Social Union (CSU)—and the Social Democrats (SPD) emerged the most popular parties by far; in the first round of *Land* elections they won some 70 percent of the total vote.

Although the parties were newly established in 1945, they all drew on important German political traditions; only Christian Democrats represented an entirely new political formation. The SPD and the Communists (KPD) were the direct successors of the SPD and KPD in the Weimar Republic (1919–33); the Liberals (later to become the Free Democrats) corresponded to the Liberal parties in the Weimar Republic.

Yet the postwar parties had changed radically from their counterparts in the Weimar Republic. Whereas in the first republic the parties were strongly ideological in character, in the second republic they have become pragmatic and much more attuned to the needs of parliamentary government. Whereas in the Weimar Republic the party system had been unstable and fragmented, the new party system was characterized by its stability and by a trend away from multipartyism. The impetus for the change came partly from the Allies' method of licensing, but it was reinforced by the imposition of the 5-percent rule brought in at the insistence of the Allies. Subsequently, it was made more stringent: in the first federal election of 1949 a party was required to obtain only 5 percent in any one *Land*, but thereafter the threshold was raised to 5 percent of the national vote. Eleven parties were represented in the first Bundestag, but the number rapidly declined in the 1950s to three in 1961, and it has remained at that level. The CDU-CSU, SPD, and FDP together won over 99 percent of the vote in 1976 as against 72 percent in 1949, although that aggregate declined slightly in 1980.

The Parties in Law

As a reaction to the political extremism of the Weimar Republic, the Basic Law was concerned to regulate the position of the parties. Article 21 of the Basic Law declares that: "The political parties shall participate in forming the political will of the people." It also places restrictions on their freedom. "Parties which, by reasons of their aims or the behavior of their adherents, seek to impair or abolish the free democratic basis order or to endanger the existence of the Federal Republic shall be unconstitutional." The question of constitutionality is decided by the Constitutional Court which banned the right-wing Socialist Reich Party in 1952 and the KPD in 1956. However, the clause has not been invoked since then: an extreme right-wing party, the National Democratic Party (NPD), still competes at elections as does the German Communist Party (DKP), which is a direct successor to the old KPD.

The full implementation of Article 21 had to await the passing of a Party Law which was delayed until 1967. The Party Law recognizes that, since the parties have a public function to perform, they are entitled to financial support from the state. The extent of public subsidy is related directly to the size of a party's vote at a federal election: the present rate is DM 3.50 (about $1.60) per vote, so that a large party with, say 15 million votes (about the total achieved by the CDU-CSU) would receive DM 52.5 million ($23.75 million) over the four-year legislative term. A party need not win seats in the Bundestag for it to qualify for assistance; it only has to obtain 0.5 percent of the federal vote. Moreover, it is possible for parties to draw on their subsidy in advance, although if their vote is lower than expected, the difference has to be repaid.

The Party Law also seeks to control the internal organization of the parties to ensure that they are democratically run. It requires the parties to publish accounts and disclose the sources of their income; it provides that there should be a democratic election of officers, and that the process of selecting candidates for elections should be open to members, either through a responsible selection committee or by holding a representative party convention.

Party Organization

West German parties lay emphasis on securing large mass memberships, but in fact the ratio of members to voters for all parties taken together is about seven per 100, and only a small percentage of members take any active part beyond paying their party dues. Membership dues are an important source of party finance, but the advent of state financing of the parties has made them less reliant on membership support. Just as for federal elections, the parties in the *Länder* receive financial support from the *Länder* governments, so they are able to maintain a strong local presence.

A major activity of party members at the local and *Land* level is the selection of candidates for elections to the municipal and district representative body and for the *Land* assembly. Candidates are chosen either by conferences of local party members or by a delegate conference. The procedures usually ensure that only party activists will exercise any direct voice. In the early 1970s the parties experienced an influx of younger members and an increase in concern with local issues, especially environmental problems. These trends led to greater internal party competition, particularly in respect of the selection of candidates, a development most evident within the SPD.

The parties maintain *Länder* organizations which in many respects function quite independently of the national organizations. This independence arises for two reasons. In the first place, each *Land* is a governing entity in its own right, so that the *Land* parties are geared to winning *Land* office and supplying the ruling minister-president. Delegates from regional organizations, meeting in convention, elect *Land* party chairmen and also decide on the selection of candidates for the *Landtag* elections. In the second place, the *Länder* parties are responsible for selecting the candidates for the federal elections, and the national party can only use influence and persuasion in the question of the choice of candidates. The selection of candidates for federal elections and, especially, the order in which they appear on the party list, are hotly contested. Major party personages will be placed high on the list, and they may also appear as district candidates as well (if successful in the district election, their names will be deleted from the list). While a candidate may be reasonably sure of election if his name appears near the head of the list, uncertainty increases the lower down it is, especially since the number of seats the party wins in the districts, an unknown factor until the results are counted, will determine the number of successful list candidates. The voter is not able to change the order in the party list, so that the *Land* convention is the all-important arena for this decision. The party will also seek to place qualified "experts" on its list, since the German political tradition relies heavily on expert knowledge.

Party organization at the federal level is concerned with securing national publicity for the party, with research in a range of policy areas, with the coordination of the *Länder* parties, and with the formulation of strategy and policy. Party policy itself is decided by national delegate conventions, usually held every other year, with the national party leadership typically in a strong position to carry the convention vote. The convention also elects the party chairman and an executive committee. For the two major parties, there is also the question of choosing the party's chancellor candidate. While the candidate may be the national party chairman, that is not necessarily the case. The party convention is a major feature in preparing for a federal election and, in other years, for mobilizing activists and publicity for the party's efforts in *Land* elections.

The national executive elected by the convention is responsible for party organization and policy between conventions. Parties have executives of about thirty members, half of whom will normally be Bundestag deputies, thus facilitating coordination between the membership party and the parliamentary bloc. There is also a smaller party presidium, consisting of a third of the executive. This body makes all the important day-to-day decisions. The relationship between the national leadership and the *Länder* parties varies. While the SPD has strong centralist traditions, the *Länder* parties of the CDU and FDP have much more independence. For all three it is important that national coalition policies should be observed in the *Länder*, since the nature of *Länder* coalitions will be reflected in the party composition of the Bundesrat. For none of the parties would it be correct to regard *Länder* politicians as purely subordinate figures, since recruitment to federal politics takes place through the *Länder*, and the path to national leadership is frequently by way of becoming minister-president of a *Land* government.

Campaigning

The frequency and importance of *Länder* elections, interspersed as they are throughout the four-year life of the Bundestag, ensures that an atmosphere of continuous election campaigning is maintained. The significance of *Länder* elections means that they will be treated as federal elections in miniature, especially when they directly precede the federal election or when party balance is about equal. There has been a considerable "nationalization" of *Länder* politics as a result, and the elections are usually dominated by national issues with the party leaders actively engaging in the *Länder* campaigns.

The normal four-year Bundestag term means that the parties are fairly certain long in advance when the federal election will occur. Campaigning therefore is fairly extensive, although intense activity is restricted to the last four weeks prior to election day. Two factors dominate the buildup to the election. One is the question of the coalition lineup: since one party rarely wins an absolute majority in the Bundestag, it is important to secure a coalition partner. In recent years it has become the practice for the parties to make known their coalition intentions before the election takes place. The consequence is that the campaign is dominated by the claims of the two rival groups for office, and from 1972 to 1980 this meant a polarization between the CDU-CSU on the one side and the SPD with the FDP on the other.

The second dominant factor relates to this bipolarity: the contest is highly personalized since both of the major parties, the CDU-CSU and the SPD, must produce convincing chancellor candidates. An incumbent chancellor is, of course, already a convincing candidate, unless his government has appeared to fail seriously. The candidates' personalities and electoral appeal are major factors affecting the outcome of the campaign. Television coverage of the party leaders is intensive, and the culmination of the campaign is marked by a marathon television program in which all four party leaders (SPD, FDP, CDU, and CSU) discuss and argue their records and policies. Since the West German parties are well endowed with money, they are able to swamp the electorate with posters and campaign literature, spending some DM 250 million (nearly $115 million) of which well over half comes from the public purse. Although the electorate remains largely passive, interest is high as shown by the turnout. Even though in actual policy terms not too much separates the parties, partisan commitment is high and the rhetoric of intense conflict is maintained often accompanied by smear campaigns and personal vilification. That climate quickly changes once the election is over.

Independent Voters

The lack of marked ideological and programmatic differences between the established parties means that party identification is not nearly as strong as it was in the Weimar Republic or in the earlier postwar years. Increasingly, the parties have to compete for the "middle ground" in the electorate which means taking account of the changing social-class composition of the electorate and the altering occupational structure. Both types of change have been particularly in evidence for West Germany, since the country has enjoyed an exceptionally long period of almost uninterrupted economic growth from the 1950s through the late 1970s. The parties therefore have to make inroads into the new middle-class and white-collar workers who have no pronounced political affiliation. It is difficult to secure their long-term allegiance so that there is a degree of electoral volatility evident from one election to another.

Unlike the two largest parties, the Free Democrats do not have a reliable "core" vote, and the central position of the FDP in the party system tends to make the party a middle road between the CDU and SPD, attracting better educated and professional people, rather than trade unionists or

FDP SUPPORT IN FIRST AND SECOND VOTES (%)		
	First Vote	Second Vote
1972	4.8	8.4
1976	6.4	7.9
1980	7.2	10.6

active church members. The position of the FDP can best be exemplified by considering the extent of "ticket splitting" which the German electoral system allows. Since the voter has two votes, one district and one party list, it is possible to vote for the candidate of one party on the first (district) vote but for another party on the second (list) vote. The great majority opt for the same party with both votes, but there is a minority of ticket splitting which predominantly involves the FDP. The high marginal vote which the FDP attracts can be seen from the difference between the party's first and second votes. The size of the party's loyal core vote is gauged from the percentage on the first ballot, and in some years, notably 1972 and 1980, there was a significant difference between the two percentages. Thus, although the party benefited in terms of Bundestag seats through ticket splitting, it did not necessarily represent a stable position. The general point to be made is that the electoral system does allow a relatively weak party identification to be shown without forcing the voter to make a complete shift in party preference.

Christian Democratic Union (*Christlich-Demokratische Union; CDU*)

History

Although the Christian Democratic Union drew on various political traditions of the pre-Nazi period, the formation of the party in 1945 represented a new departure for German politics, and it proved to have an enormous impact on the party system. In the early period of occupation, political activity was restricted, and the CDU came into existence as a loose grouping of independent zonal parties. Nevertheless, they all had a common orientation in seeking to achieve a broadly based party of Christian unity which would bring together Catholics and Protestants into one political organization. It was made easier to achieve after the experience of the Nazi dictatorship, and the pre-Nazi Catholic Center Party provided an organization model.

In the Weimar Republic, the Catholic population had been a minority, but the division of Germany and the loss of the eastern territories brought about an approximate parity of Catholics and Protestants in western Germany. Parity made it possible for the two camps to base their cooperation on equality, and strenuous attempts were made to ensure that office holders in the party represented both confessions. As the party increasingly became detached from the CDU in Berlin and the Soviet Zone, so it became more conservative in its outlook and quickly shed its transient flirtation with Christian Socialism.

By 1949, the CDU—already the strongest party in many of the *Land*—was in a position to promote its own brand of economic policy under the title of a "social market economy." The party's later electoral successes can be attributed largely to the prolonged period of economic prosperity in West Germany, and the public's perception that CDU policies were responsible. The CDU was also fortunate in having a strong leader, Konrad Adenauer (1873–66), who became the first West German chancellor in 1949, a post he retained without a break until 1963. Throughout the Adenauer era, the CDU was the dominant party, and in the 1957 election the CDU-CSU won an absolute majority of votes. However, CDU fortunes became too dependent on Adenauer's standing, and as Adenauer's authority declined in the early 1960s, the party's fortunes began to wane. In 1969, the CDU-CSU was forced into opposition for the first time in twenty years. The party had to adapt itself to the role of opposition, and, despite all its efforts, the government coalition of SPD and FDP remained intact until 1982. Furthermore, the CDU-CSU has not been able to produce a convincing leader since Adenauer's departure, a fact which can be related to the peculiarities of the CDU's organizational structure.

Organization

A feature of the CDU since its foundation has been the loose structuring of the party: the CDU still bears the impress of its origins, beginning life in the individual *Länder* rather than as a national party. As long as Adenauer was securely in power as chancellor, the underlying problems were masked, and Adenauer himself saw no reason to create a strong national organization. It is also significant that a federal CDU was not established until 1950, after Adenauer had become chancellor.

The long-term consequence has been that CDU leaders in the *Länder* have been able to carve out positions of independent power for themselves, most strikingly in Bavaria where the Christian Social Union exists as a distinct party.

The CDU is made up of a federal party and thirteen *Land* parties. Each *Land* has its own organization, but those in North Rhine-Westphalia, Lower Saxony, and Baden-Württemburg are subdivided into two groups. The federal convention of the party is the supreme authority, but in practice the *Land* parties enjoy considerable freedom. This condition reflects the heterogeneous makeup of the CDU, particularly the distinction between the predominantly Protestant northern *Länder* and the Catholic southern ones. That north-south distinction also relates in part to differences between the progressive and conservative wings of the party. Thus the framework of *Land* organizations allows differing outlooks to coexist in the party, a variety which would be more difficult to sustain in a centralized party.

National CDU headquarters are at Konrad Adenauer Haus, Friedrich Ebert Allee 73-5, D-5300, Bonn 1.

Policy

Despite its "Christian" title, the CDU has many of the traits of an orthodox conservative party. The party stands for the rights of private property and is against state intervention. Its belief in the virtues of the "social market economy" is an article of faith, as is its implacable hostility towards communism. The CDU represents itself as the party of "law and order" and opposes the employment of radicals in public service. Although the CDU bitterly opposed the SPD's *Ostpolitik* in the 1970s, which was aimed at securing a reconciliation with Germany's eastern neighbors, a future CDU government would now accept its results. Nonetheless, the party is deeply suspicious of any movement in western Germany which shows apparent friendliness towards the German Democratic Republic or the Soviet Union.

Given its interconfessional character, the Christian emphasis of the party does not mean that the CDU stands particularly close to organized religion, but it does support religious values, stresses the special place of the family in society, and is generally opposed to the liberalization of abortion laws. The CDU supports the continuation of the "church tax," that is, the collection by the state of contributions by church members (levied as a proportion of income tax) for distribution to the relevant denomination without any cost to the church bodies themselves. The CDU also staunchly defends confessional schooling.

It is evident that there is no single ideological trend within the CDU. Also the nature of Christian Democracy implies that it is an interclass party, which means that the CDU has to avoid siding too openly with the interests of private capital at the expense of organized labor. However, the CDU is opposed to the extension of social-welfare programs, especially since such schemes increase public indebtedness or raise taxation—both anathema. With the recession affecting the Federal Republic in the early 1980s and the rapid rise in unemployment, the CDU showed itself to be still in favor of fiscal and monetary stringency.

Membership & Constituency

During its long period in government, the CDU paid relatively little attention to securing a wide mass membership, since its governmental position seemed sufficient to win electoral support. During the 1970s, however, much more effort was made to build up membership. Thus in 1970, membership was only 300,000, but by 1980 it had reached almost 700,000. If CSU membership is added, this total equals that of the SPD—historically the mass-membership party par excellence.

The occupational composition of CDU membership (by percentage) is: manual workers (11); white collar and civil servants (40); independent (25); pensioners (5); housewives (11); students and apprentices (6); other (2). In addition, it is estimated that some two-thirds are Catholic, one-third Protestant, and about one-fifth women.

Electoral support for the CDU is concentrated in the older age groups and in smaller communities. The party is characterized, too, by support from people who are not trade-union members and by those, especially Catholics, who are regular churchgoers. On other variables—such as sex, schooling, and occupation—there are no great variations from the SPD, except that the CDU gains more support from farmers, the self-employed, and the professions.

Organized business interests—employers' associations, the Federation of German Industry, and the extremely well-organized chambers of commerce and industry operating at local levels—all tend to favor the CDU. But these groups have also learned to work with an SPD-led government, and the Free Democrats in coalition with the SPD can claim to represent business interests just as adequately as the CDU. The same can be said of agricultural interests, for although the CDU speaks out strongly for farmers, the FDP also identified itself with their well-being, and its position in government gave the farmers an effective spokesman. From this point of view it can be seen that the CDU's long period of opposition after 1969 probably weakened the party as a representative of leading economic interests.

Financing

The generous state financing of the parties combined with the long-term rise of party membership has meant that the CDU is relatively affluent, and its income has increased at an appreciably faster rate than for the SPD and FDP. Of its current annual income of around DM 15 million (about $6.6 million), some 30 percent comes from membership dues, 25 percent from private contributions (mainly from business), and about 30 percent from the state subsidy. Reliance on membership dues is lower for the CDU than the SPD because of the scale of business funding. Dues are fixed on a sliding-scale related to income with a basic annual contribution of DM 36, and an average payment of DM 60 (about $27). The growth in membership and state subsidization has had a beneficial effect in reducing the party's dependence on the paymasters of industry, traditionally a sinister force in German politics, but there is no sign that this source is drying up.

Leadership

Since Adenauer's departure, the CDU has failed to produce a cohesive leadership formation process. The party's chancellor candidate in the 1976 election, Helmut Kohl (born 1930), was formerly minister-president of the Rhineland-Palatinate and became party chairman in 1973. After the 1976 election, he led the CDU's parliamentary group in the Bundestag. But his position was undermined by his failure to win in 1976 and further weakened prior to the 1980 election when the party opted for Franz-Josef Strauss (CSU) as the CDU/CSU joint chancellor candidate. Strauss's failure to win again opened the question of who would lead the party into the next federal election. The sharp political shift of late 1982, which made Kohl the chancellor, also secured his position as chancellor candidate in the approaching 1983 elections.

No current leader of the CDU can take his position for granted, and Kohl has to contend with other successful *Land* leaders. In this context "success" is judged by the ability to win *Land* and federal elections. The most important contender is Ernst Albrecht (born 1931), minister-president of Lower Saxony. Briefly, the CDU favored his candidature for the chancellorship before Strauss was chosen, and he consolidated his claims in the 1982 Lower Saxony *Land* election when the CDU won an absolute majority of votes cast. Other important *Land* leaders who have to be considered are the minister-president of Schleswig-Holstein, Gerhard Stoltenberg (born 1928); the ruling mayor of West Berlin, Richard von Weizäcker (born 1920), who successfully wrested control of the city from the SPD in the 1981 election; and Alfred Dregger (born 1920) who is the right-wing leader of the CDU in Hesse.

An important positive aspect of this leadership cadre is its comparatively low average age. Against that is the fact that they are overwhelmingly provincial figures, lacking experience in federal government. For the most part they have had no service in the Bundestag, although for the CDU minister-presidents their membership in the Bundesrat provides an adequate alternative forum.

Prospects

Despite being (with the CSU) the largest political party, the CDU was in opposition for an exceptionally long period. In this situation the party tried various strategies to win back power, but without success. The party had two basic alternatives: either follow a "soft" strategy to woo the FDP away from coalition with the SPD, or a "hard" one of creating a polarized system and winning a Bundestag majority on its own account. This latter course was favored by Strauss in the 1980 election, but its failure—and the concomitant alienation of northern CDU voters—forced the CDU to take a less antagonistic line towards its opponents. The difficulties of the SPD-FDP coalition in dealing with economic problems, tension between the FDP and the SPD, and factional disputes within the SPD, all helped return the CDU to government in 1982. The party's showing in *Land* elections subsequent to the 1980 federal election indicates that its chances of remaining in government are fairly good, either in partnership with the FDP or possibly with a majority of its own.

Christian Social Union
(*Christlich-Soziale Union;* CSU)

History

The Bavarian CSU, the sister party of the CDU, reflects the particularistic traditions of Bavaria which, alone of the *Länder*, has a direct continuity with a previously independent state, the kingdom of Bavaria. Like its forerunner in the Weimar Republic, the *Bayerische Volkspartei*, which was quite separate from the Catholic Center Party, the CSU consistently has emphasized its independence from the CDU.

The success of the CSU in identifying itself with Bavarian values was shown as early as 1946 when the party won 52.3 percent of the vote in the first *Landtag* election. However, it experienced strong competition from the anticlerical Bavarian Party for some years, losing its absolute majority for a time. The failure of the Bavarian Party to maintain a presence in the Bundestag (it was excluded in 1953 when the 5 percent requirement was extended from a *Land* to a federal base) led to its decline, and from the early 1960s the CSU became the dominant party, controlling an absolute majority from 1962 until the present time. It won an unprecedented 62.1 percent of the vote in the 1974 *Landtag* election. Effectively, the CSU has become the "state party" of Bavaria.

Organization

Within Bavaria, the CSU is completely free of any obligation to the CDU. Federally, however, there are important constraints. First, the CDU and CSU form a common parliamentary group in the Bundestag, although from 1976 onwards the CSU has enjoyed concessions giving the CSU deputies freedom of action. Second, the two parties present a joint chancellor candidate at federal elections (prior to the 1980 election the chancellor candidate had invariably come from the CDU). Third, the CSU is restricted to competing within Bavaria, while the CDU competes in all *Länder* except Bavaria.

The CSU is one of the best organized of all West German parties. There are no fewer than 2,800 local CSU associations, and above these the party is organized at district, provincial, and *Land* levels. The party convention is the party's supreme authority, from which is elected an executive and a party president. The party has its own newspaper, the *Bayernkurier*.

Party headquarters are at Nymphenburger Strasse 64, 8000 Munich 2.

Policy

The outlook of the CSU can best be described as "Christian-conservative." Although generally it subscribes to the main planks of the CDU platform, especially those of an economic nature, the

CSU is marked by its clericalism, its virulent anti-socialism, and—paradoxically for Bavaria—by its uncompromising nationalistic line, particularly with regard to the *Ostpolitik*. Naturally, the CSU is also in the forefront in the defense of *Länder* rights, and it appeals to Bavarian patriotism.

Party policies put the CSU well to the right on the political spectrum, but its confrontational style is just as important in assessing the importance of the CSU in West German politics. That style is largely determined by the character of the party's long-term leader, Franz-Josef Strauss, a national rather than merely Bavarian politician whose impact gives the CSU a federal significance.

The differences between the CDU and CSU, a conflict between liberal and conservative wings, were highlighted by Strauss's criticisms of the CDU leadership after the 1976 election. Previously, Strauss had advocated a strong polarization strategy against the SPD/FDP government, and he argued that weak leadership had lost the election. Strauss's defeat in 1980, however, showed the lack of attraction for CSU policies and confrontational style in the Federal Republic as a whole. However, it left the party's standing in Bavaria unaffected.

Membership & Constituency

In 1980, CSU party membership stood at 175,000 (compared with 118,000 in 1970), a total which compares favorably with all other parties. The social makeup of membership differs from the CDU in the much larger proportion of farmers, some 20 percent, and in the active participation of Catholic priests, who make no secret of their political loyalties. In addition, there are a number of organizations which are closely related to the party and help it to permeate society—the youth movement (*Junge Union*), the women's movement, the Christian Workers' Association, and several others.

The CSU is strongest in the heartland of Upper Bavaria, and in the predominantly Catholic areas of Swabia and the Upper Palatinate. It is less powerful in Protestant regions (Upper and Middle Franconia) and in some of the larger cities, such as Munich.

If a party is able to average around 60 percent of the vote, it is clear that it has considerable interclass appeal, and the CSU—chiefly, though not exclusively, through the Catholic vote—is able to count on support from all sections of the population. It is particularly strong in rural areas, but it also combines urban middle-class support

with that of employees. The wide attraction of the CSU in Bavaria is reflected in the weakness of the SPD. In 1980, the SPD won only 32.7 percent of the Bavarian vote, far lower than in any other *Land*. Moreover, the CSU has considerable following among young voters, so that its continued hegemony appears assured.

Financing

Even though the CSU is an active-membership party, it does not rely disproportionately on membership dues, and its subscription rates are far lower than those of other parties, averaging DM 32 ($14) per member. The principal source of party funds, about a half of an annual income of DM 20 million ($9 million), comes from state subsidies, federal and *Land*. In the latter case, the CSU is the major beneficiary of the largesse provided by the CSU government of Bavaria. The other source of income (somewhat less than 20 percent) comes under the heading of contributions, a large part of which represents financing from commercial and industrial interests, which are much closer to the CSU in Bavaria than they are to the CDU elsewhere, especially in election years.

Leadership

For many years the fortunes of the CSU have been closely identified with the person of Franz-Josef Strauss (born 1915), who first became party leader in 1961. Strauss first entered the Bundestag in 1949 and has held high federal office as minister of defense and later as minister of finance. After the 1980 election, he assumed the leadership of the Bavarian government as its minister-president, a move which some saw as a decisive retreat from federal politics, but in fact that conclusion is not self-evident. A CDU-led government after the 1983 election would place itself in jeopardy if it attempted to exclude him from federal office. Within the CSU, Strauss has no serious rival, although that was not so in earlier years, and when Strauss departs, there is likely to be a sustained conflict within the party over its future direction.

Prospects

After the 1976 election, the CSU made a serious attempt to achieve full independence from the CDU by declaring the independence of the party group in the Bundestag. That revolt failed and, coupled with the Strauss debacle in 1980, the CSU is less likely to see itself as an independent force in federal politics, even though it is still an influential element in the CDU. The party's slight decline on the national stage makes no difference to the position of the CSU in Bavaria; if anything, the national rebuff of 1980 may strengthen the image of the party as the embodiment of the Bavarian spirit, with or without Strauss.

Free Democratic Party (*Freie Demokratische Partei;* FDP)

History

The FDP, formed from several liberal parties in the *Länder* of the western zones of occupation in 1948, draws on two types of German liberal tradition: one conservative, nationalist, and close to heavy industry; the other radical, favoring individual liberty, and committed to liberal democracy. Both were represented in different parties in imperial Germany and in the Weimar Republic, but the formation of the FDP brought the two streams together, although the internal politics of the party clearly show a continuing tension between the conservative and radical wings.

For a long period in the 1950s and 1960s, the FDP was in coalition with the CDU, until the formation of the "grand coalition" between the CDU and SPD in 1966. In 1969, the party joined forces with the SPD, an extremely stable coalition that has lasted until 1982. In one sense, the FDP has always been a marginal party compared with the CDU and SPD, since it has never gained more than 12.7 percent of the vote. On occasion the FDP has been perilously close to the 5-percent barrier. On the other hand, the FDP has a remarkable record of having a place in government: its total period in office since 1949 exceeds that of both the CDU and SPD. The FDP is therefore very much a government-oriented party, and its position between the CDU and SPD makes the party an eligible partner for both. Yet it would be incorrect to think of the FDP as being able arbitrarily to switch from one to the other and effectively to be in a position always to determine the nature of the federal government. In the early years of the republic, the Free Democrats' conservative tradition predominated, and the CDU was their natural ally. Gradually, the outlook of the party changed as a new generation of leaders came to the fore, and a more radical element won control when the party was in opposition from 1966 to 1969. The new leaders saw alliance with the SPD as preferable to a renewal of a CDU/FDP coalition. The shift can be related to changing FDP attitudes toward the *Ost-politik* and to a greater concern with social and political liberties rather than to any change in thinking about the role of the state in the economy and social welfare.

Once the change in the FDP became evident, the party lost much of its traditional voting support. The continuation of the socialist-liberal coalition meant that the FDP had to build a new voting base, a fact which may explain the party's modest showing in subsequent elections when it depended on ticket splitting by SPD voters to top the 5-percent hurdle. The party's win of 10.6 percent of the 1980 vote may indicate that a new base does exist. However, at the same time it also meant that fresh support was based on a continued SPD/FDP coalition, thus making the switch to a CDU coalition dangerous for the party.

Organization

As a small, nationwide party, the FDP's organization tends to be rather weak, especially in *Länder* where the party's support is low, such as Bavaria. Each *Land* has its own organization, which has a measure of independence from the federal party, especially in the matter of coalition formation. The party convention, meeting yearly, is the supreme organ. Its composition is decided on the basis of two variables: half of the 400 delegates are allocated according to size of party membership in the *Länder* and the other half according to the size of the FDP vote in the *Länder* at the previous federal election. All members have a right to attend the convention, though not necessarily to speak. The federal executive, the position of which has been strengthened in recent years, is composed of leading party officials, together with members elected by the convention, federal ministers, and the leader of the parliamentary party.

Rather at odds with the middle-class image of the FDP is the party's youth wing, the Young Democrats (*Jungdemokraten*), which is decidedly radical in its orientation. The Young Democrats membership is kept quite separate from the parent body, however. Its role in the FDP is to keep the party alert to more progressive opinion and to serve as a recruiting base for party leadership.

Federal party headquarters are at Thomas Dehler Haus, Baunscheidtstrasse 15, D 5300 Bonn.

Policy

Although the FDP has moved towards being a progressive party, its commitment to free enterprise, individual liberties, and historical anticlericalism remain leading traits of the party. In 1971, a new party program was approved which was "social liberal" in character and spoke of the "reform of capitalism," without, however, indicating the lines on which reform should proceed. The party was first to recognize the need for a conciliatory *Ostpolitik*, but its flexibility on this score did not imply any weakening of Western commitments.

Many of the FDP's policy concerns are related to the practical questions of coalition government. Its "moderate" stance between the CDU and SPD implies that the party has to constantly adjust its policies to harmonize with the coalition partner. It realizes that it will never have a free rein, but is more concerned that the "extreme" elements of its coalition partner should be kept in check.

Coalition policy also requires that there should be some uniformity between federal and *Land* coalitions, since the latter will affect federal policies and legislation through the party composition of the Bundesrat. There was a clear division between the CDU-governed *Länder* on the one hand and the SPD-FDP governed ones on the other in the early 1970s, conforming to the federal lineup of the parties. Subsequently, however, the pattern has become less clear. The FDP lost its representation in some *Länder* assemblies, and in others the FDP found itself siding with the CDU—in Lower Saxony, in the Saarland, and in West Berlin. Those cases were occasioned by problems in forming majority governments rather than by a desertion of the FDP from the SPD. Nevertheless, the FDP also wished to avoid becoming identified permanently with the SPD, which would mean losing an independent profile and robbing it of freedom of choice. From 1972 onwards, the FDP committed itself in advance of elections to federal coalition with the SPD, so that its room for maneuver was relatively limited.

The political reasons behind the FDP change of policy in late 1982 included the SPD's refusal to cut back on welfare spending in the face of rising budget deficits in a stagnant economy, a suspected SPD drift away from firm commitment to basing nuclear missiles in West Germany, and a general decline in SPD electoral fortunes since the last national elections in 1980.

Membership & Constituency

For many years the FDP reported a membership of around 80,000 which was probably well on the optimistic side. In the 1970s, an influx of new members increased the total to 85,000 in 1980. There is a striking contrast to the other parties in the small percentage of manual workers (about 5 percent) and in the larger proportion of white-collar workers and public servants (about 44 percent). About one-fifth of the membership is women.

Support for the FDP comes from Protestants, mainly from larger cities, and from professionals and the self-employed. By far the most important distinguishing feature is the higher level of education of the typical FDP voter. Yet the FDP is not able to count on stable support from any one social category, and the party has a large turnover in support from one election to another.

The FDP has always defended the interests of agriculture and industry; the party stands near to a variety of organized industrial and agricultural groups and professional associations. The FDP's almost permanent presence in government is an attraction for organized economic interests which also work with the CDU.

Financing

As a major federal party, the FDP fares poorly in comparison with the CDU and SPD because its share of the public subsidy is much smaller; the same applies to subsidies in the *Länder*. From these sources, it obtains about a third of its total income which is in the region of DM 25 million ($1.13 million). Nor is the party able to rely on membership dues, partly because its membership is fairly low, but also because each *Land* party organization is free to set its own dues, a system which tends to depress them. Contributions to the party help fill the gap, accounting for some 40 percent of the annual budget, relatively much larger than for the other parties. Most such contributions are modest amounts from individual firms or organized groups, but total a significant sum.

Leadership

The FDP relies heavily on the quality of a small group of federal leaders to enhance its national standing. It has been fortunate in being able to supply two presidents of the republic: Theodor Heuss was the first president in 1949 and Walter Scheel (born 1919) from 1974 to 1979. Scheel was the architect of the first SPD-FDP coalition formed in 1969, and he served as foreign minister and vice chancellor until elected president in 1974. He was succeeded as party leader by Hans-Dietrich Genscher (born 1927) who also became, and has remained, vice chancellor and foreign minister. Prestige to FDP leaders accrues through the holding of government office, and incumbents stay for several years in important ministries, a status quite out of proportion to the size of the party. Other important personages are Otto Graf Lambsdorff (born 1926), economics minister, and Josef Ertl (born 1925) who has been agricultural minister since 1969.

Prospects

The FDP has proved to be a "survivor" hindering the appearance of a straight two-party system and defying forecasts of impending extinction. Despite its potential attraction for young, urban, middle-class voters the party has failed to make a breakthrough electorally, and it constantly has to contend with the inherent bipolarity of the party system.

Prior to the 1983 elections, the FDP had serious problems. In October 1982, about twenty-three of its fifty-three Bundestag members refused to follow party directives to vote against the SPD government. One of those who refused charged that the arrangement, while constitutional, "had the odium of damaged constitutional decency" and "offended morality and Christian principles." At least 7 percent of the party's membership was said to have bolted by December, and the party suffered further severe defeats in elections in Hamburg and Hesse. Former elements of the party's left wing formed a new Liberal Democrats party in November. The party faces two major threats in the 1983 elections: the campaign support of the CDU may not be enough to make up for defections and the party may fail to clear the 5 percent hurdle, or the SPD may gain enough votes to put the FDP and its new partner out of government. Either event could prove fatal to the FDP's future.

The Greens
(*Die Grünen*)

The ecological movement in the Federal Republic is possibly the strongest organized political force of its kind in Western Europe. Although the Green party was only formed as a federal party in 1980, it has had a considerable impact on German politics. The Greens arose as a merger of some 250 smaller ecological and related groups which had already been active in *Länder* and communal politics. Prior to the 1980 federal election, the "Green" lists (or the associated "colored" and "alternative" lists) obtained an average of 3.46 percent of the vote in *Land* elections, winning representation in Bremen (6.5 percent) and Baden-Württemberg (5.3 percent). In the 1980 federal election, the new Green party scored only 1.5 percent, which may have indicated that the movement was only transient in its appeal. But subsequent *Land* elections, in West Berlin in 1981 and in Lower Saxony, Hamburg and Hesse in 1982, showed differently. It appears that while the

Greens (and related groups) can mobilize local support on specific issues (siting of nuclear power stations, housing conditions in West Berlin, etc.), at a federal level their appeal is diffuse; the question of political leadership and the choice of a chancellor are matters about which the Greens have little to say.

Support for the Greens is based on a number of factors. One is simply concern about the environment. Another is the mobilizing of a protest vote against the monopoly of political power wielded by the larger parties and the consensus politics they foster. A third is the advent of idealist politics in West Germany, appealing particularly to the young and well-educated. A fourth factor concerns the SPD: its long identification with government has led to dissatisfaction among younger voters who see the party as incapable of initiating radical change in German society, but who are often unwilling to commit themselves to the radical left.

It follows that the motivations of those who support the Greens are varied, and the party suffers from a diversity of ideological tensions, especially between those who wish to keep to the narrower environmental issues and those who would like to restructure German society and have a leftist inclination. Not surprisingly, those who support the Greens also rally behind the peace movement and campaign against the siting of nuclear weapons in the Federal Republic. The founder of the Green party, a CDU member of the Bundestag, Herbert Gruhl (born 1921), did not stand for election to the new party's executive because he objected to its left-wing program. The party executive practices a form of collective leadership, and the most prominent members are August Haussleiter (born 1905), Petra Kelly (born 1947), and Norbert Mann. Green *Länder* organizations are practically independent of the national party.

Party headquarters are at Friedrich-Ebert-Allee 120, 5300 Bonn 1.

Social Democratic Party of Germany
(*Sozialdemokratische Partei Deutschlands;* SPD)

History

The SPD was founded in 1875 as a merger between Ferdinand Lassalle's General German Workers' Association (formed in 1863 as a moderate, non-Marxist party) and the strongly Marxist

Social Democratic Party of August Bebel and Wilhelm Liebknecht. Despite discrimination against it, the SPD became the largest party in the Reichstag in 1912. It formed the new provisional government upon the collapse of the monarchy in 1918. At that time, the left wing of the party split off to become the KPD, and the two parties were mortal enemies throughout the life of the Weimar Republic: the SPD wishing to preserve parliamentary democracy and the KPD dedicated to its destruction. After the collapse of the Third Reich, the SPD was quickly reestablished, since many former party workers enthusiastically rallied to the party. Kurt Schumacher, who had been incarcerated by the Nazis, emerged as the indisputed leader in the western zones, but it soon became apparent that the SPD in the Soviet Zone was to be subject to Soviet pressure. The USSR was not prepared to see the KPD take second place to the SPD. In April 1946, the SPD in East Germany was merged forcibly with the KPD to form the Socialist Unity Party.

The SPD under Schumacher at first appeared to have a claim to undisputed leadership in western Germany, but the rise of the CDU meant that the two parties ran neck and neck in the first *Land* elections as well as in the first federal election in 1949. Excluded from federal government then, the SPD commenced a long spell in opposition. While the CDU went from strength to strength, the SPD appeared to stagnate, and its traditional socialism seemed to have little relevance during the period of the "economic miracle" of the 1950s. The SPD reacted by drastically changing the nature of the party with the adoption of the Godesberg Program in 1959. The party committed itself to becoming a party of the whole people rather than a class party, and explicitly supported the successful market system. It claimed to be a party with no specific attachment to Marxism and to find its roots in "the Christian ethic, humanism, and classical philosophy." Subsequent to these reforms, the SPD's vote rose gratifyingly in successive elections, but its progress was also due to the personality of Willy Brandt who eventually became party leader as well as chancellor candidate. In 1966, the SPD joined the CDU in government, with Brandt as vice chancellor and foreign minister. In 1969 it became the senior governing party in coalition with the FDP, and Brandt was the first SPD chancellor in the postwar period.

Brandt's important contribution was to implement a new *Ostpolitik*. He also appealed to the idealism of younger voters, but without actually bringing about substantial reforms. His resignation in 1974 (over a spy scandal) led to Helmut Schmidt's replacing him as chancellor, although Brandt retained his post as party leader. Schmidt and Brandt continue to hold their positions.

The SPD became the largest party in 1972, but subsequently—in 1976 and 1980—the party again had to take second place to the total vote for the CDU/CSU. For party loyalists, the satisfaction of having the SPD in government for so long was tempered by the party's stagnating vote and its loss of reforming zeal.

Organization

The SPD is a strongly centralized party, with authority securely vested in the national leadership, the party convention, and the party's parliamentary group (*Fraktion*) in the Bundestag. Thus although the *Land* leaders and minister-presidents enjoy considerable prestige, there is never any question of them challenging the national leaders.

Each *Land* has a single party organization (except Hesse which is divided into two). The SPD also emphasizes the contribution of suborganizations. By far the most important is the party's youth movement, the *Jungsozialisten* (Jusos), open to all party members up to the age of thirty-five, although in fact only a small fraction of eligible members participate. The *Jungsozialisten* represent the major ideological challenge to the party leadership, but their influence has declined since the mid-1970s. Over time, the significance of the party's ancillary organizations has declined as means of integration and mobilization, and consequently the SPD's organization is stronger on paper than it is in practice. Since the West German unified trade-union movement is by choice, officially politically neutral, the trade unions do not exist as a suborganization of the party, unlike the situation in the Weimar Republic.

Party headquarters are at Erich Ollenhauer Haus, Ollenhauer Strasse 1, 5300 Bonn.

Policy

The fount of party policy continues to be the Godesberg Program, although that document is more a statement of principles than a detailed guide to action. It has been supplemented in various ways, most notably by the middle-range working program adopted in the late 1970s, entitled *Frame Orientierungsrahmen '85* (Framework of Direction), which among other things advocated a much larger role for the government in steering and planning the economy. The party also stands for greater social-welfare provision, educational reform, and an extension of codetermination in industry. In foreign policy, the SPD still favors rescuing what it can of détente, which was ushered in by the *Ostpolitik* treaties with the Soviet bloc. In the wake of the Soviet invasion of Afghanistan and the imposition of military rule in Poland, the SPD has to take a realistic position; nonetheless it still insists in keeping the lines open, especially with the German Democratic Republic. Three policy areas are subject to increasing intraparty conflict: the position of the Federal Republic with regard to increasing the amount of nuclear armament on its territory; the nuclear power program; and the measures necessary to counter the economic recession, especially the growth in long-term unemployment. Although these policy disagreements threaten party unity, the situation was complicated by the desire to see the SPD remain in government and consequently the need to placate the FDP partners. The party leadership was able to carry the party convention with it (most recently in April 1982), but the ability of Schmidt and Brandt to win convention support hid the extent of dissension within the party.

Membership & Constituency

The SPD traditionally has been a mass-membership party; even before 1914 it had no fewer than a million members. Soon after 1945, it reached 800,000, but then declined until the early 1970s when there was a large influx of young people. By the late 1970s it again topped the million mark before declining once more. Compared with the early postwar years there has been a massive decline in the proportion of manual workers in the party, only partially reflecting the changing occupational distribution of the labor force: manual workers now account for 28 percent of members; white-collar and public-service employees for 34 percent; students and apprentices add 9 percent. Members under the age of thirty constitute half the total, and women approximately 20 percent.

Voting support is greatest in the industrial areas and large cities, with a strong concentration among trade-union members and among those who are not church members. The SPD benefited from the lowering of the voting age to eighteen in 1972 and was then generally attractive to younger voters. This support subsequently declined somewhat, particularly in *Land* elections, where the Green party has made serious inroads into the first-time and young voters. By far the most important single constituency for the SPD is the trade-union movement, which despite its formally neu-

tral position in politics nevertheless has strong links with the party chiefly through personal connections and overlapping membership. However, German trade-union membership, at around 30 percent of all employees, is on the low side compared to other industrial countries.

Financing

The SPD relies heavily on membership dues as a source of finance. The growth in membership in recent years has made this a buoyant source of income (36 percent) especially as there has been a steady rise in incomes—party dues are fixed on a sliding-scale according to declared income, an average of DM 46 ($21). All office holders (*Land* and federal) are required to pay over a proportion of their salaries to the party, and this accounts for a further 7 percent of receipts. State subsidies, *Land* and federal, amount to about 31 percent of income, while the extent of voluntary contributions (10 percent) is far lower than for the CDU and FDP. Annual party income approaches DM 15 million ($66 million) and is comparable with that of the CDU, but lower than that of the CDU/CSU combined. The inability of the party to rely on contributions makes it especially sensitive to variations in electoral performance (which affect the state subsidy) and to fluctuations in party membership.

Leadership

The new generation of political leaders which took over in the early 1960s and was responsible both for party reforms and for the winning of federal office now constitutes an aging group. The party triumvirate of party leader Willy Brandt (born 1913), Helmut Schmidt, chancellor and vice president of the party (born 1918), and Herbert Wehner (born 1906), *eminence grise* and leader of the parliamentary *Fraktion*, is likely to be replaced in the not-too-distant future, especially if the party is forced into opposition. There are no obvious and outstanding personages to succeed them, but the SPD has never found leadership succession particularly difficult. Among the senior members of the party who wield influence are: Egon Bahr (born 1922) responsible for negotiating the *Ostpolitik* and now general secretary; Hans-Jürgen Wischnewsky (born 1922) with important trade-union connections and a vice chairman of the party; Hans Koschnik (born 1929), mayor of Bremen; and Hans-Jochen Vogel (born 1926), formerly mayor of Munich and federal Minister of Justice and presently leader of the SPD in West

Berlin. Vogel was selected as the SPD's chancellor candidate for the 1983 elections when Schmidt indicated that he would not run again.

Prospects

Since 1966 the SPD has assumed the role of a natural party of government, but even before its ouster in 1982 there were signs that the party had become "tired in office" and that it might best regenerate itself in opposition. Judging by past experience, however, the SPD might then find itself out of power for a decade or more, in which case it is likely that internal party dissension would grow, for the restraining influence that the chancellor exercises would then be absent. The party's chances of winning the 1983 election appear to depend on two factors: whether voter anxiety or moral outrage over the unprecedented CDU-FDP machinations create a "sympathy" vote for the SPD, and whether elements of the party's left-wing support will resist the appeal of the Greens' policies.

Minor Parties

German Communist Party (*Deutsche Kommunistische Partei;* DKP)

The DKP is the sorry remnant and successor to the pre-Nazi Communist Party (KPD) which was one of the strongest in Western Europe. The KPD was refounded in 1945 and won representation in the 1949 Bundestag, but fell below the 5-percent level in 1953 and was banned by the Constitutional Court in 1956. The DKP was established in 1968 and steers a careful constitutional course, but its minute following—0.2 percent of the 1980 vote—makes the party electorally irrelevant. The low level of support is an index of the decline of ideology in the Federal Republic generally, but an additional handicap for the party is the indelible association in the public mind of the Communist Party with the totalitarian rule practiced by the Socialist Unity Party (SED) in the German Democratic Republic. Although the DKP claims to be Eurocommunist, it has much sympathy with the SED, and significantly it does not compete against the SED in West Berlin elections. It is generally thought that the DKP also relies on subventions from the East Germany party. Its tight organizational structure, strongest in the Ruhr industrial area, accords fully with traditional Communist parties elsewhere. It has a membership of 42,000,

mostly people under forty years of age, and manages to produce a daily newspaper, *Unsere Zeit* (Our Time), with a circulation of 60,000. Since the DKP fails to win 0.5 percent of the federal vote, it no longer qualifies for the state subsidy, a fact which makes its reliance on contributions, over 40 percent of the party's stated income, all the more important. The current leader of the party is Herbert Mies (since 1973). The DKP sees its best prospects at the local level, since it is represented on several communal councils, and at the plant level in industry. The party has to compete with a variety of minute left-wing splinter parties which generally reject the USSR and East German models of socialism.

Headquarters: Prinz-Georg Strasse 79, 4000 Düsseldorf.

Other Extreme Left Parties

Besides the DKP, there is a variety of minute extreme left parties which do contest elections but are mainly devoted to internecine warfare. The Communist League of West Germany (*Kommunistischer Bund Westdeutschlands;* KBW) seeks a restoration of the old KPD as it existed in the Weimar Republic and rejects the Soviet model. This is true also of the Communist Party of Germany (KPD), founded in 1970, which is a Marxist-Leninist-Maoist grouping. A third such formation is the Communist Party of Germany/Marxist-Leninists (KPD/ML) which specifically aims at working in both German states. There is also an International Marxist Group (*Gruppe Internationale Marxisten;* GIM) which is firmly Trotskyite in orientation. Finally, there is the Socialist Unity Party of West Berlin (*Sozialistische Einheitspartei Westberlins;* SEW) which is an offshoot of the ruling Socialist Unity Party (SED) in the German Democratic Republic. The SEW is able to compete in West Berlin because of the continuing quadripartite status of the city in international law.

Other Minor Parties

Besides the more ephemeral of the minor parties, the following regularly contest federal elections: European Labor Party (*Europäische Arbeiterpartei;* EAP), a rather shadowy organization which operates in several European countries and is led in Germany by Helga Zepp-La Rouche. It was established in 1974. It has no socialist pretensions, but claims to be technocratic, progressive, and in favor of European unification. The extreme right does not mount a serious electoral challenge in the Federal Republic, and the only party of any significance is the National Democratic Party of Germany (*Nationaldemokratische Partei Deutschlands;* NPD). The NPD was founded in 1964 and brought together a number of extreme-right fringe groups. The NPD had an important initial impact, winning representation in some *Landtage.* In the 1969 federal election, it only just missed winning seats in the Bundestag with 4.3 percent of the vote. Thereafter, however, the party declined rapidly to 0.6 percent in 1972, 0.3 in 1976, and less than 0.1 percent of the vote in 1980.

In November 1982, some 1,000 former FDP members met in Bochum and founded the Liberal Democrats (*Liberale Demokraten;* LD). Describing themselves as "social liberals," they elected Ulrich Krüger, a former Hesse *Landstag* member, as chairman and William Borm, formerly a national figure in the FDP, as honorary chairman. The party will hold its first regular conference in January 1983 to decide whether to contest the 1983 election with its own candidates or to throw its support fully to the SPD. The party does not appear to have a significant future.

National Prospects

The Federal Republic has become a byword for political stability in Western Europe, and there are few indications of substantial change in this image. The party system is exceptionally well balanced, and since the parties show only minor differences of emphasis, government alternation is unlikely to bring about sudden changes in direction. The major parties are committed to Western treaty obligations, and the Federal Republic's Western orientation is underpinned by the leading role it takes in the European Community. Some questions can be raised about the future, in partic-

ular concerning the possibly destabilizing effects of prolonged economic recession, which could destroy the political consensus. But it would be wrong to treat West Germany in this respect as being any more susceptible to political misfortune than any of her European neighbors. A complicating factor in assessing the future stability of the Federal Republic is the uncertainty surrounding the future of the "national question." While almost no one believes that German reunification is feasible and it is certainly not a live issue, nevertheless the division of Germany and the sensitivity of relationships with the German Democratic Republic have a latent potential for serious impact on West German domestic politics. This is shown in the continuing concern with the internal developments in East Germany as well as with the inter-German relations. The exposed position of West Berlin is also a permanent worry to the Federal Republic. A crisis affecting any of these would inevitably have a destabilizing effect.

Further Reading

Balfour, Michael. *West Germany: A Contemporary History.* London: Croom Helm, 1982.

Conradt, David. *The German Polity.* 2nd ed. New York: Longman, 1982.

Edinger, Lewis. *Politics in West Germany.* Boston: Little Brown, 1977.

Kaack, Heino. *Geschichte und Struktur des deutschen Parteiensystems.* Opladen: Westdeutscher Verlag, 1971.

The Law on Political Parties. Documents on Politics and Society in the Federal Republic of Germany. Bonn: Inter Nationes, 1978.

Merkl, Peter. "West Germany." In *Western European Party Systems,* P. Merkl, ed. New York: The Free Press, 1980.

Smith, Gordon. *Democracy in Western Germany.* New York: Holmes and Meier, 1979.

REPUBLIC OF GHANA

by Dayna M. Tolley, M.A.

The System of Government

Ghana, a nation of nearly twelve million people on the Gulf of Guinea in west Africa, is presently under the rule of a mixed civilian-military junta called the Provisional National Defense Council (PNDC) under the chairmanship of former flight lieutenant Jerry J. Rawlings.

A union of the British colony of Gold Coast and the United Nations mandate under British administration, Togoland, Ghana was the first former colonial black African nation to become independent (March 16, 1957). It became a republic within the British Commonwealth in 1960, with a parliamentary system which soon succumbed to the charismatic authoritarianism of Kwame Nkrumah, who installed a one-party presidential system in 1964. Since Nkrumah's ouster in 1966, Ghana had gone through five military regimes and two short-lived civilian governments before the present government took over in a coup on December 31, 1981. The country has had four constitutions (1957, 1960, 1969, 1979), the last of which was suspended by the Rawlings government.

Executive & Legislature

The PNDC has full executive and legislative powers. As announced by Chairman Rawlings on January 2, 1982, the seven-member Council included Brigadier Joseph Nunoo-Mensah, army chief of staff, as vice chairman; Joachim Armtey Kwei, an activist labor leader; two noncommissioned air force officers; an outspoken Roman Catholic priest; and a radical student leader, Chris Burkari Atim, a personal friend of Rawlings.

Rawlings asserted that he had not lead a coup, but had only lead the way for "real democracy, government of the people, by the people, for the people." He has expressed admiration for Muammar Qaddafi of Libya and envisions a "people's government" with local "people's defense committees" fashioned after the Libyan model. The two noncommissioned officers on the PNDC have

been charged with responsibility for developing and coordinating these committees.

While he was still in the air force, Rawlings had led a coup in June 1979 that threw out a military government just two weeks before elections designed to return the government to civilian control. Rawlings called his first coup "a house-cleaning exercise" to rid the government of corruption and other abuses. He ordered the execution of eight government officials, including three former military heads of state. Rawlings stepped aside for the new civilian government, but warned that he would monitor its conduct and act again "if people in power use their offices to pursue self-interest."

The new Ghanaian president, Hilla Limann, soon arranged Rawlings retirement from the air force and appointed him to a powerless advisory body. Rawlings commented frequently on the inability of the Limann government to improve the economic situation and called for investigations of corruption in government and business. During his two years out of power, Rawlings made several trips to Libya, and Limann expressed the opinion that Qaddafi was financing the Rawlings opposition. Rawlings also maintained his ties with junior officers in the military and developed close ties with student and trade-union leaders.

Rawlings moved again amid reports that members of the Limann government were under investigation for receiving masive bribes. Announcing his takeover, Rawlings denounced the civilian government for having "bled Ghana to the bone" and said it had brought the country to "total economic ruin." Unverified reports soon after the coup stated that many potential opponents of the new regime had been arrested and as many as 200 killed.

Under the 1979 constitution, a president elected by popular vote to a four-year term was to have full executive powers, assisted by a cabinet. The unicameral Parliament of 140 members, elected to five-year terms, could override a presidential veto with an absolute majority of all mem-

PRESIDENTIAL ELECTION RESULTS (1979)*

First Round		Second Round	
Dr. Hilla Limann (PNP)	631,559	Dr. Hilla Limann (PNP)	1,118,405
Victor Owusu (PFP)	533,928	Victor Owusu (PFP)	686,132
William Ofori-Atta (UNC)	311,265		
Col F. G. Bernasko (ACP)	167,775		
Alhaji Mahama Ibrahim (SDF)	66,445		
Dr. John Bilson (TFP)	49,104		
Dr. R. P. Baffour (Ind)	8,812		
Kwame Nyanteh (Ind)	8,480		
Mark Diamond Addy (Ind)	5,957		
Alhaji Imoru Ayannah (Ind)	4,874		

*Major political parties participating in 1979 election were: People's National Party (PNP), Popular Front Party (PFP), United National Convention (UNC), Action Congress Party (ACP), Social Democratic Front (SDF), and Third Force Party (TFP).

bers. In the 1979 elections, Limann's party, the People's National Party (PNP), won 71 of the seats.

Judiciary

The court system consists of the Court of Appeal and the High Court of Justice at the top of a complex system of circuit, district, and traditional courts. The courts have generally shown considerable independence.

Regional & Local Government

The country is divided into nine regions under the administration of appointees of the national government. Traditional authorities continue to exercise considerable influence in most areas.

PARLIAMENTARY ELECTION RESULTS (1979)

	PNP	PFP	UNC	ACP	SDF	TFP	Ind
Central	8	—	—	7	—	—	—
Greater Accra	6	1	3	—	—	—	—
Eastern	11	6	4	—	—	—	—
Ashanti	2	19	1	—	—	—	—
Brong-Ahafo	2	10	—	—	—	—	1
Volta	11	—	5	—	—	—	—
North	7	4	—	—	3	—	—
Upper	15	1	—	—	—	—	—
Western	9	1	—	3	—	—	—
TOTAL	71	42	13	10	3	—	1

The Electoral System

Under the 1979 constitution, voting was open to all citizens eighteen years of age and older. Candidates for Parliament ran in single-member districts and won by simple pluralities. A special decree issued a month before the election declared that a presidential candidate had to win an absolute majority or enter a runoff between the top two candidates.

The Party System

Origins of the Parties

A variety of parties developed in the pre-independence period, but they were all overshadowed by Nkrumah's Convention People's Party (CPP), which in 1964 became the sole legal party. When political activity resumed in 1966, Kofi Busia, Nkrumah's rival, organized the Progress Party. As a result of intraparty factionalization, both parties have since split.

The history of Ghanaian political parties is marked by ethnic and regional divisions rather than ideological ones. Immediately after the 1972–79 ban on parties was rescinded, some fifty parties were formed; most representing ethnic, regional, and personal interests. Only nineteen qualified to register with the Electoral Commission, which reduced the final number to six by applying strict rules requiring a national organizational base. In fact, only the PNP had a truly national identity.

Cutting across regional and ethnic lines, two major factions have been apparent since the early

1960s. One, associated with Kwame Nkrumah, represented an ideology that was socialist, populist, and anticolonial. The other, identified with Kofi A. Busia, supported a policy which encouraged private enterprise and foreign investment under a government led by an educated elite.

The Parties in Law

In 1979, through the rulings of the Electoral Commission, considerable effort was made to limit political divisions along regional and ethnic lines and to force local and ethnic leaders to cooperate with one of the major parties. However, political parties have been banned by Rawlings. Party activity has been banned for nearly a third of Ghana's twenty-five-year history of independence.

Party Organization

Party organization has been rudimentary, depending far more on personal alliances, patron-client relationships, and traditional ethnic ties than on institutionalized structure.

The parties discussed below are those which competed in the 1979 elections. Their present condition is unknown.

People's National Party (PNP)

The PNP was led by moderate and right-wing pre-1966 politicians of the CPP. Imoru Egala (died 1981) was the party's original presidential candidate, but was under a banning order and had to withdraw. He named a virtual unknown from his home village, Hilla Limann, to run in his place. The PNP was broad based, cutting across class lines. It was the only party to win seats in all nine regions, though its support in the predominantly Akan provinces of Ashanti and Brong-Ahafo was minimal. It claimed an "African view" of world politics, stressing greater cooperation with all African countries. The party emphasized a commitment to open government and full popular participation. Party economic policy stressed improving Ghana's economic condition through increased agricultural and industrial capacity.

Soon after the 1979 elections, the party splintered into several factions. The "old guard," composed of former members of the CPP, was led by Imoru Egala and the pre-1966 CPP politicians. Within this "old guard," there was a constant struggle between Nana Okutweh Bekoe, the national chairman and a rich businessman, and Imoru Egala. The Bekoe wing alleged that the Egala

wing only espoused "socialism", while using their party positions to gain access to state patronage and contracts. The Egala wing countered with the allegation that Bekoe and Kofi Batsa had misused funds. These disputes forced Limann's closest lieutenants to leave their PNP offices. In opposition to the "old guard" were two younger factions of the PNP. One, a remnant of the old CPP, was made up of ideologues. The second included those with no previous CPP affiliations, a majority of the members of Parliament.

Ghanaians viewed the inner party struggles as evidence of Limann's weakening position in his own party, which combined with deteriorating economic conditions and government scandals involving millions of dollars to diminish the government's legitimacy.

It was rumored that the PNP was financed primarily by two men, Dr. Ayeh-Kumih and Nana Okutweh Bekow, who contributed several million dollars to the 1979 campaign.

Popular Front Party (PFP)

The Popular Front party was a direct descendant of Kofi Busia's Progress Party. It advocated a liberal policy based on acceptance of market forces and willingness to encourage foreign investment and emphasized production for export. Victor Owuso, the party's candidate in the 1979 presidential elections, won less than 39 percent of the vote in the runoff against Limann. The PFP won seats from seven of the nine regions and was particularly strong in areas of Akan predominance. The party was supported by prominent men such as J. H. Mensah, B. J. da Rocha, and Jones Ofori-Atta. It gave the impression of being very wealthy, although the sources of its income are unknown.

United National Convention (UNC)

The UNC is also a descendant of Busia's Progress Party, and its leaders were members of the 1969–70 Busia government. Paa William Ofori-Atta ("Paa Willie"), a popular figure with a national following, founded the party. The party had limited resources and no well-defined character. Its major electoral successes were in Volta, Eastern, and Greater Accra regions, which have large Ewe populations.

Action Congress Party (ACP)

The ACP, led by Colonel Frank Bernasko, was a totally new party. It was not ideologically based, but relied heavily on the personality of its founder. It drew most of its support from Cape Coast in Central province, where Bernasko is a local hero. Kofi Awoonor, a Ghanaian author, said the party was for the "progressive intelligentsia."

Social Democratic Front (SDF)

The SDF was a descendant of the CPP's left, or labor, wing. The basis of the SDF was the National Democratic Front, founded and sponsored by the Trade Union Congress (TUC). This party merged with and took over the much smaller SDF. The new SDF was led by Mahama Ibrahim Issifu, the secretary general of the TUC, and espoused socialist control of the economy combined with a readiness to accept foreign investment. The SDF supported pan-Africanist ideas and liberation struggles in southern Africa, but advocated a nonaligned foreign policy. The SDF won only three seats in Parliament, all from Northern province, where Ibrahim drew some of the Muslim vote away from his coreligionist, Limann.

Third Force Party (TFP)

The Third Force Party was led by Dr. John Bilson. Locally based, it won only 4 percent of the national parliamentary vote and failed to win a seat.

Other Political Forces

Military

The armed forces consist of some 20,000 men, most of them in the army. All three branches are relatively well trained, professional, and ethnically integrated. Riven by personal and ethnic factions, the military has been generally neutral toward Rawlings, although the air force (1,400 men) and many junior officers in the army have consistently backed him. Many senior officers, however, are from the Akan ethnic group, and they are reported to be opposed to Rawlings, who along with many of his close associates, is Ewe. (Rawlings's father was Scotch.)

Students

Some 7,000 students at three universities in Accra and Cape Coast are organized in the National Union of Ghana Students (NUGS). While only a small proportion of these students are politically active, they have been intensely critical of the past Ghanaian governments and have been among the most vocal of Rawlings's supporters. Their primary complaint is that Ghana's crippled economy provides few jobs for new university graduates.

Organized Labor

Ghana's labor unions have frequently been harassed and oppressed, but have managed to maintain some degree of central organization in the Trade Union Congress. Most labor leaders have supported socialist economic concepts. Rawlings has appealed for labor support and has generated considerable enthusiasm among the working class.

Ethnic Groups

Ghana's population is ethnically diverse; over seventy-five distinct groups can be identified on the basis of language differences. Most of these groups are very small and isolated. The dominant ethnic group is the Akan people (Ashanti-Fanti) who comprise about 44 percent of the population. Other major groups are the Moshi-Dagomba (16 percent), the Ewe (13 percent), and the Ga-Adangme (8 percent). The Moshi-Dagombe are concentrated in the north, while the other four groups are much more intermingled, especially along the coast. Roughly speaking, the Ewe are concentrated in the east and the Akan in the west and central forest regions, while the Ga-Adangme are found in the middle on the coast. The coast population is predominantly Christian (about 43 percent of the population); most Ghanaians practice their traditional religions.

Primary opposition to Rawlings appears to come from the Akan and groups of northern Muslims (about 12 percent of the population). The Akan, a trading people with a feudal social structure, are apparently concerned about Rawlings's radical economic and populist ideas. There is also some Akan resentment over the execution of a former Akan chief of state, General A. A. Afrifa, during the first Rawlings government. The northern Muslims were strong supporters of Limann, Ghana's first Muslim president and a northerner himself.

National Prospects

Ghana's political difficulties are traceable, in part, to severe economic problems. Once a relatively prosperous country, serious mismanagement and declining commodity prices have ruined the economy. Gross domestic product declined an average 3 percent a year during the 1970s. Production of cocoa, Ghana's major export, fell by more than a third in the same period, while a decaying infrastructure made it increasingly difficult to get the cocoa and other products to market. The country once produced as much as 35 percent of the world's gold, but now produces only 1 percent. The balance-of-payments deficit reached 438.5 million in 1979, and the annual inflation rate hit 120 percent just before the latest Rawlings coup. Among developing nations, Ghana has one of the lowest rates of domestic savings and investment and has been unable to attract foreign investment.

The average Ghanaian faces continual shortages of consumer goods and prices that make it virtually impossible to feed a family adequately (a loaf of bread was reported to cost over $7.00 in mid-1982). At the same time, urban workers and the unemployed see sharp disparities of wealth as major businessmen and government figures live in relative luxury.

Rawlings has no intention of turning the government back to civilian control and regards his earlier withdrawal from government as "naive." He has declared, "I am prepared to face a firing squad if what I try to do for the second time in my life does not meet with the approval of Ghanaians." However, his program to root out the networks of patronage and corruption that characterize Ghanaian business and politics may damage the economy in the short run, making it difficult for him to attract experienced administrators to assist in carrying out his projects. There is also the possibility that the International Monetary Fund and World Bank may step in with demands for an austerity program to bring inflation under control. Whether Rawlings could maintain his coalition of idealists and "have-nots" under such a program is questionable. At the same time, it is doubtful that the beneficiaries of former regimes and the status quo will permit Rawlings to carry out his revolutionary program without mounting concerted opposition, probably in the form of another military coup.

Further Reading

Apter, David. *Ghana in Transition*. Princeton: Princeton University Press, 1972.

Arnold, Guy. "A New Start in Ghana." *Africa Report*. Vol. 23, No. 3, November/December, 1979.

Austin, Dennis. *Ghana Observed: Essays on the Politics of a West African Republic*. Manchester; England: Manchester University Press, 1976.

Crowder, Michael. *Colonial West Africa: Collected Essays*. London: Frank Cass and Co., Ltd., 1978.

James, C. L. R. *Nkrumah and the Ghana Revolution*. Westport, Conn.: Lawrence Hill and Co., 1977.

Kraus, Jon. "The Political Economy of Conflict in Ghana." *Africa Report*, Vol. 25, No. 5, March/April, 1981.

———. "Rawlings' Second Coming." *Africa Report*, Vol. 26, March/April, 1982.

Luckham, Robin. *Politicians and Soldiers in Ghana 1966–1972*. London: Frank Cass and Co., Ltd., 1975.

GREECE
(Elliniki Demokratia)
by Keith Legg, Ph.D.

The System of Government

The Greek Republic is a parliamentary republic and a unitary state governing nearly ten million people. The current constitution came into force on June 11, 1975, ending a period of military rule which began in 1967 and lasted until 1974. From 1832 Greece was a monarchy, and from 1843 a constitutional monarchy, except for the years 1924 to 1935 when it was a republic. Following the restoration of democratic government in 1974, a referendum on the future of the monarchy went against King Constantine II, who had been deposed in 1967 by the military regime. The constitution of 1975 established the Greek Republic and replaced the king with a presidential form of government. Complex provisions in the constitution are designed to prevent the military coups, civil wars, regime changes, arbitrary national emergencies, and other political instabilities that have characterized Greek political history in the twentieth century.

Executive

The constitution describes Greece as a presidential parliamentary system. The functions of the executive in Greece are divided between two offices, the president of the republic, who is the formal head of state, and the prime minister, who is head of government. The president, although performing mainly ceremonial functions, has important powers that can be used in both routine and extraordinary circumstances. The prime minister, as leader of the majority party, or with the support of a parliamentary majority, selects the cabinet, defines and directs general policy, and supervises the administration.

Any person who is descended from a Greek father, has been a Greek citizen for five years, is legally entitled to vote, and has attained the age of forty is eligible for the office of president. The president is elected for a five-year term (with one renewal possible) by Parliament acting in a special session at least one month before the expiration of the term of the incumbent president. The election by secret ballot requires a two-thirds majority of the total membership of the Parliament. If that number is not reached, a second ballot is taken five days later, and if necessary after five additional days, a third ballot, at which time only a three-fifths majority is required. If the third ballot is inconclusive, Parliament is dissolved, new elections held and the succeeding Parliament in another special session can elect a president with a three-fifths majority. Failing that, the president can be elected with an absolute majority.

In performing ceremonial duties, the president acts for the state, but without personal responsibility. He is head of the armed forces, but command is exercised by the government; he has the right of pardon, but it is exercised only upon the recommendation of the minister of justice; he makes formal appointments to state offices, but the selections are made by others. The president also issues acts, decrees, and regulations, but they are proposed and countersigned by the appropriate ministers. In case of war or mobilization to meet an external threat, the president, with the countersignatures of the council of ministers or the prime minister, can suspend parts of the constitution. Under extraordinary circumstances, when asked by the cabinet, he may issue decrees with a legislative content (subject to later parliamentary approval).

The president does share in legislative power, and in some contexts his political influence can be quite real. He represents the state internationally with the power to declare war and conclude treaties, but with minor exceptions these actions require the ratification of Parliament. Since all laws must be sanctioned, promulgated, and published by the president, he may return legislation to Parliament for reconsideration along with reasons for doing so. On the other hand, if Parliament approves the returned legislation with an absolute majority, the president is bound to approve it. The president on his own responsibility may proclaim a referendum on a crucial national issue. In extraordinary circumstances (which are not defined), he may address the nation directly, without the approval of the prime minister, and he may convene the council of ministers under his chairmanship.

The president appoints the prime minister and, upon the recommendation of the prime minister, the other governmental ministers. The president is required to appoint as prime minister the leader of the party with an absolute majority in Parliament, or in the absence of an absolute majority, the leader of the party with a plurality. If no party leader can gain a vote of confidence, the president has the discretion to appoint anyone (member of Parliament or not) who would be able to secure a vote of confidence. Similarly, the president may relieve a prime minister of his duties upon request or when the government is defeated in a vote of confidence. Another provision designed for extraordinary occasions permits the president to dismiss the government after consultation with the Council of the Republic (an ad hoc body made up of former prime ministers and presidents, as well as the current prime minister, the president of Parliament, and the opposition party leader). The president convenes Parliament in regular session and may also do so in extraordinary sessions. He may suspend a parliamentary session for thirty days, but only once per session. He may also dissolve Parliament upon a proposal from the government. He may also dissolve Parliament, after consulting with the Council of the Republic, if Parliament is in "obvious discord with popular feeling, or if its composition does not ensure government stability."

The powers and possibilities of the presidency have yet to be tested since the president and the prime minister—until the election of 1981—were members of the same party. Conflicts are more likely now because Constantine Karamanlis, the founder of the New Democracy Party, is the president, and the Socialist (PASOK) prime minister, Andreas Papandreou, is a political rival.

The prime minister is the head of government, the key political leader in the country. He selects the ministers who comprise the cabinet and alternate ministers or undersecretaries who make up the government. The prime minister alone may dismiss members of the government. The actual power of the prime minister varies with his control of the party. Prime ministers who lead parties (such as New Democracy) which depend heavily on locally powerful patrons and clients who support their candidacies have to appoint leading members of their party, often their personal rivals, to ministerial office. The independent power wielded by such important party chieftains limits the prime minister's control of his government. New Democracy prime ministers did not dismiss a single member of their governments during their seven years in office. Prime Minister Papandreou has already dismissed one member who did not follow orders.

There is no specified size for the government and the number of ministers and undersecretaries will vary over time. Members of the government do not have to be members of Parliament; they merely are required to meet the qualifications for parliamentary membership. The present government has three members serving in the more technical ministries who do not serve in Parliament. Papandreou appears to have rewarded many of his associates in the movement against the military regime with positions in government.

According to the constitution, the government collectively defines, directs, and is responsible for the general policy of the country. Individual ministers are responsible for actions or omissions within their sphere of authority. In practice, the importance of the government as a collective body varies. Under New Democracy governments there was little collective action; ministers ran their ministries as personal fiefdoms, without much supervision or coordination on the part of the prime minister. The present government operates quite differently, with considerably more coordination and collective discussion, even if decisions ultimately are taken by the prime minister himself. The government is responsible for the introduction of most legislation in Parliament. The constitution gives an especially important role to the minister of finance because of severe restrictions on the introduction of legislation with budgetary implications.

Legislature

Parliament at present consists of 300 deputies, the maximum permitted by the constitution (the minimum is 200); deputies are selected according to two methods. In the first method delegates are elected directly by universal secret ballot from fifty-six electoral constituencies. An electoral constituency can have from one to twenty-eight representatives depending on population. Currently, 288 delegates are elected in this way. In the second method, twelve deputies of state are nomi-

1981 PARLIAMENTARY ELECTION RESULTS*

Party	Votes	Percent	Seats
Panhellenic Socialist Movement	2,725,132	48.06	172**
New Democracy	2,033,584	35.86	115
Greek Communist Party	619,292	10.92	13
Progressive Party	95,686	1.69	—
Communist Party of the Interior	77,461	1.37	—
Party of Democratic Socialism—Agrarians (Coalition)	40,853	0.72	—
Democratic Center	23,723	0.42	—
Liberal Party	20,705	0.37	—

*This table does not include smaller parties and independents who received approximately 35,000 votes.
**One member ran on the PASOK list as a "cooperating candidate" and once in Parliament declared himself a member of the United Democratic Left, a party which has not existed since the colonels' coup.

nated by each political party, but do not actually run for election; they gain parliamentary seats in proportion to the seats gained by the party in the constituency contests. A party must gain at least 17 percent of the national vote to have a share in these seats. Individuals nominated as deputies of state have diverse backgrounds: some are prominent politicians of advanced years, others have national reputations outside of politics, and some nominations appear to repay political debts.

Parliament is elected for a four-year term, but usually new elections are called earlier. (In case of war, the parliamentary term is extended for the duration.) Parliament convenes on the first Monday in October, elects its officers, and sets its rules. It sits for at least five months, but regular sessions are automatically extended until the state budget is approved. Parliament cannot act without the presence of at least one-fourth of the total number of members.

The government must have the support of Parliament, receiving a vote of confidence (a favor-

able vote from a majority of the members) within fifteen days of taking office. Members of the government, whether members of Parliament or not, have the right to attend and speak. The Parliament may require members of the government to answer questions and provide explanations. Parliament can also withdraw confidence from a government or censure an individual member. To do this, a motion indicating the reasons must be signed by one-sixth of the members. If the motion passes, which requires a majority of the total number of deputies, the government or the individual minister must resign. If it does not pass, another such motion cannot be introduced for six months unless signed by an absolute majority of the members. In practice, the electoral system insures that one party will have an absolute majority, and unless the party fragments while in office, no motions of censure are likely to be successful.

Both the Parliament and the government can propose laws, but in practice most legislation is introduced by government ministers or on their

1977 PARLIAMENTARY ELECTION RESULTS*

Party	Votes	Percent	Seats
New Democracy	2,146,365	41.84	171
Panhellenic Socialist Movement	1,300,025	25.34	93
Union of the Democratic Center	612,786	11.95	16
Greek Communist Party	480,272	9.36	11
National Front	349,988	6.82	5
Alliance of Progressive and Leftist Forces	139,356	2.72	2
Neo-Liberal Party	˙55,498	1.08	2
Revolutionary Communist Movement of Greece	11,895	0.23	—

*This table does not include smaller parties and independents who received approximately 33,500 votes.

behalf. The time of the ordinary member is devoted to servicing constituency requests. A deputy's legislative involvement is directed to producing exceptions and loopholes to benefit particular individuals or special groups. The members are not provided with the staff or office facilities that would make real policy involvement possible. Every proposal introduced into Parliament is debated and voted on—once in principle, once article by article, and once as a whole. A committee system exists for the examination of bills, and investigating committees can also be formed. Membership on committees must reflect party strength in the Parliament. When Parliament is not in session, a section of Parliament—with membership in proportion to that of Parliament as a whole—acts in its place.

Judiciary

There are three court systems of importance: the Supreme Court, the Council of State, and the Comptrollers' Council. The Supreme Court is the highest court of appeal. The Comptrollers' Council audits government accounts and has jurisdiction in matters of fraud and negligence. The jurisdiction of the Council of State is mainly administrative; it handles petitions for the annulment of government acts based on procedural or legal violations. However, the Council of State also approves the form and constitutionality of government decrees and regulations. According to the constitution, all laws must be consistent with the broad principles and specific rules of the constitution. The government is bound to comply with an "annulling judgment of the Council of State," and courts cannot enforce an unconstitutional law. If the government does not comply, the individual office holder or employee is personally liable for damages. The military junta encountered this problem and eventually solved it by the wholesale replacement of officials in the judiciary.

A Special Supreme Court, with personnel drawn from the three separate court systems, settles conflicts over jurisdiction or inconsistent rulings among the courts. It also acts as an electoral court, validating election results, and handling litigation arising out of electoral laws. The court's judgment in all matters is irrevocable.

The Greek judiciary operates as a career service. Consequently, appointments are for life—in practice, lower-level judges serve until sixty-five years of age, and up to sixty-seven years for those in higher levels. Appointments, promotions, and transfers are formally announced by presidential decree. However, these decrees reflect the decisions of judicial councils formed of the president of the specific court system plus additional members drawn by lot from among those with a minimum of two years' service in the judiciary. The prosecutor's offices or their equivalent also influence the decisions to some extent. The minister of justice may request that a decision on personnel be referred to the entire membership of the highest court in the particular system. Promotion to the offices of president or vice president of the Council of State, the Supreme Court, and the Comptrollers' Council requires a presidential decree proposed by the cabinet.

Regional & Local Government

According to the 1975 constitution, "the administration of the States shall be organized on the basis of decentralization" and the administration of local affairs belongs to the local government agencies, the first level of which consists of municipalities and communities. Greece is divided into fifty-one administrative subdivisions called *nome*. A *nomos* is not self-governing, but is administered by a *nomarch* appointed by the central government. These administrative subdivisions are in turn divided into *deme* and communities. A *demos* must have a population over 10,000 or be designated as the administrative capital of a *nomos*; there are 256 *deme*. The second administrative subdivision, communities, number about 5,700.

In reality, the Greek state is highly centralized, and even although some discretion does exist for local and provincial administrators, most decisions are referred to central authorities. Moreover, financial constraints severely limit local independence and initiative. Government ministries have field services based on the nine traditional regional divisions: the Peloponnesus, Old Greece, Thessaly, the Epirus, Ionian Islands, Macedonia, Thrace, Crete, and the Aegean Islands. The northern-most regions receive special attention through the Ministry for Northern Greece.

Local elections are held every four years in mid-October. Communities of under 5,000 population have councils consisting of five members, one of whom is designated the president. Communities of over 5,000 (that are not classified as *deme* or cities) have eleven-member councils, of whom one is selected as president. The *deme* have a mayor elected separately plus councils of from eleven to sixty-one members.

All candidates run on lists. Each list contains at least one and one-half to twice as many names as there are seats on the council. In the communities, one person on each list will be designated as the choice for president. Council seats are allocated to the two lists gaining the most votes. The list with the most votes gets two-thirds of the council seats, and the list with the second-highest number of votes gets one-third of the seats. If no list receives an absolute majority, a runoff between the two strongest lists is held a week later. The number of votes for the list determines majority or minority status on the council; the preference votes given to the individual candidates on the list determines the order in which the individual candidates get the seats.

In larger urban areas candidates at the local level are clearly identified with national parties; in the smaller communities such identification may be lacking. In the last round of municipal elections, PASOK made strenuous efforts, largely successful, to produce single lists opposing the "establishment" candidates in a great number of local elections. The next round of municipal elections, scheduled for 1982, will be viewed as indicators of national party strength.

The Electoral System

The constitution does not specify electoral laws and no two Greek elections have been fought under precisely the same system. Each government tries to make adjustments in the electoral law likely to favor it and disadvantage the opposition.

Under the current system, seats are allocated to each of the fifty-six constituences according to population. The latest census figures (for the legal population) are divided by 288 (the number of contested seats) and the resulting quotient is divided into the population of the various constituencies to assign the number of seats. Consequently, constituencies are both single member and multimember: five districts have only one seat and the bulk of the constituencies have five or less. Athens has twenty-two seats, and the suburban Athenian district has twenty-eight. Thessaloniki, the second-largest city, has twelve seats.

All Greeks aged eighteen and above must vote unless sick or incapacitated. Special enrollment on the electoral registers is required. Once registered, the voter is given an identification booklet which is presented at the polling place as identifi-

cation. Electoral officials stamp the book, thus preventing multiple voting and proving compliance with compulsory voting laws. Turnout in the last two elections has been over 80 percent of those registered. No explanation is given for the missing 20 percent, although the severe legal penalties attached to nonvoting appear not to be enforced.

Each party or independent candidate has its own ballot. Until 1981, the party lists contained only as many names (in alphabetical order) as there were seats in the constituency. The 1981 electoral law permitted parties to add one additional candidate in districts electing up to three deputies, and two additional candidates in constituencies electing three or more. The reason for these additional candidates is apparently to relieve the pressure on party leaders from individuals who want to become candidates. Since there are minimal opportunities to run for office, the pressure on those who control nominations is substantial.

The voter, upon entering the polling place, is given copies of all the ballots. The favored party or independent ballot is selected and the rest are discarded. Voters have the right to put a single preference cross next to the name of the preferred candidate on the party list. In three districts—Athens, suburban Athens, and Thessaloniki—two preference crosses are permitted. (Any party leader or former prime minister is automatically assumed to have as many preference votes as there are party votes.) The voter in effect is voting both for a party and for a preferred candidate. In fact in many constituencies, the significant contest is not between parties, but among candidates on the same party list competing for preference votes. The completed ballot is deposited in the ballot box.

The system of reinforced proportional representation distributes seats at three levels. At the constituency level, the total number of valid votes is divided by the number of seats plus one. Parties reaching the resulting quotient or a multiple of the quotient are allocated the appropriate number of seats, and party candidates with the most preference votes receive them. In the second distribution, the constituencies are grouped into nine separate regions, and the votes in each constituency that were insufficient to secure a seat are added together. This total is divided by the number of allocated seats, and parties reaching the resulting quotient or multiple of the quotient are allocated the appropriate number of seats (and party candidates with the next highest number of preference votes get them). Any seats remaining unallocated are distributed at the third, or national, level; here the votes at the regional level that were insufficient to secure a seat are added together and divided by the number of seats left. Parties reaching the resultant quotient are allocated the remaining seats. There is one major exception to this procedure. A minimum percentage of the national vote is required to share in second and third distribution. In 1981 this was 17 percent of the national vote for single parties, 25 percent for two-party coalitions, and 30 percent for coalitions of three or more parties.

By-elections are held in the event of parliamentary vacancies, except in the last year of a parliamentary term. Even if a full 20 percent of parliamentary seats should be vacant, by-elections are held in any case. Such elections have little significance in the Greek political system.

Two features of the electoral system have had significant consequences for the party system. First, the minimum percentage of votes required for participation in the second and third distributions has effectively diminished the parliamentary representation of the far left and of other minor parties. These parties are unable to translate their votes, typically scattered in many constituencies, into parliamentary seats. Second, the system of preference crosses means that individual candidates are elected according to the preference of voters rather than party leaders. This undermines party discipline and creates incentives for the maintenance of patron-client relationships at the local level. It is significant that the current government proposes to abolish the preference feature of the electoral law.

The Party System

Origins of the Parties

In Greece little continuity in party label exists. Since ideology has been of slight importance, except for the left, politicians—while maintaining a general point of view and political tendency— have been quite able to jump from one party to another or to invent new parties. Consequently, party origins must be examined in terms of placement on a left to right spectrum, and in terms of the previous political affiliations of the parliamentary delegation.

The following table shows approximate party placement on a right to left spectrum for parties gaining parliamentary seats from 1950 to 1981. The first number after the ideological identification indicates parliamentary seats held. Parties with pluralities or majorities have a second number indicating the percentage of parliamentary deputies in the party with backgrounds in parties of a *different* ideological tendency.

The Parties in Law

The 1975 constitution gives Greek citizens of voting age the right to "freely found and join political parties." The only qualification is that the organization activities of the parties "must serve the free functioning of democratic government." State recognition and access to the ballot are achieved through registration with the public prosecutor of the Supreme Court. Even parties not actually contesting elections legally survive. Since 1950, elections have been contested by from three to fifteen parties. In 1981 there were eight parties with general public recognition and more smaller ones. The ease of party formation has contributed to the fluidity of the party system, encouraging party splits and defections based on ideological differences or personality clashes.

Article 29 of the constitution makes possible direct state financial support, but this provision has not been implemented. The state does support party activities indirectly by televising preelection rallies and providing billboard space for party advertisements. Parties controlling the government have traditionally made use of public resources to gain electoral support. Pay increases for civil servants, pension benefits, and subsidies, as well as announcements about new public works usually appear in the period before an election.

Party Organization

Formal organization rarely has been a significant party feature in Greece. The Panhellenic Socialist Movement, with a real organization based on mass membership, is a new phenomenon. It promises to alter significantly the structure of future Greek parties. Although parties on the left had long and significant formal structure, they had not had mass appeal. Until now, the most important parties have originated among members of Parliament rather than in the general public. The organizational building blocks of parties in other

PARTY AFFILIATIONS IN THE GREEK PARLIAMENT, 1950–1981

1950
New Party (minor right)—1
Independent Political Front (extreme right)—16
Populists (broad right)—62
National Reconstitution Front (minor center-right)—17
National Party (minor center)—7
Liberals (broad center)—56
George Papandreou's Party (broad center)—35
National Progressive Union of the Center (center left)—45
Agrarian Party (minor)—3
Democratic Front (left)—18

1951
Populists (extreme right)—2
Greek Rally (broad right)—114, 38.9%
Liberals (broad center)—57
National Progressive Union of the Center (center-left)—74
Agrarians (minor)—1
United Democratic Left (left)—10

1952
Greek Rally (broad right)—247, 45.7%
Liberals–National Progressive Union of the Center (broad center)—51
Independents—2

1956
National Radical Union (broad center)—165, 39.2%
Democratic Union (coalition of Liberals, National Progressive Union of the Center, and United Democratic Left) (broad center-left)—132
Independents—3

1958
United Populist Party (minor right)—4
National Radical Union (broad center)—171, 41.2%
Progressive Agrarian Democratic Union (minor center-right)—10
Liberals (center)—36
United Democratic Left (left)—79

1961
National Radical Union (broad right)—176, 35.7%
Center Union–Progressive Party (coalition of broad center and minor right)—100
Pandemocratic Agrarian Front (left)—24

1963
Progressive Party (minor right)—2
National Radical Union (broad right)—132
Center Union (broad center)—138, 15.3%
United Democratic Left (left)—28

1964
National Radical Union–Progressive Party (coalition of broad right and minor right)—107
Center Union (broad right)—171, 19.8%
United Democratic Left (left)—22

1974
New Democracy (broad right)—220, 29.7%
Center Union–New Forces (coalition of broad center and minor center-left)—60
Panhellenic Socialist Movement (center-left)—12
United Left (left)—8

1977
National Rally (extreme right)—5
New Democracy (broad right)—173, 13.5%
Neo-Liberal Party (minor center)—2
Democratic Center Union (broad center)—15
Panhellenic Socialist Movement (center-left)—92
Alliance of Left-wing and Progressive Forces (minor left)—2
Greek Communist Party (extreme left)—11

1981
New Democracy (broad right)—115
Panhellenic Socialist Movement (center-left)—172,*
Greek Communist Party (extreme left)—13

*Percentage not available.

countries—trade unions, religious organizations, or agricultural cooperatives—either did not exist or were organized and manipulated by the state apparatus itself.

Party leaders have been self-selected, able to attract and maintain support through personal connections and political bargains. These parties were fragile, lasting only as long as the bargains were kept or the personal ties remained cordial. Electoral defeats caused defections, and few parties ever survived the death or retirement of their founders. On the other hand, the leader of a successful party had real power because, controlling the government and supervising the administration, he controlled patronage, the basic medium of exchange in Greek politics.

The link between the party leader and the individual voter (and Greece has had universal manhood suffrage since 1843) ran through networks of local patrons. Given electoral districts of relatively small populations, it was easy for a single politician or a prominent local family to construct patron-client ties. (In return for his vote, the voter received material goods or the promise of future assistance.) Economic and social modernization did produce individuals without patron-client ties. Some of these individuals were attracted to the left, others developed personal allegiances to party leaders based on personality or popular appeal. Parties, then, had no individual members in the usual meaning of the term.

For the most part, the party leader had access to votes at the local level, particularly in rural areas, only through the local politician. A parliamentary candidacy began with registration with the local court by the individual himself or by the petition of twelve electors. The registration did not include a declaration of party affiliation. (A registration fee was required.) After the candidates registered, the parties made selections for their individual slates. Parties with good prospects for success had many aspirants, those with poor prospects had few or none. Although the party leader had the last word in candidate selection, national success required local candidates able to attract support. This meant party leaders selected established politicians or their political heirs. In general, party leaders had more discretion in districts where they had little strength, or in those with considerable interparty competition. They had the least control over candidacies in areas where party strength was the greatest.

The economic and social changes of the past several decades severely weakened parties based on patron-client ties. The development of a mass media has given advantages to party leaders with attractive personalities and political styles. More important, it has permitted the party leader to reach voters directly. For example, PASOK recruited candidates without the usual family connections in the constituencies. As government has become more complex and individual demands have increased in number and changed in kind, the efficiency of patron-client ties for gaining political support has decreased. The increased educational levels of the population also have made programmatic and ideological appeals more attractive.

Greek Communist Party
(*Kommunistiko Komma Elladas; KKE*)

History

The KKE renewed existence as a legal political party only in 1974. Today it is the third-largest party in Greece with 10.9 percent of the vote and thirteen Parliament seats. It was founded in 1918, but it never attracted more than 6 to 7 percent of the vote in the interwar period. It was outlawed along with other political parties by the Metaxas dictatorship in 1936. Communist activists formed the key elements in the wartime anti-German resistance movement, and the party with its front organization probably had the support of from 25 to 30 percent of the population. This support began to dissipate at war's end and was severely eroded by the eruption of full-scale civil war between the communist-led insurgents and the government in 1946 and 1947. In consequence, the party was outlawed once again in 1947. With defeat, party cadres fled to Eastern European countries, but those inside Greece operated through surrogate parties; first, the Democratic Front in 1950, and later the United Democratic Left (EDA), until it was disbanded by the imposition of military rule in 1967.

Organization

The party has survived several serious splits and defections to remain the largest party on the far left. It has competed successfully with its major rival, the Communist Party of the Interior (EKKE), for the allegiance of left-wing activists. The party maintains the standard cadre-style communist model of organization, ranging from local-level organizations to the Central Committee and Politburo. Like other communist parties, control rests firmly with the central leadership, especially the secretary general. The party presents candidate lists in most constituencies. Most of the parliamentary delegation do not have key positions with the party organization. It has a student affiliate particularly active in university elections, and party cadres are active in several major unions and agricultural organizations.

National headquarters are at 16 Odos Kapodistriou, Athens.

Policy

The party has had two goals: one, differentiating itself from other rivals on the extreme left in order to attract and maintain the support of the traditional left-wing constituency; second, contributing to the defeat of the "imperialist right-wing majority." The major organizational and propaganda effort, largely successful, was directed toward the first goal. The second goal has resulted in an equivocal relationship with PASOK, because the KKE is at once rival and ally. The party enunciates policy with particular concern for ideological justifications, yet even though Soviet-oriented, it is not merely a puppet. In foreign policy, the party calls for the elimination of American military bases in Greece and for withdrawal from NATO and from the European Economic Community (EEC). Domestically, the platform calls for national independence, democratization, the abolition of uncontrolled monopolies, and for an improvement in the life of the people. The KKE would require the nationalization of the energy sector and of other major components of the Greek economy.

Membership & Constituency

The KKE attracted approximately 600,000 votes in the last election. Most of these were from traditional left-wing supporters, but many were from younger voters. It does well among certain sections of the working class and among Greeks with refugee backgrounds (Greeks expelled from Turkey in 1922). The party received between 15 and 25 percent of the vote in major urban constituencies such as Athens, Pireaus, and Thessaloniki as well as in provincial cities such as Larissa and Volos. The KKE also received over 25 percent of the vote on the Aegean island of Lesbos, a traditional stronghold for the left. The party failed to reach its 1981 goal of 17 percent of the national vote and did not qualify for participation in the second and third distribution of parliamentary seats.

Financing

There is no information available on party finances. Most party work is done by volunteers and some revenue seems to be collected through the sale of party books and pamphlets.

Leadership

The secretary general is Harilaos Florakis (born in Navplion, 1923).

Prospects

The KKE will retain supremacy on the extreme left of Greek politics. It may even gain modest increases in voter support, particularly in rural districts previously ignored by party activists. Further expansion is severely hampered by the victory of PASOK. With its broadly socialist ideology and its extensive organization, PASOK has preempted most potential KKE support and is challenging the KKE for control of mass organizations such as trade unions and agrarian organizations. Although assured of national-level visibility, KKE is likely to remain rather stagnant, both in terms of support and policy.

New Democracy
(*Nea Democratia;* ND)

History

New Democracy, founded by Constantine Karamanlis in 1974, was a revival of the National Radical Union, a party he founded in 1955. Like others, it was disbanded after the takeover by the military in 1967. New Democracy won parliamentary majorities in 1974 and 1977.

The elections of 1981 were conducted under the leadership of George Rallis, since Karamanlis had become the president of the republic and Rallis had replaced him as prime minister. The party lost its majority, winning 35.86 percent of the vote and only 115 seats. The party is currently in crisis, with controversies over leadership, organization, policy, and ideology.

Organization

Despite formal party statutes outlining hierarchical, mass-based organization from the local to the national levels, and auxiliary organizations for students and others, the most important element of the party remains practicing politicians. These individuals, together with their close associates, operate on the basis of personal ties to constituents. Through the election of 1977, these patron-client ties plus the personality and past accomplishments of the leader, Constantine Karamanlis, were sufficient to produce electoral victories. However, diminished majorities did prompt efforts to create a mass-based party with a network of constituency organizations, and a national congress did meet in 1977. Transforming New Democracy voters into party activists has been difficult because the incentives for activism, a coherent ideology, influence on candidate selection, and participation in party decision making were all lacking. Moreover, at every level of organization, the influence of parliamentary deputies was profound.

Two features of patron-client politics have gradually become weaknesses. Because the core leadership has consisted of politicians with careers dating from the 1930s or 1940s, the party has had a generational problem. These older figures dominate the party despite efforts in the New Democracy governments of 1974 and 1977 to appoint younger men to some cabinet positions. The second problem is candidate recruitment. In the past, a high porportion of New Democracy candidates (and those of its predecessor party) virtually inherited parliamentary seats from close relatives or were associated with politically prominent local families. Consequently, formal organization could make little headway at the local level. On the basis of the 1981 election, there is evidence that New Democracy deputies elected for the first time did not have these ties.

At present, the only really viable party organization consists of the parliamentary membership. This membership is exceedingly diverse because ideological views and policy positions have never been criteria for candidate selection. Moreover, many deputies have migrated to the New Democracy Party over the years from other parties. This situation has produced deep divisions within the party, since campaign strategies with ideological dimensions were required to meet the electoral threat posed by PASOK. The elevation of Karamanlis to the presidency in 1980 resulted in an open, democratic selection of his successor by the parliamentary members of New Democracy. George Rallis, generally considered a moderate, was elected by four votes over the more conservative Evangelos Averoff. After the electoral defeat of 1981, Rallis, blamed for the disaster because of poor strategy and lackluster personality, was defeated by Averoff in a contest for party leadership.

New Democracy national headquarters are at 18 Rigillis Street, Athens.

Policy

Party policies have reflected the pragmatic political considerations of Karamanlis and his successors rather than consistent ideological or philosophical positions. In the predecessor party, the National Radical Union, Karamanlis took an extreme anticommunist position, but also projected an image of technocratic efficiency. This image was linked to the enormous economic progress and unusual government stability of Greece during the 1950s and 1960s. After Karamanlis's creation of a new political party following the collapse of military rule and his installation as prime minister, he concluded that a more moderate image was necessary to attract voter support. Simple anticommunism was no longer sufficient as the bitter memories of the 1947–49 civil war faded

and the Greek Communist Party was given legal status. A more interventionist economic and social policy produced a state takeover of several important industries and a more liberal welfare policy. The close association with the United States was balanced by overtures to other Balkan states and membership in the European Economic Community. The most profound change was the withdrawal from the military wing of NATO because of the Turkish invasion of Cyprus in 1974 and the American failure to do something about it. Paradoxically, these policies made the proposals of PASOK in 1981 seem less radical to most Greeks and may have contributed to the electoral defeat of New Democracy. The party program in 1981 emphasized "safeguarding political stability and social tranquility"; it was basically a defense of the party record rather than a challenge to the opposition. Domestic promises were geared toward preserving existing practices or instituting incremental changes. In foreign affairs, the party was committed to remaining in the European Economic Community and in NATO and to continued defense cooperation with the United States. On Cyprus, the party preferred a single, bizonal federal state, without active Greek involvement. It was not a program designed to generate voter enthusiasm, for it did not capture the imagination of voters interested in change.

Membership & Constituency

Given the preponderance of personal links among voters and deputies, formal party membership is rare and an unreliable guide to party strength. Electoral strength has been above two million votes in the past three elections. Representatives to the first (and only) party congress in 1977 were elected by some 100,000 supporters, most of whom were mobilized by sitting members of Parliament. A year earlier the party had reported a membership of 20,000. The party has been a national party with significant support in all regions of the country, although in some instances individual deputies have been able to transfer their suporters from one party to another as they themselves changed party labels. A comparison of electoral data for 1977 and 1981 shows that New Democracy lost support in virtually every area of the country, although majority support continued in constituencies in the southern Peloponnesus, parts of Macedonai and Thrace, and on the Aegean island of Samos. The party also lost support in every socioeconomic category. The strongest support was concentrated in the middle class. The party fared very badly with voters under thirty-five years of age.

Financing

There is no data available about financing. Election costs in 1981 were approximately 700 million drachmae (about U.S. $12.7 million), much of this for advertising. At the constituency level, campaign costs are borne by individual candidates.

Leadership

Evangelos Averoff-Tositsas (born Trikala, 1910) has been the party leader since fall 1981. A member of Parliament since 1946, he has held cabinet positions in most postwar governments, the last as minister of defense. He is generally considered right-wing in his political views.

George Rallis (born Athens, 1918), former party leader and prime minister, has been a member of Parliament since 1950. He held cabinet positions in many postwar governments, most successfully as minister of education. Rallis represented the more moderate, pragmatic parts of the party.

Ioannis Boutos (born Athens, 1925) was the losing candidate for party leader in 1981. He entered Parliament first in 1950, and has served continuously since 1956. His support is from younger party deputies.

Prospects

New Democracy's prospects are uncertain, especially given the magnitude of the 1981 electoral defeat. As long as Karamanlis remains president of the republic, complete collapse seems unlikely. The election of Averoff as party leader has not resolved underlying conflicts. To capture an electoral majority, the party needs to gain voter support from the far right to the center, while constructing a coherent ideology and develop a mass organization. Factionalization within the party make these developments impossible.

Since the next parliamentary election does not have to be held until 1985, it is possible that a younger member of the parliamentary party with an attractive public personality could galvanize parliamentary support and proceed either to unify the party or transform it with a new label and a personal outlook. It is more likely that New Democracy will split into two parties, one oriented toward the right wing of the political spectrum, another attempting to reconstitute the center in Greek politics.

Panhellenic Socialist Movement (*Panellenio Sosialistiko Kinema;* PASOK)

History

The Panhellenic Socialist Movement was founded in September 1974 by Andreas Papandreou. Early members included some political figures active in the Center Union Party of George Papandreou (Andreas's father) prior to the military dictatorship. Most early supporters were recruited through the resistance organization (PAK, Panhellenic Liberation Movement) founded by Andreas Papandreou to oppose the colonels.

The major asset of the party has been Andreas Papandreou himself. To the political support inherited from his father, he added an international reputation as an economist. Most important, he has a political style with enormous mass appeal. In addition, Papandreou and his close associates have a grasp of the importance of ideology and organization in creating a mass political following. The Panhellenic Socialist Movement is like other Greek parties in that it is largely the creation and instrument of its leader. It is unique, however, in that it is a populist, left-of-center party with a mass base. The party has benefitted from the massive economic and social changes occurring within Greece in the last several decades.

Organization

The party constitution outlines a hierarchical but democratic organization beginning with individuals grouped in cells through local constituency organizations to congresses at the national level. At the top, in addition to the party leader, is a central committee and a smaller executive committee. There are affiliates for youth and women, and mass organizations, often with an ephemeral existence; these are directed to particular social groups or special issues. The party is attempting to gain control of other mass organizations in Greece such as trade unions and agricultural organizations. In practice, Papandreou and his close associates determine party policies, strategies, and appointments. He has not hesitated to expel party members questioning his authority or policy, an unusual circumstance in Greek politics which has led critics to claim that Papandreou is arrogant and dictatorial. The party organization is primarily important for mobilizing support for policies and for fighting elections. Local-level organizations have been very successful in challenging the dominance of traditional political families in many rural constituencies. Party leadership has been particularly successful in encouraging younger men to seek parliamentary office. In many cases, these are individuals who were active in the youth branches of the Center Union or United Democratic Left in the period prior to the military dictatorship. The Panhellenic Socialist Movement is the first Greek party with a parliamentary majority *and* a separate and important organization outside the Parliament.

National headquarters are at 50 Charilaou Trikoupi Street, Athens.

Policy

The slogan "national independence, popular sovereignty, and social liberation" suggests the general orientation. The contradiction between privilege and underprivilege is a major theme. The basic premise is that Greece remains an underdeveloped country, politically and economically dependent upon the international capitalist system. Until the 1981 elections, according to this premise, those controlling the government did not pursue real national interests, but were subservient to foreign interests in order to enrich themselves. More specific goals were defined in July 1981, including: (1) national independence and defense of territorial integrity; (2) people's sovereignty and democracy; (3) self-supporting and balanced economic and social development; (4) cultural and spiritual revival; (5) revitalization of the countryside; (6) higher quality of life in the city and the village; (7) social justice and final social liberation of workers, women, and the nonprivileged.

In domestic policies this means greater government decentralization and popular control of public organizations formerly manipulated by government officials. The tax system is to be made more equitable, and greater expenditures for education and health will provide some income distribution. To control the economy, closer supervision of public financial institutions and foreign trade is required. Some industries are viewed as candidates for state intervention, although the undefined term "socialization" is used instead of nationalization. There is interest in foreign investment, but only if it is consistent with national economic planning.

Early foreign-policy positions called for withdrawal from NATO because it failed to guarantee Greek security in face of the Turks. There were also calls for the removal of U.S. military bases and for withdrawal from the European Economic Community. In the months since the election, the

government has taken an independent line within NATO councils. It also refused to join the U.S. and other NATO allies in imposing sanctions on the Soviet Union and Poland after the Polish military takeover in December 1981, although it did join with others in condemning Soviet pressure on the Poles. At the same time, the Papandreou government opened a Greek port to Soviet ships needing repair. The aim of this policy seems to be to demonstrate independence from the United States and to apply pressure on NATO to give more support to Greece in its dealing with Turkey. Despite the government's rhetoric, no real steps have been taken to withdraw from NATO, terminate American base privileges, or renegotiate with the EEC. Relations with Turkey have deteriorated, and the PASOK position that Cyprus become a unified republic with equal rights for all citizens neglects the realities of the Turkish occupation and the distrust between Greeks and Turks on the island. The Papandreou government also has taken a slightly stronger line in support of the Palestine Liberation Organization, giving it the same diplomatic status in Greece as Israel enjoys. Greek governments (not just PASOK) have seen Israel as an economic competitor in Western Europe and Arab states as potential allies against the Turks. In addition, the Greek Orthodox Church, with its churches and monasteries scattered across the Near East, has always supported good relations with the Arab states.

Membership & Constituency

In mid-1977, PASOK claimed 27,000 members, but the membership has since increased dramatically because of the expansion of party organization. In 1977 the party was especially strong among younger voters, gaining 45.7 percent of the vote in the 20-to-24 age group and 42.1 percent in the 25-to-34 age group. The victory in 1981 was the result of increased support from a broad cross section of voters. The party gained ground especially in the *petit bourgeois* sector, among the new managerial classes, and in rural areas. Although identified particularly with urban areas, the highest concentrations of support (over 60 percent) were on Crete in rural districts traditionally hostile to "right-wing" governments for historical reasons.

Financing

There is little information on contributions. According to estimates, the 1981 electoral campaign cost 100 million drachmae (nearly $2 million). The party relies heavily on volunteer workers.

Leadership

Andreas Papandreou (born 1919, Chios) is prime minister and party leader.

Giannis Alevras (born 1909, Messini) is president of Parliament. His background in the syndicalist movement; he is a member of the party executive committee.

Apostolos Lazaris (born 1920, Kefallonia) is minister of coordination. An economics professor, he was involved in the PAK.

Agamemnon Koutsogeorgas (born 1912, Achaia) is minister to the prime minister. A lawyer, he was involved in the PAK, and is a member of the central committee.

Ioannis Haralambopoulos (born 1919, Messinia) is minister of foreign affairs. A retired officer and leader of the PAK in Greece, he is currently a member of the central committee and executive committee.

Apostolos Tsokhatzopoulos (born 1939, Athens) is minister of public works. He is a civil engineer and economist, was involved in the PAK, and is a member of the central committee and executive committee.

Petros Moralis (born 1936, Serres) is deputy minister of education; a nonparliamentarian, a philologist, and is active in coordinating parliamentary work. He is a member of the PASOK central committee and executive committee.

Giorgos Gennimatas (born 1939) is minister of interior. He is a civil engineer and has been PASOK member since its founding. Currently, he is a member of the executive committee and central committee.

Prospects

The party is likely to be the governing party for some time and a major participant even longer. Because of its attention to ideology and organization, it is the first truly mass party in Greece. Planned changes in the electoral law will strengthen PASOK and the position of Papandreou as leader even more. The identification of younger voters with PASOK assures long-term survival. The party has effectively isolated the extreme left and overrun the center. The political right is badly shattered. Papandreou is now the commanding personality in a political culture preferring leaders with personal glamour. As long as he is party leader, major internal splits or defections are unlikely, although some conflict has surfaced between ideological hardliners in the party organization and individuals with governing responsibilities. For those not committed to the ideology or enmeshed in the organizational structure,

continued support will depend upon the success of the Papandreou government in solving national problems. If domestic problems become intractable, Papandreou is likely to emphasize foreign-policy issues.

Minor Parties

Greek Communist Party of the Interior, *Kommunistiko Komma Ellados-Essoterikou* (KKE-Interior)

This is a "Eurocommunist" faction of the Greek Communist Party led by Haralaos Dracopoulos. It has lost the battle for the support of the majority of the extreme left, gaining only 1.37 percent of the vote in 1981. One prominent member, Leonidas Kyrkos, was elected to the European Parliament.

Liberal Party, *Phileleftheron Komma*

A remnant of the center led by Nikitas Venizelos, the grandson of the great republican leader of modern Greece, the party is not likely to survive.

Party of Democratic Socialism, *Komma Demokratikou Socialistikou* (KODESCO)

Founded in 1979 by dissidents from the EDIK, it ran unsuccessfully in 1981 in cooperation with a small agrarian party, winning only 0.72 percent of the vote. Ioannis Pesmazoglou (born 1919, Chios), the party leader, was elected to the European Parliament. Despite this, there is little prospect of survival.

Progressive Party, *Proodeftikon Komma*

A minor right-wing party founded in 1955 by Spyros Markezinis (born 1909, Athens). It generally appeals to the extreme right, but over the years, it has been quite opportunistic in its willingness to form coalitions. It did not participate in the elections of 1977, and in 1981 received 1.69 percent of the vote and no parliamentary seats. One member was elected to the European Parliament.

Union of the Democratic Center, *Enosis Demokratikou Kendrou* (EDIK)

This party, led by Ioannis Zigdis (born 1913, Rhodes) is the major remnant of the old center. It held sixteen seats with 11.95 percent of the vote in 1977, but was wiped out in 1981, gaining less than one percent of the vote and no seats. It has no prospects for survival in its present form.

Other Political Forces

Military

Throughout the twentieth century, the Greek officer corps has played an important role in domestic politics, either directly or indirectly. Most recently, from 1967 to 1974, Greece was ruled by a military dictatorship, which was a disaster in both domestic and foreign policy. It also led to increasing conflict and factionalization within the military itself. After almost going to war with Turkey over Cyprus in 1974, the officers returned politics to the civilians. The major figures in the military dictatorship eventually were imprisoned or retired from active duty. Some officers, and others associated with the military dictatorship, remain attracted to authoritarian solutions and support minor right-wing parties. Other officers, especially younger ones, find the ideology of PASOK attractive. The military is not likely to intervene again soon, not only because of bitter memories, but because the ideological cohesion of anticommunism is lost. The governments of the restored democracy, whether conservative or socialist, have insisted on principles of civilian control.

Religious Groups

The prevailing religion is Eastern Orthodox Christianity. The church organization, independent of other religious authorities, is administered by the Holy Synod of Bishops. However, the church is supervised and supported by the state through the Ministry of Education and Religion. This has meant that church officials have been heavily involved in politics, usually with one political group or another, rarely as a cohesive body. The Papandreou government seeks an administrative separation of church and state, a principle not opposed by the church hierarchy. However, the potential consequences of this separation—civil marriage, easier divorces, and legal abortions—have produced unusual conflict between religious leaders and the government.

National Prospects

Greece is part of the West, and despite recent campaign rhetoric, withdrawal from NATO or from the European Economic Community seems unlikely. The major foreign-policy problems involve Turkey: the occupation of northern Cyprus and claims to the Aegean Sea. The major domestic problem is economic: integration into the EEC has created some major dislocations, and the economy is especially vulnerable to international trends.

Greeks believe that the solutions to both problems are beyond their immediate control; other states must be induced to act on their behalf. Since the other members of both NATO and the EEC see the preservation of existing membership as a major concern, the Greeks can be expected to use the threat of withdrawal as leverage to gain support against the Turks on the one hand and for economic concessions on the other. This strategy can produce only limited gains, but actual withdrawal would produce none. Consequently, public expressions of disappointment and defiance are likely to obscure the fact that basic relationships remain intact.

The electorate voted for a change in 1981. Although the election of Papandreou and PASOK may indeed produce changes in policies and even governmental structures, the most enduring result will be the change in the parties and the party system. Papandreou combined organization, ideology, and personal appeal to create a modern political party, one that appealed to large numbers of citizens dissatisfied with traditional patron-client relationships. Any political group hoping to dislodge PASOK as the governing party must adopt similar structures and carve out some identifiable ideology or program. Change planned in the electoral laws, particularly the abolition of candidate preference votes, will strengthen the control of Papandreou over his own party, and will similarly strengthen the leadership of opposition parties. The victory of PASOK also rearranged the political spectrum. The extreme left is isolated, its potential support usurped. The old governing party, unable to adjust to new political realities, is likely to fissure, producing new alternatives on the center and right. The extreme right, now in disarray with neither the monarchy nor the military to provide support may find potential alliance partners. The result of these changes in parties and in the party system will be to make Greek politics more similar to the politics of other developed Western states.

Further Reading

Campbell, John, and Sherrard, Philip. *Modern Greece*. London: Ernest and Benn, 1968.

Clogg, Richard. *A Short History of Modern Greece*. Cambridge, England: Cambridge University Press, 1979.

Couloumbis, Theodore A.; Petropulos, John A.; and Psomiades, Harry. *Foreign Interference in Greek Politics: An Historical Perspective*. New York: Pella Publishing Company, 1976.

Koumoulides, John T. A., ed. *Greece in Transition: Essays in the History of Modern Greece, 1821 – 1914*. London: Zeno Publishers, 1977.

Legg, Keith R. *Politics in Modern Greece*. Stanford: Stanford University Press, 1969.

McNeill, William H. *The Metamorphosis of Greece Since World War II*. Chicago: University of Chicago Press, 1978.

Mouzelis, Nicos. *Modern Greece: Facets of Underdevelopment*. New York: Holmes and Meier, 1978.

Penniman, Howard R., ed. *Greece at the Polls: The National Elections of 1974 and 1977*. Washington, D.C.: American Enterprise Institute for Public Policy Research, 1981.

GRENADA

by Indira Jhappan

The System of Government

Grenada, a nation of about 108,000 people in the southern Caribbean, is a one-party socialist state which has retained its ties to the British Commonwealth. The population is predominantly black, with some indigenous Arawak and Carib Indians, as well as East Indians. The economy is heavily dependent on agriculture.

Executive & Legislature

Formal executive power is vested in the British monarch represented by a governor-general. In reality, since a nearly bloodless armed revolt in March 1979, both executive and legislative power has been vested in the seven-member cabinet and the sixteen-member Revolutionary Council. This People's Revolutionary Government (PRG) is led by Maurice Bishop, leader of the former opposition party, the New Jewel Movement (NJM). Fourteen members of the Council are NJM members and two belong to another former opposition party, the Grenada National Party (GNP). The fourteen members of the first PRG were primarily drawn from the business and professional class; nine additional members from the rural working class were brought into the government later.

Judiciary

The system of justice is based on English common law and is administered by the Grenada Supreme Court, composed of a High Court and a Court of Appeal. The chief justice presides over the Court of Magisterial Appeals. The three-judge Iterant Court of Appeal sits twice a year and is the final court of appeal. Magistrates preside over courts of summary jurisdiction. Since the revolution, the government has established the Preventative Detention Tribunal which deals with political detainees and prisoners.

Regional & Local Government

The Town of St. Georges and the Corporation of St. Georges in which the town is situated are administered by the central government. District commissioners appointed by the central government administer each of the six parishes.

The Electoral System

Although the NJM government has promised that elections will be held, it has made no move to fulfill this promise, claiming that elections at this time would be inappropriate to Grenada's revolutionary development. Under the old system, the fifteen-member House of Assembly was directly elected in single-member districts by all citizens eighteen years of age and older.

New Jewel Movement (NJM)

History

The NJM is a union of two parties: the Joint Endeavour for Welfare, Education, and Liberation (JEWEL) and the Movement for Assemblies of the People (MAP). The JEWEL was founded in 1972 by Unison Whiteman, an economist, and Selwyn Strachan, a sugar factory clerk. The MAP was founded in the latter part of 1972 by Maurice Bishop, a lawyer, and Kendrick Radix. The two parties combined in 1973.

The NJM drew its leadership and membership from the professional classes opposed to the style and tactics of the governing party, the Grenada United Labour Party (GULP), led by Edward Gairy and based on a trade union of rural agricultural laborers. From its beginnings in 1970, the Gairy government and party had been repressive. GULP organized a private militia which, in concert with the police, was turned loose on demonstrators and also used to break up opposition-party meetings and rallies. Bishop's father was killed in one of these encounters in 1974. Gairy's critics accused him of turning Grenada into a "little Haiti."

In 1976, the NJM joined the GNP, an urban, middle-class party, to contest the elections of that year as the People's Alliance. The Alliance won six of the fifteen seats in the former House of Assembly in spite of GULP's alleged manipulation of the elections. On March 13, 1979, armed NJM members took over the island's main radio station and captured the police stations. Gairy had left Grenada the previous day, whether on official business or because of advance knowledge of the coup is not clear.

Organization

The government established a national student council and a number of workers' councils on the agricultural estates. These, along with local and parish councils, were intended to provide a structure of community and national organizations to serve as a command and communication network for the PRG. These councils throughout the nation were consulted and shared in the formulation of the 1982 national budget. Mass rallies are often held to encourage involvement and to convey government policy and plans to the population. The PRG also organized a 1,000-man militia, the People's Revolutionary Army, led by NJM members.

The organization of the NJM itself is unclear. It is apparently a cadre party dominated by Bishop, but it probably has considerable intraparty dialogue and debate over policy. There are some indications that factions have developed in the party from time to time. In June 1980, there was an apparent assassination attempt against Bishop, which was immediately followed by the arrest of a former NJM leader.

Policy

Once in power, the PRG immediately suspended the constitution and anounced plans to create the People's Consultative Assembly to prepare another. By late 1982, such an assembly had still not been called.

Originally, the party had a pragmatic, nationalist platform which placed little emphasis on ideology or socialism in particular. It stressed the participation of all people in the government from the bottom up. The party has since moved farther to the left, while pursuing its original goal of mass participation through the establishment of workers' local councils. Although private enterprise continues without interruption, ties with socialist countries, including Cuba, have been strengthened; those with the United States and some of the more conservative neighboring states have become strained.

Membership & Constituency

No figures are available on party membership. The party draws heavily on the support of urban professionals, intellectuals, and students. The younger elements in the party tend to be the educated children of the middle class which once was the backbone of the Grenada National Party. Before the 1976 elections, the NJM had begun to recruit support in the countryside, and by the time it took over the government was able to neutralize the power of the GULP's agricultural union.

Financing

Nothing is known of party financing. It can be assumed that it has the full resources of the government behind it.

Leadership

Maurice Bishop (born 1944) is the dominant figure in the party and appears to be in full control of both it and the government.

Opposition

No information is available on any organized opposition operating in or outside Grenada. In the months after the coup, some thirty potential opposition leaders were arrested on charges of plotting countercoups. The opposition newspaper was closed down, leaving the country with only the NJM-operated newspaper.

National Prospects

Until the new government formulates a constitution and holds elections, Grenada will continue to move farther into isolation in the region. At the present time, the government is viewed as a socialist dictatorship and is shunned for its ties with Cuba and the Communist bloc. With falling prices for its commodities and very little domestic industry, it seems unlikely that the country can long afford to remain isolated without becoming even more reliant on the Soviet camp.

Further Reading

Gooding, Earl. *The West Indies at the Crossroads: The Search for a Viable Future.* Cambridge, Mass.: Schenkman, 1981.

Jackson, Maurice. "Grenada's Revolution—The First Two Years." *Political Affairs*, Vol. 60, No. 6, June 1981.

Manuel, Sam, and Pulley, Andrew. *Grenada: Revolution in the Caribbean.* New York: Pathfinder Press, 1981.

Wesson, Robert, ed. *Communism in Central America and the Caribbean.* Stanford, Calif.: Hoover Institution Press, 1982.

REPUBLIC OF GUATEMALA
(República de Guatemala)
by Anne Nelson

The System of Government

Guatemala, a nation of nearly 7.5 million people, is a military dictatorship under the rule of General Efraín Ríos Montt. The Ríos regime dates from March 1982 when a bloodless coup overthrew the previous military regime and placed the country in the hands of a junta of young officers. The coup served as a nullification of the March 7, 1982, elections, which the ruling Revolutionary Party's candidate, General Aníbal Guevara, won amid widespread charges of fraud. Ríos Montt moved quickly to consolidate his power, discharging the other members of the junta and suspending the 1965 constitution. Ríos has announced plans for a constituent assembly and eventual presidential elections on the Honduran/Salvadoran model, but no dates have been mentioned.

The Ríos regime is continuing its predecessors' full-fledged counterinsurgency war. The guerrillas have made considerable military and political inroads since the mid-1970s in the Indian highlands to the north, and the government is further weakened by jealousies and rivalries within the army and competing economic interest groups. Although Guatemala's conflict has received less international attention than El Salvador's civil war, it promises to be equally bloody and of greater strategic importance to the developed world.

Executive

As president, General Ríos Montt, enjoys absolute power within the remaining structure of the civilian government. Other cliques in the army and the private sector continue to play a strong role in influencing policy because of their importace within the balance of forces Ríos must rely on to govern the country. Ríos's church, an evangelical sect based in the United States, is acting as a political force in support of his government. Many administrative offices are now staffed by church members.

Legislature

Under the 1965 constitution, now suspended, the Guatemalan Congress was a unicameral body with a total of sixty-one seats that were to be increased to sixty-six with the 1982 elections. Deputies were elected by direct ballot for four-year terms in districts proportioned by population and were not allowed to succeed themselves in office. In the 1978 elections, the PID/PR (Institutional Democratic and Revolutionary parties) coalition held thirty-three seats. The rightist MLN (National Liberation Movement) held twenty-one, the CAN (Authentic Nationalist Center party) three, and the DCG (Christian Democrats) two. The results of the 1982 congressional elections were disputed. The Congress itself was dissolved and the election results nullified with the March *coup d'état*. The Ríos regime has stated that the Congress will be restructured by the future constituent assembly.

Judiciary

Under the 1965 constitution, the nine members of the Supreme Court were appointed by the Congress for four-year terms. In March 1982, Ríos Montt dissolved the standing court and appointed his own. The Supreme Court will reportedly be restructured by the constituent assembly. Some aspects of the previous judiciary system appear to be functioning on a local level in some parts of the country, though many regions are under de facto military rule.

Regional & Local Government

Guatemala has twenty-two departments, each headed by a governor traditionally appointed by the president, and the central district of Guatemala City. The departments are subdivided into a total of 327 municipalities (*munícipes*). Each of these has a mayor, usually elected by direct popular vote. Some of the mayoral candidates elected in the 1982 elections have taken office, while other mayors have been appointed by the president. Mayors generally serve for two-year terms, except in the country's largest cities, where they serve for four.

The Electoral System

Under the 1965 constitution, the president and vice president were elected by direct popular vote for four-year terms and could not succeed themselves. Suffrage was universal, secret, and compulsory for literate voters and optional for illiterates (Guatemalan literacy stands at about 40 percent). All Guatemalan citizens over the age of eighteen receive a *cédula*, or voter's identity card. Separate ballots were printed for presidential, congressional, and municipal contests.

The traditional voting procedure had the voter hand over his identification to the officials, mark his ballots in secret, fold them and place them in the ballot box. He then retrieved his identification, which had been stamped to show he voted; signed or marked a registry; and had one finger stained with indelible ink.

Voting turnout is impossible to determine due to electoral fraud. The final reported results for 1978 were 839,020 votes nationwide. In March 1982, there were 2,355,064 voters registered, but final tallies were nullified with the coup. Electoral fraud in 1982 included ballot-box stuffing, confiscation of *cédulas*, and coercion of voters.

The Party System

The fundamental elements of Guatemala's party system date from the 1954 coup, in which Col. Carlos Castillo Armas overthrew President Jacobo Arbenz with the aid of the U.S. Central Intelligence Agency. It was a watershed in Guatemalan political history, since it reestablished elements of the military as the prime political movers in the country, unsettled the electoral process, and drove the Guatemalan left and center-left underground and into exile.

Although Castillo Armas was assassinated in 1957, three years before the official founding of the MLN, he was regarded as the party's spiritual godfather. The MLN and the PR are the two oldest parties in the Guatemalan political system; the PR, however, has changed ideological colors frequently over the years, while the MLN has maintained a consistent right-wing party line.

A general restructuring of the party system appears to be possible if the Ríos Montt administration continues on its present course. High-ranking officials from both the MLN and the PR were placed under arrest after the coup; they were subsequently released, but regular party activity has come to a standstill.

The 1965 constitution set strict laws for party formation. Parties were required to have a membership of at least 50,000 to acquire legal standing. Besides the parties there are civic committees, which are allowed to nominate candidates for local offices in the municipalities and occasionally evolve into full-fledged parties, such as the CAN.

Guatemala's political parties have almost invariably been led by a few personalities or interest groups with little contact with the grass roots other than at election time. Interest groups have traditionally negotiated with the national parties for a voice in choosing candidates and writing platforms. In 1982, the campaigns ranged from the official rallies of the PR/PID, where thousands of peasants were induced to participate through threats and bribes, to tours by Christian Democratic coalition candidates in small trucks through Indian villages.

Authentic Nationalist Center (*Central Auténtica Nacionalista; CAN*)

The CAN was founded by General Carlos Arana Osorio in 1979. Arana, known as "the Jackal," was the MLN-backed president of Guatemala from 1970 to 1974, following his successful counterinsurgency campaigns against guerrillas in the eastern part of the country in the late 1960s. Arana founded the CAN after a falling-out with the MLN. The CAN is regarded as Arana's personal vehicle, but his prospects were seemingly limited by the prohibition against serving two presidential terms.

In the 1982 elections, the CAN ran Gustavo Anzüeto Vielman, who had served as minister of communications and public works in the Arana administration. The party's platform stressed a "Chicago School" monetarist response to Guatemala's economic ills, which won it widespread support among the country's business community. But Arana did not offer the expected economic support to the campaign, and the 'party foundered during the contest. It claims a membership of over 53,000.

Christian Democrats of Guatemala (*Democracia Cristiana Guatemalteca;* DCG)

The DCG was organized in the late 1950s but was not legally registered until 1968. It has close ties with the Christian Democratic parties of Venezuela, Italy, Germany, and El Salvador, and is considered center-left within the Guatemalan political spectrum. The party ran a strong campaign in 1974 with Ríos Montt as its candidate. Many observers considered Ríos the winner, but General Kjell Lagerud of the PR/MLN coalition took office instead amid widespread charges of fraud.

The DCG has been a target of repression on the part of Guatemala's death squads. More than 250 Christian Democratic leaders were assassinated under the administration of General Romeo Lucas García (1978–82).

In 1982, the Christian Democrats joined forces with the PNR to form the Opposition Union (*Union Opositora*), supporting PNR founder Alejandro Maldonado for president with Christian Democrat Roberto Carpio Nicolle as his running mate. The Opposition Union claimed victory after the March 7 elections, as did the MLN. The DCG appears to have benefited from the ascendence of Ríos Montt. It claims over 55,000 members and has won particular strength among the trade-union and peasant-cooperative movements.

Institutional Democratic Party (*Partido Institucional Democratico;* PID)

The PID was founded in 1965 and joined in an alliance with the MLN to back General Arana for president in 1970. In 1974, the alliance broke up, and the PID combined with the PR to back General Kjell Lagerud, with the blessing of General Arana. The same PID-PR grouping held together to back Lucas García in 1978. The 1974 results were disputed by Mario Sandoval and his wing of the MLN. The United National Front (*Frente de Unidad Nacional;* FUN) was founded in 1978, and served as a coalition organization to link the PID and the PR. One leading Guatemalan businessman described it as "not supported by a truly popular base or by the leadership of any person in particular. . . . It was an economic convenience."

The PID has little ideological substance; it serves primarily as a vehicle for the dominant military clique that ruled the country from 1970 to 1982. The party's director, Donaldo Alvarez Ruiz, served as minister of the interior under the Lucas administration. Alvarez had an unsavory reputation for human rights abuses and fell into particular disfavor with Ríos Montt. Although the PID claimed a membership of nearly 166,000 before the coup, many of these were public employees and their relatives responding to government pressure to support the party. The PID could fade as a political force by the next election.

National Liberation Movement (*Movimiento de Liberación National;* MLN)

The MLN was a legacy of the 1954 coup and traces its origins to Castillo Armas, the leader of that coup. It has been under the leadership of Mario "Mico" Sandoval since 1970. Sandoval was the party's presidential candidate in 1970, 1978, and 1982; he was widely believed to have won the 1970 and 1978 elections.

The MLN calls itself the "party of organized violence." It advocates the elimination of all communists in the country, presenting itself as an enemy of many trade-union, church, and intellectual elements. The party's principal spokesman is Leonel Cisniega Otero, Sandoval having lost his voice to cancer some years ago. It possesses the strongest popular base of the Guatemalan parties, with most of its support in the eastern and southern provinces. Party membership is placed at close to 120,000. The MNL enjoys close relations with the ARENA party of Roberto D'Aubuisson in El Salvador.

National Renovator Party (*Partido Nacional Renovador;* PRN)

The PRN was founded by former MLN cabinet member Alejandro Maldonado Aguirre in 1978 to advance his own presidential ambitions. The 1982 alliance with the Christian Democrats represented a shift to the left for Maldonado, who was hoping for U.S. backing for his candidacy. The PRN claims nearly 51,000 members. Unlike the

Christian Democrats, it has virtually no grass-roots support of its own and may disappear before the next election.

Revolutionary Party
(*Partido Revolucionario;* PR)

The PR was founded immediately after the downfall of director General Jorge Ubico in 1944. The PR was led by Dr. Juan José Arévalo, the first elected president under the 1945 constitution, but it nearly disappeared with the coup against Arévalo's successor, Jacobo Arbenz, in 1954. The PR made a comeback in 1966 under the leadership of Julio César Méndez Montenegro, who won what is commonly regarded as Guatemala's last non-fraudulent presidential election.

The PR was shaken by its defeat in the 1970 elections and underwent a considerable reorientation to the right. It displaced the MLN in the dominant military alliance for the elections of 1974, 1978, and 1982. The corruption and violence committed in those elections and the administrations which followed in 1974 and 1978 have greatly weakened the party's credibility. Before the 1982 elections the party claimed over 248,000 members, though many belonged as a result of government pressure.

United Revolutionary Front
(*Frente Unido de la Revolucion;* FUR)

The FUR was founded in 1979 by attorney Manuel Colom Argüeta, who was assassinated shortly afterwards. The party was considered to have social democratic tendencies, and its strongest base was among the intellectual and professional circles in the capital. The FUR did not offer a presidential candidate in 1982, but gave its support to Alejandro Maldonado of the PNR-DCG coalition. The FUR claims a membership of nearly 53,000. In the late 1970s, the FUR represented the center-left of Guatemala's political spectrum, along with the Social Democrats. The assassinations of Colom and Social Democrat Alberto Fuentes Mohr drove many members of the two parties into silence, exile, or the guerrilla movement.

Other Political Forces

Guerrillas

The modern Guatemalan guerrilla movement originated with an attempted coup by a group of young army officers in 1960. The coup was put down, but several of its leaders went into hiding among the Indians and peasants. The coup was more a squabble over power than an ideological dispute, but in its aftermath the young officers established contact with labor unions and political organizations. Among them was the Guatemalan Workers Party (*Partido Guatemalteco de los Trabajadores;* PGT), the communist party founded in 1949 and briefly legalized under the Arbenz administration. As the guerrilla movement took shape, it gradually replaced the PGT's Moscow-line reformist policies with new strategies inspired by the Cuban revolution. The Guatemalan insurgents built up their strength in the eastern part of the country, with the Armed Rebel Forces (*Fuerzas Armadas Rebeldes;* FAR) as the largest organization. The FAR still exists, operating on a more restricted basis, while the PGT functions primarily as an urban guerrilla organization.

In the late 1960s, the government began a series of counterinsurgency campaigns led by Carlos Arana Osorio and Mario Sandoval with assistance from the United States. By 1968 the guerrillas were all but wiped out, and Arana and Sandoval took advantage of their victory to establish political bases, private armies, and vigilante squads to assure both legal and extralegal power. Most of the survivors of the guerrilla movement left the country, but a small band returned to the northern highlands to begin long-term recruitment of the indigenous Indian communities.

The movement emerged again in the mid-1970s with new characteristics. The largest organizations, the Guerrilla Army of the Poor (*Ejercito Guerrillero de los Pobres;* EGP) and the Revolutionary Organization of the People in Arms (*Organización Revolucionaria del Pueblo en Armas;* ORPA), developed strong political and logistical bases in the highland provinces of the Quiche, Huehuetenango, Alta Verapaz, and the Peten. For the first time, the Indian population (about 45 percent of Guatemalans) were an active and integrated part of the movement and apparently were influencing strategy and policy by their cultural emphasis on cooperation rather than competition among the guerrilla groups. The new guerrilla forces relied primarily on the local populations for support. Although Marxist rhetoric predominated in guerrilla pronouncements, ties with Moscow were actively opposed by some social democratic guerrilla leaders.

Combined armed and trained guerrilla forces in Guatemala are estimated at 4,000 to 6,000, compared to the government's army of 17,000. Although the movement has been limited by a chronic shortage of arms, it has played a profoundly destabilizing role in the country. Government attacks in guerrilla-occupied territory have led to military stalemate more often than to the "clean sweeps" which characterized the campaigns of the 1960s. Massive civilian casualties among the indigenous populations have alienated them from the government and resulted in international ostracism for Guatemala on human rights grounds. The guerrilla groups have been criticized for economic sabotage and for targeting government installations and members of government security forces in armed attacks. Right-wing vigilante groups, such as the Secret Anti-Communist Army (*Ejercito Secreto Anti-Communista;* ESA) and the Death Squad (*Esquadron de la Muerte*) have been blamed for many noncombatant deaths. In 1981, the estimate for politically motivated deaths ran between 250 and 300 a month.

Roman Catholic Church

The Roman Catholic Church as an institution is not a major political actor in Guatemala. Compared to the El Salvadoran and Nicaraguan churches, it has remained relatively silent. A few priests, mostly of foreign origin, have tried to organize and support peasant movements for self-help or openly supported the guerrillas, but most of them have been exiled or killed by right-wing death squads.

National Prospects

The possibilities for Ríos Montt to achieve his stated objectives—namely, wiping out the insurgents and establishing a constitutional government—appear extremely slim. Internal opposition runs high and includes the MLN, which counts on its own support within the armed forces and the many competing cliques within the army that could attempt further coups out of simple personal ambition and self-aggrandizement. The guerrillas have very little likelihood of winning a short-term military victory, but neither does the government have much chance of eliminating them. The Guatemalan business community has given the government a vote of no-confidence in the form of massive capital flight. United States economic and military aid has been withheld on human rights grounds, but pressure to restore the aid will mount as the Guatemalan regime weakens under the growing military, political, and economic strain.

Further Reading
Adams, Richard N. *Crucifixion by Power.* Austin, Texas: University of Texas Press, 1970.
Dombrowski, John, et al. *Area Handbook for Guatemala.* Washington, D.C.: U.S. Government Printing Office, for Foreign Area Studies, American University, 1975.
Fried, Johnathan, et al., eds. *Guatemala.* New York: Grove Press, 1983.
Friedman, Jessie A. *Labor Law and Practice in Guatemala.* Washington, D.C.: U.S. Government Printing Office, 1963.
Kinzer, Stephen, and Schlesinger, Stephen. *Bitter Fruit.* New York: Doubleday, 1982.
Manger-Cats, Sebald Godried. *Land Tenure and Economic Development in Guatemala.* Ithaca, N. Y.: Cornell University Press, 1966.
Nash, Manning. *Machine Age Maya: The Industrialization of a Guatemalan Community.* Chicago: University of Chicago Press, 1967.
North American Congress on Latin America, Guatemala. New York: NACLA, 1974.

PEOPLE'S REVOLUTIONARY REPUBLIC OF GUINEA
(République Populaire et Révolutionnaire de Guinée)
by Steven Metz, M.A.

The System of Government

Guinea, a nation of five and a half million people, is a republic with a highly centralized, one-party presidential regime. Although the constitution of Guinea, which was promulgated in 1958, is the second oldest in Africa, it has been largely superseded by the growth of the political strength of the party apparatus. Parallel party and government structures perform similar functions, but in most cases the party holds the real power.

Executive

Sékou Touré has been president of Guinea since independence in 1958. Under his leadership, the presidency has gained wide-ranging executive and legislative powers. The president is head of state and commander-in-chief of the armed forces; the prime minister, appointed by the president, is head of government.

The president initiates legislation; appoints all government officials, including the cabinet; instigates constitutional amendments; and frequently circumvents the formal legislative process by executive decrees, which carry the power of law.

The president is chosen by direct popular election for a seven-year term; there is only one candidate in the presidential election. The constitution was changed in 1974 to allow for an unlimited number of reelections for a president, thus allowing Sékou Touré to be reelected for a third term in January 1975.

Legislature

According to the constitution, the National Assembly is a legislative body with far-ranging powers. In practice, however, most political decisions are made by the president or by the policy-making organs of the party. Membership in the National Assembly is primarily an honorary position given for loyalty to the party.

The Assembly was enlarged to 210 members in 1980. Deputies to the Assembly are selected from the country at large rather than representing a particular constituency. According to the constitution, the party winning a simple majority of votes in the nation as a whole wins all seats in the National Assembly, but in practice this rule is irrelevant since, for each seat, only one candidate, chosen by the leadership of the party, appears on the ballot. The most recent election (1980) selected the National Assembly for a five-year term.

Judiciary

The constitution did not establish a particular structure for the national judiciary, but only stipulated that the president is to be the guarantor of judicial independence. Since all judges are appointed by the president, the primary judicial policy has been the implementation of party dictates.

Regional & Local Government

Guinea is divided into thirty-two regions, each governed by an officer appointed by the president. Parallel party and government structures exist at all levels, and several thousand Party-State Local Revolutionary Powers, under the direction of the party leadership, exercise control over local affairs.

The Electoral System

Elections in Guinea are direct: suffrage is universal for citizens eighteen years of age and over, and voter turnout averages over 99 percent of eligible voters. Elections are primarily a method of illustrating the legitimacy of the leadership and policies of the party elite.

Democratic Party of Guinea (*Parti Démocratique de Guinée; PDG*)

History

The PDG was founded by Sékou Touré in 1947, eleven years before independence, as a way of organizing the widespread discontent with French colonial administration. Much of the original strength of the PDG originated in the support of the communist-influenced trade unions. The PDG organized on a national, mass basis, and quickly dominated more ethnically based parties—the Guinean African Bloc (BAG) and the African Socialist Movement (MSA). These parties were later absorbed by the PDG.

Organization

In its current form the PDG is highly hierarchical and is based on the theory of democratic centralism. This type of organization allows for some degree of popular participation at the local level, but reserves matters of national policy for the party leadership. According to the leaders of the PDG, democratic centralism allows the party to represent the nation as a whole and prevents fragmentation along ethnic or tribal lines.

The primary decision-making organs of the PDG are the fifteen-member Political Bureau, national congresses which meet on an irregular basis, and the National Council of the Revolution. Sékou Touré controls the party through his positions as secretary general of the PDG and chairman of the Political Bureau. All other top party officials retain their positions on the basis of personal loyalty to Touré. Touré has stifled the discontent which was evident in the upper levels of the PDG during the 1960s, consolidating his control over nearly all aspects of party policy.

Policy

The focus of PDG policy is chiefly on the development of "African socialism" and the economic development of the country. Assimilation of the various ethnic groups into a single Guinean nation is also an important aim of the party.

Membership & Constituency

At a national congress of the PDG, it was agreed to turn the party into a cadre-type party with limited membership. Dedication to the radical transformation of Guinea into a socialist state became a prerequisite for membership. However, this change was short-lived and the previous system, which equated membership in the party and citizenship, was reinstated. Thus everyone who is an eligible elector is considered a member of the party. Only a limited number actually participates in party activities, and the number involved in making party policy is extremely small.

Financing

No data is available on party financing.

Leadership

Sékou Touré was born in 1922, the son of a Muslim peasant farmer. His career as a union organizer began at age fifteen, when he was expelled from technical college for leading a strike. He quickly became active in politics, and after he was elected secretary general of the PDG in 1952, led Guinea to independence. He was the only African leader to shun the Francophone union in West and Central Africa. He has been head of state since Guinea's independence.

Lansan Béavogui is prime minister. Although certified as a medical doctor, he has shown more of an interest in politics than in medicine. He was born in 1923, took his medical training in Dakar, and began his political career as a town councilor. He has held a variety of economic posts and has served as foreign minister.

Opposition

The repressive and highly ideological policies of Sékou Touré have driven large numbers of the most highly educated and talented Guineans into exile in neighboring states and in France. Some estimates place the total number of exiles at over one-third of the total population of Guinea.

Exile groups provide the only real opposition to Touré's regime. Many plots have been fomented by expatriate groups, with the most serious one involving an invasion of Guinea by Guinean expatriates and Portuguese soldiers in 1970. There is, however, no common ideology or organization uniting the expatriates.

National Prospects

Under pressure from the expatriate groups and from young Guineans dissatisfied with the slow rate of economic development in the country, Sékou Touré instigated a program in the late 1970s aimed at encouraging economic growth and rapprochment with France and with Guinea's West African neighbors. Based on the success of these efforts, there appears to be little chance that the Guinean political system will be seriously challenged so long as Touré remains healthy.

Further Reading

Nelson, Harold D., et al. *Area Handbook for Guinea*. Washington, D.C.: U.S. Government Printing Office for Foreign Area Studies, American University, 1976.

Rivière, Claude. *Guinea: The Mobilization of a People*, Virginia Thompson and Richard Adloff, trans. Ithaca and London: Cornell University Press, 1977.

REPUBLIC OF GUINEA-BISSAU
(*República da Guiné-Bissau*)
by Tony Hodges

The System of Government

The West African nation of Guinea-Bissau, with a population of about 800,000, has been a one-party republic, under the rule of the *Partido Africano da Independência da Guiné e Cabo Verde* (PAIGC), since its independence from Portugal in 1974. However, since a coup in 1980, the armed forces have exercised the decisive political influence in the party and the government.

Executive

The authors of the November 1980 coup established a Council of the Revolution (*Conselho da Revolução*), which has nine members, headed by a president (the head of state), with a vice-president and four advisers. Under a transitional constitutional law, published in March 1981, the president of the Council is also commander-in-chief of the armed forces. Significantly, all the Council members are black (although one of its advisers is of Cape Verdian origin), whereas the deposed president, Luiz Cabral, is of Cape Verdian descent, and Cape Verdians and mixed race *mestiços* were prominent in his regime. It is also noteworthy that six of the Council's nine members are military men and the president, João Bernardo Vieira, has had a long military career.

The provisional government is subordinate to the Council of the Revolution. It had twenty-two members in mid-1982. The prime ministry was held by the vice-president of the Council, Vítor Saude Maria. Besides ministers, vice-ministers, and secretaries of state, the governor of the national bank and the attorney general were also in the cabinet.

Legislature

The country's legislature, the People's National Assembly (*Assembleia Nacional Popular*), was dissolved at the time of the coup. Until the election of a new legislature (promised for 1982), full legislative powers are held by the Council of the Revolution under the transitional constitutional law.

Judiciary

No information is available on the country's present judicial system.

Regional & Local Government

The country is divided into eight regions and one autonomous section (the capital, Bissau), each of which is administered by a state committee and an elected council.

The Electoral System

There have been no elections since the November 1980 coup, although the new regime promised to hold elections in 1982 following the adoption of a new constitution. Under the precoup constitution, the regional councils were elected by direct suffrage, although the electorate's choice was limited to the approval or rejection of the slate of candidates presented by the party. In the only postindependence elections for the councils, held in December 1976, overall about 80 percent of voters approved the PAIGC slates though there were significant regional variations. Support for the PAIGC was lowest in the Fula regions of the northeast. The National Assembly's 150 members were selected by the regional councils.

The PAIGC is the sole legal party. However, the armed forces and the various ethnic groups have varying degrees of influence over the PAIGC and the government.

African Party for the Independence of Guinea and Cape Verde (*Partido Africano da Independência da Guiné e Cabo Verde;* PAIGC)

History

The PAIGC was founded in 1956 to lead a struggle for independence in both Guinea-Bissau and the Cape Verde Islands. In 1963, it began a guerrilla war against Portugal in Guinea-Bissau and by 1973 controlled about three-quarters of the country. Portugal retained control of the country's few towns and the northeastern savannah belt inhabited by the Islamic Fula. In 1973, the PAIGC proclaimed the Republic of Guinea-Bissau, and, a year later, in September 1974, Portugal recognized the republic and withdrew its troops.

The new PAIGC government, under President Luiz Cabral, was beset with problems. Agricultural production had fallen drastically during the war, partly because a sixth of the population had fled as refugees to neighboring territories. There was, and still is, no mining industry and almost no manufacturing. The country has to import all its oil and much of its food, including rice, Guinean's staple food. The only exports are groundnuts, fish, and palm kernels; together these pay for less than 30 percent of the import bill. The foreign debt has grown dangerously large, and there have been prolonged shortages of basic consumer goods, including rice. The shortages did much to undermine popular confidence in Luiz Cabral's regime, as did the corruption in the state administration and especially the state-run people's shops. There was resentment at the apparent privileges of the *mestiços* and Cape Verdians, who were prominent in the urban petty bourgeoisie and the regime; and there was dismay at President Cabral's personal concentration of power and the repression of dissidents, which included numerous executions.

Discontent was particularly strong among the largest ethnic group, the Balante. They had borne the brunt of the independence war and were therefore preponderant in the armed forces, but enjoyed little influence in the upper reaches of the Cabral regime, feared attempts to demobilize parts of the war-bloated army, and were disillusioned by the economic decline, shortages, and increased taxes.

The November 1980 coup, led by Prime Minister João Bernardo Vieira and supported by the army, was almost bloodless and enjoyed overwhelming popular support. Luiz Cabral was de-tained, but was allowed to go into exile in December 1981. The coup was condemned by the Cape Verdian wing of the party, which then changed its name to the *Partido Africano da Independência de Cabo Verde* (PAICV; African Party for the Independence of Cape Verde). The authors of the Guinean coup decided to retain the PAIGC organization—and the reference to Cape Verde in its name—and accused Cabral of betraying its revolutionary principles. The Council of the Revolution restructured the PAIGC as a purely Guinean party, and Council members assumed direct control of the revamped party leadership bodies.

Organization

The PAIGC's highest decision-making body, the congress, meets only about once every four years. It elects the Central Committee, but the party's most powerful body is the smaller Political Bureau, which has twelve full and four alternate members. Among these twelve full members are eight of the nine members of the Council of the Revolution; five of them are military men. The Central Committee of some sixty members is headed by the secretary general, who is elected by the congress. President João Bernardo Vieira was elected party secretary general at the first post-coup congress, held in November 1981.

The party has a pyramidal structure. Policies and guidelines are passed downwards through successive tiers of party committees at region, sector, and local (village, neighborhood, and workplace) levels. The party is flanked by three "mass organizations"—the National Union of Workers of Guinea (*União Nacional dos Trabalhadores da Guiné;* UNTG), the Amilcar Cabral African Youth (*Juventude Africana Amilcar Cabral;* JAAC), and the Women's Commission (*Comissão Feminina*).

Policy

At its third congress, in 1977, the PAIGC asserted that there is not "a proletariat in the sense of a class conscious of its interests prepared to assume its historical responsibilities." It therefore urged the "mobilization of all social forces" and stated that the "PAIGC practices a policy of national unity." The party's aim is to construct "national revolutionary democracy."

As a result, only selected foreign business interests have been nationalized. The PAIGC government, both before and after the coup, has remained committed to nonalignment, pragmatically seeking aid from as many sources as possible. In practice, most aid, including food aid, has come from Western countries. Most trade is still with the West, though military aid comes primarily from the Soviet bloc and Cuba. Guinea-Bissau has signed the Lomé Convention, which is an ecomonic and trade agreement with the European Common Market, and retains friendly relations with Portugal. It also has established close relations with neighboring Senegal and Guinea-Conakry, despite friction over disputed maritime borders. Since the November 1980 coup, the PAIGC regime has abandoned the party's old goal of unification of Guinea-Bissau and Cape Verde. It has also tried to tackle the economic crisis by scrapping some of the previous regime's prestige projects, curbing corruption, improving transport systems, and channelling more resources into agriculture.

Membership & Constituency

The PAIGC is numerically small. It is a cadre-type party, with relatively strict membership criteria.

Financing

No data on party finances are available, but the government is presumed to be the main source of party funds.

Leadership

João Bernardo Vieira (born 1939) is secretary general of the PAIGC. He is from the Pepel, one of the smaller tribes. He joined the PAIGC in 1960 and received military training in China shortly afterwards. In 1964 he was given command of the main guerrilla zone, the Balante-populated southeast. He was appointed minister of the armed forces in 1975 and principal commissioner (prime minister) in 1978.

Other Political Forces

The Front for the Liberation and National Independence of Guinea (*Frente da Libertação e da Independência Nacional da Guiné*; FLING) has opposed the PAIGC since the days of the independence war, but it has never become a significant political force. After independence, FLING and another anti-PAIGC grouplet, the Patriotic Anti-Neocolonial Union of Guinea (*União Patriótica Anti-Neocolonial da Guiné*; UPANG), recruited support from among former black soldiers of the Portuguese army and former associates of the colonial regime. But they enjoyed very little popular support, especially from the peasant population which had sustained the war for independence. They were prevented from establishing an external base when Senegal signed a security pact with the PAIGC government in 1975. The most prominent personality associated with this current is Rafael Barbosa, a former leader of the PAIGC who sided with Portugal in 1969 and has been detained by the PAIGC since 1974. Some FLING veterans have thrown in their lot with the postcoup regime.

A Front for National Unity and Growth (*Frente da Unidade Nacional e do Desenvolvimento*; FUND) was founded in November 1981 in Portugal and appears to include former officials who lost power as a result of the 1980 coup.

Ethnic Groups

The Cape Verdians and *mestiços* have only partially lost influence. As a strong component of the intelligentsia and technocracy, they remain important in the provisional government, ministries, and quasigovernment institutions. The Balante, who constitute about 40 percent of the population, grow most of the country's rice, and account for perhaps 70 percent of the army's troops, were the strongest supporters of the coup. The Muslims (30 percent of the population) and in particular the Fula of Bafatá and Gabú regions, who played no part in the PAIGC's independence war, would appear to have less influence in this largely military-based regime.

National Prospects

The country's very serious economic crisis is unlikely to be resolved in the foreseeable future. Shortages of food and other consumer commodities are likley to continue, fueling discontent. Moreover, in such conditions, army factions may well be tempted to try their luck again after the successful experience of the 1980 coup.

Further Reading
Aaby, Peter. *The State of Guinea-Bissau, African Socialism or Socialism in Africa?* Uppsala, Sweden: Scandinavian Institute of African Studies, 1978.

Andreini, J.-C., and Lambert, M. L. *La Guinée-Bissau, d'Amilcar Cabral à la Reconstruction Nationale.* Paris: Editions L'Harmattan, 1978.

"Guinea-Bissau: The Black Coup that Ended Amilcar Cabra's Dream." In *Africa Contemporary Record.* Colin Legum, ed. Vol. 13, 1980–81. New York: Holmes and Meier, 1981.

Hodges, Tony. "Guinea-Bissau, Five Years of Independence." *Africa Report,* January–February 1979.

COOPERATIVE REPUBLIC OF GUYANA

by Robert H. Manley, Ph.D.

The System of Government

Guyana, a country of nearly 850,000 people on the northeast coast of South America, is a multi-party democracy, but its political life is dominated by one party, the People's National Congress, and its founder-leader, Forbes Burnham. The population of Guyana contains several ethnic groups. At the time of independence in 1966, East Indians were estimated to comprise 50.7 percent of the population, Africans 30.8 percent, mixed 12.1 percent, Amerindians 4.7 percent, Portuguese 0.9 percent, Chinese 0.6 percent, and non-Portuguese Europeans 0.2 percent. Bloody ethnic clashes growing out of political strife were common in the late 1960s, but dropped off thereafter.

The current constitution went into effect October 6, 1980, replacing the document under which the nation became independent from Great Britain in May 1966. Transition to Cooperative Republic status was accomplished in 1970, with the enactment of amendments to the independence constitution which ended a symbolic role for the British monarch. The adjective "cooperative" was used to signify the path chosen then for achievement of a socialist system.

Executive

Under the 1980 constitution, a ceremonial presidency was replaced with a powerful office under the same name which combined responsibilities as head of state, chief executive, and commander-in-chief of the armed forces. The new post is sometimes referred to as executive president. The position was tailor-made for Forbes Burnham, who moved to it from the prime ministership, which position was continued, but made subsidiary to the presidency, as were other cabinet positions, including a number of vice presidencies. Appointments to cabinet positions, including prime minister and vice presidents, are made by the president. The presidency is now an elective rather than an appointive office.

Legislature

The constitution vests legislative power (subject to presidential veto) in a National Assembly of sixty-five elected members. Persons appointed to the cabinet who have not been elected to the Assembly may serve in the Assembly, but may not vote. The Assembly has a maximum five-year term.

Judiciary

The constitution provides for a Supreme Court of Judicature, consisting of the Court of Appeal and the High Court, Judges of the Court of Appeal are the chancellor (who serves as its president), the chief justice, and additional justices as prescribed by the Assembly. Judges of the High Court are the chief justice and additional *puisne* judges as prescribed by the Assembly. The chancellor, chief justice, and other judges are appointed by the president. The legal system is largely based on English common law. Critics from many quarters, both within and outside Guyana, have alleged that the courts have not been free from substantial influence by the dominant party.

Regional & Local Government

The new constitution provides that the nation may be divided into ten regions which can be further divided into smaller units. A regional democratic council will be elected by each region's residents, as will local democratic organs. The National Congress of Local Democratic Organs, elected by and from the local bodies, will be responsible for representing the interests of local governments.

The Electoral System

Fifty-three of the sixty-five elected members of the National Assembly are chosen in an election in which the nation as a whole is one district. Each political party contesting the election presents a list of candidates, and voters cast ballots only for a party list. Seats are allotted to the parties according to the proportion of votes cast for each list. Each party designates one person on the party list as its presidential candidate. Ten of the twelve remaining seats in the Assembly are filled in elections by and from the ten regional democratic councils. The remaining two are elected from the National Congress of Local Democratic Organs.

Subject to certain minor disqualifications, all persons may vote who are eighteen years of age or older and either citizens of Guyana or Commonwealth citizens domiciled or resident in Guyana for one year. Election of members of the National Assembly is by secret ballot, but many observers have criticized the electoral process as largely rigged and fraudulent.

In the most recent National Assembly elections (December 1980), the reported count resulted in the People's National Congress (PNC) taking forty-one of the fifty-three seats allocated in the national vote; the People's Progressive Party (PPP), ten; and the United Force (UF), two. The Working People's Alliance (WPA) refused to participate in the election, its position being that the outcome would undoubtedly be fraudulently determined by the ruling PNC. An international observer team headed by Lord Avebury, chairman of the United Kingdom Parliamentary Human Rights group, concluded that "the election was rigged massively and flagrantly." The group's report summarized reported fraud favoring the PNC in the two previous national elections in 1968 and 1973. It also pointed to aspects undercutting the credibility of the 1978 referendum held at PNC initiative to sanction a postponement of national elections and the drafting of a new constitution, noting that the referendum was opposed by all parties other than the PNC as well as by churches and civil organizations, which called for a boycott.

The Party System

Origins of the Parties

The first major political party of modern times was the Progressive People's Party, founded in 1950. With broad popular support, it pushed for Guyanese independence from Great Britain, under the combined leadership of Forbes Burnham

and Cheddi Jagan. In the mid-1950s, the party split along ethnic and ideological lines. Burnham formed the PNC with substantial support from African voters in 1957. Shortly thereafter, in 1960, the UF was formed with support from Guyanese of Portuguese and mixed descent. A movement of protest against corruption and electoral fraud and for a more effective social democratic system developed in the mid-1970s and became the formal WPA party in 1979.

The Parties in Law

The right to form political parties and their freedom of action are guaranteed by the constitution. The only stated limitation is that parties "must respect the principles of national sovereignty and democracy." Nevertheless, there are a variety of restraints placed on party activity, including government control of newsprint, which limits publication of opposition newspapers. The opposition parties and their leaders have also been subjected to various forms of harassment.

Party Organization

The PPP and PNC aim at being formal membership parties with institutionalized party structures. The PNC is apparently tightly controlled from the top, and the political leadership of the government provides the party's primary organizational scaffolding. The PPP has declared itself to be a Marxist-Leninist party, but it is unclear to what degree it has adopted a thorough-going democratic centralist organization. Both parties have been dominated by their respective leaders. There is no reliable information on the size of party memberships or on their finances.

People's National Congress (PNC)

The PNC was unable to best the PPP in the first two elections in which the two groups were pitted against one another, in 1957 and 1961. However, in 1964, the first race under a proportional representation system, its vote, when coupled with that of the United Force, surpassed that of the PPP. Accordingly, a PNC-UF coalition government was created, with Forbes Burnham as premier and the then UF leader, Peter d'Aguiar, as finance minister. The coalition ended in 1968 when the reported count in first postindependence elections gave the PNC a majority of National Assembly seats.

Following the end of the coalition with the more conservative United Force, the PNC pushed for measures to bring about a transition to socialism, beginning with the change to Cooperative Republic status in 1970 and followed in succeeding years by nationalization of all bauxite and of major sugar-producing operations. At the same time, the PNC more and more attempted to present itself and the government as synonymous, raising speculation that a one-party system was its eventual goal.

Linden Forbes Sampson Burnham (born 1923) is undisputed leader of the party. He is of African descent as are most other major party figures. Other contemporary leaders of the PNC include: Ptolemy Reid, formerly a veterinarian, a longtime party figure who since the advent of the executive presidency has served as prime minister; Hamilton Green, a hard-working party activist and a cabinet minister (now also a vice president) sometimes referred to as Burnham's most likely successor; and Desmond Hoyt, a barrister and cabinet member, also a vice president in the PNC government. Green and Hoyt both have the advantage of relative youth over Reid in respect to potential succession to party and perhaps national leadership.

People's Progressive Party (PPP)

At the time of its founding in 1950, the PPP had a broad base of support among both the East Indian and the African population, the two dominant ethnic groups, in its struggle against British rule in particular and imperialism in general. However, as Guyanese politics polarized ideologically and ethnically from the mid-1950s onward, the PPP became more and more dependent upon East Indian support and, through the years, more and more closely committed to a Marxist-Leninist approach, until in 1969 it made this its official position.

Both Cheddi Jagan (born 1918), the PPP leader, and his U.S.-born wife Janet have been in the party throughout its life. Mrs. Jagan has edited its daily newspaper, the *Mirror*, and undertaken key organizational tasks during its history. Internationally, the party has maintained warm relationships with the Soviet Union and Cuba. In mid-1975 the PPP undertook a position of "critical support" for the PNC-led government in its asserted goal of achieving socialism and undercutting imperialism. However, it has continued outspoken criticism of many aspects of government policy and implementation.

United Force (UF)

The UF was initially dependent to a considerable degree on support from Portuguese and ethnically mixed Guyanese and has been notably more conservative ideologically than either the PPP or PNC. Since Peter d'Aguiar's retirement from active politics in 1969, the United Force has been under the leadership of Fielden Singh, a barrister. The party's prospects seem limited to maintaining its very modest minority position.

Working People's Alliance (WPA)

The WPA is an ethnically diverse amalgam of opposition forces who are intensely dissatisfied with the incompetence, corruption, and party and ethnic favoritism of the PNC government. Its position is one of eclectic but dedicated socialism. Although it is only a few years old, the WPA is widely respected and was increasingly viewed as the force which might end the PNC's dominance. However, in June 1980, its most prominent leader, Walter Rodney, was killed by an explosive device, a death thought by many to have been instigated by the PNC. The party continues to have creditable leadership in Eusi Kwayana, a widely known political figure, who worked with Jagan and Burnham in the early days of the PPP.

Other Political Forces

Guyana Council of Churches

The Council of Churches has become increasingly important as a focal point for concern about the state of human rights and constitutional legitimacy during a period of evaporating support for the PNC-Burnham government. It has worked with a variety of civic groups to develop better understanding of the political-economic-social system and of alternatives for the future.

Organized Labor

While some union leadership has been relatively quiescent, leaders and rank and file in a number of unions, notably (but not limited to) those of sugar and bauxite workers, have shown vigor in carrying their demands and complaints to the government and the public.

Catholic Standard

A respected weekly newspaper, the *Standard,* has presented an ongoing, trenchant critique of the Burnham-PNC leadership in face of ongoing attempts to weaken or silence its voice.

House of Israel

This religious sect, led by "Rabbi" Washington, who left the Cleveland, Ohio, area after being charged with blackmail (he was then known as David Hill), apparently provides important "muscle" in the streets in support of the PNC government. A member of the House of Israel has been accused of killing Father Bernard Darke, a news photographer for the *Catholic Standard,* as he was covering a July 1979 Georgetown demonstration.

Guyana Defense Force (GDF)

Strengthened through the years, partly on the basis of threats posed by Venezuelan and Surinamese claims to Guyanese territory, the GDF has, along with the Guyana police forces, been a key element of PNC internal control. Financing of its operations, along with those of the police, has been a major drain on the nation's resources.

National Prospects

Incompetence and corruption, along with adverse trends in the international economic system, brought Guyana to virtual bankruptcy in 1982. The PNC government and the political system the PNC has created appears to be exhausted, at least in terms of popular support and legitimacy. Demands for Burnham's resignation and for creation of a broad coalition to form a new government and revitalize politics are heard with increasing frequency. However, PNC rule is now based on the use of repressive military and police force; with these methods, the PNC can maintain its control of government for a considerable period in spite of popular disaffection. It is impossible to foresee what circumstances or forces might bring about a change in government in the near future.

Further Reading

Constitution of the Cooperative Republic of Guyana Act 1980. Georgetown, Guyana: Ministry of Information, 1980.

Daly, Vere T. *A Short History of the Guyanese People.* London: Macmillan Education Ltd., 1975.

Despres, Leo. *Cultural Pluralism and Nationalist Politics in British Guiana.* Chicago: Rand McNally and Co., 1967.

Glasgow, Roy. *Guyana: Race and Politics Among Africans and East Indians.* The Hague: Martinus Nijhoff, 1970.

Greene, J. E. *Race vs. Politics in Guyana.* Kingston, Jamaica: Institute of Social and Economic Research, University of the West Indies, 1974.

Lutchman, Harold A. *From Colonialism to Cooperative Republic: Aspects of Political Development in Guyana.* Rio Piedras, Puerto Rico: Institute of Caribbean Studies, University of Puerto Rico, 1974.

Manley, Robert H. *Guyana Emergent: The Post-Independence Struggle for Nondependent Development.* Rev. ed. Cambridge, Mass.: Schenkman Publishing Co., 1982.

REPUBLIC OF HAITI
(République d'Haiti)
by Michel S. Laguerre, Ph.D.

The System of Government

Haiti, a country with a population of approximately 5.5 million in 1982, occupying one third of a two-nation Caribbean island, is a one-party republic and a unitary state with an autocratic presidential government. Jean Claude Duvalier inherited the office of president-for-life from his father, the late Dr. François "Papa Doc" Duvalier who was first elected in 1957 for a six-year presidential term. His reelection to a second term was announced in 1961, although elections were not due until 1963 and there was no campaign. With an amendment of the constitution of 1950 and through a manipulation of the electoral vote, he became president-for-life in 1964. Before he died in 1971, he again amended the constitution so that he could choose his own successor, his nineteen-year-old son.

Executive

The president of the republic is head of state and government. According to the constitution, any Haitian man or woman at least eighteen years old who resides in Haiti, who has never renounced his or her Haitian nationality, and who enjoys civil and political rights is eligible to become president of the republic.

The powers of the president are multiple. Responsible for preserving the internal and external security of the state, he commands the army and police. He appoints and dismisses secretaries and undersecretaries of state, all other government officials and employees, and bishops of the Roman Catholic Church. He has the legal right to dissolve the legislature when he judges it necessary. This may happen especially when there is a serious conflict between the legislative branch and the executive branch.

According to the constitution, there are some limitations to the powers of the president. He must submit all international treaties and executive orders to the National Assembly for approval. In addition, all presidential acts—except those appointing or dismissing secretaries of state—must be countersigned by the secretary of state concerned. Since the president appoints all government officers and most legislators, these restrictions on his powers are mere formalities.

Legislature

A unicameral National Assembly of fifty-eight deputies was established in 1961. Any Haitian at least eighteen years old who has never changed his nationality and who has lived for at least five years in the area that he wants to represent can be elected to the legislature. However, contractors, concessionnaires of the state in the operation of public services, and their representatives and agents are not eligible for membership in the legislature. Each member of the legislature is elected for a six-year term and can be reelected indefinitely. In fact, there have been no general elections since "Papa Doc" Duvalier became president for life; most legislators are appointed. In 1979, under pressure from the U.S. government, elections to Assembly seats were held in a few major towns. Only approved candidates ran and there was no real campaign.

The legislature meets once a year. Each session begins the second Monday of April and usually lasts three months. However, a session may be extended by the legislative branch or by a request from the executive branch. The extension can be for no more than two months.

The main role of the legislature is to enact laws for the common good and the welfare of the state. Most legislation is introduced by the deputies, often at the behest of the president. Each law or bill must be voted upon and adopted by a majority of members present before it can be sent to the executive branch for promulgation. The president reserves the right to veto any law submitted to his office. The legislature has the legal right to impose disciplinary penalties or even expel members who have not lived up to their constitutional duties.

Judiciary

The judicial branch of government is composed of three different courts: the Court of Cassation, courts of appeals, and lower courts. The Court of Cassation, comprised of a president, a vice president, and ten judges, is the highest court in the land. The judges of all the courts are appointed by the president and have no real independence. The judges of the courts of cassation and the courts of appeals are appointed for ten-year terms, while the judges of the civil courts are appointed for seven-year terms. Civil courts have jurisdictions over disputes concerning civil, political, and commercial rights, while the court of cassation rules on jurisdictional conflicts and on the constitutionality of laws.

Regional & Local Government

The republic is divided into nine *départements*; each *département* is further divided in *arrondissements* and each *arrondissement* has one or more *communes* under its jurisdiction. Each *département* and some *arrondissements* are headed by a prefect, a civilian official who is a direct representative of the executive branch. The prefect presides over technical councils of *arrondissements*. Each *commune* is administratively autonomous and is headed by a communal council, aided by a technical council of three members, all of whom are appointed by the president. The prefect oversees the political, economic, and administrative development of *arrondissements* and *communes* in his prefectural district and works toward the implementation of the policies of the central government.

The Electoral System

Suffrage extends to all citizens eighteen years of age and over. Since there have been no real elections for over two decades, there is no relevant data on voter turnout, candidate registration, or balloting. The government has manipulated the few minor elections that have been held.

National Unity Party
(*Parti de l'Unité Nationale*)

It is under the banner of the National Unity Party that François Duvalier campaigned for the presidency in 1957. The Party was created the previous year, and its rank and file as well as its leaders comprised mostly middle-class black intellectuals who had participated in the cultural-revival movement of the 1940s. Some of them were engaged in the study of Haitian folklore and published their analyses of Haitian society in *Les Griots*, a journal of culture and politics. They argued consistently and persuasively that the folk culture of the masses must be preserved and that economic progress could be achieved only through the leadership of a middle-class black intellectual.

The program of the party was to achieve national unity through economic prosperity, political stability, and social enlightenment. After the presidential elections, no effort was made to preserve the party as a distinct and independent entity. Instead, the leaders of the party were appointed as ministers, secretaries of state, and government officials. Presently, the party has no formal structure or organization.

Opposition

During the Duvalier administrations, Haitian Communist and Socialist parties have functioned as underground organizations with their leadership and ideologues living mostly in Paris, Havanna, Montreal, and Mexico. In the mid-sixties, the leadership of these various groups met to form the Unified Party of Haitian Communists (*Parti Unifié des Communistes Haitiens*). A few activists from the party returned clandestinely to Haiti in 1969 and were brutally killed by the armed forces.

The Communist Party remains a small underground organization in Haiti today. Founded in 1930 by Jacques Roumain and Max L. Hudicourt, it was outlawed in 1936. However, in 1946, the Haitian Communist Party (*Parti Communiste Haitien*) was organized once more by Félix d'Orléans Juste Constant; the Popular Socialist Party (*Parti Socialiste Populaire*) was created by Max L. Hudicourt, who was elected to the legislature the same year. All the leftist parties, including the Popular Democratic Party of Haitian Youth (*Parti Démo-*

cratique Populaire de la Jeunesse Haitienne), were again outlawed in 1950.

In the late 1970s, two new political parties were created in the capital, Port-au-Prince, because of the pressure exerted by U.S. president Jimmy Carter on Jean Claude Duvalier. The Christian Democratic Party (*Parti Démocrate Chrétien*) was headed by Sylvio C. Claude and the Haitian Christian Democratic Party (*Parti Démocrate Chrétien d'Haiti*) by Grégoire Eugène. At the end of President Carter's term in office, the Haitian government moved against those two embryonic parties. Grégoire Eugène and some of his partisans were sent into exile in New York, while Sylvio Claude and his advisors were arrested and are still in jail.

There are several other small, Haitian political groups in North America and Europe, however, they are ineffective because of factional quarrels and class conflicts. One of these, however, the new Rally of National Progressive Democrats of Haiti (*Rassemblement des Démocrates Nationaux-Progressistes d'Haiti*) shows more promise. Headquartered in Caracas, Venezuela, it is led by Professor Leslie F. Manigat, a student of Haitian politics for many years. Manigat has the ear of a large segment of the non-Marxist Haitian intellectuals, and it is likely that this new party in the years ahead will be the most challenging opposition to the administration of Jean Claude Duvalier.

Other Political Forces

Military

The armed forces have been a very important political group in Haiti. In fact, several presidents of the republic were former generals of the army. Presently the armed forces comprise the army (5,500 men), the navy (420 men including a 160-man infantry security company), and the air force (180 men including 19 pilots). The republic is divided into nine military *départements*; six of them are geographical and located in the countryside while the other three—the Dessalines Battalion, the Port-au-Prince Police, and the Presidential Guard—are functional and located in Port-au-Prince. The president in his capacity as the supreme chief of the armed forces has strategic and operational control over all of its units. There are no significant factions in the armed forces, so far

as is known. The top officers are all Duvalier loyalists and both the officer corps and the ranks are infiltrated by Duvalier men.

To counterbalance the traditional power of the military, the National Security Volunteers were created in 1961. They form a civilian militia of approximately 6,500 men. Known as *tontons macoutes* (bogeymen), their role is to maintain the Duvalier "revolution." After the death of François Duvalier, an elite corps of about 600 men, the Leopard Battalion, was formed to combat terrorism and underground communist activities in the country. They and the Volunteers receive police training. Their reputation for ruthless brutality and corruption has softened since 1971.

National Prospects

By all evidence, the political system in Haiti is stable despite the country's acute economic crisis and the continuing emigration of Haitians to North America and Europe. At present, there is no organized political party in Haiti capable of challenging the policies of the government and the opposition in exile is too weak and too divided to constitute a real threat to the regime. Except for unforeseen events, the present regime is likely to remain in office unchallenged.

Further Reading

Committee on International Relations. *Human Rights in Haiti.* Hearing Before the Subcommittee on International Organizations of the Committee on International Relations. House of Representatives. Thirty-Fourth Congress. First Session. November 18, 1975. Washington, D.C.: U.S. Government Printing Office, 1975.

Gingras, Jean Pierre O. *Duvalier, Caribbean Cyclone: The History of Haiti and Its Present Government.* New York: Exposition Press, 1967.

Laguerre, Michel S. *The Complete Haitiana: A Bibliographic Guide to the Scholarly Literature, 1900-1980.* 2 vols. New York: Kraus International Publications, 1982.

———. *Urban Life in the Caribbean. A Study of a Haitian Urban Community.* Cambridge, Mass.: Schenkman Publishing Co., 1982.

Manigat, Leslie F. *Haiti of the Sixties, Object of International Concern.* Washington, D.C.:

Washington Center for Foreign Policy Research, 1964.

Nicholls, David. *From Dessalines to Duvalier: Race, Colour and National Independence in Haiti*. Cambridge: Cambridge University Press, 1979.

Rotberg, Robert I., and Claque, Christopher K. *Haiti: The Politics of Squalor*. Boston: Houghton Mifflin, 1971.

Weil, Thomas E. et al. *Area Handbook for Haiti*. Washington, D.C.: U.S. Government Printing Office for Foreign Area Studies, American University, 1973.

REPUBLIC OF HONDURAS
(*Republica de Honduras*)
by Hewson A. Ryan, Ph.D.

The System of Government

Honduras is a constitutional republic which became independent upon the breakup of the Republic of Central America in 1838. Its present constitution—the fourteenth in its history—was approved by a constituent assembly on January 11, 1982.

Executive

Executive authority is vested in a president elected by popular vote for a single four-year term. Three vice presidents are elected simultaneously with the president; any one of them may be chosen by simple majority vote of the legislature to serve out the president's term should he leave office for any reason. The constitution provides for a Council of Ministers of approximately twelve members who serve at the pleasure of the president but who are required to countersign decrees and laws affecting their departments and who must present annual reports of their activities to the legislature.

The president must be native-born; at least thirty years of age; and may not be a pastor, priest, or member of a religious order, nor a member of the armed forces on active duty. A president cannot succeed himself or run again for the office at any time. He is titular head of the armed forces, although in practice he must exercise that function through the chief of the armed forces. He is responsible for the general administration of the nation, the direction of foreign policy, the formulation of a national-development plan, the direction of the economic and financial policy of the nation, and such other duties as may be conferred on him by the constitution. The incumbent, Roberto Suazo Córdoba, a member of the Liberal Party, was elected on November 29, 1981, with 53.9 percent of the vote and installed in office on January 27, 1982.

Legislature

The Chamber of Deputies, the unicameral legislature, is chosen by direct popular vote through a complex system of proportional representation. This involves the election of seventy-eight deputies from preferential party lists. Additional deputies may be elected to provide representatives for votes in excess of "national electoral quotients." In the 1981 elections this produced four additional seats, giving a total of eighty-two members of the present Chamber of Deputies. The basic seventy-eight seats in the Chamber are apportioned to each of the eighteen geographical divisions (departments) according to population. The largest delegations represent the departments of Morazán (the Tegucigalpa area) and Cortés (the San Pedro Sula area).

Deputies must be Honduran by birth and over twenty-one years of age. Religious leaders, members of the military and police forces, public officials and their spouses and close relatives are barred from becoming deputies. Deputies enjoy personal immunities from most legal and police actions and the premises of the legislature are declared inviolate by the constitution.

Chosen for a four-year term, each deputy is elected with a substitute (*suplente*) who may serve out his term should he vacate his seat for any reason. The Chamber is automatically convoked annually on January 21 and adjourned on October 31. Extraordinary sessions may be called by the president, the Chamber's permanent committee, or by the agreement of a simple majority of its members. Extraordinary sessions may consider only the matters specifically stated in the convocatory decree.

The Chamber is empowered to create, decree, interpret, reform, and repeal laws. It also elects the members and president of the Supreme Court, the chief of the armed forces, and the controller general; approves treaties, budgets, and loans; and controls public revenues.

ELECTION RESULTS (1981)

Party	No. of Votes	Percentage
Christian Democrats	19,163	1.6
Innovation & Unity	29,419	2.5
Liberal	636,392	53.9
National	491,089	41.6
Independents[1]	3,997	0.3
Total valid votes	1,180,060	
Null & blank	34,675	
Grand Total	1,214,735	

Note: One vote serves both to elect the president and to determine the proportion of seats for each party on municipal councils and in the Chamber of Deputies.
[1]Three independent candidates were put up by the new Honduran Socialist Party in Copan, Cortés, and Yoro departments.

The makeup of the Chamber in 1982 was forty-four Liberals, thirty-four Nationalists, three Innovation and Unity, and one Christian Democrat, giving the president's Liberal Party a clear working majority.

Judiciary

The nine-member Supreme Court and its president are elected by the legislature for periods of four years, coinciding with the terms of the Chamber and the president. Justices must by lawyers, over thirty-five years of age, with five years experience as a judge of a lower court or ten years as a practicing attorney. The Court exercises overall control of the judicial system, acts as the ultimate national judicial authority, and rules on the constitutionality of laws. The constitution provides that the annual budget of the judiciary shall not be less than 3 percent of the total government budget. The present Supreme Court, elected by the new Chamber of Deputies, is made up entirely of members of the majority Liberal Party.

Regional & Local Government

The nation's 281 municipal councils are chosen at the time of the national elections, with the parties represented proportionally as in the Chamber of Deputies. The municipalities have limited taxing and police power; in practice, they are highly dependent on the central government for authority and funding.

The Electoral System

The electoral system is based on universal suffrage for all Honduran citizens over eighteen years of age. The ballot is secret and, through the use of party symbols and colored ballots, literacy is not necessary. Registration is simple and straightforward. Official representatives of all parties are present at all polling places and must authenticate voting lists. Voting is obligatory, but is seldom enforced. Nevertheless, 83 percent of registered voters participated in the 1981 elections.

Some leaders of the losing Nationalist Party claimed fraud in the 1981 elections, but neither foreign observers, the National Electoral Tribunal, nor the Honduran armed forces seemed to take the charges seriously. The Nationalists did boycott the January 27 presidential inauguration as a symbolic protest of the alleged fraud, but they did take up their seats in the Chamber of Deputies for regular sessions.

A single ballot includes the name of a party's presidential candidate and ranked lists of that party's candidates for the Chamber of Deputies and Municipal Council in the area. A voter casts a single ballot for an entire party slate; neither substitution nor ticket splitting is possible.

The total number of votes cast in each department is divided by the number of seats to be filled to ascertain the department's "electoral quotient." The first seat is then awarded to the first name on the ballot list of the party receiving the greatest number of votes in that department. The "electoral quotient" is then subtracted from the vote total. The second seat is awarded to the party which then has the largest number of votes; the "electoral quotient" is again subtracted and the third and succeeding seats awarded in like manner until the department's delegation is completed. The votes remaining unused in the various departments are then pooled to form each party's "national remainder." The total national vote is divided by seventy-eight, the number of directly elected seats, to produce a "national electoral quotient." Each party then receives additional seats according to the number of whole times the "national quotient" is contained in its "national remainder."

The Party System

Origins of the Parties

Political parties in Honduras have existed in name since the earliest days of the republic. However, until well into the twentieth century, most of these were armed bands loyal to individual political leaders, many of whom assumed the title of general. The presidency changed hands 124 times between 1824 and 1981. Even the two major parties which have had formal national structures since the early decades of this century have split and come back together again as a result of changing loyalties to and leadership abilities of a series of strong leaders.

The Parties in Law

The constitution recognizes the role of legally inscribed political parties in providing for the effective participation of citizens in the political process. Parties are prohibited from actions against the republican, democratic system of government. Government contributions to the financing of the parties is also provided for in the constitution. Official recognition is based on presentation to the National Electoral Tribunal of petitions carrying signatures of a specified number of voters from each department. Registration traditionally has not been easily accomplished due to long delays in authenticating signatures and accusations of fraud. The two traditional parties, National and Liberal, have neither encouraged nor been particularly helpful to new parties.

At present four parties are legally recognized: the two traditional rivals, the National and Liberal parties; and two recent arrivals on the electoral scene, the Party of Innovation and Unity (PINU) and the Christian Democratic Party (PDC).

Party Organization

Party structures on a regional and local basis tend to reflect similar patterns. Political *caciques* (chieftains) organize and control local party organization, and armed clashes between rival *caciques* and their followers are still not uncommon.

All four parties are national in scope. The latest voting statistics show local party strengths in each department reflecting the national averages. There are no wholly regional parties nor departments entirely in the hands of one or another party.

The four parties have grass-roots organizations with a dues-paying membership and locally selected officials in each department capital. Many of these organizations, in addition to political organization and indoctrination, carry on programs of political education and activities such as dental and medical clinics, food distribution, etc., at the regional and municipal level.

As is the case in most countries of Hispanic tradition, party structures tend to be highly centralized with money and power generally flowing down from national party headquarters in Tegucigalpa. Traditionally, political elites have tended to develop in the capital. This may be changing, however, with the election of Suazo Córdoba, who, with some time out to serve in the legislature, has spent most of his life in a provincial medical practice and has no roots in the capital city.

Campaigning

The limited size of the country permits personal campaigning by the candidates in all areas. Personal appearances with handshaking, baby kissing, bands, and barbecues in a carnival atmosphere introduce the candidates directly to the voters. Wall posters, street banners, personal insignia, and the extensive use of newspaper, radio, and television advertising also characterize Honduran political campaigning.

Funding and direction of the campaigns are usually very centralized, with the national headquarters in control.

Expenditures are not limited or reported, but certainly exceed the amounts made available through government subsidies. The expenses are reportedly covered from funds contributed by wealthy party members and wary merchants and industrialists who are said to hedge their bets by contributing to two or more parties.

Independent Voters

Formal party membership, in the sense of paying dues and carrying a membership card, probably does not extend to more than 25 percent of registered voters. However, family traditions and loyalties extend party identification to at least double this figure. The use of a single ballot and party voting lists precludes the splitting of votes, a concept unknown in Honduras.

LIBERAL PARTY
(*Partido Liberal;* PL)

History

The present majority party, the Liberal Party (PL) traces its origins to the late-nineteenth-century leader Policarpo Bonilla whose presidential term (1894–99) was one of the more productive eras of Honduran political history. The Liberals were out of power, but retained some vestigial organization through most of the first half of this century. The party became identified with social reform and labor objectives in the 1950s under the leadership of Dr. Ramon Villeda Morales who served as president of the nation from 1957 to 1963. Villeda's overthrow in 1963 by a military coup led by General Oswaldo López Arellano took the party out of national government until its strong showing in the elections for the Constituent Assembly in 1980 and the subsequent election of its standard-bearer in the December 1981 elections.

Organization

The decision-making apparatus of the party is the annual convention, which brings together delegates from each department. In practice, an executive committee named by the convention makes most decisions. With its leader in the presidency and a working majority in the legislature, a party executive committee will probably defer to the president on most issues.

Policy

The PL's platform in the recent election campaign emphasized its determination to wipe out government corruption. It is expected to support and strengthen constitutionally mandated agrarian-reform programs and takes a liberal attitude towards the business sector. In the international field it will probably continue to support the U.S. posture on most issues. Although it has long been mildly antimilitary in its rhetoric, it must tread very carefully in this regard in view of the power of the armed forces. It has already indicated continued support for the present strong military posture regarding the Sandinistas in Nicaragua. The party has occasionally sent observers to meetings of the World Socialist Movement, but has made no move to affiliate.

Membership & Constituency

Like the other parties, the PL has a broad base throughout the country. Claims of membership figures are highly suspect, but electoral results demonstrate that it was able to win a clear majority of votes cast. Centrist in political orientation, its strength traditionally lies in the labor sector.

Financing

Financing information is not available.

Leadership

The leader of the party is the newly elected president, Roberto Suazo Córdoba, who was born in 1927 in La Paz, capital of the department of the same name. A physician trained in Guatemala, he has practiced medicine in his native city for twenty-five years, taking time out to serve as a member of the Chamber of Deputies, 1958 to 1963, and as president of the Constituent Assembly, 1980–81. His ascension to power in the party and then to the presidency was the consequence of the unexpected death of Modesto Rodas Alvarado, a leading figure in the party since the presidency of Villeda Morales (1957–63).

The other leading figure in the PL and leader of its more progressive wing is a son of Villeda Morales, Dr. Ramón Villeda Bermúdez. A veterinarian by training and a journalist and editor by avocation, Villeda Bermúdez represents a younger and more internationally minded current within the party.

Prospects

Many observers are dubious that the PL—with a weak, untested leadership and without strong ideological commitments—will be able to confront the problems of maintaining Honduras as a parliamentary democracy in the face of serious economic and social pressures. If the PL fails, still another military takeover is possible.

NATIONAL PARTY
(*Partido Nacional;* PN)

History

The second major party, the PN, claims roots in the mid-nineteenth-century Central American liberal revolution, but its origin in its present form dates from 1916. It was the party of long-term president and dictator Tiburçio Carias Andino, who ruled Honduras from 1932 to 1949, and his successors, Juan Manuel Galvez and Julio Lozano. The latter was deposed by the military coup in 1957 which paved the way for Liberal Villeda Morales' term. The PN's candidate, Ramón E. Cruz, won the 1970 elections, but his weak and aimless administration lasted little over a year before succumbing to another military coup, which in turn led to the several de facto military administrations preceding the present one. The PN was an active collaborator in most recent military governments, providing ministers for many of the cabinet posts not occupied by soldiers.

Organization

The party is nominally run by a convention and executive committee. In practice, for the past two decades the party has been under the control of Ricardo Zúñiga Augustinas, who has personally directed party strategy and dispensed funds and jobs down to the departmental level.

Policy

Like the PL, the National Party does not have a clearly recognizable ideology. It does emphasize its anticommunism and in the recent elections attempted to identify with the U.S. Republican Party. In international affairs it also follows U.S. leadership and supports the strong military stance against Nicaragua.

Membership & Constituency

The PN has traditionally been strong in rural areas and in the less developed departments. The 1981 election results showed this clearly. The party also has a history of cooperation with the military.

Financing

Accurate financial data are unavailable.

Leadership

The leading figure of the PN and its candidate for president in the 1981 elections is Ricardo Zúñiga Augustinas. Born in 1916 in Choluteca, capital of the department of the same name, he is a lawyer who has devoted most of his adult life to the PN and Honduran politics. During his term as minister of the presidency under the legal presidency of General Oswaldo López Arellano (1965–71), he controlled much of the domestic political scene and was often accused of manipulating the nation's affairs for his political and personal gain. A pragmatist and political operative of great skill, Zúñiga has no known ideology. During the presidential campaign, he attempted to associate himself with the conservative wing of the U.S. Republican Party and made much of his several visits to meet with Senator Jesse Helms in Washington and Ambassador Jeane Kirkpatrick in New York. With

his defeat it would seem that Zúñiga's position might soon be on the decline. However, no challenger has yet shown himself. Rumors, possibly inspired by Zúñiga himself, already circulate that he might make himself available to serve should the military feel the need to depose Suazo Córdoba as they did his last elected predecessor, Cruz, in 1972. Other leading figures in the PN, all proteges of Zúñiga or very much in his political debt, are Nicholás Cruz Torres, vice president of the Constituent Assembly and former PN youth leader in the 1960s; Mario Rivera López, president of the Congress in the ill-fated Cruz regime; and Irma Acosta de Fortín, a U.S.-educated engineer who is rector of the nation's only private institution of higher learning, the José Cecilio del Valle University. Two dissident movements in the PN, both led by former army officers—Armando Velázquez and Miguel Angel García—continue to attract some attention and support, but they have not threatened Zúñiga's preeminence.

Prospects

With a viable national organization and longstanding ties to the military establishment, the PN stands ready to move into government should the PL falter and/or the military carry out another coup.

Minor Parties
Christian Democrat Party (*Partido Demócrata Cristiano;* PDC)

The most recently recognized party, the PDC has existed formally for a decade or so. It claims strength in university and professional circles and probably gained some of its strength from recent Catholic "renewal" campaigns and from the Church's younger clergy, who have been active in community and labor organization in the last decade.

Comparatively little is known of the PDC's structure or policy, other than vague statements of identification with the International Christian Democratic Movement. Party claims of tens of thousands of members were belied by the mere 1.5 percent of votes (19,163) in the November 1981 elections. There is no information available on party financing. The party is led by Dr. Hernán Corrales Padilla, a physician, a former ambassador to the United States, and long-time political activist. Now in his mid-fifties, Corrales Padilla has been alternating his medical practice with politics since the 1950s.

Party of Innovation and Unity (*Partido de Inovacion y Unidad;* PINU)

Founded in 1970, principally through the efforts and persistence of an enlightened businessman, Miguel Andonie Fernández, the PINU sought to bring probity and renewal to the Honduran political scene. Finally inscribed as a legal party in 1979, PINU managed to win a three-seat balance of power position in the 1980 Constituent Assembly. However, its disappointing results (3 percent) in the 1981 vote reveal it to be still a very minor factor in Honduran politics.

Essentially middle class in outlook, the PINU has not been able to make any substantial appeal to labor or rural electorates. Ideologically moderate, it has taken no strong stand on international issues.

Financing and membership figures are not available.

The founder and principal figure in PINU, Andonie Fernández is a self-made businessman in his late fifties of Syrian-Lebanese ancestry who seeks to apply modern business-management techniques and honesty to national government.

A second major figure in the PINU during the presidential campaign was a former PN foreign minister and counselor to the military government of Colonel Melgar (1976–78), César Batres. A lawyer of repute, he brought to the PINU expertise in international negotiations and governmental administration. However, he obviously brought no substantial bloc of votes and has since apparently returned to the PN. Participation in government appears remote for the PINU.

Several unrecognized minor parties and terrorist groups are intermittently active on the political scene. None, however, has developed to a point to appear to threaten the traditional political system. They include:

The Black Hand (*Mano Negra*), a right-wing terrorist group active in 1980 against alleged Marxists, is alleged to have connections to the armed forces. It seems to have been replaced in 1981 by the Honduran Anti-Communist Movement (*Movimiento Anti-Communista Hondureño;* MACHO).

The outlawed Communist Party (*Partido Communista*) has existed in various forms since the 1930s, but has never demonstrated significant political attraction.

The Marxist-Leninist Communist Party (*Partido Communista Marxista-Leninista*)—a long-dormant, anti-Moscow group—has shown some signs of life during 1981 and 1982.

The new Honduran Socialist Party (*Partido Socialista de Honduras*) attempted to obtain access to the Chamber of Deputies by registering independent candidates in three departments. However, these candidates attracted a total of fewer than 4,000 votes. The leader of the party, Marco Virgilio Carias—a former rector of the University of Honduras—disappeared for ten days in July of 1981 and upon his reappearance alleged that he was kidnapped and threatened by the military. Military sources denied these charges and implied that the kidnapping was probably a fraud.

The Morazán National Liberation Front (*Frente Morazán de Liberacion Nacional*) is a little-known guerrilla group which took credit for shooting at the U.S. Embassy in Tegucigalpa in October of 1980.

The Lorenzo Zelaya Popular Revolutionary Command (*Comando Popular Revolucionario Lorenzo Zelaya*) is a leftist guerrilla group which took credit for shootings at U.S. military advisors and bombing the Honduran Congress building in October 1981.

The Chinchonero Movement of National Liberation (*Movimiento Chinchonero de Liberacion Nacional*) appeared in 1981. A leftist terrorist group, it took credit for the bombing of several diplomatic missions in Tegulcigalpa.

The Patriotic Renovation Movement (*Movimiento de Renovación Patriótico*) is a Honduran "Common Cause" nonideological movement favoring governmental reforms and rural development. It was formed in 1980 by former colonel and exdirector of Agrarian Reform, José Mario Montenegro.

The Revolutionary University Force (*Fuerza Universitaria Revolucionaria*) is a Marxist university student group supportive of El Salvador's guerrillas and Nicaraguan Sandinistas.

The Revolutionary Union of the People (*Unión Revolucionaria del Pueblo*) is an activist Marxist-Leninist group which split off from the Communist Party in 1980.

Other Political Forces

Military

The most significant alternative force in Honduras is the military. The evolution of a professional military establishment came in the aftermath of the Carias dictatorship in the 1950s. Prior to that period the army acted merely as an armed extension of political leaders and parties. With professionalization, the military began to exercise preponderant influence on the political establishment. Coups in 1956 and 1963 demonstrated the active political role of the armed forces. Recent constitutions have recognized this role through provisions giving the chief of the armed forces a high degree of autonomy and even political control.

The chief is named for a five-year term by the Congress from three candidates presented by the Superior Council of the Armed Forces, comprised of the generals and senior colonels. The chief may be removed only by a two-thirds vote of the legislature. The armed forces itself is governed by the Superior Council of the Armed Forces which acts in a collegial fashion. The armed forces are charged with the defense of the territorial integrity and sovereignty of the republic, the maintenance of public order, the rule of the constitution, the principle of universal suffrage, and the non-succession to the presidency. Thus much of the actual governance of the country is at the sufferance of the armed forces.

Since the military academy was not founded until the 1950s, only now are the senior ranks becoming professionalized. Under training agreements with the United States, a substantial number of officers and NCOs have received advanced training at U.S. installations in Panama and the United States. Except for one or two elite battalions, the majority of the troops are peasant conscripts who serve for a year or less. The officer corps, however, is drawn from middle-class youths, many of whom are drawn to the military academy by the prospect of a significant career.

While not immune from probably well-founded accusations of graft, corruption, and influence peddling—senior military ranks actively participate in private business—the military has also been a socially and politically progressive force in Honduran development. Military governments have supported agrarian reform, the recognition of the peasant labor organization, and the development of rural infrastructure projects. They must also be given credit for standing firm on their commitment to the return to democratic, civilian government culminating in the installation of the Suazo Córdoba regime, albeit under certain pressures from the U.S. government.

Organized Labor

Labor is another and growing force in Honduran politics. The right to organize and bargain col-

lectively was not won until 1954 after a protracted strike in the banana fields. Since that time, labor has rapidly realized other significant gains including a labor code, labor courts, a government ministry, social security, paid vacations, and agrarian reform. The oldest and strongest unions are those representing the workers of the two largest banana companies. Both later formed part of the nationwide Confederation of Honduran Workers (*Confederación de Trabajadores de Honduras;* CTH), organized in 1964 and affiliated with the Inter-American Regional Workers' Organization (*Organización Regional Interamericana de Trabajadores;* ORIT) and the AFL/CIO in the United States. A social-democratic General Central of Workers (*Central General de Trabajadores;* CGT) was formed in 1970 and, through its more militant stance, has attracted new independent unions and even some former CTH affiliates. Both confederations sponsor peasant workers' unions: the CTH, the National Association of Honduran Peasants (*Asociación Nacional de Campesinos de Honduras;* ANACH); and the CGT, the National Union of Peasants (*Unión Nacional de Campesinos;* UNC). A smaller Marxist-oriented group is the United National Front of Honduran Peasants (*Frente Unidad Nacional Campesina Hondureño;* FUNACAMH).

Low educational literacy levels make it difficult to train workers since 80 percent of the labor force has not finished primary school and the illiteracy rate approximates 50 percent. An extensive labor-training program sponsored by the AFL/CIO-supported American Institute for Free Labor Development is attacking this problem with some modest success.

Students

Student organizations at the University of Honduras tend to be more activist and strident than other national student groups. Both major parties support student federations, but the radical leftist groups seem to outnumber the traditional groups, at least in activist members. However, since most students attend the university only part time while working outside, the students do not appear to have the political power which they do at other Latin American institutions.

Banana Industry

Although its power has diminished in recent years as Honduras has diversified its exports, the banana industry still accounts for the largest single item of export earnings. Two American companies, United Brands and Castle & Cook, account for most of the bananas exported. In 1975, the Honduran Banana Corporation was established to negotiate with these two companies on production levels and prices and to insure that Honduras plays a significant role in the banana business.

Reportedly the makers and breakers of Honduran governments and politicians in the past, the companies have attempted to disengage from the local scene in recent decades. A 1976 scandal, popularly termed "Bananagate," which involved illegal payments of $1.5 million by United Brands to the then chief of state Oswaldo López Arellano, brought old memories and bitter accusations on this score once again. Since then things have been quiet, but the size and history of the U.S. involvement in the banana industry are an ever-present subject of possible political friction.

National Prospects

Social and political turmoil in all of her immediate neighbors—El Salvador, Guatemala, and Nicaragua—will undoubtedly influence developments in Honduras. Both the civilian political parties and the armed forces are fearful of the extension of Sandinista influence in Honduran labor and peasant groups. They are likewise wary of growing guerrilla influence from the Marxist-Leninist movements to their north. Refugee groups from both Nicaragua and El Salvador also place further strain on Honduras's fragile economy and political structure.

The prospects for a peaceful and orderly term for President Suazo Córdoba are limited. The growth of the military establishment to confront both internal and external armed threats, the deepening world economic crisis, the fragility of the new and inexperienced political establishment, and growing internal social tensions all combine to present the country doctor turned president with formidable if not overwhelming challenges.

Further Reading

Anderson, T. P. *The War of the Dispossessed: Honduras & El Salvador, 1969.* Lincoln, Neb.: University of Nebraska Press, 1974.

Karnes, T. L. *The Failure of Union: Central America 1824–1975.* Tempe, Ariz.: Arizona State University Press, 1976.

Martz, M. R. J. *The Central American Soccer War.* Athens, Ohio: Ohio University Center for International Studies, 1978.

Munro, D. G. *The Five Republics of Central America.* New York: Gordon Press, 1976.

Stokes, W. S. *Honduras: An Area Study in Government.* Westport, Conn.: Greenwood Press, 1974.

Wortman, M. L. *Government and Society in Central America, 1680–1840.* New York: Columbia University Press, 1982.

Woodward, Ralph. *Central America: A Nation Divided.* London: Oxford University Press, 1976.

HUNGARIAN PEOPLE'S REPUBLIC
(*Magyar Népköztársaság*)
by Emil Freund, M.A.

The System of Government

The Hungarian People's Republic is a one-party communist state in the center of Europe. It has a population of nearly eleven million people. Hungarian communists briefly ruled the country in 1919 during the period of turmoil that followed World War I when the Austro-Hungarian monarchy collapsed and Hungary was reduced to a minor state nearly surrounded by former subject nations. From 1919 to 1944, the country was ruled by a conservative regime which sought to regain some of Hungary's former territory, later flirting with fascism in pursuit of this goal. Hungary fought on the Axis side in World War II and was occupied by Soviet troops at the end of the war. The communists won less than 20 percent of the national vote in elections in 1945, but, with a variety of maneuvers and Soviet support, gained complete control of the government by May 1949.

Severe political repression and poor economic management led to social unrest and deep rifts in the party which culminated in a popular revolt in 1956. The revolt was bloodily crushed by Soviet troops and the present Hungarian ruler, János Kádár, was installed as the head of the party. Present-day Hungary's government and party reflect the major changes in organization and policy instituted by Kádár after the 1956 revolution.

Executive

De facto executive power resides in the Political Bureau of the Communist Party. What may pass for an executive in the Western sense is a collegial body elected by the National Assembly called the Presidential Council, whose chairman is the titular head of state. According to the 1949 constitution, the Presidential Council acts as an interim legislature when the full legislature is not in session, with the authority to issue decrees and interpret law. The Council of Ministers is the other half of the executive with powers equivalent to those of the Presidential Council. In theory, the

Council of Ministers is elected by the legislature and is chaired by a prime minister who is the head of government. In fact, the legislature merely gives formal approval to ministers who have been preselected by the party leadership. The ministries are responsible for the day-to-day formulation and implementation of policy, and their decisions are rubber-stamped by the legislature during its brief annual meetings. The Council of Ministers has the de facto power to override any decision made by the Presidential Council, and the individual ministers have some freedom of action, particularly in cases which involve the management of the economy. Members of both the Presidential Council and the Council of Ministers are usually high-ranking party members.

Legislature

The Hungarian National Assembly consists of 352 deputies elected to four-year terms. In theory, the legislature is the highest representative of the Hungarian people and is entrusted with the oversight of the government. Bearing the interests of the people in mind, it is supposed to generate policy for the government. However, the full Assembly meets only rarely, rubber-stamping government actions without serious debate. Nevertheless, the power of oversight and debate has been taken more seriously in recent years by the legislature's standing committees, which have specific responsibility for particular ministries.

Judiciary

The judicial system consists of three levels: the Supreme Court, the county courts, and the district courts. Judges at the county and district levels are professional jurists chosen by the Presidential Council. They are entrusted with maintaining civil order and safeguarding the process of "socialist development." The Supreme Court, elected by the legislature, has little power. Most power in the judicial branch of government is held by the chief prosecutor, who acts as the prosecutor for the entire country. The procurator's office has substantial power to enforce civil law and policy decisions made by the Council of Ministers.

Regional & Local Government

Hungary is divided into nineteen counties (*megyed*) and four urban areas with county status, which are subdivided into smaller units. All units are administered by elected councils which in turn elect executive committees for day-to-day operations. In theory, the local and county councils have more power to decide on local matters than the central government, but every council's operations are overseen by the local branch of the party secretariat to ensure that party policy is carried out. Candidates for the councils are carefully screened by the party's popular front organization, the Patriotic People's Front (PPF); occasionally, more than one candidate is allowed to compete for a council post. The largest and most influential of the local government units is the county of Budapest, the capital area.

The Electoral System

All Hungarian citizens eighteen years of age and over are eligible to vote and are required to do so under threat of substantial penalties. Turnout commonly runs over 99 percent.

The selection of candidates for the National Assembly takes place at the county level and is carefully overseen by the PPF. One of the crucial innovations made by Kádár was the opening of candidate slots to nonparty members, all of whom must nevertheless support the program of the PPF. Very few members of recent legislatures have been party members. A further Kádár innovation was to permit more than one candidate to stand for a seat in the legislature. Never widespread, this practice reached its height in the 1977 elections; in the 1981 elections only fifteen seats were sought by more than one candidate.

Hungarian Socialist Workers' Party (HSWP; *Magyar Szocialista Munkáspart*)

History

The HSWP traces its origins to the organization of a communist cell by a few Hungarian prisoners of war in Omsk, Russia, soon after the Russian revolution in 1917. Calling themselves the Hungarian International Social Democratic Party (Bolshevik), this group became active participants in Soviet government. Bela Kun, the leader of the Hungarian communist group, served under Karl Radek, a German, in the Soviet International Propaganda Department in early 1918 and used this post to aggressively agitate among other Hungarian prisoners of war. With the end of the war, several hundred communists trained in schools in Moscow and Petrograd moved into Hungary, where they published their doctrine in *Vörös Ujság* (Red Newspaper). By the end of 1918, they had established the Communist Party of Hungary (*Kommunisták Magyarországi Pártja*) and could claim several tens of thousands of members. During the winter of 1918–19, they created a tone of anarchy in the streets as they agitated for major reforms.

In March 1919, the conservative government which had taken over after the collapse of the Austro-Hungarian monarchy itself crumbled under pressure from the Allied powers to turn over all those Hungarian territories which had been promised to successor states—Czechoslovakia, Yugoslavia, Poland, and Romania. The Communist Party, in conjunction with the Social Democratic Party, thereupon proclaimed the formation of a Hungarian Soviet and a Revolutionary Government under Bela Kun. Immediate steps were taken to nationalize major industries and banks, but Kun, a doctrinaire Marxist, made no secret of the fact that he opposed any land redistribution to the peasants (largely tenant farmers on large estates owned by aristocrats) because it would support the principle of private property. This dogmatism undercut his support among the majority of the population at the same time that chaotic implementation of the nationalization program threw the economy into disarray. To forestall popular outbursts and to push their program forward, the party embarked on a policy of terror against the "enemies of the people."

At the same time, the Kun regime was hard pressed by the Romanian army which had invaded Hungary and besieged Budapest in pursuit of its claims to Transylvania. The Hungarian Soviet government collapsed in August 1919 and was replaced by the conservative authoritarian government of Admiral Miklos Horthy von Nagbánya who ruled the country until 1944. The Communist Party was outlawed and its members went underground or fled to the Soviet Union. In the Soviet Union, the party was reorganized under the direction of Stalin and the Comintern. In 1936 and 1937,

Stalinist purges largely destroyed the original leadership of the party, including Bela Kun, and loyal Stalinists were installed in the leadership.

In 1940, the Soviet government arranged for the release of the most prominent communists in Horthy's jails, including Mátyás Rákosi, who quickly gained control of the emigre party. Ernö Gerö, a Hungarian Comintern functionary, and others continued to compete for the party leadership for both personal and ideological reasons. The party chairmanship changed hands several times during the period of the Second World War.

In late 1944, as the Red Army approached Budapest, a Provisional National Assembly met in Debrecen in eastern Hungary. Under the guidance of communists, a provisional government was formed by nonfascist parties. While the Communist Party, led by Rákosi, was a distinct minority, the Russian occupation of Hungary gave the party the time and resources to develop a base of popular support; exploit divisions in the other parties; and gain control of key government ministries, such as the agriculture ministry, which under Imre Nagy undertook an extensive land-reform program. In June 1948, the Social Democratic Party was forced to merge with the communists in a new Hungarian Workers' Party (*Magyar Dolgozók Pártja*). The following year the communists gained complete control of the government.

Rákosi embarked on an ambitious program of heavy industrialization at the expense of agriculture and consumer goods. Severe economic dislocations resulted from the shift to a centrally controlled economy and the attempt to build an industrial base in a country with few of the necessary natural resources. Rákosi's dogmatism added to the country's problems. In 1953, the Russians forced Rákosi to resign as prime minister, replacing him with Imre Nagy in that position. This move institutionalized a rift in the party between hard-line Stalinists such as Rákosi and more pragmatic elements represented by Nagy, who in his brief period in office introduced several popular economic reforms.

In July 1956, after Soviet party leader Khrushchev had denounced the excesses and personality cult of Stalinism, the antidogmatists in the Hungarian party forced the resignation of Rákosi as party first secretary. Rákosi, however, had himself replaced by Ernö Gerö, another dogmatist, and Rákosi's policies were continued. The party rank and file and the general population agitated for the restoration of Nagy's reforms, and the party began to lose control of the political process. In late October, popular demonstrations of support for Nagy became violent and a fairly spontaneous

revolution began. Nagy's return to the prime ministership soon after the outbreak began did not stop the revolution, which moved rapidly toward a social democratic position with Nagy as leader. Workers' councils in Budapest, for example, called for an end to communist hegemony, democratization, and withdrawal of Hungary from the Warsaw Pact.

In early November, ostensibly at the invitation of Politburo member János Kádár, Soviet troops moved into the country and crushed the revolt. Nagy was executed and Kádár became the party's leader. He moved quickly to restore the party organization and its control of the society. As part of the reorganization, the party was given its present name. Kádár's "alliance policy" promised to make peace with the population by slight relaxations of traditional party control. In spite of continued repression and ongoing struggles with the dogmatists in the party, Kádár was able to slowly bring the country back to normal under the slogan, "Who is not against us is with us." By 1962, Kádár had gained full control of the party. The history of the party since then has been one of increasing realization of the rhetoric of the "alliance policy."

Organization

The party is organized in the classic democratic centralist mold in which decisions are made by the ruling Politburo and followed by the rank and file. Party cells are present at all levels of society and in all institutions and are organized by district throughout the country. Party congresses consisting of 400 to 800 carefully selected delegates from each district meet approximately every five years. The twelfth party congress met in March 1980. The congress elects the 125-member Central Committee from a single slate of candidates. The Central Committee in turn elects the party secretaries, who are responsible for such functional areas as economic planning, party organization, etc., and the Politburo, which usually has twelve to fifteen members. The party also maintains a variety of auxiliary organizations for children, youth, women, and others.

Policy

The party still extends its control into every facet of life, but less obtrusively than in most Soviet bloc states. Dissent is not so much repressed as smothered by silence or coopted. The party provides a variety of mechanisms to give the populace a sense of participation in the political process. Chief among these is the Patriotic People's Front which serves to mobilize nonparty members and to transmit party policy to the general public. The PPF does not have a formal membership. Its cadres organize small informal discussion groups at the neighborhood level which allow participants to express their complaints and hopes. The party in turn makes some attempt to be responsive.

The party no longer visibly intrudes in the running of the economy. In 1968, Kádár introduced his New Economic Mechanism, which granted considerable autonomy to plant managers and introduced elements of competition and other free-market processes. This policy has made Hungary one of the most prosperous of East European countries. In exchange for its independence in the economic sphere, Hungary pays total allegiance to the Soviet foreign policy line.

Membership & Constituency

From a high of 1.5 million soon after World War II, party membership fell to less than 300,000 in the wake of the 1956 revolt. Careful reconstruction and efforts to broaden the membership to include more workers, peasants, and women brought party membership up to 812,000 by the time of the party congress in 1980. Industrial workers and peasants now account for about 45 percent of the party membership.

Financing

All party members pay dues on a sliding scale related to income. Additional income is derived from party enterprises, particularly the sale of publications.

Leadership

János Kádár (born 1912) is first secretary of the party. He is the most popular party leader in Eastern Europe. No other member of the Politburo is clearly in line to succeed him, but possible candidates are György Lázár (born 1924), the prime minister since 1975; György Aczél (born 1917), the deputy prime minister; and Pál Losonczi (born 1919), chairman of the Presidential Council since 1967. There are no apparent personal or ideological factions in the Politburo. The only issue dividing the leadership is whether to extend the relaxation of party control to the intellectual and political spheres and increase the decentralization of the economy.

Other Political Forces

There are no significant political forces in Hungary apart from the party. The military is firmly under the control of the party and seems to exercise little influence in policy formulation. The National Council of Trade Unions functions more as an arm of the party than an independent force. The events in Poland may prompt the authorities to grant greater independence to the Council, and the regime has indicated that it might permit the unions a degree of autonomy in line with the developing decentralization of the economy. The Roman Catholic Church, whose former primate, Cardinal Mindszenty, was a symbol of Church resistance for many years, arrived at an agreement with the regime in 1964. The last obstacle to cooperation between the Church and the state was removed in 1974, when Mindszenty, who left Hungary in 1971, was replaced as primate. Organized dissent is sparse and confined primarily to intellectuals. Clandestine publications (*samizdat*) are tolerated, but they are not common and are not anticommunist.

National Prospects

Because Hungary relied heavily on foreign loans to finance the "miracle" of the New Economic Mechanism, the country will soon face acute economic problems as debt-service payments grow larger in relation to earnings from exports. The decentralization of the economy, with its attendant competition for financing and the requirement that enterprises show profits, generated an inflation rate of 5 percent in 1981, and it is expected that that rate will climb. Hungary thus faces many of the problems of capitalism—declining real income for workers, unemployment, and liquidity crises—as the decentralization process continues. Hungary has a long enough history of political and economic pragmatism under Kádár to see it through these problems, barring the appearance of new major disruptive forces. The key issue in Hungary's future is whether Kádár's successor will continue and extend Kádár's policies or return to more rigid party control as a way of consolidating his power.

Further Reading

Kovrig, Bennett. *Communism in Hungary: From Kun to Kádár.* Stanford, Calif.: Hoover Institution Press, 1979.

Molnár, Miklós. *A Short History of the Hungarian Communist Party.* Boulder, Colo.: Westview Press, 1978.

Toma, Peter A., and Volgyes, Iván. *Politics in Hungary.* San Francisco: W. H. Freeman and Co., 1977.

ICELAND
(Ísland)

by Ólafur Th. Hardarson, M.Sc.

The System of Government

Iceland, an island nation of some 230,000 people in the North Atlantic, is a parliamentary republic and a unitary state. The country was settled in the ninth and tenth centuries, mainly from Norway. The settlers founded a commonwealth without a king or an executive power. Its central institution, which had legislative and judicial powers, was the *Althingi*, founded in 930. In 1262 the country came under the Norwegian king, and later became a Danish colony. The *Althingi* gradually lost its legislative power and was abolished in 1800, having functioned mainly as a judicial body for centuries. It was reestablished in 1845 as a consultative assembly to the Danish king. In 1874 the king "gave" the Icelanders a constitution, which granted the *Althingi* some legislative and financial powers. In 1904 Iceland obtained home rule and an Icelandic minister, responsible to the *Althingi*. Iceland became a sovereign state in 1918, but remained in a union with Denmark under the king until 1944, when it adopted its present republican constitution.

Executive

The president (*forseti*), who is elected directly by the people every four years, has mainly ceremonial duties. As the potential political power granted to the president in the constitution (e.g., the right to refer a statute to a referendum) has never been used, the major political influence of the office has been in the bargaining process when a new coalition government is formed. The executive power in fact belongs to the cabinet, which usually represents a coalition of two or more parties and is led by the prime minister.

Legislature

The Icelandic parliament, *Althingi*, has sixty members, elected in a general election for a term of four years. During this period the *Althingi* can be dissolved at any given time, and a new election held. This is done by a decree of the president, acting upon the advice of the prime minister, who in practice dissolves the *Althingi* only with the approval of all coalition partners in the cabinet. Since 1944 there have been twelve general elections, with an average term of just over three years.

The *Althingi* has an Upper Chamber and a Lower Chamber. After each general election, one-third of the *Althingi* members are chosen in the first session of the United *Althingi* to sit in the Upper Chamber for the whole term. Both chambers proportionally reflect the party composition of the *Althingi*. The division of the *Althingi* into two houses means that a government needs the support of thirty-two members, a majority in each chamber, but only thirty votes are needed to defeat a censure motion.

The united *Althingi*, sitting as a single chamber, deals with parliamentary motions, questions, and the budget. The main role of the separate chambers is to debate and approve bills other than the budget. Bills may be introduced in either chamber, as both are on an equal footing. Bills must pass through both chambers to become law.

Formally, the *Althingi* is the most powerful institution in the Icelandic political system. It can make law on any subject it chooses (within the limits set by the constitution), it makes and breaks governments, it can make any changes it likes on the draft budget, and it elects a considerable number of people to various important posts. In practice, however, the parties are the most important units in the political system, and the cabinet plays the major role in the process of policy formation. Party discipline is normally quite strong in the *Althingi*. From 1976 to 1982 over 80 percent of passed bills were government bills. In this period, 74 percent of all government bills were passed, while the corresponding figure for private members' bills was only 23 percent, indi-

Althingi Election Results (1971–1979)
Percentages of total valid votes & numbers of elected members

	1971	1974	1978	1979
Independence Party (IP)	36.2(22)	42.7(25)	32.7(20)	35.4(21)
Progressive Party (PP)	25.3(17)	24.9(17)	16.9(12)	24.9(17)
People's Alliance (PA)	17.1(10)	18.3(11)	22.9(14)	19.7(11)
Social Democratic Party (SDP)	10.5(6)	9.1(5)	22.0(14)	17.5(10)
Union of Liberals and Leftists (ULL)	8.9(5)	4.6(2)	3.3(0)	—
Others	2.0(0)	0.4(0)	2.2(0)	2.5(1)*
Total valid votes	105.395	114.108	122.207	123.751
Percent turnout	90.4%	91.4%	90.3%	89.3%

*Two splinter-groups from the IP account for 1.9 percent. The IP splinter-group in the South constituency had one elected member. He later joined the IP parliamentary bloc.

cating the role played by the government in the legislative process.

Judiciary

The highest court is the Supreme Court of Iceland (*Haestiréttur Íslands*), established in 1920. The eight judges are appointed by the president, acting upon the advice of the minister of justice. The court can declare a statute unconstitutional and has done so on a few occasions.

The High Court of State (*Landsdómur*) can impeach cabinet ministers, but this court has never convened since it was established in 1905.

Regional & Local Government

The functions and finances of local government are decided by law. The basic units are urban municipalities, *kaupstadir* (twenty-two), and rural districts, *hreppar* (202). The rural districts are combined in counties, *sýslur* (twenty-three). Municipalities and rural districts elect their own councils (by proportional representation in most cases). The *hreppar* operate with considerable independence from the county governments, but many of the rural units are very small and relatively weak.

The Electoral System

Since mid-1959, the members of *Althingi* have been chosen by direct, proportional election in multimember constituencies. Previously a mixed system of majority representation in single-member constituences and proportional representation had been in operation. In the present system, forty-nine of the sixty *Althingi* members are elected in eight constituencies: thirty-seven in five- and six-member constituencies, and twelve in Reykjavík, the capital. In each constituency, seats are allotted to ranked lists, put forward by the political parties according to a simple proportional system (d'Hondt). The eleven remaining seats, the supplementary seats, are allotted to the parties that have won at least one seat in order to minimize the difference between each party's proportion of the vote and the party's proportion of seats in the *Althingi*. The supplementary seats are filled with candidates who were not elected in the constituencies but came next on their party's list. If an elected member cannot attend *Althingi* sessions for at least two consecutive weeks, his place is taken (temporarily, if the member returns) by the next person on the party list. Thus, by-elections are unnecessary.

The voter can only cast his vote for a list. While changes in the rank-order of candidates on the chosen list are allowed, the rules make it unlikely that such changes, even if made by a substantial proportion of the voters, will alter the ranking. Elections take place on a Sunday by secret ballot. As there are many polling places in each constituency it is easy for the voters to get to the polls. The ballot papers are counted in the constituencies. Registration is automatic, and suffrage is universal for adults twenty years of age and older. Absentee ballots can be cast in the four-week period preceding polling day. Turnout in *Althingi* elections has been stable at around 90 percent in recent decades.

The president is elected by direct, popular vote for a four-year term. There is a strong feeling at present that it is improper for the parties to put up candidates or take a stand in presidential elections. The first president, Sveinn Björnsson, was elected by the *Althingi* in 1944. In 1945 and 1949, Björnsson was the only candidate for nationwide direct election, so no actual election was held. When Björnsson died, in 1952, the Independence Party (IP) and the Progressive Party (PP) together supported one candidate, who was defeated by Ásgeir Ásgeirsson, a Social Democratic Party (SDP) member of the *Althingi* who maintained that the people, not the parties, should choose the president. (Ásgeirsson was strongly supported by his son-in-law, Gunnar Thoroddsen, an IP member of the *Althingi* and then mayor of Reykjavík. His "treason" still rankles some IP leaders.) The parties never again attempted to put up a presidential candidate. A sitting president who wishes to be reelected has never been opposed.

The Party System

Origins of the Parties

In the nineteenth and early twentieth century the question of Iceland's relationship to Denmark dominated Icelandic politics. The first political parties in the country, which emerged at the turn of the century, were cadre-style parties, mainly based on different attitudes toward independence. The independence question was largely solved in 1918, and in the 1915–30 period the party system was completely transformed. Class-based parties emerged, domestic issues became the focal point of politics, and the new parties fell neatly on the conventional left-right socioeconomic continuum. Gradually, all the parties developed the formal characteristics of mass-party organizations. After the Second World War, foreign policy became a source for a major division in the Icelandic political system. While this and other developments have made the system more complex, the four major parties are commonly ranked from right to left in the following way: Independence Party (IP), Progressive Party (PP), Social Democratic Party (SDP) and People's Alliance (PA).

The Parties in Law

While the constitution does not mention political parties, their right to operate is guaranteed by the more general clause on the right of association. The right of people of any political opinion to organize in a political party has never been seriously questioned in the present Icelandic political system. It is easy to get a list on the ballot: all that is needed is a formal recommendation by fifty to 200 registered voters.

Party Organization

The major parties are formally mass parties, organized on a regional basis. The local organizations elect representatives to the party's constituency council and to the party convention. The party convention elects a central committee, and usually also the party leader. The activity of the local organization varies; quite often they are weak and function mainly as electoral machines in campaigns. Usually the party's constituency council prepares and ranks the list of candidates; in recent years, this process has sometimes been done by primary elections. In general, the position of the leadership and the permanent politicians is quite strong. Party conferences tend to confirm the decisions made by the leadership. Usually that leadership is reelected, although challenges to the leadership, usually by a competing leadership group, have been successful at times.

Campaigning

Election campaigns to a large extent are fought on a national level through the party press; all parties are supported by at least one daily national newspaper. The major parties also get equal time on state radio and television. Local party papers bloom at election time, and local party rallies are organized. In some rural areas, the parties hold joint meetings, with speakers from all parties. The parties finance their campaigns from their own resources, but time on radio and television is free. Political advertisements in the state media are not allowed.

Independent Voters

The absence of survey data makes it hard to estimate the strength of party identification. Nevertheless, various indirect evidence and increasing electoral volatility seems to indicate that party loyalty is decreasing among the electorate.

Independence Party (IP) (*Sjálfstaedisflokkurinn*)

History

The Independence Party (IP) was founded in 1929 with a merger of the Conservative Party (founded 1924) and the Liberal Party (founded 1926). The IP united the opponents of the SDP and the PP, and has remained the largest party in the country from its foundation, usually polling around 40 percent of the votes. Until 1942, because of the electoral system then in place, the party's strength among the electorate was not reflected in seats held in the *Althingi*. The party spent most of that time in opposition. After the change, the IP became "the natural party of government"; all of its leaders have been prime ministers: Ólafur Thors (1942, 1944–47, 1949, 1953–56, 1959–63), Bjarni Benediktsson (1963–70), Jóhann Hafstein (1970–71), and Geir Hallgrímsson (1974–78). Despite considerable heterogeneity, the party has remained more united for most of its lifetime than has been the case with its socialist opponents. Nevertheless, a serious schism emerged in the party in 1980, when the deputy leader, Gunnar Thoroddsen, supported by a few IP members of the *Althingi*, formed a coalition government with the PP and the PA, leaving the bulk of the party, including party leader Hallgrímsson, in opposition. Thoroddsen and his supporters have remained in the party, however, and there are presently no signs of a permanent split.

Organization

The IP has emphasized that it is a party of independent individuals without strong party discipline (a point highly relevant in the present intraparty dispute), but it has probably been the best-organized party in Iceland in terms of electoral machinery and national coverage. From 1930 to about 1960, it was in fact the only national party in Iceland: in the towns it competed with the socialist parties, in the rural areas with the PP. The IP has combined strong leadership with a notable tolerance in party discipline. People have not been expelled from the party in times of internal strain, for example, in 1944 when five IP members of the *Althingi* refused to support a government headed by party leader Thors.

Separate organizations for women and youth are affiliated to the IP. Separate associations for working-class members have also been organized. The IP is supported by—and has close connections with—*Morgunbladid*, by far the largest Icelandic daily newspaper, with an estimated circulation of 42,000 copies, an enormous figure in a total population of 230,000 inhabitants.

The IP does not belong to any international organizations, but its youth organization is a member of the Democrat Youth Community of Europe (DEMYC) and Nordic Conservative Youth.

National headquarters are at Sjálfstaedisflokkurinn, Háaleitisbraut 1, 105 Reykjavík.

Policy

In domestic policy, the IP has combined elements from liberalism and conservatism, and emphasized nationalism and opposition to class conflict. In the 1930s, while the party was in opposition, the emphasis in party policy was more strongly directed toward economic liberalism and private initiative; after the war, as "the natural party of government," the IP increasingly accepted the welfare state, economic planning, and government involvement. The party's policy—which has been labelled "social liberalism"—has always been characterized by pragmatism. The IP has been quite sensitive toward its working-class followers and consistently tried to avoid an anti-working-class image. It has been quite successful on this score, especially in comparison to corresponding parties in Scandinavia.

In the last few years, a new emphasis on a stronger free-market approach has been put forward with considerable force inside the party, especially by younger members. This was reflected in a tough anti-inflationary program on which the party fought the 1979 election—with much less success than was expected.

The schism between Thoroddsen and Hallgrímsson, while largely personal, has some ideological overtones. Thoroddsen has maintained that his group is more supportive of the party's traditions of limited party discipline in the *Althingi* and of pragmatism (as opposed to strict free-market views) in economic policy. The Hallgrímsson group, with some justification, has rejected this analysis.

In foreign policy the IP has been the most consistent supporter of Iceland's membership in NATO and of the NATO-base in Keflavík.

Membership & Constituency

The IP claims 15,000 to 20,000 members. It has managed to secure a broad following among voters, both in rural and urban areas, and it has considerable working-class support. The party has been strongest in Reykjavík (averaging 45 percent of the vote there from 1959 to 1978) and is weakest in the East, where it averages only 20 percent of the vote. In other constituencies, the party averages 30 to 40 percent of the vote. It not only attracts some working-class voters, but has gained surprising strength in some labor unions. It is estimated that about one-fourth of delegates to recent conventions of the Icelandic Federation of Labor are IP supporters.

Financing

Very little is known about party financing. Officially, the IP, like the other parties, does not receive direct financial contributions from any interest group. The IP may receive more support from private business than do other parties, but there is no reliable evidence of this. Membership dues are low, and the party does not enforce payment strictly.

Leadership

The IP has suffered from a leadership struggle in the last decade, especially between the party leader, Geir Hallgrímsson, and his former deputy, Gunnar Thoroddsen, the present prime minister. The signs are that those disputes will be resolved in the near future. Younger men have been recruited to leading positions, and this trend is likely to continue. The following major leaders of the IP were all educated as lawyers.

Hallgrímsson (born 1925) was prime minister in 1974 to 1978 and a mayor in Reykjavík from 1959 to 1972. He has been a member of the *Althingi* for Reykjavík since 1970. Hallgrímsson's leadership has been relatively weak compared to his predecessors.

Fridrik Sophusson (born 1943) replaced Thoroddsen as deputy leader in 1981. He has been a member of the *Althingi* for Reykjavík since 1978.

Davíd Oddsson (born 1948) became mayor of Reykjavík in 1982, when the IP regained a majority in the city council, which it lost in 1978, having been in power since the party was founded.

Ólafur G. Einarsson (born 1932) is the chairman of the parliamentary bloc. He has been a member of the *Althingi* for the South West since 1971.

Prime Minister Thoroddsen (born 1910), a former professor of law, has had a long and colorful career in Icelandic politics. He has been a member of the *Althingi* (1934–37, 1942–65), mayor of Reykjavík (1947–59), and minister of finance (1959–65). In 1965, he became an ambassador. After losing the presidential election in 1968, he returned to party politics, was elected to the *Althingi* in 1971, and was minister of industry and social affairs from 1974 to 1978. Thoroddsen is likely to retire from politics with the next election.

Prospects

Compared to the postwar period as a whole, the last decade has been difficult for the IP. The party has spent more time in opposition than in government, its fortunes have been unusually bad in three elections out of four, and the party has been shaken by internal disputes. Still there are no clear signs indicating that the party will permanently lose its strong position in Icelandic politics. The IP did remarkably well in the 1982 municipal elections, and the worst intraparty disputes may well be over. Policy differences within the party, concerning its traditional pragmatism versus a more direct free-market approach, may nevertheless still produce strains within the party and affect both its electoral fortunes and its potential as a coalition partner.

People's Alliance (PA)
(*Althýdubandalagid*)

History

The People's Alliance (PA) is descended from the Communist Party (CP) and other breakaway groups from the SDP. The CP was founded in 1930 by radical SDP members as an orthodox communist party and a member of the Comintern. It won its first seats in the *Althingi* in 1937 with 8.5 percent of the vote. In line with Comintern policy, the CP demanded that the SDP join it in a Popular Front, but the SDP main body refused. Again, the left wing of the SDP broke off, and it and the CP joined to form the United Socialist Party (USP). In its first elections, in 1942, the USP polled 16.2 percent of the vote, more than the SDP. The USP was not a Comintern member, but it was clearly pro-Soviet in foreign policy, and most of its major leaders had been prominent in the CP. The party participated in the IP-SDP-USP coalition of 1944 to 1947. In 1956, after another split in the SDP, the PA was created as a loose electoral alliance between the USP and the former SDP group. The PA immediately took a role in the government coalition of 1956 to 1958. After a decade out of power, the PA re-created itself as a formal political party in 1968 and the USP was dissolved. The PA took part in the governing coalitions of 1971 to 1974, 1978–79, and 1980 to the present. It has never held the vital portfolios of prime minister, foreign affairs, or justice, but it was allotted the finance ministry in the 1980 coalition.

The 1968 reorganization of the PA led to a split in its ranks, led by former SDP leader Hannibal Valdimarsson and others, who formed the Union of Liberals and Leftists. This group had considerable success in 1971 (8.9 percent of the vote and five seats), largely at the expense of the SDP. The party lost seats in 1974 and disappeared from the *Althingi* in 1978.

Organization

Since 1968 the PA has been organized in a way similar to the other parties. The CP was Leninist in organization, and the USP, while formally a branch party like the others, was marked by the Leninist principle of "democratic centralism."

The PA is not affiliated to any international organizations. It does not operate separate organizations for youth and women as do the other parties. The party's daily newspaper is *Thjódviljinn*, with an estimated circulation of 11,000 copies.

Party headquarters are at Althýdubandalagid, Grettisgötu 3, 101 Reykjavík.

Policy

The PA defines itself as a "socialist party, based on democracy and parliamentarism. . . . The aim of the party is to establish a socialist society in Iceland." The party supports public ownership of the largest companies, while it openly rejects the Soviet model of centralized economy. The PA is farthest to the left in the Icelandic party system, but it contains a considerable variety of opinion: communists, left socialists, social democrats, environmentalists, etc. Increased government participation has given the party a more pragmatic image, and may produce some tension in the party in the near future.

The PA opposes Icelandic membership in NATO and the U.S. military base at Keflavík. It favors the dissolution of military alliances and a policy of neutrality. On the other hand, the party firmly denies being pro-Soviet and has condemned the Soviet invasions in Czechoslovakia and Afghanistan and violations of human rights in Poland and other East European countries. In recent years, the PA has been prepared to take part in government coalitions whose declared aim has been to preserve the status quo in Icelandic foreign policy.

Membership & Constituency

The PA claims only 3,000 members, but it has better national coverage than the SDP, both in terms of local organization and voting support. Nevertheless, the party is stronger in urban than in rural areas.

Financing

Very little is known about the PA's financing. Like the SDP, it may rely more on membership dues than do the PP and the IP. Each party branch has to hand over to the central organization a sum based on the number of branch members.

Leadership

In the last few years, a complete renewal of the PA leadership has taken place.

Party leader Svavar Gestsson (born 1944) became a member of the *Althingi* for Reykjavík in 1978; was minister of commerce (1978–79); and has been minister of social affairs, health, and insurance since 1980.

The chairman of the parliamentary bloc, Ólafur Ragnar Grímsson (born 1943), a professor of political science, entered the *Althingi* for Reykjavík in 1978.

Ragnar Arnalds (born 1938), educated as a lawyer, has been minister of finance since 1980. He was the chairman of the party (1968–77), a member of the *Althingi* for the North West (1963–67 and 1971 to present), and minister of education and communication (1978–79).

Hjörleifur Guttormsson (born 1935), educated as a biologist, entered the *Althingi* in 1978 and is minister of industry.

Prospects

The party's attempts to become a broad party of the left have undoubtedly met with some success, but at the same time have created some uneasiness in the party's left wing. The basic dilemma of the PA is whether it can be an acceptable coalition partner and at the same time preserve a radical, socialist identity. If it continues to develop along pragmatic lines, it risks leaving a space for a new party on its left. On the other hand, if it chooses to stress its separate identity, the party may have to spend the next years in opposition.

Progressive Party (PP) (*Framsóknarflokkurinn*)

History

The Progressive Party (PP) was founded as a parliamentary party in 1916. In its first years, the party was almost exclusively a farmer's party, and it had close ties to the cooperative movement, a considerable force, especially in rural areas. Since 1923, the PP has usually polled around 25 percent of the vote, which makes it the second-largest party in the country.

Because of the electoral system, the PP has always been stronger in the *Althingi* than among the voters. This was especially pronounced before 1942 and contributed to the strong position of the PP in the coalition system in that period: from 1917 to 1942, the PP spent only five years in opposition, and held the premiership from 1927 to 1942.

In the 1940s, the PP lost its role as "the natural party of government" to the IP. It has chaired four coalitions since 1942, but it has been in opposition for almost half of this period.

Organization

While the PP was clearly a cadre party at the beginning, it developed the formal characteristics of a mass party in the 1930s; and at present it has about 105 local party branches.

The PP has no international affiliations, but its youth movement is a member of the International Federation of Liberal and Radical Youth and the Nordic Youth Associations of Center Parties and Liberal and Radical Parties. There is also a separate women's organization within the PP. The party publishes a national daily newspaper, *Tíminn*, with an estimated circulation of 14,000 copies.

Party headquarters are at Framsóknar-flokkurinn, Raudarárstíg 18, 105 Reykjavík.

Policy

The PP may be labelled a center or an agrarian party in terms of domestic policy. For decades the party's main aims were clearly the defense of the interests of farmers and traditional culture. Party policy has changed as the PP has tried to appeal to urban voters, presenting an image as the party of "the middle ground." The party supports a "mixed economy" of private firms, cooperatives, and public enterprises. The PP emphasises rural development in which the state plays a major part.

The PP has supported Iceland's membership in NATO, but it has been critical of the Keflavík base and, at times, supported its removal.

Membership & Constituency

In its early decades, the PP's electoral support was almost exclusively in the rural areas, even though the leadership included some "urban radicals." The party did not even put up candidates in towns in several elections. As urbanization continued it was necessary for the party to broaden its appeal in order to keep its electoral strength. The party has been successful on this score. Nevertheless, the PP is still relatively weak in Reykjavík and the surrounding (mainly urban) South West constituency, where the party polled 14 to 18 percent on average from 1959 to 1978, compared to 30 to 50 percent in other parts of the country. The party's traditional strongholds are in areas where the cooperative movement has been strong.

Financing

Little is known of PP finances. The cooperative movement does not contribute directly to the party. It may place more advertisements in PP newspapers, but there is no reliable evidence that it does so. Party membership dues are relatively low and not strictly enforced.

Leadership

Party leader Steingrímur Hermannsson (born 1928, son of former PP leader and prime minister Hermann Jónasson), was educated as an engineer and has been a member of the *Althingi* for the West Peninsula since 1971. He was a minister of agriculture (1978–79) and has been minister of fisheries and communication since 1980.

Tómas Árnason (born 1923), educated as a lawyer, has been a member of the *Althingi* for the East since 1974. He was a minister of finance (1978–79) and has been minister of commerce since 1980.

Former party leader Ólafur Jóhannesson (born 1913) is minister of foreign affairs. Jóhannesson, a former professor of law, entered the *Althingi* in 1959 for the North West, was prime minister (1971–74, 1978–79), and minister of justice and church affairs and commerce (1974–78).

Páll Pétursson (born 1937), a farmer, is the chairman of the parliamentary bloc. He has been a member of the *Althingi* for the North West since 1974.

Prospects

The PP has been a government party continuously since 1971. Electorally, the party has been close to its norm in the last decade, except in 1978, when it suffered badly. The PP has enjoyed some two extra members in the *Althingi* due to the electoral system, but this is likely to be changed. Increasing electoral volatility may produce some difficulties for the PP, especially in the urban areas, as the party tries to reconcile rural interests and the expectations of its urban voters.

Social Democratic Party (SDP) (*Althýduflokkurinn*)

History

The Social Democratic Party (SDP) was founded in 1916 as the political arm of the labor movement. The party was organizationally tied to the Icelandic Federation of Labor (founded at the same time) until 1942.

The SDP was founded as a democratic socialist party and was clearly a working-class party. It maintained that politics were about economic distribution and the living conditions of the working class—a very radical conception in a period when politics was dominated by the struggle for independence from Denmark.

The SDP grew continuously in strength for its first two decades, and polled over 20 percent of the vote in 1934. The party lost some ground in the 1937 election, and since 1942 it has usually been the smallest of the four major parties, receiving 14 to 16 percent of the vote. This history is in stark contrast to the development of the social democratic parties in Scandinavia. The socialist bloc in Iceland has been smaller than in the other Nordic countries, and the Icelandic Social Democrats have been the smaller of the two major socialist parties within that bloc. This can partly be explained by the splits the SDP has suffered, losing its left wing each time.

The SDP first joined a coalition government (with the PP) in 1934, having supported the PP government 1927 to 1931. The party has been in government for almost two-thirds of the remaining period, holding the premiership in one coalition (Stefánsson, 1947–49) and two minority cabinets (Jónsson, 1958–59; Gröndall, 1979–80). The SDP has worked with all other parties in coalitions. Of special interest is the extraordinarily long coalition partnership of the SDP with the IP 1959 to 1971, an unusual political combination by European standards. After that partnership, the SDP showed unusually poor performance at the polls in 1971 and 1974, but the party won the greatest victory in the electoral history of the republic in 1978, when its share of the vote increased from 9.1 to 22 percent. The SDP has been in opposition since 1971, except for the 1978-to-1980 period.

Organization

The SDP was the first formal mass party and to some extent showed the way toward present party organization and intraparty democratic procedures. The party has suffered more from intraparty disputes than the other parties. In 1952 the party leader even lost his post in a vote in the party convention, a unique case in Icelandic party history. The stormy 1980 party convention showed tensions continue to exist in the party.

In 1975, the SDP added a clause to its constitution making open primaries compulsory before every *Althingi* election. Other parties have experimented with primaries in the last decade, but no other party has taken this radical step. (Open primaries are virtually unknown in parliamentary systems, and they tend to loosen the party structure, and give more room for free play by individuals.) It is too early to say what effects primaries will have on the Icelandic party system in general and the SDP in particular, but the signs are that it will lead to a weakening of the parties as organizations.

The SDP is a member of the Socialist International. The party's youth and women's associations are also affiliated to international and Nordic Social Democratic organizations. The party's daily newspaper, *Althýdubladid*, has an estimated circulation of 4,000 copies.

Party headquarters are at Althýduflokkurinn, Althýduhúsinu, Hverfisgötu 8–10, 101 Reykjavík.

Policy

The domestic policy of the SDP has evolved along lines similar to many other European social democratic parties: nationalization and class struggle have been deemphasized, and a "mixed" economy and the welfare state have become core issues in the party program. The fact that the SDP has three times lost its left wing has probably put its mark on SDP policy, which seems to be closer to the political center than is the case with the Scandinavian social democrats. The party has tried to renew its image in recent years. It fought the 1978 election, in which the party presented many new candidates, with the slogan: "SDP—a new party on an old base." The party tried to combine "new politics"—emphasis on various populist issues; an anti-establishment image; and new forms of participation, such as the primaries—with "old politics" such as commitment to welfare, industrial democracy, and a new anti-inflationary program. This mixture brought electoral success in 1978, but the party has not been able to maintain that momentum. It was not clear in mid-1982 which direction the party would take in terms of domestic policy.

The SDP has been closest to the IP on the foreign-policy dimension. It has supported Iceland's membership in NATO and the base in Keflavík, but the party's youth association has been critical of that policy. In the last few years, the SDP seems to have followed the policies of the Socialist International in international affairs more closely than previously.

Membership & Constituency

The SDP claims 5,000 members. As a working-class party, its support was mainly in the urban areas. The party has never been able to win a considerable following in rural districts, but it is likely that its urban support now comes from a broader range of classes than it used to.

Financing

No reliable data on party financing exists. Like the PA, the party's central organization collects established sums based on membership from its branches, relying more on membership dues than the other parties. The SDP does not receive any direct support from the trade unions.

Leadership

A new generation has taken over the leadership in the last few years. The Party leader Kjartan Jóhannsson (born 1939), educated in engineering and economics, entered the *Althingi* for the South West in 1978 and was minister of fisheries from 1978 to 1980.

Sighvatur Björgvinsson (born 1942), the chairman of the parliamentary bloc, has been a member of the *Althingi* for the West Peninsula since 1974 and was minister of finance (1979–80).

Vilmundur Gylfason (born 1948), educated as a historian, played a major part in developing the SDP's new style before the 1978 election. He was elected to the *Althingi* for Reykjavík in 1978 and was minister of education, justice, and church affairs (1979–80). Gylfason, the *enfant terrible* of the SDP, has caused several hot disputes in the SDP leadership. He lost his challenge for the deputy leadership in the 1980 party convention.

Magnús H. Magnússon (born 1922), the deputy leader of the party, has been a member of the *Althingi* for the South since 1978. He was a minister of social affairs, health, and insurance (1978–80).

Prospects

The SDP has suffered its worst electoral disaster and its greatest victory at the polls within the last decade. It has uncharacteristically spent most of this time in opposition, experienced a change of style and leadership, and suffered from some internal strain. Reversing the party's electoral fortunes in the late 1970s was a major achievement, but because that gain has not been consolidated, it is extraordinarily hard to predict anything about the role the SDP will play in Icelandic politics in the next few years.

Minor Parties

Minor parties have frequently put up candidates for *Althingi* elections in the postwar period, but only two of these have won seats: the National Preservation Party in 1953 and the Union of Liberals and Leftists in 1971 and 1974. Most other minor "parties" have in fact only been active in one election campaign and then disappeared, with the exception of the very small but active Trotskyites and Maoists, which have had virtually no success at the polls.

Other Political Forces

Besides the political parties and the administration, major interest groups play an important role in the political system. Most important are the Federation of Labor (ASÍ) and the Federation of Employers (VSÍ). The ASI has formally been independent of parties since 1942, but the parties have competed for influence in the organization, especially the USP/PA, the IP, and the SDP. While the interest organizations have become more autonomous, various informal links with the parties remain. In 1977–78, the PA and the SDP joined hands in the ASÍ, when the labor movement strongly opposed the economic measures of the IP-PP government; it is very likely that this contributed to the heavy losses of the government parties in 1978. The Federation of Employers and the Board of Commerce have in recent years advocated their own economic policies, which have considerable similarities to the IP platform. While the decision-making structure of Icelandic government cannot be termed corporatist, it is clear that the cabinets have to take serious account of the interest organizations in the formation of economic policy, and the government is frequently involved in the bargaining between ASI and VSI.

National Prospects

Iceland has in recent years combined a very high standard of living and economic instability, notably a very high rate of inflation (around 50 percent). The country is still to a large extent dependent on the export of fish and fish products. The other major natural resource is hydro-electric energy. Despite grave economic difficulties at present, the country is likely to keep its relatively prosperous economic standing.

While the parties have experienced decreasing power, increasing electoral volatility, and less internal cohesion in the last few years, they will continue to function as the basic units of the political system, which—despite some strains—is likely to remain fundamentally unchanged in the near future.

Further Reading

Elder, N., A. H. Thomas, and D. Arter. *The Consensual Democracies? The Government and Politics of the Scandinavian States.* Oxford, England: Martin Robertson, 1982.

Grímsson, Ólafur Ragnar. "Iceland: A Multilevel Coalition System." In *Government Coalitions in Western Democracies*, E. C. Brown and J. Dreijmanis, eds. New York and London: Longman, 1982.

———. "The Icelandic Power Structure 1800–2000." *Scandinavian Political Studies*, Vol. 11, 1976.

Kristjánsson, Svanur. "The Electoral Basis of the Icelandic Independence Party 1929–1944." *Scandinavian Political Studies*, Vol. 2 (new series), No. 1, 1979.

Nordal, Jóhannes, and Kristinsson, Valdimar, eds. *Iceland 874–1974.* Reykjavík: Central Bank of Iceland, 1975.

Tomasson, Richard F. *Iceland: The First New Society.* Reykjavík: Iceland Review, and Minneapolis: University of Minnesota Press, 1980.

Wisti, Folmer, ed. *Nordic Democracy.* Copenhagen: Det danske selskab, 1981.

REPUBLIC OF INDIA
(*Bharat*)

by M. Glen Johnson, Ph.D.

The System of Government

India is a federal parliamentary democracy with a single dominant political party and many factionalized, but significant, smaller parties.

Though its roots are much deeper, the contemporary Indian political system dates from August 15, 1947, when its long and unique struggle for independence from British rule finally succeeded. Independence brought partition on religious lines between secular but predominantly Hindu India and Muslim Pakistan. Even truncated in this way, the new India became the second largest state in the world in population. According to the 1981 census, the population of India was almost 684 million; approximately one out of every six persons on earth is an Indian.

Newly independent India drafted a constitution modeled on the British and other existing constitutions. The constitution, which entered into force on January 26, 1950, provides for a democratic republic, secular, parliamentary, and federal in character. It is one of the longest and most detailed written constitutions in the world and one of the most frequently amended.

Executive

The president of the republic is the head of state and supreme commander of the military forces, but exercises the executive power only formally. The president is elected to a five-year term by an electoral college composed of the elected members of both houses of the national Parliament and of the lower houses of the state legislatures. Voting is weighted to allow for population differences between the states. The president is supposed to be a nonpartisan figure, but in practice candidates have been elected only if they were acceptable to the prime minister.

From the beginning, the president was intended to exercise his power only with the closest advice of the prime minister and the cabinet. His primary role was to be symbolic, much in the manner of the British monarch, although there was considerable discussion of the extent of the president's discretionary powers. Any ambiguity was removed by the Forty-second Amendment to the constitution in 1976 and the Forty-fourth Amendment in 1978 which explicitly required the president to act in accordance with the advice of the cabinet.

Thus, effective executive power belongs to the prime minister and the cabinet (formally the Council of Ministers). The prime minister is appointed by the president and must be able to command majority support in the Lok Sabha, the lower house of the Parliament. If there is a recognized leader of a party or coalition which commands a majority in the Lok Sabha—as has normally been the case—the president has no discretion. Only in 1979, when the governing Janata Party coalition under Prime Minister Morarji Desai disintegrated in office, was the president able to exercise any discretion. At that time, he asked Charan Singh, leader of the Lok Dal, to form a government. Singh was unable to mobilize majority support in the Lok Sabha, and recommended that the president dissolve the Lok Sabha and call elections, which he did.

The prime minister is responsible to the Lok Sabha, which may force the prime minister from office at any time by demonstrating the lack of majority support for him. In practice, this has happened only in 1979, when the Janata coalition split and Prime Minister Desai resigned in face of an impending vote of no confidence.

The president appoints the members of the Council of Ministers on the advice of the prime minister and removes them in the same way. Within the cabinet, the prime minister has evolved into the strongest figure; the collective decision-making process of the British system of cabinet government is much less characteristic of India where the prime minister and his formal and informal advisers (who may or may not be members of the cabinet) predominate. Cabinet ministers, therefore, mainly are occupied with implementation of policy decisions affecting their governmental ministries and with day-to-day administrative responsibilities. In addition, most ministers are responsible for political liaison between the ruling party at the Centre (the national government) and in particular states.

Ministerial departments are staffed by a powerful and prestigious civil service, the modern successor to the almost legendary Indian Civil Service of British colonial days. At the apex of the modern civil service is the Indian Administrative Service, an elite cadre of highly qualified, competitively selected administrators who exercise wide-ranging power over implementation and administration of government policy subject only to the supervision of politically responsible ministers. In recent years, the power exercised by civil servants has become controversial.

India has had only five prime ministers in more than thirty-five years of independence, and Jawaharlal Nehru and his daughter, Indira Gandhi, have governed for thirty of those years. Nehru served from 1947 to 1964 and his successor, Lal Bahadur Shastri, from 1964 to 1966. Mrs. Gandhi served from 1966 to 1977, when her Congress Party, until then the only governing party India had known at the Centre, suffered severe reverses in national elections after eighteen months of authoritarian rule under the draconian emergency provisions of the Indian constitution. The 1977 elections brought together a number of opposition parties in a coalition which took the name Janata (People's) Party. The constituent parties of the coalition were the Congress (O—Organization), the Bharatiya Lok Dal, the Jana Sangh, and the Socialists (since dissolved). The Janata Party won an overwhelming victory and formed a government under Prime Minister Morarji Desai who served from 1977 to mid-1979 when the party split. Charan Singh then became the prime minister. New national elections resulted in Mrs. Gandhi's return to power in January 1980.

Since her reelection, there has been discussion in governmental and political circles about a shift to a presidential form of government somewhat on the French model. Though such a shift has been advocated by highly placed individuals both in Mrs. Gandhi's ruling Congress (I) Party and in some of the opposition parties, Mrs. Gandhi herself regularly has argued that no significant modification in the cabinet/parliament form is to be expected in the foreseeable future.

Legislature

The Indian Parliament is bicameral. The more important lower house is called the Lok Sabha or "house of the people." It has 542 members directly elected from single-member district constituencies based on population. Elections are normally held at five-year intervals. The five-year limit has been abridged only once. In 1976, operating under the emergency provisions of the constitution and on the recommendation of Prime Minister Gandhi, the Lok Sabha's life was extended by one year. The extension was renewed a year later, although Prime Minister Gandhi surprised everyone by calling elections in May 1977. Parliamentary elections may be called at less than five-year intervals by the president acting on the advice of the prime minister; this has happened twice, the elections of 1971 and 1980.

Seventy-nine Lok Sabha seats are reserved for members of the Scheduled Castes, those who, as untouchables or outcasts, historically have been at the economically depressed and socially degraded bottom of the Hindu caste system. Forty seats are reserved for members of the Scheduled Tribes, tribal groups which historically have been depressed economically or otherwise deprived of full participation in Indian society. The reserved seats are allocated among the states on the basis of the proportion of their populations which fall into the respective Scheduled category. Electorates for the reserved seats are made up of all classes of Indian citizens, but only Scheduled Caste or Scheduled Tribe members may stand for such seats. These provisions for special representation are constitutionally temporary, but they have been regularly extended. In another special category, the president of India is empowered to appoint up to two Anglo-Indians (descendants of mixed British-Indian marriages or liaisons) to the Lok Sabha if, acting on the advice of the prime minister, he finds that this community is insufficiently represented as a result of the election process.

By constitution, the Lok Sabha must meet at least twice each year with no more than six months between sessions. In practice, it usually meets three times a year.

The upper house of Parliament is the Rajya Sabha or "council of the states." It has 250 members, twelve of whom are appointed by the president from among Indians distinguished in the arts and professions. The remainder is elected by the state legislatures to fixed terms, with approximately one-third retiring every second year. Thus it is possible that the partisan majority in the Lok Sabha will not coincide with the majority in the Rajya Sabha, which has happened on two occasions, in 1977 and 1980.

The two houses of Parliament have the same

power over ordinary legislation; both must pass bills in agreed form. However, money bills may be introduced only in the Lok Sabha, and the Rajya Sabha has only the power of delay. If a money bill is amended or rejected by the Rajya Sabha, it needs to be merely repassed by the Lok Sabha in the original form to be sent to the president for assent. The Rajya Sabha exercises independent jurisdiction in a limited range of issues relating to the states.

Judiciary

India's constitution makers took the notion of parliamentary supremacy from the British model, but tried to graft onto it an independent judiciary and judicial-review system based largely on the American model. At the apex of an integrated national judicial system is the Supreme Court of India. It consists of a chief justice and not more than thirteen other judges appointed by the president. Judges of the Supreme Court serve until they reach the age of sixty-five, unless removed by an elaborate and difficult parliamentary procedure. The chief justice is normally the most senior judge in terms of age although there have been one or two controversial cases of "supersession," i.e., the appointment of a less senior judge as chief justice.

The Supreme Court has broad original and appellate jurisdiction which extends to civil and criminal matters and especially to matters of constitutional interpretation and Centre–state relations. The exercise of these powers has led to considerable conflict between governments committed to greater or lesser degrees of social reform and a court equally committed to the protection of fundamental rights outlined in the constitution. The conflict between court and government has been waged in a variety of ways over the years. Many of the forty-four amendments to the Indian constitution have been designed to reverse some Supreme Court ruling striking down an act of Parliament. The most substantial attack on the court came in 1976 when Mrs. Gandhi's government pushed through Parliament the very detailed and extensive Forty-second Amendment Act which, among other things, placed very stringent limitations on the power of the Supreme Court to review acts of Parliament on constitutional grounds. The Supreme Court itself struck down part of this amendment and the Janata Party government further altered it in the Forty-fourth Amendment in 1978. The fundamental difficulty of reconciling parliamentary supremacy with judicial review remains one of the troublesome issues facing the Indian political system.

Regional & Local Government

India is a federation composed of twenty-two states and nine union territories. However, Indian federalism is weighted heavily toward the central government. The union territories include Delhi (India's capital city), Chandigarh (the joint capital of the states of Punjab and Haryana), and several smaller or isolated territories some of which came to India from European colonial powers other than the United Kingdom. The union territories are ruled by the central government under a variety of arrangements.

The states are organized mainly along language lines. The central government may and occasionally has reorganized state boundaries. The structure of state government is similar to that of the Centre. The executive power is vested in a governor who is appointed by the president of India on the advice of the prime minister. The governor is appointed for a five-year term and is largely a figurehead whose powers and role are analogous to those of the president at the Centre.

Real political and administrative power is exercised by a chief minister (analogous to the prime minister at the Centre) and his council of ministers who are appointed by the governor and are collectively responsible to the legislative assembly. Most states have a unicameral legislature. The legislative assemblies are composed of between 60 and 500 members chosen by direct election from territorial constituencies based on population. The legislative assemblies function in a manner similar to the Lok Sabha at the Centre. Seven states have bicameral legislatures with a smaller legislative council functioning alongside the legislative assembly. Members of the legislative council are elected indirectly by the assembly or appointed by the governor to fixed terms with approximately one-third retiring every second year.

The Indian constitution divides the functions of government between the states and the Centre through three detailed lists. The Union List contains areas which are exclusively reserved to the Centre, including defense and military forces, atomic energy, foreign affairs, railways, shipping, air transport, posts and telegraph, currency, international trade, banking, insurance, mining, and nonagricultural income and corporate taxation. The State List contins items reserved to the states, including public order, police, prisons, local government, public health, agriculture, land and land tenure, property tax, and tax on agricultural income. The Concurrent List contains items on which either the states or the Centre may act, including criminal law, preventive detention, marriage and divorce, contracts, economic and social planning, social security, labor, education, and civil procedure. In the event of conflict between Centre and state action on matters on the Concurrent List, the Centre position prevails. Moreover, a reserve clause grants the Centre exclusive jurisdiction over all areas not enumerated in one of the lists. In periods of emergency or with the concurrence of two-thirds of the Rajya Sabha, the Centre may act on matters on the State List.

Finally, if the president "is satisfied that a situation has arisen in which the government of the State cannot be carried on in accordance with the provisions of this Constitution" (Art. 356), he may, on the advice of the prime minister, suspend the state government and rule directly from Delhi. This is referred to as President's Rule and has been used with increasing frequency since the 1960s.

The Electoral System

Although the Rajya Sabha and the legislative councils are indirectly elected, the more important Lok Sabha and the legislative assemblies are elected directly. Since 1967, all electoral constituencies have been single member. Candidates must be Indian citizens at least twenty-five years of age. Most successful candidates are nominated by recognized parties, although a large number of independents (2,830 in 1980) always stands for election. A candidate must put up a deposit of 500 rupees (about $65) to run for a Lok Sabha seat and 250 rupees for a legislative-assembly seat. A candidate must poll at least one-sixth of the votes cast in that constituency in order to have his deposit refunded. The candidate receiving a simple plurality of the valid votes cast in the constituency wins.

Vacancies caused by death, resignation, or removal from office are filled in by elections which are watched carefully as signals of political trends.

Since the majority of the electorate is illiterate, political parties and independent candidates have developed symbols which are used in all campaign materials. Ballots list candidates by symbol, in English and in the local language(s). Voting is secret and carefully supervised. Although there have been charges of corruption, intimidation, and "booth capturing," most observers agree that Indian elections are remarkably free, fair, and orderly considering the levels of literacy and development in the country.

All Indian citizens twenty-one years of age and over are eligible to vote. Registration rolls are kept by the Election Commission, an independent agency charged with responsibility for the fair and efficient conduct of elections, and are updated regularly at the initiative of the commission.

Since illiterate voters may feel intimidated by officials in the polling booths, parties are permitted to set up booths at a distance from the actual polling booth to assist voters in identifying their names on the electoral rolls. Activity at these booths on election day is often considered a clue to electoral trends.

India is so large that the 1980 national election required two separate polling days. Voters' fingers are marked with indelible ink to insure against double voting. Votes are not counted until the final polling day is underway, and returns are not released until all polling is completed. The entire operation is supervised by the Election Commission.

With approximately 300 million eligible voters, India has the largest democratic electorate in the world. Voter turnout has been relatively high. Since 1962, between 55 and 65 percent of the eligible voters have exercised their franchise in each national election.

The Party System

Origins of the Parties

Most—but not all—Indian political parties grew out of the independence struggle. The Congress Party, which has held power at the Centre for all but three of the thirty-five years since independence, is the direct descendant of the Indian

LOK SABHA ELECTIONS, 1980

Parties	Number of Candidates	Number of Seats Won	% of Seats	% of Votes
Congress (I)	489	351	66.9	42.66
Lok Dal	292	41	7.8	9.43
CPM	62	35	6.7	6.03
Janata	431	31	5.9	18.94
DMK	16	16	3.0	2.15
Congress (U)	212	13	2.5	5.31
CPI	50	11	2.1	2.60
AIADMK	24	2	0.4	2.38
Akali Dal	7	1	0.2	0.71
Others	200	16	3.0	3.24
Independents	2,830	8	1.5	6.54
TOTAL	4,611	525*		

* Polling was postponed for 17 seats.

LOK SABHA ELECTIONS, 1980

State	Total Seats	Cong (1)	Lok Dal	Janata	Cong (U)	CPM	CPI	Others	Ind.	Polling Postponed
Andhra Pradesh	42	41			1					
Assam	14	2								12
Bihar	54	30	5	8	4		4		3	
Gujarat	26	25		1						
Haryana	10	5	4	1						
Himachal P.	4	3								1
Jammu and Kashmir	6	1			1			3		1
Karnataka	28	27		1						
Kerala	20	5			3	6	2	3	1	
Madhya Pradesh	40	35		4					1	
Maharashtra	48	39		8	1					
Manipur	2	1					1			
Meghalaya	2	1								1
Nagaland	1								1	
Orissa	21	19	1							1
Punjab	13	12						1*		
Rajasthan	25	18	2	4	1					
Sikkim	1							1		
Tamil Nadu	39	20						19*		
Tripura	2					2				
Uttar Pradesh	85	51	29	3			1		1	
West Bengal	42	4				27	3	7		1
Andaman and Nicobar	1	1								
Arunachal P.	2	2								
Chandigarh	1	1								
Dadra, Nagar Haveli	1	1								
Delhi	7	6		1						
Goa, Daman Diu	2				1				1	
Lakshadweep	1				1					
Mizoram	1								1	
Pondicherry	1	1								
TOTAL	542	351	41	31	13	35	11	35	3	17

* In Punjab: Akali Dal, 1; in Tamil Nadu: AIADMK, 2; DMK, 16.

National Congress, the umbrella organization which directed the mainstream of the independence struggle from 1885 until independence in 1947. As an umbrella organization focused on the quest for greater autonomy and then independence, the Congress was highly aggregative, seeking to unite disparate ideologies and personalities in service of self-rule. With independence at hand, it was inevitable that ideological and personal differences would loom larger. Eventually, these differences led to defections from the dominant Congress Party.

An early ideological split led to the establishment of the Socialist Party in 1947. Personality differences created a break between Charan Singh and the Congress in Uttar Pradesh, India's largest state, and the establishment of the Bharatiya Kranti Dal in 1967. A combination of ideology and personality led to a major "split" in the Congress in 1969 and the establishment of the Congress (O). Almost all of the Indian parties—except the Communist Party, the Jana Sangh (forerunner of today's Bharatiya Janata Party), and some of the regional and state parties—arose from defections or splits in the Congress Party.

The Parties in Law

Political parties are not given significant treatment in the constitution of India and have little special status in Indian law. Independent candidates have essentially the same legal rights and

INDIAN PARTY SYSTEM SINCE INDEPENDENCE*

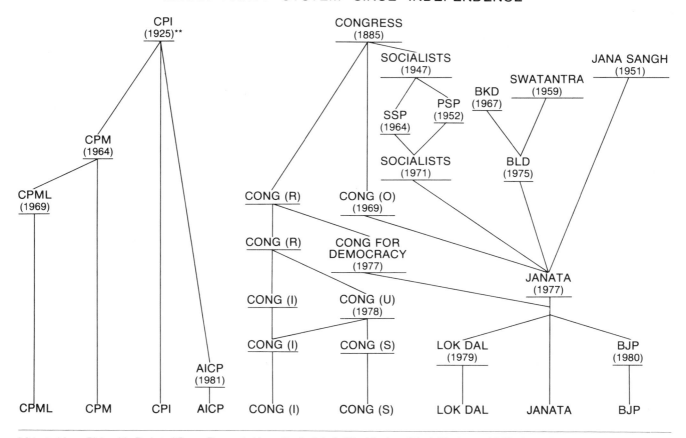

* Adapted from Richard L. Park and Bruce Bueno de Mesquita, *India's Political System*, 2d ed. (Englewood Cliffs, N. J.: Prentice-Hall, 1979).
** Numbers in parentheses indicate date of founding.

responsibilities as party candidates: nomination procedures, financial limits, and reporting requirements are the same.

Parties recognized by the Election Commission have reserved symbols. Considering the limited literacy among Indian voters, the allocation of symbols by the commission becomes an important function, especially when splits in important parties result in competing claims to the traditional party symbol.

To be recognized at the national level, a party must have received a minimum of 3 percent of the national vote in the last preceding election. A similar requirement obtains at the state level. In the 1980 elections, there were six recognized national parties and twenty-seven recognized state parties with reserved symbols. In addition, there were thirteen unrecognized parties registered with the Election Commission.

Party Organization

Most Indian parties profess to be mass organizations based on dues-paying members; in reality,

few are. Only the Congress, the Jana Sangh, and the Communist parties have sustained such a mass character over any length of time, and the Congress has been the most successful of the three. The Jana Sangh and the Communists are numerically smaller and confined to a narrower geographical area than Congress. One of the reasons for the relative success of the Congress is that it generally has been a coalition party composed of disparate groups espousing different emphases in government policy. Over the years, however, the Congress has become less coalitional and more personalistic in character, reflecting Mrs. Gandhi's policies.

None of the other parties has been of the coalition type, except the Janata briefly during its incumbency from 1977 to 1979. Other parties tend to be either ideological (the Socialists, the Communists, and the Jana Sangh) or personalistic (the Lok Dal, the Democratic Socialist Party); ideological elements can be found in the personalistic parties and vice versa.

The main parties maintain national organizations and organizations in the states. Real power usually is divided between these two sets of organizations in shifting measures. The real work of running local campaigns rests with the state or local units of the party. While a state or local unit's ability to mobilize voters and their role in state and local government often carry substantial political power, the national organization usually exerts major influence over the allocation of tickets (nominations). Although the details of party organization and the distribution of power between central organization and the states differ from party to party and from time to time, all the main national parties are structured to reflect the division of electoral and administrative structures into states and districts.

Mahatma Gandhi envisioned partyless government at the self-sufficient village level, and most parties continue to pay lip-service to this ideal. Indeed, the main local government institution, the *Panchayati Raj*, or council of five, is based on traditional systems of local government and is intended to be non-partisan. However, political operatives of all parties at the local level constantly use traditional aspects of village power such as caste, economic status, and religion in their struggle to mobilize voters and political workers. Thus the high-minded national goals espoused by party leaders are frequently at odds with the practical political activities of the village operatives.

As in most parliamentary systems, there is a certain amount of tension and conflict between the parliamentary and organizational wings of the parties. Such conflict has been most pronounced in the Congress because it has the longest history as a ruling party. However, the Janata also experienced differences when in power from 1977 to 1979. Such differences often have been seen at the state level, for example, in the Communist parties of West Bengal over the hostile reaction of the Communist-controlled coalition state government to the peasant uprisings in Naxalbari District in 1967. Generally, where parties are out of office and have little prospect of gaining power, strains between the parliamentary and organizational wings are less apparent.

Campaigning

Indian political campaigns have a festive air. People turn out in large numbers for political rallies and other appearances by candidates. Candidates circulate extensively in their constituencies, usually travelling from village to village by jeep, sometimes on foot or by elephant. In urban areas, parties canvas door to door and put up gaily decorated stands from which campaign literature is circulated. Signs, banners, and graffiti play a prominent role in campaigns. Party notables move extensively around the state or country making personal appearances in tightly contested constituencies.

Radio and television are government controlled and have not played prominent roles in campaigning. However, beginning in 1977 in some state elections and in the 1980 national elections, all recognized parties were provided with equal amounts of campaign time on radio and television.

Campaign expenditures are sharply limited by law. In 1980, each candidate for the Lok Sabha was permitted to spend between 15,000 rupees ($1,875) and 100,000 rupees ($12,500), depending on the size and nature of the constituency. Each candidate is required to maintain a daily documented account of expenditures which must be submitted to the relevant election official. Failure to comply with these regulations may result in a candidate being disqualified from serving in either house of Parliament for three years.

However, it is widely agreed that these limits are wholly unrealistic and that Indian elections are vastly more expensive. A well-known Indian news magazine (*India Today*; June 16–30, 1981) reported that more than 20 million rupees ($2.5 million) was spent by the winning candidate in a hotly contested by-election in June 1981, and suggested that this was far from a record.

Political finances are the subject of much rumor and speculation and little hard data. Parties devote a good deal of effort to raising money. Some of the devices used include the collection of membership dues, the sale of advertisements in party publications, the sale of space and decorations at party functions, requests for direct donations, and, it has been charged, pressures bordering on extortion and solicitation of bribes. The large industrial families—the Birlas, the Tatas, etc.—have a tradition of financial support for political movements that goes back to well before independence. The tradition continues today. The Congress (now the Congress [I]) has been the main beneficiary of financial support from the business houses, but other parties also have sought such support with varying degrees of success.

Communist parties are widely believed to receive support from outside India, and there have been repeated charges that other parties, including the Congress, have received covert monies from the U.S. Central Intelligence Agency. However, hard evidence about sources of financial support for Indian parties is fragmentary at best and should be approached with extreme caution.

Independent Voters

Party-membership figures in India are highly unreliable. Personalist parties rarely have any formal membership outside Parliament. Even in mass-based parties, frequent defections, splits, and factional conflicts make available figures highly unreliable. Voting rolls do not indicate party identification, but public-opinion studies indicate that a suprisingly large proportion of the voters expresses identification with parties. Recent elections suggest that party identification may be less indicative of voting behavior that orientation to personalities and issues. Since 1971, Lok Sabha and state Assembly elections have generally occurred at different times. Therefore, since voters usually cast only one ballot for one member of the Lok Sabha, ticket splitting is normally impossible.

Indian People's Party
(Bharatiya Janata Party; BJP)

History

The BJP was founded in 1980 after the breakup of the governing Janata Party coalition. It is the current manifestation of the former Jana Sangh (People's) Party with its long tradition of militant Hindu nationalist politics. Two principal Hindu nationalist organizations developed in the pre-independence period—the Rashtriya Swayamsevak Sangh (RSS), or National Volunteer Organization, a paramilitary cadre organization, and the Hindu Mahasabha, a related political party. After independence, the Hindu Mahasabha became ever more narrowly sectarian, and the RSS called for the establishment of a more broadly based party. Dr. S. P. Mookerjee, a former leader of the Hindu Mahasabha and a former member of Nehru's cabinet, responded by founding the Bharatiya Jana Sangh (usually called Jana Sangh). Beginning with the first general election in 1952, the Jana Sangh gradually replaced the Hindu Mahasabha as the voice of Hindu cultural militancy.

The Jana Sangh gained sufficient electoral strength in the Hindi-speaking areas of north central India in the 1960s to participate in some coalition governments at the state level and to control some municipal governing bodies including the Delhi Municipal Corporation.

As the leading proponent of Hindu cultural nationalism, the Jana Sangh was particularly repugnant to the secularists in the Congress and was frequently the main target of Congress politicians.

After a former RSS activist assassinated Mahatma Gandhi in 1948, the organization was banned for a time. At the time of emergency rule in 1975 to 1977 Jana Sangh leaders were imprisoned and the RSS was again banned.

The Jana Sangh became one of the four main coalition partners in establishing the Janata Party in 1977. The Janata won most heavily in the north Indian Hindi belt—where the Jana Sangh had its main strength and where its cadre affiliate, the RSS, had its most extensive organization.

The first defections from the Janata coalition, however, came over the issue of whether the Janata was sufficiently secular, a euphemism for questioning the role of the Jana Sangh and the RSS in the party. The bulk of the former Jana Sangh members stuck with the Janata until after the 1980 elections, but then left to form the BJP under the leadership of former Jana Sangh leader and former Janata foreign minister, Atal Bihari Vajpayee.

Organization

The party's organizational strength depends on the RSS, the paramilitary cadre group. The cadres of RSS can be seen training in the early hours in open areas in many Indian towns, but the organization's actual strength is hard to gauge. The RSS provides a tightly knit, well-organized, disciplined body of workers which can be mobilized for campaigns and other party work. The connection has been a mixed blessing, however, for it also creates tension over control of party policy and strategy. It also has limited the success of efforts to develop alliances with other parties and handicapped attempts to broaden the base of the party.

Party headquarters are at 11 Ashoka Road, New Delhi 110 001.

Policy

The main concern of the BJP has been to foster Indian culture. The party has maintained that it has no desire to impose orthodox Hinduism (it even has some Muslim members), but is concerned with Indian culture. However, it tends to emphasize Hindu issues such as the prohibition of cow slaughter. As a nationalist party, the BJP is devoted to Indian self-sufficiency and to severe limits on the incorporation of alien influences into the Indian culture. Less importance has been attached to economic policy. The Jana Sangh originally took a rather conservative position on economic issues, at one point even discussing merger possibilities with the free-enterprise Swatantra

Party. In time, however, the Jana Sangh moved more to the left on economic issues, and its BJP successor supports a moderately socialist economic policy.

In foreign policy, the Jana Sangh took a militantly anti-Pakistan position, rejecting the legitimacy of the 1947 partition, and advocating reunification of the subcontinent by force if necessary. The responsibilities of office seemed to alter Jana Sangh perspectives, especially those of A. B. Vajpayee, who took a more benevolent approach to neighboring countries including Pakistan, a stance which created some intra-party conflict. Now out of power again, some of the old militancy has returned in the rhetoric of BJP leaders. Janata supports nonalignment in the Nehru sense and claims that the Congress under Indira Gandhi has slipped into a tacit alliance with the Soviet Union. Vajpayee advocates a closer relationship with the United States coupled with continued good relations with the Soviet Union. The BJP shares the Congress concern about possible effects of United States–China–Pakistan cooperation on Indian security interests. The BJP supports a strong national defense, including the development of an effective nuclear capability.

Membership & Constituency

The BJP, like the Jana Sangh before it, draws its main support from middle-class Hindus living in urban areas. It has proved remarkably attractive to urban youth; the RSS has an estimated one million members. Geographically, its main strength has been in the Hindi-speaking areas of north India, although the 1980 election results seemed to cast some doubt on the solidity of this strength. The current leadership of the party is making a determined effort to broaden the geographical base of the party. Special attention is focused on eastern and western regions where Hindu nationalism has some roots; there are also efforts to organize in traditionally less responsive southern areas.

Financing

The BJP appears to rely heavily on dues and contributions from its ideological supporters. Participation in government from 1977 to 1979 probably increased its ability to attract funds from traditional sources.

Leadership

The BJP leadership is young by Indian standards, reflecting in part the traditional attractive-

ness of the RSS to the youth. The most prominent leader is the party president, A. B. Vajpayee (born 1926), who has been responsible for the strategy of broadening the geographical base of the party. His most important colleague is former RSS leader and Janata minister, L. K. Advani (born 1927).

Prospects

Most observers believe that the BJP has the best prospect to become a viable alternative to the Congress (I) among the opposition parties. Its organization, the breadth of its appeal, and the relative youth of its leadership set it apart from most other Indian parties. If it is to challenge seriously the Congress (I) at the Centre, however, the BJP will have to broaden its base and construct alliances with other opposition parties. The essential prerequisite to either of these developments is a softening of the BJP's image of linguistic and cultural narrowness. But that very softening, if it comes, could cost the BJP some of its ideological support and add to the difficulties of the BJP-RSS relationship.

At the state and local level, BJP prospects are somewhat better in the short term. Political and economic difficulties of incumbent Congress (I) governments may provide some opportunities for a well-organized BJP to participate in new governments in the northern region, especially at the municipal level.

Communist Party of India (CPI)

History

Founded in 1925, the Communist Party of India was initially a part of the Communist International and soon became closely connected with the Communist Party of Great Britain. In the 1930s it collaborated with the Congress in the independence movement and was especially involved with the Congress Socialists. This relationship was never an easy one and broke down completely during the Second World War. The Communists advocated collaboration with the British (and the Soviets) in the "anti-fascist war," while the Congress launched an anti-British non-cooperation movement and demanded immediate independence. Legalization of the Communist Party in 1942 gave it the opportunity to broaden its organization while the Congress leaders were immobilized in British jails.

After the war and with the coming of independence, the Communists were divided over the appropriate approach to parliamentary democracy and to the Congress government. This has been a basic issue inhibiting the unity of the Communists throughout the postindependence period.

When the Soviets, after the death of Joseph Stalin in 1953, began to woo the international nonaligned movement and its most prominent leader, Nehru, the CPI opted for competitive electoral politics within the parliamentary framework. In 1957, the CPI led a coalition government in the southern state of Kerala. Congress-led street agitation forced that government from office in 1959, and President's Rule was imposed.

In 1964, the party split, with the more moderate group under the leadership of S. A. Dange retaining the party label and a close relationship with the Soviet Union. The more militant wing, led by E. M. S. Namboodiripad, a former chief minister of Kerala, and Jyoti Basu, later to become chief minister of West Bengal, left to form the Communist Party of India (Marxist) or CPM. The basic cause of the split was a long-standing difference over how to relate to the ruling Congress. Dange, adhering to the Soviet view, argued that the Congress represented an anti-imperialist force and should be opposed only on domestic issues and, then, without intent to bring down the government. Namboodiripad and Basu were deeply disturbed by the fiercely anti-Chinese foreign policy Congress had adopted after the Sino–Indian border war in 1962 and by the Congress role in overturning the CPI-led government in Kerala in 1959. They argued for implacable opposition to the Congress.

The CPI never regained the strength it had possessed before the split, but it did play a prominent role in national politics again in 1969 when its support for Mrs. Gandhi's faction of the Congress provided the necessary parliamentary margin to permit her to retain the prime ministership. The support for Mrs. Gandhi openly tied the fortunes of the party to her. Since then, the party's electoral successes have depended largely on the support CPI candidates have received from the Congress (I) and on Mrs. Gandhi's popularity. Where she has supported them, they have won; where Congress (I) candidates have also run, CPI candidates generally have lost.

The relationship to Mrs. Gandhi led to yet another split in the CPI in 1981. The general secretary of the party, C. Rajeswara Rao, argued that the party's support for Mrs. Gandhi during the emergency period had been a mistake. Dange and some of his followers disagreed, and Dange left the party to join the newly formed All-India Communist Party (AICP)—essentially the pro–Indira Gandhi faction of the CPI—leaving those who had come to doubt the wisdom of the Congress (I) alliance in what was left of the CPI.

Organization

The CPI claims to have a highly organized structure operating on the basis of democratic centralism. In fact, the state organizations have considerable autonomy, and there is a substantial amount of fragmentation and factionalism. To the extent that power is centralized, it is lodged with the general secretary.

The party has an extensive publication program which includes journals, such as *New Age*, which are published directly by the party; the widely read *Link*, a newsmagazine which generally follows a Marxist line; and books on technical as well as political subjects. In addition, the party distributes subsidized publications from the Soviet Union.

It has acquired control of the All-India Trade Union Congress and operates youth, peasants', and women's organizations.

Party headquarters are at 15 Kotla Marg, New Delhi 110 002.

Policy

The CPI always has had a close relationship with the Soviet Union, and its attitudes toward existing Indian governments have often been a function of Soviet relations with the particular government. The party is not simply a tool of the Soviets, however; Soviet views are only one among several factors influencing CPI policy and actions.

On domestic issues, the CPI follows classic Marxist policy positions favoring secularism, rapid industrialization, nationalization of large-scale industry, land reform, and collectivized agriculture. In foreign policy, the CPI favors a pro-Soviet position on global issues and an anti-imperialist posture on regional issues. It tends to support Mrs. Gandhi on relations with neighboring states, especially Pakistan. It supports a strong defense capability.

Membership & Constituency

The CPI electoral strategy emphasizes a broad rural constituency and the urban working class. In Kerala and Bengal, the CPI has done well among middle peasants and is the dominant Communist influence in the fragmented urban trade-union movement. The CPI lost much of the traditional Communist support in West Bengal and Kerala to the CPM, but retains important support among left voters in some areas of Bihar, Andhra Pradesh, and Uttar Pradesh.

Financing

The CPI uses all the customary devices to raise money. In addition, it apparently raises substantial funds through the sale of subsidized Soviet publications. There are persistent and generally accepted rumors that the CPI receives substantial direct funding from the Soviet Union. No official confirmation of this rumor has ever come from either the CPI or the Soviets.

Leadership

S. A. Dange's dominant role in the party precluded the rise of other important leaders. His age—he was born in 1899—had already begun to lessen his grip even before he left the party. The present general secretary, C. Rajeswara Rao, is, like most of the CPI leadership, a veteran of union activity.

Prospects

Dange's departure offers an opportunity for younger leaders to begin to forge some sort of left unity, though it is far too early to tell how successful the effort will be or even how much of an effort will be made. If unity were established, the Communists would be a powerful force indeed in West Bengal and Kerala and would begin to be a significant force in parts of Uttar Pradesh, Andhra, and Bihar. Failing that, the CPI will continue on the fringes of Indian politics, important only in intermittent coalitions in Kerala and, perhaps, West Bengal and in its influence in trade union circles. Its ties to Moscow also give it an importance to the Congress (I) foreign policy which cannot be ignored.

Communist Party of India (MARXIST); CPM

History

The CPM split from the CPI in 1964 over issues of militancy, ideology, and personality. It favored a more militant opposition to the Congress government. It felt the Maoist notion of peasant-based revolution was more relevant to the Indian situation than the worker-based ideas of Marx and Lenin advocated by a CPI heavily influenced by the British communists.

The CPM gained credibility among Marxist voters when the CPI sided openly with Mrs. Gandhi after 1969. The CPM position of firm opposition to her rule, especially during the emergency period in the mid-1970s, resulted in considerable electoral success among left voters, especially in the election of 1977 when the CPM was allied loosely with the Janata coalition. While the CPI generally has been able to win seats only where the Congress permitted, the CPM has been highly successful in challenging Congress (I) candidates, especially in West Bengal. In state politics, the CPM has been even more successful. It has headed the state government in West Bengal with Jyoti Basu as chief minister since 1977 and gained an enhanced majority after May 1982 elections. After leading the Kerala government under E. M. S. Namboodiripad from 1967 to 1969, the CPM continued to be a major factor in that state throughout the 1970s.

Organization

The organizational structure of the CPM is similar to that of the CPI—strongly centralized on paper but state-based in practice. In West Bengal, Jyoti Basu has managed to retain a more disciplined control over his party than is usual in India.

Headquarters are at 4 Ashoka Road, New Delhi 110 001.

Policy

In foreign policy, the CPM tends more toward nonalignment with an anti-imperialist cast and is suspicious of the pro-Soviet disposition of the CPI. The ideological predisposition of CPM toward the Chinese version of Marxism has stimulated a policy of advocating rapprochement between New Delhi and Peking, but the CPM does not have close links with Peking.

Membership & Constituency

The CPM has done better than the CPI in the traditional Communist strongholds of West Bengal and Kerala, but less well in Uttar Pradesh, Andhra, and Bihar. It has targeted landless laborers in rural areas and has done well in that constituency. It has had less success with organized urban workers.

Financing

As a sometime participant in the government in West Bengal and Kerala, the CPM has access to traditional sources of funds in these states. There have been occasional rumors of financial support from the People's Republic of China, but these are given less credence than the reports of Soviet support for the CPI.

Leadership

The two principal CPM leaders, Jyoti Basu (born 1914) and E. M. S. Namboodiripad (born 1909), are among the most highly regarded active political leaders in India. Both are veterans of left-wing and union politics. Basu, trained in law, comes from a prominent elite Bengali family. Namboodiripad is widely regarded as the most intellectually sophisticated of contemporary politicians. Although they have dominated the party since the 1964 split from the CPI and are now aging, their prominence has attracted a highly competent younger group of leaders.

Prospects

Since the 1964 split there has been recurring talk of "unity of the left forces" in India. The latest split in the CPI has led to renewed speculation that the new anti-Gandhi CPI might be able to establish some degree of cooperation with the CPM. International and ideological ties, however, will work against unity.

Indian National Congress (I)

History

The Indian National Congress was founded in 1885 as an organization of prominent Englishmen and members of the Indian elite devoted to expanding opportunities for Indians in the colonial regime and incorporating Indian elite opinion in policy making.

The first two decades of the twentieth century brought a deep struggle over philosophy and direction between the early great Congress leaders, B. G. Tilak (1856–1920) and G. K. Gokhale (1866–1915). Gokale was highly educated in the Western tradition and believed deeply that India must absorb and utilize Western ideas and technology. He struggled to maintain the moderate, elitist, secular character of the Congress.

Of the two, Tilak was the more radical. A prominent scholar of the Hindu scriptures, Tilak wanted to mold the Congress in the Hindu tradition, broaden its appeal to include the masses, and transform it into a more militant organization. The growing importance of the Tilak view within the Congress gave it an increasingly Hindu character in spite of continuing professions of secularism.

Mohandas K. Gandhi became the dominant Congress leader in 1920 and remained its preeminent figure until his assassination in 1948. Gandhi was convinced that Congress had to retain its secular character in order to succeed as an umbrella organization, directing the many strands of the independence movement. But he realized that the movement also depended on the mobilization of mass participation in the freedom struggle. Hindu symbolism and philosophical principles provided ready tools for mobilizing the masses. Throughout his years at the helm of the Congress, Gandhi struggled to balance the commitment to secularism with the necessity of mobilizing the Hindu masses. In the end, however, the predominently Hindu character of the Congress so frightened significant Muslim elites that independence could only be won at the price of partition.

Gandhi's leadership and philosophy left a profound mark on the postindependence party. He came to be revered as a saint by the Hindu masses. He was universally called Mahatma, "great soul." His philosophy and strategy of nonviolence (*ahimsa*) and noncooperation based on soul force (*satyagraha*), and his commitment to secularism, mass participation, village self-sufficiency, and reform of the most discriminatory features of the Hindu caste system continue to be touchstones for the modern Congress party.

The two principal lieutenants of Gandhi, Jawaharlal Nehru and Sardar Vallabhai Patel, presided over the transformation of the national movement into a modern political party. As expected, the Congress formed the first independent government under Nehru. Although Congress never won a majority of the popular vote, the electoral system and the fragmentation of the opposition parties insured that Congress usually would have a majority in the Lok Sabha. Congress has received between 41 percent and 48 percent of the vote in each national election, except in 1977 when it polled only 34.5 percent.

At the state level, Congress has been less dominant. It has often lost control of state governments to regional parties or to coalitions. In 1967, Congress lost control of nearly half the state governments while retaining control at the Centre. After a comeback in 1972, Congress again lost badly in 1977, retaining control of only one state and participating in a coalition in one other. The 1980 elections again restored Congress power in most states other than those which have developed a tradition of other-party government—West Bengal, Kerala, Kashmir, Tamil Nadu, and some of the smaller frontier states. Elections in May 1982, resulted in a victory for a coalition led by Congress (I) in Kerala and Congress (I) minority governments in Haryana and Himachal Pradesh.

During these years there have been frequent splits and defections in the party, but the main leadership has shown remarkable continuity. Nehru was the preeminent leader from 1948 until his death in 1964 and unchallenged between 1951 and 1962. Lal Bahadur Shastri was prime minister from 1964 until his sudden death in 1966, but much real power in the party rested with a group of party bosses known as the "Syndicate" led by K. Kamaraj of Tamil Nadu. The "Syndicate" played a prominent role in the selection of Nehru's daughter, Mrs. Indira Gandhi (no relation to Mahatma Gandhi), as Shastri's successor, and struggled with her for power until a major split occurred in 1969 between pre-Syndicate and pre-Gandhi factions. Her victory over the "Syndicate" was confirmed by the electorate in 1971, and she has remained the dominant figure in the party since then, although there were some temporarily successful challenges to her leadership during the 1977–80 period when the Congress was out of office. In fact, her role has become so overwhelming that the party is now officially and universally labeled Congress (I) for Indira Congress to distinguish it from the various offshoots of the original Congress.

Congress (I) alone retains the dominant position, the national scope, and the range of support which characterized the undivided Congress, and Mrs. Gandhi is the only party leader in India with genuine national stature.

Organization

Congress (I) is a highly structured party. Basic organizational units exist at the district, the state, and the national levels. The annual conference of the party is composed of the members of the Congress committees at the state and district levels. The conference elects the Congress president to a two-year term and chooses the All-India Congress Committee (AICC). Real power, however, is in the Congress Working Committee (CWC), often called the Congress High Command, which has twenty members, thirteen of whom are appointed by the Congress president.

The Congress president is usually selected by the prime minister if the Congress is in power. Sometimes, expecially after periods of some tension between the organization party and the parliamentary party, the prime minister may assume the Congress presidency, as Nehru did in the early 1950s and Indira Gandhi did in 1980. At other times, the prime minister will insure that a trusted loyalist holds the position.

The daily newspaper, the *National Herald*, was founded by Nehru and is closely tied to the Congress (I). After the CPI gained control of the All-India Trade Union Congress, the Congress Party organized the Indian National Trade Union Congress (INTUC). Congress (I) also has women's and youth organizations. The Youth Congress became very important in the party in the 1970s as the organizational base from which Mrs. Gandhi's younger son, Sanjay, launched his political career. Under his leadership, the Youth Congress provided large numbers of party workers and actively recruited new members. When Sanjay died in 1980, the Youth Congress lost some of its importance.

Headquarters are at 24 Akbar Road, New Delhi 110 001.

Policy

Congress (I) espouses moderate socialism and a planned mixed economy aimed at rapid economic growth, self-sufficiency, and industrialization. It supports a secular state with egalitarian values and special programs for victims of discrimination. Land-reform and national-integration planks have been consistently incorporated into its party manifestos. In spite of egalitarian and socialistic rhetoric, however, Congress (I) policy also has been geared to expansion of the private sector.

Under Nehru, the Congress developed a foreign policy based on nonalignment, i.e., active participation in international affairs while refraining from alliance with either superpower bloc. That policy has continued, although American support for Pakistan and the development of warmer relations between the United States and China have encouraged a closer relationship between India and the Soviet Union. Although the Congress government signed a long-term Treaty of Friendship with the Soviet Union in 1971 (in the midst of the Bangladesh crisis), the Congress (I) still adheres to a fiercely nationalistic form of nonalignment. Congress (I) favors a strong defense posture with as much self-sufficiency as possible.

Under Indira Gandhi, Congress seems to have attached a lower priority to a prominent global role for India than was the case under Nehru.

Congress (I) has professed a desire for friendly relations with India's neighbors in south Asia, but has expected them to acknowledge and accept India's leading role in the area. The party attaches special importance to relations with Pakistan. While desiring more normal relations, Congress (I) clearly expects Pakistan to recognize India's dominant role in the subcontinent and opposes international military assistance to Pakistan.

Membership & Constituency

In the past, Congress has claimed as many as 10 million primary members and over 300,000 active members, although most observers agree such claims probably overstate the facts. Both membership categories contribute to party finances by payment of dues, although the amount for primary members is nominal. Active members may be assigned specific party duties and are eligible to hold party office.

Congress success has rested on the maintenance of the traditional if incongruous coalition of Muslims, Scheduled Castes, Brahmins, industrialists, landless laborers, and well-to-do landowners. The loss in 1977 was apparently the result of the defection of large numbers of Muslim and Scheduled Caste voters, especially in north India. In addition, large numbers of women voters seem to vote Congress in response to Mrs. Gandhi's emphasis on the deterioration of law and order. Minority groups of all sorts, especially religious minorities, have joined the Congress coalition, reflecting the widespread perception that the opposition parties' commitment to secularism is suspect.

Some evidence indicates that the Congress is having difficulty recruiting new support among young voters, who do not remember the Congress role in the independence movement. Age distribution in India is skewed toward the youthful end of the scale, so it is imperative for any Indian party to seek the support of the youth. The prominent role played by Mrs. Gandhi's younger son, Sanjay, and his Youth Congress in the 1977 and 1980 elections may have been partly designed to address this problem.

Geographically, Congress always has enjoyed strong support in the south except in Tamil Nadu. However, it has built its power on solid support in the Hindi belt of north India. Congress has had to fight more competitively in the eastern and western regions of the country.

Financing

As the ruling party for most of India's independent history, the Congress has had a decided advantage over other parties in raising funds. It uses the usual devices, of course, and many observers have asserted that Congress fund-raising efforts, especially during the emergency period, have sometimes been rather like extortion. In the early days of independent India, Congress enjoyed a near-monopoly over political contributions from businesses and still receives substantial support from such sources. Party dues also provide significant funds.

Leadership

Mrs. Gandhi's increasing insistence on personal loyalty to her within the party has meant gradual exclusion from power or ouster from the party for all former Congress leaders with any independent political base. It is now clear that the Congress has one leader and one leader only.

Mrs. Gandhi was born in 1917 into a prominent Kashmiri Brahmin family in Allahabad in Uttar Pradesh. She grew up in the political struggle for independence in which her father and grandfather played leading roles. She suffered long family separation while her father and her mother and, eventually, she herself, were in British jails. She married Feroze Gandhi, a lawyer and politician, who died in 1960. She served as her father's hostess and confident while he was prime minister. Few democratic political leaders in history have had such long experience at the center of momentous political events.

Mrs. Gandhi's closest advisors change frequently. She apparently trusts few people in the top ranks of the party. In the mid-1970s, she began to rely more and more on her younger son, Sanjay. It was widely assumed that he was being groomed to succeed his mother. However, Sanjay was killed in June, 1980, when the light plane he was piloting crashed in New Delhi. After Sanjay's death, his older brother Rajiv, who had been a commercial airline pilot, entered political life and was elected to the Lok Sabha in 1981. Whether Rajiv will now follow the path that had been set out for his brother is uncertain since he had previously avoided politics.

Prospects

As the only truly national party with the only truly national leader, Congress (I)'s prospects for retaining power appear bright. The lesson of the 1977 and 1980 elections, as well as a large number of state elections, is that the Congress will do well as long as the opposition remains fragmented. Responsibility for governmental performance in difficult economic, political, and international circumstances may permit opposition parties to chip away at Congress power in some local and perhaps even state situations. In spite of constant talk of national unity of opposition parties, such unity seems unlikely, and Congress (I) dominance at the Centre seems assured for the foreseeable future. The increasing personalization of the party under Mrs. Gandhi could pose leadership problems, if she were to suddenly leave political life.

Indian Peoples' Party (Bharatiya Lok Dal)

History

The Lok Dal is primarily a personalist vehicle for former prime minister Charan Singh, a leader of the Jats, a middle peasant caste scattered across north India.

The Lok Dal was formed in 1975 by the merger of seven parties, the largest of which was Singh's Bharatiya Kranti Dal (BKD). Also participating in the merger were the Swatantra (Freedom) Party (a classical free-enterprise, business-oriented party), a splinter from the Congress, and a socialist faction led by Raj Narain. The Lok Dal in turn became one of the major constituents of the Janata Party in 1977, but did not surrender its own identity. Indeed, the Lok Dal and the Jana Sangh (forerunner of the BJP) were the main competitors in the struggles which led to the collapse of the Janata government in 1979. Since then, the Lok Dal has suffered defections from members who are not pleased with Charan Singh's dominance. In the 1980 election, the Lok Dal returned forty-one representatives to the Lok Sabha, making it Parliament's second-largest party.

Policy

The Lok Dal's main policy concerns relate to India's economic-development strategy. It argues that the strategy followed to date has favored the urban industrial sector at the expense of the rural agricultural sector. The Lok Dal would redress this alleged imbalance, barring large-scale industrial development whenever village and cottage industries could produce the same items. It opposes increased urbanization. Foreign policy has a much lower priority for the Lok Dal; it supports nonalignment.

Organization

The Lok Dal organization consists primarily of its parliamentary bloc. Organizational structure at the regional and local level is rudimentary and ad hoc, and consists of little more than the personal followers and clients of the members of Parliament.

The location of party headquarters is 15 Windsor Place, New Delhi.

Membership & Constituency

The Lok Dal draws its support mainly from the increasingly prosperous middle agricultural castes of north India, which have benefitted from land redistribution and the "green revolution." They see Lok Dal as a way to add some measure of political power to an improved economic situation. The party has almost no support among the high castes, the landless, urban dwellers, or in other sections of the country.

Financing

Lok Dal funds are derived primarily from the contributions of relatively prosperous agricultural castes in north India.

Leadership

Although it is the personalist party of Charan Singh (born 1902), the Jat leader and former prime minister, the Lok Dal has been able to attract a handful of other prominent leaders of the Janata coalition. The most important of these are the former socialist leaders, Madhu Limaye, who is Lok Dal general secretary, and George Fernandes (born 1930).

Prospects

In the near term, the Lok Dal will play a significant role in the politics of rural north India and, in the unlikely event of some sort of opposition unity, on the national scene as well. The Lok Dal is heavily dependent on its aging leader who is in uncertain health. Nevertheless, the consituency it represents has been politically mobilized and will seek outlets for political action regardless of personalist developments in the party. The forms these outlets will take are extremely difficult to predict.

Minor Parties

Akali Dal

The Akali Dal is a Sikh communal party confined to the Punjab. Its roots go back to early Sikh nationalism. It has supported greater autonomy for Sikhs and there have been charges that some groupings of unspecified strength within the Akali have supported Sikh secessionist activity. The Akali Dal has never commanded large-scale support among the Sikhs in the Punjab and has managed to participate in government only briefly in coalitions.

Communist Party of India (Marxist-Leninist; CPML)

In 1967, an apparently spontaneous peasant revolt broke out in the Naxalbari District of West Bengal. The West Bengal state government, dominated by Communists, adopted a policy of crushing the rebellion. Some leftists—believing the government's actions contrary to the dictates of Marx, Lenin, and Mao—joined forces with the Naxalbari peasants. Dubbed Naxalites, they vowed violent actions against authority, especially in the rural areas of Bengal and Andhra. The central and state governments have made determined efforts to stamp out this movement and incarcerate its leaders.

In 1969, several factions of Naxalites came together to form the CPML. Factionalism within the CPML centers on the issue of violent revolution versus an electoral strategy. The latter has yielded little success at the polls. The People's Republic of China has given verbal and, perhaps, financial encouragement to this party.

Democratic Socialist Party

The Democratic Socialist Front is the personalist party of H. N. Bahugana, former chief minister of Uttar Pradesh, who has developed some personal following among Muslims and other groups which feel themselves disadvantaged in Indian society. Bahugana left the Congress with Jagjivan Ram to form the Congress for Democracy in 1977. When the Janata coalition disintegrated, he rejoined Mrs. Gandhi and briefly became a general secretary of the Congress (I). Never able to exert as much influence over Mrs. Gandhi as he had hoped, Bahugana left Congress (I) again to form the Democratic Socialist Party with some defectors from the Lok Dal. He won a hotly contested by-election in Uttar Pradesh in 1982. The party is vigorously engaged in coalition building. In the unlikely event of a major success on this front, Bahugana and the party could play a significant role in the future of Indian politics.

Dravida Munnetra Kazhagam (DMK)—Dravidian Progressive Federation & All-India Anna-Dravida Munnetra Kazhagam (AIADMK)

The heir to the anti–Brahmin Dravidian nationalist movement in south India, the DMK was founded in 1949 by C. N. Annadurai to press the claims of Tamil cultural and linguistic autonomy. Its platform of radical populist economics and cultural nationalism bordered on secessionism, but served to gain the party control of the Tamil Nadu state government in 1967.

Rivalries which were primarily personal in nature but related to the party's relations with Mrs. Gandhi's Congress followed Annadurai's death in 1969 and led to a split in 1972. Two factions emerged. The old title of DMK was retained by the group led by M. Karunanidhi. A new group, under the leadership of film idol M. G. Ramachandran (universally known as M.G.R.), claimed to be the true followers of Annadurai and called itself the All-India Anna DMK (AIADMK). These two parties have dominated the politics of Tamil Nadu for the last fifteen years, with the DMK controlling the state government until 1976 when President's Rule was imposed. M.G.R.'s AIADMK has controlled the government since 1977.

Responsibilities of office have muted whatever secessionist zeal lingered in these parties, though they both continue to champion states rights and to resist the spread of Hindi cultural and linguistic preeminence.

Shifting relationships between these two parties and various groups at the Centre, including the Congress, have had a reciprocal impact on state and national politics. Dravidian parties are likely to continue to dominate the politics of Tamil Nadu, but are unlikely to spread to other areas.

Indian National Congress (J)

The Congress (J) is the personalistic party of Jagjivan Ram, a senior figure in Indian politics as the self-styled leader of India's ex-untouchables. Ram has held cabinet positions in India longer than any other living person, serving Nehru as minister of railways, Mrs. Gandhi as minister of agriculture and of defense, and in the Janata government as deputy prime minister and minister of defense. His resignation from Mrs. Gandhi's government in February 1977, to form the Congress for Democracy, provided one of the earliest clues to the seriousness of her difficulties. Ram tried to claim the prime ministership for himself in 1977 and again when the Janata coalition fell apart in 1979, but he failed in both attempts. He then tried to gain control of the remnants of the Janata Party. Failing that, he sought an invitation to rejoin Mrs. Gandhi's government, but she was not in a generous mood. Finally, Ram (born 1908), in uncertain health and apparently losing whatever hold he once had on his ex-untouchable constituents, formed his own Congress (J). Most observers agree it is no more than a structure from which Ram will try to form political alliances, perhaps with the Muslims, to facilitate his return to power.

Indian National Congress (Socialist and Secular)

The Congress (S) Party is the remnant of a group which split from Mrs. Gandhi in 1978 while she was out of power. Immediately after the split, the group was known as Congress (R) after Bramananda Reddy, its president. Then, in 1978, Swaran Singh, who had been Mrs. Gandhi's foreign minister, became president of the group, and it took the name Congress (S). When Singh was replaced by Devraj Urs, the former chief minister of Karnataka, in 1979, the party became known as Congress (U). Under this label, it fought the 1980 elections, winning thirteen seats in the Lok Sabha. Its main leaders at that time were Urs, Singh, and Y. B. Chavan of Maharashtra, another of Mrs. Gandhi's former ministers. Mrs. Gandhi's electoral triumph proved too much of an attraction for many of her former colleagues, including Chavan, who applied to rejoin the Congress (I). This left a remnant, which reconstituted itself Congress (Socialist and Secular).

Congress (S) considers itself the inheritor of the "true" Congress. It adheres to traditional Congress policies, but rejects the authoritarian leadership of Mrs. Gandhi and her unrepentant attitude toward her emergency rule.

As reconstituted, the Congress (S) is untested in a national election, but its main support appears to lie along the western coast of India in Maharashtra and Kerala with, perhaps, an isolated pocket in West Bengal.

With the return of Chavan to the Congress (I) and the death of Urs, the leadership of Congress (S) has passed to younger and more dynamic leaders. The two most prominent are Sharad Pawar, once briefly chief minister of Maharashtra, and A. K. Anthony, former chief minister of Kerala.

It seems unlikely that the Congress (S) will become a major force at the national level. More likely it will take on the role played by the Congress (O) from 1972 to 1977, that is, to provide a political home for Congress politicians who object to Mrs. Gandhi's leadership. The skill and prominence of some of its leaders may make it a force with some potential for coalition building in the states where it retains its major support.

Janata Party

The present Janata (People's) Party is the remnant of the coalition which governed India from 1977 to 1979. At that time it was composed of the Jana Sangh, the Bharatiya Lok Dal, the Socialists, and the Congress (O). Jagjivan Ram's Congress for Democracy later joined this group. Although each of these groups was supposed to submerge its separate identity into the new party, the entire period of Janata rule was characterized by factional infighting. After the Janata government collapsed, the Lok Dal and the BJP left to form or reform separate parties. Some more or less prominent leaders left to form their own personalist parties or join others. The rump comprises the Janata Party of today.

Having lost Hindu nationalist support to the BJP and prosperous landowning agriculturalists to the Lok Dal, Janata was left with pieces of the old Congress (O) support in states like Gujarat and Maharashtra.

The contemporary Janata Party is led by Chandra Shekar, former Young Turk of the Congress, and Morarji Desai, the octogenarian former leader of the Congress (O) and former Janata prime minister.

Barring the success of coalition or merger talks, which seems unlikely, the Janata Party will play an insignificant role in electoral politics at the national or state level. It seems likely to remain the ideological home of fairly orthodox Gandhian socialists, for example, the followers of Jayaprakash Narayan.

Muslim League

The remnants of the major Muslim political organization of preindependence days, most of whose leaders went to Pakistan, the Muslim League of today is a small party devoted to the welfare of Muslims in Kerala. It occasionally has participated in coalition governments at the state level.

National Conference

The party of Sheik Mohammed Abdullah which controls the state government in Jammu and Kashmir, the National Conference has been a tool for giving Kashmiri Muslims a special role in their government in a state which Pakistan claims as its territory. Although Sheik Abdullah was earlier imprisoned by Congress governments at the Centre, he became chief minister of Jammu and Kashmir in the 1970s with Mrs. Gandhi's blessing. His party has maintained a somewhat uneasy alliance with the Congress (I) at the Centre. While retaining the chief ministership, the aging sheik (born 1905) turned the party leadership over to his son in 1981.

Peasants and Workers Party (PWP)

The Peasants and Workers Party is a radical Marxist party with some influence among landless laborers in Maharashtra.

Other Political Forces

Organized Labor

The twenty million organized workers in India are highly politicized. Most political parties have union affiliates, and the competition among parties for worker allegiance extends into most industrial work forces. Nevertheless, fragmentation limits the importance of unions, which lies chiefly in their ability to disrupt industrial production and transportation and to provide political workers at election time. The main labor federations and their political affiliations are Indian National Trade Union Congress (INTUC)—Congress (I); All-India Trade Union Congress (AITUC)—CPI; Centre of Indian Trade Unions (CITU)—CPM; Hind Mazdoor Sabha—originally Socialist, now Janata.

Students

University campuses in India are extensively politicized, and Indian parties try to use student activism and unrest for their own ends. Indian student activism tends to be spontaneous and sporadic. The largest student organization is the All-India Students Organization (Akhil Bharatiya Vidyarthi Parishad—ABVP), which is affiliated with the RSS and dominates many of the campuses of north India, including Delhi University. It provided an important source of campaign workers for the Jana Sangh and the Janata Party, and now provides valuable assistance to the Bharatiya Janata Party. The Congress (I), through the Youth Congress, and the Marxists also have been able to attract periodic activity on their behalf from groups of students.

Business

Private business in India is organized through several federations, the largest and best known of which is the Federation of Indian Chambers of Commerce and Industry (FICCI). Through financial contributions and extensive lobbying, Indian business has developed sustained access to the top echelons of the cabinet, the civil service, and the Congress (I) Party. Students of business and politics in India consider business to be the best-organized and most frequently consulted interest group in the country. However, they conclude that business has been unable to turn organization and access into effective influence on questions of public policy.

Peasants

Indian peasants have not been able to organize effectively on a national level, but the middle landowning peasant castes often have been able to influence political activity significantly at the local and, in some cases, at the state level. Most major parties have peasant organizations. The Congress's Farmer's Forum and Bharat Sevak Samaj have been handicapped by the connections between local Congress organizations and the large landholders whose interests are in conflict with those of the peasants. There are two All-India Kisan (peasant) Sabhas affiliated respectively with the CPI and the CPM. The Socialists' Kisan Panchayat (council) was transferred to the Janata Party coalition. The most important peasant political force, however, is found in the Lok Dal followers. In 1978, Charan Singh founded the All-India Kisan Sammelan (AIKS), which became a mobilization tool for his peasant-based Lok Dal.

Caste

Caste is a hierarchical ordering of status groups, membership in which is based on birth. Caste groups have been *the major institution* organizing human relationships and interactions in India for centuries. Individual decisions are made in a framework of caste relationships. Inevitably, a system so deeply imbedded in Indian society has influenced and been influenced by the modern political system. No single factor influences politics in India more deeply than caste, but this influence is felt most fully at the local level.

Caste groupings and more formal Caste Associations have become mediating and mobilizing insitutions in Indian politics. They use and are used by political parties at the local level. They interpret political issues and positions to their members, and convey caste political interests to the parties and administration. They mobilize voters, workers, and sometimes money and candidates. Their importance to the political process cannot be exaggerated, but since they work most intensively at the local level, it is difficult to generalize about their impact on the national parties.

Scheduled Castes

Historically the most economically and socially degraded groups in Indian society, the Scheduled Castes are separate castes grouped together for legal and administrative purposes. The Indian constitution outlaws the most extreme form of discrimination against members of these groups—untouchability—and provides special protections in parliamentary representation, civil-service employment, and education. In spite of such legal protection and government efforts, untouchability is still widely practiced in rural India, and members of the Scheduled Castes remain heavily overrepresented among the poorest, least employed, and most illiterate in Indian society.

Like other Indians, untouchables generally have looked to the Congress (I) Party as the source of protection for their interests. However, there have been significant untouchable political movements. The most important of these was the Scheduled Caste Federation, founded in 1942 by Dr. B. R. Ambedkar, the most prominent untouchable leader of the modern period, who was the chairman of the Drafting Committee of the Indian Constitution and the law minister in Nehru's first cabinet. The Scheduled Caste Federation, like Ambedkar's movement of religious protest involving the conversion of untouchables from Hinduism to Buddhism, was largely confined to Maharashtra and central Uttar Pradesh.

Attempting to broaden its appeal to non-Scheduled oppressed groups, the Scheduled Caste Federation took the name Republican Party of India (RPI) in 1956. It achieved considerable success at

the state level in Maharashtra and at the municipal level in Agra City in the late 1950s and 1960s, but factionalism has reduced its importance in more recent times.

A more militant student-based group called the Dalit (oppressed) Panthers emerged in Maharashtra in the 1960s and developed some influence by forging links between rural and urban groups.

In the late 1970s, another organization, the All-India Backward and Minority Communities Employees Federation (BAMCEF), began to organize the Scheduled Castes and other oppressed groups on a broader geographical basis. It used the now-significant number of Scheduled Caste government employees—holders of reserved posts in the civil service—as an organizing base.

Muslims

The most important political minority in India is the Muslim minority. With over 80 million Muslims, India, after Bangladesh and Indonesia, has the third largest Muslim population in the world. Yet, Muslims are only about 12 percent of the Indian population. The more militant Muslim elite migrated to Pakistan, and the remaining Muslims are fragmented politically, geographically, and culturally. Most of them have supported the Congress Party, except in 1977 when significant numbers defected to other groups.

Militant Muslim communalism is represented by the Jamaat-e-Islami, a tightly organized paramilitary organization which is the counterpart of the Hindu RSS. Like the RSS, it was banned during the emergency, but has made a strong comeback since.

National Prospects

Predictions about future developments in the Indian political system have been notably risky; for more than sixteen years Indira Gandhi has made a career of being unpredictable. Nevertheless, several characteristics and trends are apparent and seem likely to be a part of the Indian system in the near term.

Congress (I)'s hold on power at the Centre is secure so long as Mrs. Gandhi remains politically active and the opposition remains fragmented. The personalization of the Congress (I) leadership is likely to continue and will probably pose serious problems for the Indian systems when Mrs. Gandhi leaves the political scene. Opposition unity is likely to be achieved only sporadically, if at all, and is, therefore, unlikely to seriously challenge Congress dominance at the Centre, although there may be some opposition successes at the state and local level.

The technological sophistication and productive scale of the economy make India an increasingly significant and successful participant in the international economic system, especially among the developing countries, but the domestic economy continues to be plagued by seemingly intractable problems of population growth, industrial unrest, lagging productivity, and serious inequities in the distribution of income, all of which seem destined to place continuing strains on the political system.

Foreign policy is characterized by continued concern over the bilateral Indo-Pakistan relationship. Increasing intrusion of the superpowers into the region will make the relationship much more difficult to manage and will complicate India's overall foreign policy problems.

These various economic, political and foreign policy problems will continue to strain the capabilities of India's political system. Facing such strains in the past, the system has demonstrated an ability, unusual among newly independent countries, to function with modest effectiveness as a relatively open, free, competitive, and stable democratic polity. That pattern seems likely to continue.

Further Reading

Barnett, Marguerite Ross. *The Politics of Cultural Nationalism in South India.* Princeton, N. J.: Princeton University Press, 1976.

Baxter, Craig. *The Jana Sangh: A Biography of an Indian Political Party.* Philadelphia: University of Pennsylvania Press, 1969.

Brass, Paul. *Factional Politics in an Indian State: The Congress Party in Uttar Pradesh.* Berkeley: University of California Press, 1966.

———. *Language, Religion and Politics in North India.* Cambridge, England: Cambridge University Press, 1974.

——— and Franda, Marcus, eds. *Radical Politics in South Asia.* Cambridge, Mass.: MIT Press, 1973.

Burger, Angela S. *Opposition in a Dominant Party System.* Berkeley: University of California Press, 1969.

Erdman, Howard L. *The Swatantra Party and Indian Conservatism.* Cambridge, England: Cambridge University Press, 1967.

Franda, Marcus. *Radical Politics in West Bengal.* Cambridge, Mass.: MIT Press, 1971.

Frankel, Francine. *India's Political Economy, 1947–77.* Princeton, N. J.: Princeton University Press, 1978.

Hardgrave, Robert L., Jr. *India: Government and Politics in a Developing Nation.* 3rd. ed. New York and London: Harcourt, Brace, Jovanovich, Inc., 1980.

Hart, Henry C., ed. *Indira Gandhi's India: A Political System Reappraised.* Boulder, Colo., Westview Press, 1976.

Kochanek, Stanley A. *Business and Politics in India.* Los Angeles and London: University of California Press, 1974.

———. *The Congress Party of India: The Dynamics of One-Party Democracy.* Princeton, N. J.: Princeton University Press, 1968.

Kothari, Rajni. *Politics in India.* Boston: Little, Brown and Co., 1970.

Nayar, Baldev Raj. *Minority Politics in the Punjab.* Princeton, N. J.: Princeton University Press, 1966.

Overstreet, Gene D. and Windmiller, Marshall. *Communism in India.* Berkeley: University of California Press, 1959.

Park, Richard L. and Bueno de Mesquita, Bruce. *India's Political System.* 2d. ed. Englewood Cliffs, N. J.: Prentice-Hall, Inc., 1979.

Ram, Mohan. *Maoism in India.* New Delhi: Vikas, 1971.

Sen Gupta, Bhabani. *Communism in Indian Politics.* New York: Columbia University Press, 1972.

Sisson, Richard. *The Congress Party in Rajasthan.* Berkeley: University of California Press, 1972.

Weiner, Myron. *India at the Polls: The Parliamentary Election of 1977.* Washington, D.C.: American Enterprise Institute, 1978.

———. *Party Building in a New Nation.* Chicago: University of Chicago Press, 1967.

REPUBLIC OF INDONESIA
(*Republik Indonesia*)
by R. William Liddle, Ph.D.

The System of Government

In formal terms, Indonesia is a unitary state with a constitutional government comprising the sovereign People's Consultative Assembly, an executive branch headed by a president chosen by the members of the Assembly, and an elected legislature. Beneath this carefully constructed facade of constitutionalism is an authoritarian regime dominated by a president whose power is based primarily on the support of the armed forces.

The basic document of government is the constitution of 1945, adopted at the beginning of the war for national independence (1945–49) against the Netherlands. In 1950, this document was replaced by a provisional constitution instituting a Western-style parliamentary democracy. In 1959, however, President Sukarno reinstated the original 1945 document. The present regime, called the New Order, dates from March 11, 1966, when President Sukarno was forced to turn over executive authority to his army commander, General Suharto.

Indonesia has a population of about 150 million people (fifth in the world) who live on over 6,000 islands. The Indonesian archipelago consists of over 13,000 islands which stretch 3,000 miles along the equator from Singapore to Papua New Guinea. It includes the islands of Java, Sumatra, Bali, Sulawesi (Celebes), and the Moluccas, and parts of Borneo and New Guinea. Over 250 distinct languages are spoken on the islands; the official language is Bahasa Indonesia, a Malay tongue now understood by nearly all the population.

Executive

Under the 1945 constitution, the president is the head of state, chief executive, and supreme commander of the armed forces. He may also declare a state of domestic emergency. Legislative powers and the powers to declare war and make treaties are shared by the president and the Parliament. The president is chosen for a five-year term by the People's Consultative Assembly. President Suharto was elected for a third term in March 1978.

Within the New Order executive, the three most important institutions—all closely controlled by the president—are *Bappenas*, *Pertamina*, and *Kopkamtib*. *Bappenas*, the national economic-planning body under the direction of Prof. Wijoyo Nitisastro, has been responsible for preparing the development plans that have produced an average real per capita growth rate of about 5 percent per year during the decade of the 1970s. The conservatism and expertise of *Bappenas* officials have also been the principal guarantee to foreign bankers, investors, and governments of the economic soundness of the New Order.

Pertamina is the national oil company, a crucial enterprise in an economy where petroleum and petroleum-related products account for more than half of exports and state revenue. Though it produces only a small proportion of Indonesia's oil itself, *Pertamina* controls the industry through such devices as production-sharing agreements with foreign companies (the split is now 85 percent/15 percent) and a monopoly over domestic distribution.

Kopkamtib is the Operations Command for the Restoration of Security and Order, an extraconstitutional device used by the president to legitimize emergency repressive actions against dissident groups and individuals. It was created by General Suharto on October 10, 1965, and was intended for use against the Communist Party in the wake of assassinations of six senior army generals. *Kopkamtib's* existence long after the end of any communist threat reflects its continuing importance as a symbol of Suharto's personal power and right to hold executive authority.

Legislature

There are two legislative bodies at the national level. The People's Consultative Assembly (*Majelis Permusyarawatan Rakyat*) meets once in five years to elect the president and vice president and to set the "broad outlines of state policy." Its 920 members include the 460 members of Parliament plus another 460 members appointed by the president and by the provincial governors to represent regional, military, political party, and other interests.

The People's Representative Council (*Dewan Perwakilan Rakyat*), or Parliament is elected for a five-year term. Of its 460 members, 364 are elected and ninety-six are appointed by the president, mostly to represent the armed forces, whose personnel do not have the right to vote. During the New Order, the Parliament has acted as a legitimator of presidential initiatives. Only government-sponsored legislation has been discussed, and the Parliament has not been allowed to engage in independent investigations or to build the staff that would enable it to become a co-equal in power with the executive.

Judiciary

The Supreme Court (*Mahkamah Agung*) is appointed by the president. It has both original and appellate jurisdiction, but no power of judicial review. The Court has never played a significant autonomous political role. In 1981, for the first time in the history of the republic, the president appointed an army general to be chief justice.

Regional & Local Government

Regional government is the responsibility of the Department of Home Affairs. Indonesia is divided into twenty-seven provinces and three hundred and sixty-four districts, each of which has a legislature plus an executive who, in principle, is nominated by members of the regional legislature but, in practice, is appointed by higher officials. All provinces and districts are headed by loyalists of the government party (*Golkar*), although one province in the 1982 elections (two in 1977) and several districts did not have *Golkar* pluralities. Until recently, the subdistrict, a purely administrative unit without a legislature, was the lowest level of national government, but under a 1979 law on village government previously autonomous village leaders have become state officials as well.

The Electoral System

The popular acronym for the New Order electoral system is *luber*—*langsung*, u*mum*, b*ebas*, r*ahasia:* direct, general, free, and secret. Most observers agree that this is a reasonably accurate description of the formal structure and procedures of the system, but not of the informal means by which the government secures its desired result.

The same electoral system has been used for all three New Order elections in 1971, 1977, and 1982. Elections for members of Parliament and the two levels of regional legislatures are held simultaneously. The provinces are multimember districts for Parliament and the provincial legislatures, with the province constituted as a single multimember district for its own legislature.

All citizens aged eighteen and over (or married) are eligible to vote, except for members of the armed forces, persons involved in the 1965 "thirtieth of September movement" (which resulted in the kidnapping and murder of six senior army officers on October 1), and other categories such as convicted criminals and the mentally incompetent. Registration is conducted several months before the election by local government officials and is virtually universal. Shortly before the election, each registered voter receives an authorization card which he or she presents to election officials at the polling place on election day in exchange for ballots.

Voting is by party list. Each voter is given three paper ballots containing the parties' names and ballot symbols, one ballot for each legislative level. In the secrecy of the voting booth, the voter punches a hole in the symbols of the party of his or her choice, then deposits the ballots in boxes, labelled with the three legislative levels, placed in front of the election officials and in full view of the public. Seats in national and provincial legislatures are distributed according to the percentage of votes each party receives—a simple system of proportional representation.

In all three elections held during the New Order, the voter turnout has been more than 90 percent.

The Party System

Origins of the Parties

Today's three-party system has its roots in the open politics of the late 1940s and early 1950s which culminated in the 1955 elections for Parliament and Constituent Assembly. Dozens of political parties and independent candidates contested the 1955 elections, but four dominated the results: the Indonesian Nationalist party, with 22.3 percent; *Masyumi*, a modernist Muslim party with considerable support outside of Java, with 20.9 percent; *Nahdlatul Ulama*, a traditional Islamic party based in East and Central Java, with 18.4 percent; and the Indonesian Communist Party, with 16.4 percent. *Masyumi* was banned in 1960 by President Sukarno, who accused its leaders of complicity in a series of regional rebellions; President Suharto allowed a successor, Indonesian Muslims' Party (*Partai Muslimin Indonesia*), to be formed in the late 1960s, but kept it weak by prohibiting the old leadership from playing an active role. The Communist Party was banned in 1966 by General Suharto, who accused its leaders of responsibility for the assassination of several high-ranking officers on September 30, 1965.

In 1969 President Suharto's New Order government decided to hold elections as a means of legitimizing his personal rule and that of the armed forces *cum* bureaucratic polity he had established. The nine parties then in existence were permitted to compete. To ensure its own dominance of Parliament and the People's Consultative Assembly, the government created its own political party, *Golkar*, and equipped it with a number of organizational and other advantages over its competitors. The result was an overwhelming victory for *Golkar*, which obtained 63 percent of the vote compared to 19 percent for *Nahdlatul Ulama*, its nearest competitor.

In 1973 the nine political parties were forced by the government to fuse into two: the Indonesian Democracy Party, comprising the old Nationalist Party, the Protestant and Catholic parties, and two small nationalist parties; and the Development Unity Party, which contains the old *Nahdlatul Ulama*, the Indonesian Muslims' Party, and two small Islamic parties. In the 1977 elections, *Golkar* received 62 percent of the vote; Development Unity, 29 percent, and Indonesian Democracy, 9 percent. In 1982, the results were *Golkar*, 64 percent, Development Unity, 28 percent, and Indonesian Democracy, 8 percent.

The Parties in Law

The current three-party system is regulated by a 1975 law. No other parties are permitted to exist. The state provides some funds to maintain party offices, assists the parties with campaign financing, and gives salaries and perquisites to party leaders who sit in Parliament.

Party Organization

The three parties are allowed by law to maintain a central leadership structure in Jakarta and branches at the provincial and district levels. The doctrine of a "floating mass" (protection of the mass public from politics except during election campaigns) is used to justify a prohibition on organization below the district.

In formal terms, the two nongovernmental parties are mass parties with dues-paying membership; however, the informal structures more closely approximate federations of cadre parties. It is important to note that the federations have been forced on the parties, and that many of the leaders owe their positions to support from government intelligence operatives. Development Unity, based on Islam, is the most clearly ideological party. Indonesian Democracy's constituent groups are more diverse, but cohere around a secular or at least non-Islamic position. In the 1950s, three cleavages, corresponding to important mass constituencies, divided the parties. First, the secular versus Islamic cleavage opposed the nationalist, communist, and Christian parties to the Islamic. Second, the outer islands versus Java cleavage opposed the *Masyumi* and Christian parties to the nationalists, traditional Muslims, and communists. Third, the cleavage between the lower and upper classes opposed the communists to the nationalists, traditionalist Muslims, and modernist Muslims. The respective leaderships of the last three groups tended to come from the bureaucracy, the village landowners and religious teachers, and the urban traders. Today's party system, dominated by *Golkar*, only weakly articulates the interests of groups outside the bureaucracy.

Implementation of the "floating mass" concept has meant that, with the exception of the quinquennial national election campaigns, there is virtually no political party activity at the village level. This is in sharp contrast to the politicization of the 1950s and 1960s, when party organizational efforts were continuous and intense. Especially in Java, party penetration of the villages was pervasive and national politics was often played on the village stage; for example, during 1964–65, "one-sided actions" of the Communist Party implemented national land-reform legislation against the interests of *Nahdlatul Ulama* landowners. Today, partisan politics does not, as far as is known, have much effect on the election of village officials (who until recently have served for life). In these elections, relatives, friends, and neighbors, not parties, provide the candidates' typical support. There are also frequent reports of vote-buying and other forms of bribery, since village government positions carry both high status and great economic potential for the officeholder.

All three political parties are run by their national leaderships with little influence from below but considerable influence from the New Order government. Party leaders are chosen at infrequent national congresses held under close government supervision and effectively penetrated by the state intelligence and security apparatus. Candidates for legislative office are selected by the national party leadership, but must undergo screening by the government. In the 1982 screening, several Development Unity party members of Parliament known for their willingness to oppose the government on important policy issues were not permitted renomination or were placed so low on the party's list that they had no real chance of election. The national party organizations are in principle superior to the parliamentary parties, but again in practice the government has on occasion intervened to support a parliamentary leader against his party.

Campaigning

In its campaign regulations, the government's primary concern is security. A successful election is one in which the political temperature is raised by as few degrees as possible.

The election law specifies a limited campaign period of about six weeks followed by a "quiet week" without campaigning immediately prior to election day. Party campaigners are restricted in what they may say—they may not challenge *Panca Sila*, the state philosophy of five fundamental principles (belief in God, humanitarianism, national unity, democracy, and social justice); nor may they criticize another party or oppose the policies of the government. There are also elaborate rules ostensibly designed to prevent conflicts among supporters of different parties, but in fact used to restrict the campaign activities of the nongovernment parties. For example, permits for rallies must be obtained weeks in advance; one party may not hold a rally on the same day as another within a certain radius of kilometers; parades cannot be held separately but must be connected with and end at the site of a rally; and so on.

All three political parties run highly centralized campaigns with national speakers who tour the country or visit the region of their origin. Each party also sponsors entertainers—from rock groups (Islamic rock bands are extremely popular among Development Unity supporters) to traditional singers, dancers, and puppet shows—whose principal duty is to attract and warm up audiences for the speakers. The heart of the campaign, however, is in the relationship between the voter and the party representative who directly solicits his vote.

In the case of *Golkar*, the party representative is the hamlet head or other village official who has been charged with the responsibility by his civilian and military superiors and is under their surveillance. The rule for all officials is *monoloyalitas*—one supports *Golkar* or leaves government service. In the 1971 elections, when many officials still felt close to one of the nine nongovernmental parties, supervision from above and by the armed forces component of the bureaucracy was close. Today, most civil servants have adjusted to the system and also recognize the material and status benefits the New Order's economic development policies have brought them. Development Unity's campaigns, particularly in the case of the *Nahdlatul Ulama* component, are based on the close links between devoutly Islamic voters and the network of rural religious teachers who are virtually the only significant Indonesian leadership group not easily manipulated by the government. Indonesian Democracy has no comparable local influentials (until the emergence of *Golkar*, its nationalist party component's leadership structure was filled with civil servants) and as a result the party receives very few votes.

Independent Voters

Little is known about party identification in Indonesia. It is assumed that in the 1950s and early 1960s there was a high degree of identification with what were clearly defined ideological parties. Today, devout Muslims continue to identify strongly with Development Unity. It is also certain that many more devout Protestants and Catholics vote for *Golkar* than for Indonesian Democracy, which incorporates their confessional parties. A few nationalist concentrations remain, particularly in Jakarta and Central Java, but for the most part identification with the old Nationalist Party has been lost in the New Order.

Ticket splitting, in the sense that one may vote for a different party list for Parliament and the provincial and district legislatures, is possible in Indonesia. Province-wide totals for the three elections suggest that few voters exercise this option, although some opposition-oriented intellectuals have recommended it as a strategy for building up the nongovernmental parties at the local level.

Development Unity Party (*Partai Persatuan Pembangunan;* PPP or P3)

History

The founding of the Development Unity party in 1973 represented the first time in the history of the republic that all Islamic groups were brought under a single roof. Islamic political unity had been a long-term goal of many Muslim politicians and political intellectuals, but the 1973 fusion of *Nahdlatul Ulama, Partai Muslimin Indonesia*, and two small parties of only regional and historical significance was imposed upon them by a government seeking greater control of the party system through simplification. Though clearly an Islamic organization, the party was not permitted to give itself an Islamic name, and only after extended and intense negotiations was it allowed to adopt the Ka'abah (the most important Islamic shrine, in Mecca, Saudi Arabia) as its ballot symbol. In the new Parliament created by the 1982 elections, Development Unity has ninety-six members. It has no cabinet ministers.

Organization

There has been no serious attempt at genuine fusion within the Development Unity Party. Each of the four constituent parties continues to exist as a "nonpolitical association," and it is the leaders of these associations who make up the leadership of the party as well. Most conflicts have been between the *Nahdlatul Ulama* and *Muslimin Indonesia* components and have involved the assignment of positions on the party's election lists, leadership positions in Parliament, and similar issues. In 1981, a dispute over list assignments also brought to light a rupture within *Nahdlatul Ulama* (NU) that threatened to end in that organization's withdrawal from the party. Idham Chalid, general chairman of NU since 1956, appears to have cooperated with government intelligence officials and *Muslimin Indonesia* leaders in preparing a list that removed or ranked very low a number of the most militant NU leaders, including some of its prominent younger faces. Idham's action was opposed not only by those directly affected, but by prominent members of NU's religious council, a body of highly respected religious teachers whose authority, according to the organization's constitution, is superior to that of the executive leadership. Of greatest concern to the religious council has been the growing evidence of successful government penetration not just of the Development Unity Party, which they recognize is unavoidable, but of NU itself. One attempted solution has been a move to oust Idham leadership; another has been withdrawal from partisan politics altogether. In late 1982 these battles were still in progress.

Development Unity has no affiliated organizations for youth, women, farmers, or other functional categories, though its components do. The most important of these are *Gerakan Pemuda An-*

sor, the NU youth group and a major source of future leaders and campaign activists, and *Muslimat NU*, the women's organization.

Policy

Development Unity's major policy concern is religion. In 1973, it opposed a government-sponsored marriage bill and succeeded in obtaining some concessions. It has also consistently opposed government attempts to elevate Javanese mysticism (see below, *Religious Organizations*) to the status of an official religion. Another policy area in which it differs with the government is over the electoral system and political party organization laws, where it has pushed for greater openness and more meaningful competition. On economic issues, the party has attempted somewhat tentatively to position itself on the distribution side of option between distributing resources to the populace and investment for growth. In foreign policy, internal party sentiment is anti-Israel, but since the government officially also takes an anti-Israel position, the issue is rarely debated.

On policy issues, the major cause of intraparty opposition within NU and between NU and *Muslimin Indonesia* is the struggle between hard-liners and soft-liners. Muslimin Indonesia's leaders are virtual government appointees without an independent mass base, unable to offer a strong challenge to government policy positions. Within NU, the Idham leadership also cooperates closely with the government. The two most prominent NU opposition groupings, led by Jusuf Hasjim and Abdurrahman Wahid, are in favor of NU's withdrawal from Development Unity: the former for tactical purposes to force the government to respond more positively to NU demands or to await a more pro-Islamic government, and the latter to restore NU to its original role as an educational organization with a broadly social rather than narrowly political purpose.

Membership & Constituency

As befits a cadre party, Development Unity's leaders pay slight attention to questions of membership and consequently little is known about party demographics. *Nahdlatul Ulama*'s principal stronghold continues to be the dense network of religious teachers and their followers in East Java centered around the *Tebu Ireng* school at Jombang, with important additional concentrations in Central Java and South Kalimantan. *Muslimin Indonesia* claims credit for the remainder, but its leaders do not have comparable roots anywhere. Other factors influencing the party's vote include the tendency of devout Muslims in Indonesia to punch an Islamic ballot symbol and a widespread impression that Development Unity is the party of protest against the government and *Golkar*.

With the combined support of the traditionalist Muslims of East and Central Java and the modernists of much of the rest of the archipelago, Development Unity enjoyed a wide vote distribution in the 1982 election. The party's highest percentage, 59 percent, was in Indonesia's westernmost province of Aceh, often called the front yard of Mecca, and its lowest, less than 1 percent, in the Catholic and tightly government-controlled province of East Timor. Overall, Development Unity won more than 20 percent of the total vote in seventeen of twenty-seven provinces, doing especially well in West Sumatra (41 percent), Jakarta (40 percent), South Kalimantan (39 percent), South Sumatra (38 percent), and East Java (37 percent). Between 1977 and 1982, the party increased its vote by 5 percent and 8 percent, respectively, in Bengkulu and West Sumatra, lost 4 percent in Jakarta, and lost between 4 percent and 12 percent in seven additional provinces located mostly in Kalimantan and Sulawesi.

Financing

Little information is available on party financing. The pattern is one of heavy state support designed to make party officials dependent on the government. *Nahdlatul Ulama*, which can obtain funds from its rural constituency of religious teachers and their landowning followers, is undoubtedly freer than other party components of the constraints which state largesse imposes.

Leadership

The most prominent *Nahdlatul Ulama* leaders include:

Dr. K. H. Idham Chalid (born 1921, in South Kalimantan), president of Development Unity and general chairman of the NU National Executive, has his power base in East Java and, reportedly, in support from the government.

K. H. Ali Ma'shum has been general chairman of NU's Religious Council since 1981 and is head of the Krapyak Muslim school in Yogyakarta. His power base is among religious teachers in Central Java.

H. M. Jusuf Hasjim (born 1929 in Jombang, East Java) is first chairman of the NU National Executive. He is a former member of Parliament and an opponent of Idham Chalid. His power base is in East Java. He leads an NU faction most of whose

members have been associated with him since their days as guerrilla fighters in East Java during the war for independence.

Abdurrahman Wahid (born 1940 in Jombang, East Java) is the secretary of the UN National Executive and founder and head of the Ciganjur Muslim School, South Jakarta. A prominent columnist, his power base is in family connections with the founding fathers of NU.

Chalid Mawardi (born 1936 in Sala, Central Java) is general chairman of NU's *Ansor* youth movement.

H. Nuddin Lubis (born 1919 in Panyabungan, North Sumatra) is the chairman of Development Unity's parliamentary delegation and vice chairman of the party's National Executive. A follower of Idham Chalid, he has no mass base of his own.

Muslimin Indonesia leaders do not have independent power bases but are closely tied to the government. The best-known leader, Dr. H. John Naro (born 1929, Palembang, Sumatra), is the general chairman of Development Unity and chairman of *Muslimin Indonesia*.

Prospects

Under the New Order, the Development Unity Party has no chance of obtaining power or a significant share of power. Though partially colonized by the government, it is and will almost certainly remain the principal opposition party. In recent years there has been a revival of religious interest among Indonesian Muslims. While there are many reports of increasing militancy and growing frustration, this has not yet been translated into political action at the polling booth or elsewhere. If *Nahdlatul Ulama* leaves the party, Islamic politics may be increasingly conducted outside the system, but it is more likely that an uneasy *modus vivendi* will prevail.

Golongan Karya; Golkar

History

Golkar is the vehicle by which President Suharto has maintained his personal dominance, and the dominance of his allies in the armed forces and civilian bureaucracy, over the Indonesian political system within the framework of the constitution of 1945. It is not so much a political party as it is the political arm of the bureaucracy and a means by which the number of legislative seats occupied by Development Unity and Indonesian Democracy can be reduced to the bare minimum.

Golkar was founded in 1964 by senior army officers to combat growing communist and radical nationalist strength in Parliament and the regional legislatures. From 1964 to 1969, it was built around a core of army-sponsored labor unions and cooperative organizations for ex-soldiers, and also included a diverse and loosely coordinated group of nonparty legislative representatives. In 1969, at President Suharto's direction, it was turned into a state party in order to contest the 1971 elections. It now has an overwhelming majority in Parliament, holding 244 elected and ninety-six appointed seats. All cabinet ministers are *Golkar* members.

Organization

Golkar's structure mirrors the state's structure. Its leadership boards at the national, provincial, and district levels are made up of high-ranking officials, including active-duty military officers or their representatives. While *Golkar* legislative delegations reflect the spectrum of state agencies, civil and military, there is no evidence of voting blocs or factions based on members' affiliations with specific segments of the bureaucracy. Instead, they act for the most part as a unified voting bloc for government legislation. Because it is the political arm of the state, *Golkar*'s national coverage is complete.

Policy

Economic growth is the major domestic policy orientation of the Suharto government and thus of *Golkar*. Emphasis has been placed on foreign assistance (about a fifth of annual revenues) and to a lesser extent on foreign investment (about $4 billion realized between 1967 and 1981). *Golkar* also emphasizes the development of natural resources: first, oil and natural gas; second, other resources, such as tin and lumber, as well as plantation or small-holder agricultural products (coffee; rubber; palm oil; and self-sufficiency in rice, nearly achieved in 1981 and 1982). In the present (third) five-year plan, attention is being paid to questions of equity, including assistance to large and small indigenous entrepreneurs and a range of welfare programs from school building to village health centers. Foreign investors, though still welcome, are now more closely regulated than in the early New Order days. Several industries are run by the state.

The Suharto government's foreign policy is markedly pro-Western on Cold War issues and moderately supportive of the position of underde-veloped nations on issues relating to the international economic order. Indonesia is a member of OPEC and of the United Nations' Group of 77. Despite American urging, the Suharto government has not recognized the People's Republic of China, which it accuses of support for the Indonesian Communist Party and involvement in the September 30, 1965, assassination of generals. Within Southeast Asia, Indonesia is a strong supporter of ASEAN (the Association of Southeast Asian Nations, including Thailand, Malaysia, Singapore, Indonesia, and the Philippines) and considers itself the major (if not hegemonic) power in the region.

Membership & Constituency

Although in principle a mass-membership party, *Golkar* in practice does not compile membership lists except prior to elections, when village officials are required by their superiors to obtain voters' signatures on *Golkar* membership forms as a campaign tactic. Election results for the three elections show consistency over time and across provinces, though there is some tendency for *Golkar* to enjoy overwhelming margins of victory in the more sparsely populated and isolated regions and also where devout Muslims are fewest. The party's lowest vote total in 1982 was in strongly Islamic Aceh (39.6 percent); its highest in Southeast Sulawesi (96.9 percent). Fourteen provinces, none of them in Java, gave *Golkar* 70 percent or more of their votes.

Financing

All of *Golkar*'s finances come via the state but are nonbudgetary in origin. Some of these funds are reportedly skimmed from *Pertamina* and other state company profits, and some are collected from Chinese and other businessmen with lucrative state contracts. The United States government has also contributed at least small amounts to *Golkar* campaigns, as in a 1971 gift of radio equipment to link the central *Golkar* headquarters to its provincial branch offices.

Leadership

Golkar's most important "leaders" are officials assigned party responsibilities. Two officials who have had much to do with *Golkar*'s election victories are:

General (ret.) H. Amirmachmud (born 1923 in Cimahi, West Java) is minister of home affairs and is assigned the duty of ensuring the loyalty of the territorial civil service which is the backbone of *Golkar* campaigns.

Lieutenant General (ret.) Ali Murtopo (born 1924 in Blora, Central Java) is minister of information and honorary chairman of the Center for Strategic and International Studies, where *Golkar*'s initial campaign strategy was devised and which continues to be the nerve center of the party's national campaign organization.

Two figures who hold at least formally important positions within *Golkar* are Major General (ret.) Amir Murtono (born 1924 in Kertosono, East Java), who is general chairman of *Golkar;* and Ir. [Engineer] Sarwono Kusumaatmadja (born 1943 in Jakarta), who is secretary and principal spokesperson for the *Golkar* parliamentary delegation.

Satellite Organizations

Legally, *Golkar* may not have affiliates, but there is nonetheless a plethora of organizations with strong *Golkar* connections. These include every organization for state officials, most prominently, the Officials' Corps of the Republic of Indonesia (*Korps Pegawai Republik Indonesia;* KORPRI); the Indonesian Armed Forces Veterans Association (*Persatuan Purnawirawan Angkatan Bersenjata Republik Indonesia;* PEPABRI); the associations of civilian officials' and armed forces officers' wives; and the association of retired military officers. State-sponsored organizations for farmers, workers, youth, fishermen, etc. all declare their support for *Golkar* during each election campaign, as do a number of quasicorporate private organizations.

Prospects

Golkar is the central mechanism chosen by the New Order to create the illusion of popular sovereignty and democratic control while maintaining the reality of rule by a small, primarily military elite. The probability is very high that it will remain in power for the duration of the regime.

Minor Parties

Indonesian Democracy Party (*Partai Demokrasi Indonesia;* PDI)

Though it incorporates the once-mighty Indonesian Nationalist Party (along with the Protestants, Catholics, and two small nationalist organizations), Indonesian Democracy is today a minor party. Its highest vote in 1982 was in Yogyakarta (16 percent), where it ran third to *Golkar* and Development Unity; it received less than 5 percent of the vote in fourteen provinces and less than 10 percent in an additional eight. In its traditional Central Java stronghold, it won only 12 percent.

Like Development Unity, PDI is the product of a 1973 shotgun marriage and its components have maintained their separate identities. Internecine conflict has been continuous, mostly between factions of the old Nationalist Party over positions that give them access to elite status and income. The party is thoroughly penetrated by the president's intelligence operatives.

In the 1950s, the Indonesian Nationalist Party's main strengths were its closeness to the charismatic President Sukarno; its radical nationalist or populist ideas; and its support by a large segment of the bureaucracy, especially the provincial, district, and subdistrict officials of the Department of Home Affairs. The last category was required to support *Golkar* before the 1971 election and must continue to do so. Sukarno was discredited in the mid-1960s and died in 1970. Though there are signs of the continuing popularity of his ideas, and of renewed interest in the late president's career and role in modern Indonesian history, no new leadership with the capability of mobilizing the nationalist base has emerged either within or outside the party. If radical nationalist ideas are again to play a role in Indonesian politics, it is likely that they will be articulated either by dissident army officers or by a totally new nationalist party following the collapse of the New Order.

Other Political Forces

Military

From the beginning of the New Order, the central actor in Indonesian politics has been not the political parties but the military. President Suharto, in office since 1967, is a retired general. Eight of seventeen heads of cabinet departments are military officers, as are the occupants of fifty-two of 106 second-echelon departmental positions and a large majority of provincial governors and district heads. Both the Parliament and the People's Consultative Assembly are led by one four-star general; and generals hold the top positions in the Supreme Court, Supreme Audit Board, and the Public Prosecutor's office. This participation is legitimated by the doctrine of *dwi-fungsi*, the twin functions of the armed forces to provide for national defense and to play a positive social and political role.

There are two competing explanations for this massive armed forces involvement in political life. One stresses the incompetence of civilian politicians and traces the rise of the military's political role to the multiparty Parliament and cabinet instability of the early 1950s, followed by the threat of a growing Communist Party in the late 1950s and early 1960s and the collapse of civilian government in 1965. A second explanation emphasizes the influence of the war for independence, when the newly created army was forced by the circumstances of guerrilla warfare and governmental disarry to shoulder many nonmilitary responsibilities. The *dwi-fungsi* doctrine, it is argued, grew directly out of the sense of national responsibility engendered during this period. Since 1957, when all Dutch enterprises in Indonesia were nationalized and given to the army to run, the military has also had an economic stake which has propelled it to ever deeper participation.

The origins of the senior generation of today's armed force officers, including the retired officers closest to the president, are the immediate pre–World War II period, the 1942–45 Japanese occupation, and the 1945–49 war for independence. Suharto himself was a Dutch army sergeant and a Japanese army lieutenant before joining the nationalist cause after the declaration of independence in August 1945. Among active duty officers, this so-called "Generation of 1945" is rapidly being replaced by a small "transitional generation" which received its training in the 1950s in a variety of schools and courses in Indonesia and abroad. Just moving into important divisional command positions is the "Academy" or "Magelang" generation, officers graduated from the armed forces' academy in Magelang, Central Java, after 1960. In comparison with their seniors, members of the Academy generation are politically inexperienced, but they are thought to be better trained technically and more sophisticated in military matters and general administration.

Serious factionalism does not now appear to exist within the Indonesian armed forces. During the war for independence, the military consisted largely of semi-autonomous guerrilla bands under the command of charismatic leaders, a pattern that continued into the independence period and played, together with the ethnic and regional base of army divisions, a major role in the regional army rebellions of the late 1950s. Partisan politics and a drive for rationalization at the end of the guerrilla struggle were also factors in internal armed forces disunity in the 1950s. Divisional tensions, especially among the Java-based Siliwangi, Diponegoro, and Brawijaya (located in West, Central, and East Java respectively) divisions, continued into the late 1960s, but those tensions have since been dissipated by policies of centralization of command in the Department of Defense and Security in Jakarta and by promotion policies that cut across divisional lines for younger officers, who as a result do not develop loyalties to any particular unit.

The main visible cleavage today is between the Suharto loyalists and a small number of retired generals who have long been at odds with the president on a range of issues including internal military affairs, the role of the army in politics, the New Order's treatment of Islam, governmental corruption, and so on. Of greater ultimate concern, however, are the attitudes of the Academy generation. Because of the secrecy in which the strongly nationalist officers' corps wraps itself, little is known of the younger officers' plans or activities, but the consensus among observers is that they are motivated mainly by personal career ambitions, which they are pursuing through established channels of advancement, and have not moved to form factions in opposition to their seniors.

For economic reasons, troops are still mostly recruited and serve in their area of origin. The exceptions are elite troops such as the Army Paracommando Command and the Army Strategic Reserve's Airborne Division. Within the armed forces leadership there has been considerable concern over discipline since the badly executed takeover of the former Portuguese colony of East Timor in 1975. The present minister of defense, Mohammed Jusuf, has since 1978 conducted well-publicized campaigns to improve both battle-readiness and food, housing, and other amenities for his troops.

Students

Students' political activity has been effectively suppressed since 1978 by the present minister of education, Daoed Joesoef, whose policy of Normalization of Campus Life has outlawed student councils and instituted close surveillance of the campuses and summary expulsion of activists.

The history of student involvement in politics extends to the first decades of the century when Mohammad Hatta, later to become first vice president of the republic, and other students founded the early nationalist organization, *Perhimpoenan Indonesia* (Indonesian Association), in the Netherlands. More recently, students at the major universities (especially the University of Indonesia in Jakarta and the Bandung Institute of Technology) played an important role in support of General Suharto and other New Order forces between 1965 and 1969.

In the 1970s, the universities were centers of debate and demonstrations critical of the government. Troops were frequently used against students, particularly in late 1973 and early 1974, when students demonstrated against corruption and foreign investment, and again in late 1977 and early 1978, when they protested the reelection without opposition of President Suharto by the People's Consultative Assembly. Major student leaders were arrested in 1978 and put on trial. Several of them clandestinely published their summary pleas, written as indictments of the New Order political system and its economic policies.

Religious Organizations

Islam, Protestantism, Catholicism, Buddhism, and Confucianism are the five officially recognized religions. Throughout the twentieth century, Indonesian Islam has been split doctrinally into conservative or traditional and modern or reformist wings. The principal organization of traditional Islam since 1926 has been *Nahdlatul Ulama*. The chief modernist organization is *Muhammadiyah*, in the 1950s closely associated with the *Masyumi* political party but, since the early 1960s, firmly committed to a nonpolitical educational and social role. Another important modernist organization is *Himpunan Mahasiswa Islam* (Islamic Students' Association), historically a major source of cadre for student opposition politics and Islamic political parties.

The other four recognized religions have peak organizations, such as the *Dewan Gereja Indonesia* (Indonesian Council of Churches), which play a quasicorporate role in linking their constituencies to the government via the Department of Religion's directorates-general for *pembinaan* (guidance) of religious group affairs. In the case of Islam, a government-sponsored Council of Islamic Teachers performs this function.

Throughout the 1970s, the major religious issue in Indonesian politics was the tension between Islam and Javanese mysticism. Among the Javanese, perhaps as many as two-thirds of the population are only nominally Muslim, and many of these are followers of indigenous and Hindu beliefs which long antedate the arrival of Islam in the archipelago. The religious practices of many high government officials, including the president and several of his closest advisors, are more influ-

enced by this Hindu-Javanese tradition than by Islam. Mystical organizations, their national association, and their supporters in high places have sought greater recognition and opposed the Development Unity party and Islamic leaders on many issues. In 1978, the Broad Outlines of State Policy passed by the People's Consultative Assembly accorded "beliefs" equal status with "religion," but in deference to Muslim opposition placed the office for guidance of beliefs in the Department of Education.

Ethnic Groups

Ethnic groups do not play an overt role in New Order politics, and little is known of their covert influence. The pre-New Order pattern was one of much greater participation. During the colonial period many nationalist organizations had an ethnic or regional base and in some cases used regional names, as in the *Jong Sumatranen Bond* (Young Sumatran Association). Ethnic cleavages were also marked in the political parties and the armed forces of the 1950s and early 1960s. Regional army rebellions in the late 1950s briefly raised the prospect of national disintegration.

During the New Order, and for several years prior to it, the trend has been toward centralization of government and political life in Jakarta and of increasing Javanization of the center and extension of Javanese influence to the other islands. About 50 percent of the 150 million Indonesian people are members of the Javanese ethnic group, whose homeland is the provinces of Central and East Java and the Special Region of Yogyakarta; another 15 percent are Sundanese (West Java). The remainder include several relatively large groups (two million or more) such as the Acehnese, Bataks, and Minangkabau of Sumatra; the Madurese; the Balinese; and the Bugis/Makasar people of Sulawesi; and as many as five hundred smaller groups (including an estimated two hundred and fifty minuscule isolated groups in the easternmost province of Irian Jaya). There are also about four million Chinese, most of whom live in the cities and towns.

In contrast to this pattern of relative ethnic diversity, some 80 percent of the Indonesian military elite (including most of the territorial commanders outside Java) and probably a similar proportion of the higher civilian bureaucracy are Javanese. Because factionalism within the bureaucracy is based on close personal relations between patrons and clients, the system almost necessarily discriminates against non-Javanese, although one can find clusters of non-Javanese as well as patron-client networks based on university and other ties that link Javanese and non-Javanese in a variety of combinations. Indonesian Chinese, regardless of citizenship, are widely regarded as political pariahs, outside the "national" community. The Chinese business elite seeks security from the Indonesian military elite by trading money, favors, and business opportunities for political and personal security.

The overall tone of this system is perhaps set by President Suharto. Although quintessentially Javanese in culture (in contrast to the cosmopolitan Sukarno), he is surrounded by clients who are mostly but not entirely Javanese (the non-Javanese, he knows, have no chance to replace him), and is reputed to have built a personal and family fortune through his Chinese business associates.

Organized Labor

During the 1950s and early 1960s most political parties had their own labor unions. The largest by far was the communist party's All-Indonesian Central of Labor Organizations, (*Sentral Organisasi Buruh Seluruh Indonesia;* SOBSI), banned in 1966. Today all labor unions are in principle independent of politics, but they combined in the All-Indonesia Labor Federation, (*Federasi Buruh Seluruh Indonesia;* FBSI), which is in practice closely controlled by the government and a part of the Big Family (*Keluarga Besar*) of *Golkar*.

Interest-Group Organizations

The great majority of interest groups in Indonesia have been effectively penetrated by *Golkar* and/or the state security and intelligence apparatus. These include associations for doctors, lawyers, journalists, businessmen, women, farmers, youth, and even athletic organizations. In exchange for political support, leaders and members of these organizations have access to government officials, receive special treatment and facilities, and in some cases exercise monopoly control over their professions.

Within associations, or among associations in a particular functional area, there is often competition for government favors. Businessmen, for example, are very dependent on government contracts, and as competition has become more intense in recent years, the number of organizations, each tied to a high-level official as patron, has mushroomed. In addition to the Indonesian Chamber of Commerce, the Association of Young Indonesian Entrepreneurs, the Association of Indigenous Indonesian Entrepreneurs, and so on,

there appeared in 1982 the frankly named Association of Companions of the Government (*Asosiasi Rekanan Pemerintah*).

National Prospects

There are two schools of thought on the prospects for political stability in Indonesia. One school points to the number and severity of cleavages—along ethnic/regional, religious, and social-class lines—in this archipelagic nation whose motto is *Bhinneka Tunggal Ika* (Unity in Diversity), and to the intense and sometimes violent political expression of those cleavages in the 1950s and 1960s. These observers conclude that Indonesia today must be like its famous volcanic island Krakatau in the late nineteenth century—quiet on the surface but building internally toward a massive explosion.

A second school sees the domination of the center over the regions, the Javanese over the non-Javanese, the secular over the religious forces, the military over civilians, the newly rich over the still poor as likely to continue for some time. They point to the exhaustion of opposition forces in the political (and military) battles of the 1950s and 1960s, to the government's continuing readiness to suppress any opposition that dares raise its head, and to the ameliorative effects of the genuine prosperity which the New Order has brought to perhaps two thirds of the population of all social and cultural groups. The weight of evidence accumulated during sixteen years of the New Order seems increasingly to support the latter view.

Further Reading
Anderson, Benedict R. O'G. "The Idea of Power in Javanese Culture." In *Culture and Politics in Indonesia*, Claire Holt, ed. Ithaca and London: Cornell University Press, 1972.
Booth, Anne, and McCawley, Peter, eds. *The Indonesian Economy During the Soeharto Era.* Kuala Lumpur: Oxford University Press, 1981.
Crouch, Harold. *The Army and Politics in Indonesia.* Ithaca and London: Cornell University Press, 1978.
"Current Data on the Indonesian Military Elite." *Indonesia,* No. 18, October, 1974; No. 23, April, 1977; No. 26, October, 1978; No. 29, April, 1980; No. 33, April, 1982.
Emmerson, Donald K. "The Bureaucracy in Political Context: Weakness in Strength." In *Political Power and Communication in Indonesia,*

Jackson, Karl D., and Lucian W. Pye, eds. Berkeley, Los Angeles, and London: University of California Press, 1978.

Feith, Herbert, and Castles, Lance, eds. *Indonesian Political Thinking: 1945–1965.* Ithaca and London: Cornell University Press, 1970.

Geertz, Clifford. *The Religion of Java.* Glencoe, New York: Free Press, 1960.

Liddle, R. William. "Participation and the Political Parties," In *Political Power and Communication in Indonesia.* Jackson, Karl D., and Lucian W. Pye, eds. Berkeley, Los Angeles, and London: University of California Press, 1978.

McDonald, Hamish. *Suharto's Indonesia.* Blackburn, Victoria, Australia: Fontana Books, 1980.

MacDougall, John. "Patterns of Military Control in the Indonesian Higher Central Bureaucracy." *Indonesia*, No. 33, April, 1982.

Mackie, J. A. C., ed. *The Chinese in Indonesia: Five Essays.* Honolulu: University Press of Hawaii, 1976.

McVey, Ruth. "The Post-Revolutionary Transformation of the Indonesian Army" (Parts I and II). *Indonesia*, No. 11, April, 1971 and No. 13, April, 1972.

Ricklefs, M. C. *A History of Modern Indonesia, c. 1300 to the Present.* Bloomington: University of Indiana Press, 1981; and London: Macmillan, 1981.

Weinstein, Franklin B. *Indonesian Foreign Policy and the Dilemma of Dependence: From Sukarno to Soeharto.* Ithaca and London: Cornell University Press, 1976.

"White Book of the 1978 Students' Struggle." Translated by the editors. *Indonesia*, No. 25, April, 1978.

ISLAMIC REPUBLIC OF IRAN
(*Jomhuri-ye Eslami-ye Iran*)
by Lawrence G. Potter, M.Phil.

The System of Government

Iran, a country of some forty million people, has been an Islamic republic, governed by the Islamic Republic Party, since April 1, 1979. Before then, the country was a constitutional monarchy governed by the late Shah Mohammad Reza Pahlavi (reigned 1941–79; died July 27, 1980). A coalition of groups (Muslim clergy allied to merchants of the bazaar, liberal reformists, and leftists) overthrew the Pahlavi regime in February 1979. Leadership of the country was then assumed by the *ulema* or Muslim clergy, united behind Ayatollah Rouhollah Khomeini. The country's first constitution, granted in 1906 by the reigning monarch of the Qajar dynasty, was replaced by the present constitution of December 1979. The new constitution provides for clerical control of all branches of government. The current political structure and the constitution itself could change at any time, as the country is still in a state of revolutionary upheaval.

The acknowledged leader of the country is Ayatollah Khomeini, who is referred to as the *faqih* or guide of the revolution. In his conception of Islamic government (sometimes referred to as *velayat-e faqih*), the state is to be guided by a learned religious jurist who rules in the absence of the Twelfth Imam. This Imam, descendant of the Prophet Muhammad, went into "concealment" in the ninth century and is expected to return at the end of the world to establish a golden age. Until that time, the Imam's will is transmitted through *ayatollahs* or *mujtahids* to the people. The position of Khomeini as *faqih* is ambiguous: it is provided for in the constitution, but it is not formally a part of the government.

Executive

The apogee of the political system was until recently the Shah, who governed with the aid of a small group of trusted advisors. Power was highly centralized in the monarchy. The Shah governed by a "politics of distrust," making all important political decisions himself and assigning overlapping responsibilities to underlings who reported directly to him and competed with each other. Loyalty was the key criterion for service, and anyone who threatened to develop his own power base was removed. As the linchpin of the system, the Shah was the only person who had access to all the information. The system fostered great personal insecurity because everyone's position depended on the will of the Shah. In the words of a study written in 1976 for the CIA, "Although surrounded, the Shah is alone, to the best of any observer's knowledge. He seeks information. He does not seek advice, and few in Iran would dare to give him any. He decides; others execute." When he was deposed there was no individual or institution capable of replacing him.

The Revolutionary Council, now disbanded, was the most important decision-making body in Iran before the formation of the present government. It was a committee of thirteen, appointed by Khomeini, formed on Jan. 13, 1979, and dissolved on Sept. 11, 1980, after President Rajai's government was installed. Its membership was secret.

According to the new constitution, it is the responsibility of the executive branch to open the way for the creation of an Islamic society. The *faqih*, or leader, of the country should be a religious jurist who enjoys the confidence of the majority of the people. Very extensive powers are placed at his disposal: he appoints the religious jurists on the Council of Guardians, appoints the highest judicial authorities, and has command of the armed forces including the revolutionary guards. He can declare war. He must sign the order formalizing the election of the president and can dismiss the president for the good of the country if the Supreme Court finds him politically incompetent (a fate that befell the former president Abolhassan Bani-Sadr in June 1981).

Should there be no decisive majority of the people in favor of one *faqih*, three to five candidates are to be appointed by a Council of Experts to serve on a Leadership Council. Any *faqih* who is unable to carry out his duties is to be removed by the Council of Experts.

The president holds the highest position after the *faqih.* He is responsible for carrying out constitutional laws and acts as a link between the three branches of government. He is elected for a four-year term, by an absolute majority of the votes cast, and can be reelected for one additional term. Only the *faqih* can dismiss him.

The president nominates the prime minister, who must be approved by the Parliament. The prime minister stays in office as long as he has the confidence of the Parliament. This system prevented President Bani-Sadr from appointing the prime minister of his choice.

Legislature

The *Majlis* (the National Consultative Assembly or Parliament) is composed of 270 members elected for four-year terms. The *Majlis* holds open sessions, except under exceptional conditions: its discussions are made public by radio, and its minutes are published in newspapers. It is empowered to make laws and approve international agreements. Its powers, however, go beyond legislation: it is also authorized to conduct investigations into all the affairs of the country.

Council of Guardians

This council is an extremely powerful twelve-member group that determines whether laws passed by the Parliament conform with Islamic principles and can be ratified. It is responsible for interpreting the constitutional law and supervising elections. Six clergymen are appointed by the *faqih* or Leadership Council. The other six, whose selection must be voted on by the *Majlis*, are nominated by the High Judicial Council and are lawyers from different branches of the law. According to the constitution, members are elected for six-year terms, but after a three-year period half the Council is to be changed by lottery. Such a change has not yet taken place. Because this group has at times refused to go along with Khomeini's directives (for example, on land reform), he has now authorized laws passed by Parliament to take effect even if the Council has vetoed them.

Council of Experts

The first Council of Experts was a seventy-five-member group (sixty of whom were clergymen) elected in August 1979 to draft the new constitu-tion. These elections were boycotted by opposition groups when it became obvious that their viewpoints would be excluded. Candidates were qualified by nine-member provincial committees (each including five religious leaders). When the constitution was completed, that first Council disbanded. A second Council of Experts was due to be elected in the summer of 1982 to choose Khomeini's successor (or more likely a Leadership Council), but election was repeatedly postponed. It was announced, however, that nominees for membership did not have to be a resident of the locality they wished to represent. It was also announced that the new Council would become a permanent revolutionary institution and would not disband after choosing the successor. What its function might be remained unclear.

Judiciary

The judiciary is in principle supposed to be an independent force. Its responsibilities are to be overseen by the five-member High Judicial Council, made up of the head of the Supreme Court, the attorney general, and three judges. They serve for five-year terms, with the possibility of extension for another five. Trials are to be held openly and the public is allowed to attend, unless this is incompatible with public order, which it often is. Judges must issue findings on cases (i.e., they cannot claim lack of precedent) which must be based on Islamic principles. In March 1982, the prosecutor general gave Iranian judges the authority to ignore laws of the previous regime if they were un-Islamic.

Regional & Local Government

There has always been a strong tradition of local government in Iran, although power was increasingly centralized in Tehran under the Pahlavis. Provincial heads, as well as the mayor of Tehran, were appointed directly by the Shah, and the minister of the interior was the main influence in selecting provincial officials. The only authority elected on a local level was the village headman.

The administrative divisions of Iran have frequently been changed, and the new government will undoubtedly modify the arrangements that have prevailed since May 1977. Iran is currently divided into twenty-three provinces (*ostan*), headed by governor generals (*ostandar*). Provinces are divided into 472 districts (*shahrestan*) headed by governors (*farmandar*). Districts are divided into 499 subdistricts (*baksh*) administered by lieutenant governors (*bakshdar*). Subdistricts are divided into townships (*dehistan*) led by sheriffs (*dehdar*). Townships are divided into villages (*deh*), which are led by a headman (*kadkhoda*).

The Electoral System

Members of Parliament are elected by direct and secret ballot. The first elections were held in two rounds, in March and May 1980. A candidate had to have an absolute majority to win on the first ballot, otherwise there were more rounds of voting. This system made it difficult to fill seats in many constituencies. In the first Parliament, which convened on May 28, 1980, 213 deputies were seated (out of 270 places), about a quarter of whom were clerics.

Candidates that wish to run for office must be approved by the Council of Guardians, which pares the list of aspirants drastically. Thus, of the seventy people who registered to run in the presidential election of July 24, 1981, sixty-seven were disqualified. In the presidential election of Oct. 2, 1981, forty-four people registered to run, and the Council disqualified thirty-nine. Khomeini barred clergymen from running for president in the first two elections, but then changed his policy. The third president was a clergyman.

The voting age is sixteen, although it was lowered to fifteen in the October 1981, presidential election, because a low turnout was expected. Clergymen are on hand at polling places to advise illiterates.

Accurate figures on voter turnout are not available; estimates suggest up to twenty-three million are eligible voters. In the election of Bani-Sadr as president on January 25, 1980, he received nearly eleven million votes or 75.7 percent of the total vote. When Rajai was elected as president, he won thirteen million votes, or 88 percent of the total votes cast. However, Bani-Sadr claims that the latter election was rigged and actually only 2.7 million people voted. In the election of Khamene'i as president, preliminary returns indicated that he received 14.8 million votes, or 95 percent of the total. These figures are very high, however. In the last parliamentary elections held under the Shah (1975), the electorate was estimated at fourteen million and only about seven million voted.

The government is clearly worried about low voter turnout, and Khomeini has announced that it is "a divine and religious obligation to vote." However, most, if not all, opposition groups have boycotted the various elections. Voting procedures were never taken seriously under the Shah—the results were predictable—and the same attitude remains; now the candidate of the Islamic Republic Party always wins.

The Party System

Iran has political parties and elections, but participation in them implies no meaningful choice. Rather, the ruler or ruling elements utilize them to bolster the regime. Elections are rigged and are not taken seriously by the people. Electoral politics in Khomeini's Iran thus resemble those under the Shah; only the ruling group is different.

Origins of the Parties

Although political parties have existed in Iran since 1906, they only achieved some degree of freedom in periods when the central government was too weak to impose its will on the country—notably 1906 to 1923, 1941 to 1948, 1951 to 1953, and in early 1979. Most Iranians are now too young to remember the great burst of political activity in the country from 1951 to 1953. This period was dominated by the National Front, a coalition of nationalists which received support both from the communist Tudeh and the *ulema* (especially Ayatollah Kashani). It was led by the immensely popular Dr. Mohammad Mosaddeq, who by presiding over the nationalization of the oil industry caused a confrontation with Great Britain. He strongly opposed the Shah and even forced him briefly into exile in August 1953, after which the Shah was restored in a countercoup.

In 1957, the Shah decided to establish a system with two officially sponsored parties. A "progovernment" party was formed called *Mellioun* (replaced in 1963 by *Iran-e Novin*), which was countered by a "loyal opposition" party called *Mardom*. They were both led by trusted friends of the king. There were a few smaller parties of lesser importance, such as the Pan-Iranists. In 1975 the Shah abolished the existing parties and created a new official party called the *Rastakhiz-e Iran*, which was intended to mobilize the people behind the government. This was the only legal party in Iran until shortly before the overthrow of the Shah in 1979.

Parliament was traditionally dominated by landlords and other powerful local interests, although their representation was much reduced after the introduction of the Shah's "White Revolution" in the early 1960s. All candidates were screened by SAVAK, the secret police. The Shah's wishes were never opposed; only the details of implementing his policies were discussed. Despite its lack of real power, membership in the *Majlis* was desirable because it confirmed elite status. The body as a whole was very highly educated. In the twenty-fourth *Majlis* (1975–79), the last to be elected under the Shah, out of a total 270 seats 160 members were college graduates and fifty held doctorates.

A major reason for the anarchy that has enveloped Iran since the departure of the Shah is the people's lack of experience in free political expression. To this might be added a lack of responsible political leadership. The public has a cynical attitude towards party politics, which is seen as a foreign import which will not work in Iran. Iranians rally around individuals, not party platforms, and membership figures do not necessarily indicate the amount of support for party platforms. In fact, large segments of the Iranian population do not seem to be represented by any political party at present. Those parties currently active in Iranian politics take extreme positions, and the only centrist parties are located abroad. This tends to obscure the existence of more moderate elements, notably the Westernized intelligentsia and *bazaaris*, who constitute a significant factor in the country.

The Parties in Law

The freedom to form and participate in political parties is guaranteed in the new constitution, but parties may be banned if they violate "principles of independence, freedom and national unity, or are contrary to the principles of Islam or the Islamic Republic."

Party Organization

Parties, as such, are a relatively recent innovation in Iran. They do not accurately reflect Iranian political behavior, which has developed over the course of many centuries. In Iran power resides in individuals, not institutions. It is exercised informally through personal networks, and personal connections and influence are commonly needed to get things done. The real holders of power may therefore not have any formal position at all. Iranian politics are characterized by intense factionalism, and interpersonal relations are marked by constant rivalry, tension, and maneuvering. In this system there was, nevertheless, always the possibility of upward social mobility given the right patron or connections.

The importance of family in Iran is pervasive, and power has long been exercised by a political elite notable for its small size, cohesion, and historical continuity. A study of membership in the *Majlis* from 1906 to 1967 revealed that there were forty elite families who were important at the national level, and many of these also had been significant during most of the Qajar dynasty (1779–1925). In addition, there are 150 to 160 elite families who were important at the provincial level.

Personal ties and power networks are developed through informal meetings of groups called *dowrehs* (circles). *Dowrehs* are made up of individuals from many different occupations who meet regularly on a social basis. A typical grouping might include a government minister, a prominent businessman, a doctor, etc. Through *dowrehs*, an individual can count on friends strategically placed throughout society to help him get things done.

The clerical elite or *ulema* ("learned in religious law") that now holds power in Iran is, like the secular elite, an extremely small group that has developed extensive social and economic relationships among themselves. Clerical status tends to run in families, and there are extensive marriage alliances. One study has shown that the six grand ayatollahs can be placed on one geneology of two generations. These connections can run across party lines. Nureddin Kianuri, leader of the Tudeh Party, which supports Khomeini, is the grandson of a famous ayatollah and is also closely related to Khomeini.

In addition to family relationships, student-teacher ties are key factors. Three of the most eminent ayatollahs, Khomeini, Shariatmadari, and Golpaygani, all studied together under the same master at Qom in the 1920s and 1930s. Many clerics in prominent positions today are former students of Khomeini, including Khamene'i, the current president, and Montazeri, Khomeini's brother-in-law and his choice as his successor.

Islamic Republic Party
(*Hezb-e Jomhuri-ye Eslami*)

History

The Islamic Republic Party (IRP), dominated by Shi'a clergy, has been the most prominent political party in Iran since the ouster of the Shah. It regards Ayatollah Khomeini as its main source of inspiration, deriving its legitimacy from close association with him. Since the summer of 1981, it has consolidated its position and now has supporters throughout the government apparatus and holds the majority in the *Majlis*.

The party was established in early 1979 by Ayatollah Mohammad Ali Beheshti, Hojjatoleslam Hashemi-Rafsanjani, and Hojjatoleslam Ali Khamene'i. The IRP was, however, largely regarded as the creation of Beheshti, then perceived to be the second most powerful cleric after Khomeini.

Ayatollah Mohammad Beheshti died at the age of fifty-two in an explosion in Tehran on June 28, 1981, that wiped out most of the party leadership. At the time, he was officially head of the IRP and chief justice of the Supreme Court, but he also wielded great influence in the Revolutionary Council and with the revolutionary committees (*komitehs*) and the revolution's paramilitary forces (*pasdaran*). Beheshti had a much broader awareness of the world outside Iran than most other clerics, having directed the Islamic Center in Hamburg, Germany, from 1965 to 1970, serving as spiritual advisor to exiled Iranians. It is above all his unique organizational genius that has been missed by the party.

From its foundation until June 1981, the party was engaged in a struggle against moderates and secularists; a struggle that it finally won. After the removal from power of Bani-Sadr and other centrists, the religious right dominated the government. The IRP spent the next six months battling the Mojahedin and again prevailed. By the spring of 1982, the regime felt confident enough to release thousands of prisoners in a New Year amnesty.

Like the Communist Party in the Soviet system, the IRP is more than a political party. Its supporters control the executive, legislative, and judicial branches of government. In the election for president in January 1980, their candidate only got 10 percent of the vote. However, they won a solid majority in the parliamentary elections that took place later that spring. At present about two-thirds of the members of Parliament are IRP members.

Organization

Although the IRP is the governing party, it lacks clear-cut structure or ideology. Because of its loose structure and the factional differences within the clergy, there is no real central direction by the party. Khomeini is apparently remote from day-to-day activities, and in some cases has had to ratify actions taken by extremist supporters. The

IRP has a unique organizational advantage, though, in that policy decisions can be rapidly propagated throughout the country through the network of *mullas*.

The resilience of the IRP and the ruthless determination with which it has eliminated opponents has surprised observers. It has been suggested that, fearing the death of Khomeini, the party wants to entrench itself quickly. The party has managed to institutionalize the revolution and assure its own survival by creating organizations which parallel government agencies and hold the real power. These include armed groups such as the *pasdaran* and *hezbollahis* (clergy-led mobs), civilian organizations such as Islamic Associations (*anjoman-e eslami*), the *komitehs*, and the revolutionary courts.

The Revolutionary Guards (*pasdaran*) are a militia of zealous young Muslims that was designed to counterbalance the army, police, and gendarmes, who were regarded as pro-Western and of doubtful commitment to the regime. They sometimes enforce decisions made by the *komitehs*. They have played a key role in fighting leftist groups, particularly the Mojahedin. The *pasdaran* have recently won new prestige on the battlefield, where they worked in uneasy if effective alliance with the army to achieve battlefield successes over Iraq.

The Party of God (*hezbollahis*) is not a political party in the usual sense, but street mobs, allied to the clergy, that patrol large cities like Tehran and maintain order "in the name of the Imam" (i.e., Khomeini). Referred to by Bani-Sadr as "the club-wielding thugs of the clergy," they were particularly active in the summer and fall of 1981 in battles with leftists. Many IRP members of Parliament sympathize with them.

Islamic Associations (*anjoman-e eslami*) have been established by supporters of the government in schools, workplaces, and many neighborhoods. They monitor others for ideological purity and may harass those who decline to attend prayers or rallies for the regime. They play a key role in distributing goods and food ration coupons through local mosques, particularly in poorer neighborhoods, and through this process have achieved a measure of social control.

Hundreds of Revolutionary Committees (*komitehs*) sprang up throughout the country in the early revolutionary period, and they have become much resented de facto local governments. They act as tribunals and assume police functions. Their decisions are often enforced by the *pasdaran*. As the police forces have slowly been reconstructed, the *komitehs* have yielded some power, but they continue to monitor activities they consider to be counterrevolutionary.

Revolutionary courts led by *ulema* appeared throughout the country after the fall of the Shah and displaced the formal system of justice. Initially, central direction of the courts was minimal. Wide disparities in sentences for the same crime were common. These courts were undoubtedly used to settle many old scores. A recent attempt to merge these courts with the Ministry of Justice was rejected by Khomeini, who has emphasized the necessity for their independence.

Policy

The main policy of the IRP is to provide an Islamic government for Iran. The clerical elements that make up the party are sharply divided, however, on how to do this (see further discussion under *Other Political Forces*). Lack of clear-cut policy has led critics to charge that the only policy of the IRP is to cover up women in Islamic garb (*hijab*).

Khomeini's express intention to export the revolution has caused shudders in neighboring countries, particularly those with significant Shi'a minority groups, such as Iraq and Bahrain. To spread their philosophy throughout the Islamic world, the revolutionary government has set up eighty broadcast and relay stations which broadcast thirty-seven hours of programs a week in twelve languages, and they plan to expand this network.

Membership & Constituency

The main supporters of the IRP are the deeply religious, extremely poor, lower classes of society. It should be pointed out, however, that the party has so far also received support from wealthy *bazaaris*, while some poor people are dissatisfied with it. It should also be noted that the number of government workers swelled from 700,000 before the revolution to about 1.2 million by mid-1982; these workers may constitute an IRP voting bloc.

The party's stronghold is Tehran, particularly in the slums in the southern part of the city. The degree of support in other cities is unclear. In fact, it has been reported that many people have left Tehran and retreated to villages where they feel safer. Most party supporters are illiterate and look to their local *mullas* for guidance. It is from this milieu that the *pasdaran* and *hezbollahis* are drawn.

The enormous size of this segment of the population has ensured huge turnouts in support of the revolution and the IRP, although the allegience of the people is probably primarily to Khomeini. Hundreds of thousands sometimes attend mass Friday prayer meetings in Tehran. Nevertheless, support for the IRP has declined since the heady early days of the revolution. The third anniversary celebrations, held in Tehran in April 1982, drew a crowd of only about 100,000, which is not considered large for Iran.

Financing

Because of the close identification of the IRP with the government, the party is presumably assured adequate income and patronage. The Foundation for the Oppressed (*Bonyad-e Mostazafin*) is in charge of all property and business enterprises confiscated by the regime and can presumably assist party sympathizers with jobs. The clergy also receives money collected in mosques all over Iran.

Leadership

The IRP has had three leaders so far: Beheshti (January 1979 to June 28, 1981), Bahonar (June 30 to August 30, 1981), and Khamene'i (September 1, 1981 to the present). The most prominent members are:

Hojjatoleslam Ali Akbar Hashemi-Rafsanjani (forty-eight years old, from Kerman) served on the Revolutionary Council after Khomeini's return to Iran. He was shot and seriously wounded on May 25, 1979. He was appointed minister of the interior on July 19, 1979, and has served as speaker of the *Majlis* since July 20, 1980. He is a half-brother of Khomeini.

Hojjatoleslam Seyyed Ali Hossein Khamene'i (forty-two years old) studied under Khomeini at Qom and is now his close confidant. He took up anti-Shah activities in 1963 and was arrested seven times. An extremist who does not compromise, he has moved up rapidly in the hierarchy. He was a member of the Revolutionary Council and was Khomeini's personal representative to the Supreme Defense Council, which oversees the war with Iraq. He also headed Revolutionary Guard units on the battlefield. While *Imam Jom'eh* (Friday prayer leader) of Tehran, he was gravely wounded in an attack while he was speaking on June 27, 1981. He has been the leader of the IRP since September 1981, and the president of Iran since October 2, 1981. He is now also president of the Supreme Defense Council. In the first stage of the elections for the *Majlis* (spring 1980), he polled more votes than any other clerical candidate. He is considered pro-Soviet.

Behzad Nabavi (thirty-nine years old) is one of the few top leaders of the IRP who is not a clergyman. He studied in the United States and has a background in law, literature, and electrical engineering. He was imprisoned for anti-Shah activities from 1970 to 1978. After the revolution, he served on the committee which supervised the government-controlled radio and television networks. He was the government's chief spokesman for some time and was in charge of the negotiations that led to the freeing of the American hostages. He was minister of state for executive affairs from September 11, 1980, until June 1, 1982, during which time he was thought to be responsible for much of the government's day-to-day business. He leads a political faction in the Parliament known as the Mojahedin of the Islamic Revolution.

Ali Akbar Velayati (thirty-seven years old) is a layman from Tehran who studied medicine at Tehran University and completed postgraduate studies in the United States in 1976. While in the United States, he was active as a member of the Moslem Students Association. Upon his return to Iran, he served as a member of Parliament from Tehran and was an aide to the speaker, Rafsanjani. He was originally proposed as prime minister by President Khamene'i in the fall of 1981, but the *Majlis* refused to confirm him, apparently due to his inadequate record as a revolutionary—he did not play a prominent role in the Shah's downfall. He has served as foreign minister since December 14, 1981.

Ayatollah Rouhollah Khomeini, born about 1900 in the village of Khomein in central Iran, while not formally an IRP leader, became the symbol of the revolution against the Shah and since then has been the main unifying force behind the Islamic Republic. He had long opposed the Pahlavi dynasty, first publishing criticism of it in 1944. His prominent political role dates from 1963, when he played an active part in instigating antigovernment riots. He was in exile, primarily at the Shi'a holy city of Najaf, Iraq, from 1964 to 1978. In January 1978, the Shah's government made the mistake of trying to discredit him and thus sparked the riots that became a revolution.

Khomeini is one of the six grand ayatollahs, but he is distinguished more for his political activity than his religious scholarship. He is in fact somewhat suspect in religious circles because of his experiments in mysticism.

Khomeini has proven himself a master politician characterized by his uncompromising tactics and strong belief in his own mission. His version of Islamic government is now enshrined in the Iranian constitution. His suspicion of foreign countries (particularly the United States and Israel), which he blames for Iran's troubles, strikes a responsive chord in many Iranians.

Khomeini has kept aloof from day-to-day activities, tending to issue only those orders that he knows will not be disobeyed. At present, his position is unassailable, and his major goals have been accomplished: he expelled the Shah, released the American hostages when he was ready, and so far his forces have prevailed in the war with Iraq.

Prospects

The IRP seems likely to remain in control of the government for the forseeable future. However, its early cohesiveness has broken down, and after the death of Khomeini, differences among the *ulema* may become much more pronounced. Attention may increasingly focus on mismanagement of the economy, rather than being diverted by foreign crises such as the hostage crisis or war with Iraq.

Opposition

Organization of the Crusaders of the Iranian People
(*Sazman-e Mojahedin-e Khalq-e Iran*)

History

The Mojahedin is the largest leftist group in Iran today and is regarded by the Khomeini regime as its most dangerous opponent. The Shah referred to them as "Islamic Marxists," and the name has stuck, much to their dismay. Their leader, Mas'ud Rajavi, is in exile, and the group has gone underground in Iran.

The Mojahedin (the name refers to soldiers in a holy war, or *jihad*) arose at the same time as the Fedayan in the early 1960s. There is, however, a major difference in their origins: whereas the Fedayan arose out of the secular communist Tudeh Party, the Mojahedin's roots were in the religious wing of the National Front, particularly the Liberation Movement of Iran (*Nehzat-e Azadi-ye Iran*). The Liberation Movement had been formed in 1961 by Mehdi Bazargan and Ayatollah Taleqani, both former supporters of Mohammed Mossadeq, and attempted to fuse Iranian Shi'a precepts and European socialism into a new ideology that would appeal to the mass of Iranians.

The Mojahedin was formed in 1966 by a circle of nine young militants led by Mohammad Hafeznejad and Sa'id Mohsen. It took up military operations in August 1971, six months after the Fedayan. Mojahedin targets were, however, more ambitious than those of the Fedayan: they tried to interrupt the Shah's 2,500 year anniversary celebrations at Persepolis, tried to hijack an Iran Air jet, robbed banks, bombed airline offices, and assassinated (in 1973, 1975, and 1976) several American military officials working in Iran.

In May 1975, the Mojahedin split into two organizations. The smaller group became known as the Battle Organization or *Paykar* (*Sazman-e Paykar Barye Azadi-ye Kargar*). It decided that a Marxist orientation was more important than an Islamic one, and renounced armed action in favor of political activity. They have recruited in factories and oilfields and among the urban proletariat.

The other group emphasizes its Islamic orientation and continues to use the name Mojahedin. They voted in favor of the Islamic Republic in March 1979, but not for the new constitution. After the revolution, the IRP did not allow the Mojahedin any significant positions within the government. Khomeini declared Rajavi ineligible to run for president of Iran in January 1980 on the grounds that he had opposed the constitution. Observers believe that he would have received several million votes.

After the two and a half years of uneasy cooperation with Khomeini, the Mojahedin broke decisively with the government on June 20, 1981, after authorities fired on a huge demonstration the Mojahedin had organized to protest the dismissal of Bani-Sadr. For the next several months they carried out armed resistance to the regime, which blamed them for a number of fatal bombings. The most violent phase of the revolution so far was in the summer and fall of 1981, when thousands of suspected Mojahedin were executed by the authorities. Mojahedin activity has been much less in evidence since then, although in June 1982 the group claimed to be carrying out fifty to 100 resistance operations daily. Rajavi has recently placed the Mojahedin within the framework of a new coalition, the National Council of Resistance (NCR).

Organization

The Mojahedin have recently focused on strengthening their organization and recruiting more members. The group has always been noted for being well organized, with authority passing from a central committee through a broader central council and on to a number of cells around the country. With their leader in exile, it is unclear how policy is being made in Iran.

The Mojahedin, like the Fedayan, has always had strong links with Palestinian groups, particularly Yasir Arafat's Al-Fatah. Some early Mojahedin took part on the Palestinian side in the "Black September" events in Jordon in 1970.

Mojahedin newspapers published in Kurdistan circulate clandestinely in Iran. A pro-Mojahedin newspaper, *Iran Liberation*, is available in the United States.

Policy

The majority Mojahedin group, led by Rajavi, cooperated with Khomeini at first, but broke with the regime in June 1981; since then they have been engaged in armed resistance. Their violent activities are reminiscent of their tactics under the Shah, and are undoubtedly intended to provoke strikes and open dissatisfaction, leading to the downfall of the regime. Their actions, however, did not produce much public support. They have recently cooperated with tribal groups such as the Qashqai in antiregime activities. Aside from guerrilla activities, they try to keep themselves in the public consciousness by writing slogans on walls and bus seats and distributing their propaganda clandestinely.

The Mojahedin claim to be working for a progressive, democratic, and Islamic government. All political parties could operate freely, although they would exclude the Tudeh and monarchists from power. They support the internal autonomy of Kurdistan within the state of Iran, persuading the Kurdish Democratic Party to join them in their Paris-based alliance, the NCR.

The Mojahedin look for inspiration to the writings of Ali Shari'ati (1933–77), often considered the ideologist of the revolution. Shari'ati combined a Western education and concern for anticolonial struggles with a sharp consciousness of his identity as a Shi'a Muslim. He believed that the true Shi'a faith was a revolutionary ideology which called for political activism to end oppression and injustice. His goal was to create a just and classless society. He believed that the intelligentsia, not the conservative *ulema*, should lead the revolution. His writings and speeches found a ready audience in the early 1970s when Iran was in the throes of rapid modernization.

In terms of foreign policy, Rajavi is aware of the importance of Western opinion and has attempted to shake the Mojahedin's image as "Islamic Marxists." He now emphasizes the moderation of the group, in contrast to his intended platform for the presidency in 1980 which was strongly anti-Western and anticapitalist.

Membership & Constituency

Because it is a guerrilla group, the active membership of the Mojahedin was always small, although popular support swelled in the postrevolutionary period, particularly among students. In early 1980, it was thought to have 5,000 hard-core members and 50,000 supporters, with the *Paykar* faction capable of attracting 10,000 in university areas. In June 1980, at perhaps the height of their popularity, the Mojahedin attracted 150,000 sympathizers to a rally in Tehran. In the summer of 1981 their strength was estimated at 100,000, and the party newspaper, *Mojahed*, had a circulation of 500,000. Support has declined since the party went underground and engaged in violent antiregime activity. It is now trying to rebuild; by early 1982 the number of active Mojahedin in Iran was estimated at several thousand.

The group's ideology, emphasizing Shi'a Islam, socialism, and Iranian nationalism, has proved highly appealing to many important groups in the country. The Mojahedin compete directly with the IRP for the allegiance of the poor and highly religious masses, the students, industrial workers, and former communists. Because of their emphasis on Islam, they can attract a much broader base of support than the Fedayan. They claim to have substantial sympathy among the armed forces, although this is impossible to prove. The Mojahedin are particularly strong in the north (Azerbaijan and the Caspian area) and in the outskirts of Tehran and Shiraz.

Financing

No information is available on Mojahedin funds. Their headquarters in Paris are presumably funded by sympathetic Iranian exiles. The Mojahedin in the United States solicit money, but it is unclear whether any of this is forwarded to Iran.

Leadership

Mas'ud Rajavi (born 1937) is the leader of the Mojahedin. He joined the group shortly after its formation and is the only original member to have survived. He fought for the Palestinians in Jordan in September 1970. He was imprisoned by the Shah from 1971 to 1978 and sentenced to death, but the sentence was commuted to life after his trial attracted international attention. In 1975, at the time the Mojahedin split into two factions, Rajavi actively continued in the Islamic faction, even from prison. He escaped from Iran with Bani-Sadr on July 28, 1981 and now lives in Paris. By removing himself from active struggle in Iran, Rajavi has discredited himself in the eyes of some former followers in Iran.

The top leadership of the Mojahedin in Iran suffered a severe blow after a shootout with the authorities on February 8, 1982. Among those killed were Musa Khiabani, the commander of the resistance forces in Iran, and Ashraf Rabi'i, wife of the exiled Rajavi.

Prospects

The Mojahedin is a respected organization in Iran; it has prestige because of its long guerrilla struggle against the Shah at a time when the *ulema* were either acquiescent or in exile. Its ideology has proven to have strong appeal to the lower classes that made the revolution. It is possible that the Mojahedin will be able to rebuild its ranks and offer a real alternative to the *ulema's* brand of Islam. Although the Mojahedin could operate openly in the early days of the revolution, they were careful never to fully expose their military organization. Despite their failure to provoke the downfall of the regime, they continue to mount small actions against it; for example, they assassinated one of Ayatollah Khomeini's representatives in Yazd on July 2, 1982, and another in Kermanshah on October 15. Key factors in the group's future will be the amount of tribal support it receives; the susceptibility of young *mullas* to its ideology; and the attitude of the *bazaaris*, who are apprehensive about Mojahedin socialist notions.

Organization of the Guerrilla Devotees of the Iranian People
(*Sazman-e Cherik-ha-ye Fada'i-ye Khalq-e Iran*)

History

Popularly known as the Fedayan, this secular Marxist coalition was formed in March 1971 from three different groups which originated in the mid-1960s. The real founder and theoretician of the Fedayan, Bijan Jazani (died 1975), was previously a member of the Soviet-backed Tudeh, but became disillusioned with that party's restriction of its activities to the political arena. He formed his own group in 1964 which later merged with two groups, one led by Mas'ud Ahmadzadeh and the other by Behruz and Ashraf Dehqani (brother and sister). These groups, inspired by guerrilla movements in other countries, such as that led by Che Guevara, decided to take up guerrilla warfare against the government of the Shah.

The Fedayan began the leftist guerrilla campaign against the Shah in the village of Siahkal in the Caspian forests on February 8, 1971. Although their attack on a gendarmerie post there failed, this action announced their existence to the authorities. It also persuaded them of the inadvisability of mounting actions in rural areas for the benefit of an unsympathetic peasantry. Future attacks were carried out in cities, primarily Tehran, but also in Mashhad, Isfahan, and Tabriz.

As a coalition representing diverse ideological elements, it split into three parts in June 1980. The majority group, called the *Aksariyyat*, decided to acquiesce in the IRP's rule in order to protect themselves. The minority group, called the *Aqaliyyat*, believe in the necessity of continuing armed struggle against the Khomeini regime. A third group, which follows Ashraf Dehqani, also believes in armed struggle. The Fedayan has always operated underground, except for the first six months of 1979.

Organization

As an underground group, it has been tightly organized through an autonomous cell structure. Activities have been concentrated in the northern urban centers of Iran—Tehran, Tabriz, Rasht, Gorgan, Qazvin, and Enzeli (formerly Bandar Pahlavi).

Policy

During the period 1971 to 1977, the Fedayan followed Jazani's policy of attempting to politicize the people through armed struggle. They carried out sudden violent operations, such as assassinations, bombings, bank robberies, and attacks on police stations. They were willing to suffer a high casualty rate in order to demonstrate their dissatisfaction with the Shah.

The Fedayan were opposed to the strong Islamic orientation of the Khomeini regime and did not support the idea of an Islamic Republic. They

refused to turn in their weapons in February 1979 as Khomeini ordered, and were among the group that occupied the American Embassy in Tehran in that month. Their policy at this time called for a complete restructuring of the state and the establishment of a free and democratic classless society. They were particularly concerned with the rights of workers. They wanted to expel foreign workers, nationalize foreign banks, and establish a people's army. They share with the Tudeh a commitment to autonomy for the nationality groups, supporting the Turkmans, Kurds, and Azerbaijanis in their struggles with the authorities.

Since the group split into factions in 1980, the majority, following the ideas of Jazani, has given up armed confrontation for open political activity. In this they resemble the Tudeh. They believe in the necessity of mass mobilization, achieved by means of strikes and demonstrations. The minority groups continue armed activity against the regime as they did under the Shah.

Membership & Constituency

The number of members has always been small and a tightly held secret. At the time of the revolution in early 1979, the Fedayan were estimated to have about 5,000 hard-core members, and a rally they organized in Tehran in February 1979 drew an estimated 70,000 supporters. In the summer of 1981, its strength was estimated at 80,000. However, support probably declined when the majority group was discredited by accommodating with the regime.

The Fedayan has appealed to educated urbanites, particularly from cities with universities. Students, teachers, and workers in factories and in the oilfields have shown support. Its members are young, in contrast to the older generation that tends to join the Tudeh. An analysis of those killed by the Shah's government up to January 1979 showed that half were students; 30 percent were government and office workers; and 20 percent were engineers, manual workers, etc. Response appears to be much lower in rural areas.

Financing

International support has been very important to the Fedayan, as it has to the Tudeh. However, while the Tudeh has been long sustained by Moscow, the Fedayan's ties are with the Palestine Liberation Organization (PLO). Two of the founders of the Fedayan were trained by the PLO in 1963, and after 1969, the PLO provided training for Fedayan cadres in Lebanon. Training was also provided to about 1,200 Fedayan by China, Cuba, and South Yemen. While the Shah was still in power, Libya supplied arms and money via the Popular Front for the Liberation of Palestine (PFLP); this connection apparently still continues.

Leadership

The original leaders of the Fedayan were practically all young intellectuals with a university background. About 10 percent were women. Bijan Jazani, the group's founder, was born in 1937 in Tehran. He was arrested in 1967 and died in prison in 1975. His book, *Capitalism and Revolution in Iran* (London: Zed Press, 1980), is still influential among the Fedayan. The present leadership of the Fedayan in Iran is not known.

Prospects

A basic problem of the Fedayan is that they lack an Islamic dimension and appeal to a small base; many urban workers that it might attract have been coopted by the Mojahedin or the IRP. The Fedayan will undoubtedly continue to survive as an opposition group and continue to mount actions against Khomeini's Islamic Republic. However, the majority Fedayan has lost credibility, it is difficult to say how much, and the minority Fedayan is not a political party in the normal sense, but rather a small group dedicated to guerrilla activity. There is no program or provision for large-scale political activity. The regime announced in March 1982 that the *pasdaran* had crushed the minority Fedayan in a series of raids in Tehran. Two months later, however, the government announced that a large number of Fedayan had been arrested in Shiraz, where they had robbed twenty banks and a jewelry store.

Party of the Masses
(*Hezb-e Tudeh*)

History

The Tudeh Party, formed in the fall of 1941, is the oldest existing Communist Party in the Middle East and has been active in Iranian politics longer than any other party that still functions. A Dr. Arani is regarded as its founder; he died in prison for his Marxist beliefs before his disciples formed the party after their release.

The party was strongest in the northern zone of Soviet occupation (1941–46), particularly Azerbaijan, and the Caspian provinces of Mazandaran and Gilan. (After the First World War, there had been a short-lived communist movement in Gilan, where the establishment of an Iranian Soviet Socialist Republic was announced in 1920.) There were also branches of the Tudeh in industrial areas, such as the city of Isfahan and the oil-producing area of Khuzistan.

The Tudeh was active in organizing trade unions, and was able to mount a major general strike in the oil fields in July 1946 (similar to the tactics used in the fall of 1978 that helped bring down the Shah). Tudeh members were part of the Iranian cabinet in the fall of 1946, when three were briefly included. In elections for the fourteenth Parliament (1944–46), the party won eight out of 136 seats.

The Tudeh's chief liability has always been its close identification with the Soviet Union. It gained a reputation for serving as a Soviet agent when, after World War II, it supported Soviet demands for an oil concession. This was opposed by most Iranians, as well as the Western powers. The Tudeh also supported two autonomous republics which were formed briefly in Azerbaijan and Kurdistan.

The Tudeh declined after 1946 and was banned in 1949 when an attempted assassination of the Shah was blamed on one of its members. However, it operated freely during the Mossadeq period (1951–53), and the Western powers feared the influence that they supposed the Tudeh had over Mossadeq. The party, however, did nothing to prevent the return of the Shah in August 1953, after he had been forced out of the country. This passivity is regarded in retrospect as one of their greatest miscalculations.

The Tudeh was vigorously suppressed after the restoration of the Shah. The leadership fled to Eastern Europe, and despite revival in the early 1960s, the party in Iran remained moribund until the onset of the revolution in the late 1970s, when it enjoyed a rebirth. The IRP has kept the Tudeh out of government; for example, in July 1981, the Council of Guardians refused to allow party leader Kianuri to run for parliament in a by-election.

Organization

The Tudeh is the best organized and most tightly disciplined of the parties in revolutionary Iran. It is thanks to this, and support from the Soviet Union, that it was able to survive a thirty-year period of exile and return to rebuild its ranks. It has apparently been divided into two factions from the beginning: one wanted to pursue a more independent revolutionary strategy, and the other was more amenable to Soviet direction. Since the mid-1940s, the latter group has prevailed, led by Nureddin Kianuri and his brother-in-law, Abdolsamad Kambakhsh (died 1971). As to who or what really rules the party, there is disagreement, but the party is widely perceived to be subject to Soviet bidding.

The party had at its disposal, in its period of exile, a radio station called Iran Courier (*Peik-e Iran*) which began broadcasting from Baku in the Soviet Union in 1959 and moved to Sofia, Bulgaria, in the 1960s. It was closed down by the Bulgarians in 1976, after they completed a trade agreement with the Iranian government. An "unaffiliated" radio station called the National Voice of Iran (NVOI), which supports the Tudeh Party and Soviet policy objectives in Iran, now broadcasts from Baku in Persian and Azeri. This station is used to criticize policies of the Khomeini regime, something which has been avoided in the official Soviet media. For example, the NVOI has criticized harassment of local communists and Iranian demands for the overthrow of the Iraqi government. The party publishes a newspaper, *Mardom* (The People), and a theoretical journal, *Donya* (The World).

Policy

The domestic policies of the Tudeh Party have been remarkably consistent over the last forty years. The Tudeh opposed armed struggle, was critical of groups that attempted to fuse Islam with Marxism, and took a reserved attitude towards clerics such as Khomeini. They preferred quiet political activity, such as organizing factory workers.

A major shift in policy took place when the party leadership was changed in early 1979. The Tudeh then decided to support Khomeini, calling for a United Front of all parties opposed to the Shah's regime. This appeal, which presumably would have increased the Tudeh's respectability, was refused by Khomeini and Karim Sanjabi, leader of the National Front. However, the Tudeh did maintain close links with members of the Fedayan, some of whom joined the Tudeh.

Support for the government is justified on the grounds that Khomeini ousted the Shah, broke links with Israel, and maintains an anti-imperialistic stance. The Tudeh's differences with the government are muted and turn on objections to the religious nature of the new constitution and the attitude displayed towards women. The Tudeh also differs on the nationalities question: it has always favored self-government for tribal and ethnic groups. The party has been a faithful supporter of the Islamic Republic Party, particularly its more radical faction, and has attacked Ayatollah Shariatmadari and the Hojjatiyyeh faction of the clergy.

In foreign policy, the Tudeh has always been pro-Soviet and does not criticize Moscow. It has sought to accentuate the anti-American tone of the revolution, particularly after the hostages were taken. It has ties with other communist parties, and cooperated with the Khalq faction in Afghanistan.

Membership & Constituency

The Tudeh has experienced only three periods of open activity, which correspond with periods of largest membership: 1941 to 1949, 1951 to 1953, and from 1979 on.

During the wartime period, the party is estimated to have had about 25,000 members, with perhaps 400,000 sympathizers in the trade unions. In the Mossadeq period, crowds of from 50,000 to 100,000, large for that time, turned out for Tudeh demonstrations. The party's ranks were decimated after 1953. Until the mid-1960s, when the party was infiltrated by SAVAK, there were about 500 members in exile and about 300 in Iran. Afterwards, there were virtually no members in Iran.

Tudeh membership increased in the 1970s, although by 1976 it still had less than 1,000 members. In August 1979, the Tudeh candidate to the Council of Experts attracted 50,000 votes in Tehran, and the party won 60,000 votes (3 percent) in that city in the parliamentary elections of March 1980. In the spring of 1980, readership of their newspaper, *Mardom*, was estimated at 40,000, twice that of the IRP newspaper. In early 1982, the CIA estimated Tudeh strength at perhaps 1,000 to 2,000 hard-core supporters and 15,000 to 20,000 sympathizers.

The constituency that the Tudeh appeals to is the same today as when it was first formed: urban workers and the industrial proletariat, particularly in the oilfields, and Westernized intellectuals. The party has not done well in rural areas or among non-Persian ethnic groups, with the exception of the Azerbaijanis. Its members tend to be older than the members of the Fedayan and Mojahedin.

Financing

It is generally believed that the Soviet Union finances party activities. The extent of indigenous support is not clear.

Leadership

The present party leadership is still drawn from the original leaders of the 1940s, who were long in exile. The longtime secretary general, Iraj Eskandari, was abruptly replaced in January 1979 by his deputy, Nureddin Kianuri. The reason for the change was that Eskandari had seriously underestimated the religious nature of the revolution. Kianuri immediately announced support for Ayatollah Khomeini and said that the program of the Ayatollah coincided with that of the Tudeh. Other important figures in exile are Reza Radmanesh, secretary general before Eskandari, and Ehsan Tabari, a leading Tudeh theoretician and historian, who has edited the journal *Donya*.

Prospects

The Tudeh Party has several problems. For the last decade, it has not been the only leftist party in Iran, but has had to compete with the Fedayan (who are not tainted by the Russian connection), and the Mojahedin (who seek to integrate Islam into their Marxism). The Tudeh represents an atheism that is unacceptable to the majority of Iran's population today. Also, the leaders are in their sixties or over and have been absent from Iran for many years. In a country where more than half of the population is under twenty years of age, they may seem increasingly irrelevant.

The Tudeh Party will survive, however, because the leadership has shown that it is willing to make pragmatic accommodation to the existing power structure. Its small size is made up for by its tight organization. Its members, who tend to be activists, have persistently, if unobtrusively, worked their way into the government. They are periodically purged. In January 1982, Prime Minister Mousavi charged that Tudeh members had gained control of vital industries, and he initiated a crackdown that forced more than 1,000 individuals out of the foreign, oil, and finance ministries. Hundreds more were purged in July 1982. The Tudeh presumably is organizing in the oilfields, factories, and armed forces, and reportedly assists the regime in security matters. However, the party is regarded with suspicion by most Iranians, who consider it too responsive to Soviet desires. The

clerical regime, believing that the Tudeh is discredited, tolerates its existence. The Tudeh has apparently tried to recruit sympathetic *mullas* to serve in leadership positions, but it is doubtful they have had much success.

The Tudeh's role in the revolution was essentially that of a bystander, and it can take little credit for the overthrow of the Shah. Although the rebirth of the party is an impressive achievement, the Soviets understand the limited appeal of the Tudeh. They may in the future draw closer to the Fedayan and particularly the Mojahedin, which will probably prove to be a much more significant force in the politics of Iran.

Minor Parties

National Front (*Jebhe-ye Melli*)

The National Front played an important role in the early days of the revolution, but now appears to be defunct inside Iran. It was not a political party as such, but rather a coalition that was originally formed in 1951 by Dr. Mohammad Mossadeq. It experienced a period of revival from 1961 to 1963 and was revived again from December 1977 until the spring of 1979.

Its ideology has been seen as secularist and slightly left of center; it was opposed to the establishment of an Islamic Republic. The National Front's longtime policy called for a restoration of the constitution of 1906; nationalization of major industries; and creation of a nationalist society that would be neither capitalist nor communist, but distinctively Iranian.

Support was drawn from professionals and the educated middle class and from *bazaaris*. The party was led by the secular supporters of Mossadeq, notably Karim Sanjabi (born 1909) and Shapur Bakhtiar (born 1917), both lawyers. There was a rift between the two in the fall of 1978. Sanjabi concluded a pact with Khomeini, then in exile in Paris, to work together for the overthrow of the Shah. He went on to become foreign minister in Khomeini's first government, although he resigned in April 1979. Bakhtiar, who did not oppose the idea of a constitutional monarchy, severely criticized Khomeini, and served as the last prime minister under the Shah. The National Front expelled him from the party as a traitor, and he left Iran in February 1979 after trying to prevent the return of Khomeini.

While there still appears to be some moderate, centrist constituency for the program of the National Front, the party has been squeezed out by more radical groups. Also, its aging leadership may seem less relevant to young Iranians today. The party never had a strong organizational structure, but existed more as a range of ideas held by many. The Front's secular viewpoint puts it at odds with Islam, the strongest mobilizing force in Iran today.

National Democratic Front (*Jebhe-ye Democratic-e Melli*)

After the demise of the National Front in early 1979, the National Democratic Front arose as a left-liberal offshoot. It was founded in February 1979 by Hedayatollah Matin-Daftari (Hedayatollah here is a given name, not a clerical title), a noted lawyer and grandson of Mossadeq, and existed openly only until August of that year. It accused Khomeini of trying to establish a religious dictatorship, called for a boycott of the elections for the Constituent Assembly, and protested the shutdown of the independent newspaper *Ayandegan* in June. It also supported rights for minority groups, especially the Sunni tribes. The party has now gone into exile and has joined the National Council of Resistance in Paris.

The Opposition in Exile

There are many Iranian groups outside the country that oppose the current government in Iran and seek its overthrow. Paris has become the center of antiregime activity; in late 1981 more than sixty such groups were active there. Most of the movements have crystallized around prominent personalities who refuse to work with each other. The opposition in exile therefore remains fragmented and is characterized by constantly shifting alliances. The programs of these groups span the political spectrum: from royalists who want to restore the Pahlavi family to the throne to those who argue for a constitutional monarchy to secularists and leftists.

National Council of Resistance (NCR)

The NCR, which claims to represent a majority of the popular, democratic, and independence-seeking forces, was established in Paris in July 1981 and may be considered the most significant exile grouping at present. It is an unwieldy coalition of four groups who fought together to bring down the Shah and now seek to depose Khomeini. Included are the Mojahedin and the Kurdish Democratic Party (KDP)—both of which have sec-

tions in Iran actually fighting the regime—the National Democratic Front and the group associated with Bani-Sadr. Monarchists are excluded.

The NCR represents an alliance of convenience which may not be able to hold together in the future. Its two leaders, the Mojahedin's Rajavi and former president Bani-Sadr, have sharply differed in the past. Bani-Sadr is suspect in the eyes of the Mojahedin and the KDP because of his long cooperation with Khomeini and his association with the government's warfare against the Kurds and the Mojahedin. The Mojahedin, for their part, have been criticized for their alliance with Bani-Sadr. The Mojahedin's policy of tribal autonomy, on the other hand, makes it a natural ally for the KDP.

After achieving power, the NCR (which is against the monarchy) would establish a Democratic Islamic Republic based on a nationwide system of locally elected councils. Their program emphasizes equal rights, freedom for the media and political parties, and a nonaligned foreign policy. They propose to nationalize foreign trade and carry out radical land reforms. They would guarantee the rights of women, national minorities (especially the Kurds), trade unions, and other professional organizations.

Front for the Liberation of Iran

The Front for the Liberation of Iran is a coalition of moderate nationalists and monarchists who accept a program drawn up by Ali Amini (born 1905), a former Iranian prime minister who is considered pro-American. Formed in January 1982, this group was conceived as an alternative to the NCR's antimonarchism. It wants to include everyone, including the Shah's son, Reza II, and the left. They believe that their immediate task is to start a series of armed initiatives. After restoring law and order, they would hold an election to determine what kind of government Iran would have. Their economic program combines public ownership of major industries with free enterprise. They stress reestablishment of civil liberties and international nonalignment.

National Iranian Resistance Movement

The National Iranian Resistance Movement is led by Shahpur Bakhtiar and seeks to establish a social democratic government in Iran. This was the first exile group to be formed in Paris (in 1979) and is now one of the largest and best-funded groups. It has several newspapers, branches in different countries, and a radio station that transmits to Iran. Bakhtiar's close ties to monarchists have dissuaded some from joining his group.

Royalists

Royalist groups are primarily directed by the family of the late Shah (who never abdicated) or his former top military officers. Some support the return to the throne of the Shah's son, who declared himself Reza Shah II upon reaching the age of twenty on October 31, 1980. Many, however, doubt his capacity to lead. Since the revolution, Reza has lived primarily in Cairo with his mother, Empress Farah Diba. The Shah's twin sister, the widely disliked Princess Ashraf Pahlavi (born 1919), lives in New York and is the main representative of the family in the United States.

Several small groups work for the royalist cause, funded apparently by wealthy exiles and Western intelligence agencies. Reports are occasionally made that they are organizing military forces in eastern Turkey, reports vehemently denied by the Turkish government.

The most prominent of these groups are Free Iran (*Iran-e Azad*), which is led from Paris by Princess Azadeh Shafiq, the daughter of Ashraf; and Born Free (*Azadegan*), led by General Bahram Aryana (born 1905), who was chief of staff in the Iranian army under the Shah. *Azadegan* achieved notoriety in August 1981 when some of its members hijacked a French-built gunboat in the Mediterranean that was being delivered to the Iranian government. The Iranian Salvation Movement is led by General Gholam Ali Oveissi, former army commander. Oveissi is discredited by many because of his role in suppressing dissent in the last months before the fall of the Shah. Admiral Ahmad Madani (born 1930) heads one of the more significant groups. Trained in the West as a naval officer, he was commander in chief of the Iranian Navy under the Shah, but was forced out in 1972. He was one of the few military men accepted by Khomeini and served as governor of Khuzistan in the early revolutionary period. He was the first defense minister in Bazargan's government, and lost to Bani-Sadr in elections for the presidency in January 1980. He was later elected to the *Majlis*, but left the country soon afterward on being implicated in an antiregime plot.

Other Political Forces

Shi'a Clergy

The clerical group, which is primarily of rural origin, has been estimated to include 150,000 to 180,000 persons. Of this perhaps 14,000 to 15,000 are lower-ranking *mullas* who are active on a local level, preaching in mosques throughout the country and providing religious leadership and education. Higher ranking clerics are called *mojtahids* and are capable of giving *fatwas* (legal rulings). The title *hojjatoleslam* ("proof of Islam") is below the rank of *ayatollah* and is used by most clerics in the Parliament. The leading *mojtahids* are accorded the title *ayatollah* ("sign of God"), of which there are thought to be about 100 at present. The highest-ranking *ayatollahs* are called the *ayatollah ozma* ("grand ayatollahs"), of which there are six, including Ayatollah Khomeini.

The image of the Iranian *ulema* generally conveyed by the foreign media is that of a fanatically intolerant, monolithic establishment. This image, however, is very misleading, for it does not take into account the serious personal and ideological disagreements that characterize intraclergy politics. In Shi'a Islam, every individual can choose the ayatollah whose interpretation of Islam he wishes to follow. There are about 100 ayatollahs in Iran competing for the allegiance of the rest of the clergy and close to thirty-six million Shi'a Muslims. The atmosphere of extremism that has dominated Iran since the revolution has tended to highlight the attitudes of extremists like Khomeini, obscuring those who take more moderate positions.

Such disagreements take on added importance since Khomeini is aged and in failing health, and the struggle for the succession has clearly begun. The question of the succession is, however, only part of much larger battles currently dividing Iran's clerics. Other important issues are the nature of clergy-state relations, land reform, nationalization of industry and trade, relations with the Soviet Union, and the role of women.

Attempts have been made by outsiders to classify the leading clergymen into different factions and ideologies, but no consensus has been reached. There are, nevertheless, two main trends that can be discerned at present, and many *Majlis* deputies incline to one or the other. The trends are associated with the most important centers of Shi'a learning in Iran, Mashhad, and Qom.

Although labels can be misleading, the group associated with Qom, led by Khomeini, has been characterized as a radical and populist one that calls for a significant restructuring of Iranian society. This group has been referred to as Followers of the Imam's (Khomeini's) Line. Qom is seen as attracting lower-class, rural students who are receptive to a populist form of Islam and who may turn into radical clerics like Khamene'i. They tend to endorse the concept of a strong *faqih*, are in favor of some land reform, and want to nationalize industry. An important adherant is Ayatollah Montazeri, Khomeini's choice as his successor.

The Hojjatiyyeh group has emerged as a powerful political force since the summer of 1981. This group represents a more traditional Shi'a faith, in which the different viewpoints of many ayatollahs are all seen as equally acceptable. It is led by Shaikh Mahmud Halabi and Ayatollah Tabataba'i Qomi. It opposes the concentration of power in the hands of the *faqih* and believes the clergy should not be directly involved in government. This group strongly favors private property and is opposed to central control of the economy. They are also opposed to land reform and are associated with wealthier elements of the bazaar. They are strongly anticommunist and therefore oppose any accommodation with the Tudeh Party. They insist on the strict application of religious laws, particularly regarding women.

In terms of relative strength in the Parliament, the Followers of the Imam's line and the Hojjatiyyeh are closely matched, but the majority of the IRP are believed to sympathize with the Hojjatiyyeh. Several government ministers are aligned with the group, including the foreign minister, Ali Akbar Velayati, government spokesman and labor minister Tavakkoli, and defense minister Salimi. They are also well represented in courts and mosques around the country.

The Mojahedin of the Islamic Revolution (not to be confused with the *Mojahedin-e Khalq*) is in favor of central control of the economy and the nationalization of banks and industry. This group is led by Behzad Nabavi, minister of heavy industries.

The conflict between the Qom and Mashhad groups bears directly on the question of the succession. From Khomeini's point of view, it is not enough to have a respected religious figure succeed him; it must be a person who is ideologically compatible. This is where difficulties arise, because Khomeini's version of Shi'a Islam is different from and more radical than that of his peers. The other five grand ayatollahs all have serious differences with his policies.

Two important areas in which Khomeini's position departs from more traditional ones is his view of the monarchy and the role of the clergy in government. Khomeini has attacked monarchy as "un-Islamic." He also believes that the clergy should rule directly, which has never been generally accepted before in Iran. Along with this, Khomeini envisions an all-powerful role for the *faqih*.

Ayatollah Kazem Shariatmadari, who is probably the most-respected cleric in Iran, has strong differences with Khomeini. Shariatmadari would be satisfied with a constitutional monarchy guided by clerics, as envisioned in the 1906 constitution. At the time the 1979 constitution was being drafted, he vigorously protested the strong role outlined for the *faqih*. Shariatmadari, who has been living under house arrest in Qom since 1979, has a strong base of support in Azerbaijan among Turkish-speaking Iranians.

In April 1982 Khomeini's faction attempted to undercut Shariatmadari by implicating him in a rather unlikely plot to assassinate Khomeini. The Society of Qom Religious Teachers announced that they would strip him of his title as *marja at-taqlid* (source of imitation). But because titles are not formally given in Shi'a Islam, they cannot be formally taken away, and the effect of this announcement is questionable. In Tabriz and other cities, shops in the bazaar closed down to indicate their support of Shariatmadari.

Khomeini has indicated that he would like his former student, Ayatollah Hossein Ali Montazeri, age sixty, to succeed him. Montazeri, however, is not regarded as possessing sufficient stature for the job, and the idea of his succession has recently been downplayed. Other clerics who hold high positions in the IRP, such as Rafsanjani and Khamene'i, are not of the first rank and are still relatively young.

It seems highly unlikely that another individual can inherit Khomeini's role as *faqih*. The powers Khomeini holds, for the most part, are not derived from the constitution, and no successor could inherit them. It seems much more likely that a committee of three to five clergymen, as provided for in the constitution, will guide the state. There is a serious question, therefore, whether Khomeini's policies will survive his death.

Military

The two shahs of the Pahlavi dynasty were both authoritarian figures closely identified with the army. They pampered it and used it as their primary instrument for modernizing the nation and asserting central control from Tehran. Before the revolution, the Shah's armed forces (413,000 men in uniform, plus 300,000 reserves) were equipped with the best military hardware available, and many officers received training in the United States. A disproportionate number of troops were drawn from the Turkish and Kurdish minority groups. Considering how formidable this force appeared to be, observers were shocked by its impotence during the revolution. Afterwards, the officer corps was discredited for having supported the Shah, and the army was severely weakened.

The new constitution calls for an Islamic army religiously educated and faithful to the goals of the revolution. Its primary role is external defense. The Revolutionary Guards or *pasdaran*, which adhere to Khomeini's ideological position, serve as a counterweight to the more Western-oriented army. The total armed forces now amount to about 150,000 regulars plus some 40,000 *pasdaran*.

Khomeini as *faqih* has command of all the armed forces and can name the heads of both the army and the *pasdaran*. He delegated his power as commander-in-chief to President Bani-Sadr from February 19, 1980, to June 10, 1981. The post was delegated to General Zahirnejad on October 15, 1981.

The main operations of the army in the early days of the Islamic Republic consisted of subduing dissident tribesmen, particularly the Kurds, Turkmans, and Baluchis. The top army leadership, particularly General Zahirnejad and Colonel Sayyad-Shirazi, were promoted to their present positions after achieving distinction in battles against the Kurds.

With the onset of the war against Iraq, the army and *pasdaran* were forced to work together, and the intrusion of *mullas* into military affairs caused great confusion. However, the religious fervor of the *pasdaran* helped demoralize the enemy, and the two groups eventually fought well together. After a long stalemate, the Iranian troops won a string of victories in the spring of 1982 and finally drove the Iraqis from their main prize, the port city of Khorramshahr.

After the Iranian victory in expelling the Iraqis from their territory, tensions between the *pasdaran* and the army once again became evident. The *pasdaran* were eager to advance into Iraq, while the army had reservations. However, an Iranian invasion of Iraq did take place on July 13, 1982. When the Iran-Iraq conflict ends, the army and *pasdaran* will likely be employed in further warfare against the Kurds.

The current top military leadership was installed after a disastrous plane crash near Tehran on September 29, 1981, killed thirty-seven top-ranking officers, including General Valiollah Fallahi, the army chief of staff. The army is now led mostly by officers in their thirties. Colonel Mohammad Salimi (born 1938) was named defense minister on November 2, 1981. Previously, he was a representative of Khomeini on the Supreme Defense Council. General Qassem Ali Zahirnejad was named commander of the joint forces on October

1, 1981; he had been chief of the ground forces. Colonel Ali Sayyad-Shirazi was named chief of the ground forces to replace Zahirnejad. A civilian, Mohsen Reza'i, is chief of the *pasdaran;* Ali Shamkhani is deputy chief. Finally, Hojjatoleslam Ali Akbar Nateq-Nuri, born 1943, was named, on April 8, 1982, commander-in-chief of the (internal) security forces (i.e., the police, gendarmerie, and revolutionary committees in the cities and villages, but not the *pasdaran*). He has also been interior minister since December 14, 1981.

The army enjoyed new prestige because of its successes, although this could quickly be tarnished if the invasion of Iraq settles into another long stalemate. Speculation is now focused on the future role in government of the army and its leaders. Khomeini recently warned the army and *pasdaran* to stay away from politics and political parties, even the IRP. He has also told politicians and Islamic groups not to intervene in military affairs. Although many had predicted a military coup before now, the army has stayed out of domestic politics. Small detachments of both forces were sent to Syria in June 1982 to fight Israeli troops in Lebanon.

The ruling clergy associated with Khomeini undoubtedly remain suspicious of the army's loyalty. The regime has publicly announced that 2,000 secret agents keep army personnel under surveillance. During the long course of the Iran-Iraq war, accusations were made that the clerical leadership in Tehran was holding the army back and did not want it to win the war lest it return to Tehran emboldened to intervene in domestic politics.

The *pasdaran* are now undergoing increasing institutionalization. A bill was recently approved to form a separate ministry for them (in addition to the ministry of defense), thus perpetuating two separate armed forces in the country.

Bazaaris

One of the most significant political forces in Iran is the merchants of the bazaar, or *bazaaris*, who might be characterized as moderate right. "The bazaar" refers to a nationwide network of merchants and shops which has historically played a key role in financing the clerical establishment, including Islamic schools and social welfare activities. The *bazaaris* distrusted the Shah, believing that he wanted to destroy their power base by adopting economic policies (such as import/export quotas) that favored more Westernized merchants. *Bazaaris* played a crucial role in organizing anti-Shah demonstrations in 1978.

The traditional hostility of the *bazaar* to the government, which has persisted for 150 years, may again assert itself. *Bazaaris* are uncomfortable with the ruling radical wing of the Islamic Republic Party, and a few prominent *bazaaris* have been executed on charges of profiteering. Their increasing alienation would be a serious development for the Khomeini regime.

Intelligentsia

Under the Shah a rather large group of Westernized intelligentsia arose. Such people were often educated abroad, and most did not hold the Muslim clergy in esteem, although some were religious (e.g., Mehdi Bazargan). They generally supported the Shah in his efforts to modernize the country, and his policies enabled them to become a new elite. The top military leaders may be included in this group. Although the intelligentsia participated in the revolution, they hoped that the new government would be a liberal, if not secular regime. The intelligentsia have been a favorite target for removal by the Khomeini regime, and many have fled abroad (one estimate is that 200,000 have left). Their skills, however, will be needed in the future, and eventually they may be able to exercise a moderating influence on the government.

Organized Labor

Trade unions as such do not now exist in Iran. In the earlier part of the century, workers and employers were united in traditional guilds. Between 1945 and 1953 trade unions were formed, particularly in Tehran and the oilfields, and there were many strikes. However, from 1953 until 1979, any attempt to organize a labor movement was strongly suppressed. After 1959, the Shah permitted the formation of "official" trade unions, which were not allowed to strike or engage in political activity (unless it was to support the regime). There were about 1,000 such unions by 1978. They were not industry-wide, but were confined to single factories.

After the fall of the Shah, many owners fled the country and workers took over in the factories, which they ran through workers' councils. The IRP has taken an ambivalent position towards the workers' councils; the Mojahedin and Fedayan are favorable; and the Tudeh is against them (it would prefer one large, general union). Many Iranian workers were arrested in April and May 1982 following strikes in car factories and telecommuni-

cations offices. Workers were protesting the replacement of workers' councils by Islamic Associations, which they regarded as government attempts to infiltrate their ranks.

Students

Iranian students abroad long criticized the Shah's regime, and now many (particularly the Mojahedin) oppose Khomeini. While students in Iran played a prominent role in the ouster of the Shah, the extent of their support for Khomeini's government is unclear at the moment (it appears to be stronger among high school students than college-age ones). Students in Iran today constitute a large, potentially disaffected group. All colleges and universities have been closed since the spring of 1980 (when there was rioting), and many students have nothing to do. The schools are supposed to develop a new "Islamic curriculum" in all disciplines before reopening. Medical schools were partially reopened in February 1982. Even when the schools were open, there was severe competition to get in (in 1977, 290,000 applied and 60,000 were accepted). Some pressure on the system was relieved by sending tens of thousands of students abroad, but now few are permitted to study abroad unless they are training in fields the country needs, such as engineering.

Minority Religious Groups

About 90 percent of the people of Iran are Muslims of the Shi'a sect. The minority religious groups include Sunni Muslims, (nearly all tribal people), and non-Muslims, (primarily Baha'is, Christians, Jews, and Zoroastrians). The Pahlavis restrained the Shi'a clergy from harassing these groups and protected the non-Muslim minorities in particular, abolishing overt forms of discrimination and permitting them freedom of worship. They were all very apprehensive at the prospect of a militant Shi'a regime coming to power, and their fears have proven well founded, for an atmosphere of religious intolerance has prevailed since the revolution.

According to the new constitution, Zoroastrians, Jews, and Christians are the only recognized non-Muslim minorities and are to be left free to follow their religious precepts. Jews and Christians have traditionally been protected in Islamic societies, which regard them as "People of the Book," sharing a similar heritage to the Muslims. They are represented in the *Majlis* as follows: Zoroastrians and Jews each have one representative, the Assyrian and Chaldean Christians together have one representative, and the Armenian Christians of the north and south each have one representative. There is a provision for a small increase in representation, should their numbers increase in the next ten years.

The Baha'is, probably the largest minority (around 300,000), are reviled for being apostates from Islam and are not recognized as a legitimate religious group. They are not mentioned in the constitution and have no seat in Parliament. A peaceful community, they have been subject to severe oppression since their faith was founded in Iran in 1844. The Shah was assured of their loyalty, and many high officials in his government were believed to be Baha'is, although they are forbidden by their religion to accept political posts.

After the fall of the Shah, many Baha'is lost jobs, had property confiscated, and were imprisoned or executed when they refused to recant their faith. The holiest Baha'i shrine in Iran, the House of the Bab in Shiraz, was destroyed by mobs in September 1979. They have frequently been charged as being agents of Zionism or aiding Israel (the world center of their faith is in Haifa); collaboration with the Shah, particularly with his secret police, SAVAK; immorality (Baha'i marriages are not recognized by Muslim clergy); and opposition to the Khomeini regime. The state regards them as a political faction and has condoned the violent acts directed against them.

There are about 300,000 Christians in Iran, consisting primarily of Armenians (270,000) and Nestorians or Assyrians (30,000), with much smaller numbers of Roman Catholics, Greek Orthodox, and Anglicans. The Armenian community is well established in the quarter of Julfa in Isfahan, where they have a cathedral. Many young Armenians joined leftist groups, especially the Fedayan, at the time of the revolution. Many older Armenians owned shops selling imported food and liquor that were burned by mobs. The Armenian community, however, is noted for its tenaciousness and will doubtless survive the revolutionary period. The situation among the Anglicans is much worse. Although their community (which has been in Iran for 150 years) is tiny, numbering only 1,000 to 2,000, they are associated in the popular mind with the British and have been regarded as agents of imperialism. Anglican hospitals and schools have been seized, an Anglican priest in Shiraz was murdered, and in February 1980, Anglican Bishop Dehqani-Tafti fled the country.

The Jewish community is primarily located in Tehran, with smaller groups in Hamadan, Kashan, Isfahan, and Shiraz. In 1978, it numbered about 100,000, but a steady stream of emigration, mostly to Israel and the United States, has now reduced this number to about 40,000. Jews have lived in Iran for over twenty-five centuries and have become well integrated into Persian society, although often subject to discrimination. Ayatollah Khomeini's strong denunciations of Zionism and Israel and the execution of a few prominent Jews caused sharp anxiety in the community and encouraged many to leave.

The Zoroastrian community is located primarily in Tehran, Yazd, and Kerman and is estimated to number 40,000. Zoroastrianism was the official religion of the Persian Empire for hundreds of years before the introduction of Islam in the seventh century. Because of the Shah's desire to glorify pre-Islamic Iran, some Zoroastrians became loosely associated with the imperial court. Zoroastrians are a genuinely Iranian group with no foreign ties, so they have not been particularly subject to harassment during the revolution.

Ethnic Groups

The tribal groups of Iran live in mountainous and peripheral areas of the country, far from the reach of the central government. Most tribal people do not speak Persian as a first language, and, while they are Iranians, feel remote from urban Persian culture. They have long desired autonomy within Iran, although not actual independence. Several of the largest Iranian tribal groups (especially the Kurds, Baluchis, and Turkmans) are part of larger populations which live in adjacent countries. There are no accurate figures on tribal populations, and calculation is difficult because many people who are ethnically tribal now live in urban areas. The major tribes include the Kurds (about four million in Iran), the Baluchis (about 500–750,000 in Iran), Bakhtiaris (600–800,000), Lurs (500–800,000), Qashqai (400,000), Turkmans (315,000), and Arabs (about 150,000 tribal out of a much larger population in Iran of 600,000 to two million).

Although it is usually asserted that the tribes in Iran are Sunni, in fact only the Baluchis and Turkmans have a Sunni majority. Among the Kurds, Sunnis constitute a plurality; Arabs and Lurs are majority Shi'a; Bakhtiaris and Qashqai are totally Shi'a.

The tribes have not played a significant role in national politics since the early part of the twentieth century, and this fact does not seem likely to change. They had a long history of hostility to the Pahlavi regime, which attempted to integrate them into a modern state by disarming and set-tling them and forcing them into the state educational and military systems.

The tribes, however, have retained considerable freedom. The central government is still obliged to delegate its authority in tribal areas and in doing so attempts to influence tribal leadership. Tribes are economically important because they provide foodstuffs such as meat and milk to urban areas.

The tribes played a small part in the revolution, but most had no desire to see the imposition of a militant Shi'a regime. Although the new constitution stipulates that tribal people shall enjoy equal rights, this has been limited to cultural rather than political autonomy. The Khomeini regime represents an urban, centralized Persian government, like that of the Shah. By seeking in similar ways to extend central control to tribal areas, it has met with the same resistance.

It was the practice of the Shah to appoint officials to areas where they had no ties, to prevent the formation of local power centers. Likewise in the summer of 1980 Khomeini's government appointed a Shi'a Muslim who was not a Baluch to govern the province of Sistan and Baluchistan, where Sunni Baluch tribesmen are in the majority. In the spring of 1979, violence flared in the Turkman areas of northeast Iran when tribesmen complained that they were denied membership in the local revolutionary committee, which was dominated by Shi'a.

Khomeini rejects the idea of tribal political autonomy, as did the Shah, and has excluded tribesmen from national political participation. For example, the secretary general of the Kurdish Democratic Party, Abdol-Rahman Qasemlou, was elected in August 1979 to the Council of Experts, but the Revolutionary Council barred his participation. In June 1980, a leader of the Qashqai, Khosrow Qashqai, was elected to the Parliament, but was not permitted to take his seat. He was executed in the fall of 1982.

While the weakness of the central government has for the time being allowed the tribes greater autonomy, since the summer of 1979 armed clashes have occurred between central government forces and Kurds, Baluchis, Turkmans, and Qashqai. The government did acknowledge the help of what it referred to as "the brave tribal irregular warfare combatants" in the liberation of Khorramshahr in May 1982 in the war with Iraq, presumably referring to the Bakhtiaris and Lurs.

Two tribal groups, the Kurds and the Baluchis, have their own political parties, and both have armed factions in Iran opposing the regime. All of the major leftist parties—the Tudeh, the Mojahedin, and the Fedayan—support the idea of tribal autonomy.

The main political party supported by the Kurds is the Kurdish Democratic Party, led by Abdol-Rahman Qasemlou (born about 1930), whose slogan is "democracy for Iran, autonomy for the Kurds." It has now joined in an alliance with the Mojahedin and is part of the umbrella National Council of Resistance. The Komala is a small Marxist-Leninist party akin to the Tudeh and is important in urban areas, especially Sanandaj. The Fedayan also have a Kurdish section. The Baluch Liberation Movement is allied with the Fedayan minority group, and the Qashqai have connections with the Mojahedin.

Khomeini has blamed tribal opposition on leftist instigation and foreign interference. Outside powers have in the past sometimes supported tribal autonomy, but historically they have preferred to deal with a strong central government if possible. Many predicted that the Soviet Union would seek to "stir up the tribes" in an attempt to destabilize the country, but it has not done so thus far.

National Prospects

For the last several years Iran has been undergoing momentous political, social, and economic changes. The country experienced a genuinely popular revolution, as opposed to the kind of palace *coup d'état* more common in the Middle East. Further upheaval seems certain in the years ahead, particularly after Khomeini dies. The aura of violence that was never present in Iran before the revolution is now widespread and does not augur well for the future. The problem of legitimate succession, which has always afflicted Islamic countries, will once again come to the forefront. Conflict between the different groups and parties will likely break out and other *ulema*, who do not share Khomeini's views, may withdraw the clergy from actual exercise of power.

Predictions of Iran's imminent collapse due to economic problems, bureaucratic paralysis, or military invasion have not been borne out. The lower classes, who were the backbone of the revolution, are still behind the government, but their patience with it may run out as the country experiences serious economic difficulties. A social group to watch is the *bazaaris*, for should they turn against the government, it would be in serious difficulty. The Westernized elite which ran the country under the Shah has largely fled or kept quiet; eventually they must be lured back to help reconstruct the country. The influence of exile groups on a future government is questionable, despite the earlier triumphial return of Khomeini to Iran from Paris.

Further Reading

Abrahamian, Ervand. *Iran Between Two Revolutions.* Princeton, N. J.: Princeton University Press, 1982.

Akhavi, Shahrough. *Religion and Politics in Contemporary Iran: Clergy-State Relations in the Pahlavi Period.* Albany, N. Y.: State University of New York Press, 1980.

Bill, James. "The Patterns of Elite Politics in Iran." In *Political Elites in the Middle East,* George Lenczowski, ed. Washington, D.C.: American Enterprise Institute for Public Policy Research, 1975.

_____. "Power and Religion in Revolutionary Iran." *The Middle East Journal,* Vol. 36, No. 1, Winter 1982.

Blaustein, Albert P., and Flanz, Gisbert H., eds. "Iran". *Constitutions of the Countries of the World.* Dobbs Ferry, N. Y.: Oceana Publications, April 1980.

Chubin, Shahram. "Leftist Forces in Iran." *Problems of Communism,* Vol. 29, No. 4, July–August 1980.

Cottam, Richard. *Nationalism in Iran.* Rev. ed. Pittsburgh: University of Pittsburgh Press, 1979.

Fischer, Michael. *Iran: From Religious Dispute to Revolution.* Cambridge, Mass.: Harvard University Press, 1980.

Halliday, Fred. *Iran: Dictatorship and Development.* New York and Harmondsworth, Middlesex, England: Penguin Books Ltd., 1979.

Hooglund, Eric. *Land and Revolution in Iran, 1960–1980.* Austin, Texas: University of Texas Press, 1982.

Keddie, Nikki R. *Roots of Revolution: An Interpretive History of Modern Iran.* New Haven and London: Yale University Press, 1981.

Lenczowski, George, ed., *Iran Under the Pahlavis.* Stanford, Calif.: Hoover Institution Press, 1978.

Rubin, Barry. *Paved with Good Intentions: The American Experience and Iran.* New York and Oxford: Oxford University Press, 1980.

REPUBLIC OF IRAQ
(Al-Jumhuriyya al-'Iraqiyya)
by Reeva Simon, Ph.D.

The System of Government

Iraq, a nation of over thirteen million people, is a one-party unitary socialist state. The current regime came into power on July 17, 1968, after a Ba'thist coup led by General Ahmad Hasan al-Bakr.

Executive

The president of the republic is the head of state and government and the chairman of the Revolutionary Command Council (RCC) of the Ba'th (Renaissance) party—the "supreme organ of the state." He is elected by a two-thirds majority vote of the RCC from among its members. There are no provisions in the constitution for the term of the office of president, but he must be a native-born Iraqi. If the president is absent or incapacitated, his duties are taken over by the vice-chairman of the RCC, who also is elected from among its members.

The head of state exercises power directly or through a Council of Ministers which he appoints. By convention, this cabinet has consisted of one-third Ba'th party members who hold the key portfolios. In August 1979, there were thirty cabinet members. The president appoints local officials and the head of the Kurdish Executive Council, who is technically vice-president of Iraq.

First established in July 1968, the Revolutionary Command Council remains, in 1982, the top decision-making body of the state. Its mission is to carry out the popular will and the tenets of the Ba'th party: "unity, freedom, and socialism."

Individual members of the RCC are answerable only to the Council of Ministers as a whole, which can dismiss an RCC member by a two-thirds vote. It can send to trial any member of the RCC, any deputy to the president, or any cabinet minister. In September 1977, a constitutional amendment stipulated that all members of the Ba'th party Regional Command were to be regarded as members of the RCC, increasing the membership of the RCC from the original five members to twenty-two. Since 1979, however, the number has been reduced to sixteen.

The functions of the RCC are executive and legislative. The RCC approves government recommendations concerning national defense and internal security. It declares war, orders general mobilization, concludes peace, ratifies treaties and agreements, approves the general budget of the state, sets rules for the impeachment of RCC members, and can set up a special court to try the impeached. The RCC can authorize the chairman or vice-chairman to exercise some of its powers, except for legislative ones. The chairman of the RCC, who is also the president, signs all laws and decrees issued by the RCC and supervises the work of the cabinet ministers and the operations of state institutions.

Legislature

The provisional constitution of 1970 provided for the election of the National Assembly, but elections did not take place until 1980. The government amended the constitution in July 1973, to provide for an assembly of 100 members to be selected by the RCC. This amendment was abrogated in March 1980 when the RCC promulgated laws instituting a National Assembly for all of Iraq and a Legislative Assembly for the autonomous region of Kurdistan.

The National Assembly which was elected on June 20, 1980, consists of 250 representatives; 175 of them are Ba'th party members. According to the constitution, the National Assembly's members are elected proportionally, one deputy for every 50,000 citizens, to a four-year term. Those elected tended to be young—approximately forty years of age—and from low socioeconomic backgrounds. They tended to have more than a high school education and no military background.

The National Assembly, which technically shares legislative powers with the RCC, can introduce and pass laws, approve treaties and international agreements, discuss domestic and foreign policy, and is empowered to question ministers and propose their dismissal to the RCC. However, it has no veto power, cannot interfere in matters of defense and internal security, and cannot question RCC members. A dispute between the Assembly and the RCC over the Assembly's rejection of an amendment is resolved by a two-thirds majority of the combined membership of the two bodies, sitting in a joint session.

As of mid-1982, the National Assembly seems to provide a semblance of popular participation in government and to be an agent of legitimization for the one-man rule of President Saddam Hussein, who uses it as a platform for his policy announcements. In September 1980, for example, the president used the Assembly to announce the abrogation of the 1975 treaty with Iran, thus initiating the Iraq-Iran war.

Judiciary

The highest court is the Court of Cassation which is the court of last resort. It has a president, a vice-president, no fewer than fifteen permanent members, deputized judges, reporting judges, and religious judges. In addition to being the court of last appeal, the Court of Cassation has original jurisdiction over crimes committed by high government officials, including judges. Within its organization, the Penal Body, consisting of three judges, is the highest court for criminal matters. It does not try cases of offenses against the state which are defined as security matters. These are tried by the Revolutionary Court.

The Revolutionary Court consists of three judges who sit permanently in Baghdad. Crimes against the security of the state include economic and political crimes such as trade in narcotics, rebellion, and espionage. The sessions are held *in camera* and there is no appeal. After the attempted coups against the regime in 1970 and in 1973, and after the riots in Najaf and Karbala in 1977, the RCC established temporary tribunals to try large numbers of security offenders. These trials were presided over by three or four high government officials who were not bound by the ordinary provisions of criminal law and who meted out swift, severe decisions.

Regional & Local Government

Iraq is divided into eighteen administrative provinces, each under a governor appointed by the president. The provinces are divided into districts and districts into subdistricts, headed by district officers and subdistrict officers. Cities and towns are headed by mayors. All chief administrative officers except those of minor cities and towns are appointed by the president. Baghdad, the capital, has a special status.

Although the government's National Action Charter of November 15, 1971, mentions "popular councils" as a means to narrow the gap between the government and the people, by 1979 as far as could be determined, these councils existed only in Baghdad, in other major cities, and in a few of the smaller administrative units. Their members seem to be government appointed and their function is to channel popular grievances and needs to the proper authorities, as well as educating and encouraging the people to support Ba'th government policies.

The Electoral System

The June 20, 1980, elections were the first since the 1958 overthrow of the monarchy. A government order of March 1980 authorized the elections to the National Assembly by secret ballot under direct universal suffrage. At least 840 candidates stood for election in 250 electoral districts. Nominations were open to all but communists and property owners. A special election committee screened the candidates to certify that they were civilian native Iraqis whose father or mother were born in Iraq, not "bourgeois capitalists." Any military personnel who wished to run had to resign from the military, as the Iraqi government stresses the authority of the civilian sector over the military. Although one of the provisions for candidacy was that a candidate had to believe in the principles of the July 17 Revolution, he did not have to be a Ba'th party member. Of the 250 representatives elected, some 175 were Ba'th party members; eight were women.

Arab Socialist Ba'th (Renaissance) Party
(*Hizb al-Ba'th al-'Arabi al-Ishtiraki*)

History

The Ba'th party in Iraq is a regional branch of the Arab Socialist Ba'th party which was established in the 1940s in Damascus, Syria, by Michel Aflaq and Salah al-Bitar. Its secular ideology combines socialism with Arab unity—the union of the Arab states into one Arab entity. Iraqi students, inspired by the Syrian leaders, founded a local party in Iraq. Early supporters were primarily high school and college students, and some army officers, most of them urban Sunni Arabs. Some early members who were to play leading political roles in the party were Ahmad Hasan al-Bakr, Salih Mahdi Ammash, and Saddam Hussein. Ahmad Hasan al-Bakr emerged as head of the military wing of the party, while Saddam Hussein led the civilian wing.

The Iraqi Ba'th played a minor role in the 1958 coup which overthrew the Iraqi monarchy, and the party at first supported the coup leader, Abd al-Karim Qasim. In 1959, however, because of the regime's support of the communists, Ba'thists participated in an attempted assassination of Qasim. The party was suppressed and Saddam Hussein, one of the plotters, was exiled. In February 1963, leading members of the party led the Ba'th to power, overthrowing Qasim. Shortly after the coup, the Syrian Ba'thists also came to power in that country. The party's National Command and the Syrian Regional Command were located in Damascus. The Iraqi Regional Command was seated in Baghdad.

In November 1963, a non-Ba'thist military coup, led by Abd al-Salam Arif, ousted the Ba'th government. Arif's coup was possible because of the disintegration of the Ba'th party; party moderates influenced by Arif—including Talib Shabib and Hazim Jawad—had been expelled. The leader of the Marxist wing of the Ba'th, 'Ali Salah Saadi, also severed ties with the Ba'th and formed the Arab Revolutionary Workers Party.

In early 1966, the radical wing of the Syrian Ba'th overthrew the Syrian government of General Amin al-Hafez, which had been supported by Salah al-Bitar, and established a rival National Command in Damascus. Ahmad Hasan al-Bakr and Saddam Hussein remained faithful to the leadership of al-Bitar and Aflaq, who moved to Baghdad in 1966. On July 17, 1968, al-Bakr and Saddam Hussein in conjunction with non-Ba'th army officers overthrew the government of Abd al-Rahman Arif. Three weeks later, the Ba'thists took complete control, purging the non-Ba'thist officers.

Bakr and Saddam dominated the RCC after purging the top echelons of the party in the early 1970s. Additional purges in 1977 left only Saddam's close associates in the Baghdad National Command and in the RCC. In 1978, there was an extensive purge of the middle ranks of the party. On July 16, 1979, Bakr resigned for reasons of health and Saddam Hussein took over full control of the party. Following an attempted coup by the military wing of the party two weeks later, Saddam purged the armed forces and reshuffled the RCC, five of whose members were tried and executed for their alleged involvement in a Syrian Ba'thist plot. Saddam used the abortive coup as a pretext to attempt to concentrate his power by appointing relatives and close friends from his home town, Tikrit, to nearly all key posts.

Organization

The Iraqi Ba'th party is a highly structured, disciplined, elitist party. The basic unit of the party is the cell or circle (*khalwa*), followed by the section (*firqa*), the branch (*shu'ba*), and the major branch (*far'*). The cell is an urban living quarter or a village. A few sections form a branch which is usually a small town, while a major branch comprises an entire district or a large city. The districts are represented in the party's Regional Command, whose sixteen members compose the core of the party leadership. Although members of the Regional Command are supposed to be elected by a regional congress which is to meet annually to discuss and approve policy, they are, in reality, chosen by the top leaders in the party.

Party influence emanates from Baghdad and the party penetrates into every segment of society. Party cadres are in the government, in rural and urban mass organizations, and in the army. Their role is to educate and indoctrinate, to provide guidance according to the party's prinicples and policies, to improve the party's image, and to monitor the activities of various groups so that infractions can be corrected. Party members attend regular meetings for ideological discussions, and participate in general "popular" activity such as the construction of houses and the eradication of illiteracy. The party is portrayed as the intermediary between the state and people, the true advocate of the people, and the conduit through which grievances are channeled. The party fosters professional organizations for lawyers, doctors, and teachers, and has organized peasants, women, and youth.

The daily newspaper *al-Thawra* (Revolution) is the organ of the Ba'th party. The English-language daily *Baghdad Observer* is state sponsored.

Policy

The economic orientation of the Ba'th party is socialism. Once in power, the party nationalized the Iraq Petroleum Company in June 1972, and by 1975 all foreign interests in the IPC were eliminated. Petroleum revenues finance Iraq's economic plan, which emphasizes industrial development, agricultural self-sufficiency, and a variety of social welfare programs including housing, education, and medical services for the poor.

There has been a shift of population from rural to urban areas, causing a reorientation in the government's agricultural program. Saddam Hussein has been encouraging people to return to the farm, offering plots and subsidies to farmers. In addition, some collective farms are being dismantled and private farming encouraged.

The Ba'th party is opposed to "imperialism, Zionism, and reactionary" forces. Its espoused policy is nonalignment. Baghdad was scheduled to host the nonaligned nations' conference in September 1982, a role which automatically would make Saddam Hussein the unofficial spokesman for the nonaligned movement for the following three years.

Iraq's relations with the Soviet Union have deteriorated since 1975, despite the April 1972 Treaty of Friendship and Cooperation and another agreement signed between the two countries in December 1978, whereby Iraq received arms and technical aid in return for allowing the Iraqi Communist Party to participate in a National Front. Since 1979, Saddam has not hesitated to purge communists from the army. In 1980, Iraq denounced the Soviet invasion of Afghanistan and Soviet activities against "Arab Somalia" in the Horn of Africa. Although a declared neutral in the war between Iran and Iraq, the Soviet Union refused to sell Iraq arms and has become increasingly involved in Iran.

Iraq's trade with Soviet bloc countries has declined while trade with the United States and imports from Europe and Japan have increased. Since 1977 arms sales have increased from France, which has provided Iraq with Mirage combat aircraft, tanks, and antitank missiles. The French provided the nuclear reactor at Osirak which was destroyed by Israel in June 1981. The French government has decided to replace the reactor, although under close supervision.

Iraq is a founding member both of the Organization of Petroleum Exporting Countries (OPEC; 1960) and of the Organization of Arab Petroleum Exporting Countries (OAPEC; 1968). For many years Iraq has advocated higher crude prices, but in 1980, as part of Saddam's moderation policy, Iraq joined Saudi Arabia in its oil policy.

The Camp David Agreement (1978) and the fall of the Shah of Iran (1979) catapulted Iraq into a pivotal position in the Persian Gulf and the Arab world. Saddam Hussein saw Iraq as the likely successor to Egypt for leadership in the Arab world because of Iraq's population, wealth, military po-

tential, and its consistent espousal of the Palestinian cause. Iraq was a major "rejectionist" power and hosted the Baghdad summit conference against the Camp David Agreement. Since then, however, Iraq has shifted to a more moderate postion, withdrawing support from the radical Palestine groups and giving it to Yassir Arafat's Palestine Liberation Organization.

Relations with Syria have been bitter since 1966. A brief rapprochement, despite conflicts over the use of the headwaters of the Euphrates River and competition for leadership of the National Command of the Ba'th party, began with the unity scheme proposed in October 1978 and ended in July 1979. Once Saddam took full control of the government, he disclosed that the plotters against the regime in July 1979 had contact with a "foreign power," namely Syria.

The war with Iran was initiated by Iraq in September 1980. A basic cause of the war was attempts by the new Shi'a Muslim regime in Iran to arouse the majority Shi'a population of Iraq against the secular Ba'th government. Baghdad also hoped to take advantage of Iran's domestic turmoil to nullify the 1975 Algiers agreement which gave the two countries an equal share in the Shatt al-Arab waterway between the two countries. Syrian support for Iran and Saudi and Jordanian support for Iraq has further moderated Ba'th policy in the Gulf, where the party no longer lends support to revolutionary movements.

Membership & Constituency

The Ba'th claimed a total of 1.5 million supporters or 12 percent of the population in mid-1978, with party regulars estimated at approximately 50,000, of whom the majority was Arab Sunni. The Ba'th has emphasized selectivity: a supporter may give ten years of active service before becoming a regular member. However, early in 1979, Saddam Hussein began encouraging everyone either to join the party or to consider himself a Ba'thist even if he were not in the organization. Membership, nevertheless, remains a key to social and political mobility in Iraq, and the practical consequences of the party's new membership policy remain to be seen.

Leadership

From 1968 to 1977, RCC members were in their thirties and forties. Increasingly, the leaders of the party are Arab Sunni, from lower-middle-class families, whose origins are in the small towns northwest of Baghdad, notably the town of Tikrit.

Many RCC members are related by marriage or by tribal origin.

The two leaders to emerge in control of the Ba'th party in the early 1970s were Ahmad Hasan al-Bakr and Saddam Hussein. Al-Bakr was born in Tikrit in 1914 and served as president from 1968 until he resigned in July 1979. Hussein was born in Tikrit in 1937. Saddam's brother, Barzan, controls the intelligence service; his brother-in-law, Adnan Khairallah, was made deputy commander of the armed forces; and another fellow Tikriti, Sa'dun Shakir, is minister of the interior.

Satellite Organizations

In 1977 there were thirteen trade unions with a total membership of some 900,000 members. These are under direct control of the Ba'th party and are organized under a federation of unions. The function of trade unions is to mediate between labor and management; there have been no strikes in Iraq since 1968.

The paramilitary organizations are more significant. The People's Militia (*al-Jay'ish al-Sha'bi*) of the Ba'th party was formed in 1970. In 1978 its estimated strength was 100,000. The original goal of the regime was a militia of 200,000 by 1980 to be organized in armed units in every town and village in Iraq. It is estimated that there were more than 500,000 militiamen in March 1981.

The militia's functions are to protect the regime, to back up the regular armed forces in war, and to carry political indoctrination to the general population. Personnel are armed with light and medium arms including heavy machine guns and antitank weapons. They are positioned in the cities and could be used to thwart any coup attempt. Evidence exists that the militia fought in 1975 against the Kurds and in Lebanon on the side of the Palestinians. In the early 1980s, it was used both on the Iranian and the Kurdish fronts. Before the Iraq-Iran War only party members over the age of eighteen who had completed their army service were recruited for service in the militia. With the active participation of the militia in the war, recruitment has increased and membership includes foreign volunteers.

The paramilitary youth organization for secondary-school students is the *Futuwwah* (Youth Vanguard). Boys and girls from the ages of fourteen to eighteen are organized into youth platoons.

In order to broaden its base, the Ba'th regime formed a National Progressive Front (NPF) on July 17, 1973, to include the Iraqi Communist Party (ICP) and the Kurdish Democratic Party (KDP). The NPF was to be directed by the High Council controlled by the Ba'th: three of the members were to be Communists, three Kurds, and two others were to represent the remains of the pre-Ba'th liberal parties such as the National Democratic Party and the Independence Party. Eight members, including the NPF secretary general, were to be Ba'th. The NPF, which did not have official Kurdish support, was fairly ineffectual throughout its existence. It has not met since the suppression of the Iraqi Communist Party in mid-1979. The Communists, who numbered some 2,000 in 1978, went underground, and are said to be allied with the Kurds fighting against the regime.

Other Political Forces

Military

The army has been involved in Iraqi politics since the creation of the state in 1921. The Iraqi army and major civilian posts were in the hands of the Iraqi Arab officers who had supported the Amir Feisal in his revolt against the Ottoman Turks in 1916. In 1936 army officers perpetrated the first of a series of military coups which finally brought Arab nationalist officers to power.

Britain intervened when some of these officers attempted to side with the Germans in 1941. The army was purged and reorganized, but in 1958 a new group of nationalist officers overthrew the monarchy in a particularly bloody coup. These "Free Officers" were led by Abd al-Karim Qasim and Abd al-Salam Arif. Qasim seized control of the government, but was subsequently overthrown in 1963 by the coalition of Arif and the Ba'thists.

The Ba'thist officers who took over in 1968 were determined to end the cycle of coups. Although the military (or "right") wing of the party, headed by Bakr, enabled the Ba'th to take power, Saddam Hussein does not have a military background. In anticipation of his accession to full power, Saddam had Bakr, as president and commander-in-chief, confer upon him the highest rank in the army—lieutenant general—thus merging the military and civilian wings of the party under Saddam's sole, and civilian, authority.

Saddam Hussein has tried to control the army by increasing financial benefits in order to improve morale and ensure the loyalty of the troops to the Ba'th regime. To counteract morale problems, the regime offered amnesty in 1975 and 1979 to deserters during the conflicts against the Kurds.

In 1975 the Military Service and Pension Law was passed, raising pay and pension allowances and increasing benefits, the goal being to make the military an attractive career.

At the same time, there have been on-going purges of the officer corps, most notably in 1978 when communist officers were arrested and executed. Since 1977, Ba'thist officers have held all of the top military commands, loyalty to the regime being the prerequisite for advancement. Political "commissars" in all units report to the party, which controls all security forces. Officers' commands are frequently changed, and the names of commanders at the Iranian front are not mentioned in published reports in order to prevent any officer from building a popular following.

Historically, Arab Sunnis have dominated the Iraqi officer corps. Since its establishment in 1924, the Military College has favored Arab Sunnis over Shi'a and Kurds, who are represented in the officer corps far below their proportion of the population. The military remains a means of advancement for urban lower-middle-class sons of minor government officials and small traders. Most officers have close family and tribal ties, and most top commanders now hail from the Tikrit area. While the professionalism of the army has improved greatly in the last twenty years, it remains a potential threat to the Ba'th government and to Tikriti dominance.

Kurds

The Kurds are non-Arab, Kurdish-speaking, Sunni tribesmen living primarily in the Irbil, al-Sulaimaniyya, and Kirkuk areas. Their claim to be a majority in Kirkuk is disputed by the government, which would like to minimize Kurdish claims to this oil area. The estimated two million Iraqi Kurds (approximately 12 percent of the population) are part of larger group of Kurds numbering some ten million who inhabit an area divided between Turkey, the Soviet Union, Iraq, and Iran. Since the emergence of Kurdish nationalism in the twentieth century, the Kurds have been working for the establishment of an independent Kurdistan.

Under the Iraqi monarchy (1921–58), there were intermittent Kurdish uprisings against the government. At first the Kurds supported Abd al-Karim Qasim (1958–63), but in 1961 they formally opposed the government when Qasim turned against them. After 1961 there was large-scale fighting between the Kurds, led by Mulla Mustafa Barzani and his *Pesh Merga* (Those Who Face Death), and the central government.

Ba'th policy has been to recognize Kurdish cultural rights while undertaking military offensives against the tribesmen. In March 1970, Barzani and Saddam Hussein agreed to autonomy for the Kurds; in July, a constitutional amendment recognized two principal nationalities in Iraq; Arab and Kurd. The Autonomy Plan of March 1974 granted the Kurds cultural autonomy, but the government simultaneously issued the Kurds an ultimatum to accept the plan. The Kurds refused, turning again to open rebellion.

The Iraqi army was not able to subdue the Kurds until the Ba'th reached an understanding with the Shah of Iran. In March 1975, the two parties signed an agreement in Algiers which, in return for Iraqi concessions including the reestablishment of the Iraq-Iran border in the middle of the Shatt al-Arab waterway, the Shah agreed to stop supplying the Kurds. By April, the Iraqi army was able to break the rebellion. The government began a resettlement plan, transferring an estimated one-third of the Kurdish population to the south away from the Iranian frontier. In addition a "dead" area was established along the border— water sources were filled in and vegetation destroyed—in order to prevent movement across the border. Despite these measures, Kurdish forces have engaged Iraqi troops in the north since the outbreak of the Iraq-Iran war.

Formally, Kurdish affairs are directed by the Executive Council and the Legislative Assembly, as stipulated by the constitutional amendment enacted in 1974 providing limited self-rule for the Kurdish areas. Officials must be Kurds or Kurdish-speaking, and Kurdish is the official language of all local government communication. The Executive Council, consisting of up to twelve members, is approved by a majority of the Legislative Assembly. Its president is chosen by the head of state and has cabinet rank. During its first session in 1974, the Legislative Assembly of eighty members was dominated by the seventy-two RCC-appointed members. The other eight were co-opted from various Kurdish groups. In the September 1980 elections to the Assembly, 194 candidates ran for fifty seats. Most of those elected to the three-year terms held positions in mass organizations linked to the Ba'th party. The Assembly's powers are limited to economic and social programs. It has no power over justice, police, internal security, or the administration of frontier areas. The Assembly can question members of the Executive Council and can withhold a vote of confidence. The central government oversees Kurdistan through the minister of state for regional autonomy and other officials who supervise local Kurdish governments.

The Iraqi Kurdish parties, all of which advocate Kurdish autonomy and varying degrees of "progressivism," differ on leadership. The Kurdish Democratic Party of Iraq is a remnant of the old party of Mullah Mustafa Barzani. It has split over succession with the sons of Barzani, Mas'ud and Idris, leading the major part of the party. The Patriotic Union of Kurdistan controls the countryside of Kirkuk and Sulaimaniyya. It is led by Jalal Talabani. The Unified Socialist Party of Iraqi Kurdistan is led by Dr. Mahmud Osman. All of these parties are in armed opposition to the government.

Shi'a

Iraq is generally described as a country composed of a Shi'a majority ruled by a Sunni minority. The Shi'a comprise approximately 55 percent of the population and are concentrated in the rural areas south of Baghdad and in certain Baghdad neighborhoods. Historically, the Shi'a have had little contact with the state and have not been represented proportionately either in the ruling elite or in the military. Despite their reputation for being the underprivileged of Iraq because of the large numbers of rural Shi'a and urban slumdwellers, Shi'a comprise a large part of Iraq's middle class, and are strongly represented in the professions and the civil service.

The most holy shrines of Shi'a Islam are in the Iraqi cities of Najaf and Karbala, and visits to them are incumbent on observent Shi'a. Thus, there has been constant intermingling between the faithful Shi'a of Iraq and Iran. Followers of Shi'a doctrine see the successor of the Prophet Mohammed, or his representatives, as more than religious leaders; they also are supposed to be the final arbiters of political policy. Traditionally, they have regarded all non-Shi'a regimes as unworthy of any loyalty.

Shi'a were attracted both to the Communist Party and to the Ba'th. Since 1963, their numbers in the Ba'th have declined because some defected to join Sa'adi's leftist group, and many received long jail terms under the Arif regimes.

The Ba'th has followed a two-pronged policy with regard to the Shi'a. The secular regime has tried to recruit Shi'a members by emphasizing its nonsectarian ideology and by stressing the "Arabness' of the Iraqi Shi'a. In 1979, three Shi'a were purged from the RCC because of their alleged complicity in a Syrian plot against the regime. Saddam has deported Iranian residents of Iraq and Iraqis of Iranian origin and arrested more than 10,000 people since the Khomeini regime came to power in Iran. Some 178 Shi'a intellectuals, professionals, and religious functionaries, including the religious leader Ayatallah Muhammad Baqr al-Sadr, have been executed.

There are two newly emergent Shi'a parties. The *al-Da'wah al-Islamiyyah* (The Islamic Call) was founded in Najaf in the late 1960s as an attempt to counteract Shi'a support for the Communist Party. It is split over doctrine. Some follow the more conservative Kazim Shari'at Madari of Qum, Iran, who stood for reform rather than the overthrow of the Shah. Others support Iran's Ayatollah Khomeini and engage in sabotage within and outside of Iraq. In March 1980, the RCC declared membership in the *al-Da'wah* illegal and subject to the death penalty.

The *al-Mujahidin* (Muslim Warriors) was founded in Baghdad in 1979. It has no links with Iran. Members are religiously oriented graduates of modern schools opposed to the intervention of religious leaders in the life of the country.

National Prospects

Iraqi reverses in the Iraq-Iran War have brought Saddam's effectiveness into question. But despite the presence of diverse opposition groups—Shi'a, Kurds, supporters of the Syrian Ba'th—to date none of them is as well organized as the firmly entrenched Iraqi Ba'th party. Saddam's political acumen and his control of the party apparatus via relatives and supporters will not make it easy to remove him from power.

Further Reading
Baram, Amazia. "The June 1980 Elections to the National Assembly in Iraq: An Experiment in Controlled Democracy." *Orient*, September 1981.
_____. "Saddam Hussein: A Political Profile." *Jerusalem Quarterly*, No. 17, Fall 1980.
Batatu, Hanna. "Iraq's Underground Shi'a Movements: Characteristics, Causes, and Prospects." *Middle East Journal*, Vol. 35, Autumn 1981.
_____. *The Old Social Classes and the Revolutionary Movements of Iraq: A Study of Iraq's Old Landed and Commercial Classes and of its Communists, Ba'thists, and Free Officers.* Princeton, N.J.: Princeton University Press, 1978.
Devlin, John F. *The Baath Party.* Stanford, Calif.: Hoover Institution Press, Stanford University, 1976.
Kelidar, Abbas. *Iraq: The Search for Stability.*

500 Iraq

Conflict Study No. 59. London: Institute for the Study of Conflict, 1975.

Khadduri, Majid. *Socialist Iraq: A Study in Iraqi Politics Since 1968.* Washington, D.C.: Middle East Institute, 1979.

Marr, Phebe A. "The Political Elite in Iraq." In *Political Elites in the Middle East.* George Lenczowski, ed. Washington, D.C.: American Enterprise Institute for Public Policy Research, 1975.

Springborg, Robert. "Baathism in Practice: Agriculture, Politics, and Political Culture in Syria and Iraq." *Middle Eastern Studies*, Vol. 17, April 1981.

IRELAND
(*Eire*)
by Cornelius O'Leary, Ph.D.

The System of Government

The Republic of Ireland is a parliamentary republic and a unitary state. Legislative power is vested in the *Oireachtas* (Parliament), consisting of two chambers, the *Dail* (Assembly) and *Seanad* (Senate), both of which are elected at least every five years.

The constitution, adopted by popular referendum in June 1937, established a republic called the Irish Free State in what was previously (1922–37) a British dominion. One attribute of sovereignty was, however, missing: the president could not accredit diplomats abroad or receive the credentials of foreign diplomats—these functions were reserved (as with the other dominions) to the British king. However, in 1949, when the Republic of Ireland Act became effective, these functions were transferred to the president of Ireland and sovereignty was complete.

Executive

The head of state, the president, is elected by the people for a term of seven years. He cannot serve more than two terms. His functions are largely formal or ceremonial. In fact, all but one of his powers are exercised subject to advice from the cabinet: the exeception is the right of the president at his absolute discretion to refuse a dissolution to a *taoiseach* (prime minister) who has lost the support of a majority of the *Dail*. (This power has not been exercised.) The *taoiseach* as head of government is the chief executive officer who, through his control of the cabinet and the Parliament, exercises immense influence over the development, passage, and administration of the law.

Legislature

The Parliament (*Oireachtas*) of Ireland is bicameral. The lower house, or *Dail Eireann*, consisted of 166 deputies in 1982, elected by the single transferable vote system (STV) of proportional representation in forty-one constituencies which, according to their population, have three, four, or five deputies. (See Electoral System, below.)

The *Dail* elects its own speaker; usually the speaker comes from a party in the government, but there is no fixed convention. The *Dail* also elects its standing committees, generally in proportion to party distribution in the chamber. The chairmen come from the government parties, except the chairman of the Public Accounts Committee who, as in the British Parliament, is always a member of the opposition. The committees, apart from dealing with routine business (as the Committee of Procedure and Privileges) scrutinize broad areas of administration. However, they so faithfully reflect the party balance in the *Dail* that they have rarely embarrassed the government, even when its majority is precarious.

Most legislation is initiated by the government, although time is allowed for private members' bills. A vote on a government bill is a vote of confidence and party discipline is enforced (as in the House of Commons), except when a bill raises a question of conscience. In 1973, for example, the *taoiseach* and another minister voted against a bill dealing with contraception, which the government as a whole had backed. It was defeated.

The Senate (*Seanad*) is coequal to the *Dail*. However, if the Senate rejects a bill passed by the *Dail*, and if the bill is repassed by the *Dail* and then returned to the Senate not later than ninety days afterwards, it will become law notwithstanding a second Senate defeat. Only in one case (a 1959 bill to amend the constitution by abolishing the single transferable vote system; see *Electoral System*) has the Senate rejected a *Dail* bill. The intention of the constitution makers in 1937 was to create a second chamber on broad vocational lines, but in practice most of those elected (excluding the university senators) have party affiliations. The nominating power of the prime minister

IRISH ELECTION RESULTS (1982)

	Votes	Pct.	Seats
Fianna Fail	786,951	47.3	81
Fine Gael	621,088	37.3	63
Labour	151,875	9.1	15
Workers' Party	38,088	2.3	3
Others	67,131	4.0	4*
	1,665,133	100.0	166

* Including the outgoing speaker, who is automatically returned from the constituency of his choice.

generally (though not always) ensures that the governing party or coalition has a majority of Senate seats.

The Senate comprises sixty members recruited by three distinct methods. *First,* forty-three are elected from various occupational panels—agriculture, industry and commerce, labor, culture and education, and administration—to which they have been nominated by the appropriate nominating bodies in the community and by members of the *Dail.* These forty-three are chosen by an electorate comprising all the members of the *Dail* and of the major local authorities (county, borough, and urban councils). In 1982, the total electorate was 884. *Second,* three are elected by graduates of the National University of Ireland (electorate: 49,695) and three by graduates of Trinity College, Dublin (electorate: 9,164). *Third,* eleven are nominated directly by the prime minister.

The Senate elected in April 1982 had the following party distribution: Fianna Fail—28; Fine Gael—19; Labour—6; independent university representatives—4; independent Fianna Fail—1; others—2. Since the constitution prescribes that an election to the Senate shall take place not later than ninety days after the *Dail* election, the new *Dail* and new *taoiseach* participate in the Senate election.

Judiciary

Ireland's court of final appeal is a Supreme Court of five judges and a chief justice appointed by the president on the advice of the government. Neither Supreme Court judges nor those of lesser courts can be removed from office except by resolution of both houses of the legislature and then only for express misconduct or incapacity. The president may refer bills passed by the legislature to the Supreme Court for a determination of their constitutionality. Money bills and a few others are excluded from this provision.

Regional & Local Government

Local government in Ireland is handled by 115 elected bodies ranging from county councils down to town commissions. Elections to these bodies take place at least every five years and are hard fought by the national parties, which win seats in proportion to their share of the vote. The councils, particularly those of the counties, have considerable independence, including the right to collect taxes.

The Electoral System

The members of the *Dail* and the Senate are elected by the single transferable vote (STV) method of proportional representation. This system allows the voter to indicate a second choice, which is counted if the voter's first choice has more than enough or too few votes to get elected. The system requires that a candidate must win a certain quota of votes to be elected. The quota equals the total district vote divided by the number of district seats to be filled, plus one additional vote. For example, a candidate running for a seat in a three-member district in which 3,000 people have voted, must win 1,001 votes to be elected. It does not require the creation of ranked party lists, permits voting for individuals, and increases the ties between the elected representative and the constituency.

The STV system was adopted for elections in various British dominions in the early twentieth century; in 1922, when the Irish Free State was established, STV was prescribed both for parliamentary and local elections. A similar provision was inserted in the constitution of 1937 and has remained in force ever since, in spite of two attempts by Fianna Fail governments in 1959 and 1968 to carry constitutional amendments abolishing STV and reverting to the British method of the single nontransferable vote in single-member constituencies.

The standard argument used against STV is that by accurately representing smaller parties it tends to produce a multiparty system and thereby makes stable government more difficult. In fact, in the twenty general elections since the establishment of the Irish Free State, only seven have produced an overall *Dail* majority for a single party; but the consequence has not been government instability. Since 1923 there have been only nine changes of government.

Under the constitution, the constituencies are

represented by at least three deputies, since 1947 they have been represented—based on population—by three, four, or five members. A candidate for Parliament need not be a resident of the constituency in which he runs, a fact which has permitted candidates from Northern Ireland to run on occasion. The constitution provides that constituency boundaries be revised not less than every twelve years to take account of population movements, and that the ratio of deputies to population be not less than one per 30,000 or more than one per 20,000. All such revisions up to 1981 were made by the government of the day; the last revision was made by an independent commission chaired by a judge. The present distribution is fifteen five-seat, thirteen four-seat and thirteen three-seat constituencies—a lower proportion of the last category of constituencies than at any time since 1947.

The ballot lists the names of all candidates in the constituency alphabetically, with the party designation noted after the name. All those over age eighteen who are on the register (based on an anual house-to-house survey) and not subject to any prohibitive disability are entitled to vote. In 1981, the total number on the register was the highest ever, 2,275,450. Although the average turnout in general elections held since the end of the Second World War has been 74.5 percent, it slumped to 73.8 percent in the general election of February 1982. By-elections take place in the whole constituency, regarded as a single-seat area for the purpose.

The Party System

Origins of the Parties

The two main parties, Fianna Fail and Fine Gael, owe their origin to the split in the nationalist movement *Sinn Fein* (We Ourselves), which having fought a succesful guerrilla war against British rule between 1919 and 1921 could not agree on the terms of the Anglo-Irish Treaty of December 1921. The larger faction (Cumann na nGael, later Fine Gael) accepted the treaty and dominion status within the British commonwealth; the minority, led by Eamon de Valera, founder of Fianna Fail, refused to settle for less than a republic. For the first twenty-five years of the Irish state, the electoral struggle was essentially between these two parties, but with the increasing ascendancy of Fianna Fail, other parties, including Labour and

various farmers' groups, made headway. In 1948, a coalition of five parties including Fine Gael and Labour ousted de Valera. After 1951, however, the minor parties gradually declined, and in all general elections since 1961, Fianna Fail, Fine Gael, and Labour have secured well over 90 percent of the votes cast. In 1981, there was a minor resurgence of small parties and independents, who together secured 8.3 percent of the national poll.

The Parties in Law

The Irish constitution does not take cognizance of the existence of political parties, but their activities are governed by several statutes, including the Electoral Act of 1963. That act conferred on registered parties certain rights, including the right to advertise in the telephone directory, to include the party designation on the ballot paper (previously not allowed), to receive a subsidy fom public funds in proportion to the seats won at the previous election, and to share in the allocation of broadcast time during an election campaign. Whether a party is registered or not depends on the clerk of the *Dail*, who determines if it is a bona fide organization. (The Provisional Sinn Fein party, believed to be the political wing of the Provisional I.R.A., has been refused recognition.) Television advertising by political parties is prohibited by law. A candidate for election to the *Dail* must put up a sizable deposit (about $139), which is lost if he fails to get one-third of the quota of votes required for election.

Party Organization

Parties have a three-tier organizational structure—branch, constituency, and national. The constituencies are divided by law into district electoral divisions, comprising parishes (the basic local unit) or clusters of parishes. These districts provide the appropriate areas for the party branches. The function of the branch, apart from fundraising and disseminating party propaganda, is to provide a supply of candidates for elections to local authorities (county, borough, and urban district councils) and also delegates to the next-highest party body, the constituency association.

At the constituency level, delegates from each party branch select the party candidates for *Dail* elections. The constituency association has the sole responsibility for running the election campaigns in the constituency and linking up efficiently with the national organization. All parties, in their rules, confer on the national organization the power to refuse to ratify a candidate selected by a constituency association. This rarely happens, but when it does it is a cause of serious intraparty dissension. In 1981, for example, when the Labour Party governing body refused to ratify the candidacy of an outgoing deputy, Dr. John O'Connell, in the new Dublin South-Central constituency, on the ground that he would be competing against the party leader, Frank Cluskey. Eventually O'Connell stood successfully as an independent and Cluskey was defeated. In recent years, party rules have been changed to allow the leader to nominate his own additional candidate in any constituency he deems fit. Several such additions were made in 1981 and 1982.

On the national level, parties meet annually in an *Ard-Fheis* (Fianna Fail and Fine Gael) or Annual Conference (Labour). These massive gatherings contain two or three delegates from every branch and sometimes delegates also from the constituency bodies, i.e., 6,000 to 7,000 in all. The *Ard-Fheis* (High Meeting) is the major party propaganda exercise in the year—especially when elections are not in the offing. The *Ard-Fheis* is the top policy-making body, although considerable latitude is allowed to a parliamentary bloc in government, which is not bound by conference decisions. On the other hand, all parties regard the national organization as superior to the parliamentary organization, particularly in the Labour Party.

The *Ard-Fheis* also elects the party National Executive Committee—Administrative Council in the Labour Party—which is the governing body of the party between annual conferences. The National Executive is a body of between twenty and forty members, including the party officers. About half of the members of the Executive are also members of the *Oireachtas*. In all parties the leader is elected by the parliamentary bloc. The party bloc leader, the general party leader, and the party president are all one person, except in the Labour Party, where there is a party chairman (equivalent to party president), who presides at the annual conference and Administrative Council meetings.

Campaigning

The most important focus of campaigning is clearly the general election, which must take place every five years, but may occur more frequently. The last three were in 1977, 1981 and 1982. During election campaigns the bulk of party spending goes to newspaper advertising with several full-page advertisements in the same daily newspapers for the two major parties. In recent years extensive use has been made of television and public-relations techniques in projecting the party image. Party appearances on television and radio during an election campaign are limited by law and subject to agreement between the parties.

The state subsidy is for ordinary party expenses, not electioneering. All parties have separate arrangements for raising campaign funds, and there are no legal restraints on the amount spent. Estimated expenditures for all parties in the 1981 election were about IR £1.8 million (about $2.5 million).

Independent Voters

In the early years of the republic, independent candidates and minor parties flourished. Two separate agrarian parties successfully contested *Dail* elections between 1922 and 1933, and 1943 and 1961, respectively. Other minor parties won seats in the elections between 1927 and 1933 and between 1943 and 1957.

Some of these parties were extreme republican groups anxious to reunify the country by force, if necessary; others were middle-class groups. Since the election of 1961, the votes for independent and minor-party candidates have declined sharply, and the number of independent deputies in *dails* elected between 1965 and 1981 never exceeded four. However, in 1981 a small urban Marxist group called Sinn Fein—The Workers' Party, which was descended from a militant republican Sinn Fein group that had secured representation in 1957, won 1.7 percent of the vote and one seat, which increased to 2.3 percent of the vote and three seats in 1982.

An independent candidate, pledged to inner-city renewal, was also elected in Dublin in 1982. While in 1981, the wave of public sympathy following the prolonged hunger-strikes by prisoners in Northern Ireland led to the election of two prisoners in Belfast jail—one of whom subsequently died. Candidates with similar extreme republican leanings gained a mere 1 percent of the national vote in 1982 and none were elected. It would appear that the 1981 vote was largely a sympathy vote and therefore evanescent. However, the increase in the number of five-seat constituencies in the 1980 revision helps minor party and independent candidates. The tradition of hard work by the *Dail* deputy in the constituency—especially acting as an intermediary between the citizen and government departments—has been a dominant feature of the Irish political culture. Independents who win election are generally strong "constituency men" with efficient local machines.

PARTY VOTE IN DAIL ELECTIONS
(percent) (1965–1982)

	'65	'69	'73	'77	'81	'82
Fianna Fail	47.7	45.7	46.2	50.6	45.3	47.3
Fine Gael	34.1	34.1	35.1	30.5	36.5	37.3
Labour	15.4	17.0	13.7	11.6	9.9	9.1
Others	2.8	3.2	5.0	7.3	8.3	6.3

In the past, voter identification with one or another party has been strong, but the parties can no longer rely on voter loyalty. Younger voters in particular show a tendency to vote for personalities or policies regardless of party.

Fianna Fail (Soldiers of Destiny)

History

This party, originally composed of the anti-Treaty wing of Sinn Fein, was formally constituted in 1926 under the leadership of Eamon de Valera, who had been president of the clandestine Irish Republic from 1919 to 1921. From the beginning it was a party of radical republicanism, committed to advancing from the dominion status conferred in 1922 to full independence, restoration of the Irish language, encouragement of Irish industry, and a minimal welfare program for what was then the poorest democracy in Europe. In the fifty years between 1932, when it first came to power, and 1982, Fianna Fail has always been the largest party in the *Dail* and has never fallen below 41 percent of the total national poll in any general election; it has been the party of government for a total of thirty-nine years.

De Valera, a great charismatic leader, retired from active party work on his election to the presidency in 1959. His successor as party leader, Sean Lemass, was a much more pragmatic politician, dedicated to raising the level of economic growth, improving relations with Britain and Northern Ireland, and bringing Ireland into the EEC—an aim delayed by French opposition until 1972. Lemass's successor, Jack Lynch, continued to pursue these objectives. The onset of the disturbances in Northern Ireland in the late 1960s caused the first break in party solidarity. In 1970, two ministers (including Charles Haughey) were dismissed from the cabinet for allegedly helping to smuggle arms into Northern Ireland. The ministers were acquitted at a subsequent trial, but a rift

was opened up between the extreme republican and moderate wings of the party. In June 1977, the moderate Lynch won a great electoral victory, (over 50 percent of the total poll). When Lynch retired in December 1979 on the grounds of ill health, he was succeeded by Haughey, who, in a contested election among the members of the parliamentary party, secured forty-four votes to thirty-eight for a staunch supporter of Lynch.

Haughey narrowly lost the election of 1981 and was replaced by a Fine Gael–Labour coalition under Garret FitzGerald, leader of Fine Gael. However, the life of the coalition was precarious, depending on support from four independents. When the budget of 1982, which imposed heavy taxes on clothing and footwear, was defeated, ensuing elections gave Fianna Fail three more seats—just two short of an overall majority. Fianna Fail formed a government (March 9, 1982) with the support of two independents, but not before an attempt was made to replace Haughey as leader by a former Lynch supporter, Desmond O'Malley.

Organization

From its outset Fianna Fail has claimed to be a national movement, not just a party, and its organization has been structured accordingly. The branch (or *cumainn*) established at parish level in the rural areas, or ward level in the towns, since the 1930s has extended throughout the country. Fianna Fail *cumainn* are strongest in the west of Ireland and weakest in the Dublin region.

Above the *cumainn*, the constituency associations (*comhairli*) perform the clearly defined functions of recruitment and propaganda. The *Ard-Fheis*, the supreme party body, generally rubber stamps the policies proposed by the party leadership. Its support of Jack Lynch in 1971 greatly strengthened his hand against the dissidents of the time. This, the most serious dispute in the history of the party, was settled by the mass party, not just the parliamentary group. In 1974 the *Ard-Fheis* established a youth committee in every constituency. Party headquarters are on Upper Mount Street, Dublin 2.

Policy

Fianna Fail is identified with policies of law and order, support for the EEC, neutrality, Irish reunification by consent, economic cooperation with the United Kingdom, and a high level of public expenditure to cope with the growing unemployment rate. These policies are not mutually consistent.

The neutrality policy, born of Ireland's purely pragmatic neutrality during the Second World War, is held by Fianna Fail's opponents to inhibit a full commitment to the EEC. The policy on Northern Ireland, which presently involves opposing any British initiative which does not explicitly provide for eventual reunification, has worsened relations with Great Britain. The public-expenditure policies under the last Fianna Fail government led to increasing budget deficits and a level of borrowing which in 1982 would have amounted to almost one-quarter of the estimated gross national product. These policies were denounced by the Fine Gael–Labour government as leading the country into bankruptcy and tacitly replaced with a policy of fiscal conservatism when the Haughey government of March 1982 accepted the targets of the abortive budget of the previous January. The only significant exception is a program of over $139 million for inner-city development in Dublin—the price charged by a newly elected independent deputy to support Haughey's return to power.

Membership & Constituency

In 1981 Fianna Fail had about 55,000 members in 2,676 cumainn, an increase of 200 cumainn over 1979. Party members comprised about one of every fourteen Fianna Fail voters in February 1982.

According to a February 1982 survey, Fianna Fail electoral support broke down into the following categories: 48 percent of men, 46 percent of women, 42 percent of youth under twenty-five years of age, 51 percent of persons over sixty-five, 35 percent of the top social classes, 49 percent of the working classes, and 48 percent of farmers. The Protestants in the republic are so few—4 percent of the population—that they are not included in sample surveys. It is believed that they divide in roughly equal proportions between Fianna Fail and Fine Gael, with a minority supporting Labour.

Surveys in Ireland do not investigate the socioeconomic characteristics of party members, merely the partisan cohorts in the electorate. However, from observation it can be said that Fianna Fail activists are predominantly middle class, with a sprinkling of trade unionists. Although most trade-union leaders profess adherence to the Labour Party, some of the most prominent support Fianna Fail. The leadership of Fianna Fail consists of prosperous professionals and businessmen.

Financing

Fianna Fail receives financial support in three ways. Membership dues of 50 pence to £1 ($0.70 to $1.40) annually, which are used to support the cumainn throughout the country. The total is not published. A national collection taken up annually (in rural areas, at church gates on Sunday), produced over $400,000 in 1980. This is used to pay for the headquarters staff, and organize the Ard-Fheis and other central activities. The balance (about $154,000 in 1980) is returned to the constituency associations. Lastly, the party receives a government subsidy (about $150,000 in 1981). Election fund-raising is kept separate from the day-to-day running of the party. Parties do not publish the details of their campaign expenditures, but it is believed that Fianna Fail gets considerable help from large firms. Expenditures on newspaper advertising and the leader's helicopter tours of the country during the election campaign of 1981 would suggest a total campaign budget approaching $1.5 million.

Leadership

Until the retirement of Eamon de Valera in June 1959, after a total of twenty-one years as head of government, virtually all the Fianna Fail leaders were of the "Treaty generation." Lemass quickly promoted younger men of whom Lynch, Haughey, and the current president of Ireland, Dr. Patrick Hillery, were the most prominent. By the time Jack Lynch succeeded to the leadership in 1966, the Treaty generation had passed from the scene. All of Haughey's cabinet are under sixty and the average age is forty-seven. Present leaders are:

Charles Haughey (born 1925 in Dublin) is prime minister. The party leader since 1979, his power base is in Dublin City.

Raymond MacSharry (born 1938 in Sligo) has been deputy prime minister and minister for finance since March 1982. His power base is in Sligo-Leitrim.

Brian Lenihan (born 1930 in Dundalk) is director of elections and minister for agriculture. His power base is in Dublin City.

Bertie Ahern (born 1951 in Dublin) has been chief whip in Parliament since 1982. The minister of state for defense, he was elected from Dublin West.

Desmond O'Malley, Haughey's most likely replacement, was born in Limerick in 1939. He is minister for trade, commerce, and tourism.

Prospects

The position of Fianna Fail in government remains precarious. Whether it will last the four-year term (1982–86) remains problematical, although after the expense of two general elections within a year, no party would wish for another in the near future. Nevertheless, Fianna Fail would appear certain to remain the largest party in the Dail for some years to come, and there is no sign of the leadership deviating from its consistent aversion to a coalition with any other party. Haughey's hold on the party leadership is still insecure, and Desmond O'Malley, who is openly backed by the former leader, Jack Lynch, remains an obvious rival.

Fine Gael (Irish Tribe)

History

Fine Gael is descended from Cumann na nGael (Society of the Irish), a party formed around the first government to which the British handed over control of the Irish Free State in 1922. Its leader was W. T. Cosgrave, president of the Executive Council (prime minister) of the Irish Free State (1922–32). Cumann na nGael was supported by the propertied and professional classes who wanted a stable regime and looked askance at the revolutionary potential of the anti-Treatyites under de Valera. Unfortunately, the party was very loosely structured and, when supplanted in office by Fianna Fail, found it impossible to recover its previous level of electoral support. In 1933 the party merged with a smaller group, the Centre Party, to form the new Fine Gael under Cosgrave's leadership.

Fine Gael was from its inception a typically conservative party, favoring balanced budgets and low taxation. Its support of the British Commonwealth connection remained, but proved a dwindling asset, especially after the outbreak of the Second World War. While Fianna Fail won six successive general elections, Fine Gael's electoral support declined from 39 percent in 1923 to just under 20 percent in 1948. In 1948, it was mainly a big farmers' party, with a sprinkling of lawyers and professional men in the big cities.

Fine Gael's recovery started in 1948, with the formation of the first coalition government under John A. Costello; the coalition, comprised of five parties, lasted until 1951. In the 1950s Fine Gael proceeded to mop up the electoral support of the smaller parties, and by 1954 it secured 32 percent of the national poll. Fine Gael consolidated its new position with a modern party structure.

From 1965 Fine Gael tried to change its image from a conservative to a socially progressive party with the adoption of a program to expand the very inadequate social services of Ireland. The most outspoken advocate of the change was a young economist, Garret FitzGerald, then a senator. In 1973, Fine Gael formed another coalition, this time with Labour alone, under the leadership of Liam Cosgrave, son of the founder of the party. When Fianna Fail returned to office in 1977, Garret FitzGerald became leader and headed the short-lived coalition with Labour.

Organization

Fine Gael was until 1948 very loosely structured. There was some rudimentary organization in each constituency, but outside the large cities no local organization to speak of. After the party's return to power in 1948, a director of organization was appointed, but the network of branches covering the country was not completed until the 1960s. At present its three-tier structure closely resembles that of Fianna Fail, except that it is particularly strong in the Dublin region and also in Cork. It is weakest in some rural areas on the western periphery (e.g., Kerry and Clare).

The Fine Gael parliamentary party remains relatively uncontrolled by the mass organization and, especially since 1977, the role of the *Ard-Fheis* has become largely that of a sounding board for the leadership. This has caused some murmurings about FitzGerald's decisive and authoritarian style of leadership.

Party headquarters are on Upper Mount Street, Dublin 2.

Policy

Fine Gael is identified with policies of stern repression of subversive organizations, fiscal orthodoxy, protecting the lowest-paid workers by maintaining the level of social services and by tax credits, cultivating good relations with the pro-British Unionist community in Northern Ireland, and continuing in coalition with the Labour Party against Fianna Fail.

The most distinctive feature of Garret FitzGerald's short term as *taoiseach* (June 1981–March 1982) was a "crusade" to educate the public on the necessity of purging the Irish constitution of features that might be repugnant to Ulster Protestants, such as the constitutional ban on divorce, and thereby to hasten the eventual reunification of the country. The downfall of the government brought the crusade to a speedy end, but it still remains Fine Gael policy.

Membership & Constituency

In 1981 the party had approximately 35,000 paid-up members, or about one of every eighteen Fine Gael voters in February 1982.

According to a February 1982 survey, the electoral support of Fine Gael broke down as follows: 33 percent of men, 38 percent of women, 33 percent of youth under age twenty-five, 35 percent of those over age sixty-five, 51 percent of the top social classes, 30 percent of the working classes, and 40 percent of the farmers.

Fine Gael is still the party of the propertied classes—although the very wealthy tend to support Fianna Fail. It has among its activists a high level of barristers, solicitors, and other professionals, and more academics than any other party. Its support is weakest among semiskilled and unskilled workers. Currently, the sole Protestant deputy in the Dail is a Fine Gael member.

Financing

In 1981, Fine Gael secured financial support through membership dues of £1 (about $1.40) per member per year, totaling over $51,000; contributions from deputies and senators, totaling $25,000; a levy on constituency associations for the support of the national organization, totaling $180,000; and the state subsidy, which amounted to nearly $93,000 in 1981. There is no national collection as in Fianna Fail and branches are allowed to raise funds in their own way. Election funds are raised by the "Capital [Dublin] branch"; according to party headquarters, some $834,000 was spent on the 1981 elections and $556,000 in those of 1982.

Leadership

W. T. Cosgrave, founder of Fine Gael, retired in 1944, long before his great rival, de Valera. Subsequent leaders were of the "Treaty generation" until James Dillon (1959–65). Dillon's successor, Liam Cosgrave (1965–77), son of W. T. Cosgrave, embodied the conservative outlook of the party and was not at all sympathetic to the progressive orientation of the party associated with Dr. Garret FitzGerald. FitzGerald succeeded to the leadership in 1977 and seems set to lead the party in the foreseeable future. He is easily the most successful of contemporary Irish politicians in projecting a favorable media image. In the 1982 election, he ran far ahead of Haughey in public esteem. In a poll in February 1982, 56 percent of the sample preferred FitzGerald for prime minister to 33 percent for Haughey. Present leaders are:

Garret FitzGerald (born 1926 in Dublin) has been party leader since 1977. His power base is in Dublin City.

Peter Barry (born 1928 in Cork) is deputy leader. His power base is in Cork.

Sean Barrett (born 1944 in Dublin) has been chief whip since March 1982. He is also based in Dublin.

Prospects

With only eighteen seats less than Fianna Fail, Fine Gael is obviously its main rival for power. The only question is whether the next government will be a coalition with Labour, as has happened four times before, or a one-party government. Generally, Fine Gael is committed to the idea of such a coalition, but the idea is now less popular with Labour than before. At least one prominent Fine Gael member has argued that the party should try to aim at forming a government on its own. Such an objective would of course have been quite unrealistic before the great increase in seats in 1981.

Irish Labour Party

History

The Labour Party is the oldest of the three main parties in the *Dail*. It was founded in May 1912 by James Larkin, who also founded the biggest Irish trade union, the Irish Transport and General Workers' Union, and James Connolly, afterwards executed for his part in the Easter rising of 1916. Until the 1960s, the Irish industrial working class was largely confined to the big cities, Dublin and Cork, and the agricultural laborers and small farmers held aloof. However, even in the 1920s, Labour seemed a significant party, securing over 10 percent of the vote in the first two general elections after independence. After the coming of Fianna Fail to power (with Labour support), the party declined, its support going almost exclusively to Fianna Fail. The party made a significant recovery in 1943, but in the following year a "red scare" caused a split in its ranks which was not healed until 1950. Nevertheless, Labour participated in the 1948–51 and 1954–57 coalitions. Under the leadership of Brendan Corish (1960–77), the party tried to change its character from a simple trade unionists' party to a social-democratic party, and for the first time some prominent intellectuals (Dr. Conor Cruise O'Brien, for example) secured election as Labour deputies. However, the effort to become a major party on the left failed through electoral apathy and Labour entered two coalitions as the minor party with Fine Gael in 1973 and again in 1981. The poor performance of Labour in the February 1982 elections (winning little over 9 percent of the poll) was attributed by some deputies to too close an identification with the conservative fiscal policies of Fine Gael. On the day before the new *Dail* met, the party's Administrative Council voted by a majority of one not to enter a new coalition. The issue of a coalition is likely to be discussed at the next annual conference, but procoalition forces in the party appear to have lost ground in a recent by-election in Dublin when the Labour candidate lost his deposit (failed to get one-third of the quota of votes required for election).

Organization

Labour Party organization is similar to that of Fianna Fail and Fine Gael, except that the constituency associations have no independent life of their own and are merely groups of branches. The organization is strongest in Dublin (120 branches) and weakest in the two provinces of Connacht and Ulster, where there is a total of only twenty branches.

As in social-democratic parties elsewhere, the parliamentary party is deemed to be the servant of the mass party. The annual conference of some 1,200 delegates is the supreme policy-making body, and when, in 1957, it decided against coalitions, the decision had to be rescinded by another conference (1973). The Administrative Council runs the party between annual conferences and the party chairman, not the party leader, presides at its sessions. Of the thirty-five council members only fourteen are parliamentarians and two are trade unionists. The party leader is elected after every general election by majority vote of the Dail deputies. When, as in 1982, the party leader is in favor of Labour joining a future coalition and the party chairman is vehemently opposed, there is considerable tension within the party.

Party headquarters are at 16 Gardiner Place, Dublin 1.

Policy

Labour is identified with the usual social-democratic package: high taxation, extensive social services, public ownership (where possible, especially of the commercial banks), and public expenditure to promote employment. Labour takes an extreme neutralist view and opposes EEC membership. In relation to Northern Ireland, the party is closer to Fine Gael than Fianna Fail, advocating a gradual rapprochement with the Ulster Unionists rather than a commitment to an all-Ireland state. It is also in favor of the FitzGerald "crusade" to rid the Irish constitution of elements that alienate Protestants.

The party suffered considerable heart-searching over its support for the budget of January 1982, and this is one of the causes of the subsequent disillusionment with Fine Gael.

Membership & Constituency

In 1982, the Labour party had 5,500 members (an increase of 1,500 over 1972) organized in 510 branches. Of the branches, 300 are in Dublin and the province of Munster. Party members comprised about one of every twenty-eight Labour voters in February 1982.

According to a February 1982 survey, Labour support in the electorate broke down as follows: 8 percent of men and 6 percent of women; of the age groups it had its greatest support among the 25-to-34-year-old cohort (11 percent); and of the social classes, its greatest support came from semi-skilled and unskilled workers (10 percent).

The Labour Party has always had close links with the Irish trade-union movement. In fact its original title was the Irish Trade Union Congress and Labour Party. At present seventeen unions, including the largest in the country, the Irish Transport and General Workers' Union, are affiliated with the party, and the party secures a proportion of union dues from every affiliated organization. Election returns, however, show that the trade unions are unable to deliver their votes solidly to the Labour party.

Financing

Labour's finances come from party dues; at about $4 per member per year, they total nearly $23,000 per year. Trade-union affiliation fees amount to some $18,000, and the state subsidy was about $44,000 in 1981. Labour has no separate election fund as is the case with the other parties, but party headquarters state that the total party expenditure on the election of 1981 was about $116,000 and on that of 1982, $62,500.

Leadership

The early leaders of the party were all trade unionists. Brendan Corish was a local union government officer and his successor, Michael O'Leary, the education officer for the trade-union movement. Although the intellectual leavening provided by the elections of 1969 and 1973, which concentrated on the party's social-democratic potentials, has all but disappeared, the party leadership is more occupationally mixed than twenty years ago. The party chairman in 1982 was a university lecturer and the chief whip, a lawyer. Present leaders are:

Michael O'Leary (born 1936 in Cork) has been leader since 1977, briefly deputy prime minister in 1981–82. His power base is in Dublin.

Michael D. Higgins (born 1941 in Limerick) is party chairman (1978 to present) and is based in Galway.

Mervyn Taylor (born 1931 in Dublin) became chief whip in 1982.

Prospects

With its persistent failure to secure even 20 percent of the national vote (falling to less than 10 percent in 1981 and 1982) Labour is now threatened from two sides. On the one hand, some of its previous support has swung to Fine Gael; and on the other, it is in danger from the Workers' Party as a party of the radical left, especially in Dublin.

Minor Parties

Only one minor party secured representation in the elections of 1981 and 1982. Other fringe parties participated but secured merely 1 percent, or less, of the national vote.

The Workers' Party (formerly Sinn Fein—The Workers' Party), evolved slowly out of the Official Sinn Fein Party. It is the only party in the republic to have a branch—also called the Workers' Party—in Northern Ireland. Its membership in the republic is about one thousand. It is generally committed to a Marxist program, but is totally opposed to violence. It won one seat in 1981 and three in 1982. Its leader, Thomas MacGiolla, fared quite respectably in a 1982 Dublin by-election and is expected to enter the *Dail* at the next election. The Workers' Party is a radical alternative to Labour.

National Prospects

Between 1960 and 1980, the Irish republic experienced the greatest period of growth in its history. Through a succession of schemes for state-aided industrial investment, the national output was more than doubled, and living standards improved by well over two-thirds for a population which increased by about a fifth. The process of Irish decline, in train since 1850, was thus dramatically reversed.

However, by the election of 1981, all the economic indicators were unfavorable: low growth, high inflation, high unemployment, and excessive borrowing. To cope with this situation (which they blamed on their predecessors), the short-lived coalition turned back to fiscal conservatism. The coalition failed, but Fianna Fail is now still applying its remedies. It remains to be seen whether the next stage—an incomes policy—can be achieved without labor unrest. Fianna Fail is a minority government, but the unlikelihood of Fine Gael and Labour coalescing again in the near future and the impecunious state of all parties after two general elections within a year, probably means that the present government will last its term.

The other major problem for the republic arises from the disturbed state of Northern Ireland, which has spilled over into the republic, depressing tourist earnings and causing much heavier expenditure on the army and police forces. Although violence in Northern Ireland has declined in recent years, there is little promise of real stability. The issue weighs heavily on Irish politics, with the two parties sharply, though quietly, divided over the problem. Fine Gael and Labour see a rapprochement between Protestants and Catholics in Northern Ireland as the necessary condition of any political progress; while the Fianna Fail, true to its Irish republican traditions, refuses to believe that any solution confined to the six counties alone can possibly succeed and argues that any solution must have a built-in "Irish dimension." The outcome, if any of the Northern Ireland struggle could, in the long run, sharply affect the positions of Ireland's parties.

Further Reading
Busteed, M. A. "The 1981 Irish General Election." *Parliamentary Affairs*, Vol. 35, No. 1, 1982.

Chubb, Basil. "Ireland." In *European Political Parties*, S. Henig and J. Pinder, eds. London: Allen and Unwin/PEP, 1969.

Gallagher, Michael. *Electoral Support for Irish Political Parties*. London and Beverly Hills: Sage Publications, 1976.

Garvin, Tom. *The Evolution of Irish Nationalist Politics*. Dublin: Gill and Macmillan, 1981.

Manning, Maurice. *Irish Political Parties*. Dublin: Gill and Macmillan, 1972.

O'Leary, Cornelius. *Irish Elections 1918–1977: Parties, Voters and Proportional Representation*. Dublin: Gill and Macmillan, 1979.

Mair, Peter. "The Autonomy of the Political: The Development of the Irish Party System." *Comparative Politics*, Vol. 11, No. 4, 1979.

———. "Muffling the Swing: STV and the Irish General Election of 1981." *West European Politics*, Vol. 5, No. 1, 1982.

Penniman, Howard R., ed. *Ireland at the Polls*. Washington, D.C.: American Enterprise Institute for Policy Research, 1978.

Whyte, J. H. "Ireland, Politics Without Social Bases." In *Electoral Behavior: A Comparative Handbook*, R. Rose, ed. New York: The Free Press, 1974.

STATE OF ISRAEL
(Medinat Yisrael)
by Bernard Reich, Ph.D.

The System of Government

Israel is a multiparty parliamentary republic of some four million people, of whom 11 percent are Muslim Arabs, 2.5 percent Christians (mostly Arabs), and 1.2 percent Druze, an Arab sect. Among the Jewish population, approximately 55 percent were born in Israel and 45 percent were born elsewhere. An estimated 55 percent are Sephardic Jews, mostly of Middle Eastern and North African origins, while 45 percent are Ashkenazic Jews of European and New World origins. In addition to Israel itself, the Israeli government administers two occupied territories: the West Bank with 700,000 Arabs and the Gaza Strip with 400,000 Arabs. In 1981, Israel extended its law and jurisdiction to the Golan Heights (formerly Syrian) with a population of several thousand Druze. Approximately eighty Israeli settlements have been established on the West Bank.

Although Israel achieved its independence in May 1948, the origins of the political system predate the founding of the state. During the period of the British mandate (1922–48), the Jewish community in Palestine (the *Yishuv* or settlement) established institutions for self-government, including the Assembly of the Elected (*Asefat HaNivcharim*), a representative body chosen by secret ballot. The party system appeared with the first election to the Assembly in 1920, and a system of proportional representation was used to distribute the Assembly's seats.

The Assembly met annually and elected the National Council (*Vaad Leumi*) to exercise administrative responsibility for Jewish communal affairs between Assembly sessions. The National Council functioned alongside the Jewish Agency for Palestine, which was created on the authority of the League of Nations mandate and which included Jewish organizations sympathetic to the idea of a Jewish national home. The Jewish Agency acted as the international diplomatic representative of the *Yishuv*, conducting negotiations with Great Britain, the mandatory government, and the League of Nations, in addition to fund raising and establishing a network of communications with foreign governments. After the United Nations adopted a plan for the partition of Palestine in 1947, a National Council of State was chosen from the National Council and the Jewish Agency executive. This provisional government consisted of a state council (which served as a legislature), a cabinet elected from along the state council's members, and a president elected by the state council. The executive of the National Council became the cabinet. The provisional government functioned from May 14, 1948 (Israel's Independence Day) until February 14, 1949, at which time the state council's authority was transferred to the first *Knesset* (Assembly), a popularly elected, unicameral parliament.

Although Israel has no formal written constitution, a number of Basic Laws have been passed which are intended in time to form portions of a consolidated constitutional document: The *Knesset* (1958); The Lands of Israel (1960); The President (1964), The Government (1968); The State Economy (1975), The Army (1976); and Jerusalem, The Capital of Israel (1980).

Executive

The president is the head of state and is elected by the *Knesset* for a five-year term. He may be reelected. His powers and functions are primarily formal and ceremonial; his actual political power is very limited. Potentially, his most important role is selecting a member of the *Knesset* to form a government. The political composition of the *Knesset* has so far determined this selection, but it is possible that different combinations of parties could gain the support of the *Knesset*, thereby giving the president a crucial role in determining which person might form the next cabinet.

The prime minister as head of government is the chief executive officer and wields considerable power. He or she determines the agenda of cabinet meetings and has the final word in policy

KNESSET ELECTION RESULTS (1961–1981)

	1961		1965		1969		1973		1977		1981*	
	%	Seats	%	Seats	%	Seats	%	Seats	%	Seats	%	Seats
Herut	13.8	17	—	—	—	—	—	—	—	—	—	—
Liberal	13.6	17	—	—	—	—	—	—	—	—	—	—
Gahal[a]	—	—	21.3	26	21.7	26	—	—	—	—	—	—
Ind. Liberals	—	—	3.8	5	3.2	4	3.6	4	1.2	1	0.6	0
Shlomzion[b]	—	—	—	—	—	—	—	—	1.9	2	—	—
Free Center[c]	—	—	—	—	1.2	2	—	—	—	—	—	—
Likud[d]	—	—	—	—	—	—	30.2	39	33.4	43	37.1	48
Tehiya	—	—	—	—	—	—	—	—	—	—	2.3	3
Telem	—	—	—	—	—	—	—	—	—	—	1.6	2
Mapai	34.7	42	—	—	—	—	—	—	—	—	—	—
Mapam	7.5	9	6.6	8	—	—	—	—	—	—	—	—
Rafi[e]	—	—	7.9	10	—	—	—	—	—	—	—	—
Achdut HaAodah	6.6	8	—	—	—	—	—	—	—	—	—	—
State List[f]	—	—	—	—	3.1	4	—	—	—	—	—	—
Alignment[g]	—	—	36.7	45	46.2	56	39.7	51	24.6	23	36.6	47
Nat. Religious Party	9.8	12	9.0	11	9.7	12	8.3	10	9.2	12	4.9	6
Agudat Yisrael	3.7	4	3.3	4	3.2	4	—	—	3.4	4	3.7	4
Paolei Agudat	1.9	2	1.8	2	1.8	2	—	—	1.4	1	0.8	0
Torah Religious Front[h]	—	—	—	—	—	—	3.8	5	—	—	—	—
Arab Parties	3.5	4	3.4	4	3.5	4	2.4	3	1.4	1	—	—
Communist Parties	4.2	5	3.4	4	4.0	4	3.4	4	4.6	5	3.4	4
Haolam Hazeh	—	—	1.2	1	1.2	2	—	—	—	—	—	—
Citizens Rights	—	—	—	—	—	—	2.2	3	1.2	1	1.4	1
DMC	—	—	—	—	—	—	—	—	—	—	11.6	15
Moked	—	—	—	—	—	—	1.4	1	—	—	—	—
Shelli[j]	—	—	—	—	—	—	—	—	1.6	2	0.5	0
Flatto-Sharon[k]	—	—	—	—	—	—	—	—	2.0	1	—	—
Tami	—	—	—	—	—	—	—	—	—	—	2.3	3
Shinuy	—	—	—	—	—	—	—	—	—	—	1.5	2

*Nineteen-eighty-one election data: eligible voters, 2,490,014; total voters, 1,954,609; turnout, 78.5 percent; total valid votes, 1,937,366; votes for parties not winning seats, 99,903 (5 percent); quota to enter *Knesset,* 18,375; number of votes earning one seat, 15,312. First-round distribution allocated 113 seats; of the remainder, Likud received two; the Alighment, Shinuy, Telem, Tehiya, and Tami received one each.

[a] 1965 alliance of Herut and Liberals.

[b] Joined Likud after 1977.

[c] Formed 1968 as a splinter from Herut.

[d] 1973 alliance of Gahal, Free Center, and State List.

[e] Formed 1965 as a splinter from Mapai.

[f] Joined Likud alliance in 1973.

[g] 1965 alliance of Mapai and Achdut HaAvodah; incorporated Rafi in 1968 to form Israel Labor Party; 1969 alliance of Labor and Mapam.

[h] Joint list of Agudat Yisrael and Paolei Agudat Yisrael.

[i] Party of Yigael Yadin, included portions of Yadin's Democratic Movement, Shinuy, the Free Center, and members of the Labor Alignment; dissolved before 1981 elections.

[j] Formed 1977, from Moked, Haolam Hazeh, and independent socialists.

[k] A one-man party founded by Shmuel Flatto-Sharon.

decisions, although such decisions are often arrived at by hard bargaining and compromise among the coalition of parties participating in the government. The prime minister's ultimate weapon in controlling the coalition is the threat to resign, which would mean the fall of the government. A more common tool of prime ministerial power is the principle of collective responsibility: once a policy is determined, cabinet members must support it in the *Knesset* or resign, although exceptions in specific policy areas are sometimes agreed to in advance as the price a minor party exacts for joining the cabinet and supporting the government.

The prime minister's powers are limited by the fact that he cannot dismiss a cabinet member or dissolve the Parliament without its approval. Even the prime minister's resignation does not mean new elections for the *Knesset*, but only the formation of a new cabinet, perhaps with a slightly different coalition of parties. A new government is constitutionally established when it receives a vote of confidence from the *Knesset*. The maximum term of a government and the *Knesset* is four years.

From the outset, Israel's governments have been coalitions of several political parties. This is the result of several factors: the intensity with which political views are held, the proportional representation voting system, and the multiplicity of parties. These factors have made it all but impossible for a party to win an absolute majority of seats in the *Knesset*. Despite the constant need for coalition governments, they have proved to be quite stable; no government has been forced from office by a vote of no confidence.

The stability of Israel's cabinets and political life has several bases. Political life in Israel has been dominated by a small and relatively cohesive elite that has held positions in government and other major institutions since the period preceding independence. The strength of the Labor Party until 1977 and, thereafter, Prime Minister Begin's political skills have also contributed to stability. Rigorous party discipline in the *Knesset* has helped to curb irresponsible action by individual *Knesset* members.

The coalition system has resulted in the acceptance of bargaining as a procedure for the allocation of government portfolios and the distribution of power, as well as being a factor in determining government policy. This has permitted the religious parties, particularly the National Religious Party, to play strong roles in government decision-making because they are essential components of any parliamentary majority.

Legislature

The *Knesset*, a unicameral body of 120 members, is the supreme authority in the state. The *Knesset*'s main functions are similar to those of other modern parliaments and include votes of confidence or no confidence in the government, legislation, participation in the formulation of national policy, approval of budgets and taxation, election of the president, and generally supervising the activities of the administration. Legislation is usually presented by the cabinet, although a member of the *Knesset* (MK) can initiate private bills. Bills are drafted by ministerial committees in consultation with the Ministry of Justice, approved by the cabinet, and sent to the speaker of the *Knesset* who sends the bill to the appropriate committee for consideration. The legislation is read and voted on three times and is passed by a simple majority of MKs present at the time of the vote. An absolute majority is required for the election of the president and state comptroller and for changes in the system of proportional representation and the Basic Laws.

The state comptroller's office, which functions as an arm of the *Knesset*, oversees the accounts and operations of government ministries and other state bodies. Critical reports from the controller usually bring reforms.

Judiciary

The judiciary consists of two court systems, secular and religious. Judges for both types of courts are appointed by the president upon recommendation by the nominations committee chaired by the justice minister. This committee consists of the president of the Supreme Court and two other Supreme Court justices, two MKs, one other cabinet member, and two members of the Chamber of Advocates (Israel's bar association). The Supreme Court is the highest court in the land. It hears appeals from lower courts in civil and criminal cases, issues writs of *habeas corpus*, protects the rights of the Israeli citizen, and protects the individual from arbitrary actions by public officials. The Supreme Court does not have the power of judicial review, but it may invalidate administrative actions and ordinances it regards as contrary to *Knesset* legislation. There are five district courts and numerous municipal and magistrate courts on the local level. The military courts are under the purview of the Military Court of Appeal, which is responsible to the Supreme Court.

Religious courts have jurisdiction over personal matters including marriage and divorce, alimony, inheritance, etc. The High Rabbinical Court of Appeal is the highest Jewish religious court and is overseen by the Ashkenazic and Sephardic chief rabbis. Its decisions are final. Christian and Muslim courts function in the same capacity.

All judges are tenured, holding office until death, resignation, mandatory retirement at age seventy, or removal for cause.

Regional & Local Government

Israel is divided into six administrative districts under the jurisdiction of district commissioners and fourteen subdistricts overseen by district officers. These officials are appointed by and responsible to the interior minister. A district official drafts legislation pertaining to local government, approves and controls local tax rates and budgets, reviews and approves by-laws and ordinances passed by locally elected councils, approves local public works projects, and decides matters of grants and loans to local governments.

Local and regional councils are elected by universal, secret, direct, proportional balloting. Mayors are chosen from among these councilmen with the same sort of coalition bargaining as occurs in the *Knesset*. *Kibbutzim* (collectives), *moshavim* (cooperatives), and other types of settlements are also governed by elected councils. Local governments are responsible for providing education, health and sanitation services, water, road maintenance, park and recreation facilities, fire houses, and setting and collecting local taxes and fees.

The Electoral System

Elections for the *Knesset* are national, general, equal, secret, direct, and proportional. Every citizen eighteen years of age or older has the right to vote, but must be twenty-one years old in order to run for a *Knesset* seat. The same rules apply to local elections.

The individual voter casts his ballot for a party list, not for an individual candidate. The list is prepared by each party, which ranks from one to 120 candidates on the list. The list stands for the entire country as a single constituency; there are no by-elections. If a seat in the Knesset becomes vacant, the next person on that party's list takes the seat. Elections are held by law at least every four years, but can occur more frequently. Participation is very high, averaging about 80 percent of eligible voters.

Elections are supervised by the Central Election Committee, composed of representatives of each political party in the outgoing *Knesset*, and chaired by a justice of the Supreme Court.

The proportional representation system is based on the d'Hondt system. Parties receiving at least 1 percent of the valid votes cast are entitled to a seat in the *Knesset*. The distribution is determined by dividing the total number of valid votes for all the lists that obtained at least 1 percent of the valid vote by the number of *Knesset* seats, the result being the quota required to obtain one seat. Each list receives the largest number of seats which can be determined by this process. The remaining seats are then distributed to those parties with the largest number of surplus votes. Any leftover seats go to the parties which have already won the greatest number of seats.

The Party System

Origins of the Parties

Israel's political parties trace their origins to the 1920s and 1930s when three categories of parties developed in the *Yishuv*: the labor or socialist left, the center and rightist nationalist grouping, and the religious parties. These formal parties, in turn, grew out of movements, clubs, and other groups that began to develop around the Zionist movement in Europe at the turn of the century. A few new parties, mostly small, have developed directly out of Israel's recent political experiences, e.g., Sephardic parties and parties taking a "dovish" stand on the Arab-Israeli conflict.

The Parties in Law

The only restriction on the formation of a new party is that its list may be disqualified if its candidates espouse the aim of destroying the state or the political system. New parties must collect signatures of supporters and post a bond before being allowed to campaign. These requirements, which are easily met, have permitted the creation of a large number of parties. The bond is forfeited if the party does not win at least one seat. Access to radio and television is provided by the government in proportion to the parties' strength in the outgoing *Knesset*, with a minimum set aside for each party and each new list. The state also provides some financial assistance to the parties according to the number of seats held in the previous *Knesset*. New parties get a set amount.

Campaign expenditures are limited by law. All election expense accounts are audited by the state comptroller but are made public only in aggregate.

Party Organization

Political activity in Israel is highly ideological, often personalistic, and often based upon alliances of two or more parties. Charismatic individuals often contribute to a party's success (Ben-Gurion, Begin), and the formation of electoral alliances (Gahal, Likud, Israel Labor–Mapam Alignment) help the individual parties maximize their strength and influence on policy without losing their ideological identities. Smaller parties may consist of no more than one or two *Knesset* members and their loyal supporters, who are generally highly organized.

Israeli parties are marked by centralized leadership. The Central committee and party oligarchs are chosen by party elections, but control of the party machinery, determining the rankings on the party's national election list and thus the candidates' chances of winning a seat in the *Knesset*. This central control extends to the local-government level. Party branches are often permitted more flexibility in choosing candidates for local office, but party necessities may also require that such candidates be chosen by the party nominating committee or be imposed by the requirements of an alliance or government coalition agreement. The parties are highly disciplined. All viewpoints may be aired in annual conventions and intense bargaining can occur between factions, but once a policy is decided upon, members are expected to support it, keep silent or quit the party.

In addition to campaigning and party business in the *Knesset*, the major parties engage in a great variety of other activities: publishing; housing projects; recreational facilities; various types of cooperatives; banking; and in the case of the religious parties, large educational systems. All the major parties maintain a variety of auxiliary organizations for youth, women, and other special groups.

Israeli party membership as a percentage of eligible voters is unusually high. Membership is not required, but many voters join a party as a matter of civic duty and "fraternal" responsibility, and to participate in intra-party elections. There are also some practical advantages to party membership and activity as the parties have considerable patronage to distribute. Their economic activities can provide both employment and security for party members.

Within the major groupings of left, center-right, and religious parties, the life of parties and alignments is fluid. Parties form, merge, split, dissolve, change names, and reform. Many small parties are formed primarily to advocate a special point of view on a very narrow subject and have little hope of winning a *Knesset* seat. Others are the personal followings of major political figures who can lead their supporters into and out of alliances and mergers as necessary to further their effect on policy or advance their personal ambitions. Some of these small parties do not clearly fit into the three major groupings, but from time to time may become aligned with one of them. Many parties form in preparation for national elections and dissolve or merge soon after. In 1981, some thirty-eight parties prepared to contest the elections; thirty-one finally ran candidates. Outside of the Likud alliance and the Labor Alignment, only eight of those parties won seats.

Campaigning

Political campaigning takes place both within the parties and between the parties on the national scene. Within the parties, the goal is to achieve leadership positions and high positions on the election list; nationally, it is to secure as many votes as possible for the party. Campaigning focuses more on parties than individuals, although at times individuals have been made the focus of opposition efforts. The campaigns involve television and radio appeals, substantial use of newspaper and magazine space, and rallies. Generally, the parties seek to rally their traditional supporters and to sway the small number of uncommitted voters. Domestic issues have tended to be the focal points of discussion, but foreign and security policy developments have often affected the outcome, such as in 1981. Given the small size of the country and its population, extensive appearances of the parties' leading candidates throughout the state are an important aspect of the campaign.

Independent Voters

Party loyalty and voter identification with specific parties is very high. Electoral patterns in national and local elections are very largely the same. Voter identification within the three blocs—left, center-right, and religious—is even stronger, and voters crossing from one bloc to another are relatively rare. Within the two secular blocs, there are small groups of uncommitted voters who may shift from one party to another in support of a particular personality or policy.

Because of the diversity and fluidity of party formation, the discussion of parties below will concentrate on the three general groupings, providing detailed data only for Herut, Labor, and the National Religious Party. Additional paragraphs will briefly cover minor parties which do not clearly fit into the major groups.

THE RIGHT-CENTER
Likud (Union)

Likud was established in 1973 and the present form of the alliance crystalized at the time of the 1977 elections. It consists of the Gahal alliance (Herut and Liberals); the La'am alliance (the State List and the Free Center); Achdut (a one-man faction in the *Knesset*); and Shlomzion, Ariel Sharon's former party. Likud came to power in Israel in 1977, ousting the Labor government for the first time since Israel became independent. Although it retained its government position after the 1981 elections, its majority in the Knesset seldom exceeds two or three votes. Likud is right of center, strongly nationalist, and assertive in foreign policy. All the Likud parties, including those previously allied in Gahal, retained their own organizational structures and memberships, except Shlomzion. Menachem Begin's Herut party is the dominant force in Likud.

Tenuat HaHerut
(Freedom Movement)

History

Herut is descended from the Revisionist movement of Vladimir Zeev (Jabotinsky; 1880–1940), who settled in Palestine after World War I and is regarded by many as the leading Zionist figure after Theodore Herzl, Zionism's founder. The Revisionists advocated militant ultranationalistic action as the means to achieve Jewish statehood. Revisionism called for the creation of a Jewish state in "Greater Israel" (all Palestine and Jordan), rapid mass immigration of Jews into Palestine, formation of a free-enterprise economy, rapid industrialization—as opposed to agricultural settlements—to increase employment opportunities, a ban on strikes, and a strong army. In order to effect these policies, and because they were outnumbered by leftist and moderate ele-

ments in the Zionist Organization, the Revisionists formed the New Zionist Organization in 1935. Their rejection of the socialist and liberal Zionist leadership and its conciliatory policy toward the mandatory power led Revisionists to form two paramilitary groups: Irgun Zvai Leumi (Etzel), founded 1937, and the even more radical Lechi (Stern Gang), founded 1939–40. The Irgun was commanded by Menachem Begin after 1943. Betar, the Revisionist youth movement, was founded by Jabotinsky in 1920 and continues as the Herut youth wing today. Begin founded Herut in June 1948 to advocate the Revisionist program within the new political context of the State of Israel.

Organization

Herut organization is highly complicated, varying from place to place, institution to institution, and election to election. While democratic procedures are used within the party and rank-and-file members can influence minor decisions, a small leadership group dominated by Begin determines party policy.

Herut and Likud headquarters are at 4 Etzel Street, Tel Aviv.

Policy

Herut's political orientation has changed little over the years. It advocates the "inalienable" right of Jews to settle anywhere in Israel, in its historic entirety, including Judea and Samaria (the West Bank). Other policies include a minimum of economic controls, a restructured free enterprise system to attract capital investment, and the right to strike.

Membership & Constituency

Israeli political parties are reluctant to reveal membership figures for fear that changes over the years might reveal negative trends in a party's fortunes. There is no reliable estimate of the numbers of Herut members. Herut's electoral strength comes mainly from the Ashkenazic poor and from the Sephardim. The latter generally have a lower level of education, are more traditional in religion and culture, and are less familiar with socialist theory than most Ashkenazim. It has been suggested that Begin's uncompromising attitude toward the Arabs, his strong leadership qualities, and his personal combination of both the national and religious elements in Judaism have attracted many of Herut's voters.

Financing

No reliable information is available on Herut finances or sources of income. Most income derives from membership dues and donations.

Leadership

Within Herut and Likud, the primary force remains Menachem Begin (born 1913 in Poland), regarded by many as an heroic figure because of his role as a leader of the underground in the Israeli struggle for independence. Begin is extremely skillful as a politician and has managed to maintain his governments (1977–81, 1981 to present) with only a thin majority in face of several votes of no confidence and, at times, decreased public confidence in his leadership.

In the event of Begin's retirement or death, a strong contender for the position of prime minister and leader of Likud is Ariel (Arik) Sharon (born 1928), former general and minister of agriculture and minister of defense. Sharon has advocated a policy of expansion of Israeli settlements throughout the occupied territories, especially the West Bank. Much of Sharon's political support comes from the conservative wing of Likud, as well as from ultranationalist religious factions in and outside of Likud. He is a controversial figure, particularly since the massacre by Christian Phalangists of Palestinians in refugee camps in Lebanon. He is, nevertheless, likely to remain a major figure in the party, although his many detractors see him as abrasive, headstrong, and unpredictable. Sharon established his own party, Shlomzion, which won two seats in 1977, but later merged it with Likud.

Sharon's chief rival within the party is Yitzhak Shamir, the present foreign minister, who belongs to the original nucleus of Herut and is a close confidant of Begin. Shamir is in his late sixties.

Prospects

Likud under Menachem Begin's leadership seems likely to remain in power in the near future, barring a major scandal over the war in Lebanon and the massacre in Beirut. Begin has said that he would retire from public life at age seventy (in 1983). His health has been of some concern. His successor as leader of the Likud (and the government) would likely be either Foreign Minister Yitzhak Shamir, Ariel Sharon, or Deputy Prime Minister and Minister of Construction and Housing David Levy. Current indications are that such a change (especially if elections are needed) would increase the strength of Likud at the expense of both the Labor opposition and the smaller parties. This prospect may well be altered, perhaps substantially, by the potential scandal noted above. The constituency of Likud appears to be a solid and growing portion of the population while that of Labor appears to be on the decline.

Liberal Party
(HaMiflagah HaLiberalit)

The Liberal Party's beginnings can be traced to middle-of-the-road Zionists who wanted to unify Zionists without regard to socialist, Revisionist, or religious feelings. They stressed industrial development and private enterprise. This group split into two wings in 1935: General Zionists A, the larger of the two groups, on the left and General Zionists B on the right. Both were comprised of industrialists, merchants, landlords, white-collar professionals, and intellectuals. The two factions merged in 1946 to form the General Zionist Party; split again in 1948, when the one group formed the Progressive Party; and merged again in 1961 as the Liberal Party. The party won seventeen seats in the 1961 election, the same as Herut. In 1965, Herut and the Liberals set up an electoral alliance, Gahal.

Seven Liberals in the *Knesset* refused to join Gahal and formed the Independent Liberal Party. From 1965 to 1977, the Independent Liberals averaged about 3.5 percent of the vote and retained four or five *Knesset* seats. In 1971, they won only one seat, and in 1981, with only 0.6 percent of the vote, they disappeared from the *Knesset*.

In the meantime, in 1973, retired general Ariel Sharon, then a member of the Liberal Party within Gahal, advocated a wider union of parties which could present itself as a genuine alternative to the Labor Alignment. Sharon and former air force commander Ezer Weizmann successfully brought the Free Center Party, the State List, and the Land of Israel Movement (a nonparty group advocating immediate Israeli settlement and development of the occupied territories) into the Herut-Liberal alliance to form Likud. The Liberals are presently led by Simcha Erlich (born 1915). Party headquarters are at 48 HaMelech George Street, Tel Aviv.

Free Center Party
(HaMerkaz HaHofshi)

This party was founded by Shmuel Tamir (born 1923) in 1967, when he and two other *Knesset* members split from the Herut party. The Free Center rejoined Herut in 1973. Subsequently, the larger portion of the former Free Center, excluding Tamir, joined the La'am faction (organized in 1977) within Likud. Tamir joined Yadin's Democratic Movement.

State List

Originally founded in 1968 by David Ben-Gurion, Israel's first prime minister, when he and a few of his followers refused to join in the new Israel Labor Party, the State List won four seats in 1969 when it could still be considered a party of the left. In 1973, sizable remnants of the party joined the Likud alliance, eventually merging with other groups to form La'am. The group is led by Yigal Hurvitz.

Telem

Telem was Moshe Dayan's party for the 1981 elections. Dayan died in October 1980, but the party won two seats in the *Knesset*. Those two members joined the Likud and the party dissolved.

Tehiya (Renaissance)

Tehiya is a party of "true believers" focusing on the Land of Israel with an ideological fervor reminiscent of Israel's political parties in the early years of independence and before. It is composed of both religious and secular elements and appeals strongly to Israel's youth. It has a component from *Gush Emunim* (Bloc of the Faithful), but various secularists and secular-oriented groupings are also involved. Tehiya includes old associates of Menachem Begin from the anti-British underground. Former Herut Knesset members (Geula Cohen) and Land of Israel Movement personalities have also joined. Tehiya's origins are in the Camp David Accords (which they would like to see revised in favor of a more hardline stance) and the Egypt-Israel Peace Treaty, which called for total withdrawal from Sinai and commitment to autonomy for the Palestinians. They believe that Begin has sold out and that the occupied territories must remain in Israel's hands. The party's head is Professor Yuval Ne'eman (a physicist from Tel Aviv University), a leading nuclear scientist with a long-standing role in the defense establishment. In July 1982, Tehiya joined the ruling coalition of Menachem Begin's Likud. This move seemed to help ensure Tehiya's future and to help strengthen the opposition in the government to concessions concerning Palestinian autonomy in the West Bank. Ne'eman became Minister of Science and Technology.

THE LEFT
Alignment (*Maarach*)

The Alignment is an alliance between the Israel Labor Party and Mapam formed in 1969. The Labor Party in turn was formed in 1968 by Mapai, the dominant partner, *Achdut HaAvodah*, and most of Rafi. Mapam and the Labor Party retain their own organizations and memberships.

Israel Labor Party
(*Mifleget HaAvodah HaYisraelit*)

History

Mapai (*Mifleget Poalei Yisrael;* Israel Workers Party), originated with the union of two smaller parties in 1930, but the roots of the movement can be traced back to the turn of the century in Europe, especially Russia. Mapai soon became the dominant party in Israel. The two parties which formed it had established the trade-union federation Histadrut in 1920, and under their leadership Histadrut became the embodiment of Jewish Palestine. Mapai controlled it as well as the National Assembly and the Jewish Agency. Many of the noted figures in the creation of Israel came out of Mapai—Ben-Gurion, Moshe Sharett (Shertok), Golda Meir (Myerson), Moshe Dayan, and others.

After Israel became independent, Mapai consistently won the largest number of votes in *Knesset* elections, usually about one-third of the total. It was the leading member of all government coalitions and ordinarily held the key portfolios of defense, foreign affairs, and finance, as well as the prime ministership. The party permeated the government, the bureaucracy, the economy, and most of the other institutions of Israel. It joined with two other parties to form the Israel Labor Party.

One of these, *Achdut HaAvodah*, originally the party of Ben-Gurion in the 1920s, was militantly class conscious in its early years. It was merged with Mapai from 1930 to 1944, when it left in disagreement with Mapai's gradualist policies, the prohibition of party factions, and the general exclusion of more radical elements from Mapai leadership. It rejoined Mapai in 1965.

The other group, Rafi, appeared in 1965, when Ben Gurion and his proteges, Moshe Dayan and Shimon Peres, left Mapai, partly out of dissatisfaction with the leadership of Levi Eshkol. Rafi advocated more technocratic efficiency in government, the transfer of some of the Histadrut's functions to the state, and reform of the electoral system in favor of single-member districts with simple plurality elections. Rafi stood alone for only one election (1965) and gained a respectable ten seats in the *Knesset*. It merged with Mapai and *Achdut HaAvodah* in 1968 to form the Israel Labor Party. The new party retained Mapai's dominant position until 1977, when lackluster leadership, corruption scandals, and the founding of the Democratic Movement for Change made way for the Likud victory.

Organization

Labor Party organization, like that of Herut, varies considerably. It too uses highly democratic procedures within the party, but is really run by a small leadership group. Its headquarters are at 110 HaYarkon Street, Tel Aviv.

Policy

Labor's policies are Zionistic and socialistic. They include support for the immigration of Jews to Israel, establishment of a social welfare state, a state-planned and publicly regulated economy with room for the participation of private capital, full employment, minimum wages, and the right to strike. Labor stands for the separation of religion and the state, although it has historically made major concessions to the religious parties in this area. It supports equality for minorities, including the Arabs, and believes in a negotiated settlement with the Arab states without prior conditions, i.e., it has not rejected the possibility of returning some of the occupied territories to Arab sovereignty.

Membership & Constituency

No accurate data on the party's membership are available. The party's support comes mainly from lower- and middle-class Ashkenazim, with a smattering of Sephardic support. The *kibbutz* and *moshav* movements primarily support Labor, and Histadrut remains a Labor Party stronghold.

Financing

Data on the party's financing are unavailable. Most income is derived from membership dues and contributions.

Leadership

Shimon Peres (born 1923) remains the party's titular head despite strong criticism of his pallid performance in the 1981 election campaign. Peres, once an ally of Dayan and Ben-Gurion in Rafi, served as defense minister in Rabin's government (1974–77). His political and government experience has focused on his specialty, defense policy. Yitzhak Rabin (born 1922) remains Peres's chief rival for the leadership of the Labor Party and the Alignment. A former prime minister, chief of staff during the 1967 Six Day War, and former ambassador to the United States, Rabin aims to return to his former pre-eminence, in spite of the taint of corruption that touched his 1974–77 government. Although Rabin agreed before the 1981 elections to serve as defense minister in a Peres government should the Alignment prevail, Peres and Rabin remain hostile to each other.

Prospects

The Alignment faces a number of problems in its efforts to regain the government. Its internal divisions are well known, and the clash between Rabin and Peres for leadership (as well as their mutual animosity) is a major factor affecting Labor's leadership. The party also faces a decrease in its constituency compared to Likud due to demographic changes in the country. Peres's lackluster performance in the 1981 elections still plagues Labor's image. But its prospects may well be improved by the changes wrought in Israel by the Lebanon War of 1982 and its political fallout.

Mapam (*Mifleget HaPoalim HaMeuhedet;* United Workers Party)

Mapam was organized in 1948 when HaShomar HaTzair merged with radical elements from *Achdut HaAvodah*. From its beginnings, the party was more Marxist than Mapai. The former *Achdut HaAvodah* members left in 1954 because of Mapam's pro-Soviet orientation and acceptance of

Arabs as party members. Although the party's domestic policy was essentially indistinguishable from Mapai's, Mapam's share of the vote in national elections declined steadily before it joined the Alignment for the 1969 elections. The party is led by Victor Shemtor (born 1918). The party headquarters are at 4 Itamar ben Avi, Tel Aviv.

Communists

The communist movement began during the Palestine mandate and has existed continuously since that time, although it has been plagued by internal divisions and splits. Although they are isolated from the mainstream of political life, communist parties have been legal in Israel since independence and have been represented in the *Knesset* continuously. They generally secure a large portion of their support from Israel's Arab population, not apparently out of ideological commitment but as a form of dissent. On average, the communists secure four or five seats in the *Knesset*. The Israel Communist Party (*Miflaga Kommunistit Yisraelit*; Maki) was founded in 1948 and split in 1965. The splinter group, the New Communist List (*Reshima Kommunistit HaDasha*; Rakah) was pro-Moscow, strongly anti-Zionist, and primarily Arabic in membership.

In the 1981 elections, the Rakah-led Democratic Front for Peace and Equality (DFPE) won four seats in the Knesset. Its platform called for the total withdrawal of Israel from the occupied territories; equal rights for the Arab community; the establishment of a democratic, socialist, secular state in Palestine; peace with the Arab states; and a nonaligned foreign policy. Meir Vilner (born 1918) is the party's general secretary; Tawfiq Toubi is deputy secretary general.

Shelli (*Shalom LeYisrael;* Peace for Israel)

After the split with the New Communist List in 1965, Maki became more moderate in its opposition to government policies and became primarily Jewish in membership. In 1975, it merged with *Moked* (Focus), a socialist party, and in 1977, Moked united with other noncommunist groups to form Shelli. The new party was founded by Arye Eliav, a former Labor Party secretary general. The party's platform calls for the establishment of a Palestinian Arab state, the withdrawal

of Israel to its pre-1967 borders, and political negotiations with the Palestine Liberation Organization on the basis of mutual recognition. Shelli's campaign for the 1977 election secured it two seats—Arye Eliav (born 1921) and Meir Pail (born 1926), the former Moked leader—but the party was unsuccessful in the 1981 election.

RELIGIOUS PARTIES
National Religious Party; NRP (*Miflaqa Datit-Ieumit;* Mafdal)

History

Founded in 1956, the NRP was a full merger of Mizrachi (short for "spiritual center"), formally established as a party in Palestine in 1918, and *HaPoel HaMizrachi* (Mizrachi Worker), founded in 1922. The *HaPoel* retained a degree of independence as the trade-union section of the party responsible for immigration and absorption, labor and vocational affairs, housing, settlement, culture, pension funds and economic affairs, etc. The central NRP organization was responsible for policy, party organization, religion and rabbinical relations, and publications. From its beginning, this party of Orthodox religious Zionists began to have an impact on the movement, electing 19 percent of the delegates to the Twelfth Zionist Congress in 1921. Since Israel became a state, the NRP has served in every government except for a brief period from 1958 to 1959, when it left the coalition over the question of who should be considered a Jew for purposes of immigration.

Organization

The party is overseen by the World Center, a council elected by the world conference of the party. (In spite of the word "world," the conference is overwhelmingly Israeli as is the World Center.) The conference also elects the chairman of the World Center, the party leader. Delegates to the conference are elected from local party branches by the party members. The World Center supervises the party's women's and youth organizations. The former has over 50,000 members in Israel and is active in providing nurseries and kindergartens and cultural and vocational education for its members. The best known of the party's youth organizations is *Bnai Akiva*. The NRP also has a sports organization, *Elitzur*. In addition, the United Mizrachi Bank and the Mishav construction company are also NRP enterprises. Bar Ilan University and the Mosad HaRav Kook publishing house were established by Mizrachi and are a part of the NRP operation. Party headquarters are at 108 Ahad Haham Street, Tel Aviv.

Policy

The NRP was founded to emphasize the need for legislation based on Judaic religious law (*Halacha*) and protective of a "Torah true" tradition. It actively supports Jewish immigration, the development of the private sector, and government support of all Halachically necessary religious activities, including a religious school system and rabbinical councils in every city and town. These aims have been constant since the founding of NRP's predecessors, and they have been realized to a large degree. With only some minor intraparty disagreement, the NRP view was that it was organized for religious purposes and had no particular role to play in political, economic, or foreign affairs. It was able to cooperate effectively with Mapai and Labor primarily because of its willingness to defer to the left on foreign and defense questions in return for support in religious matters.

With the Israeli capture of the West Bank and Sinai in 1967, however, NRP attitudes began to change. The capture of ancient Israeli cities—Hebron, Shechem (Nablus), and Old Jerusalem—was seen as a miraculous achievement in fulfillment of the covenant between God and the Jewish people. The NRP believed that the return of any of the territory of historic Israel would be a repudiation of that covenant. On that basis, NRP "hawks" sought to focus the party's efforts on the rapid settlement of the new territory with the aim of securing it for Israel in perpetuity.

Although "hawks" are to be found in all of the NRP factions, they appear to be concentrated in the Youth Faction, which originally sought to reform the party organization, in part to increase the opportunities for newer and younger members in the party and government. They also wanted to increase NRP's independence in the coalition with the Labor Party. After 1967, the Youth Faction sought to appeal to nontraditional voters with the slogan "no return of any part of Eretz [historic land of] Israel." Largely because both groups are composed of the same people, the Youth Faction has strong but informal ties with *Gush Emunim* (Bloc of the Faithful), the leading movement of West Bank settlers. In some respects, the Youth Faction considers itself the political representation of the *Gush Emunim*. Youth Faction leaders have come to increasing prominence in both the

NRP and the government. Nevertheless, the NRP also encompasses other factions which represent more flexible (i.e., moderate) points of view on the future of the West Bank.

Membership & Constituency

No reliable data on NRP membership are available. Voting support comes primarily from Orthodox Jews (the vast majority of religiously active Jews in Israel, where the U.S. Conservative and Reform movements are barely represented). While traditional Sephardic Jews also support the party, it is from the Ashkenazic community that the party draws most of its support and its leadership.

Financing

No reliable information on NRP financing is available. Membership dues and donations provide the bulk of the party's income.

Leadership

The factionalism of the NRP reflects both personal conflicts and differing policy perspectives. Yosef Burg (born 1909) has been the party leader since its founding and has served in most Israeli cabinets. A man of great political skills, he has worked successfully to maintain and expand the religious foundation of the state. His seniority and role as head of the largest faction (*Lamifneh*) secures his dominant position in the party, but he does not dictate its positions or policies. His influence is, in part, the result of his shrewd use of patronage in allocating jobs in the party and the party-controlled institutions. As a government minister, he has also been able to distribute many public jobs in the religious and educational establishments and a variety of posts controlled by the Ministry of the Interior. In mid-1982, Burg was both minister of religious affairs and of interior.

The Youth Faction leaders are Zevulon Hammer (born 1936) and Yehuda Ben-Meir (born 1939). Hammer is minister of education and Ben-Meir is deputy minister of foreign affairs.

Prospects

The NRP is very likely to continue to play a key role as a coalition partner in government regardless of the fortunes of other parties.

Association of Israel (*Agudat Yisrael*)

The world organization of Orthodox Jews, founded in 1912 by various rabbis and other religious leaders in Europe, *Agudat Yisrael* was at first opposed to Zionism, believing that Israel should wait for divine redemption and the coming of the Messiah, and that the establishment of a political state in Palestine was heretical. Although it boycotted the institutions of the Jewish community in Palestine, it eventually became a political party in 1948. It now accepts the state, but without ascribing any religious significance to it. It has been represented in Parliament since 1948 and has supported most of the coalition governments, but since 1952 it has refused to accept a cabinet portfolio. Its voting strength lies in Jerusalem and Bnei Brak, and consists mostly of Ashkenazim.

All crucial decisions on policy are made not by the party's *Knesset* members or its membership, but by a twelve-member Council of Torah Sages, composed of revered rabbis, heads of yeshivas (religious schools), and members of Hasidic dynasties. (Hasidism comprises several ultra-orthodox, somewhat mystical sects, whose leadership tends to be hereditary.) Beside the Council, the party's central institutions are the Great Assembly composed of representatives of the local branches, the Central World Council, and the World Executive Committee. It has a youth movement (*Tzeirei Agudat Yisrael*), a women's movement (*Neshei Agudat Yisrael*), and its own school network in which religious instruction is a major part of the curriculum. The government supplies most of the funds for the school system.

Agudat Yisrael is primarily concerned with enhancing the role of religion in the state and is opposed to all forms of secularism. Its support for the Begin coalition was secured only after the construction of a lengthy coalition agreement containing numerous concessions to the group's religious perspectives, e.g., strict Sabbath laws and revision of legislation to accommodate orthodox Jewish principles. The parliamentary leader is Avraham Shapiro, in his early fifties in 1982, a highly successful and pragmatic businessman. Party headquarters are at 17 Hadaf HaYomi Street, Tel Aviv.

Workers of the Association of Israel (*Poalei Agudat Yisrael*)

Founded in 1922 to counteract the growth of secularism, socialism, and antireligious tendencies among workers, this organization was the labor wing of *Agudat Yisrael*. Within *Agudat Yisrael*, it fought for the development of the land and the building of a Jewish state in the spirit of the Torah and tradition.

In 1946, it founded the World Union of *Poalei Agudat Yisrael*, in effect seceding from *Agudat Yisrael*. Its members joined the Haganah to fight the Arab invasion in 1948. It joined the trade-union department of Histadrut under a special arrangement. It continued to accept the advice of the Council of Torah Sages until 1960, at which time it joined the government and officially split from *Agudat Yisrael*.

TAMI (*Tenuah LeMassoret Israel; Movement for Jewish Tradition*)

Tami is a small *Knesset* faction which was founded in May 1981 by then Religious Affairs Minister Aharon Abu Hatzeira (born 1938). The party is based on Sephardim, but it was created primarily because of Abu Hatzeira's personal political ambition and his antipathy to NRP's leaders, especially Yosef Burg. Abu Hatzeira left the NRP after receiving what he regarded as insufficient support during his trial on various criminal charges. He accused the NRP leadership of "ethnic discrimination." Tami sought to appeal to followers of the NRP and *Agudat Yisrael* by stressing the Moroccan connection, intending thereby to draw voters from Israel's large Moroccan community to fellow Moroccan Abu Hatzeira. Abu Hatzeira had strong support from Nessim Gaon, a Swiss-Jewish millionaire of Sudanese origin, who has been active in Sephardic causes. He had hoped for a sizable victory which would give him significant bargaining power after the election, but his efforts suffered a number of crucial setbacks, including repudiation by his venerable uncle, Rabbi Yisrael Abu Hatzeira, a leader of Moroccan Jews in Israel. In addition, it became clear that he had created a party with a narrow, sectarian base—and thus lost any chance for a broader appeal to others, especially Sephardim of non-African origin. Other negative factors also emerged; Abu Hatzeira still faces trial on charges of embezzlement of funds when he was mayor of Ramle, although he was acquitted of bribery charges in May 1981.

The party's main concerns revolve around the specific interests and ambitions of Abu Hatzeira (born 1938), despite statements that the party seeks to eliminate anti-Moroccan sentiments in

Israel. The number-two candidate on Tami's list, Aharon Uzan (born 1924), a former agriculture minister in Labor governments, has noted that the party's purpose "is to right the glaring wrongs perpetrated against us North Africans and against the Sephardim in general."

Minor Parties

Citizens' Rights Movement (HaTenua LeZechuyot HaEzrah UleShalom; Ratz)

Led by Shulamit Aloni (born 1928), a former Labor Party member and civil rights activist, Ratz did well following the 1973 war when there was substantial discontent with the Labor Party. It won three seats in the 1973 elections and joined the government coalition for a brief period in 1974. Its position declined in the 1977 and 1981 elections, and, following the latter, Aloni pledged her party's support to Labor in an effort to block Likud's efforts to form the new government.

Shinuy (Change)

In the wake of the 1973 war, a small protest group called Shinuy was founded by Professor Amnon Rubinstein of Tel Aviv University. It sought to effect changes in the Israeli political system and political life. It developed a party organization, but did not have a candidate of imposing stature. In 1976, it joined with others to form the Democratic Movement for Change (DMC) which secured fifteen seats in the 1977 election. The DMC was constituted under the leadership of archeology professor Yigael Yadin, who served as deputy prime minister under Begin after the 1977 elections. The party included Shinuy, Yadin's own Democratic Movement, and individuals and groups from both within and outside the existing political parties. Although composed mostly of elements from the center-left, the party could not be neatly classified in terms of traditional Israeli political ideology. It focused on the need for electoral reform and general improvement in the political life of the country.

The DMC's initial success was not enough to make it an indispensable element in the new government, and failing to achieve its major goals, it dissolved itself just prior to the 1981 elections. Shinuy again emerged as an independent unit and won two seats in the 1981 elections.

Arab Parties

Arab political parties have been a part of the Israeli political scene since independence, and Arabs have been represented on a regular basis in the Knesset. In the elections for the Knesset between 1949 and 1969, the majority of Israeli Arabs supported the dominant Jewish party or the Arab lists affiliated with it. In 1973 and 1977, this support declined; the communists gained nearly 50 percent of Arab votes in 1977. To a great extent, this reflected growing Arab nationalism and support for the Palestinians—causes espoused by the communists. Overall Arab participation in the political process also declined during the same period. In 1981, the Alignment tripled its vote among the Arabs of Israel compared to 1977; this was seen as a vote for the best of the bad alternatives. Much of the turn to Labor was seen as anti-Begin and anti-Likud out of disappointment with Begin's ignoring of the Arab problem in Israel. There was an unexpectedly low turnout of voters and a sharp decline in support for Rakah. Five Arab and Druze members were seated in the 1981 Parliament: two in the Alignment, two in Rakah, and one Druze in Likud.

Other Political Forces

Histadrut (General Federation of Labor)

The General Federation of Labor in Israel was founded in the 1920s as a federation of Jewish Labor. It later admitted Arabs to full membership. The purpose was to unite and organize all workers, to raise their standard of living, and to defend their economic interests, as well as to represent their interests in other areas. Histadrut provides a wide range of services to its members and is also a substantial employer. It cooperates with the government in numerous areas related to foreign and domestic policy and carries out many functions which are normally government activities in other modern states. Many of its leaders have served in major government posts (including that of prime minister) before and after working in Histadrut. Its decision-making bodies are organized along partisan political lines, with Labor predominating. The organization as a whole has long been closely aligned with the leaders and policies of the Labor Party.

National Prospects

Israel's political system has been substantially tested both before and since independence. Despite political diversity, party politics, and coalitions, governments in Israel have remained remarkably stable. Although electoral reform has been discussed, on and off, for more than two decades, no major overhaul of the system has occurred and is unlikely in the near future. The major change will be in the electorate—the growing majority of the Sephardic community of Israel. This Jewish community of non-Western origin will increasingly utilize its strength to affect the results of elections. This seems to suggest a loss of support for the left-of-center parties (with their primarily Ashkenazic constituency) and a growth for Likud and the religious parties, which have traditionally drawn much of their support from the Oriental Jewish community.

Further Reading

Arian, Alan. *The Choosing People: Voting Behavior in Israel.* Cleveland and London: Case Western Reserve University Press, 1973.

———, ed. *The Elections in Israel—1969.* Jerusalem: Jerusalem Academic Press, 1972.

Freudenheim, Yehoshua. *Government in Israel.* Dobbs Ferry, N. Y.: Oceana Publications, Inc., 1967.

Isaac, Rael Jean. *Party and Politics in Israel: Three Visions of a Jewish State.* New York and London: Longman, 1981.

Medding, Peter Y. *Mapai in Israel: Political Organization and Government in a New Society.* Cambridge, England: Cambridge University Press, 1972.

Penniman, Howard R., ed. *Israel at the Polls: The Knesset Elections of 1977.* Washington, D.C.: American Enterprise Institute, 1979.

Rackman, Emanuel. *Israel's Emerging Constitution, 1948–51.* New York: Columbia University Press, 1955.

Reich, Bernard. *Quest for Peace: United States-Israel Relations and the Arab-Israeli Conflict.* New Brunswick, N.J.: Transaction Books, 1977.

Sachar, Howard M. *A History of Israel: From the Rise of Zionism to Our Time.* New York: Alfred A. Knopf, 1976.

Safran, Nadav. *Israel: The Embattled Ally.* Cambridge, Mass.: The Belknap Press of Harvard University Press, 1981.

Yaacobi, Gad. *The Government of Israel.* New York: Praeger, 1982.

Zidon, Asher. *Knesset: The Parliament of Israel.* New York: Herzl Press, 1967.

REPUBLIC OF ITALY
(*Repubblica Italiana*)
by Martin Slater, Ph.D.

The System of Government

The Republic of Italy, a nation of over fifty-seven million people, is a parliamentary democracy and unitary state. The present republican constitution dates from 1948. It was prepared by the 1946 Constituent Assembly which replaced the transitory regime that had been established following the fall of Mussolini's Fascist dictatorship in 1943.

Executive

The cabinet, known as the *Consiglio dei Ministri* (Council of Ministers), is the chief executive authority within the state. With over forty governments since the Second World War, the Italian political system has been characterized by high cabinet instability. One of the major causes of this instability has been the proliferation of political parties, none of which has an absolute majority of seats in Parliament.

The head of government is the president of the Council of Ministers, or prime minister. He is formally appointed by the head of state, the president of the republic. The prime minister must also receive the support of a majority in Parliament. In reality, since no party has a majority, the prime minister's nomination and acceptability are very much the result of hard bargaining among the parties' leaders. For an individual to be acceptable as prime minister, it is often advantageous that he not be perceived as too powerful a figure within one of the major parties. Thus, Giovanni Spadolini, prime minister in 1982, was acceptable to Socialist and Christian Democratic members of the government because the small Republican Party, of which he is leader, has less than 4 percent of the seats in Parliament. A previous prime minister, Francesco Cossiga, was a middle-ranking Christian Democrat at the time of his appointment. The power brokers behind the scenes are the secretaries of the governing political parties. They also negotiate among themselves in order to put forward a list of names for appointment to various ministerial positions. A person may be selected for a ministerial position who is not a member of the legislature, but it is not the normal practice.

Once the cabinet has been appointed, the prime minister must present it to Parliament within ten days for a vote of confidence. The cabinet is collectively responsible to Parliament and must resign if defeated by a vote of censure. But, unlike countries such as Britain, a fall of government does not automatically lead to new elections. Instead, the round of interparty bargaining and negotiation begins again.

The president of the republic, though regarded as a figurehead by many, does, in fact, possess some important executive functions. He nominates the prime minister, and in cases where the party bargaining has ended in deadlock, this nomination may be decisive. He may dissolve Parliament after consulting with the leaders of the two chambers. The present incumbent, Sandro Pertini, on more than one occasion has threatened to use this power if party deadlocks over government formation could not be resolved. The president also has the right of pardon and the power to make various judicial, legislative, and military appointments. Finally, the president can suspend the promulgation of legislation, although he cannot veto it. Instead, he may ask Parliament to reconsider. As one of Italy's few symbols of national unity, the president is in a unique position to make a popular appeal over the heads of party leaders. In this capacity, President Pertini has used his position to good effect.

The increasing importance attached to the presidency is evidenced by the growing level of competition in presidential elections. The president, who must be at least fifty years old, is elected for a period of seven years by a joint session of both houses of Parliament and three delegates from each of the country's twenty regions, except Val d'Aosta which sends only one. To be elected in one of the first three ballots, a candidate needs a two-thirds majority. After the third ballot, he needs only an absolute majority. Only once, in 1946, was a president elected on the first ballot. Since then, a large number of ballots has normally been necessary. The greatest number thus far was the twenty-one ballots needed to elect the Christian Democrat, Giovanni Leone, in December 1971. President Pertini, a Socialist, was elected on the sixteenth ballot on July 8, 1978.

Legislature

Italy has a bicameral parliamentary system. The lower house, known as the Chamber of Deputies (*Camera dei Deputati*), has 630 members elected on a basis of proportional representation from large multimember constituencies. The total number of deputies once fluctuated, but was fixed at 630 in 1963. The minimum age for candidates is twenty-five. The upper house, known as the Senate (*Senato*), has 315 elected members and five members appointed for life by the president of the republic. Former presidents of the republic are also senators for life. Each region has a minimum of seven elected senators, except Friuli-Venezia-Giulia which has three, Molise which has two, and Val d'Aosta which has one. The minimum age for Senate candidates is forty.

The Chamber and the Senate meet in two sessions per year, beginning in February and October. There is no specified length of sessions, and in recent years the chambers have been in almost continual session. In addition to the two mandatory sessions, a special session may sometimes be called by the president of each chamber, in consultation with the president of the republic.

Formally, the two chambers have equal powers. The prime minister usually sits in the lower chamber, but this is not a hard and fast rule. The last two prime ministers (Spadolini and Fanfani) have been senators. Each chamber elects its own president. Usually this election is a matter for negotiation between the governing parties. In the past, the Christian Democrats retained control of these offices. But in recent years, a Socialist and a Communist have, in turn, been elected to the presidency of the lower house.

There are between eleven and fourteen standing committees in each chamber. The committees are important for it is here that legislation is first introduced and considered. The president of each committee is in the powerful position of controlling the legislative agenda. Having been considered in committee stage, bills are usually sent to the full legislature, where they must be passed separately by both the Senate and the Chamber of Deputies. Uniquely, though, for a West European parliamentary system, the committees also have the power to pass legislation in certain matters in committee without sending it to the floor of the house.

As in most other legislatures, the executive is the main initiator of legislation, but many other groups have the right to introduce bills. These include members of Parliament, chamber committees, regional councils, and the electorate on presentation of a petition. Members of Parliament are, in fact, quite active in putting forward bills.

One further important method of initiating legislation is through referendum. If either one-third of the legislature, five regional assemblies, or 500,000 electors demand that a law be repealed, a

LEGISLATIVE ELECTION RESULTS (1979)*						
	Senate			Chamber of Deputies		
	Votes	%	Seats	Votes	%	Seats
Christian Democrats (DC)	12,001,669	38.3	138	14,007,594	38.3	262
Communists (PCI)	9,851,437	31.5	109	11,107,883	30.4	201
Socialists (PSI)	3,251,678	10.4	32	3,586,256	9.8	62
Social Movement (MSI)	1,781,341	5.7	13	1,924,251	5.3	30
Social Democrats (PSDI)	1,320,351	4.2	9	1,403,873	3.8	20
Republicans (PRI)	1,051,699	3.4	6	1,106,766	3.0	16
Liberals (PLI)	691,514	2.2	2	708,022	1.9	9
Radicals (PR)	413,217	1.3	2	1,259,362	3.4	18
South Tyrol People's (SVP)	172,552	0.5	3	206,264	0.6	4
Val d'Aosta Union	37,080	0.1	1	33,250	0.1	1
Proletarian Unity (PDUP)	—	—	—	501,431	1.4	6
Per Trieste	—	—	—	62,602	0.2	1

*Includes only parties which won seats.

referendum must be held. The first such referendum to be held was the 1974 Divorce Referendum, which resulted in the repeal of the antidivorce laws.

Under normal circumstances, the term of office of both Chamber and Senate is five years, running concurrently. The last three terms, however, have ended prematurely. Early elections were held in 1972, 1976, and 1979 as a result of the failure of political parties to agree on the composition of a new government.

Judiciary

The 1948 constitution provided for the establishment of the Constitutional Court (*Corte Costituzionale*). Like many other constitutional privisions, it was not immediately acted upon, and the court finally came into existence in 1956. It consists of fifteen members (with an additional sixteen to be appointed by Parliament in the event of impeachment proceedings). Five members are appointed by the judiciary; five by the president of the republic; and five are elected by joint session of Parliament. The president of the court is elected for a three-year term by its members.

It is the highest court in the land, with the power to judge the constitutional validity of laws promulgated by Parliament; conflicts of administrative competence, for example, between regional and national government; impeachment of the executive; and the admissibility of petitions for referendums. The court has, in fact, played a radicalizing role in sweeping away much legislation which was a legacy of Mussolini's fascist administration.

Regional & Local Government

Of Italy's twenty regions, five have held a special status as autonomous regions since World War II. The reasons had to do with cultural and/or linguistic and/or geographic distinctiveness. These regions are Friuli-Venezia-Giulia, Sardinia, Sicily, Trentino-Alto Adige, and Val d'Aosta. Since 1969, the German speaking province of Bolzano in Trentino-Alto Adige has had special status as an autonomous province. This status gives it greater independence from central government than that enjoyed by the regions.

Although the 1948 constitution also provided for regional government in Italy's fifteen other regions, it was not until 1970 that regional reform legislation was passed. Historically, the Christian Democrats had opposed regional reform as they saw it providing important power bases for the

opposition Communist Party. For the same reasons, the Communists campaigned strongly for regional reform. Elections to the new regional assemblies and the creation of regional governments have indeed given the Communists a much more extensive role in the governmental process.

Other levels of government include the province and the commune. Provincial government powers are very limited, but the local, or communal, elections are important because they determine the composition of relatively important governments in Italy's cities, towns, and villages. At present, the Communists have control of many of Italy's major cities.

The Electoral System

A system of proportional representation is used for elections to the Italian Parliament. The system differs for the Chamber of Deputies and the Senate. For the Chamber of Deputies, the country is divided into thirty-two constituencies, each grouping two to three provinces. Of these constituencies, thirty-one are multimember, ranging in size from two to forty-seven seats. The number of seats varies according to the size of the population in each constituency. The Val d'Aosta forms the only single-member constituency. At the general election, each party presents a list of candidates up to but not exceeding the number of seats allocated to the constituency. Joint lists are permissible. Thus the Communists and Socialists presented a joint list at the 1948 elections. The voter votes for a party list, but under the so-called *panachage* system, the voter may also indicate between three and four preferences among the candidates, depending upon the size of the constituency. The voter may also strike out candidates, which cancel out other voters' preferences. The candidate who receives the most preferences in each party moves to the top of the party list. There is thus a rank ordering of candidates in each list, with those at the top having a better chance of being elected.

Seats are allocated according to a quota system. The quota is calculated by dividing the number of votes by the number of seats in the constituency plus two. Fractional remainders go into a national pool, where unassigned seats are allocated on a proportional basis. Parties are only eligible for the allocation of seats in this pool if they have met two conditions: a minimum of

300,000 votes nationally and achievement of the minimum quota in at least one constituency. In the 1972 elections, the Party of Proletarian Unity won 648,000 votes (over 2 percent of the national total), but failed to gain any seats because they had not won a constituency seat. Their vote was distributed too widely. Normally, however, the Italian electoral system tends to ensure the representation in Parliament of a large number of small parties. In the single-member Val d'Aosta constituency, election is by simple majority.

In contrast to the Chamber of Deputies, the Senate is elected on the basis of a modified proportional system. Each of the country's twenty regions is divided into single-member constituencies, roughly equal in terms of population size. A candidate may run in up to three constituencies. Candidates receiving 65 percent of the poll are automatically elected. The remaining seats are distributed on a proportional basis within the region, using the d'Hondt method.

There are no by-elections in Italy. When a member of Parliament dies or retires, he is replaced by the next person in line on the party list in the case of the Chamber of Deputies, and the next in line of the regional candidates in the case of the Senate. In the Chamber of Deputies, the Radical Party has used resignations to spectacular effect. In 1980, all the Radical deputies resigned to be replaced by a new set.

Italians are automatically registered to vote in their place of residence. Since there are no postal ballots and no proxies, everyone, including temporary migrants and Italians living abroad, must return to their place of residence in order to vote. Members of the armed forces, however, are allowed to vote where they are stationed. The government offers inexpensive fares and special train services for voters to return home at election time. Though nonvoting is *not* illegal, many Italians believe it to be so, because the 1948 constitution states that voting is a civic duty and a public record of those people who fail to vote is kept for five years. The consequence is that turnout in all postwar elections has been extraordinarily high, never dropping below 92 percent.

Universal male suffrage was first introduced in 1919 and a decree of March 10, 1946, extended suffrage to women. Until 1975, all men and women over the age of twenty-one were eligible to vote for the Chamber of Deputies; the age requirement for the Senate was thirty. In 1975, the age requirements were reduced to eighteen for the Chamber of Deputies and twenty-five for the Senate.

The Party System

Italy has a multiparty system, in which no party has an absolute majority. Twelve parties are currently represented in Parliament, but the majority have no more than a handful of seats. The two parties that dominate the party system are the Christian Democrats, with 38.3 percent of the popular vote in 1979, and the Communists, with 30.4 percent. The next-largest parties are the Socialist Party, with 9.8 percent of the vote, and the rightwing Italian Social Movement, with 5.3 percent. The dominance of the Christian Democrats and the Communists led one commentator, Giorgio Galli, to describe Italy as having an "imperfect two-party system." Giovanni Sartori has described it in another way as a case of "polarized pluralism." The Communists and Neo-Fascists are perceived respectively as antisystem parties of left and right, while the Christian Democrats occupy the center of the political spectrum. Whatever the merits of these various models, what is not in dispute is that there are two major political subcultures in Italy—Catholicism and socialism. The Christian Democrats and Communists are an outgrowth of these subcultures. The problems of governability in the 1970s have to do with the fact that there has never been an accommodation between the two.

Origins of the Parties

In view of the current dominance of the Catholic and socialist traditions, it may seem surprising that they played no role in the founding of the modern Italian state. At the time of unification in 1861, liberalism dominated politics. Unification had been achieved by the small bourgeois elite of Piedmont. The electorate was initially less than 2 percent of the population, leaving no scope for the development of mass parties. Indeed, the path was only opened to the development of mass parties after the electoral reform of 1882, which gave voting rights to the middle classes and a small section of the working class. (Universal male suffrage was not introduced until 1919.) Parliamentarians did not belong to highly organized political parties. Rather, governing coalitions were created through the dispensation of patronage to local notables. Among the political elites, there was a broad ideological consensus. Any political group not accepting the rules of the party game was regarded as anti-system.

The Radicals constituted the early opposition. With their support coming from the northern petite bourgeoisie, they were the first mass political organization. In 1892, with the founding of the Socialist Party, the Radicals drifted towards an accommodation with the parliamentary regime. There was no serious attempt by the political elite to integrate the working class into the political system. The Socialist Party, drawing its support from the working class, remained antisystem. To be a socialist was to be an opponent of the regime.

Catholics, for their part, were also excluded from the parliamentary system. But, in their case, the exclusion was partly voluntary. The nature of Italian unification in the 1860s had served to alienate Catholics from the new state, and the pope, losing his temporal powers, forbade Catholics to participate in politics. It was only when faced with the threat of a powerful Socialist Party that Catholicism began to develop as a mass political movement. By 1919, the Catholic Popular Party had become the second-largest party in terms of voting strength. The Popular Party represented a tradition of social and radical Catholicism. Accordingly, the Popular Party, like the Socialist Party, was considered antisystem and was never integrated into the pre-1919 system.

Following the First World War, the traditional political elite no longer enjoyed legitimacy with the newly enlarged electorate. The introduction of universal male suffrage benefited the Socialist and Popular parties, and after the 1919 elections, they held a majority of seats in Parliament. However, socialism and Catholicism remained as alienated from one another as they both were from the traditional political elite. With growing social unrest within the country, the reaction of the political elite was to surrender any political initiative it had left to the emerging Fascist Party of Benito Mussolini. Although the Fascists then barely qualified as a mass movement, their nationalism and vigorous antisocialism struck a responsive chord with the bourgeois political elite and their supporters. The Fascists were the answer to socialism. Following the Fascist march on Rome in 1922, Mussolini was invited to form an administration. By 1926, he had consolidated his dictatorship, outlawing all political opposition.

The Fascist period was important for the future development of party politics. First, the advent of the dictatorship discredited the traditional political elites. Though they survived the period in the guise of the present-day Liberal and Republican parties, they never again enjoyed widespread political support, which meant that a bourgeois party could not dominate post — World War II politics.

Fascism also resulted in the consolidation of the Catholic political tradition. The signing of the Lateran Pacts in 1929 established Catholicism as the state religion, giving the Church a privileged position in the cultural life of the nation. It also ended the sixty-year isolation of the Catholics. Far from compromising Catholicism with Fascism, the Lateran Pacts consolidated the strength of Catholicism and allowed it to emerge from the Fascist period with a solid social and organizational base from which it could develop its own political organization—the Christian Democratic Party.

The Socialists had entered the Fascist period as a divided movement, a division that was formalized in 1921 with the creation of the Communist Party. After 1920, in fact, the Socialist Party had shown little appetite for revolutionary action, although this was not always apparent from the rhetoric of the party leaders. The division of the socialist movement was important in so far as it paved the way for the eventual integration of the Socialist Party into the postwar political system.

Fascism affected the socialist movement in other ways, too. First, both Communists and Socialists emerged from the period with considerable moral authority, having led the opposition to the dictatorship and participated in the Resistance movement, the Communists, in particular. The martyrdom of their leader, Antonio Gramsci, who died in prison, and his own great intellectual contribution to the socialist movement aroused both popular and intellectual support for the Communists. Second, the experience of Fascism fostered within the Italian socialist movement a strong commitment to political liberties.

The final legacy of the Fascist era was the continued existence in Italy of the nondemocratic right. Drawing its support from the lower ranks of the civil service, parts of the south, and more recently, discontented youth, the extreme right remains an isolated group.

By the end of the Second World War, patterns of political loyalties had been firmly established. Cooperation between Catholicism and Socialism, based on common opposition to Fascism, was possible for a short period of time, but Christian Democracy had emerged from Fascism as the dominant political force. With the advent of the Cold War, the Communists were excluded from government. The isolation of the Communists was followed by a further split of the Socialist Party. In 1948, a majority of Socialists joined ranks with the Communists in opposition to the Christian Democratic government. A smaller group broke away, forming the Social Democratic Party.

The Parties in Law

Article 49 of the 1948 constitution sets out the legal position of political parties, stating that all citizens have the right to associate freely in political parties in order to participate in the democratic process of determining national policy. Although this provision appears to allow the widest latitude to the formation of political groups, the reference to democratic procedure is important. Thus political parties engaged in terrorism, such as the Red Brigades (*Brigate Rosse*) can be outlawed and, indeed, have been. The prohibition also applies to the Fascist Party. In the case of the Fascists, Article XII of the Transitory Provisions (made after the fall of the Fascist dictatorship) forbids the reorganization of the Fascist Party in any form.

Other important legislation relevant to the legal position of political parties is the 1974 bill providing for public financing of parties according to their share of the national vote.

Party Organization

Italian political parties are mass-membership parties. The largest parties, the Christian Democrats and the Communists, each have between 1.5 and 2 million members, and the smaller parties between 100,000 and 500,000 members. All members have to pay party dues, which are usually no more than a few thousand liras. Membership is high relative to party membership in other countries, with between 15 and 20 percent of the electorate party members. The active membership, however, is very low, probably less than 5 percent of the membership.

Since the parties see themselves as representing distinctive ideologies, joining one is an ideological decision. Prospective members must be proposed by existing members and are required to make an ideological commitment to the party. With the emphasis on ideology, one might expect Italian political parties to be internally cohesive. In fact, nearly every party is highly factionalized, with the factions having a semiformal status with rights of representation. The one major party that is not publicly factionalized is the Communist Party. But in recent years, it, too, has shown increasing signs of factionalism. Factions are not always based on ideology; they are also based on personal ties.

The ideological divisions of the party system are reflected in everyday life. Most parties have links with a wide range of organizations and associations: unions, cooperatives, youth movements, women's organizations, even taverns and sports associations. In addition, the major parties organize cultural festivals and publish their own national newspapers and magazines. Thus, political ideologies reach deep into the daily life of Italians; parties are fully integrated into social and cultural life.

The view of the Italian party system as highly ideological is complicated to some extent by the existence of clientelistic political structures, especially in the southern part of the country. Many people join and vote for political parties as a means of access to employment, housing, etc. There are no purely clientelistic parties as such, but all the parties to a greater or lesser extent engage in clientelistic activities in certain parts of the country.

In terms of formal organization, all Italian parties have tended to copy the organizational model of the Communist Party, that is, organized in a branching structure with communal, provincial, regional, and national levels, corresponding to the administrative levels of the Italian state.

At the local level is the party section, although not all parties have sections in every city, town, and village. Whether or not a party section exists in a particular location depends on the size of the party and the community. At the provincial and regional levels, there are federations; and at the national level, there is the national executive of the party. The only parties that do not share this organizational pattern are the small ethnoregional parties.

Formally, the organization is democratic from the base upwards: section members elect section heads; section heads elect a provincial committee, which elects a regional committee; which elects the national committee. The elections take place during provincial, regional, and national congresses. The national congresses—held every one to two years—determine the broad policies of the party. The national executive, elected by the congress, meets every few months and consists of approximately 100 members. To carry out the day-to-day running of the party, the executive elects a secretariat or executive bureau. The secretariat consists of the secretary general, his assistants, and a number of full-time officials who have responsibility for particular policy areas.

Most parties use a system of proportional representation for election to the various committees. This system ensures the representation of the various factions at all levels of the party. Clearly, though, the election of the secretary general means that some factions lose out. To be elected, a secretary general needs to organize a coalition of factions. The one major party that does not follow this system is the Communist Party, where factions are not formally recognized.

Despite the democratic organization of the parties, the party bureaucracies dominate the lower levels. In many cases, national political leaders have important local bases which ensure their own standing within the party, and which they control through the use of patronage. Even without such patronage, the general pattern is for decisions to be made at the top, possibly by the party secretary acting unilaterally. The decisions are then endorsed at the lower levels. Even major decisions, such as the Communists' "historic compromise" of a proposed alliance with Italy's other democratic parties, are often presented to the party as a *fait accompli*.

The main functions of party members at the local level are to elect local officials of the party and government. The level of interference by the central party bureaucracy in these decisions depends on the importance of the local community. Party members at the local level play an important role distributing party tracts and propaganda material, selling party newspapers, collecting membership dues, and getting out the vote in elections.

At the provincial level, one finds full-time party officials alongside volunteers. Provincial officials coordinate the activities of local sections and determine the party lists for provincial elections. The influence of the central party bureaucracy on the composition of these lists is considerable. The regional federations also have a number of full-time officials, concerned with the preparation of lists for the regional elections. They are also concerned with the politics of regional governments, which in the last few years have so grown in importance that some regional party leaders would regard it as a step down to run for national office.

At the national level, the party executives share some power with the members of Parliament. Much is made of the dominance of the party bureaucracy over deputies and senators, and indeed, it is the party executive that generally determines the formation of the government, but it is also true that the party executive is drawn, in large part, from the parliamentary bloc.

Campaigning

All political parties in Italy publish an electoral program or manifesto prior to the national legislative elections. They are the centerpieces of the electoral campaigns and are published in the party newspapers. The campaign as a whole is closely controlled by the national executives. Senior committees within the executives prepare the manifestoes. To some extent, the fact that the last three elections have been held prematurely has excluded rank-and-file influence in the campaign, because there has been little time for broad consultation on the content of the party programs.

Campaigns are highly ideological. But the evidence shows that parties tend to talk past one another, rather than engaging in a debate over particular policies. In recent years, while the Communism-versus-Catholicism issue has dominated election campaigns, the arguments have been general not specific. Speeches by political leaders play a major part in electoral campaigns, and extensive use is made of radio, television, and newspapers. In addition, wall posters are very common.

It is estimated that campaign expenses represent 10 percent of the expenditure of the major political parties, and up to 50 percent of the smaller parties. Since 1974, public funds have been made available to partially offset these expenses.

Independent Voters

Given the high party membership levels and the ideological commitments membership entails, ticket splitting in local, regional, and national elections has been rare. However, increased education and social mobility combined with growing skepticism and distrust of the political process among most voters has led some observers to believe that party loyalties are declining, and that most votes are being cast from more issue-oriented, sophisticated, and independent standpoints.

Italian Social Movement (*Movimento Sociale Italiano;* MSI)

History

Under the law of June 20, 1952, the Fascist Party is specifically outlawed. The Italian Social Movement, established in 1946, is an extreme right-wing party that, despite its claims to the contrary, shares the ideological outlook of the old Fascist Party. In 1972, the party formed an electoral alliance with the Monarchist Party (*Partito Democratico Italiano di Unita Monarchica;* PDIUM). The success of this alliance in the 1972 elections encouraged the merger of the two parties in January 1973, when the party became known as *Movimento Sociale Italiano—Destra Nazionale* (Italian Social Movement—National Right). Failure in the 1976 elections led to a more moderate group of MPs breaking away to form *Democrazia Nazionale* (National Democracy). The new party won no seats in the 1979 election.

The MSI has been in opposition throughout most of the postwar era. It has been an active organizer of extraparliamentary activity, although it disclaims direct connections with right-wing terrorists.

Organization

The organizational pattern of the MSI is similar to other parties. Membership is allowed at age fourteen, and the MSI lays stress on gaining the support of discontented youth.

The party has a number of affiliated organizations, including a trade union, the Italian Confederation of National Workers' Unions (*Confederazione Italiana dei Sindacati Nazionali dei Lavoratori;* CISNAL). Its daily newspaper is *Il Secolo d'Italia.*

Party headquarters are at Via Quattro Fontane 22, 00184 Rome.

Policy

The MSI is strongly anti-Communist and also opposes Italy's various international alliances. Despite its heavy emphasis on law and order, the party has itself contributed to political lawlessness in Italy with its encouragement of extraparliamentary political activity. The party is Catholic but of a different tradition to that of the Christian Democrats.

Membership & Constituency

The MSI claims a membership of 400,000, many of whom are the young unemployed and uneducated. The MSI's greatest electoral success—8.7 percent of the vote—occurred in 1972. In some southern cities, such as Catania, it overtook the Christian Democrats, becoming the largest party. In the north, it receives less popular support.

Financing

The MSI is financed by membership dues and public funds, of which it receives the fourth-largest share. It is also likely that it receives contributions from a number of clandestine sources.

Leadership

Giorgio Almirante (born 1914, in Salsomaggiore, Parma) has been secretary since 1969. Pino Romualdi (born 1913 in Predadappio, Forli) is vice secretary.

Prospects

Despite social, economic, and political crises in Italy, the MSI has declined over the past few years. Public concern about right-wing terrorism, such as the bombing of the Bologna Railway Station in 1980, has left the party increasingly isolated. There is little likelihood of electoral gains in the near future, and no likelihood of participation in coalition government with other parties.

Italian Communist Party (*Partito Communista Italiano;* PCI)

History

The PCI is Western Europe's largest Communist Party. It was founded in 1921 after a split in the ranks of the Socialist Party at its Leghorn Congress. The reformists stayed in the Socialist Party, while the maximalists led by Antonio Gramsci formed the Communist Party.

During the period of the Fascist dictatorship (1926–43), the Communist Party went underground. Some of its leaders escaped abroad, such as Palmiro Togliatti, who settled in Moscow. Others, such as Antonio Gramsci, were imprisoned. Gramsci, the party secretary, died as a result of illness contracted during his imprisonment. At the end of the Fascist period, Togliatti returned to take over the party leadership.

The Fascist period was important for the future development of the PCI for several reasons. First, the fact that the PCI was an underground movement fighting for civil liberties during the 1930s isolated it from what was happening in world communism at the time. Thus, the PCI was never involved in defending Stalinist excesses. At the end of the war, the PCI was and remained the least Stalinist of Europe's Communist parties. It was relatively autonomous. The *via italiana al socialismo* (Italian way to socialism) proclaimed by Togliatti in 1956 was a natural manifestation of this autonomy.

Second, the experience of Fascism fostered within the PCI a strong belief in the importance of political freedom. Thus, the PCI could accept the notion of alternance in government far more easily than some other European Communist parties. Third, because of the PCI's heroic role in the Resistance, the appeal of Gramsci's *Prison Notebooks*, and PCI organizational survival during Fascism (made easier by the party's cell-like structure), after the war, the party emerged as the dominant force on the left and the second-largest party in Italy.

The early postwar years saw the PCI participate in a tripartite government with Socialists and Christian Democrats, but the advent of the Cold War soon put an end to this political cooperation. The PCI went into opposition and became increasingly isolated during the 1940s and 1950s. At first, the Socialists joined the Communists in isolation. The two parties formed an electoral alliance in 1948, but by the 1960s, the Socialists had moved towards an accommodation with the Christian Democrats, joining the center-left coalition of 1963.

It was to some extent the participation of the Socialists in government, combined with the social problems of the late 1960s, that opened up certain political opportunities for the PCI, since the party now stood as the only substantial voice of opposition on the left. Their share of the vote increased slowly but steadily during the 1960s.

The PCI made a conscious effort to broaden its appeal by a strategy of alliances with other social and political groups. This policy reached its culmination in 1973 with Enrico Berlinguer's announcement of the strategy of "historic compromise." The compromise was to be an alliance between the Communists and all the other democratic parties in Italy. Such an alliance, argued the Communists, was the best way to tackle Italy's pressing social and economic problems.

There were several reasons why the Communists' saw the "historic compromise" as their best strategy. First, the experience of the Marxist Allende government in Chile had shown the difficulties faced by a democratically elected left-wing regime in holding on to power against right-wing forces. Second, the increase in terrorism combined with the success of neo-Fascist parties in the 1972 elections pointed towards a need for solidarity among democratic parties, i.e., the lessons of the interwar years had been learned well. Third, social conflicts in the late 1960s had shown the irrelevance of ideological divisions to the basic problems—low pay, poor housing, lack of schools, etc.—which working people had to face. Finally, the "historic compromise" was an admission that Catholicism *did* exist in Italy. If the Communist Party wished to solve the problems of working people, it had to admit that many members of the working class were Catholic and supported the Christian Democratic Party.

The "historic compromise" strategy was spectacularly successful. In the 1976 elections, the Communists increased their share of the vote from 27.6 percent to 34.4 percent. The problem for the Communists was what to do with their success. The Christian Democrats, having fought the election on an anti-Communist plank, were intransigent in their unwillingness to accept the Communists as full coalition partners. In the end, under pressure from the Socialists, a DC minority government was formed with the conditional support of five parties, including the Communist Party. In return, the Communists were able to participate in committees determining government policy. They were also able to sponsor such policies as a fair-rent law.

The PCI's support for the government came to an end in 1979 when the Communists realized that their strategy had begun to backfire. Continued support of the government would mean further dissatisfaction among their own supporters, who were suffering under government austerity measures. On the other hand, a retreat would be to deny the alliance strategy. In the end, the latter option seemed the lesser of two evils. In the 1979 elections, the PCI vote slipped back to 30.4 percent, and the Communists returned to their old popular-front strategy aimed at allying the leftist parties.

Organization

Officially, there are no factions in the Communist Party, and it is run according to the policy of democratic centralism. When an issue is discussed in party meetings, people may take sides and argue over particular policies. Once a decision has been made, however, party policy must be loyally supported. Continued dissent will result in expulsion. Members of the party have been expelled for refusing to follow the party line, but it is also true that the top leadership of the party has shown increasing divisiveness in recent years, with moderate, centrist, and hard-line wings.

The party is organized throughout Italy at all four levels. The supreme party body is the Congress which meets every four years. The Congress debates broad policy issues, and also elects the party's Central Committee. The Committee in turn elects the political bureau of thirty-two members. The Secretariat, drawn from this body, consists of seven members, headed by the general secretary. It is the latter who directs the day-to-day running of the party.

The PCI is a member of the Communist International, but in recent years has become increasingly estranged from the East European members and from the French Communist Party. The PCI is also a member of the Communist Group in the European Parliament.

The party's major publications include a daily newspaper, *L'Unità*, the weekly *Rinascita*, and two bimonthly journals, *Critica Marxista* and *Politica ed Economia*. The party owns its own publishing house.

Outside organizations associated with the party include Italy's largest trade union, the Italian General Labor Confederation (*Confederazione Generale Italiana di Lavoro;* CGIL). The party also has youth and women's sections, social clubs, cooperatives, and farmers' associations.

PCI headquarters are at Via delle Botteghe Oscure 4, 00186, Rome.

Policy

As part of its alliance strategy, the main target of the PCI's attacks has not been the free enterprise of small-scale businesses, but that of monopoly capital. Many of the PCI's policy stances have been quite uncontentious. In recent years, the party has called for increased government efficiency, peace, more spending on social services, and the protection of civil liberties.

The party has assiduously avoided deep discussion of foreign policy issues, given the sensitivity of the subject matter. Generally, the party accepts Italian membership in NATO and the European Community for the forseeable future. In the longer term, the party favors a middle way for Europe between the two superpowers.

Since 1979, the party's "historic compromise" strategy has been effectively abandoned. The Communists now call for a government of the left.

Membership & Constituency

The PCI claims to have over 1.5 million members, approximately one sixth of its electorate. There are three important demographic characteristics of PCI membership and support. First, it is predominantly male; second, approximately two-thirds of the PCI's support comes from the working class; and, third, the main regions of Communist strength are in the so-called red zone of central Italy.

Financing

Communist Party funds are derived from a wide range of sources: membership dues, ac-

counting for perhaps 10 percent of party income; Communist parliamentarians' salaries, half of which are paid into the party coffers; public funds made available for electoral and organizational expenses; profits from the party-owned companies that enjoy a monopoly of Soviet-Italian trade; profits from party cooperative enterprises; and fund-raising activities. As a highly organized party, the Communists have higher organizational expenses than other Italian parties.

Leadership

Although it is a working-class party, the party leadership of the PCI is predominantly middle class.

Enrico Berlinguer (born 1922) has been general secretary since 1972. Giorgio Napolitano (born 1925) is the member of the Secretariat responsible for organizational affairs, and Eugenio Peggio (born 1929) is secretary of the PCI's economic-policy unit.

Prospects

The PCI was not successful in the 1979 elections, compared to 1976, and is unlikely to be successful in future elections, unless the leadership is able to give the party a new sense of direction. So far, it has not.

Christian Democratic Party (*Partito della Democrazia Cristiana;* DC)

History

The party was first formed in 1943 as a combination of a number of non-Fascist Catholic groups active or semiactive under Fascism, including Catholic Action (*Azione Cattolica*) and the Milanese Guelph movement (*Movimento Guelfo*). These groups were heirs to the Popular Party (*Partito Popolare Italiano*).

The role of Catholics in Italian political life had long been complicated by the "Roman question"—the pope's refusal to accept the status of the Vatican under the terms of the Law of Guarantees issued by the new Italian state in 1872. The pope's ban on Catholic participation in Italian politics meant that Catholics were late arrivals on the political scene in the early twentieth century. The Popular Party was the first manifestation of mass political Catholicism. Led by the left-wing Sicilian priest, Don Sturzo, it concentrated on social issues, irritating the Vatican which was still more interested in resolving the Church's status. Ousted in 1923, Don Sturzo was replaced by Alcide de Gasperi, who emerged in 1943 as the leader of the Christian Democrats. The Christian Democratic Party was then, and is today, much broader than the old Popular Party. It aggregated the traditions of liberal and social Catholicism, as well as more conservative Catholic groups.

In the first postwar election of 1946, the Christian Democrats emerged as the largest party with 35.4 percent of the vote. They participated in a tripartite government with Socialists and Communists until 1947. The advent of the Cold War led directly to the break-up of this coalition and the isolation of Italy's second- and third-largest parties as antisystem parties. The Christian Democrats played on this theme, opposing both Communists and Socialists. Their reward was a 48.5 percent share of the vote in the 1948 legislative elections. They also convinced the public and themselves that the Christian Democratic Party was the only party that could govern Italy. It was not choice that led them into government; it was a moral duty.

The postwar success of the Christian Democrats was not just due to their anti-Communism, other factors were important as well. First, under the terms of the Lateran Pacts of 1929, Catholic groups had been able to organize throughout the Fascist period. When Fascism came to an end, they were swiftly able to set up a political party. Second, the traditional nonsocialist parties had been discredited by their weak response to the rise of Fascism, leaving the Christian Democrats as the main rallying point for the anti-Fascist middle classes. Finally, the Christian Democrats were able to appeal to Catholic elements among the working class.

Portraying themselves as the natural party of government, the Christian Democrats have dominated all postwar governments. From 1948 to 1963, they formed a number of coalitions with the small parties of the center and right. De Gasperi who was prime minister in eight successive governments, exercised strong central control in the party. Following his death in 1954, the party became more factionalized, with first Amintore Fanfani and then Aldo Moro as leaders. In 1963, it was Moro who led the first administration to include the Socialist Party. In 1962, the Naples Congress of the DC had approved an "opening to the left" (apertura a sinistra).

By 1968–69, increasing social conflicts revealed the center-left coalition's lack of success in coping with Italy's social and economic problems. The DC's coalition partners were increasingly concerned about their own electoral prospects. Too few concessions had been made by the DC to reforms advocated by the coalition partners. A series of minority and coalition governments followed, but rifts between the parties forced an early election in 1972. The Communist and Fascist gains in this election made the political situation even more unstable. The DC responded by moving to the right under the renewed influence of Fanfani. The limitations of this move became clear when the DC's antidivorce position was defeated in the referendum of May 1974, and the party suffered losses in the provincial and regional elections of 1975. In the premature elections of 1976, the DC held its own, but only with a virulently anti-Communist campaign, despite which the Communists made startling gains. Thus, whether they liked it or not, the Christian Democrat leaders were obliged to seek some kind of accommodation with the Communists. This accommodation took the form of a six-party agreement in 1977 in which the Communists, Socialists, Republicans, Social Democrats, and Liberals gave external support to a DC government.

The withdrawal of the Communists in 1979 precipitated new elections, followed by a series of minority and coalition governments. Although the coalitions excluded the Communists, the Christian Democrats found that they had to make far greater concessions to their coalition partners than they had hoped. Thus, in 1981, the Christian Democrats were obliged, for the first time in the postwar era, to cede their traditional control of the prime ministerial office. They reacquired this office in November 1982, when Amintore Fanfani became prime minister for the sixth time.

Organization

The DC is above all a party of factions (correnti). In the early days, the strong leadership of de Gasperi ensured that the party was relatively unified. But, by the 1954 party congress, the faction under the leadership of Fanfani and Taviani, Democratic Initiatives (Iniziativa Democratica), was successfully able to challenge the traditional dominance of de Gasperi's "centrist" followers. In recent years, the major factions have been Base, Nuova Sinistra (New Left), and Forze Nuove (New Forces) on the left; the Morotei, now disbanded, an influential group on the center-left which followed the assassinated politician, Aldo Moro; the Dorotei, Iniziativa Popolare (Popular Initiative), and Impegno Democratico (Democratic Commitment) in the center; and *Nuove Cronache* (New Chronicles) on the right. The *Dorotei*, with origins in the Catholic northeast, have been the dominant faction. The placing of factions on this ideological spectrum should be treated cautiously. They depend also on personality and patronage.

In terms of its formal organization, the DC follows the pattern of other Italian political parties. At the national level, the party Congress meets biannually. The National Council has 120 members elected by the Congress; others are coopted from government, party, and affiliated organizations. The day-to-day running of the party is entrusted to the Central Directorate and the Secretariat. The Central Directorate has thirty-five members of whom twenty-seven are elected by the National Council. The Council elects the political and administrative secretaries who form part of the party executive.

The Christian Democrats have international affiliations to the Christian Democratic World Union; the European Christian Democratic Union; and the European People's Party, which is the Euro-parliamentary group of European Community Christian Democratic parties.

The party has a wide range of publications. They include the daily newspaper *Il Popolo* and the weekly *La Discussione.*

The party is also closely tied to a number of Catholic organizations that involve many aspects of the nation's social and cultural life. These organizations include a Catholic trade-union organization, the Italian Confederation of Workers' Unions (*Confederazione Italiana dei Sindacati dei Lavoratori;* CISL); a workers' association, the Christian Association of Italian Workers (*Associazione Cristiana dei Lavoratori Italiani*); Catholic Action (*Azione Cattolica*), which once had almost three million members, but now has only about 750,000; and women's, youth, and teachers' organizations. In addition there are strong links with the conservative Small Farmers' Association (*Coltivatori Diretti*), which includes 1.75 million families. Finally, the Church has extremely close ties with the party at all levels. These ties have diminished only slightly with the election of a Polish pope.

Party headquarters are at Piazza del Gesú 46, 00186 Rome.

Policy

The Christian Democrats are strongly associated with NATO and European Community membership. It was a Christian Democratic government that took Italy into these organizations. Italy also houses the headquarters of the southern flank of NATO. Related to this international outlook is the party's stand against Communism. The party lays great emphasis on freedom and democracy, and the Communist Party is portrayed as the enemy of those values.

True to its multiclass traditions, the Christian Democrats identify themselves with programs to achieve social justice. And, true to their Catholic traditions, they have opposed divorce and abortion, both unsuccessfully. These specific policies are part of a more general emphasis on traditional morality and a Christian way of life.

Despite considerable state involvement in the economy, the Christian Democrats have never seriously developed economic planning. Instead, successive governments have had a laissez-faire view of the economy, stemming not from any fixed ideological doctrine, but more from inertia and incompetence in decision making. Only in the last few years have there been serious attempts by Christian Democratic governments to follow through on rigorous economic policies, including fiscal reform and various austerity measures.

Membership & Constituency

The DC claims to have almost two million members. That is one member for every six votes it received, or 6 percent of the entire electorate. In 1945, membership stood at 537,582. It increased to over 1.5 million by the 1950s, and has stayed at that level since.

Overall, the occupational composition of DC membership shows the party to have been successful in appealing to all social classes. The early drive to increase membership was particularly successful in southern Italy. The majority of members now live in the south and the islands, the reverse of what was previously the case. Part of the reason for the DC's success in attracting new members, particularly in the south, has been its control of patronage, which is important for those working in the public sector (over one-third of the party's members work in the public sector).

The Christian Democratic vote has three major characteristics. First the party has a broad electoral appeal, with all social classes well represented. Second, far more women than men vote for the Christian Democrats. Third, the Christian Democratic vote is not evenly spread throughout the country. The DC is strongest in those areas of the country with strong clerical traditions, mainly the northeast and some provinces in Lombardy, such as Bergamo and Brescia. It is also strong in the southern part of the country where the party has successfully engaged in the politics of patronage.

Financing

The main sources of DC finance are state funds, of which the DC receives approximately 40 percent of the total; contributions from private industry, state agencies, and Catholic organizations; income from social clubs, etc.; and membership dues, which account for approximately 10 percent of the total.

Leadership

The DC leadership is predominantly middle class and Catholic. Leaders also tend to come from regions of traditional DC strength, the northeast and the south. Having a local power base is very important to advancement within the party hierarchy, and gaining control of a government ministry has been an important method of passing along patronage to local supporters. Highway construction is the most commonly cited form of patronage.

Ciriaco De Mita (born 1928) has been party secretary since 1982. His power base is in Avellino, his birthplace not far from Naples. Amintore Fanfani (born 1908), former party secretary and prime minister in six governments. Giulio Andreotti (born 1919) has been prime minister on several occasions and has represented Lazio, outside of Rome, since 1948. Emilio Colombo (born 1921) has served as foreign secretary and prime minister. His power base is in Potenza, his birthplace. Francesco Cossiga (born 1928 in Sardinia) was prime minister from 1979 to 1980.

Prospects

The future is somewhat uncertain for the Christian Democrats. They successfully resisted the Communist challenge in the late 1970s, but they now must face a vigorous challenge from the two Socialist parties. Socialist gains are likely to be at the expense of the Christian Democrats in future elections. Having lost the premiership in 1981 and 1982, the Christian Democrats will be hard pressed to exert their dominance again on future coalitions. However, the Christian Democrats should never be underestimated. Their great experience in government and control of so much patronage is likely to put them at the center of government for many years to come, as they demonstrated by regaining the premiership in late 1982.

Democratic Party of Proletarian Unity for Communism (*Partito Democratico di Unità Proletaria per il Communismo; PDUP*)

History

PDUP was established in 1974 by Lucio Magri, a dissident Communist who had left that party in 1969 and set up the left-wing newspaper *Il Manifesto*. PDUP consisted of a number of political groupings to the left of the Communist Party. In 1976, it contested the elections as part of Proletarian Democracy (*Democrazia Proletaria*), winning six seats with 1.5 percent of the vote. In 1979, it contested the elections alone and won the same number of seats.

Organization

The party is organized at national, regional, provincial, and local levels on the same basis as other parties. Its newspaper is *Il Manifesto*. The party is especially active in universities and large factories.

PDUP headquarters are at Via Tomacelli 146, 00186 Rome.

Policy

The party opposes any coalition with the bourgeois parties, thus opposing the Communists' "historic compromise" strategy. It opposes NATO and the role of the armed forces, and supports changes in traditional morality. It believes in a controlled economy.

Membership & Constituency

The party is effectively one of intellectuals, and some of the younger and more radical members of the working class. It has some 8,000 members.

Financing

Membership dues and public funds provide most of the party's funds.

Leadership

Lucio Magri and Giorgio Foa are the main figures associated with the party.

Prospects

The prospects of the party are poor. The renewed leftward movement of the Communist Party in the last few years has taken away much of the PDUP's *raison d'etre.*

Italian Liberal Party
(*Partito Liberale Italiano;* PLI)

History

The PLI dominated Italian politics in the early years of the new Italian state following unification in 1861. The party was founded in 1848 by Count Camillo di Cavour, the architect of Italian unity. The decline of the PLI as a political force occurred in the early part of the twentieth century, with the extension of the suffrage and the rise of the Popular and Socialist parties. Its weak response to Fascism discredited it in the eyes of the postwar electorate.

The PLI participated in a number of Christian Democratic–led coalitions in the postwar era. During the 1950s, the party suffered a decline in popular support, moving into opposition. By the 1963 election it had recovered its strength, gaining 7.4 percent of the popular vote. Since then, the Liberals have suffered a steady decline, which was halted in the 1979 election, when their share of the vote stood at 1.9 percent.

Organization

Despite its small size, the Liberal Party is seriously factionalized. Some elements, for instance advocate an alliance with parties of the left, including the Communists; for others, such an idea is anathema.

In terms of formal organization, the PLI follows the pattern of other parties. The party publishes *La Nuova Tribuna* monthly.

PLI headquarters are at Via Frattini 89, 00187 Rome.

Policy

The party is liberal in the sense that it stands for free enterprise. No other Italian party makes free-enterprise policies an important part of its party program. The Liberals also favor political freedoms and democratic rights. In the international arena, they strongly support Italy's membership in the European Community.

Membership & Constituency

The Liberal Party claims to have 150,000 members. With declining electoral support, membership too has plummeted. Traditionally, the Liberals have been associated with big business, particularly the *Confindustria,* the employers' association. These links still exist, but are no longer so strong. Many of the Liberals' new supporters in the 1960s came from the petty bourgeoise, especially those who regard the Church with some antagonism.

Financing

Because of their declining electorate, the Liberals have received a declining share of public funds that are made available to political parties. They receive additional finance from membership dues and business and industrial contributions.

Leadership

Valerio Zanone (born 1936) has been party secretary since 1976.

Prospects

Despite their slight recovery in the last elections, the Liberal Party's prospects are not particularly bright. Parties in the center-left of the political spectrum currently hold the political initiative. Only the spectacular success of conservative economic policies in other parts of the industrialized world might convince Italians to take notice once again of the Liberals.

Radical Party
(*Partito Radicale;* PR)

History

The Radical Party was founded in 1955 as a break-away group of the Liberal Party. It did not come to national prominence until the 1970s, by which time it had moved considerably further to the left under the influence of Marco Pannella. The party has been an outspoken critic of the political establishment, both Christian Democrat and Communist.

Organization

The Radical Party has a decentralized democratic structure and insists on the rapid rotation of party officials and representatives.

Party headquarters are at Via Torre Argentina 18, 00186 Rome.

Policy

The party is identified with civil libertarian policies. It was very active in organizing the campaigns against the antidivorce and antiabortion laws. The Radicals also aggregate demands of ecologists, nuclear disarmers, etc. They could be termed the new left of Italy's postindustrial society.

Membership & Constituency

The Radicals have a membership of approximately 20,000. Their popularity increased dramatically in the 1979 elections when their share of the vote jumped from 1.1 percent to 3.4 percent. Much of this increase came from young voters and voters, including members of the working class in northern Italy, disillusioned with the radicalism (or lack of it) of the Communist Party.

Financing

Like all other parties, the Radicals receive public finance in proportion to their share of the vote. They have no affiliated organizations and must rely on membership dues and their own fund-raising activities for additional finance.

Leadership

Leadership rotates regularly in the Radical Party. The person most associated with their success is Marco Pannella.

Prospects

It seems probable that with the rise of the peace movement in Europe as a whole, the growing strength of the ecologists, etc., the popularity of the Radicals will increase. They have seized on the issues which many young people today regard as important and have made them their own. Their future will depend on how the more established parties respond.

Italian Republican Party
(*Partito Repubblicano Italiano;* PRI)

History

The PRI was founded in 1894 as the outgrowth of the early radicals. It owed its inspiration to Giuseppe Mazzini, an early advocate in the 1880s for a unified republican state. Though the Republicans had initial pretensions to become a radical, populist party, the party gained and still retains the character of a liberal, intellectual group. Except in a few localized areas, the party never succeeded in establishing a mass base.

Like the Liberals, the Republicans were reconstituted in 1943, but remained somewhat discredited by the events leading up to the Fascist dictatorship. This discredit was partially offset by the Republicans' active role in the Resistance movement.

Although a small party, never with much more than 3 percent of the vote, the Republicans, because of their strategic position in the center-left of the political spectrum, have been in and out of coalition governments throughout the postwar era. The main figure for much of this time was Ugo La Malfa, who died in 1980 after having been the first Republican to be given the opportunity to form an administration in 1980. He failed, and it was left to the leader of the party, Giovanni Spadolini, to form the first Republican-led administration one year later.

Organization

The PRI has the same branch organization as other Italian parties. It is more organized in urban than in rural areas. It publishes a daily newspaper, *La Voce Repubblicana.* It is connected with the Italian Union of Labor (*Unione Italiana di Lavoro;* UIL).

Republican headquarters are at Piazza dei Caprettari 70, 00186 Rome.

Policy

The party emphasizes the need for government efficiency, democracy, and human rights. It believes in economic planning and greater productivity and also favors decentralization of government. Social justice is also high on the party's list of priorities. The Republicans favor both NATO and EEC membership.

Membership & Constituency

The party has approximately 100,000 members. Both in membership and elections, it appeals predominantly to the urban middle classes.

Financing

The party receives some public funds as well as contributions from commerce and industry and membership dues.

Leadership

Giovanni Spadolini (born 1921), an historian, has been party secretary since 1979. Bruno Visentini (born 1914) has been party president since 1979. Giorgio La Malfa (born 1939), an economist, is a PRI deputy and has been a government minister in recent coalitions.

Prospects

Although Spadolini lost the premiership in late 1982, the prospects for the PRI look favorable. Spadolini was adept at holding an unstable coalition together, and that should pay off at the next elections. A possible danger to the Republicans is the growing strength of the two Socialist parties. Their success could be at the partial expense of the Republicans.

Italian Social Democratic Party (*Partito Socialista Democratico Italiano;* PSDI)

History

The PSDI was founded in 1947 as a result of a split in the Socialist Party at its Congress that year. Until 1952, it was known as the Workers' Socialist Party (*Partito Socialista dei Lavoratori Italiani;* PSLI). The source of the split was the Saragat faction's opposition to an electoral alliance with the Communist Party. In choosing to set up their own party, the Social Democrats allied themselves with the bourgeois parties of the center and right. Their reward has been regular participation in Christian Democratic-led coalitions during the post-war era.

During the 1960s, the "opening to the left" brought about a rapprochement between Socialists and Social Democrats. At a joint congress in 1965, the parties formally merged into the United Socialist Party (*Partito Socialista Unificato;* PSU). In 1969, however, as a result of increasing ideological divisions, made worse by electoral losses, the unified party broke up, and the PSDI was reconstituted. Giuseppe Saragat was the founder and leader of the PSDI for many years and was also president of the republic from 1964 to 1971.

Organization

The PSDI has an organizational structure similar to other Italian parties. The party is affiliated internationally with the Socialist International. Its main publications include the weekly magazine *L'Umanita* and a monthly journal, *Ragionamenti* (Reasonings).

The main parapolitical organization associated with the PSDI is the Union of Italian Labor (*Unione Italiano di Lavoro;* UIL). It was founded in 1948, following an ideological split in the Communist CGIL. Republicans and Socialists are also active in the UIL, which is the smallest of Italy's three main labor unions.

Party headquarters are at Via Santa Maria i Via 17, 00187 Rome.

Policy

Despite its socialist origins, the PSDI is a relatively conservative party. It is a strong supporter of NATO, law-and-order policies, and the mixed economy. Since 1981, the PSDI has agreed to collaborate more closely with the Socialists.

Membership & Constituency

The PSDI claims a membership of 200,000. With only 3.8 percent of the vote in the 1979 elections, it can hardly be considered a party with a mass base. It does not receive significant working-class support, with most of its support coming from the white-collar sector. Recent opinion polls show its popularity to be on the increase ending a long decline which began 1960s.

Financing

The PSDI's three major sources of funding are public funds, membership dues, and private contributions.

Leadership

Pietro Long (born 1935) has been national secretary since 1978.

Prospects

With the Christian Democrats and the Communists on the defensive, and with a new understanding between the Social Democrats and the Socialists, the prospects of the PSDI are brighter than they have been for some time. In the next elections, due no later than 1984, they should increase their share of the vote and have greater weight in future government coalitions.

Italian Socialist Party
(*Partito Socialista Italiana;* PSI)

History

The first mass party in Italy, the PSI was formally established in 1892 by Filippo Turati. Although it was an antisystem party, it became the largest party with the expansion of the franchise in 1919.

In the early days, the party was deeply divided between reformists and maximalists. And in 1921, the latter split away at the Leghorn Congress to found the Communist Party. In 1922, right-wing reformists also split from the party to found their own organization, but returned to the fold in 1930.

The Socialists had an underground organization during the Fascist period and were active in the Resistance. After the war, they emerged in the 1946 elections as the largest party on the left with 20.7 percent of the vote. But the Communists were close behind with 18.9 percent. When the Social Democrats split from the Socialists over the policy of an electoral alliance with the Communists, the PSI lost about one-third of its support.

During the 1950s, the Socialists' ties to the Communist Party isolated them from other parties within the political system. It was under the leadership of Pietro Nenni that the Socialists moved somewhat reluctantly to an accommodation with Catholicism and the parties of the center. This accommodation was finally achieved in 1963 when the Socialists entered a center-left coalition led by the Christian Democrats. This period also saw a rapprochement with the Social Democrats. The two parties merged in 1965, but separated again in 1969. The Socialists' move to the right in the 1960s also precipitated a left-wing break-away movement, the Italian Socialist Party of Proletarian Unity (*Partito Socialista Italiano di Unità Proletaria;* PSIUP), founded in 1964. It finally disbanded in 1972; some members returned to the Socialists, but the majority joined the Communist Party.

The experience of government was a mixed blessing to the Socialists. On the one hand, they were able to gain access to large areas of public patronage; a Socialist, for example, became minister of public works. On the other hand, the Socialists also became tarred with the brush of corruption and immobilism. As junior coalition partners, the reforms they were able to achieve were very limited. Meanwhile, the Communists became the main voice of opposition on the left.

Throughout the various crises of the 1970s, the Socialists played a cautious role between the two major parties. By the late 1970s, however, the leadership had fallen into the hands of the right-wing factions, led by Bettino Craxi, who has brought dynamic leadership to the Socialists. Following the 1979 elections, he imposed tough demands on the Christian Democrats for future Socialist participation in coalitions. One of these demands has been for greater ministerial representation for the Socialists, who have also refused to accept the Christian Democrats' hold on the premiership. Now that they have agreed on greater collaboration with the Social Democratic Party, the Socialists see and sell themselves as a "third force" in Italian politics.

Organization

Like other Italian parties, the Socialist Party is highly factionalized. At the present time, the right-wing faction under Bettino Craxi is in the ascendant. The leader of the left, Claudio Signorile, was recently deposed as vice secretary of the party.

In terms of its formal organization, the PSI has a branchlike structure similar to that of other parties. The party has a number of associated organizations, including the Italian Union of Labor (UIL) and the General Confederation of Italian Labor (CGIL). These are not exclusively socialist, but have socialist representation. The party also has women's and youth organizations.

The PSI publishes a daily newspaper, *Avanti.* It also has a number of other publications including a monthly journal, *Mondo Operaio.*

In its international affiliations, the party, like the PSDI, belongs to the Second International.

Party headquarters are at Via del Corso 476, 00186 Rome.

Policy

The Socialist Party has undergone a considerable change over the postwar era. From initial opposition to NATO and the European Community, the party has become an active supporter.

In domestic economic policy, the party has moved from a belief in a centralized planned economy to an endorsement of more orthodox economic policies in the 1970s and 1980s. The Socialists, unlike the Communists, have seldom made reference to nationalization. More generally, the Socialists emphasize the need to improve social services, social justice, and government efficiency. Under Craxi, the party has steered a rightward course with the object of presenting the party as an alternative to the doctrinaire socialism of the Communists and to the inefficiency and corruption of the Christian Democrats.

Membership & Constituency

The Socialists claim a membership of approximately 500,000, approximately one-sixth of their electorate. Membership has remained relatively stable over the past thirty years. However, there has been a gradual decline of membership in traditional socialist strongholds in the northern industrial regions. Similarly, there has been an increase in membership in the south. These changes have been most noticeable since the 1960s. Today, the membership and the electorate of the Socialist Party is remarkably heterogeneous in terms of its socioeconomic characteristics. It is a party that appeals as much to the middle classes as it does to the working classes.

Financing

The Socialist Party receives about 10 percent of the total public funds distributed to the parties. Membership dues, private contributions, and money earned from cooperative enterprises make up the bulk of the party's income.

Leadership

Bettino Craxi (born 1934) has been secretary of PSI since 1976. His power base is in Milan, his birthplace.

Claudio Signorile (born 1937) is leader of a leftist faction.

Prospects

The Socialist Party's prospects appear to be favorable. If the Socialists make substantial electoral gains in the next election, it seems likely that they may gain the premiership of a coalition government, which could initially include Christian Democrats and later Communists.

Minor Parties

There are two kinds of minor parties that play a significant role in Italian politics: ethnoregional and armed terrorist parties.

South Tyrol People's Party (*Sudtiroler Volkspartei;* SVP)

The SVP has long been the dominant party in the German-speaking South Tyrol, where it ob-

tains 70 percent of the local vote. It governs in the province of Bolzano in coalition with the Christian Democrats. Essentially, the SVP is a conservative, Catholic party seeking to maintain German cultural dominance of the area. The party finances a trade union and a newspaper. It no longer calls quite so loudly for union with Austria. It maintains close foreign links with the North Tyrol in Austria and with the Bavarian Christian Social Union. Party headquarters are in Bolzano (Bozen).

Val d'Aosta Union (*Union Valdotaine*)

With two parliamentary seats, the *Union Valdotaine* represents the French-speaking minority in the Val d'Aosta. It is an amalgamation of several regional groups.

For Trieste (*Per Trieste*)

Per Trieste is a nonparty list calling for greater autonomy for this city on the Yugoslav border.

Other regional parties have gained representation only in regional councils.

Red Brigades (*Brigate Rosse*)

The best known of the armed parties is the Red Brigades (*Brigate Rosse*) whose leader, Renato Curcio, is now in prison. The party had its origins in the late 1960s among disaffected university students. Universities in Trento and Padova were important training grounds. The party believes in the need for armed struggle in order to achieve socialism. In 1978, the party kidnapped and murdered the prominent Christian Democrat, Aldo Moro. The party is financed through kidnapping and bank raids. Its precise membership is not known, but it is thought to have perhaps 200 activists and as many as 100,000 sympathizers.

National Prospects

The resignation of the Spadolini government in November 1982 may be regarded by some observers as indicating a certain continuity in Italian politics. A pattern of unstable governments has not heretofore threatened the existence of the state. Yet viewed from another angle, it could be argued that Italy is now in a deeper and more serious political crisis than it has ever faced before. This political crisis is a reflection of social and economic crises. The immediate economic problem is an estimated budget deficit for 1982 equal to 15 percent of GNP. Public expenditures are wildly out of control. Huge wage increases won by the unions in the 1970s are indexed to the cost of living, which further aggravates the economic crisis. Inflation is currently running at close to 2 percent per month, and a further increase in the money supply could lead to run-away inflation. The ability of the government to finance the public debt is seriously in doubt. Thus, the Italian state is close to bankruptcy, which would mean the breakdown of the social security system, the public administration, and the enormous state enterprises which dominate the Italian economy. Such a breakdown would entail severe social costs and probably provoke extensive social unrest.

The long-term solution depends on the formation of a government that is prepared to make hard choices, for example, cutting public expenditure and abolishing indexed wage increases. Work on pressing social problems, such as the development of Italy's economically depressed south, would have to be postponed. Such choices would not be popular, and no political party has so far shown any willingness to take on the challenge. The new Fanfani government has made the usual promises to deal with the crisis, but significantly has made no promise to deal with indexation. It is doubtful that Fanfani will be better able than previous governments to cope with pressing problems. To an outside observer, there seems to be little doubt that only the cooperation of the Communists will enable a government to pursue an austerity plan without provoking severe social unrest. But the Communists, for their part, are wary of supporting any austerity plan unless they are part of the government. After the failed cooperation of the 1970s, both major parties are in a quandary as to their future strategy. The problem remains one of accommodation between Catholicism and Communism. The threat of terrorism adds a further dimension of uncertainty.

Should the Fanfani government not prove equal to its task, early elections are the most likely outcome, perhaps in the spring of 1983 if not sooner. If the Socialist parties increase their vote at the expense of the major parties, as is currently predicted, there could be a greater possibility for some form of broad interparty cooperation. Such developments will determine the future of the Italian state.

Further Reading

Allum, P. A. Italy: *Republic Without Government?* London: Wiedenfeld & Nicolson, 1973.

Amyot, Grant. *The Italian Communist Party.* London: Croom Helm, 1981.

Barnes, Samuel H. *Representation in Italy.* Chicago: University of Chicago Press, 1977.

Blackmer, D. L. M., and Tarrow, S., eds. *Communism in France and Italy.* Princeton, N. J.: Princeton University Press, 1975.

Graziano, L., and Tarrow, S., eds. *La Crisi Italiana.* Vol. I, II. Torino: Einaudi, 1979.

Penniman, Howard, R., ed. *Italy at the Polls, 1979.* Washington, D.C.: American Enterprise Institute, 1979.

Pridham, Geoffrey. *The Nature of the Italian Party System.* London: Croom Helm, 1981.

Zariski, R. *The Politics of Uneven Development.* New York: Holt, Rinehart, and Winston, 1981.

Zuckerman, Alan S., *The Politics of Faction.* New Haven, Conn.: Yale University Press, 1979.

REPUBLIC OF IVORY COAST
(*République de la Côte d'Ivoire*)
by Steven Metz, M.A.

The System of Government

Ivory Coast has a presidential form of government built on a separation of powers. The system is based on the constitution adopted at independence in 1960.

The real key to politics in Ivory Coast, however, lies with one man—President Félix Houphouët-Boigny. Houphouët-Boigny led Ivory Coast to independence, wrote the constitution, and has totally dominated Ivorian politics for the past three decades.

Ivory Coast is the most prosperous nation in Black Africa and retains very close ties with the former colonial metropole, France. Because of the stability of the economy and the use of many French experts in the government and economy, Ivory Coast has one of the most efficient, stable, and smooth-running governments in Africa.

Executive

Most political power lies with the presidency, as stipulated by the constitution. The president is head of state, head of government, and the embodiment of national unity. In addition, he has the power to initiate legislation, which is almost invariably approved by the National Assembly. He may appoint, dismiss, and outline the functions of the cabinet members and may appoint most other high-ranking civil, judicial, and military leaders. The president is also commander-in-chief of the military. Since Houphouët-Boigny also leads the sole national party, his real power exceeds even that granted by the constitution. He further consolidated his political power in 1977 with a cabinet reshuffle that replaced many of the older ministers with younger technocrats.

The president is chosen by a direct national election for a five-year term of office. The constitution stipulates that the president be at least forty years old, an eligible voter, and not the holder of one of several high political offices which could affect the outcome of an election.

The president is elected if he receives a majority of votes cast on the first ballot, or, if no candidate receives a majority, through a runoff election between the two top candidates. The most recent election was in October 1980, when Houphouët-Boigny was elected to a fifth five-year term. Although he ran unopposed, voter turnout was over 80 percent, with Houphouët-Boigny receiving 99.9 percent of the votes cast.

Before 1980, the president of the National Assembly had been designated the successor of the president in case of death or incapacitation, but in November of that year the National Assembly unanimously adopted a constitutional amendment creating the position of vice president. A vice president is to be elected in 1985 in the same manner and at the same time as the president. Until that election, Houphouët-Boigny has no official successor.

Legislature

The legislative branch of Ivory Coast government is made up of a National Assembly of 147 members. Deputies to the National Assembly are selected from a national slate presented by the party. Although candidates for a seat in the National Assembly do not represent a single district or constituency, there is an attempt by the party nominating committee to create a ticket balanced geographically, ethnically, and by occupation.

A deputy to the National Assembly must be at least twenty-three years old and an eligible elector. He must not be the holder of certain high government positions, the employee of a foreign government or international organization, or a high-ranking employee of a firm receiving a government subsidy.

According to the constitution, the National Assembly meets in two regular sessions, each lasting about three months. The first session opens in April and the second in October. The primary powers of the National Assembly are the voting of laws and the authorization of taxes. The constitution requires that the National Assembly present a balanced budget, which means that any bill which would require an increase in spending must be accompanied by a statement either showing how revenues could be increased or how other spending could be cut to compensate for the new spending.

The constitution stipulates that any power not expressly given to the National Assembly is outside its domain. This serves to augment the power of the president, who has fewer constitutional limits on his power. In fact, Houphouët-Boigny's control of the party, which nominates all deputies to the National Assembly, means that the actions of the president are almost never opposed by the National Assembly.

The most recent elections for the National Assembly were held in November of 1980, when deputies were elected for a new five-year term. The 1980 election was the first in which a multicandidate slate was presented, and the results expressed widespread discontent with the old Assembly. Although voter turnout was only around 30 percent, fifty-four of eighty incumbents standing for reelection were defeated.

Judiciary

The legal system of Ivory Coast is a mixture of customary and French law. The Supreme Court's constitutional section may rule on the constitutionality of bills which have been proposed or passed by the National Assembly, but not promulgated. The court's administrative section is the court of final appeal for cases dealing with government administration and the bureaucracy; and the audit and control section oversees state expenditures and audits state accounts. The High Court of Justice, composed of deputies to the National Assembly, rules on crimes committed by government officials within the line of duty, and on charges of treason against high officials, including the president.

While the judiciary of Ivory Coast plays a valuable role in the administration of the government, the fact that the president controls appointments to the courts means that the judiciary seldom opposes the president on political issues.

Regional & Local Government

Local government in Ivory Coast is modeled after the French system. The country is divided into twenty-five departments, each governed by a prefect appointed by the president. The thirty-seven largest towns and cities are governed by municipal councils which, since the 1980 election reforms, are elected from a multicandidate slate presented by the party.

The Electoral System

Elections in Ivory Coast are direct; suffrage is universal for those twenty-one years of age and older. The electoral process is by secret ballot and follows a campaign limited by law to a two- or three-week period.

All elections are by the slate system in which the party gaining the majority of votes wins all the seats in the National Assembly or local council. A further obstacle to the rise of an opposition party is a system of expensive filing fees required of candidates for political office. While any qualified citizen is free theoretically to run against the Democratic Party of Ivory Coast (PDCI) slate, he will not get his money back unless he gains at least 10 percent of the vote.

The Party System

Although the constitution of Ivory Coast states that parties may be formed and may compete openly, the country is in practice a one-party state. Even when candidates who are not formally members of PDCI compete in elections, they do so with the approval of the party.

Besides the slate system and the expensive filing fees for candidates, the PDCI has prevented the rise of formal opposition by giving prominent persons, who might conceivably lead such an opposition, high and demanding positions in the government. The institution in 1980 of a multicandidate-slate system was designed in part to overcome a tendency on the part of politicians to show greater concern for their immediate party ties than for their responsibilities as legislators.

The total domination of the government by the PDCI has helped to make it an unofficial fourth branch of the government. Most important decisions affecting government policy actually are made by the elite of the PDCI, and Houphouët-Boigny has utilized his control of the party to insure his control of the government.

Democratic Party of Ivory Coast (*Parti démocratique de la Côte d'Ivoire;* PDCI)

History

The PDCI was formed in the late 1940s as the Ivorian branch of the African Democratic Rally (*Rassemblement Démocratique Africain* [RDA]). The RDA was an organization formed to encourage independence for French West Africa. Although the French opposed the efforts of the RDA prior to 1951, after that date the French withdrew their support of other African groups, and then allowed the RDA—and its branch, the PDCI—to dominate politics in the region. Both the RDA and the PDCI were founded by Houphouët-Boigny. The PDCI has won every election since independence.

Organization

The organization of the PDCI is highly centralized. While party organs exist down to the local level, all policy is formed at the national level. Local party organs serve more to mobilize support than as policymaking bodies.

Policy

In effect, the PDCI is a nonideological party dedicated to free enterprise and to a very close relationship with the West in general and with France in particular. Rather than proposing long-range political schemes, the PDCI follows a pragmatic approach which emphasizes solving current problems and preserving the balance among the various ethnic groups which make up Ivory Coast.

Except for occasional student unrest and an attempted military coup d'état in 1973, there have been few challenges to Houphouët-Boigny's control of the party and the government. His strict repression of violence, his policy of co-opting the opposition, his emphasis on "dialogue" with those who disagree with his policies, and the prosperity of Ivory Coast have all combined to augment his control of Ivorian politics. Since the late 1970s, Houphouët-Boigny has concentrated on making the party and the government more democratic through actions such as the electoral reforms and on diminishing political corruption. Both efforts appear to have succeeded.

Membership

The party claims universal membership. Through village-level organs of the party, all eligible voters participate in party activity, although this activity is more an expression of support than real input into policymaking.

Financing

Although no data is available on party finances, it can be assumed that substantial funds come directly from the government.

Leadership

Félix Houphouët-Boigny (born 1905) was trained as a physician, but he was always more interested in politics than in the practice of medicine. His prestige as a tribal chief and wealthy planter have added to his effectiveness.

Philippe Yace was the heir-apparent until a period in 1978 to 1979 when he was removed from public view for what was seen as mishandling of duties dealing with a local election. The most frequently mentioned successors now are two ministers of state, Mathieu Ekra and Jean-Baptise Mockey, and the Ivorian representative at the World Bank, Henri Konan-Bédié. Whoever the successor, it is likely that Houphouët-Boigny's policies will be carried on after his death—at least in the short run—in order to preserve the precarious yet successful political and economic equilibrium which these policies have fostered.

Other Political Forces

Ethnic Groups

There is no single dominant tribe in Ivory Coast. Three major groups make up over 50 percent of the population. They are distributed as follows: Akan, 25 percent; Mande, 15 percent; Kru, 18 percent. Cabinet positions are distributed more or less according to these proportions. In general Ivorian politics is centered less on tribal divisions than on class lines or on rural–urban splits, neither of which would provide a workable basis for political fragmentation following Houphouët-Boigny's death.

French Influence

The influence of the French in the Ivorian government is considerable, but generally unopposed, primarily because nearly all segments of Ivorian society realize that much of the smoothness which typifies the political and economic administration of the country is due to French help. While there is occasional public grumbling about the role of the French, the relationship will probably continue after Houphouët-Boigny's death.

National Prospects

As long as Houphouët-Boigny controls the government, political stability seems assured. Because of his age, however, the problem of the succession makes prediction difficult.

Most opposition to the government appears centered around personal grievances and general student discontent, rather than focusing on specific ideological issues or on ethnic or regional differences.

Since so much of the stability and efficiency of the Ivorian government depends on the prosperity of the economy, the government is very conscious of the need for continued economic growth. The policy of encouraging foreign investment, while causing some degree of discontent among the local middle class, appears to have created a stable rate of growth. Any serious setback in the economy could have lasting repercussions in the political system.

Further Reading

Roberts, T. D., et al. *Area Handbook for the Ivory Coast.* Washington, D.C.: U.S. Government Printing Office for Foreign Area Studies, American University, 1973.

Foster, Philip and Zolberg, Aristide R. *Ghana and the Ivory Coast.* Chicago: University of Chicago Press, 1971.

Zolberg, Aristide R. *One-Party Government in the Ivory Coast.* Princeton: Princeton University Press, 1974.

JAMAICA

by Indira Jhappan

The System of Government

Jamaica, a Caribbean island nation of nearly 2.25 million people, is a parliamentary democracy which gained its independence from Great Britain in 1962 after eighteen years of self-government. The population is predominantly of African descent with small groups of East Indian, Arab, Jewish, and mixed heritage. There is a small elite group of wealthy families and businessmen, but the majority of the population is poor. The economy rests on bauxite mining and processing, industry, tourism, and to a lesser extent, agriculture.

Executive

Executive power is formally vested in the British monarch represented by a governor-general appointed by the monarch on the advice of the prime minister of Jamaica. The governor-general is advised by the six-member Privy Council. The real executive officer of the nation is the prime minister, who is the leader of the majority party in the House of Representatives, to which he and his cabinet are responsible.

Legislature

The bicameral Jamaican Parliament consists of the House of Representatives and the Senate. The House presently has sixty members elected by direct universal suffrage to five-year terms. The twenty-one-member Senate is appointed by the governor general: thirteen members on the advice of the prime minister and eight on the advice of the leader of the opposition. Cabinet members may be appointed from either the House or the Senate. Although the Parliament is the preeminent authority, it is effectively under the control of the prime minister.

Bills may be introduced by either body, with the exception of money bills which can only be introduced in the House. While the Senate may delay the passage of a bill by voting it down, the House can override that action by passing the bill a second time. Senate approval is required for constitutional amendments. Parliamentary standing committees handle legislative business under the direction of the prime minister and his cabinet. On the advice of the prime minister, the governor-general may dissolve the Parliament and call for new elections at any time.

Judiciary

The judicial system is based on English common law and procedures. The courts of superior record are the Supreme Court and the Court of Appeal. The Supreme Court consists of the chief justice and other judges. The chief justice is appointed by the governor-general on the recommendation of the prime minister in consultation with the leader of the opposition. The other judges are also appointed by the governor-general on the advice of the Judicial Service Commission, which is chaired by the chief justice. Appeals from the Supreme Court go to the Court of Appeal, which is the highest court in Jamaica. Appeals from the Court of Appeal may be sent to the Privy Council in London, which is the ultimate court of appeal. Judges retire after sixty-five years of age and can only be removed on the request of the governor-general to the Privy Council in London and after an investigation by that body.

Regional & Local Government

For administrative purposes, Jamaica is divided into fourteen parishes and the Kingston and St. Andrew Corporation, which includes the principal urban area. Each parish has an elected council which administers local affairs.

RESULTS OF ELECTIONS (1972–1980)			
	1972	1976	1980
People's National Party (PNP)	37	48	9
Jamaica Labour Party (JLP)	15	12	51
Independents	1	—	—

The Electoral System

Jamaica has held national elections since 1944; all Jamaicans eighteen and over are eligible to vote. Elections to the House of Representatives are held at least every five years, and seats are won by simple plurality in single-member constituencies. A candidate must make a nominal deposit to run for office and forfeits it if he or she fails to gain 12.5 percent of the constituency vote. The boundaries of the constituencies are reviewed by a standing committee in the Parliament. Elections in the past have been fairly conducted.

The Party System

Modern party activity began in Jamaica in 1938 with the founding of the PNP. From the beginning, political parties and labor unions have had intertwined histories. The two major political leaders of the previous generation both gained prominence in association with the labor movement: Alexander Bustamente first gained nationwide stature when he was arrested and imprisoned during a period of labor unrest in 1938; Norman Manley was his defense lawyer. The unions and parties compete with each other for members, and the electoral success of a party often brings increased membership to its associated unions. The trade-union movement not only supplies party support, but also party leadership. The present JLP leader is an exception in not having come up through union leadership.

The party system is open and well developed. There are no barriers to the entry of new parties or independents, but they have seldom fared well in face of the disciplined organizations of the two major parties. Both the PNP and JPL are organized by constituency. Initially, union organization was the armature on which party organization was built, but in the 1950s, more organized and independent party structures were developed. While the constituency organizations have some say in the formation of policy and name the party candidates, a charismatic party leader generally determines policy and important candidacies in consultation with party notables. Both parties maintain youth organizations which provide the core of their forces during campaigns.

Campaign expenditures are limited by law. No details of party financing are available, but it is generally believed that both parties receive sizable contributions from business and industrial interests.

Election campaigns are well organized and hard fought, but have been marked by serious violence in recent years. Over 500 people reportedly died in campaign-related violence preceding the 1980 election. Much of this violence stems from the youth wings of the parties, which attempt to control sections of Kingston so that opposition candidates will find it virtually impossible to campaign in those sections.

These areas of violence are often those housing the poorest of the population. Each party competes most strongly for this section of the vote, which has been the deciding factor in Jamaican elections. The 1972 and 1976 successes of the PNP under Michael Manley were due to his left-wing appeal to the urban poor, while his failure to improve their lot and unemployment rate of 30 percent was decisive in the PNP's rout in 1980.

Jamaica Labour Party (JLP)

The JLP was founded by Alexander Bustamante in 1943 after he took his Bustamente Industrial Trade Union (BITU) out of association with the PNP in a dispute over that party's advocacy of Jamaican independence. Most of the JLP's support came from the working classes, while the leadership was primarily from the middle and professional classes. Initially opposed to independence, the JLP first came to power in 1944, when Jamaica achieved self-government. It was out of power from 1955 to 1962, but presided over the transfer of sovereignty in 1962. It was out of power again from 1972 to 1980.

In its early years, the party was dominated by Bustamante, but with his retirement in the mid-1960s, the strength of the constituency organizations was increased and more democratic procedures were developed. The party's political perspective has always been right of center, emphasizing free enterprise, foreign investment, and economic expansion as the best route to improved conditions to the island's poor. Strongly based in the rural areas of the island, the JLP also draws on the social elite, as well as on a sizable portion of small business interests and the urban poor.

The present JLP leader, Edward Seaga (born 1930), is a white businessman who was born in the United States of Jamaican parents. First elected to the House in 1962, he became leader of the party in 1974. He has a reputation as an expert in financial management. The continuance of the party in power will depend almost entirely on Seaga's success in resolving the nation's economic problems through increased foreign investment and rising employment.

People's National Party (PNP)

The PNP was founded in 1939 by Norman Manley. It was primarily a middle-class party which sought Jamaican independence and an end to the dominance of British capital on the island. It relied heavily on Bustamante's union in its early years, but developed as a well-organized party with relatively little union buttressing when Bustamante split with the party in 1943. In the 1950s, Manley organized the National Workers' Union to provide a strong base of labor support for the PNP.

While the party's strength in its early years was based primarily on the middle and professional classes, the party moved sharply to the left after the founder died in 1969 and his son, Michael Manley (born 1923), took over. The younger Manley had been a UNW organizer and leader, and he increased the appeal of the party to the urban poor and to younger voters. As prime minister from 1972 to 1980, Manley pursued a socialist policy, stressing nationalization of foreign interests and a variety of social programs, of which the best known was a literacy campaign. Manley associated Jamaica with the Third World and nonaligned movements and expressed solidarity with the governments of Cuba and Grenada.

Manley's term of office saw a 17 percent decline in the Jamaican economy, an increase in the unemployment rate from 20 percent to 30 percent, and the accumulation of a foreign debt amounting to about one billion dollars. As a result, many of the party's major figures were defeated in the 1980 elections, although Manley retained his seat. At the moment, the party's future does not appear to be promising, but it will undoubtedly remain a serious opposition party, ready to challenge any failure by the Seaga government. To this end, although Manley was reelected party leader in September 1982, the party appears to be moving to the right and cutting its ties to the left.

Minor Parties

Several small parties have competed in most elections, without success. Most of them also have their own trade-union detachments. For example, the Worker's Liberation League (WLL), a Marxist-Leninist party, is associated with the University and Allied Workers' Union. The party leader, Dr. Trevor Munroe, is vice president of the union.

National Prospects

Seaga's cautious economic policies, if they receive a quick assist from foreign investors and the United States' Caribbean Basin development proposals, may put the island on the road to recovery. The continuing world economic slowdown, however, places limits on the speed and degree of that recovery even with the best possible planning and execution of development programs. While the party system has proven itself stable and transfers of power have been orderly for nearly forty years, it is not inconceivable that further deterioration in the economy could bring an abrupt and violent change in the political system.

Further Reading

Brown, Aggrey. *Colour, Class, and Politics in Jamaica.* New Brunswick, N. J.: Transaction Books, 1978.

Gooding, Earl. *The West Indies at the Crossroads: The Search for a Viable Future.* Cambridge, Mass.: Schenkman, 1981.

Kuper, Adam. *Changing Jamaica.* London: Routledge and Kegan Paul, 1976.

Stone, Carl. *Democracy and Clientelism in Jamaica.* New Brunswick, N. J.: Transaction Books, 1980.

———. "Democracy and Socialism in Jamaica, 1962–1979." *Journal of Commonwealth and Comparative Politics*, Vol. 19, No. 2, July 1981.

———, and Brown, Aggrey, eds. *Perspectives on Jamaica in the Seventies.* Kingston: Jamaica Publishing House, 1981.

JAPAN
(*Nihon*)
by Martin E. Weinstein, Ph.D.

The System of Government

Japan, a nation of about 117 million people, is a unified constitutional monarchy with a parliamentary cabinet form of government. Japan has been governed by its cabinet and has had an elected Parliament and competitive political parties since 1889, but the government did not become fully representative and responsible until 1947. Under the Meiji constitution of 1889, the emperor was nominally sovereign and the cabinet was legally responsible to the emperor, not to the popularly elected lower house of the National Diet. In practice, before World War II, prime ministers and their cabinets were usually selected by agreement between the leaders of the majority political parties in the Diet and the emperor's extraconstitutional advisers, including elder statesmen, court officials, and military leaders. Under the 1947 constitution, (promulgated during the U.S. occupation, 1945 – 52), the emperor is defined as "the symbol of the State and of the unity of the people," with no powers related to government. The prime minister is now elected by the popularly elected Diet and is responsible to it.

Although the emperor's duties as head of state are purely symbolic and ceremonial, it would be a mistake to conclude that the imperial institution is empty or meaningless. The imperial family represents 2,000 years of continuity in Japanese life. It is the central, unifying element in the Japanese national consciousness.

The 1947 constitution also broadened and more firmly guaranteed the civil liberties of Japanese citizens, making Japan among the most free and open nations in the world today.

Executive

The constitution vests executive power in the cabinet, composed of about twenty ministers, headed by the prime minister. The constitution stipulates that all members of the cabinet be civil-ians and that a majority of the ministers, including the prime minister, be members of the Diet. In practice, since 1947, almost all the cabinet members and all prime ministers have been members of the House of Representatives (lower house) of the Diet. The constitution provides that the prime minister be selected by a formal resolution of the Diet. Since a majority of those present and voting is required for selection, the post goes to the leader of the majority party or coalition in the Diet. If the House of Representatives and the House of Councillors (upper house) cannot agree on a prime minister, the majority vote of the lower house prevails.

The prime minister selects and can dismiss the members of his cabinet. Twelve of the ministers preside over ministries; the others, without portfolio, include the deputy prime minister, the director of the Economic Planning Agency, the director general of the Defense Agency, and the director of the Environmental Agency.

The constitution makes the cabinet responsible for preparing and submitting the annual government budget to the Diet, managing the nation's foreign and domestic affairs, concluding treaties, administering the civil service, and reporting to the Diet on both national affairs and foreign relations. The cabinet formulates and executes all major policies of state. Despite the prime minister's authority to appoint and dismiss ministers, the cabinet operates by collective responsibility. All members of the cabinet are jointly responsible for their policies or decisions. The cabinet usually meets several times a week. Formal votes are rarely, if ever, taken. Issues are discussed until a consensus is reached. Any dissenting minister is expected to resign.

The formidable powers of the cabinet are limited by its relationship to the Diet, especially the lower house. Cabinet ministers are legally required to attend sessions of both houses of the Diet, and of their committees, and to reply to questions. Bills submitted by the cabinet to the

Diet are subject to amendment and rejection; rejection is rare. The cabinet is dependent on the Diet for appropriations of funds. Cabinet members may also be impeached by resolution of either house of the Diet, although no such impeachment has yet occurred. Finally, the lower house may adopt a resolution of no confidence in the cabinet. Then the cabinet either must resign *en masse* within ten days, or the cabinet must dissolve the lower house and call for a general election. In the latter case, the cabinet must still resign following the convocation of the new Diet, thus giving the Diet the opportunity of either replacing or reinstating the prime minister who called the election.

In practice, no-confidence resolutions have been rare. There have only been three since 1947: two against Prime Minister Yoshida Shigeru* (1948 and 1953) and one against Prime Minister Ohira Masayoshi (1980). Conservative members of the lower house, who have been in the majority since 1948, are reluctant to engage in expensive, impromptu election campaigns. Moreover, they tend to cooperate with and support their faction leaders, who sit in the cabinet. Thus, although the cabinet is responsible to the Diet and is subject to continual influence and control by both its own party and, to some extent, the opposition parties in the Diet, the cabinet generally holds the initiative and the upper hand in the cabinet-Diet relationship.

It should be noted that Japanese prime ministers usually reorganize their cabinets several times in the course of their terms in office. A prime minister can expect to remain in office from two to six years, while other cabinet ministers will generally hold their posts for less than two years. Since the prime minister's position depends on his ability to forge and maintain a dominant coalition among the powerful, well-organized factions within his own party, he reorganizes his cabinet to adjust to shifting factional alignments, as well as to maximize his support within his party by awarding cabinet posts and, thus, their patronage opportunities to as many deserving faction leaders as he can. While frequent cabinet reorganizations do weaken ministerial authority, they do not lead to instability in Japanese policy. The major policymaking ministries and agencies—finance, foreign affairs, international trade and industry, and economic planning—are headed by administrative vice ministers who are career civil servants. These vice ministers meet regularly and frequently with the director of the cabinet secretariat

and the director of the cabinet's Bureau of Legislation, constituting what is known as the "little cabinet." Because they usually hold office longer than their ministers and are extremely well informed and tactful, the administrative vice ministers exert a powerful influence in shaping cabinet policy.

Although the prime ministership is the highest political office in Japan and the cabinet, in comparative international terms, a powerful executive, their authority is hedged by continual checks by the Diet, by intraparty politics, and by the bureaucracy, as well as by the media and the opposition parties. As a result, with few exceptions, such as Prime Minister Yoshida (1946–47, 1948–54)—known as "one man Yoshida"—and Prime Minister Tanaka Kakuei (1972–74)—known as the "computerized bulldozer"—Japanese prime ministers have not been dramatic, take-charge leaders. Their style is one of quietly seeking and building agreements on policy within their government and party, in the Diet, and among the voters, with a minimum of open controversy and confrontation. Consequently, although the competition among conservative faction leaders for the prime ministership and cabinet posts is intense—and provides the Japanese media and public with continual, frequently dramatic power struggles—the central issue in Japanese politics has not been one of deciding among alternative, conflicting policies, but rather who shall get what office and when.

Legislature

The constitution describes the Diet, or legislature, as "the highest organ of state power" and "the sole law-making organ of the State." It provides for a popularly elected bicameral Diet consisting of the 511-member House of Representatives (lower house) and the 252-member House of Councillors (upper house). The basic constitutional provisions have dramatically strengthened the present Diet as compared to its pre-1947 predecessor. The pre-1947 Diet was only one of several groups involved in selecting the cabinet and only one of several sources of law. Under the Meiji constitution both the emperor and the cabinet could and did issue edicts and decrees that had the force of law. No such circumvention of the Diet's legislative powers is now possible.

Ordinary Diet sessions must be convened at least once a year, beginning in mid-December, and

*Japanese personal names in this article are presented in the Japanese style; i.e., surname first.

last for 150 days, unless extended by the Diet. The vote on extension is frequently a major political issue. The ruling party generally favors extension in order to pass legislation that was not completed in the regular session. The opposition parties resist extension as a means of blocking this legislation and impeding cabinet policy. Extraordinary sessions can be called at any time by the cabinet or upon petition by one-fourth of the members of either house. Special sessions are mandated by the constitution and must be convoked within thirty days following a general election. In Japan, as in most modern representative governments, the Diet is now normally in session for the greater part of the year.

Although the lower house conducts its deliberations in both plenary sessions and committees, the committees are usually more important. There are sixteen standing committees largely paralleling the principal ministries and agencies of the government. Membership in the committees is allocated in accordance with relative party strength. Although the majority party has kept control of the chairmanships of all major committees, some committee chairmanships have occasionally been awarded to opposition members. Assignment to committees is made by the parties. Special committees, such as those on the election

system or the Northern Islands (occupied by the Soviet Union in 1945 and still claimed by Japan), are created to deal with particular problems, supposedly of temporary duration. As the two examples mentioned suggest, however, "temporary" can mean decades.

The scheduling and flow of legislative business in the lower house is controlled by the important Committee on House Management, composed of senior representatives of each political party in numbers proportional to their strength in the house. Since the tightly disciplined ruling Liberal Democratic Party (LDP) can count on a majority to pass whatever bills reach a vote in the house, drawing up the house calendar is a politically crucial operation. Generally, when the ruling party encounters determined opposition to a bill in the management committee, the bill in question is either revised to make it palatable to the opposition or it is shelved. In extreme cases, the opposition parties will threaten to boycott the Diet. Although the ruling party could legally ignore a boycott and pass its bill, it rarely does so. Japanese custom requires that important decisions be reached by consensus, not imposed by fiat. To railroad legislation through the Diet would be to call into question the propriety and even the legitimacy of the government, issues which the media would not

HOUSE OF REPRESENTATIVES ELECTIONS, 1960–1980

Party	1960 Percent of Vote	Seats	1963 Percent of Vote	Seats	1967 Percent of Vote	Seats	1969 Percent of Vote	Seats
Liberal Democrats (LDP)	57.5	296	54.7	283	48.8	277	47.6	288
Socialists (JSP)	27.5	145	29.0	144	27.9	140	21.4	90
Democratic Socialists (DSP)	8.7	17	7.4	23	7.4	30	7.7	31
Communists (JCP)	2.9	3	4.0	5	4.8	5	6.8	14
Komeito	—	—	—	—	5.4	25	10.9	47
Independents & Others	3.1	6	5.0	12	5.5	9	5.5	16
Total Seats		467		467		486		486

Party	1972 Percent of Vote	Seats	1976 Percent of Vote	Seats	1979 Percent of Vote	Seats	1980 Percent of Vote	Seats
Liberal Democrats (LDP)	46.8	271	41.8	249	44.6	248	47.9	286
Socialists (JSP)	21.9	118	20.7	123	19.7	107	19.3	107
Democratic Socialists (DSP)	6.9	19	6.3	29	6.8	35	6.6	32
Communists (JCP)	10.5	38	10.4	17	10.4	39	9.8	29
Komeito	8.5	29	10.9	55	9.8	57	9.0	33
New Liberal Club (NLC)	—		4.1	17	3.0	4	3.0	12
Independents & Others	5.3	16	5.8	21	5.6	21	5.0	12
Total Seats		491		511		511		511

fail to dramatize. Thus, the compromises negotiated in the management committee are of great importance in running the Diet.

Members of the lower house are elected for four-year terms. There have been twelve general elections since 1947, however, which indicates that members of the lower house seldom serve a full term before being tested at the polls. Intervals between general elections have varied from six months to the full four years, but usually range about two to three years.

House of Councillors members are popularly elected from two types of constituency. One hundred and fifty-two are chosen from local constituencies. The number of councillors for each local constituency is roughly proportional to population. The remaining 100 members are chosen at large by the national constituency. Councillors serve six-year terms, and the upper house cannot be dissolved. Terms are staggered, so that one half of the upper house stands for election at three-year intervals.

The composition of the upper house is the result of a compromise negotiated between the U.S. occupation officials and the senior Japanese constitutional lawyers who drafted the 1947 constitution. The Americans proposed a unicameral, popularly elected Diet. The Japanese strongly resisted this proposal and advocated instead a corporate upper house representing the professions and selected interest groups, as distinct from the political parties. The existing upper house was supposed to combine the advantages of less partisan, better informed local representation with those of a panel of nationally eminent and also less partisan candidates. In practice, however, the upper house has become as partisan as the lower, and most of the national candidates are drawn from well-known figures in the arts, sports, and the media.

The internal organization of the upper house parallels that of the lower, and so do its deliberations. When the lower house is dissolved for a general election, the upper house suspends its session until the convocation of the postelection Diet. In the case of ordinary bills, if the upper house disapproves a bill passed by the lower house, the lower house can legally enact this bill by passing it a second time by a two-thirds majority of the members present. In practice, such conflicts have occurred rarely, and when they have, they were settled in joint conference committees. In the case of the budget bill, the selection of the prime minister, or the ratification of a treaty, the lower house prevails against the upper by a simple majority. The apparent weakness of the House

of Councillors and the duplication in it of what is essentially a partisan vote has led to recurrent calls for abolition or reform. In the absence of a major crisis, however, the house will endure.

In addition to its powers to make the laws, (including most importantly the budget), to impeach ministers and judges, and to ratify treaties, the Diet is also responsible for auditing the government's accounts and is empowered to appoint committees, with full powers of subpoena, to investigate the efficiency and honesty of the government. It was just such a committee which vigorously pursued the Lockheed scandals in 1976, leading to the arrest and trial of former prime minister Tanaka.

Since the ruling conservatives had enjoyed uninterrupted control of the government since 1948, the question naturally arises of how significant the work of the Diet has been. Is it simply a rubber stamp for the conservative LDP, or are meaningful deliberations conducted in the Diet between the ruling and opposition parties? Although the seemingly permanent LDP majority has rendered the Diet a less significant deliberative body than the British Parliament or the U.S. Congress, the Diet does fulfill a central deliberative and mediating function in Japanese government and politics. As noted, the conservatives habitually refrain from using their majority to railroad legislation through the Diet. Both the conservatives and the opposition know that the media and the voters will judge them harshly if they blatantly disregard the national preference for consensual policymaking. The Diet, providing the central forum for negotiations and compromises, is an essential binding element holding together the Japanese body politic.

Because the Diet is an effective deliberative body, the opposition rarely, and only in desperation, resorts to boycotts, street demonstrations, or violence. In 1960, when the Kishi cabinet, despite a Diet boycott, pushed through ratification of the revised U.S.-Japan Security Treaty, huge street demonstrations and violence in the Diet provoked a national crisis which led to the prime minister's resignation and a general election. Although the conservatives maintained their majority in that election, the "treaty riots" were widely interpreted as evidence of the fragility of representative government in Japan, and forecasts of the early demise of Japanese democracy abounded. More than two subsequent decades of relatively successful, peaceful representative government have refuted those gloomy forecasts. Nevertheless, while the Japanese have managed it for almost thirty-five years, the question of whether a representative political system can long endure with apparently permanent ruling and opposition parties still remains open.

Finally, the nature and significance of the relationship between the Diet standing comittees and the career bureaucracy should be considered, for example, the link between the Diet Committee on Commerce and Industry and the Ministry of International Trade and Industry. It is generally believed in Japan that the bureaucrats initiate and powerfully influence the committee's work. To those who believe that the Diet should control and supervise the bureaucracy, and who see the bureaucracy as antidemocratic, this state of affairs is deeply objectionable. It provides a source for continual criticism in the media and the numerous intellectual journals. The question of how a large, powerful, nonelected bureaucracy is to be made responsive to popular interests and needs is serious, and it is not unique to Japan. It is common to all the industrialized democracies in which electioneering has become more time consuming, while the volume of legislative business has swelled and the technical expertise and judgment required to manage this legislation clearly surpass any one person's grasp.

Judiciary

The 1947 constitution vests "the whole judicial power" in the Supreme Court and in such lower courts as may be established by law, thus creating a judicial branch independent of and equal to the executive and legislative branches. The Supreme Court has administrative control of the lower courts and is explicitly given the power of judicial review. It can determine the constitutionality of any law, government order, regulation, or official act. The fifteen judges of the Court are appointed by the cabinet, with the exception of the high judge, who is appointed by the emperor upon nomination by the cabinet. The judges serve until legal retirement age, subject to popular referenda at ten-year intervals. Beneath the Supreme Court is a hierarchy of eight high courts; fifty district courts (with attached family courts); 575 summary courts; and numerous paralegal civil and family conciliation commissions, composed of one judge and two respected laymen, to provide for out-of-court settlement of disputes.

The courts and the legal system, however, play a lesser role in Japan than this extensive judicial organization might suggest. By tradition, Japanese prefer to settle disputes informally by means of mediation and negotiation and are reluctant to dramatize and publicize their conflicts in the courtroom. The number of civil suits per capita in Japan is between one-tenth and one-twentieth of that in the United States or the United Kingdom. The legal profession is smaller and less prominent politically. There is approximately one lawyer per 10,800 people in Japan, as compared to one per 587 in the United States, or one per 1,700 in the United Kingdom.

In keeping with this reluctance to seek legal remedies, the Supreme Court has made infrequent and tentative use of its power of judicial review. However, in 1976 the court ruled that the then existing apportionment of seats in the House of Representatives was unconstitutional—a decision which may have marked the beginning of a more interventionist role for the Court. It should be noted that in a substantial number of cases involving political issues such as freedom of expression, especially by organized mass demonstrations, versus the authority of the police to regulate such activity in the public interest, the court has ruled in favor of the public interest over the private right.

Regional & Local Government

The 1947 constitution provides for "local public entities" to be governed "in accordance with the principle of local autonomy," with their own elected executives and asemblies. Theoretically, each of Japan's forty-seven prefectures (including the metropolis of Tokyo, the urban prefectures of Kyoto and Osaka, and the district of Hokkaido), and each of the cities, towns, and villages within the prefectures, could legally govern itself, make its own laws, raise its own revenues, and provide its own services. The U.S. occupation officials who participated in the drafting of the constitution, and who advocated its local autonomy provisions, favored local self-government as a means of strengthening democracy in Japan. In practice, however, although local governments are elected, do collect taxes, make laws, and provide local services, they are highly homogeneous, generally follow the national government's lead in both law and policy, and are dependent on national government funds for about half their budgets. Consequently, fiscal dependency and long-ingrained habits of looking to Tokyo for guidance make Japan more of a unified state than the constitution implies.

Local governments, however, have been the arena for two noteworthy political phenomena. The opposition, frequently operating as a progressive coalition of the Socialist and Communist parties, has at one time or another won the governorships in several important urban prefectures, such as Tokyo, Osaka, Kyoto, Okayama, and Saitama. They have also been more successful in winning seats in local assemblies than in the national Diet. Before the June 1980 general election, local trends favoring the opposition were frequently interpreted as the beginning of a groundswell that would carry the opposition to a majority coalition in the national Diet. Since the 1980 election, however, in which the conservatives regained a number of lost seats and reversed a two-decade pattern of gradual decline, political analysts have been more inclined to interpret local support for the opposition as a protest vote or a strictly local arrangement and not as evidence of a grass-roots shift among the Japanese voters away from the conservatives.

A related phenomenon is the development at the local level of environmental protection groups. In the 1960s, the Japanese government began encouraging industry to decentralize by offering tax breaks, free land, and inexpensive utilities to companies that would locate in the more rural, lightly populated regions of the country. One consequence of decentralization was that many of the residents of the new industrial zones, who had previously either favored industrialization or had been indifferent, organized themselves into politically effective local groups to work for pollution control. Initially, the opposition showed decidedly more sympathy for these local groups than did the conservatives, but by the middle 1970s, the conservatives had made impressive strides both in cleaning up industrial pollution and in linking themselves with local environmental protection groups.

The Electoral System

The 511 members of the House of Representatives are returned from 130 medium-sized, multi-member election districts. Each district returns from three to five members, with the exception of the Amami Islands special district, which is represented by a single member. In the general election, each voter casts a single vote for a single candidate. The three to five candidates who win the most votes are elected.

For the House of Councillors, 152 members are chosen from forty-seven electoral districts on the same basis as representatives: the top vote getters in the multimember districts win. The other 100 councillors are elected by the nation at large, a

procedure which confronts the voter with a formidable ballot of several scores of names at least. The voter thus has two votes to cast for the House of Councillors—one for a local constituency candidate and one for a national candidate. While the national candidate elections are not as partisan as other elections, parties and interest groups do instruct their supporters as to which of the many national candidates to vote for.

The Election Law provides that any eligible Japanese voter over the age of twenty-five can stand for election to the lower house. A person becomes a candidate by notifying the chairman of the local election board and filing a deposit of 100,000 yen (about $500), which is forfeit unless the candidate polls one-fifth of the valid votes cast divided by the number of seats in the district. Since general election campaigns are very expensive and party endorsements are very important, there are usually only two to three candidates for each lower-house seat in each district.

The Election Management Commission of each city, town, and village is required by law to prepare each year a basic list of voters. This list constitutes the role of registered voters and includes all eligible voters. The list is publicly posted during each November, for correction of errors and omissions. On December 20, the list becomes legally valid and remains so until it is superseded one year later.

Under the Public Offices Election Law, voter qualifications are kept to a minimum. All Japanese citizens who have attained the age of twenty, and who have established residence in a particular city, town, or village for a period of three months are eligible to vote in all elections. There are no poll taxes or literacy requirements, (Japan is the most-literate country in the world). Only those judged legally incompetent or who are serving prison sentences and convicted violators of the election law are denied the franchise.

In Japan, especially in the rural areas, voting is regarded not only as a right, but as a duty. In the 1976 general election, for example, 78,244,787 Japanese were entitled to vote. This represented 70 percent of the total population. Of the eligible voters, 56,602,755 or 73.5 percent cast valid ballots. Voting is by secret ballot, and elections have been relatively peaceful and honest since the early 1900s.

The number of seats in the House of Representative was increased from 467 to 486 in 1967; to 491 in 1972; and to the present 511 in 1975. From 1950 until 1976, there were 124 election districts. Six districts were added that year bringing the total to the present 130. The addition of both lower-house seats and election districts was an effort to roughly apportion lower-house seats by population as Japanese voters migrated from rural to urban districts. Since the shrinking rural districts were loathe to surrender their seats, additional seats were created for the growing urban districts. Nevertheless, if one applies the one-person, one-vote criteria, the urban districts in Japan continue to be underrepresented in the lower house. The voters also vote in regular referenda on the Supreme Court justiceships. The 1947 constitution also provides for special referenda on proposed constitutional amendments, although no such case has yet occurred.

The Party System

Origins of the Parties

Political parties are not new to Japan. In one form or another, they have existed since 1874, when a group of disaffected samurai left the newly organized Meiji government and organized themselves into an opposition party calling for representative government and popular elections. The antecedents of the Liberal Democratic Party can be traced back to at least the early 1880s. The major opposition party, the Japan Socialist Party, was formally organized in 1925 and the much smaller Japan Communist Party in 1922. Both these parties trace their common Marxist-labor ancestry back to the turn of the century.

Under the Meiji constitution, from 1889 to 1947, the political parties competed for control of membership in the lower house of a Diet which possessed only limited and partial powers. In the 1930s, the revolutionary left-wing parties were declared illegal, and in 1940, the remaining parties agreed to a government proposal to disband and merge themselves into the Imperial Rule Assistance Association, in order to give the government more unified support in its prosecution of the war against China. Nevertheless, party loyalties and the local organizations of individual politicians remained intact through the war. When the U.S. occupation authorities began their democratization program, they discovered that Japan was already equipped with energetic, experienced political parties.

The Parties in Law

Political parties are legally established and regulated in accordance with the Political Finance Control Law. As the existence of the Japan Com-

munist Party (JCP) and the Clean Government Party (KMT) indicates, this law imposes no ideological, philosophical, or religious restrictions on political parties. Any group of candidates for either national or local government can register with the Ministry of Home Affairs as a political party by filing a petition stating the party's name, purpose, organization and leadership, responsible financial officer, and location of headquarters. Having registered, a party is eligible to collect dues and receive political donations and is required to report its income and expenditures to the ministry. The Political Finance Control Law does not regulate the campaign activities or finances of individual candidates. These matters come under the Election Law.

Under the Election Law, any Japanese voter twenty-five years or older may get on the ballot for the lower-house election by registering as a candidate with the local election board and filing a deposit of 100,000 yen (about $400–$500, depending on exchange rate). A candidate must register within four days of the official announcement of a lower-house election. Since this announcement must be made twenty-one days before the election, the official, legal campaign for a general election is limited to twenty-one days.

Party Organization

Japan has a multiparty system in which six parties are currently most important: the Liberal Democratic, New Liberal Club, Socialist, Democratic Socialist, Communist, and Clean Government parties. Except for the smaller Communist and Clean Government (Komeito) parties, which are membership organizations, these parties are essentially parliamentary parties. Public participation in politics, except during the weeks preceding an election, is limited to Diet members and professional politicans, whose primary focus is the Diet.

The link between the parties and the voters are the local support organizations (koenkai) built and maintained by candidates and members of the Diet. These local support organizations, which owe their loyalty primarily to an individual politician, are clearly stronger than local branches of the national parties. The Japanese voter expects that his Dietman will respond to local needs for roads, bridges, new schools, price supports for rice, and so on; and that the Dietman himself will also present gifts at business openings, funerals, weddings, and graduations. The constituents also expect to get help and advice from their Dietman when looking for jobs, medical treatment, and loans. In may respects, the modern Dietman plays a role in his district, among his supporters, comparable to that of a fuedal lord among his retainers, or an American turn-of-the-century ward heeler among his ward residents.

The Dietman's national party affiliation is significant, but not crucial. The voters persist in their "conservative" or "progressive" preferences, and so long as their champions do not cross these ideological lines, the Dietman can enjoy a certain flexibility in party affiliation. This accounts for the relative ease with which both the conservative and progressive parties split and re-form. In January 1960, for example, a small group of moderate, right-wing Socialist Dietmen walked out and formed the Democratic Socialist Party. In 1976, young, dissident conservative Dietmen left the Liberal Democratic Party and formed the New Liberal Club. In both cases, the Dietmen held on to their seats and took their local support groups with them into the new party, thus demonstrating the organizational weakness of both the Socialist and Liberal Democratic parties at the grass-roots level.

Moreover, in all the parties, with the exception of *Komeito* and the Communists, perhaps, individual candidates and Dietman tend to give their primary allegiance *not* to their national party directly, but to a faction within the party. These factions are typically led by seasoned, successful Dietmen, who can make political funds available to faction members. Among the conservatives, a faction leader is seen by his followers as a potential prime minister or cabinet minister, with patronage at his disposal. Factionalism of this type is traditional in Japan, and it is strongly buttressed by the existing multimember, single-vote electoral system. This system pits the candidates of any one party against each other as much or even more than it pits them against opposition-party candidates. A candidate, therefore, looks beyond the evenly distributed party funds and his almost always insufficient personal funds to a source of funds and support that will give him an edge over his competitors within the party. This source is the faction leader. The faction leader is the party leader, and the political parties are essentially coalitions of well-organized, disciplined Dietmen's factions. The current leadership and membership of the factions are regularly listed and discussed in the Japanese media.

Campaigning

Japan's multimember districts and the factional structure of its political parties create an election campaign problem that is common to all parties: essentially, one of how many candidates to endorse and financially assist in each district. Frequently, competing factions within each party work to increase their membership by getting party endorsement for their faction's candidate. But too many candidates would inevitably divide the party's vote in the district, causing the weaker candidates to defeat each other, losing seats to the opposition, weakening the party's position in the Diet.

The Liberal Democrats have generally shown the best judgment and control in awarding endorsements. Although there is considerable variation from election to election, the 1963 figures are reasonably representative. In 1963 the Liberal Democrats elected 78 percent of their endorsed candidates; the Socialist 72 percent; the Democratic Socialist 38 percent; and the Communists only 4 percent. Since a candidate usually competes with members of his own party in the multi-member districts, a candidate's personal connections with local organizations and his personality tend to be more important for his electoral success than the positions he takes on policy issues.

The Election Law places narrow limits on the expenditures, speechmaking, and publicity of candidates. Expenditure restrictions are calculated by a complex formula which takes into account the number of registered voters and the number of candidates in a district. A candidate's expenses for the legal three-week campaign period are usually well under $10,000, but these are only a small fraction of the costs of the overall campaign which begins informally several months before the announcement of an election.

The Election Law prohibits door-to-door canvassing; only one campaign vehicle per candidate is permitted; serving food or beverages as part of the campaign is prohibited; and the number of mailings, posters, speeches, and media appearances are all limited. Candidates cannot buy television time during the campaign. Instead, the Election Law provides for each candidate to make three television apearances of four-and-one-half minutes each, free of charge. These legal restrictions are circumvented by candidates from all the parties by a variety of devices: for example, by using social clubs for political gatherings and by having "friends" make donations to local interest groups such as taxi drivers' associations or housewives' clubs. In spite of the ingenuity of the candidates in circumventing campaign restrictions, the legal campaign period is relatively colorless and dull.

The object of the Election Law is to have a

short, inexpensive, fair campaign in which the importance of money and campaign gimmicks is minimized. The actual result is to put the main burden of campaigning into the period before the official campaign when speeches, meetings, and advertising are not regulated. Consequently, election campaigning goes on for 365 days (and nights) of the year and is extremely expensive. Some idea of the cost of campaigning may be gathered from a 1970 media slogan, *go-to-yon-raku*, which meant that 500 million yen (about $2.3 million) won an upper-house seat, while 400 million yen (about $1.8 million) lost.

Independent Voters

Since voters give their primary loyalty to individual politicians rather than to parties, the usual questions of voter identification and independence are not clearly relevant to Japanese politics. The individual politician can take his supporters with him, with little or no loss, if he switches party loyalty. Voter identification with the broad "conservative" and "progressive" tendencies is relatively stable, but voters do shift their party preferences within those tendencies. This is particularly true on the left, where a major gain for either the Communists, Socialists, or Democratic Socialists usually means a major loss for one or both of the other two parties.

Clean Government Party (*Komeito*)

History

Komeito is the political branch of one of Japan's new religions, the Value Creation Society (*Sokagakkai*). *Sokagakkai* was formed in the 1930s, ostensibly as an offshoot of the Nichiren sect of Buddhism. In 1962, *Sokagakkai* established the League for Clean Government (*Komei Seiji Renmei*), which was transformed into the Clean Government Party in 1964. The party's initial election effort and successes were in the national constituency of the House of Councillors, where its small but disciplined vote could be used with maximum effect. In 1967, the *Komeito* jumped to national prominence by winning twenty-five seats in the House of Representatives in its first general election campaign, once again showing fine judgment in running the correct number of candidates in the appropriate districts.

In 1971, *Komeito* officially severed all connections with *Sokagakkai*, in an effort to establish itself as a secular political party rather than as the political branch of a religious sect with a reputation for extreme nationalism and militancy. Nevertheless, most of *Komeito's* votes continue to come from *Sokagakkai*, and most of the Japanese public still identify the party with the religion. Consequently, while the party has been able to count on a reliable block of voters, its religious affiliation has also been an obstacle to its growth.

Organization

Not only is *Komeito* unique among Japanese political parties in its religious connection, it is also unusual for being a membership, mass-based party. To the extent that it has remained associated with *Sokagakkai*, *Komeito* has available to it a voting bloc of hierarchically and geographically organized members, based on small neighborhood cells led by activist missionary leaders. This network engages in both devotional and political campaign activities.

Party headquarters are at 17 Minami-Moto-machi Shinjuku-Ku, Tokyo.

Policy

In its party platform, *Komeito* advocates more honesty in politics and improvement of the quality of life for less affluent Japanese. In a recent election, for example, it called for lower utility rates, complete tax exemptions for citizens in low-income brackets, old-age pensions for all, increased subsidies for farmers, and national self-sufficiency in principal food crops. In foreign affairs, the party has shifted gradually from opposition to the U.S.-Japan Security Treaty to favoring treaty revision and the conclusion of nonaggression pacts with the Soviet Union and the People's Republic of China.

Membership & Constituency

Sokagakkai claims a membership of close to fifteen million dues-paying members. Critics believe its followers number from eight to ten million. In general elections, *Komeito* has been able to count on five to seven million votes. Most of the party's adherents come from lower-income, blue-collar city dwellers who have migrated from the countryside. These people find the intimate, hierarchical *Sokagakkai* neighborhood cells a natural substitute for the rural village and extended family.

Financing

Compared to the other parties, *Komeito* probably gets an unusually high proportion of its funds from membership dues, which are paid through *Sokagakkai*, but it also taps sources in the business world. No reliable information is available on party financing.

Leadership

Komeito has been authoritatively led for more than a decade by chairman Takeiri Yoshikatsu (born 1926).

Prospects

Unless *Komeito* succeeds in breaking away from its identification with *Sokagakkai*, it is unlikely to substantially increase its voter support (9 to 10 percent of the votes cast), or its strength in the lower house, which has fluctuated from twenty-five to fifty-seven seats, and presently stands at thirty-three seats. Given its ambiguous ideological orientation, however, *Komeito* could enter into a coalition government with almost any party or faction, ranging from the ultraright to the Socialists on the left.

Japan Communist Party (JCP; *Nihon Kyosanto*)

History

The Japan Communist Party (JCP) shares a common ancestry with the Socialists in the Marxist-labor groups founded at the beginning of the century. A Communist Party was officially organized in 1922, in the heyday of Japan's post–World War I liberalism, but within a few years the party's revolutionary program and its repudiation of the imperial institution led to its abolition as a legal organization. Most of the party's leading members either converted to more acceptable political faiths; spent the 1930s and 1940s in prison; or escaped abroad, like Nozaka Sanzo, who spent the war years with the Chinese Communists in Yenan. In 1945, the U.S. occupation authorities freed the imprisoned Communists and recognized them as a legal party. The JCP has participated in every postwar general election. After a weak showing in 1947, the JCP enjoyed a surge of popularity in the 1949 election, in which it won 9.7 percent of the vote and thirty-five seats in the lower house. In 1952, its share of the vote dropped

to 2.6 percent and it lost all its seats. From 1960 to 1972, the party's share of the vote grew and has held fairly steady at 10 percent since 1972. The JCP's position in the lower house has fluctuated even more than its voter support, to a large extent because a small but influential number of progressive voters swing between left-wing Socialist candidates and Communists. In the 1976 election, for example, the Japan Socialist Party won 140 seats and the Communists five seats. In 1979, the Socialists took 107 seats and the Communists thirty-nine. In the 1980 election, the JCP slipped to twenty-nine seats while the JSP held at 107, because the JCP ran an excessive number of candidates, gambling that its popular vote would increase when in fact it declined slightly.

Organization

The JCP is headed by a hierarchical committee structure based on a 168-member Central Committee which elects the thirty-eight-member Presidium and the fourteen-member Presidium Standing Committee. The last is equivalent to the political bureau (politburo) in a standard communist party organization, and it alone determines policy. The party is tightly disciplined and operates on democratic-centralist principles; i.e., once a policy decision is made, it must be faithfully adhered to by all members.

Party headquarters are at 4-26 Sendagaya Shibuya-ku, Tokyo.

Policy

The Sino-Soviet dispute had a deeply divisive effect on the party throughout the 1960s. In the early 1970s, however, the leadership decided to clearly assert the JCP's independence of both Moscow and Peking, to stop calling for violent revolution, and to focus on economic and social issues rather than Marxist doctrine. This shift in orientation and tactics apparently has paid off in both voter support and Diet seats. The JCP has campaigned vigorously against inflation and in support of improved social security and public health care and has been a champion of environmental protection. In foreign policy, which it does not emphasize as much as it did before 1970, the party calls for abrogation of the U.S.-Japan Security Treaty and friendly, cooperative relations with Japan's neighbors, China and Russia.

Membership & Constituency

The JCP is a mass-membership party, claiming about 300,000 registered, dues-paying members.

The party can also count the readership of its newspaper *Akahata*, among its reliable supporters. *Akahata's* Sunday circulation is close to two million. In addition, there is a contingent of left-wing Sohyo labor-union members who are staunch JCP supporters. Membership in these three groups overlaps considerably. The JCP does not have the backing of a labor-union federation, as do the Socialist and the Democratic Socialist parties.

Financing

No complete, reliable information is available on party finances, but it is known that *Akhata* and other profitable party publications provide a substantial part of its income. Rumors also abound of funds contributed by the Russian and Chinese Communists.

Leadership

For more than a decade, Miyamoto Kenji (born 1908) has chaired both the Pesidium and its Standing Committee. The party general secretary is Fuwa Tetsuzo (born 1930).

Prospects

Election statistics suggest that JCP voter support has peaked and leveled off at about 10 percent, and that like the DSP and *Komeito*, its future as a small, minority party will be determined by how efficiently it uses its voter support to maximize its seats in the lower house and by its prospects of entering a coalition government. Since the DSP and *Komeito*, as well as all the conservatives, have announced that they will not cooperate with the Communists, and since even the Socialists are sharply divided on this issue, the JCP's prospects are not bright. It is possible, however, that another decade of politically astute leadership and concentration on nonideological issues will make the JCP more acceptable.

Japan Democratic Socialist Party (DSP; *Nihon Minshu Shakaito*)

History

The Japan Democratic Socialist Party (DSP) was established in January 1960, when a right-wing faction of the Socialist Party led by Suehiro

Nishio, along with several members of the DSP Kawakami faction, resigned their party membership over a doctrinal and tactical dispute and asserted their political independence. At the time, the DSP had the support of thirty-five to forty Socialist members of the lower house. However, in the November 1960 general election, the DSP candidates fared poorly, emerging with only seventeen seats. In subsequent elections the DSP came back up to more than thirty seats in the lower house while its share of the popular vote gradually declined from 8.7 to 6.6 percent, evidence of careful electoral management.

Organization

The DSP has avoided factionalism by virtue of the fact that it has operated like a single faction. Officially, the party leadership is elected at regular conventions. In practice, the DSP leader operates like a faction leader. The DSP Diet members have their local support groups (*koenkai*) and have enjoyed a high rate of return to the Diet in elections.

Party headquarters are at 4th Mori Building, 1 Sakuragawa-cho, Shiba-Nishikubo, Minato-ku, Tokyo.

Policy

The DSP advocates a moderate, pragmatic socialism in which a welfare state and nationalized industries would operate side-by-side with a free-enterprise sector. In foreign policy, the DSP favors continuation of close security and economic relations with the United States, but advocates revision of the Security Treaty to limit stationing of U.S. forces in Japan only in time of emergency. The DSP also favors closer relations with Moscow and Peking.

As its programs suggest, the DSP has viewed itself as a bridge between the Liberal Democrats and the right wing of the Socialist Party. It has sustained itself on the expectation of either entering a centrist coalition government with a minority Liberal Democratic Party, or with a new centrist party composed of right-wing Socialists, the DSP, NLC, and several conservative factions.

Membership & Constituency

The party draws its support from the moderate, right-wing labor federation known as *Domei* (2.3 million members). The party constituency sees itself as moderately progressive.

Financing

No reliable information on DSP finances is available, but the party is believed to get most of its funds from the labor federation, *Domei*.

Leadership

Kasuga Ikko (born 1910) has been the party leader since the death of Suehiro Nishio in 1981.

Prospects

Given the gradual but cumulative decline in its popular vote, the DSP's prospects are not bright. The Liberal Democratic victory in 1980 dimmed DSP prospects of coalition-government participation. It will either have to strengthen or at least consolidate its voter support, or face a decline in its lower-house membership and its political clout.

Japan Socialist Party (JSP; *Nihon Shakaito*)

History

The Japan Socialist Party (JSP) traces its history back to the Marxist-labor groups in turn-of-the-century Tokyo and to the prewar Socialist Party, which was formally organized in 1925. In prewar Japan, the Socialists were viewed as only marginally legal and played only a small role in the Diet and electoral politics. Under the U.S. occupation, the labor-union movement was greatly strengthened, and a number of well organized Socialist parties, based on the unions, emerged to form the major opposition to conservative rule. From May 1947 to March 1948, the Socialists led a coalition cabinet headed by Katayama Tetsu, a moderate Socialist. Conservative elements in the coalition and occupation policy combined to prevent the Socialists from implementing their nationalization program, and they had virtually no impact on government policy. The present Japan Socialist Party (JSP) was established in October 1955, by the amalgamation of several postwar Socialist parties. The JSP's electoral strength and the number of its seats in the lower house peaked in the late 1950s, at 32.9 percent of the popular vote, and 166 seats. JSP electoral strength has declined gradually since then. It is, however, still the major opposition party, with about twice the electoral

support and lower house seats as the next strongest party, *Komeito*.

Organization

The seemingly permanent opposition role of the JSP has done much to shape its organization, leadership, and policies. With virtually no control over government policy and no government patronage to dispense, a rigid, old-fashioned Marxism has remained the core of party allegiance. Intraparty doctrinal disputes have been intense and bitter. Policy positions have frequently been more responsive to doctrine than to voter preferences.

The JSP has an elaborate party headquarters in Tokyo and local party branches throughout Japan. However, it is actually governed by its factions and faction leaders. The JSP Dietmen and candidates maintain their own local support organizations (*koenkai*). The faction leaders are senior Dietmen with access to political funds from friendly labor unions. In recent decades the factions have grouped themselves into left, center, and rights wings, with the left representing the extremes of doctrinal rigidity and electoral weakness. The party conventions, which elect the chairman of the party executive committee and the secretary general, are dominated by party staff and professional organizers and not by the more moderate Diet members. This has perpetuated the party's ideological orientation and accounts for the fact that the JSP has sometimes been farther to the left than the Communists in insisting on the necessity of class struggle and a proletarian takeover of the government.

Party headquarters are at 1-8-1 Nagata-cho Chinjoda-ku, Tokyo.

Policy

The JSP's program calls for the prompt nationalization of all industry and banking and vaguely implies that a JSP election victory would represent an irreversible step in Japan's historical development. Both these positions embarrass moderate Socialist politicians as well as many people who vote for the Socialists. In foreign policy, the JSP has opposed the U.S.-Japan Security Treaty since its inception in 1951. The party advocates an unarmed, neutral foreign policy and calls for dramatic improvement in relations with Japan's socialist neighbors. The JSP has been especially sympathetic and supportive of Peking in the Sino-Soviet dispute.

Membership & Constituency

The party's seemingly self-destructive policy is largely accounted for by the peculiar relationship between the JSP and its supporting unions. The core of JSP financial and voter support is centered in the massive (4.3 million member) national confederation of labor unions known as *Sohyo*. While *Sohyo's* member unions engage in pragmatic collective bargaining on wages and working conditions, *Sohyo's* more politically committed and ideologically rigid staff and members have gravitated toward the JSP, dominating the party's conventions, publicity and election campaigns.

Financing

Although no reliable, complete information on financing is available, *Sohyo* is believed to furnish the bulk of the JSP's funds, as well as many of the party's staff and services.

Leadership

The party chairman is Ichio Asukata (born 1915).

Prospects

Despite its slow electoral decline, the JSP remains the most powerful of the opposition parties. In the event of a conservative defeat, one would naturally expect the JSP to assume a central role in a possible leftist coalition government. However, the party has been deeply divided over the propriety of cooperating with either the Communists or *Komeito*, and it is quite conceivable that an LDP disintegration would trigger a parallel fracturing of the JSP. In that case, the moderate, pragmatic wing of the party would move toward a centrist coalition with the DSP, NLC, *Komeito* and liberal conservative factions, while the more doctrinaire JSP factions would gravitate toward the Communists.

Liberal Democratic Party (LDP; *Jiyuminshuto*)

History

The Liberal Democratic Party (LDP) was established in November 1955, when two conservative parties, the Liberals and the Japan Democratic Party, merged. It traces its origins back to the earliest Japanese parties of the 1870s. The LDP and its predecessors have ruled Japan since 1947, with the exception of the short-lived, Socialist-led coalition cabinet of Katayama Tetsu (1947–48). The merger of the Liberals and Democrats was in response to the unification of the JSP earlier that year and to the urgings of the business community, which hoped to reduce conservative political infighting and to more efficiently channel its contributions into a single conservative party.

Organization

The LDP has national and local party organizations and a sizable secretariat; however, its affairs are largely conducted by the powerful faction leaders in the Diet, who constitute an informal, collegial governing body. The key objective of LDP factional politics is the party presidency. As long as the LDP controls a majority in the lower house, the party presidency is tantamount to the prime ministership of Japan. Under current party rules, which went into effect in 1979, the president is chosen for a renewable, three-year term by means of a complicated process that combines a primary-style vote among LDP registered voters, with a convention vote by Dietmen and party professionals. The primary-style vote was introduced to weaken the factions and "democratize" the party. In 1979, it led to an expensive primary-style campaign in which the politically dominant and better-funded Ohira and Tanaka factions used their connections and their money to carry the primary vote. As was generally anticipated, the Ohira-Tanaka coalition then went on to complete its victory at the convention vote. The results of 1979 suggest that the factions still rule in the LDP, with the primary-style campaign simply making the party presidency more expensive.

Conservative prime ministers, although primarily dependent on their majority "mainstream" factional coalition, are careful to keep their lines open to the minority, "anti-mainstream" factions in the LDP. Dissatisfaction over cabinet appointments, the search for new factional combinations, and occasional differences over policy lead to disintegration of the "mainstream" coalition; opportunities are then created for the "anti-mainstream" factions to bargain their way into the government. This kind of factional, coalition politics is not conducive to bold, decisive leadership; on the contrary, it produces a cautious, carefully hedged approach to both politics and policy-making.

Party headquarters are at 1-11-23 Nagata-cho Chiyoda-ku, Tokyo.

Policy

The LDP has no elaborate program. The party was established to keep the Socialists out of power and to maintain a probusiness climate in Japan. Since business in Japan includes almost every imaginable enterprise—from small retail outlets to enormous international firms and ranges from the most sophisticated technology to traditional mat-weaving—it is a mistake to conclude that the LDP represents a narrow, parochial interest group. By American or European standards, the LDP is left of center. It has implemented environmental protection policies that are still considered radical in the occident, and it has unblushingly co-opted welfare policies proposed by the Socialists. In foreign affairs, the party has firmly supported close security and economic ties with the United States and the West, while attempting to gradually improve relations with the People's Republic of China and the Soviet Union.

Membership & Constituency

In many respects, the LDP is a conservative Dietman's club supported by an enormously heterogeneous conglomeration of constituencies. The rural prefectures and middle-aged and older voters are predominantly conservative and pro-LDP. But the 1980 election showed that LDP efforts to cultivate younger, urban, and semi-urban voters had not been wasted.

Financing

The almost complete absence of reliable information about LDP finances has not in the least inhibited public discussion of them. It is generally agreed that big businesses provide the bulk of the party's funds. The Citizen's Association, a fund-raising arm of the LDP, regularly duns businesses for anonymous contributions to support the party organization. These contributions are evenhandedly distributed among endorsed party candidates at election time. While substantial, these party funds only cover a fraction of an LDP Dietman's or candidate's expenses. The remainder of these expenses are met from personal sources with the help of a faction leader.

LDP FACTIONS: LEADERS AND RELATIVE STRENGTHS		
Leader	Lower House Members	Upper House Members
Suzuki Zenko (born 1911)	60	27
Nikkaido Susumu (born 1910)*	63	40
Fukuda Takeo (born 1905)	47	32
Nakasone Yasuhiro (born 1918)	44	8
Komoto Toshio (born 1911)	31	12

*Tanaka Kakuei (born 1918), former prime minister, was asked to resign from the LDP following his indictment in connection with the 1975 Lockheed scandal. Nikkaido nominally assumed the leadership of the Tanaka faction, but Tanaka is still a member of the lower house and is believed to be the de facto leader of the faction.

Leadership

Ohira remained as prime minister until his sudden death in June 1980, in the midst of the general election campaign. His successor as party president and prime minister, Suzuki Zenko, who had been an Ohira faction lieutenant, was chosen by the faction leaders to complete Ohira's term of office. The ruling factional coalition upon which Suzuki's position as prime minister rested was a combination of the Suzuki, Nikkaido (Tanaka) and Nakasone factions. In late October 1982, Suzuki announced his intention to resign, setting off a new leadership struggle in the party.

Prospects

The LDP's surprising success in the 1980 election dampened forecasts of its imminent defeat and collapse, but did not guarantee its future. The LDP's strongest assets are the sharp and bitter divisions among the opposition progresssive parties and a residual belief among most Japanese that, while the progressives stand for high ideals, they are not solid and responsible enough to govern the nation. A dramatic loss of public confidence in the LDP, combined with greater harmony and realism among the opposition parties, could quickly dissipate the LDP's assets.

New Liberal Club (NLC; *Shin Jiyu Kurabu*)

History

The New Liberal Club was established in June 1976, when Kono Yohei and five younger, dissident conservative Dietmen announced their resignation from the ruling Liberal Democratic Party and declared themselves an independent party. The New Liberal Club enjoyed a dramatic initial success in the 1976 general election, in which it won seventeen seats in the lower house. In the November 1979 general election, however, the party's share of the popular vote slipped and it was reduced to four seats, which cast doubts on its viability. Fortunately for the NLC, a crisis in the Liberal Democratic Party led to an unexpected general election in June 1980, only eight months after the NLC's debacle. In the 1980 election the NLC carefully apportioned its reduced vote to win twelve seats in the lower house and a firmer grip on political life.

Organization

Like most of the other parties, NLC organization consists of the loosely structured *koenkai* of individual Dietmen.

National party headquarters are at 1-11-28 Nagato-cho Chiyoda-ku, Tokyo.

Policy

The NLC originated in Kono's outspoken criticism of the Liberal Democratic Party's involvement in the Lockheed scandals in 1976 and to his view that the party's leadership was too old and rigid. The NLC has called for higher standards of political morality and for correcting social inequities in Japan's free-enterprise economy. They favor close security and economic cooperation with the United States. The NLC calls itself a conservative-reformist party.

Membership & Constituency

The NLC's constituency reflects the same variety as the DLP's.

Financing

No reliable information is available on NLC financing. Kono Yohei probably derives most of his political funds from connections in the business world, some of which he inherited from his father, who had been an LDP faction leader.

Leadership

Kono (born 1937) continues to be the dominant voice in the NLC.

Prospects

The politicians who formed the NLC felt that the LDP was on the verge of defeat and possibly disintegration, and that they would be better placed to participate in a new conservative or centrist governing coalition if they had their own organizational base. The Liberal Democratic victory in 1980 upset this calculation. Kono and his followers can either continue to gamble on Liberal Democratic decline, at the cost of denying themselves Liberal Democratic patronage, or they may attempt to bargain their way back into the parent party.

Other Political Forces

Big-Business Interests

The conventional wisdom is that Japan is governed by a tripartite alliance of the LDP, the bureaucracy, and big-business interests. Many Japanese political writers have attributed enormous influence to big businesses, (referred to as the *zaikai*), assuming that they speak with a single voice and exercise an omnipresent, but invisible control over politicians and bureaucrats. To some extent this exaggerated view reflects the Marxist influence in Japanese education. There is no doubt, however, that big businesses are the major source of LDP funds, that they are engaged in perpetual lobbying, and that business executives have numerous links—school, family, and social ties—with politicians and bureaucrats. What is more difficult to determine is precisely what big business gets in return for its contributions. The LDP clearly believes that it should promote a good climate for business; with the help of the bureaucrats, it has done so with a degree of success that is the envy of American and European businessmen. On the other hand, despite perpetual scandalmongering in the more sensational Japanese weekly journals, there is little evidence of illegal deals or influence peddling between politicians and business executives. Such deals appear to be the exception rather than the rule.

Big business is organized into four lobbying organizations: the Federation of Economic Organization (*Keidanren*), the Committee for Economic Development (*Keizai Doyukai*), the Federation of Employer's Organizations (*Nikkeiren*), and the Japan Chamber of Commerce (*Nissho*). *Keidanren* is the best funded and most influential of these. Its membership is limited to about 800 of Japan's largest corporations and the biggest banks and trading groups. *Keidanren* has consistently called for abolition of the LDP factions—on the grounds that the factions are unsavory and unduly expensive—but has not been successful in this effort.

Bureaucracy

Although the 1947 constitution declares that "all public officials are servants of the whole community," the notion of a high official being a humble and compliant servant to the public is alien to Japanese history and culture. In practice, the Japanese higher civil service is a carefully selected, highly trained governmental elite, with powerful influence across the entire range of government and politics. The national government employs close to a quarter of a million civil servants. Of these, between 15,000 and 20,000 attain the first, second, and third grades, which comprise the higher civil service. Only about 1,000 of these bureaucrats attain the most prestigious and powerful first grade.

Government service has traditionally been one of the most desirable careers open to young Japanese. Access to its higher levels is achieved through academic excellence and not by virtue of wealth or family. Beginning in elementary school, the brighter students are tested in a series of difficult examinations. Excellent performance in these examinations provides entrance to the best middle and higher schools and eventually to the best of the public universities, the most prestigious in Japan. The equivalent of an honors degree from one of these universities is essential to anyone applying for the higher civil service examination. This provides Japan with a bureaucratic elite characterized by the highest intelligence, literacy, industry, and discipline.

After about twenty years of detailed, patient work in their respective ministries, several thousand of these higher civil servants assume positions in which their rank and expertise give them a powerful influence on a variety of vital political issues, including taxation, bank rates, availability of credit, foreign trade, subsidies in industry and agriculture, and the location and construction of public works. In their early or middle fifties, these experienced and well-connected bureaucrats are required by law to retire. A substantial number of them enter politics, running for the Diet as conservatives. Those who win Diet seats and survive several elections stand a good chance of gaining cabinet posts. Of the fourteen prime ministers since 1947, seven have been former bureaucrats, most of them having served either in the Ministry of Finance or the Ministry of Foreign Affairs.

National Prospects

Japan enjoys a high degree of social and political stability in an open and free society. If there is no major disruption of Japan's Middle East petroleum supplies, no dramatic failure of the international trading system, and no war directly involving Japan, the nation's prospects for the next four or five years are relatively good. In a period when the American and Western European economies have been bogged down in stagflation, Japan has continued to generate impressive economic growth. Japan's economic policymakers have demonstrated resiliency and ingenuity in the face of rising energy costs, international monetary instability, and recent threats of protectionist measures against Japan's exports. Unless Japan is overcome by international disaster, it is most likely that it will hold to its present stable, prosperous, peaceful course.

Further Reading

Ike, Nobutaka. *Japanese Politics: Patron-Client Democracy.* New York: Alfred A. Knopf, Inc., 1972.

McNelly, Theodore. *Politics and Government in Japan.* Boston: Houghton Mifflin Company, 1972.

Tsuneishi, Warren M. *Japanese Political Style.* New York: Harper and Row, Inc., 1966.

Tsurutani, Taketsugu. *Political Change in Japan.* New York: David McKay Company, Inc., 1977.

Ward, Robert E. *Japan's Political System.* Englewood Cliffs, N. J.: Prentice-Hall, Inc., 1978.

HASHEMITE KINGDOM OF JORDAN
(Al-Mamlaka al-'Urduniyya al-Hashemiyya)
by Joseph M. Hiatt, Ph.D.

The System of Government

The Hashemite Kingdom of Jordan, a country of over three million people, is technically a constitutional monarchy. In practice, however, the king functions as an absolute monarch, consulting with a council of ministers appointed by him and backed by the loyalty and effectiveness of the Jordanian army, the Arab Legion.

In the immediate aftermath of World War I, the territory was part of Syria. At that time, Britain and France agreed on a division of their spheres of interest in the Middle East, France taking control of Syria proper and Britain creating the area of Transjordan ("across" or east of the Jordan river), attached to but administered separately from its Palestine mandate. In 1921, the British installed Abdullah ibn Hussein as leader of the territory. Abdullah was the brother of Faisal, the Arab leader who, with some British help, had led the Arab revolution against the Ottoman Turks during World War I. Faisal had hoped to become king of all Arab lands north of the Arabian peninsula, from which the Hashemite family, once the rulers of Mecca, had been driven by the Sa'udis. The creation of Transjordan, with Abdullah at its head, was intended in part as a sop to Faisal when the Anglo-French deal over Syria dashed his hopes. (Faisal was subsequently installed as king of British-mandated Iraq.)

Transjordan and its Hashemite leadership thus came into being as accidental by-products of diplomatic maneuverings by European powers. Geographically, the territory is an extension of the Arabian peninsula desert up to its natural northwestern boundary at the Jordan River valley. Economically, it was the outer fringe of the Levant with commercial connections to Jerusalem, Beirut, and Damascus. Culturally, with the exception of the sedentary farmers of the east bank of the Jordan valley, it was part of a bedouin sphere which extended into western Iraq, southern Syria, and the Hejaz of Saudi Arabia. Thus, Jordan was and is an artificial construction, pulled and pushed in different directions and alternately threatened and sustained by its neighbors.

Britain relinquished its mandate over Transjordan on March 22, 1946; Abdullah proclaimed himself king on May 25; and the new nation's constitution was adopted December 7. (The current constitution, adopted January 1, 1952, is essentially a revision of the first, with additions to include the territory and population of the West Bank.) The country was not economically self-sufficient and was propped up with liberal British subsidies. When Britain withdrew from Palestine, Abdullah sent the Arab Legion across the Jordan, capturing the West Bank and most of Jerusalem. In April 1949, the country changed its name to Jordan in recognition of its new position on both banks of the river. The new territory was formally annexed in April 1950, an act that outraged Palestinians and Arab leaders who had sought to establish a Palestinian state on the West Bank. King Abdullah was assassinated by a Palestinian in Jerusalem in July 1951. His mentally ill son, Talal, succeeded him, but was replaced a year later by Talal's son, Hussein, born in 1935 and seventeen years old at the time of his accession to power.

The young king, who had been educated at Harrow and Sandhurst in England and was thoroughly Westernized, faced a formidable array of problems. With the acquisition of the West Bank, the country's population was doubled. The estimated 450,000 Palestinians consisted of destitute refugees from the new state of Israel, settled farmers on the West Bank, and many educated and cosmopolitan businessmen and intellectuals whose attitudes toward the desert kingdom ranged from scorn to hatred. Jordan had also acquired the role of protector of the holy places of the three great Western religions, a role that brought it under some pressures from foreign nations, particularly in the Islamic world. While possession of Jerusalem brought in considerable tourist receipts, Jordan was almost wholly dependent on foreign subsidies from Britain and later from the U.S. Finally, rising currents of Arab nationalism and radicalism in Egypt, Syria, and Iraq challenged both the idea of monarchy and the right of Jordan to exist as a separate Arab entity. The positive elements in the situation were the determination of the Western powers and Israel that Jordan should remain independent and the well-deserved reputation of the British-trained and equipped Arab Legion as an efficient fighting force.

The survival of the country and the monarchy depended in large part on Hussein's ability to negotiate his way among the contending forces inside and outside the country. The task required the subtle balancing of conflicting demands, the ability to change course quickly, and great steadiness of purpose. None of these qualities are readily provided by a democratic system, and Hussein kept a firm grip on the levers of power, while making some effort to encourage a working democracy.

Executive

As head of state the king approves and promulgates all legislation. As commander-in-chief of the armed forces, he alone can declare war and conclude peace. He can sign treaties, though the constitution requires that treaties be approved by the legislature. He appoints the members of the upper house of the legislature and selects its speaker. He can order elections of members of the lower chamber, which he can convene, adjourn, and dissolve at will. In 1976, he was empowered by constitutional amendments to suspend indefinitely the election and convening of the lower chamber. Succession to the throne is confined to the male descendants of Abdullah; the crown prince is Hussein's younger brother, Hassan.

The Council of Ministers consists of the prime minister and the ministers whom he selects on the recommendation of the king. The prime minister is appointed by the king and may be dismissed by him, in which event the Council must resign. The top executive arm of the government, the Council is charged by the constitution with administering all affairs of the state, internal and external, except those matters statutorily allocated to other agents. Under the constitution, the Council is required within a month of its formation to submit a statement of its program and policies to the House of Deputies for approval and is obliged to resign should it fail to obtain a vote of confidence by a two-thirds majority.

In his appointments to the Council, Hussein has generally tried to ensure that all population groups and a range of political opinions are repre-

sented. Council membership also tends to reflect foreign-policy considerations. The prime minister is usually a known conservative or a leftist, depending on Hussein's shifting policies. Also, even though Jordan lost the West Bank to Israel in 1967, West Bank residents continue to comprise about one-third of the Council members, a clear message that Hussein has not relinquished Jordan's claim to the territory.

Legislature

The constitution provides for a National Assembly with an upper chamber, the House of Notables, and a lower chamber, the House of Deputies. The upper chamber, constitutionally limited to half the size of the lower chamber, has thirty members who must be Jordanians over forty years of age and unrelated to the king. They are selected for four-year terms by the king from among ministers and government officials, retired high-ranking military officers, and other prominent figures. The House of Deputies, a representative body, was doubled in size to sixty members by the constitution of 1952 to provide the then newly annexed West Bank with representation equal to that of the East Bank. Deputies had to be at least thirty years of age with no criminal record or active business interests and were elected by popular ballot for four-year terms. The House was dissolved in 1974, then briefly reconvened and dissolved again in 1976, when the king and his ministers assumed primary legislative responsibility. The legislature was, in part, replaced by a National Consultative Council (NCC) established by royal decree in 1978.

The NCC has sixty members who must be Jordanian citizens at least thirty years of age and mentally sound; they are appointed by the king, not elected by popular vote, and serve for only two years. They "study and debate all bills" and advise the Council of Ministers, but they cannot influence legislation or policy nor override the King's veto, as the National Assembly was empowered to do. The NCC has gained little popular support, but seems to be a permanent feature of Jordanian government; in April 1980, it was reappointed for a second term.

Judiciary

The judicial system plays no obvious role in Jordanian political life. The Muslim and Christian communities have their own religious courts, which handle mostly family-related matters. Legal procedure in civil and criminal matters is based on Islamic law and operates through a system of magistrate's courts, courts of first instance, courts of appeal, and the Court of Cassation, the last sitting as a supreme court of appeal.

Regional & Local Government

Regional government in Jordan acts effectively as an arm of the national government, communicating its programs and policies to local administrative districts. The current regional structure includes five provincial units or governates; three others were lost with the West Bank in 1967. These units are subdivided into smaller administrative divisions down to the village level, with an appointed head or administrator at each level.

The Electoral System

Direct secret election of members of the House of Deputies was constitutionally guaranteed in 1946. Representation was to be proportioned according to each district's population size and ethnic composition. At the time the House was dissolved in 1976, ten seats were reserved for nomadic and seminomadic groups, Circassians and Chechans, and Christians, while the remaining fifty were for the majority Muslim Arabs. The Provisional Law of 1960 reaffirmed the right of franchise for Jordanian males twenty years or older. Non-Jordanians, bankrupts, the insane or imbecile, or anyone related to the king within the limits defined by the Royal Family were not enfranchised. Women obtained the franchise in 1973. Voters registered in their home districts, and the electoral rolls were approved by a committee which was selected by the provincial governor and included the local head or heads of the town, tribe, or city section, with an official of the national government as chairman. The list was then posted for public challenges or approval. Parliamentary elections have not been held since 1967. The National Assembly, it is argued, cannot legally be convened if West Bank Palestinians are unable to elect and send representatives. But even before the 1967 suspension, Jordanian elections had displayed a troubled irregularity. Only one legal party was represented in the first parliamentary election in 1947. In the 1950s, illegal parties fielded "independent" candidates in several elections and won seats. Various parties were legalized and participated in elections during the 1960s, but their activities were short lived, and in the 1970s the king indefinitely suspended elections. That state of affairs continued into the early 1980s.

The Party System

Origins of the Parties

Among the parties active during the British Mandate period, some were of foreign origin, such as the Iraqi Istiql-al (Independence) Party, which advocated unification of Transjordan with Iraq, Syria, and Palestine. Others were indigenous, including a succession of six nationalistic parties arising in 1927 and the years following and two loyalist parties recognized in 1947 by King Abdullah to foster support for his dream of a greater Syria based on the Hashemite Kingdom. Generally, the parties were either parochially naitonalistic, pan-Arab, or pan-Islamic in outlook; those themes reemerged in the parties that developed after independence.

The Parties in Law

Following the Arab-Israeli war of 1948, the Jordanian monarchy restricted political activity to safeguard national security, and parties either dissolved or went underground. The constitution of 1952 again granted citizens the right to form political parties; and in 1953 a law provided for their licensing. But to be licensed the parties were required to register with the Ministry of Interior, a measure which gave the government the power to exclude any group it chose. Official recognition was granted first to the National Socialist Party in 1954, and later extended to others. The Socialists came to power in the 1956 parliamentary elections and initiated a program that challenged both the monarchy and its policies. In 1957 a plot among the military leadership to overthrow King Hussein was uncovered and crushed. To restore security and safeguard the throne, parties were again made illegal and, with one exception, have remained so until the present.

That exception was the Jordanian National Union established in 1971 by King Hussein. It was not a political party as such, but a forum for political debate and activity; membership was forbidden to advocates of "imported ideologies." It had a constituent congress with Hussein as president and in theory represented both the East and West Bank populations. It was renamed the Arab National Union in 1972, reduced in size, and reorganized into an executive committee and a council in 1974. It was abolished with the approval of the Council of Ministers in 1976. At its demise, its membership was estimated to be about 100,000. As for the banned parties, the government still retains the 1957 prohibition on their official existence and restricts the activities of their leaders.

Because they are illegal, parties do not play a visible role in Jordanian politics today, and details on organization, policy, size, and range of appeal are not available. The paragraphs that follow discuss the major political parties of the past which give some indication of the political viewpoints which have appeared in Jordan.

Arab Constitutional Party
(Al-Hizb al-Arabi al-Dusturi)

Officially recognized in 1956, this was a loyalist party headed by Tawfiq Abul Huda, a palace politician, and it drew strength mainly from the influence and feudal power of its leaders. The least anti-Western of Jordanian parties, it also had a great affinity for Nasser and advocated renunciation of the Anglo-Jordanian treaty which gave Britain certain rights of access to and control over Jordanian territory. Its political program amounted to little more than slogans calling for the liberation of Palestine, promotion of Arab unity, and support of the constitution.

Communist Party of Jordan
(Al-Hizb al-Shuyui al-'Urduni)

Communism was outlawed in Jordan in 1948, but in 1951 a Soviet-oriented party was formed in a tight network of small cells under the leadership of Fariq Warrad. The party has been forced to adopt various identities and functions in association with other groups. Membership was punishable by imprisonment for up to fifteen years. It has drawn most of its support from lower-middle-class students, teachers, and professionals. In 1954, it applied again for official recognition under the name of the National Front. The movement has also appealed to Palestinians, but it is suspicious of the Palestine Liberation Organization (PLO) and has made no alliances with militant groups. The party has been anti-Hussein and has posed as the champion of social justice and the enemy of imperialism. It has advocated coop-

eration with socialist states as well as rapid industrialization and social-welfare legislation on housing, education, and employment. In 1971, it split into pro-Soviet and pro-Chinese factions. By the end of the 1970s, the party's total membership was estimated at only 500 and was regarded as posing no particular threat to the stability of the Kingdom.

National Socialist Party
(Al-Hizb al-Watani al-'Ishtiraki)

This group, under the leadership of Suleiman Al-Nabulsi, first appeared in October 1950 when it petitioned the government for recognition also under the name of the National Front. The petition was finally granted in July 1954, when the group began official operation as the National Socialist Party. It drew its membership from prosperous and progressive businessmen, landowners, and professionals. Its non-Marxist brand of socialism emphasized social reform and integration of classes, including the guarantee of equal opportunity and individual property ownership; elimination of feudalism, poverty, and illiteracy; and government control of the forces of production. It identified imperialism as the source of Jordan's problems and demanded abrogation of the Anglo-Jordanian treaty. It further believed that Jordan was too poor in resources to survive alone and should unite with Iraq as a first step toward pan-Arab union. It was the anti-Western and anti-monarchist programs of the National Socialist Party that led to the crisis of 1957.

Socialist Renaissance Party
(Hizb al-Ba'th al-Ishtiraki)

The Socialist Renaissance or Ba'th Party was started by a group of Transjordanian and Palestinian intellectuals in 1952 and, after three government refusals, finally obtained official recognition in August 1955. It was formed independently of the Ba'th in Syria and only later combined with that party. One of the most highly organized of Jordanian political parties, it drew its support from intellectuals, students, and liberal professionals. Its democratic socialist program emphasized redistribution of wealth and protection of private property. Pan-Arab in orientation, it initially espoused a broadly xenophobic ideology, later narrowed to anti-Western focus, and advocated neutralism and nonalignment.

Other Political Forces

Muslim Brotherhood (*Al-'Ikhwan al-Muslimin*)

The Muslim Brotherhood was imported into Jordan in 1946 from Egypt, where it had been founded two decades earlier. King Abdullah admitted it on the belief that it was a religious group with no political interests, but over the years it sought and won continuous representation in the legislature. Its greatest support has come from the lower classes and conservative elements of the upper classes. The Brotherhood is based on membership units which are represented in a legislative assembly; this body in turn elects the executive branch, which is governed by a general director. Strongly nationalistic and xenophobic, the Brotherhood bases its program on the principles of Islam, insisting on a return to pure Islamic practice. It advocates unification of the Muslim world and rejects capitalism and communism as incompatible with Islam. The Brotherhood continues to operate in Jordan under an agreement with the king that it will restrict its political activity.

Military

The military was created under British auspices during the mandate period and was initially associated with the settled population from which it drew its recruits. The army protected the settled population against raiding bedouin nomads who distrusted central government and refused enrollment in the army. In the 1930s, a military unit created specifically for patrolling the deserts succeeded in attracting bedouin recruits, and bedouins eventually became a major component of the army. Fiercely loyal to the king, they have been the mainstay of the monarchy, backing Hussein when he crushed the military conspiracy of 1957 and during subsequent attempted assassinations and coups.

Palestinians were excluded from serving in the Arab Legion until the early 1970s. They were instead organized into a National Guard, which consisted of some 30,000 men by the late 1960s. Following the exclusion of the Palestine Liberation Organization from Jordan in 1970, however, a draft was introduced, and Palestinians were brought into the army. By 1974, it was estimated that one-third of the Legion was composed of Palestinians. There are some indications that the Palestinians' views are being adopted by the bedouin forces on the one hand, while their increased influence in the Legion is resented on the other. There have been signs of dissatisfaction with the Hussein government among the bedouin ranks, but it is difficult to tell if this is anything more than the "give-and-take" dialogue which Hussein has usually enjoyed with his bedouin subjects.

Palestinians

The Palestinians burst onto the Jordanian political scene in 1948 when they fled in hundreds of thousands from the Arab-Israeli fighting in Palestine and doubled the Jordanian population virtually overnight. They were granted Jordanian citizenship along with the right to vote and representation in the National Assembly. Palestinians provided labor and professional skills for Jordan, and many attained high-level positions in government. Many Palestinians also went abroad to work and sent money home to their families, providing Jordan with an important source of foreign exchange (an estimated $700 million in 1980).

The formation of the Palestinian Liberation Organization (PLO) in 1964 marked a turning point in the relations between the government and the Palestinians. In areas where Palestinians had settled in great numbers, the PLO gradually assumed de facto administrative control, adjudicating local disputes and controlling traffic in and out of the Palestinian areas. The 1967 war brought Jordan another 250,000 Palestinian refugees, cut off the profits of its richest agricultural area and from the Holy Land tourist trade, and severely crippled the Arab Legion.

The PLO moved quickly to take advantage of the situation. By 1970, their intrusion into Jordanian life was widespread and threatening. The PLO's incursions into the West Bank were flagrant and drew Israeli retaliation against Jordan. Hussein initiated a series of military campaigns against the PLO that culminated in the events of Black September 1970, when the PLO was pushed out of Jordan. Not until ten years later were the first tentative steps taken to explore restoration of official contacts between the PLO and Jordan. Palestinians, however, have remained in Jordan throughout this period, drawing on its services and contributing to its economy.

Foreign Nations

Jordan has never been economically self-sufficient and can survive only with liberal transfusions of cash. These were supplied for years by Britain and then by the United States. In 1978, however, in the aftermath of the Camp David accords between Israel, Egypt, and the United States, other Arab states undertook to contribute the necessary cash to keep Jordan afloat and end its dependence on the United States. Approximately $1.25 billion annually was pledged by an unlikely collection of Arab oil-producing nations: Iraq, Saudi Arabia, Kuwait, Libya, and Algeria. Libya has never paid, and Algeria tends to pay only part of its commitment; the three Gulf nations, particularly Iraq, pay regularly and on time. While this shift to Arab financing has given Hussein greater freedom of action vis-a-vis the West, it also has given the Arab nations greater influence on Jordanian policy. Jordan has generously supported Iraq in its war with Iran, for example, even at the cost of considerable disruption to the Jordanian economy as it has supplied dock facilities and trucking to ensure a smooth flow of materiel to the Iraqi army. Its support for Iraq has, in turn, worsened Jordan's relations with Syria, never good even in the best of circumstances. The two countries nearly went to war in late 1980 and Syria tacitly admitted direct involvement in an attempted assassination of Hussein in early 1981.

National Prospects

The imminent demise of Jordan as a country and/or of the Hashemite monarchy has been predicated regularly ever since the 1920s. Their continued survival is a testament not only to the astuteness of the Hashemites and their advisors, but indicates that Jordan plays an essential role in the balance-of-power equations in the region. Any pessimistic view of the country's future must face down sixty years of contrary evidence.

Given the delicate position of the government, both domestically and internationally, political liberalization is unlikely in the near future. Besides several coup and assassination attempts directed against Hussein, there have been political assassinations of other public figures. During the 1970s, discontent arose in the military over the

quality of army life and low pay. Incidents reported as "mutinies" or "abortive coups" have occurred frequently. In that same period, Hussein seemed to prefer traveling to Europe and living in high style. Recent reports, however, show that he is again concerned about his popular image and has been traveling among his subjects. He will have to use that traditional gesture consistently and continually if he hopes to retain his popular support. He must also manage the problem of the Palestinians, who make up about 40 percent of Jordan's population, contribute heavily to the economy, and thus have a major role to play in the nation's future. Any political agreement that suggests significant Jordanian concessions to the Israelis and a threat to Palestinian interests could provoke this disaffected group. The government must be seen to work for improving the lot of Palestinians and resolving internal Jordanian problems, if it is to continue to withstand disruptive forces.

Further Reading
Abidi, Aqil Hyder Hasan. *Jordan: A Political Study, 1948–1957*. New York: Asia Publishing House, 1965.
Aruri, Naseer H. *Jordan: A Study in Political Development (1921–1965)*. The Hague: Martinus Nijhoff, 1972.
Bannerman, M. Graeme. "The Hashemite Kingdom of Jordan." In *The Government and Politics of the Middle East and North Africa*, David E. Long and Bernard Reich, eds. Boulder, Colo.: Westview Press, 1980.
Gubser, Peter. *Politics and Change in Al-Karak, Jordan*. London: Oxford University Press, 1973.
Hiatt, Joseph M. *Between Desert and Town: A Case Study of Encapsulation and Sedentarization among Jordanian Bedouin*. Ph.D. dissertation, University of Pennsylvania, 1981.
Nyrop, Richard F., ed. *Jordan: A Country Study*. 3rd ed. Washington, D.C.: U.S. Government Printing Office, for Foreign Area Studies, American University, 1980.
Sinai, Anne and Pollack, Allen, eds. *The Hashemite Kingdom of Jordan and the West Bank: A Handbook*. New York: American Academic Association for Peace in the Middle East, 1977.
Vatikiotis, P. J. *Politics and the Military in Jordan, 1921–1957*. New York: Praeger Publishers, 1967.

PEOPLE'S REPUBLIC OF KAMPUCHEA
(Satheanarakraot Pracheameanit Kampuchea)
by Stephen Heder, M.A.

The System of Government

The People's Republic of Kampuchea (PRK; formerly known as Cambodia) is a one-party state officially said to be "gradually advancing towards Socialism." The PRK was proclaimed on January 10, 1979, following the overthrow of the radical, disastrous, and immensely unpopular Democratic Kampuchea regime of Pol Pot by a Vietnamese invasion force. It is dominated militarily and politically by the Socialist Republic of Vietnam as part of the three-nation Indochinese (Vietnam, Laos, Kampuchea) "unity bloc of militant solidarity."

The government and party situation remain somewhat fluid as Kampuchean and Vietnamese forces attempt to bring together the complex elements of an unusually tangled history to form a relatively orthodox Marxist-Leninist regime. The leading political figures of the PRK come from three sources. First and foremost is a group of so-called ex-Khmer Viet Minh, the survivors of a group of approximately 1,000 Kampucheans who participated in the Vietnamese communist-sponsored Khmer Issarak (Free Khmer) anticolonial movement during the First Indochina War from 1945 to 1954 and who went into exile in Vietnam in 1954. Most of them returned to Kampuchea in 1970 to fight on the communist side against the U.S.-sponsored Lon Nol regime during the Second Indochina War. From 1971 to 1976, these Khmer Viet Minh were subjected to an increasingly thorough and murderous purge by the local Kampuchean communist organization, the so-called Khmer Rouge, headed by Pol Pot. There are fewer than 100 survivors of the Khmer Viet Minh; they either managed to escape the purges by going back to Vietnam or remained safely in exile there after 1970.

The second and leading group, numbering several hundred, consists of former Khmer Rouge cadres and army combatants who fled to Vietnam, mostly during 1977–78, to escape even more massive and bloody purges carried out against the Khmer Rouge party and army by the Pol Pot leadership following the collapse of the Lon Nol regime in 1975 and the foundation of the ultraradical and self-destructive Democratic Kampuchea regime.

Finally, there are members of the elite of the prewar, prerevolution society—upper-class civil servants, military men, and intellectuals—who either took refuge in Vietnam from Democratic Kampuchea starvation, epidemic disease, and executions, or were co-opted into the PRK regime shortly after January 1979.

All three groups were represented in three institutions responsible for attempting to bring the nation into some sort of political order. The National United Front was established with Vietnamese help on December 2, 1978, apparently to accomplish two things: first, to provide a general structure for coordinating all Kampuchean political activity, including that of noncommunists, in order to build a state organization; and, second, to allow time to build a communist party uncontaminated by old-regime elements which were still active and necessary in the state administration. The Front Central Committee at its founding was headed by Heng Samrin, an ex-Khmer Rouge military commander. The other two institutions were the Communist Party, organized on the Kampuchean-Vietnamese border in January, 1979, and the People's Revolutionary Council (PRC). The latter was the ostensible Kampuchean government from January 1979 to June 1981. The main source for the new civil service was surviving bureaucrats and intellectuals of the old elite. The most prominent and politically reliable of these new-regime functionaries were included on an expanded Front Central Committee which was formed at the Front's second national congress in September 1979.

The state and party organizations were formally consolidated in the first half of 1981, and a draft constitution was published in March. This was a much-revised version of an earlier draft circulated in 1980, evidently rejected by the Vietnamese as too sophisticated and advanced for the

Kampuchean context. The revised constitution simplified the state structure and reduced the autonomy and formal representativeness of local administration. From June 24 to 27, 1981, after a national party congress, the first plenary session of the National Assembly, elected earlier in the year, met to approve the new state's first constitution.

Executive

According to the 1981 constitution, executive power is vested in the Council of State, with direct administrative control in the hands of the Council of Ministers. The chairman of the Council of State, and thus chief of state, was Heng Samrin; the chairman of the Council of Ministers, or cabinet, was Pen Sovann, an ex-Khmer Viet Minh who had received military training in Hanoi and had lived in Vietnam from 1954 to 1979. Almost all the politically important ministerial portfolios—including defense, planning and economy, interior, trade, finance, communications, and industry—were held by ex-Khmer Viet Minh. The only two portfolios of significance held by ex-Khmer Rouge were foreign affairs and justice. Old-elite civil servants, who had either taken refuge in Vietnam in 1978 or had been co-opted into the regime shortly after January 1979, were given the portfolios of agriculture, education, health, and information.

On December 4, 1981, Pen Sovann was ousted from all his state and party posts, ostensibly for reasons of health, but more likely because of his autocratic methods in dealing with his colleagues. Another ex-Khmer Viet Minh, Chan Si, was named to the chairmanship of the Council of Ministers in January 1982. A recipient of a Vietnamese military education, Chan Si was curiously low ranking in the party, only number eight on the Central Committee. His leap to the prime ministership was perhaps an indication of an unstable situation among the top party leadership.

Legislature

National Assembly elections were held on May 1, 1981. Eighty-one of the 117 seats were filled by party members. The primary work of the Assembly was the approval of the constitution prepared by the party and the election of officers to the Council of State and Council of Ministers. In addition, the Assembly elected the Presidium, charged with carrying out the Assembly's work when it was not in session. Chea Sim, a former Khmer Rouge who went to Vietnam in 1978, was elected chairman of the Presidium.

Judiciary

The PRK has yet to establish a functioning judicial system. The elimination of a provision for the establishment of a Supreme People's Court was part of the simplification entailed in the revision of the original draft constitution.

Regional & Local Government

In January and February 1979, Vietnamese troops installed provincial people's revolutionary councils (PRCs) in each of the country's eighteen provinces and its two independent municipalities, Phnom Penh and the port of Kompong Som. As far as can be determined, all provincial and municipal PRC chairmen were brought in from Vietnam, and almost all were ex-Khmer Viet Minh or ex-Khmer Rouge. The Vietnamese and the newly established provincial PRCs, usually working together but sometimes acting separately, also established PRCs in most of the country's 199 districts by mid-1979. The majority of district PRC chairmen were chosen from among the local population, with preference given to persons with some formal education or administrative experience, but as free as possible from connections with previous regimes. At the subdistrict (khum) and village levels, so-called self-management committees (SMCs) were set up by elections which were more or less strictly supervised and controlled by the Vietnamese and/or provincial and district PRC cadres. Many of the district, subdistrict, and village cadres appointed and elected in the chaos of early 1979 soon proved insufficiently loyal to the PRK regime. Some were implicated in opposition activities. Thus, a fair number of district PRCs and subdistrict and village SMCs were purged or dissolved before the end of 1979. They were then reestablished with persons who had been more carefully screened and indoctrinated. By mid-1980, it seemed that district PRCs and local SMCs were generally stabilized, although many problems of political loyalty remained, especially among the SMCs.

In early 1981, new elections of village and subdistrict committees (and urban precinct committees) were carried out in selected areas. Elections at these levels were continued in waves throughout the country through July. Party cadres and core-group members (see below under *Membership*) from provincial and district PRCs appraised the candidates and managed the elections to make sure the proper persons were elected, arousing some popular resentment over interference in local affairs.

The Electoral System

The candidates for the 1981 National Assembly elections were carefully screened by the central party leadership, which selected 148 candidates for 117 seats in the eighteen provinces and the two independent municipalities. Although the number of candidates exceeded the number of seats, candidate lists were arranged and voting results manipulated so that in fact there was little real choice; those at the top of candidate lists in each constituency invariably won by ridiculously overwhelming margins. The population was largely indifferent and sometimes hostile to the predestined results of the elections.

Kampuchean People's Revolutionary Party (KPRP; *Pak Pracheachon Pativoat Kampuchea*)

History

From January 5 to 8, 1979, sixty-six exiled Kampuchean communists, approximately half ex-Khmer Viet Minh and half ex-Khmer Rouge, held an ad hoc congress under Vietnamese auspices to form the Committee to Reorganize the Party and a temporary party standing committee of seven members to handle party affairs until a more formal party organization could be established. At the time of the congress, approximately two hundred Kampucheans were recognized by it as genuine Communists and members of the party, which for the moment was known by the same name as the Khmer Rouge Party headed by Pol Pot, namely, the Communist Party of Kampuchea (*Pak Kommunis Kampuchea*). It seems that neither all the surviving Khmer Viet Minh nor all the Khmer Rouge who had reached Vietnam were considered party members. Five of the seven members of the temporary Standing Committee were evidently ex-Khmer Viet Minh, while two were ex-Khmer Rouge. The head of the committee, apparently holding the title of first secretary, was the ex-Khmer Viet Minh Pen Sovann.

The ad hoc party congress was still in session when Vietnamese forces captured the Kampuchean capital of Phnom Penh on January 7. On January 8, the congress closed and the national People's Revolutionary Council (PRC) of eight members was proclaimed to act as the provisional government of the "newly liberated" Kampuchea.

The ex-Khmer Rouge Heng Samrin was named chairman of this Council and Pen Sovann its vice chairman charged with national defense. Heng Samrin's ex-Khmer Rouge colleagues held the portfolios of foreign affairs and interior, while Pen Sovann's fellow ex-Khmer Viet Minh were in charge of the economy, health, and information portfolios. A schoolteacher of the old-elite class, who had taken refuge in Vietnam in 1978, was given the education portfolio.

From 1979 to 1980, the state, party, and front organizations of the PRK were extended and developed, at first fitfully and then more solidly, with the assistance and under the protection of more than 100,000 Vietnamese troops and a corps of several thousand Vietnamese political advisors and technical experts.

The party developed slowly. Almost immediately after January 1979, it was beset with serious internal recriminations, with charges of corruption, incompetence, and political unreliability being made publicly by party First Secretary Pen Sovann against many party cadres. Continuing controversies between the ex-Khmer Viet Minh and the ex-Khmer Rouge in the party leadership were openly expressed in public statements by members of the two factions.

Organization

The first post-1979 party congress (officially enumerated as the fourth) was held from May 26 to 29, 1981. By this time party membership had grown to perhaps 700 persons (including candidates), of which 162 attended the congress. Core-group membership (see below under *Membership & Constituency*) had reached more than 3,000. The congress changed the name of the party from the Communist Party of Kampuchea to the Kampuchean People's Revolutionary Party, setting 1951 as the year of the party's foundation. This was a symbolic refutation of the Khmer Rouge brand of Communism and a symbolic return to the "tradition" of a Communism based on Vietnamese tutelage. (The party organization established under Vietnamese control in Kampuchea during the First Indochina War was called the Khmer People's Revolutionary Party and was formed in 1951.) The congress elected the Central Committee of nineteen full members and two alternatives, the Political Bureau of eight members, and the Secretariat of seven members. Pen Sovann was elevated from first secretary to the more prestigious position of general secretary, head of both the Political Bureau and the Secretariat. Twelve of the twenty-one Central Committee members and alternatives were fellow ex-Khmer Viet Minh. The rest were former Khmer Rouge who had been in Vietnam in 1978.

It was widely believed that Pen Sovann's concurrent holding of the posts of party secretary general and prime minister and the dominance of ex-Khmer Viet Minh on the Central Committee and Council of Ministers confirmed their hegemony over the party and state. It turned out, however, that serious conflict had been developing under the facade of consolidation, pitting Pen Sovann against many of his fellow ex-Khmer Viet Minh and probably against most ex-Khmer Rouge leaders as well. Indications are that Pen Sovann was ever more deeply alienating his comrades by attempting to create a myth of his sagacity and by his penchant for unrelenting criticism of their performance. In the second half of 1981, several ranking ex-Khmer Viet Minh cadres were shunted out of important posts by Pen Sovann for what most members of this fraction saw as little or no reason. The Vietnamese, too, evidently disagreed with Pen Sovann's "undemocratic" political style. It has been reported that he attempted to shore up his position by making a play for support from the Soviet Union.

On December 4, 1981, Pen Sovann was suddenly removed from all of his party and state posts by the party Central Committee. The official cover story that he had become ill was later supplemented with officially inspired rumors that he had gone insane. He was replaced as secretary general by Heng Samrin. The choice of the ex-Khmer Rouge Heng Samrin was evidently a compromise that indicated that the ex-Khmer Viet Minh group was afflicted by further internal disputes and weaknesses which made it impossible for them to put forward one of their own faction.

Policy

The general outlines of the party's domestic and foreign policies were laid down at the party's May 1981 national congress. The congress resolution declared that the Party's basic domestic tasks were economic and political: "to rebuild the country, restore the force of the revolution, and strengthen the latter in such a way as to make it sufficiently strong to defend and rebuild the country"; and to lead the people to "build the fatherland through a period of transition" of "gradual advance toward socialism." The resolution candidly admitted that this would be "a long struggle indeed" which would require "much time" to carry out.

The resolution defined restoration of agriculture as the main economic task, emphasizing the need to achieve food self-sufficiency. It stated that semicollective "solidarity groups" composed of ten to twenty peasant families must be the basic organizational form of agricultural production. It also called for the "restoration and development of big and small industry and craftsmanship by relying on the available local raw materials." It proclaimed state ownership of "all the bases of industrial production, all the networks of communications and transportation and the networks for exchange and distribution of goods."

The emphasis in the political sphere was not on quantitative expansion but on qualitative strengthening and consolidation of the party, core groups, army, mass organizations for workers, youth and women, the Front, and the organs of state administration. Particular emphasis was given to the need for more and better "ideological work," that is, political indoctrination aimed at increasing loyalty to the regime, at all levels in all these institutions. In what can be read as an admission of serious problems in the key institution of the party, the resolution called for struggle against a long list of party shortcomings: elitism, authoritarianism, and aloofness from and oppression of the masses. The party rank and file were criticized for divisive and factionalist tendencies and acts, failure to hold orderly chapter meetings and to constantly practice criticism/self-criticism, lack of respect for the principle of democratic centralism, recruitment of new members in ways not conforming to party regulations, and Maoist tendencies. The leadership was criticized for tendencies toward the implementation of both libertarian and dictatorial systems and toward a cult of personality. The Central Committee was charged with failure to maintain solidarity and political and organizational independence within the party as well as failure to act as the genuine leading core and the center of unity within the party. The purge of Pen Sovann may have been an attempt to solve some of these problems.

The resolution's section on foreign policy proclaimed Kampuchea "an integral part of the great family of Socialist countries." It characterized strengthening "solidarity with the Soviet Union and other fraternal Socialist countries" as Kampuchea's foremost foreign-policy goal and, in this context, went on to declare that Kampuchea would "always strengthen the relations of fraternal friendship and militant solidarity with Viet Nam and Laos." This formulation seemed designed to give pride of place to the Soviet Union as the head of the socialist camp while at the same time putting Kampuchea's relations with Vietnam and Laos on a higher plane than its relations with the Soviet Union. It nevertheless failed to designate Kampuchea's relationship with its Indochinese neighbors as a "special relationship," thus implying that Kampuchea's ties to Vietnam were not as intimate and fully developed as those of Laos to Vietnam. There are some indications that the ouster of Pen Sovann has been followed by a shift towards a declaration of the existence of a Kampuchea-Vietnam special relationship.

Membership & Constituency

It is unlikely that party membership went much above the 300 mark by the end of 1979, if it even reached that level. In 1980, internal party strife was muted, or at least hidden, and more attention was paid to recruitment activities. A system of "core groups" (krom snoul) was instituted to function as a seedbed from which to select promising persons as party cadres. Core groups were formed inside the state and Front organs as well as inside army units and included the most active and politically trustworthy administrators and combatants. Members of the core group were given special political indoctrination in party-run schools. They also received certain political and economic privileges in an attempt to tie them more closely to the regime. If they performed satisfactorily, they could be nominated for candidate party membership after a period of from six to nine months. It seems that by the end of 1980, 2,000 to 3,000 core-group members had been recruited, with core groups established in most departments of central PRC ministries, many district PRCs, and a few subdistrict SMCs. Also by the end of 1980, a good number of core-group members had been nominated as candidate party members, so that total party membership probably approached and may have surpassed the 500 mark. In some districts there were now enough party members to form district party cells (three or more party members). Elsewhere, party members at the district level were members of provincial party cells. About one-half of the new party members were inside the state and Front organs at the central, provincial, and district levels and one-half in the army, which by the end of 1980 had probably grown to a size of 30,00 men (in regular units). The majority of those in the state and Front organs were of petty-bourgeois or upper-class background, while the majority of those in the army were of peasant background. The large proportion of nonproletarian and upper-class elements enter-

ing the party was likely a matter of some concern to the party leadership.

Financing

Nothing is known of the party's finances.

Leadership

Heng Samrin (born 1934) was formally in control of the party leadership in mid-1982, but the key posts at the highest level of the party were predominantly in the hands of ex-Khmer Viet Minh. There were, moreover, clear signs of continuing factionalism among the top party leadership, and abrupt leadership changes could not be ruled out. The unusual promotion of Chan Si to the premiership in early 1982 illustrates the impossibility of predicting who may rise to major leadership positions.

Opposition

The PRK faces organized opposition from three groups. The armed remnants of the Khmer Rouge, the discredited party of Pol Pots' Democratic Kampuchea regime, lack popular support but carry out small-scale guerrilla warfare in several outlying parts of the country, especially in areas adjacent to the Thai border, with the help of generous military aid from China. The republicanist and anticommunist Khmer People's National Liberation Front (KPNLF) led by former prime minister Son Sann, appeals mainly to the prerevolution elite, has infiltrated the middle and lower ranks of the PRK's political and administrative apparati, and maintains a number of semiguerrilla military units in several bases along the Thai border. The Kampuchean National Liberation Movement (better known by its French acronym, MOULINAKA) is associated with the country's charismatic former monarch, Norodom Sihanouk, and with his name appeals primarily to the Kampuchean peasantry. MOULINAKA lacks a coherent underground network inside the country and has no visible military arm.

On June 22, 1982, after three years of difficult and often bitter negotiations, these three groups formed a loose union, the Coalition Government of Democratic Kampuchea (Roathaphibal Chamroh Kampuchea Pracheathipatay), with Sihanouk as president, former Khmer Rouge chief of state Khieu Samphan as vice president in charge of foreign affairs, and Son Sann as prime minister.

The coalition was formed under intense pressure from the five members of the noncommunist Association of Southeast Asian Nations or ASEAN (Thailand, Singapore, Malaysia, Indonesia, and the Philippines), China, and the United States. These nations feared that Democratic Kampuchea would lose United Nations recognition if it remained a purely Khmer Rouge entity. The KPNLF and MOULINAKA had always resisted coalition with the Khmer Rouge because of the certain damage such an association would do to their popularity inside the country. They ultimately gave in to the external pressure, partly in the hope of receiving diplomatic and material support from ASEAN, China, and the United States, which they see as a necessary counterbalance to massive Vietnamese and Soviet aid to the PRK. The terms of the coalition agreement allow them to maintain their political and organizational identities and to receive aid independently of the Khmer Rouge.

National Prospects

The formation in June 1982 of the Coalition Government of Democratic Kampuchea grouping the Khmer Rouge, the KPNLF, and MOULINAKA under a single internationally recognized umbrella suggests that political and armed conflict will continue in Kampuchea. While the PRK's administrative structures have become increasingly consolidated since 1979, so have resistance organizations, and these resistance forces have put themselves in a position to receive increased external diplomatic and material support by their acquiescence to the coalition. Although the immediate effect of the formation of the coalition may well be to weaken the KPNLF and MOULINAKA politically by associating them more closely with the hated Khmer Rouge, their access to external aid may allow them to mobilize more effectively popular anti-Vietnamese sentiment in the longer

run. There is no prospect that they could militarily oust the Vietnamese, with or without the help of the Khmer Rouge armed forces; however, if they can overcome the negative effects of the coalition on their popularity, they may be able to threaten the PRK politically to a greater extent than in the period 1979 to 1982. Their ability to do so will probably be facilitated by further infighting among the three factions in the PRK leadership, as well as by Kampuchea's continuing difficulties in achieving food self-sufficiency and in improving the economic situation in the country generally. ASEAN, China, and the United States will certainly attempt to take advantage of any gains by the resistance to increase pressure on Vietnam to agree to give up its hegemony over Kampuchea. Vietnam, in any case, will continue to have the option, albeit risky, of concerted military action against all resistance forces.

Further Reading
"Cambodia." *Far Eastern Economic Review 1982 Yearbook.* Hong Kong: Far Eastern Economic Review Press, 1982.
Carney, Timothy. "Kampuchea in 1981: Fragile Stalemate." *Asian Survey*, Vol 22, No. 1, January 1982.
Chanda, Nayan. "Now a Non-Person." *Far Eastern Economic Review*, 18 December 1981.
"Kampuchea." *Far Eastern Economic Review 1980 Yearbook.* Hong Kong: Far Eastern Economic Review Press, 1980.
"Kampuchea." *Far Eastern Economic Review 1981 Yearbook.* Hong Kong: Far Eastern Economic Review Press, 1981.
Leifer, Michael. "Kampuchea in 1980: The Politics of Attrition." *Asian Survey*, Vol 21, No. 1, January 1981.
_____. "Kampuchea 1979: From Dry Season to Dry Season." *Asian Survey*, Vol. 20, No. 1, January 1980.

REPUBLIC OF KENYA
(*Djumhuri ya Kenya*)
by Thomas Paul Ofcansky, Ph.D.

The System of Government

Kenya, a nation of more than 16.5 million people, gained its independence from Great Britain on December 12, 1963. It is a one-party, partially democratic state. The basis of the country's government is the 1963 constitution as amended in 1964, 1967, and 1982. The 1964 amendment, known as the republican constitution, established a republican form of government with a strong executive and a powerful central government. The 1982 amendment established the one-party system.

Since independence, Kenya has had the reputation of being one of the most stable nations in Africa. However, serious opposition to the government has emerged on at least two occasions. In 1978, an elaborate conspiracy to assassinate President Daniel arap Moi was discovered in the police force (the "Ngoroko affair"). The plot leader, Joseph Mungai, a former police officer, was arrested, but he was released after Moi called on the country to forgive and forget. No information on the forces behind the plot has been revealed, nor has there been any adequate explanation as to why the plotters were not prosecuted.

Then, on August 1, 1982, a group of discontented, ill-trained, and poorly led enlisted members of the country's 2,200-man air force attempted a coup against the Moi regime. Although the rebels enjoyed widespread support among university students and the urban poor, loyalist elements from the Kenyan army and the General Service Unit (a paramilitary force) rallied to stop the revolt and to restore order. Within a month the government announced that it had disbanded the air force and had made plans to reorganize it under the command of Major General Mahamoud Mohamed, who had been deputy commander of the Kenyan army.

Executive

The chief executive officer, since 1978, is Daniel Teroitich arap Moi. He is president (head of state), prime minister (head of government), and commander-in-chief of the armed forces. The president appoints the vice president and other members of the cabinet from among members of the National Assembly. The president must command a majority vote in the National Assembly, and if he loses a vote of confidence must resign or dissolve the legislature and call for new elections. The president is elected to a five-year term by popular vote. He also must be an elected member of the National Assembly and is entitled to attend its meetings and vote on legislation. The president's successor is the vice president who may be removed from office at any time at the former's discretion.

Legislature

The national legislature is the unicameral National Assembly. The body consists of 171 members: 158 elected by popular vote for five-year terms, twelve nominated by the president, and the attorney-general as an ex officio member. Since 1969, all members of the National Assembly have belonged to the country's sole political party, the Kenya African National Union (KANU).

According to the constitution, the National Assembly is the supreme state organ. Since independence, however, the executive has exerted tremendous political influence over the legislature. This influence is due mainly to the fact that of the Assembly's present members, fifty-three hold ministerial posts and fifty-four more have positions in state-owned corporations or on the boards of government commissions.

Nearly all legislation is drafted and introduced by the government. Indeed, ministries rarely consult Assembly members or committees about a particular bill in advance of its presentation on the floor. Although the government has never suffered an outright defeat on any important legislative measure, it has changed or withdrawn numerous bills because of staunch parliamentary opposition.

The National Assembly can force the resignation of the entire cabinet by a vote of no confidence. Opposition in the Assembly consists mainly of backbenchers who use the right of interpellation to question ministers and to register complaints of their constituents. National Assembly debates, however, are rather subdued even though many of them reflect a high degree of public concern over major social, political, and economic issues.

Judiciary

Kenyan jurisprudence is based on English common law, African customary law, legislative acts by the National Assembly after 1963 and by the British Parliament before independence, and judicial precedent. A chief justice and eleven *puisne* (associate) judges—all of whom are appointed by the president—comprise Kenya's High Court, which sits continuously in Nairobi, Mombasa, Nakuru, and Kisumu. The Judicial Service Commission advises on all other judicial appointments. Because of a chronic shortage of law school graduates, many positions in the judiciary still are held by foreigners.

Kenya's legal system is noted for its independence and integrity. The courts are empowered to review all government acts and legislation and to declare laws and acts null and void. The state also may be sued for damages caused by its illegal acts.

Regional & Local Government

Kenya is divided administratively into provinces, districts, divisions, locations, and sublocations. Provincial commissioners, who answer directly to the president, govern the country's eight provinces (Coast, Northeastern Eastern, Central, Rift Valley, Nyanza, Western, and Nairobi). The commissioners are accountable for education, transport, and health in their provinces. District commissioners are responsible for Kenya's various districts, while district officers head divisions within each district. As of 1978, there were forty districts and 215 divisions. Chiefs and subchiefs represent the government in locations and sublocations.

The entire nation is under the jurisdiction of five levels of local authorities: municipal councils, town councils, county councils, urban councils, and area councils. There are eleven municipal councils, including Nairobi City Council; six town councils; thirty-eight county councils; eighteen urban councils, and fifty-four area councils.

These local councils, which fall outside the regional administrative structure, raise revenue by levying taxes, build and maintain roads, guard the public's health and welfare, supervise education, build homes, and provide various agricultural and social services.

Municipal councilors and aldermen are elected directly by the people. The central government also appoints members to each council. As political power in Kenya becomes more centralized, many of the local councils' functions are being transferred to ministries and regional administrations. Apart from the councils, the only means of participation for rural people in governmental processes is through meetings, called *barazas*, convened by chiefs, subchiefs, or district officers.

The Electoral System

Kenya's electoral system is generally free, with the president and members of the National Assembly being elected by direct popular vote. Candidates are selected in primary elections. National elections have been held in an orderly fashion since independence (1963, 1966, 1969, 1974, and 1979), and the government has fully supported their results. The only exception occurred in 1979 when ten candidates—most of whom were former Kenyan People's Union members—were barred from running for the Assembly for political reasons. The constitution provides for universal suffrage for all citizens over the age of 18.

Although Kenya is a one-party state, there has been tolerance of dissenting political activity. In the 1974 elections, for example, eighty-eight sitting National Assembly members, including a number of cabinet ministers, lost their seats. In the 1979 elections, multiple candidacies resulted in the defeat of 60 percent of the incumbents; moreover, thirty-one candidates challenged the election results and five of them were successful.

Kenya African National Union (KANU)

History

In 1982, the National Assembly unanimously approved a constitutional amendment making KANU the sole legal political party in Kenya. Originally a Kikuyu organization, KANU—which was preceded by the Kenya African Union (KAU)—commenced nationwide operations in 1960 to broaden its base of support. In the years just prior to independence, the Kenya African Democratic Union (KADU), which had been formed in 1960 by leaders of some of the country's smaller ethnic groups to guard against Kikuyu/Luo (the major ethnic groups) domination, opposed KANU. To facilitate the movement toward complete independence and to produce the country's first African government, Jomo Kenyatta engineered a coalition between the two parties.

In 1963, KANU won an absolute majority in the pre-independence general elections and Kenyatta became prime minister; nineteen months later (December 1964) he became executive president of the Republic of Kenya. After the voluntary dissolution of KADU in 1964, KANU became the country's sole political party. Many former KADU officials, including Daniel Moi, then obtained positions within KANU. The Kenya People's Union (KPU), formed in 1966 by Luo leader Oginga Odinga, was banned in 1969.

Organization

Largely because it has never developed an effective, popular political ideology, KANU has failed to become a mass party or to enlist widespread grass-roots support. It is mainly an electoral party, functioning only in times of stress, turmoil, or elections. KANU's party institutions also are weak. National congresses are rarely held and most national party officials are appointed by the president. The party's local office holders are elected by a delegate conference, which includes all members of the National Assembly. There also is a tacit understanding that the eight seats on KANU's national executive should go to representatives of the country's eight provinces. On the local level, party units are largely ineffective and function only intermittently.

Policy

KANU's political principles include centralized government, racial harmony, Kenyanization of the economy, industrialization and general development on a free-enterprise basis, and "positive nonalignment" in foreign affairs.

Membership & Constituency

According to one report, KANU—which claims to represent all political, economic, and ethnic elements in Kenya—had at least three million members by January 1979. During the same year, party officials launched a vigorous membership drive to attract an additional two million supporters. Although precise figures are unavailable, and Nathan Munoko (born 1922), the party's national organizing secretary and the *Daily Nation* have questioned the effectiveness of the campaign, it is almost certain that KANU's membership roll has increased significantly over the past three years.

Financing

Since its inception KANU has been plagued with financial difficulties. To help rejuvenate the party, officials announced in 1979 that all KANU life members had to re-enroll for 1,000 Kenya shillings (about $120) each. At the same time, fundraising drives added Ksh. 308,000 (about $37,000) to KANU's treasury. It remains to be seen whether these measures will have a meaningful, long-term impact on the party's ailing financial condition.

Leadership

KANU's top leadership closely parallels the country's political elite. Daniel Teroitich arap Moi (born in Baringo in 1924) is party president; Mwai Kibaki (born 1931) serves as vice president. Robert Matano (born 1924) is KANU's secretary general.

Other Political Forces

Military

Kenya's armed forces number approximately 14,750. President Moi heads the defense structure as commander-in-chief. The minister of defense presides over the Defense Council, while the chief of defense staff is commander of the army.

Kenya's small military force has virtually no capacity for projecting power beyond its borders. Its combat worthiness has never been tested in the field, making its possible effectiveness against the highly trained Somali forces in some future conflict a matter of grave concern.

With the Soviet Union building up its "bluewater navy," the United States has become increasingly sensitive to eastern Africa's strategic value. It therefore has concluded a series of agreements with Kenya to gain facilities for its navy in Mombasa. In exchange, the United States will supply the Moi regime with about $79.5 million, half of which will be used to dredge Mombasa harbor and improve the airfields at Nanyuki and Embakasi. The rest of the money will provide Kenya's military establishment with an impressive array of American equipment, including Phantom fighters, transport aircraft, and antitank guns. The growing American presence has been extremely unpopular with many of the country's more radical elements.

Traditionally, Kenya's armed forces have been relatively nonpolitical and have exerted very little influence on national affairs. On August 1, 1982, however, a group of air force enlisted men and junior officers—many of whom were Kikuyu—revolted against the Moi regime. According to a radio broadcast from the "National Redemption Council," the coup was necessary because "rampant corruption and nepotism have made life almost intolerable in our society. The economy is in shambles, and the people can't afford food, housing, and transport." During the time they occupied the official Voice of Kenya radio station, the rebels promised to replace the present government with "a regime of socialist complexion."

As news of the coup spread throughout Nairobi, university students and destitute shantytown dwellers joined the airmen. Many of them turned to looting on an extensive scale.

Within six hours loyalists suppressed the revolt and quickly restored law and order. In the aftermath, President Moi disbanded the air force and placed all former personnel under arrest, detained about 1,000 civilians, closed the University of Nairobi and ordered the students to return home. It remains to be seen whether these measures will prevent future violent outbursts led by disgruntled military men.

Urban Poor

Since independence, Kenya's cities, especially Nairobi and Mombasa, have grown at a tremendous rate. Most of the new inhabitants were peasants fleeing the poverty of the countryside. A vast majority of these urban residents (70 percent in Nairobi and 67 percent in Mombasa) live in slums and squatter settlements. Most are also unemployed. Although the government has tried to pacify this increasingly alienated population with artificially low food prices, it is clear that the visible disparities of wealth and the evidence of widespread corruption have convinced many of the urban poor that radicalism and violence are the only answers to their problems.

Ethnic Groups

Interethnic rivalries among the country's numerous groups also have troubled the Moi regime, primarily by obstructing national integration. Since 1978, the most serious ethnic problems have been Somali separatism, Kikuyu dominance in politics and business, and Luo dissatisfaction with the government's overall performance.

Somalia's traditional advocacy of Somali self-determination in part of Kenya's North-Eastern Province has been a constant threat to the region's stability. After repeated attempts to placate the Somali minority, the Kenya government decided to use force to try to solve the problem. In May 1982, the provincial commissioner of North-Eastern Province declared a protracted war against the banditry of armed ethnic Somalis (Shiftas). He "ordered security forces now combing the province not to return until they had wiped out Shifta bandits from the area." According to a local KANU spokesman, "neighboring countries" had fueled Somali banditry by smuggling arms into the area on camels and donkeys. Over the next few years it should become evident whether this new policy will destroy the separatist movement or merely strengthen the rebel's resolve.

Until Jomo Kenyatta's death, the Kikuyu dominated nearly all aspects of political, economic, and social life in Kenya. Since that time, however, there has been a gradual but steady loss of Kikuyu influence in the country's affairs. Nowhere is this erosion of power more evident than in Kenyatta's own family.

Problems began when president Moi refused to give Dr. Njeroge Mungai, a nephew of the late president, a ministerial post even though he had been returned to the National Assembly. In 1979, Ngengi Muigai, another nephew, left the board of Mackenzie (Kenya) Ltd., while Udi Gecaga, Kenyatta's son-in-law, lost his position as chairman of the board of the *Standard* newspaper. Rumors also persist that the government is investigating the tax returns of Kenyatta's widow, Mama Ngina.

To make matters worse, the Kikuyu lost four seats in Nairobi—a city traditionally considered to be part of their area of influence—in the 1979 general election. So far, Kikuyu dissatisfaction has been confined to some minor disturbances in Central Province; but this situation could change radically and without warning at any time.

The Luo community of Western Region is the most numerous and powerful ethnic group after the Kikuyu. Primarily, many Luo leaders complain that their region of Kenya contributes significantly to the nation's food supplies and to its growing agricultural industries in sugar, tea, and wood pulp—which bring in valuable foreign exchange—but has had less than its fair share of development projects. Even when the government announced two major schemes for Western Region in 1979—the establishment of the Lake Victoria Basin Development Authority and the Kericho Valley Development Authority—it was clear that president Moi was solidifying his grass-roots support among the Kalenjin-speaking peoples rather than trying to improve the standard of living in the Luo community.

The other Luo grievance against the Moi regime concerns the activities of Oginga Odinga (born 1911), a prominent Luo leader who was Kenya's first vice president after self-government. After forming the KPU in 1966, Odinga repeatedly spoke out against the government, claiming, among other things, that economic independence still had to be won, and that the KANU machine was unable to solve the country's problems. When a group of Luo dissidents stoned Jomo Kenyatta's motor car in Kisumu in 1969, the government outlawed the KPU and detained Odinga without trial on grounds of subversion. When Moi became president, he released Odinga and welcomed him back into KANU, hoping his benevolence would lessen discontent among the fractious Luo.

Odinga, however, continued to attack the Kenya government, saying that "for the common man, African governments are evidently more ruthless than the colonial regimes we struggled so hard against." Consequently, in 1982 Moi expelled Odinga from KANU on the grounds that he had rejected "the strategies, philosophy, and ideology" pursued by the KANU government. The Odinga affair undoubtedly will provide Luo dissidents with yet another reason for opposing what they perceive to be an anti-Luo government.

Students

Relations between the University of Nairobi student body, which numbers more than 5,000 and the government have also steadily deteriorated. Troubles began in October 1979 when a group of students launched a protest march through the streets of Nairobi against a KANU decision to bar former KPU members from standing in the general elections. As punishment, Moi promptly sent the students home for a premature Christmas vacation ostensibly "to enable them to take part in the election campaign." After one month, the students were allowed to return to complete their examinations. The university was closed again in February 1980, after students who claimed poor food was served to them smashed several cars and vehicle showrooms in Nairobi. Although the

present atmosphere appears to be calm, it is unlikely that the intensity of the past few years has dissipated completely.

Organized Labor

Approximately 390,000 workers are members of Kenya's thirty-one major labor unions. These organized workers represent about 43 percent of the country's wage earners. With the exception of the Kenya National Union of Teachers and the Kenya Union of Civil Servants, all principal unions are affiliated with the Central Organization of Trade Unions (COTU). The government, through the ministry of labor, dominates labor-management relations, beginning with the authority to register trade unions. The ministry also supervises union representation elections, and certifies winners before they can officially sit down at the bargaining tables. Strikes, which can be banned by the ministry or the president, usually are short and infrequent. From 1966 to 1976, for example, the most strikes reported in any one year was 155. Normally, there are less than 100 strikes a year, each lasting about three or four days. Because of the government's role in organized labor, most unions are staunch supporters of the Moi regime.

National Prospects

Apart from the 1974–76 period, Kenya's economy displayed a healthy growth rate until 1978. President Moi, like his predecessor, has conducted economic policy pragmatically, and the political climate has been favorable to overseas investment and to foreign aid.

However, serious questions have been raised about the distribution of Kenya's relative prosperity. The main problem is a continuing population explosion which is placing serious strains upon the economy in terms of public expenditure. Moreover, the labor force has been growing far more rapidly than employment opportunities. Kenya could very well experience a serious degree of political and social instability.

Another major difficulty concerns Kenya's foreign-exchange position, which has deteriorated because of the oil crisis and the international economic recession. To help resolve this problem, the government has introduced changes into its budget, including the establishment of an export bonus for manufacturers and measures to limit demands on foreign exchange for the importation of luxury consumer goods and oil. Although increased coffee prices produced a temporary improvement in the foreign-exchange position, continued high oil prices will cause serious economic problems for the Kenya government for the foreseeable future.

Further Reading

Arnold, Guy. *Modern Kenya.* London: Longman, 1982.

Barkan, Joel D., and Okumu, John J. *Politics and Public Policy in Kenya and Tanzania.* New York: Praeger, 1979.

Brown, Jeremy M. *Kenyatta.* London: Allen and Unwin Ltd., 1973.

Hazelwood, Arthur. *The Economy of Kenya: The Kenyatta Era.* London and New York: Oxford University Press, 1979.

Heyer, Judith. *Agricultural Development in Kenya: An Economic Assessment.* London and New York: Oxford University Press, 1977.

Holtham, Gerald, and Hazelwood, Arthur. *Aid and Inequality in Kenya: British Development Assistance to Kenya.* London: Croom Helm, 1976.

Kitching, Gavin. *Class and Economic Change in Kenya: The Making of an African Petite Bourgeoisie.* New Haven, Conn.: Yale University Press, 1980.

Oyugi, Walter O. *Rural Development Administration: A Kenyan Experience.* Bombay: Vikas India, 1980.

Rempel, Henry, and Hourse, William J. *The Kenyan Employment Problem.* London and New York: Oxford University Press, 1978.

Swainson, Nicola. *The Development of Corporate Capitalism in Kenya.* Berkeley, Calif.: University of California Press, 1980.

DEMOCRATIC PEOPLE'S REPUBLIC OF KOREA

(Chosun Minju-jui Inmin Kongwa-guk)

by Donald M. Seekins, Ph.D.

The System of Government

The Democratic People's Republic of Korea, or North Korea, is a one-party socialist state in control of the northern half of the Korean peninsula, which has been divided between rival governments in the north and south since the country, a colony of Japan from 1910 to 1945, was occupied by Soviet and United States military forces at the end of World War II. North Korea, with a land area of 122,370 square kilometers, about 55 percent of the total land area of the peninsula, shares a 1,025-kilometer border with the People's Republic of China along the Yalu and Tumen rivers, and a 16-kilometer border with the Soviet Union at the mouth of the Tumen River. Since the end of the Korean War in July 1953, the Demilitarized Zone (DMZ), a 4,000-meter wide "no man's land" along the 38th parallel, has divided the Democratic People's Republic of Korea from the Republic of Korea (South Korea). North Korea has a population estimated in 1980 at between seventeen to nineteen million, no official figures on population having been published by the government since 1963. This is about half the population of South Korea. Given the antagonistic relationship between the governments of the north and south, the "demographic gap" is of great concern to the North Koreans for both economic and military reasons.

An examination of the history, both ancient and modern, of the Korean peninsula sheds much light on the character and the preoccupations of the North Korean regime. Korea is an ancient country, which, like Poland in the west, has been a marching-ground for the armies of its more powerful neighbors (China, Japan, the Mongols, the Manchus, and, since the nineteenth century, Russia) and yet has managed, with great tenacity, to preserve its national identity. A tragic history has given the Korean people great determination and strength of character, and yet has also made them highly suspicious of outsiders and at times, rigidly conservative. The Yi Dynasty, which despite foreign invasion and bitter internal rivalry between political factions lasted from 1392 to 1910, sought protection by becoming a tributary of China, assiduously copying its political institutions and social practices, and by closing itself off from all other foreign influences, becoming what Westerners in the nineteenth century called the "hermit kingdom."

In 1876, however, Japan forcibly opened the country, in much the same manner as Japan itself was opened by Commodore Perry in 1853. The next three decades saw intense rivalry between Japan, China, and Russia for dominant influence in Korea, but it was Japan, through its victories in the Sino-Japanese War (1894–95) and the Russo-Japanese War (1904–05) which gained control, abolishing the Yi Dynasty and making Korea a colony in 1910. Japanese rule, which combined policies of economic exploitation and cultural assimilation, was bitterly resented.

The dream of Korean independence after the defeat of Japan gave way to the tragedy of dismemberment with the occupation of the peninsula by Soviet and American armed forces. Although the United Nations planned for Korea's reunification after nationwide elections, these never occurred. The Democratic People's Republic of Korea, with its own constitution, was established on September 8, 1948, claiming control over the entire peninsula and accusing the rival Republic of Korea, established in August 1948, of being a "puppet" regime. The Korean War (June 1950 to July 1953), which resulted in the death and dislocation of millions of people and the desolation of virtually the entire peninsula, locked the governments of the north and south into a stance of rigid hostility. For over three decades the region has been one of the most militarized in the world, while the goal of reunification grows ever more distant.

Executive

As in other socialist countries, the state organization of the Democratic People's Republic of Korea is defined as subordinate to the ruling Marxist-Leninist party, the Korean Workers' Party (KWP): the state is the implementer of the policy lines formulated by the party, which owes its dominant position to its role as representative and "vanguard" of the revolutionary working class. State structure is outlined in the 1972 constitution, which replaced the original constitution ratified in 1948 at the time of the establishment of the DPRK.

The head of state is the president, who has been, since the office was established in 1972, Kim Il Sung. The president, though elected for renewable four-year terms by the national legislature, the Supreme People's Assembly, is in practice accountable to no one, being at once commander of the armed forces, chief executive with control over the State Administration Council (cabinet), and supreme legislator through his power to issue edicts with the force of law and the requirement that all other legislation be approved by him. The president is also responsible for approving treaties and agreements with foreign countries. The creation of this office in 1972 marked the unrivalled supremacy of Kim Il Sung, secretary general of the Korean Workers' Party (KWP). The president is assisted by a first vice president and, in 1982, two other vice presidents. In that same year, the premier, head of the State Administration Council, was Li Jong Ok.

Legislature

Delegates to the unicameral Supreme People's Assembly (SPA) are chosen for four-year terms in direct elections based on universal suffrage, each delegate representing a constituency of 30,000 persons. There were 615 deputies elected in 1981. North Korea reported that 34.6 percent of the deputies are workers, 10.2 percent cooperative farm workers, and 49 percent are "doctors, professors, scientists, technicians and other specialists." Some 19 percent are women. The powers of the SPA include not only the election of the president and the passing of laws, but amendment of the constitution and approval of the national budget and economic plans. Sessions are held twice a year, in spring and late fall. When the SPA is not in session, its Standing Committee, elected by the deputies, acts in its name. Although the 1972 constitution defines the SPA as the "highest organ of state power," it is, in fact, neither an initiator of legislation nor an effective monitor or critic of government policies or leadership.

The Central People's Committee, elected by the SPA for a four-year term, functions essentially as the link between party and state, the great majority of its members being members of the Central Political Bureau (Politburo) of the KWP. Its powers and responsibilities are broad, including the definition of domestic and foreign policy lines and control over the State Administration Council and Central People's Commissions dealing with national defense, foreign policy, state control, internal matters, and justice and security.

Judiciary

Central Court judges are elected by the SPA for three-year terms. They thus fall under the control of the state and party and have no independence. Furthermore, the procurator general, appointed by the SPA, exercises supervisory control over the court system down to the provincial and local people's courts.

Regional & Local Government

The country is divided into nine provinces and four "special cities" (the capital, P'yongyang; Kaesong; Namp'o and Ch'ongjin). Subnational units are divided into urban districts (in the "special cities" and other large cities), regular cities, and some 152 countries. Each of these units has its own local people's assembly, local administration committee, and local people's committee, corresponding to the SPA, the State Administration Council, and the Central People's Committee on the national level. On the village level, there are no formal government organizations: administrative matters are the responsibility of the chairman of the local agricultural collective.

The Electoral System

Elections are managed by the party's umbrella organization, the Democratic Front for the Reunification of the Fatherland. A single slate of candidates approved by the party is presented to the electorate and election is automatic. Voter turnout routinely runs close to 100 percent according to North Korean sources; in the 1982 elections, the turnout not only reached that absolute figure, but all candidates were elected unanimously. Most candidates are KWP members; other political groupings receive a few seats.

The Party System

The Democratic People's Republic of Korea is one of the most tightly regulated countries on earth, far closer in fact to the model of a "totalitarian" state than the Soviet Union or the People's Republic of China. North Korea's small size facilitates efficient surveillance. Its continuing confrontation with South Korea creates a pervasive atmosphere of military discipline and mobilization, and the special role of Kim Il Sung as the nation's supreme and uncontested leader has created what appears to be an almost totally controlled society. Political power, on both the national and local levels, is monopolized by the Korean Workers' Party and no other group, not even the army, is capable of maintaining an independent power base.

Korean Workers' Party (KWP; *Chosun Nodong Dang*)

History

The Korean Workers' Party (KWP) was established in August 1946 as a coalition of diverse elements, including Korean communists who had been based in the Soviet Union before and during World War II, particularly in the Maritime Province bordering Manchuria and Korea. Others had been in China and were closely associated with the Chinese communist movement. A third group consisted of underground resistance fighters who had operated within Japanese-occupied Korea itself. The party's structure and principles were modeled on those of the Soviet Communist Party; a number of its most prominent members had been members of the Soviet party. Its development since 1946, however, has been unambiguously in the direction of one-man rule under Secretary General Kim Il Sung. In the early years, Kim, who owed his position as KWP leader to Soviet support, had to recognize and deal with the somewhat divergent viewpoints of other party leaders even if no one seriously challenged his

supremacy. A series of purges, however, eliminated factions formed by former underground fighters and returnees from the Soviet Union and China, so that by 1956 all sources of potential opposition were eliminated. Kim reorganized the KWP, and subjected it to intense and unremitting doses of ideological remolding. In the 1960s, a campaign to idolize Kim and his revolutionary achievements was initiated and has remained the dominant theme of North Korean political life.

Organization

The highest organ of the Korean Workers' Party is its party congress, whose delegates, numbering 3,220 full and alternate members at the Sixth Party Congress in October 1980, are elected by members of provincial and "special city" party congresses. Although it is supposed to be convened every four years, the Congress has in fact met much less frequently: the previous two congresses were held in September 1961 and November 1970. As is the case in other one-party systems, the congress, meeting so infrequently and with such a large membership, is not the effective locus of decision-making, but only a platform for the promulgation of decisions made by a much smaller group of leaders.

Power is concentrated in ever smaller concentric circles. The Central Committee, with a membership of 248 in 1981, convenes the congress and acts in its name when it is not in session. The largest single group in the Central Committee following the Sixth Party Congress was what could be called "technocrats."

The Political Bureau (Politburo), with thirty-four members in 1981, is elected by the Central Committee. The Standing Committee of the Political Bureau, with only five members in 1981, is composed of North Korea's most powerful leaders: Kim Il Sung, Kim Il, Kim Jong Il (Kim Il Sung's son), O Jin U, and Li Jong Ok.

National-level party organs included the Secretariat, with nine secretaries heading different party departments, including the Inspection Committee, responsible for party discipline; an Audit Committee, responsible for finances; a Military Committee, headed by Kim Il Sung; and a Liaison Bureau in charge of relations with underground "revolutionary" elements in South Korea. Several Central Committee departments deal with a variety of matters such as agriculture, fisheries, science and education, and propaganda and agitation. The party publishes Nodong Sinmum (Workers' News), a daily newspaper, and *Kulloja* (The Laborer), a theoretical journal.

There are party congresses, committees, and secretariats on all subnational levels as well as smaller party units in rural villages. The basic unit of the party on the local level is the cell, to which all party members must belong.

Important mass organizations include the Socialist Working Youth League, which schools future party members, and the Young Pioneer Corps for children.

The Democratic Front for the Reunification of the Fatherland comprises a spectrum of groups coordinated by the party. Among them are the General Association of Korean Residents in Japan, which organizes support for the P'yongyang regime among Japan's more than 600,000 Korean nationals. Also included are the Korean Social Democratic Party and the Chondogyo Chongu (Young Friends) Party, which are permitted a limited existence under the supervision of the KWF, the leading force in the Front. (Chondogyo is a "new religion" founded in the nineteenth century.)

Policy

Kim is revered not only as the revolutionary leader who liberated Korea from the Japanese (the role of the Soviets being glossed over), but as the creator of the *Juche* ("self-reliance" or "independence") ideology, originally conceived of as the adaptation of Marxist-Leninist theory to the Korean context. In recent years, *Juche* has become increasingly nationalistic rather than proletarian internationalist in tone and has emphasized the importance of cultural and social, as well as economic and political self-sufficiency. Some observers suggest that Kim's bitter experiences as a Korean in a Chinese middle school in Qilin may have steeled his nationalist resolve almost as much as resistance against the Japanese. But, on the broadest historical level, *Juche* represents a reaction against *sadaejui*, subservience or "flunkeyism," the tendency of some Koreans to admire and copy the ways of more powerful foreign countries, as the ruling classes copied China during the Yi Dynasty.

Although Kim elaborates on *Juche* in the seven volumes of his *Selected Works* published to date, it is difficult to define in precise terms. Two ideas are prominent and interrelated. One is straightforwardly nationalist: the imperative of taking from Korean history and culture those elements which will contribute to the building of a new revolutionary society. The second is described as "the independent stand of rejecting dependence on others and of using one's own brains, believing in one's own strength, and displaying the revolutionary spirit of self-reliance."

Juche has implications for policy. Economic self-reliance is stressed, although it is sometimes honored in the breach when the government finds it necessary to seek credits from abroad. Economic plans have emphasized industrialization, technical innovation, and the maximum utilization of domestic resources.

Constant military preparedness is emphasized in *Juche*. Relations with China and the Soviet Union are formally friendly, but care is taken not to seem dependent on either. *Juche* has also served as Kim's weapon in intraparty power struggles, pro-Soviet and pro-Chinese opponents being purged as "flunkeyists."

Juche, at times, has not only involved a repudiation of Soviet and Chinese models of socialist construction, but also has shown a tendency to depart from the theoretical foundation of the revolution, Marxism-Leninism. This is indicated by the fact that while Kim discussed Marxism-Leninism and its importance to the Korean revolution in his November 1970 Fifth KWP Congress, he failed to mention it at all in his October 1980 Sixth Congress address. While the Chinese communists have always modestly described "Mao Zedong Thought" as only an application of universal Marxist-Leninist truths, in the DPRK the thought of Kim is styled *Kim Il Sung Jui*, a full-class "ism" equal and perhaps superior to Marxism-Leninism and one with universal application. Seminars and discussion groups dedicated to "the study of the *Juche* idea" have been established around the world in places as disparate as New York, New Delhi, Lima, and Tokyo. It is advertised to people in the Third World as an alternative road to development superior to those proposed by the superpowers. A number of Third World leaders, like President Didier Ratsiraka of Madagascar, have been attracted by the Kim Il Sung model of national independence and one-man rule.

The great preoccupation of the P'yongyang government since the end of the Korean War has been its hostile and competitive relationship with the Republic of Korea. Technically, the peninsula is still in a state of war, with armistice talks being carried on at Panmunjom since July 1953. The conflict has made the north a tightly disciplined armed camp, and the supremacy of Kim Il Sung is based in large part on his role as a national leader in time of protracted war. DPRK policies toward the south have alternated between the support of antigovernment activities in the Republic of Korea, culminating in the January 1968 attempt to assassinate South Korean President Park Chung

Hee, and gestures of conciliation, expressed in its reiterated commitment to peaceful reunification of Korea and the proposal that a "Democratic Confederal Republic of Koryo" be established. This proposal envisages a union of the two halves of the peninsula in a system which would respect their social, economic, and political differences. Given the numerical disparity between the populations of the two Koreas, the DPRK position has been that both should be represented equally in some kind of confederal assembly, rather than on the principle of "one man one vote." Dialogue between the DPRK and the south was initiated in 1971, but there has been little in the way of concrete results. Hostile acts against the south continue, such as the building of secret tunnels under the DMZ and the murders of American officers in August 1976.

Membership & Constituency

It is estimated that the number of KWP members could have been as high as 3.2 million at the time of the Sixth Party Congress (1980), a sharp rise from the two million announced by the KWP in 1976. This could have been due to the induction of a large number of the "Three Revolution Workteams," a recent mass movement for political mobilization. Overall, party members compose about fifteen percent of the total population. Recruits must be recommended by members in good standing and must serve a probationary period of one year.

Criteria for party membership include personal commitment to its ideology, loyalty to Kim Il Sung, and proper class background. Former revolutionary fighters, workers, and poor peasants have generally been perceived as the most revolutionary classes and thus most eligible for party membership. In recent years, however, technical and administrative expertise has been seen as, if not more, important than class background and such criteria play an increasingly central role in the selection of party cadres and management personnel. The leadership's emphasis on rapid modernization has created a special need for cadre trained in economics. Schools for the training of KWP cadres include the College of People's Economic Management, the Kim Il Sung Higher Party School, and the Kumsong Political College.

Financing

Information on party financing is unavailable. It can be assumed that, as in other communist states, party members pay a portion of their income in dues and that direct government support is considerable.

Leadership

Kim Il Sung, who was born near P'yongyang on April 15, 1912, fought with guerrilla units against the Japanese on the Soviet-Manchuria border between 1932 and 1945, led the Korean Workers' Party since its founding in 1946, has been premier since 1948, and, after the adoption of the 1972 constitution, president of the DPRK. He has dominated the North Korean political scene in a manner unmatched even by Mao Zedong in China and Stalin in the Soviet Union.

Visitors to North Korea are struck—some would say stunned—by the degree to which Kim is idolized by his countrymen as a heroic, almost divine figure. The village where Kim was born and the places where he lived or travelled are treated virtually as holy shrines, and statues of Kim abound throughout the country. North Korea's only university is named after him. The near worship of Kim is an odd phenomenon, but observers point to precedents in the traditional Confucian principle of filial piety (*hyo* in Korean; Kim is described as a benevolent father to all his people), or even in the prewar Japanese emperor ideology, with the idea that all people owe him unquestioning loyalty as recipients of his benevolence. The almost mystical character of the Kim personality cult suggests the spirit of a messianic religion, with which Kim seen as a prophet bringing his people out of the wilderness. "New religions" in South Korea, such as the Unification Church of Sun Myung Moon, have similar themes. The grooming of Kim's son, Kim Jong Il, as his successor marks a hitherto unprecedented phenomenon: a Marxist (or formerly Marxist) hereditary ruling dynasty. Although not regarded as the equal of his father, Kim Jong Il, born on February 16, 1942, is described as the ideal leader of a new generation of revolutionaries, and has already taken on significant responsibilities in the party.

It was expected that Kim Jong Il would be given a top government position, most likely a vice presidency at the opening of the new Supreme People's Assembly in April 1982. The fact that he was not, and indeed was not even made a member of the Central People's Committee, has been interpreted by some observers as revealing an attempt by old guard leaders to block the too-rapid rise of the younger Kim. Yet others have suggested that it was deemed improper to promote Jong Il in April since that would divert attention from the seventieth birthday of the "Fatherly Leader."

National Prospects

Kim Il Sung is reported to be unwell and speculation was rife over North Korea's course once he passes from the scene. Many believe that once Kim Jong Il takes over, assuming that he does, he may be more actively belligerent toward South Korea than his father in recent years. Yet it is difficult to make predictions, given the small amount of reliable information which reaches the outside world from North Korea and the perhaps exaggerated apprehensions of many in the Korea-watching field, particularly in Seoul, for whom the memories of the Korean War remain vivid. Both North and South see themselves as locked in bitter competition in the ideological, military, and economic fields, and it is unlikely that this feeling will subside in the near future.

One important issue is the future of *Juche* ideology. Although the North Koreans, unlike the more radical of China's leaders, have not seen a serious contradiction between the values of revolutionary consciousness and technological expertise, *Juche* presupposes the establishment of a self-sufficient economic system. This predilection for autarky is necessarily in conflict with the need for economic and technical modernization, one of the government's basic goals. Whether a controversy over the conflicting values of self-reliance and modernization will develop, as it did in China, remains to be seen.

The passing of a charismatic, revolutionary leader has usually brought profound changes in the countries where it has occurred. Given the extremes of the Kim "cult," his death may have traumatic consequences in terms of regime stability and legitimacy. A new generation (or an old generation without Kim) will have to learn to make decisions and command the people's loyalty without him.

Further Reading

Bunge, Frederica M., ed. *North Korea: A Country Study*. Washington: U.S. Government Printing Office, for Foreign Affairs Studies, American University, 1982.

Kim, Alexander Joungwon. *Divided Korea: The Politics of Development*. Cambridge: Harvard University Press, 1975.

Koh, Byung Chul. "Political Leadership in North Korea: Toward a Conceptual Understanding of Kim Il Sung's Leadership Behavior." *Korean Studies*, Vol. 2, 1978.

Nahm, Andrew C. *North Korea, Her Past, Reality and Impression*. Kalamazoo: Center for Korean Studies, Western Michigan University, 1978.

Scalapino, Robert A., and Lee, Chong-sik. *Communism in Korea*. 2 vols. Berkeley: University of California Press, 1972.

Shinn, Rinn-sup. "North Korea in 1981: First Year for De Facto Successor Kim Jong Il." *Asian Survey*, Vol. 22, No. 1, January 1982.

Tharp, Mike. "North Korea: An Eclipse of the Son." *Far Eastern Economic Review*, April 16, 1982.

REPUBLIC OF KOREA
(*Daehan Minguk*)
by Donald M. Seekins, Ph.D.

The System of Government

The Republic of Korea, or South Korea, is a military regime with a centralized, presidential system of government. It is in control of the southern half of the Korean peninsula which has been divided between rival governments in the north and south since Korea, a colony of Japan after 1910, was occupied by United States and Soviet military forces at the end of World War II. The Republic of Korea, with a land area of 98,477 square kilometers, about 45 percent of the total area of the peninsula, is separated from the Democratic People's Republic of Korea, or North Korea, by the Demilitarized Zone, a 4,000-meter-wide strip of land running from the east to the west coast both north and south of the thirty-eighth parallel, the boundary before the outbreak of the Korean War in June 1950. The Demilitarized Zone was fixed after the ceasefire of July 27, 1953. According to the government census of 1980, the population of the Republic of Korea in that year was 37,448,836 (about twice that of North Korea), with Seoul, the capital, one of the largest cities in the world with 8,366,756 inhabitants. Given the intense antagonism between north and south, the disparity in population gives the latter some advantage in terms of labor force and economic potential. (For a brief review of Korean history prior to 1945, see **Korea, North.**)

On August 15, 1945, with the advance of Soviet troops into the peninsula, U.S. president Harry Truman proposed dividing Korea into two occupation zones separated by the thirty-eighth parallel. Stalin accepted the proposal, and in December of that year, the Allies agreed on a five-year trusteeship period with the United States and the Soviet Union responsible for establishing a viable government for a unified and independent Korea. Growing Cold War suspicions on the part of the superpowers and the antagonisms of different political groups within Korea itself created a deepening fissure between north and south. In November 1947, the United Nations General Assembly laid the groundwork for nationwide elections. These were carried out only in the south, however, and the Republic of Korea was established on August 15, 1948. The republic has its own constitution, promulgated in July 1948, which remains in force although it has been much amended to suit the purposes of both civilian and military leaders since that time.

The Korean War, which began in June 1950 with the invasion of the south by the armed forces of the north, intent on "liberating" the entire peninsula, had a formative influence on the development of the political system of the Republic of Korea. Millions of people were dislocated, a cause of great social and political instability in the postwar years. The threat of further aggression from the north led political leaders to establish a highly centralized, authoritarian order under which dissent and opposition were linked with communist subversion, often without real justification. American military support of the Seoul government made South Korea the keystone of the United States defense perimeter in East Asia. South Korea remained, even during periods of East-West detente, on the front lines of the Cold War.

During the period from 1948 to 1960, known as the First Republic, Syngman Rhee—an accomplished scholar, with advanced degrees from prestigious American universities—was president of the Republic of Korea. Rhee was one of the most important leaders of the struggle for national independence, having been the first president of the Korean government-in-exile in Shanghai in 1919. He had tremendous prestige; that he was descended from Yi Song-gye, founder of the Yi Dynasty, gave him an added aura of legitimacy, particularly among South Korea's tradition-oriented peasants who formed the majority of the population. His administration, however, was marked by pervasive corruption and favoritism, and Rhee himself had no tolerance for critics or political opponents. Rhee refused to support the establishment of a parliamentary system of government in which the legislature would have supreme power.

He insisted instead on a centralized, presidential system which would give him broad powers as chief executive. Rhee's first four-year term was to end in August 1952, and the National Assembly had defeated a constitutional amendment sponsored by him which would allow for a popularly elected president, rather than one chosen by the Assembly. Rhee declared martial law in May and forced the assemblymen to pass the amendment. In 1955, a second constitutional amendment was passed, also through the use of dubious methods, which allowed Rhee to succeed himself indefinitely. In 1960, however, popular outrage over his autocratic and often brutal methods (some 142 students were killed by the police during demonstrations early that year), forced him, now an old man of eighty-five years, to retire.

South Korea experienced a brief period of democratic rule during the Second Republic, which lasted from April 1960 to May 1961. The constitution was revised once again, this time to provide for a parliamentary form of government. Chang Myon, a leader of the opposition Democratic Party, was chosen prime minister. Bitter struggles between Democratic Party factions and continued instability in the nation as a whole gave a small group of military officers under Major-General Park Chung Hee the opportunity to seize power on May 16, 1961.

These officers established the Supreme Council for National Reconstruction, headed by Park, which ruled the country after the National Assembly was dissolved. Military officers took over high-level administrative positions in the government. Under martial law, all political activities were suspended, and many politicians of the Rhee era were "blacklisted." In June 1961, the Korean Central Intelligence Agency (KCIA) was established to carry out surveillance of civilian and military opponents of the new regime. Its founder and first director was Colonel Kim Jong-pil, a member of the junta and relative of Major-General Park through marriage. Kim was to play a central role in organizing the government-sponsored Democratic Republican Party. A by-now familiar tactic, the proposal and approval of a new constitutional amendment in the National Assembly, allowing for popular election of the president, enabled Park to retire from the military and run for election as the Democratic Republican Party candidate, winning narrowly in October 1963 against Yun Po-sun of the opposition New Democratic Party.

Spectacular economic growth, comparable to that of Japan, during Park's sixteen-year rule as president transformed South Korea from a predominantly rural, agricultural country into an urbanized, industrial one exporting manufactured products to world markets. The South Korean "miracle" insured support for Park's regime, as individual incomes steadily rose, particularly during the 1970s. Close links with Japan were seen as essential for economic development, and thus a South Korea-Japan treaty normalizing relations between the two countries was ratified in June 1965. There had, however, been substantial opposition, particularly among students, given the history of Japanese colonialism; violent demonstrations led to the imposition of martial law. Park won presidential elections in 1967 and 1971, but with only narrow margins of votes against New Democratic Party candidates Yun Po-sun and Kim Dae Jung. Like Rhee, Park had the constitution amended in 1969 to allow himself a third term in 1971.

The decade of the 1970s saw Park establish dictatorial, one-man rule. In October 1972, he proclaimed martial law and dissolved the National Assembly. A month later, he held a national referendum in November on a new constitutional revision which established what he called the *yushin* or "revitalization" reform.

Political institutions as defined by the 1972 *yushin* constitutional revision were tailored to fit Park Chung Hee's preference for centralized, one-man rule. The president was given broad powers. He was head of state; commander of the armed forces; chief executive; and chairman of the National Conference for Unification, a body consisting of some 2,359 members elected by the people, which was responsible for choosing the president. Park controlled the powerful KCIA and a number of other important executive agencies. The National Assembly had little power, because the *yushin* reforms denied it the previously guaranteed right to investigate the activities of the executive branch. The power of the president to declare martial law during "emergencies" and dissolve the Assembly at will also curtailed its powers.

Continued popular opposition caused Park to enact Emergency Measure Number Nine (May 1975), which made it a crime to criticize the *yushin* system or advocate revision. The KCIA became increasingly powerful and feared as it used harsh methods to silence opposition, even among Koreans overseas. The most spectacular example of this was the alleged KCIA kidnapping of New Democratic Party leader Kim Dae Jung from a Tokyo hotel in August 1973, an event which caused a serious rupture in South Korean-Japanese relations and underlined the regime's increasingly poor human rights record. Thousands in South Korea were jailed or put under house arrest, including Second Republic president Yun Po-sun and dissident poet Kim Chi Ha; many were subjected to brutal treatment.

Park was assassinated on October 26, 1979, by Kim Jae Gyu, then director of the KCIA. The motives were apparently more personal than political. Kim bitterly hated Park's closest confidante, Cha Ji Chul, whom he also shot, and had hatched a desperate plot to seize power with the aid of a small circle of KCIA operatives. The assassination of Park led to the collapse of the *yushin* system and the brief restoration of civilian rule under acting president Choi Kyu Ha. In December 1979, Choi abolished Emergency Measure Number Nine, and released a large number of political prisoners who had been jailed under its provisions. These included Kim Dae Jung, who had been under house arrest following his kidnapping from Tokyo to Seoul. The political scene was enlivened as both the Democratic Republican Party under Kim Jong-pil and the New Democratic Party under Kim Young Sam and Kim Dae Jung began jostling in anticipation of presidential and National Assembly elections following the promised establishment of a more liberal constitutional order.

Factional struggles within the parties, strikes by workers demanding higher wages and better working conditions, and a wave of student unrest, however, provided the military with yet another opportunity to establish its dominance over the political system. Major-General Chun Doo Hwan, head of the Defense Security Command, established his control over the military by leading younger generals in a successful move to oust chief of staff General Chong Seung Hwa and other Park-era senior military officers on December 12, 1979. On May 17, 1980, Chun reacted to increased student militancy, aimed at getting the military out of politics, by proclaiming martial law. His decree banned all forms of political activity, closed the headquarters of political parties, outlawed strikes, and muzzled journalists. The universities were closed, and the National Assembly suspended. Opposition leaders were arrested on charges of corruption and sedition. In Kwangju, the capital of South Cholla Province, Kim Dae Jung's home region and long a center of opposition sentiment, the brutal treatment of student demonstrators by the police and army paratroopers sparked a revolt by the general populace

which lasted for nine days and reportedly resulted in the death of up to 2,000 persons. The official death toll was 189. A similar revolt broke out in Mokpo on the south coast, Kim's home town.

The junta established the Special Committee for National Security Measures with power in the hands of four men: generals Chun Doo Hwan, Cha Gyu Hon, No Tae Wu, and Chong Ho Yong. A campaign of "social purification" was initiated. Some nine thousand people—members of the National Assembly, government officials, managers of state-run corporations, and educators—were fired from their posts. Nearly two hundred magazines and newspapers were closed, and several hundred journalists sacked for promoting "corrupt influences." Kim Dae Jung and a number of his supporters were tried by a military court; Kim was sentenced to death on charges of subversion in September 1980.

President Choi Kyu Ka resigned on August 16, and Chun, now a five-star general, retired from the military to run for the presidency. With the support of the military, he was approved as interim president by the National Conference for Unification, which acted as an electoral college. His draft constitutional amendment, establishing a new political order, that of the Fifth Republic, was ratified in a referendum on October 22, 1980. It was reported that more than 95 percent of the voters turned out, and that 91.6 percent approved the new document. The Chun constitution abolished the National Conference for Unification, limited the presidency to a single, nonrenewable seven-year term, and made it more difficult for the president to proclaim martial law and dissolve the National Assembly. Both the Chun and *yushin* constitutions, however, provided for indirect, rather than direct election of the chief executive. Thus, at the end of 1980, the South Korean people found themselves under the iron rule of a general who had been unknown to most of them just a few months before.

Executive

The president, under the Chun constitution, continues to have broad powers as chief executive, commander of the armed forces, and head of state, but is nonetheless limited in two important respects. First, he can declare an emergency and assume special powers, suspending normal civil and political rights, only with the approval of the National Assembly, which can, with a majority vote, revoke the emergency decree. Second, he cannot dissolve the National Assembly during the first three years of its mandate and even then must first consult with the cabinet ministers and the Assembly speaker.

Chun declared his opposition to "one-man rule" and limited the president to a single seven-year term, promising not to run again after his term ran out in 1988. Given recent South Korean history, however, his promise is viewed with some skepticism.

Important executive agencies include the Presidential Secretariat and the State Council, which in 1982 were headed by the president and included the prime minister and twenty-two cabinet ministers defined by function. By law, the cabinet must number between fifteen to thirty, excluding the president and prime minister. The prime minister and other ministers are chosen by the president. Other important executive bodies include the Agency for National Security Planning (the KCIA, until its name was changed in December 1980); the Advisory Council for Peaceful Unification Policy, a large body of some 9,000 members from all walks of life responsible for formulating views on eventual unification with the north; the Advisory Council on State Affairs, composed of what one observer calls "elder statesmen," headed by the former president (Choi Kyu Ha in 1982); and the National Security Council, concerned with defense planning and foreign policy.

Legislature

In 1981, the National Assembly, a unicameral body, had 276 members serving four-year terms. Its responsibilities include the passage of bills to be approved by the president and the approval of the national budget. The power to investigate executive-branch activities and question govern-

ment officials, denied by the *yushin* system, was restored with the 1980 constitution. The Assembly can, in theory, call for the impeachment of the president, the prime minister, and other high officials if they violate the constitution.

Judiciary

The 1980 constitutional revision in principle gives greater autonomy to the judicial branch of government, since the chief justice of the Supreme Court, rather than the president (as in the *yushin* system), is responsible for appointing lower-level judges. He is, however, appointed by the president and approved by the National Assembly, serving a nonrenewable five-year term. The Supreme Court can review the constitutionality of administrative decrees, but not laws passed by the National Assembly, which is the responsibility of the Constitutional Committee. This body has a nine-year term and consists of nine persons: three nominated by the president, three by the National Assembly, and three by the chief justice. The Committee also has final judgment regarding the impeachment of public officials and the dissolution of political parties.

Regional & Local Government

The Republic of Korea is divided into nine provinces and four province-level special cities, Seoul, Pusan, Taegu, and Inchon. The four special cities and other large cities are divided into wards and precincts, while the provinces are divided into cities and counties. Counties are divided into towns, townships, and villages.

The military coup of May 1961 brought the dissolution of elected local councils and ended local

NATIONAL ASSEMBLY ELECTION RESULTS (1981)

Party	Candidates	Seats Won Direct	Seats Won Proportional
Democratic Justice Party (DJP)	92	90	61
Democratic Korea Party (DKP)	90	57	24
Korean National Party (KNP)	75	18	7
Civil Rights Party (CRP)	81	2	
Democratic Socialist Party (DSP)	50	2	
New Political Party	54	2	
Democratic Farmers' Party (DFP)	15	1	
Human Welfare Party (HWP)	12	1	
Independents		11	

self-government. Regional and local government is thus under the control of the national government, with local and regional officials being appointed by the level directly above them. Although there has been talk of restoring provincial and local popularly elected assemblies, the limited financial resources of the provinces and local jurisdictions hamper progress in this direction. The mayor of Seoul, the capital, is appointed by the president, while the governors of the provinces and the other special cities are nominated by the ministers of home affairs and approved by the president. Lower-level officials such as the mayors of towns are appointed by the provincial governors.

The Electoral System

There are two types of popular elections in the Republic of Korea: elections for members of the electoral college which select the president of the republic and elections for two-thirds of the members of the National Assembly.

The presidential election involves two stages: popular elections of deputies to an electoral college, which last took place on February 11, 1981, and selection of the president by the deputies (February 25). The 1981 electoral college contained 5,278 members, chosen from 1,905 districts, with two to five deputies each, depending on population. Both party candidates and independents could run. Although electoral college deputy candidates were expected to make known in advance the presidential candidate of their choice, once elected they had the right to support a different candidate.

In the February 25 election, 4,755 deputies voted for Chun Doo Hwan, the Democratic Justice Party candidate; 404 deputies voted for Yu Chi Song, the Democratic Korea Party candidate; eighty-five for Kim Chong Chol of the Korean National Party; and twenty-six for Kim Ui Taek of the Civil Rights Party.

Two-thirds (184 in the 1981 election) of the Assembly are chosen by popular vote from ninety-two regional electoral districts, each district returning two representatives. The remaining ninety-two seats are allocated to the different political parties in proportion to the number of votes each received in the general election. Only parties with a minimum of five elected seats are entitled to nonelected, proportionally allocated seats. Suffrage is extended to all citizens twenty years of age and over.

The Party System

Origins of the Parties

Political parties first appeared in South Korea at the end of World War II. The decade of the 1950s was marked by the struggle between the Liberal Party, which Syngman Rhee established in 1951, and the Democratic Party which originally supported Rhee but opposed his altering of the constitution to establish a strong presidency. The short-lived Second Republic saw the Democratic Party in power, but much weakened by factional infighting. Between 1963 and 1972, the first decade of Park Chung Hee's presidency, the dominant group was the government-sponsored Democratic Republican Party (DRP). During this period, relatively fair and open competition existed between the DRP and the opposition New Democratic Party (NDP). The establishment of the *yushin* system in 1972, however, undercut party politics. The president was now selected by the National Conference for Unification whose members could not be affiliated with political parties, and the powers of the National Assembly were curtailed. The DRP itself became, in a sense, superfluous, and a battery of emergency regulations put a tight lid on the activities of opposition groups.

The unsettled period between the assassination of Park and the ratification of the 1980 constitutional amendment saw increased activities by political parties, particularly the NDP, although at this time it was split into antagonistic factions led by Kim Young Sam and Kim Dae Jung. In October 1980, however, the martial-law regime of Chun Doo Hwan abolished all the old political groupings. The following month it enacted the Political Party Law which provided the framework for the establishment of entirely new parties with new leaders. Under the Special Law for Political Renovation, 835 of the most prominent politicians were prohibited from engaging in political activity until June 30, 1988. Subsequently 268 were "rehabilitated," but the exclusion of the remaining 567 underlined the basic discontinuity between the old and new parties.

The Parties in Law

Under the Political Party Law, new parties could be founded with as few as twenty "promoters," as opposed to thirty previously. Park regime rules—which prohibited party affiliations for all teachers, government officials, and journalists—were abolished. Parties were required to have at least twenty-six branch chapters throughout the country, a measure designed apparently to prevent the rise of regionally based groupings. A party could be disbanded if it failed to receive a minimum of 2 percent of the popular vote or elect one National Assembly representative.

To register as candidates, party nominees needed nomination letters and a deposit of 7 million won ($10,500). Independent candidates were at a decided disadvantage, being required to submit recommendations from between 500 to 700 voters and a 15 million won ($22,500) deposit.

The Political Fund Law of December 1980 was passed to regulate campaign contributions. It allowed for the organization of support groups of no more than 1,000 members to raise funds. Political parties could collect membership dues and donations from nonmembers. Parties were required to report their finances in detail to the Central Election Management Committee. They receive government subsidies in proportion to their popular support as reflected in election returns. Foreign corporations, state-run enterprises, religious bodies, educational institutions, and the mass media cannot make contributions to parties.

Party Organization

While the Political Party Law sets down some strict rules for party organization, e.g., the requirement that a party have twenty-six branch chapters around the country, it is doubtful if these rules are strictly followed or enforced. With the exception of the government party, little is known about the formal organization of the parties. The basic structure of all of them continues to be informal networks of patron-client relationships based on traditional regional and local loyalties and dependence.

Campaigning

Campaigning during the elections is strictly regulated, in principle at least, by the Central Election Management Committee, which sets down guidelines for exposure at "joint speech rallies," at which all candidates speak, in the mass media, and on election posters. Individual campaigning by candidates is prohibited. The National Assembly Election Law provided for a twenty-day campaign period in 1981 (March 5 to March 25), which, like the presidential electoral college campaign, was tightly regulated. Individual candidates had to register with local election management committees by March 10, and 605 "joint speech rallies" were scheduled between March 13 and March 23.

Although "clean" elections was a much-reiterated theme in 1981, observers reported that both the Democratic Justice Party and opposition party candidates were prone to vote-buying and "pork barrel" tactics. The decision to make the city of Taegu, a center of support for opposition politicians, a "special city" in July 1981 was interpreted as a DJP move to buy Taegu support, as special-city status would bring Taegu more tax revenue. The *Far Eastern Economic Review* reported on March 27, 1981, that in some cases voters had demanded 100,000 won ($150) before joining a particular party. Strong-arm methods apparently were also occasionally employed. Thus, according to the *Review*, one candidate running as an independent from Kwangju, a former general who had gained much respect for refusing to order in his troops to put down the uprising in May 1980, disappeared ten days before the election. He later turned up to announce that he was quitting the race.

Democratic Justice Party (DJP)

History

On November 2, 1980, 105 people, led by fifteen prominent legislators, government figures, labor leaders, academicians, and businessmen, met to establish a new government party, the Democratic Justice Party. Regional and local party chairmen were named to organize local support. The new chairman, Lee Chai Hyung, had been a leader of the old opposition New Democratic Party, but since the new DJP reportedly has relied heavily on the local networks of the old government party, there appears to be little break with the past.

Organization

At the party's convention on January 15, 1981, some 3,162 delegates approved a party constitution which set up a "unitary party leadership" consisting of the Central Executive Committee of thirty members chaired by the party president. The delegates chose Chun Doo Hwan for that job. The party intends to develop a mass membership, tightly organized down to the local level. This program suggests that the DJP leaders see their principal competition not in the South Korean opposition, but in Kim Il Sung's Korean Worker's Party in North Korea.

Policy

Chun and other leaders have stressed a number of themes in their pronouncements: the establishment of a "welfare state" in which the people's standard of living would be improved; the reform of the highly competitive and costly education system to provide more equal educational opportunity; the "purification" of society to abolish corrupt practices; and the need for constant vigilance against the north. Like Park, Chun has emphasized the need to adapt universal democratic principles to the specific circumstances of South Korea, although "Korean-style democracy" continues in practice to be synonymous with centralized, authoritarian rule.

Membership & Constituency

Figures on party membership were not available in mid-1982. The National Assembly election of March 1982 showed that popular support for the party was generally balanced throughout the nation; the party gained at least half the seats in each of eight provinces and in the two special cities which existed at that time (Seoul and Pusan). In South Cholla province, it gained less than half and on Cheju island none.

Financing

Of the 6 billion won (about $9 million) collected by all political parties in 1981, over 90 percent reportedly went to the DJP. Businessmen and other interest groups were apparently apprehensive about the consequences of supporting even the conservative opposition. No details of the party's financing were available.

Leadership

The DJP is Chun's party and takes its direction solely from him. The upper ranks of the leadership are apparently dominated by military officers, while middle ranks and administrative offices are filled with prominent civilians from all walks of life.

Minor Parties

The 1980 Political Party Law is seen as encouraging the establishment of a large number of small parties, which has been interpreted as a government tactic to fragment the opposition. Thus, the old system, in which the Park's Democratic Republican Party faced concerted opposition from the broadly supported New Democratic Party, has been replaced with virtually a one-party system. The viability, even the genuineness, of the new opposition parties is much in doubt. Active opposition elements, primarily student and Christian groups, regard them as "window dressing." Since most major opposition leaders are either in jail or barred from political activity until 1988, the new parties are led by second and third stringers who are inexperienced newcomers or old timers who are widely seen as co-opted by the government. By and large, the new party leaders seem to be people who want to continue their political careers, but do not want clear identification with the DJP or will not accept direct dictation from it. The parties remain under tight government control and are thought to be under thorough surveillance by the security apparatus. Opposition figures who step out of line are penalized. A Korean National Party leader who spoke with members of the North American Committee for Human Rights in Korea while on a visit to the United States was arrested and charged with "adultery" on his return to Korea. Little is known about the parties; they are considered so peripheral to the political process that their activities are seldom reported.

Democratic Korea Party (DKP)

The largest opposition group, the DKP, was formally established on December 1, 1980. On January 17, 1981, the party chose Yu Chi Song, a former legislator and New Democratic Party leader, as its president and candidate for president of the republic. The DKP leadership is composed of the remnants of the old New Democratic Party, although some 70 percent of the old NDP leadership are among those barred from political life until 1988. The party has called for the establishment of a two-party rather than a multiparty democratic system, greater respect for human and civil rights, a more powerful National Assembly, and self-government on the provincial and local levels. The National Assembly election revealed that its strength lay principally in the urban areas; in the special cities of Seoul and Pusan; and in Kyonggi Province, surrounding Seoul. Support was also strong in the Honam region (North and South Cholla Provinces). Yet in all these areas, the DKP could not win more seats than the DJP and by early 1982, the party was divided over the quality of its leadership and its direction. A *Far Eastern Economic Review* correspondent quotes one DKP assemblyman as saying that "ours is the most carefree opposition in the most difficult time in the nation's history."

Korean National Party (KNP)

The KNP was formed in December 1980 by former Democratic Republican Party legislators and chose Kim Chong Chol as its president and presidential candidate. Election data reveal that it is relatively strong in the Yongnam region (North and South Kyongsang Provinces), where Park Chung Hee had his power base.

Other minor parties include the Civil Rights Party, headed by Kim Ui Taek; the New Political Party, headed by Kaup Su; the Democratic Socialist Party headed by Ko Chang Hun; the Democratic Farmers' Party, and the Human Welfare (Anmin) Party. Government tolerance of the Democratic Socialists and another noncommunist leftwing group, the Socialist Party of Korea, headed by Kim Chol, has been interpreted as an attempt on its part to appear "liberal" to the outside world, particularly Western Europe. In any event, the effectiveness of the two socialist parties was greatly inhibited by the bitter rivalry between their leaders. Both are veteran socialist campaigners who had spent many months in jail during the Park era. Ko's Democratic Socialists drew the most support.

Four parties were disbanded after the March National Assembly elections, having failed to elect a single representative: Kim Chol's Socialist Party of Korea, which ran twenty candidates; the Korean Christian Democratic Party, which ran fifteen candidates; the Wonilminlip Party, which ran thirteen candidates; and the Unification National Party, which ran ten candidates.

Opposition

Students

Students have had a long history of political activism, going back to the Confucian *sowon* (private academies) of the Yi Dynasty. They have characteristically seen themselves as the nation's "conscience," fighting force with principle. During the Japanese colonial period, they were an important element in the struggle for independence, and their opposition to the autocratic practices of Syngman Rhee contributed to his downfall in April 1960. They opposed Park's plan to extend military rule for four more years in 1963, the normalization of relations with Japan in 1965, and the establishment of the *yushin* system after October 1972. The Chun regime has been unable to neutralize them. The Kwangju uprising seemed particularly ominous to the regime, since it represented one of the few times when the general populace joined the students in opposing the military.

University students are the most active politically, given the fact that high school students—at least in the middle classes—are preoccupied with studying for the highly competitive college entrance examinations. Until recently, academic requirements have been lenient; very few college students failed to receive their degrees and had free time to devote to political activities. The Chun government has introduced a "graduation quota system" under which universities are allowed to admit 30 percent more students than there are places for graduation (a quota set by the Ministry of Education). Universities are thus required to fail the academically poorest 30 percent of their student body, a measure designed in part to obtain higher-quality graduates, but also to hamper student political activity.

Christian Churches

South Korea's Roman Catholic and Protestant Christians numbered some 7,165,000 in 1979, and leaders of the Christian community have been active in criticizing the government for human rights violations and the perpetuation of social injustices. They have also played an important role in the labor-union movement.

President Chun, in 1982, encountered increasing opposition from church groups. Both Catholics and Protestants have called for his resignation, citing the illegality of his seizure of power in 1980, and his failure to eliminate corruption and irregularities in the enforcement of law and order. The trial of sixteen defendants, including a Catholic priest and several theology students, charged with involvement in the burning of a United States cultural center in the city of Pusan, increased tension between church and state in mid-1982, with the government accusing the church of sheltering subversives friendly to North Korea.

Regional

Another important aspect of opposition is regional. Although Korea is a small country compared to its neighbors, and there has been much movement of the population during the twentieth century, regional consciousness remains strong. Park, Chun, and their closest followers have come from the Yongnam region (North and South Kyongsang Provinces) in the southeast. This area has been consistently favored in terms of investment and development projects. The Honam region (North and South Cholla Provinces) of the southwest is the poorest part of the country and has been largely neglected. It has a long history of antigovernment opposition going back to the Yi Dynasty, and it was no surprise that the strongest resistance to the imposition of Chun's new regime should appear in Kwangju, capital of South Cholla Province. Factional rivalry between Kim Dae Jung and Kim Young Sam of the New Democratic Party was in part based on the fact that the former's following was from Honam and the latter's from Yongnam.

Other Political Forces

Military

Military officers, both active and retired (occupying civilian posts), continue to be the central component of what observers call the "power strata," controlling the state bureaucracy and occupying top positions in the Democratic Justice Party.

The dominant role of the military in the political system is a feature the Republic of Korea shares with many developing countries; yet in light of Korea's long history, it is something of an aberration. Traditionally, it has been civilian scholar-officials versed in the Confucian classics rather than military officers who have held political power. Popular disapproval of the military, particularly among students and intellectuals, grows out of the conviction that military rule is per se illegitimate, no matter what its accomplishments. That both Park and Chun have attempted to cover the reality of military power with the mantle of a government-sponsored political party reveals that they, too, are responsive to this attitude. Yet the ruling military circle also sees itself as the only group in society with the training, discipline, and organization needed to run the state in an efficient manner. It has taken credit, with much justification, for the spectacular modernization of South Korea in the past two decades.

Under the Japanese, Korea had no armed forces of its own, and the United States occupation authorities had to build up a military establishment virtually from scratch. A small number of Korean officers had served in the Japanese army or had led anti-Japanese resistance forces in China. They were given training at the American-sponsored Military English Language School starting in December 1945, which became the following year the Constabulatory Officers' Candidate School. The army was established in November 1948. All male youths are required to undertake some form of military service. In 1981, South Ko-

rea had the world's sixth-largest armed forces, with some 600,000 personnel on active duty, augmented by 39,000 American troops. The North, however, possesses the world's fifth-largest armed forces.

Park Chung Hee had studied at a Japanese military academy and served as a lieutenant in Japan's Kwantung Army in northeast China during World War II. His demise and the takeover by Chun Doo Hwan marked the passing of a generation within the military elite. Chun, born in 1931, graduated in 1955 from the Korean Military Academy, the top school for military officers founded in 1950 on the model of American's West Point. Chun drew upon his fellow academy alumni for support during the months when he maneuvered himself into a position of power.

In contrast to the situation in the early 1960s, when South Korea lacked trained administrators and professionals and officers took over a broad range of functions, there is now a large, highly educated class of civil servants, technocrats, and managers with whom the military must cooperate in the national interest. Accord between the military and what are called the "special privileged strata," including South Korea's top businessmen and entrepreneurs, is especially vital. It remains to be seen whether Chun can balance a former military man's concern with discipline and order—echoed in his repeated calls for "social purification"—and the increasingly complex demands of an industrial society with close links to the international economic system.

United States and Japan

The Republic of Korea's most important relations are with the United States and Japan. The United States has supported South Korea militarily and economically since before the outbreak of the Korean War, and a continued U.S. commitment to the peninsula has been seen both in Washington and in Seoul as essential to the country's survival. During the administration of President Jimmy Carter, there was talk of a phased withdrawal of ground troops, the most visible sign of that commitment. But when intelligence reports in 1978 and 1979 revealed that North Korea had greater military strength than was previously estimated, this idea was dropped. Carter's criticism of human rights violations under the *yushin* system, however, continued to chill U.S.-South Korean relations. Added to this was American reluctance in 1980 to support a new military regime which had bloodied its hands at Kwangju and earned international criticism for the death sentence imposed on Kim Dae Jung. When Chun Doo

Hwan visited Washington in February 1981 to confer with newly inaugurated President Ronald Reagan, he found the new administration gratifyingly sympathetic to his position, in marked contrast to its Democratic predecessor. Continued U.S. support of Chun has aroused some anti-American feeling among intellectuals and dissidents.

Despite cultural heritages that have much in common, relations between Korea and Japan have been marked by much bitterness, culminating in the colonial occupation. Yet the years since 1965 have seen close cooperation between South Korea and Japan, particularly in the economic sphere. In 1981, 75 percent of all foreign companies in South Korea were Japanese, accounting for more than 50 percent of all foreign investment. Although leaders of Japan's Liberal Democratic Party have acknowledged the importance of South Korea for Japan's own security, recent Korean demands for a $6 billion loan from the Japanese government, tied to the assertion that South Korea was in the front line of Japan's defense, were regarded with little enthusiasm by Japanese officials. As in the United States, the fate of Kim Dae Jung was a major issue in Japan, and the commutation of his death sentence to life imprisonment removed a major obstacle in South Korea-Japan relations.

National Prospects

South Korea's remarkable progress in social and economic development is to a great extent the result of the government's success in harnessing and directing the energies of the people toward modernization under far from ideal conditions. The growth of a more complex society, however, puts pressure on the leadership to develop a broad base of popular support beyond the "power strata" of top military officers and bureaucrats. The greatest challenge will be a gradual transfer from military rule to a more settled political process dominated by civilians. If Chun keeps his promise to step down from the presidency in 1988, the legitimacy of the system he has established will clearly be strengthened. Yet in mid-1982, conditions remained unsettled. The credibility of the Chun government, with its puritanical emphasis on the theme of "social purification," has been severely shaken by a financial scandal, a one billion dollar loan fraud which brought two large steel corporations to the brink of bankruptcy and involved relatives of Lee Soon Ja,

Chun's wife. The links between the thirty persons arrested in connection with the scandal and the leadership circle around the president remained, as of June 1982, unclear. Public confidence in the government, however, was eroded.

Even in the best of times, South Korea's prospects have been uncertain. They depend to a great extent upon external, as well as internal, factors: international economic conditions and the receptivity of world markets to Korean exports; the behavior of the North; and the attitude of leaders in the United States, Japan, and other countries concerning South Korea's status. Attaining internal stability and consensus and a secure place for South Korea in the international environment, remain the country's greatest challenges.

Chun Doo Hwan has stated his willingness to meet with North Korean president Kim Il Sung on the issue of peaceful reunification, an ever-more-distant goal which both north and south nonetheless continue to affirm. In January 1982, Chun proposed a blueprint for reunification which called for a halt in the north-south arms buildup, resident liaison missions in each capital, and respect for each government's international agreements including the north's alliances with the People's Republic of China and the Soviet Union and the south's security ties with the United States. Chun's proposal was rejected by the North Koreans, however, and the atmosphere of tension and confrontation continues.

Further Reading

Asia 1981 Yearbook. Hong Kong: Far Eastern Economic Review Publications, 1980.

Bunge, Frederica W., ed. *South Korea: A Country Study.* Washington, D.C.: U.S. Government Printing Office, for Foreign Area Studies, American University, 1982.

Han Sungjoo. *The Failure of Democracy in South Korea.* Berkeley and London: University of California Press, 1974.

Kim Se-Jin. *The Politics of Military Revolution in Korea.* Chapel Hill, N. C.: University of North Carolina Press, 1971.

Suh, Dae-Sook. "South Korea in 1981: the First Year of the Fifth Republic." *Asian Survey,* Vol. 22, No. 1, January 1982.

U.S. Congress, 97th, 2nd session. *Country Reports on Human Rights Practices.* Washington, D.C.: U.S. Government Printing Office, 1982.

Vreeland, Nena, ed. *South Korea: A Country Study.* Washington, D.C.: U.S. Government Printing Office, for Foreign Area Studies, American University, 1975.

KUWAIT
(*Dawlat al-Kuwayt*)
by Jill Crystal, M.A.

The System of Government

Kuwait, a nation of nearly 1.5 million people at the northwest end of the Persian Gulf, is a semi-constitutional monarchy governed by an emir from the Sabah family who rules in conjunction with senior family members through an appointed Council of Ministers. Kuwait first emerged as a semi-autonomous political unit in the early eighteenth century when it was settled by the Bani Utub branch of the Arabian Anazah confederation. The ascendancy of the Sabah family dates from about 1756 when the leading families appointed a Sabah shaikh to represent them in dealings with the Ottoman Empire. In the nineteenth century, Kuwaiti rulers, caught on the fringes of empires and fearing Ottoman, Persian, and Wahhabi incursions, acquiesced to the growing British influence in the Gulf region. In 1899, Shaikh Mubarak (founder of the current ruling line) negotiated a treaty with Great Britain, which secured Kuwait's independence from the Ottomans in exchange for British control over its foreign relations. The association with Great Britain, which continued until independence in 1961, consolidated the Sabah family's control over domestic politics. The Kuwaiti constitution was promulgated on November 11, 1962. In international politics, Kuwait's existence as an independent state remained tenuous. Its current borders were established at the 1922 Uqair Conference attended by Britain, Iraq, and Saudi Arabia. Kuwait remains threatened by its neighbors, however, particularly by Iraq which laid claim to the shaikhdom's territory in a 1961 proclamation.

Kuwait, originally a pearling and trading economy, became increasingly dependent on oil after World War II. In 1936 Shaikh Ahmad had granted a concession to the Kuwait Oil Company (jointly owned by British Petroleum and Gulf Oil). In 1973, Kuwait acquired a 25 percent share in the company and took over full ownership in 1976. Production rose to 1.076 billion barrels a year by 1972, but fell to 607 million barrels in 1980 in line with the state's conservationist policy following the 1973 price increases. Current reserves, among the highest in the world, are estimated at 68 billion barrels and, at current production levels, will last for over a century. The consequences of a transformation to an oil-based economy were to give Kuwait one of the highest per capita incomes in the world (almost $20,000) and to increase its dependence on foreign trade and foreign laborers (who now comprise almost 60 percent of the population). The large revenues, paid directly to the rulers, freed the Sabahs from much of their historical dependence on merchant allies and financed a large bureaucracy to administer new welfare and development projects and to redistribute wealth through state employment.

Executive

In accordance with the 1962 constitution, Kuwait's chief executive, the emir, is chosen from male descendants of Shaikh Mubarak. Since 1915, Kuwait's emirs have all been chosen (with one exception, alternately) from the Salim and Jabir branches of the Sabah family. The actual selection is made privately by senior family members. In this manner, Kuwait's present emir, Shaikh Jabir al-Ahmad al-Sabah (born 1928 in the Jabir line) was named heir apparent and crown prince in 1966. He acceded to power peacefully in December 1977, on the death of the emir Shaikh Sabah al-Salim al-Sabah (of the Salim line). The present crown prince (a Salim), appointed February 1978, is Shaikh Jabir's second cousin, Prime Minister Sa'ad Abdullah al-Salim al-Sabah.

The emir has very broad powers, but governs within the informal constraints set by family consensus. Intrafamily disagreements are managed and family control assured by the direct recruitment of family members into the highest and most sensitive administrative posts. In the current Council of Ministers (appointed March 1981), seven of the sixteen ministers are Sabahs. Besides Prime Minister Sa'ad, these include the emir's

The Al-Sabah Emirs

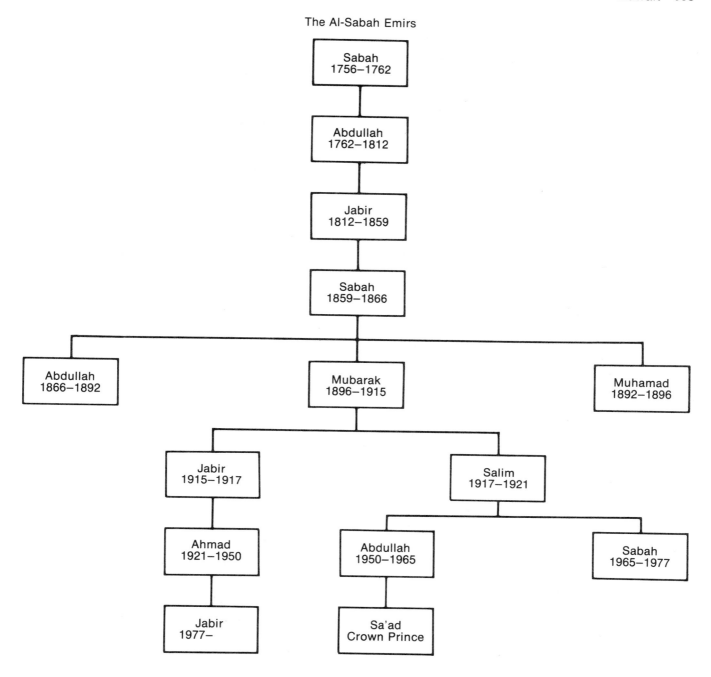

brothers Shaikh Sabah al-Ahmad al-Jabir al-Sabah (deputy prime minister, foreign affairs, information) and Shaikh Nawaf al-Ahmad al-Jabir al-Sabah (interior). Shaikh Salim al-Sabah al-Salim al-Sabah (defense) is Crown Prince Sa'ad's cousin.

Legislature

Kuwait's National Assembly (*Majlis al-Umma*), was first elected in 1963. Subsequent elections were held in 1967, 1971, and 1975. In August 1976, the Assembly was dissolved and several articles

of the constitution suspended by decree of the emir. The Assembly's functions were assumed by six appointed legislative committees under the Council of Ministers.

Several factors led to the suspension of the National Assembly in 1976. The Assembly had grown popular as a forum for public opinion and criticism of government policies. Debates over oil company agreements and production levels and over social policy (especially housing) sometimes included verbal attacks on members of the Sabah family. The government also had become concerned about internal security problems, precipitated by terrorist activity and the rise of a leftist opposition. The Assembly had also become an effective forum for Middle Eastern issues, of particular importance to the country's non-Kuwaiti majority, which includes 300,000 resident Palestinians. Just prior to its dissolution, the Assembly adopted pro-Palestinian resolutions condemning Syrian involvement in the Lebanese civil war, in opposition to the government's officially neutral position. The dissolution of the Assembly was accompanied by press curbs; the introduction of new censorship rules; the arrest of several leftists; and the dissolution or suspension of several newspapers, social clubs, and professional and trade unions.

In February 1981, new elections were held and the Assembly reconvened with new guidelines. The current Assembly consists of fifty seats, two in each of twenty-five constituencies. Election is by simple plurality. The majority of seats are filled, as in previous elections, by conservative government loyalists and members of traditionally allied families. Within this group, some observers saw a shift in predominance from the established commercial elite towards tribal bedouin leaders (who took twenty-three of the fifty seats), towards younger technocrats (who took thirteen seats), and towards Sunni Muslim "fundamentalists" (five seats). The election was viewed as a defeat for more radical Arab nationalists who, under the leadership of Dr. Ahmad al-Khatib of the Arab Nationalist Movement, had held a third of the seats in the 1976 Assembly but won no seats in the 1981 election. It was also a defeat for the Shi'a Muslims, who ran several candidates but won only four seats. This realignment was partly attributable to a redistricting which affected many previously radical and Shi'a areas. The level of dissent the emir will tolerate in the new Assembly has yet to be tested.

Judiciary

Kuwait's judicial system, as reorganized in 1980, has three levels. The highest court is the Supreme Court of Appeals, although the emir can act as a de facto final appeals court. There is the national Court of First Instance and summary courts in each administrative district. The legal code is drawn primarily from the Egyptian and Ottoman codes, with the constitutional stipulation that legislation not conflict with the shari'ah (Islamic law). "Acts of Government" are outside the jurisdiction of the courts.

Regional & Local Government

Kuwait's administration is highly centralized. However, Kuwait City, Ahmadi, Jahra, and Hawalli are, administratively, provincial governates, with governors and municipal councils appointed by the emir. Smaller administrative divisions are the same as electoral constituencies.

The Electoral System

Suffrage is restricted to adult (age twenty-one), literate, male Kuwaiti citizens. Citizens are defined as persons whose families lived in Kuwait before 1921. Members of the police and armed forces cannot vote nor can foreigners, some 60 percent of the population. In January 1982, the Assembly defeated a bill to enfranchise women. The electorate thus comprises less than 10 percent of Kuwait's total population. Of this group, less then half (42,000) are registered to vote. In the 1981 election, about 90 percent of the registered voters (or less than 3 percent of the total population) voted for 448 candidates. Candidates ran on individual platforms, since political parties are illegal.

Ruling Family, Tribal, and Merchant Leaders

Kuwait has had more success than neighboring Gulf shaikhdoms in settling intrafamily disputes peaceably. Since the time of Mubarak, succession has been confined, relatively smoothly, to the Jabir and Salim lines. Personal ambitions within the family, loosely associated with either traditionalist or more modern points of view, are the primary sources of dispute.

Tribal and merchant families, whose input into the decision-making process has declined since the development of an oil economy, have not presented an overt challenge to the regime. Nonetheless, these somewhat overlapping groups may offer the greatest potential threat to regime stability. They have been mollified, economically, by the business opportunities associated with increased oil revenues. Politically, they have been partially co-opted into the state through the Assembly and ministerial posts. Still, their autonomous corporate existence and historical claim to political participation could provide the basis for a loyal or disloyal opposition.

Other Political Forces

Military

The military is subject to firm, and personal, Sabah control. Disturbances have been reported in recent years within the police force and at the Infantry School. There is some potential for a disenchanted prince within the military establishment to use his position in alliance with other groups to create opposition for the regime.

Shi'a Muslims

Estimates of the number of Shi'a in Kuwait vary. Some 10 percent of the total population may be Shi'a, while the number of Kuwaiti nationals who are Shi'a may be as high as 20 percent. Most of these latter are probably Persian in origin. While a small portion of the Shi'a community is influentially placed in commerce, the community's impact on policy has been slight and appears to be diminishing as the power of Shi'a Iran grows.

Non-Nationals

According to the 1980 census, 58 percent of Kuwait's population of 1.4 million is foreign. Palestinians and Indians form the two largest groups. Crucial to the economy, these non-nationals, some now of several generations standing, have few political rights and little chance of acquiring them through citizenship. They cannot organize independent trade unions; they cannot own property, stock in Kuwaiti businesses, or companies without a Kuwaiti partner. They enjoy only limited access to the benefits of the welfare state.

Non-nationals, however, have so far provided only sporadic opposition to the regime. Their capacity to organize is minimized by internal cleavages (language, culture, occupation), fear of deportation, and self-interest in keeping lucrative if insecure jobs. Their long-term threat to the regime lies, first, in their potential nuisance value in alliance with other disaffected groups, and second, in their contacts abroad. The Kuwaiti border with Iraq is difficult to close effectively against the movement of people, money, weapons, and ideas. Activities of the Palestine Liberation Organization, while financially supported by Kuwait outside its borders, are particularly worrisome inside the emirate, given the large Palestinian population.

Kuwait's rulers are well aware of the trade-offs involved. In the months surrounding the constitutional crisis of 1976, the government deported thousands of foreign (primarily Arab) workers. At the same time, it made some social services available to foreigners and opened a few loopholes for acquiring Kuwaiti citizenship.

National Prospects

Thus far, Kuwait has maintained a high degree of political stability through a combination of cautious leadership, a cohesive ruling alliance, and government largesse. Merchant and tribal allies have profited from business ventures, while the bulk of the Kuwaiti population has benefitted from the massive distribution of oil wealth in the form of direct transfer payments; guaranteed state employment (the state is Kuwait's largest employer); and free or subsidized housing, health care, and education. As extensive social services become the norm, however, they may be seen less as examples of the rulers' largesse and more as rights that the individual, as citizen, can claim from the state.

Kuwait's leaders also face possible trouble from the internalization of external threats. Iraqi claims to Kuwait and its oil have been a recurrent problem in the past, although Kuwait's firm support of Iraq in its war with Iran has defused this issue for the moment. The Arab-Israeli conflict, which insinuated itself into local politics most notably in the 1976 Assembly suspension, continues to be monitored closely by Palestinians and other Arabs. Since the Iranian revolution and subsequent Gulf war, Kuwait has also had to contend with growing Shi'a unrest (manifested in demonstrations and bombing incidents) and with security problems associated directly with the war itself. Iran has bombed Kuwaiti refineries three times during the war, as a warning against aid to Iraq. Saudi Arabia, too, keeps a watchful eye on its small neighbor and has expressed concern that four of those involved in the 1979 Mecca mosque attack were Kuwaitis. Kuwait's small size, vulnerable strategic location, and dependence on foreign labor all render it particularly susceptible to these regional disputes.

Further Reading

Dickson, H. R. P. *Kuwait and Her Neighbors*. London: George Allen and Unwin Ltd., 1956.

Ismael, Jacqueline. *Kuwait: Social Change in Historical Perspective.* Syracuse, N. Y.: Syracuse University Press, 1982.

Long, David, *The Persian Gulf: An Introduction to Its People, Politics, and Economics.* Boulder, Colo.: Westview Press, 1976.

Nyrop, Richard, ed. *Area Handbook for the Persian Gulf States.* Washington, D.C.: U.S. Government Printing Office, 1977.

Winstone, Harry and Freeth, Zahra. *Kuwait: Prospect and Reality.* New York: Crane, Russak, 1972.

PEOPLE'S DEMOCRATIC REPUBLIC OF LAOS

(Sathalanalao Paxithipaty Paxaxon Lao)

by H. Monte Hill, Ph.D.

The System of Government

Laos, a nation of nearly four million people, is a one-party communist state. The present government was established December 2, 1975, after King Savang Vatthana abdicated the throne held by his family for over 500 years. The republic is ruled by the Lao People's Revolutionary Party (LPRP), an outgrowth of the Pathet Lao (technically, the Lao People's Liberation Army), a communist military force founded in 1951 to combat French colonial domination with northern Vietnamese help. The state does not have a written constitution, though the Supreme People's Council is said to be writing one.

Executive

The president's powers are formal only. Real executive power resides in the prime minister, whose source of strength lies with the LPRP of which he is the secretary general.

Legislature

Originally appointed to draw up a constitution, the Supreme People's Council functions as a quasilegislative body chaired by the nation's president. All or almost all of its forty-five members are also members of the LPRP.

Judiciary

The Central Supreme Court is supposed to have final judicial authority. Numerous people's courts operate at the local level.

Regional & Local Government

There are thirteen provinces governed by LPRP cadres under direction from the capital, Vientiane. In the northern highlands, non-Lao ethnic groups manage their own affairs with little interference from the central government.

The Electoral System

Laos is one of the areas of the world least touched by Western political processes. No national elections of any sort have ever been held there.

Lao People's Revolutionary Party (LPRP; Phak Paxaxon Tapivad Lao)

History

The LPRP traces its origins to the Pathet Lao founded in 1951 by Prince Souphanouvong, a scion of the royal family. Organized and sustained with the help of communist Viet Minh forces from northern Vietnam, Pathet Lao guerrillas were soon able to establish a provisional government in northern Laos. Soon after the defeat of the French in Vietnam (1954) and the establishment of an independent communist government in Hanoi, real control of the Pathet Lao movement was taken over (1955) by Kaysone Phomvihan, who had the full support of the North Vietnamese government. Souphanouvong, however, continued to serve as the leading figure in negotiations with the legal government.

From 1955 to 1975, the Pathet Lao maintained continuous pressure against the United States-backed government in Vientiane, even during periods when Souphanouvong joined that government in flimsy coalitions. By 1961, the Pathet Lao controlled about half the country. Ten years later, with the help of some 60,000 North Vietnamese troops, the revolutionaries controlled nearly two-thirds of Laos, restricting the sway of the Vientiane government to the Mekong River valley around the capital.

It was at this time, about 1972, that the LPRP was formally established in anticipation of taking full control of the central government. The contending forces signed a ceasefire agreement in 1973 and in 1974 formed a coalition government. With the communist victory in Vietnam, the LPRP took over the government of Laos, though it maintained the facade of the coalition until the following December.

Organization

Local, district, and provincial administrative committees, which function as both party and government bodies, are directly managed by the elite national Central Committee of twenty-three people who also occupy all key government positions. At the apex of the LPRP and government structure is a seven-member Politburo which determines policy for the party and the nation.

The Leninist system of democratic centralism prevails. Disagreement and debate within the Central Committee is limited; decisions made in the Politburo and the Central Committee are binding on all members. Lower levels of the party apparently are not consulted on such decisions. Party discipline is strict; violations are punished by expulsion and/or imprisonment in "re-education" camps.

The major party publication is *Siang Paxaxon* (Voice of the People).

Policy

The party aims at creating a model communist state. Most peasant holdings have been collectivized, and heavy taxes have been imposed on both the collectives and the few remaining private farms. One of the party's primary aims is to achieve self-sufficiency in agricultural production. All major industry has been taken over by the government.

No political opposition is permitted; since 1975, over 50,000 people have been interned in "re-education" camps in Laos and Vietnam. Among recent dissidents sent off for "re-education" were a government minister and the chairman of the Vientiane Administrative Committee, both of whom had opposed the party's pro-Hanoi policy.

There are unconfirmed reports that a faction of the party leadership advocates a slower, moderate, and pragmatic approach to building the communist society and a nonaligned "Tito-style" foreign policy. Real dissension within the top ranks, however, is minimal; cohesion and unity is one of the strengths of the LPRP leadership.

Membership & Constituency

LPRP has an estimated 15,000 members. Little is known of their social or educational background. The party does not actively recruit new members, and requirements for admission to the party are rigorous. As a result, the party leadership can rely on relatively well-disciplined and dedicated cadres to carry out its instructions.

Financing

Nothing is known of party financing. It can be assumed that party cadres are required to return a portion of their income to the party and that state support is considerable.

Leadership

The most powerful party figure is the radical ideologue Kaysone Phomvihan (born 1920), LPRP secretary general and prime minister of Laos. His chief ally and probable successor is Nouhak Phongsavan, deputy prime minister in 1982. The party founder, Souphanouvong (born 1909) is president of the party and the nation, chairman of the Supreme People's Council, and president of the party's front organization. Souphanouvong and Phoumi Vongvichit, education minister in 1982, are reportedly the leaders of the moderate faction.

Mass Organization

The party's only auxiliary organization is the Lao Front for National Reconstruction (formerly the Lao Patriotic Front), designed to mobilize nonparty support for government policy. It has not been successful.

Opposition

The radical policies of the Phomvihan government have evoked widespread but disorganized resistance among the multi-ethnic Buddhist and animistic Laotians. Most Laotians have refused to join the Lao Front for National Reconstruction or cooperate in the current regime's economic programs. Over 200,000 Laotians have fled into neighboring Thailand and many have joined guerrilla groups remaining within the country.

The only organized opposition to the current regime among Laotian refugees is the government in exile of former royal minister Sanikone in France. Established on October 14, 1978, the Sanikone group has considerable financial support from West European right-wing organizations, but it is small in numbers (about 300) and has little apparent influence within or outside Laos.

Internally, there are in the southern lowlands of Laos an unknown number of small obscure bands of former royal government soldiers, LPRP defectors, and others who oppose the Phomvihan administration. Some of these groups formed a Laotian Popular Front in 1976 and claim to have combat strength of 4,000. Little is known about their finances, leadership, and organization apparatus, but they are believed to be formed around the personalities of individual leaders rather than ideology.

The most noticeable opposition comes from isolated and autonomous ethnic groups of Upland Tai, Lao Theung, Mien (Yao), and Hmong (Meo) which live in the mountainous region of northern Laos. Numbering about 2.6 million (60 percent of the Laotian population), these communities are feudal and patrilineal. Leadership typically is determined by kinship, seniority, and, in some cases, wealth. Decision making is democratic with participation by all heads of village households.

The 60,000 Hmong have a more highly developed political system extending beyond the villages to recognized district and provincial leaders. Moreover, the Hmong are excellent fighters and well financed by, among other things, profits generated from opium production. The most influential Hmong leader is believed to be former royal general Vang Pao who commanded the CIA-sponsored mercenary Hmong army prior to the communist takeover in 1975. Vang Pao, in spite of living in exile in the United States, still maintains close contact with other Hmong leaders both inside and outside Laos.

These groups—lowland and highland—are reputed to receive limited American, Thai, and Chinese aid. Nevertheless, with the exception of the Hmong, they remain poorly financed, trained, disciplined, and equipped.

Other Political Forces

Vietnam

As a satellite of Vietnam, the Laos government is overseen by Vietnamese officials. Vietnamese hegemony is assured, among other things, by the presence in Laos of 70,000 Vietnamese troops, 6,000 civilian officials, and 800 secret police. In addition, as part of a program to control rebellious Laotian highlanders, an estimated 100,000 Vietnamese citizens have been settled in the northern mountains along the Vietnamese border. Vietnamese influence in Laos is buttressed by large amounts of Soviet aid, including 1,000 Russian police and military training advisers.

National Prospects

The Vietnamese-backed Phomvihan regime is stable and very likely to remain so. The organized opposition may be an annoyance, but it is not a serious threat. The regime's real difficulties are economic. Industrial production, all small scale, is hampered by lack of funds and skilled personnel, while plans for the development of collectivized agriculture face stiff passive resistance from the peasantry. Given the government's consolidation of power, however, and its willingness to use that power ruthlessly, even economic disaster is unlikely to topple the LPRP in the foreseeable future.

Further Reading

Brown, MacAlister and Zasloff, Joseph J. "Dependency in Laos." *Current History* (December 1979).

———. "Laos 1977: The Realities of Independence." *Asian Survey*, Vol. 18, Feb. 1978.

———. "Laos 1978: The Ebb and Flow of Adversity." *Asian Survey*, Vol. 19, Feb. 1979.

Chandra, N., "Laos Back to the Drawing Board." *Far Eastern Economic Review*, September 8, 1978.

Gunn, Geoffrey C. "Foreign Relations of the Lao People's Democratic Republic: The Ideological Imperative." *Asian Survey*, 20 (October 1980).

Neher, Clark D. *Politics in Southeast Asia*. Cambridge, Mass.: Schenkman Publishing Company, 1979.

Stuart-Fox, Martin. "Factors Influencing Relations Between the Communist Parties of Thailand and Laos," *Asian Survey*, Vol. 19, Apr. 1979.

Vanderkroef, Justus M. "Laos: Paradoxes and Dilemmas of Survival," *Asian Survey*, Vol. 20, Sept. 1980.

Whitaker, Donald P., et al., *Area Handbook for Laos*. Washington, D.C.: U.S. Government Printing Office for Foreign Area Studies, American University, 1972.

REPUBLIC OF LEBANON
(*Al-Jumhouriya al-Lubnaniya*)
by Judy Barsalou, M.Phil.

The System of Government

Lebanon, a nation of over three million people, is a multiparty democracy where competition for political power and office, until the 1975–76 war, was limited and channeled by a confessional agreement known as the National Pact. The pact was designed to minimize conflict and competition among the seventeen recognized religious confessions or communities by guaranteeing each a place in the governing of the state. This confessional system failed in the early 1970s in part because it did not recognize that Muslims in Lebanon had become more numerous than Christians. But while the confessional system demonstrably has failed the Lebanese, national consensus on its modification or its replacement by another governing principle has not been achieved. Although the worst fighting ended in 1976, the government has yet to restore order and exercise its authority. The very existence of Lebanon as a unified state remains in question.

Since the founding of the Lebanese state on August 30, 1920, the question of its identity has never entirely been resolved. None of the religious communities constitutes an absolute majority of the population, and the presence of a large European-oriented Christian community (now somewhat less than half the population) has meant that Lebanon's identification with the Arab world has never been complete. Complicating matters is the fact that Lebanon, part of the Ottoman Empire until World War I, in 1920 was carved out of what was known as Greater Syria, then under French mandate. From the first, many of Lebanon's Muslim citizens thought of Lebanon as an unwelcome but temporary product of French imperialism, ultimately fated to become an integral part of an organic Arab nation comprised of the whole of the Arab world. Others in Lebanon, predominantly members of the various Christian communities, regarded the new state as a nation in its own right based on a unique Phoenician heritage.

Despite this profound difference in perception, confessionalism served the infant Lebanese state very well. It provided the basis for the reconciliation of the largely autonomous sects while it legitimized, but limited, competition and rivalry. Instead of imposing on Lebanon an alien political system, it recognized the tradition of leadership by *zu'ama* (feudal chieftains) on behalf of their "flocks." The details of the confessional system were delineated in the unwritten National Pact agreed upon by the representatives of the combined Muslim and Christian communities in 1943. It appeared to resolve Lebanon's conflict over its identity by declaring Lebanon an independent, secular, and neutral state with an Arab "face." Accordingly, neither the Christian nor Muslim Lebanese were to look to the West or to the Arab states, respectively, for factional support. The second part of the National Pact endorsed the so-called confessional system, in use in one form or another since the 1860s. According to the established formula, the president of the republic must be Maronite Christian, the prime minister Sunni Muslim, the speaker of the Chamber of Deputies Shi'a Muslim, the deputy speaker Greek Orthodox, the defense minister Druze, and the commander of the military Maronite Christian. Furthermore, seats in the Chamber of Deputies were divided among Christians and Muslims in a 6 to 5 ratio based on the official census of 1932, the last one conducted. The various communities were also proportionally represented in the cabinet, the civil service, and the military. In addition, the Lebanese constitution guaranteed freedom of religion and respect for the religious interests of each community.

With the major exception of the 1958 civil war precipitated by the reluctance of Camille Chamoun to give up the presidency at the end of his six-year term, Lebanon appeared to prosper as a democratic state from 1943, the year of its independence, until the mid-1970s when it was overcome by one of the most virulent civil wars of the century. Known as the "Switzerland of the Middle

East" because of its prosperity and apparent success at balancing the demands of its many communities, Lebanon was famous for its outstanding uncensored press, its literacy rate of over 90 percent (the highest in the Arab world), and the charm and sophistication of Beirut, its capital. Also unusual was its success in maintaining civilian-led governments in a region where military coups abounded. But there was another side of Lebanon of which few cared to take note: the gap between the rich and poor was widening rather than shrinking. By 1960 over 80 percent of the population was estimated to be at or below the poverty level. The coincidence of religious and economic cleavages exacerbated ethnic divisions in Lebanese society. Christians tend to enjoy a higher standard of living than Muslims; and the largest Muslim sect, the Shi'a, unrecognized in the confessional distribution of power, is the poorest and most socially disadvantaged of all the sects. The refusal of the Christians to participate in a new national census that does not count Lebanese living outside Lebanon, which would reveal their own relative decline in numerical strength, has meant that the outdated 1932 census continues to provide the basis for the distribution of power among the sects. Estimates now indicate that approximately 60 percent of two million citizens living in Lebanon (excluding the 370,000 Palestinian residents) are Muslim, and that the Shi'a sect is slightly larger than the Sunni.

The changing composition of the population, the impoverishment of the middle class, inflation, land speculation, and general economic uncertainty were problems that the Lebanese government failed to address effectively. Student unrest and repeated incursions by Israeli troops into southern Lebanon since 1973 in pursuit of Palestinian *fedayeen* further eroded government legitimacy. Pressured by Israel and by the disruptive presence of politically active Palestinians within its borders, in addition to its own internal discontents, the overburdened confessional system simply collapsed. The result was an eighteen-month civil war (April 1975 through October 1976), and the death of an estimated 30,000 to 60,000 Lebanese and Palestinians inside Lebanon.

Lebanon has been in upheaval ever since. In March 1978, the general anarchy plaguing the country was punctuated by an Israeli invasion of southern Lebanon, resulting in massive civilian casualties and physical destruction. Then, on June 6, 1982, an invading Israeli army entered Lebanon, declaring its intention to "cleanse" southern Lebanon up to 25 kilometers north of the Israeli-Leba-

THE LEBANESE POPULATION, 1932*		
Muslim	383,180	48.7 %
Sunni	175,925	22.4
Shi'a	154,208	19.6
Druze	53,047	6.7
'Alawi	—	—
Isma'ili	—	—
Christian	392,544	49.9
(Catholic)		
Maronite	226,378	28.8
Greek Catholic	45,999	5.8
Armenian Catholic	5,694	.7
Syrian Catholic	2,675	.3
Latin (Roman)	—	—
Chaldean	528	.06
(Non-Catholic)		
Greek Orthodox	76,522	9.7
Armenian Orthodox	25,462	3.2
Protestant	6,712	.8
Syrian Orthodox	2,574	.03
Other Jewish, Baha'i, etc.	9,819	1.2
Total Population	785,543	

*Official census.

nese border. Having achieved this objective, the Israelis then encircled Beirut, cutting off for weeks supplies of food and water to West Beirut, and subjecting its population to shelling and bombing estimated by one Lebanese official to have destroyed twenty-five percent of the structures in West Beirut. Massive destruction was also reported in villages and cities throughout the south; Palestinian refugee camps, in particular, were targeted for Israeli fire. By September 2, the respected Lebanese daily, *an-Nahar*, estimated 17,825 Lebanese and Palestinians had died throughout Lebanon, and 31,103 had been wounded. The Israelis admitted to the loss of 326 soldiers and 1,900 wounded by the end of August. Since then many more soldiers and Lebanese civilians have died, notably over 300 Palestinian and Lebanese civilians living in the ruins of the Shatila and Sabra refugee camps south of Beirut, massacred by soldiers of the Phalange (Kata'ib) while the Israeli army ringing the camps looked on.

Executive

Ostensibly a parliamentary system, the government historically has been dominated by its president, who is chief executive and head of state. Elected by secret ballot in the Chamber of Deputies, the president cannot run for consecutive six-year terms. He selects and dismisses his ministers, who are carefully chosen to preserve a fragile sectarian balance in the cabinet. And he also appoints the Muslim prince minister after extensive and sometimes protracted consultations with the traditional leaders (*zu'ama*) of each community and other prominent politicians. The president cannot dissolve the Chamber of Deputies without the approval of the cabinet. He can grant pardons, appoint civil servants, propose bills, and enact emergency legislation on which the Parliament has failed to act for forty days.

Lebanese presidents on the whole have enhanced their power by enlarging administrative departments over which they have undiluted authority and by building coalitions of important politicians who will support their administrations. Typically, the president will pass the office of prime minister around among prominent Sunni Muslims so as not to alienate powerful individuals within that community. The president's choice of a prime minister is crucial, for he must be a man who can compromise with the president and bring broad Muslim support to the government. But the number of cabinets in a twenty-eight–year period between 1926 and 1964—forty-six in all—reflects more than the president's inclination to co-opt important politicians by including them at one time or another in his cabinet. While this practice institutionalized and dampened sectarian rivalry and caused each leader to identify his own well-being with that of the government, it often generated conflict sufficient to bring down governments.

Legislature

The ninety-nine seats of the Chamber of Deputies were contended for by candidates seeking four-year terms in direct elections. The number of seats in the Chamber of Deputies was always a multiple of eleven, and seats were apportioned among the communities in such a way that Muslims had five-elevenths of the seats and Christians, six-elevenths. The seats were further distributed among the sects to reflect their size in the 1932 census: Maronites (30); Sunni (20); Shi'a (19); Greek Orthodox (11); Greek Catholic (6); Druze (6); Armenian Orthodox (4); Armenian Catholic (1); Protestant (1); other minorities (1). Because of the 1975–76 civil war, the 1976 parliamentary elections were not held; representatives elected in 1972 continue to occupy their seats. Six of the ninety-nine representatives have since died, and new elections were scheduled for 1982. The Chamber of Deputies ordinarily met in two sessions each year: from March 15 to May 31 and from October 15 to December 31.

The Chamber of Deputies had the potential to exert significant control over the policy-making process, but in the final analysis it did not. It could amend the constitution by a three-quarter–majority vote (subject to possible executive veto), question and recall government ministers, and propose and act on legislation. It was also capable of indirectly exercising judicial power through the constitutional provision of a seven-person Supreme Court whose members were elected by the Chamber of Deputies. This court, however, was never convened.

Much of Parliament's potential to play a wider role in Lebanese politics was neutralized not just by disproportional presidential power but by the complex factional politics engaged in by the Parliament's members. Intense rivalries exist not only among the different communities represented in the Chamber of Deputies, but among parliamentary representatives of prominent families and the myriad political blocs emanating from them. Because less than one-third of the members of the Chamber belong to political parties, they are relatively free to switch alliances as need dictates. The fragility and fluidity of coalitions in Parliament diminished the capacity of this institution to act decisively on national problems. Only rarely did the Chamber of Deputies summon up sufficient support among its own ranks to vote against a president's bill. Its role was passive—stabilizing rather than innovating.

Judiciary

The secular court system of Lebanon, akin to that of France, coexists with the confessional courts of each religious community. The latter consider matters of personal status, such as inheritance and marriage. In the secular court system, fifty-six single-judge courts decide civil and criminal cases in the first instance. Eleven courts of appeal, each consisting of three judges, receive their appeals. Three of the four higher courts of appeal—the courts of cassation—take commercial and civil cases, while the fourth decides criminal cases. Courts of cassation also have three presiding judges. The Court of State (*Majlis Al-Shura*) is the highest functioning court of appeal. Theoretically independent of the government, the judiciary actually is linked to it through the minister of justice who sits in the cabinet. Lebanese courts do not possess the power of judicial review, except with respect to policies adopted by the cabinet and the civil service. The 1975–76 civil war caused major disruptions in the judicial process through the destruction of prisons, the escape of prisoners, and the difficulties involved in notifying individuals involved in judicial proceedings.

Regional & Local Government

In theory, Lebanon is administratively divided into five prefectures (*muhafazat*): Beirut, Mount Lebanon, South Lebanon, North Lebanon, and the Baqaa. Councils for each are headed by a prefect appointed by the cabinet, and consist of prominent community members, also appointed. Municipalities hold local elections in which mayors, members of municipal councils, and *mukhtars* are chosen. *Mukhtars* resolve minor judicial disputes and serve as equivalents of U.S. county clerks.

The national civil service is subject to the constraints of the confessional system. Individuals often are chosen for posts less on the basis of their individual merit than because of their ability to meet a confessional quota. Accordingly, the civil service, especially since the civil war, operates inefficiently and morale is low.

The Electoral System

Representatives to the Chamber of Deputies are chosen through direct, single-round, secret elections from multiple-member districts. The confessional system in Lebanon really operates as a "pre-set" proportional representational system in which the number of seats each community holds in Parliament is fixed in advance. Because in some districts up to eight candidates will win seats, most candidates join slates or "lists" of candidates usually headed by a member of a prominent family who they hope will help carry them to power. Lists are drawn up with an eye to putting together the most attractive combination of persons representing strategic families and important cities and villages. Less than 2 percent of the independent candidates running for office—that is, those who do not join lists—are actually elected.

In casting their ballots, voters choose as many candidates as there are seats in their district. And they may vote for all or only part of a list. They need not vote for a candidate who is of the same religion, although many voters do. Voters are not required to register to vote, but they must be twenty-one years of age. Suffrage is universal. The archaic requirement that voters must cast their ballots in the villages or cities from which their families originated, without regard to current place of residence, probably reduces voter turnout; in the 1972 elections approximately 55 percent of the electorate voted.

The Party System

Lebanon is a country of many political parties and factions, most fairly recent in origin and none possessing a majority in the Chamber of Deputies or enjoying the support of a broad cross-section of the population. Until the 1970s none of the parties exerted much influence on the Chamber of Deputies or the political system in general. Only recently have coalitions of parties and political "forces," including the rightist Lebanese Front and the leftist Lebanese National Movement, garnered national constituencies. Because of the localized, largely single-sect nature of most of the parties, it is misleading to speak of a Lebanese party system. Rather than providing the mechanism through which broad public interests are represented, with few exceptions the parties tend to reinforce sectarian and regional differences. They provide the power bases of traditional leaders and have served as building blocks of transitory parliamentary alliances.

Political parties in Lebanon generally are of two types: regional or transnational parties which exist not only in Lebanon but also in other countries in the Middle East (such as the Ba'th party and the Syrian National Social Party); and parties entirely Lebanese in character (such as the Progressive Socialist Party and the Kata'ib, also known as the Phalange). Many of the parties, including the Lebanese Communist Party, the Syrian National Social Party, and the Kata'ib party, have been illegal at one time or another in their history, but in the current anarchic Lebanese political order all political groups and parties operate openly. They recruit new members, publish newspapers, levy their own taxes on the citizenry, and maintain standing militias. The Kata'ib, for example, taxes the property and income of East Beirut residents, and collects levies on imports entering the country through Junieh. It also takes a percentage of gasoline sales, movie tickets, and restaurant checks in East Beirut. Government revenue has declined commensurately. In the absence of crucial public services in the wake of the war, including garbage collection and policing in areas of Beirut, some parties took over these functions or organized citizens to do so.

Party organization varies. The Lebanese Communist Party and the Organization for Communist Action, for example, are cadre-type organizations whose members are organized and indoctrinated in cells. Other parties, such as the Progressive Socialist Party, resemble more the mass-party model of organization and do not exert the same degree of control over their members. Even some transnational parties have memberships in which one religious sect dominates, such as the Lebanese Communist Party, which is almost half Shi'a Muslim.

Many of the parties ostensibly choose their leaders in a democratic manner through regular elections. But in the main, especially in those exclusively Lebanese, parties are led by the scions of wealthy, well-connected families who rise to power in part by virtue of their social position. These *zu'ama* traditionally have served as links between ordinary persons and the government. In return for a favor—a loan of money, the arrangement of a job interview, or, since the war, the protection of one's home or business from preying militias, etc.—the notable may expect to receive in return the vote and political loyalty of the citizen. Not all *zu'ama* belong to the aristocratic feudal families of Lebanon. Others, having gained positions of prominence through intellectual achievement or business success, serve in a similar manner as patrons to less well-connected clients. Even in the transnational parties, patron-client interactions of this sort are to be found among the elite of the party and the rank and file.

The many Lebanese political parties and forces defy easy classification and ranking by importance. The distribution of parliamentary seats among them tells us little, not only because in the last decade less than one-third of the parliamentary representatives have claimed to belong to a party, but because overall party strength is also determined by the party's military might. Second, while the pressures generated by the 1975–76 civil war temporarily polarized the political spectrum into a right-left dichotomy, not all the parties, particularly those of a sectarian nature, can be easily classified in terms of ideology. Finally, many of the "parties" behave more like factions—seeking their narrow interests rather than securing collective benefits—and yet call themselves parties. Others, such as the Independent Nasserist Movement (more commonly known as al-Murabitun) and the Movement of the Disinherited (a Shi'a political-military organization) do not have such pretensions. But since the early 1970s, these groups have exerted their influence in much the same way as the traditional parties—through expedient coalition-making, large-scale demonstrations, and military force.

To reduce the complexity of the Lebanese political system, parties and forces are considered here as they appear in the Lebanese polity, grouped in right- and left-wing configurations. Those parties which lie outside these configurations are treated separately. The discussion begins with the parties and forces on the right.

Lebanese Front

In March 1976 in the midst of the civil war, several of the leading right-wing Christian personalities and their militias and parties formed a coalition called the Lebanese Front. Initially, it consisted of Pierre Gemayel and his Kata'ib party (now the only powerful force in the Front); the National Liberal Party led by former president Camille Chamoun; former president Sulayman Frangieh and his militia; Father Sharbel Kassis, head of the Order of Maronite Monks; and Charles Malik, Edward Honein, Jawad Boulos, and Fuad Boustani, all leading figures in the Christian community. Christian organizations remaining outside the Front included the National Bloc led by Raymond Eddé, the three Armenian parties (Tashnak, Ramgavar Azadagan, and Hunchak), the Guardians of the Cedar, and the Destourian (Constitutional) Party of Michel al-Khoury. Sulayman Frangieh and his supporters withdrew from the Front May 11, 1978.

The Lebanese Front has studiously avoided calling for the partition of Lebanon. But leftist forces in Lebanon contend that the Front's platform, adopted at a meeting at Saydet al-Bir convent in February 1977, amounts to as much. The platform endorses a confederacy for Lebanon in which each religious community is free to establish its own military, financial, educational, judicial, religious, and cultural institutions. The platform also expresses the Front's commitment to the "liberation of all national territories," and its intention to prevail upon the other Arab states to help relocate in their countries the approximately 370,000 Palestinians living in Lebanon—many of whom entered the country after the 1970 civil war in Jordan. Bashir Gemayel, son of Pierre Gemayel, was commander of the Lebanese Forces—the combined militias of the constituent members of the Lebanese Front. Although funding of the Front remains secret, it is thought that the organization is supported by contributions collected at home and abroad, particularly in West Germany and the United States. The Front has openly carried weapons supplied by the Israelis, especially since the June 1982 invasion. Ammunition boxes of obvious Israeli origin were found in Sabra and Shatila Palestinian refugee camps after Front troops slaughtered more than 300 there in September 1982.

Phalangist Party
(Al-Kata'ib)

History

This party was established in November 1936 by a group of young nationalists impressed by the fascism of Nazi Germany and intent on ending French mandate rule and discrediting pan-Syrianism. Pierre Gemayel and his collaborators also conceived of the party as a means of infusing Lebanese youth with a spirit of discipline and responsibility, a reverence for private enterprise, and a sense of their Phoenician heritage. Because of the party's agitation against French rule, it was banned by French authorities throughout most of its existence during the mandate period.

Often described as the only Lebanese party which has played a significant role in Lebanese politics, it is true that Gemayel and other party members have held numerous portfolios in the cabinet, establishing themselves as a force with which every Lebanese government must contend. Yet the party has never held more than nine of the ninety-nine seats in the Chamber of Deputies, and its share of seats following the 1972 elections declined to seven. The deployment of its military forces, however, provided the mainstay of the right-wing military effort in the 1975–76 civil war.

Organization

The party's pyramidal structure reveals an authoritarian bias. Its president, for many years now Pierre Gemayel, is elected to renewable three-year terms by members of the Central Council. A twenty-three–member Political Bureau, nine members of which are chosen by the Central Council, formulates party policy and appoints lower-level party officials. The Central Council, larger than the Political Bureau and consisting of lower-level officials representing regional branches of the party, acts as a rubber stamp for decisions made in the Political Bureau. It also supervises five regional departments which are in turn subdivided along municipal lines. The party's military council directs the party's regular militia, perhaps as many as 6,000 men, and its semiregular and backup forces whose combined total is approximately 13,500 men. Three publications are produced by the party: an Arabic daily, al-'Amal; a French daily, Le Reveil; and a French monthly, Action-Proche Orient.

Policy

The Kata'ib is the most important member of the Lebanese Front. At the head of the Front, the Kata'ib has spoken out repeatedly against socialism, the institutional reforms proposed by the leftist Lebanese National Movement, pan-Arabism, and the presence of Palestinians in Lebanon. The party called for a withdrawal of Palestinian fedayeen from southern Lebanon, where they engaged the Israeli military and irregular right-wing forces of Sa'ad Haddad (supplied by Israel). The inability of the government to control the military activities of the Palestinians, and the party's rising concern about broad leftist and Muslim support for the Palestinians in Lebanon, led the Kata'ib in the early 1970s to undertake an intensive program of military buildup.

Although Lebanon has experienced de facto partition as a result of civil war, the Kata'ib maintains that it has not sought and does not approve of this solution. Pierre Gemayel, however, argues for the decentralization of government to accommodate de facto partition and suggests that a confederated Lebanon might logically follow. The party's militia has refused to allow the Lebanese army to take over areas under its control until the leftist Lebanese and Palestinian forces do the same.

Membership & Constituency

In 1970 the party's membership was approximately 70,000 and may have been twice that during the civil war. Most of its supporters are young Christian Maronite and Greek Catholic (the latter a distant second) petit-bourgeois who are concentrated in Mount Lebanon. Additional supporters are organized in the party's numerous branches abroad. In the 1960s almost 10 percent of its members were female.

Complete information about party financing is not available. It is known that the Kata'ib is supported, at least in part, by the following means: the taxation of citizens in regions under the party's military control, including east Beirut and much of northern Mount Lebanon; excise taxes imposed on goods brought through the ports of Beirut and Junieh; membership contributions; and economic and military aid from Western Europe and the United States.

The party's hierarchy is dominated by members of the Gemayel family. The president of the party, Pierre Gemayel, was born November 6, 1905, in Bikfaya to a prominent family of the Christian Maronite faith. Elected to Parliament in 1960, he has held the same seat ever since. His youngest son, Bashir, born November 10, 1947, in Beirut, became the commander of the Kata'ib Military Council in July 1976. In August that same year, Bashir assumed command of the combined militias of the Lebanese Front. In September 1982, Bashir Gemayel was elected president of the republic at a session of parliament held in Israeli-occupied territory in Lebanon. He and party followers were killed a few days later in a massive explosion at Kata'ib headquarters. Pierre Gemayel's eldest son, Amin, born in 1941, represents the Metn region in the Chamber of Deputies, and became a ranking member and major spokesman of the party. Following the assassination of his brother, Amin was elected president of Lebanon in October.

National Liberal Party (NLP)

Created by Camille Chamoun after he reluctantly stepped down from the presidency at the end of his term in 1958, the National Liberal Party serves primarily as his mouthpiece. Chamoun, born in 1900 to a Maronite family living in the Shouf region of Mount Lebanon, exercises almost complete control over the party as its president. His son Dory (born 1932) is secretary general of the party.

In the 1960s the National Liberal Party's loosely organized membership, according to unreliable party statistics, numbered 60,000 to 70,000, and in the 1968–72 Chamber of Deputies eight deputies represented the party. Up-to-date membership figures are not available, but party membership is drastically reduced. Now as then, most of the party's members are Maronite Christians. Although

the party claims to represent the liberal interests of all Lebanese, it has become more narrowly identified since the early 1970s with the goals of the Christian right-wing forces for which its militia, the Tigers, fought in the 1975–76 civil war. Despite their earlier cooperation, the Kata'ib launched a successful military operation against the NLP in July 1980 for control over primarily Christian east Beirut. The Kata'ib's preminence over the NLP and a sizable portion of the country is now well established, and the NLP's very existence stands in question. Pierre Gemayel has suggested that the two parties merge, with himself as secretary general and Chamoun as president. Whatever Chamoun's inclinations, such a move is opposed by members of the party, particularly his son Dory. The party's headquarters are located in Rue du Liban, Beirut, Lebanon.

The parties and forces of the left are more numerous and perhaps more mecurial than those of the right. They are considered next.

Lebanese National Movement (LNM)

The current Lebanese National Movement, which includes sixteen parties and six individuals who are important figures in Lebanese politics in their own right, can be viewed as a successor to two earlier attempts to form a broad front among the left-of-center Lebanese parties. A leftist coalition first emerged in 1964 under the name of the Front of Patriotic and Progressive Parties and Personalities. Initiated by Kamal Jumblat of the Progressive Socialist Party, the Front included four reformist members of Parliament (including Jumblat), as well as two extraparliamentary groups—the radical Arab Nationalists' Movement and the Lebanese Communist Party. This coalition lost momentum in mid-1967 because of profound differences in the political outlooks of its members. The Front was brought to life again late in 1968 in response to a December 28, 1968, raid by eight Israeli helicopters on Beirut International Airport. All Lebanese flag carriers, thirteen planes worth $4.3 million, were destroyed on the ground in retaliation for an attack on Israel's El Al airlines in Athens a few days earlier by two Palestinian *fedayeen* belonging to the Beirut-based Popular Front for the Liberation of Palestine. Popular outrage over the failure of the Lebanese army to defend Lebanon from outside attack eventually led to the collapse of the cabinet. The Israeli attack and a common interest in organizing in defense of the Palestinian movement in Lebanon led to the ad hoc reconstitution of the leftist front, which has come to be known as the Lebanese National Movement. Another critical factor contributing to the formation of the LNM was the common awareness among its members that none of the constituent parties alone had the strength to oppose the right-wing militias. As the political forces in Lebanon became increasingly polarized in the early 1970s, small groups and parties on both sides of the political spectrum joined alliances simply to survive.

In the summer of 1975, representatives of leftist groups met in Beirut where they adopted the "transitional program" of the Lebanese National Movement. This document calls for a revision of the current government structure and the abolition of confessional representation. To achieve this the LNM would delete all confessional clauses from the constitution and the National Pact of 1943 and replace them with a system of proportional representation. The program endorses the strengthening of the Chamber of Deputies and the cabinet at the expense of the president in order to further secularize the system. It also stresses the need for a strong secular army capable of defending the country and sharing the "responsibility" of the other Arab armies in promoting the Palestinian cause and other Arab interests. Finally, the program advances the idea of an elected "founding Assembly," which will engage in a dialogue on the future constitutional direction of the country and prepare legislation for the adoption of necessary reforms.

By no means homogeneous ideologically, the LNM encompasses parties and personalities whose positions range from liberal democratic to revolutionary communist. But to characterize the LNM as a leftist-Muslim alliance is not entirely correct. Many individual Christians belong to the LNM, although it is true that the majority of persons and parties grouped within the LNM are Muslim. More importantly, all the constituent groups of the LNM support an entirely secular reform program for Lebanon. The institutional members of the LNM include six major parties and groupings (named first) and ten minor organizations. The institutional members are the Progressive Socialist Party; the Organization for Communist Action; the Lebanese Communist Party; the Movement of Independent Nasserists (al-Murabitun); the Syrian National Social Party; the Ba'th party (pro-Syria branch). The minor members of the Movement are the Ba'th party (pro-Iraq branch); the Arab Socialist Union-Arab Brigades; the Arab Socialist Union (led by Kamil Yuncs); the Arab

Socialist Union (led by Munir Sayyad); the People's Nasserist Organization; the Union of Working People's Forces; the Kurdish Democratic Party Organization; the Arab Socialist Action Party; the Patriotic Christian Front; and the Lebanese Democratic Movement (supporters of al-Fateh). The ten minor organizations are too small to deserve further discussion. The influential individuals who belong to the LNM, unrepresented by any party, are Ussma Fakhuri; Fuad Shbaklo; Muhammad Kabbuni; M. Alber Mansour; Issam Noaman; and Issat Harb.

The number of individuals who are affiliated with the LNM through their parties is unknown. The size of the LNM budget and its sources of income are secret. The LNM has a joint military command but no army or militia of its own. Instead, the Joint Military Command coordinates the military units of each constituent party. The total number of soldiers at the disposal of the LNM before June 1982 probably ranged from 5,000 to 10,000 men and women.

Formally, the Central Political Council, in which every party of the LNM has its representative, is the supreme decision-making body of the Movement and possesses both executive and legislative powers. Each party in the Central Political Council theoretically has veto power over every measure it considers. In reality, the Council is dominated by the four most influential parties in the LNM—the Organization for Communist Action, the Lebanese Communist Party, the Progressive Socialist Party, the Syrian National Social Party—with some input from the Syrian Ba'th, and al-Murabitun. The LNM Executive Committee, which consists of representatives from the six parties named above and five rotating members, is guided by an inner circle made up of the representatives of the four dominant parties. That inner circle formulates the actual policies of the Movement, using the Central Political Council as a rubber stamp. Indicative of the relationship between these two organs is the fact that on the average, the Executive Committee meets at least once a week and the Central Political Council once a month. Until his assassination in March 1977, Kamal Jumblat was chairman of the LNM, a substantial power center in the Movement which was left vacant until his son, Walid, assumed the position in 1980. The executive secretary-general of the LNM, since 1976 Mohsen Ibrahim (also secretary-general of the Organization of Communist Action), conducts the day-to-day business of the Movement and oversees the work of seven central bureaus and approximately fifteen regional councils. The LNM Central Political Council was located on Wata al-Musseitbeh St., Beirut, before the Israeli invasion.

Lebanese Communist Party (LCP)

Established in October 1924 but not openly active until 1936, this party subsequently was banned between 1948 and 1971. Throughout much of its existence, however, the LCP has been intensely active in labor organizing, in unsuccessful attempts to win a seat in the Chamber of Deputies, and, more recently, in its leadership role in the LNM. Until 1944 the Syrian and Lebanese communists were organized into one party. Their split reflected the independent status of each country, and later the two parties fell out over various issues—including whether or not to support the Nasserist movement in Syria and Lebanon. Ideological disagreements within the LCP, as well, have produced the fracturing of the party. In 1963, for example, disenchanted Trotskyist and Maoist members of the party's youth branch founded a short-lived rival organization called the Union of Lebanese Communists.

The base of the party's pyramidal structure is comprised of party "groups," each group consisting of seven to ten members. Elected representatives from these groups form regional committees which take responsibility for party work in different regions. A central committee, comprised of elected members of the regional committee, is the highest party organ between party congresses and chooses the leader and secretary-general of the party. Because the Central Committee meets only twice a month, activities are supervised on a daily basis by the party's Political Bureau, whose members are also chosen by the Central Committee. The party publishes a daily, *al-Nida*; a weekly, *al-Akhbar* (now temporarily suspended); a monthly, *al-Tarik*; and an Armenian weekly, *Gantch*.

Following the lead of the Soviet Union in 1947, the LCP accepted the partition of Palestine. This position alienated many of its followers and was reconsidered by the party in the late 1960s. The LCP gave its full support to the Palestinian movement after the October 1973 Arab-Israel war. Since World War II, the LCP has not called for the establishment by revolutionary means of a socialist state in Lebanon. And from the early 1970s, it has asserted that limited reform of the existing political system is necessary before sweeping economic and social reforms can be achieved. Its Middle East policy calls for a just solution of the Palestinian problem and strongly criticizes the Camp David accords as a separate Egyptian peace with Israel which disregards the interests of the Palestinians.

Estimates of party membership before the Israeli invasion range from 8,000 to 10,000. Approximately 60 percent of the members are Muslim (Shi'a, 45 percent; and Sunni and Druze, 15 percent). The Christians who constitute the remaining 40 percent of the party are comprised of Greek Orthodox (25 percent) and other Christians (15 percent). The party's standing militia of approximately 1,200 men played an important military role in the civil war and fought side-by-side with Palestinian forces against the Israeli sweep into Lebanon.

The important military role played by the party in the civil war, its strong support for the Palestinian movement, and its successful moderation of its own radical inclinations have attracted to it socially and economically disadvantaged persons disenchanted with the political leadership offered to them by their traditional *zu'ama*. The LCP is only one of several secular parties to benefit from the declining popularity of traditional leaders (such as Sunni leader Saeb Salam and the Shi'a leader Kamal al-As'ad). It appears to have understood more quickly the opportunities inherent in this development. The LCP's leadership of the Shi'a in particular has not been uncontested—as the August 1981 battles between al-Amal (a Shi'a militia) and the LCP demonstrate.

The party's top leadership includes George Hawi who is secretary-general of the party. Information about party financing is unavailable. Party headquarters were located on Abu Shakr St., Beirut, before the Israeli invasion.

Organization for Communist Action (OCA)

Created in 1970 from the amalgamation of two leftist organizations—the Movement of Lebanese Socialists and Socialist Lebanon, the former a direct descendant of the Arab Nationalists' Movement—OCA has become more moderate than its forebears. Since 1972 OCA has turned its attention away from such ideologically contentious issues as the rift between the Soviet Union and China, focusing instead on regional and local problems. Highly supportive of the Palestinian movement, OCA was one of the first leftist organizations in Lebanon to suggest that a Palestinian state confined to the West Bank and the Gaza Strip might be acceptable. It also has endorsed the adoption of limited reform of the current Lebanese system rather than its immediate and complete overthrow.

Organizationally similar to the Lebanese Communist Party, this group displays all the classic features of a cadre party. Yet OCA declines to describe itself as a party because, although it claims to defend the interests of the Lebanese working class, its members feel they cannot yet assert that they fully represent the working class as a whole. Members are organized in small cells that form the base of the organization; regional committees administer OCA policy adopted by the Central Committee. The organization's Political Bureau, which meets more frequently than the Central Committee, the secretary-general (Mohsen Ibrahim), and the members of the Secretariat of the Central Committee (notably Fawaz Trabulsi) all play instrumental roles in the formulation of OCA policy.

Membership and financial statistics for the organization are unavailable. The party's militia fought against Israeli troops in Lebanon. The Organization of Communist Action's headquarters were located on Rue de l'Université Arabe, Beirut, before the Israeli invasion.

Progressive Socialist Party (PSP)

This anomalous party was founded in 1949 by Kamal Jumblat, the feudal leader of the schismatic Muslim Druze sect. Jumblat was able to call upon the personal loyalty of many of his followers to support the party. Yet, while most of its members are Druze, the party has exercised an influence on Lebanese politics disproportionate to the relatively small size of the Druze community. Jumblat's leadership qualities and the party's secular, socialist ideology largely account for this; these two factors also provided the basis for Jumblat's leadership of the Lebanese National Movement. Jumblat's son, Walid (born 1949), assumed the presidency of the PSP in 1977 and the chairmanship of the LNM in 1980.

The party has participated in numerous governments and currently holds four seats in the Chamber of Deputies, down from the six it won in the 1960 and 1964 elections. Since 1951 it has always had at least three seats in the Chamber of Deputies, and prominent members of the party have held numerous cabinet portfolios.

The president of the party, along with the Leadership Council consisting of the president and eleven top party officials, set policy for the party. The General Committee, which meets annually, has a limited consultative role; it elects the president and half the members of the Leadership Council to renewable four-year terms. The basic party unit is a branch; three branches constitute a

district. The party's rank and file exercise little power over decision making.

Believing that confessionalism disrupted the unity and harmony inherent in Lebanese society, Kamal Jumblat opposed the confessional distribution of power and the communal court system of Lebanon. In their stead he proposed a nonaligned, secular, socialist society in which class and communal competition would have no place. Although he had misgivings about the structure of the legislative system, he believed in parliamentary government and did not propose its elimination, only its reconstitution. Jumblat, and now his son Walid, are also identified with support for the Palestinian movement.

In the late 1960s the party claimed to have 10,000 members, half of them living in the Shouf region of Mount Lebanon. Estimates indicate that the current membership may be slightly larger. The party publishes the weekly, *al-Anba'*. Information regarding party financing is unavailable.

The unique leadership of Kamal Jumblat is sorely missed by the party. However, Walid Jumblat has readily assumed the responsibilities of his inherited social and political position. The party has demonstrated its resiliency through two civil wars and shows every sign of continuing to constitute an important component of the combined leftist forces in Lebanon. Party headquarters could be reached at P.O. Box 2893, Zkak al-Blat, Beirut, before the Israeli invasion.

Syrian National Social Party

Established in November 1932 by Antoun Sa'adeh, this party was banned from political life for many years. Its opposition to French mandate rule, its call for armed rebellion against the Lebanese government in July 1949 (for which Sa'adeh was executed), and a failed coup attempt in December 1961 did little to endear the party to the authorities. The Lebanese government was especially alarmed by Sa'adeh's promotion of the concept of a single "natural" Syrian nation consisting of Lebanon, Palestine, Jordan, Syria, Iraq, Kuwait, and Cyprus. And the party's connection with Italian fascism and German Nazism (the party's symbol is based on the swastika) was also a source of concern.

While Antoun Sa'adeh was alive, he functioned as the party's absolute leader. Today, the party is led by its Supreme Council and the party's leader, elected by the Supreme Council to a three-year term. The Supreme Council's nine members are elected to three-year terms by the party's "trustees" (life members). An administrative Council of Commissioners supervises the work of several bureaus in charge of foreign affairs, defense, and so forth. At the local level, party members are organized into neighborhood sections. Information about party financing is not available. The party publishes a weekly, *Sabah al-Khayr*, and a monthly, *Fikr*.

In the early 1970s, liberal tendencies within the party began to appear, precipitating the alienation and departure of the dissident right-wing from the party in March 1975. The left wing of the party, led by Ina'am Ra'ad, joined the Lebanese National Movement. Its 2,000-strong militia fought in the fiercest battles of the civil war, losing perhaps as many as a quarter of its soldiers. The right-wing faction remained unaffiliated with either the right or the left in the war.

A reconciliation between the two wings was achieved after the civil war, and the combined membership, according to inflated party statistics, numbers approximately 27,000. Although the party's ideology has always been nonsectarian and the membership multiconfessional, it is widely believed that Greek Orthodox and Druze appear in strong numbers in the organization.

Movement of Independent Nasserists (*al-Murabitun*)

This organization took shape during the 1958 Lebanese civil war after then-president Camille Chamoun denounced Egyptian president Nasser, accusing him of interfering in Lebanon's internal affairs. The organization did not become prominent, however, until after Nasser's death in 1970.

Named after some legendary troops in North Africa, al-Murabitun (The Vigilant) from its inception has been headed by Ibrahim Qulaylat, who promotes a pan-Arab socialism. The organization is administered by a Leadership Council, which directs a few regional branches and a militia of several hundred. The radio station, Voice of Arab Lebanon, and the organization's weekly, *al-Murabitun*, disseminate its views. The party headquarters were destroyed by Israeli forces, along with the entire block on which they were located.

Al-Murabitun competes with the traditional Sunni and Shi'a leaders for members, attempting, with little success, to organize the myriad Nasserist groups in Lebanon into one front. Its exact membership is unknown, but almost all members are Sunni Muslims. The party has little strength outside Beirut. No financial information about the group is available.

Other Political Forces

Numerous other small organizations, militias, and prominent individuals play minor but not inconsequential roles in the Lebanese system. Some of them, along with various military forces, are considered here.

Armenian Parties

Three Armenian parties operate in Lebanon—the Tashnak Party, founded in 1890 in Russian Transcaucasia; the Hunchak Party, founded in 1887 in Geneva; and the Ramgavar Azadagan Party, established in 1921. The Tashnak Party, the most influential of the three, is pro-Western and promotes free enterprise; the other Armenian parties have leftist leanings. In the late 1960s the Tashnak Party had 2,000 members, all of them Armenian Orthodox, and five representatives in the Chamber of Deputies. In the same period, the Hunchak Party had approximately 5,000 members; and the Ramgavar Azadagan Party had 1,500 members. Although Armenians are Christian, most tried to remain neutral throughout the civil war, and their reluctance to aid the predominantly Christian right-wing forces led to severe clashes. Financial information about the parties is unavailable. The Tashnak Party publishes the daily, *Aztaq*.

Movement of the Disinherited

This organization represents the interests of the largest and most deprived sect in Lebanon, the Shi'a Muslims. It was created in the early 1970s by the religious head of the community, Imam Musa Sadr, who was born in Qum, Iran, March 15, 1928, and took up residence in Lebanon in 1960. Sadr was elected president of the Supreme Shi'a Council in May 1969, a post which he held until his disappearance following a trip to Libya in September 1978.

In the early 1970s, on behalf of not only the Shi'a but other disadvantaged people in Lebanon, Sadr organized a series of demonstrations to draw attention to what he considered government neglect of the south, where many of the Shi'a live. These demonstrations culminated in a huge rally of more than 75,000 in Ba'albek in March 1974. Under Sadr, the Shi'a community became recognized not only as a religious community on equal standing with the Sunni and Christian sects, but as a military force as well with the establishment of the movement's militia, al-Amal (diminutive of Afwaj al-Muqawah al-Lubnaniah, or Contingency of Lebanese Resistance). Amal tended to stay out of the fighting during the civil war, but it has enforced an annual observance of Sadr's disappearance by closing down roads and shops in west Beirut. Membership and financial statistics for the movement are not available.

Sulayman Frangieh

Born June 15, 1910, Frangieh is a former president of the republic (1970–76) and heads the Christian Maronite political group known as al-Maradah (the Giants) based in Northern Lebanon. Once part of the Lebanese Front, Frangieh and his followers fell out with the Kata'ib over Frangieh's determination to eliminate from his stronghold in Zghorta all right-wing military forces other than his own. Frangieh has also accused the Kata'ib of seeking to partition Lebanon and of collaboration with Israel. Pierre Gemayel of the Kata'ib, on the other hand, contends that Frangieh has collaborated with the Syrian-dominated Arab Deterrent Force. Their mutual animosity took on the dimension of a blood feud when members of the Kata'ib killed Frangieh's son, Tony, and thirty-one of his followers June 13, 1978.

Rashid Karamah

Born December 30, 1921, Karamah is a traditional leader of the Sunni Muslim community. He has served as prime minister in several governments, most recently in 1975–76 during the Frangieh presidency. A moderate, Karamah's repudiation of the National Liberal Party and the Kata'ib, and his good relations with Syria and the PLO, have alienated the right wing and many of his traditional supporters. In a similar position are other prominent traditional leaders, including Saeb Salam (born 1905, Sunni, several times prime minister), and Kamal al-As'ad (born 1929, Shi'a, former minister of education and speaker of Parliament). All have found a good many of their disenchanted followers joining secular parties, such as the Lebanese Communist Party and al-Murabitun, which are perceived to be less accommodating to the right wing and less self-interested than the *zu'ama*. However, with the scattering of left-wing forces by the Israeli invasion, Saeb Salam—almost by default—has returned to a position of some prominence.

Military

Lebanon's military forces, because of their confessional composition, have always been hostage to any acute political or military crisis in the country. In the 1958 civil war, for example, the military was withheld from major participation for fear that it would disintegrate along sectarian lines. During the 1975–76 civil war, the 18,000-strong Lebanese army did collapse when the predominantly Muslim rank and file refused to obey the orders of their predominantly Christian officers, including the Maronite commander, Iskander Ghanem. The rival Army of Arab Lebanon was formed when Lieutenant Ahmad Khatib (Sunni) deserted the army with many of his men and their equipment. By the end of the 1975–76 war, more than 50 percent of the military had joined rival militias or had simply gone home. Many continued to collect their salaries even as they fought the army from which they had defected. The government has attempted to reconstruct the military, partly with American aid, but this institution still lacks the physical presence and the prestige to assert itself decisively.

Arab Deterrent Force

The ADF was created at the Riyadh summit of Arab leaders in October 1976 to bring about a general ceasefire that would end the civil war. Consisting of almost 30,000 troops from six Arab states, the force is dominated by a 24,000-man Syrian contingent. The establishment of the ADF and its financial support by the Arab League (with Saudi Arabia footing most of the bill) legitimized the Syrian entry into the civil war with more than 5,000 troops in late May 1976. Although Lebanese president Ilias Sarkis is the titular commander of the ADF, Syrian president Hafez al-Asad, for obvious reasons, has decisive control over the force. Since late 1976 the ADF has clashed with the militias of both the right and the left but has essentially maintained the de facto partition of the country.

Israeli Military

Up to 70,000 Israeli soldiers invaded Lebanon in June 1982 and by early October at least 40,000 remained in the country. At that time they occupied southern Lebanon and portions of the Beqaa Valley and had just withdrawn from all of West Beirut which they took over after the departure of some 14,000 Palestinian fighters, dispersed to eleven countries in the region. Although spokesmen of the U.S. administration expressed hope that both Syrian and Israeli forces would soon withdraw from Lebanon, the ordering of winter uniforms for Israeli troops, and the building of more permanent facilities for them in the south, point to a long-term Israeli occupation of much of the country.

Army for the Defense of South Lebanon

Organized by a former officer in the Lebanese army, Major Sa'ad Haddad (Maronite Christian), this militia was formed in much the same way as the Army of Arab Lebanon. With the help of the Israelis, Haddad controls a 700-square-kilometer area in southern Lebanon, along the Israeli border, which he has declared "the State of Free Lebanon." Haddad's militia carried on running skirmishes with the leftist-Palestinian forces dug in throughout the south below the Litani River and occasionally engaged the Lebanese army and UN forces stationed there. It also assisted the Israeli invasion of Lebanon. Haddad refuses to return control of the territory to the Lebanese government until it evicts the 24,000 Syrian soldiers in the ADF and the Palestinian *fedayeen* operating in Lebanon. Israel remains Haddad's primary source of weapons, ammunition, medical supplies, and money to pay his troops. The recently established radio station of the militia is also supported by millions of dollars in contributions from evangelical groups in the United States.

United Nations Interim Force in Lebanon (UNIFIL)

Established by UN Security Council Resolution 425 in March 1978, UNIFIL has been renewed every six months since then. The force consists of 6,000 men from several countries. It was put into place following the massive Israeli invasion of south Lebanon in March 1978, which resulted in widespread destruction of property and hundreds of civilian deaths. The force has occupied most of the territory from which the Israeli forces withdrew in June 1978. Although UNIFIL has condemned Israeli support of Haddad's militia and has tried to prevent fighting in this area, it generally has failed to maintain peace in the south or reimpose Lebanese-government control there.

National Prospects

The short-term future of Lebanon promises to be dominated by the anarchy which has gripped the country since 1975. Although six years have elapsed since the civil war ended, the government has been unable to reassert its control over the country. Lebanon still suffers from the partial administrative collapse of the government and from the ravages of the Israeli and Syrian armies and the more than forty private militias roaming the country. The failure of the government to establish a nonsectarian army capable of exercising credible force makes unlikely the rapid reimposition of government authority. As long as thousands of Syrian and Israeli troops continue to occupy the country, Lebanon does not control its own destiny. Dismemberment of the Lebanese state into spheres of influence controlled by these outside forces is now a reality for the Lebanese people.

Further Reading

Baaklini, Abdo. *Legislative and Political Development: Lebanon, 1842–1972.* Durham, N. C.: Duke University Press, 1976.

Barakat, Halim. *Lebanon in Strife: Student Preludes to the Civil War.* Austin and London: University of Texas Press, 1977.

Entelis, John P. *Pluralism and Party Transformation in Lebanon: al-Kata'ib, 1936–1970.* Leiden: Brill, 1974.

Hudson, Michael C. "The Lebanese Crisis and the Limits of Consociational Democracy." *Journal of Palestine Studies,* Vol. 5, Nos. 3–4, 1976.

———. *The Precarious Republic: Political Modernization in Lebanon.* New York: Random House, 1968.

Khalidi, Walid. *Conflict and Violence in Lebanon.* Center for International Affairs. Cambridge, Mass.: Harvard University Press, 1979.

Koury, Enver M. *The Crisis in the Lebanese System: Confessionalism and Chaos.* Washington, D.C.: American Enterprise Institute for Public Policy Research, 1976.

Nasr, Nafhat, and Palmer, Monte. "Alienation and Political Participation in Lebanon." *International Journal of Middle East Studies,* Vol. 8, No. 4, 1977.

Salibi, Kamal. *Crossroads to Civil War: 1958–1976.* Delmar, N. Y.: Caravan Books, 1976.

Suleiman, Michael. *Political Parties in Lebanon: The Challenge of a Fragmented Political Culture.* Ithaca, N. Y.: Cornell University Press, 1967.

KINGDOM OF LESOTHO

by Jack Parson, Ph.D.

The System of Government

Lesotho, a nation of 1.5 million people entirely surrounded by South Africa, is a constitutional monarchy. However, since 1970 crucial sections of its constitution have been suspended and power is now exercised by and through the prime minister, Chief Leabua Jonathon. Chief Jonathon's regime dominates a largely nominated Parliament, which includes selected members of opposition parties. Through the army and civil service, the regime has maintained itself in power despite significant continuing political, sometimes violent, opposition.

Lesotho's political system is conditioned by its history and geopolitical position. In the late nineteenth century, the Basotho tribe under King Moshoeshoe I maintained its independence against the expansionist Afrikaner Voortrekkers. The price for survival was the loss of their most fertile land and the acceptance of a British protectorate, leaving the kingdom as a small British colonial island surrounded by South Africa.

Stripped of its more productive agricultural land, the kingdom is dominated by the rugged Maluti mountains. The unproductive land, in conjunction with colonial policy, caused the population to depend upon wages from migrant employment. Today, more than half of Lesotho's adult males, and a significant number of females, work in the mines and factories and on the farms of South Africa. Further, Lesotho imports a major proportion of its food and other consumer goods from South Africa.

The rather harsh colonial period gave way to a period of party politics and elections leading to independence in 1966 under the leadership of Prime Minister Leabua Jonathon and the Basutoland National Party (BNP). The last national election was held in 1970. The BNP appeared headed for defeat when the prime minister suspended the elections, charging the opposition with manipulating the outcome. Since that time the prime minister and BNP have ruled without popular mandate. Although the prime minister has promised a new constitution and elections, he and a small elite supported by the army retain tight control of the state.

Executive

Formally, the king, as head of state, appoints the prime minister and cabinet. The latter is composed of members of both houses of Parliament. In effect, the king, as a constitutional monarch, is obliged to appoint a prime minister and cabinet enjoying majority support in the National Assembly.

The prime minister is executive head of the government and is assisted by the cabinet. Policymaking within the national government is largely consensual, centered on the prime minister's office. A small elite within the BNP together with senior civil servants determine policy which is then approved in Parliament. Implementation of policy is effected in a rather autocratic manner.

Legislature

The constitution provides for a Parliament composed of a National Assembly and Senate. The National Assembly was composed of sixty popularly elected members. The Senate was composed of twenty-two principal chiefs and eleven others nominated by the king.

Following the annulment of elections in 1970, an interim Assembly of ninety-three members was created with a BNP majority, but including twenty-six opposition party representatives. In 1980, Jonathon's government of national unity included three members of opposition parties. However, it is clear that this is representation for an officially sanctioned opposition and does not necessarily represent an accurate assessment of popular feelings.

Judiciary

The High Court is the Superior Court of Record with unlimited original jurisdiction and is also a court of appeal for subordinate courts. There is an appeal beyond the High Court to a court of appeal.

Subordinate courts include nine district magistrates courts as well as fifty-eight local courts and thirteen central courts which are also courts of appeal.

Regional & Local Government

Central government links to the local level are conducted through ministerial administrative officers and the 1,084 chiefs owing allegiance to the principal and ward chiefs.

The Party System

Lesotho has a multiparty system. Three political parties are represented in the Assembly and cabinet. However, given the present semiofficial nature of party representation and the constraints on party activity, it is difficult to assess the relative popular strength or organizational capacity of any of the three major parties.

Basutoland Congress Party (BCP)

The BCP was formed in 1952 under the leadership of Ntsu Mokhele. Its program was strongly nationalist, anti-South African and antichief. Under Mokhele's leadership it won the 1960 elections but lost to the BNP in 1965. It was on the verge of regaining power in 1970 when the elections were suspended. Since that time, the BCP has been in a state of crisis, and is now represented by three factions. Mokhele claims the leadership of the party in exile in Zambia, a "parliamentary" BCP participates in Jonathon's government of national unity, and the BCP "Proper" favors negotiations with the BNP to widen participation in the government. Some sections in exile are presumed to be involved in periodic incidents of political violence in Lesotho attributed to the Lesotho Liberation Army.

Basutoland National Party (BNP)

The BNP was formed in 1958 under the leadership of Leabua Jonathon, a minor chief. The party's original program sought backing from chiefs and their followers and was anticommunist. It is supported informally by a strong and well-organized Roman Catholic Church. The original BNP flirtation with South Africa has turned to vocal opposition to the South African apartheid system.

The party maintains a network of regional and local committees parallel to the hierarchy of chiefs. It is centrally controlled. The BNP derives its strength from its ruling position. Whether the party could win a free general election is questionable.

Marematlou Freedom Party (MFP)

The MFP was formed in 1957, partially over a dispute concerning succession to the kingship. Its support historically has been from sections of the chiefs and its role has been that of a third and minor party.

Other Political Forces

In addition to organized political parties, a number of internal and external groups impinge upon the political process. An elite stratum, based on education and bureaucratic position—and located in the civil service, parastatal bodies, and the educational system—constitutes a pressure group concerning the allocation of resources and Lesotho's South African policy. Some within this stratum wish to see a more radical domestic system including systematic attempts to lessen dependence on South Africa. Others are more concerned to maintain the relatively privileged position of the civil service in the economy which rests upon Lesotho's ties with South Africa.

Migrant workers and their families, although not systematically organized, constitute the largest grass-roots pressure group. Almost all households in Lesotho depend either directly or indirectly on one or more members' employment in South Africa. Domestic and foreign policies must take this fact into account.

The Catholic Church, although perhaps less powerful than formerly, still constitutes an important influence on politics.

The most pervasive entity influencing the political process in Lesotho is South Africa. Its ability to influence Lesotho ranges widely—from the provision of transportation facilities and consumer goods to the imposition of quotas, formal and informal, on the number of Basotho allowed to immigrate on short-term labor contracts. Since independence, Lesotho's foreign policy toward Pretoria has moved from a degree of cordiality to a more assertive and cautiously hostile stance. This foreign-policy position causes certain problems, but also attracts considerable international aid to Lesotho.

National Prospects

Given the constellation of political forces and processes in Lesotho, the future is highly uncertain. Internally, much depends upon the country's ability to resolve the long-standing constitutional crisis and to construct a set of political institutions that can accommodate a diverse array of interests. But doing so would require that the external factor of South Africa be manageable; however, that is beyond the capacity of any internal political actor in Lesotho.

Further Reading

Hirschmann, David. "Changes in Lesotho's Policy Towards South Africa." *African Affairs*, Vol. 78, No. 311, April 1979.

Kowet, Donald. *Land, Labour Migration and Politics in Southern Africa: Botswana, Lesotho and Swaziland.* Uppsala: Scandanavian Institute of African Studies, 1978.

Leys, Roger. "Lesotho: Non-Development or Underdevelopment. Towards an Analysis of the Political Economy of the Labour Reserve." In *The Politics of Africa: Dependence and Development,* Timothy Shaw and Kenneth Heard, eds. London: Longman and Dalhousie University Press, 1979.

"Lesotho." In *Africa South of the Sahara 1981–82.* 11th Ed. London: Europa Publications Limited, 1981.

"Lesotho." In *African Contemporary Record.* New York: Africana Publishing Company, annual publication.

REPUBLIC OF LIBERIA

by Joseph P. Smaldone, Ph.D.

The System of Government

Liberia has been governed by a military regime since the April 12, 1980, army coup which ousted President William R. Tolbert, Jr. Tolbert and twenty-seven others were killed at the presidential mansion; thirteen other high officials were executed ten days later. Some 300 others were arrested. This watershed event abruptly ended a unique 133-year republican tradition, the oldest in Africa, and rule by the True Whig Party (TWP), which had governed continuously since 1877. The coup ended domination of Liberian politics by the Americo-Liberian oligarchy. These descendants of free-born American Negroes, former slaves, and West African ex-slaves who settled the territory in the nineteenth century constitute about 5 percent of Liberia's 1.9 million people.

Executive

The country is ruled by a twenty-two–member People's Redemption Council (PRC) under its chairman, commander-in-chief and head of state Samuel K. Doe. Supreme executive and legislative authority is vested in the PRC, which is composed mainly of former noncommissioned officers who staged the 1980 coup. The PRC rules by decree, the 1847 constitution having been voided and then partly reinstated. All other laws remain in force. Martial law has been in effect since the coup. All civil and political rights have been suspended, and political parties and activities have been banned.

The PRC governs through a seventeen-member cabinet. The original PRC cabinet was comprised of a balance of military personnel, former opposition leaders, and even some of Tolbert's ministers. The civilian cabinet members were given military commissions and rank in July 1981, but subsequent cabinet appointees have not been commissioned. In April 1981 a twenty-five–member national commission was appointed to revise the constitution in preparation for a return to democratic rule, which Head of State Doe has since set for April 12, 1985, the fifth anniversary of the coup.

The suspended constitution, which was based on the American model, provided for a unitary republican form of government with strong executive power vested in a popularly elected president whose term of office was limited after a 1975 constitutional amendment to a single eight-year term.

Legislature

Legislative power under the constitution was vested in a bicameral legislature. The House of Representatives, whose seventy-odd members were elected on the basis of proportional representation, served four-year terms; the eighteen-member Senate (two from each county) had six-year terms. The legislature was more a channel for the distribution of party and political patronage than a law-making body. It initiated no major legislation, never challenged the executive, and often passed important laws without debate. The True Whig Party had no effective political opposition for more than a century, and won elections virtually uncontested.

Judiciary

Before the 1980 coup, the Liberian judicial system was based on a Supreme Court with a chief justice and four associate justices; ten circuit courts with criminal, civil, and probate jurisdiction; numerous subordinate magistrate and justice-of-the-peace courts; and tribal courts to administer customary law in civil matters. All judges were appointed for life by the president.

In April 1980 the PRC dissolved the Supreme Court and established a People's Supreme Tribunal with seven judges appointed by the PRC. It has original jurisdiction over matters of state and is the court of last resort. Renamed the People's Supreme Court in January 1982, it also has jurisdiction over the established people's courts system. Although the circuit and inferior courts initially were disestablished, the PRC restored them in May 1980. The PRC also created a five-member Supreme Military Tribunal to try persons accused of political crimes against the state. As under the republic, all judges are appointed and serve at the pleasure of the head of state.

Regional & Local Government

Liberia is divided into nine counties and six territories, each administered by a superintendent and subordinate officers appointed by the head of state. This structure was adopted in the 1963–64 administrative reorganization which abolished the distinction between the five coastal counties and the three interior provinces, which were transformed into four counties. The counties are further subdivided into districts, subdistricts, territories and their districts, commonwealth districts, and townships. The capital city, Monrovia, is administered directly by the central government. Now as before, local government in Liberia enjoys little fiscal or administrative autonomy, and serves as an extension of a highly centralized government.

The Electoral System

The electoral system was effectively suspended with the April 1980 coup. Until then, the president, vice-president, and members of the legislature were elected by the suffrage of property-owning citizens eighteen years of age or older by secret ballot. Citizens are defined constitutionally as "persons of Negro descent," and only citizens can own land. Elections were the principal mechanism by which the True Whig Party dominated Liberian politics. Handpicked candidates regularly won office virtually uncontested.

The Party System

Although the suspended constitution did not expressly provide for political parties or the right to form them, for more than a century Liberia was effectively a one-party state dominated by the True Whig Party. Opposition parties were not legally proscribed, but organized political dissent was short-lived and usually took the form of a TWP splinter group challenging an incumbent president for reelection.

In the years immediately preceding the coup, the most significant public opposition came from the Progressive Alliance of Liberia (PAL) and the Movement for Justice in Africa (MOJA). The socialist-oriented PAL was founded by Liberian students in the United States in the mid-1970s. It began activity in Liberia in early 1978 and, after a court battle, registered legally in January 1980 as the People's Progressive Party (PPP). However, within three months it was banned after it sought to contest the nationwide municipal elections. It was PAL-sponsored demonstrations against a proposed increase in the price of rice, the country's staple food, that resulted in widespread rioting and looting in April 1979. Police and military units reacted poorly, firing indiscriminately into the crowds; discipline disintegrated as the police themselves turned to looting. In March 1980 PPP's call for a general strike to force Tolbert's resignation led to the arrest of PAL and PPP leaders on charges of sedition and treason. Their trial was to begin on April 14, ironically the anniversary of the Easter 1979 riots, but they were freed in the wake of the coup. The PPP's chairman, Gabriel Baccus Matthews—who envisioned PAL as a revolutionary mass movement of workers, peasants, and students—served as foreign minister in the PRC government until November 1981, and in March 1982 was named director general of the cabinet.

Formed in Liberia in 1973 as a campus-based intellectual movement, MOJA was more organized and ideologically coherent than PAL/PPP. Its leaders—Dr. Togba Nah Tipoteh, former chairman of the Economics Faculty at the University of Liberia, and Dr. Amos Sawyer, a former political science chairman and dean at the university—focused on labor grievances and endorsed industrial action. Sawyer ran as an independent candidate in the Monrovia mayoral election scheduled in November 1979, but the government, doubtless worried about the prospect of a MOJA victory over the previously unchallenged True Whig candidate, postponed the election. After the coup, Tipoteh became minister of economic affairs and planning, but resigned in August 1981 and went into exile. Sawyer was appointed head of the national constitutional commission by the PRC government.

Other Political Forces

Americo-Liberian Elite

Perhaps the most significant yet unpredictable political force in Liberia is the Americo-Liberian elite whose status and interests were so conspicuously identified with True Whig Party dominance.

Although politically intimidated and deprived of political organization since the coup, this group has retained its privileged socioeconomic position. The PRC government has not carried out wholesale political or bureaucratic purges, nor has it appropriated and redistributed the property and wealth of the former political elite. In short, the Americo-Liberians have been stripped of formal political power, but not of the socioeconomic basis of power. It remains to be seen whether this historic and relatively homogeneous elite will reconstitute itself as a coherent political force when the ban on political parties and activities is lifted in preparation for the 1985 elections.

Military

The military, which deliberately had been kept small, poorly equipped, and politically isolated under the republic, has clearly and abruptly become the most decisive institution in Liberian politics. Known as the National Guard after 1962, and now as the Armed Forces of Liberia, the army traces its history to the early days of the republic and its organizational identity to the creation of the Liberian Frontier Force in 1908. Trained and equipped almost exclusively by the United States, the 5,000-man army reflects the basic cleavage in Liberian society, with the officer corps drawn mainly from the Americo-Liberian elite and the enlisted ranks from the tribal population. Until the April 1980 coup, its functions had been limited to frontier defense, internal security, and occasional international deployments such as World War I and II and the United Nations Congo operation. Despite the existence of a 1959 U.S.-Liberian mutual defense pact, between 1950 and 1980 the United States provided only $15.5 million in military material and training to Liberia. However, since the 1980 coup the United States has significantly increased its military-assistance program, which amounted to $12.6 million in fiscal year 1982. The bulk of the funds provides housing for the soldiers. The crucial question now is whether the coup has transformed the military into a permanent political actor.

Organized Labor

The Liberian labor force consists of about 600,000 workers of whom about 120,000 are wage earners. Seventy percent of the labor force is in agriculture, 11 percent in services, 5 percent in industry and commerce, and 14 percent in other occupational categories. Foreigners hold most of the top-level managerial jobs. Most of the indigenous labor force is unskilled and highly mobile, seeking intermittent wage employment to supplement subsistence farming. There was no organized-labor movement to speak of until 1963, when the first labor legislation was passed and labor-management negotiations on the basis of collective bargaining were introduced.

Most of the industrial and commercial workers are organized in occupational unions affiliated with the new Liberian Federation of Labor Unions, a 1980 merger of the Labor Congress of Liberia (founded 1953) and the Congress of Industrial Organizations (founded 1959). These traditionally were headed by well-connected members of the Americo-Liberian elite, many of whom were government officials (President Tubman's son formerly headed the CIO). Hence under the republic, the government sought to control the unions through patronage and paternalism. However, MOJA and PAL managed to mobilize workers in Monrovia against the Tolbert government.

Since the coup the PRC has banned strikes, but removed a long-standing prohibition on the organization of agricultural workers by industrial unions. Despite the ban, several strikes have occurred, which the PRC has thus far successfully contained with a combination of persuasion, threats, and dismissals. Organized labor is now more highly politicized and could become a source of opposition, especially as economic conditions have deteriorated.

Students

Liberian students represent an elite in a society in which only 24 percent are literate and 16 percent attend secondary school. Despite a remarkable increase in budgetary support during the Tolbert years, the government-operated University of Liberia continued to suffer from inadequate resources and facilities, low standards, and political interference. University students, organized since 1955 as the Liberian National Union of Students (LINSU), have been prone to political dissent. This tendency became more pronounced in the late 1970s as both PAL and MOJA sought to mobilize student support.

In December 1981 Head of State Doe expressly extended the ban on political organizations and activity to include students, and authorized university administrators to select student representatives "to coordinate student activities with the faculties on each campus." In January 1982, LINSU formally appealed to Doe to reconsider the ban and restore the students' right to select their own leaders. The PRC, making an object lesson for all, ordered the six student leaders arrested and tried by the Supreme Military Tribunal. The six were sentenced to death by firing squad, but Doe granted them executive clemency. The released students gratefully pledged their cooperation with the PRC.

Students remain a latent political force which the PRC hopes to neutralize.

National Prospects

Political conditions and prospects in Liberia are uncertain at best. The PRC has no particular ideology or program. Although it has survived two years and plans a restoration of elected government in 1985, many formidable problems and obstacles remain. Coordination within the PRC government is poor; personal rivalries threaten to escalate into open political turmoil; and frequent resignations, purges, and plots continue unabated. Economic and social problems are even more intractable, requiring heavy dependence on external assistance.

Further Reading

Clapham, Christopher. "Liberia." In *West African States: Failure and Promise*, John Dunn, ed. Cambridge and New York: Cambridge University Press, 1978.

Hlophe, Stephen S. *Class, Ethnicity and Politics in Liberia: A Class Analysis of Power Struggles in the Tubman and Tolbert Administrations from 1944–1975*. Washington, D.C.: University Press of America, 1979.

Legum, Colin, ed. "Liberia." *Africa Contemporary Record: Annual Survey and Documents 1979–80*. Vol. 12. London and New York: Africana Publishing Co., 1981.

"Liberia." *Africa South of the Sahara 1981–82*. 11th ed. London: Europa Publications, 1981.

Liebenow, J. Gus. "The Liberian Coup in Perspective." *Current History*, Vol. 80, No. 463, March 1981.

Lowenkopf, Martin. *Politics in Liberia: The Conservative Road to Development*. Stanford, Calif.: Hoover Institution Press, Stanford University, 1976.

Okolo, Julius Emeka. "Liberia: The Military Coup and Its Aftermath." *World Today*, Vol. 37, No. 4, April 1981.

U.S. Department of State, *Background Notes: Liberia*, publication 7991. Washington, D.C.: U.S. Government Printing Office, August 1967, May 1973, May 1977, April 1979, December 1981.

U.S. Department of State, *U.S. Policy Toward Liberia*, Current Policy no. 210. Washington, D.C.: U.S. Government Printing Office, August 19, 1980.

SOCIALIST PEOPLE'S LIBYAN ARAB JAMAHIRIYA
(Al-Jamahiriyah al-Arabiya al-Libya al-Shabiya al-Ishtirakiya)

by Ronald Bruce St John, Ph.D.

The System of Government

The Socialist People's Libyan Arab Jamahiriya, a nation of three million people, is a unitary state governed by a unique organization of congresses and committees. This system of government evolved slowly after the Libyan Free Unionist Officers Movement, led by a Central Committee of twelve officers, executed a well-planned *coup d'état* on September 1, 1969, and overthrew the monarchy which had ruled the United Kingdom of Libya since independence in 1951.

The Central Committee soon renamed itself the Revolutionary Command Council (RCC), and on December 11, 1969, it replaced the 1951 constitution with a Constitutional Proclamation, which described the Libyan Arab Republic as a free Arab democratic republic constituting part of the Arab nation. Islam is the religion of the state and its objective is overall Arab unity.

The RCC is designated the highest authority in the Libyan Arab Republic and exercises both executive and legislative functions. As such, it is empowered to take whatever measures it deems necessary to protect the regime or the revolution. Such measures may take the form of proclamations, laws, orders, or resolutions. The Constitutional Proclamation specifically gives the RCC power to declare war, conclude and ratify treaties, appoint diplomatic envoys and receive diplomatic missions, proclaim martial law, and control the armed forces.

The RCC is further empowered to appoint a Council of Ministers consisting of a prime minister and ministers; the Council's function is to implement the state's general policy as defined by the RCC. The RCC may also dismiss the prime minister and ministers; the prime minister's resignation automatically results in the resignation of the entire Council of Ministers.

The 1969 Constitutional Proclamation was to remain in force until the completion of the so-called nationalist democratic revolution, when it would be superseded by a permanent constitution. This has never occurred; and since Libya's political system has experienced continuous change since the overthrow of the monarchy, the system functioning today bears little resemblance to the one detailed in the proclamation. Moreover, there is some doubt as to whether the Constitutional Proclamation will *ever* be replaced by a constitution. The *Green Book*, the economic and political manifesto of Colonel Muammar al-Qaddafi, de facto ruler of Libya, describes man-made law, including constitutions, as illogical and invalid, concluding that the genuine law of any society is either tradition (custom) or religion.

Executive

Colonel Qaddafi, initially chairman of the RCC, is the head of state. The general secretary of the General People's Congress (GPC) is the chief executive, and the General Secretariat of the GPC is the chief executive's staff and advisory body. The General People's Committee (or General Popular Committee), comprised of a general secretary and twenty secretaries, serves as a cabinet, replacing the former Council of Ministers, abolished in 1977.

Colonel Qaddafi was the general secretary of the GPC from 1977 until early 1979, when he relinquished the post to concentrate on what he described as "revolutionary activities with the masses." He has retained his position as de facto commander-in-chief of the armed forces and adopted the new title of leader of the revolution. During Qaddafi's tenure as general secretary of the GPC, the remaining members of the RCC initially formed its General Secretariat. They also resigned their posts in 1979 to focus on revolutionary activities. Regardless of position or title, Qaddafi and the former members of the RCC control and direct the Libyan government. Members of the General Secretariat of the General People's Congress are selected by them and serve at their convenience. Members of the General Secretariat, in turn, appoint members of the General People's Committee who serve three-year terms.

The objectives of the revolution have remained constant since the overthrow of the monarchy and can best be summarized within the major goal statements of freedom, socialism, and unity. The emphasis on freedom is the result of Libya's long history of foreign domination and exploitation. In practical terms, it means complete political and economic independence from any foreign direction or control. Through socialism, more often referred to as social justice, the revolution seeks to insure equal access to law and justice, to achieve a more equitable distribution of wealth, and to eliminate class differences. With the issuance of part two of Qaddafi's *Green Book* in 1977, the socio-economic revolution in Libya became increasingly radical and pervasive. Unity is sought both domestically and internationally. On the national level, the objective is to unite society in purpose and effort by a centralized political authority. Internationally, the goal is overall Arab unity, and in pursuit of it, the government repeatedly has proposed mergers with neighboring Arab states.

Legislature

The national-level representative body is called the General People's Congress (GPC), which was created in 1976. Delegates to the GPC are usually the chairmen of the basic people's congresses and the branch or municipal people's committees, as well as representatives from the university student unions and the national federation of unions and professional associations. The number of delegates varies from session to session, but generally approximates 1,000.

Scheduled to meet annually, normally for two weeks in November or December, the GPC is the major arena in which the plans, programs, and policies of the government are discussed and ratified. Formal ratification carries with it the responsibility for implementation by the people's committees, people's congresses, and trade unions and associations. At its first session in 1976, the General Secretariat of the GPC began submitting major government policies and plans to the GPC for review and authorization. Both the general administrative budget and the 1976–80 development budget were submitted, for example, as well as several major domestic and foreign policy items. Thereafter, this practice was continued. At the fifth session of the GPC (January 1–6, 1980), for example, a progress report on the 1976–80 five-year plan and a draft of the 1981–2000 national socio-economic plan were discussed, as were a wide range of other domestic- and foreign-policy questions ranging from an amendment to the social security law to the bilateral pacts which Libya had concluded with other states in 1979. Nevertheless, there are limits to the subjects the head of state will allow on the GPC agenda. Libya's intervention in Chad, for example, was not discussed at the sixth session of the GPC (January 3–7, 1981).

With the abolition of the RCC and the Council of Ministers in 1977, both executive and legislative power was theoretically vested in the GPC. In reality, the GPC has delegated much of its major responsibility to the General Secretariat and the General People's Committee. In December 1978, for example, the GPC authorized the General People's Committee to appoint ambassadors and the secretary of foreign affairs to receive the credentials of foreign diplomats.

The fourth session of the GPC (December 1978) illustrated some of the limits of its power and authority. In the first two days of the congress, several representatives called for an increase in salaries, although the recently published second part of the *Green Book* had called for their abolition. Other representatives demanded an end to the military draft after the General Secretariat had announced universal conscription for all young people. As a result of these and similar actions, the meeting was adjourned on the third day, officially out of respect for the death of the president of Algeria. Unofficially, delegate independence convinced the general secretary and the General Secretariat that they had to reassert their control over the revolution. After the adjournment, several People's Committees were told to select new members before the GPC reconvened, and mobile election teams representing the government were dispatched to monitor those reelections.

While the general secretary and General Secretariat closely supervise the activities of the GPC, the latter does serve as a clearing house and sounding board for the views of the Libyan people as transmitted by their representatives on the congresses, committees, and functional organizations. Moreover, for the first time in the nation's history, subnational government requires popular participation in the selection of local leadership and allows popular involvement in the local policy-making process. At the same time, it provides an effective organization for the national leadership to communicate their ideas and objectives to the people. In this regard, while Colonel Qaddafi and the former members of the RCC remain the primary decision makers, the current political system has produced a level of representation and participation hitherto unknown in Libya.

Judiciary

From the beginning, the RCC indicated that it intended to place the nation's entire juridical system in an Islamic context. On October 28, 1971, the RCC established a Legislative Review and Amendment Committee, composed of the leading legal experts in Libya, to make existing laws conform with the basic tenets of the Islamic code of law, the Shari'ah. Two years later, the RCC promulgated a law which merged the existing civil and Shari'ah courts into a single juridical system.

The revised court system consists of four levels: partial court, court of first instance, appeals court, and the Supreme Court. The Partial court, existing in most villages and towns, is the primary level of the system. The Court of first instance serves as a court of appeal for the partial court. In addition, it is the court of original jurisdiction for all matters involving more than 100 Libyan dinars. An Appeals Court sits at each of three cities: Tripoli, Benghazi, and Sabhah. As its name suggests, it hears cases referred from a court of first instance. The Appeals Court has no original jurisdiction except for cases involving felonies or high crimes. The Supreme Court sits in Tripoli and is composed of five chambers specializing in civil and commercial, criminal, administrative, constitutional, and personal matters. Each chamber consists of a five-judge panel with the majority establishing a decision. Before its formal abolition, the RCC appointed all judges; now, they are appointed by the GPC with the General Secretariat

and the secretary of justice probably making the actual decision. With the exception of political cases, both judicial independence and due process of law generally appear to have been respected since 1969.

In addition to the regular court system, certain other bodies are involved in the administration or enforcement of justice. The Supreme Court for Judicial Authorities plays an administrative role, supervising and coordinating the various courts. The prime responsibility of the Council of State is to deliver advisory legal opinions for government bodies on draft legislation or other actions or regulations they are contemplating. A People's Court has been convened periodically to try crimes against the state. Plots and conspiracies against the state have also been referred to special ad hoc military courts convened for that purpose.

Regional & Local Government

There are three levels of subnational government in Libya: the zone, the municipality or branch municipality, and the national. At the lowest level, zone residents elect a zone people's committee (or popular committee) to administer the affairs of the zone. The zone does not include a congress or legislative body.

The next echelon of government is the municipality. In the case of Libya's larger urban areas, municipalities are divided into branch municipalities; Tripoli, for instance, is divided into five branches. There were approximately 190 municipalities or branch municipalities in 1980, although the total number fluctuates. All zones are components of either a municipality or a branch municipality.

Each municipality or branch municipality elects a legislative assembly known as the basic people's congress (BPC). Meeting quarterly, the BPC makes recommendations or decisions on administrative matters within its jurisdiction, such as roads, sewage, water, and public clinics. The BPC also debates the agenda of the GPC in advance of its annual meeting. The BPC selects its own chairman as well as a five-member people's committee, which has day-to-day administrative responsibility. All voting in the BPC is public—either a show of hands or a division into yes-or-no camps.

In those instances where a municipality is divided into two or more branches, a municipal People's Leadership Committee is established to coordinate the activities of the branch people's committees. The municipal people's leadership commitee is made up of the chairman and deputy chairman of the branch people's committees. They select one of their number to be chairman— effectively, the mayor of the municipality. In those municipalities not large enough to be divided into branches, the chairman of the municipal people's committee serves as mayor of the municipality.

In 1978, the General People's Committee at the national level was decentralized to include a similar structure at the municipal level. Municipal general people's committees are elected by the BPC for a term of three years. They are responsible for the coordination of activities between the General People's Committee and the BPC.

In addition to the zone and municipal committees and congresses, Libyan workers are organized into unions or professional associations. Each union or professional association elects its own people's committee (also known as popular committee) to administer its affairs. In turn, these People's Committees participate in the federation of unions at the national level. The national federation of unions and professional associations sends representatives to the GPC to address issues of special relevance to the unions, but these representatives are not allowed to vote on major policy issues. While the unions and professional associations bring necessary expertise to selected issues, Colonel Qaddafi has insisted that their views as citizens be represented through the people's committees and the BPCs.

Libyan universities are managed to a large degree by student unions. Under this system, each college or faculty in Libya's three universities (Tripoli, Benghazi, and Beida) elects a chairman and a committee (also known as cabinet) to administer the college. Representatives of these committees form the university student union which, along with the president of the university, is responsible for running the university. The president of the university serves at the pleasure of the members of the student union. Like unions and professional associations, university student unions attend the GPC in a nonvoting capacity.

A completely new echelon of subnational government, the revolutionary committee, was also established in 1979. Revolutionary committees now exist in virtually all government departments and agencies as well as within the BPCs, the people's committees of the union and professional associations, the university student unions, and the armed forces.

The revolutionary-committee system was established to raise the political consciousness of the people, especially in those areas which seemed to be influenced by traditional or petit-bourgeois ideas or individuals. It was also ex-

pected to counter the growing tendency of BPCs to advocate parochial interests and concerns instead of taking a broader view of the nation's needs. Examples of this latter tendency were the excessive budgetary demands made by BPCs at the Fourth General People's Congress and the reluctance of people's committees west of Tripoli to support the reallocation of coastal farming land.

Revolutionary committees report directly to Qaddafi. Colonel Qaddafi convenes the revolutionary committees both individually and en masse. Since all members are self-proclaimed zealots, the revolutionary committees have become the true cadres of the revolution. In the words of Colonel Qaddafi, "the People's Committees exercise administrative responsibilities while the Revolutionary Committees exercise revolutionary control."

The Electoral System

The Declaration of the Establishment of the People's Authority declares that direct popular authority is the basis for the political system in the Socialist People's Libyan Arab Jamahiriya. The people exercise their authority through the people's committees, people's congresses, unions and professional associations, and the General People's Congress. Elections are direct, and all voting consists of a show of hands or a division into yea-or-nay camps. Suffrage and committee/ congress membership are open to all Libyan citizens eighteen years of age or older in good legal and political standing.

In theory, the residents of each zone elect their own people's committee. Similarly, the residents of each branch municipality or municipality elect their own basic people's congress. The members of a BPC then elect a chairman and a five-member branch or municipal people's committee. The General People's Congress is made up of the chairmen of the BPC, the branch and municipal people's committees, and representatives of the people's committees for unions, professional associations, and student unions.

In reality, the revolutionary committees severely limit the democratic process by closely supervising committee and congress elections at the branch and municipal levels of governments. Revolutionary committees scrutinize the professional and revolutionary credentials of all candidates for the basic people's congresses, professional people's committees, and the municipal General People's Committees; only approved candidates actually stand for election.

The Party System

The RCC continued the monarchy's ban on the organization and operation of political parties. The December 1969 Decision on the Protection of the Revolution, the Penal Code, and Law No. 71 of 1972 effectively render political-party activity of any sort a crime and constitute a strict legal injunction against unauthorized political activity.

Like many Islamic thinkers, Colonel Qaddafi rejects the political-party system—not because it is fundamentally incompatible with the Koran or the Shari'ah—but rather because he is unfavorably impressed with party organization and competition. In the *Green Book*, he describes the political party as the modern dictatorial instrument of governing and the party system as an overt form of dictatorship.

Qaddafi's condemnation of the political-party system is multifaceted. He argues that political parties, because they are generally made up of people of similar beliefs, represent and promote the interests of only a segment of society. Such segments form parties to attain their ends and impose their doctrines on society as a whole. Moreover, in such a system, competition between parties frequently escalates, often resulting in the dominant party or parties ignoring the rights and interests of minority-party members. In a final criticism, Qaddafi argues that political parties, in their struggle to gain power, often destroy the accomplishments of their predecessors, even if those accomplishments were for the general good. His solution to these dilemmas is the system of congresses and committees which he has established.

General People's Congress System

The development of Libya's current political system has been an evolutionary process which very likely is still incomplete. To understand this system and how it functions, it is necessary to trace its progress from the traditional, tribal-based monarchy, which the RCC overthrew in 1969, to the formal Declaration of the Establishment of the People's Authority in 1977.

The members of the Revolutionary Command Council shared similar backgrounds, motivations, and world views. Most were from lower-middle-class families and minor tribes and attended the Libyan military academy at a time when a military career offered opportunities for higher education and upward socio-economic mobility. The language of the RCC was the language of Arab nationalism guided by the precepts of the Koran and Shari'ah, strengthened by a conviction that only the revolutionary government understood and spoke for the masses.

The September 1 *coup d'état* was completed without the participation of any organized civilian groups, and, initially, the RCC maintained the military character of the revolution. In the early days, it exercised both executive and legislative functions, enshrining its right to do so in the December 1969 Constitutional Proclamation. Later, the RCC appointed civilians to the Council of Ministers to help operate the government, but even then it reserved supreme authority in all fields for itself. It sat at the top of the pyramid, issuing proclamations, laws, and resolutions; insuring support of the armed forces; overseeing the activities of the government; and creating new institutions to promote the objectives of the revolution.

The RCC's chairman, Colonel Qaddafi, quickly became the dominant figure in the revolutionary government. While never given formal authority over his RCC colleagues, Qaddafi was able to impose his will through a combination of personality and argument. In theory, the RCC functioned as a collegial body with the members discussing issues and policies until enough of a consensus evolved to establish a unified position. In practice, as the revolution unfolded, Qaddafi increasingly exercised the final choice in major decisions, and Libyans increasingly looked to his public statements to guide their own behavior. By 1975, for example, Qaddafi had become the only member of the RCC to initiate major political programs or policies. In this manner (as Fathaly and Palmer point out), Qaddafi attempted both to generate support for the revolution and legitimize its new political institutions through increasingly charismatic leadership. In late 1975, he issued part one of the *Green Book* entitled "The Solution to the Problem of Democracy." Part two followed in the fall of 1977 and part three in early 1979; more parts are expected in the future.

The executive-legislative system comprised of the RCC and the Council of Ministers operated into 1977; however, on September 1, 1976, the seventh anniversary of the revolution, Colonel Qaddafi introduced a plan to reorganize the government. The key feature of his proposal was the creation of a new, national-level representative body called the General People's Congress (GPC) to replace the RCC as the supreme instrument of government.

The details of the plan were included in the Declaration of the Establishment of the People's Authority issued on March 2, 1977. This declaration was not a constitution, as some observers suggested, but its central principle relating to people's authority, coupled with other resolutions adopted at the same time, fundamentally revised the governmental organization described in the 1969 Constitutonal Proclamation. The March 1977 Declaration also changed the name of the country to the Socialist People's Libyan Arab Jamahiriya. *Jamahiriya* was a newly coined Arabic word which has no official definition, but unofficially has been translated as "people's power" or "state of the masses."

Colonel Qaddafi was designated general secretary of the GPC, and the remaining members of the now-defunct RCC comprised the General Secretariat. A General People's Committee was also named to replace the Council of Ministers, whose twenty-six members were termed secretaries instead of ministers.

As soon as the RCC had seized control, it moved to solidify its power base by reducing tribal and regional power and identification, increasing political participation, and implanting new local leadership supportive of revolutionary goals.

In 1970 and 1971, laws were promulgated which established a Ministry of Local Government, increased the power of local authorities to implement the policies of the national government, and redesignated some of the names and boundaries of the existing ten *muhafaza* (provinces or governorates). In this last move, former tribal areas were divided into administrative zones based on population density and geographic divisions. The new zones crossed old tribal boundaries and combined different tribes into a single zone. Rezoning reduced regional identity and accompanying social and political power and relocated traditional administrative centers. It was especially effective when buttressed by supportive actions, such as changing the title of local leadership from shaikh to zone administrator, and replacing traditional leaders with new ones who qualified for leadership on the basis of standardized civil service examinations. The RCC began to replace traditional leaders with modernizing leaders as early as October 1969.

The RCC scrapped this policy of building a core of revolutionary administrators less than two years after its initiation. The fatal weakness of these newly appointed leaders was that they generally lacked the socio-economic background and attitudes towards change necessary to generate popular representation or participation. Consequently, subnational government continued to function largely as a hierarchical administrative system rather than the popular system the RCC desired. In this sense, the performance of the revolutionary administrators mirrored a failure of the RCC both in underestimating the power base of the traditional leadership and in overestimating the appeal of its own socio-economic and political reforms.

On June 11, 1971, Colonel Qaddafi announced the formation of the Arab Socialist Union (ASU), an official mass-mobilization organization patterned after the Egyptian counterpart of the same name. The RCC intended the ASU to become the primary link between the government and the people, filling the void left by the abolition of the tribal system. The ASU system was envisioned as an organization from local to national level which would provide the masses with an opportunity to participate in the establishment and execution of local policies. At the same time, the ASU promised a pervasive network of organizations throughout Libyan society capable both of monitoring citizens at all levels and becoming a source of support for revolutionary policies whenever such support was required. The ASU was conceived of as an organization which mirrored government policy and interests while remaining sensitive to public demands and aspirations.

The ASU was organized at the national, governorate, and basic (local) levels. Both the basic and *muhafaza* units consisted of two main organizations: a congress (or conference) representing the general membership and a committee for leadership. Membership was based both on geography (places of residence) and function (occupation or workplace). Application for membership was made either where the individual lived (a *mudiriya* or *mahalat*) or at the workplace; however, the individual could not join the ASU at both levels. The basic committee consisted of ten people elected by and from the basic congress to serve as its executive body. The governorate congress consisted of two or more representatives elected from each basic unit, with the actual number elected depending on the size of the basic unit's membership. The governorate committee consisted of twenty people elected by and from the congress members. Colleges and universities were considered the equivalent of a single governorate and were treated accordingly. Basic units were created among staff and faculty. Committees at both basic and governorate levels elected secretariats and appointed subcommittees to investigate issues and suggest policies. Membership in the ASU was open to any Libyan citizen of the working people who was eighteen or more years of age, in good legal standing, sound mental health, not a member of the royal family, associated with the previous monarchical government, or specifically barred by the RCC. Working people were defined as farmers, workers, soldiers, intellectuals, and owners of nonexploitive national capital. The charter of the ASU specified that 50 percent of all ASU members must be workers and farmers.

The ASU structure at the national level was the National General Congress (or Conference), a forerunner of the General People's Congress. The Congress was made up of ten, fourteen, or twenty representatives from each governorate depending on the size of the membership of that body. It also included members of the RCC, the Council of Ministers, and delegates from certain functional organizations—such as the army, police, youth and women's organizations—professional associations, and trade unions. The term of the National General Congress, scheduled to meet every two years, was six years. The ASU was firmly controlled by the RCC with Qaddafi serving as president and the other members of the RCC designated the Supreme Leading Authority of the Arab Socialist Union.

The first National General Congress of the ASU, held in March 1972, was attended by representatives from 286 geographical basic units and 85 functional basic units. Membership at that time (according to Habib) was over 300,000 persons out of an eligible membership of some one million. Speakers at the Congress described the ASU not as a political party, but as an alliance of the people's working forces and declared it to be the only organization in Libya permitted to engage in political activity. In addition, Qaddafi and other RCC members openly admitted that they would circumvent normal democratic processes in the transitional stage of the revolution to promote revolutionary change and safeguard against counterrevolutionary action. The probable length of this transitional stage was not discussed.

To a large degree, the ASU was stillborn. The rigid direction and control insisted on by the RCC stifled local initiative and suffocated local leadership. Moreover, the organization was never able to resolve its fundamental contradiction of seeking simultaneously to reflect government interests and articulate local demands. Finally, the ASU was undercut by existing government ministries and orgainzations which viewed it as a competitor for authority.

The year 1972 also marked the passage of Law No. 130, a comprehensive piece of legislation which attempted to rationalize and simplify subnational government. The former district and subdistrict divisions were abolished, thus reducing subnational administration to the governorate and municipality. The principal organ of local government at both levels became the council, which had both executive and legislative powers. At the governorate level, executive power was exercised by the governor; at the municipal level, by the mayor. Both governors and mayors were appointed by the RCC.

A council was created at each of the ten governorates and forty-six existing municipalities. Members on the governorate and municipal councils comprised both appointed and elected seats—many members also belonged to the ASU. Governorate and municipal councils were given the responsibility for implementing the policies of the central government as well as local planning for areas such as health, education, social assistance, agriculture, local industry, and transportation services. All council decisions were subject to review by the prime minister, who could reject them. He was also empowered to dissolve councils. Finally, the Ministry of Local Government was abolished, and its functions were taken over by the Ministry of the Interior.

On April 15, 1973, Colonel Qaddafi proclaimed a popular revolution and called for the Libyan people to elect people's committees. Like the ASU, the people's committee structure was given both a geographical and functional basis. Geographically, committees were formed at the zone, municipal, and governorate levels. At the zone level, direct popular elections were used to fill the seats on the people's committee. Zone committees then elected representatives to constitute the municipal people's committee, and, similarly, municipal people's committee members selected representatives to form the governorate people's committee.

Later in 1973, the RCC promulgated Law No. 78 to clarify the administrative responsibilites of the people's committees. The law transferred the functions and authority of the governorate and municipal councils established in 1972 to the people's committees at the same levels. The chairmen of the governorate people's committees, in effect, became the governors and the chairmen of the municipal people's comittees became the mayors. The RCC also authorized the election of people's committees in public corporations, institutions, companies, and universities as well as in other sectors, such as hospitals, convalescent homes, and government printing plants.

The term of the people's committees were set at three years. Committee members could be removed by a two-thirds vote of the membership. In addition, the RCC reserved for itself the right to dissolve a people's committee at any time or expel one or more of its members. In fact, this had already happened several times during the summer and fall of 1973. In some cases, as many as three or four elections had to be held before a suitably revolutionary group of lower-level employees had emerged as members of the people's committee. The government security services also used the elections to expose and denounce individuals opposed to or simply ambivalent about the objectives of the revolutionary government. The law also empowered the RCC to create new people's committees whenever and wherever needed.

The creation of the people's-committee system was a significant stage in Libya's political evolution. For the first time in Libya's history, the subnational political system actively encouraged popular participation in the selection of local leadership and allowed substantial local involvement in the local policy-making process. With its formation, the RCC increased the political involvement and experience of the Libyan people and focused their attention on the issues of most importance to the local community.

Still not satisfied with the level of popular involvement and participation, at the 1974 National Congress Qaddafi called for a further refinement of the subnational administrative machinery. The Congress responded by stressing the primacy of the people's committees in administrative affairs and by recommending the elimination of the governorates. In February 1975, the RCC issued a law abolishing the governorates and reestablishing a Ministry of Municipalities. Two months later, another RCC law formally established the municipality as the single geographical and administrative subdivision in Libya.

Other Political Forces

Military

The September *coup d'état* was totally military in conception, planning, and execution. It was accomplished without the participation or even knowledge of organized civilian groups. In the early years the RCC insisted on maintaining the military direction of the revolution. Under attack from all facets of the former elite structure, the RCC worked to create a reliable coercive arm capable of sustaining the revolution.

To a certain degree, the military has become the most representative institution in the country; it now draws its membership from all strata of society. Recognizing this fact, Qaddafi has integrated the armed forces and sought to instill in them a spirit of unity, discipline, and professionalism.

Within a year, the military establishment tripled in size, largely due to the merger of regional and specialized security forces; it continued to grow in quantity and quality throughout the 1970s. In May 1978, the government issued a conscription law making military service compulsory; in January 1979, it was announced that women would be conscripted along with men. Expenditures for equipment also increased dramatically throughout the decade and Libya's armed forces entered the 1980s with the highest ratio of military equipment to manpower in the Third World.

The military has rewarded Qaddafi's paternalism with a general absence of major upheavals or open dissension, although there were serious coup attempts in 1970 and 1975. Since then, military opposition has been relatively minor and seldom surfaces except in the form of small unit rebellions such as that staged by an air force unit in Tobruk in August 1980. The motivation for such discontent varies, but has increasingly centered on dissatisfaction with Qaddafi's domestic and foreign policies. While opposition within the armed forces has not been widespread, most observers agree that any significant challenge to the revolution would probably originate within the armed forces, particularly the army, as the military is the only group in the country with the required power and organization.

Petit Bourgeoisie

After 1977, the regime followed an increasingly radical socio-economic policy which included housing redistribution and currency exchange, leading to the state takeover of all import, export, and distribution functions by the end of 1981. The resultant widespread redistribution of wealth and power has directly affected the economic well-being of different sectors of the population, activating dormant political opposition. Particularly affected were the members of the petit-bourgeoisie, which prospered after 1969 as the revolutionary government's emphasis on the service and housing sectors created lucrative opportunities in trade, real estate, and small consumer manufacture.

Opposition is not limited to a single socio-economic group; it also includes farmers, the educated elite, and middle-level and senior-level government officials. Outside the country, opposition exists among student groups and self-imposed exiles with a number of organized opposition groups operating in Western Europe and the Middle East. Few details are known about the organization and activities of these groups.

However, the opposition is badly fragmented and must deal with considerable regime support, especially among the younger, less well-to-do elements of society. This support has been generated by Qaddafi's charismatic leadership and the regime's distributive economic policies. Moreover, in recent years, Qaddafi had taken extraordinary and often violent measures to stifle opposition at home and abroad and to limit any collaboration between domestic and foreign opponents.

National Prospects

After more than twelve years in power, Colonel Qaddafi is now one of the longest established rulers in the Middle East. Assisted by oil revenues, which have generally accounted for some 99 percent of Libya's export earnings since the mid-1960s, he has implemented a series of radical policies which have drastically—and permanently—modified Libya's social, cultural, and material life. Regardless of changes in national leadership, the former socio-economic and political system has been destroyed and the people cannot return to it. In any case, Qaddafi's political position now seems more secure than at any time

in the last decade. In the future, he can be expected to continue to use the revenue from oil reserves, currently estimated at more than thirty years at present allowed production, to maintain and buttress his political position.

Further Reading

Alexander, Nathan [Ronald Bruce St John]. "The Foreign Policy of Libya: Inflexibility Amid Change." *Orbis*, Vol. 24, No. 4 (Winter 1981).

————. "Libya: The Continuous Revolution." *Middle Eastern Studies*, Vol. 17, No. 2 (April 1981).

Allan, J. A. *Libya: The Experience of Oil*. London: Croom Helm, 1981.

el-Fathaly, Omar I., and Palmer, Monte. *Political Development and Social Change in Libya*. Lexington, Mass.: Lexington Books, 1980.

————. Palmer, Monte, and Chackerian, Richard. *Political Development and Bureaucracy in Libya*. Lexington, Mass.: Lexington Books, 1977.

First, Ruth. *Libya: The Elusive Revolution*. Harmondsworth, England: Penguin, 1974.

Habib, Henri Pierre. *Politics and Government of Revolutionary Libya*. Ottawa, Canada: Le Cercle du Livre de France, 1975.

Khadduri, Majid. *Modern Libya: A Study in Political Development*. Baltimore: Johns Hopkins University Press, 1963.

Nelson, Harold D., ed. *Libya: A Country Study*. American University Foreign Area Series. Washington, D.C.: U.S. Government Printing Office, 1979.

al-Qaddafi, Muammar. *The Green Book, Part I: The Solution to the Problem of Democracy*. London: Martin Brian and O'Keefe, 1976.

St John, Ronald Bruce. "Libya's Foreign and Domestic Policies." *Current History*, Vol. 80, No. 470 (December 1981).

GRAND DUCHY OF LUXEMBOURG
(*Grand-Duche de Luxembourg*)

by Gordon Smith, Ph.D.

The System of Government

Luxembourg, a nation of about 360,000 people, is a constitutional monarchy with a parliamentary form of government. The Grand Duchy was created in 1815 with the Dutch king as the first grand duke. Following the Belgian succession from the Netherlands (1830), a portion of the duchy became autonomous (1839), while the rest became the county of Luxembourg in Belgium. Full independence was achieved in 1867; the nation's constitution dates from 1868. The present grand ducal family, the House of Nassau, ascended the throne in 1890.

Executive

The position of the grand duke is hereditary, but the powers of the office are primarily formal. Real executive power lies with the prime minister and his cabinet who are responsible to the Chamber of Deputies.

Legislature

The fifty-nine-member Chamber of Deputies is the sole legislative body. However, the constitution requires legislation approved by the Chamber to be reaffirmed after a three-month interval; this guards against rash or arbitrary action. If this procedure is not followed, the Council of State, a purely administrative body, may impose a suspensory veto on the legislation. The Council of State, consisting of twenty-one members appointed for life by the grand duke, also gives an advisory opinion on all bills before they are put to the Chamber as well as on any subsequent amendments.

Judiciary

The supreme court is the Superior Court of Justice, with sixteen full members, appointed for life by the grand duke as advised by the Superior Court itself. The Superior Court also nominates judges for the lower courts, and members can only be removed by action of the Superior Court. The Superior Court, when sitting as a Court of Cassation, has jurisdiction over questions of law, but no general power of judicial review of legislation.

Regional & Local Government

Luxembourg is divided into twelve cantons which are administrative districts of the central government. Below the cantonal level, each municipality (commune) has a council elected for a six-year term and a mayor (burgomaster) appointed by the council majority. In the larger communes, politics resembles national politics in miniature, with elections based on proportional representation and party lists. As a result, interparty cooperation and coalition are essential. In smaller communes, council members are elected by simple majorities, and personality is usually more significant than party affiliation.

The Electoral System

The Chamber of Deputies is chosen at five-year intervals, although elections may be called sooner if the prime minister chooses, or if the government loses the confidence of the Chamber. In practice, early elections have not been called in recent times, since all postwar governing coalitions have lasted the full legislative period.

Seats are allocated according to a system of proportional representation from lists of candidates presented by the parties. For election purposes the country is divided into four electoral districts; proportionality is determined within the four districts, not nationally.

Voting is compulsory for all citizens age eighteen and older. Each voter has the same number of votes as there are seats for the district. The voter may cast all his votes for a single party list *or* choose specific candidates from several parties. This latter option, known as *panachage*, has the effect of helping to determine both the representation of parties and the final ranking of candidates on the party lists. This possibility of "personalization" benefits parties which present well-known politicians. In this respect, the bourgeois parties appear to gain at the expense of the left-wing parties.

The Party System

Origins of the Parties

The modern party system dates from the beginning of the century with the formation of the Socialist Workers' Party (LSAP) in 1902. Under electoral pressure from the LSAP, the previously unstructured personalist coalitions of bourgeois interests coalesced into the Party of the Right in 1914, and the oldest political formation in Luxembourg, the Liberals, followed suit.

The Parties in Law

The parties are not specifically referred to in the constitution, although their position is safeguarded by its general provisions. A series of electoral laws, beginning with the adoption of proportional representation in 1919, determines in detail the conduct and form of elections, especially the presentation of party lists. Otherwise, the parties are free concerning matters of their internal organization and financing.

Party Organization

Parties in Luxembourg are organized at both a local (communal) and national level. Annual party congresses constitute the primary authority. (The congress of the Communist Party meets every three years.) The strength of cantonal politics means that even the smaller parties are active locally. However, in no case is party membership very high, so that activists tend to determine party policy. The relationship with nonparty organizations—the Catholic Church, and the competing trade union organizations (confessional, secular, and the separate association for salaried employees)—is very important.

Campaigning

Despite the coalition basis of politics, campaigns are hard fought. Partly, given the electoral system, competition is a matter of personality, but there are sharp ideological differences between left and right. The 1979 campaign in particular was marked by charges of a "socialist plot" to turn Luxembourg into a trade-union state. Party newspapers play a significant part in campaigns; the press tends to be markedly partisan.

Independent Voters

The influence of the Catholic Church and the organized labor movement ensures that party identification is high. The flexible system of vote casting, however, does mean that voters can cross party lines, for they have as many votes as there are seats to be filled in the electoral district. The tendency is for voters to give some votes to attractive candidates in parties not strongly opposed to the party of their first choice.

Christian Social People's Party (*Chreschtlich-Sozial Vollekspartei; CSV*)

Originally founded as the Party of the Right (*Partei der Rechten*) in 1914, the CSV took its present name in 1944. It has been the "natural" party of government for many years; until 1974 it had been represented in every government since 1919 and had supplied every prime minister since 1945—with the smaller LSAP and Democratic Party (DP) alternating as junior partners in coalition. However, its dominant electoral position has been declining since the 1950s, and in 1974 it was forced into opposition by a center-left coalition.

In an overwhelmingly Catholic country (94 percent), the CSV enjoys widespread support which is fairly evenly distributed among all ages and classes throughout the country, although the party is affected adversely by urban encroachment and the declining importance of the agricultural sector. Party membership, at 8,000, is higher than for the other parties. Party finance depends partly on membership dues, but there are close links with paraparty organizations, such as the Christian trade-union movement, and the party benefits from its close association with the Catholic Church and the support of the country's leading daily newspaper.

The CSV is fortunate in having a strong, experienced leader in Pierre Werner (born 1913). Werner first became prime minister in 1959 and held the post continuously until 1974, returning once more after the 1979 election. The CSV's proven record in office and its unswerving antisocialist policy may, in the more conservative 1980s, help to stem a long-term decline in the social bases of its support.

Party headquarters are at 38 rue du Cure, Luxembourg-Ville.

Democratic Party
(*Demokratesch Partei; DP*)

The Democratic Party was founded in 1945 and was based partly on the anti-German resistance movement. It was characterized by a strong anti-clericalism which it inherited from its forerunner, the prewar Liberal Party. The DP is now fully in the mainstream of European progressive liberalism, and this change enabled the DP to join forces with the LSAP in 1974 to implement a program of social reform. The party appears to have a secure electoral base in the middle classes and among white-collar employees, especially in the urban area of Luxembourg-Ville. The party is also attractive to floating voters who make use of the *panachage*. Party membership, at about 3,500, is not very high, and finance from this source is low. The party favors free enterprise and, in the tradition of liberalism, stands close to industry. The DP publishes its own daily newspaper.

Until 1980 the DP had a widely popular leader in Gaston Thorn (born 1928), prime minister from 1974 to 1979. In 1981 he became president of the Commission of the European Communities. His successor as leader of the DP, and deputy prime minister in the CSV-led government, is Mme. Colette Flesch (born 1937). The fact that the DP was ready to enter a coalition with the CSV in 1979 suggests the possibility that the center-left experiment was only a temporary arrangement and that governing with the CSV is more suited to the DP's nature. In any case, it is rare for a DP-LSAP combination to have an overall majority in the assembly.

Party headquarters are at 46 Grand rue, Luxembourg-Ville.

Luxembourg Socialist Workers' Party
(*Letzeburger Sozialistisch Arbrechterpartei;* LSAP)

Founded in 1902, the LSAP is a determinedly "working class" party with little sign of ideological weakening. The party has very close links with the trade-union movement, especially with the

Letzeburger Arbechterverbund (Luxembourg Workers' Association), the left wing of a union movement which is sharply divided along ideological and confessional lines. (During the 1974–79 coalition period, the LSAP actively promoted programs to increase the authority and unity of the trade-union movement.) In spite of its proworker stance, the LSAP joined several governments with the CSV prior to its 1974 coalition with the DP, a fact less surprising considering the affiliation of the Christian unions to the CSV. Party support and membership comes largely from trade unionists, especially manual occupations. Party membership is 6,000. Party finance relies on membership dues and trade-union support. The LSAP also publishes its own daily newspaper with a relatively large circulation.

Unlike the CSV and the DP, the LSAP fails to project a significant personality as leader and this reflects the nature of the party. The present leader (president) of the LSAP is Mme. Lydie Schmit. The party has only once (1964) overtaken the CSV in the share of the vote, and it appears that its rather traditional socialist image may prevent the LSAP from ever becoming a dominant force.

Party headquarters are at 63 rue de Bonnevoie, Luxembourg-Ville.

Minor Parties

Communist Party of Luxembourg
(*Kommunistesch Partei vun Letzeburg;* KPL)

The KPL was founded in 1921 as a breakaway from the LSAP. For many years the KPL had the reputation of being the most intransigent of all communist parties in Western Europe; it alone welcomed the Soviet invasion of Czechoslovakia in 1968. Subsequently, it adopted a more critical stance, but its share of the vote has steadily declined since the "pre-Czechoslovakia" election of 1968. The KPL's strongest support comes from the area of heavy industry in the south of Luxembourg.

Social Democratic Party
(*Sozial-Demokratesch Partei;* SKP)

The Social Democratic Party split from the LSAP in 1971 over the latter's willingness to cooperate with the communists in local government and over the extent of trade-union influence on the LSAP. Though the SDP deprived the LSAP of several of its leading members, the party does not appear to threaten the older organization: the SDP

Elections to the Luxembourg Chamber of Deputies (1959–1979)					
	1959 %	1964 %	1968 %	1974 %	1979 % Seats
CSV	38.9	35.6	37.4	29.8	36.4 24
LSAP	33.0	35.9	30.9	26.9	22.5 14
DP	20.3	12.2	18.0	23.3	21.9 15
KPL	7.2	10.4	13.1	8.7	4.9 2
SDP	—	—	—	10.1	6.4 2
Others	—	5.9	—	—	8.3 2

has not participated in government and its vote fell sharply in 1979. Membership is about 2,000, and its support comes mainly from middle-class and nonunionized voters.

Other minor parties have not been of particular importance for Luxembourg politics, and they are usually ephemeral. The "Alternative List," a loose coalition favoring the "new politics" of environmental and antinuclear concerns, attracted only about one percent of the vote in 1979. More significant—and ususual—for a protest movement was the support given independent socialists and the *enrolés de force* when they fought on a common list in 1979 and obtained 7 percent of the vote. The *enrolés* represent a single-issue group seeking compensation from West Germany for those who were forcibly recruited into the German army during World War II.

National Prospects

Luxembourg presents a picture of relative political stability, and its position as a founding member of the European Economic Community (with Gaston Thorn now president of the Communities Commission) means that the duchy has an international influence quite disproportionate to its size. Domestic politics, after the center-left coalition ended in 1979, have reverted to the traditional Christian-Social style of rule. Nonetheless, the economic difficulties of recent years, in particular the long-term decline of the steel industry, have led to tensions in labor relations which are likely to be exacerbated with the LSAP out of government.

Further Reading
Herchen, A. *History of the Grand Duchy of Luxembourg.* Luxembourg: Linden, 1950.
Hirsch, M. "European Elections: Luxembourg." *West European Politics*, May 1980.
——— "Luxembourg." In *Political Parties in the European Community*, S. Henig, ed. London: George Allen and Unwin, 1979.
Holt, S. *Six European States.* London: Hamish Hamilton, 1970.
Weil, G. L. *The Benelux Nations: The Politics of Small Country Democracies.* New York: Holt, Rinehart and Winston, 1970.

DEMOCRATIC REPUBLIC OF MADAGASCAR

(République Démocratique de Madagascar [French]; Repoblika Demokratika Madagasikara [Malagasy])

by Philip M. Allen, Ph.D.

The System of Government

Madagascar, a sparsely populated island country of nine million people in the western Indian Ocean, has a strong presidential system which relies on informal compromises and accommodations among ethnic, economic, and bureaucratic interests. These interests are largely represented by several parties which make their influence felt more in the bureaucracy and state corporations than in the legislature.

The French conquest of the island in 1886 imposed a regime of mercantile exploitation on what had been a relatively well-developed centralized monarchy dominated by the Merina aristocracy of the island's central plateau. As the Malagasy Republic, the island became autonomous within the French Community in 1958. Under the independent First Republic, led by President Philibert Tsiranana from 1960 to 1972, the Merina continued to control intellectual and professional life, the civil service, and those sectors of commerce not monopolized by French companies and their resident Indian and Chinese partners. Both the French and Tsiranana, however, favored the various coastal ethnic groups in a divide-and-rule policy designed to deprive the Merina of significant political power.

In 1972, popular unrest forced Tsiranana to turn over the government to his army commander in chief who supported a relatively peaceful but revolutionary nationalist resurgence, hitherto associated with the Merina middle class. The complex French colonial fabric of banking, plantation agriculture, oligopolist trade, and controlled industrial projects was gradually abolished; the French military presence on the island was ended; and the country adopted a conscientiously non-aligned foreign policy.

While the break with France was never as complete as rhetoric made it seem, Madagascar began to develop a bureaucratic structure of state corporations and interlocking political institutions dominated by a congeries of Malagasy elites who agreed with one another only on the nationalist purpose of the program.

Executive

Following a three-year transition in which three military chiefs of state sought to implement the revolutionary idea of 1972 without sacrificing continuity, the Second Republic took shape in a new constitution submitted to referendum on December 21, 1975. An executive president, elected by direct universal suffrage for a seven-year term, governs through a Supreme Council of the Revolution (CSR); two-thirds of the twenty-one Council members are appointed by the president, who chairs its sessions and approves the list of remaining members submitted to him by the legislature. The president also appoints his prime minister and endorses the list of government ministers who carry out CSR policy.

Having served the first three years of the revolution as foreign minister and leader of its so-called radical wing, Didier Ratsiraka, a navy captain, was named chief of state by the CSR on June 15, 1975, and was subsequently confirmed by 92 percent of the voters in a referendum. Ratsiraka was reelected to a seven-year term in November 1982.

Ratsiraka does not have a popular power base. His political position depends in part on his capacity to divide and rule a fractious coalition called the Advance Guard of the Malagasy Revolution (AREMA). Policy formation consists of compromises between the practical and ideological requirements of nationalist interests and the interests of bureaucratic and business classes still tied to French and other international arrangements, many of them necessary. France remains Madagascar's principal trade partner and source of capital. An unpublicized but evident arrangement with the Bank of France provides backing for the nonconvertible Malagasy franc (FMG) despite dissolution of formal links with the franc zone.

Secluded in his fortified residence and protected by security agencies and their secret police, the president regularly denounces domestic and foreign conspiracies against him. In January 1982, true to the typical Malagasy blend of fact, reticence, and imagination, the president's brother-in-law, commander of one of the presidential security services, reported the discovery and abortion of a plot against Ratsiraka that allegedly involved foreign mercenaries, local politicians, and a Catholic priest. Close Malagasy affinities with the Seychelles archipelago suggested to the government that the plot was somehow related to the commando team that had failed to overthrow the Seychelles government the previous November. At the same time, Ratsiraka is responsible for Madagascar's assertion of its African and Indian Ocean affinities and has developed openings to the Soviet Union, North Korea, Cuba, and other socialist states without entirely sacrificing French interests in the island.

Legislature

The 137-seat National People's Assembly is renewed every five years by direct suffrage. The legislature has limited powers, meeting for only four months in the year, and requiring a two-thirds majority to overturn a government budgetary or other proposal. Although the body is relegated to an essentially rhetorical utility in the complex Malagasy system, its debates have occasionally dramatized national problems and executive deficiencies. In June 1981 and May 1982, parliamentary leaders called general attention to inefficiencies and corruption in public services, managing even to penetrate the otherwise suffocated national press. New elections, technically due before the end of June 1982, were postponed for a year on a financial pretext which served to protect the 1982 presidential reelection from the complications of a recriminatory legislative campaign.

Judiciary

Civil and criminal procedures in Madagascar conform largely to French legal codes and juris-

prudence; the High Constitutional Court determines the constitutionality of laws, electoral disputes, and conflicts between central and local authorities. High Constitutional Court judges are elected by the National Assembly, but most appeals to the court must first be approved by the president. A parallel system of courts, which makes its own rules, handles political and security cases, using the several intelligence agencies and the gendarmerie for enforcement. Madagascar has encountered steady criticism in international human rights commentary for its lengthy detention periods, the torpor of its military-trial system, and alleged torture of political prisoners.

Regional & Local Government

Coordination between the central authority and local populations has eluded all regimes in this large island of relatively isolated and autonomous regions linked only by extraordinarily deficient road, rail, air, and radio ties. The First Republic had sought to knit the provinces to the capital, Antananarivo, by a dominant political party network that permitted mandarinates for local leaders in alliance with overseas French and local Chinese and Indian entrepreneurs. The inefficacy of this structure became increasingly apparent through the 1960s, inviting a dramatic peasant revolt in 1971 and the alliance of urban intellectuals and labor which brought down the Tsiranana government a year later.

Even before the accession of Ratsiraka in 1975, the revolutionary solution for Madagascar's structural incoherence took the form of a revival of the *fokonolona* (village council) system implemented by the Merina monarchy of the nineteenth century. Genuine powers of taxation, public borrowing, rural production and marketing control, police and public services are bestowed on 11,400 village and urban-district councils (*fokontany*) of directly elected officials. The councils are grouped into a hierarchical structure of representative bodies—*firaisana* or cantons, *fivondrono* which correspond to prefectures, and six *faritany* or provinces. In theory, this decentralized system replaces the old apparatus of appointed prefects and sub-prefects who supervised elected communal officials. In actuality, the president's coalition, AREMA, holds 89.5 percent of the 73,000 electoral positions at the several levels of local government, and central policies are conveyed from national party headquarters through these channels to the putatively autonomous local apparatus. Central government technical expertise, attached to the local economic committees (*vatoeka*), also enforces a Malagasy version of "democratic centralism."

Disputes have arisen between the local administrative units and the state enterprises which are held responsible for interregional and foreign trade. A recent proposal for the institution of a coffee project in Antananarivo province on the plateau was rejected by the central government because of an unspoken agreement that coffee growing was the monopoly of the coast *faritany*.

Marketing inefficiencies, profiteering, and black market operations have contaminated the division of national and local responsibilities and diminished popular participation. In early January 1982, voters in Antsiranana province (formerly Diego-Suarez) voted to recall the *faritany* chief and seven of nine *fivondrono* presidents because of corruption and malfeasance. Refusal by the Interior Ministry to honor this constitutional recourse led to violent confrontations between police and rioting citizens in several northern towns.

The Electoral System

Political participation revived in 1976 after four years of transitional military rule. Respecting the vast diversity of Malagasy loyalties—regional, ethnic, and class—Ratsiraka restricted participation only by requiring overt acceptance of his generally socialist and anti-imperialist program. Elections for legislative and local government representation took place in 1977, with the traditionally acquiescent electorate (universally enfranchised at eighteen years of age) supporting candidates proposed by central authority. The government claimed an 88 percent turnout, although other sources estimate the participation as somewhat lower. With 60 percent illiteracy, the electorate chooses ballots marked by party symbols and colors.

The Party System

Malagasy parties first appeared in preparation for the 1958 elections. Most were formed as affiliates of mother parties in France. Chief among these was the *Parti Social Démocrate* (PSD) of Philibert Tsiranana, the first president of Madagascar. The primary Malagasy party without immediate ties to France was the Congress Party for the Independence of Madagascar (AKFM), a coalition of several pro-independence groups.

In 1982, authorized political parties were grouped for purposes of national unity into a loose National Front for the Defense of the Revolution (FNDR). Each party may share power within the CSR and other institutions of state. In practice, however, the vast divergence between interests and personalities has tended to neutralize the FNDR as a genuine political body. Two parties (National Movement for the Independence of Madagascar and Militants for Power to the People) have entered and left the Front on several occasions, and Ratsiraka has usually had to govern through his own coterie of loyal Advance Guard of the Malagasy Revolution adherents.

Advance Guard of the Malagasy Revolution
(*Avant-Garde de la Révolution Malagasy;* AREMA)

AREMA holds 112 of the 137 National Assembly seats and almost 90 percent of local elected offices. A personal creation of President Ratsiraka, AREMA is far from a monolithic power bloc. It includes a strong militant wing, cutting across age and geographical lines, with ideological influence from North Korea and other socialist models. However, the party also contains prominent representatives of the Merina bourgeoisie and other more "pragmatic" (albeit nationalistic) interests, as well as sheer opportunists and unreconstructed Social Democrats from the Tsiranana First Republic. In early 1982, the Merina moderate faction seemed to lose considerable influence with the disappearance from the cabinet of former finance and planning minister Rakotovao Razakaboana, a liberal economist once regarded as a potential rival to the president.

Congress Party for the Independence of Madagascar
(*Antokon'ny Kongresy ho'any Fahaleovantenan'i Madagasikara;* AKFM)

The AKFM was formed in 1958 to campaign for outright independence, rather than the French Community solution proposed in General de Gaulle's Fifth Republic constitution. It lost that vote, but remained as the principal opposition party in the First Republic, usually holding three seats in the old National Assembly, as well as the city administration of the capital, Antananarivo. Its leader since 1958, Pastor Richard Andriamanjato, has been repeatedly reelected as mayor of the capital. Still limited primarily to the Merina intellectual and professional elite of the city, the AKFM nevertheless defines itself as a "scientific socialist" party of Soviet inspiration, which earns the antagonism of large numbers of the population opposed to the Merina or the Soviet features. Where it has appeal, the party is well organized. It holds sixteen of the 137 Assembly seats and received 7.3 percent of the vote in the 1977 local elections.

Militants for Power to the People (*Militants pour le Pouvoir au Peuple;* MFM)

The MFM formed as a coalition of labor, unemployed urban workers, students, and intellectuals in the aftermath of the anti-Tsiranana street revolts of 1972. The party's influence remains restricted to the capital, but it was accused of successful manipulation in the Antsiranana recall vote in early 1982.

The MFM hesitated to join the FNDR, but having done so in 1977 it continues to oppose the dominance of the AREMA and its tendency to favor the elites of both the coast and the Merina. Alleging discrimination in earlier local balloting, the MFM refused to contest the 1977 elections. Its leader, sociologist Manandafy Rakotonirina, spent periods of 1973 and 1976 in prison for his disputes with the prevailing power.

National Movement for the Independence of Madagascar (*Mouvement National pour l'Indépendence de Madagascar;* MONIMA)

MONIMA has been a regional-based advocate for the interests of the rural south since the late 1950s. Its leader, Monja Jaona, has been an outspoken critic of both republics and has suffered persecution from both sources of authority. The aged (eighty years or more) but charismatic Monja, who is held responsible for the peasant

jacqueries of 1971, broke from the FNDR in 1977 and boycotted the elections of that year. It rejoined the FNDR in 1981, but quarreled again with Ratsiraka in mid-1982 over government control of agricultural production and marketing. Monja is the oldest in the CSR and theoretically the second-strongest person in the republic, but his party's role remains that of critic and dissenter within the ranks, rather than a policymaker.

People's Movement for National Unity (*Vonjy Iray Tsy Mivaky*)

Vonjy grew out of the old Tsiranana PSD, which had survived the 1972 revolution as the Malagasy Socialist Union, headed until 1976 by Tsiranana's former vice president, André Resampa. The *Vonjy* held seven seats in the 1982 Assembly. It appeals to the more conservative cultural traditions of the island's west coast. Its leader in 1982 was Dr. Marojaima (Jerome) Razanabahiny.

Union of Christian Democrats (*Union des Démocrates-Chrétiens;* UDECMA)

UDECMA is a tiny party of the Catholic proletariat along the east coast. It holds two seats in the Assembly and is led by Norbert Randriamorasata.

Other Political Forces

Military

The army and gendarmerie have been politicized and given important roles in national policymaking. A Military Development Committee acts as a watchdog agency of the CSR, and the enlarged, well-trained army (9,500 men) serves in development projects. Internal security outside Antananarivo is the responsibility of the gendarmerie, which has clashed with citizens' groups on a number of occasions, most recently in a tragic "massacre" of over a hundred villagers in the south who had been mistaken for cattle rustlers.

Students

The number of university students quadrupled to 15,000 in the decade after 1972, and student restiveness remains troublesome for the regime. Student-led riots in February 1981 touched off demonstrations by unemployed and other discontents, threatening a repetition of the movement that toppled Tsiranana's regime in 1972. Leaders of the riots were imprisoned until late June of 1982.

Ethnic Groups

Madagascar's ethnic groups do not differ greatly in either language or culture. They are distinguished rather by strong clan loyalties and relative isolation from each other. The Merina, nearly twice as numerous as any of the other groups, are dominant both culturally and economically, a position that makes them suspect in the eyes of the rest of the population. The Merina intellectuals tend to support the MFM, while the business and landholding elite support the AKFM. The Betsileo, the most Indonesian of all the remaining groups, live on the plateau south of the Merina and do not favor one party. Among the more African groups, the Betsimisaraka, who live in the Tamatave area, support AREMA and the UDECMA, while the Tsimihety of the northwest support both *Vonjy* and AREMA. The Sakalawa of the west coast support MONIMA and AREMA, and the Antandroy in the far south support MONIMA. These and the other ethnic groups play some role as such in the political system, but class and economic interests as well as party loyalties cut across ethnic group lines.

Opposition in Exile

Remnants of the former regime and some of their dispossessed French sympathizers have gathered around the figure of André Resampa in exile. Resampa and other social democrats had been arrested for implication in the assassination of former president Richard Ratsimandrava in February 1975, but were subsequently acquitted and allowed to go to France. If Ratsiraka's program continues to fail to stimulate production and employment, and if the Malagasy social climate remains afflicted by disillusion with government in general, the divisive forces in the FNDR, and even in the president's own party, could move the system in Resampa's direction.

National Prospects

For the time being, Ratsiraka seeks to balance his revolutionary strategy and nonaligned foreign policy against urgent needs for balance of payments support (from France and the International Monetary Fund) and for productive capital, which has not appeared in the domestic economy. Given some assistance from French Socialist sources and an opportunity to restore confidence in a badly mismanaged economy, Ratsiraka will probably neutralize the challenge to his leadership from the right. Nevertheless, failure to increase production, assure orderly distribution of goods and services, and knit the sprawling social fabric into harmony has encouraged rebelliousness in the population. Urban vandalism expands frequently into mortal riot; peasant discontent expresses itself in criminal truculence and resistance to production exhortations; and corruption and mismanagement are regularly denounced despite tight security controls and press censorship.

Further Reading

Heseltine, Nigel. *Madagascar.* New York: Praeger, 1971.

Legum, Colin, ed. *Africa Contemporary Record.* London and New York: Holmes and Meier, annual.

Leymarie, Philippe. "Madagascar: la course de vitesse des socialistes." *Le Monde Diplomatique,* No. 340, July 1982.

REPUBLIC OF MALAWI

by Timothy Dunmore, Ph.D.

The System of Government

Malawi, a country of some six million people, is a single-party republic and a unitary state. It was formerly the British protectorate of Nyasaland. In 1953 Malawi became part of the British-ruled Federation of Rhodesia (the present Zimbabwe and Zambia) and Nyasaland. After a period of active native opposition to both the federation and the colonial power, the former was dissolved in December 1963. Six months later the independent state of Malawi was created.

In 1966, Malawi became a republic under a constitution that remains in effect. The first and current president of Malawi is Dr. Hastings Kamuzu Banda. Both constitutionally and in practice the political system is dominated by Banda and his Malawi Congress Party (MCP).

Executive

The executive branch consists of a president and a cabinet. The president is both head of state and head of the government. He appoints all the members of the cabinet, and they are responsible directly to him rather than to the legislature. In 1981, Banda was also minister of external affairs, agriculture and natural resources, justice, and works and supplies. He appoints senior civil servants and leading officers in the armed forces. The cabinet, the civil service, and the army do not present any real challenge to President Banda's position. He dominates the legislature through the MCP of which he is president. In addition, the president has an unlimited right to declare a state of emergency.

In spite of his advanced age (mid-seventies) and his consequently increased reliance on his senior advisers, the president still determines the basic lines of Malawi government policy, particularly with regard to its most powerful neighbor, South Africa. The only active opposition to Banda comes from political organizations in exile.

According to the constitution, the president is directly elected every five years. However, in 1971 Banda was elected president for life by the people

of Malawi. On his death, he is to be succeeded by a three-man Presidential Council chaired by the head of the ruling Malawi Congress Party and staffed by two members of the cabinet.

Legislature

The National Assembly is a single chamber consisting of up to 102 members; every member belongs to the Malawi Congress Party. Eighty-seven members are elected from approximately equal electoral districts. In addition to the elected members, the constitution allows the president to nominate up to fifteen people to the Assembly. Furthermore, he can participate in Assembly debates whenever he wishes. The president can also veto any bill passed by the Assembly. In the unlikely event of the legislature repassing the same bill within a six-month period, the president is supposed to call new elections. Both constitutionally and in view of the party system, the legislature is dominated by the executive in Malawi. Its real powers are consultative and advisory rather than legislative.

The normal parliamentary term is five years, although the president may dissolve the Assembly before that time, as he did in 1978 after only a two-year term.

Judiciary

Formally, the highest court in Malawi is the Supreme Court of Appeal which hears appeals against decisions of the High Court. It is the High Court, however, that makes the most important judicial decisions in all civil and criminal matters. It is headed by the chief justice, who is a presidential appointee. It does not challenge the executive's powers or decisions.

Regional & Local Government

Malawi is divided into three major areas, the Southern, the Central, and the Northern regions. Each is represented in the national cabinet by an appointed regional minister. The regions in turn are divided into a total of twenty-four districts, the cities of Blantyre and Lilongue, and six towns. While local councils are elected, all are supervised by the Ministry of Local Government, which also controls the allocations of money to all levels.

The Electoral System

Deputies to the National Assembly are directly elected in single-member districts. The ballot is secret, although a high level of illiteracy requires voters to show their preferences by placing voting slips in a separate box for each candidate.

The 1971 and 1976 elections were uncontested, but in 1978 forty-seven of the eighty-seven electoral districts were contested by two or three candidates; candidates in the other forty were returned unopposed. All candidates were from the MCP, and all were personally approved by the president. Candidates were not allowed to campaign or to spend any money for political purposes. In contested constituencies, all the candidates were presented to the voters at the same mass meeting. The only speeches were made by Banda himself.

No less than thirty-one sitting MPs were defeated, including two cabinet ministers. However, President Banda had previously announced that he would use the elections to reshuffle his cabinet and expressed himself content at the defeat of so many MPs. Malawi's first experiment at single-party electoral competition was skeptically regarded by Western journalists at the time, but it did provide Malawi citizens with something of a choice among personalities, although not among policies.

Malawi Congress Party (MCP)

History

The MCP was established in 1959 under Banda's leadership to fight for the end of the federation with Rhodesia and for independence from British colonial rule. The party's position benefited from Banda's personal success in securing independence and from his successful program of economic development. Since 1965, the only opposition to the MCP has come from small minorities within the country and from former cabinet ministers in exile.

Organization

The party is more of an organization for promoting support for the regime than a forum for debating policy issues. Officially, party policy is made by the annual party convention which is composed of party officials from national, regional, and district levels; members of Parliament; some traditional chiefs; chairmen of the district councils; and representatives of other organizations, such as the League of Malawi Youth and the League of Malawi Women. In practice, the convention's role is at best advisory and at worst merely ceremonial. In fact, the party is organized along democratic-centralist lines, with all appointments and elections controlled by Banda.

Policy

The policy of the MCP is basically that of Banda. In foreign affairs, Malawi is distinguished from other black African states by its willingness to remain on good terms with South Africa. Only in 1975, when a black government came to power in Mozambique, did Banda temporarily modify his friendship with Pretoria. Even then, the modification lasted less than two years.

MCP policy toward South Africa is based primarily on economic necessity. The Malawi economy relies heavily on the earnings of its citizens— more than 100,000—who work in South Africa. Malawi's army also depends heavily on South Africa for its arms. Opposition to Malawi's economic and military reliance on South Africa has come mainly from outside rather than inside Malawi.

Internally, Banda has sought to encourage the growth of private industry, especially agriculture, by providing state financing and advice to farmers and industrialists through the Malawi Development Corporation.

Membership

All Malawi adults are members of the MCP, but few take an active part in it.

Financing

Much of the party's income appears to come from the government itself.

Leadership

Dick Tennyson Matenje became secretary general of the party in January 1982, replacing Elson Bakili Muluzi, who had been regarded as Banda's most likely successor. Officially, Muluzi resigned for "personal reasons." Banda (born 1906) is president of the party, but takes little direct part in running it. Whether Matenje is now first in line to succeed him is unclear.

Opposition

There are three opposition parties in exile, two based in Tanzania and one in Mozambique. They all claim to be socialist and are encouraged by the governments of Tanzania and Mozambique, which dislike Malawi's ties with South Africa.

The Congress for the Second Republic is based in Dar es Salaam, Tanzania, and is led by Kanyama Chiume, a former prime minister. The Malawi Freedom Movement (MAFREMO) is led by another former cabinet minister, Orton Chirwa; its policies are perhaps more populist than socialist. The most left wing of these parties is the Socialist League of Malawi (LESOMA) led by Dr. Attati Mpakati. It has the support of the Cuban and Russian governments, and in 1980 established a military organization, the Peoples' Liberation Army of Malawi (PLAM), to overthrow the Banda regime.

Other Political Forces

Military

Malawi's army has no great history of political involvement, although it did suppress the rebellion of Harry Chipembere in 1965. Its leaders are appointed by the president, and its direct ties with the South African Armed Forces isolate it from any links with opposition groups.

Organized Labor

The Malawi Trades Union Congress unites three unions which in 1981 had a total membership of 6,500. The only other labor organization is the Teachers' Union. These unions are not politically active. In any case, the vast majority of the population is not unionized. Most work in agriculture or abroad.

Ethnic Groups

The vast majority of the population is African. Since Banda values their role in his country's economic development, the small European minority is well treated. As in Kenya and Uganda, however, the Asian minority has been subjected to repression. They have been driven out of their positions as traders in the villages, but there is no firm indication that they are to be expelled from the country. The Africans come from many different tribes including the Chewa, the Ngoni, and the Yao.

After many years of preparation, the capital of Malawi was moved in 1975 from Zombe in the Southern Region to Lilongwe in the Central Region. Banda announced that this move would promote the development of the Central Region, but it caused some resentment among the ethnic groups in the more developed and prosperous Southern Region, notably the Nyanja. They viewed the decision as showing bias towards particularly the Chewa people, who are more concentrated in the Central Region and whose language has become dominant in the country.

Religious Groups

About half the population is Christian, one fourth Hindu, one fifth Muslim. Jehovah's Witnesses are officially proscribed because of their refusal to acknowledge the government's authority.

National Prospects

In spite of the claims of its opponents, the Banda regime is generally accepted within Malawi. There are now few, if any, political prisoners. The competitive element was introduced into the 1978 elections partly because of the stability of the regime. This stability, however, depends heavily on continuing good relations with South Africa and a continuing economic success. Any change in the political climate to the south could endanger Malawi's economy and its political system, especially if it coincided with Banda's death. It seems unlikely that any accommodation will be reached with the opposition groups in exile until the president's demise.

Further Reading

McMaster, Carolyn. *Malawi: Foreign Policy and Development.* London: Julian Freedman, 1974.

Pachai, B. *Malawi: The History of a Nation.* London: Longman, 1973.

Pike, John G. *Malawi: A Political and Economic History.* London: Pall Mall Press, 1968.

Short, Philip. *Banda.* London: Routledge and Kegan Paul, 1974.

Williams, T. David. *Malawi: The Politics of Despair.* Ithaca, N.Y.: Cornell University Press, 1978.

MALAYSIA

by Peter Dawson

The System of Government

Malaysia is a parliamentary federation comprising the eleven states of the Malay peninsula together with the federal territory of Kuala Lumpur, the capital, which comprise West Malaysia, and the states of Sabah and Sarawak on the island of Borneo, which comprise East Malaysia. The country has a population of nearly 14.5 million people of whom about 47 percent are Malay, 32 percent Chinese, and 9 percent Indian. It achieved independence from British colonial rule on August 31, 1957, as the Malayan Federation, then consisting of the states of the peninsula only. In September 1963, Sabah, Sarawak, and Singapore joined the federation, but Singapore seceded on August 9, 1965. The federal territory of Kuala Lumpur was created in 1974. The present constitution has been effective from 1957, with only limited subsequent alterations. It provides for a parliamentary and cabinet system closely modeled on that of the United Kingdom.

Executive

The head of state is the *Yang di-Pertuan Agong* (or king) who serves for a term of five years. The office rotates according to precedence among the royal rulers of nine of the thirteen states of the federation, but accession to the office is confirmed by election among these nine rulers. The office thus constitutes a unique combination of monarchic, rotational, and elective principles. Although formally the head of government, the king is in practice a constitutional monarch with only very limited discretionary powers. The effective head of government is the *Perdana Mentri* (prime minister), working with and through the *Juma'ah Mentri* (cabinet). The king appoints as prime minister the member of the *Dewan Ra'ayat* (House of Representatives) likely to command the confidence of a majority in the House, normally the leader of the majority party. Members of the cabinet are appointed by the king from either of the two houses of Parliament on the advice of the prime minister. The cabinet is required by the

constitution to be collectively responsible to the parliament.

Legislature

The legislature consists of the king and the two *majlis* (councils): the *Dewan Negara* (Senate) and the *Dewan Ra'ayat* (House of Representatives). The king, however, takes no active part in the proceedings of Parliament.

The Senate, which is the less powerful of the two houses, has sixty-eight members. Two members are elected by each state legislature, while the king, acting on advice from the prime minister, appoints an additional forty-two, including two to represent the federal territory. Senators serve for three years, their term being unaffected by a dissolution of the House of Representatives. Senators tend to be prominent older figures in public life, representative of occupational and ethnic groupings, although in recent years Senate seats have sometimes been used to groom younger, rising politicians. Despite the minority group of territorial representatives, the Senate has never been active in promoting states' rights against those of the federation.

The House of Representatives has 154 members directly elected from single-member constituencies by simple majorities. The minimum qualifying age for membership is twenty-one. Dual membership of the two federal houses is forbidden as is simultaneous representation of two federal constituencies, but several federal legislators also hold seats or office in their state assemblies. The maximum life of the House of Representatives is five years, but it may be dissolved at any time by the king acting upon the request of the prime minister. The king does have the power, never used so far, to refuse such a request. In recent years, Parliament has met for about eleven weeks in each year.

A simple majority in both houses is sufficient to carry legislation. The Senate has a delaying power of one month over money bills and of one year over other bills. Most constitutional amendments require a two-thirds majority while certain articles of the constitution cannot be amended without the consent of the *Majlis Raja Raja*.

The *Majlis Raja Raja* (Conference of Rulers), which meets three or four times a year, comprises the thirteen rulers of the states of the federation including the nine hereditary royal rulers and the governors of Penang, Malacca, Sabah, and Sarawak. It acts as a third house of the Parliament on amendments to certain sections of the constitution (especially Article 153 which protects the position of Malays), the extension of Islamic religious practices, the making of certain major state appointments (such as judges of the Federal Court), as well as on legislation affecting the position of rulers and the boundaries of states. The nine royal rulers, sitting within the Conference of Rulers, are responsible also for the election of the king and his deputy.

Since independence the government coalition, dominated by the United Malays National Organization, has always held an absolute majority of the seats in the House of Representatives. In the 1982 general election, the Democratic Action Party (DAP) was able to win seats in the federal territory and in only four states including Sabah and Sarawak. The Pan-Malaysian Islamic Party (PAS) won seats in only two states, while the independents were all elected in Sabah and Sarawak. The dominance of the National Front and the very limited territorial base of the opposition parties was

---

HOUSE OF REPRESENTATIVES ELECTION RESULTS (1982)

National Front		
United Malays National Organization (UMNO)	70	(69)
Malayan Chinese Association (MCA)	24	(17)
Berjaya	10	(9)
United Bumiputra Party (PPBB)	8	(8)
Sarawak National Party (SNAP)	6	(9)
Sarawak United People's Party (SUPP)	5	(6)
Gerakan	5	(4)
Malayan Indian Congress (MIC)	4	(3)
Others	—	(6)
	132	(131)
Opposition Parties		
Democratic Action Party (DAP)	9	(16)
Pan-Malaysian Islamic Party (PAS)	5	(5)
Independents	8	(—)
Others	—	(2)
	22	(23)
Total Seats	154	

* Figures for 1978 are in parentheses.

---

confirmed by the results of the elections to state assemblies which were held at the same time.

Judiciary

The Federal Court is the highest judicial authority in Malaysia with the power to interpret the constitution and to adjudicate in disputes between states or between any state and the federal government. It is also the highest court of appeal in criminal cases for the federation. In civil cases there remains an appeal from the Federal Court to the Privy Council sitting in London. Beneath the Federal Court are two High Courts, one for West and one for East Malaysia, which have original jurisdiction in their areas in both civil and criminal cases as well as appeal from subordinate courts. The lord president, who heads the Federal Court, is appointed by the king who must act on the advice of the prime minister after consulting the Conference of Rulers. Other senior judges are similarly appointed with the lord president also being consulted. The independence of the judiciary is maintained by this means as well as by the stipulation of legal qualifications, a high security of tenure and remuneration, and restrictions on discussion of judicial conduct in the legislatures. In numerous cases, the judiciary have displayed a very high standard of independence from political influence.

Regional & Local Government

Each state is governed by a *Mentri Besar* (chief minister) who is responsible to a unicameral legislative assembly whose members are directly elected, except in Sabah which retains a limited number of nominated members. The relations among the state ruler or governor, the chief minister, and the assembly are broadly similar to those which prevail at federal level among the king, prime minister, and the Parliament. But the powers of states are limited, being confined principally to land and natural-resource management and the oversight of local government. Sabah and Sarawak, however, enjoy some powers not available to the states of West Malaysia. The federal government is the main taxing authority and controls the borrowing powers of states so that apart from land revenue, states enjoy no significant sources of income. Since state legislatures are now dominated by political parties that are members of the governing coalition at federal level, a further degree of state and federal harmonization is achieved.

The Electoral System

All members of the House of Representatives are directly elected by a simple majority within each of the 154 single-member constituencies. Twenty-six of the sixty-eight members of the Senate are elected by their state legislatures. All citizens over the age of twenty-one (other than those detained as being of "unsound mind" or serving a prison sentence or who have been sentenced to death or imprisonment of more than twelve months) are eligible to vote by secret ballot in elections for the House of Representatives or legislative assemblies. The Election Commission conducts elections and prepares and annually revises electoral rolls. It is also responsible every eight to ten years for reviewing and recommending changes to the boundaries of state and national constituencies. Registration of voters is neither automatic nor compulsory. The ballot paper in each constituency lists all the candidates and their party symbols; voters indicate their choice by marking an *X*. Votes are counted centrally within each constituency in the presence of candidates and their agents. Turnout is high, usually above 70 percent. The system is in the main fair and equitable, although various technical factors relating to voter registration and constituency delimitation together with the effects of the simple-majority method have produced in all national elections a highly disproportionate number of seats for the governing coalition.

The Party System

Origins of the Parties

The most distinctive feature of Malaysian political parties is that they are all communally based, but a second major feature is a tendency towards consociation and coalition. The communal divisions are not only racial, but are also reinforced by language, religion, culture, and to a considerable extent, economic role. With Malays constituting approximately half of the total population, Chinese approximately one-third, and people of Indian descent one-tenth, parties which represent the interests of these groups are assured of substantial support. The three major parties (UMNO, MCA, and MIC) all came into existence in the late 1940s specifically to defend their respective ethnic communities against threats perceived in the various constitutional proposals advanced by the colonial government. Well before independence in

1957, they had formed a coalition which was formally registered as the Alliance Party in 1958. The Alliance collapsed in the wake of communal rioting after the 1969 election, which had shown a growth in support for non-Alliance parties and thus an erosion of the claim by the Alliance to represent a national interest.

After a period of emergency rule, during which electoral and parliamentary activity were suspended, the coalition was reconstituted in 1971 as the National Front (*Barisan Nasional*). At the same time, it was broadened to include several smaller parties, previously in opposition, so that the Malay and Chinese communities were now represented by more than one party within the Front. The United Malays National Organization (UMNO) has always been the dominant participant. With intercommunal harmony the overriding aim of government throughout Malaysia's history, the National Front has achieved this aim by private interparty compromise. However, resentment among some sections of the population against this process of elite adjustment has sustained support for several opposition parties.

The Parties in Law

The constitution makes no reference to political parties, but under separate legislation (the Societies Act 1966) all organizations seeking to contest elections must be formally registered. On a few occasions, the refusal of registration has effectively suppressed the activities of some smaller opposition parties. A 1981 amendment to the Societies Act requires all clubs, societies, and associations to register as either political or nonpolitical. This has been seen as limiting the capacity of pressure groups to campaign and lobby to secure changes in government policy. From time to time, security and sedition laws have been used to detain members of opposition parties either because of suspected communist links or because their activities were deemed to be subversive. Parties receive no direct, formal state support. Any qualified election candidate whose nomination has been properly made can be included on the ballot whether or not he is a representative of a political party.

Party Organization

Malaysian parties are too numerous, too different in size, and in several cases too limited to particular regions for many substantial generalizations to be possible. The parties are permanent associations sustained by membership dues and private donations. Most maintain a three-tiered organization at constituency, state, and national level. They are identifiable principally by communal characteristics, although different parties drawing their membership from the same community may be distinguished by socioeconomic and, to a limited degree, ideological differences. The major support for the DAP, for example, comes from the poor stratum of Chinese, while the MCA is more substantially supported by the better off.

The participation of the major parties in the National Front and the dependence of all on that membership, except UMNO, for access to cabinet office and the consequent benefits to their communities necessitates the maintenance of close central control over subordinate levels. A major instrument of this control for parties within the National Front is the patronage exercised by the chief ministers of states. Although the principal parties hold annual conferences at which major policy issues are determined and national officers are chosen, these processes are usually closely and successfully regulated. Nevertheless, despite this consistent pattern of central and elite domination, some opportunity remains for local leaders to develop local support. For the wealthier, especially within Chinese communities, contributions to community projects, such as schools and places of worship, may generate prestige and power. For all aspirants to party office or candidacy, the role of broker—representing constituents' interests within the multiple and many-layered processes of governmental bureaucracy—is universally expected. Thus, education and experience of working within bureaucracies are important factors determining election at the local level.

Campaigning

Fear of threats to public order have led the government, in recent elections, to ban large public rallies by any party. The preferred method of campaigning has been to hold meetings within private houses at which a largely invited audience participates in a process akin to a seminar, with an address by a speaker followed by questions and discussion. This method, where it is used, permits issues to be presented in a way which is specific to particular areas or occupational groups. In addition, door-to-door canvassing occurs, and pamphlets and posters are widely distributed and displayed although their influence, if any, is difficult to assess. The press has an important role. Seven newspapers, published in English as well as the vernacular languages, have an influence that is generally felt to be substantial, their effect being usually to enhance support for candidates representing the ruling National Front.

It is difficult to determine accurately the full expenditure of parties during election campaigns. Local party branches are in all cases dependent on central party funds derived either from voluntary contributions or from levies on holders of well-paid posts which have been secured by party intervention. The larger parties, most of which are in the National Front, are by far the richer and can thus readily afford the costs of publicity, transport for party workers, and other necessary expenses.

There is usually not any close national party control of local campaigns. With the larger parties, pre-existing party cohesion encourages a uniformity of approach, although the fact that state assembly elections are held at the same time as those for the national legislature will often ensure that wholly local issues may be promoted in a manner which conflicts with the national party's line.

Independent Voters

The existence of the National Front as an electoral, as well as a governing, coalition may present some voters with a dilemma when the NF-endorsed candidate is not from their own ethnic community. In that event, if a candidate from their own community is standing for an opposition party a conflict arises between the desire to vote for the coalition—which almost inevitably enjoys a national majority and which is regarded as the source of many material benefits—and the wish to assert communal solidarity. There has been some evidence of differential voting for national and for state assemblymen.

National Front (Barisan Nasional)

Although registered for legal purposes as a political party, the Front is an electoral and governing coalition comprising eleven parties and has no organizational structure of its own. Its constituent parties (each of which has a separate entry) are UMNO, Berjasa, Berjaya, MCA, MIC, Gerakan, PPBB, PPP, SNAP, SUPP, and USNO.

United Malays National Organization (UMNO; *Pertubohan Kebangsaan Melayu Bersatu*)

History

The UMNO was founded in May 1946, with Dato Onn bin Jaafar as its first president, in order to resist the introduction, by the British colonial administration, of a unitary form of government throughout Peninsular Malaya. This was seen by Malays and especially by their hereditary rulers as detrimental to Malay interests. The UMNO was not formally registered as a political party until April 1950. Throughout Malaysia's history, it has been the largest national party and the dominant party of government. All four of Malaysia's prime ministers since 1957 have been the leaders of UMNO. Data Onn's attempts in 1950 to widen UMNO membership to include non-Malays and to introduce other reforms were strongly opposed and led to his resignation and replacement as party president in 1951 by Tunku Abdul Rahman. An ad hoc coalition between UMNO and the MCA to fight the Kuala Lumpur municipal elections in 1952 led to the establishment a year later of the Alliance coalition which also included the MIC. Tunku Abdul Rahman became prime minister following the first general election in 1955 and led his country to independence in 1957. Throughout the 1960s, his attempts to hold the Alliance together and placate ultranationalist Malays in his own party weakened his position. The decline in support both for UMNO and the Alliance which was revealed by the 1969 election results and the communal rioting which followed led to his resignation, both as prime minister and as party president, and his replacement by Tun Abdul Razak.

After a period of emergency rule during which Parliament was suspended, Razak was able to put together a wider governing coalition of nine parties, including some which had previously been in opposition. This National Front was registered as a political party on June 1, 1974. In the parliamentary elections which followed the Front won 135 out of the 154 seats.

Other major measures taken during the emergency period were the introduction of the New Economic Policy (NEP) which sought to promote substantially the economic advancement of the Malay population and the passing of a constitutional amendment which declared seditious any questioning of Malay privileges, the status of Malay as the national language, and as such issues as citizenship and the position of traditional rulers. Important controversies were thus barred from public debate, even in Parliament, and the grounds on which opposition parties might base their criticisms were denied to them.

The death of Tun Abdul Razak in 1976 and the succession of Datuk Hussein Onn was followed by a brief period of factional fighting within UMNO. In part, the conflict was between older members of the party who had been associates of Tunku Abdul Rahman and younger men, technocratically inclined, who had been brought to prominence by Tun Abdul Razak. The outcome involved the arrest of several of the latter group for alleged communist activities, although much of the evidence, including their confessions, appeared fragile. At the same time others of Razak's protegés, untainted by any communist association, survived. Of this group, Dr. Mahatir bin Mohamad, who in 1970 had been expelled from the party's supreme council, was appointed to the deputy premiership over the heads of more senior men. A major casualty of this period was Datuk Harun, the chief minister of Selangor. His control over the massive patronage of his state and his support in the youth wing of the party constituted a threat to the leadership of Razak and then of Datuk Hussein Onn. He was charged with corruption in late 1975. Over the next two years, he was successively stripped of office, expelled from the party, and tried and sentenced to a term of imprisonment, thus demonstrating Hussein Onn's gathering control of the party.

In July 1981, Hussein Onn was succeeded as prime minister by Dr. Mahatir Mohamed who, within a year, led his party into a general election, the results of which reemphasized UMNO's continuing dominance in the political life of Malaysia.

Organization

The UMNO is a cadre party, exclusively Malay in membership, which has succeeded through its extensive organization in every state and penetration to village level in uniting Malay interests across region and class. As an exclusively Malay party, UMNO enjoys a high degree of homogeneity. It is distinguished also by being the only party with branches throughout the federation, including Sabah and Sarawak. It is relatively highly structured with a president, deputy president, and five vice presidents. The heads of the party's youth wing and its women's wing (*Wanita* UMNO) are automatically vice presidents, the remaining three being elected by the party's general assembly. Together with other appointed and elected members, including a secretary-general, treasurer, and publicity chief, they constitute the principal power center of the party. The dual roles of party president and prime minister have been employed in a mutually enhancing manner by all four incumbents, whose positions have usually been supported by the senior party officers who are also cabinet ministers.

The youth and women's wings enjoy a semi-autonomous status, at times acting as pressure groups within the party. They have both performed vitally important functions during elections in organizing campaigns at the local level.

Policy

The principal objectives of UMNO policy have consistently been UMNO dominance and Malay unity. The one is seen as reinforcing the other. These aims are secured by maintaining tight central control of the party while securing the widest possible electoral and governing coalition with Malay and non-Malay parties. These two strategies have at times been felt to conflict, leading to strains within the party, notably in 1969. Over the past decade, the party has promoted the New Economic Policy (NEP), which uses active discriminatory measures to advance the material well being of Malays. This policy has coincided with a more strident assertion of economic nationalism which has led the government to buy its way into many of the large expatriate corporations, especially in the mining and plantation industries. Determinedly anticommunist both at home and abroad the party's and government's foreign policy has been characterized by active membership in the Association of South East Asian Nations, an increasing concern to promote cooperation among Islamic countries, very cautious relations with China, and of late, the assertion of ostensibly anti-British sentiment.

Membership & Constituency

No information is available on the size of the membership of UMNO. The party's supporters include most of the Malays of West Malaysia and many in Sabah and Sarawak. Only those Malays whose political views are most influenced by their Islamic faith support other parties in any appreciable number.

Financing

No information is available on details of UMNO financial sources or expenditures.

Leadership

Dr. Mahatir Mohamed (born 1925) is in firm control of the party. He is the first prime minister to have been educated locally (in medicine), and unlike his predecessors, he is not a member of a Malay royal house. Once identified with the radical right, he is thought by many observers to retain an inclination in that direction.

Prospects

While the party's leadership remains acutely sensitive to any threat to its hegemony, especially from rival Malay parties, it is extremely difficult to envisage UMNO being displaced as the governing party.

Malayan Chinese Association (MCA)

The MCA was founded in 1949 to protect the interests of the Chinese people, approximately one-third of the population, in the face of what were regarded as markedly pro-Malay policies of the British colonial government. Officially registered as a party in 1952, the MCA cooperated with UMNO at an electoral level and, in 1953, became a member, together with the MIC, of the Alliance coalition. The MCA was again a member of the Front, but the inclusion in the Front of Gerakan, a rival Chinese party, has reduced the MCA's standing, since it can no longer claim to be the sole representative of Chinese interests in the government. While it has a widespread organization throughout Malaysia, it does not control any state assembly, unlike Gerakan which controls Penang. Although from its inception it attempted to be a mass membership party, it is seen as representing the interests of the better off among the Chinese community and is vulnerable to the more populist appeal of some of the opposition parties among the poorer Chinese. These difficulties were reflected in a sharp factional struggle through the 1970s between some of the older founding members of the party and younger and more radical elements. With twenty-four seats in the federal Parliament, it is the second-largest coalition partner, but its freedom to formulate policy is powerfully circumscribed by its membership in the Front. In order to protect its position and that of its members it must acquiesce in policies, especially with regard to Malay advancement, which cannot always be regarded as being in the immediate interest of its members.

Organizationally, the MCA is very similar to UMNO, with a powerful central committee comprising members elected by a general assembly or nominated by the party president. It has a strong state-level organization with subordinate levels down to ward branches. The party is lead by Datuk Lee San Choon (born 1935) who first entered Parliament in 1959 and has held several senior ministerial posts.

Gerakan
(Parti Gerakan Rakyat Malaysia)

The party is universally known as Gerakan, but its full name can be loosely translated as Malaysian People's Movement. It was founded in 1968 by Dr. Lim Chong Eu and pledged to a program of noncommunalism, moderate socialism, and democracy. Despite the presence of Malays on the party committee it is still seen as a Chinese party. Its power base is in Penang, where it controls the state government with the patronage which that entails, but it also has a few branches elsewhere. It entered the Front in 1972.

Malayan Indian Congress (MIC)

From its inception in 1946, the MIC has been faced by the difficulty of sustaining unity in the face of divisions within the Indian community, which constitutes less than 10 percent of the population and which is clustered in geographically scattered locations or thinly spread in urban centers. Although a member of the Alliance and subsequently of the National Front, it is the weakest partner with only four seats in the federal Parliament. Since the Indian population nowhere comprises more than 25 percent of the voters in any constituency, without the constituencies and seats allocated to it by the Front it could not hope to survive as a significant group.

Sabah People's Union
(Bersatu Rakyat Jelata Sabah; Berjaya)

Berjaya was founded in 1975, with the encouragement of the Front, largely in order to isolate the chief minister of Sabah, Tun Mustapha, and his USNO party, who were at odds with the prime minister. It was successful in achieving this end. In 1976, it formally entered the Front and in 1981 secured forty-three of the forty-eight seats in the elections to the state assembly. In 1982, it won ten of the sixteen Sabah seats in the federal Parlia-

ment. Berjaya is one of the few multicommunal parties in Malaysia.

United Sabah National Organization (USNO)

The party of the former chief minister of Sabah, Tun Mustapha, USNO was severely undermined when Berjaya was established in 1976. With the resignation of Tun Mustapha and his departure from the country, both USNO and Berjaya were admitted to the National Front in 1976, although USNO remained in opposition to Berjaya in the state assembly. It has no seats in the federal Parliament.

United People Party
(Parti Pesaka Bumiputra Bersaut; PPBB)

The PPBB is a Sarawak-based party established in 1973 within the Front. It obtained eight of the twenty-four Sarawak seats in the 1982 federal election. Its appeal is to the Malay population of that state.

Sarawak United People's Party (SUPP)

The oldest Sarawak party in the Front was founded in 1959. Its support is predominantly from the Chinese population. It has five seats in the federal Parliament.

Sarawak National Party (SNAP)

Founded in 1961 this Sarawak-based party, whose support comes mainly from the indigenous peoples of the state, came into the National Front in 1976. In 1982, it won six of the twenty-four federal parliamentary seats in Sarawak and together with its Front allies, the PPBB and the SUPP, secured that territory's interests within the NF.

People's Progressive Party of Malaysia (PPP)

Originally founded in 1953 as the Perak Progressive Party, it changed to its present name in 1956. Its appeal is restricted mainly to non-Malays in the Ipoh area. It survives as a party within the Perak state assembly where its appeal to poorer

Chinese offsets some of the advantage which might otherwise accrue to the DAP, one of the two opposition parties in that state.

Berjasa
(*Barisan Jama'ah Islamiah Semalaysia*)

Most commonly known by its Malay acronym, Berjasa, the party's name could be translated as the Malaysian Islamic People's Front. It was formed in 1977 as a splinter group from the PAS and has served to weaken that party's electoral support within the state of Kelantan in which both are based. A more assertively Islamic party than UMNO, it holds no seats in the federal Parliament, but is represented in the Kelantan state assembly.

Opposition Parties

Democratic Action Party (DAP)

Founded in 1966 in the wake of Singapore's secession from the federation, the DAP was the Malayan version of the People's Action Party, Lee Kuan Yew's Singapore-based party. DAP's objective was and is to establish a democratic and socialist society in Malaysia. It analyzes Malaysian society in class rather than communal terms, and while its support comes mainly from urban, working-class Chinese, it retains an appeal for many disaffected non-Malays including some of the intelligentsia. Although efficiently organized, the competition from rival Chinese parties, MCA and Gerakan, and its inability to secure any substantial support in rural areas have denied it control of any state assembly and thus substantially limited its capacity to secure federal parliamentary seats. The party chairman is Chen Man Hin (born 1924 in China), who was educated at the University of Malaya in Singapore and has worked as a medical practitioner.

Pan Malaysian Islamic Party
(*Partai Islam Se Malaysia;* PAS)

Known variously by its English or Malay/Arabic acronyms, PAS originated in the early 1950s as an Islamic promotional group within UMNO. In 1955, alienated by UMNO concessions to non-Malays, it was established as a separate party. A Malay nationalist party, its primary appeal is to poorer, especially rural, Malays. It seeks to combine Islamic traditions with a modernizing thrust and some elements of socialism. Islam is regarded as a force for national unity. Religious teachers are active in its campaigning and religious themes are interwoven with political assertions. PAS may represent the only significant potential threat to UMNO's dominance, partly because the rural poor as a whole have derived the least benefit from the substantial economic changes since independence, partly because PAS is least ready to accommodate the interests of other racial groups, and partly because its appeal echoes the success of radical Islamic movements elsewhere. For a short period between 1973 and 1977, PAS was a member of the National Front, but since then its power in Kelantan, the one state where it was dominant, has been eroded. In 1982, it won only five seats in the federal Parliament, four of them in Kelantan, and only eighteen state assembly seats. The ten seats in the Kelantan assembly were insufficient to secure a majority. The party president is Dato Haji Mohamed Asri bin Haji Muda (born 1923), a former farmer and teacher. He has been a major figure in the party since it began and held ministerial office when the PAS was in the National Front.

Minor Parties

There are a number of very minor parties, most of which are active only in state assembly elections.

Other Political Forces

Formal groups other than political parties are not of significance in Malaysian politics. The principal parties are capable of articulating within themselves and within the governing coalition many of the demands and pressures which would elsewhere find separate institutional expression. Traditional social structures within the main communal groups provide a further channel for meeting demands, while extensive networks of patronage and clientelism within and outside the public sector perform the same function. Another important factor inhibiting the rise of other political organizations has been the 1981 amendment to the Societies Act, which forbids political activity to groups not registered as political. This has severely inhibited overt political activities on the part of all nonparty groups.

Organized Labor

Trade unions provide only a very limited exception to these generalizations. Their membership is drawn principally from the Chinese and Indian communities. Subject to strict government control, not affiliated with any political party, and with the joint holding of union and political party office forbidden, their role is restricted to localized place-of-work bargaining with employers. They have no impact on national political activity.

Ethnic occupational groups also exist, such as the Chinese Chambers of Commerce or the United Chinese School Teachers' Association, but a largely overlapping membership with the MCA ensures that collective interests are promoted within and through the party.

Briefly, during the early to mid 1970s, student organizations, notably the University of Malaya Students Union, were active in making political assertions especially on behalf of poor peasant communities, but separate legislation making political activity on university campuses a punishable offense and the more general restraints referred to above have served to preempt any further student role in national or local parties.

National Prospects

Malaysia's political system is remarkably stable and relatively peaceful, even though it is based on Malay dominance and Chinese acquiescence. The government and the unique political arrangement of the National Front will continue to maintain communal peace by any means necessary. The most serious threat to that peace remains the ideals of ultranationalist and fervently Islamic Malays who object to the declining but still major role the Chinese continue to play in the economy.

A separate but possibly associated threat could arise among poor, especially rural, Malays, many of whom see the benefits of the New Economic Policy accruing to a relatively small and mainly urban middle class. Were they able to make common cause with the poor Chinese, who are mostly to be found in rural areas, the National Front would be faced with a more serious challenge than that which culminated in violence in 1969.

Further Reading

Crouch, Harold; Lee Kam Hing; and Ong, Michael, eds. *Malaysian Politics and the 1978 Election.* Oxford and New York: Oxford University Press, 1980.

Kassim, Ismail. *Race, Politics and Moderation: A Study of the Malaysian Electoral Process.* Singapore: Times Books International, 1979.

Means, Gordon P. *Malaysian Politics.* 2nd. ed. London: Hodder & Stoughton, 1976.

Milne, R. S., and Mauzy, Diane K. *Politics and Government in Malaysia.* Singapore: Federal Publications, 1978.

Milne, R. S., and Ratnam, K. J. *Malaysia—New States in a New Nation. Political Development of Sarawak and Sabah in Malaysia.* London and Portland, Ore.: Frank Cass, 1974.

Sheridan, L. A., and Groves, Harry E. *The Constitution of Malaysia.* 3rd ed. Singapore: Malayan Law Journal (Pte) Ltd., 1979.

Suffian, Tun Mohamed; Lee, H. P.; and Trindade, F. A. *The Constitution of Malaysia. Its development: 1957–1977.* Oxford and New York: Oxford University Press, 1978.

Von Vorys, Karl. *Democracy Without Consensus: Communalism and Political Stability in Malaysia.* Princeton, N. J.: Princeton University Press, 1975.

REPUBLIC OF MALI
(République du Mali)
by Valerie Sanford Griffith

The System of Government

Mali, a country of seven million people in the heart of west Africa, is a one-party unitary state with a mixed military-civilian government. The present government came to power in 1968 in a bloodless military coup led by then-lieutenant Moussa Traoré, who ousted the one-party leftist civilian regime of Modibo Keita. The country's present constitution was approved by referendum in 1974.

Executive

Brigadier General Moussa Traoré is head of state, head of government, and minister of defense. He presides over a cabinet composed largely of civilians, but in which army officers control the key ministries of justice, interior, and defense. Traoré was elected president in June 1979 without opposition and soon thereafter dissolved the Military Committee of National Liberation (*Comité Militaire de Libération Nationale;* CMLN) which had previously exercised all executive and legislative powers. Under the 1974 constitution, the president is elected by direct popular vote to a five-year term and may be reelected only once. Traoré's power is sharply limited by military and bureaucratic factions, apathy and corruption, and by his inability to form a coalition able to pursue a long-term policy.

Legislature

The National Assembly of eighty-two members was elected to a four-year term in June 1979. It appears to have been stillborn, while the single party's national congress functions as a legislature, approving and disapproving Traoré's proposals. The congress is composed of close to 400 delegates selected by local and regional party organizations. Since the public appears to be extremely apathetic toward the party, it is unclear how representative the congress delegates may be of the country's populace.

Judiciary

The nineteen-member Supreme Court supervises a judicial system consisting of the Court of Appeal and lower courts. Supreme Court justices are appointed to five-year terms by the president. Few signs of judicial independence have been observed.

Regional & Local Government

Mali is divided into seven administrative districts governed by appointees of the president. The capital district of Bamako is administered directly by the central government. The regions are further divided into *cercles* and *arrondissements.* Larger towns and cities have elected councils with some ability to administer local affairs and influence the regional administration. Regional governors have apparently found their authority undercut by regional leaders of the government party. To improve their position, they have been made ex officio members of the party's National Council.

The Electoral System

Candidates for the National Assembly are supposed to be selected by local committees of the party. No details of the electoral system have been reported in available sources.

The Party System

Political parties first appeared in Mali in the pre-independence period. The anticolonial, leftist

Sudanese Union (*Union Soudanaise-Rassemblement Democratique Africain;* US-RDA) was founded by Modibo Keita in the late 1940s. It was opposed by the Sudanese Progressive Party (*Parti Soudanaise Progressiste;* PSP), which was supported by merchants in towns along the Niger, veterans of the French colonial army, and the nomad chieftans of the semiarid north. The PSP was banned in the early 1960s when Keita turned Mali into a one-party state. The radical socialist and anti-French policies of the US-RDA had disastrous effects on the Malian economy, and, in 1967, Keita sought a reapproachment with France. Radical elements in his own party opposed this move, and Keita was forced to rely on a private militia to suppress opposition. The 1968 coup ended all overt political activity in the country.

Democratic Union of the Malian People
(*Union Democratique du Peuple Malien;* UDPM)

History

The UDPM was officially chartered as Mali's only party in the constitution of 1974. The party was not actually organized on the grass-roots level, however, until 1978 when local branches were organized in preparation for the 1979 elections. The party has not been a success. Set up as part of a five-year transition to civilian rule, its initial leadership was predominantly military. Hampered by apathy, factionalism, and poor organization, it has had no grass-roots appeal. Efforts to put new life in the party from late 1980 to early 1982 appear to have failed. By mid-1982, the party probably consisted of no more than its national and regional leaders and their clients.

Organization

Although the UDPM is organized along Marxist-Leninist lines, it is not a Marxist party. At the top is the Central Executive Bureau (*Bureau Executif Central;* BEC) of some nineteen members. Most BEC members are now civilians. The BEC, equivalent to a communist party politburo, is elected by the party congress, which consists of some 400 delegates selected by regional and local committees. Between congresses, party affairs are in the hands of the elected National Council of over 125 people. With the exception of the BEC and the congress, which Traoré has increasingly relied upon to generate support for his policies and enthusiasm for the party, most party organs appear to be moribund, coming to life only to select delegates to the congress. Local and regional party organs are probably little more than the personal political vehicles of local notables. The discipline usually associated with this form of party and state is absent in Mali.

Policy

Under Traoré's leadership, party and government policy is pragmatic. Mali, although potentially wealthy in mineral resources and agriculture, has never recovered from the economic disruptions of the Keita regime and the disastrous Sahelian drought of the 1970s. A foreign debt of some $600 million, a severe shortage of foreign exchange, and the necessity of relying on foreign subsidies (mostly French) determine Traoré's policies.

Traoré's major aims are to end the stranglehold which thirty state companies have on the national economy and to revive Mali's agriculture to the point where the country is at least self-sufficient in food, if not a net exporter. The 1981–85 economic plan gave priority to agricultural development, but failed in its early years due to the bad management and marketing practices of the largest state company, the Malian Office of Agricultural Products (*Office des Produits Agricoles Maliens;* OPAM). Present policy calls for the phasing out of most of the state companies by 1986 and returning most of their functions to the private sector.

In foreign policy, Mali is heavily reliant on the Soviet Union for arms, takes a nonaligned position, and seeks assistance from any quarter. Traoré has sought to end the economic isolation of the country by fully rejoining the West African Monetary Union, which Mali left in 1962. The other members of the Union will not accept Mali currency at face value, but the necessary 50 percent devaluation would further undermine Traoré's capacity to govern. By mid-1982, France and the International Monetary Fund appeared to have reached agreements with Mali and the Union that would make integration possible without serious domestic consequences; i.e., France will underwrite the Malian franc.

Membership & Constituency

No figures are available on UDPM membership. Given the general public apathy toward the party, it is likely that it consists of only a small number of paid functionaries and opportunists.

Financing

Information on UDPM finances does not exist. At an extraordinary session of the party's first congress in late 1980, Traoré was able to persuade the members of the National Council to forgo their expense accounts, which suggests that the party is not well financed and relies on state subsidies for its work.

Leadership

Moussa Traoré (born 1936) is party president, but is unable to command the full support or loyalty of its major organs. For example, his attempt to reshape the BEC was rejected by the extraordinary congress session. The BEC, once mostly made up of military officers, is now mostly civilian. The outstanding exception is Colonel Amadou Baba Diarra, one of the few members of the original Traoré group to remain in formal politics, and even he reportedly wants to leave. The secretary of the party, Sory Coulibaly, has control of the party's daily affairs and is reputed to be its most powerful figure. There are indications that Traoré would like to oust him from the post. An ally of Traoré, Lieutenant Sekou Ly, is deputy secretary.

Other Political Forces

Military

Little is known of the factions within the army. Nearly all the officers formerly in government have returned to the barracks or settled into comfortable roles in the bureaucracy. Promotion in the army is slow and has tended to occur only after failed coups, when rebellious officers are cashiered. There are signs that a young officer plotted to assassinate Traoré and return the country to a more socialist course. The officer's uncle, Filifing Sissoko, the leading figure in the president's cabinet at the time and reputedly pro-Soviet, remained in office after the incident.

Bureaucracy

The thirty state companies have been a major drain on the country's finances because of poor productivity, lax supervision, and large and chronic deficits. Traoré has repeatedly accused their officials of disloyalty and personal enrichment at the expense of the nation. Nevertheless, the companies employ over 20,000 people and constitute a major source of patronage for an even larger number. Attempts to dissolve most of these companies will provoke sharp resistance from politicians, organized labor, students (who hope to be employed in them), and businessmen with vested interests in their incompetence and corruption.

Organized Labor

Trade unions are federated in the National Union of Malian Workers (*Union Nationale des Travailleurs Maliens;* UNTM) which is supposed to be controlled by the ruling party. Nevertheless, the union's official publication, *Barakela* (The Worker), is often critical of the government and Traoré. The largest single component of the UNTM, the National Union of Education and Culture (*Syndicat Nationale de l'Education et de la Culture;* SNEC), agitated for higher wages and better conditions in 1980, and several SNEC leaders were arrested. Shortly thereafter, the UNTM leadership itself called on state employees to protest the plans to dissolve the state companies.

Students

The party controls the National Union of Mali Youth (*Union Nationale de la Jeunesse Malien;* UNJM), but a breakaway faction sparked major demonstrations against the government in 1979 and 1980. The dissident organization, the National Union of Students and Pupils (*Union Nationale des Etudiants et des Eleves Maliens;* UNEEM) protested against the severity of examinations, the inflexibility of the educational system, poor teaching, and lack of student grants. They also demanded that corrupt officials be brought to trial and that the country return to Keita's socialist policies. Schools were closed for several months after students fought with police and soldiers in the streets. Hundreds of students were arrested and the UNEEM leader was killed in prison. The sharp repression of the students was seen as the responsibility of the BEC and further alienated youth from the party. The government has since spoken of reforms, but they are likely to be too little to satisfy the students.

Ethnic Groups

Although Mali has several different ethnic groups, there is little ethnic rivalry. About two-thirds of the population is Muslim, and only 2 percent is Christian. The remainder practice traditional religions. About 80 percent speak a common language, Bambara. Only the nomadic Taureg in the north are not fully integrated into the society. Both Libya and Algeria have encouraged Taureg distrust of the central government.

National Prospects

Moussa Traoré has been president of Mali for over a decade. He took over a crippled economy from Modibo Keita and was immediately faced with the severe social and economic consequences of the Sahelian drought. By mid-1982, the economy showed little sign of recovery. Increased foreign investment in mineral-resource development—gold, uranium, iron, oil—will not be profitable for several years. Agricultural recovery, while proceeding slowly, is still hampered by continuing drought in some areas and by low prices and poor roads that discourage farmers from producing an excess for export. What excess is produced is frequently smuggled into neighboring countries where prices are higher.

Throughout his rule, Traoré has shown considerable willingness to pursue a moderate course, consult with and bow to the will of the various interest groups, and encourage the development of civilian government and a more open political system. However, his base of support appears to be narrowing at just the time he needs greater cooperation to carry out necessary reforms. Overall, significant portions of the population seem to be lacking in any sense of civic responsibility to the needs of the country as a whole and appear to tolerate the Traoré government only because it has not threatened major interests. It seems doubtful that Traoré can push through the major reforms he wants without losing what little support his government still has.

Further Reading
Harrison Church, R. J. *West Africa* 7th ed. London: Longman, 1974.
Imperato, Pascal James. *Historical Dictionary of Mali.* Metuchen, N. J.: Scarecrow Press, 1977.
"Mali." In *Africa Contemporary Record, Annual Survey and Documents,* Harrison Church, R. J., et al., eds. New York and London: Africana Publishing Co., 1981.

REPUBLIC OF MALTA

(*Repubblika ta Malta*)

by Charles R. Foster, Ph.D.

The System of Government

Malta, an island nation of 360,000 people south of Sicily, Italy, has a two-party parliamentary system. The republic gained its independence from Great Britain in September 1964. Until 1974, the monarch of England was titular head of state, represented in Malta by a governor general. In that year, Malta became a republic within the Commonwealth.

Executive

The head of state is a president elected to a five-year term by the legislature. Miss Agatha Barbara became president on February 15, 1982. The head of government and chief executive officer is the prime minister, a post filled by the Labour Party's Dom Mintoff since 1971. The prime minister, as leader of the majority party in the legislature, determines legislative policy and names his own cabinet, which is formally appointed by the president.

Legislature

Malta's unicameral legislature, the House of Representatives, consists of sixty-five members, elected to five-year terms by universal suffrage. In 1976, the Labour Party won 51.2 percent of the vote and thirty-four seats; in 1981, it won only 49.1 percent of the vote, but retained its thirty-four seats. The opposition Nationalist Party won 48.8 percent of the vote in 1976 and 50.9 percent of the vote in 1981, but won only 31 seats each year. Charging that the Labour Party had skillfully readjusted the boundaries of constituencies to deprive the Nationalists of their rightful majority in the House, the Nationalists boycotted the new legislative session in February 1982. In April, the speaker of the House announced that the Nationalist seats had been formally vacated under a rule that forbids a member to be absent more than two months. Thus, Mintoff operates the government with the approval of a legislature consisting solely of the thirty-four Labour Party members. The Nationalist Party has called for new elections.

Judiciary

As originally constituted, Malta's judicial branch was independent of the executive. Nine judges, appointed by the president on the advice of the prime minister, serve in the superior courts. A constitutional court of three judges is supposed to review laws and executive acts. All judges are entitled to serve until age sixty-five. In 1980, however, after four private persons filed suit against the government over the closure of a private hospital, the government suspended the superior judges and announced the resignation of the chief judge. In early 1981, the courts resumed their work under a new law which barred the courts from ruling on the validity of government actions. The legislation set up a five-member panel to supervise the administration of justice. The panel was to consist of two members of the Labour Party, and one of the Nationalist Party, one representative of organized labor, and one representative of the bar. The bar representative and the Nationalist boycotted the new panel.

Regional & Local Government

Malta has no local government and few regional branches of the central government. The country is administered as a unit from the capital, Valletta.

The Electoral System

Malta uses the single transferable vote system of proportional representation. Candidates run in multimember districts. Their names appear on the ballot in alphabetical order with their party affiliations noted. The voter is required to rank the candidates in order of preference. To be elected, a candidate must reach a quota of votes—the total votes in the district divided by the number of seats to be filled, plus one additional vote. Votes in excess of the quota are distributed to candidates ranked second on the ballots for first-ranked winners. If a voter's first choice does not reach the necessary quota, his or her vote goes to the highest-ranked candidate who can achieve the quota. While this system does not guarantee proportionality, it does mean that every vote counts.

Citizens age eighteen and over are eligible to vote, and turnout is very high. In the last three elections, it has exceeded 90 percent.

The Party System

The first Maltese political groups were born out of a controversy over language which followed the publication of a British government report on education in 1880. The report recommended that English replace Italian in the primary schools. The pro-English faction ultimately evolved into the present Labour Party, while the more conservative Italian faction later became the Nationalist Party. By 1930, the language issue had become irrelevant as English and the native Maltese (a Semitic language) came to predominate, but the liberal versus conservative tendencies sharpened in the dispute continue to mark the two parties.

There are no restrictions on party activity, but the Nationalists charge that the state-controlled broadcasting system is manipulated by the Labour government, and that the Labour Party employs organized violence against their opponents and the press. The 1981 campaign was marked by some violence on both sides, but the election results, although anomalous, were accepted with relative passivity by the populace.

Malta Labour Party (MLP)

History

The Labour Party was founded officially in 1921 by Dr. Paul Boffa. It came to power for the first time in 1955. After a period out of power, it returned to government in 1971 and has remained in power since then.

Organization

The MLP is organized at the national, district, and village level; virtually every village has its own MLP committee, which is elected annually by the local dues-paying members. Every local committee elects one member to sit on the district committee, which acts as a clearing house for party propaganda and campaign work. At the apex of the pyramid is the National Executive composed of representatives of the district committees and of the Labor League of Youth, party members in the legislature, and additional members elected by the annual National Conference. Conference delegates are representatives of the local committees of each village and town. While the party is highly democratic, the leadership is cohesive and there are no signs of serious party divisions or factions.

Policy

The MLP intends to transform Malta into a socialist state and has gone far toward achieving this aim. Important sectors of the economy, including commercial banks, have been nationalized, taxation is high and wealth disparities are low. The party has long been anticlerical and, in 1974, pushed through a constitutional amendment which prohibited the Roman Catholic Church from speaking out on political issues.

In foreign policy, the party has adopted a neutralist stance and the Labour government is seeking international recognition of Malta as a formally neutral state. That neutrality has been recognized by Italy, France, Saudi Arabia, Algeria, Iraq, the United Arab Emirates, and the Soviet Union. The government permits NATO forces to use Maltese facilities, but it also provides supply and repair services to Soviet ships. The party also pursues a variety of economic and trade policies aimed at making Malta as economically independent as possible.

Membership & Constituency

No reliable data is available on party membership, but the party draws its members and electoral support from nonprofessionals and the working class. It also draws much of its support from anticlericals in the villages who see themselves engaged in a daily struggle against the conservative social teachings of the Roman Catholic Church.

Financing

The party is largely financed by membership dues and other personal contributions.

Leadership

Dominic Mintoff (born 1916) has been the dominant figure in the party since the late 1940s. An energetic and self-assertive man, Mintoff presents himself as the embodiment of the proudly independent and often beleaguered Maltese.

Prospects

The possibility of Malta becoming a one-party state led by the MLP cannot be discounted, but the fact that the majority of the electorate did not support the party in the 1981 elections means that any open move in that direction might provoke considerable popular resistance. It is more likely that the MLP will continue to try to remain in control of the government by continued use of more or less subtle government measures to undercut the strength and effectiveness of the opposition.

Nationalist Party
(*Partit Nazzjonalista*)

History

During the dispute over language, the conservative faction was led by Dr. Fortunato Mizzi and later by his son, Dr. Enrico Mizzi, who was a founder of the Nationalist Party in the 1920s. The Nationalists were in power in 1964 when independence from Great Britain was negotiated and led the government until 1971.

Organization

The Nationalists are less formally organized than the MLP. The primary elements of the party are the personal organizations of the party's candidates and members in the House, most of whom are local notables. A party executive group selected by local party leaders serves as a policy- and strategy-making body. There are no permanently organized village committees or party clubs, although some do exist at the township and district level.

Policy

The Nationalist Party subscribes to a modern liberal and free-enterprise policy. While it does not reject the socialist measures taken by the Labour Party, it wants to ease trade-restriction policies imposed by the Mintoff government to enhance Malta's economic independence. The Nationalists are prepared to rely on the economic and political support of the West, call for rapid formal association with the European Economic Community, and support the NATO military alliance. The party is also supportive of the Roman Catholic Church's role in education and hospital operation.

Membership & Constituency

Support for the party comes primarily from devout churchgoers in the villages, businessmen and small entrepreneurs, and white-collar professionals.

Financing

No information is available on party financing.

Leadership

Dr. Edward Fenech Adami (born 1934) is the party leader. He is noted for a quiet urbane manner and for his tactful negotiating skills.

Prospects

The party called for a one-day general strike on June 30, 1981, to protest the formal ouster of its delegates from the legislature. While most shops closed in Valletta and major towns and school attendance by students and teachers was reported to have fallen to 20 percent in some areas, there was no mass response to the strike call. Government offices and factories continued to function at near-normal levels. This lack of major response suggests that the Nationalists cannot rely on popular pressure to halt the trend to MLP dominance of the state. Nevertheless, if elections are held as constitutionally scheduled in 1986, the party may receive a sufficient number of votes in protest against MLP tactics to return it to government. The party's future would appear to depend on whether Mintoff can avoid alienating those Labour Party voters who are committed to a competitive democratic political system.

National Prospects

Malta has been sharply affected by the European economic decline, and has experienced a fall off in exports and in the trade of the shipping services it provides. However, the impact of these trends appears to have been lessened by the government's policy of tight import restrictions which has kept the balance-of-payments deficit under control and increased the country's self-reliance. There is some hope that an area of the Mediterranean seabed south of Malta may contain oil. This relative economic stability and hopeful outlook should mitigate the likelihood of serious political violence between the two dominant political groups.

Further Reading

Austin, Dennis. *Malta and the End of Empire.* London: F. Cass Co., 1971.

Blouet, Brian. *The Story of Malta.* London: Faber & Faber, 1972.

Boissevain, Jeremy. *Saints and Fireworks: Religion and Politics in Rural Malta.* London: University of London, 1965.

Owen, Charles. *The Maltese Islands.* New York: Praeger, 1969.

ISLAMIC REPUBLIC OF MAURITANIA

(République Islamique de Mauritanie; Joumhouriyyat Mouritania Al-Ishamiyya)

by Valerie Sanford Griffith

The System of Government

Mauritania, a country of nearly two million people in northwest Africa, has been ruled by a military junta since the July 1978 overthrow of the one-party regime led by Moktar Ould Daddah, who had been president since the country gained independence from France in 1960. The immediate cause of the coup was military and popular dissatisfaction with a hopeless war with the Polisario guerrillas in the Western Sahara, which Mauritania had annexed in 1976. A ceasefire was signed with the Polisario in 1979. Mauritania recognized the right of Western Sahara to be independent and proclaimed its neutrality in the continuing war between the Polisarios and Morocco. The country continues to be sharply divided between pro- and anti-Polisario forces and by ethnic, tribal, and regional divisions.

Executive

Full executive and legislative powers are vested in the Military Committee for National Salvation (*Comité Militaire des Salut National;* CMSN), led by Lieutenant Colonel Mohammed Kouna Ould Haidalla, who became president in January 1980. (The junta had had two other leaders between the time of the coup and Haidalla's appointment.) The CMSN is assisted by a cabinet of over twenty members of whom nearly half are army or police personnel. Early in 1981, a draft constitution was published. It provided for a multiparty state with a presidential system of government. The president would be elected by direct universal suffrage for a six-year term and could be reelected only once. The prime minister and cabinet would be appointed by the president. No date has been set for a referendum on the proposed constitution.

Legislature

Mauritania is presently without a legislature. In March 1979, the government announced the establishment of a National Consultative Council of eighty-seven Moors and seventeen black members appointed by the CMSN. This attempt to meet black demands for increased formal representation collapsed when the black members resigned. The draft constitution provides for a popularly elected National Assembly.

Judiciary

Mauritania's High Court of Justice consists of twelve judges named by the president. The Supreme Court, also appointed by the president, administers the civilian court system and is the last court of appeal. The Special Military Court investigates and tries cases which threaten the security of the government and state. The Islamic Court was founded in 1980 to administer traditional Islamic law (shari'ah) in crimes against people and property and in family matters.

Regional and Local Government

Mauritania is divided into thirteen regions administered by appointees of the central government. In September 1978, the interior minister, who is responsible for regional administration, stated that the military government would seek to decentralize regional government and asked the regional governors to prepare independent development plans for their regions. Nouakchott, the capital, is administered directly by the central government. Traditional tribal structures and loyalties remain in place over most of the country.

The Electoral System

No information on the electoral provisions of the draft constitution have been published in available sources.

The Party System

The country has not had a multiparty system since 1964 when Ould Daddah made his Mauritanian People's Party (*Parti du Peuple Mauritanien;* PPM) the sole legal party. No party activity has been permitted since the 1978 coup. The new draft constitution guarantees free political association and a multiparty system, but it is thought that new parties would appeal to ethnic divisions and that the CMSN will not allow parties to form on such lines. The CMSN has set up a new organization, Structure for the Education of the Masses (*Structure de l'Education des Masses*), that could serve as a future political party. Its organizational efforts are led by Mustapha Ould Abeidarrahamane.

In spite of the ban on political organization, the government and army are divided by factions (discussed below) which represent various social divisions within the country and points of view on the Saharan war.

Haidalla Faction

Composed of nationalist army officers of various stripes, this group dominates the government. It supports neutrality in the Saharan war and tries to maintain a balance between the contending interests of Libya, Algeria, and Morocco in the Western Sahara and in Mauritania. It is relatively moderate and pragmatic in policy. Besides Haidalla, the faction includes his closest advisors: prime minister Lieutenant Colonel Maaouya Sid Ahmed Taya; Lieutenant Colonel Yall Abdoulaye, commander in chief of the military; and many other army officers, who it is said, tend to give their loyalty to Taya rather than to Haidalla. The government itself is made up of representatives of most of the factions. Frequent government changes are in part dictated by Haidalla's concern that no one faction gain too much strength by long association with the government and by shifts in relations with Algeria, Libya, and Morocco. While Haidalla is careful to preserve Mauritania's neutrality and to keep pro-Polisario factions in line, his position in the predominantly pro-Polisario government is undoubtedly aided by his birth in and close family ties to Western Sahara.

Haidallah must not only keep a balance between the political factions, but must also forge working alliances with Moorish tribal groups and with key black political figures. The latter have held five to eight cabinet seats in the Haidalla regime. As for tribal alliances, Haidalla briefly tried an alliance between his own region of Adrar in the northwest and the Hodh region in the extreme southeast. By mid-1982, he had developed a working alliance with the Trarza region (Ould Daddah's home area), east of Nouakchott.

The 10th of July Movement (*Le Mouvement du 10 Juillet*)

The army group which originally overthrew the Ould Daddah regime, this faction is pro-Polisario and leans toward Libyan and Algerian interests. It supported former prime minister Sid Ahmed Bneijara (from the Hodh region), who was ousted in April 1981 after getting too close to Libya's Muammar Qaddafi. Two men associated with the group, Mahmoud Ould Boye and Mohammed El Moktar Ould Zamel, were in the cabinet appointed in July 1982.

Nasserites

This pan-Arab group favors union with the Polisario's Saharan Arab Republic and the full Arabization of Mauritania. It is opposed to the pro-Iraqi Ba'ath party faction in the army. The director of the Mauritanian press agency, Hassan Ould Saleh, is a major figure in this faction.

National Democratic Movement (*Mouvement National Démocratique;* MND)

Once a strongly pro-Chinese leftist group, the MND is still a major, if partly clandestine, force among army officers and bureaucrats. It is pro-Polisario, but its major concern in mid-1982 was to end the conflict and distrust between the black Mauritanians of the south and the Arabic Moors of the north. Blacks, led by Traore Ladji, are a major element in the movement. The MND has been an important source of support for moves toward a more open and democratic system.

Free Man (*El Hor*)

El Hor is an organization of the Harratine, former slaves of the Moorish upper class. (Slavery was not abolished in Mauritania until 1980 and still exists in some isolated pockets; under the Ould Daddah, slaves theoretically were free to leave their masters, but the institution remained untouched.) *El Hor* is led by educated ex-slaves who now hold high positions in the army, government, and trade unions, chiefly Boubakar Ould Messoud and Breika Ould M'Barek. The position of *El Hor* on the Saharan issue is not clear.

Opposition

Alliance for a Democratic Mauritania (*Alliance pour une Mauritanie Démocratique;* AMD)

The AMD was the vehicle by which Ould Daddah hoped to return to power with the help of Morocco and funding from Persian Gulf oil states. Based in Senegal and Morocco, AMD sponsored an unsuccessful coup attempt in March 1981 and since then has suffered serious setbacks: Senegal expelled known AMD activists, the major AMD military leaders captured in Mauritania were executed, and Ould Daddah apparently gave up the leadership. Now based in Paris, the group is still supported by exiles in Morocco and conservative business and military leaders in Mauritania. It favors resuming the alliance with Morocco against the Polisario and the re-annexation of the southern Western Sahara by Mauritania.

Other Political Forces

Military

The 7,500-man army is ethnically integrated, although Moorish officers and troops predominate. It is supplied primarily by France, and a small group of French military advisers works with the army. Most officers are associated with one or another of the factions listed above. In addition, a number of officers are associated with the Iraqi Ba'ath party. Published opinion differs as to their political orientation, but they are thought to lean more toward Morocco than to Algeria and Libya, which tend to support the Syrian Ba'ath party.

Ethnic Groups

About 75 percent of Mauritanians are Arab-speaking Moors of Arab-Berber stock. They are divided in turn into numerous tribal groups and into the "white" Moors, the dominant class, and "black" Moors, the ex-slaves, or Harratine. The

Harratine now constitute a sizable portion of the free labor force and urban shanty-town dwellers, along with poorer classes and drought refugees of both black and Moorish descent. Some 25 percent of the population is black and belongs to the Toucouleur, Soninke, Bambara, and Wolof ethnic groups. The blacks are primarily settled farmers in the Senegal River basin on the southern border, while the Moors are primarily nomadic pastoralists.

Sharp differences in national income exist between the north and south: the per capita gross domestic product (GDP), from southern agriculture amounts to about $150 per year, while the annual GDP per head from mineral extraction in the north is some $1,300. The great Sahelian drought of the 1970s accentuated this disparity. Nevertheless, southern blacks had far more contact with the French colonial system, and educated blacks have been consistently overrepresented in the bureaucracy. Arabization of education is designed, in part, to reduce the black role in government. The draft constitution designates Arabic as the sole official language, but a few concessions have been made to permit education in French and black ethnic languages. Periodically, organizations are formed in the south to seek an independent black state.

Organized Labor

The Mauritanian Labor Union (*Union Mauritanienne du Travail;* UMT) is the only organized force in the country outside of the army. Until October 1981, the leadership of the UMT remained in the hands of Ould Daddah appointees; they were ousted only with the combined force of all the factions and a powerful bureaucrat. The Sahelian drought sharply increased the size of the available labor force and the population of the urban centers (Nouakchott's population nearly doubled between 1976 and 1978). With this potential increase in numbers, trade-union militancy could become a major problem for the military regime.

Bureaucracy

A number of state companies have control of extensive portions of the economy with all the opportunities for patronage and graft such control provides. A major state company in charge of food distribution (*Sominex*) is now largely run by private businesses; whether the state gets its share of the revenues from *Sominex* is unclear. The state insurance firm, *Smar*, is a major source of investment funds; its support, both economic and political, is courted by all. Mixed private-state organizations are responsible for mineral development (copper, iron, tungsten, uranium) with the help of foreign investors, while the National Industrial and Mineral Society (*Société Nationale Industrielle et Minèrie;* SNIM) operates the country's mines, which produce most of Mauritania's foreign exchange.

While Haidalla and his immediate associates are considered honest, corruption is a serious problem. Many army officers, government figures, and heads of state companies display obvious signs of new wealth. Haidalla's brother, who became visibly wealthy in a short time, has been nicknamed "Billy" after former U.S. president Carter's younger brother.

Religious Leaders

About 95 percent of the population is Muslim. The dominant religious figures, the marabouts, gain their position partly by inheritance and partly by their reputations for wisdom and piety. Most Mauritanians, black and Moor, are followers of one or another marabout and frequently consult that marabout on all matters. The rise of Islamic consciousness in the Arab world has increased the influence of the marabouts and several, including Haidalla's marabout, Ely Cheikh, have become politically significant on both regional and national levels. Barring a future clash between modern and traditional values on the scale of that in Iran, however, the rise of a single dominant religious leader is very unlikely.

National Prospects

In spite of numerous coup attempts, shifts in military leadership, and factionalism since 1978, Mauritania's potential for political stability appears fairly strong. Most of the country's leaders are pro-Polisario and view the successful Polisario campaign against Morocco as an aid to Mauritanian national integrity, which Morocco has often threatened in the past. The Haidalla government is overcoming the worst effects of the Sahelian drought, aided by rapid development of the country's mineral resources and capital investments in those resources by France, Japan, the United States, and others. Agricultural development is proceeding more slowly, partly because of the feudal system of land holding prevalent in most of the country.

The primary destabilizing factor in the future is likely to be the continuing process of urbanization with its attendant poverty and breakdown of family and tribal ties. Potential "have-not" coalitions of organized labor, the Harratine, and the populist and leftist MND could mount serious challenges against the government if progress falters.

Further Reading
Gerteiny, A. C. *Mauritania.* London: Pall Mall, 1967; and New York: Praeger, 1967.
"Mauritania." In *Africa Contemporary Record, Annual Survey and Documents*, R. J. Harrison Church et al., eds. Vol. 12, 1979–80. New York and London: Africana Publishing Co., 1981.

UNITED MEXICAN STATES
(*Estados Unidos Mexicanos*)
by Marvin Alisky, Ph.D.

The System of Government

Mexico's constitution officially designates this nation as the "United Mexican States," indicating a federal republic in form. However, in practice Mexico remains a centralized or unitary republic with token states' rights. For example, while a governor is popularly elected within each of the thirty-one states, the dominant Institutional Revolutionary Party (*Partido Institucional Revolucionario;* PRI) always wins in every state. The president of Mexico unofficially selects all PRI gubernatorial candidates on the basis of their loyalty to his cabinet ministers, whose directives they must carry out. The constitution reserves for the federal government all authority over commerce, banking, land use, public health, labor laws, corporations, and licensing of professionals.

Any understanding of Mexican public life must begin with the concept of the Revolution, always spelled with a capital *R* to distinguish this ongoing struggle for social justice from the various revolts for political power which preceded it.

Prior to the Revolution General Porfirio Díaz had ruled Mexico as a repressive dictator from 1876 to 1911. The army and police maintained order through force. Díaz took land from political opponents and peasant villages, concentrating large farm-ranch-plantations (called *haciendas*) among a ruling elite. A few hundred *hacienda* owners controlled half of the nation's arable area. Some 90 percent of the rural population spent their lives working on the *haciendas* at marginal pay, perennially in debt to their employers, virtually under feudal conditions.

The military phase of the Revolution began in November 1910; during the ten years of civil war one million lives, out of a population of fifteen million, were lost. With the federal constitution of 1917 in force, the Revolution became a program of continuing social and economic reforms to redress the inequities of centuries. Intellectual Francisco Madero, the first Revolutionary president (1911–13), provided the political theme: "Effective suffrage, no reelection." Peasant leader Emiliano Zapata provided the social theme: "Land, bread, and justice." Zapata's goals have been translated into welfare benefits in a mixed public-private economy.

The "no reelection" protection against extended dictatorship limits the president and the governments to one six-year term, with no second term ever, and prohibits members of Congress, state legislatures, and municipal councils from serving two consecutive terms. After an intervening term, these lesser officials can run again for the same office. Thus the Mexican political structure is a "musical chairs" system under which PRI leaders rotate horizontally as well as vertically from one government position to another.

In 1980 Mexico's population reached seventy million, after sixty years of relatively nonviolent government by a self-replenishing leadership which uses the PRI to win election to the most powerful offices. A coalition of government, party, industrial, labor, and agrarian leaders dominates public life.

Executive

Executive power is vested in a president as head of government and head of state. The president must be a native-born Mexican of native-born parents, indicating the nationalism in the constitution, and at least thirty-five years of age.

Unofficially, he must have had experience as a cabinet minister, be physically vigorous, and able to mediate between the left and right wings of the dominant PRI. Since its founding, the PRI has always elected its presidential candidate. Its inner circle chooses the nominee, with the incumbent president having the most influential vote in picking the cabinet minister most likely to hold together the Revolutionary coalition. During the last year of his six-year term, the incumbent strives to inculcate in his successor his personal concept of the ongoing Revolutionary goals. From 1913 to 1946, presidents had been army generals as well as civilian administrators; since 1946 every president has been a civilian.

There is no vice president. In the event of the death or resignation of the president, the federal Congress elects an interim president.

Presidential powers are extensive and allow the chief executive to dominate the legislative branch. The president can introduce bills directly into both houses of Congress and can assign legislative priorities. The president can veto legislation; he has never had to do so, however, as no law opposed by him has ever been enacted.

The president appoints the cabinet ministers, diplomats, high-ranking officers of the armed forces, and all federal judges, with Senate confirmation. One-party dominance assures approval of his choices. The president can pardon anyone convicted of any felony, and chief executives have used this right freely in political matters to co-opt former opponents.

The constitution allows the chief executive to issue decree laws in most areas of public life. For example, the income tax was created by presidential decree, followed years later by congressional action. Presidential decrees have created cabinet ministries, government corporations, major public-works projects, significant budget changes, and public policies ranging from family planning to nuclear energy, followed later by congressional legislation.

The senior cabinet officer is the *Secretario de Gobernación* (minister of internal affairs), who controls federal-state-municipal relations, liaison with Congress, elections, voter and party registration, immigration and emigration, motion picture production and theaters, television and radio noncommercial air time, the federal police, and federal prisons.

The next most important members of the cabinet are the ministers of planning and budget, finance and public credit, and commerce. These three help the president formulate economic and other domestic policies. Ranking next is the minister of foreign relations, who helps the president conduct foreign policy in conjunction with the aforementioned four ministers.

Presidents Lázaro Cárdenas (1934–40) and Manuel Avila Camacho (1940–46) had been minister of defense. Presidents Miguel Alemán (1946–52), Adolfo Ruiz Cortines (1952–58), Gustavo Díaz Ordaz (1964–70), and Luis Echeverría (1970–76) had been *Secretario de Gobernación*. President Adolfo López Mateos (1958–64) had been minister of labor, and President José López Portillo (1976–

MINORITY-PARTY DEPUTIES		
	1979	1982
PAN	38	56
PCM	18	16
PPS	12	10
PARM	12	0
PST	11	9
PDM	9	9

82), minister of finance. President Miguel de la Madrid (1982–88) was minister of planning and budget.

Legislature

The federal Congress consists of a Senate and a Chamber of Deputies. There are sixty-four senators, two from each of the thirty-one states and two from the Federal District surrounding the national capital, Mexico City. A senator's term runs six years and coincides with the presidential term. The PRI has always won every Senate seat except one, in 1976, which went to a candidate of the opposition Popular Socialist Party (*Partido Popular Socialista;* PPS) from the state of Oaxaca.

The Chamber of Deputies has 400 members, of which 300 are elected from congressional districts based on population. In each congressional district, the candidate with the most votes, plurality or majority, wins the seat. In 1979, the PRI won 296 district seats, and the PAN won the other four. In 1982, the PRI won 299 of the seats, while PAN kept only one.

The remaining 100 seats are for the six minority parties, chosen on the basis of proportional representation. A deputy's term runs three years, every other election coinciding with the presidential election.

The PRI dominates Congress regardless of slight shifts in the number of minority-party deputy seats. Since the legislative branch debates the form rather than the substance of new laws, changes in bills received from the executive branch are cosmetic rather than substantive. Both houses put legislation in final form in committee hearings which follow the guidelines set down by the appropriate cabinet ministry. Floor debate serves as an escape valve for frustration, but has little effect on legislation. The bandwagon journalism of the pro-establishment media filters congressional criticism of the government, making it appear more moderate than it really is.

Sessions run from September 1 to December 31 annually. Each year, the president calls Congress into special sessions for two months or more sometime during a period in January to August. When Congress is not in session, each chamber furnishes half of the thirty members of the Congressional Commission (*Gran Comisión*), which functions in place of Congress, including the confirmation of presidential appointments.

Without consecutive terms, senators and deputies cannot acquire seniority in Congress. Committee, subcommittee, and chamber leaders are chosen instead on the basis of party seniority.

Judiciary

Mexico's federal court system has exclusive authority for all important civil litigation, leaving to the court system of each state civil jurisdiction over minor sums of money and divorce cases. Suits involving contracts, finance and banking, labor-management relations, corporations, and interstate and intrastate commerce are handled by federal courts.

In criminal law, federal courts handle bank robberies, kidnappings, and most major felonies. Murder cases, however, are heard in state courts.

The one major restraint on presidential power is judicial, the writ of *amparo* (relief), which can be issued by any federal judge on behalf of a citizen claiming his constitutional rights have been violated by a government official. The *amparo* can be directed against a government official at any level, but can be obtained only from a federal court.

This writ stays the disputed governmental action until an appeal can be heard by the federal Supreme Court. The *amparo* combines some of the judicial powers found in the Anglo-Saxon writs of injunction, mandamus, and habeas corpus. It may halt official action, compel officials to carry out constitutional obligations, or force judges to tell a defendant the specific charges against him in a criminal case. Political disputes over elections and campaigns are excluded from the authority of *amparos*.

From 1917 to 1980, some 5,500 writs of *amparo* involved the president and his cabinet ministers as defendants. In one-third of these cases, private citizens or groups won their Supreme Court appeal over presidential action.

The federal Supreme Court has twenty-six members: a chief justice and twenty-five justices who divide into five divisions (*salas* or chambers) of five members each. The *salas* consider penal, civil, labor, administrative, and *amparo* appeals cases, respectively.

Supreme Court justices must be native-born Mexicans and be at least thirty-five years old. The president appoints them with Senate confirmation. A justice must retire at age sixty-five or at any time after age sixty if he has completed ten years of service. Since 1929 every justice has been a member of the dominant party, the PRI.

The intermediate federal judicial level is circuit courts of appeal, which there are six. The Supreme Court selects appellate judges from among Federal District Court judges to serve four-year terms. The president can grant an appellate judge tenure until age sixty-five.

Each of the thirty-one states has a state supreme court (*Supremo Tribunal de Justicia*), ranging in size from three to eight justices. The governor selects these justices for six-year terms.

Regional & Local Government

In each of the thirty-one states, a governor is popularly elected for a six-year term and can never serve a second term. Since 1929, every governor has been a member of the PRI. Despite the formality of state party conventions, the dominant party's inner circle in Mexico City preselects the candidate most likely to carry out the national administration's wishes. Except in six states, gubernatorial terms do not coincide with the presidential term. Thus, each incoming president "inherits" twenty-five governors who were selected by his predecessor, albeit unofficially.

Under Article 76 of the constitution, the president can have the Senate remove the governor of any state in which law and order cannot be maintained. The chief executive then designates an interim governor to finish the term. From 1917 to 1964, presidents have removed an average of one governor per year. Since 1964, presidents have averaged only one removal per presidential term. However, each chief executive has pressured one to three other governors to voluntarily resign when political crises got out of control.

Each state has a one-chamber legislature, with members elected for three-year terms, every other election coinciding with the election of the governor. State constitutions reserve most of the powers for the governor, making the legislature a rubber-stamp committee formalizing details of his programs. Legislatures vary from nine to twenty-five members.

In each state the legislature must approve all municipal budgets, which the governor's finance director coordinates.

Mexico has 2,359 municipalities (*municipios*), which are like countries in the United States. Every town and city within the *municipio* is governed by the municipal council (*ayuntamiento*). Councils range in size from five to eleven members who serve three-year terms. Mayors (*presidente municipal*) have the constitutional powers to dominate the councils. During any three-year period, fewer than twenty local governments are controlled by minority parties, the remainder being held by the PRI.

The Electoral System

Elections at all levels of government are popular and direct and provide representation by a simple majority winner, except for the 100 seats in the federal Chamber of Deputies which are reserved for minority parties on the basis of proportional representation. Federal Chamber of Deputies districts and state legislative districts each have a single representative. Two Senators are elected statewide from each state. For each senator and deputy, as well as state legislators and municipal council members, a substitute is also elected. This allows each party to reward its workers with nominations as substitutes. In the event of a vacancy between elections, the substitute immediately fills the post, obviating the need for a by-election.

For purposes of determining minority-party winners by proportional representation, Mexico is divided into three regions. Each minority party prepares lists of candidates for the proportional-representation ballot of each electoral district. All voters receive two ballots, one with congressional-district candidates and one with minority-party candidates. Each voter may choose one name on the ballot listing the minority-party candidates. After the count, each minority party's vote in the three regions is totaled and proportional representation of each party in each region is determined. If it is determined that a minority party is entitled to five seats, for example, in one of the regions, the top five vote getters of that party in that region will get those seats. The system does not systematically favor one minority party over any other.

Voting is secret in booths. Each voter gets a separate ballot for local, state, and federal races should these occur simultaneously. Voters cannot split their ballot but must choose an entire party slate. When given the paper ballot, the voter has his or her thumb coated with indelible yellow ink, which will not wear off for twenty-four hours,

thereby preventing voting twice. All Mexican federal elections must be held on the first Sunday in July, and all state and local elections must be on Sunday.

With the PRI dominant, voter indifference characterizes most elections. Half of the eligible voters do not go to the polls in presidential elections; in congressional or municipal races with strong minority-party candidates, the turnout may reach 70 percent of the registered voters. PRI leaders encourage PRI voter turnout with promises of continuing welfare programs and patronage.

The Federal Electoral Commission protects PRI interests in tabulating disputed congressional elections. Opposition charges of fraudulent vote counting arise in fifteen to twenty-five congressional districts every three years and in several municipalities each year.

The Party System

Origins of the Parties

After Mexico achieved independence from Spain in 1821, its party system consisted of several small parties, each a personalistic group following a strong leader. The real impetus for the institutionalization of parties and the end of purely personalistic movements was the formal uniting of the Agrarian, Labor, and Peasant parties in March 1929 as the National Revolutionary Party (*Partido Nacional Revolucionario;* PNR), now the PRI.

The Parties in Law

The federal Law of Political Organizations and Electoral Processes (*Ley Federal de Organizaciones Politicas y Procesos Electorales* or LOPPE) gives Congress the authority to set requirements for a party to qualify for a place on the ballot.

The 1978 LOPPE requires a party to have at least 65,000 members, with at least 3,000 in each of half of the states. While a new party is awarded temporary recognition for the next federal election, it must win 1.5 percent of the total national vote to retain its legal status. In the 1982 congressional elections, five minority parties retained their official recognition. A new party must be active for four years before it can petition the Federal Electoral Commission for recognition. To get on the ballot for any office, a candidate must have a party affiliation.

Party Organization

The LOPPE requires each party to maintain a permanent national headquarters and a national executive committee. At least six months before an election, a party must hold a national convention to publicly announce its candidates for all offices it intends to contest. In practice, each party's inner circle chooses its candidates.

National officers of each party dominate state and local committees. The only party with active municipal committees throughout the republic is the dominant PRI, which maintains them with government patronage and informal, extralegal use of contingency funds from federal and state budgets.

Campaigning

The Federal Electoral Commission awards each party free postage and telegraph service proportional to the party's percentage of the total vote in the previous election. The government furnishes each party with an equal number of political posters; in 1979, each of the six minority parties got one million posters, the same number the PRI received.

The ministry of internal affairs requires television and radio networks and stations to give free air time to be shared equally by all recognized parties in congressional races. No additional air time can be purchased, and no air time is allotted to state and local contests. All parties must share four hours of television and four hours of radio time per month for three months preceding elections. In 1979, the seven parties equally divided that time. Campaign broadcasts must deal with issues and policies and not individual candidates.

Independent Voters

Independent voters constitute less than 10 percent of the registered voters.

Authentic Party of the Mexican Revolution
(*Partido Auténtico de la Revolución Mexicana;* PARM)

History

The PARM was founded in 1954 by General Jacinto B. Trevino, former minister of industry.

PARM elected its first two deputies to the federal Congress in 1958; adding seats each three years thereafter, it elected twelve deputies in 1979. PARM usually wins from 2 to 2.5 percent of the total congressional vote in each federal election, but in 1982 did so poorly (1.33 percent) that it won no seats and lost its status as a recognized party. Besides deputy seats, its only other officeholders have run six municipal governments since 1958.

Organization

PARM organization is rudimentary. It is primarily a loose association of retired generals who manage the party from Mexico City. There is very little local organization.

National headquarters are at Rio Nazas 168, Colonia Cuahutemoc, Mexico, D.F.

Policy

This party calls for a moderate approach to the ongoing social Revolution, with protection of private property and welfare programs. It wants increased government aid to small farmers.

Membership & Constituency

PARM claims a membership of 200,000, most of whom are middle-aged, middle-class men. Its strength centers in Mexico City and the states of Nuevo León, Jalisco, and Tamaulipas.

Financing

PARM's financing comes from dues, contributions from conservative retired generals, and from government subsidies. In return for subsidies, PARM always supports the PRI presidential candidate.

Leadership

Retired general Antonio Gómez Velasco (born 1920) was PARM president from 1976 to 1982. He directed physical education for the Education Ministry in the 1970s.

The 1982–83 PARM president, Jesús Guzmán Rubio (born 1940), is a retired army general with a law degree. He was a deputy in the federal Congress from 1973 to 1976 and 1979 to 1982.

Carlos Enrique Cantú Rosas (born 1922), PARM secretary general, is a former mayor of Nuevo Laredo and was a deputy in the federal Congress from 1973 to 1976.

Prospects

PARM will have to petition the Federal Election Commission for rerecognition as a party if it is to compete in the 1985 congressional elections. The party may disappear before then.

Communist Party of Mexico (*Partido Comunista de México;* PCM); or Unified Socialist Party of Mexico (*Partido Socialista Unificado de México;* PSUM)

History

Francisco Cervantes López—publisher of a weekly socialist newspaper, and Manabendra N. Roy, a Marxist from India—founded the PCM at a Mexico City socialist conference in September 1919. Roy became PCM secretary general and José C. Valadés, head of the Politburo.

In 1920, the PCM began publishing its official organ, *Vida Nueva,* twice a month. In 1921, the party launched its Communist Youth of Mexico group, sent delegates to the Third Comintern Congress in Moscow, and held its own First Party Congress.

In 1922, the famous painters Diego Rivera and David Siqueiros joined the PCM and began its magazine, *El Machete.* From 1930 to 1935, the party was outlawed for its violence against the government. The Hitler-Stalin nonaggression pact in 1939 cost the PCM 1,000 of its 30,000 members. In 1940, the PCM helped French Stalinist Jacques Mornard assassinate Soviet dissident Leon Trotsky in Mexico City. In the 1950s, the PCM lost members to the Popular Socialist Party. The party helped organize student riots in 1968 which provoked excessive government force, cost 200 lives, and got 2,000 rioters prison sentences. The riots failed to achieve their goal, which was to force the government to cancel the Summer Olympics in Mexico City that year. PCM's intention was to discredit the government.

Organization

The PCM's Central Committee has sixty-five members. In 1976, the eleven-member Executive Committee replaced the Politburo. A party congress is held every two to three years. Arnoldo Martínez Verdugo has been PCM secretary general since 1964 and dominates the party. The Central Committee publishes a weekly, *Oposición.*

An auxiliary, Communist Youth of Mexico, (*Juventud Comunista de México;* JCM) is active on all Mexican university campuses. Since 1978, the PCM has publicly disavowed its former support for the 23rd of September Communist League guerrillas, whose bombings and kidnappings in the states of Guerrero, Morelos, and Jalisco provoked military counterinsurgency. The guerrillas were suppressed in all three states and are no longer active.

PCM controls the Socialist Revolutionary Party, the Mexican People's Party, the Mexican Workers Party, and the Socialist Action and Unity Movement, none of which have legal status on the ballot. In November 1981, the PCM adopted the name Unified Socialist Party of Mexico (*Partido Socialista Unificado de México;* PSUM) for the 1982 elections so that its candidates and those of its unregistered satellite groups could run as a coalition on the ballot. The party's JCM controls the Student Federation of the National Autonomous University of Mexico.

Party headquarters are at Montery No. 159, Colonia Roma, Mexico, D.F.

Policy

PCM's domestic policy calls for expropriation of all privately owned businesses, industries, and services under a Marxist government; party ownership of all media; and abolition of nonsocialist schools. Its foreign policy is anti-United States and pro-Soviet Union. PCM supports Cuba, the Sandinista government in Nicaragua, and the Democratic Revolutionary Front in El Salvador.

Membership & Constituency

PCM claims a membership of 120,000. However, not until the 1979 congressional elections—when it got 703,068 votes or 5.2 percent of the total vote, winning eighteen deputy seats in Congress—did it qualify for the ballot. It lost two of those seats in 1982.

Financing

The party collects dues from members. In addition, it receives grants from the Communist Party of the Soviet Union, the Cuban Women's Federation, the government of Libya, the Palestine News Agency, and other unspecified foreign sources. The PCM owns and rents out office buildings in Mexico City, Tepic, and Veracruz.

Leadership

Secretary General Arnoldo Martínez Verdugo was born in 1925 in Sinaloa state and was a clerk in the Sinaloa state government from 1940 to 1955. He was head of the JCM from 1945 to 1949. He has been a member of the Central Committee since 1955. Valentín Campa, PCM political secretary, and Alejo Méndez García, another prominent leader, were born in 1930 in Mexico City.

Prospects

PCM will continue to rival the Popular Socialist Party as the voice of Mexican Marxists and will continue to dominate the Socialist Workers Party deputies, who follow the lead of PCM deputies in Congress. The party hopes that high unemployment and inflation will discredit the PRI so that the PCM can gain a foothold in the executive branch of government in the late 1980s. Depending on its future success, the PCM may remain permanently, the PUSM.

Institutional Revolutionary Party (*Partido Revolucionario Institucional;* PRI)

History

With the institutionalizing of the social Revolution under the constitution of 1917, the Agrarian, Labor, and Peasant parties clustered in an alliance under presidents Albaro Obregón from 1920 to 1924 and Plutarco Calles from 1924 to 1928.

The dominant party of Mexico, the PRI, was founded as the National Revolutionary Party (*Partido Nacional Revolucionario;* PNR) by former Mexican president Plutarco Calles on March 4, 1929, in Querétaro. The PNR brought together regional and national leaders from the agrarian, labor, bureaucratic, and military sectors.

In 1933, the PNR established the practice of putting forward six-year plans for the country; each subsequent president has adopted the existing plan as the program of his government. The party's national assembly changed the name to the Institutional Revolutionary Party in 1946 to emphasize the continuing social and economic reforms to which it is committed.

President Manuel Avila Camacho in 1943 created the National Federation of Popular Organizations (*Confederación Nacional de Organiza-*

ciones Populares; CNOP) as the sector for bureaucrats, professionals, housewives, merchants, and others of the growing middle class. CNOP subsequently became a dominant force in the party, overshadowing the labor and agrarian sectors in policymaking.

In 1963, the party created an Institute of Political, Economic, and Social Studies (*Instituto de Estudios Politicos, Economicos, y Sociales;* IEPES) to research national needs and policy priorities. The IEPES coordinates PRI and government policy formulation.

In 1964, the PRI elected as its president attorney Carlos Madrazo, former governor of Tabasco. He got the PRI to adopt a policy of party primaries to open nominations for state and local offices to those not tied to political cliques. Madrazo arranged party primaries in two states, Baja California Norte and Chihuahua. However, since its 1929 founding, the PRI has relied on an elite inner circle to select nominees. The inner circle, therefore, got the party's National Executive Committee to cancel the policy of primaries and forced Madrazo to resign. Since 1966, the Revolutionary coalition elite have continued to choose nominees privately.

In the 1982 elections, the PRI won 69.1 percent of the total vote for the 300 congressional districts, taking 299 of the seats, plus all the seats in the Senate. The PRI won 72 percent of the vote in the presidential race, electing Miguel de la Madrid for the 1982–88 term. Inasmuch as the PPS and the PARM also listed him as their candidate, de la Madrid got 75 percent of the presidential vote.

Organization

At the apex of the PRI's organization is the National Executive Committee (*Comité Ejecutivo Nacional;* CEN). The CEN includes the party president, the secretary general, and secretaries for agrarian, labor, popular, and social action. CEN also has two secretaries of political action, always one federal deputy and one senator. CEN also has a secretary of finance and one for media and public relations.

The next level is the National Council, which has fifteen representatives from each of the agrarian, labor, and popular sectors, plus the heads of the state committees from the thirty-one states and the Federal District. The CEN dominates the Council. The Council guides state and municipal PRI assemblies and reports on them to four staff officers of the CEN: the director of administrative services, the director of adjudication, the director of electoral action, and the director of social activities.

The lowest nationwide entity is the National Assembly, in which 1,500 representatives chosen in municipal and state assemblies represent the general PRI membership. National assemblies meet every three or four years and merely ratify CEN policies. In addition, the PRI convenes a national convention every six years to formally ratify the presidential candidate which the CEN already has announced.

The agrarian sector is dominated by the National Federation of Peasant-Farmers (*Confederación Nacional de Campesinos*). The labor sector includes four federations and independent unions, all dominated by the Mexican Federation of Labor (*Confederación de Trabajadores de México*). The secretary general of the National Federation of Popular Organizations (CNOP) always comes from the unions of civil servants.

PRI publishes a monthly magazine, *La República*, which circulates to party municipal committees, federal and state government agencies, and public libraries. PRI publishes a semimonthly journal, *Proyección Politica*, for party leaders at every level. The party owns jointly with the federal government the Mexico City daily newspaper, *El Nacional*. Every six years the CEN appoints its publisher.

The party's women's group is the Revolutionary Feminine Association (*Asociación Nacional Femenina Revolucionaria;* ANFER). The PRI's youth group is the National Movement of Revolutionary Youth (*Movimiento Nacional de la Juventud Revolucionaria;* MNJR). The ANFER and MNJR directors attend CEN meetings.

National headquarters are at Insurgentes 59, Z.P.3, Mexico, D.F.

Policy

PRI's domestic policy stresses "no reelection," a Revolutionary ban on continuation in one office. The party supports the right to strike, even for those working for the government in essential services (except for the military). Minimum wages for all trades and for unskilled labor, social security, basic health care for the poor, public housing for workers, communal or individual farms for peasants, and profit sharing for private-sector workers are PRI policies.

PRI's foreign policy stresses Mexico's independence from the United States, the Soviet Union, and Europe. It favors cooperation with the Organization of American States to promote Latin American regional common markets. The party favors left-of-center Latin American governments.

Membership & Constituency

PRI members hold all executive government posts from minister down through middle-level bureaucrats, all federal judgeships, all governorships, all Senate seats, and 299 of the 300 congressional district deputy seats. Before the 1982 elections, it also held 478 of the 483 seats in state legislatures and controlled 2,341 of the 2,359 municipal governments. PRI members hold 99 percent of all federal, state, and local executive-branch jobs and all diplomatic appointments.

Civil service merit systems are only token, with the PRI's political patronage being the rule in public life. Government jobs are filled on the basis of the political clique (*cammarilla*) system. A successful PRI politician's entourage is horizontal among peers who were classmates in school and vertical among rising administrators and their trusted assistants. Since a *cammarilla* is based on close friendships, as a *cammarilla* leader rises in the PRI and in government, he has his associates promoted into higher-level offices.

Among rank-and-file PRI members, extended family relationships form clusters within the party, based on lifelong friendships within each age group, class, and community.

Financing

Bureaucrats pay party dues equal to three days' pay a year. Other members pay token dues or are given credit for dues by performing various services for the party. Prominent politicians fund banquets and entertainment within their own cities and states. At every level of government, unaudited government contingency funds are used for PRI activities.

Leadership

In March 1981, Mexican President José López Portillo and the CEN chose Javier García Paniagua as PRI president. Born in Jalisco in 1935, García Paniagua, an economist, had managed a government agricultural bank, been a senator, assistant minister of internal affairs, then Lopez Portillo's minister of agrarian reform. He will probably be replaced by an appointee of de la Madrid.

Miguel de la Madrid (born 1934 in Colima), the president of Mexico, is the real leader of the party. De la Madrid has a law degree from the National

University and a degree in public administration from Harvard University. He has been assistant director of finance for the national oil company (PEMEX), the Mexican envoy to several international economic conferences, and a director of the National Bank for Foreign Trade. He was minister of planning and budget from May 1979 to September 1981.

The PRI secretary general is Guillermo Cossío Vidaurri, (born 1934) a former assistant minister of agrarian reform. ANFER director is Yolanda Sentíes de Ballesteros (born 1941), a daughter of a former head of the Chamber of Deputies. She was a deputy from 1979 to 82 and head of the women's caucus in Congress. MNJR director is Hugo Díaz Thomé (born 1951), a former party Social Action administrator in the Federal District.

Prospects

The PRI has run the government since 1929 and dominates most facets of public life. Opposition minority parties receive substantial, although slanted, media coverage as they challenge PRI legislation in Congress and government daily operations, but the policy changes they occasionally coax the PRI to adopt have been more cosmetic than substantive.

In the 1960s and the 1970s, communist guerrilla kidnappings and killings did selective damage to the PRI in a few cities. The most serious challenge to the PRI came during July–October 1968 when the far left organized student riots designed to provoke bloodshed, hoping to force the government to cancel the Olympics. Such a cancellation might have discredited the PRI enough to drive it from power, but the ploy failed.

Even with the pressures of inflation, high unemployment, massive foreign debt, and a declining currency, the government of the PRI continues to command the support of a majority of citizens and likely will remain in power for the foreseeable future.

Mexican Democrat Party
(*Partido Demócrata Mexicano;* PDM)

History

In the city of Irapuato on May 23, 1971, Juan Aguilera Aspeitia founded the right-wing PDM. Aguilera, a business executive in the state of Guanajuato, is head of the Sinarquista National Union (*Union Nacional Sinarquista;* UNS), a fas-

cist group which began in Guanajuato in 1937. In addition to UNS members, he assembled other rightists who wanted parochial education to replace public schools.

Organization

PDM's National Executive Committee and its twenty-three regional committees include secretaries for finance, membership, public relations, and campaigns. Each committee has representatives of artisans, proprietors of small businesses, and peasants. PDM publishes a party monthly magazine, *El Demócrata*, distributed to members throughout the republic.

Party headquarters are at Edison No. 89, Colonia Revolucion, Mexico, D.F.

Policy

PDM's domestic policy calls for a reduction of state-owned enterprises, reduction of welfare programs, an end to PRI cronyism in government, and a "union of Church and State." Its foreign policy favors alliances with anticommunist nations.

Membership & Constituency

PDM's membership of 100,000 in twenty-two states and the Federal District includes many middle-class religiously oriented urbanites. On the ballot for the first time in the 1979 congressional elections, the PDM won nine deputy seats. In the 1982 elections, PDM won 2.5 percent of the proportional representation congressional, sufficient for it to retain its nine seats.

Financing

PDM does not make public its party financing.

Leadership

Since 1978, a business executive from Irapuato, Gumersindo Magaña Negrete, has been PDM president. Its executive committee includes founder Aguilera; Ignacio González Gollaz, a business executive of San Luis Potosí; and José Valencia González, a financier from Mexico City.

Prospects

PDM's chances for growth are almost nil. Catholic lay leaders favor the National Action Party. The party dominates no municipalities, but may continue to retain a few deputy seats.

National Action Party
(*Partido de Accion Nacional;* PAN)

History

The PAN was founded on September 14, 1939, by Manuel Gómez Morín, on a platform of Catholic social principles within the framework of the institutionalized Revolution. Gómez Morín (1897–1972) was dean of the law school of the National University of Mexico and University president.

PAN's roots went back to the National Catholic Party, which was active in Congress from 1911 to 1913. When PAN got on the ballot in 1940, it was the first time since 1914 that a conservative party could fully participate in Revolutionary Mexico.

In 1946, PAN won four deputy seats in Congress and its first two municipal governments. In 1947, PAN won its first seat in a state legislature in Michoacan.

Organization

The party president and secretary general direct the National Executive Committee, which has secretaries for political action, public relations, finance, recruitment, and campaigning. The Committee guides state and municipal chairmen.

In 1958, PAN presidential candidate Luis H. Alvarez introduced into Mexico the first open party convention; an obvious contrast to the PRI's inner-circle selection of candidates. PAN's subsequent conventions also have been open contests. In 1976, the necessary 80 percent of delegates could not agree to nominate Pablo Emilio Madero, nephew of the father of the 1910 Revolution Francisco Madero. The party then voted not to offer a 1976 presidential candidate.

PAN publishes a monthly magazine, *La Nación.* The daily newspapers *El Heraldo* in Mexico City and *El Norte* in Monterrey editorially support it. PAN has a youth sector and a women's association.

Party headquarters are at Serapio Rendon 8, Mexico, D.F.

Policy

Its domestic policy calls for multiparty policy formulation in the government, less government investment in industrial and commercial corporations, and effective suffrage by ending fraudulent vote tabulations favoring the PRI in some congressional districts. Its foreign policy calls for an anticommunist stance to replace the pro-Castro, pro-Sandinista position of the government.

Membership & Constituency

PAN has 500,000 members, a majority being from the middle class and upper class. In percentage of total presidential votes, PAN improved from 7.9 percent in 1952 to 13.9 percent in 1970, when it got two million votes. In the 1964 and 1970 presidential elections, PAN got 31 percent of the vote in Mexico City.

In the 1979 congressional elections, PAN won four districts plus thirty-eight minority-party seats, for a total of forty-two deputies, getting 11.4 percent of the total vote.

In the 1982 congressional elections, PAN won 18 percent of the total vote, getting fifty-six of the 100 minority party seats. It won only one of the 300 congressional district seats. PAN candidate Emilio Madero won 16.5 percent of the total presidential vote, getting 3.7 million votes to sixteen million for PRI candidate De la Madrid. Five other minor presidential candidates shared the remaining two million presidential votes.

Since 1946, PAN has won twenty-nine of the mayor's races and seats in thirty-seven Municipal Councils. Key victories came in 1967 when PAN took over local government in two state capitals, Hermosillo in Sonora and Mérida in Yucatan. Up to 1979, PAN had won seats in seven state legislatures.

Financing

Three-fourths of the members pay voluntary, locally set dues. Catholic Action groups make contributions. The party holds fund-raising raffles, dances, and concerts.

Leadership

National Committee members include José Angel Conchello, an attorney from Monterrey and a deputy in Congress; Manuel González Hinojoa, 1976–78 PAN president; and Efraín González Morfín, the 1970 PAN presidential candidate. Since 1978, the PAN president has been Abel Vicencio Tovar. Born in 1925 in Mexico City, he is an attorney, former deputy, and former PAN secretary general.

Prospects

Because of longtime Church-state conflicts in Mexico, PAN will not affiliate with Christian Democratic parties of Europe, but accepts Catholic social reforms, especially papal encyclicals calling for increased social justice. If fraud were removed from congressional districts in which the PRI barely wins, PAN could win twenty-five or more deputy seats over its current total. It cannot win the presidency, although its candidate is the principal opponent of the PRI candidate.

Popular Socialist Party
(*Partido Popular Socialista;* PPS)

History

On September 25, 1947, labor leader Vicente Lombardo Toledano founded the Popular Party. In 1948, he added "Socialist" to its name, trying to unite Marxists and noncommunist leftists.

A union organizer, Lombardo Toledano was ousted as head of the Mexican Federation of Labor in 1940 because he organized the communist-oriented Latin American Workers Federation. He was the unsuccessful PPS presidential candidate in 1952 and a PPS deputy in Congress from 1964 to 1967. He died in 1968.

Since 1958 the PPS has supported the PRI presidential candidate, but fields its own candidates for Congress and for state and local office.

Organization

PPS has a National Executive Committee and state and municipal committees. It publishes a monthly magazine, *Nueva Democracia,* and a weekly newspaper, *El Combatiente.* Its auxiliaries are the National Socialist Youth and the Socialist Women's Association.

Party headquarters are at Alvaro Obregón No. 185, Colonia Roma, Mexico, D.F.

Policy

PPS wants to nationalize all privately owned industries and businesses, creating a socialist economy. Its foreign policy supports all leftist and Marxist developing nations.

Membership & Constituency

PPS claims 300,000 members. Its strongholds are the states of Oaxaca, Nayarit, and the Federal District. Most members pay voluntary dues, and it receives grants from European Socialist parties.

In 1968 Jorge Cruickshank, without opposition in the state of Oaxaca, became the first PPS senator, breaking the thirty-nine-year PRI monopoly on senate seats. Every three years from 1964

through 1976, PPS won from five to eight deputy seats in Congress. In 1979 it won 2.9 perent of the total congressional vote and twelve deputy seats. Since 1948 PPS has won ten municipal governments.

Financing

The PPS owns office buildings which it rents, and a printing company which accepts nonpolitical business. Profits go into the party treasury. PPS does not make public the status of its income from contributions.

Leadership

The head of the party is the secretary general, a post filled by Jorge Cruickshank since 1968. Born in 1915 in Oaxaca, he was a mechanical engineer and taught at the National Polytechnic Institute. From 1943 to 1951, he led the National Union of Education Workers. He was a deputy in Congress from 1964 to 1967 and 1970 to 1973 and a senator from 1976 to 1982.

Prospects

PPS's influence on government remains indirect, through its ties to the leftists within the dominant PRI. As a result of the 1982 elections, that influence seems to have diminished. The party won only 2.15 percent of the total vote for minority-party seats, slightly less than in 1979.

Socialist Workers Party
(*Partido Socialista de los Trabajadores;* PST)

History

This Marxist party was founded in July 1973. In the 1979 elections, it got 2.3 percent of the congressional vote, winning eleven of the minority-party seats in Congress. In 1982, it won only 2 percent of the vote and nine seats.

Organization

The PST is well organized, directed from the center, and highly disciplined. Headquarters are at Avenida Mexico No. 199, Colonia Condesa, Mexico, D.F.

Policy

The PST calls for government expropriation of all industries and businesses, with each enterprise to be headed by a workers committee. Municipal governments would operate all utilities.

Membership & Constituency

The PST claims 110,000 members, primarily working class, including some Indians.

Financing

The party does not report any financial information.

Leadership

The PST was founded and is still led by Rafael Aguilar Talamantes. Born in 1940 in Baja California Sur, he studied economics at the National University from 1958 to 1964. He was in prison for six years (1964–70) for leading riots which resulted in student deaths.

Prospects

The party's main chance for survival and expansion depends on its organizational efforts among groups of Indians, especially the Maya Aztec, Zapotec, and Tarascan, to which the PST devotes more energy than any other party.

Other Political Forces

Organized Management

Under a 1941 law, every retail store or commercial company must join the local chamber of commerce. These chambers in turn must unite in the Federation of National Chambers of Commerce (Confederación de Cámaras Nacionales de Comercio; CONCANACO). It has an executive council, annual general assemblies, and assesses dues on a scale based on annual sales.

Under that 1941 law, every manufacturer, wholesaler, and distributor within a nationwide industry must belong to that industry's national chamber. For example, every shoe manufacturer must belong to the National Chamber of the Shoe Industry; every radio and television station must belong to the National Chamber of Broadcasters. These industrywide chambers in turn must unite in the Federation of Industrial Chambers (Confederación de Cámaras Industriales; CONCAMIN). It, too, has an executive council, an annual general assembly, and assesses dues on a scale based on annual sales.

Neither CONCANACO nor CONCAMIN are part of the PRI, but individual business and industrial executives usually join the PRI. CONCAMIN and CONCANACO have full-time staffs of economists, lawyers, and other specialists who draft suggested policies, regulations, and procedures. They then lobby directly with the highest appropriate level of government concerned, such as the ministers of commerce, labor, finance, or foreign relations.

Organized Bureaucracy

All federal government employees below the top five levels of administrators belong to unions. Thirty-one unions have members throughout the agencies and departments of the executive branch and among staff employees of the judicial and legislative branches. Since 1936, these unions have been united in the Federation of Unions of Workers in the Service of the State (Federación de Sindicatos de los Trabajadores en el Servicio del Estado; FSTSE). It has one million members.

The FSTSE dominates the popular sector of the PRI and helps formulate major government policies. Its well-disciplined members turn out for political rallies, campaign speeches, and elections. The FSTSE has its own Social Security Institute, which provides better pensions and health services than the social security system for workers in the private sector.

Following the lead of the FSTSE in political activities is the separate National Union of Employees in Service to State and Municipal Governments.

Organized Labor

The largest group of unions is the Mexican Federation of Labor (Confederación de Trabajadores de México; CTM), which helps formulate labor policy for the PRI and the government.

Other federations less politically powerful are the Revolutionary Federation of Workers and Peasants (Confederación Revolucionario de Obreros y Campesinos; CROC) and the National Workers Federation (Confederación Nacional de Trabajadores; CNT).

The Railroad Workers, Petroleum Workers, and Telephone Workers Unions are semi-autonomous, having loose links to the CTM but operating independently. All federations and autonomous unions meet annually in the Congress of Labor, whose key committees articulate organized labor's needs and goals.

National Prospects

Mexico's political prospects during the six-year term of President Miguel de la Madrid are linked to the economic condition of the republic. For twenty-two years (1954–76), during steady economic growth, the peso remained at 12.5 to the dollar. Since 1978, Mexico has been the fourth-largest petroleum exporter in the world; however, most oil profits have gone to service a huge foreign debt rather than to elevate living standards.

In 1982 the peso slipped from 48 to the dollar to more than 100. In August the government for the first time used currency controls, preventing dollars from leaving the country except for vital payments. Inasmuch as the government had periodically promised not to use such controls, their imposition engendered discernible political cynicism.

The International Monetary Fund, private United States and European banks, and foreign governments renegotiated Mexico's loans on condition that the government adopt austerity measures, including reduction of subsidies for food and fuel purchased by Mexicans. With the largest foreign debt of any developing nation in the world, $80 billion, Mexico had to finally adopt measures to reduce deficit spending, a move which was politically unpopular among most Mexicans. The alternative was national bankruptcy, so the severe standards which the government imposed were accepted, with disgruntlement, by a majority of citizens. Nevertheless, political stability likely will continue during the 1980s.

Further Reading

Alisky, Marvin. "Mexico's Population and Migration Problems." *Current History*, Vol. 80, No. 469, November 1981.

———. *Latin American Media: Guidance and Censorship.* Ames, Iowa: Iowa State University Press, 1981.

Briggs, Donald C. and Alisky, Marvin. *Historical Dictionary of Mexico.* Metuchen, N. J.: Scarecrow Press, 1981.

Camp, Roderic A. *Mexico's Leaders: Their Education and Recruitment.* Tucson, Ariz.: University of Arizona Press, 1980.

Cornelius, Wayne A. *Politics and Migrant Poor in Mexico City.* Stanford, Calif.: Stanford University Press, 1975.

Grindle, Merilee S. *Bureaucrats, Politicians, and Peasants in Mexico.* Berkeley: University of California Press, 1977.

Hansen, Roger D. *The Politics of Mexican Development.* Baltimore: Johns Hopkins Press, 1971.

Johnson, Kenneth F. *Mexican Democracy: A Critical View.* 2nd ed. New York: Praeger, 1978.

Meyer, Michael C., and Sherman, William L. *The Course of Mexican History.* New York: Oxford University Press, 1979.

Padgett, L. Vincent. *The Mexican Political System.* 2nd ed. Boston: Houghton Mifflin, 1976.

Ross, Stanley R., ed. *Is the Mexican Revolution Dead?* 2nd ed. Philadelphia: Temple University Press, 1975.

Wilkie, James W. *The Mexican Revolution: Federal Expenditure and Social Change Since 1910.* 2nd ed. Berkeley: University of California Press, 1970.

MONGOLIAN PEOPLE'S REPUBLIC
(*Bugd Nairamdakh Mongol ard Uls*)
by Paul Hyer, Ph.D.

The System of Government

The Mongolian People's Republic, a nation of nearly two million people, is a communist state politically patterned after the Soviet Union. It is generally characterized as a satellite of the Soviet Union; indeed, it was the prototype of the satellite system that later emerged in the Soviet bloc in Eastern Europe.

Mongolia had been under Chinese control from 1691 to 1911, when the Mongolian nobility declared it an independent monarchy under a "reincarnated" Buddhist lama. In 1921, Outer Mongolia was the scene of the first communist revolution in Asia when it revolted against renewed Chinese domination. With Soviet aid, it became an independent republic in 1924. Most, although not all, Mongols continue to believe that their independence from China requires a strong link to the Soviet Union.

The constitution of 1960 theoretically places government in the hands of the people acting through representatives elected to the Great National Khural (*soviet* or assembly). In fact, government is in the hands of a Presidium and Council of Ministers, whose election by the Khural is assured by direct or indirect manipulation by the Central Committee of the single party, the Mongolian People's Revolutionary Party (MPRP) which monopolizes power and administers it through the party Politburo.

Executive

The highest executive body of government through which party policies are implemented is the Council of Ministers which directs the work of the ministries, guides the planned economy, directs foreign affairs, supervises the state monopoly of foreign trade, directs the national defense, and maintains public order through the police.

Legislature

The Grand National Khural is a single house with 354 members elected for a term of three years. The Khural meets annually for about one week to rubber stamp party policy and decisions. When the Khural is not in session, the nine-member Presidium rules in its name. The president of the Presidium, Yumjhagiin Tsedenbal, is head of state; Tsedenbal is also the party secretary.

Judiciary

Supreme Court justices are elected for terms of four years by the Khural. In courts at province, town, and district levels, lay assistants, usually party members, sit with professional judges to hear cases.

Regional & Local Government

The administrative system consists of eighteen provinces, with over 350 districts, and twenty separate municipalities. The boundaries of the districts and the agricultural collectives are the same. Each subdivision is nominally administered by People's Deputies Khurals, which, in fact, are controlled by local party secretaries.

The Electoral System

The party controls elections to the Khurals by creating single-candidate election lists. To indicate approval, a voter simply places an unmarked ballot in the box. The only other option is to cross out names. Suffrage is universal for those eighteen years of age and over. In the national election in 1980, 99 percent of the electorate was reported to have turned out to give their near-unanimous approval to the party's candidates.

Mongolian People's Party (*Mongol Ardyn Nam*)

History

Mongolian politics were traditionally characterized by fragmented political power in the hands of a hereditary nobility which was paralleled and complemented by a powerful monastic clergy of lamaist Buddhism. Politics were dominated by these elites and the people had no active role.

The declaration of independence in 1911 was followed by a decade of nationalistic fervor and continued political turbulence. Radical Mongolian nationalists, encouraged by the victory of the Bolsheviks in Russia, organized the vanguard of the MPRP in January 1920. The party itself emerged in 1921 with the rise of a small group of procommunist leaders who looked to the Soviet Union for direction and institutions to revolutionize the nation. Their success was insured by Moscow's decision in 1921 to set up a satellite government in Ulan Bator. Support from the Red Army and the introduction of Soviet political directors consolidated the party's power. During the 1920s there were great internal divisions between left-wing radicals and right-wing moderates and conservatives. The late 1920s and the 1930s saw violent purges and a forced collectivizing of the countryside. The nobility and clergy were neutralized, but covert competition for personal power continued within the party for many years.

Finally, Khorlain Choibalsan emerged as the strong man in 1939 and the institutions of the party and government were firmly established in, more or less, their present form. A dominating personality not unlike Stalin, Choibalsan ran the government with virtually no consultation with formal government bodies. Only two party congresses were convened between 1939 and 1952, the year when Choibalsan died. He was succeeded by Yumjhagiin Tsedenbal, whose administrative style is much more moderate and conventional.

Organization

The party's structure follows the conventional communist model. A party congress nominally appoints the Central Committee to handle the day-to-day affairs of the party. This pattern is duplicated in the eighteen provincial administrative jurisdictions, called *aimaks*. The party secretary, Tsedenbal, is also president, thus combining the top party and state posts. (This represents more personal concentration of power than is usually found in Moscow.) Tsedenbal is unrivaled, but he shares power with the party's Politburo, the leading collective decision-making group in the system. A nine-man body, the Politburo effectively controls the party's Central Committee.

There is a system-wide tendency for party members to simultaneously hold government jobs. By one recent count, almost half the full membership of the Central Committee also held government posts, a pattern repeated at each lower level. At the same time, there appears to be little participation of lower-level party members in higher party councils; few regional party leaders or officials are represented on the Central Committee.

Since Tsedenbal took over in 1952, the party congress has met six times. By last count, the congress included 708 delegates and forty-four alternates. Selected by various organizations to represent them, roughly 50 percent of the delegates are from party and state organs; 25 percent from the combined areas of industry, construction, and communications; and 25 percent from the livestock and agricultural sector.

The party congress, if not the elite, generally reflects the ethnic divisions of the country. About 80 percent of the delegates are from the Khalka Mongolian ethnic group which makes up about 76 percent of the population. Most of the rest of the congress comes from two other Mongolian ethnic groups, about 13 percent of the population. Kazakhs are the largest single minority in the country, but they comprise only 2 percent of the population and are not a source of friction. They are represented in the party congress. Chinese are a tiny urban minority, and unlike their unassimilated counterparts in Southeast Asia, have little impact on policy and no power to disrupt.

Two satellite associations of the party are the association of labor unions with well over 100,000 members, and the party's youth organization, the *Revsomols*, with 80,000 to 100,000 members. The youth organization was once a major independent force within the party, but has now become thoroughly subordinate to party leadership.

Policy

Party policy has been strongly pro-Russian and anti-Chinese. Top party leadership pushes for solid integration of the country into the Council for Mutual Economic Assistance (COMECON), the other members of which are the USSR and the Eastern European countries. (Mongolia is not a member of the Warsaw Pact organization, but Soviet troops are stationed within the country along its border with China.) Soviet Union party decisions are invariably echoed in Ulan Bator.

Intraparty disputes continue over such problems as overdependence on the Soviet Union, support for particular Soviet policies, and relations with China. A nationalist element in the party has been the object of recent purges and tightening of party controls to eliminate the "narrow nationalists" who were anathema to Moscow and potential rivals of Tsedenbal.

Recent purges have not led to the execution of the opposition figures, but only to their removal from office. In fact, in recent years the party has had considerable stability in its structure, dynamics, and personnel, and there has been a fair amount of intraparty mobility or "changing of the guard."

Membership & Constituency

Total party membership probably exceeds 70,000, about 4 percent of the population. Some 50 percent of the membership consists of the "intelligentsia" and government employees, another 30 percent is made up of urban workers, and the remaining 20 percent consists of *arats*, members of the livestock cooperatives. Projections indicate that the relative number of workers is increasing and that of the *arats* decreasing. The word "intelligentsia" is commonly used in Mongolia to refer to the so-called "working intelligentsia" which includes many poorly educated and inarticulate persons. The party elite are virtually all true intelligentsia—bureaucrats, officials, and professionals.

Financing

No information is available on party finances. Presumably, membership dues and state support cover party expenses.

Leadership

The leadership is relatively young; Tsedenbal, for example, was born in 1916, and the head of government, Jambiin Batmunkh, was born in 1926. In part, this reflects the lack of education among older Mongolians, which, in turn, also partly explains why party power is so narrowly concentrated.

Yumjhagiin Tsedenbal was chairman of the State Planning Commission (1944–48) before he became head of the state and party. The personality cult which marked his predecessor's reign has not been continued, but personality and personal differences appear to be of as much importance in the alignments of the elite as policy and ideology.

Tsedenbal was educated in the Soviet Union and has a Russian wife. Many of the elite have similar personal as well as political ties to the Soviet Union.

Tsedenbal is an economist, and Soviet-educated economists predominate at the top levels of the party. Among other leaders, one is the author of a widely used book on livestock finances, one is a planning specialist, and a third is a financial expert. Apart from the group of economists, a group of party officials who specialize in foreign affairs has remained especially strong.

A third group of leaders is composed of military men, although professional soldiers do not seem to have great influence in the party outside of the area of their immediate expertise. Nevertheless, the army is generally regarded as a key element in both the integration and indoctrination of a once-fragmented society. It has also played a major role in the spread of literacy. The structure and dynamics of the internal-security apparatus, the Ministry of State Security, is modeled closely on that of the Soviet Union, but it is not important as a separate leadership group.

Opposition

There is some evidence of irritation among artists and teachers over party controls and censorship, but there are no signs of consistent or organized dissent.

National Prospects

The political system of Mongolia is totalitarian in intent, but less so in fact and effectiveness. The majority of the people are less than a generation removed from an almost completely nomadic society, and while the change to an industrial and agricultural society has proceeded rapidly, it is by no means complete. The nomadic spirit of free-wheeling independence is still alive in Mongolia. The slow development of education, communications, and transportation also make the classic formula for communist control difficult to apply effectively. Bureaucratic incompetence and inefficiency are endemic: party policy is often not carried out, not because of deliberate opposition, but because of the ineptitude and lethargy of those who must deal directly with the people and the problems.

At the same time, the last quarter of a century has seen a major increase in the percentage of the population involved in the political life of the country. It is the consensus of specialists that a higher percentage of the Mongolian people are represented in the power structure of Mongolia than is the case in any other communist nation, or indeed of most other Asian nations. This is due in part to the sparse and relatively homogeneous population; but it also reflects the growth of education, communication and transportation—developments which are essential to the communist recipe for totalitarian control.

Further Reading

Bawden, Charles R. *The Modern History of Mongolia.* New York: Praeger, 1968.

Friters, Gerard M. *Outer Mongolia and Its International Position.* New York: Octagon Books, 1978.

Ginsburg, George. "Local Government in the Mongolian People's Republic 1940–1960." *Journal of Asian Studies*, Vol. 20, No. 4, August 1961.

Jagchid, Sechin and Hyer, Paul. *Mongolia's Culture and Society.* Boulder, Colo.: Westview Press, 1980.

Shirendev, B. and Sanjdorj, M. *History of the Mongolian People's Republic.* Translated and annotated by William A. Brown and Urgunge Onon. Cambridge, Mass.: Harvard University Press, 1977.

Lattimore, Owen. *Nomads and Commissars; Mongolia Revisited.* New York and London: Oxford University Press, 1962.

———. "Satellite Politics: The Mongolian Prototype." *Western Political Quarterly*, Vol. 9 (1956).

Rupen, Robert A. *How Mongolia Is Really Ruled.* Stanford, Calif.: Hoover Institution Press, Stanford University, 1979.

———. *Mongols of the Twentieth Century.* 2 Vols. Bloomington, Ind: Indiana University Press, 1964.

KINGDOM OF MOROCCO
(*Al-Mamlaka al-Maghrebia*)
by Tony Hodges

The System of Government

The Kingdom of Morocco, with a population of nearly 20.5 million, is a traditional monarchy. Although there is a constitution, the reigning Alawite dynasty is not a "consitutional monarchy" in so far as all three of Morocco's postindependence constitutions (adopted in 1962, 1970, and 1972) have enhanced rather than limited the king's power.

The Monarchy

The pivotal role of the monarch is spelled out in the 1972 constitution: "The King is the Commander of the Faithful, the Supreme Representative of the Nation, the Symbol of her Unity and the Guarantor of her existence and continuity. He is the Defender of the Faith and the Guardian of respect for the Constitution."

The constitutional powers of the king are wide-ranging: he appoints and dismisses the prime minister and the other ministers; he has the right to address the Chamber of Representatives and "the content of his address shall be above comment"; he is commander-in-chief of the armed forces and appoints the senior military officers; and he controls the judiciary by virtue of his powers to appoint the judges and preside over the Higher Judicial Council.

The king has the right to dissolve the Chamber of Representatives by decree and exercise its legislative powers until new elections, which must be held within three months. However, by virtue of Article 35 of the constitution, the king may declare a state of exception under which he may rule by decree for an indefinite period. This right was first invoked by Hassan II in 1965. The state of exception lasted almost five years, until the promulgation of the 1970 constitution. Hassan II was able once again to rule by decree without any elected legislative body between 1972 and 1977

simply by refusing to call general elections after the adoption of the 1972 constitution.

Constitutional revision, which can be initiated by the king without reference to the Chamber of Representatives, requires approval in a referendum, but the consitution specifies that "the monarchical system, and provisions relating to Islam, shall not be subject to revision."

The king claims a divine right to rule, as *Amir al-Muminin*, or Commander of the Faithful; and it is this presumption to both the spiritual and temporal leadership of his subjects which sanctions his claim to ultimate control over the nation's political life.

A rule of primogeniture is established in the constitution. If the king dies or abdicates before his successor reaches the age of sixteen, the king's powers are exercised by a regency council, composed primarily of royal appointees. Until the heir reaches his twentieth birthday, it acts as a consultative body.

Executive powers are delegated by the king to the Council of Ministers, which is headed by the prime minister. Since the last general elections, in 1977, the government has been a coalition of pro-royalist "independents," the Istiqlal (Independence) Party, the Popular Movement (*Mouvement populaire;* MP), and nonparty technocrats. Since March 1979, the premier has been Maati Bouabid, who has no party affiliation.

Although its influence on the process of decision making is considerable, the Council of Ministers is subordinate and responsible to the king, who personally makes the most important policy decisions. The king is advised by a small, influential royal cabinet, a group of four or five royal counselors headed by a director-general, who are among the king's most trusted political allies.

Legislature

Since 1977, when the first parliamentary elections were held under the 1972 constitution, Morocco has had a unicameral legislature, known as the Chamber of Representatives. Two-thirds of its seats are elected directly, and the remaining third by provincial and prefectoral assemblies and by corporate groups representing commerce, industry, agriculture, crafts, and labor. Originally, representatives were to serve four-year terms, but a consitutional amendment, approved by referendum in May 1980, extended the life of the Chamber to six years, thereby postponing the elections due in 1981.

The Chamber's legislative competence is relatively narrow. The consitution bars the Chamber from adopting bills or amendments which reduce the state's revenue or raise public expenditure. If, by December 31, the Chamber has not approved the following year's budget, the government can simply proceed as if the budget had been approved. The deputies have the right to vote on the development plan but cannot amend it. With regard to the broad objectives of economic, social, and cultural policy, the Chamber can pass *lois cadres* (framework laws), but the details of such laws and all other subjects not specified as falling within the Chamber's competence are considered to come under the government's admininstrative authority. The government is entitled to reject any legislative proposal passed by the Chamber which it deems to be outside its legislative competence. In the event of a disagreement between the Chamber and the government in such a case, a ruling is made by the constitutional chamber of the Supreme Court.

In fact, the Chamber has engaged in very little legislative activity since 1977, and there has been a high rate of absenteeism on the part of the deputies, possibly because of the Chamber's relative lack of importance in the political system.

Judiciary

Although formally independent of the executive and the legislature, the judiciary is under the strong influence of the king, who appoints the judges and presides over the Higher Judicial Council, which supervises the judicial system. In political trials, sentences often appear to be predetermined by the Ministry of Justice; and Amnesty International has claimed that political prisoners frequently are not given a fair trial, often subjected to torture, and may be held incommunicado for months or years.

The court system includes communal and district courts for minor offenses, thirty tribunals of first instance, nine appeal courts, a Supreme Court (with criminal, civil, administrative, social, and constitutional chambers), social courts for labor cases, the High Court for crimes committed by ministers in the exercise of their public functions, the Special Court of Justice for crimes committed by civil servants, and the Court of Justice which judges serious state security and political cases.

Regional & Local Government

At the local level, Morocco is divided into several hundred rural and municipal communes, which are administered by state officials known as *caids* in the rural areas and *pashas* in the municipalities. They are appointed by and responsible to the Ministry of the Interior. The communal councils, which have between nine and fifty-one members each, directly elected with a six-year mandate, have neither the funds nor the authority to be more than "rubber stamp" bodies for the decisions of the local *caid* or *pasha* and his administration. Several communes comprise a *cercle*, which is headed by a *supercaid*.

The highest unit of of subnational administration is the province or, in large conurbations, the prefecture. They are administered by governors, appointed by the king, and responsible to the Ministry of the Interior. Each province and prefecture has an indirectly elected assembly of eleven to thirty-three members selected by the communal councillors. Like the communal councils, the provincial assemblies have little real power, their decisions being subject to the approval of the governor.

The Electoral System

The Chamber of Representatives has 267 seats, 264 of which were filled at the last general election, in 1977, and three in May 1981 to represent the formerly Mauritanian sector of Western Sahara, Oued ed-Dahab, which was annexed by Morocco in 1979. Of these 267 seats, 178 are filled by direct elections in single-member constituencies. Suffrage is universal for Moroccan citizens age twenty-one and over. The remaining eighty-nine seats are elected indirectly. Of these, forty-nine are elected by the provincial and prefectoral assemblies, which are in turn elected by the municipal and rural communal councils; fifteen are elected by the Chambers of Agriculture; ten by the Chambers of Commerce and Industry; ten by the

THE 1976–1977 PARLIAMENTARY ELECTIONS

Party	Communal Council Elections Nov 12, 1976 Seats	Provincial/ Prefectoral Assembly Elections Jan 25, 1977 Seats	Direct Stage June 3, 1977 % Votes	Seats	Indirect stage June 21, 1977 Provincial/ Prefectoral Assemblies Seats	Chambers of Agriculture Seats	Chambers of Commerce & Industry Seats	Chambers of Crafts Seats	Salaried Employees Seats	Total Seats	Total Seats
Independents (Royalists)	8,582	369	44.46	81	32	10	10	7	1	60	141
Istiqlal Party	2,184	50	21.62	46	4	—	—	—	1**	5	51
MP	1,054	45	12.40	29	10	5	—	—	—	15	44
USFP	874	27	14.63	15	—	—	—	—	—	—	15
MPDC	452	15	2.02	2	1	—	—	—	—	1	3
UNFP/UMT*	113	3	—	—	1	—	—	—	6	7	7
PPS	26	1	2.30	1	—	—	—	—	—	—	1
Action Party	58	2	1.80	2	—	—	—	—	—	—	2
Others	19	1	0.77	—	—	—	—	—	—	—	—
TOTAL	13,362	513	100.00	176	48	15	10	7	8	88	264

* The UNFP was the only major party to boycott the June 1977 elections. However, some independent UNFP candidates stood for election. The UMT labor federation, which is close to the UNFP, won six of the eight seats representing salaried employees.

** A seat won by the Istiqlal Party's labor federation, Union Generale des Travailleurs Marocains (UGTM).

Chambers of Crafts; and eight by representatives of salaried employees.

The largely urban-based left-wing parties are at a decided disadvantage to the overtly proroyalist forces in this system. First, rural voters greatly outnumber urban voters: in 1977, only 30.5 percent of the six and one-half million registered voters were in the urban areas. Secondly, the anti-monarchical parties generally have failed to penetrate the countryside, partly because the king's religious prestige is greater there than in the cities, but also because the Ministry of the Interior, through its network of *caids*, effectively bars the more radical urban parties from campaigning in many rurl areas. Thirdly, the system of indirect election artificially reinforces the royalist majority in the Chamber of Representatives.

Thus, the royalist *Mouvement Populaire* (MP) won only 12.4 percent of the votes in the direct elections to the Chamber on June 3, 1977, but won twenty-nine rural seats, while the left-wing Socialist Union of Popular Forces (*Union Socialiste des Forces Populaires;* USFP) won only fifteen seats with 14.6 percent of the poll. Since the MP won an additional fifteen indirectly elected seats and the USFP won none, the MP ended up with almost three times as many seats as the USFP (forty-four compared to fifteen) despite getting fewer votes. With only 44.5 percent of the votes, the "independents" won eighty-one of the directly elected seats, but with their additional sixty indirectly elected seats, they enjoyed a disproportionately large majority in the Chamber of Representatives—141 of the 264 seats. The Istiqlal Party came second in terms of popular support (21.6 percent) and forty-six seats, but was also at a disadvantage in the indirect stage of the elections, winning only five of the eighty-eight seats, and so ended up with only fifty-one seats in the Chamber of Representatives. Over 82 percent of registered voters went to the polls in the June 1977 elections.

Accusations of election-rigging frequently have been levelled against the government by opposition parties. The official returns for referenda held to legitimize successive constitutions and constitutional amendments in particular have been viewed skeptically by independent observers. It hardly seems credible, for example, that 96.7 percent of the votes cast in the May 1980 referendum supported the constitutional amendment extending the life of a parliament from four to six years despite the vigorous opposition of the two main opposition parties, the USFP and the Party of Progress and Socialism (*Parti du Progrès et du Socialisme;* PPS).

The King

Hassan II (born 1929) has displayed remarkable skill in defending the monarchy's grip on power, which he codified when he finally drew up the country's first constitution in 1962.

Like his father, he tried to undermine the UNFP and the Istiqlal Party (which was forced to leave the government in 1963) by building up rival ultra-royalist movements, like the MP and a royalist coalition, the Front for the Defense of Constitutional Institutions (*Front pour la Défense des Institutions Constitutionelles;* FDIC) which was formed to contest the first general elections, in 1963. Although the FDIC itself was short-lived, royal support for such loyalist movements has been a constant theme of Hassan II's political strategy. Thus, it was the MP and the "independents" who received the palace's support in the 1977 elections.

It has been in the countryside, where the king still enjoys considerable religious prestige and the Ministry of the Interior's *caids* can prevent effective penetration by the opposition parties, that the king has been able to rely on solid electoral support for these loyalist movements.

Hassan's control of state resources, including radio and television, is an important political advantage of which he makes full use. Press circulations rarely exceed 50,000, but there are 1.7 million radios and 465,000 television sets (1977), and the king commands an audience whenever he makes a speech, which he does frequently. The educational system is also used to inculcate loyalty to the monarchy, which is portrayed in textbooks as the country's bastion against foreign rule.

The king also uses his powers of appointment and patronage to buy support and placate critics. Indeed, favoritism and corruption are an integral part of his strategy of rule. He is also a renowned master of creating and exploiting divisiveness; a political juggler who has successfully orchestrated the political system by playing up the rivalries and mutual suspicions of the country's main factions—political parties, trade unions, and the armed forces—and so diminished the threat to the throne from each.

Additionally, he has been careful to include "safety valves" in the political system—outlets for the expression of grievances and protest which, although circumscribed, discourage most opposition politicians from dropping out of the established system altogehter and engaging in more radical forms of opposition. Thus, within certain bounds, political parties are allowed to exist legally, publish newspapers, and, from time to time, contest elections and express their views in Parliament.

This does not, however, prevent the king from repressing his political opponents or curbing civil liberties when he finds it opportune or necessary to defend his rule. In July 1963, for example, his government announced the discovery of a "plot" against the monarchy, arrested 130 members of the UNFP, including twenty-one of its twenty-eight deputies, and sentenced ten party members, among them its exiled leader, Mehdi Ben Barka, to death. In October 1965, Ben Barka was murdered in mysterious circumstances in Paris. The previous March, hundreds of slum-dwellers were killed in Casablanca when the army suppressed antigovernment riots. The riots, and the factional squabbling with the FDIC, prompted Hassan to declare a state of exception in June 1965 and to rule by decree for the next five years. Opposition newspapers frequently have been censored or suppressed; opposition parties have sometimes been banned (a fate suffered at times by both the communists and the socialists); and over the years thousands of oppositionists have been detained, sometimes to be tortured and occasionally executed.

An additional weapon in the king's armory is his populism. After narrowly thwarting two military coups in 1971 and 1972, for example, he rallied popular support by ordering the Moroccanization of the remaining French landholdings, sending troops to fight in the October 1973 Middle East war and, above all, launching his great campaign to annex Spanish-ruled Western Sahara. Spain's cession of its desert colony in 1976 allowed the king to recoup his lost popularity, neutralize the opposition parties, and so permit a relative liberalization, which culminated in the calling of the 1977 general elections.

However, as the enthusiasm generated by the "recovery" of Western Sahara gave way to renewed mass agitation over the country's chronic domestic problems, the king resorted once again to the stick. In June 1981, the king ordered the army to suppress riots in Casablanca sparked by huge rises in food prices. More than 600 are believed to have been killed and 2,000 arrested. More than 200 leaders of the USFP and its trade unions received jail terms in a series of political trials, and the party's newspapers were shut down.

During his two decades of rule, King Hassan generally has aligned his foreign policy with the West. He has maintained especially close relations with France and the United States. While condemning Zionism, he has tended to favor detente between Israel and the Arab world. He has allied with the most pro-Western regimes in Africa and sent troops to help crush the Shaba uprisings in Zaire in 1977 and 1978. In the Maghreb (North Africa, excluding Egypt), he abandoned Morocco's traditional claims to Mauritania and the Algerian Sahara in 1969 to 1972, but maintained the claim to Western Sahara. Since 1975, the war against the Western Saharan nationalist guerrillas of the Polisario Front has been his major preoccupation. Domestically, he favors retaining an important place for private business and foreign investment in the economy, though many large industries, including the key phosphate mines, are in public hands. A pragmatic and flexible politician, King Hassan is, above all, committed to the maintenance of his rule and the survival of his dynasty.

The fate of many monarchies in the Third World suggests that eventually the Alawite dynasty will be overturned. The progressive urbanization and modernization of Moroccan society bring greater questioning of the monarch's claim to a divine right to rule. His religious prestige is lowest in the urban areas, where 44 percent of Moroccans now live (compared to only 14 percent at the time of independence).

The Party System

Parties first emerged in Morocco as a consequence of the nationalist struggle against French and Spanish rule, which began under the leadership of French-educated intellectuals and religious reformists (*Salafis*) and reached a mass scale in the late 1930s. In 1943, Ahmed Balafrej and other nationalists founded the Istiqlal Party, which was to spearhead the struggle for independence under the leadership of Allal el-Fassi.

The Istiqlal Party formed a close alliance with Sultan Mohammed V, whose Alawite dynasty had been forced to accept a Franco-Spanish "protectorate" in 1912. After about 1946, he refused to cooperate with the French authorities, who retaliated by exiling him to Madagascar in 1953. This step only fanned the flames of nationalist revolt. An Army of Liberation began guerrilla attacks in 1955, and France, which was already facing a rebellion in Algeria, decided to come to terms with the Moroccan nationalists. Mohammed V returned to Morocco as a national hero and, in 1956, France and Spain ended their protectorate.

In granting Morocco independence, France and Spain returned full sovereignty to the sultan, who acquired the title of king. A struggle for primacy then ensued between the monarch and the more radical factions of the nationalist movement. The king retained all legislative powers and refused to hold elections or allow a constitution to be drafted. He also encouraged the emergence of royalist political movements. The king's enormous prestige stood him in good stead in this contest, as did the practical support of France, which helped to build up the king's Royal Armed Forces (*Forces Armées Royales;* FAR) and provided many of his government's civil servants for serval years. Between 1956 and 1959, the irregulars of the Army of Liberation were gradually forced to hand over their arms, join the FAR, or disband. Though the Istiqlal Party was included in the postindependence government, the king tried to weaken it by giving cabinet posts to royalist independents and the small Democratic Independence Party (*Parti Démocratique de l'Indépendance;* PDI) and by encouraging the Berber-based MP after its creation in 1957. As little more than a loose alliance of factions united in support of independence, the Istiqlal Party was unable to check Mohammed V's tightening grip on power; and in 1959 the party split, the more radical nationalists setting up the National Union of Popular Forces (*Union Nationale des Forces Populaires;* UNFP). By the time of Hassan II's ascent to the throne, in 1961, upon Mohammed V's death, the monarchy was well entrenched in power.

Istiqlal (Independence) Party

History

Founded in 1943, the Istiqlal Party led the struggle for independence, in close alliance with Sultan Mohammed V. As a broad alliance united in pursuit of independence, it enjoyed overwhelming popular support, but it had no agreed program of policies for independent Morocco. It was unable to offer effective resistance to the consolidation of political power in the hands of the monarch. The party was greatly weakened by the split with the UNFP in 1959, as well as by the palace's encouragement of ultraloyalist factions. In 1963 it was forced out of the government, in which it had participated since 1956, and it remained in opposi-

tion until 1977, when it reentered the government with eight cabinet posts.

Organization

Between party congresses, which are held every two or three years, with over 5,000 delegates attending, the party is headed by a 510-member National Council. Day-to-day leadership is provided by the much smaller Executive Committee. The party publishes two daily newspapers, *Al-Alam* in Arabic and *L'Opinion* in French.

Policy

Party policy is strongly nationalist. In the immediate postindependence years, it championed the idea of "Greater Morocco"—the incorporation into Morocco of Western Sahara, Ifni, Mauritania, the Algerian Sahara, and northwestern Mali. The party objected strongly to King Hassan's recognition of Mauritania and to the de facto border with Algeria in 1969 to 1972. Istiqlal would be the most resistant to concessions to the Polisario Front in Western Sahara. The party is noted for supporting full Arabization of education, strict adherence to Islamic principles, rejection of birth control, and denigration of "foreign ideologies" like Marxism. It accepts royal primacy, despite irritation at the king's refusal to share real power. Since 1977, it has loyally backed government policies and so muted its support for such causes as rapid Arabization and the nationalization of banks.

Membership & Constituency

The party is primarily urban and middle class and enjoys the support of much of the country's religious officialdom. It is weak among students and unionized workers, though it has a very small student organization and a labor organization.

Financing

Istiqlal's funding traditionally has come from prominent bourgeois families. This support, however, has declined significantly since the early 1960s.

Leadership

Since Allal el-Fassi's death in 1974, M'hammed Boucetta (born 1925 in Marrakesh) has been Secretary general. He has been foreign minister since 1977.

Prospects

Because of its association with unpopular government policies, the party is likely to continue losing support to forces on its left, in particular the USFP, and perhaps also to Islamic fundamentalist groups.

National Assembly of Independents (*Rassemblement National des Independants;* RNI)

History

Founded in October 1978, the RNI was initially a loose coalition of the royalist "independents" who won the 1977 general elections. It had much in common with the earlier FDIC, the bloc of proroyalist forces which held half the seats in the 1963–65 Parliament, although, unlike the FDIC, it did not include the MP. Like the FDIC, the RNI was soon beset by internal squabbles. Two rival factions emerged in 1980; and, in April 1981, fifty-nine of the RNI's deputies announced that they were forming a new parliamentary group, known as the Democrat Independents (*Indépendants Démocrates;* ID). The RNI rump then suffered a serious setback when its six members in the government lost their ministerial posts in a cabinet reshuffle in November 1981.

Organization

The RNI remains a loosely structured bloc of royalists. It has two daily newspapers—*Al-Mihttaq* in Arabic and *Al-Maghrib* in French.

Policy

The RNI is strongly proroyalist. It is supportive of private business, strongly antisocialist, and pro-Western in foreign policy.

Membership & Constituency

The party's top leaders come mainly from the wealthiest strata of Moroccan society. Many have important commercial or industrial interests or have served as senior technocrats in successive governments. The party enjoys support from members of the chambers of commerce and industry and such bodies as the employer's General Economic Confederation of Morocco (*Confedera-tion Generale Economique du Maroc;* CGEM). Its electoral support is primarily rural.

Financing

The RNI is supported by the personal funds of its leading members.

Leadership

Ahmed Osman (born 1930 in Oujda) is the RNI's president. He is a brother-in-law of King Hassan and was prime minister from 1973 to 1979.

Prospects

Deprived of the advantages of participating in the government, yet lacking in credibility as a real opposition party, the RNI rump is unlikely to prosper and may suffer new factional crisis.

Democrat Independents (*Indépendants Démocrates;* ID)

History

Registered as a parliamentary group in April 1981 and as a political party a few weeks later, the Democrat Independents are a breakaway from the RNI. In the November 1981 cabinet reshuffle, they increased their number of ministerial posts from three to five, while the RNI rump left the government.

Organization

Organization remains rudimentary and consists primarily of the parliamentary bloc and the network of patron-client relationships of its rural leaders.

Policy

Like the RNI, the ID are strongly proroyalist. They are antisocialist, pro-Western in foreign policy, and supportive of private business. But, whereas the RNI rump tends to represent the interests of industry and commerce, the ID are supported by many of the large landowners and therefore support policies favorable to the development of large-scale commercial farming.

Membership & Constituency

The leaders of the ID are generally wealthy and are often large landowners. Their electoral base is overwhelmingly rural.

Financing

The financial support of its wealthy constituency covers ID expenses.

Leadership

Arsalane el-Jadidi (minister of labor), Khalihenna Ould Rachid (secretary of state for Saharan affairs), Moussa Saadi (minister of energy and mines), and Abdelhamid Kassimi are the principal leaders of the ID.

Prospects

Probably, ID will continue as the king's ally until Hassan II once again feels the need to create a scapegoat or undercut a potential rival power.

Party of Progress and Socialism (Parti du Progres et du Socialisme; PPS)

History

Founded in 1974, the PPS is the direct successor of two previous Communist parties—the Moroccan Communist Party, which was founded in 1943 and banned in 1952 and 1959, and the Party of Liberation and Socialism, which was founded in 1968 and banned in 1969. The pro-Moscow communists were allowed by the king to reorganize as the PPS in 1974 as a result of the relative liberalization that accompanied the campaign to annex Western Sahara. Since then, the party has managed to retain its legality. In contrast to the USFP, it did not face severe repression after the June 1981 Casablanca riots, apparently because of the moderation of its leadership, the party's small size, and its relatively limited audience.

Organization

The party is tightly knit and headed by a central committee and political bureau. It publishes two daily newspapers, one in French, the other in Arabic, both titled Al-Bayane. They were banned for four weeks after the June 1981 riots. Since 1974, the party has been able to consolidate organizationally and extend the circulation of its press.

Policy

The PPS faithfully toes the Moscow line on major international issues, with the single important exception of the Western Saharan question, on which the USSR is a supporter of Saharawi self-determination, while the PPS defends Morocco's annexation of the territory and supports the war against the Polisario Front. For defensive reasons, the party avoids overt criticism of the monarchy. With Stalinist orthodoxy, it adheres to the notion of revolution by stages, i.e., before the socialist revolution there must first be a "national democratic revolution" carried out by a broad alliance of classes to achieve land reform, democratization, and the end of imperialist domination.

Membership & Constituency

The PPS is an urban-based party; most of its members are students, teachers, and other intellectuals. It has some working-class electoral support and is active in the unions affiliated with the Moroccan Union of Labor (Union Marocaine du Travail; UMT). It decries the other major labor confederation as divisive. The party is represented in the leadership of the National Union of Moroccan Students (Union Nationale des Etudiants Marocains; UNEM).

Financing

Membership dues and sales of its publications may cover some of PPS's needs. Nothing is known about its finances.

Leadership

Ali Yata, who was secretary general of the earlier communist parties, has been secretary general of the PPS since its founding.

Prospects

Though Morocco's economic and social crises might increase the party's audience, popular discontent is more likely to benefit the larger USFP. Moreover, the party faces competition from other Marxist groups to its left. In the event of a military coup or a shift in the palace's political strategy, the party could be banned again.

Popular Movement
(*Mouvement Populaire;* MP)

Created in 1957 and legalized in 1959, the MP exploited local rural grievances that lay behind rural rebellions in 1957 to 1959. It presented itself in the Berber-populated mountainous regions as an alternative to the Arab-dominated, urban-based Istiqlal Party. It received encouragement from the palace, which saw the movement as a useful counterweight to the urban parties. It gave loyal support to the king and joined the FDIC in the sixties. It received four posts in the government after the 1977 elections.

The MP's distinctive features are its royalism and Berberism. It has no prospect of extending its popular appeal beyond the Berber rural regions. The party is very loosely organized and publishes only a weekly newspaper, *Al-Haraka,* in Arabic. The secretary general is Mahjoubi Aherdane (born 1921), the founder of the party and minister of cooperation in the current government.

Socialist Union of Popular Forces
(*Union Socialiste des Forces Populaires;* USFP)

History

Founded in 1974, the USFP emerged from a split in the UNFP in 1972. The UNFP had itself split from the Istiqlal Party in 1959. Led by the more radical Istiqlal leaders, among them Mehdi Ben Barka, the UNFP was immediately harassed by the palace—first by its expulsion from the government in 1960, then by the mass trial of UNFP leaders in 1963. Two years later, Ben Barka was assassinated. Although originally backed in its breakaway from the Istiqlal Party by the UMT, the party was further weakened by the UMT's refusal to back its political initiatives in the mid-sixties.

The loss of the party's most radical leaders led to the emergence of a more compromise-prone leadership, while the uneasy relations between the UNFP and UMT leaders led to a party split in 1972. One faction, led by Abderrahim Bouabid, broke ranks with a rival faction led by Abdallah Ibrahim and the UMT's leader, Mahjoub Ben Seddik. Bouabid's "Rabat wing" of the UNFP was briefly banned in 1973 and 1974, but was relegalized as a result of the liberalization initiated by the king in 1974, changing its name to the *Union Socialiste des Forces Populaires* the same year.

The party accused the government of fixing many of the results in the 1977 elections and has since remained in opposition. It was severely repressed after the June 1981 Casablanca riots and massacre. Its newspapers were immediately suppressed and had still not been allowed to restart publication a year later. Some 200 leaders of the party and its allied Democratic Labor Confederation (*Confederation Démocratique du Travail;* CDT) were jailed. Abderrahim Bouabid and two other members of the party's political bureau were imprisoned between September 1981 and March 1982.

Organization

The USFP has held a national congress about once every two to three years. Its leadership consists of a thirty-five–member national administrative commission and a nine-member political bureau. Until the repression unleashed against the party in June 1981, it published two newspapers— an Arabic-language daily, *Al-Moharrir,* and a French-language weekly, *Liberation.* It has a youth wing known as the *Jeunesse Ittihadia* (United Youth) and has close relations with the Socialist International. The party is politically heterogeneous and includes a revolutionary socialist tendency known by the name of its clandestine newspaper, *Alikhtier Athaouri* (Revolutionary Option), inspired by one of the UNFP's historic leaders, Mohammed Basri, who has lived in exile in Paris since the early sixties.

Policy

The USFP's political outlook is, broadly speaking, social democratic. It advocates reform of the constitution, civil liberties, and the liberation of political prisoners. It calls for the nationalization of the principal means of production, transport, exchange, and credit; land reform on the basis of "land to the tiller"; large-scale housing programs and the control of urban rents and property speculation; anticorruption measures; and wage increases. Strongly nationalist, it supports the war against the Polisario Front and, like the PPS, tends to criticize the government for alleged weakness in prosecuting the war effort.

Membership & Constituency

Primarily urban-based, the USFP draws most of its members from the educated middle class. It is particularly strong among students, teachers, and lower-level civil servants, but it also recruits through the trade unions affiliated with the CDT, which it controls. In elections, it enjoys wide support in the cities from workers, the unemployed poor, students and the middle class. It has a majority on several municipal councils, including Rabat.

Financing

The USFP has been liberally supported by its wealthier adherents.

Leadership

Abderrahim Bouabid (born 1920) is the party's first secretary.

Prospects

As the major left-wing party, the USFP could be expected to be the principal beneficiary of the widespread discontent in the cities. However, the repression it has suffered since June 1981 has seriously handicapped the party and prevented it from capitalizing effectively on its political opportunities.

Minor Parties

Action Party (*Parti de l'Action;* PA)

Founded in 1977 and led by Abdallah Senhaji, the PA is Berber based, proroyalist, and conservative.

Forward (*Ilal-Amam*)

Founded in 1970 in a split from the PPS's predecessor, the Party of Liberation and Socialism, this group supports self-determination in Western Sahara and the Polisario Front. It is outlawed and many members, including its principal leader, Abraham Serfaty, are in jail.

March 23 (*23 Mars*)

Founded in 1970 in a split from the UNFP, March 23 is led by Mohammed Ben Said. It is Marxist-Leninist. In 1978 and 1979, it split over attitudes towards the USFP and the Western Saharan war: one faction joined the USFP; other factions remained outlawed, with some members in jail. It is active and influential in the UNEM.

National Union of Popular Forces (*Union Nationale des Forces Populaires;* UNFP)

The rump of UNFP since the split by forces which founded the USFP in 1974, this group is led by Abdallah Ibrahim. It is social democratic in viewpoint and has close links with the UMT. It boycotted the 1977 parliamentary elections.

Popular Democratic and Constitutional Movement (*Mouvement Populaire Démocratique et Constitutionel;* MPDC)

Founded in 1967 in a split from the MP, this royalist group is led by Abdelkrim Khatib.

Other Political Forces

Military

The Royal Armed Forces (*Forces Armées Royales;* FAR) were formed in 1956, primarily with Moroccan troops that had served in the French and Spanish armies. Crown Prince Hassan, who became chief of staff in 1957, used these troops to put down several localized rural rebellions in 1957 to 1959 and to disband and partially absorb the irregular forces of the Army of Liberation. Hassan integrated the officers into the royal patronage system, using his position as chief of staff to determine promotions. The FAR came to be seen as one of the pillars of the monarchical regime.

In 1971 a group of senior military officers, angered by corruption, attempted a coup. It failed, but the attempt revealed that the armed forces could no longer be considered a secure bastion of royal power. In August 1972, there was a second unsuccessful coup attempt, this time by air force officers.

The king's reaction to these challenges was diverse. The officer corps was purged. The post of defense minister was abolished, and the king again became chief of staff of the armed forces. Part of the army was dispatched to the Middle East in 1973, while most of the rest was virtually disarmed until the outbreak of the war in Western Sahara.

Since 1972 there has been no centralized command structure between the king and the army battalion and brigade commanders and the chiefs of the air force and the navy. This, the king hopes, will make the planning of another coup much more difficult. A military inspectorate keeps the king directly informed of the FAR's activities, as do such parallel security forces as the *Forces Auxiliaires*, the *Gendarmerie Royale*, and the *Sureté Nationale*.

Traditionally, most of the FAR's officers and men were Berbers from the Atlas and Rif mountains, which had been the main recruiting grounds for the French and Spanish armies in Morocco. However, the composition of the officer corps was transformed by the events of 1971 and 1972. Most senior postindependence officers have been recruited from Arab urban bourgeois families. The composition of the ranks has been changed by the introduction of selective conscription in 1967, though voluntary enlistment by rural Berbers remains important.

Organized Labor

Though French unions had had affiliates in Morocco for some years, the first Moroccan labor federation, the Moroccan Union of Labor (*Union Marocaine du Travail;* UMT) was founded in 1955 by supporters of the Istiqlal Party. Under Mahjoub Ben Seddik, the federation supported the UNFP's split from the party in 1959; but, from 1962, relations between the UMT and the UNFP were strained. The UMT, which was subsidized by the government, was generally unwilling to back the UNFP's political campaigns and concentrated on narrow trade-union matters. After the split in the UNFP in 1972, Ben Seddik retained links with the rump led by Abdallah Ibrahim. In consequence, the larger faction, which went on to form the USFP in 1974, set about building a rival trade-union movement. From the beginning it had the support of the National Education Union (*Syndicat National de l'Enseignement;* SNE) which had been independent of the UMT since its creation in 1965, and the postal workers' union, which had split from the UMT in 1963. In 1978, eight USFP-led unions, representing teachers, phosphate workers, postal workers, health employees, sugar and tea workers, water and electricity workers, petroleum and gas workers, and some railwaymen, founded the Democratic Labor Confederation (*Confederation Démocratique du Travail;* CDT). By 1979 there were three more affiliates, representing workers in the tobacco industry, agriculture, and municipal administration; and, although the UMT retained some of its traditional strength in basic industries, notably the railway and the electricity-generating industry, the CDT had become the more powerful of the two federations by 1981. Both the UMT and the CDT called general strikes in June 1981 to protest the massive increases in food prices decreed by the govern-

ment; and it was the CDT's strike, on June 20, which ended in widespread rioting and the army's bloody intervention. Almost all the CDT's top leaders, including its secretary general, Noubir el-Amaoui, were jailed. A year later most remained in jail, and Noubir el-Amaoui was still awaiting his trial.

Student Movements

Since the founding of the National Union of Moroccan Students (*Union Nationale des Etudiants Marocaines;* UNEM) in 1955, the student movement has been one of the most radicalized sectors of Moroccan society. In 1970 to 1973, student protest reached a peak, with many universities almost permanently on strike; and, at UNEM's fifteenth congress in 1972, Marxist-Leninist *frontistes* from the March 23 movement and Ilal-Amam displaced the UNFP leadership which had headed the union since the 1950s. The government reacted by banning UNEM in January 1973 and jailing many of its leaders. Some remain in jail to this day. The government relegalized UNEM in November 1978, but ensured that it would be reconstituted by "responsible" socialists of the USFP and the PPS. However, UNEM has resumed its tradition of militant opposition to government policies, mainly over specific student grievances such as grants, university entrance requirements, and Arabization, and on the charged issue of political prisoners. At the seventeenth congress in August 1981, the UNFP withdrew from UNEM's executive commission, leaving the leadership in the hands of the PPS, the March 23 movement, and the *Groupe des Martyrs* faction. Strikes became frequent in 1981; and in December three of the union's executive members were detained.

National Prospects

Much of the educated elite in the universities, the state administration, the officer corps of the armed forces, and the political parties is alienated by the corruption and favoritism of the patronage system, the failure to provide reward based on merit, and the king's unwillingness to allow a real dispersal of decision-making power. The scale of Morocco's economic and social problems—the oil-import bill, fluctuating prices for phosphate ore (the main export), soaring food imports and agricultural failings, the ongoing rural exodus into the cities, and the swelling unemployment and shantytowns—suggests that discontent with the established order will grow. It is doubtful that any of the political parties could overthrow the monarchy. The one organized force that would be capable of doing so is the army, and its political ambitions may hinge on the outcome of the war in Western Sahara which, in 1982, its seventh year, still showed few signs of coming to an end.

Further Reading

Amnesty International Briefing: Morocco. London: Amnesty International, 1977.

Gellner, Ernest, and Micaud, Charles, ed. *Arabs and Berbers, From Tribe to Nation in North Africa.* Lexington, Mass.: Lexington Books, D.C. Heath, 1972.

Knapp, Wilfrid. *North West Africa, A Political and Economic Survey.* 3rd ed. New York: Oxford University Press, 1977.

Nelson, Harold D., ed. *Morocco, A Country Study.* Foreign Area Studies. Washington, D.C.: American University, 1978.

Waterbury, John. *The Commander of the Faithful: The Moroccan Political Elite, A Study in Segmented Politics.* New York: Columbia University Press, 1970.

———. "Corruption, Political Stability, and Development: Comparative Evidence from Egypt and Morocco." *Government and Opposition* (London), VII, Autumn 1976.

Zartman, William, ed. *Man, State and Society in the Contemporary Maghrib.* New York: Praeger, 1973.

SAHARAN ARAB DEMOCRATIC REPUBLIC
(*República Árabe Saharaui Democrática*)
by Tony Hodges

The System of Government

The former Spanish colony of Western Sahara has been disputed territory since 1975–76 when, upon Spain's withdrawal, it was annexed and partitioned by Morocco and Mauritania. An indigenous nationalist movement, the Polisario Front, with support from Algeria, put up strong resistance to the annexation and finally forced Mauritania to withdraw in 1979. Since then, the Polisario Front has continued its war against Morocco; by 1982 its forces controlled approximately nine-tenths of the territory, though Morocco retained the main centers near the coast, and about half the area's total population of some 80,000. A large part of the population lives under Polisario administration in refugee camps in southwestern Algeria.

In February 1976, a pro-Polisario assembly of notables, the Provisional Saharawi National Council, proclaimed the founding of the Saharan Arab Democratic Republic (SADR). By 1982, the new state had been recognized by fifty foreign governments and admitted to the Organization of African Unity (OAU). Morocco's claim to sovereignty in Western Sahara has not been recognized by any nation.

The government is, in reality, synonymous with the political movement, the Polisario Front, which inspired its creation. Under the constitution, which was adopted in August 1976, the Front's leaders automatically fill the main executive posts in the government.

Executive

The Council for the Command of the Revolution (CCR) is "the supreme organ of executive power of the SADR." It is constituted, for the duration of the war, by the Polisario Front's Executive Committee. It has nine members and is presided over by the Polisario Front's secretary general, who is therefore head of state. The Council of Ministers, which had eleven members in 1982, is designated by the CCR, headed by a prime minister who must be a member of the CCR, and carries out the CCR's "directives."

Legislature

The Saharawi National Council has "legislative and consultative power," according to the constitution. However, it appears to have little real power, since the CCR has wide-ranging legislative as well as executive powers. Of its forty-one members, twenty-one are ex officio by virtue of their membership in the Polisario Front's political bureau. The remaining twenty members are elected by "popular base congresses." The council has three commissions, responsible for political and social affairs, foreign relations, and military matters, respectively.

Judiciary

Primary tribunals, an appeals court, and a people's supreme court, whose judges are appointed by a Judicial Council, presided over by the minister of justice comprise the judiciary. There is also a special State Security Court, designated by the CCR.

Regional & Local Government

The SADR is divided into three *wilayat* (sing., *wilaya*), which are administered by wilaya people's councils. Each council is headed by a *wali*, or governor, and is comprised of the officials who head the people's councils of the lower administrative units, the *dairat* (sing., *daira*), whose members are elected by the popular-base congresses. In current practice, this administrative structure exists only in the Saharawi refugee camps in southwestern Algeria.

The Electoral System

Elections are "nonparty" in character. The members of the Daira People's Councils are elected directly in the *dairat*, that is to say in the refugee camps at present, but the higher wilaya people's councils are elected indirectly. Of the forty-one members of the theoretical legislature, the Saharawi National Council, only twenty are elected directly, from the *dairat*, as noted above. The others are ex officio, as members of the Polisario Front's Political Bureau.

Popular Front for the Liberation of Saguia el-Hamra and Río de Oro (Polisario Front)
(*Frente Popular para la Liberación de Saguia el Hamra y Río de Oro; Frente Polisario*)

History

The Polisario Front was founded in May 1973 and began a guerrilla war against Spain the same month. At its second congress, in August 1974, it officially adopted the goal of independence. After Spain's withdrawal in 1975–76, it fought a guerrilla war against Morocco and (until 1979) Mauritania.

Organization

The Front's highest decision-making body is the congress, which has been held five times between 1973 and 1982. Between congresses, the top leadership body is the nine-member Executive Committee, which is elected by the congress and headed by the secretary general. A subordinate body, also elected by the congress, is the Political Bureau, whose twenty-one members include the SADR's three *walis* and the secretaries general of auxilliary movements for women, students, and workers: the National Union of Saharawi Women (*Unión Nacional de Mujeres Saharauis;* UNMS), the General Union of Saharawi Workers (*Unión General de Trabajadores Saharauis;* UGTS), and the General Union of Students of Saguia el Hamra and Río de Oro (*Unión General de los Estudiantes de Saguia el Hamra y Río de Oro;* UGESARIO). In the Polisario-run refugee camps, all adult Saharawi refugees belong to eleven-member cells headed by an *arifa* (pl., *arifat*) who is responsible to the *wilaya*'s Department of Training and Orientation.

The Polisario Front publishes a fortnightly newspaper, *Sahara Libre,* and a monthly magazine, *20 de Mayo,* in Spanish, Arabic, and French editions.

Policy

The Front's overriding and unifying objective is the achievement of full independence. It supports the holding of a referendum on self-determination under United Nations or Organization of African Unity auspices, and it calls on Morocco to hold bilateral peace talks. The Front officially embraces socialism, Islam, Arabization, the unification of the Arab world, and the improvement of the status of women. After the war, a Polisario Front government would be likely to pursue a pragmatic, nonaligned foreign policy and would probably cooperate with foreign companies to exploit the country's phosphates and other mineral wealth.

Membership & Constituency

The Front is not a "vanguard party." Rather it is a mass movement of which all Saharawis, except those who have allied with Morocco, are members. Hence, the entire adult refugee population is enrolled in the Front's cells.

Financing

The Algerian and Libyan governments are presumed to be the main sources of funds, as well as armaments.

Leadership

Mohammed Abdelaziz (born c. 1947) is secretary general of the Polisario Front. He comes from the territory's largest *gabila* (tribe), the Reguibat, and was educated in Morocco. A founder-member of the Front, he was elected secretary general at the third congress, in August 1976. As such, he is also president of the CCR and so head of state of the SADR.

Bachir Mustapha Sayed (born c. 1950–52), also a member of the Reguibat, was educated in Morocco and was elected deputy secretary general at the third congress in August 1976. He is a member of the Front's executive committee and of the SADR's CCR.

Mohammed Lamine Ould Ahmed is prime minister of the SADR. Born c. 1947, he is a member of a small tribe, the Taoubalt. He was educated at Mohammed V University in Rabat, Morocco. He was appointed prime minister in March 1976. He is a member of the Front's executive committee and of the SADR's CCR.

Other Political Forces

A small minority of Saharawis have declared support for Western Sahara's integration into Morocco. These are mainly traders who have sided with Morocco to preserve their business interests in the Moroccan-controlled towns. A number of Saharawis have joined Moroccan political parties—notably the Istiqlal Party, the proroyalist "independents," and the *Mouvement Populaire*—and some have been elected to the communal councils and provincial assemblies in the Moroccan-controlled areas and to the Moroccan Chamber of Representatives.

National Prospects

As of 1982, Morocco controlled about one-tenth of the land area of Western Sahara—notably a zone in the northwest known as the "useful triangle" because it includes the old Spanish colonial capital, El-Ayoun; the important phosphate mines at Bou-Craa; and the country's only precolonial city, Smara. The SADR's forces, the Saharawi People's Liberation Army (SPLA), controlled the rest of the territory, but seemed unlikely to have the military means to evict the Moroccan army from the heavily defended enclaves it controlled near the coast. A total Moroccan withdrawal seems unlikely in the absence of far-reaching political change in Morocco, since King Hassan II has effectively staked his prestige and credibility as a ruler on the annexation of the territory. However, Morocco is under very powerful military, diplomatic, and economic pressures to resolve the conflict. These pressures may ultimately be sufficient to force a complete Moroccan withdrawal. Hence the Polisario Front and its main external ally, Algeria, are likely to continue what is, in essence, a war of attrition.

Further Reading

Barbier, Maurice. *Le Conflit du Sahara Occidental.* Paris: Editions L'Harmattan, 1982.

Hodges, Tony. *Historical Dictionary of Western Sahara.* Metuchen, N. J.: Scarecrow Press, 1982.

Hodges, Tony. "Whither Western Sahara?" *Africa Research Bulletin*, Political Series, Vol. 19, No. 2, 15 March 1982.

Mercer, John. *Spanish Sahara.* London: George Allen and Unwin, 1976.

PEOPLE'S REPUBLIC OF MOZAMBIQUE
(*Republica Popular de Moçambique*)
by Michael Radu, Ph.D.

The System of Government

Mozambique, a nation of more than 10.5 million people, is a communist state, with a one-party presidential political system. The country became independent on June 25, 1975, following more than a decade of guerrilla war against Portuguese colonial rule. Between September 20, 1974, and June 25, 1975, the country was ruled by a transitional government led by Joaquin Chissano and composed of Portuguese officers and representatives of the guerrilla movement, the Front for the Liberation of Mozambique (*Frente de Libertação de Moçambique*; FRELIMO). After independence, the post of prime minister previously occupied by Chissano was abolished, and a presidential system introduced. FRELIMO's leader, Samora Moises Machel, was appointed president, an office he retains today. The country was proclaimed a people's republic, with Marxism-Leninism the official ideology and FRELIMO the only legal party.

The control exerted by FRELIMO over the entire society, provided for in the 1977 Constitution (amended in August 1978), is implemented directly, through its power over the government, and indirectly, through the government role played by the Politburo members and the party's use of mass organizations.

Executive

The president of FRELIMO, is the sole nominee for presidency. The president's powers are extensive: he chairs and controls the government and appoints or removes ministers; appoints and recalls the president and vice-president of the People's Supreme Court and the general prosecutor of the republic; appoints and removes from their offices the governors of the ten provinces, the governor of the National Bank, the commander of the police, and the rector of the university; he is the supreme commander of the armed forces, and has the right to void the decisions of the provincial assemblies.

Legislature

The powers of the National People's Assembly, the supreme legislative institution, are purely formal. The 226 deputies for the National People's Assembly were appointed by the party in 1977. They included the entire Central Committee, the members of the government, the provincial governors (appointed by the president), members of the military selected by the Central Committee, all the Politburo members, and a small number of cadres selected by the party. With such membership, it is natural that the assembly rubber stamps the actions of the government and approves all laws proposed to it. Legislative initiative belongs to the Central Committee, the Politburo, the president, the government, the Permanent Commission of the Assembly itself, and to its committees—all under direct control of the FRELIMO leadership. Between the two annual sessions of the Assembly, the president and the Permanent Commission, selected from among the deputies nominated by the Central Committee of FRELIMO and chaired by the president, govern by decree.

Judiciary

The judiciary consists of elected judges at the local level, of a combination of professional and elected judges at the district and provincial levels, and by appointed professional magistrates at the national level. Formally, the judges are independent, but in reality, by virtue of the president's power to remove Supreme Court judges, they are under party control. In 1979, as a result of increased opposition and antigovernment guerrilla operations, the Military Revolutionary Tribunal was established, with jurisdiction over crimes against state security; its decisions cannot be appealed. The trials in this court are always extremely brief and in many cases the sentence of death is carried out the following day.

Regional & Local Government

The powers of the governors of the ten provinces mirror, on a local level, those of the president. The governors are responsible to FRELIMO only, and their decisions can only be overruled by the president.

Local, district, municipal, and provincial assemblies were elected in 1977 by universal vote from candidates nominated by FRELIMO's local organizations.

Front for the Liberation of Mozambique
(*Frente de Libertação de Moçambique;* FRELIMO)

History

The party was founded in 1962 by the American-educated Eduardo Mondlane, who united three small anti-Portuguese groups in the new front. Following Mondlane's assassination in February 1969, a sharp factional conflict developed between his colleagues. A nationalist and moderate faction led by Uria Simango was opposed by a Marxist-Leninist group led by Machel, Chissano, and Marcelino dos Santos. After a brief period of compromise, when the movement was under the collective leadership of a Machel–Simango–Dos Santos coalition, Machel was able to eliminate Simango and become the undisputed leader of FRELIMO in 1970.

FRELIMO began the anti-Portuguese war in 1964, with most of its guerrillas at the time coming from the northern Makonde tribe. Following the expulsion from the front of the Makonde chief, Lazaro Kawandame, in 1968, most of the group's insurgents came from the central regions, while the leadership remained largely of southern origin. Militarily, FRELIMO never represented a real threat to the Portuguese, and the "liberated zones" under its control by 1974 were largely lim-

ited to the remote and sparsely inhabited northern and northwestern provinces, where the movement established a rudimentary political structure. Despite such unimpressive successes, FRELIMO obtained widespread international support and contributed to the weakening of the Portuguese colonial rule, two factors which explain its recognition by the Portuguese, in September 1974, as the sole representative of the Mozambican people.

Until 1977, FRELIMO persisted in calling itself a movement rather than a party, that is, it was a coalition of disparate groups united by their anticolonial stand. However, the February 3–6, 1977, Congress, FRELIMO's third, proclaimed the movement a "vanguard party" closely modelled after those in Eastern Europe and the USSR.

Organization

Formally, the supreme organ of FRELIMO is the congress, which elects the Central Committee, and which in turn selects the ten members of the Politburo. Since the congress is convened irregularly and its delegates are selected from among those proposed by the Central Committee, its role is to approve and legitimize the decisions taken by the leadership. The Central Committee itself only convenes in plenary session about once a year, at the request of the Politburo. It is the latter body which has concentrated power. All FRELIMO members are expected to obey leadership decisions according to the Leninist principle of democratic centralism.

The ten Politburo members are all comrades linked by personal ties of friendship, similar backgrounds, and strong dedication to Marxism-Leninism; nine of them also had some guerrilla experience. In 1980 they were appointed senior officers, although most no longer have ties to the military. Thus, Machel appointed himself field marshal; foreign minister Chissano and two of the party ideologues, Dos Santos and Jorge Rebelo, became major-generals, as did the interior and security ministers, Joaquin Veloso and Mariano Matsinhe, respectively; Defense Minister Alberto Chipande, national Political Commissar Armando Guebuza, and the secret political police director, Sebastiao Mabote, were appointed lieutenant-generals. Only the tenth-ranking member, Planning Minister Mario de Graca Machungo, remained a civilian.

Immediately after the establishment of the 1974 provisional government, FRELIMO created a large number of "dynamizing groups" (*grupos dinamizadores*)—voluntary village, factory, or neighborhood vigilante groups—which allowed the party to take advantage of a wave of denunciations, to expand its still-small forces, and to control the activities of most of the population. By 1978, when the reliability of these groups, in light of FRELIMO's transformation into an elite party, became doubtful, they were replaced by "groups of popular vigilance." These were also vigilante groups but under stricter party control, organized around a secretariat responsible to the National Service of People's Security (SNASP), the political police. SNASP has the right to make arrests; its national director is ex officio a member of the government; and ever since its inception in 1976, SNASP has been directed by a Central Committee or Politburo member.

In addition to its control over the government and the secret police, FRELIMO also supervises and directs national life through its use of mass organizations, such as the Organization of Mozambican Women, the Youth Organization, and the party cells in enterprises.

Policy

The internal policies of FRELIMO since 1975 have been a direct result of its ideology. All private enterprise, from the large English-owned SENA sugar estates to the offices of Portuguese doctors and lawyers down to funeral parlors and street vendors' tables, were nationalized or, in most cases, confiscated. Rental property was forbidden, all banks were nationalized, and a state monopoly over internal and foreign trade was established. One of the results of these policies was the mass exodus of the over 200,000 Portuguese who represented the majority of the skilled manpower, professionals, and even small traders in the rural areas. Another result was that the Mozambique economy was badly damaged: the GNP declined year after year and shortages of all basic commodities became widespread.

The situation was worsened by Mozambique's undeclared war with Rhodesia—waged between March 1976 and December 1979—which included devastating Rhodesian raids against Mozambican territory and the sending of Mozambican "volunteers" to Rhodesia disguised as local guerrillas. All this was a concrete implementation of FRELIMO's "internationalism." At the same time, the country became increasingly dependent on South Africa for most of its hard currency revenues.

FRELIMO's foreign policy is consistently anti-Western, despite the fact that Mozambique receives most of its foreign economic aid from the Scandinavian countries and the members of the European Economic Community. On the other hand, Mozambique has signed treaties of friendship and cooperation with the Soviet Union, East Germany, Bulgaria, and Romania. It supports the Vietnamese occupation of Kampuchea, the Soviet invasion of Afghanistan, and the imposition of martial law in Poland. East German, Soviet, and Cuban advisers train SNASP and army personnel; Bulgarians advise on agricultural matters; and East Germans and Romanians are involved in the mining industry.

Membership & Constituency

The immediate practical result of the decision to convert FRELIMO into a true party was to decimate the membership, since the new statutes imposed strict membership requirements. While at the time of independence FRELIMO may have had as many as 10,000 members, by 1979 Machel was vaguely estimating the membership at a few thousand. A drive began in 1979 to increase membership.

Financing

Nothing is known of party finances. It can be assumed that direct state subsidies cover most of FRELIMO's expenses.

Leadership

Samora Moises Machel was born in 1933 in Gaza province, the son of a local chief. He had only four years of formal education. Until 1963, when he joined FRELIMO, he worked as an orderly at a Maputo hospital. He underwent military training in Algeria and, in 1964, led the first FRELIMO raid inside Mozambique. Machel became the movement's secretary for defense in 1966 and commander-in-chief in 1968. In 1971, Machel received the Lenin Centenary Award in Moscow.

Marcelino dos Santos was born in 1931 in Maputo. He studied at the universities of Lisbon and Paris. In April 1961, he became secretary of the umbrella organization of the anti-Portuguese groups in Portugal's African colonies, the Conference of Nationalist Organizations of the Portuguese Colonies (*Conferencia des Organizações Nacionalistas des Colonias Portuguesas*; CONCP) and the following year became one of FRELIMO's founders. In 1965, Dos Santos became responsible for FRELIMO's foreign affairs. Since May 1970, he has been FRELIMO's vice-president. Between 1975 and 1979, he was planning minister, and thereafter secretary for economic affairs and the Politburo's second-ranking member. Of all

FRELIMO leaders, he is certainly the closest to the Soviets and to the Portuguese Communist Party, with which he was formally associated in the late 1950s.

Joaquin Chissano was born in 1939 in Gaza province and studied in Mozambique and Portugal. Between 1964 and 1974, he was FRELIMO's representative in Tanzania and minister of defense. Between September 20, 1974, and June 25, 1975, Chissano was prime minister of the transitional government of Mozambique and since then has remained the third-ranking Politburo member and foreign affairs minister.

Opposition

Many of FRELIMO's policies, domestic as well as foreign, have resulted in a significant development of internal opposition. The undeclared war with Rhodesia served as a catalyst for such opposition to increase its activities with Rhodesian support. By 1978 the Makonde people in the north were involved in a sporadic insurgency which provoked the dispatch of Tanzanian units to help FRELIMO, and by 1979 a new armed group, the Mozambican National Resistance, was formed. This group is increasingly active in the densely populated central provinces, is largely made up of former FRELIMO guerrillas disappointed with the orientation of the regime, and led by former FRELIMO commanders. Although discreetly backed by South Africa since 1980 and partly financed by Portuguese businessmen whose properties were confiscated by FRELIMO, the antigovernment group seems to enjoy widespread rural and urban support.

National Prospects

While it is highly unlikely that factionalism will develop within the tightly structured top leadership of FRELIMO, the party's inability to solve the economic and internal-security problems of Mozambique can be expected to become more evident. The threat of national economic collapse and of increasingly effective antigovernment guerrillas could easily lead FRELIMO's leaders to divert attention from these domestic difficulties by adopting a more aggressive policy toward South Africa. Such a policy might well be abetted, even encouraged or required, by the Soviet bloc, upon which FRELIMO depends for its survival. The consequence could be a condition of persistent violent conflict involving not only Mozambique and most of its neighbors, but the major powers as well.

Further Reading

Alpers, Edward A. "The Struggle for Socialism in Mozambique 1960–1972." In *Socialism in Sub-Saharan Africa.* Carl G. Rosberg and Thomas M. Callaghy, eds. Berkeley: Institute of International Studies, University of California, 1979.

Machel, Samora. *Le processus de la révolution démocratique populaire au Mozambique.* Paris: Editions l'Harmattan, 1977.

Ottaway, David and Ottaway, Marina. *Afrocommunism.* New York: Africana Publishing Company, 1981.

Saul, John S. *The State and Revolution in Eastern Africa.* New York: Monthly Review Press, 1979.

Young, Crawford. *Ideology and Development in Africa.* New Haven and London: Yale University Press, 1982.